The New Encyclopædia Britannica

in 32 Volumes

FOUNDED 1768
15 TH EDITION

Encyclopædia Britannica, Inc.

Robert P. Gwinn, Chairman, Board of Directors
Peter B. Norton, President
Philip W. Goetz, Editor in Chief

Chicago
Auckland/Geneva/London/Manila/Paris/Rome
Seoul/Sydney/Tokyo/Toronto

THE UNIVERSITY OF CHICAGO

"Let knowledge grow from more to more
and thus be human life enriched."

First Edition   1768–1771
Second Edition   1777–1784
Third Edition   1788–1797
Supplement   1801
Fourth Edition   1801–1809
Fifth Edition   1815
Sixth Edition   1820–1823
Supplement   1815–1824
Seventh Edition   1830–1842
Eighth Edition   1852–1860
Ninth Edition   1875–1889
Tenth Edition   1902–1903

Eleventh Edition
© 1911
By Encyclopædia Britannica, Inc.

Twelfth Edition
© 1922
By Encyclopædia Britannica, Inc.

Thirteenth Edition
© 1926
By Encyclopædia Britannica, Inc.

Fourteenth Edition
© 1929, 1930, 1932, 1933, 1936, 1937, 1938, 1939, 1940, 1941, 1942, 1943,
   1944, 1945, 1946, 1947, 1948, 1949, 1950, 1951, 1952, 1953, 1954,
   1955, 1956, 1957, 1958, 1959, 1960, 1961, 1962, 1963, 1964,
   1965, 1966, 1967, 1968, 1969, 1970, 1971, 1972, 1973
By Encyclopædia Britannica, Inc.

Fifteenth Edition
© 1974, 1975, 1976, 1977, 1978, 1979, 1980, 1981, 1982, 1983, 1984, 1985,
   1986, 1987
By Encyclopædia Britannica, Inc.

© 1987
By Encyclopædia Britannica, Inc.

Library of Congress Catalog Card Number: 85-82101
International Standard Book Number: 0-85229-443-3

ENCYCLOPÆDIA BRITANNICA

PHILIP W. GOETZ
Editor-in-Chief

ROBERT McHENRY
Managing Editor

ENCYCLOPÆDIA BRITANNICA, INC.

ROBERT P. GWINN, *Chairman, Board of Directors*

PETER B. NORTON, *President*

The New Encyclopædia Britannica

PROPÆDIA

Outline of Knowledge
and
Guide to the Britannica

How to use the PROPAEDIA

As its title indicates, the PROPAEDIA, or Outline of Knowledge, is intended to serve as a topical guide to the contents of the *Encyclopædia Britannica,* enabling the reader to carry out an orderly plan of reading in any field of knowledge or learning chosen for study in some depth. The PROPAEDIA's table of contents gives the reader an overview of the Outline of Knowledge as a whole; the introductory essays for each of the ten parts illuminate the major concerns of that part of human knowledge; the headnotes that are affixed to parts and divisions prepare the reader for examination of the subjects being covered there; and the outlined presentations of these subjects, with their lists of related article titles, enable the reader to carry on a course of study that may be more or less extensive and detailed in accordance with individual interests and desires.

Structure. Each of the 10 parts, 40 divisions, and 176 sections that make up the PROPAEDIA is marked in the table of contents by a heading, which is followed by the number of the page on which that unit of the PROPAEDIA begins. This structure provides three ways to utilize the outline: (1) one may turn to any of the parts as a whole and examine the contents of that part; (2) one may select a particular division of a part and examine the contents of that division; or (3) one may focus on a single section or several sections of such a division and examine the contents of that section or those sections.

Sectional outlines. The sectional outlines present, in an orderly arrangement of topics, subjects that are treated in articles in the MACROPAEDIA and MICROPAEDIA. Each section number incorporates the numbers of the part and division to which it belongs. For example, Section 725 is the fifth section in Part Seven, Division II; Section 96/10 is the tenth section in Part Nine, Division VI. In each sectional outline the major subjects are indicated by

capital letters ("A," "B," etc.). There are always at least two major subjects, but there may be many more in a given section. When it is necessary to subdivide a major subject, up to three additional levels may appear in the outline; the first is indicated by Arabic numerals, the second by lowercase letters, and the third by Roman numerals, as shown below:

B. Metallurgy

    1. Mineral dressing: crushing and grinding, concentration or mineral preparation

    2. Process metallurgy

        a. Pyrometallurgy: metallurgical processes that involve the use of heat

          i. Gas–solid reactions; *e.g.,* roasting

         ii. Distillation: processes for refining metals by condensing metal vapours

The INDEX, with its alphabetically arranged subject headings, is indispensable in finding where a given subject appears in the Outline of Knowledge. These headings, where appropriate, carry specific citations pointing to the part, division, or section of the PROPAEDIA that covers the subject in question. A subject referred to in a sectional outline is, in many cases, treated fully in an article of the same title in the MACROPAEDIA or MICROPAEDIA, each such title being included in the list of suggested reading at the end of the section. These titles, as well as significant references to the subjects in other contexts, are cited in the INDEX. It may be helpful to compare the functions of the PROPAEDIA and the INDEX: Both are guides to the contents of the *Encyclopædia Britannica,* but the PROPAEDIA's primary purpose is to indicate *what* subjects are covered, while the INDEX's primary purpose is to indicate *where* they are covered.

THE CIRCLE OF LEARNING

"The alphabetical system of arrangement," observed the Editors of the Eleventh Edition of the *Encyclopædia Britannica* (1910–11), "with its obvious advantages, necessarily results in the separation from one another of articles dealing with any particular subject." Consequently, "the student who desires to make a complete study of a given topic must exercise his imagination if he seeks to exhaust the articles in which that topic is treated." This result is certainly a serious defect in the system for anyone who feels—as did the Editors of the Eleventh Edition—that an encyclopaedia should not be merely a "storehouse of facts," but should also be "a systematic survey of all departments of knowledge." To remedy this defect, the Editors constructed a "Classified Table of Contents," which they believed to be "the first attempt in any general work of reference at a systematic subject catalogue or analysis of the material contained in it."

Remarkable as it was at the time, that Table of Contents did not fully succeed in achieving its objective of overcoming the defects of an alphabetical organization of encyclopaedic articles by means of a topical presentation of their content. A quick glance at the 24 major categories into which the Table of Contents was divided will reveal that the alphabet was still the thread on which the parts were strung: I. Anthropology and Ethnology; II. Archaeology and Antiquities; III. Art; IV. Astronomy; V. Biology; VI. Chemistry; VII. Economics and Social Science; VIII. Education; IX. Engineering; X. Geography; XI. Geology; XII. History; XIII. Industries, Manufactures and Occupations; XIV. Language and Writing; XV. Law and Political Science; XVI. Literature; XVII. Mathematics; XVIII. Medical Science; XIX. Military and Naval; XX. Philosophy and Psychology; XXI. Physics; XXII. Religion and Theology; XXIII. Sports and Pastimes; XXIV. Miscellaneous. In each of these categories, the only further subdivisions involved the distinction of general from particular subjects, and the distinction of both of these from biographical entries. Under each of these headings, titles of the encyclopaedia's articles were listed in strictly alphabetical order.

In planning this Fifteenth Edition of *Encyclopædia Britannica,* the Editors, while deciding to retain the alphabetical ordering of the articles in the set, sought to improve upon the effort that their predecessors had made to overcome the defects of an alphabetical organization by giving the reader a truly topical, and totally nonalphabetical, Table of Contents. It would serve the purpose that the Editors of the Eleventh Edition had in mind, which was to enable the reader to "make a complete study of a given topic"—that is, a department of knowledge or field of learning.

It may be asked why it was not thought better to abandon the alphabetical principle entirely and construct a purely topical encyclopaedia, in which all the articles would be assembled, volume after volume, according to some general schema for the organization of human knowledge. The answer is twofold. First, a purely topical organization of the articles themselves cannot avoid the appearance of a certain tendentiousness or arbitrariness in the editorial commitment to one rather than another organizing schema or set of principles. The reader is, therefore, provoked to ask: Does this order, volume by volume and article by article, reflect the only right or proper exposition of the whole of human knowledge?

Second, a purely topical encyclopaedia provides its readers with only one mode of access to its contents. This may be alleviated somewhat, perhaps, by the addition of an alphabetical index; but an index, by its very nature, serves the purpose of enabling the reader to look up *particular* items of information; it does not provide a general and systematic mode of access to the contents of the encyclopaedia.

The basic plan of the new *Britannica,* therefore, aims to give its readers access to its contents by both the topical and the alphabetical modes. General and systematic topical access is provided by the Outline of Knowledge contained in this volume, called the "Propædia" because it is a kind of preamble or antechamber to the world of learning that the rest of the encyclopaedia aims to encompass. Alphabetical access is provided not only by the two-volume Index but also by the alphabetical ordering of the short articles in the Micropædia.

Unlike the Classified Table of Contents in the Eleventh Edition, which was alphabetically organized by categories and subjects, the Outline of Knowledge in this Fifteenth Edition is a purely topical presentation of the subjects covered in the articles to be found in both the Macropædia and the Micropædia. It is, therefore, reasonable to ask how such a purely topical outline of encyclopaedic content avoids the tendentiousness or arbitrariness that is attributable to an encyclopaedia in which the articles themselves are topically rather than alphabetically arranged. Does not the Outline of Knowledge here presented reflect, perhaps even conceal, a commitment to one set of organizing principles rather than another? Does it not embody biases or preconceptions that are not universally acceptable?

It is hardly possible to say "No, not at all" to these questions. Two points, however, can be made affirmatively that tend to reduce or alleviate whatever degree of arbitrariness remains unavoidable in a topical outline of the whole of human knowledge. One is that the Outline of Knowledge, while conceived by the Editors, was constructed and corrected in the light of detailed recommendations, directions, and analytical contributions from scholars and experts in all the fields of knowledge represented. A list that includes the advisers who worked with the Editors in the construction of the Outline of Knowledge follows Part Ten of the Propædia.

The second point is that the Outline of Knowledge is conceived as a circle of learning. To say that the contents of an *en-cyclo-paedia* form a circle of learning is more than a literal transliteration from Greek to English. In Greek or English, reference to the circle introduces a powerful metaphor, the understanding of which should help the reader to overcome whatever arbitrariness still resides in the Outline of Knowledge in spite of determined efforts on the part of all concerned to minimize this defect. A circle is a figure in which no point on the circumference is a beginning, none is a middle, none is an end. It is also a figure in which one can go from any point, in either direction, around the circumference; in addition, one can go across the circle from any point to any other; or, by any number of transecting lines, starting from a given point, one can go to any number of other points on the circumference, near or far.

The 10 parts into which the Outline of Knowledge is divided are disposed not along a finite straight line beginning at this point and ending at that; they are disposed rather as segments of the circle. While it is true that, in this arrangement, one part may lie next to another and at some distance from still another, it is also true that, since the circle can rotate around its axis, any one of the 10 parts may be regarded as standing at the top of the circle, or at the left or right side of it, or at the bottom. In other words, with the circular arrangement of the parts, and with the rotation of the circle, the reader can begin anywhere in the circle of learning and go to adjacent parts around the circle; or, moving along interior transecting lines, the reader can go from any part across the circle to parts that are not adjacent on the circumference. This view of the Outline of Knowledge can be represented in a number of diagrams.

For a synopsis of the subject matter covered in each of the 10 parts of the outline, the reader is referred to the Table of Contents set forth on pages 9–15 of this volume. The titles of the individual parts are given in the following list:

Part One.	Matter and Energy
Part Two.	The Earth
Part Three.	Life on Earth
Part Four.	Human Life
Part Five.	Human Society
Part Six.	Art
Part Seven.	Technology
Part Eight.	Religion
Part Nine.	The History of Mankind
Part Ten.	The Branches of Knowledge

The pair of diagrams below shows the 10 parts as segments of a circle. Part One is placed at the top of the diagram to the left, and Part Nine is at the top of the diagram to the right, to illustrate the effect achieved by rotating the circle.

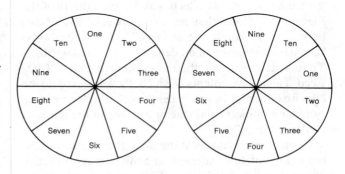

The second pair of diagrams, following, places one of the 10 parts at the centre of the circle with the remaining nine parts as segments of the circle formed by lines radiating from the centre. The point being made here is that any part can occupy the central position—the place in the circle of learning at which one begins, going thence in all directions to the remaining nine parts. To illustrate this, Part Five occupies the centre in the diagram to the left; Part Three, the centre in the diagram to the right.

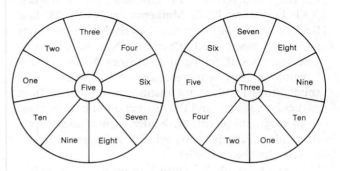

The final diagram offers still another approach to the circle of learning. In this diagram, Part Ten occupies the central position; and here there is only one diagram rather than a pair because the reason for placing Part Ten in the central position applies to it alone and to none of the other nine parts.

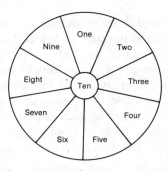

The reason for this special placement of Part Ten stems from the one organizing principle to which the Editors were explicitly committed in planning and producing this new *Britannica*. Briefly stated, that principle involves a distinction between (a) what we know about the world of nature, of man and society, and of human institutions *by means of* the various branches of learning or departments of scholarship; and (b) what we know about the branches of learning or departments of scholarship—the various academic disciplines themselves. For the most part—there are a few exceptions—Parts One through Nine represent the knowledge of nature, of human society, of human institutions, and their history. In clear contradistinction, Part Ten mainly covers the disciplines themselves—the branches of knowledge or fields of scholarship—by which one inquires into, thinks about, or comes to have knowledge of the world in which he lives. Part Ten examines the nature, methods, problems, and history of the various branches of knowledge or scholarly disciplines, the actual content of which is set forth in Parts One through Nine.

Thus, for example, Section 10/34 in Division III of Part Ten examines the nature, methods, problems, and history of the biological sciences; but the knowledge of life that the biological sciences afford is outlined in Part Three. Or, to take another example, Section 10/41 in Division IV of Part Ten examines historiography and the study of history; but the actual history of mankind is outlined in Part Nine.

There are, however, three departments of learning that are exclusively treated in Part Ten—both with regard to the nature and history of the disciplines themselves and also with regard to the knowledge or understanding afforded by these disciplines. They are logic (in Division I of Part Ten), mathematics (in Division II), and philosophy (in Division V). The reason for this exceptional treatment of these three disciplines is given in the Introductory Essay to Part Ten.

The special character of Part Ten thus explains the diagram in which it occupies the centre of the circle of learning, but that must not be interpreted as attributing prime importance to it. This diagram simply indicates the special function Part Ten performs in relation to the other parts. It alone stands in close relation to all the rest; there are varying degrees of relatedness among the other parts. For example, Parts Three and Four, dealing with Life on Earth and with Human Life, are closely related; Parts Four and Five, dealing with Human Life and with Human Society, are also closely related; but Part Four has a different relatedness to Part Three, on the one hand, and to Part Five, on the other. In the presentation of the Outline of Knowledge, the headnotes and the cross-references give the reader an indication of these interrelationships.

Anyone who is in a position to compare the classified list of articles in the Eleventh or even the Fourteenth Edition with the Outline of Knowledge will be persuaded, the Editors think, that whereas the immediately preceding editions of *Britannica* represented a 19th- and early 20th-century view of the state of human knowledge, the new *Britannica,* in its Fifteenth Edition, is an encyclopaedia that reflects the many changes and innovations in man's knowledge and understanding that are emerging at the end of this century and will continue into the next.

The reader's attention should be called to the following features of the Propædia, or Outline of Knowledge:

1. It serves as a Table of Contents for 681 long articles in the Macropædia and also for the tens of thousands of shorter articles in the Micropædia.

2. Each of the 10 Parts of the Outline and the several Divisions of each of those Parts is prefaced by a brief summary of the topics covered.

3. The Divisions of each Part are followed by a number of Sections in which each of the topics covered is outlined.

4. At the end of each sectional outline, there is a list of Suggested Readings, first in the Macropædia, second in the Micropædia, which is followed by a list of the biographical articles that are relevant to the subjects covered in the outline of that Section.

5. In the topical outline of each Section, cross-references are made, when relevant, to other Sections in the Propædia on which related subjects are treated.

Because it is constructed in this manner, the Propædia provides the reader who wishes to pursue the study of a whole field of knowledge with an easily used guide. The Propædia thus offers readers a more comprehensive and detailed study guide for the use of the *Encyclopædia Britannica* than has ever been furnished before.

To facilitate their use of the Propædia as a study guide, readers should turn to pages 9–15, which follow. Here they will find a synoptic Table of Contents of the Propædia itself, set forth in the order of the 10 Parts, under each of which the component Divisions are listed, and under each Division, the component Sections.

This synoptic Table of Contents gives readers an overview of the Outline of Knowledge as a whole. The introductory essays for each of the 10 Parts, each written by an authority in that field, illuminate the major concerns of that area of human knowledge.

The Propædia, or Outline of Knowledge, helps readers answer for themselves the question that, in its most general form, is as follows: *What can I learn from the Britannica concerning one or another area of human knowledge?* More specifically, the question might be: *What can I learn about the Earth?* or *What can I learn about art?* The reader's interest may be even more specific. In the field of the Earth sciences, the question might be: *What can I learn about the Earth's constituent minerals and rocks?* or *What can I learn about weather and climate?* In the field of art, the question might be: *What can I learn about the theory and classification of the arts?* or *What can I learn about music?*

Another point should be mentioned because, in the view of the Editors, it distinguishes the Fifteenth Edition from all preceding editions.

The Outline of Knowledge presented in this Propædia volume was constructed *before* those articles themselves were named, outlined, commissioned, written, and edited. The outline served as the basis for determining what articles should be written, what their scope should be, how they should be related to other articles, and so on. It was, therefore, in origin a table of *intents* rather than a table of *contents*. It represented the intentions of the Editors in laying down a comprehensive plan for producing a new encyclopaedia, appropriate to the state of human knowledge and learning at the end of the 20th century and looking forward to emergent developments in the century to follow. What was originally, or in the planning stage of the work, a Table of Intents, then subsequently became, after the writing and editing of the articles was completed, a Table of Contents that tries to reflect accurately and faithfully the actual content of the articles.

All preceding editions of *Britannica,* as most other encyclopaedias, have been constructed from classified lists of articles. Such classified lists may vary from one edition to another, as they have from the First Edition of *Britannica* through the Fourteenth, but the variations are relatively minor as compared with the fact that they are all the same in form—nothing but classified lists of articles, as exemplified by the one presented in the Eleventh Edition, already referred to. In sharp contrast to such editorial procedures, the Fifteenth Edition has the distinction of being planned not in accordance with a classified list of articles, but rather in the light of an orderly topical outline of the whole of human knowledge, in the form of the circle of learning that is an *en-cyclo-paedia.*

MORTIMER J. ADLER
Director of Planning

CONTENTS

Part Three. Life on Earth

Part Four. Human Life

Part Five. Human Society

Part Six. Art

Part Seven. Technology

Part Eight. Religion

Part Nine. The History of Mankind

14 Contents

Part Ten. The Branches of Knowledge

Introduction to Part One:
The Universe of the Physicist, the Chemist, and the Astronomer

by Nigel Calder

"Give me matter and I will build a world from it." For 200 years since the philosopher Immanuel Kant uttered it, physicists, chemists, and astronomers have striven to make good that boast. That they can now tell an almost unbroken story of events from the birth of the universe to the origin of life on Earth is the cumulative result of many lifetimes spent in careful observation and experiment. Yet even amid this success in updating the first verses of Genesis, new questions nag. Why does familiar matter adopt the forms it does? Are the laws of nature that are known to us enforced throughout the vast, tumultuous universe? What unimaginable worlds of fire or blackness can nature conjure up, quite different from our own?

When men presume to take the fire of the Sun and put it experimentally in a bottle, they forfeit all hope of certainty and repose. Yet the great quest for control over nature starts gently enough. A child at play with building blocks or sand or a rubber ball is a human mind engaged in discovering how matter behaves. Experiments with the rubber ball, for example, reveal laws of reflection. The child finds that the ball will come back to him only if he projects it accurately at a right angle to a flat surface (wall or floor); otherwise it bounces away from him and another child may grab it and interrupt the research program.

If all grown-up children had abandoned this kind of play, the human species would still believe that the Earth was at the centre of the universe, that the planets were propelled by angel-power, and that thunder was the voice of God. But some adults retained the boundless inquisitiveness of the young. Isaac Newton, not the most modest of discoverers, likened himself to a child playing on the seashore. Critics nowadays refer scathingly to the "expensive toys" of the physicists who want many millions of dollars to build a particle accelerator. Not unfairly—a particle accelerator, for all its awesome complexity and cost, is simply a modern way of continuing the experiments with the rubber ball, to see what happens when the ball is very small and travels almost at the speed of light.

By strange paths, play leads to far-reaching results. After the discovery that an electric current creates magnetism, Michael Faraday made a note to look for electricity from magnetism. He played repeatedly with magnets and wires until, ten years later, he discovered electromagnetic induction. Today, giant turbogenerators confirm his discovery 60 times a second, as they feed electric power to our factories and kitchens. In James Clerk Maxwell's hands, Faraday's ever-changing electric currents transformed themselves into mathematical equations predicting the existence of waves that traveled at the speed of light—indeed *were* light and invisible radiations of a similar kind, including radio waves. Other researchers who were unwittingly taking atoms to pieces came up with a beam of electrons, which inventors turned into a magic pencil;

today those waves and electrons enable lesser men to preen themselves on television screens in 260,000,000 homes.

In this latter part of the 20th century, a word-association test for *physicist* may very well evoke *bomb*. By coincidence, investigators of the nature of matter and energy stumbled upon a way of breaking open the storehouse of energy in the nucleus of the atom just at the time the human species was entering a period of unprecedented warfare. The swarms of nuclear-powered submarines that cruise with nuclear-tipped, city-killing missiles are a grim enough outcome of the "game." The fact remains that the heart of physics itself is not directed to any such purpose but is an open, cooperative effort by scientists of all nations to understand the material universe we live in.

We inhabit an electric world. It is true that gravity stops us from falling headfirst into the abyss of space; true also that the daylight that powers all life comes from the nuclear reactor that we call the Sun. But of the great set of natural forces known to the physicist—gravitational, nuclear, and electromagnetic—the last, electromagnetism, is the chief governor of events on Earth.

It operates so discreetly, though, that when men started rubbing amber on their sleeves and found it attracted dust, or considered the seeming magic of the north-pointing lodestone, nothing suggested that these were more than curiosities. There was laughter when Benjamin Franklin said that lightning was electric—until he proved it. Nothing suggested that the colour, quality, and chemical behaviour of all familiar matter would be explained by research in electricity and magnetism. But that is in the nature of physics: you ponder the falling of an apple and realize what holds the planets in their courses; you look to see what happens when you pass electric currents through a gas and, in due course, you find out what holds a stone together and why grass is green.

A series of discoveries in the late 19th and early 20th centuries illuminated the hidden mechanisms of our electric world like star shells on a dark night. Diligent work by chemists had shown that all matter was composed of vast numbers of atoms, different for each chemical element and capable of combining in predictable ways to make molecules and crystals. Indeed there was a remarkable pattern in the so-called "periodic table": when the chemical elements were listed by weight, it turned out that elements 3, 11, and 19 . . . all had similar properties; 4, 12, and 20 . . . were also very much alike, and so on.

This pattern made sense only when the physicists discovered the construction of atomic matter. An atom consists of a heavy nucleus surrounded by a number of lightweight electrons exactly neutralizing the electric charge on the nucleus. The electrons group themselves around the nucleus in "shells," like the layers of an onion, each shell being capable of accommodating a definite number of electrons. The outward face of the atom, its outermost shell of electrons, is crucial in determining its chemical behaviour. The number of electrons to be fitted in depends on the charge on the nucleus. In some elements, the metals, there are only one or two easily detachable electrons in the outermost shell. Other elements, the most reactive nonmetals, fall short by only one or two electrons in having a complete outermost shell. These "surplus" and "missing" electrons create a supply-and-demand situation in which atoms combine chemically by exchanging or sharing electrons. The repetition of chemical properties throughout the periodic table arises as one shell of electrons is completed and the next one begins to fill.

The mechanisms sketched in these last few sentences account for almost all the chemical behaviour of all the matter on Earth. The electrical and magnetic behaviour of materials also depends on the arrangements of electrons in their atoms and, in some cases, on the combined effects of many atoms packed together in a crystal. The strength of the chemical bonds formed by electrons, and the related forces between molecules, determine whether materials are solids, liquids, or gases; and they help to fix the strength and flexibility of solids, but in this case the explanations are complicated by the invisible flaws that exist in all materials. The colour of materials is explicable by the "jumps," from one position to another in the vicinity of an atom, which the rules allow an electron to make as the atom, molecule, or crystal absorbs or emits light of particular energy, or colour. Make the same electrons in vast numbers of atoms "jump" the same way simultaneously and you have a very intense laser beam.

Light and its invisible counterparts—radio waves, infrared, ultraviolet, and X-rays—are the purest form of energy. These "electromagnetic radiations" are created by the jerking of electrons, sometimes quite gently, as in a radio antenna, and sometimes very fiercely, as when a beam of fast-moving electrons is suddenly halted by the target in an X-ray tube. The normal "jumps" of electrons in atoms are of intermediate intensity. All these radiant forms of energy can travel through empty space, for example from the Sun to the Earth.

But energy can readily change from one form to another. Sunlight captured by green leaves is converted into the chemical energy of plant-stuff. Coal is plant-stuff buried millions of years ago when continents collided, and a boiler can convert the chemical energy of coal into a scalding jet of steam that turns the blades of a turbine—these are forms of kinetic energy, the energy of directed movement. Using Faraday's trick, the turbine can generate electrical energy. At the end of this chain of transformations, you can switch on the electrical energy and reconvert it to light energy, thereby enjoying the benefits of sunlight after the Sun has set.

The vibrations of sound and the gravitational energy of water about to cascade down a mountainside are other forms of energy. Sooner or later, though, a shout dies away, water comes to rest, the light from your electric bulb is absorbed in the wallpaper. Where has the energy gone? It has been taken up in those random motions of atoms and molecules that we call heat. All energy degrades to meaningless heat eventually.

Unless there were continuous supplies of new energy,

life and indeed all interesting activity in the universe would quickly cease. For example, your brain is kept functioning by food—chemical energy produced by sunlight just in the past few months. Those new supplies of energy come from the transformation of matter into energy.

The Sun is a very ordinary star, lying in the suburbs of a galaxy consisting of about 100,000,000,000 stars; we see the rather flat cross section of the galaxy as the Milky Way, a brushstroke of light across the night sky. There is nothing special, even, about our Galaxy; it is just one of vast numbers of galaxies scattered like ships in a great ocean of space.

The universe is a battleground between gravity and nuclear forces. To make a star, gravity sweeps together a mass of hydrogen gas; it becomes hot and nuclear reactions begin. The nuclei of hydrogen atoms combine together to make heavier elements almost, but not quite, as heavy as the sum of the hydrogen nuclei that went into them. The little bit of matter that is lost is converted into a relatively immense amount of energy. It would blow the star apart but for the strenuous restraint of gravity. A balance is struck, and the size and brightness of a star depends on its mass and on how much of its nuclear fuel has been burned. Fortunately, our star, the Sun, is a slow-burner; nevertheless, inexorable physical changes billions of years from now will make the Sun grow to fill the whole of our sky and swallow the Earth.

In a star more massive than the Sun, this "burning" of nuclear fuel proceeds faster and culminates in a vast explosion called a supernova. In the explosion, nuclear reactions proceed apace and make all the different chemical elements. The diverse atoms, heavier than hydrogen, of which our own bodies are constructed, were made in stars that exploded before the Sun was formed. Some of the heavy material was left swirling around the newborn Sun and made the Earth. Radioactive energy stored in some of the elements provided an internal source of heat for the Earth that accounts for volcanoes, earthquakes, and the slow movements of continents. Sunlight stirred the materials on the surface of the Earth into chemical activity. Eventually this activity became organized in peculiar ways, and life began.

So far, so good. But there are new mysteries that are "out of this world," in the sense that matter and energy are involved in events far more violent than anything normally encountered on the Earth or even in the Sun. The paramount questions with which physicists are now wrestling can be paraphrased as follows: Why is hydrogen the raw material of the universe? Experiments with the nucleus of the hydrogen atom—the proton— are undertaken in the big accelerators that transform the stuff of the atomic nucleus into bizarre, short-lived particles. These particles have properties, similar to electric charge, called the hypercharge and the baryon number. For example, the proton itself has, besides an electric charge of +1, a hypercharge of +1 and a baryon number of 1. However the particles may transform themselves in violent interactions, the totals of charge, hypercharge, and baryon number do not change.

Attempting to find out why this partial order remains amid the confused varieties of nuclear matter, theorists are led to the idea that the particles we see consist of combinations of other, quite different particles that they have named quarks. An early success of this theory was the prediction of the existence of a new combination, a particle called the omega minus that eventually turned up in 1964 during an experiment with the big machine at the Brookhaven National Laboratory, Long Island, N.Y. The quarks themselves have not been discovered at the time of writing.

The next big leap in understanding may well come when the theory of how small pieces of matter behave is blended with the theory of gravity, which at present concerns the huge pieces of matter that make up our universe of galaxies, stars, and planets. With such a "unified" theory physicists may at last be able to answer that question about the raw material of the universe—why hydrogen? At the same time, we shall perhaps come to understand why matter was formed in the "big bang," with which (as many astronomers now suppose) the universe came into existence some 10,000,000,000 years ago, or why the "big bang" was not merely a "big flash."

Even so fundamental an advance would not exhaust the opportunity for fresh discovery in the physical sciences. Another set of pregnant problems results from very strange objects recently discovered in the sky, namely "hot" galaxies, quasars and pulsars. The quasars, in particular, are compact objects of such extraordinary energy that existing laws of physics seem scarcely able to account for them. The pulsars, which flash many times a minute, are also very odd, but less baffling. They are evidently remnants of exploded stars that have collapsed to the enormous density of the material of the atomic nucleus. If an ocean liner were compressed to the density of a pulsar, it would be no bigger than a grain of sand.

The evidence of the pulsars encourages a further idea—one of the strangest in the whole history of man's study of matter and energy. In a pulsar, nuclear forces prevent collapse to even greater densities. But if the collapsed star were even more massive, gravity would be stronger and it would overwhelm even the nuclear forces. Then there would be nothing to stop the process until the whole star had collapsed to smaller than a peanut. Through the intense gravitational field thus set up, no light could escape, and the star would in effect disappear from the universe. Only its gravity would remain, like the grin of the Cheshire Cat in *Alice in Wonderland,* and, if a space traveler ran into one of these "black holes," he too would be drawn to the same invisible kernel, there to disappear forever—or at least until the laws of physics change.

The possibility that such black holes exist holds out a hope of explaining the quasars as objects of this kind from which material somehow "bounces" out. But that is only a little comfort when scientists have now to reexamine the theory of gravity, which they thought Einstein had cleared up 60 years ago, and to work out the implications of a universe peppered with black holes where the familiar laws of nature are unlikely to apply. There is even the uncomfortable suggestion that our whole universe may be just a big black hole in someone else's universe! Physics, the master science, cannot evade these new battles of the mind.

Part One. Matter and Energy

Three points should be noted about the scope of Part One and its relations to other parts.

The sciences of physics, chemistry, and astronomy have themselves been the object of historical and analytical studies regarding their nature, scope, methods, and interrelations. Part Ten, on the branches of knowledge, is concerned with such studies. The outline in Section 10/32 of Part Ten deals with the sciences of physics, chemistry, and astronomy and treats their history, their nature and scope, and their principal problems and interrelations.

The design and operation of observational and experimental instruments are important in the development of the physical sciences. The treatment of scientific instrumentation is placed in Section 723 of Part Seven, on technology.

Accounts of the several kinds of mathematics used in observation and experiments, and in the derivation and application of physical theories, are set forth in Division II of Part Ten.

The three increasingly complementary physical sciences of physics, chemistry, and astronomy house the knowledge and the organizing theories about matter in all its dimensions, from subatomic particles to the cosmos, about all the states of matter, all the forms of energy, and all the interrelations of matter and energy.

Division I. Atoms: Atomic Nuclei and Elementary Particles

The outlines in the two sections of Division I deal with subatomic and atomic physics.

Section 111. The Structure and Properties of Atoms

A. The atomic nature of matter

  1. The atom as consisting of the nucleus surrounded by electrons, the arrangement and behaviour of which determine atomic interactions

  2. Early philosophical speculations on the possible atomic nature of matter

  3. The scientific evidence for the existence and the nature of atoms

    a. Developments in chemistry

    b. The development of spectroscopy and the discovery of atomic spectra

    c. The discovery of the electron as a particle and as a component of all matter

    d. The discovery of X-rays

    e. The discovery of the radioactive transformation of one element into another

    f. The Brownian movement of suspended particles

    g. The development of mass spectrometry

    h. The development of scattering and resonance studies with atomic and molecular beams

  4. Models of atomic structure

    a. The Rutherford model of the atom

    b. The Bohr–Sommerfeld model

    c. The wave-mechanical theory of the electronic structure of the atom

B. Atomic weights

1. Variations in atomic weight as a result of variations in isotopic composition

2. Significance of atomic weights in chemistry

3. Atomic weight scales

4. Methods used for determining atomic weights: chemical methods, physical methods

C. Atomic spectra and the electronic structures of the atom

1. Atomic spectra: their significance and interpretation

   a. The spectrum of the hydrogen atom

   b. The emission spectra of singly and multiply ionized atoms

   c. Atomic absorption spectra

   d. The effects of magnetic fields and the effects of electric fields on atomic spectra

   e. Intensities, isotope shifts, and fine and hyperfine structures of atomic spectral lines as related to atomic structure

2. Theories of the origin of atomic spectra in quantized electronic transitions: the classical Bohr theory, wave-mechanical interpretations

D. X-rays and atomic structure

1. General X-ray phenomena

2. The theory of X-rays and their spectra

   a. The structure of the atom as related to the emission of characteristic X-rays, absorption edges, fluorescence yield, mesic atoms

   b. Continuous X-rays and bremsstrahlung; *i.e.,* the radiation produced by the sudden retardation of a fast-moving charged particle in an intense electrical field

3. Detection and measurement of X-rays

4. Applications of X-rays in biological, medical, industrial, and scientific fields
   [see 423.B. and 723.G.8.]

5. Diffraction of X-rays by crystals
   [see 125.A.2.]

E. The concept of antimatter

1. General properties of antimatter

2. Production of antiparticles in high-energy collisions

3. Invariance of the laws of physics under charge conjugation, an operation in relativistic mechanics that transforms every particle into its antiparticle

4. Speculations about the possible existence and role of antimatter in the universe

F. The fundamental physical constants: dimensional and dimensionless constants

1. Measurement of the physical constants

2. Interrelationships among the constants

3. Standards of measurement

Suggested reading in the *Encyclopædia Britannica:*

MACROPAEDIA: Major articles dealing with the structure and properties of atoms

Analysis and Measurement, Physical and Chemical
Atoms: Their Structure, Properties, and Component Particles
Physical Principles and Concepts
Physical Sciences, The

MICROPAEDIA: Selected entries of reference information

<u>General subjects</u>

atom models:
Aufbau principle
Bohr atomic model
electronic
 configuration
octet
Rutherford atomic
 model
shell atomic model

*experimental effects
 results:*
Auger effect
Brownian
 movement
electron
 paramagnetic
 resonance

Franck–Hertz
 experiment
Fraunhofer lines
ionization
 potential
magnetic
 resonance
spectral line series
Stark effect
Stern–Gerlach
 experiment
Zeeman effect

*fundamental
 constants:*
molar gas constant
Planck's constant

laws and principles:
Bose–Einstein
 statistics
complementarity
 principle
Fermi–Dirac
 statistics
Pauli exclusion
 principle
quantum
 mechanics
Schrödinger
 equation
selection rule
uncertainty
 principle

wave–particle
 duality
other:
antimatter
atom
atomic mass
atomic radius
energy state
excitation
matter
orbital
positronium
quantum
quantum number
transition
X ray
zero-point energy

<u>Biographies</u>

See Section 10/32 of Part Ten

INDEX: See entries under all of the terms above

Section 112.   The Atomic Nucleus and Elementary Particles

A. The structure of the atomic nucleus and general nuclear phenomena

  1. General properties of atomic nuclei

    a. Mass

    b. Charge: atomic number

    c. Radius

    d. Spin

    e. Magnetic moment: nuclear magnetic resonance phenomena

    f. Electric quadrupole moment

  2. Components of atomic nuclei

    a. Neutrons
      [see D., below]

    b. Protons

    c. Other possible short- and long-lived components

  3. Isotopes: atomic species with the same atomic number but with different atomic masses
    [see B., below]

  4. Systematic relationships between nuclear masses and nuclear binding energies

  5. Nuclear models and the properties of nuclear states

  6. Theories of nuclear structure and nuclear binding force

  7. General nuclear phenomena and reactions
    [see C. and E., below]

  8. The formation and evolution of the atomic nuclei in the universe

B. Isotopes: atomic species with the same atomic number but with different atomic masses

  1. Classification of isotopes or nuclides

  2. Isotopic composition of the elements

  3. Formation of isotopes by nuclear reactions
    [see E., below]

4. Effects of isotopic substitution on physical and chemical properties of substances

5. Chemical and physical separation of isotopes

    a. Mass spectrometry

    b. Other methods of separation; *e.g.,* diffusion, centrifugal separation, thermal diffusion

6. Applications of radioactive and stable isotopes
[see 242.D.2 and 723.G.8.]

C. Radioactive nuclei: their properties and their radiations

1. The phenomenon of radioactivity

2. Types of radioactivity

3. Sources of radioactivity: naturally occurring radioactive elements, particle bombardment

4. Interaction of radiation with matter
[see I., below]

5. The energy release associated with radioactive decay

6. Nuclear models used to explain nuclear binding: the liquid drop model, the shell model, the unified model

7. Rates of radioactive transitions

    a. Exponential decay law

    b. Alpha decay

    c. Beta decay

    d. Gamma transition

8. Applications of radioactivity
[see 723.G.8.]

9. Measurement and characterization of radioactivity
[see I.4., below]

D. The neutron as a component of the nucleus and in nuclear reactions

1. Properties of neutrons

2. Sources of neutrons

3. Manipulation and control of neutrons

4. Nuclear reactions produced by neutrons

5. Neutron detection based on the secondary effects of nuclear reactions

E. Reactions of atomic nuclei

1. The classification of nuclear reactions

    a. The types of nuclear reactions classified according to the kind of bombarding radiation or particles

    b. The types of nuclear reactions classified according to the nuclear processes involved or according to their products

2. The energy relationships of nuclear reactions

3. Theories and models of nuclear reactions

F. The splitting of atomic nuclei by nuclear fission

1. Phenomena of nuclear fission

    a. Spontaneous and induced fission reactions

    b. Products of nuclear fission

    c. The energy released in fission

2. Fission chain reactions: the critical mass

    a. Nuclear explosions: nuclear, or atomic, bombs

    b. Controlled nuclear fission

3. Nuclear models and theories of nuclear fission: liquid drop model, adiabatic models, statistical models

G. The fusion of atomic nuclei

   1. Phenomena of nuclear fusion

   2. Nuclear fusion reactions

     a. General types of fusion reactions

     b. The energy released in fusion reactions

     c. Requirements for intensive fusion reactions

   3. Occurrence of thermonuclear reactions

     a. Thermonuclear reactions in the Sun and the stars

     b. Thermonuclear explosions: the hydrogen, or thermonuclear, bomb

   4. Basic conditions required for a thermonuclear reactor

     a. The formation of a suitable plasma

     b. The confinement and control of high-temperature plasma

   5. The possible approaches to controlled fusion: prospects for the future

H. Subatomic, or elementary, particles

   1. Development of the concept of subatomic particles as the fundamental units of matter and energy

     a. The discovery of the various particles

     b. Yukawa mesons and the theory of nuclear forces

     c. Advances in quantum field theory: renormalization theory, dispersion theory

     d. The known elementary particles

   2. The basic forces associated with particle interactions

   3. Systems for classifying the elementary particles

     a. According to the forces that influence them

     b. According to the kind of statistics they follow

     c. According to their particle–antiparticle symmetries

     d. According to stability

     e. According to charge multiplets

     f. According to unitary symmetry, or the SU(3) classification

     g. According to charged-hypercharge multiplets

   4. Elementary particles and the laws of conservation and symmetry

     a. The theory of subatomic particles and the quantum mechanical symmetry operations

     b. Dynamic symmetries: space and time inversion

     c. Violation of conservation laws: charge conjugation, time reversal, parity

     d. Internal symmetries

   5. Sources of the unstable elementary particles

     a. Formation of resonances in high-energy accelerators

     b. Production by cosmic ray interactions

   6. Relations of the weak interactions to strong and electromagnetic interactions described by conserved current and algebra of current

   7. Other particles suggested by contemporary theoretical ideas

   8. Reactions of elementary particles with atoms

   9. Theories of nuclear structure and nuclear forces involving the elementary particles

I. Effects of the passage of nuclear, or elementary, particles, nuclear radiations, or ionizing radiation through matter

   1. The fundamental processes involved when energetic particles or radiations interact with or pass through matter

     a. The passage of electromagnetic waves and their interaction with atomic structure

b. The passage of particles or radiations through matter

2. Secondary and tertiary effects of radiation: physical effects, molecular activation and related phenomena, chemical effects, biological effects

3. Utilization of high-energy radiation in biological, medical, and technological fields

4. The use of fundamental processes of interaction between radiation and matter for the detection and characterization of nuclear and elementary processes

a. Mechanisms of detection systems: ionization and charge collection, conversion of the distributed energy of the primary ionizing particle into light

b. Properties of ionization media

c. Major types of radiation detectors: scintillation counters, ionization detectors, spark chambers, cloud chambers, bubble chambers
[see 723.F.7.]

d. Applications of radiation detectors in science, technology, and industry
[see 723.G.8.]

Suggested reading in the *Encyclopædia Britannica:*

MACROPAEDIA: Major articles dealing with the atomic nucleus and elementary particles

Analysis and Measurement, Physical and Chemical
Atoms: Their Structure, Properties, and Component Particles
Physical Principles and Concepts
Physical Sciences, The
Radiation
Subatomic Particles

MICROPAEDIA: Selected entries of reference information

General subjects

conservation laws and symmetry:
charge conjugation
charge conservation
CP violation
Eightfold Way
energy, conservation of
gauge theory
isospin
momentum, conservation of
parity
spin
time reversal
nuclear interactions:
excitation
fission product
neutron capture
nuclear energy
nuclear fission
nuclear fusion
nuclear reaction
nucleosynthesis
spallation
spontaneous fission
thermonuclear reaction
transmutation
nuclear structure:
binding energy

collective model
compound-nucleus model
isotope
liquid-drop model
magic number
magnetic resonance
nuclear magnetic resonance
nuclear model
nuclide
shell nuclear model
particle interactions:
cross section
fundamental interaction
pair production
proton–proton reaction
scattering
radiation detection:
cloud chamber
coincidence counting
ionization chamber
scintillation counter
solid-state detector
spark chamber

radioactivity:
activity
alpha decay
background radiation
beta decay
decay constant
fallout
gamma decay
gamma ray
half-life
isomer
metastable state
radioactive isotope
radioactive series
radioactivity
subatomic particles:
alpha particle
antiparticle
antiproton
baryon
boson
electron
hadron
hyperon
J/psi particle
lepton
magnetic monopole
meson
muon
neutrino

neutron
photon
positron
proton
quark
quasiparticle
subatomic particle
thermal neutron
W particle
zeta particle
other:
bremsstrahlung
Cherenkov radiation
Compton effect
de Broglie wave
electron diffraction
electron optics
Millikan oil-drop experiment
neutron optics
quantum electrodynamics
radiation
Stern–Gerlach experiment
synchrotron radiation
unified field theory
wave function

Biographies
See Section 10/32 of Part Ten

INDEX: See entries under all of the terms above

Division II.   **Energy, Radiation, and the States and Transformation of Matter**
[For Part One headnote see page 21.]

Division I deals with modern advances in subatomic and atomic physics.

The outlines in the first three sections of Division II treat, respectively, chemical elements, chemical compounds, and chemical reactions. The last five sections of this division are concerned with heat, thermodynamics, and the nonsolid states of matter; with the solid state of matter; with the mechanics of particles, rigid bodies, and deformable bodies; with electricity and magnetism; and with waves and wave motion.

Section 121.   **Chemical Elements: Periodic Variation in Their Properties**

A. The systematic classification of the elements on the basis of their chemical and physical properties and atomic structures: the periodic law of the elements

B. The groups of the chemical elements in the long form of the periodic table: their occurrence, history, physical and chemical properties, principal compounds, production, and uses

  1. Hydrogen, its forms, isotopes, and compounds: water, its structure, forms, and physical and chemical properties

  2. The alkali metals, or the Group Ia elements of the periodic table: lithium, sodium, potassium, rubidium, cesium, francium

  3. The alkaline-earth metals, or the Group IIa elements of the periodic table: beryllium, magnesium, calcium, strontium, barium, radium

  4. The boron group of the elements, or the Group IIIa elements of the periodic table: boron, aluminum, gallium, indium, thallium

  5. The carbon group of the elements, or the Group IVa elements of the periodic table: carbon, silicon, germanium, tin, lead

  6. The nitrogen group of the elements, or the Group Va elements of the periodic table: nitrogen, phosphorus, arsenic, antimony, bismuth

  7. The oxygen group of the elements, or the Group VIa elements of the periodic table: oxygen, sulfur, selenium, tellurium, polonium

  8. The halogen elements, or the Group VIIa elements of the periodic table: fluorine, chlorine, bromine, iodine, astatine

  9. The noble gases, or the Group 0 elements of the periodic table, formerly called the inert gases: helium, neon, argon, krypton, xenon, radon

  10. The zinc group elements, or the Group IIb elements of the periodic table: zinc, cadmium, mercury

  11. The transition elements: elements with partly filled d or f orbitals occupying the middle portion of the periodic table

    a. Individual elements of the first transition series: titanium, vanadium, chromium, manganese, iron, cobalt, nickel, copper

      b. Individual elements of the second and third transition series: zirconium and hafnium, niobium and tantalum, molybdenum and tungsten, technetium and rhenium, ruthenium and osmium, rhodium and iridium, palladium and platinum, silver and gold

      c. The lanthanide elements
[see B.12., below]

      d. The actinide elements
[see B.13., below]

  12. The rare-earth, or lanthanide, elements of the periodic table: scandium, yttrium, lanthanum, cerium, praseodymium, neodymium, promethium, samarium, europium, gadolinium, terbium, dysprosium, holmium, erbium, thulium, ytterbium, lutetium
[see 724.C.3.u.]

  13. The actinide elements of the periodic table: actinium, thorium, protactinium, uranium, neptunium, plutonium, americium, curium, berkelium, californium, einsteinium, fermium, mendelevium, nobelium, lawrencium

  14. The transactinide elements of the periodic table: rutherfordium (or kurchatovium), hahnium (or nielsbohrium), element 106, element 107

C. Other classifications of the elements or groups of them

  1. Metals; semimetals, or metalloids; nonmetals

  2. Stable and radioactive elements

  3. Native and combined elements

  4. Noble metals, including the platinum group of metals

  5. Synthetic elements: transuranium elements

  6. Biologically active or essential elements
[see 335.A.3.]

  7. Technologically significant elements
[see 724.C.3.]

D. The origin of the elements and their relative abundances in nature

  1. On Earth

      a. In the crust
[see also 214.C.]

      b. In the hydrosphere
[see also 214.F. and 222.B. and C.]

      c. In the atmosphere
[see also 214.G. and 221.A.1.c.]

      d. In the biosphere

  2. In the solar system
[see also 133.A.]

  3. In the stars
[see also 132.D.7.b.]

  4. In the rest of the universe
[see also 131.A.1.a.]

Suggested reading in the *Encyclopædia Britannica:*

MACROPAEDIA: Major articles dealing with chemical elements: periodic variation in their properties

    Chemical Compounds
    Chemical Elements

MICROPAEDIA: Selected entries of reference information

General subjects

actinide elements:	cerium	nobelium	cesium
actinide	einsteinium	plutonium	francium
actinium	fermium	protactinium	lithium
americium	lawrencium	thorium	potassium
berkelium	mendelevium	uranium	rubidium
californium	neptunium	*alkali metals:*	sodium
		alkali metal	

Biographies
  See Section 10/32 of Part Ten

INDEX: See entries under all of the terms above

Section 122.   **Chemical Compounds: Molecular Structure and Chemical Bonding**

A. The theory of molecular structure: its history and development

  1. Early concepts of molecular structure

  2. Quantum mechanical and electrostatic approaches to the theory of molecular structure

  3. Molecular bonds and shapes

    a. Spatial arrangement of atoms: chains, rings, chelates, polymers

    b. Isomers: structural isomers, stereoisomers

  4. Time-dependency properties of molecules

  5. Molecular structure and its relation to the properties of bulk matter

    a. The physical properties of matter as affected by molecular size, shape, and interactions, and interactions of molecules with radiations and fields

    b. The chemical behaviour of matter as determined by the nature of molecular bonds

    c. The chemical, physical, and biochemical properties of a substance inferred from its known or postulated molecular structure

B. Experimental and theoretical procedures for the determination of molecular structures

   1. The separation, isolation, and purification of chemical substances based on chemical equilibria and rate phenomena

      a. By volatility differences: distillation, sublimation, evaporization

      b. By chromatography: liquid phase, gas phase, thin layer

      c. By solubility differences: precipitation, crystallization, zone melting, solvent extraction

      d. By ion-exchange reactions

      e. By electrophoresis and electrolytic methods

      f. By mechanical methods: filtration, sedimentation, sieving, flotation, centrifugation

   2. Classical methods of qualitative and quantitative analysis

   3. Instrumental methods used to identify functional groups, molecular sub-units, and structural features

      a. Spectrochemical methods: microwave, infrared, ultraviolet, Raman spectroscopy, colorimetry, atomic absorption spectroscopy

      b. Mass spectrometry

      c. Magnetic resonance spectrometry

      d. Thermometric methods: thermogravimetry, calorimetry, cryoscopy

      e. Radiochemical methods: radiometric analysis, activation analysis, isotopic dilution

      f. Electrochemical methods: potentiometry, polarography, electrodeposition, oscillometry

   4. Diffraction methods for determining molecular structures: electron, X-ray, and neutron beam diffraction

   5. Physical methods used to determine optical activity, magnetic susceptibility, calorific values, heat of combustion, activation energy, and reaction rates

   6. The synthesis and characterization of derivatives, or specifically modified molecules

   7. The determination of molecular weight based on thermodynamic theory, on transport phenomena, and on known spatial arrangements of atoms in the solid state

   8. The principles of conformational analysis as related to molecular structure

   9. The scattering of molecular beams and its usefulness in the study of molecular interactions

C. Spectra of molecules

   1. The theory of molecular spectra

   2. Types of molecular spectra: microwave, infrared, Raman, visible, and ultraviolet spectra

   3. The interpretation of molecular band spectra in determining molecular structure

D. The theory of chemical bonding: its development and experimental bases

   1. Nonquantum treatments of chemical bonding

      a. Early ideas and concepts of chemical bonding: valence

      b. The early electronic theory of bonding

         i. The nature of ionic bond: shell theory, ion pairs

         ii. The nature of covalent and coordinate bond: the octet

      c. Application of the quantum theory to atomic structure

   2. Quantum-mechanical treatment of chemical bonding

      a. Atomic and molecular orbital concepts

      b. Bonding in the hydrogen molecule

      c. Bonding in simple polyatomic molecules

      d. Quantum-mechanical calculations

   3. Other bonding effects: hydrogen bonding; metallic bonds in metals, intermetallic compounds, and coordination compounds; bonds in crystals, in weak associations, and in electron-deficient compounds

   4. Experimental observation of chemical bonding

     5. Anomalous molecular structures, or molecular fragments with apparently anomalous valences: free radicals, carbenes, carbanions, carbonium ions

E. Systems of classification of chemical compounds or substances

     1. By their elemental composition or molecular structure: organic, inorganic, organometallic, and nonstoichiometric compounds

     2. By their bond type: ionic, covalent, and coordination compounds

     3. By their chemical reactivity: acids, bases, and salts; oxidizing and reducing agents

     4. By their physical state: gas, liquid, and solid

     5. By their origin: natural and synthetic

F. Inorganic compounds

     1. Nomenclature of binary, ternary, and coordination compounds

     2. Structural classification of inorganic compounds

         a. Salts

         b. Oxides, anhydrides, acids, and bases

         c. Coordination compounds

         d. Organometallic compounds
           [see G.1.c., below]

         e. Catenates

         f. Inorganic polymers

         g. Special nonmetallic derivatives

     3. Methods of preparation of inorganic compounds

     4. Reactions of inorganic compounds; *e.g.,* acid–base, substitution, isomerization, oxidation–reduction, addition

G. Organic compounds

     1. The major groups of organic compounds: their nomenclature, chemical and physical properties, synthesis, occurrence, reactions, and analysis

         a. Hydrocarbons: aliphatic and aromatic

         b. Organic halogen compounds: alkyl, alkenyl, and alkynyl halides; aryl halides

         c. Organometallic compounds

         d. Alcohols, phenols, and ethers

         e. Carboxylic acids and their derivatives

         f. Aldehydes, ketones, and their derivatives

         g. Organic nitrogen compounds

         h. Organic sulfur compounds

         i. Organic phosphorus compounds

         j. Organic silicon compounds

         k. Heterocyclic compounds

         l. Oils, fats, and waxes

         m. Carbohydrates

         n. Amino acids, proteins, and peptides

         o. Isoprenoids and terpenes

         p. Steroids and their derivatives

         q. Nucleotides and nucleosides

         r. Nucleic acids: DNA and RNA

         s. Alkaloids

         t. Dyestuffs and pigments

         u. Organic polymers

2. Preparation and purification of organic compounds

3. Physical properties of organic compounds

4. Reactions of organic compounds: addition, substitution, displacement, hydrolysis, pyrolysis, condensation, polymerization, molecular rearrangement

Suggested reading in the *Encyclopædia Britannica:*

MACROPAEDIA: Major articles dealing with chemical compounds: molecular structure and chemical bonding

Biochemical Components of Organisms
Chemical Compounds
Molecules: Their Structure, Properties, and Forms
Physical Principles and Concepts

MICROPAEDIA: Selected entries of reference information

General subjects

alcohols and phenols:
alcohol
amyl alcohol
butyl alcohol
catechol
cetyl alcohol
chlorophenol
cresol
ethyl alcohol
fusel oil
glycerol
glycol
methyl alcohol
naphthol
phenol
phytol
picric acid
propyl alcohol
pyrogallol
resorcinol
aldehydes and
ketones:
acetone
aldehyde
benzaldehyde
ethyl acetoacetate
formaldehyde
ketone
alkaloids:
alkaloid
atropine
caffeine
cocaine
codeine
curare
ephedrine
heroin
ibogaine
mescaline
morphine
nicotine
piperine
quinidine
quinine

scopolamine
theophylline
amino acids, proteins,
and peptides:
amino acid
collagen
glutamic acid
glutamine
gluten
histidine
histone
hydroxyproline
insulin
keratin
myoglobin
pepsin
peptide
prolamin
protein
proteolytic enzyme
renin
scleroprotein
serotonin
transaminase
carbides:
carbide
silicon carbide
tungsten carbide
carbohydrates:
carbohydrate
cellulose
disaccharide
glucose
glycoside
monosaccharide
pectin
polysaccharide
sugar
carboxylic acids:
acetic acid
benzoic acid
butyric acid
carboxylic acid
citric acid
fatty acid

formic acid
gallic acid
lactic acid
maleic acid
malonic acid
oxalic acid
peroxy acid
salicylic acid
soap
stearic acid
succinic acid
tartaric acid
coordination
compounds:
chelate
coordination
compound
coordination
number
effective atomic
number
ligand
ligand field theory
metal carbonyl
dyes and pigments:
alizarin
anthraquinone
anthraquinone dye
auxochrome
azo dye
carmine
chlorophyll
chromophore
cochineal
cyanine dye
dye
flavonoid
indigo
lake
melanin
porphyrin
Prussian blue
quercitron bark
triphenylmethanedye
ultramarine

esters:
ester
ethyl acetoacetate
lactone
polyester ethers:
ether
ethylether
polyether
heterocyclic
compounds:
coumarin
furan
imidazole
indole
lactone
melamine
purine
pyran
pyrazine
pyrazole
pyridine
pyrimidine
pyrrole
quinoline
thiazine
thiazole
thiophene
hydrocarbons:
acetylene
benzene
biphenyl
butadiene
butane
butene
ethane
ethylene
hydrocarbon
methane
naphthalene
olefin
paraffin
hydrocarbon
propane
styrene

toluene
xylene
inorganic acids and
  oxides:
  acid
  carbon dioxide
  carbon monoxide
  Dry Ice
  hydrogen chloride
  hydrogen cyanide
  hydrogen ion
  nitric acid
  nitric oxide
  nitrous acid
  nitrous oxide
  oxide
  phosphoric acid
  phosphorous acid
  rare-earth metal
  silica gel
  silicic acid
  sulfur oxide
  sulfuric acid
  water glass
inorganic nitrogen
  compounds:
  ammonia
  ammonium
    hydroxide
  azide
  hydrazine
  hydroxylamine
isoprenoids and
  terpenes:
  abietic acid
  camphor
  carotene
  isoprene
  limonene
  menthol
  pinene
  terpene
methods of chemical
  analysis:
  assaying
  chemical
    precipitation
  chromatography
  colorimetry
  countercurrent
    distribution
  differential thermal
    analysis
  electrophoresis
  gas
    chromatography
  gel
    chromatography
  gravimetric
    analysis
  iodine value

nephelometry and
  turbidimetry
paper
  chromatography
polarimetry
polarography
qualitative
  chemical analysis
quantitative
  chemical analysis
spectrochemical
  analysis
thin-layer
  chromatography
titration
volumetric
  analysis
molecular bonds and
  shapes:
  configuration
  conformation
  diastereoisomer
  enantiomorph
  isomerism
  optical activity
  racemate
  resolution
  strain theory
  tautomerism
nucleic acids and
  their components:
  adenine
  adenosine
    triphosphate
  cytosine
  deoxyribonucleic
    acid
  guanine
  nuclease
  nucleic acid
  nucleoside
  nucleotide
  ribonucleic acid
  thymine
  uracil
oils, fats, and waxes:
  babassu palm
  castor oil
  Chinese wax
  cod-liver oil
  cohune oil
  copra
  cottonseed
  essential oil
  fat
  fish oil
  grease
  lard
  linseed
  lipid
  oil
  phospholipid

pine oil
sperm oil
spermaceti
tallow
triglyceride
turpentine oil
wax
whale oil
organic halogen
  compounds:
  acid halide
  aldrin
  benzene
    hexachloride
  carbon
    tetrachloride
  chloral
  chloral hydrate
  chlordane
  chlorobenzene
  chloroform
  chlorotrifluoro-
    ethylene
  cyanogen halide
  DDT
  dichlorobenzene
  ethyl chloride
  ethylene bromide
  ethylene chloride
  Freon
  halocarbon
  halon
  iodoform
  methyl bromide
  methyl chloride
  methylene chloride
  phosgene
  polychlorinated
    biphenyl
  tear gas
  tetrachloroethane
  tetrachloroethylene
  tetrafluoroethylene
  Toxaphene
  trichloroethane
  trichloroethylene
  vinyl chloride
  vinylidene chloride
organic nitrogen,
  sulfur, or
  phosphorus
  compounds:
  amide
  amine
  aniline
  azo compound
  benzidine
  biotin
  choline
  diazonium salt
  dimethoate
  ethanolamine

isocyanide
nitrile
nitro compound
nitrobenzene
nitroglycerin
nitroso compound
oxime
parathion
PETN
phorate
picric acid
polysulfide
sulfide
sulfonamide
sulfonic acid
sulfoxide
thiol
thiourea
urea
xanthate
organometallic
  compounds:
  carborane
  ferrocene
  Grignard reagent
  metal carbonyl
  tetraethyllead
peroxy compounds:
  hydrogen peroxide
  peroxide
  peroxy acid
petroleum, gasoline,
  oil, and coal:
  diesel fuel
  gasoline
  kerosine
  microcrystalline
    wax
  napalm
  naphtha
  paraffin wax
  petrochemical
  petroleum
polymers and resins:
  balsam
  copal
  copolymer
  dammar
  dragon's blood
  elastomer
  frankincense
  gamboge
  initiator
  latex
  Lucite
  macromolecule
  mastic
  monomer
  neoprene
  polyacrylonitrile
  polychlorotri-
    fluoroethylene

Biographies

INDEX: See entries under all of the terms above

Section 123. Chemical Reactions

A. General considerations of chemical reactions

1. Basic concepts involved in the study of chemical reactions: transformation, conservation of mass and energy, law of simple multiple proportions in compounds

2. Growth of major theories concerning chemical reactions

3. Classification and nomenclature of the principal kinds of chemical reactions

  a. According to the relationship involved between the starting materials and the final products

   i. Decomposition reactions

   ii. Polymerization reactions

   iii. Chain reactions

   iv. Substitution reactions

   v. Addition and elimination reactions

   vi. Oxidation–reduction reactions
    [see F., below]

   vii. Acid–base reactions
    [see E., below]

  b. According to the energy changes involved
   [see B.1., below]

  c. According to the reaction rates or chemical kinetics involved
   [see C.6., below]

  d. According to the reaction mechanism involved
   [see D.4., below]

B. Energy changes in chemical reactions

    1. The classification of chemical reactions according to energy changes involved: exothermic and endothermic

    2. The significance of activation energy in chemical reactions

    3. Thermodynamic relations in chemical reactions: chemical equilibrium, free energy and entropy changes

C. Rates of chemical reactions

    1. Factors that affect the rate or direction of chemical reactions

       a. Solvents

       b. Temperature

       c. Pressure

       d. Catalysts

       e. Collisions

       f. Light

       g. Isotopic substitution

       h. Molecular structure

    2. Factors that affect the kinetic order of chemical reactions: concentration of reactants, mechanism of reaction, conditions of the reaction

    3. Factors that affect the extent of chemical reactions: equilibrium constant

    4. Complex reactions: reactions governed by more than one reaction rate

    5. Experimental methods for studying chemical kinetics

       a. Measurement of reaction rates

       b. Determination of the order of reactions

       c. Relaxation methods

    6. Kinetic studies as a means of elucidating reaction mechanisms

D. Mechanisms of chemical reactions

    1. Factors influencing the course of a reaction: reactants, transition state, solvent, catalysts, products, reaction conditions

    2. Energy changes through single-stage and multi-stage processes

    3. Factors that reveal the mechanisms of a reaction: chemical and stereochemical nature of the reactants, intermediates, and products; kinetics of the reaction

    4. Classification of reaction mechanisms based on the nature of electron pairing in the transition state, on the nature of the attacking species, on the nature of catalysis, on the number of components of the transition state

    5. Mechanisms of the principal types of reactions: nucleophilic and electrophilic substitution, addition and elimination reactions

E. Acid–base reactions and equilibria

    1. General properties of acids and bases

    2. Theoretical approaches to acid–base concepts

       a. The definition of an acid as a substance that gives rise to hydrogen ions and of a base as a substance that gives rise to hydroxyl ions in aqueous solutions

       b. The Brønsted–Lowry concept defining an acid as a proton donor and a base as a proton acceptor

       c. The Lewis electronic theory defining an acid as an electron acceptor and a base as an electron donor

    3. Acid–base reactions

       a. Proton-transfer reactions

       b. Lewis acid reactions

       c. Acid–base catalysis

4. Quantitative aspects of acid–base equilibria

    a. Equilibria in aqueous solutions

    b. Equilibria in nonaqueous solvents

    c. Equilibria involving Lewis acids

    d. The effect of molecular structure on acid–base equilibria

5. The experimental study of acid–base reactions and equilibria

F. Oxidation–reduction reactions

1. Major classes of oxidation–reduction reactions: oxygen atom transfer, hydrogen atom transfer, electron transfer

2. Definitions of oxidation and reduction based on the reaction's stoichiometry

3. Theoretical aspects of oxidation–reduction processes

    a. The concept of oxidation state

    b. Half reactions and the determination of redox potentials

    c. Oxidation–reduction equilibria and reaction rates

    d. Mechanisms of redox reactions

4. Electrochemical reactions: chemical changes associated with the passage of an electrical current

    a. The electrochemical process: types of reactions

    b. Complex electrochemical reactions

    c. The Nernst and Butler–Volmer equations

5. Oxidation–reduction reactions in biological systems

6. Oxidation–reduction reactions in combustion and flames

G. Photochemical reactions

1. The photochemical process

2. Experimental methods used in the study of the photochemical process and photochemical reactions

3. The application of photochemical processes

H. Chemical reactions and chemical theory in the synthesis of chemical compounds

1. Factors that affect the choice of a specific synthetic path

2. Factors that affect the choice of reaction conditions

3. The separation and purification of reaction products
[see 122.B.1.]

4. The identification, characterization, and analysis of reaction products
[see 122.B.2. through 9.]

Suggested reading in the *Encyclopædia Britannica:*

MACROPAEDIA: Major articles dealing with chemical reactions

    Chemical Reactions
    Physical Principles and Concepts

MICROPAEDIA: Selected entries of reference information

General subjects

acid-base reactions and equilibria:	Lewis theory	*electrochemistry:*	electromotive series
acid–base reaction	pH	anodizing	Faraday's laws of
amphoterism	*catalysis of reactions:*	electrical double	electrolysis
Brønsted–Lowry	acid–base catalysis	layer	*kinetics and*
theory	catalysis	electrochemical	*mechanism:*
buffer	catalyst	reaction	activation energy
hydrogen ion	catalyst poison	electrochemistry	Arrhenius equation
hydroxide	Ziegler–Natta	electrolysis	chain reaction
	catalyst	electrolytic cell	

Biographies

See Section 10/32 of Part Ten

INDEX: See entries under all of the terms above

Section 124.   **Heat, Thermodynamics, and the Nonsolid States of Matter**

A. The principles of thermodynamics

1. The description of physical phenomena based on the concepts of system, state of a system, and changes of state

2. The first law of thermodynamics

3. The second law of thermodynamics

4. Stable equilibrium

   a. Equations relating properties of systems that are in, or are passing through, stable equilibrium states

   b. Temperature considered as the potential governing the flow of energy between systems

   c. Heat

      i. The definition of heat as a form of energy transferred from one body to another under the influence of a difference in temperature

      ii. Theories of heat: the phlogiston theory, the caloric theory, the kinetic molecular theory

      iii. Heat transfer in matter: heat conductivity in solids, convection in liquids and gases, heat transfer in boiling liquids, evaporation and condensation

      iv. Technical applications of heat energy
         [see 721.B.7. and 725.A.5.a.]

      v. Heat and its relation to entropy, work, and change of energy

5. Thermodynamic relations in simple systems

   a. The Carnot cycle

   b. Maxwell's equations relating entropy to pressure, volume, and temperature for closed systems that assume only stable equilibrium states

   c. Phase changes and equilibria

   d. Simple one-component systems: processes at constant volume and at constant pressure; the equation of state, which relates pressure, volume, and temperature for stable equilibrium states

   e. Simple multicomponent systems: Gibbs equation for entropy change, the Gibbs–Dalton rule for mixture of gases, Raoult's law and Henry's law for ideal solutions

   f. Bulk flow

   g. Equilibrium in chemical reactions
      [see 123.B.3.]

6. The third law of thermodynamics

7. The effects of applied force fields on simple systems

8. Steady rate processes; *e.g.,* systems approaching stable equilibrium, flow of a substance through a barrier

9. Statistical thermodynamics

   a. The laws of thermodynamics that consider the detailed microscopic structure of physical systems and the states of such systems

   b. Statistics of grand systems

B. The gaseous state of matter

   1. The nature and properties of a gas

   2. The thermodynamic approach to gases: the macroscopic view that deals with bulk measurable properties

      a. The simple gas laws

      b. The thermal equation of state for perfect gases

      c. Empirical equations of state for real gases

   3. The particle-description approach to gases

      a. The distribution function

      b. The Boltzmann transport equation, the single-particle distribution function

      c. The N-particle distribution function and the thermodynamic-equilibrium properties and transport properties of dense gases

      d. The behaviour of a gas at the hydrodynamic and thermal relaxation stages

C. The liquid state of matter

   1. The behaviour and properties of liquids at equilibrium

   2. The molecular structure of liquids based on distribution functions, which measure the probable distribution of some property of molecules through the liquid

   3. Properties of liquids

      a. Transport properties

      b. Acoustical properties: propagation of sound waves

      c. Electrical and magnetic properties

      d. Thermodynamic properties

      e. Optical properties

      f. Surface tension

D. Solutions and solubility

   1. General classes of solutions: electrolytes and nonelectrolytes, solutions of weak electrolytes, endothermic and exothermic solutions

   2. Properties of solutions

      a. Composition ratios: molarity, molality, mole fraction

      b. Equilibrium properties: correlation of the vapour pressure of a solution to its composition

      c. Colligative properties: rise in boiling point, decrease in freezing point, osmotic pressure

      d. Transport properties: viscosity, thermal conductivity, diffusivity

   3. Thermodynamic and molecular aspects of solvent and solute interactions

      a. Energy considerations: entropy, enthalpy, Gibbs free energy

      b. Effects of molecular structure and weak intermolecular forces

      c. Effects of chemical interactions; *e.g.,* hydrogen bonding, chemical combinations

   4. General theories of solution: the prediction of solubility and solution properties

a. Solutions of nonelectrolytes: Raoult's law and Henry's law for ideal solutions; theoretical expressions for the excess properties of regular athermal, associated, and solvated solutions

b. Solutions of electrolytes: Debye–Hückel theory and modifications, Arrhenius dissociation theory

5. Effects of temperature and pressure on the solubility of solids and gases

E. Physical effects at surfaces

1. Surface tension and surface energy: cohesion and adhesion

2. Adsorption on liquid and solid surfaces

3. Tribological phenomena, the mechanical and physical effects at interfaces: friction, wear, lubrication

4. Colloids: the kinds of dispersions and their properties and preparation

a. Irreversible colloidal systems: lyophobic sols, emulsions, foams, pastes, gels

b. Reversible colloidal systems: solutions of polymers and proteins, solutions of soaps and dyes

F. The plasma state of matter: completely ionized gases interacting with magnetic and electric fields

1. Basic plasma properties and parameters: electrical quasineutrality, electron density, kinetic temperature, particle velocities, magnetic and electric field strengths

2. Elastic and inelastic collisions of plasma particles

3. Radiation from plasmas; *e.g.,* X-rays, synchrotron radiation, excitation radiation

4. The formation of plasmas

5. The behaviour of plasmas in magnetic and electric fields

6. The determination of plasma variables

7. Fluidlike behaviour in plasmas

8. Applications of plasmas; *e.g.,* power production, jet propulsion
[see 112.G.4., 721.B.8.a., and 721.C.3.]

9. The existence of plasmas in nature: in the extraterrestrial medium, in the Sun and stars, on Earth

G. The properties of matter at extreme conditions

1. Properties of matter at low temperatures

a. Effects of low temperature on entropy, heat capacity, magnetic properties, and conductivity

b. Special physical phenomena at very low temperatures: superconductivity, superfluidity

c. Special methods for obtaining and characterizing low temperatures: adiabatic cooling, adiabatic dilution

2. Special properties of matter at high temperatures

3. Effects of high pressure on the physical, chemical, electronic, and magnetic properties of matter

H. Transport phenomena

1. The kinetic molecular theory of the transport properties of gases, liquids, suspensions, and polymers

2. Phenomenological expressions of transport

3. Hydrodynamic aspects of transport phenomena

4. Transport phenomena in macrosystems

Suggested reading in the *Encyclopædia Britannica:*

MACROPAEDIA: Major articles dealing with heat, thermodynamics, and the nonsolid states of matter

Matter: Its Properties, States, Varieties, and Behaviour
Physical Principles and Concepts
Physical Sciences, The
Thermodynamics, Principles of

MICROPAEDIA: Selected entries of reference information

General subjects

colloids:
  aerosol
  colloid
  dialysis
  emulsion
  foam
  gel
gaseous state of matter:
  Avogadro's law
  Boyle's law
  Dalton's law
  degenerate gas
  diffusion
  fluid
  gas
  kinetic theory of gases
  Maxwell–Boltzmann distribution law
  mean free path
  perfect gas
  van der Waals forces
heat transfer in matter:
  adiabatic demagnetization

caloric theory
convection
heat transfer
thermal conduction
liquid state of matter:
  capillarity
  detergent
  diffusion
  fluid
  glass
  liquid
  osmosis
  superfluidity
  surface-active agent
  surface tension
phase changes and equilibria:
  boiling point
  condensation
  critical point
  distillation
  eutectic
  freezing point
  latent heat
  melting point
  phase
  phase diagram

phase rule
thermal fusion
vaporization
solutions and solubility:
  amalgam
  Arrhenius theory
  exsolution
  Henry's law
  ideal solution
  saturation
  solid solution
  solution
thermodynamics and statistical mechanics:
  absolute zero
  canonical ensemble
  carnot cycle
  energy, equipartition of
  enthalpy
  entropy
  free energy
  freedom, degree of
  Hamiltonian function
  heat

heat capacity
internal energy
Lagrangian function
Maxwell's demon
Rankine cycle
reversibility
specific heat
temperature
thermodynamics
other:
  adsorption
  cohesion
  friction
  liquid crystal
  plasma
  Stefan–Boltzmann law
  thermal expansion
  transport phenomenon
  tribology
  wear

Biographies
  See Section 10/32 of Part Ten

INDEX: See entries under all of the terms above

Section 125.   The Solid State of Matter

A. Crystals and crystallography

  1. Patterns of atoms in crystals

     a. The three-dimensional periodic arrangement of atoms in crystals: crystal planes and their notation

     b. Symmetry considerations in the classification of crystal systems

  2. Diffraction of X-rays, electrons, and neutrons by crystal structures

  3. Processes of crystal growth

     a. Theoretical aspects of crystal growth: energy considerations, growth of eutectics, constitutional supercooling, nucleation

     b. Preparation of crystals: monocomponent and polycomponent crystal growth

  4. Imperfections and dislocations in crystalline materials and their effects on the properties of the crystals

  5. Effects of temperature, pressure, and alloying on the strength and hardness of crystals

B. The theory of the crystalline solid state

  1. The classification of solids according to their electronic structure and bonding: ionic solids, covalent solids, metallic solids, molecular solids, hydrogen-bonded solids

2. The arrangement of atoms in crystalline solids
   [see A.1.a., above]

3. The elastic and plastic properties of solids

4. The thermal and thermodynamic properties of solids: specific heat, thermal conductivity

5. The electronic structure of solids

   a. The nature and mobility of electrons in conductors, insulators, and semiconductors

   b. Electron emission: thermionic emission, photoelectric emission, field emission

   c. The nearly free electron approximation

   d. The energy-band theory of the solid state

6. The principal types of magnetic behaviour exhibited by solids: paramagnetism, diamagnetism, ferromagnetism

7. The interaction of light with solids

   a. The behaviour of solids illuminated with radiation: reflection, absorption, or transmission of photons

   b. The generation of electromagnetic radiation from the energy supplied to the solid

   c. The photoelectric effect

C. Ionic crystals

   1. Bonding in ionic crystals

   2. The structure of ionic crystals

      a. Perfect ionic crystals

      b. Defects in ionic crystals: Frenkel defect, Schottky defect, colour centres

   3. Properties of ionic crystals

      a. Vibrational and electronic properties

      b. Thermal properties

      c. Polarizing and diffusion properties and the nature of ionic conduction

      d. Optical properties

D. Metals

   1. Structural aspects of metals and alloys

   2. Elementary description of metals: the use of the free electron model to explain thermal and electrical conductivity of metals

   3. The electronic structure of metals and related effects

      a. The interaction between the periodic lattice and the conduction electrons: the weak pseudopotential

      b. Electron motion in a magnetic field and conduction-related effects

   4. Band structure and properties of metal groups: alkali metals, semimetals, noble metals, transition metals

   5. Lattice vibrations: interaction between ions; interaction between electrons, phonons, and dispersion

   6. Metal surface phenomena: thermionic and field emission of electrons, electron tunnelling, photoemission, free carrier absorption and interband transitions

   7. Many-body effects: plasma oscillations, spin waves, Fermi liquid theory, dynamic effects and shake-off electrons

   8. Superconductivity in metals

      a. Thermal properties of superconductors: transition temperature, specific heat and thermal conductivity, energy gaps

      b. Magnetic and electromagnetic properties of superconductors: critical field, Meissner effect, phase coherence effects

   9. Magnetic phenomena in metals: diamagnetism, paramagnetism, ferromagnetism, antiferromagnetism, nuclear magnetic resonance

E. Semiconductors and insulators

   1. General properties of semiconductors and insulators

   2. Mechanisms of conduction: mobility of charged particles and electrons in solids

   3. Electrical conduction in semiconductors

      a. Chemical approach: impurity conduction, hopping process

      b. Physical approach: energy band and gaps, lattice vibrations, statistical properties

      c. Extrinsic and intrinsic semiconductors

      d. Measurement of conductivity and of energy gaps

   4. Principles involved in semiconductor applications

      a. Optical effects: photoelectric effect, photovoltaic effect, luminescence

      b. Electrical and related effects: hot electron effects, thermoelectric effects

      c. Junction effects

      d. Pressure and stress effects

F. The glassy or amorphous state of matter

   1. Effects of temperature and composition on glass properties

   2. The structure of glass

   3. General properties of glasses: mechanical, chemical, optical, and electrical properties

---

Suggested reading in the *Encyclopædia Britannica:*

MACROPAEDIA: Major articles dealing with the solid state of matter

   Matter: Its Properties, States, Varieties, and Behaviour
   Physical Principles and Concepts

MICROPAEDIA: Selected entries of reference information

General subjects

Biographies

  See Section 10/32 of Part Ten

INDEX: See entries under all of the terms above

Section 126.   Mechanics of Particles, Rigid Bodies, and Deformable Bodies: Elasticity, Vibrations, and Flow

A. The principles of classical mechanics

   1. The fundamental parameters and concepts of classical mechanics: matter, space, motion, time

   2. Statics, the equilibrium of systems at rest: force, friction

   3. Dynamics: motion of systems

     a. Kinematics: motion of particles and rigid bodies without consideration of the forces producing the motion

       i. Velocity and acceleration

       ii. Rotation about a fixed axis

       iii. Motion in a circular path

       iv. Simple harmonic motion

       v. Relative motion

     b. Kinetics: motion of bodies under the action of forces upon them

       i. Newton's laws of motion: the law of inertia, the law of force, the law of action and reaction

       ii. Motion under a constant force

       iii. Ballistics: phenomena and laws of projectiles and their propulsion, flight, and impact

       iv. The motion of the pendulum

       v. Newton's law of universal gravitation

       vi. Kepler's laws of planetary motion

     c. Impulse and momentum

     d. Work and power

     e. Energy

       i. The concepts of energy and energy conservation

       ii. Forms of energy and examples of energy transformations associated with each energy form

       iii. The equivalence of mass and energy

     f. The conservation of momentum

   4. Mechanics of nonrigid bodies

     a. The collision of bodies or particles: centre of mass system, elastic collisions, inelastic collisions

     b. Stiffness in mechanical vibrations

   5. Motion in a rotating frame of reference: inertia forces and Coriolis forces

   6. Mechanics of complex systems

     a. The principle of virtual work

     b. The rotation of spinning tops and gyroscopes

     c. The precession and nutation of rotating bodies

     d. Lagrange's and Hamilton's equations of motion

B. Relativistic mechanics in inertial systems of reference

   1. Mechanical foundations of special relativity

   2. Relativistic kinematics

   3. The relationship between gravitational mass and inertial mass

C. The stress dynamics of elastic materials

   1. The phenomenon of elasticity: stress-strain relationships

   2. Elasticity in viscous and crystalline bodies

3. Elastic constants

4. The theory of elasticity: mathematical expressions defining elastic properties

D. Vibrations of elastic bodies

1. The nature of vibrations: natural or free vibrations, damped and forced vibrations

2. Vibrators and their sources of energy

3. Types of vibrational waves: their properties and modes of propagation

4. The behaviour of materials undergoing vibration

5. Detection and utilization of vibrations
   [see 723.F.6. and 735.K.2.]

E. Fluid mechanics, including gas dynamics

1. General properties of fluids, ideal and actual: mechanical and thermodynamic properties

2. Fluid statics and equilibrium

   a. The basic equation of fluid statics

   b. Fluid forces on plane and curved surfaces: analysis of forces, buoyancy, stability of floating and submerged bodies

3. Fluids in motion: hydrodynamics and aerodynamics

   a. Frictionless one-dimensional fluid flow

   b. Flow in pipes and channels: laminar flow, turbulent flow, special types of flow

   c. General two- and three-dimensional flow: mathematical conditions, vorticity, boundary layers, drag

   d. Compressible fluid flow: isentropic flow, shock waves

F. Rheological phenomena: deformation and flow

1. Continuum mechanics

   a. Kinematics of deformation and flow: strain, shear, compression, elongation

   b. Dynamics: balance of forces and torques

2. Constitutive equations: stress-deformation relations in different media

3. Yield strength of materials: fracture and fatigue

4. The application of molecular theories to explain rheological phenomena

---

Suggested reading in the *Encyclopædia Britannica:*

MACROPAEDIA: Major articles dealing with the mechanics of particles, rigid bodies, and deformable bodies: elasticity, vibrations, and flow

Energy, The Concept of
Mechanics: Energy, Forces, and Their Effects
Physical Principles and Concepts

MICROPAEDIA: Selected entries of reference information

General subjects

deformation and	yield point	kinetics	statics
elasticity:	Young's modulus	mass	velocity
bulk modulus	*elementary classical*	mechanics	*energy:*
deformation and	*mechanics:*	momentum	energy
flow	acceleration	motion	kinetic energy
elasticity	collision	motion,	mechanical energy
Hooke's law	d'Alembert's	equation of	potential energy
plasticity	principle	Newton's law of	power
shear modulus	dynamics	gravitation	work
slip	force	Newton's laws of	*fluid mechanics:*
strain	gravity, centre of	motion	Archimedes'
stress	inertia	particle	principle
tensile strength	kinematics	position vector	

austausch	Magnus effect	precession	ballistics
coefficient	Pascal's principle	reduced mass	celestial mechanics
Bernoulli's	Reynolds number	torque	density
theorem	terminal velocity	uniform circular	equilibrium
boundary layer	Torricelli's	motion	equivalence
capillarity	theorem	*vibrations:*	principle
cavitation	turbulent flow	damping	escape velocity
convergence and	viscosity	pendulum	Kepler's laws of
divergence	*rotary motion:*	periodic motion	planetary motion
eddy	angular	reduced mass	pressure
fluid	momentum	resonance	reference frame
fluid mechanics	angular velocity	simple harmonic	specific gravity
Froude number	centrifugal force	motion	statistical
hydraulics	Coriolis force	vibration	mechanics
laminar flow	couple	*others:*	
Mach number	inertia, moment of	action	

Biographies

See Section 10/32 of Part Ten

INDEX: See entries under all of the terms above

Section 127.   Electricity and Magnetism

A. The static electrical charge

1. General phenomena of static electricity

a. The basic laws of electrostatics that relate the interaction of charged bodies at rest

b. The electrostatic field

c. The electric dipole

d. Electrostatic energy and force

e. Electricity in the atmosphere
[see also 212.C., 221.A.4., and 223.B.2.]

2. Electrostatics of dielectrics and capacitors: polarization

3. Electrostatic potential

a. High-voltage phenomena

b. Electrical fields and potential distributions in two and three dimensions

4. Measurement of electrostatic forces and fields
[see 723.D.1.e.]

B. Moving charges and electric currents

1. Direct electric current: current that flows in one direction

a. General phenomena of moving electrical charges: definitions of electrical quantities and their units

b. Electromotive force

c. Behaviour of direct currents in electrical circuits: Ohm's law; Kirchhoff's laws; the principles of devices that measure or indicate the presence of current, potential difference, and resistance

2. The conduction of electricity

a. The motion of charged particles in an electric field

b. The mechanisms of the conduction of electricity: in a vacuum, in gases, in liquids and solids, in metals and semiconductors

c. Thermoelectric effects: phenomena in which electrical energy is transformed into thermal energy or vice versa

d. Electron emission: thermionic emission, secondary emission, photoelectric emission

3. Alternating electric currents: current that reverses itself with uniform frequency

    a. Faraday's law of electromagnetic induction

    b. The mathematical and graphical representation of alternating currents

    c. Basic laws of alternating current circuits

    d. The detection and measurement of alternating currents and voltages
       [see 723.D.1.e.]

    e. Parallel resonant circuits

    f. Alternating current bridges for determining impedance

    g. Propagation of electric waves in cables

    h. Filters that select signals

    i. Transient phenomena of alternating circuits

    j. Eddy currents and skin, or surface, effects

    k. Principles of generation and transmission of ac single- and multiphase power

4. Primary effects and properties of electric fields and currents

    a. Magnetic effects of steady electric currents
       [see C.2., below]

    b. Magnetic effects of changing currents
       [see C.4., below]

    c. Force, energy, and power associated with electromagnetic fields

    d. The generation of electromagnetic radiation by the changing of currents in circuits

5. Effects of electricity on matter

    a. Piezoelectricity and applications of the phenomenon

    b. Optical effects: electroluminescence, Kerr effect, Stark effect

    c. Thermal effect: resistance heating

    d. Chemical effects: electrolysis, electro-osmosis, electrophoresis

    e. Bioelectric effects: effects associated with nerve, brain, and muscle action in which potential differences occur and can be influenced by applied potential

C. Magnetism

  1. General phenomena of magnetic systems

  2. Magnetic effects of steady electrical currents

    a. The magnetic field of steady currents: Ampère's law, the law of Biot and Savart

    b. The magnetic moment of a current loop

    c. The magnetic field of a solenoid

  3. Motion of charged particles in magnetic and electric fields

    a. The force on a moving charge

    b. Motion of charges in uniform flux density

    c. Motion of charges in combined electric and magnetic fields

    d. Magnetic dipole moments: atomic moments, nuclear moments, magnetic resonance

  4. Magnetic effects of varying currents

    a. The laws of electromagnetic induction

    b. Inductance and magnetic energy

  5. Properties of magnetic materials

    a. The classification of magnetic substances

    b. Induced and permanent atomic magnetic dipoles

    c. Magnetism of matter

       i. Diamagnetism

      ii. Paramagnetism

     iii. Ferromagnetism

     iv. Antiferromagnetism

   v. Ferrimagnetism

   vi. Terrestrial magnetism
    [see also 212.B.]

  d. Atomic structure and magnetism

D. The theory of fields in physics

 1. The definition of a field in physics: the scope of field theory

 2. Mathematical treatment of fields

 3. Classification of fields: material and nonmaterial fields; scalar, vector, and tensor fields

 4. Examples of scalar, vector, and tensor fields in ordinary space

 5. Fields with distributions in more than three dimensions

E. The electromagnetic field and the theory of electromagnetic radiation

 1. The classical theory of radiation

  a. The development of concepts and theories concerning the nature of light

  b. Semiquantitative treatment of electromagnetic radiation: Maxwell's equations for the electromagnetic nature of light

  c. The electromagnetic spectrum

 2. The quantum theory of radiation

  a. Evidences of the particle nature of electromagnetic radiation: Compton effect, photoelectric effect, Raman effect

  b. The wave–particle duality of the photon

  c. The interaction of electromagnetic radiation with atomic and molecular structures: absorption, emission, and scattering processes

  d. The relation of electromagnetic radiation to quantum theory and relativity

 3. The mathematical formulation of electromagnetic theory

  a. Maxwell's equations for electromagnetic fields and radiation

  b. Transmission of radiation in free space

  c. Wave equations in space bounded by conductors

  d. Scattering of electromagnetic waves

  e. Electromagnetic waves in material media

  f. The functions of antennas

F. Relativistic electrodynamics

 1. Electrodynamics in four-dimensional notation

 2. Applications of relativistic principles in the treatment of electromagnetic and nuclear force fields of relativistic particles

---

Suggested reading in the *Encyclopædia Britannica*:

MACROPAEDIA: Major articles dealing with electricity and magnetism

 Electricity and Magnetism
 Electromagnetic Radiation
 Physical Principles and Concepts

MICROPAEDIA: Selected entries of reference information

General subjects

stationary electric	dielectric constant	electric field	electrostatic
charges and related	electret	electric	induction
phenomena:	electric charge	polarization	Stark effect
capacitance	electric dipole	electric potential	*electric currents and*
Coulomb force	electric	electric	*related phenomena:*
dielectric	displacement	susceptibility	alternating current

cathode ray	*electricity in the*	polarization	diamagnetism
charge carrier	*atmosphere:*	Poynting vector	ferrimagnetism
direct current	atmospheric	radiation	ferromagnetism
electric current	electricity	Raman effect	hysteresis
electrical	ball lightning	Stefan–	magnet
impedance	lightning	Boltzmann law	magnetic dipole
electricity	Saint Elmo's fire	thermal radiation	magnetic
electromotive force	*electromagnetic fields*	ultraviolet	permeability
Faraday's law of	*and the theory of*	radiation	magnetic pole
induction	*electromagnetic*	*magnetic effects of*	magnetic
inductance	*radiation:*	*electric currents:*	susceptibility
Joule's law	electromagnetic	Ampère's law	magnetostriction
Kirchhoff's circuit	field	Biot–Savart law	paramagnetism
rules	electromagnetic	Gauss's theorem	*other:*
Lenz's law	radiation	displacement	electrostriction
Ohm's law	electromagnetic	current	ferroelectricity
Peltier effect	spectrum	magnetic circuit	Leyden jar
reactance	ether	magnetic field	permittivity
resistance	infrared radiation	magnetic force	piezoelectricity
resistivity	Maxwell's	magnetism	Zeeman effect
Seebeck effect	equations	magnetometer	
Thomson effect	Michelson–Morley	*magnetism of matter:*	
	experiment	anti-ferromagnetism	
	Planck's	Barkhausen effect	
	radiation law	Curie point	

Biography

Maxwell, James Clerk
See also Section 10/32 of Part Ten

INDEX: See entries under all of the terms above

Section 128.   Waves and Wave Motion

A. General wave phenomena and the theory of wave motion

   1. General properties of waves: frequency, amplitude, wavelength, phase

   2. Classification of waves

      a. Waves classified by the medium supporting the transmission of wave motion: water waves, sound waves, electromagnetic waves

      b. Waves classified by the motion of particles in a wave: transverse, longitudinal, torsional, and cylindrical waves

      c. Other classifications: bow waves and shock waves

   3. The theory of waves

      a. General characteristics of vibratory motion: periodicity, group velocity, energy content

      b. The velocity of waves

      c. The wave equation: the space–time description of wave motion

      d. Transport of energy and momentum

   4. The principle of superposition of waves

      a. Standing waves: waves with stationary nodes

      b. Modulation of waves

      c. Pulse and wave trains

   5. The behaviour of waves at boundaries or interfaces: reflection, transmission, refraction

   6. The diffraction and interference of waves

   7. The interaction of waves with matter: absorption, dispersion

B. Electromagnetic waves

1. General properties of electromagnetic waves

2. Waves of the electromagnetic spectrum and their properties

    a. Electric current waves

    b. Radio waves

    c. Microwaves

    d. Infrared waves

    e. Visible light
       [see C., below]

    f. Ultraviolet waves

    g. X-rays
       [see 111.D.]

    h. Gamma radiation

3. Sources of incoherent electromagnetic waves

    a. Sources of radio waves: oscillators, antennas

    b. Sources of microwaves: klystrons, travelling wave tubes

    c. Sources of infrared, visible, and ultraviolet waves

        i. Black-body radiation

        ii. Luminescence, fluorescence, phosphorescence

        iii. The passage of electrical current through a resisting medium

    d. Sources of X-rays: X-ray tubes, nuclear and astronomical sources

    e. Sources of gamma rays: nuclear sources, Mössbauer radiation

4. Sources of coherent electromagnetic waves: lasers and masers
   [see 725.B.5.g. and 735.G.3.]

5. The transmission of electromagnetic waves: through matter, through space, by wave guides and transmission lines

C. Light waves

1. Light as a wave motion: the wave theory of light

    a. The properties of light consistent with the wave theory: diffraction, interference, polarization, dispersion

    b. The spectrum of light: the description of colour in terms of wavelengths

2. The velocity of light and its measurement

3. Interference of light

4. Diffraction phenomena

5. Polarization

    a. Superposition of polarized beams: plane, circularly, or elliptically polarized light

    b. Double refraction: waves in anisotropic media

    c. Characterization of polarized light by Stokes's parameters and Poincaré sphere

6. Properties and behaviour of light waves based on Maxwell's equations of electromagnetic theory

7. The interaction of light with matter

    a. Reflection and refraction

    b. Dispersion and scattering

    c. Absorption: mechanical and chemical effects of light

8. The quantum theory of light: the photon

    a. Observed photon phenomena: photoelectric effect, Compton scattering, Rayleigh scattering

    b. The uncertainty principle in relation to the study of the phenomena of light

    c. The detection and counting of photons

9. The separation of light into its constituent wavelengths, the analysis of light spectra

10. Sources of light

11. The biological effects of light, including photosynthesis
    [see 322.A. and 335.B.]

D. The focusing and imaging of light waves

   1. Geometrical optics: the geometry of light rays and their image-forming properties through optical systems

     a. Theoretical considerations: law of reflection, law of refraction, Lagrange theorem, Gauss theory of lenses

     b. Optical systems: components, applications, lens aberrations, brightness of image formed

   2. Optics and information theory

     a. Optical data processing

     b. Holography: a two-step image-forming process using coherent light

E. Sound waves

   1. The nature and properties of sound waves

   2. Shock waves and their characteristics

   3. Sources of sound waves

   4. The reception of sound

   5. Applications of acoustics

     a. Recording and reproduction
       [see 735.F.]

     b. Architectural and acoustical design
       [see 733.A.8.]

     c. Speech and music
       [see 514.D.1. and 624.B.]

     d. Military acoustical detectors
       [see 735.J.2.]

     e. Noise control
       [see 733.A.8.]

   6. Physical aspects of musical sound
     [see 624.B.1.]

     a. The special properties of musical sound: pitch, timbre, loudness; fundamentals and overtones

     b. The production of sound waves by musical instruments

Suggested reading in the *Encyclopædia Britannica*:

MACROPAEDIA: Major articles dealing with waves and wave motion

   Colour
   Electromagnetic Radiation
   Light
   Optics, Principles of
   Sound

MICROPAEDIA: Selected entries of reference information

General subjects

behaviour and properties of waves:	Doppler effect	line broadening	Snell's law
absorption	double refraction	longitudinal wave	standing wave
amplitude	Faraday effect	moiré pattern	total internal
beat	Fermat's principle	Newton's rings	reflection
Brewster's law	frequency	phase	transverse wave
diffraction	Huygens' principle	Rayleigh scattering	wave front
dispersion	interference	reflection	wave motion
	interference fringe	refraction	wave number

wave velocity	thermoluminescence	magnification	sound intensity
wavelength	ultraviolet	mirror	timbre
Young's	radiation	optical image	tone
experiment	X ray	optics	whistler
electromagnetic	*lasers and masers:*	periscope	white noise
waves:	laser	prism	*other:*
chemiluminescence	maser	projection screen	aureole
colour	optical pumping	projector	Cellini's halo
electroluminescence	stimulated	pupil	halo
electromagnetic	emission	relative aperture	Michelson–Morley
radiation	*manipulation of light*	spectroscopy	experiment
electromagnetic	*waves:*	stereoscopy	mirage
spectrum	aberration	*sound waves:*	Mössbauer effect
ether	aperture	combination tone	Munsell colour
gamma ray	collimator	loudness	system
infrared radiation	critical angle	overtone	photoelasticity
light	diffraction grating	pitch	pleochroism
luminescence	diopter	resonance	Poynting vector
phosphor	fibre optics	resonator	Stokes lines
phosphorescence	Fresnel lens	shock wave	wave–particle
radiation	holography	siren	duality
rainbow	lens	sound	
spectrum	light modulator	sound barrier	

Biographies

See Section 10/32 of Part Ten

INDEX: See entries under all of the terms above

Division III.   **The Universe: Galaxies, Stars, the Solar System**
[For Part One headnote see page 21.]

The outlines in the three sections of Division III deal with the subject matter of cosmology and cosmogony, of astronomy, and of astrophysics.

Accounts of the complex instrumentation involved in these disciplines are set forth in Section 723 of Part Seven. Historical and analytical studies of the nature and scope of astronomy and astrophysics are set forth in Section 10/32 of Part Ten.

Section 131.   **The Cosmos**

A. The structure and properties of the universe

   1. Basic data for the universe

      a. The estimated chemical composition of the universe
       [see also 121.D.]

      b. The large-scale structure and behaviour of the universe: evidence that the universe is expanding, Hubble's law and the theory of the red shift

      c. The age of the universe

      d. The clustering of galaxies

      e. Cosmic microwave background radiation

      f. The missing mass problem

      g. Space–time: a four-dimensional continuum used to describe the universe

   2. Cosmological models: theoretical representations of the original behaviour of the universe
     [see E.1., below]

3. The known and postulated components of the universe

   a. Distant galaxies
      [see 132.A.]

   b. The Local Group of galaxies
      [see 132.A.1.c.]

   c. Quasars and related objects, including such hypothetical phenomena as supermassive black holes at the centres of galaxies

   d. Nebulae

   e. Stars and stellar groups
      [see 132.C. and 132.D.]

   f. Planetary systems: solar and extrasolar systems
      [see 133.A.]

B. Gravitation: a universal force of mutual attraction that is postulated as acting between all matter

   1. Development of gravitational theory

      a. Early concepts: the Aristotelian viewpoint, contributions of Kepler and Galileo

      b. Newton's law of gravity
         [see also 126.A.3.b.v.]

   2. Interpretation of gravity measurements

      a. Potential theory: mathematical representation of the gravitational fields of irregular mass distributions
         [see also 10/22.D.2.c.]

      b. Effects of local mass differences: measurement of small gravity anomalies

   3. Modern gravitational theory and its relation to other aspects of physical theory

      a. Field theories of gravity and their general properties and predictions

      b. Gravitational fields and the general theory of relativity: principles and consequences
         [see D.2., below]

   4. Acceleration of gravity on the Earth's surface
      [see 212.A.]

   5. The gravitational constant, G: methods of measurement, possible variation in time and space

C. Celestial mechanics
   [see also 126.A.]

   1. The scope and history of celestial mechanics

   2. The two-body problem and perturbations that cause the orbits of planets and satellites to deviate from ellipses

   3. The unsolved three-body problem

   4. The general *n*-body problem

D. Properties of the space–time continuum: the astronomical implications of relativity theory

   1. The special theory of relativity

      a. Historical background: the search for the ether

      b. Relativity of space and time

      c. Consequences of the special theory

   2. The general theory of relativity

      a. Use of relativity to interpret gravitational phenomena

      b. Experimental confirmation of the theory

      c. Implications of general relativity

E. The origin and development of the universe

   1. The development of the universe as a whole

      a. Big-bang versus steady-state models of the universe

b. Primordial nucleosynthesis

c. The early universe: extrapolations backward in time to the beginning of the universe

2. The formation and development of components of the universe: galaxies, stars, the solar system
[see also 132.B., 132.D., and 133.A.]

a. The origin and development of galaxies: protogalaxies

b. The formation and development of stars

c. The origin of the solar system

3. Time scale of the universe: dating of significant events in the history of the universe

4. Theories of the possible fate of the universe

Suggested reading in the *Encyclopædia Britannica:*

MACROPAEDIA: Major articles dealing with the cosmos

Analysis and Measurement, Physical and Chemical
Cosmos, The
Gravitation
Physical Sciences, The
Relativity

MICROPAEDIA: Selected entries of reference information

General subjects

cosmology:	*element synthesis:*	free-fall	Lorentz–Fitzgerald
big-bang model	carbon cycle	gravitation	contraction
cosmology	nucleosynthesis	gravitational radius	relativistic mass
cosmos	proton–proton	Newton's law of	relativity
expanding universe	reaction	gravitation	time dilation
Hubble's constant	*extraterrestrial life:*	weight	*other:*
Mach's principle	Green Bank	weightlessness	cosmic ray
Olbers' paradox	equation	*relativity:*	ephemeris
quasar	Ozma, Project	Einstein's mass–	Scorpius X-1
steady-state	*gravitation:*	energy relation	supernova
hypothesis	Cavendish	equivalence	
	experiment	principle	

Biographies

See Section 10/32 of Part Ten

INDEX: See entries under all of the terms above

Section 132.   Galaxies and Stars

A. Galaxies in general

1. Statistical properties

a. Classification of galaxies

b. Observational methods of determining the distances to galaxies

c. Distribution of galaxies

2. Physical properties: size, mass, luminosity, age, composition

3. Structural features

4. Clusters of galaxies

a. Types and distribution

b. Interactions between cluster members

5. Extragalactic radio and X-ray sources

   a. Radio galaxies

   b. X-ray galaxies

   c. Quasars

6. The origin and evolution of the galaxies
   [see also 131.E.2.]

B. The Galaxy: the Milky Way system

1. Distance determinations in the Galaxy

2. Stellar velocities: the motions of stars with respect to the Sun, the motion of the Sun with respect to the Local Standard of Rest (LSR)

3. The stars and star clusters nearest the Sun

4. The classification of stars according to the Hertzsprung–Russell diagram

5. The galactic composition

   a. The stellar populations

   b. Emission nebulae: composition and physical characteristics of H II regions

   c. Planetary nebulae

   d. Supernova remnants

   e. Dust clouds

   f. The general interstellar medium: principal components and their distribution throughout the various galactic regions

      i. Grains of interstellar dust

      ii. Interstellar regions of neutral hydrogen (H I regions)

      iii. Interstellar molecules and radicals

   g. Primary cosmic rays

   h. Interstellar magnetic field

6. Structure and dynamics of the Galaxy

   a. The spatial structure of the Galaxy: the dimensions of the Galaxy

   b. Regions of the Galaxy: the nucleus, the central bulge, the dish, the spiral arms, the spherical component, the massive halo

   c. The magnetic field of the Galaxy: its origin and its effects on cosmic rays, radio waves, and light

   d. The rotation of the Galaxy: the differential rotation of stars, gas about the galactic centre

7. The evolution of the Galaxy
   [see also 131.E.2.]

   a. Hydromagnetic and gravitational theories of the formation of spiral structure

   b. Chemical evolution: the problem of the distribution of heavy elements

   c. Star formation: theories concerning the gravitational condensation of galactic dust and gas clouds

C. Star clusters and stellar associations

1. Globular clusters: systems containing many thousands to a million old stars in a symmetrical, roughly spherical form

2. Open clusters: systems containing about a dozen to hundreds of stars, usually in an unsymmetrical arrangement

3. Stellar associations: loose groupings containing dozens to a few hundred stars of similar spectoal type and common origin

4. Relationship of clusters to the Galaxy: the formation and dispersion of clusters and their locations in the Galaxy

5. Clusters in external galaxies

D. Stars

    1. The identification and nomenclature of the stars

        a. The celestial sphere and celestial coordinate systems

        b. The constellations and other sky divisions

        c. Star names and designations

        d. Modern star maps and catalogs

    2. Observable stellar characteristics

        a. Stellar positions and motions

        b. The apparent brightness or apparent luminosity of the stars: the UBV and other systems

        c. Stellar spectra
          [see also 111.C.]

    3. Derived, or calculated, stellar characteristics

        a. Intrinsic stellar brightness: absolute magnitudes, total luminosities

        b. Stellar masses

        c. Stellar diameters

        d. Stellar temperatures

        e. The average characteristics of main-sequence, or dwarf, stars

    4. Stellar variability

        a. Geometric variables; *e.g.,* eclipsing binaries

        b. Intrinsic variables

            i. Pulsating stars; *e.g.,* Cepheid, RR Lyrae, and Beta Canis Majoris variables

           ii. Explosive variables; *e.g.,* novae, supernovae, and novalike variables

    5. Statistics of stars

        a. Correlations between luminosity, spectrum, mass, and radius: the Hertzsprung–Russell diagram and other relations

        b. Statistics of binary star systems

        c. Statistics of special types of stars

    6. Stellar structure

        a. Stellar atmospheres

        b. Internal structure of stars

    7. Stellar evolution
        [see also 131.E.2.]

        a. The life history of a typical star

            i. Formation of a protostar by gravitational contraction

           ii. Attainment of the main sequence

          iii. Evolution away from the main sequence

          iv. Estimates of stellar ages

        b. Formation of chemical elements in stars

        c. Probable fates of stars: white dwarfs, neutron stars, black holes

---

Suggested reading in the *Encyclopædia Britannica*:

MACROPAEDIA: Major articles dealing with galaxies and stars

    Cosmos, The
    Galaxies
    Nebula
    Physical Sciences, The
    Stars and Star Clusters

MICROPAEDIA: Selected entries of reference information

Underline: General subjects

astronomical catalogs and instruments:
AG catalog
Almagest
armillary sphere
astronomical map
Carte du ciel
celestial globe
Henry Draper Catalogue
Hertzsprung–Russell diagram
Messier catalog
New General Catalogue of Nebulae and Clusters of Stars
star catalog
star gauges

constellations:
Aquarius
Aries
Cancer
Capricornus
constellation
Crux
Gemini
Leo
Orion
Pisces

Sagittarius
Scorpius
Taurus
Ursa Major
Virgo

galaxies:
Andromeda Galaxy
galaxy
Maffei I and II
Magellanic Cloud
Milky Way Galaxy
Seyfert galaxy
Virgo A

individual nebulae:
Crab Nebula
nebula
Strömgren sphere
30 Doradus

radio and X-ray emission:
cosmic ray
forbidden lines
pulsar
radio source
red shift
Sagittarius A
Scorpius X-1
synchrotron radiation

21-centimetre radiation

star pairs and groups:
binary star
eclipsing variable star
Pleiades
star cluster
stellar association

stars:
Algol
Alpha Centauri
Barnard's star
Betelgeuse
Bethlehem, Star of
colour index
Eta Carinae
Fomalhaut
Harvard classification system
Kepler's Nova
magnitude
Mira Ceti
Sirius
star
Sun
Tycho's Nova

stellar evolution:
black hole
carbon cycle
Chandrasekhar limit
giant star
neutron star
nova
Population I and II
supernova
white dwarf star

variable stars:
Cepheid variable
eclipsing variable star
light curve
long-period variable star
T Tauri star
U Geminorum star
variable star

other:
galactic coordinate
H I region
H II region
infrared source
interstellar medium
limb darkening

Underline: Biographies

See Section 10/32 of Part Ten

INDEX: See entries under all of the terms above

Section 133.   The Solar System

A. A survey of the solar system

1. The Sun
[see B., below]

2. The major planets of the solar system, their surfaces and atmospheres, their satellites
[see also C., D., and E., below]

3. Other constituents of the solar system

a. Minor planets, or asteroids

b. Comets

c. Meteoroids, meteors, and meteorites

d. The interplanetary medium

4. Regularities of the solar system: the distances of the planets from the Sun, the distribution of natural satellites

5. Interactions among various bodies in the solar system: gravitational perturbations, actual physical encounters

6. Theories of the origin of the solar system: origin by an orderly process, origin by catastrophe
   [see also 131.E.2.c.]

B. The Sun

1. The Sun's surface layers and their features: the quiet Sun

   a. Solar data derived from observations of the photosphere, the visible luminous surface of the Sun

   b. The chromosphere, the relatively transparent layer that forms a transition zone between the Sun's photosphere and corona: the flash spectrum, spicules, supergranulation

   c. The corona, the luminous, high-temperature, rarefied gas envelope of the Sun: form, structure, physical properties; the solar wind

2. Solar features that occur with increased frequency during the active phase of the solar cycle: the active Sun

   a. Centres of activity: areas of localized strong magnetic fields at the Sun's surface

   b. Sunspots: their physical nature, the sunspot cycle of about 11 years

   c. Other features; *e.g.,* faculae, prominences, flares, coronal condensations

3. The solar interior: energy generation, the evolution of the Sun
   [see also 132.D.7.]

4. Solar radiation, including light, radio waves, and particles

5. Solar-terrestrial relationships and interactions

C. The planets and their satellites

1. The terrestrial planets

   a. Mercury

   b. Venus

   c. Earth
      [see D., below]

   d. Mars

2. The minor planets, or asteroids
   [see A.4.a., above]

3. The giant planets and Pluto

   a. Jupiter

   b. Saturn

   c. Uranus

   d. Neptune

   e. Pluto

D. The Earth as a planet

1. The distance of the Earth from the Sun: the astronomical unit and solar parallax

2. The orbital motion of the Earth around the Sun and the rotation of the Earth on its axis: the year, the day, the precession of the equinoxes
   [see also E.6.a., below]

3. Effects of the Earth's orbital position and speed on astronomical observations

   a. Astronomical parallax

   b. Aberration of light

4. The Earth's magnetism, temperature, and other physical properties
   [see 212]

5. The structure and composition of the Earth's interior
   [see 213]

6. The origin of the Earth, its atmosphere, hydrosphere, and surface features
   [see 232 and 241]

E. The Moon

1. The shape, radius, mean density, and varying brightness of the Moon

2. The motion of the Moon

    a. The apparent motion: the month, or sidereal and synodic periods of the Moon; optical and physical librations
    [see 6.a.ii., below]

    b. The actual motion

3. The mass and gravitational field of the Moon

    a. Underlying theory: basic gravitational properties of the Moon

    b. Discovery of lunar mascons: gravity anomalies on the Moon

4. The physical nature of the Moon

    a. Observations from Earth and from space vehicles: results of remote lunar photography, manned lunar landings, and close-up photography
    [see also 738.C.]

    b. The lunar surface features: craters, lineaments (*e.g.,* mare ridges, the lunar grid system, rilles), temporary or transient features

    c. Theories of origin of the Moon's surface features: the volcanic and impact theories

5. The origin and evolution of the Moon

    a. Probable development of the Moon's orbit

    b. Evidence from the composition and physical properties of the Moon

6. The chemical nature of the Moon

    a. Surface composition: findings of the chemical analysis of lunar rock samples

    b. Possible zonal variations of the interior

7. The Sun–Earth–Moon system

    a. Relative motions of the Sun, Earth, and Moon

        i. The geometry of the Sun–Earth–Moon system: the celestial equator, the apparent motion of the Sun along the ecliptic, the inclination of the Earth's axis to its orbit

        ii. Motions of the Sun–Earth–Moon system as the astronomical basis of chronology: the day, month, and year; the Sothic cycle, Metonic cycle, and other complex cycles

    b. Eclipses of the Sun and Moon

    c. Tides in the Earth and in the Moon
    [see also 222.F.3.]

Suggested reading in the *Encyclopædia Britannica:*

MACROPAEDIA: Major articles dealing with the solar system. See also Section 211 of Part Two

Calendar
Earth, The: Its Properties, Composition, and Structure
Eclipse, Occultation, and Transit
Physical Sciences, The
Solar System, The

MICROPAEDIA: Selected entries of reference information

General subjects

calendars:	Dionysian period	Gregorian calendar	Julian calendar
Aztec calendar	Egyptian calendar	intercalation	Julian period
calendar	French republican	international date	leap year
Chinese calendar	calendar	line	lunar calendar
day	Greek calendar	Jewish calendar	Mayan calendar

month
Muslim calendar
perpetual calendar
Roman republican
  calendar
solar calendar
Tibetan calendar
week
year
comets:
  Arend-Roland,
    Comet
  comet
  Encke's comet
  Halley's comet
Jupiter:
  Amalthea
  Callisto
  Europa
  Ganymede
  Great Red Spot
  Io
  Jupiter
Mars:
  Chryse Planitia
  Deimos
  Mars
  Olympus Mons
  Phobos
  Syrtis Major
  Tharsis
  Utopia Planitia
Mercury:
  Caloris
  Mercury
minor planets:
  asteroid
  Eros
  Icarus

Pallas
Ra–Shalom
Trojan planets
Moon:
  Cassini's laws
  Copernicus
  libration
  Linné
  Mare Orientale
  Moon
  Tycho
Neptune:
  Neptune
  Nereid
  Triton
*objects of
  extraterrestrial
  origin:*
  achondrite
  ataxite
  carbonaceous
    chondrite
  chondrite
  chondrule
  Hraschina
    meteorite
  meteor
  meteor shower
  meteorite
  meteorite shower
  meteoritics
  Orgueil meteorite
  tektite
  Tunguska event
planetary motion:
  aberration,
    constant of
  anomaly
  conjunction

Copernican system
eclipse
ecliptic
equinox
equinoxes,
  precession of the
heliocentric system
nutation
occultation
orbit
orbital velocity
parallax
phase
Ptolemaic system
retrograde motion
solstice
synodic period
tidal friction
tide
Tychonic system
zodiac
Pluto:
  Charon
  Pluto
Saturn:
  Dione
  Enceladus
  Iapetus
  Mimas
  Phoebe
  Rhea
  Saturn
  Titan
  Tethys
Sun:
  chromosphere
  corona
  facula
  flash spectrum

heliopause
limb darkening
photosphere
solar cycle
solar energy
solar flare
solar nebula
solar
  prominence
solar radiation
solar wind
Sun
sunspot
Uranus:
  Ariel
  Miranda
  Oberon
  Titania
  Umbriel
  Uranus
Venus:
  Venus
other:
  albedo
  Bode's law
  celestial mechanics
  Forbush effect
  gegenschein
  interplanetary
    medium
  mare
  planet
  Planet X
  planetesimal
  quadrature
  rille
  satellite
  solar system

Biographies
  See Section 10/32 of Part Ten

INDEX: See entries under all of the terms above

Introduction to Part Two:
The Great Globe Itself

by Peter J. Wyllie

We all have a sense of awareness and appreciation of the Earth; we all admire the scenery. One of the rewards of studying and understanding the Earth is the development of this sense to a greater extent. This development brings us closer to nature, closer to an awareness of some transcendental power, closer to God if we choose to define God in these terms. To "commune with nature" is to seek peace, but of course the Earth is not always peaceful and benevolent; sometimes it is powerful and savage. Even cities, the culmination of man's domination of the landscape, are not immune to the ravages of nature. They have been devastated by floods, wracked and ripped by tornadoes and hurricanes, ruined by ash or lava from volcanoes, and demolished by earthquakes. These events, too, we wish to understand.

Man's appreciation of the Earth begins with physical contact. This immediate experience of the senses is followed by the spiritual desire and need to understand where the Earth and its human observers came from, and why. The third stage of appreciation comes from scientific analysis and interpretation. Before we examine the relationship between man and the Earth in more detail, we should consider our position in the solar system and the universe.

Human civilization has developed and flourished in a small niche in space. Our home is perched on the surface of a sphere, enormous to us but tiny compared to the universe, that spins around its axis once each day while moving at a fantastic speed around the Sun, completing an orbit once each year. Although normally unaware of it, we too are spinning and moving at the same speed as the Earth, but we are held securely on the surface by the gravitational attraction of the mass of rocks beneath us.

The Sun, a huge globe of burning gas, provides the energy that fuels the activities and processes of our immediate environment, the boundary layer between the rocky surface of the Earth and the fluid envelope of air and water that separates the Earth from the starkness of space. The air and water nurture life and simultaneously protect it from the potentially damaging radiation and particles that approach the Earth from other parts of the solar system and beyond.

A view of the Earth from space differs markedly from what we see from within our own restricted environment at the Earth's surface. From where we stand, it appears that the Sun, the Moon, and the stars are moving in great arcs around the Earth, and it was once believed that this was the way of the universe. Man on his world was surely the centre of all things. But we know now that this is only a relative picture; although the Moon does orbit the Earth, the Earth–Moon system moves around the Sun, which is itself speeding through the universe.

We exist because the Earth exists, and we claim the Earth as our own by referring to it as Mother Earth, the universal provider. The Earth provides all of our material needs and satisfies some of our spiritual needs: "I will lift up mine eyes unto the hills, from whence cometh my help." A day in the mountains, at the seashore, or in the countryside sharpens that sense of awareness of the Earth which was compared above with an awareness of God.

Since he first appeared on Earth, man has wondered at nature's awesome beauty and trembled at its indomitable power. The dread engendered by the physical experience of nature on the rampage, in storms, floods, or earthquakes, has shaped the development of primitive religions. Mystical or sacred attributes were assigned to natural objects and phenomena, and ceremonies were devised to honour and placate the unknown powers. Modern man has become increasingly insulated from his natural surroundings, partly because he is separated from them by masses of concrete, partly because scientific investigation tends to dispel the mystery of nature. This is not to imply that no problems remain to be solved, but we have learned enough to be reasonably sure that all are ultimately explicable in terms of rational science. Therefore, we no longer feel the need to populate the sky, mountains, trees, and winds with gods, spirits, and souls. But we can still enjoy the sensuous and spiritual appreciation of the Earth and retain or rediscover the intimacy with our natural surroundings that was experienced by primitive man.

One of the appealing aspects of Earth study is that wherever we go, our favourite subject is right there with us. There is always something new to be seen, to be admired, or to be examined in detail. While traveling in a commercial airliner, a meteorologist can examine the upper portions of the clouds as a change from his normal ground-based view and can track the flight right through the fronts and the high- and low-pressure regions charted on the newspaper weather map in his lap. An oceanographer flying over the coastline can see at a glance the large-scale patterns in the waves rolling shoreward and the effect of coastal prominences on these patterns. A geologist peering through the plane window can examine the distribution of hills and valleys laid out below him, gaining a bird's-eye view to supplement the pattern of features that he had previously seen only on maps. These pleasures are not reserved for the professional Earth scientist. Anyone can observe the Earth and Earth processes in action, almost anywhere.

Man is a curious species; he needs to know how and why things happen. The simple, visual pictures of nature are beautiful, awe-inspiring, and on occasion terrifying, but they can be more satisfying if they invoke a series of additional images. Just as one's appreciation of any work of art is enhanced by knowing something of the artist and his position in art history, so one's appreciation of nature's pictures is enhanced by knowing something about natural history. For a full appreciation of the splendour of mountain peaks rising abruptly from the plains, reaching

61

for the puffs of cloud that ride above them, we need to know something of the processes that raise mountains— or were they always there? We need to know something of the winds that carry moisture from the oceans to the skies, because we see that the clouds come, change their shapes, and then disappear. We can gain a great deal by learning a little about the scientific approach to appreciation of the Earth. And it is not at all difficult for the nonprofessional to read about and to understand many of the necessary concepts.

Two of the most troublesome concepts are time and size—dimensions that distinguish the Earth sciences from any other Earth-bound subject. It is very difficult for us to grasp the meaning of the statement that the Earth formed 4,600,000,000 years ago. Similarly, the enormous volume of water in the oceans or the volume of rocks in a mountain range almost defy comprehension. We have been considering the Earth and scenery as it is exposed to us at the present. But when we study the Earth, we realize that the present scenery is merely a transient feature in the immense span of geological time. Early students of the Earth were hampered by the belief that the Earth was only a few thousand years old. Many of them were seeking answers to two recurrent questions that we find throughout human history. How and when was the Earth formed? How and when was man formed? Attempts to answer these questions are responsible for many myths and religions in various cultures, both ancient and modern.

In the early part of the 19th century the study and interpretation of rocks led geologists to conclude that the Earth must be of far greater antiquity than the age implied by a literal interpretation of the Bible. They realized that the layers of rock now exposed at the surface contain records of the history of the Earth during the times that each layer was formed. One major branch of the Earth sciences is devoted to the discovery, translation, and interpretation of the "record of the rocks." Many rock layers enclose fossils, and these remnants of animals and plants serve as illustrations in the historical book of nature, making it possible to trace the development and changes of species through time.

Fossil hunting has been a popular pastime for many generations. With a little experience and a little knowledge, an amateur fossil hunter can add interpretation to his discoveries. From a few fossil shells and corals in a limestone, he can reconstruct in his mind's eye the whole flourishing community of life that once existed on a coral reef, now frozen into the rock record. A piece of coal, with fossil imprints of leaves, ferns, and other plant remains from which the coal was formed, can conjure up a picture of a luxuriant swamp of 300,000,000 years ago, populated by strange beasts long since vanished from the Earth. The history of the Earth, the evolution of life, and the origin of man, at least in part, are preserved in the rocks. It is here that fundamentalists still supporting "creationism" will find much evidence for the evolution of life forms, if they care to examine it. This aspect of Earth study has almost universal appeal. Earth history and human history overlap in archaeology, and the records of early civilizations exposed in excavation sites always excite public curiosity.

The scientific approach to the appreciation of nature informs us that the key to interpretation of the past history of the Earth from the record of the rocks lies in processes occurring at the present time. These processes have been grouped into great cycles. Two of the most important are the hydrologic cycle, concerned with the circulation of water, and the mountain-building cycle.

The oceans constitute a vast reservoir for the hydrologic cycle. The atmosphere and the oceans are in constant motion, driven by the energy from the Sun and the rotation of the Earth. Masses of humid air, carrying water that has evaporated from sun-drenched tropical oceans, migrate to cooler latitudes, where the water is precipitated as rain or snow and thus returned to the ocean reservoir either directly or indirectly, over or through the ground. The moving air masses and ocean currents bring to the continental masses rain or drought, heat or cold, making them hospitable, habitable, or uninhabitable for human colonies. Minor changes in atmospheric circulation have converted fertile plains to barren deserts and caused major changes in the development of ancient civilizations.

The hydrologic cycle shapes our local environment. The features that we know collectively as scenery are produced mainly by flowing water, although ice, wind, and solar energy also contribute. The force of gravity and the rivers together carry the products of weathering downhill to the ocean reservoir. The average rate at which the surface of the land is being worn down and the land dispersed into the oceans is a trivial 1.5 inches per 1,000 years, but the dimensions of geological time gives significance to small numbers. At this rate, all of the continents would be worn down to sea level within 20,000,000 years. This means that during the 4,600,000,000 years since the Earth was formed, the continents could have been worn down to sea level at least 200 times. By now there should be no land rising above sea level, but we still see high mountains.

The mountains exist and persist because the effects of the hydrologic cycle are offset by the mountain-building cycle. Forces within the Earth cause large regions of the surface to rise very slowly, imperceptibly in human terms. Imperceptible, that is, until an earthquake signals an abrupt movement in the continuing process of mountain building. While some parts of the Earth rise, other regions sink. This slow rhythm has been termed "the pulse of the Earth." Although we do not understand the details of what is happening within the Earth, we are now confident that internal forces are responsible for shaping the major features of the Earth's surface, such as the distinction between continents and ocean basins and the persistence of mountain ranges on the land and beneath the ocean. The detailed sculpture of the surface results from the conflict between the mountain-building cycle and the hydrologic cycle.

The internal forces do more than cause the land surface to rise and fall; they cause the land to move sideways as well. It is now generally believed by most scientists that the continents drift. There is persuasive evidence that the surface of the Earth is covered by a small number of very large shell-like plates, about 60 miles thick, across which the continents are scattered rather like logs frozen into the ice on a lake. The rigid shells of rock slide over the Earth's interior, carrying the continents with them and grinding against each other along their edges like ice floes. The plate boundaries are sites of geological activity: earthquakes and volcanoes are concentrated along them. Because of these movements, supercontinents have been rifted apart, and ocean basins have opened, expanded, and closed again as continents collided. Collisions of continents have thrust up great mountain ranges such as the Himalayas. The continents are still drifting at rates of an inch or two per year: the Atlantic Ocean is increasing in size, and the Pacific Ocean is becoming smaller. Most people are fascinated by the theory of continental drift. The theory is not only aesthetically pleasing but also has practical applications.

What stokes the subterranean fires that drive the Earth's engine, causing continental drift, mountain building, volcanic eruptions, and earthquakes? We have no satisfactory answer to this question, but we do know that an enormous amount of energy is involved in the activity along the plate margins. One major earthquake releases more energy than a hydrogen bomb. Modern man is a powerful animal, thanks largely to his exploitation of the Earth for material and energy, and he dominates the landscape like no species before him. He feels reasonably secure in his command of the environment while contemplating the urban scene, because the landscape is largely a product of

his industry, and it is clearly subservient to his wishes and his computer-operated control panels. But when the Earth releases a minute fraction of its internal energy in a major earthquake, man becomes helpless. All control is lost while the surface of the Earth rises and falls in solid waves.

Man cannot live in harmony with his environment during an earthquake. It has become clear, however, that he must learn to do so at other times if he is to avoid the dire predictions of those who evaluate such factors as projected world populations, the material and energy resources of the Earth, projected rates of consumption of these resources, and the volume and toxicity of waste materials discarded. We live in a restricted environment with finite space and resources, and we have become a force producing major modifications in the environment at rates very rapid compared with normal rates of Earth evolution. Social decisions about the continued exploitation of the Earth should be made with full information about the problems, and social decisions are based on votes, in theory at least. This alone is sufficient reason for any intelligent person to inform himself about the Earth, quite apart from the fascination of the subject, because his future depends upon it.

Part Two. The Earth

Several points about the relations of this part to other parts should be noted. The consideration here of the Earth's physicochemical properties presupposes the physical and chemical knowledge and theories set forth in Part One. Knowledge of the Earth is in turn presupposed by Parts Three, Four, and Five, which are Life on Earth, Human Life, and Human Society, respectively. The several Earth sciences have themselves been the objects of historical and analytical studies concerned with their nature, scope, methods, and interrelations. These studies are set forth in Section 10/33 of Part Ten. The instrumentation used in the Earth sciences is dealt with in Section 723 of Part Seven.

Division I.   The Earth's Properties, Structure, and Composition

The outlines in the four sections of Division I treat the Earth as a planet; the Earth's physical properties; the structure and composition of the Earth's interior; and the Earth's constituent minerals and rocks.

Section 211.   The Planet Earth

A. The orbital motions of the Earth

1. The revolution of the Earth about the Sun, the rotation of the Earth on its axis

2. Forces and dynamic effects related to the rotation of the Earth

   a. The Coriolis force

   b. The effects of centrifugal force

   c. Tidal friction

B. The figure of the Earth

1. The conventional definition of the figure of the Earth: the geoid

2. The development of improved approximations to the Earth's size and shape

3. The world geodetic system: the measurement of geodetic parameters

   a. The astrogravimetric method

   b. Satellite measurements

   c. Correlation of data from different methods

4. International reference systems: standard reference figures, precision measurements and their implications concerning global structure and processes

Suggested reading in the *Encyclopædia Britannica:*

Section 212.   **The Earth's Physical Properties**

A. The Earth's gravitational field
[see also 131.B.]

  1. The factors that determine the gravitational field at the Earth's surface

  2. Measurement of gravity
     [see also 723.D.2.d.]

  3. Interpretation of gravity data: inferences about the Earth's interior

    a. Isostasy: the approximate balance between the elevation of the Earth's surface and the density of the rocks below

    b. Irregularities in the gravitational field

B. The Earth's magnetic properties
[see also 127.C.]

  1. The Earth's main geomagnetic field and its variations
     [see also 4.b., below]

  2. Transient and short-term geomagnetic fields

  3. Origin of the geomagnetic field

  4. Rock magnetism
     [see also 127.C.5.]

    a. Magnetization of rocks: induced and remanent magnetism

    b. The Earth's paleomagnetic field: the record of variation and polar reversal

C. The Earth's electrical properties
[see also 127.B.]

  1. Currents produced by the motion of charged particles in the Earth's ionosphere
     [see also 221.A.4.]

  2. Electrical conductivity and dielectric behaviour of the Earth's rocks and minerals

  3. Currents induced by geomagnetic field variations, currents generated by the Earth's core

D. The Earth's thermal properties
[see also 124.A.4.c.]

  1. Sources of the Earth's heat
     [see also 112.C.5.]

2. Transmission of heat from the Earth's interior to its surface: thermal conductivity and gradients, heat flow data

3. Geological aspects of heat flow: convection currents in the Earth, rock metamorphism, and mountain building

4. Surface manifestations of heat flow: volcanoes and volcanism

E. The mechanical properties of the Earth

1. The fundamental mechanical properties of the Earth's body and the indirect evidence used to determine them

2. Nature of deformable media: stress and strain, models of the stress–strain behaviour of materials, seismic waves
[see also 126.C. and F.]

3. The basic internal mechanical properties of the Earth

4. The Earth's departures from spherical symmetry: oblateness, lateral variations associated with crustal structure, isostasy and its effects
[see also 211.A.2.b.]

5. Anelasticity in the Earth

6. Response of the Earth to stresses of long duration
[see also 241.G.]

F. Physical properties of Earth materials

1. Volumetric properties: rock density and porosity

2. Mechanical properties
[see also 126.C.,D., and F.]

3. Thermal properties: specific heat and thermal conductivity, thermal expansion and rock melting

4. Magnetic and electrical properties
[see also B.4. and C.2., above]

5. Hydraulic properties: porosity and permeability, the capacity to store and transmit fluids

6. Optical properties: colour, lustre

G. The deformation of materials in the Earth's crust

1. Stress and strain of rocks

2. Folding of rocks

    a. Tectonic folding

    b. Foliation, lineation

    c. Nappes

    d. Salt domes and other diapiric structures
    [see also 724.B.1.b.]

    e. Nontectonic folding; *e.g.,* slumping of recently deposited sediments

3. Fracture in rocks: joints, faults

4. Structural interference: the superposition of strains produced by the tectonic events of different ages

5. The deformation of ice in sheets and glaciers
[see also 222.A.3.a.]

Suggested reading in the *Encyclopædia Britannica:*

MACROPAEDIA: Major articles dealing with the Earth's physical properties

Earth, The: Its Properties, Composition, and Structure
Minerals and Rocks
Volcanism

MICROPAEDIA: Selected entries of reference information

<u>General subjects</u>

continental drift	earthquake	isostasy	seafloor spreading
dipolar hypothesis	fault	orogeny	telluric current
dynamo theory	fold	plate tectonics	volcanism
Earth	geosyncline	polar wandering	
Earth tide	gravitation	remanent	
		magnetism	

<u>Biographies</u>

See Section 10/33 of Part Ten

INDEX: See entries under all of the terms above

Section 213.   **The Structure and Composition of the Earth's Interior**

A. The Earth's concentric layers

1. Physical properties and zonal structure of the Earth
   [see also 212]

2. The basic divisions of the solid Earth

   a. The crust: the Earth's outer layer, which may be differentiated into continental and oceanic crust

   b. The Mohorovičić Discontinuity: the zone that separates crust from mantle

   c. The mantle: the layer between crust and core that comprises the bulk of the Earth's volume

3. The development of the Earth's structure and composition
   [see 241.A.]

B. Earthquakes: sources of seismic waves within the Earth

1. Causes of earthquakes

2. Distribution of earthquakes

3. Magnitude, motion, and energy of earthquakes
   [see also 126.C. and 128.A.]

4. Seismic measurements and their interpretation
   [see also 723.F.6.]

C. Distribution of elements in the Earth's core, mantle, and crust
   [see 214.C.]

D. The indirect geophysical and geochemical evidence used to infer the structure and composition of the Earth's interior
   [see also 133.A.4.d., 212.E., and 214.A.5.]

1. Geophysical evidence, mainly from earthquake analyses
   [see also 212.E.]

   a. Seismic wave velocities

   b. Other geophysical evidence; *e.g.*, the Earth's moment of inertia, density distribution

2. Geochemical evidence

   a. Investigations of geochemical equilibria at high temperatures and pressures: phase transitions in the Earth's interior
      [see also 214.A.5.]

   b. The composition and mineralogy of meteorites that may correspond to rocks forming the Earth's interior
      [see also 133.A.4.d.]

   c. Evidence from crustal igneous rocks that are derived from the upper mantle; *e.g.*, andesite lava flows, peridotite and eclogite inclusions in lava flows and some igneous rocks

Suggested reading in the *Encyclopædia Britannica:*

MACROPAEDIA: Major articles dealing with the structure and composition of the Earth's interior

Earth, The: Its Properties, Composition, and Structure
Earthquakes

MICROPAEDIA: Selected entries of reference information

General subjects

Earth	Mohorovičić	Richter scale	seismic wave
earthquake	Discontinuity	seismic belt	

Biographies

See Section 10/33 of Part Ten

INDEX: See entries under all of the terms above

Section 214.   **The Earth's Constituent Minerals and Rocks**

A. The mineral constituents of the Earth

1. The chemical composition, internal structure, and external morphology of minerals

2. The physical properties of minerals: hardness; cleavage; specific gravity; magnetic, electrical, optical, and thermal properties

3. Classification of minerals in terms of crystal structure and chemical composition
   [see also 122.F.]

   a. The principal nonsilicate minerals

      i. Native elements

      ii. Sulfides, including arsenides and antimonides
         [see also 4.c., below]

      iii. Sulfosalts

      iv. Oxides and hydroxides

      v. Halides

      vi. Carbonates

      vii. Nitrates and iodates

      viii. Borates

      ix. Sulfates

      x. Chromates

      xi. Phosphates, including vanadates and arsenates

      xii. Tungstates and molybdates

   b. The silicate minerals

      i. Silicate structure and composition

      ii. Isolated or double tetrahedral group silicates

      iii. Chain silicates

      iv. Sheet silicates

      v. Framework silicates

4. The occurrence of minerals in nature

   a. The major rock-forming mineral groups

      i. The olivines

      ii. The pyroxenes

      iii. The amphiboles

   c. Formation of metamorphic rocks

   d. Rocks of the principal facies

   e. Distribution of metamorphic rocks

4. The rock associations formed in different environments of the Earth's crust

   a. In the oceanic regions: basaltic lavas, reef limestones, abyssal sediments of the deep oceans

   b. In the stable continental regions: conglomerates, sandstones, evaporites, coal measures

   c. In the continental borderlands: sandstones, shales, limestones

   d. In the island arcs: andesite and spilite lavas, ultrabasic intrusive rocks, graywackes, shales

   e. In the major mountain ranges: regionally metamorphosed rocks, granitic batholiths, early-stage basalts and peridotites, late-stage andesite lavas

   f. In the piedmont regions that are adjacent to mountain ranges: gabbros, basalts, arkoses

C. Distribution of chemical elements in the Earth
   [see also 121.D.1.]

D. Distribution of mineral fuels

   1. Coals
      [see also 724.B.1.b. and C.2.]

   2. Petroleum
      [see also 122.G.1.a. and 724.B.2. and C.1.]

   3. Tar sands and oil shales
      [see also 122.G.1.a. and 724.B.2. and C.1.]

   4. Natural gas
      [see 724.B.2.]

E. Distribution of elements in soils

F. Distribution of elements in the hydrosphere
   [see 222.B. and C.]

G. Distribution of elements in the atmosphere
   [see 221.A.1.c.]

H. The selective concentration of elements by plants and animals

 I. The geochemical cycle: the primary geochemical differentiation of the Earth; the migration of elements throughout the atmosphere, hydrosphere, and solid Earth

---

Suggested reading in the *Encyclopædia Britannica:*

MACROPAEDIA: Major articles dealing with the Earth's constituent minerals and rocks

   Chemical Elements
   Earth, The: Its Properties, Composition, and Structure
   Fuels, Fossil
   Minerals and Rocks
   Volcanism

MICROPAEDIA: Selected entries of reference information

General subjects

borate minerals:	nahcolite	aventurine	perthite
borate mineral	rhodochrosite	celsian	plagioclase
borax	*feldspar and*	feldspar	sanidine
ulexite	*feldspathoid*	feldspathoid	scapolite
carbonate minerals:	*minerals:*	labradorite	sodalite
aragonite	adularia	microcline	wairakite
bastnaesite	albite	micropegmatite	*halide minerals:*
calcite	alkali feldspar	nepheline	calomel
carbonate mineral	analcime	orthoclase	cerargyrite
magnesite	anorthite	peristerite	fluorite

halide mineral
halite

*igneous rocks and
formations:*
alkaline rock
amygdule
andesite
anorthosite
aplite
basalt
basanite
batholith
dacite
diabase
dike
diorite
dunite
felsic rock
gabbro
granite
granodiorite
greisen
igneous rock
ijolite
Kimberlite
laccolith
lamprophyre
latite
leucitite
limburgite
magma
monzonite
myrmekite
nephelinesyenite
nephelinite
obsidian
pegmatite
peridotite
perlite
phonolite
picrite
pitchstone
pumice
pyroxenite
rhyolite
roof pendant
sill
spilite
syenite
tachylyte
teschenite
theralite
tinguaite
trachyte
tuff
volcanic glass
xenolith
*metamorphic rocks
and their formation:*
amphibolite facies
anatexis
cataclastite

charnockite
eclogite
epidote-amphibolite
  facies
glaucophane schist
  facies
gneiss
granitization
granulite facies
greenschist facies
hornfels facies
induration
marble
metamorphic rock
metamorphism
metatexis
migmatite
phyllite
sanidinite facies
schist
skarn
slate
zeolitic facies
*mineral fuels and
deposits:*
anthracite
asphalt
asphaltite
bitumen
bituminous coal
brown coal
cannel coal
coal
crude oil
gas reservoir
Gilsonite
lignite
maceral
natural gas
oil shale
ozokerite
peat
petroleum
petroleum trap
pitch lake
pyrobitumen
shale oil
subbituminous
  coal
tar sand
wet gas
*molybdate and
tungstate minerals:*
molybdate
  and tungstate
  minerals
scheelite
wolframite
wulfenite
native elements:
diamond
electrum
graphite

industrial
  diamond
native element
*oxide and hydroxide
minerals:*
anatase
bauxite
boehmite
cassiterite
chromite
chrysoberyl
columbite
corundum
cuprite
emery
gibbsite
goethite
gossan
hematite
ilmenite
limonite
magnetite
oxide mineral
pitchblende
psilomelane
pyrochlore
pyrolusite
ruby
ruby spinel
rutile
sapphire
spinel
thorianite
uraninite
phosphate minerals:
amblygonite
apatite
arsenate mineral
carnotite
descloizite
erythrite
fluorapatite
lazulite
mimetite
phosphate mineral
pyromorphite
scorodite
triphylite
turquoise
vanadate mineral
variscite
*sedimentary rocks
and their formation:*
arkose
armoured mud ball
black shale
breccia
cementation
conglomerate
diagenesis
diatomaceous earth
dolomite

evaporite
flysch
geode
gravel
graywacke
hälleflinta
limestone
lithification
loess
lutite
marl
molasse
nodule
oölite
phosphorite
porcellanite
quartzite
sand
sandstone
sedimentary facies
sedimentary rock
shale
siliceous rock
silt
siltstone
stratification
stylolite
subgraywacke
tillite
tripoli
silica minerals:
agate
amethyst
aventurine
carnelian
chalcedony
chert and flint
chrysotile
citrine
coesite
cristobalite
fulgurite
jasper
lechatelierite
moss agate
onyx
opal
phillipsite
quartz
rock crystal
rose quartz
sard and sardonyx
sepiolite
serpentine
silica
silica mineral
smoky quartz
tridymite
silicate minerals:
actinolite
aegirine
almandine
amphibole

andalusite	pyrophyllite	sulfide mineral	hydraulic
andradite	pyroxene	sulfosalt	equivalence
augite	rhodonite	supergene sulfide	hydrothermal ore
beryl	Riebeckite	enrichment	deposit
biotite	silicate mineral	tetrahedrite	iridescence
chlorite	staurolite	*zeolite minerals:*	kaolin
clay mineral	talc	apophyllite	lapis lazuli
cordierite	topaz	chabazite	metallogenic
diopside	tourmaline	clinoptilolite	province
emerald	vermiculite	epistilbite	metasomatic
enstatite	vesuvianite	erionite	replacement
epidote	wollastonite	faujasite	mineral
forsterite–fayalite	zircon	heulandite	Mohs hardness
series	zoisite	laumontite	nitrate and iodate
garnet	*sulfate minerals:*	mordenite	minerals
grossular	alunite	natrolite	nuée ardente
hornblende	anhydrite	zeolite	ore
humite	barite	*other:*	paragenesis
jadeite	celestite	accessory mineral	phase diagram
kaolinite	gypsum	amphibolite	phase rule
kyanite	halotrichite	bentonite	placer deposit
lepidolite	sulfate mineral	chromate mineral	pleochroic halo
melilite	*sulfide minerals:*	clay mineralogy	porphyry copper
mica	antimonide	cleavage	deposit
monticellite	argentite	colour index	primary mineral
montmorillonite	arsenide	crocoite	pseudomorph
nephrite	arsenopyrite	devitrification	pyroelectricity
olivine	galena	Eh-pH diagram	Riecke's principle
orthopyroxene	marcasite	filter-pressing	rock
peridot	orpiment	fuller's earth	saussuritization
phenakite	pyrite	gemstone	sinter
phlogopite	sphalerite	geochemical facies	vein
phyllosilicate	stibnite	grade scale	

INDEX: See entries under all of the terms above

Division II.   **The Earth's Envelope: Its Atmosphere and Hydrosphere**
[For Part Two headnote see page 65.]

The outlines in the three sections of Division II treat the Earth's atmosphere, its hydrosphere, and weather and climate.

Section 221.   **The Atmosphere**

A. The structure, composition, and physical properties of the atmosphere
[see also 241.B. and 723.G.5.]

   1. Regions of the atmosphere

      a. The lower atmosphere: the troposphere, the stratosphere, the mesosphere

      b. The upper atmosphere: the thermosphere and the exosphere

      c. The composition of the atmosphere: the gross composition and regional variations

         i. Water cycle
[222.D.3 and 223.A.1.]

        ii. Carbon budget

       iii. Nitrogen budget

       iv. Sulfur budget

   2. The homosphere

   a. The effects of ultraviolet radiation: photodissociation of molecules

   b. The role of the ozone layer: the absorption of ultraviolet radiation of wavelengths harmful to plant and animal life and the heating of the stratosphere and mesosphere

   c. Mechanisms of air mixing: molecular and turbulent diffusion

3. The heterosphere

   a. Oxygen dissociation in the lower thermosphere

   b. Effects of vertical transport: the distribution of atmospheric constituents

   c. Variations in atmospheric densities

   d. The escape of helium and hydrogen from the upper atmosphere

   e. Ionization mechanisms
      [see also 4.b., below]

4. The ionosphere
   [see also 127.B.2.]

   a. The gross features of the ionosphere

   b. Formation and characteristics of the ionosphere

   c. Ionospheric variations and disturbances of atmospheric origin

   d. Ionospheric variations and disturbances of solar origin: magnetic and auroral storms, the Northern Lights
      [see also 133.B.]

   e. The effects of the ionosphere on radio waves
      [see also 735.I.5.]

5. The exosphere

   a. Effects of low particle density on the properties of the exosphere

   b. Determination of the critical zone, the layer above which the number of particle collisions is negligible

   c. Particle trajectories in the exosphere

   d. The Van Allen radiation belts
      [see also 133.B. and 212.B.]

B. The large-scale motions of the atmosphere
   [see also 223, 232.A.5., and 723.G.5.]

   1. The general nature and relative scales of atmospheric motions: the resolution of winds into zonal (east–west), meridional (north–south), and vertical components

   2. The relation of wind to pressure and temperature: the cause of winds, the effect of Coriolis force, idealized winds derived from simplified models—the geostrophic and thermal winds
      [see also 211.A.2.a.]

   3. Jet streams

   4. The westerlies of the mid-latitudes

      a. Standing waves of the mid-latitude westerlies and related systems

      b. Mid-latitude traveling disturbances: cyclones, anticyclones
         [see also 223.B.1.]

   5. Tropical wind systems

      a. Trade winds

      b. Tropical disturbances: noncyclonic storms, hurricanes and typhoons
         [see 223.B.4.]

      c. Monsoons

   6. Stratospheric and mesospheric wind systems

      a. Polar Night Westerlies

      b. Summer Easterlies of the mesosphere and stratosphere

   7. The mean meridional circulations of the atmosphere

   8. The driving mechanism of the atmosphere: the energy balance and the transport of heat and momentum

Suggested reading in the *Encyclopædia Britannica*:

MACROPAEDIA: Major article dealing with the atmosphere

Atmosphere

MICROPAEDIA: Selected entries of reference information

General subjects

atmospheric motion and disturbances:	Hadley cell	aureole	*other:*
anticyclone	hurricane	aurora	air
atmospheric circulation	jet stream	halo	air mass
	monsoon	*regions and zones of the atmosphere:*	atmosphere
atmospheric turbulence	polar anticyclone	D region	atmospheric pressure
cyclone	Rossby wave	E region	greenhouse effect
cyclostrophic wind	Siberian anticyclone	exosphere	lapse rate
doldrums	thunderstorm	F region	magnetic storm
eddy	tricellular theory	ionosphere	solar wind
extratropical cyclone	tropical cyclone	magnetosphere	temperature inversion
	updraft and downdraft	mesosphere	whistler
Ferrel cell	wind	ozonosphere	
geostrophic motion	*atmospheric optical phenomena:*	protonosphere	
gradient wind	airglow	stratosphere	
Greenland anticyclone	atmospheric corona	thermosphere	
		troposphere	
		Van Allen radiation belt	

Biographies

See Section 10/33 of Part Ten

INDEX: See entries under all of the terms above

Section 222. **The Hydrosphere: the Oceans, Freshwater Bodies, and Ice Masses**

A. The distribution of water in the hydrosphere

   1. Saltwater bodies

      a. Oceans and marginal seas

      b. Gulfs and bays

   2. Freshwater bodies

      a. Rivers, lakes, and marginal bodies such as estuaries and swamps
[see 232.C.1., 2., and 3.]

      b. Groundwater contained within the pores of rocks

   3. Ice

      a. Ice sheets and glaciers
[see also 212.G.5. and 232.C.6.]

      b. Icebergs and pack ice

      c. River ice and lake ice

   4. Water in the biosphere
[see 351]

B. The physical and chemical properties of seawater
[see 241.C.]

C. The physical and chemical properties of freshwater
[see also 214.A.5.]

D. The hydrologic cycle

    1. The general nature of the hydrologic cycle: the types of processes involved and their complex interaction, scales of magnitude of the interrelated components of the global hydrologic system, influences of climate and other factors

    2. The roles of evaporation and transpiration in the hydrologic cycle
    [see also 336.B.4.]

    3. The role of water vapour in the hydrologic cycle: condensation, precipitation
    [see also 223.A. and D.1.e.]

    4. Runoff and subsurface water in the hydrologic cycle
    [see also 232.A.4.]

    5. The role of ice in the hydrologic cycle
    [see also A.3., above]

    6. Water resources and supply
    [see also 737.A.1.]

E. Ocean–atmosphere interaction

F. Waves in the hydrosphere
[see also 126.E., 128.A., and 232]

    1. Surface waves: simple waves, ocean waves, tsunamis

    2. Internal waves

    3. Tides
    [see 133.E.6.c.]

G. Ocean currents

    1. The distribution of ocean currents

    2. The forces that cause and affect ocean currents: pressure gradients, Coriolis force, frictional forces
    [see also 211.A.2.a.]

    3. The general surface circulation

    4. The general deep sea circulation

    5. Tidal currents: periodic currents associated with tides in the sea

    6. Density currents down continental slopes, produced by differences in temperature, salinity, or sediment concentration
    [see also 231.C.3.]

    7. The influence of ocean currents on weather and climate
    [see also 223.D.1.d.]

Suggested reading in the *Encyclopædia Britannica*:

MACROPAEDIA: Major articles dealing with the hydrosphere: the oceans, freshwater bodies, and ice masses

    Earth, The: Its Properties, Composition, and Structure
    Hydrosphere, The
    Ice and Ice Formations
    Lakes
    Oceans
    Rivers

MICROPAEDIA: Selected entries of reference information

General subjects

freshwater resources:	river	glacier	*motions of the sea:*
aquifer	spring	ice formation	density current
groundwater	water resource	ice shelf	ocean current
ice	well	iceberg	rip current
lake	*ice masses:*	pack ice	seiche
reservoir	firn	permafrost	tide

tsunami	halocline	lagoon	hydrologic cycle
undertow	thermocline	ocean	hydrosphere
wave	*saltwater bodies:*	*other:*	sea level
whirlpool	bay	air–sea interface	water mass
ocean zones:	estuary	bore	
bottom water	gulf	fetch	

Biographies

See Section 10/33 of Part Ten

INDEX: See entries under all of the terms above

Section 223.   Weather and Climate

A. Condensation of water in the atmosphere producing clouds, fogs, and precipitation

   1. Moisture in the atmosphere
      [see also 221.A.1.c. and 723.G.5.]

      a. Humidity indices: absolute, specific, and relative humidity; dew-point temperature

      b. Climatic aspects of atmospheric humidity
         [see D.1.e., below]

      c. Effects of atmospheric humidity on the life and health of mankind and other organisms
         [see D.4., below]

   2. Condensation of atmospheric water vapour

      a. Convection, air mass convergence, and other processes that lead to condensation
         [see also 221.B.]

      b. Condensation nuclei: atmospheric ions, salt and dust particles

      c. Dew

      d. Frost

   3. Clouds and fogs
      [see also 723.G.5.]

      a. Formation and growth of clouds

      b. Description and classification of clouds

      c. Clouds and weather

      d. Fog

      e. Artificial modification of clouds and fogs

   4. Precipitation
      [see also 222.D. and 723.G.5.]

      a. Origin of precipitation in clouds, mechanisms of precipitation release
         [see A.3.a., above]

      b. Types of precipitation: drizzle, rain, freezing rain; snow; sleet, hail

      c. The world distribution of rainfall

      d. Effects of precipitation

B. Winds and storms
   [see also 221.B.]

   1. Development and distribution of cyclones and anticyclones

   2. Lightning and thunderstorms
      [see also 127.A. and B.]

   3. Tornadoes, hail, and other severe phenomena associated with organized storms or squall lines

   4. Tropical cyclones: hurricanes and typhoons
      [see 221.B.5.b.]

C. Weather forecasting and weather lore

D. Climate: the aggregate of weather
[see also 133.B.5., 221, and 723.G.5.]

1. Factors that generate climate

a. Solar radiation

b. Temperature

c. Atmospheric pressure

d. The world's oceans

e. The moisture cycle

2. Climatic variation

a. Seasonal changes resulting from the north–south migration of belts of cyclonic activity and other cyclic processes

b. Local effects: modification of climate by local terrain and surface conditions

c. Effects of mankind's activities on global climate
[see also 737.C.1.]

3. Climatic types: the Köppen classification system, world climates and their distribution

4. Influences of climate on terrestrial life

5. Microclimates
[see also 351.B. and 723.G.5.]

6. Paleoclimates
[see also 242.E.]

Suggested reading in the *Encyclopædia Britannica*:

MACROPAEDIA: Major article dealing with weather and climate

Climate and Weather

MICROPAEDIA: Selected entries of reference information

General subjects

atmospheric humidity and precipitation:
aerosol
cloud
condensation
  nucleus
dew
fog
frost
hail
hoarfrost
humidity
precipitation
rain
rime
snow

atmospheric pressure and wind:
anticyclone
atmospheric
  circulation
atmospheric
  pressure
bora
breeze
Buys Ballot's law
convergence and
  divergence
cyclone

cyclostrophic wind
etesian wind
foehn
geostrophic motion
gradient wind
Greenland
  anticyclone
gregale
haboob
Hadley cell
harmattan
horse latitude
jet stream
katabatic wind
khamsin
lee wave
levanter
lightning
mistral
monsoon
polar anticyclone
Siberian
  anticyclone
subtropical high
surge
tricellular theory
updraft and
  downdraft
wind

climate and climatic variation:
autumn
climate
drought
Indian summer
Köppen climatic
  classification
microclimate
pluvial regime
season
snow line
spring
summer
timberline
urban climate
winter
meteorological measurement and weather forecasting:
Beaufort scale
hygrometry
isentropic chart
isobar
isotherm
psychrometric
  chart
temperature–
  humidity index

weather bureau
weather forecasting
weather map
weather station
windchill
World Weather
  Watch
weather disturbances and related phenomena:
atmospheric
  turbulence
blizzard
extratropical
  cyclone
hurricane
lightning
storm
thunder
thunderstorm
tornado
tropical cyclone
weather fronts:
cold front
equatorial front
front
occluded front

polar front | Saint Swithin's | atmospheric | urban dust
stationary | Day | electricity | weather
front | weather lore | greenhouse effect | weather
warm front | *other:* | smog | modification
weather lore: | almanac | sunshine |
Groundhog Day | | |

<u>Biographies</u>

See Section 10/33 of Part Ten

Division III.   The Earth's Surface Features
[For Part Two headnote see page 65.]

The outlines in the two sections of Division III deal with the basic physical features of the Earth's surface and with the features produced by geomorphic processes acting on the Earth's surface.

Section 231.   Physical Features of the Earth's Surface

A. Vertical relief of the Earth's surface

1. Hypsography of the Earth's surface: distribution of land and sea, elevation of the continents, coastlines

2. Physiography of the continents: Europe, Asia, Africa, Australia, North America, South America, Antarctica

3. The oceanic regions

   a. Principal oceanic features: mid-ocean ridges, continental margins, abyssal depressions
   [see also 723.G.3. and 735.J.2.]

   b. Oceanic physiography

B. The stable platform regions of the continents

1. The continental shield areas and their age, structure, and constituent rocks
   [see also 214.B.4.]

2. Uplift, downwarp, and fracture of continental platforms

   a. Plateaus and basins

   b. Rift valleys

   c. Water bodies occupying fault-bounded structural depressions: lakes and landlocked seas; inland seas with outlets to the oceans; elongated seas formed by crustal separation, such as the Red Sea or the Gulf of California
   [see also 241.G.]

C. The continental shelf and slope

1. Composition: evidence from bottom samples, geophysical techniques

2. Structure and origin

3. Submarine canyons incising the continental terrace

D. The oceanic deeps

1. Components of ocean basins

   a. The oceanic crust

   b. Major features of the deep-ocean floor: mid-ocean ridges, trenches, fracture zones, seamounts and guyots, abyssal hills and plains, sediments of the ocean floor
   [see G., below, and 241.G.]

   c. Basin boundaries: the continental slope, the continental rise
   [see C., above]

2. The origin of ocean basins

E. Coral islands, coral reefs, and atolls
[see also 354.B.]

F. The major mountain ranges and fracture zones of the Earth's crust on the continents and beneath the oceans

1. Types of mountains

2. The worldwide system of folded mountain ranges, fracture zones, and volcanic island arcs

a. The Circum-Pacific System

b. The Tethyan System

c. Subsidiary mountain ranges

d. The volcanic island arc systems

e. The rock types constituting the folded mountain ranges and island arcs
[see also 212.G. and 214.B.4.]

G. Oceanic ridges
[see also 241.G.]

1. Classification of ridges

a. The mid-ocean ridge system

b. Other ridges: lateral, linear, and boundary ridges; microcontinents

2. Origin and growth of ridges

a. General geophysical properties

b. Mid-oceanic ridges as manifestations of divergent lithospheric plate boundaries
[see also 241.F.]

3. Occurrence and distribution of ridges in the Atlantic, Pacific, and Indian oceans
[see also A.3., above]

Suggested reading in the *Encyclopædia Britannica*:

MACROPAEDIA: Major articles dealing with the physical features of the Earth's surface

Continental Landforms
Earth, The: Its Properties, Composition, and Structure
Oceans
Plate Tectonics
Volcanism

MICROPAEDIA: Selected entries of reference information

General subjects

continental shelf and slope:	cuesta	volcano	oceanic trough
continental shelf	dome	*oceanic structures and features:*	seamount
continental slope	drumlin		submarine gap
submarine canyon	esker	abyssal hill	*other:*
submarine fan	meteorite crater	abyssal plain	continent
submarine slump	mountain	archipelagic apron	density current
landforms and surface features:	pediment	atoll	landform
	plain	cay	lake
alluvial fan	plateau	coral reef	marine sediment
basin	playa	guyot	ocean
beach	rift valley	island	ooze
canyon	saline flat	island arc	
cave	salt dome	oceanic plateau	
continental shield	sand dune	oceanic ridge	
	volcanic dome	oceanic trench	

Biographies

See Section 10/33 of Part Ten

INDEX: See entries under all of the terms above

Section 232. **Features Produced by Geomorphic Processes Acting on the Earth's Surface**

A. The action of the hydrosphere and atmosphere on the Earth's surface features

1. The process of weathering: the disintegration and alteration of rocks at or near the Earth's surface

2. Soil formation as a result of weathering

   a. Processes and factors in soil formation
   [see also 354.A.2.b.]

   b. Classification and distribution of soils

   c. Soil crusts

3. Gravitational processes: earth movements on slopes

4. Fluvial processes
   [see also 126]

   a. The flow of water in a natural channel

   b. Entrainment and transport of materials

   c. Erosion, deposition

   d. River forms and fluvial processes in different environments

   e. The flow of rivers in estuaries
   [see C.3.b., below]

   f. The flow of ephemeral streams
   [see C.1.d., below]

   g. The relationship of rivers and groundwater

   h. The sediment yield of drainage systems

   i. The erosion of canyons and valleys

   j. The formation of hillslopes

5. Eolian processes

   a. Transportation of rock debris by wind

   b. Effects of wind transport

   c. Deposition by wind: formation and migration of dunes, the role of vegetation

   d. Wind action and the works of mankind

6. Marine processes

   a. Erosion and deposition of coastal materials by waves and currents

   b. Transport of sediment by density flows

7. Glacial processes: erosion, transport, deposition, glacial loading and unloading, periglacial processes
   [see also C.6., below]

8. Lacustrine processes

   a. Erosion and deposition by waves and currents

   b. Sedimentation in lakes

   c. Effects of flora and fauna on lakes and lake systems
   [see 354.B.3.a.]

B. The actions of the biosphere, exosphere, and lithosphere upon the Earth's surface features

1. Biological processes
   [see 351]

   a. Effects of plants and organisms on rock weathering and soil formation
   [see A.1., above]

   b. Effects of animal trails, tracks, and burrows on the erodibility of Earth materials and on sediment yield
   [see A.4.h., above]

   c. Effects of vegetation type and density on sediment yield
   [see A.4.h., above]

   d. Effects of mankind on the Earth's surface features
      [see also 355, 731, 733.B., 734, 736, and 737]

  2. Extraterrestrial processes: the occurrence of meteorite craters
     [see also 133.A.4.d.]

  3. Volcanic-tectonic processes
     [see also 212.D.4., 212.G., 231.F., and 241.E.]

C. The characteristic features of the Earth's major environments

  1. The fluvial environment
     [see also 354.B.3.b.]

     a. Distribution of rivers in nature

     b. Drainage patterns

     c. The geometry of river systems

     d. Streamflow and fluvial landforms: peak discharge and flooding, river floodplains and terraces, river deltas, ephemeral streams, waterfalls

     e. The development of river systems through geological time

  2. The lacustrine environment
     [see also 354.B.3.a.]

     a. Lake basins

     b. Lake waters: chemical composition, thermal properties

     c. Lake hydraulics: lake currents, surface waves, seiches, effects of wave and current action
        [see also 222.F.]

     d. The hydrologic balance of lakes

     e. Lakes in arid regions
        [see C.5.c., below]

     f. Glacial lakes
        [see C.6.e. below]

     g. Swamps, marshes, and bogs

  3. The estuarine environment

     a. The formation of estuaries

     b. Hydrologic features of estuaries

  4. The marine environment
     [see also 354.B.4.]

     a. Coastal features resulting from depositional processes

         i. Beaches: materials, morphological features, physical processes

        ii. Sand dunes and sandbars

       iii. River deltas
            [see C.i.d., above]

        iv. Coral reefs
            [see 231.E.]

         v. Lagoons

        vi. Marshes
            [see C.2.g., above]

     b. Coastal features resulting from erosional processes: sea cliffs and related landforms

     c. Coastal features dependent on bedrock type, bedrock structure, or local topography: grottoes, spouting holes, fjords, peninsulas, islands

     d. Submerged coastal features: the continental shelf and slope, submarine canyons
        [see 231.C.]

  5. The desert environment
     [see also 354.A.1.c.]

     a. General aspects of deserts: basic types of deserts and their climatic features, areal extent of the major deserts of the world today, economic importance of deserts

     b. The aridity of deserts
        [see also 223.D.]

Suggested reading in the *Encyclopædia Britannica*:

MACROPAEDIA: Major articles dealing with the features produced by geomorphic processes acting on the Earth's surface

Continental Landforms
Earth, The: Its Properties,
    Composition, and Structure
Geomorphic Processes
Ice and Ice Formations

Lakes
Oceans
Rivers
Soils
Volcanism

MICROPAEDIA: Selected entries of reference information

General subjects

*effects of fluvial
    processes:*
  alluvial fan
  arroyo
  bajada
  delta
  desert pavement
  drainage basin
  floodplain
  fluvial process
  inselberg
  meander
  oxbow lake
  river
  river terrace
  valley
  waterfall
effects of weathering:
  calcrete
  cave
  duricrust
  exfoliation
  ferricrete
  pediment
  pepino hill
  sinkhole
  weathering
*glacial features and
    landforms:*
  chatter mark

cirque
drumlin
esker
estuary
fjord
glacial valley
ice cave
kettle
moraine
moulin
outwash
roche
  moutonnée
till
*gravitational
    processes on
    hillslopes:*
  avalanche
  creep
  landslide
  mass movement
  mudflow
  rock glacier
*marine features
    produced by wave
    action:*
  beach
  beach cusp
  chenier
  lagoon

sandbar
sea cave
wave-cut
  platform
*physiographic effects
    of eolian processes:*
  barchan
  desert varnish
  playa
  saline flat
  sand dune
  seif
*soil formation and
    major soil types:*
  alfisol
  aridisol
  chernozem
  clay
  entisol
  histosol
  humus
  inceptisol
  kaolisol
  laterite
  mollisol
  oxisol
  podsol
  podsolic soil
  soil
  spodosol

ultisol
vertisol
*volcanic structures
    and related
    phenomena:*
  cinder cone
  fumarole
  geyser
  hot spring
  lava cave
  mud volcano
  volcanic dome
  volcano
other:
  astrobleme
  meteorite crater
  morphogenetic
    region
  peneplain
  permafrost
  pingo
  polder
  residual landform
  thermokarst

Biographies
  See Section 10/33 of Part Ten

INDEX: See entries under all of the terms above

Division IV.   The Earth's History
[For Part Two headnote see page 65.]

The outlines in the three sections of Division IV deal with the origin and development of the Earth and its envelopes; the interpretation of the geological record; and the eras and periods of geological time.

Section 241.   Origin and Development of the Earth and Its Envelopes

A. The origin and development of the lithosphere
[see also 213.A.]

   1. Theories of the origin of the Earth
[see also 133.A.7.]

   2. The development of crust from mantle: processes involved in the geochemical differentiation of the Earth's outer layers

B. The origin and development of the atmosphere
[see also 133.A.7. and 221.A.]

   1. The relation of the development of the Earth's atmosphere to the origin of the solar system, the development of other planetary atmospheres

   2. The original atmosphere of the Earth

   3. Development of the present terrestrial atmosphere
[see also 112.C. and 335.B.]

   4. Effects of mankind's activities

   5. The present atmosphere
[see 221.A.]

C. The origin and development of the hydrosphere

   1. The early oceans

   2. The transition stage from about 3,500,000,000 to 1,500,000,000 years ago

   3. The chemical view of the modern oceans

   4. The present hydrosphere
[see 222]

D. The formation and growth of the continents

   1. The Earth's crust and upper mantle
[see also 212.D.2., 213.A., 214.B.1.c., and 232]

   2. Endogenic regimes of the continents: geosynclines, platforms, rifts, continental margins
[see also 231]

   3. The relation between endogenic regimes and deep-seated Earth processes

E. The formation and growth of mountain ranges and belts

   1. The distribution of mountain belts in relation to global tectonics

   2. The tectonic mountain belts
[see also 212.G., 214.B., and 231.F.]

   3. The geosynclinal hypothesis of mountain building

   4. The development of mountain systems

F. The theory of plate tectonics

   1. Early speculations about the existence of a single supercontinent and its fragmentation into the present-day landmasses

2. Wegener's concept of continental drift

3. Hess' seafloor spreading model

4. Plate tectonics as a unifying theory

    a. A Lithospheric plate boundaries as sites of volcanism, seismicity, and orogeny

    b. The impact of continental drift on the evolution of life forms

---

Suggested reading in the *Encyclopædia Britannica*:

MACROPAEDIA: Major articles dealing with the origin and development of the Earth and its envelopes

    Atmosphere
    Earth, The: Its Properties, Composition, and Structure
    Plate Tectonics
    Volcanism

MICROPAEDIA: Selected entries of reference information

General subjects

atmosphere and hydrosphere:	*landmasses and ocean basins:*	plate tectonics	orogeny
atmosphere	continental drift	sea-floor spreading	sedimentation
Earth	Gondwanaland	*evolution of the Earth's crust:*	subsidence
hydrosphere	Laurasia	epeirogeny	uplift
ocean	Pangaea	erosion	volcanism
			weathering

Biographies

    See Section 10/33 of Part Ten

INDEX: See entries under all of the terms above

Section 242.   **The Interpretation of the Geological Record**

A. The stratigraphic interpretation of the geological record

1. The layered rocks of the Earth's crust and their depositional environments: the nature of the rock record
[see also 214.B.2.]

    a. Clastic sedimentary rocks

    b. Carbonate rocks

    c. Volcanic rocks

    d. Cyclic deposits: cyclothems, varved deposits

2. Stratigraphic classifications and their historical development: criteria for the correlation of layered deposits

    a. The principle of uniformitarianism

    b. The principle of superposition of strata

    c. The idea of a fossil succession

    d. The facies concept

    e. The stage concept

    f. The recognition of zones

    g. Radiometric dating
    [see D.2., below]

3. Stratigraphic nomenclature in theory and practice

a. Stratigraphic terminology and its standardization

b. Stratigraphic boundary problems: Lower and Upper Paleozoic boundaries, Cenozoic boundaries

c. Special stratigraphic terminologies and divisions

B. The interpretation of the geological record

1. The nature of fossils and fossilization processes

2. The fossil record

a. Precambrian life: the Cryptozoic fossil record

i. The primitive atmosphere and oceans, the origin of life
[see also 241 and 312.A.]

ii. Precambrian protists, plants, and animals: the Gunflint Chert deposits, Ediacara fauna, and other remains

b. Post-Precambrian life: the Phanerozoic fossil record
[see also 313]

i. The occurrence and evolution of the plants

ii. The occurrence and evolution of the Protista

iii. The occurrence and evolution of the Porifera

iv. The occurrence and evolution of the Cnidaria (Coelenterata)

v. The occurrence and evolution of the Mollusca

vi. The occurrence and evolution of the Conodonta

vii. The occurrence and evolution of the Bryozoa

viii. The occurrence and evolution of the Brachiopoda

ix. The occurrence and evolution of the Arthropoda

x. The occurrence and evolution of the Echinodermata

xi. The occurrence and evolution of the Graptolithina

xii. The occurrence and evolution of the fishes

xiii. The occurrence and evolution of the Amphibia

xiv. The occurrence and evolution of the Reptilia

xv. The occurrence and evolution of the birds

xvi. The occurrence and evolution of the mammals

3. The appearance and disappearance (mass extinctions and background extinctions) of species revealed in the fossil record
[see also 312.C.]

4. The paleontological criteria for the correlation of layered rocks

a. Index fossils

b. Faunal and floral assemblages

c. Organic microfossils: pollen, spores, tests

C. Relative age dating

1. Application to geological problems: the relative geological time scale

2. Application to archaeological problems
[see 10/41.B.2.b.]

D. Absolute dating

1. General considerations: the meaning of absolute age, requirements for absolute dating, the rate of record accumulation

2. Radiometric dating
[see also 723.G.8.]

a. Radioactivity and radioactive decay
[see 112.C.]

b. Principles of radiometric dating

    c. Definition of time zero, sources of error in radiometric dating

    d. Major dating methods; *e.g.,* uranium–thorium to helium–lead, potassium-40 to argon-40, carbon-14

    e. Minor dating methods

  3. Non-radiometric dating: biological and geological processes as absolute chronometers

  4. Applications of absolute dating

    a. The absolute geological time scale

    b. Determination of the age of the Earth and the ages of rocks and meteorites

    c. Determination of the rates of sea-floor spreading

    d. Lunar history

E. The paleogeographical interpretation of the geological record

F. The reconstruction of the geological history of the Earth based on the global correlation of the accumulated evidence from the geological record
[see 241 and 243]

Suggested reading in the *Encyclopædia Britannica:*

MACROPAEDIA: Major articles dealing with the interpretation of the geological record

    Earth, The: Its Properties, Composition, and Structure
    Geochronology: The Interpretation and Dating of the Geological Record

  MICROPAEDIA: Selected entries of reference information

General subjects

carbon-14 dating	fossil	polychaete	sedimentary facies
common-lead	geochronology	hypothesis	tephrochronology
dating	helium dating	potassium–argon	uniformitarianism
dating	horizon	dating	varved deposit
dendrochronology	index fossil	protactinium-231–	
Earth	ionium–thorium	thorium-230	
faunal succession,	dating	dating	
law of	lead-210 dating	radiation-damage	
fission-track dating	paleogeography	dating	

Biographies

    See Section 10/33 of Part Ten

INDEX: See entries under all of the terms above

Section 243.   **The Eras and Periods of Geological Time**

A. Precambrian time: from the time of formation of the oldest rocks to 570,000,000 years ago

B. The Lower Paleozoic Era: from 570,000,000 to 395,000,000 years ago

  1. The Cambrian Period

  2. The Ordovician Period

  3. The Silurian Period

C. The Upper Paleozoic Era: from 395,000,000 to 225,000,000 years ago

  1. The Devonian Period

  2. The Lower Carboniferous Period

  3. The Upper Carboniferous Period

  4. The Permian Period

D. The Mesozoic Era: from 225,000,000 to 65,000,000 years ago

1. The Triassic Period

2. The Jurassic Period

3. The Cretaceous Period

E. The Cenozoic Era: from 65,000,000 years ago to the present

1. The Tertiary Period

2. The Quaternary Period
    [see also 411.B. and 412]

    a. The Pleistocene Epoch
        [see also 232.A.7. and C.6.]

    b. The Holocene, or Recent, Epoch
        [see also 412]

Suggested reading in the *Encyclopædia Britannica*:

MACROPAEDIA: Major articles dealing with the eras and periods of geological time

Earth, The: Its Properties, Composition, and Structure
Geochronology: The Interpretation and Dating of the Geological Record
Volcanism

MICROPAEDIA: Selected entries of reference information

General subjects

Cenozoic period:
Aftonian
  Interglacial Stage
Allerød
Ancylus Stage
Aquitanian Stage
Astian Stage
Auversian Stage
Bartonian Stage
Blancan Stage
Blytt–Sernander
  system
Boreal Climatic
  Interval
Bracheux Sands
Bronze Age
Calabrian Stage
Cenozoic Era
Chattian Stage
Cromerian
  Interglacial Stage
Eemian Interglacial
  Stage
Elsterian Glacial
  Stage
Eocene Epoch
Florissant
  Formation
Gamblian Pluvial
  Stage
Gipping Glacial
  Stage
Great Drought
Günz Glacial Stage
Günz-Mindel
  Interglacial Stage

Helvetian Stage
Holocene Epoch
Holstein
  Interglacial Stage
Hypsithermal
  Climatic Interval
ice age
Illinoian Glacial
  Stage
Ipswichian
  Interglacial Stage
Iron Age
Irvingtonian Stage
Kamasian Pluvial
  Stage
Kanjeran Pluvial
  Stage
Kansan Glacial
  Stage
Lattorfian Stage
Laurentide Ice
  Sheet
London Clay
Ludian Stage
Luisian Stage
Lutetian Stage
Mauer
Mesolithic Period
Mindel Glacial
  Stage
Mindel-Riss
  Interglacial Stage
Miocene Epoch
Montian Stage
Nebraskan Glacial
  Stage

Neogene Period
Neolithic Period
Oligocene Epoch
Paleocene Epoch
Paleogene Period
Paleolithic Period
Pleistocene Epoch
Pliocene Epoch
Pontian Stage
Puercan Stage
Quaternary Period
Rancholabrean
  Stage
Riss Glacial Stage
Riss-Würm
  Interglacial Stage
Rupelian Stage
Saale Glacial Stage
Salpausselkä ridges
Sangamon
  Interglacial Stage
Sannoisian Stage
Sarmatian Stage
Scandinavian Ice
  Sheet
Siwalik Series
Sparnacian Stage
Stampian Stage
Sub-Atlantic
  Climatic Interval
Sub-Boreal
  Climatic Interval
Tertiary Period
Tongrian Stage
Tortonian Stage
Trinil Faunal Zone

Villafranchian
  Stage
Waal Interglacial
  Stage
Weichsel Glacial
  Stage
Wisconsin Glacial
  Stage
Würm Glacial
  Stage
Yarmouth
  Interglacial Stage
Ypresian Stage
Lower Paleozoic era:
Arenig Series
Ashgill Series
Cambrian Period
Canadian Series
Caradoc Series
Cayugan Series
Champlainian
  Series
Chazyan Stage
Cincinnati Arch
Cincinnatian Series
Dalradian Series
Franconian Stage
Holmia Series
Idamean Stage
Lancefieldian Stage
Lipalian interval
Llandeilo Series
Llandovery Series
Llanvirn Series
Ludlow Series

Medinan Series
Mindyallan Stage
Nashville Dome
Niagaran Series
Oeland Series
Ordovician Period
Paleozoic Era
Paradoxides Series
Queenston Delta
Silurian Period
Soussien Stage
Tremadoc Series
Trempealeauan
 Stage
Wenlock Series
Williston Basin
Mesozoic era:
 Albian Stage
 Anisian Stage
 Aptian Stage
 Barremian Stage
 Berriasian Stage
 Clarence Series
 Coniacian Stage
 Cretaceous Period
 Great Oolite Series
 Gulf Series
 Hauterivian Stage
 Hell Creek
  Formation
 Jurassic Period
 Karnian Stage
 Lance Formation
 Maestrichtian
  Stage
 Mata Series
 Mesozoic Era
 Niobrara
  Limestone

Pierre Shale
Purbeck Beds
Raukumara Series
Rhaetian Stage
Solnhofen
 Limestone
Stormberg Series
Sundance
 Formation
Taitai Series
Triassic Period
Turonian Stage
Valanginian Stage
Wealden Series
Precambrian era:
 Animikie Series
 Belt Series
 Bitter Springs
  microfossils
 Bruce Series
 Cobalt Series
 Coutchiching
  Series
 Fig Tree Series
 Grand Canyon
  Series
 Grenville Series
 Gunflint
  microfossils
 Huronian System
 Katangan Complex
 Keewatin Series
 Keweenawan
  System
 Knife Lake Series
 Lewisian Complex
 Longmyndian
 Onverwacht Series
 Phanerozoic Eon

Precambrian time
Proterozoic
Seine Series
Sturtian Series
Swaziland System
Timiskaming
 Series
Torridonian Series
Transvaal System
Ventersdorp
 System
Witwatersrand
 System
Upper Paleozoic era:
 Alberta Basin
 Allegheny Series
 Atokan Series
 Avonian Stage
 Beaufort Series
 Carboniferous
  Period
 Catskill Delta
 Cazenovian Stage
 Chemungian Stage
 Chesterian Series
 Coal Measures
 Conemaugh Series
 Deerparkian Stage
 Desmoinesian
  Series
 Devonian period
 Devonian Series
 Dittonian Stage
 Downtonian Stage
 Dunkard Group
 Dwyka Series
 Ecca Series
 Eifelian Stage
 Emsian Stage

Famennian Stage
Finger Lakes Stage
Frasnian Stage
Givetian Stage
Guadalupian Stage
Helderbergian
 Stage
Karoo System
Kungurian Stage
Leonardian Stage
Meramecian Series
Mississippian
 Period
Missourian Series
Monongahela
 Series
Morrowan Series
Namurian Series
Ochoan Stage
Old Red Sandstone
Osagian Series
Pennsylvanian
 Period
Permian Basin
Permian Period
Pottsville Series
Sakmarian Stage
Salado Formation
Siegenian Stage
Springeran Series
Stephanian Series
Tioughnioga Stage
Virgilian Series
Westphalian Series
Wolfcampian Stage

Biographies

See Section 10/33 of Part Ten

INDEX: See entries under all of the terms above

Introduction to Part Three:
The Mysteries of Life

By René Dubos

We take for granted the existence of life on Earth. Yet, as far as we now know, life exists nowhere else in the solar system, its origin is still a mystery, and its effects on our planet have been little short of miraculous. Without life the surface of the Earth and its atmosphere would be very different from what they are now. We are both spectators and actors in a continuing performance where life is both author and producer, and for which the Earth serves as an ever-changing stage.

Cataclysms give us now and then a glimpse of what our planet would look like without life. In 1883, a series of stupendous volcanic eruptions destroyed two-thirds of Krakatoa Island in the Malay archipelago and covered what was left of it with a thick layer of lava. All living things were killed, not only on Krakatoa itself, but also on the neighbouring islands that were in the path of the tidal wave generated by the explosion and of the volcanic fallout. What had once been a luscious tropical forest suddenly became a gray and lifeless landscape, as desolate as the surface of the Moon.

Pictures taken of Krakatoa in the months following the disaster help us to realize that what we regard as the surface of the Earth is less a geological structure than a living mantle. Our planet would be drab and dusty, an insignificant object in space, if it were not for the myriad of living forms that have generated its atmosphere and its soil out of gases and rocks. In fact, the phrase "life on Earth" is somewhat misleading because the surface of the Earth as we experience it, with its entrancing diversity and colourful warmth, is literally a product of biological activities—a creation of life.

Krakatoa remained a desolate landscape for a long time after the 1883 volcanic explosion. But progressively the wind and the sea brought back to its sterilized surface a multiplicity of living things, some of which managed to establish a permanent foothold on the lava. Today, the island harbours once more a rich flora and fauna, not very different from that of the native forest of the Malay archipelago.

There is a paradox in the marvelous resiliency of nature. On the one hand, all individual forms of life are extremely delicate. And yet life itself has been capable of prevailing over brute physical forces for several billion years, and has generated immensely diversified ecosystems that have remained viable even under the most inhospitable conditions. Life probably emerged from inanimate matter, but it is now more powerful than inanimate matter.

All biological phenomena are of practical importance because they determine the characteristics of the Earth's surface and therefore affect the quality of human life. Men have always been concerned with the contributions that living things make to their immediate environment and to the global economy; they have wondered how the flora and fauna become more or less stabilized under normal conditions, and manage to reestablish stable ecosystems after cataclysms; in our times they worry to what extent living things can be disturbed or eliminated by urbanization and industrialization without thereby threatening human welfare.

But the phrase "life on Earth" also raises other questions of a more philosophical character, questions that have been in the minds of humble, uneducated people even before they became the preoccupation of scholars. In the universe at large, lifelessness is the rule, life the puzzling exception. How do living things differ from inanimate matter? How did they originate? And can life be created *de novo*? Is man qualitatively different from the rest of the living world or merely a higher, or the highest, specimen in its evolution, the paragon of animals?

It is clear from the geological record that life has been at home on the Earth for immense periods of time. The types of fossils found in rock formations indicate that all major groups of animals and plants were already represented by recognizable ancestors some 400,000,000 years ago. Furthermore, microscopic structures closely related to the present forms of blue-green algae have been found in geologic formations that are even very much older—some 3,000,000,000 years old. Since these fossils of algae-like organisms have a complex cellular organization, it can be assumed that they had been preceded by simpler forms, and that the origin of life is more ancient than the oldest traces of it which have been detected. In fact, there is no way to know when life first appeared on Earth, because its earliest manifestations were certainly so minute, fragile, and undifferentiated that none of them have survived as fossils.

There is a peculiar fascination to the phrase "the origin of life" because it means different things to different men, and reaches into the deepest layers of their beliefs. For the religious man, it implies the mysteries of divine creation—whether expressed as biological species in their final forms, or as the potentialities posited by Aristotelian philosophers and medieval theologians. For the student of myths, it evokes Aphrodite emerging fully developed from the foam of the sea. The myth may have a factual basis if it is true, as it is commonly believed, that the cradle of life was to be found in the primitive oceans. For the modern scientist the phrase "origin of life" refers to the kind of chemical reactions that first generated complex organic molecules and assembled them in such a manner that they could duplicate themselves—thus converting inanimate matter into living substance.

Whatever the mystical or rational basis of a person's beliefs, there is a universal poetic quality in the thought that life once arose from matter, and has been perpetuating itself ever since. But the only real clue to the origin of life is that all its forms—at least all the living things we know—have many physicochemical characteristics in common. In particular, they all transfer their hereditary endowment from one generation to the next through the agency of a peculiar kind of molecule known as nucleic acid, the now famous DNA. This uniformity of fundamental structure holds true irrespective of the size, shape, and complexity of the organism—whether it be microbe, plant, animal, or man. Indeed, the similarity in structure of the genetic apparatus throughout the living world is so perfect that it cannot possibly be a matter of chance. The conclusion seems inescapable that all the living forms that now exist have had a common origin.

The simplest hypothesis to account for the origin and evolution of life is that all biological phenomena are caused by the physicochemical forces that govern the inanimate world. Some scientists believe, indeed, that there is nothing very unusual in the emergence of a living molecule from matter. According to them, it is probable that life repeatedly emerged *de novo* on Earth and that it is still emerging today somewhere in the cosmos. By making the reasonable assumption that one of the living forms that appeared on Earth proved more vigorous than the others, it is easy to account for the single origin of all surviving species. If an entirely new genetic form of life were to appear today on Earth, it would have no chance of success, because it could not compete with the established form and all its variations.

The hypothesis that life is nothing more than a special manifestation of ordinary physicochemical forces has the merit of being economical of thought; in addition, it is supported by the fact that all biological phenomena go hand in hand with the kind of reactions observed in the inanimate world. But even if we grant that living phenomena always obey physicochemical laws, this does not constitute decisive evidence that life is merely an expression of these laws. Other theories are conceivable. One of them, rarely voiced because it is not scientifically fashionable, is that some unknown principle runs like a continuous thread through all living forms and governs the organizations of their physicochemical processes. The illustrious Danish physicist Niels Bohr, for example, suggested that "the very existence of life must be considered an elementary fact, just as in atomic physics the existence of a quantum of action has to be taken as a basic fact that cannot be derived from ordinary mechanical physics."

Uncertainties concerning the fundamental nature of life and its origin would disappear if it were possible to generate at will self-reproducing molecules from inert material. Some experimental findings have recently been quoted as evidence of this possibility.

A fully developed virus, which had been naturally produced by a living organism, was separated into its component parts by chemical procedures. When these separate parts were tested for biological activity, they were found to be inert, that is, they were unable to multiply in a susceptible organism. This biological activity was restored, however, when the parts of the virus were chemically reassembled in the test tube under the proper conditions. Spectacular as this achievement is from the chemical point of view, it does not constitute—as has been claimed—the production of life *de novo*. Since the virus first had to be produced by a living organism, and since its reassembled parts showed activity only when introduced into a living susceptible organism, all the biological machinery essential for its reproduction had to be provided by preexisting life.

In a completely unrelated kind of experiment, several complex molecules similar to those found in living things have been produced in the laboratory by exposing simple chemicals to the kind of radiation that probably existed in the primitive atmosphere. But this chemical feat does not constitute production of life *de novo* because the molecules so produced have not been assembled—*organized*—in a way enabling them to duplicate themselves and to develop. An organic molecule, however complex and similar to the kind found in living things, still belongs to the realm of inanimate matter if it cannot reproduce and evolve.

To become "living," an assembly of biogenic molecules must contain the information needed for its further development and must be able to transmit this information to its progeny. Even in its simplest manifestations, life is historical; it embodies the past and carries instructions for the future.

More than a century ago, the French physiologist Claude Bernard gave a clear formulation of the now classical view that the earmark of a living thing is not the chemical composition of its parts but their organization. He wrote: "Admitting that vital phenomena rest upon physicochemical activities, which is the truth, the essence of the problem is not thereby cleared up; for it is no chance encounter of physico-chemical phenomena which constructs each being according to a preexisting plan, and produces the admirable subordination and the harmonious concert of organic activity.

"There is an arrangement in the living being, a kind of regulated activity, which must never be neglected, because it is in truth the most striking characteristic of living beings. . . ."

In this celebrated passage, Bernard used the word "arrangement" to denote the interdependence and integration of the structures and properties of any given living organism. But biological organization applies also to the ecological system of which the organism is a part. All living things, without exception, depend on other living things for their survival and development. Furthermore, the higher the organism is on the evolutionary scale, the more exacting is its dependence on a complex web of life.

One of the major trends of evolution has thus been the emergence of more and more complex ecosystems, exhibiting high degrees of integration. But, paradoxically, an opposite trend can also be detected as one ascends the evolutionary scale—namely, a trend toward freedom or at least toward increasing independence of the individual organism within the constraints of the ecosystem. Freedom becomes more and more apparent as one proceeds from the protoplasmic jelly of biological beginnings to warm-blooded animals roaming in the wild, and finally to man who modifies his environment according to his views of the future. In a real way, evolutionary development is associated with the gradual insertion of more and more freedom into matter and into individual lives.

In the *Outline of Knowledge*, Part Three, concerned with life on Earth, is placed between Parts Two and Four, concerned, respectively, with the Earth itself and with human life. This positioning is reasonable enough, but one could read into it an assumption that reaches far deeper than the logical ordering of concepts and facts. The tacit assumption is that human life has emerged from the inanimate matter of the Earth through the same kind of evolutionary continuum that links all the other living forms in a great chain of being. In reality, however, the theory of evolution does not provide decisive evidence for this assumption. What is *known* of biological evolution applies only to the anatomical structures and physiological functions of organisms that have lived in the past or are living now. The successive steps from matter to life, and from life to consciousness, have not yet been shown to have taken place through the kind of mechanisms that account for the evolutionary changes of anatomical structures of physiological functions. There exists a continuum from one form of life to another, but extending this continuum to inanimate matter on the one hand, and to human consciousness on the other, is a matter of faith rather than of scientific knowledge.

Even the most cursory observation of nature reveals that all living forms are conditioned by environmental forces, and that reciprocally they shape the environment, thereby contributing to the triumph of life. But it must be realized that the word "life" encompasses different kinds of relations to nature. At its lowest level, "life" implies, as mentioned above, the deterministic and blind chemical reactions through which an organism—simple or complex as it may be—transmits its distinctive characteristics to its descendants and reacts adaptively to its environment. At its highest, "life" involves man's consciousness and free will and refers to the deep reality of the world within and the affirmation of the individual self, irrespective of the external world.

There is no way at present to link these two extreme and apparently incompatible manifestations of life—biological determinism and human freedom. Yet both are real, and both have been immensely influential in giving the present characteristics to our planet.

The surface of the Earth reflects the activities of countless living things. Even though these operate chiefly through blind, deterministic mechanisms, life introduces on Earth a degree of order, organization, and diversity not found anywhere else in the cosmos, not even in the movement of the celestial bodies. Man emerged, not on the bare planet, but in this orderly and diversified biological world. As soon as he achieved his identity as *Homo sapiens*, he began to insert his free will into ecological determinism. For good or evil, he has now become the most powerful influence in changing the face of the globe. His conscious choices will determine not only his own fate, but also the fate of life on Earth.

Part Three. Life on Earth

Several points about the relations of Part Three to other parts should be noted. The separation of Part Three from Part One, on matter and energy, and from Part Two, on the Earth, reflects a traditional division of labour among the natural sciences. However, the separation is not rigid. The borderline disciplines of biophysics and biochemistry appear throughout Part Three, especially in Division II, concerned with the molecular basis of vital processes. The effects of the Earth's atmosphere and hydrosphere on living things are reflected throughout Part Three, especially in Division V, which is concerned with the biosphere and with ecosystems.

Some fundamental biological knowledge of humans is involved in the treatment throughout Part Three of what is common to all life and to all animals. And Section 355, the last section of Part Three, deals with mankind's place and activities in the biosphere. However, what is specific to human life, human health, and human behaviour is separately dealt with in Part Four, on human life.

The biological sciences have themselves been the object of historical and analytical studies. Such studies are dealt with in Section 10/34 in Part Ten, which treats the historical development of the biological sciences; the methodology, scope, and conceptual structure of biology as a whole; and the several component disciplines at the different levels of biological research.

The design and operation of observational and experimental instruments are important in the development of the biological sciences. Such scientific instrumentation is dealt with in Section 723 of Part Seven.

Division I.   The Nature and Diversity of Living Things

The outlines in the three sections of Division I deal with the nature, the origin and evolution, and the classification of living things.

Section 311.   Characteristics of Living Things

A. The general conception of life

1. Definitions of life: physiological, metabolic, biochemical, genetic, and thermodynamic definitions

2. Mechanism and vitalism: the adequacy of physics and chemistry for the explanation of living phenomena

3. The successive and emergent levels of biotic organization: the molecular, cellular, organismic, individual, and population levels

B. The distinctive properties of living things

1. The common occurrence of nucleic acids and metabolic and genetic regulators in all living things

2. Metabolism

3. Homeostasis

4. Reproduction and development

5. Variation among organisms

6. Sensory and behavioral reactions to external stimuli

C. The search for life beyond the Earth

1. The notion of extraterrestrial life and its chemistry

2. The significance of the search for life beyond the Earth

3. Exobiological survey of the solar system: its physical environments and biological prospects

---

Suggested reading in the *Encyclopædia Britannica*:

MACROPAEDIA: Major article dealing with the characteristics of living things

    Life

MICROPAEDIA: Selected entries of reference information

General subjects

    cell   life

    evolution   life cycle

    homeostasis   metabolism

Biographies

    See Section 10/34 of Part Ten

INDEX: See entries under all of the terms above

Section 312.   **The Origin of Life and the Evolution of Living Things**

A. Stages in the emergence of life

1. Hypotheses about the origin of life

2. Steps in the production of chemical precursors of life

    a. Formation of the Earth's primitive reducing atmosphere

    b. Production of simple organic molecules

    c. Production of long-chain molecules consisting of repeating units

    d. Origin of the genetic code

3. The earliest living systems

    a. Evolution of enzymatic reaction chains

    b. Origin of procaryotic and eucaryotic cells

    c. Evolution of photosynthesis

4. The antiquity of life: evidence of biological activity in the geological record
[see also 243]

5. Adaptive radiation of organisms: phylogeny

    a. The basis of phylogeny: use of the fossil record, comparative anatomy, and other evidence to indicate phylogenetic relationships

    b. Early stages of phylogeny: chemical evolution of early living systems, the probable main lines of descent
[see A.2. and 3., above]

    c. Major trends in the phylogeny of plants: algal predecessors, land plants, seed plants

    d. Major trends in the phylogeny of animals: origin of multicellular animals, changes in the body plan of the lower metazoans, theories of linear descent from lower to higher forms and of descent along two principal lines

    e. Life as the product of a historical process
[see also 243]

B. The theory of evolution

　　1. The history of evolutionary theory

　　2. The evidence for evolution

　　3. The synthetic theory of evolution

C. The process of evolution

　　1. Natural selection

　　　　a. Adaptation

　　　　b. Aspects of the process of natural selection: coloration, mimicry, polymorphism

　　　　c. Implications of natural selection: the coefficient of selective advantage, imperfect or excessive adaptation, and extinction

　　2. Heritable variation: the raw material of evolution

　　　　a. Mutation: sudden changes in genes

　　　　　　i. The nature of mutation

　　　　　　ii. Types of mutation

　　　　　　iii. Significance of mutation

　　　　b. Gene recombination

　　3. Theories about the rate of evolution: slow evolution and "punctuated" evolution

D. The establishment of species and the process of speciation

　　1. The distinctiveness of species

　　2. The criterion of reproductive isolation

　　3. The properties of species

　　4. The evolution of species: allopatric speciation, sympatric speciation, stasipatric speciation

　　5. The relationship between species and other taxonomic categories: family, order, class, phylum

---

Suggested reading in the *Encyclopædia Britannica:*

MACROPAEDIA: Major articles and a biography dealing with the origin of life and the evolution of living things

　　Coloration, Biological
　　Darwin
　　Evolution, Human
　　Evolution, The Theory of
　　Mimicry

MICROPAEDIA: Selected entries of reference information

General subjects

adaptation	coloration	Lamarckism	phylogeny
aggressive mimicry	concealing	melanism	polymorphism
analogy	coloration	mimicry	selection
auxochrome	Darwinism	mosaic evolution	species
biopoiesis	dialectic	Müllerian mimicry	spontaneous
carotene	eobiont	mutation	generation
chromophore	evolution	Origin of Species	
clone	homology	orthogenesis	

Biographies

　　See Section 10/34 of Part Ten

INDEX: See entries under all of the terms above

Section 313.   **The Classification of Living Things**

 A. Systematic classification of organisms in a hierarchical arrangement

  1. The objectives of biological classification: identification and the making of natural groups

  2. History of biological classification: from Aristotle to Linnaeus and Darwin

  3. The process of establishing taxonomic relationships

  4. Current systems of classification

 B. The viruses

 C. The monerans: the procaryotes

  1. Blue-green algae
   [see D., below]

  2. Bacteria and allies

 D. The protists: the simpler eucaryotes

  1. The algae

  2. The slime molds

  3. The true fungi

  4. Algal-fungal partnerships: lichens

  5. The protozoans

 E. The nonvascular plants, or bryophytes

  1. Liverworts

  2. Mosses

 F. The vascular plants, or tracheophytes

  1. Whisk ferns, or psilopsids

  2. Club mosses, or lycopsids

  3. The horsetails, or sphenopsids

  4. The true ferns

  5. The nonflowering seed plants, or gymnosperms

   a. Early gymnosperms

   b. Conifers

  6. The flowering plants, or angiosperms

   a. Dicotyledonous plants

   b. Monocotyledonous plants

 G. The invertebrates: animals without backbones

  1. The lower invertebrates

   a. The mesozoans

   b. The sponges

   c. The coelenterates

   d. The ctenophores

   e. The flatworms

   f. The ribbonworms

   g. The spiny-headed worms

   h. The aschelminthes

   i. The entoprocts

2. The lophophorates

    a. The "moss animals," or ectoprocts

    b. The phoronid worms

    c. The lamp shells, or brachiopods

3. The schizocoelomates

    a. The mollusks

    b. The peanutworms

    c. The annelid worms

    d. The spoonworms

    e. The oncopods

    f. The arthropods
       [see H., below]

H. The arthropods

1. Trilobites

2. Arachnids

3. Crustaceans

4. The myriapods

5. The insects, or hexapods

I. The enterocoelomate invertebrates: echinoderms through protochordates

1. Nonchordate enterocoelomates

2. The chordates

J. Vertebrates

1. Fishes

2. Amphibians

3. Reptiles

4. Birds

5. Mammals

Suggested reading in the *Encyclopædia Britannica*:

MACROPAEDIA: Major articles dealing with the classification of living things

Amphibians	Bacteria	Fishes	Mollusks
Angiosperms: The	Birds	Flatworms:	Moss Animals:
Flowering Plants	Bryophytes and	Phylum	Phylum Bryozoa
Annelids: Phylum	Primitive	Platyhelminthes	Protophytes
Annelida	Vascular Plants	Gymnosperms	Protozoa
Arachnids	Chordates	Insects	Reptiles
Arthropods:	Cnidarians	Lamp Shells:	Sponges: Phylum
Phylum	Crustaceans	Phyllum	Porifera
Arthropoda	Echinoderms	Brachiopoda	Viruses
Aschelminths	Ferns	Mammals	

MICROPAEDIA: Selected entries of reference information

Underline {General subjects}

  amphibians:

amphibian	Cacops	frog	Leptodactylidae
amphiuma	caecilian	green frog	midwife toad
arrow-poison frog	clawed frog	hellbender	mud puppy
axolotl	Diadectes	Ichthyostega	Myobatrachidae
bullfrog	Eryops	Labyrinthodontia	narrow-mouthed
	fire-bellied toad	leopard frog	toad

newt
salamander
Seymouria
siren
spadefoot toad
Surinam toad
tadpole
toad
tree frog

angiosperms—beech order:
beech
black oak
bur oak
chestnut
chestnut oak
chinquapin
English oak
live oak
oak
pin oak
red oak
tanbark oak
white oak
willow oak

angiosperms— bellflower order:
balloonflower
bellflower
Campanulales
harebell
Lobeliaceae
rampion
tuftybell

angiosperms—birch order:
alder
Balanopales
Betulaceae
birch
filbert
gray birch
hop-hornbeam
hornbeam
paper birch
river birch
sweet birch
white birch
yellow birch

angiosperms— buttercup order:
anemone
baneberry
barberry
Berberidaceae
bugbane
buttercup
Christmas rose
Clematis
columbine
globeflower
hellebore
Hepatica

larkspur
mayapple
meadow rue
monkshood
Oregon grape
Ranunculaceae
Ranunculales

angiosperms—cactus order:
barrel cactus
cactus
chin cactus
cholla
Christmas cactus
Easter cactus
fishhook cactus
hedgehog cactus
leaf cactus
living-rock cactus
Mammillaria
melon cactus
night-blooming
  cereus
old man cactus
Opuntia
organ-pipe cactus
peyote
pincushion cactus
prickly pear
Rhipsalis
saguaro
Schlumbergera
sea-urchin cactus

angiosperms—caper order:
Brassicaceae
broccoli
Brussels sprouts
cabbage
candytuft
Capparales
cauliflower
charlock
Chinese cabbage
collard
cress
kale
Kerguelen cabbage
kohlrabi
marsh cress
mustard
peppergrass
radish
rape
rock cress
rocket
spiderflower
stock
toothwort
turnip
wallflower
whitlow grass

angiosperms— composite order:
artichoke
Asteraceae
basket-flower
boneset
chamomile
Chrysanthemum
cineraria
coneflower
dandelion
endive
fleabane
goldenrod
groundsel
guayule
Jerusalem
  artichoke
lettuce
marigold
pussy-toes
safflower
sunflower
thistle
zinnia

angiosperms— dogwood order:
angelica
anise
Apiaceae
Araliaceae
carrot
Cornales
cow parsnip
dogwood
fatsia
ivy
parsnip
poison hemlock
schefflera
tupelo

angiosperms—ebony and primrose orders:
Bumelia
Diospyros
Ebenales
ebony
persimmon
pimpernel
primrose
Primulales
sapodilla
storax

angiosperms— euphorbia order:
boxwood
Buxaceae
cassava
castor-oil plant
copperleaf
croton
crown of thorns

Euphorbiaceae
Euphorbiales
Jatropha
jojoba
manchineel
mercury
Omphalea
Phyllanthus
poinsettia
redbird cactus
sandbox tree
spurge
tung tree

angiosperms—figwort order:
Acanthaceae
belladonna
Bignoniaceae
bladderwort
broomrape
eggplant
figwort
foxglove
Gesneriaceae
henbane
Indian paint brush
jacaranda
mullein
nightshade
petunia
potato
sausage tree
Scrophulariales
Solanaceae
toadflax
tobacco
tomato
witchweed

angiosperms— gentian order:
Apocynaceae
Asclepiadaceae
bedstraw
buckbean
carrion flower
coffee
Gentianaceae
Gentianales
Indian hemp
Loganiaceae
oleander
partridgeberry
periwinkle
Rubiaceae

angiosperms— geranium order:
Barbados cherry
flax
Geraniales
geranium
Impatiens
lignum vitae

nasturtium
Oxalis
shamrock
wood sorrel
angiosperms—ginger order:
  abaca
  arrowroot
  banana
  bird-of-paradise
   flower
  Cannaceae
  ginger
  ginger lily
  Marantaceae
  Musaceae
  plantain
  prayer plant
  Strelitziaceae
  Zingiberaceae
  Zingiberales
angiosperms—grass order:
  agrostology
  Arundinaria
  bamboo
  barley
  beach grass
  bent grass
  bluegrass
  bluestem
  bromegrass
  cordgrass
  corn
  crabgrass
  esparto
  fescue
  foxtail
  grass
  love grass
  millet
  muhly
  needlegrass
  oat grass
  oats
  panicum
  Paspalum
  Pennisetum
  Poaceae
  quack grass
  reed
  Restionales
  rice
  rye
  ryegrass
  sorghum
  sugarcane
  wheat
  wild rice
angiosperms—heath order:
  Arbutus
  azalea

bilberry
blueberry
Clethra
cranberry
crowberry
Ericales
Gaultheria
heath
heather
huckleberry
Indian pipe
Kalmia
Labrador
 tea
leatherleaf
Lyonia
Pieris
pipsissewa
rhododendron
Vaccinium
wintergreen
angiosperms—laurel order:
  avocado
  California laurel
  greenheart
  lambkill
  Laurales
  laurel
  sassafras
  sweet shrub
angiosperms—lily and iris orders:
  Agavaceae
  Alliaceae
  Amaryllidaceae
  Asparagus
  asphodel
  bear grass
  blue-eyed
   grass
  cantala
  chive
  Colchicum
  Crocus
  Dioscoreaceae
  Dracaena
  elephant's-foot
  Erythronium
  fritillary
  garlic
  Gladiolus
  henequen
  Iridales
  Iris
  leek
  Liliaceae
  Liliales
  mariposa lily
  Mauritius
   hemp
  Narcissus

onion
phormium
pickerelweed
Sansevieria
Smilax
ti
tulip
water hyacinth
yam
angiosperms—magnolia order:
  Annonaceae
  champac
  cherimoya
  lancewood
  magnolia
  Magnoliaceae
  Magnoliales
  Myristicaceae
  pawpaw
  tulip tree
  Winteraceae
  ylang-ylang
angiosperms—mallow order:
  Abutilon
  balsa
  baobab
  Bombacaceae
  cacao
  cotton
  durian
  Hibiscus
  jute
  kapok
  kenaf
  linden
  mallow
  Malvaceae
  Malvales
  okra
  roselle
  sisal
  Sterculiaceae
  Tiliaceae
  urena
angiosperms—mint order:
  balm
  Coleus
  dittany
  dragonhead
  glory-bower
  Lamiaceae
  Lamiales
  Lantana
  lavender
  lemon verbena
  Mentha
  peppermint
  rosemary
  Salvia

spearmint
teak
Verbenaceae
angiosperms—myrtle order:
  allspice
  cannonball tree
  Cuphea
  Epilobium
  Eucalyptus
  Eugenia
  feijoa
  fireweed
  Fuchsia
  guava
  jaboticaba
  Leptospermum
  loosestrife
  mangrove
  mare's-tail
  Myrtales
  myrtle
  Onagraceae
  paperbark tree
  pomegranate
  water chestnut
angiosperms—nettle order:
  Cannabis
  elm
  Ficus
  fig
  hackberry
  hemp
  India rubber plant
  jackfruit
  Moraceae
  mulberry
  Osage orange
  Pilea
  ramie
  Ulmaceae
  Urticaceae
  Urticales
angiosperms—orchid order:
  bucket orchid
  Dendrobium
  Epidendrum
  greenhood
  helleborine
  jewel orchid
  ladies' tresses
  lady's slipper
  Odontoglossum
  Oncidium
  Ophrys
  orchid
  Orchis
  Pogonia
  twayblade
  Vanda

vanilla
*angiosperms—palm
and related orders:*
  Anthurium
  Arales
  Arisaema
  Arum
  babassu palm
  calla
  coco de mer
  coconut palm
  Cyclanthales
  date palm
  dumb cane
  oil palm
  palm
  Pandanales
  Philodendron
  skunk cabbage
  Typhales
*angiosperms—pea
order:*
  Acacia
  Albizia
  bean
  bluebonnet
  broom
  chick-pea
  Clianthus
  clover
  cowpea
  crown vetch
  Fabales
  honey locust
  indigo
  laburnum
  lentil
  locoweed
  locust
  logwood
  lupine
  mesquite
  Mimosa
  narra
  pagoda tree
  palo verde
  pea
  peanut
  redbud
  rosewood
  senna
  sensitive plant
  smoke tree
  soybean
  sunn
  vetch
  Wisteria
*angiosperms—pepper
and birthwort
orders:*
  birthwort
  Peperomia
  Piperaceae

Piperales
wild ginger
*angiosperms—phlox
order:*
  alkanet
  bindweed
  borage
  Boraginaceae
  bugloss
  Convolvulaceae
  dodder
  forget-me-not
  Hydrophyllaceae
  Ipomoea
  Lennoaceae
  Loasaceae
  Mertensia
  Phlox
  Polemoniales
  Rivea
  sweet potato
  waterleaf
*angiosperms—
pineapple and
related orders:*
  Aechmea
  Bromeliaceae
  Commelinales
  Cryptanthus
  Cyperales
  Dyckia
  Eriocaulales
  Juncales
  papyrus
  pineapple
  Puya
  Spanish moss
  spiderwort
  Tillandsia
  umbrella plant
  Zebrina
*angiosperms—pink
order:*
  Amaranthaceae
  baby's breath
  beet
  Bougainvillea
  campion
  carnation
  Caryophyllaceae
  Caryophyllales
  Celosia
  chard
  chickweed
  goosefoot
  Halogeton
  Lychnis
  Nyctaginaceae
  pigweed
  pink
  poke
  Portulacaceae

purslane
spinach
sugar beet
*angiosperms—poppy
order:*
  bleeding heart
  bloodroot
  bush poppy
  California poppy
  celandine
  Corydalis
  Fumariaceae
  fumitory
  horned poppy
  Hypecoaceae
  Papaveraceae
  Papaverales
  poppy
  prickly poppy
*angiosperms—rose
order:*
  almond
  Amelanchier
  apple
  apricot
  attar of roses
  blackberry
  boysenberry
  cherry
  chokecherry
  cinquefoil
  cotoneaster
  crab apple
  firethorn
  hawthorn
  loganberry
  loquat
  medlar
  nectarine
  peach
  pear
  plum
  quince
  raspberry
  Rosales
  rose
  spirea
  strawberry
  sweetbrier
*angiosperms—rue
order:*
  Anacardiaceae
  bel fruit
  burning bush
  Burseraceae
  cashew
  citron
  grapefruit
  kumquat
  lemon
  lime
  mahogany

mango
Meliaceae
myrrh
orange
pili nut
Pistacia
poison ivy
Rhus
Rutaceae
Rutales
shaddock
Simaroubaceae
sumac
tree of heaven
*angiosperms—
sandalwood order:*
  Australian
   Christmas tree
  Balanophoraceae
  bastard toadflax
  dwarf mistletoe
  Loranthaceae
  mistletoe
  sandalwood
  Santalaceae
  Santalales
  Viscaceae
*angiosperms—
saxifrage order:*
  Astilbe
  currant
  Echeveria
  gooseberry
  houseleek
  hydrangea
  Kalanchoe
  Pittosporaceae
  Ribes
  Saxifragaceae
  Saxifragales
  saxifrage
  stonecrop
*angiosperms—
soapberry order:*
  Aceraceae
  akee
  box elder
  buckeye
  guarana
  horse chestnut
  litchi
  maple
  red maple
  Sapindales
  silver maple
  sugar maple
*angiosperms—
staff-tree, buckthorn,
olive orders:*
  alder buckthorn
  ash
  bittersweet

buckthorn
Ceanothus
Celastraceae
Celastrales
Euonymus
Forsythia
holly
jasmine
jujube
lilac
Oleaceae
olive
privet
Rhamnales
tea olive
Vitaceae
angiosperms—
tamarisk order:
  boojum tree
  ocotillo
  Tamaricales
  tamarisk
angiosperms—tea
order:
  Camellia
  Clusiaceae
  Dipterocarpaceae
  Elatinaceae
  franklinia
  Gordonia
  mammee apple
  mangosteen
  Ochnaceae
  Saint-John's-wort
  stewartia
  Theaceae
  Theales
angiosperms—teasel
order:
  bush honeysuckle
  Caprifoliaceae
  Dipsacaceae
  Dipsacales
  elder
  feverwort
  field scabious
  honeysuckle
  scabious
  snowberry
  teasel
  Valerianaceae
  Viburnum
angiosperms—violet
and related orders:
  Begonia
  Begoniales
  bottle gourd
  bryony
  cucumber
  Cucurbitales
  Datiscaceae
  dishcloth gourd
  Flacourtiaceae

gourd
melon
pansy
papaya
Passiflorales
passion-flower
pumpkin
rock rose
squash
sun rose
Violales
violet
watermelon
angiosperms—walnut
order:
  butternut
  hickory
  Juglandales
  pecan
  walnut
angiosperms—water
lily order:
  fanwort
  hornwort
  Nymphaeales
  Rafflesiales
  water lily
  water shield
angiosperms—
water-plantain and
related orders:
  Alismales
  arrowhead
  Elodea
  Hydrocharitales
  Najadales
  pondweed
  water plantain
angiosperms—
witch-hazel and
related orders:
  Casuarinales
  Cercidiphyllales
  Didymelales
  Eucommiales
  Eupteleales
  Fothergilla
  Hamamelidaceae
  Hamamelidales
  katsura tree
  Myricales
  plane tree
  sweet gum
  Trochodendrales
  winter hazel
  witch hazel
angiosperms—other:
  aspen
  barbeya
  buckwheat
  buffalo berry
  Calycerales

carnivorous plant
cobra plant
Connarales
Daphne
Diapensiales
dicotyledon
Dilleniales
everlasting
Glossopteris
hardwood
Hippuridales
Illicales
Leitneriales
lotus
macadamia
monocotyledon
Nelumbonales
Nepenthales
Nepenthes
Paeoniales
peony
pitcher plant
Plumbaginales
Podostemales
Polygalales
Polygonales
poplar
Proteales
Rafflesiales
rhubarb
Salicales
Sarraceniales
sundew
taro
Theligonales
Thymelaeales
Triuridales
Venus's-flytrap
wild flower
willow
arthropods—
arachnids:
  arachnid
  black widow
  brown spider
  chigger
  crab spider
  false scorpion
  funnel weaver
  funnel-web spider
  garden spider
  giant water
    scorpion
  harvestman
  jumping spider
  mite
  nursery-web spider
  red spider
  scorpion
  silk spider
  spider
  sunspider

tarantula
tick
trap-door spider
whip scorpion
wolf spider
arthropods—
crustaceans:
  amphipod
  barnacle
  blue crab
  branchiopod
  brine shrimp
  clam shrimp
  copepod
  crab
  crayfish
  crustacean
  crustacean louse
  decapod
  Dungeness crab
  fiddler crab
  fish louse
  gammarid
  ghost crab
  gribble
  hermit crab
  hooded shrimp
  horseshoe shrimp
  isopod
  krill
  land crab
  lobster
  malacostracan
  mantis shrimp
  mantle
  mussel shrimp
  mustache shrimp
  opossum shrimp
  pea crab
  pill bug
  robber crab
  sand flea
  scampi
  shellfish
  shrimp
  skeleton shrimp
  sow bug
  spider crab
  tadpole shrimp
  tanaid
  water flea
  whale louse
arthropods—
other:
  arthropod
  centipede
  eurypterid
  horseshoe crab
  insect
  millipede
  myriapod
  Paradoxides

pauropod
sea spider
symphylan
trilobite
bacteria and allies:
actinomycete
Bacillus
bacteria
biochemical
oxygen
demand
blue-green algae
Clostridium
denitrifying
bacteria
episome
eubacteria
gram stain
Haemophilus
Lactobacillus
Micrococcus
mycoplasma
Pasteurella
pneumococcus
pseudomonad
rickettsia
Salmonella
sheathed bacteria
Spirillum
spirochete
Staphylococcus
Streptococcus
Streptomyces
sulfur bacteria
Vibrio
birds—anseriform
order:
Anatidae
anseriform
black duck
bufflehead
Canada goose
canvasback
dabbling duck
diving duck
duck
eider
gadwall
goldeneye
goose
magpie goose
mallard
merganser
néné
perching duck
pintail
pochard
redhead
ring-necked duck
scaup
scoter

screamer
sheldgoose
shelduck
shoveler
snow goose
steamer duck
stifftail
swan
teal
whistling duck
white-fronted
goose
wigeon
wood duck
birds—
caprimulgiform and
apodiform orders:
apodiform
caprimulgiform
chuck-will's-widow
crested swift
frogmouth
hummingbird
nighthawk
nightjar
oilbird
owlet frogmouth
poorwill
potoo
swift
swiftlet
whippoorwill
birds—charadriiform
order:
auk
auklet
avocet
charadriiform
courser
curlew
dotterel
dowitcher
godwit
great auk
greenshank
guillemot
gull
jacana
jaeger
killdeer
knot
lapwing
murre
murrelet
oystercatcher
painted snipe
phalarope
plover
pratincole
puffin
redshank

ruff
sandpiper
seedsnipe
sheathbill
skimmer
skua
snipe
stilt
surfbird
tattler
tern
thickknee
turnstone
willet
woodcock
yellowlegs
birds—columbiform
and psittaciform
orders:
bristlehead
cockatoo
columbiform
conure
dodo
domestic pigeon
lovebird
macaw
parakeet
parrot
passenger pigeon
pigeon
psittaciform
sandgrouse
turtledove
wood pigeon
birds—coraciiform
and piciform orders:
barbet
coraciiform
flicker
honey guide
hornbill
ivory-billed
woodpecker
jacamar
kingfisher
kookaburra
motmot
piciform
piculet
puffbird
roller
sapsucker
toucan
woodpecker
birds—cuculiform
and owl orders:
ani
barn owl
coucal
cuckoo

cuculiform
eagle owl
fish owl
ground cuckoo
hawk owl
horned owl
owl
roadrunner
screech owl
short-eared owl
turaco
wood owl
birds—extinct:
Aepyornis
Archaeopteryx
Diatryma
Hesperornis
Ichthyornis
birds—falconiform
order:
accipiter
bald eagle
bateleur
bird of prey
buzzard
caracara
condor
eagle
falcon
falconiform
golden eagle
goshawk
gyrfalcon
harrier
hawk
hobby
kestrel
kite
lammergeier
merlin
osprey
peregrine falcon
secretary bird
sparrowhawk
turkey vulture
vulture
birds—galliform and
gruiform orders:
bustard
button quail
coot
crake
crane
curassow
finfoot
galliform
gallinule
grouse
gruiform
guinea fowl
hoatzin

jungle fowl
limpkin
megapode
mesite
partridge
peacock
pheasant
ptarmigan
quail
rail
seriema
trumpeter
turkey
whooping crane
birds—passeriform
order:
accentor
Aegithalidae
antbird
becard
bell-magpie
bellbird
bird-of-paradise
bishop
blackbird
Bombycillidae
bowerbird
broadbill
buffalo weaver
bulbul
bunting
butcherbird
Callaeidae
Campephagidae
canary
Carduelidae
catbird
Certhiidae
chat
chat-thrush
chough
cisticola
cock-of-the-rock
cordon bleu
Corvidae
Cotingidae
creeper
crow
cuckoo-shrike
currawong
Dendrocolaptidae
dipper
drongo
Emberizidae
Estrildidae
fairy bluebird
false sunbird
fantail
flowerpecker
flycatcher
forktail
Furnariidae

Galápagos finch
gnatcatcher
goldfinch
grackle
Grallinidae
grass finch
grosbeak
ground thrush
Hawaiian
  honeycreeper
helmet-shrike
Hirundinidae
honeycreeper
honeyeater
house sparrow
hypocoly
Icteridae
Irenidae
jay
kingbird
kinglet
kiskadee
lark
laughing thrush
Leiothrix
lyrebird
magpie
magpie-robin
manakin
mannikin
martin
meadowlark
Mimidae
mockingbird
monarch
Muscicapidae
myna
Nectariniidae
nightingale
nightingale thrush
nuthatch
oriole
oropendola
ovenbird
Panuridae
Paridae
Parulidae
passeriform
pewee
Philepittidae
phoebe
pipit
pitta
Ploceidae
prinia
quelea
raven
redstart
Remizidae
robin
rockfowl
rosefinch

scrub-bird
seedeater
sharpbill
shrike
shrike-vireo
silky flycatcher
song-babbler
songbird
sparrow
starling
Sturnidae
sunbird
swallow
Sylviidae
tailorbird
tanager
tapaculo
thickhead
thrush
tit
tit-babbler
tityra
towhee
treecreeper
Turdidae
tyrannulet
tyrant flycatcher
umbrellabird
vanga-shrike
vireo
wagtail
warbler
wattle-eye
waxbill
waxwing
weaver
white-eye
whydah
woodcreeper
woodswallow
woodwarbler
wren
Xenicidae
birds—others:
albatross
aviary
aviculture
bird
bittern
booby
cassowary
casuariiform
ciconiiform
coly
Colymbiformes
cormorant
diving petrel
egret
emu
flamingo
frigate bird
fulmar

gannet
grebe
hammerhead
heron
ibis
kiwi
loon
moa
ornithology
ostrich
pelecaniform
pelican
penguin
petrel
plumage
prion
procellariiform
rhea
shearwater
shoebill
snakebird
spoonbill
stork
storm petrel
syrinx
tinamou
trogon
tropic bird
bryophytes:
Bryophyta
bug-on-a-stick
carpet moss
cord moss
cushion moss
granite moss
hair-cap moss
horned liverwort
leafy liverwort
liverwort
luminous moss
Marchantia
moss
peat moss
screw moss
tree moss
wind-blown moss
classification:
classification
nomenclature
taximetrics
taxon
taxonomy
enterocoelomates:
acornworm
amphioxus
arrowworm
beardworm
bêche-de-mer
blastoid
brittle star
cake urchin
carpoid

chordate
crinoid
crown-of-thorns
  starfish
cystoid
echinoderm
echinoid
graptolite
heart urchin
hemichordate
protochordate
pterobranch
sand dollar
sea cucumber
sea lily
sea squirt
sea urchin
shellfish
starfish
tunicate

fishes—atheriniform
and related orders:
  atheriniform
  dealfish
  dory
  flying fish
  grunion
  killifish
  lantern-eye fish
  live-bearer
  molly
  oarfish
  silversides

fishes—
batrachoidiform and
related orders:
  anglerfish
  batfish
  brotula
  cave fish
  clingfish
  cod
  frogfish
  goosefish
  grenadier
  hake
  paracanthopterygian
  pearlfish
  pollock
  toadfish
  whiting

fishes—
cartilaginous:
  basking shark
  blue shark
  carcharhinid
  chimaera
  chondrichthian
  Cladoselache
  devil ray
  dogfish
  electric ray

guitarfish
hammerhead shark
mackerel shark
mako shark
monkfish
ray
saw shark
sawfish
shark
skate
stingray
thresher shark
tiger shark
white shark

fishes—cypriniform
and siluriform
orders:
  barb
  bitterling
  bullhead
  carp
  catfish
  characin
  chub
  corydoras
  dace
  electric catfish
  electric eel
  goldfish
  hatchetfish
  knifefish
  labeo
  loach
  madtom
  minnow
  ostariophysan
  pencil fish
  piranha
  roach
  sucker
  tench
  tetra
  tigerfish
  wels
  zebra fish

fishes—
gasterosteiform
order:
  cornetfish
  gasterosteiform
  pipefish
  sea horse
  shrimpfish
  stickleback
  swamp eel
  trumpet fish

fishes—jawless fish
and placoderms:
  Agnatha
  antiarch
  Arctolepis
  arthrodire

Bothriolepis
Cephalaspis
hagfish
lamprey
ostracoderm
Palaeospondylus
placoderm
spiny shark
swim bladder

fishes—perciform
order:
  angelfish
  archer fish
  barracuda
  bass
  bigeye
  black bass
  blenny
  bluegill
  bonito
  butterfish
  butterfly fish
  carangid
  cichlid
  crappie
  damselfish
  darter
  discus fish
  dragonet
  drum
  fingerfish
  glassfish
  goatfish
  goby
  gourami
  grouper
  grunt
  hind
  hogfish
  jack
  jewfish
  labyrinth fish
  mackerel
  marlin
  mojarra
  moonfish
  mudskipper
  mullet
  Nile perch
  parrot fish
  perch
  perciform
  pikeperch
  pomfret
  pompano
  porgy
  prickleback
  rabbitfish
  ragfish
  remora
  runner

sailfish
scad
scat
sea bass
sheepshead
Siamese fighting
  fish
sleeper
slipmouth
snapper
snook
soapfish
spadefish
spearfish
spiny eel
stargazer
sunfish
surfperch
surgeonfish
swordfish
threadfin
tilefish
tripletail
tuna
weakfish
weever
wolffish
wrasse

fishes—
pleuronectiform
and tetraodontiform
orders:
  boxfish
  dab
  filefish
  flatfish
  flounder
  halibut
  mola
  plaice
  porcupine fish
  puffer
  sole
  tetraodontiform
  triggerfish
  turbot

fishes—salmoniform
order:
  Atlantic salmon
  bristlemouth
  brook trout
  brown trout
  capelin
  char
  coho
  hatchetfish
  king salmon
  lake trout
  mudminnow
  pike
  rainbow trout
  salmon

salmoniform
sandfish
scaleless dragonfish
smelt
spookfish
trout
viperfish
whitefish
fishes—scorpaeniform
and related orders:
 dragonfish
 flathead
 flying gurnard
 greenling
 lion-fish
 lumpsucker
 poacher
 redfish
 scorpaeniform
 scorpion fish
 sculpin
 sea robin
 snailfish
 stonefish
 zebra fish
fishes—others:
 alewife
 anchovy
 bichir
 bony fish
 bowfin
 Cheirolepis
 chondrostean
 clupeiform
 coelacanth
 crossopterygian
 deep-sea fish
 Dipterus
 eel
 elopiform
 Eusthenopteron
 fish
 gar
 gulper
 herring
 holostean
 ladyfish
 lungfish
 menhaden
 moray
 mormyrid
 notopterid
 osteoglossomorph
 paddlefish
 Rhipidistia
 sardine
 shad
 sturgeon
 tarpon
 teleost
 wolf herring

gymnosperms:
 alerce
 American
  arborvitae
 Araucariaceae
 arborvitae
 bald cypress
 big tree
 California nutmeg
 cedar
 conifer
 Cordaitales
 Cupressaceae
 cycad
 Cycadeoidales
 Cycas
 cypress
 cypress pine
 dawn redwood
 Douglas fir
 eastern red cedar
 English yew
 Ephedra
 false cypress
 fir
 giant arborvitae
 ginkgo
 Gnetaceae
 Greek fir
 hemlock
 incense cedar
 Japanese cedar
 Japanese torreya
 Japanese yew
 juniper
 larch
 Lebachia
 Pinaceae
 pine
 Podocarpaceae
 redwood
 seed fern
 Sequoia
 spruce
 stinking yew
 Taxaceae
 Taxodiaceae
 Torreya
 umbrella pine
 Welwitschiaceae
 yellowwood
 yew
insects—coleopteran
order:
 alfalfa weevil
 bark beetle
 beetle
 bess beetle
 billbug
 blister beetle
 boll weevil

branch and twig
 borer
carrion beetle
casebearing beetle
chafer
checkered beetle
click beetle
coleopteran
Colorado potato
 beetle
cucumber beetle
darkling beetle
dermestid beetle
dung beetle
elm bark beetle
firefly
flat bark beetle
flea beetle
flower chafer
glowworm
ground beetle
Japanese beetle
June beetle
ladybird beetle
leaf-rolling weevil
long-horned beetle
metallic
 wood-boring
 beetle
net-winged beetle
plum curculio
potato beetle
predaceous
 diving beetle
primitive weevil
rhinoceros beetle
rove beetle
seed beetle
shining leaf chafer
soldier beetle
spider beetle
stag beetle
strepsipteran
tiger beetle
tortoise beetle
tumbling flower
 beetle
unicorn beetle
water scavenger
 beetle
weevil
whirligig beetle
insects—fly order:
 anthomyiid fly
 bee fly
 biting midge
 black fly
 blow fly
 bot fly
 crane fly
 dipteran

flesh fly
fly
fruit fly
fungus gnat
gall midge
Hessian fly
horse fly
housefly
hover fly
leaf miner
louse fly
midge
mosquito
robber fly
tachinid fly
tsetse fly
vinegar fly
warble fly
insects—
hymenopteran order:
 ant
 Apocrita
 bee
 braconid
 bumblebee
 chalcid
 cuckoo wasp
 fig wasp
 gall wasp
 honey ant
 honeybee
 horntail
 hymenopteran
 ichneumon
 leaf-cutter bee
 sand wasp
 sawfly
 spider wasp
 Symphyta
 thread-waisted
  wasp
 velvet ant
 wasp
 wood wasp
insects—lepidopteran
order:
 bagworm moth
 blue butterfly
 bollworm
 brush-footed
  butterfly
 butterfly
 carpenter moth
 casebearer
 clearwing moth
 copper butterfly
 diamondback
  moth
 flour moth
 forester moth
 gelechiid moth

geometrid moth
gossamer-winged
  butterfly
gypsy moth
hairstreak
harvester
hawk moth
lappet
leaf roller moth
lepidopteran
measuring worm
milkweed butterfly
monarch butterfly
morpho
moth
olethreutid moth
owlet moth
painted lady
parnassian
  butterfly
peppered moth
pyralid moth
regal moth
saturniid moth
silkworm moth
skipper
slug caterpillar
  moth
sulfur butterfly
swallowtail
  butterfly
tent caterpillar
  moth
tiger moth
tineid moth
tussock moth
white butterfly
yucca moth
zebra swallowtail
  butterfly

insects—others:
alderfly
ambush bug
antlion
aphid
apterygote
assassin bug
back swimmer
bedbug
bristletail
bug
burrower bug
caddisfly
chewing louse
chinch bug
cicada
cockroach
cone-headed
  grasshopper
coreid bug
cottony-cushion
  scale
cricket

dipluran
dobsonfly
dragonfly
earwig
ephemeropteran
flea
flower bug
froghopper
giant water bug
grape phylloxera
grasshopper
harlequin
  cabbage bug
heteropteran
homopteran
human louse
jumping plant
  louse
katydid
lace bug
lacewing
leaf insect
leafhopper
locust
long-horned
  grasshopper
louse
lygaeid bug
mantid
mantispid
marsh treader
mayfly
meadow
  grasshopper
mealybug
mole cricket
neuropteran
odonate
orthopteran
plant bug
proturan
psocid
pygmy grasshopper
red bug
San Jose scale
scale insect
scorpionfly
shield-backed
  grasshopper
short-horned
  grasshopper
smaller water
  strider
snakefly
springtail
stinkbug
stonefly
sucking louse
termite
thrips
treehopper
walkingstick
water boatman

water scorpion
water strider
webspinner
whitefly

lopophorates:
Atrypa
horseshoe worm
lamp shell
lingulid
moss animal
Tetractinella

lower invertebrates:
archaeocyathid
Ascaris
aschelminth
Aurelia
bread-crumb
  sponge
Cassiopea
Chrysaora
clionid
cnidarian
coral
ctenophore
eelworm
entoproct
eye worm
filarial worm
flatworm
fluke
freshwater jellyfish
gastrotrich
Gonionemus
guinea worm
hookworm
horny sponge
Hydra
Hydractinia
hydroid
jellyfish
Leucosolenia
Liriope
lungworm
medusa
mesozoan
millepore
nematocyst
nematode
Obelia
pinworm
planarian
polyp
Portuguese
  man-of-war
priapulid
ribbonworm
rotifer
Rugosa
sea anemone
sea fan
sea gooseberry
sea pen
sea walnut

siliceous sponge
spiny-headed
  worm
sponge
tapeworm
threadworm
trichina
Venus's flower
  basket
worm
zoanthid

mammals—
  artiodactyl order:
alpaca
antelope
aoudad
artiodactyl
aurochs
babirusa
bighorn
bison
boar
bongo
bontebok
bovid
brocket
buffalo
bush pig
camel
cattle
chamois
chevrotain
deer
dibatag
duiker
eland
fallow deer
gaur
gazelle
gerenuk
giraffe
gnu
goat
guanaco
hartebeest
hippopotamus
ibex
impala
Kobus
kudu
llama
moose
mountain goat
mule deer
muntjac
musk deer
musk-ox
nyala
okapi
oryx
peccary
Père David's deer
pig

pronghorn
red deer
reedbuck
reindeer
roe deer
ruminant
saiga
sheep
sika
springbok
tahr
vicuña
wapiti
warthog
water buffalo
white-tailed deer
yak

*mammals—bat
order:*
bat
brown bat
bulldog bat
disk bat
false vampire bat
free-tailed bat
Hipposideridae
horseshoe bat
Jamaican fruit bat
New Zealand
  short-tailed bat
Phyllostomatidae
Pteropodidae
sheath-tailed bat
vampire bat
Vespertilionidae

*mammals—carnivore
order:*
aardwolf
African
  hunting dog
Arctic fox
Asiatic black bear
badger
bat-eared fox
bear
bearded seal
binturong
black bear
bobcat
brown bear
bush dog
cacomistle
Caffre cat
canine
caracal
carnivore
cat
cheetah
civet
clouded leopard
coati
coyote

crabeater seal
dhole
dingo
dog
elephant seal
fennec
ferret
fisher
flat-headed cat
fossa
fox
fur seal
genet
golden cat
gray fox
grison
grizzly bear
harbour seal
harp seal
hooded seal
hyena
jackal
jaguar
jaguarundi
kinkajou
leopard
leopard cat
linsang
lion
lynx
margay
marten
mink
mongoose
monk seal
mustelid
ocelot
olingo
otter
ounce
Pallas's cat
panda
polar bear
polecat
procyonid
puma
raccoon
raccoon dog
ratel
sable
sea lion
seal
serval
skunk
sloth bear
South
  American fox
spectacled bear
stoat
sun bear
suricate
tayra

tiger
viverrid
walrus
weasel
Weddell seal
wildcat
wolf
wolverine

*mammals—cetacean
order:*
ambergris
baleen whale
beaked whale
beluga
blue whale
bottlenose whale
dolphin
fin whale
gray whale
humpback whale
killer whale
narwhal
pilot whale
porpoise
right whale
sei whale
sperm whale
whale

mammals—extinct:
Baluchitherium
Barylambda
Brontotherium
Camelops
cave bear
Chalicotherium
Condylarthra
Coryphodon
Creodonta
dawn horse
Dinohyus
Dryopithecus
Elasmotherium
Glyptodon
Irish elk
Litopterna
mammoth
mastodon
Merychippus
Miacis
Moeritherium
Moropus
multituberculate
Mylodon
Notoungulata
Oreopithecus
Phenacodus
sabre-toothed cat
Thylacosmilus
titanothere
Toxodon
Triconodon
Uintatherium

woolly rhinoceros
*mammals—
insectivore and
edentate orders:*
anteater
armadillo
edentate
elephant shrew
golden mole
hedgehog
insectivore
mole
otter shrew
short-tailed shrew
shrew
sloth
solenodon
tenrec

*mammals—
monotremes and
marsupials:*
bandicoot
cuscus
echidna
glider
kangaroo
koala
marsupial
marsupial mole
marsupial mouse
monotreme
native cat
numbat
opossum
phalanger
platypus
rat kangaroo
rat opossum
Tasmanian devil
Tasmanian wolf
wallaby
wombat

*mammals—
perissodactyl
order:*
ass
donkey
Equidae
horse
mule
perissodactyl
Przewalski's horse
rhinoceros
tapir
zebra

*mammals—primate
order:*
ape
avahi
aye-aye
baboon
capuchin monkey

Celebes black ape
chimpanzee
colobus
diana monkey
drill
durukuli
galago
gelada
gibbon
gorilla
guenon
hamadryas
howling monkey
indri
langur
lemur
loris
macaque
mandrill
mangabey
marmoset
monkey
orangutan
patas monkey
potto
primate
proboscis monkey
rhesus monkey
saki
siamang
sifaka
spider monkey
squirrel monkey
tarsier
titi
tree shrew
uakari
woolly monkey
woolly spider
   monkey

*mammals—rodent
order:*
agouti
bamboo rat
bandicoot rat
beaver
cane rat
capybara
cavy
chinchilla
chipmunk
cloud rat
cotton rat
dormouse
field mouse
flying squirrel
gerbil
gopher
grasshopper
   mouse
ground squirrel
guinea pig

gundi
hamster
harvest mouse
hutia
jerboa
jumping mouse
kangaroo rat
lemming
maned rat
marmot
mole rat
mouse
muskrat
nutria
paca
pocket mouse
porcupine
pouched rat
prairie dog
rat
rice rat
rock rat
rodent
sewellel
spiny rat
springhare
squirrel
tuco-tuco
viscacha
vole
water rat
white-footed
   mouse
wood rat
woodchuck

mammals—others:
aardvark
colugo
dugong
elephant
hare
hyrax
lagomorph
mammal
manatee
pangolin
pika
proboscidean
rabbit
sea cow
sirenian
ungulate

protists—algae:
Acetabularia
agar
algae
algology
brown algae
Chlorella
desmid
diatom
dulse

Fucus
green algae
Irish moss
kelp
laver
Nostoc
Oedogonium
phytoplankton
Pleurococcus
red algae
Sargassum
sea lettuce
seaweed
Spirogyra
stonewort
Ulothrix
Vaucheria
water bloom
water net

protists—fungi:
Agaricales
Amanita
Ascomycetes
Basidiomycetes
Boletaceae
cup fungus
Deuteromycetes
fungus
Lycoperdales
mushroom
mycorrhiza
Oomycetes
Polyporales
Pyrenomycetes
stinkhorn
truffle
water mold
yeast
Zygomycetes

*protists—
   protozoans:*
actinomyxidian
amoeba
astome
Balantidium
Ceratium
Chlamydomonas
chloromonad
chrysomonad
ciliate
cilium
cnidosporidian
coccolith
cryptomonad
dinoflagellate
Entamoeba
entodiniomorph
Euglena
flagellate
flagellum
foraminiferan
fusulinid

gregarine
Gymnodinium
gymnostome
haplosporidian
helioflagellate
heliozoan
heterochlorid
heterotrich
Holomastigotoides
hymenostome
hypermastigote
hypotrich
Leishmania
microsporidian
myxosporidian
Nosema
odontostome
oligotrich
opalinid
Paramecium
peritrich
Plasmodium
proteomyxid
protomonad
protozoan
pseudopodium
radiolarian
rhizomastigote
Sarcocystis
sarcodine
sporozoan
suctorian
testacean
tintinnid
trichocyst
trichomonad
trichostome
Trypanosoma
volvocid
Volvox
Vorticella

protists—others:
beard lichen
Iceland moss
lichen
manna
Myxomycetes
oak moss
Parmelia
Plasmodio-
   phoromycetes
protist
slime mold

*reptiles—
   crocodilians:*
alligator
caiman
crocodile
gavial

reptiles—extinct:
Allosaurus
Anatosaurus
Ankylosaurus

Apatosaurus
Bradysaurus
Camptosaurus
Clidastes
Cynognathus
Dicynodon
Dimetrodon
Dimorphodon
dinosaur
Diplodocus
Edaphosaurus
Euparkeria
Gorgosaurus
ichthyosaur
Iguanodon
Limnoscelis
Mesosaurus
mosasaur
Moschops
Nothosaurus
Ornitholestes
Oviraptor
Pachycephalo-
  saurus
Pentaceratops
phytosaur
Plateosaurus
Plesiosaurus
Podokesaurus
Protoceratops
Psittacosaurus
Pteranodon
pterodactyl
pterosaur
Rhamphorhyn-
  chus
sauropterygian
Stegosaurus
Struthiomimus
therapsid
Triceratops
Tritylodon
Tyrannosaurus
reptiles—lizards:
anole
Calotes
chameleon
gecko
Gila monster
glass snake
horned toad
iguana
Komodo dragon
lizard
monitor lizard
racerunner
skink
reptiles—snakes:
adder
anaconda

Aniliidae
black snake
blind snake
boa
boomslang
brown snake
bull snake
bushmaster
Cerastes
coachwhip
cobra
colubrid
copperhead
coral snake
egg-eating snake
elapid
fer-de-lance
flying snake
garter snake
green snake
hognose snake
indigo snake
king snake
krait
mamba
mangrove snake
moccasin
python
racer
rat snake
rattlesnake
sea snake
shieldtail snake
sidewinder
snake
taipan
tree snake
vine snake
viper
wart snake
water snake
reptiles—turtles:
Blanding's turtle
box turtle
Emydidae
mud turtle
musk turtle
painted turtle
pond turtle
sea turtle
side-necked turtle
snake-necked
  turtle
snapping turtle
softshell turtle
terrapin
tortoise
turtle
wood turtle
reptiles—others:
reptile

tuatara
schizocoelomates—
  annelids:
annelid
earthworm
fanworm
feather-duster
  worm
fireworm
leech
lugworm
oligochaete
palolo worm
peacock worm
polychaete
rag worm
sea mouse
schizocoelomates—
  mollusks:
ammonoid
ark shell
belemnoid
bivalve
bubble shell
cephalopod
chiton
clam
cockle
conch
cone shell
coquina clam
cowrie
cuttlefish
ear shell
gaper clam
gastropod
geoduck
jingle shell
land snail
mantle
mollusk
monoplacophoran
murex
mussel
nautilus
nudibranch
octopus
olive shell
opisthobranch
oyster
periwinkle
piddock
prosobranch
pteropod
pulmonate
razor clam
scallop
seashell
shellfish
shipworm

slug
squid
top shell
triton shell
tusk shell
whelk
worm shell
schizocoelomates—
  others:
oncopod
onychophoran
peanutworm
pentastomid
spoonworm
tardigrade
trochophore
tracheophytes:
Adiantaceae
angiosperm
Aspleniaceae
bracken
cliffbrake
club moss
fern
gymnosperm
horsetail
Lepidodendron
Lycopsida
Marattiaceae
Ophioglossaceae
Osmundaceae
Pleuromeia
Polypodiaceae
prefern
Psilopsida
quillwort
Rhynie plants
Salviniales
Schizaeaceae
Sphenopsida
spike moss
staghorn fern
tracheophyte
whisk fern
viruses:
adenovirus
arbovirus
lysogeny
myxovirus
picornavirus
plant virus
polyoma virus
poxvirus
virion
virology
virus

Biographies

See Section 10/34 of Part Ten

INDEX: See entries under all of the terms above

Division II. The Molecular Basis of Vital Processes

[For Part Three headnote see page 95.]

The outlines in the three sections of Division II deal with the molecular level of biotic organization and set forth theories of the chemical transformations and the exchanges of energy that occur in the distinctively vital processes treated in Section 311 of Division I.

Section 321. Chemicals and the Vital Processes

A. The inorganic milieu of living systems

B. Organic chemicals participating naturally in the life processes

   1. Carbohydrates

   2. Lipids

   3. Proteins and peptides

   4. The major carrier of chemical energy: ATP

   5. Nucleic acids

      a. General features

      b. Deoxyribonucleic acid (DNA)

      c. Ribonucleic acid (RNA)

   6. Biological pigments and coloration

   7. Enzymes

   8. Vitamins

   9. Hormones

      a. General features of hormones: relationship between endocrine regulation and neural regulation, the evolution of hormones

      b. The hormones of vertebrates

      c. The hormones and hormonelike substances of invertebrates: neurohormones, molting hormones, pheromones

      d. The hormones of plants

  10. Other natural products: alkaloids, steroids and sterols, isoprenoids and terpenes

C. Drugs: chemicals administered to an organism to change its physiological state or to combat pathogens

   1. Sources and development of drugs

   2. General aspects of drug action

   3. Absorption, distribution, metabolism, and excretion of drugs

   4. Classification of drugs by organ or organ system of principal effect

      a. Drugs affecting the cardiovascular system

      b. Drugs affecting smooth and skeletal muscle systems

      c. Drugs affecting the central nervous system

d. Drugs affecting the autonomic nervous system and the eyes

e. Drugs affecting the excretory system

f. Drugs affecting the digestive system

g. Drugs affecting the reproductive systems

h. Drugs affecting the immune response system

i. Drugs affecting the histamine response system

5. Drugs directed against disease organisms

    a. Drugs derived from living microorganisms: antibiotics

    b. Chemical compounds used to treat infectious diseases: chemotherapeutic drugs

6. Drugs directed at the suppression of cancer

7. Drug use and abuse: the nature of drug addiction and dependence
[see 522.C.9.]

D. Ethyl alcohol, alcohol consumption
[see 522.C.9.]

E. Biocides and biorepellents

1. Antiseptics and disinfectants

2. Biocides directed by mankind against animal and plant pests

3. Biotoxins produced by microorganisms, plants, and animals: microbial toxins, phytotoxins, zootoxins

4. Biological and chemical warfare agents

F. The selective concentration of chemicals by organisms

Suggested reading in the *Encyclopædia Britannica:*

MACROPAEDIA: Major articles dealing with chemicals and the vital processes

    Biochemical Components of Organisms
    Cells: Their Structures and Functions
    Chemical Compounds
    Drugs and Drug Action
    Poisons and Poisoning

MICROPAEDIA: Selected entries of reference information

General subjects

biocides:	rodenticide	sugar	*drugs—analgesics:*
Agent Orange	Toxaphene	*drugs affecting the*	acetaminophen
aldrin	*biotoxins:*	*autonomic nervous*	acetanilide
biological control	lambkill	*system:*	acetylsalicylic acid
chemosterilant	mycotoxin	adrenergic drug	analgesic
chloral	poison	anticholinesterase	antipyrine
chlordane	toxin	atropins	salicylic acid
DDT	venom	beta blocker	*drugs—anesthetics:*
dichlorobenzene	*carbohydrates:*	cholinergic drug	anesthetic
dimethoate	carbohydrate	ganglion blocking	chloroform
fumigant	cellulose	agent	cocaine
fungicide	disaccharide	neuromuscular	curare
herbicide	glucose	blocking agent	cyclopropane
insecticide	glycoside	*drugs affecting the*	procaine
Malathion	monosaccharide	*cardiovascular*	hydrochloride
parathion	pectin	*system:*	
phorate	polysaccharide	digitalis	
		nitroglycerin	

drugs—antibiotics:
  allopurinol
  antibiotic
  cephalosporin
  erythromycin
  penicillin
  streptomycin
  tetracycline
drugs—antiseptics:
  Dakin's solution
  iodoform
  melachite green
  merbromin
  silver nitrate
drugs—
  chemotherapeutic:
  allopurinol
  anthelmintic
  aspidium
  catechu
  chloroquine
  diethylcarbamazine
    citrate
  diethylstilbestrol
  isoniazid
  pamaquine
  Prontosil
  quinacrine
  quinine
  sulfa drug
  sulfadiazine
  sulfanilamide
  sulfonamide
  tryparsamide
drugs—hallucinogens:
  bufotenine
  Cannabis
  DMT
  hallucinogen
  hashish
  ibogaine
  LSD
  marijuana
  mescaline
  PCP
  peyote
  psilocin and
    psilocybin
drugs—narcotics:
  codeine
  fentanyl
  heroin
  methadone
  morphine
  narcotic
  opium
drugs—sedatives:
  barbiturate
  chloral hydrate

  paraldehyde
  sedative–hypnotic
    drug
  thalidomide
drugs—stimulants:
  amphetamine
  caffeine
  imipramine
  iproniazid
  isocarboxazid
  methamphetamine
  stimulant
  tranylcypromine
drugs—tranquillizers:
  chlordiazepoxide
  chlorpromazine
  diazepam
  lithium carbonate
  meprobamate
  reserpine
  tranquillizer
drugs—other drugs
  and drug action:
  adjuvant
  antacid
  antagonism
  antihistamine
  antimicrobial agent
  astringent
  cytotoxic drug
  diuretic
  drug
  ephedrine
  laxative
  phenol coefficient
  promethazine
  quinidine
  scopolamine
  synergism
  theophylline
  urethane
enzymes and enzyme
  action:
  allosteric control
  amylase
  cofactor
  cooperativity
  enzyme
  feedback inhibition
  hydrolase
  induction
  inhibition
  ligase
  lipase
  Michaelis–Menten
    hypothesis
  nuclease
  pepsin
  proteolytic enzyme

  renin
  serotonin
  transaminase
  zymogen
hormones:
  adrenaline and
    noradrenaline
  aldosterone
  androgen
  corticoid
  cortisol
  enterogastrone
  estrogen
  hormone
  insulin
  luteinizing
    hormone (LH)
  neurohormone
  progesterone
  testosterone
isoprenoids and
  terpenes:
  abietic acid
  camphor
  isoprene
  limonene
  menthol
  pinene
  terpene
lipids:
  capsaicin
  fatty acid
  lecithin
  lipid
  phospholipid
  prostaglandin
  sphingolipid
  triglyceride
nucleic acids:
  adenine
  cytosine
  deoxyribonucleic
    acid
  guanine
  nucleic acid
  nucleoside
  nucleotide
  ribonucleic acid
  thymine
  uracil
pigments and
  coloration:
  auxochrome
  carotene
  chlorophyll
  chromophore
  flavonoid
  melanin
  phytol

  porphyrin
  quinone
proteins and
  peptides:
  actin
  amino acid
  collagen
  glutamic acid
  glutamine
  gluten
  histidine
  histone
  hydroxyproline
  keratin
  myoglobin
  peptide
  prolamin
  protein
  scleroprotein
steroids and
  sterols:
  cholesterol
  cortisone
  ergosterol
  saponin
  steroid hormone
vitamins:
  biotin
  carnitine
  choline
  folic acid
  lipoic acid
  nicotinic acid
  pantothenic acid
  para-aminobenzoic
    acid
  vitamin
  vitamin A
  vitamin B complex
  vitamin B_1
  vitamin B_2
  vitamin B_6
  vitamin B_{12}
  vitamin C
  vitamin D
  vitamin E
  vitamin K
other:
  adenosine
    triphosphate
  denaturation
  histamine
  piperine
  sapogenin
  secretion

Section 322.   **Metabolism: Bioenergetics and Biosynthesis**

A. Photosynthesis: the initiation of energy conversion in the biosphere
[see also 335.B.]

1. The biological importance of photosynthesis

2. Factors that influence the rate of photosynthesis and the energy efficiency of photosynthesis

3. Determination of the mechanism of photosynthesis

4. The site of the photosynthetic process in green plants: the chloroplast

5. The photosynthetic pigments

6. The energetics of photosynthesis: photoelectron transfer, photophosphorylation

7. The metabolic path of carbon in photosynthesis: the carbon reduction cycle

B. Metabolism: the totality of all chemical processes in the living organism

1. The fragmentation of complex molecules: catabolism

2. The combustion of food materials and the conservation of part of the energy in them: cellular respiration, oxidation and transduction

3. The biosynthesis of cell components: anabolism

4. Regulation of metabolism

C. The nitrogen cycle: nitrogen fixation, nitrification and denitrification

---

Suggested reading in the *Encyclopædia Britannica*:

MACROPAEDIA: Major articles dealing with metabolism: bioenergetics and biosynthesis

Cells: Their Structures and Functions
Metabolism
Photosynthesis

MICROPAEDIA: Selected entries of reference information

General subjects

adenosine triphosphate	catabolism	feedback inhibition	metabolism
anabolism	cellular respiration	gluconeogenesis	photosynthesis
antimetabolite	chloroplast	induction	tricarboxylic acid
	cytochrome	inhibition	cycle

Biographies
See Section 10/34 of Part Ten

INDEX: See entries under all of the terms above

Section 323.   **Vital Processes at the Molecular Level**

  A. The cell membrane

    1. The nature of membranes

    2. Compartmentalization of the cell

    3. Movement of water across cell membranes: osmosis

    4. Movement of solutes through membranes in response to a concentration gradient

    5. Movement of solutes through membranes independent of concentration gradients: active transport, pinocytosis

  B. Bioelectricity

  C. The nerve impulse

    1. The structure of the neuron

    2. Characteristics of artificially stimulated nerve fibres

    3. Nature of the nerve impulse

    4. Transmission of the nerve impulse: the synapse

  D. Muscle contraction

    1. Contractile or motile activity of some type as a characteristic of all living things

    2. Striated, or skeletal, muscle in higher animals

    3. Cardiac muscle

    4. Smooth muscle

  E. Bioluminescence

    1. The significance of bioluminescence in behaviour, metabolism, and research

    2. The range and variety of bioluminescent organisms

    3. The biochemical events of light emission: enzymic and nonenzymic systems

---

Suggested reading in the *Encyclopædia Britannica*:

Division III.   **The Structures and Functions of Organisms**
[For Part Three headnote see page 95.]

Division I deals with the nature, origin, evolution, distinctive properties, and classification of living things. Division II deals with the molecular level of biotic organization. The outlines in the nine sections of Division III deal with life at the cellular level and at the organismic level.

Section 331.   **The Cellular Basis of Form and Function**

A. Cell theory and classification

  1. The cell theory

    a. Historical background

    b. Challenges to and revisions of the cell theory in the light of later knowledge

  2. Classification of cells

    a. General features: comparisons between cells and viruses and between procaryotic and eucaryotic cells, tissues as providing a functional classification of cells

    b. Cells and tissues of animals: absorptive cells, secretory cells, nerve cells, sensory cells, muscle cells, cells in supporting tissues, circulating cells, reproductive cells

    c. Cells and tissues of higher plants: outstanding features of the plant cell; meristematic, epidermal, and other types of plant cells

    d. Comparison between animal cells and plant cells

B. Cell design and cell organization

  1. The cell as a molecular system

    a. Macromolecules in cells: nucleic acids, proteins, polysaccharides

    b. Small molecules in cells: lipids, nucleotides, porphyrin derivatives, water

  2. Form and structure of the cell

    a. Sizes and shapes of cells

    b. Morphological elements: parts of cells—cell membrane, extracellular membrane system, mitochondria, ribosomes, microtubules, microfilaments, nuclear envelope, chromosomes, nucleolus

    c. Procaryotic and eucaryotic cells
    [see 312.A.3.]

C. Functional aspects of cells

  1. The internal environment and the cell matrix: the concept of the cell as a "protoplasm," the concept of the cell as a "bag" containing a water solution of molecules

  2. Cell membranes

  3. Interplay of nucleus and cytoplasm

  4. Cell movement: ciliary, flagellar, and amoeboid

  5. Cells in combination: extension of the cell concept for multicellular life

D. The cell cycle

  1. Cell growth: doubling of size, genetic replication, preparation for mitosis

2. Mitosis: the separation of sister chromosomes to opposite poles of the mitotic apparatus, a spindle-shaped structure in the cytoplasm

    a. Special structures in mitosis: the centrioles and the kinetochores (centromeres)

    b. The chromosome cycle

    c. Telophase

    d. Cytokinesis

3. Meiosis: reduction division that produces daughter cells with half the number of chromosomes of the parent cells

4. Differences between meiosis and mitosis

E. Fertilization

    1. Characteristics of the mature egg

    2. Events of fertilization

    3. Biochemical analysis of the events of fertilization

    4. Mechanisms that aid in the union of gametes

Suggested reading in the *Encyclopædia Britannica:*

MACROPAEDIA: Major article dealing with the cellular basis of form and function

    Cells: Their Structures and Functions

MICROPAEDIA: Selected entries of reference information

General subjects

cell	fission	ploidy
chromosome	gamete	protoplasm
cytology	meiosis	receptor
cytoplasm	mitosis	recombination
cytoplasmic	multicellular	
streaming	organism	
fertilization	nucleus	

Biographies

    See Section 10/34 of Part Ten

INDEX: See entries under all of the terms above

Section 332.   **The Relation of Form and Function in Organisms**

A. Biological form and function

B. Plant tissues and fluids: classification, organization, main functions

    1. Relatively undifferentiated tissues of nonvascular plants

    2. Well-differentiated tissues in vascular plants

        a. Meristematic (cell-producing) tissues: apical, lateral, intercalary

        b. Mature tissues

            i. Dermal (protective) tissues: the epidermis of the primary plant body, the periderm of the secondary plant body

            ii. Vascular (conducting) tissues: the xylem, the phloem

            iii. Fundamental (ground) tissues: the parenchyma, the supportive collenchyma and sclerenchyma, the endodermis

    3. Cells of plant tissues
       [see 331.A.2.c.]

C. Organs of plants: tissue organization, functions, and types

1. Development of organs in vascular plants: internal and external morphology, tissue organization, functions, types, and modifications; the stem; the leaf; the root

2. Physiology of organs in vascular plants

3. Diverse sizes and forms of organ systems in vascular plants: potential for unlimited growth

   a. Varieties of shoot systems

   b. Varieties of root systems

   c. Varieties of reproductive organs and organ systems

4. Organs of nonvascular plants: analogues of stem, leaf, and root

5. Evolution of plant organs and organ systems into the complex, multicellular state

D. Animal tissues and fluids: classification, organization, and main functions

1. Classification of tissues: anatomical, embryological, functional

2. Tissues for assimilation, storage, transport, and excretion: alimentary, liver, kidney, and lung tissues; blood and lymph

3. Tissues for coordination: nervous and sensory tissues, endocrine tissues

4. Tissues for support and movement: connective tissues, cartilage, bone, muscle

5. Other tissues: reproductive tissues, hemopoietic tissues, tissue fluids

6. Cells of animal tissues
   [see 331.A.2.b.]

E. Animal organs and organ systems

1. Specialized organ systems

   a. Relating to the environment primarily: integumentary, skeletal, muscular, nervous, and endocrine systems
      [see also 333.C. and D.; 334.A., B., and C.]

   b. Serving cell metabolism primarily: digestive, respiratory, circulatory, and excretory systems
      [see also 335.C.; 336.A., B., and C.]

   c. Serving genetic continuity primarily: the reproductive system

2. Interrelationships between organ systems: functional interdependence, feedback mechanisms

3. Development of organ systems
   [see also 338.D.]

4. Evolution of organ systems

Suggested reading in the *Encyclopædia Britannica:*

MACROPAEDIA: Major articles dealing with the relation of form and function in organisms

   Organs and Organ Systems, Plant and Animal
   Tissues and Fluids

MICROPAEDIA: Selected entries of reference information

General subjects

bark	growth ring	phloem	symmetry
cambium	inflorescence	pistil	tissue
connective tissue	leaf	placenta	vascular bundle
cork	lignin	root	vascular system
cortex	meristem	sclerenchyma	vessel
epithelium	mucus	sieve tube	wood
flower	organ	stomate	xylem
	parenchyma		

Biographies

   See Section 10/34 of Part Ten

INDEX: See entries under all of the terms above

Section 333. **Coordination of Vital Processes: Regulation and Integration**

A. Maintenance of steady states in biological systems: homeostasis

1. The nature of homeostatic systems

2. Homeostatic processes

3. Homeostatic control hierarchies: homeostatic subsystems that serve either organisms or natural communities

4. Origin and evolution of homeostasis

5. Individual adjustments to gradual changes in the physical environment: acclimatization

6. Inactive states accompanied by a lower than normal rate of metabolism: dormancy

B. Information reception and processing: sensory reception

1. Classification of sensory systems

a. According to location of receptors: exteroceptors, interoceptors

b. According to type of stimulus: photoreceptors, thermoreceptors, chemoreceptors, mechanoreceptors, electroreceptors, sound receptors

2. Evolution of sensory systems: specialized organs and information-processing structures

3. Sensory information: interactions between adjacent sense cells and sensory neurons

C. Endocrine systems in animals

1. General features of hormonal coordination: the relationships between endocrine and neural regulation

2. Vertebrate endocrine systems

a. Relationships of endocrine glands to each other and to the blood

b. Structure and function

3. Invertebrate endocrine systems: insects, crustaceans, annelid worms

4. Comparative, adaptive, and evolutionary aspects of endocrine systems: the neurosecretory cell, hypothalamus-pituitary control systems

5. The human endocrine system
[see 421.E.]

D. Nervous systems in animals

1. Comparison of chemical and nervous regulation: control mechanisms located between the stimulus and the response

2. Nervous coordination

a. Intracellular coordination: general cytoplasmic responsiveness, or irritability, to a stimulus

b. Organelle systems: the channeling of responsiveness at the subcellular level within more complex protozoans

c. Nervous systems: the channeling of responsiveness at the cellular level within multicellular organisms

i. The neuron, or nerve cell

ii. The transmission of the nerve impulse and the synapse
[see 323.C.]

3. Invertebrate nervous systems

a. Theories of the evolutionary origin of the nervous system

b. Diffuse nervous systems

c. Centralized nervous systems

4. Vertebrate nervous systems

a. The central nervous system: the brain and its components; the spinal cord; the brain coverings (meninges), cavities, cerebrospinal fluid, and neuroglia (nonnervous tissue)

b. The peripheral nervous system

c. Embryonic development of the vertebrate nervous system

d. Evolution of the vertebrate nervous system

e. Biodynamics of the vertebrate nervous system

5. The human nervous system
[see 421.J.]

E. The biological clock: periodicity

1. Rhythms without apparent external correlates: brain waves, breathing, heartbeat

2. Rhythms correlated with natural geophysical cycles: solar-day rhythms, lunar-tidal rhythms, monthly rhythms, annual or seasonal rhythms, epochal rhythms

3. The mechanism of the biological clock

4. Factors affecting biological periodicities

5. The amplification and superimposition of individual rhythms in communities
[see 352.C.1.b.]

Suggested reading in the *Encyclopædia Britannica*:

MACROPAEDIA: Major articles dealing with the coordination of vital processes: regulation and integration

Endocrine Systems
Nerves and Nervous Systems
Sensory Reception
Tissues and Fluids

MICROPAEDIA: Selected entries of reference information

General subjects

endocrine systems:
adrenal gland
endocrine system
parathyroid gland
pituitary gland
secretion
thyroid gland
nervous systems:
adrenergic nerve
fibre
autonomic nervous
system
brain
cerebral fissure
cerebrospinal fluid
cranial nerve

ganglion
meninges
nervous system
neuron
reflex
spinal cord
synapse
vagus nerve
sensory reception—
photoreception:
cone
eye
eyespot
macula lutea
photoreception
rhodopsin

rod
visual pigment
sensory reception—
sound reception:
ear
echolocation
external auditory
canal
sound reception
tympanic
membrane
vestibulocochlear
nerve
sensory reception—
other:
chemoreception

lateral line system
mechanoreception
receptor
sense
smell
taste
thermoreception
touch reception
other:
acclimatization
biological rhythm
diapause
hibernation
homeostasis
tropism

Biographies

See Section 10/34 of Part Ten

INDEX: See entries under all of the terms above

Section 334. **Covering and Support: Integumentary, Skeletal, and Musculatory Systems**

A. The body covering

1. General features of the body covering, of integument: comparisons among unicellular organisms, plants, and animals

2. Plant integuments: organization and function

3. Invertebrate integuments: organization and function

   a. Cellular components and their derivatives

   b. Noncellular coatings of the integument

4. Vertebrate integuments: cellular components and their derivatives

   a. Skin layers: the epidermis, the dermis

   b. Skin derivatives and appendages: skin glands and pigment; epidermal scales; claws, nails, and hoofs; horns and antlers; feathers and hair; dermal derivatives

5. Skin variations among vertebrates

6. Embryology and evolution of the vertebrate skin

7. The biodynamics of vertebrate skin

8. Human integument and derivatives: skin, hair, nails, teeth, gums

B. The body skeleton

1. The roles of the body skeleton

2. Description and composition of the skeletal elements

   a. Cuticular structures: bone, crystals, cuticle, ossicles, spicules

   b. Semirigid structures: flexible cuticular structures, calcareous spicules that are not tightly packed, keratin, notochord, cartilage

   c. Other elements: connective tissue, the hydrostatic skeleton, elastic structures, buoyancy devices

3. The invertebrate skeleton: organization and function

4. The vertebrate skeleton: structure and function

   a. General features

   b. Embryology of vertebrate skeletons

   c. Vertebral column and thoracic skeleton

   d. Appendicular skeleton: pectoral girdle, pelvic girdle, limbs

5. Joints in vertebrates and invertebrates permitting various types of movement

6. Properties of bone and its development

7. The human skeletal system

C. The body musculature

1. General features of muscle tissue: its role in movement, support, colour changes, temperature regulation, and discharge of certain glands; arrangement and gross function

2. Muscle contractile systems

   a. Simple contractile systems: simple contractile fibrils and epithelio-muscular cells

   b. Complex contractile tissues: striated muscle, smooth muscle

3. Muscle contraction
   [see 323.D.]

4. Invertebrate muscle systems

5. Vertebrate muscle systems

   a. Embryonic development and divisions of the muscular system

   b. Evolution of the vertebrate musculatory system

    c. Function and regulation of muscle action

    d. Electric organs in certain fishes

  6. The human musculatory system
[see 421.H.6. and 7.]

Suggested reading in the *Encyclopædia Britannica*:

MACROPAEDIA: Major articles dealing with covering and support: integumentary, skeletal, and musculatory systems

    Integumentary Systems
    Muscles and Muscle Systems
    Supportive and Connective Tissues
    Tissues and Fluids

MICROPAEDIA: Selected entries of reference information

General subjects

integument:	extensor muscle	fibula	tibia
bark	flexor muscle	fontanel	ulna
beak	gluteus muscle	humerus	vertebral column
claw	iliocostalis muscle	joint	zygomatic arch
dermis	latissimus dorsi	ligament	*other:*
epidermis	levator muscle	mast cell	arm
exoskeleton	muscle	metacarpal	digit
feather	pectoralis muscle	occipital	face
hair	sphincter muscle	parietal	foot
horn	trapezius muscle	pelvic girdle	hand
integument	triceps muscle	radius	heel
scale	*supportive and*	rib	hip
test	*connective tissues:*	sacrum	jaw
musculature:	bone	scapula	leg
abdominal muscle	carpal bone	skeleton	shoulder
abductor muscle	cartilage	skull	tail
adductor muscle	clavicle	sternum	thorax
biceps muscle	femur	tarsal	

Biographies

  See Section 10/34 of Part Ten

INDEX: See entries under all of the terms above

Section 335.   **Nutrition: the Procurement and Processing of Nutrients**

A. The basic features of nutrition

  1. The various nutritional patterns; *e.g.,* autotrophism and heterotrophism, phototrophism and chemotrophism

  2. Methods of ingestion or penetration
[see C., below]

  3. The essential nutrients: compounds that cannot be synthesized by an organism and must be supplied in food; the nutritional needs of organisms

  4. Syntrophism: nutritional interrelationships in which the immediate or end products of metabolism of one organism may provide essential nutrients for another

B. Photosynthesis: the production of food in green plants
[see also 322.A.]

C. Digestion and digestive systems

  1. The contrast between autotrophs and heterotrophs

2. The alimentary system in animals other than man

    a. Invertebrate digestive systems: vacuolar systems, channel-network systems, saccular systems, tubular systems

    b. Vertebrate digestive systems: oral cavity, teeth, and pharynx; esophagus and stomach; small intestine, pancreas, and liver; the large intestine

    c. Embryology and evolutionary development of the vertebrate digestive system

    d. Biodynamics of the vertebrate digestive system: control of secretions and intestinal movements

3. The human alimentary system
[see 421.D.]

Suggested reading in the *Encyclopædia Britannica:*

MACROPAEDIA: Major articles dealing with nutrition: the procurement and processing of nutrients

    Digestion and Digestive Systems
    Nutrition

MICROPAEDIA: Selected entries of reference information

General subjects

digestive system:	pharynx	swallowing	molar
alimentary canal	plica circularis	*nutrients and*	palate
anal canal	pylorus	*nutrition:*	periodontal
anus	rectum	carbohydrate	membrane
argentaffin cell	small intestine	fat	permanent tooth
cecum	stomach	nutrition	premolar
colon	vermiform	nutritional type	primary tooth
digestion	appendix	protein	saliva
digestive nerve	villus	vitamin	salivary gland
plexus	*ingestion and*	*oral cavity:*	tongue
esophagus	*digestion:*	canine tooth	tooth
gallbladder	appetite	cementum	*other:*
gastric gland	chewing	dentine	bile
large intestine	defecation	enamel	bilirubin
liver	digestion	gum	chyme
pancreas	peristalsis	incisor	feces
Paneth cell	satiety	ivory	intestinal gas

Biographies

    See Section 10/34 of Part Ten

INDEX: See entries under all of the terms above

Section 336.   **Gas Exchange, Internal Transport, and Elimination**

A. Respiration and respiratory systems

1. The process of extracting oxygen and releasing carbon dioxide

2. Gases in the environment: the range of respiratory problems faced by aquatic and terrestrial animals

3. Basic types of respiratory structures

    a. Respiratory organs of invertebrates: tracheae and gills

    b. Respiratory organs of vertebrates: gills and lungs

4. Dynamics of respiratory mechanisms

5. The control of respiration: neural reflexes, muscular feedback, chemically sensitive controls

6. Adaptation to special environmental conditions

7. The human respiratory system
   [see 421.C.]

B. Circulation and circulatory systems

  1. Circulation and transport patterns: general aspects common to all circulatory systems

    a. Circulation in single cells: streaming movements within the protoplasm

    b. Circulation in multicellular animals

  2. The fluid media involved in circulation: blood and lymph

    a. Evolutionary origins of circulating fluids

    b. Plasma

    c. Formed elements of the circulating fluid: red cells, white cells, platelets, thrombocytes

    d. Lymphocytes and lymph in vertebrates

  3. Transport systems in animals

    a. Invertebrate circulatory systems

    b. Vertebrate circulatory systems

    c. Coronary circulation

    d. Embryonic development of the circulatory system

    e. Biodynamics of vertebrate circulation

    f. The human cardiovascular system
   [see 421.A.]

  4. Plant internal transport

C. Elimination: the disposal of wastes

  1. General features of elimination

  2. Excretion and excretory systems

    a. Excretory mechanisms

    b. Invertebrate excretory systems

    c. Vertebrate excretory systems

    d. The evolution of the vertebrate excretory system

    e. The human excretory system
   [see 421.G.]

Suggested reading in the *Encyclopædia Britannica:*

MACROPAEDIA: Major articles dealing with gas exchange, internal transport, and elimination

  Cells: Their Structures and Functions
  Circulation and Circulatory Systems
  Excretion and Excretory Systems
  Respiration and Respiratory Systems
  Tissues and Fluids

MICROPAEDIA: Selected entries of reference information

General subjects

blood and lymph:	platelet	cardiac output	heartbeat
agglutinin	serum albumin	cardiovascular	hepatic vein
blood	thymus	system	lung
complement	*circulatory and*	circulation	lymph node
erythrocyte	*respiratory systems:*	coronary artery	lymph nodule
hemoglobin	aorta	diaphragm	portal vein
hemolysis	artery	diastole	pulmonary
leukocyte	atrium	gill	circulation
lymph	blood pressure	heart	renal vein
lymphocyte	capillary	heart valve	respiration

systemic	*excretory systems:*	perspiration	phloem
circulation	cloaca	renal capsule	root
systole	excretion	renal pelvis	sieve tube
trachea	kidney	renal pyramid	translocation
valve	loop of Henle	urinary bladder	transpiration
vein	malpighian tubule	urine	transport
vena cava	nasal gland	*plant internal*	vascular bundle
venous sinus	nephridium	*transport system:*	vessel
ventricle	nephron	mass flow	xylem

Biographies

See Section 10/34 of Part Ten

INDEX: See entries under all of the terms above

Section 337.   Reproduction and Sex

A. The forms of reproduction and their comparative adaptive significance

   1. Levels of reproduction

      a. Molecular replication and reproduction

      b. Cell reproduction: binary and multiple fission

      c. Reproduction of organisms
        [see A.2., below]

      d. Life cycles of plants and animals

   2. Reproduction of organisms: sexual and asexual reproduction

   3. Natural selection and reproduction: the evolution of reproduction and variation control
      [see also 312.C.1.]

B. Sex and sexuality

   1. The distinctions between sex, sexuality, and reproduction

   2. Transduction and transformation as sexlike recombination in viruses and bacteria

   3. The adaptive significance of sex: establishment of genetic diversity

   4. The origin of sex and sexuality

   5. Sex patterns

   6. Determination of the sex of individuals

      a. The sex chromosomes

      b. Abnormal chromosome effects

      c. The effect of parthenogenetic development

      d. Environmental and hormonal influences

C. The reproductive system in plants: its organization and function

   1. General features: asexual systems that create new plants identical to the parent plant, sexual systems that create new plants different from either of the two parents

   2. The sex organs of bryophytes

      a. In liverworts and hornworts

      b. In mosses

   3. The variations of sex organs in tracheophytes

      a. In spore plants

      b. In seed plants

   4. Variations in reproductive cycles: apogamy and apospory (apparent secondary loss of capacity for sexual reproduction)

5. The physiology of reproduction: the influence of internal and environmental factors on the maturation of sporophytes and gametophytes as manifested by their ability to produce spores and gametes

D. The reproductive system in animals: its organization and function

1. General features

2. Reproductive systems of invertebrates

   a. Gonads, associated structures, and products in monoecious and dioecious types

   b. Mechanisms that aid in the union of gametes

   c. Specializations associated with parthenogenesis

   d. Provisions for the developing embryo
   [see 338.D.2.b.]

3. Reproductive systems of vertebrates

   a. Gonads, associated structures, and products

   b. Adaptations for internal fertilization; *e.g.,* the cloaca, intromittent (copulatory) organs, accessory structures

   c. Role of gonads in hormone cycles

   d. Provision for the developing embryo
   [see 338.D.2.b.]

   e. The human reproductive system
   [see 421.F.]

Suggested reading in the *Encyclopædia Britannica:*

MACROPAEDIA: Major articles dealing with reproduction and sex

Behaviour, Animal
Reproduction and Reproductive Systems
Sex and Sexuality

MICROPAEDIA: Selected entries of reference information

General subjects

plant reproduction:	fission	ovary	testis
gametophyte	gestation	ovulation	*other:*
ovary	incubation	ovum	alternation of
ovule	meiosis	placenta	generations
pistil	parturition	uterus	courtship
pollen	recombination	vagina	gamete
pollination	reproduction	*reproductive*	gonad
propagation	self-fertilization	*system—male:*	hermaphroditism
pseudocopulation	sexual intercourse	bulbourethral	orgasm
spore	viviparity	gland	sex
sporophyte	*reproductive*	ductus deferens	sex chromosome
reproductive	*system—female:*	epididyme	sexual
processes:	egg	penis	differentiation
budding	estrus	prostate gland	sexual dimorphism
conjugation	fallopian tube	seminal vesicle	
cross-fertilization	menopause	sperm	
fertilization	menstruation	spermatogenesis	

Biographies

See Section 10/34 of Part Ten

INDEX: See entries under all of the terms above

Section 338.   **Development: Growth, Differentiation, and Morphogenesis**

A. The nature and scope of biological development

B. The constituent processes of development and their control

 1. Growth

 2. Morphogenesis

 3. Differentiation

 4. Control and integration of development

C. Development of plants

 1. General features: types of life cycles, alternation of generations as independent phases of the life cycle

 2. Preparatory events

 a. Formation of sex cells

 b. Pollination

 c. Fertilization

 3. Early development: from fertilized egg (zygote) to seedling

 a. Embryo formation

 b. Independent dormant stages and germination of the seeds and fruits of higher plants, dispersal

 4. Later development: the sporophyte plant body

D. Development of animals

 1. Preparatory events: the egg and its activation by normal fertilization or by parthenogenesis

 2. Early development

 a. Embryo formation: cleavage, gastrulation

 b. Embryonic adaptations for the maintenance of the developing embryo: shell, yolk stores, membranous sacs, placenta

 3. Organ formation

 4. Postembryonic development: transformation of the newborn into the adult

E. Aging and decline in animals: life span, death
 [for aging in man, see 422.A.]

 1. Senescence in mammals

 2. Causes of aging

 3. The duration of life

F. Specialized patterns of development

 1. Biological regeneration

 2. The healing processes and scar tissue formation

 3. Biological malformation

 4. Twinning: multiple births

 5. Development in vitro: cell and tissue cultures

 6. Development of transplanted tissues and organs

Suggested reading in the *Encyclopædia Britannica:*

MACROPAEDIA: Major articles dealing with development: growth, differentiation, and morphogenesis

 Death
 Growth and Development, Biological
 Tissue Culture

MICROPAEDIA: Selected entries of reference information

General subjects

animal development:	incubation	umbilical cord	*plant development:*
amnion	larva	*development*	endosperm
blastocyst	metamorphosis	*processes:*	germination
chorion	neural crest	aging	fruit
cleavage	notochord	death	parthenocarpy
ectoderm	nymph	development	seed
embryo	paedomorphosis	histogenesis	*other:*
endoderm	parturition	morphogenesis	blastema
fetus	placenta	organogenesis	dysplasia
gastrula	pupa	regeneration	monster
gestation	segmentation		

Biographies

See Section 10/34 of Part Ten

INDEX: See entries under all of the terms above

Section 339.   Heredity: the Transmission of Traits

A. Basic features of heredity

   1. Early speculations on the nature of heredity

   2. Mendelian genetics: Mendel's experiments and their significance, the universality of Mendel's laws, interactions among genes and their variant forms (alleles)

   3. The combined action of heredity and environment in producing an organism

B. The physical basis of heredity

   1. Chromosomes and genes: the cellular basis of heredity

   2. Molecular genetics: the chemical and molecular nature of genes, the genetic code and its mutations, the expression and regulation of genes, applications of molecular genetics

C. Heredity and evolution
[see also 312.C.]

   1. Population genetics: the gene pool, the Hardy–Weinberg principle, changes in gene frequencies

   2. Natural selection as an agent of evolutionary change

   3. Artificial selection for genetic improvements of selected organisms: domesticated animals, cultivated plants, humankind
[see also 355.B.3.]

   4. Outbreeding and inbreeding: the effects of consanguinity on the vigour of offspring

---

Suggested reading in the *Encyclopædia Britannica:*

MACROPAEDIA: Major article dealing with heredity: the transmission of traits

Genetics and Heredity, The Principles of

MICROPAEDIA: Selected entries of reference information

General subjects

albinism	genotype	Mendelism	testcross
allele	Hardy–Weinberg	mutation	transformation
character	law	operon	variation
chromosome	heredity	pedigree	
dominance	hybrid	phenotype	
gene	inbreeding	plasmid	
genetic code	Lamarckism	polyploidy	
genetic drift	linkage group	recessiveness	

Biographies
See Section 10/34 of Part Ten

INDEX: See entries under all of the terms above

Division IV. **Behavioral Responses of Organisms**
[For Part Three headnote see page 95.]

Several of the sections in Division III deal with the structure and internal functioning of organisms. The outlines in the two sections of Division IV deal with the external actions and reactions of living things in relation to changes in their environment.

Section 341. **Nature and Patterns of Behavioral Responses**

A. Diverse conceptions of animal behaviour

1. The variety of animal behaviour

2. Classification of animal behaviour

3. Components of animal behaviour

B. Patterns of stereotyped response: unlearned behavioral reactions of organisms to some environmental stimulus

1. Plant movements: tropic and nastic movements, nutation, other autonomous movements

2. Animal movements: reflex and reflexlike activities, taxes, fixed action patterns and instinct

3. Photoperiodism

C. Hormonal and nervous control of behaviour

1. Interaction of endocrine and nervous systems

2. Hormonal influences on behaviour; e.g., by sex hormones

3. The nervous system and behaviour: the role of the nervous system in receiving information, processing it in the brain and spinal cord, and initiating the appropriate response

D. Evolution of behaviour

1. Evidence of the genetic determination of behaviour

2. The influence of experience on behaviour: phyletic patterns in the evolution of learning

3. Evolutionary origins and evolutionary consequences of behaviour patterns

---

Suggested reading in the *Encyclopædia Britannica*:

MACROPAEDIA: Major article dealing with the nature and patterns of behavioral responses
    Behaviour, Animal

MICROPAEDIA: Selected entries of reference information
General subjects

animal behaviour	instinct	play	tropism
behaviour genetics	photoperiodism	reflex	

Biographies
See Section 10/34 of Part Ten

INDEX: See entries under all of the terms above

Section 342.   Development and Range of Behavioral Capacities: Individual and Group Behaviour

    A. Basic behavioral activities of individuals

        1. Food getting

        2. Locomotion

        3. Avoidance behaviour

        4. Aggressive behaviour: attack and defensive threats

        5. Behaviour related to habitat

        6. Behaviour related to reproduction

    B. Higher behavioral characteristics of individual animals

        1. Simple nonassociative learning; *e.g.,* habituation, sensitization

        2. Associative learning; *e.g.,* classical and instrumental, or operant, conditioning

        3. Spatial learning; *e.g.,* maze learning, navigation

        4. Perceptual learning: imitation and observational learning; *e.g.,* song learning, imprinting

        5. Complex problem solving

            a. Discriminations of relational and abstract stimuli

            b. Generalized rule learning

            c. Insight and reasoning

            d. Language learning

    C. The behaviour of animals in groups

        1. Distinctions between groups of social animals and groups of nonsocial ones

        2. Animal communication

        3. The range of social behaviour among social and nonsocial animals

        4. Dynamics of social behaviour

    D. Evolution of behaviour
       [see 341]

Suggested reading in the *Encyclopædia Britannica:*

MACROPAEDIA: Major articles dealing with the development and range of behavioral capacities: individual and group behaviour

      Behaviour, Animal
      Learning, Animal

MICROPAEDIA: Selected entries of reference information

General subjects

adjustment	brachiation	habit	scavenger
aggressive	brooding	habituation	social learning
behaviour	cannibalism	homing	sound production
alarm signal	cleaning behaviour	imprinting	submissive
animal behaviour	colony	learning	behaviour
animal	conditioning	locomotion	suckling
communication	courtship	motivation	terrestrial
aquatic locomotion	display behaviour	nest	locomotion
associative learning	dominance	pheromone	territorial
avoidance	hierarchy	predation	behaviour
behaviour	feeding behaviour	reproductive	Weber's law
bird song	flight	behaviour	

Biographies
See Section 10/34 of Part Ten

INDEX: See entries under all of the terms above

Division V. **The Biosphere: the World of Living Things**
[For Part Three headnote see page 95.]

Division I of Part Three deals with the nature, origin, evolution, distinctive properties, and classification of living things. Divisions II, III, and IV deal with life at the molecular, cellular, organismal, and behavioral levels.

The outlines in the five sections of Division V deal with the world of living things taken as a single system of biotic and environmental interactions and interdependencies.

Section 351. **Basic Features of the Biosphere**

A. The extent of the biosphere

1. Preconditions of the biosphere: the Earth as an ideal medium for life
[see 312.A.2.]

2. The levels of organization within the biosphere: the biocycle, the ecosystem, the community, the population
[see 352.A. and C.; 354]

3. Energy flow in the biosphere

4. Cycling of matter in the biosphere

a. The general pattern of chemical cycles in nature
[see also 214.E., F., and G.]

b. The carbon and oxygen cycles

c. The nitrogen cycle

d. The sulfur cycle

e. The water cycle
[see also 222.D.]

f. The sedimentary cycles of essential minerals

5. The concept of the noosphere: mankind's place in the biosphere
[see 355.B.]

B. The ecosystem: a collection of integrated communities and their environment

1. Definition of an ecosystem

2. The biotic components of the ecosystem

a. Producers

b. Consumers

c. Decomposers

3. The abiotic components of the ecosystem

a. Pressure and temperature
[see 223.D.]

b. Radiation

c. Illumination

d. Water and soil characteristics, salts
[see 222]

e. Wave action: wind and water
[see 222.F. and 223.B.]

f. Fire as a limiting factor

4. The conditioning of the abiotic environment by living organisms

5. The effect of micro-environments on the ecosystem

6. Processes that determine the nature and productivity of the ecosystem

7. Types of ecosystems
[see 354]

Suggested reading in the *Encyclopædia Britannica*:

MACROPAEDIA: Major articles dealing with the basic features of the biosphere

Biosphere, The
Ecosystems

MICROPAEDIA: Selected entries of reference information

General subjects

biochemical oxygen demand	biosphere body heat	eutrophication food chain	oxygen cycle phosphorus cycle
biogeochemical cycle	carbon cycle ecosystem	microclimate nitrogen cycle	sulfur cycle vernalization

Biographies
See Section 10/34 of Part Ten

INDEX: See entries under all of the terms above

Section 352.   **Biological Populations and Communities**

A. Biological populations

1. The study of populations
[see 10/34.B.4.]

2. The measurable characteristics of biological populations

a. Age, sex, and genetic differences and their distribution

b. Numbers and density: the effects of natality and mortality, the reproductive rate and death rate

3. Growth of populations: growth form and carrying capacity

4. Fluctuations in stable populations: variations in population size

5. Movements: migration; emigration; dispersion; dispersal; the influence of topographical, climatic, and biological barriers

6. Interactions of populations
[see B., below]

7. Factors affecting the structure of human populations
[see 524.A.]

B. Biotic interactions

1. Intraspecific interactions: positive and negative interactions of individuals within a species

2. Interspecific interactions: interactions among members of different species

a. The range of interspecies associations

b. Negative interactions, in which one or both populations are harmed: consumption, parasitic interactions, amensalism and antagonism

        c. Positive interactions, in which one or both populations are benefited: commensalism, mutualism

        d. Neutralistic interactions

    3. Interactions between populations of different species and the ecological, evolutionary, and biogeographical aspects of interaction on the population level

C. Biological communities

    1. Community structure

        a. Vertical and horizontal patterns: the influence of variations in environmental conditions on the stratification and zonation of organisms

        b. Time relations: periodicity and population changes in the community

        c. Interactions in the community: heterotrophic nutrition, predation, symbiosis

        d. Niches and species diversity

        e. Ecotones and the "edge effect"

    2. Community function: energy flow

    3. Community succession: growth toward a stable, mature condition

    4. Communities in space

        a. Landscape patterns: the habitats of a landscape as forming a pattern of environmental gradients

        b. Climax interpretation: monoclimax theory, polyclimax theory, and climax pattern hypothesis

        c. Community gradients: coenclines

    5. Community classification and its bases

        a. The association as the unit of classification

        b. The biome or formation as the unit of classification

        c. Other bases for classification: *e.g.,* ecological succession, habitat, community metabolism

    6. Community structure in past ages: biogeographical succession
       [see 242.B. and 243]

Suggested reading in the *Encyclopædia Britannica:*

MACROPAEDIA: Major articles dealing with biological populations and communities

    Behaviour, Animal
    Ecosystems

MICROPAEDIA: Selected entries of reference information

General subjects

amensalism	competition	epiphyte	niche
biome	ecological	flyway	parasitism
carnivore	succession	herbivore	parasitology
climax	ecology	homing	predation
commensalism	ecosystem	migration	symbiosis
community	ecotone	mutualism	trophic level

Biographies
    See Section 10/34 of Part Ten

INDEX: See entries under all of the terms above

Section 353.   Hazards of Life in the Biosphere: Disease and Death

A. Disease as a departure from the "normal" state, or a disruption of homeostasis; death as the irreparable disruption of life processes

1. The nature of noncommunicable disease: metabolic defects, environmental hazards

2. The nature of communicable, or contagious, disease

   a. The multifactorial concept of contagious disease

   b. Endemic disease and epidemic disease

   c. Immunity: defense against biotic invasion

3. Control of disease: prevention, treatment

B. Plant diseases

C. Animal diseases

D. Human diseases
[see 423]

Suggested reading in the *Encyclopædia Britannica:*

MACROPAEDIA: Major articles dealing with hazards of life in the biosphere: disease and death

Death
Disease
Immunity

MICROPAEDIA: Selected entries of reference information

General subjects

animal diseases and	mastitis	autoimmunity	Dutch elm disease
zoonoses:	mycosis	drug allergy	ergot
actinomycosis	myopathy	immunity	fruit spot
anthrax	nagana	immunization	leaf blister
ascariasis	pox disease	interferon	mosaic
aspergillosis	Q fever	interleukin	Panama disease
bloat	rabies	phagocytosis	powdery mildew
brucellosis	Rift Valley fever	toxoid	psorosis
canine distemper	rinderpest	transfer factor	rot
cestodiasis	salmonellosis	vaccine	rust
coccidiosis	scrapie	variolation	scab
equine encephalitis	strangles	*plant diseases:*	scorch
erysipelothrix	swine fever	aster yellows	smut
infection	toxoplasmosis	black knot	snow mold
feline distemper	trichomoniasis	black spot	sunscald
foot-and-mouth	tularemia	blight	wilt
disease	vibriosis	bulb rot	*other:*
glanders	yellow fever	bunt	bacteria
histoplasmosis	zoonosis	canker	disease
hookworm disease	*immunity and*	clubroot	epidemic
hyperkeratosis	*immunization:*	crown gall	germfree life
leptospirosis	antibody	curly top	prion
listeriosis	antigen	damping-off	quarantine
lungworm	antitoxin	dieback	veterinary science
malaria	autoantibody	downy mildew	virus

Biographies
See Section 10/34 of Part Ten

INDEX: See entries under all of the terms above

Section 354.   **Biogeographic Distribution of Organisms: Ecosystems**

    A. Terrestrial ecosystems

       1. The land environment

          a. Land as a medium for life and the comparison of the terrestrial and aquatic ecosystems

          b. Limiting factors to living on land

          c. Major terrestrial biomes: the tundra, the coniferous forest, the middle-latitude forest, the tropical rain forest, the grassland and savanna, the scrublands, the desert

          d. Specialized biomes: polar biomes, subterranean biomes

       2. Major life-forms

          a. Growth habits and indicator organisms

          b. Classification by habitat: soil organisms, trees and other rooted plants, epiphytes and periphytes, permeants

          c. Classification by niche: producers, consumers, decomposers

       3. Productivity in terrestrial ecosystems

    B. Aquatic ecosystems

       1. The aquatic environment

       2. The ocean and its communities: communities of the open sea

          a. The sea as a biological environment

          b. Character of oceanic populations: benthos, plankton, nekton

          c. Adaptations to marine conditions

          d. Productivity of marine communities as judged by biological oxygen consumption or by nutrient concentration

       3. Inland waters and their communities: freshwater communities

          a. Lacustrine, or standing-water, communities: in lakes and ponds; in swamps, marshes, and bogs

          b. Riverine, or flowing-water, communities: in rivers and streams, in springs

       4. Boundary ecosystems: between waters or between water and land

          a. Estuarine communities: communities in brackish water

          b. Neritic communities: life along seacoasts

       5. Productivity in aquatic ecosystems: the problem of determining productivity, comparisons of productivity

    C. The distribution of organisms

    D. Biogeographic regions and their inhabitants: regional floras and faunas

       1. The Megagaean realm

          a. Holarctic region: the nontropical parts of Eurasia, northern Africa, and North America

          b. Ethiopian region: Africa south of the Sahara, southwestern Arabia, Madagascar

          c. Oriental region: tropical southern and southeastern Asia

       2. The Notogaean realm: Australia, New Guinea, New Zealand, tropical Pacific islands

       3. The Neogaean realm: Central and South America

       4. The Antarctic realm: Antarctica and most of the sub-Antarctic islands

Suggested reading in the *Encyclopædia Britannica:*

Section 355. The Place of Humans in the Biosphere

A. The qualities that set human beings apart in the biosphere

1. Structural characteristics and physical capabilities providing humans with a versatility unparalleled in the biosphere

2. Physiological characteristics underlying the unique behaviour of humans: lack of a definite breeding season, long life span with slow development and lengthy dependency to maturity

3. Behavioral capacity as the basis of the unique culture of humans: communication through propositional speech, intellect and conceptualization

B. The effects of human action upon the biosphere

1. The influence of the human species on the modification of the environment

2. The influence of the environment on the modification of the human species

3. The attempts to change genetic endowments through deliberate selective measures: eugenics

C. The utilization of organisms by humans

1. Domestication of plants and animals: distribution and development

2. The cultivation of plants: plant breeding and growing

3. The uses of plants

4. The cultivation of animals: animal breeding and raising

5. Major uses of animals

6. The maintenance of public and private collections of live and preserved animals and plants

    a. Museums of natural history

    b. Zoological gardens and aviaries

    c. Institutional and private aquariums

    d. Botanical gardens and arboretums

D. The conservation and management of natural resources

    1. The nature and scope of conservation management

    2. Types of natural resources

    3. Management of natural resources

Suggested reading in the *Encyclopædia Britannica:*

MACROPAEDIA: Major articles dealing with the place of humans in the biosphere

Biosphere, The

Conservation of Natural Resources

Ecosystems

Farming and Agricultural Technology

Gardening and Horticulture

Horses and Horsemanship

Pets

MICROPAEDIA: Selected entries of reference information

General subjects

conservation and
management of
natural resources:
  conservation
  desalination
  drainage
  ecosystem
  flood
  forestry
  Greenpeace
  hunting
  irrigation
  national forest
  national park
  nature reserve

surface mining
terrace cultivation
wildlife
  conservation
domestication and
raising of plants and
animals:
  animal breeding
  animals, cruelty to
  aquarium
  arboriculture
  botanical garden
  breed association
  cereal
  dog

domestic cat
domestication
fowl
fruit
gardening
genecentre
horse
horticulture
hydroponics
livestock
oceanarium
pet
plant breeding
studbook
terrarium

vegetable
zoological garden
pollution and
pollution control:
  acid rain
  emission control
    system
  greenhouse effect
  pollution
  refuse disposal
    system
  sewage system
  smog
  water purification

Biographies

  See Section 10/34 of Part Ten

INDEX: See entries under all of the terms above

Introduction to Part Four:
The Cosmic Orphan

by Loren Eiseley

When I was a young lad of that indefinite but important age when one begins to ask, Who am I? Why am I here? What is the nature of my kind? What is growing up? What is the world? How long shall I live in it? Where shall I go? I found myself walking with a small companion over a high railroad trestle that spanned a stream, a country bridge, and a road. One could look fearfully down, between the ties, at the shallows and ripples in the shining water some 50 feet below. One was also doing a forbidden thing, against which our parents constantly warned. One must not be caught on the black bridge by a train. Something terrible might happen, a thing called death.

From the abutment of the bridge we gazed down upon the water and saw among the pebbles the shape of an animal we knew only from picture books—a turtle, a very large, dark mahogany-coloured turtle. We scrambled down the embankment to observe him more closely. From the little bridge a few feet above the stream, I saw that the turtle, whose beautiful markings shone in the afternoon sun, was not alive and that his flippers waved aimlessly in the rushing water. The reason for his death was plain. Not too long before we had come upon the trestle, someone engaged in idle practice with a repeating rifle had stitched a row of bullet holes across the turtle's carapace and sauntered on.

My father had once explained to me that it took a long time to make a big turtle, years really, in the sunlight and the water and the mud. I turned the ancient creature over and fingered the etched shell with its forlorn flippers flopping grotesquely. The question rose up unbidden. Why did the man have to kill something living that could never be replaced? I laid the turtle down in the water and gave it a little shove. It entered the current and began to drift away. "Let's go home," I said to my companion. From that moment I think I began to grow up.

"Papa," I said in the evening by the oil lamp in our kitchen. "Tell me how men got here." Papa paused. Like many fathers of that time, he was worn from long hours, he was not highly educated, but he had a beautiful resonant voice and he had been born on a frontier homestead. He knew the ritual way the Plains Indians opened a story.

"Son," he said, taking the pattern of another people for our own, "once there was a poor orphan." He said it in such a way that I sat down at his feet. "Once there was a poor orphan with no one to teach him either his way, or his manners. Sometimes animals helped him, sometimes supernatural beings. But above all, one thing was evident. Unlike other occupants of Earth he had to be helped. He did not know his place, he had to find it. Sometimes he was arrogant and had to learn humility, sometimes he was a coward and had to be taught bravery. Sometimes he did not understand his Mother Earth and suffered for it. The old ones who starved and sought visions on hilltops had

known these things. They were all gone now and the magic had departed with them. The orphan was alone; he had to learn by himself; it was a hard school."

My father tousled my head; he gently touched my heart. "You will learn in time there is much pain here," he said. "Men will give it to you, time will give it to you, and you must learn to bear it all, not bear it alone, but be better for the wisdom that may come to you if you watch and listen and learn. Do not forget the turtle, nor the ways of men. They are all orphans and they go astray; they do wrong things. Try to see better."

"Yes, papa," I said, and that was how I believe I came to study men, not the men of written history but the ancestors beyond, beyond all writing, beyond time as we know it, beyond human form as it is known today. Papa was right when he told me men were orphans, eternal seekers. They had little in the way of instinct to instruct them, they had come a strange far road in the universe, passed more than one black, threatening bridge. There were even more to pass, and each one became more dangerous as our knowledge grew. Because man was truly an orphan and confined to no single way of life, he was, in essence, a prison breaker. But in ignorance his very knowledge sometimes led from one terrible prison to another. Was the final problem then, to escape himself, or, if not that, to reconcile his devastating intellect with his heart? All of the knowledge set down in great books directly or indirectly affects this problem. It is the problem of every man, for even the indifferent man is making, unknown to himself, his own callous judgment.

Long ago, however, in one of the Dead Sea Scrolls hidden in the Judaean Desert, an unknown scribe had written: "None there be, can rehearse the whole tale." That phrase, too, contains the warning that man is an orphan of uncertain beginnings and an indefinite ending. All that the archaeological and anthropological sciences can do is to place a somewhat flawed crystal before man and say: This is the way you came, these are your present dangers; somewhere, seen dimly beyond, lies your destiny. God help you, you are a cosmic orphan, a symbol-shifting magician, mostly immature and inattentive to your own dangers. Read, think, study, but do not expect this to save you without humility of heart. This the old ones knew long ago in the great deserts under the stars. This they sought to learn and pass on. It is the only hope of men.

What have we observed that might be buried as the Dead Sea Scrolls were buried for 2,000 years, and be broken out of a jar for human benefit, brief words that might be encompassed on a copper scroll or a ragged sheet of vellum? Only these thoughts, I think, we might reasonably set down as true, now and hereafter. For a long time, for many, many centuries, Western man believed in what we might call the existent world of nature; form as form was seen as constant in both animal and human guise. He believed in the instantaneous creation of his world by the Deity; he believed its duration to be very short, a stage upon which the short drama of a human fall from divine estate and a redemption was in progress.

Worldly time was a small parenthesis in eternity. Man lived with that belief, his cosmos small and man-centred. Then, beginning about 350 years ago, thoughts unventured upon since the time of the Greek philosophers began to enter the human consciousness. They may be summed up in Francis Bacon's dictum: "This is the foundation of all. We are not to imagine or suppose, but to *discover,* what nature does or may be made to do."

When in following years scientific experiment and observation became current, a vast change began to pass over Western thought. Man's conception of himself and his world began to alter beyond recall. "'Tis all in pieces, all coherence gone," exclaimed the poet John Donne, Bacon's contemporary. The existing world was crumbling at the edges. It was cracking apart like an ill-nailed raft in a torrent—a torrent of incredible time. It was, in effect, a new nature comprising a past embedded in the present and a future yet to be.

First, Bacon discerned a *mundus alter,* another separate world that could be drawn out of nature by human intervention—the world that surrounds and troubles us today. Then, by degrees, time depths of tremendous magnitude began, in the late 18th century, to replace the Christian calendar. Space, from a surrounding candelabrum of stars, began to widen to infinity. The Earth was recognized as a mere speck drifting in the wake of a minor star, itself rotating around an immense galaxy composed of innumerable suns. Beyond and beyond, into billions of light years, other galaxies glowed through clouds of wandering gas and interstellar dust. Finally, and perhaps the most shocking blow of all, the natural world of the moment proved to be an illusion, a phantom of man's short lifetime. Organic novelty lay revealed in the strata of the Earth. Man had not always been here. He had been preceded, in the 4,000,-000,000 years of the planet's history, by floating mollusks, strange fern forests, huge dinosaurs, flying lizards, giant mammals whose bones lay under the dropped boulders of vanished continental ice sheets.

The Orphan cried out in protest, as the cold of naked space entered his bones, "Who am I?" And once more science answered. "You are a changeling. You are linked by a genetic chain to all the vertebrates. The thing that is you bears the still aching wounds of evolution in body and in brain. Your hands are made-over fins, your lungs come from a creature gasping in a swamp, your femur has been twisted upright. Your foot is a reworked climbing pad. You are a rag doll resewn from the skins of extinct animals. Long ago, 2,000,000 years perhaps, you were smaller, your brain was not so large. We are not confident that you could speak. Seventy million years before that you were an even smaller climbing creature known as a tupaiid. You were the size of a rat. You ate insects. Now you fly to the Moon."

"This is a fairy tale," protested the Orphan. "I am here, I will look in the mirror."

"Of course it is a fairy tale," said the scientists, "but so is the world and so is life. That is what makes it true. Life is

indefinite departure. That is why we are all orphans. That is why you must find your own way. Life is not stable. Everything alive is slipping through cracks and crevices in time, changing as it goes. Other creatures, however, have instincts that provide for them, holes in which to hide. They cannot ask questions. A fox is a fox, a wolf is a wolf, even if this, too, is illusion. You have learned to ask questions. That is why you are, an orphan. *You are the only creature in the universe who knows what it has been.* Now you must go on asking questions while all the time you are changing. You will ask what you are to become. The world will no longer satisfy you. You must find your way, your own true self."

"But how can I?" wept the Orphan, hiding his head. "This is magic. I do not know what I am. I have been too many things."

"You have indeed," said all the scientists together. "Your body and your nerves have been dragged about and twisted in the long effort of your ancestors to stay alive, but now, small orphan that you are, you must know a secret, a secret magic that nature has given to you. No other creature on the planet possesses it. You use language. You are a symbol-shifter. All this is hidden in your brain and transmitted from one generation to another. You are a time-binder, in your head the symbols that mean things in the world outside can fly about untrammeled. You can combine them differently into a new world of thought or you can also hold them tenaciously throughout a lifetime and pass them on to others."

Thus out of words, a puff of air, really, is made all that is uniquely human, all that is new from one human generation to another. But remember what was said of the wounds of evolution. The brain, parts of it at least, is very old, the parts laid down in sequence like geological strata. Buried deep beneath the brain with which we reason are ancient defense centres quick to anger, quick to aggression, quick to violence, over which the neocortex, the new brain, strives to exert control. Thus there are times when the Orphan is a divided being striving against himself. Evil men know this. Sometimes they can play upon it for their own political advantage. Men crowded together, subjected to the same stimuli, are quick to respond to emotion that in the quiet of their own homes they might analyze more cautiously.

Scientists have found that the very symbols which crowd our brains may possess their own dangers. It is convenient for the thinker to classify an idea with a word. This can sometimes lead to a process called hypostatization or reification. Take the word "Man," for example. There are times when it is useful to categorize the creature briefly, his history, his embracing characteristics. From this, if we are not careful of our meanings, it becomes easy to speak of all men as though they were one person. In reality men have been seeking this unreal man for thousands of years. They have found him bathed in blood, they have found him in the hermit's cell, he has been glimpsed among innumerable messiahs, or in meditation under the sacred bô tree; he has been found in the physician's study or lit by the satanic fires of the first atomic explosion.

In reality he has never been found at all. The reason is very simple: men have been seeking Man capitalized, an imaginary creature constructed out of disparate parts in the laboratory of the human imagination. Some men may thus perceive him and see him as either totally beneficent or wholly evil. They would be wrong. They are wrong so long as they have vitalized this creation and call it "Man." There is no Man; there are only men: good, evil, inconceivable mixtures marred by their genetic makeup, scarred or improved by their societal surroundings. So long as they live they are *men,* multitudinous and unspent potential for action. Men are great objects of study, but the moment we say "Man" we are in danger of wandering into a swamp of abstraction.

Surveying our fossil history perhaps we are not even justified as yet in calling ourselves true men. The word carries subtle implications that extend beyond us into the time stream. If a remote half-human ancestor, barely able to speak, had had a word for his kind, as very likely he did, and just supposing it had been "man," would we approve the usage, the shape-freezing quality of it, now? I think not. Perhaps no true orphan would wish to call himself anything but a traveler. Man in a cosmic timeless sense may not be here.

The point is particularly apparent in the light of a recent and portentous discovery. In 1953 James D. Watson and Francis H.C. Crick discovered the structure of the chemical alphabet out of which all that lives is constituted. It was a strange spiral ladder within the cell, far more organized and complicated than 19th-century biologists had imagined; the tiny building blocks constantly reshuffled in every mating had both an amazing stability and paradoxically, over long time periods, a power to alter the living structure of a species beyond recall. The thing called man had once been a tree shrew on a forest branch; now it manipulates abstract symbols in its brain from which skyscrapers rise, bridges span the horizon, disease is conquered, the Moon is visited.

Molecular biologists have begun to consider whether the marvelous living alphabet which lies at the roof of evolution can be manipulated for human benefit. Already some varieties of domesticated plants and animals have been improved. Now at last man has begun to eye his own possible road into the future. By delicate excisions and intrusions could the mysterious alphabet we carry in our bodies be made to hasten our advancement into the future? Already our urban concentrations, with all their aberrations and faults, are future-oriented. Why not ourselves? It is in our power to perpetuate great minds *ad infinitum?* But who is to judge? Who is to select this future man? There is the problem. Which of us poor orphans by the roadside, even

those peering learnedly through the electron microscope, can be confident of the way into the future? Could the fish unaided by nature have found the road to the reptile, the reptile to the mammal, the mammal to man? And how was man endowed with speech? *Could* men choose their way? Suddenly before us towers the blackest, most formidable bridge of our experience. Across what chasm does it run?

Biologists tell us that in the fullness of time more than ninety percent of the world's past species have perished. The mammalian ones in particular are not noted for longevity. If the scalpel, the excising laser ray in the laboratory, were placed in the hands of some one person, some one poor orphan, what would he do? If assured, would he reproduce himself alone? If cruel, would he by indirection succeed in abolishing the living world? If doubtful of the road, would he reproduce the doubt? "Nothing is more shameful than assertion without knowledge," the great Roman statesman and orator Cicero once pronounced as though he had foreseen this final bridge of human pride—the pride of a god without foresight.

After the disasters of the second World War when the dream of perpetual progress died from men's minds, an orphan of this violent century wrote a poem about the great extinctions revealed in the rocks of the planet. It concludes as follows:

> I am not sure I love
>   the cruelties found in our blood
>   from some lost evil tree in our beginnings.
> May the powers forgive and seal us deep
>   when we lie down,
> May harmless dormice creep and red leaves fall
>   over the prisons where we wreaked our will.
> Dachau, Auschwitz, those places everywhere.
> If I could pray, I would pray long for this.

One may conclude that the poet was a man of doubt. He did not regret man; he was confident that leaves, rabbits, and songbirds would continue life, as, long ago, a tree shrew had happily forgotten the ruling reptiles. The poet was an orphan in shabby circumstances pausing by the roadside to pray, for he did pray despite his denial; God forgive us all. He was a man in doubt upon the way. He was the eternal orphan of my father's story. Let us then, as similar orphans who have come this long way through time, be willing to assume the risks of the uncompleted journey. We must know, as that forlorn band of men in Judaea knew when they buried the jar, that man's road is to be sought beyond himself. *No man there is who can tell the whole tale.* After the small passage of 2,000 years who would deny this truth?

Part Four. Human Life

The outlines in the three divisions and fifteen sections of Part Four treat stages in the development of human life on Earth; human health and diseases; and human behaviour and experience.

Several points should be noted about the relations of Part Four to preceding and subsequent parts.

The fundamental physical and chemical properties of matter are dealt with in Part One. The treatment of the Earth in Part Two encompasses those properties of the Earth that are supportive of human life. Much fundamental biological knowledge concerning human life is involved in the treatment—in Part Three, Life on Earth—of what is common to all animal life; the last section of Part Three deals with mankind's place in the biosphere.

Knowledge of the biomedical and psychological aspects of human life is not wholly separable from, and is germane to, the subjects covered in Parts Five through Ten, which treat human society, the fine arts, technology, religion, the history of peoples and civilizations, and man as logician, mathematician, scientist, historian, and philosopher.

The biological, medical, and psychological sciences have been themselves the object of historical and analytical studies concerned with their nature, methods, and interrelations. These studies are set forth in Sections 10/34, 10/35, and 10/36 of Part Ten. The instrumentation involved in these sciences is dealt with in Section 723 of Part Seven.

Division I.   **Stages in the Development of Human Life on Earth**

The outlines in the two sections of Division I present studies in historical comparative anatomy that place *Homo sapiens* within a general taxonomy; the theory of human evolution; and studies, in genetics and physical anthropology, of human heredity and the races of mankind.

Section 411.   **Human Evolution**

A. The evolutionary process

B. Estimates of the antiquity of mankind and of the chronology of hominid evolution

C. Human evolutionary relationships with living and fossil primates

    1. The primates

      a. Distinguishing characteristics of the primates

      b. The natural history of primate life

      c. Evolution and paleontology

      d. Classification of the primates: the two main groups or suborders, the prosimians (principally lemurs, lorises, and tarsiers) and the anthropoids (monkeys, apes, and man)

    2. Distinguishing characteristics of the Hominidae

      a. Morphological characteristics

      b. Inferred behavioral characteristics

      c. Contrasting adaptations of Hominidae and Pongidae

D. The fossil record of the Hominidae

1. The discovery and recognition of the hominid fossil record
2. Classification of the Hominidae
   a. *Ramapithecus*
   b. *Australopithecus*
   c. *Homo erectus*
   d. *Homo sapiens*
      i. Fossil remains from Europe and Africa: Vértesszőllős man, Swanscombe man, Steinheim man, Fontéchevade man, Omo man
      ii. The Neanderthal peoples of Europe
      iii. Populations of sub-Saharan Africa
      iv. Populations of Asia
      v. Cro-Magnon man

Suggested reading in the *Encyclopædia Britannica*:

MACROPAEDIA: Major articles dealing with human evolution

Evolution, Human
Life

MICROPAEDIA: Selected entries of reference information

General subjects

cultural stages:	Krapina remains	Homo	Ibero-Maurusian
Mesolithic Period	Laetolil remains	transvaalensis	industry
Neolithic Period	Lantian man	Hominid	Levalloisian
Paleolithic Period	Makapansgat	Neanderthal man	stone-flaking
hominid fossils:	Olduvai Gorge	*tools and tool*	techniques
Amud remains	Omo remains	*industries:*	Magdalenian
Arago remains	Peking man	Abbevillian	culture
Boskop skull	Peninj mandible	industry	Maglemosian
Chad	Petralona skull	Acheulian industry	industry
australopithecine	Piltdown man	Aterian industry	Mousterian
Chancelade	Ramapithecus	Aurignacian	industry
skeleton	Saccopastore skulls	culture	Oldowan industry
Ehringsdorf skull	Solo man	Azilian industry	Osteodontokeratic
Ferassie	Sterkfontein	Chopper	tool industry
skeletons, La	Swanscombe skull	chopping-tool	Perigordian
Hadar remains	Telanthropus	industry	industry
Heidelberg jaw	capensis	Clactonian	Solutrean industry
Java man	*hominids:*	industry	Stillbay industry
Kabwe man	Australopithecus	Ertebølle industry	stone-tool industry
Kafzeh	Cro-Magnon man	Fauresmith	*other:*
Kanapoi fossil	Homo erectus	industry	evolution
Koobi Fora	Homo habilis	flake tool	Gigantopithecus
remains	Homo sapiens		missing link

Biographies

See Section 10/36 of Part Ten

INDEX: See entries under all of the terms above

Section 412.   Human Heredity: the Races of Mankind

A. Heredity in humans

    1. The biological basis of human heredity: genetic reproduction

    2. Inheritance of behavioral traits

        a. Fraternal and identical twins and the inferences that can be made from twin studies

        b. Genetic explanations for abnormalities: chromosome variations, mutation

    3. Applications of human genetics

    4. Specific behavioral traits affected by inheritance

    5. Consanguinity and its effects

B. The nature and origin of human races

    1. Aspects of racial diversity

    2. Hallmarks of race

        a. Old hallmarks; *e.g.,* colour, hair form, body measurements, features such as eyes and nose

        b. New hallmarks; *e.g.,* blood traits, amino acids, enzymes

    3. Modern measures of race: blood groups and genetic evidence

    4. A geographical taxonomy of the living races: Caucasoids; Congoids and Capoids; Australoids and Oceanic peoples; peoples of East Asia; peoples of the Indian subcontinent; peoples of the Western Hemisphere—North, Central, and South American Indians

    5. Present distribution of human populations

Suggested reading in the *Encyclopædia Britannica*:

Division II.   **The Human Organism: Health and Disease**
[For Part Four headnote see page 143.]

The outlines in the four sections of Division II treat the structures and functions of the human body; human health; the manifestation, recognition, and treatment of human disease; and the practice of medicine.

The outline referred to in Section 421 deals with the structures and the functions of the several organ systems, the proper coordination and regulation of which constitute the health of the human body. It treats the cardiovascular system; the lymphatic system; the reticuloendothelial system; the respiratory system; the digestive system; the endocrine system; the reproductive system; the excretory system; the supportive-protective system; body cavities and membranes; the nervous system; and the composition and properties of body fluids and tissues.

The outline in Section 423 first treats the general characteristics, causes, and classifications of human disease. It then treats the concepts, principles, and methods of the medical art, in the two stages of diagnosis and therapy. The outline encompasses detailed studies of the diseases of the human body. They treat the symptoms, diagnosis, and treatment of diseases that affect the body as a whole, and of diseases that affect each of the organ systems dealt with in their healthy state in Section 421.

The outline in Section 424 deals with issues relating to the professionalization of the practice of medicine—not only those internal to the profession but also those arising from the educational, economic, social, political, and legal dimensions of institutionalized medicine.

Section 421.   **The Structures and Functions of the Human Body**

A. The structures and functions of the cardiovascular system

   1. The heart

   2. The blood vessels: arteries, veins, and capillaries

   3. Human blood

      a. Components of blood: plasma, red blood cells (erythrocytes), white blood cells (leukocytes), platelets (thrombocytes)

      b. Blood groups

   4. Blood circulation: the central pump, the systemic circulation, the pulmonary circulation

B. The structures and functions of the lymphatic system: lymphocytes, lymphatic vessels, lymph nodes, and the lymph

C. The structures and functions of the respiratory system

   1. The upper portion of the respiratory tract: nasal cavity, pharynx, larynx, and trachea

   2. The lungs and bronchi

   3. The regulation, control, and dynamics of breathing

D. The structures and functions of the digestive system

   1. Structure of the components of the digestive tract

      a. Mouth and related structures

      b. Pharynx and esophagus

      c. Stomach

      d. The small intestine and the small bowel mucosa

      e. Large intestine, rectum, and anus

      f. Associated glands and structures: pancreas, liver, gallbladder, and bile ducts

   2. The digestive process

E. The structures and functions of the endocrine system

Principal Parts of
THE HUMAN BODY

This Plate on gross anatomy comprises 14 Views, 12 of which are transparent, showing all principal parts of the human anatomy. Below is a list in English (insofar as this is possible) of the names of the parts illustrated. The number immediately following the name is the code number for that part; the other number or numbers indicate the View or Views on which it is shown. A key to the Plate, with Latin names, is given on the last page.

Abdominal oblique muscle, external, 87: 1, 8
Abdominal oblique muscle, internal, 88: 1
Adductor longus muscle, 68: 6, 7, 14
Adductor brevis muscle, 67: 7
Adrenal gland: see Suprarenal gland
Aorta, 3: 5, 6, 10, 11, 14
Aponeurosis of external abdominal oblique muscle, 4: 1
Appendix, vermiform, 5: 4, 12, 13
Atrium, left, 19: 11
Axillary artery, 6: 5, 6, 14
Axillary vein, 178: 3, 10, 11
Biceps brachii muscle, 69: 5, 6, 10, 11
Bile duct, common, 35: 4, 5, 10, 11, 13
Brachial artery, 7: 5, 6, 14
Brachial muscle, 70: 14
Brachial plexus, 140: 5, 6, 7, 14
Brachial vein, 179: 3, 8, 10, 11
Brachiocephalic trunk, 164: 5, 14
Brachiocephalic vein, 180: 3, 4, 10, 11
Brachioradialis muscle, 71: 12, 13, 14
Breastbone, 160: 1, 2, 8, 9
Bronchus, left, 20: 5, 14
Buccinator muscle, 72: 1
Carotid artery, common, 8: 5, 14
Celiac trunk, 165: 5, 10, 12, 14
Cephalic vein, 183: 3, 4, 8, 9, 11, 12, 13, 14
Cerebellum, 22: 11, 14
Cerebrum, 23: 11, 14
Cheekbone, 134: 1
Collarbone, 24: 1, 2, 7, 8, 9, 14
Colon, ascending, 25: 3, 4, 12, 13
Colon, descending, 26: 3, 4, 12, 13
Colon, sigmoid, 27: 3, 4, 12, 13
Colon, transverse, 28: 3, 4, 11
Coracobrachialis muscle, 73: 5, 14
Corpus callosum, 32: 11, 14
Deltoid muscle, 74: 5, 6, 8, 9, 14
Depressor anguli oris muscle, 75: 1, 10
Diaphragm, 34: 2, 3, 4, 5, 6, 9, 10, 11, 14
Digastric muscle, 76: 3
Ductus deferens, 36: 5, 6
Duodenum, 37: 5, 12, 13
Epigastric vessels, deep, 169: 5, 8, 9
Esophagus, 122: 5, 6, 12, 13, 14
Extensor carpi radialis longus muscle, 77: 14
Falx cerebri, 38: 12, 13
Femoral artery, 9: 5, 6, 14
Femoral nerve, 114: 7, 14
Femoral vein, 184: 5, 6, 14
Femur, 39: 7
Flexor carpi radialis muscle, 78: 14
Fossa ovalis, 40: 8
Frontal bone, 126: 3, 7
Gall bladder, 200: 3, 4, 10, 11
Gastric vessels, 170: 11
Gastro-omental vessels, 171: 10
Glans penis, 46: 1
Gluteus medius muscle, 79: 1, 5, 6, 7, 14
Gluteus minimus muscle, 80: 7
Gracilis muscle, 81: 6, 7, 14
Heart: see Atrium; Pericardium; Ventricle
Humerus, 48: 7
Ileum, 49: 12
Iliac artery, common, 10: 5, 6, 14
Iliac artery, external, 11: 5, 6, 14
Iliac artery, internal, 12: 5, 6, 14
Iliac spine, anterior superior, 159: 1, 2, 7, 8, 14
Iliacus muscle, 82: 7, 14

Iliac vein, common, 185: 5, 6, 14
Iliac vein, external, 186: 5, 6, 14
Iliac vein, internal, 187: 5, 6, 14
Iliohypogastric nerve, 115: 7
Ilioinguinal nerve, 116: 7
Inguinal ligament, 55: 1, 2, 3, 5, 6, 8, 13, 14
Inguinal ring, deep, 1: 1, 2
Inguinal ring, superficial, 2: 1
Innominate artery: see Brachiocephalic trunk
Innominate vein: see Brachiocephalic vein
Intercostal muscle, external, 83: 1
Intercostal muscle, internal, 84: 2, 9
Intestine, large: see Colon
Intestine, small, 50: 3, 4, 10, 11
Ischium, 127: 7
Jaw, lower, 61: 1, 2, 3, 4, 5, 6, 7, 11, 14
Jaw, upper, 62: 2, 3, 4, 5, 6, 7, 11, 12, 13, 14
Jugular vein, internal, 188: 3, 4, 5, 10
Kidney, 149: 5, 6, 14
Lacrimal gland, 41: 2
Larynx, 51: 4, 7, 11, 14
Ligament of the liver, falciform, 53: 3, 9
Ligament of the liver, round, 56: 2, 9
Ligament of the penis, fundiform, 54: 1
Line, arcuate, 58: 2
Line, semilunar, 59: 1, 2, 8, 9
Linea alba, 57: 1, 2, 8
Liver, 47: 3, 4, 9, 10, 11
Mammary vessels, internal: see Thoracic vessels, internal
Masseter muscle, 85: 1
Median nerve, 117: 5, 6, 14
Medulla oblongata, 63: 11, 14
Mesenteric artery, inferior, 14: 5, 6, 14
Mesenteric artery, superior, 15: 14
Mesenteric vein, inferior, 189: 13
Mesenteric vein, superior, 190: 5
Mesenteric vessels, inferior, 173: 12, 13
Mesenteric vessels, superior, 174: 5, 12, 13
Mesentery, 65: 4, 11, 12
Mesocolon, transverse, 66: 11, 12
Mylohyoid muscle, 86: 2, 3
Nasal concha, inferior, 29: 4, 7, 11, 14
Nasal concha, middle, 30: 4, 7, 11, 14
Nasal concha, superior, 31: 4, 7, 11, 14
Nasal septum, 152: 5, 6, 12, 13
Obturator nerve, 118: 7
Occipital bone, 128: 4, 5, 7
Omentum, greater, 123: 10
Omentum, lesser, 124: 3, 4, 9, 10, 11
Omohyoid muscle, 89: 1, 2, 9
Orbicularis oris muscle, 90: 1
Ovarian vessels, 175: 14
Ovary, 135: 14
Pancreas, 136: 5, 12, 13
Parietal bone, 129: 3, 7
Parotid gland, 42: 1, 2
Pectoralis major muscle, 91: 1, 2, 5, 8, 9, 14
Pectoralis minor muscle, 92: 2, 5, 9, 10, 11
Penis, 137: 2, 3, 5
Pericardium, 138: 10
Phrenic nerve, 119: 10
Platysma muscle, 139: 8, 9
Pons, 144: 11, 14
Portal vein, 191: 5, 11, 12, 13
Pronator teres muscle, 93: 14
Prostate, 145: 6

Psoas major muscle, 94: 7, 14
Pterygoid muscle, internal, 95: 2
Pubis, 130: 3, 6, 7, 13, 14
Pulmonary artery, 16: 5, 10, 11, 14
Pulmonary vein, 192: 11, 14
Pylorus, 147: 12, 13
Quadratus lumborum muscle, 96: 14
Quadriceps femoris muscle, 97: 3, 4, 5, 6, 14
Rectum, 148: 7, 14
Rectus abdominis muscle, 98: 1, 2
Renal artery, 17: 6, 14
Renal vein, 193: 6, 14
Rib, 125: 1, 2, 7, 9
Sacrum, 131: 7
Saphenous hiatus: see Fossa ovalis
Saphenous vein, greater, 194: 8, 9
Sartorius muscle, 99: 1, 2, 9
Scalene muscle, anterior, 100: 14
Scrotum, 151: 1, 2, 5
Seminal duct: see Ductus deferens
Seminal vesicle, 202: 6
Serratus muscle, anterior, 101: 1
Shoulder blade, 150: 7
Sinus, frontal, 153: 2, 3, 4, 5, 6, 7, 11, 12, 13, 14
Sinus, inferior sagittal, 156: 12, 13
Sinus, maxillary, 154: 2, 3
Sinus, sphenoidal, 158: 4, 5, 6, 7, 11, 12, 13, 14
Sinus, straight, 155: 12, 13
Sinus, superior sagittal, 157: 12, 13
Skull, 33: 2
Sphenoid bone, 132: 7
Spinal cord, 64: 7, 14
Spleen, 52: 5, 12, 13
Splenic artery, 13: 5
Splenic vessels, 172: 12, 13
Sternohyoid muscle, 103: 1, 2, 9
Sternomastoid muscle, 102: 1, 2, 8, 9, 10
Sternothyroid muscle, 104: 2, 9
Stomach, 196: 3, 4, 10, 11
Styloglossus muscle, 105: 3
Subclavian artery, 18: 5, 6, 14
Subclavian vein, 195: 3, 4, 10, 11
Submandibular gland, 43: 1, 2
Suprarenal gland, 44: 5, 6, 14
Temporal bone, 133: 3, 7
Temporal muscle, 106: 1
Tensor fasciae latae muscle, 107: 1, 5, 6, 14
Tentorium cerebelli, 161: 11, 14
Testicle, 162: 5
Testicular vessels, 176: 5, 6
Thoracic vessels, internal, 177: 9, 10
Thyrohyoid muscle, 108: 2
Thyroid cartilage, 21: 3
Thyroid gland, 45: 3, 4, 10, 11
Tongue, 60: 3, 4, 5, 6, 7, 11, 14
Transversus abdominis muscle, 109: 1, 2
Transversus thoracis muscle, 110: 2, 9
Trapezius muscle, 111: 5, 6, 10, 14
Triceps brachii muscle, 112: 5, 6, 14
Turbinate bones: see Nasal concha
Ulnar nerve, 120: 5, 6, 14
Umbilical fold, medial, 142: 9
Umbilical fold, median, 143: 9
Ureter, 166: 5, 6, 13, 14
Urinary bladder, 201: 3, 4, 5, 6, 12, 13
Uterus, 167: 14
Vagina, 168: 14
Vagus nerve, 121: 14
Vena cava, inferior, 181: 5, 6, 11, 14
Vena cava, superior, 182: 4, 5, 10, 11
Ventricle, left, 198: 5, 10, 11
Ventricle, right, 197: 5, 10, 11
Vertebra, 199: 6, 7, 11, 14
Windpipe, 163: 5, 6, 14
Womb: see Uterus
Zygomaticus major muscle, 113: 1, 10

Abbreviations: A. (Arteria); L. (Ligamentum);
M. (Musculus); N. (Nervus); and V. (Vena).

KEY TO VIEW 14

3. Aorta
6. A. axillaris
7. A. brachialis
8. A. carotis communis
9. A. femoralis
10. A. iliaca communis
11. A. iliaca externa
12. A. iliaca interna
14. A. mesenterica inferior
15. A. mesenterica superior
16. A. pulmonalis
17. A. renalis
18. A. subclavia
20. Bronchus principalis
22. Cerebellum
23. Cerebrum
24. Clavicula
29. Concha nasalis inferior
30. Concha nasalis media
31. Concha nasalis superior
32. Corpus callosum
34. Diaphragma
44. Glandula suprarenalis
51. Larynx
55. L. inguinale
60. Lingua (tongue)
61. Mandibula
62. Maxilla
63. Medulla oblongata
64. Medulla spinalis
68. M. adductor longus
70. M. brachialis
71. M. brachioradialis
73. M. coracobrachialis
74. M. deltoideus
77. M. extensor carpi
    radialis longus
78. M. flexor carpi radialis
79. M. gluteus medius
81. M. gracilis
82. M. iliacus
91. M. pectoralis major
93. M. pronator teres
94. M. psoas major
96. M. quadratus lumborum
97. M. quadriceps femoris
    (rectus)
100. M. scalenus anterior
107. M. tensor fasciae latae
111. M. trapezius
112. M. triceps brachii
114. N. femoralis
117. N. medianus
120. N. ulnaris
121. N. vagus
122. Oesophagus (esophagus)
130. Os pubis
135. Ovarium (ovary)
140. Plexus brachialis
144. Pons
146. Pulmo (lung)
148. Rectum
149. Ren (kidney)
153. Sinus frontalis
158. Sinus sphenoidalis
159. Spina iliaca anterior superior
161. Tentorium cerebelli
163. Trachea
164. Truncus brachiocephalicus
165. Truncus coeliacus
166. Ureter
167. Uterus
168. Vagina
175. Vasa ovarica
181. V. cava inferior
183. V. cephalica
184. V. femoralis
185. V. iliaca communis
186. V. iliaca externa
187. V. iliaca interna   193. V. renalis
192. V. pulmonalis   199. Vertebra

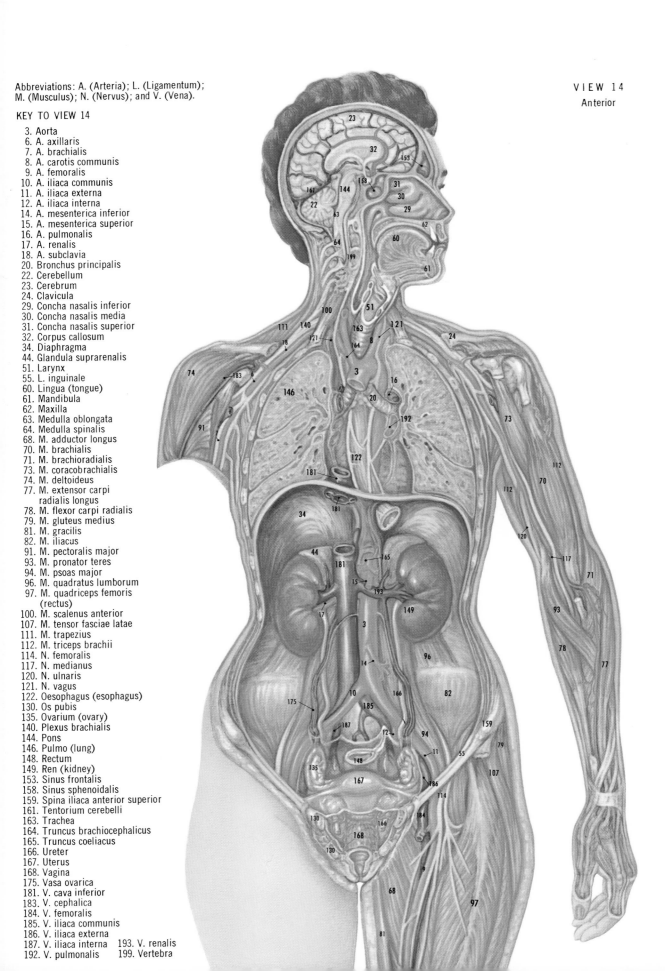

Principal Parts of
THE HUMAN BODY

KEY TO PLATE, VIEWS 1-14

On the list below, the number at left is a code number for the part of the body named.
The number or numbers at right indicate the View or Views on which that part of the body is shown.

Abbreviations: A. (Arteria); L. (Ligamentum); M. (Musculus); N. (Nervus); and V. (Vena).

1. Annulus inguinalis profundus, 1,2
2. Annulus inguinalis superficialis, 1
3. Aorta, 5,6,10,11,14
4. Aponeurosis m. obliquus externus abdominis, 1
5. Appendix vermiformis, 4,12,13
6. A. axillaris, 5,6,14
7. A. brachialis, 5,6,14
8. A. carotis communis, 5,14
9. A. femoralis, 5,6,14
10. A. iliaca communis, 5,6,14
11. A. iliaca externa, 5,6,14
12. A. iliaca interna, 5,6,14
13. A. lienalis (a. splenica), 5
14. A. mesenterica inferior, 5,6,14
15. A. mesenterica superior, 14
16. A. pulmonalis, 5,10,11,14
17. A. renalis, 6,14
    A. splenica: see 13
18. A. subclavia, 5,6,14
19. Atrium sinistrum, 11
20. Bronchus principalis, 5,14
21. Cartilago thyroidea, 3
22. Cerebellum, 11,14
23. Cerebrum, 11,14
24. Clavicula, 1,2,7,8,9,14
25. Colon ascendens, 3,4,12,13
26. Colon descendens, 3,4,12,13
27. Colon sigmoideum, 3,4,12,13
28. Colon transversum, 3,4,11
29. Concha nasalis inferior, 4,7,11,14
30. Concha nasalis media, 4,7,11,14
31. Concha nasalis superior, 4,7,11,14
    Cor (heart): see 19,138,197,198
32. Corpus callosum, 11,14
33. Cranium, 2
34. Diaphragma, 2,3,4,5,6,9,10,11,14
35. Ductus choledochus, 4,5,10,11,13
36. Ductus deferens, 5,6
37. Duodenum, 5,12,13
    Esophagus: see 122
38. Falx cerebri, 12,13
39. Femur, 7
40. Fossa ovalis (hiatus saphenus), 8
    Gall Bladder: see 200
    Gaster: see 196
41. Glandula lacrimalis, 2
42. Glandula parotidea, 1,2
43. Glandula submandibularis, 1,2
44. Glandula suprarenalis, 5,6,14
45. Glandula thyreoidea, 3,4,10,11
46. Glans penis, 1
    Heart: see 19,138,197,198
47. Hepar (liver), 3,4,9,10,11
    Hiatus saphenus: see 40
48. Humerus, 7
49. Ileum, 12
50. Intestinum tenue, 3,4,10,11
    Kidney: see 149
51. Larynx, 4,7,11,14
52. Lien (splen; spleen), 5,12,13
53. L. falciforme hepatis, 3,9
54. L. fundiforme penis, 1
55. L. inguinale, 1,2,3,5,6,8,13,14
56. L. teres hepatis, 2,9
57. Linea alba, 1,2,8
58. Linea arcuata, 2
59. Linea semilunaris, 1,2,8,9
60. Lingua (tongue), 3,4,5,6,7,11,14
    Liver: see 47
    Lung: see 146

61. Mandibula, 1,2,3,4,5,6,7,11,14
62. Maxilla, 2,3,4,5,6,7,11,12,13,14
63. Medulla oblongata, 11,14
64. Medulla spinalis, 7,14
65. Mesenterium, 4, 11, 12
66. Mesocolon transversum, 11,12
67. M. adductor brevis, 7
68. M. adductor longus, 6,7,14
69. M. biceps brachii, 5,6,10,11
70. M. brachialis, 14
71. M. brachioradialis, 12,13,14
72. M. buccinator, 1
73. M. coracobrachialis, 5,14
74. M. deltoideus, 5,6,8,9,14
75. M. depressor anguli oris, 1,10
76. M. digastricus, 3
77. M. extensor carpi radialis longus, 14
78. M. flexor carpi radialis, 14
79. M. gluteus medius, 1,5,6,7,14
80. M. gluteus minimus, 7
81. M. gracilis, 6,7,14
82. M. iliacus, 7,14
83. M. intercostalis externus, 1
84. M. intercostalis internus, 2,9
85. M. masseter, 1
86. M. mylohyoideus, 2,3
87. M. obliquus externus abdominis, 1,8
88. M. obliquus internus abdominis, 1
89. M. omohyoideus, 1,2,9
90. M. orbicularis oris, 1
91. M. pectoralis major, 1,2,5,8,9,14
92. M. pectoralis minor, 2,5,9,10,11
93. M. pronator teres, 14
94. M. psoas major, 7,14
95. M. pterygoideus medialis, 2
96. M. quadratus lumborum, 14
97. M. quadriceps femoris, 3,4,5,6,14
98. M. rectus abdominis, 1,2
99. M. sartorius, 1,2,9
100. M. scalenus anterior, 14
101. M. serratus anterior, 1
102. M. sternocleidomastoideus, 1,2,8,9,10
103. M. sternohyoideus, 1,2,9
104. M. sternothyroideus, 2,9
105. M. styloglossus, 3
106. M. temporalis, 1
107. M. tensor fasciae latae, 1,5,6,14
108. M. thyrohyoideus, 2
109. M. transversus abdominis, 1,2
110. M. transversus thoracis, 2,9
111. M. trapezius, 5,6,10,14
112. M. triceps brachii, 5,6,14
113. M. zygomaticus major, 1,10
114. N. femoralis, 7,14
115. N. iliohypogastricus, 7
116. N. ilio-inguinalis, 7
117. N. medianus, 5,6,14
118. N. obturatorius, 7
119. N. phrenicus, 10
120. N. ulnaris, 5,6,14
121. N. vagus, 14
122. Oesophagus (esophagus), 5,6,12,13,14
123. Omentum majus, 10
124. Omentum minus, 3,4,9,10,11
125. Os costate, 1,2,7,9
126. Os frontale, 3,7
127. Os ischii, 7
128. Os occipitale, 4,5,7
129. Os parietale, 3,7
130. Os pubis, 3,6,7,13,14
131. Os sacrum, 7

132. Os sphenoidale, 7
133. Os temporale, 3,7
134. Os zygomaticum, 1
135. Ovarium (ovary), 14
136. Pancreas, 5,12,13
137. Penis, 2,3,5
138. Pericardium, 10
139. Platysma, 8,9
140. Plexus brachialis, 5,6,7,14
141. Plexus lumbosacralis, 7
142. Plica umbilicalis medialis, 9
143. Plica umbilicalis mediana, 9
144. Pons, 11,14
145. Prostata, 6
146. Pulmo (lung), 3,4,5,6,10,11,14
147. Pylorus, 12,13
148. Rectum, 7, 14
149. Ren (kidney), 5,6,14
150. Scapula, 7
151. Scrotum, 1,2,5
152. Septum nasi, 5,6,12,13
153. Sinus frontalis, 2,3,4,5,6,7,11,12,13,14
154. Sinus maxillaris, 2,3
155. Sinus rectus, 12,13
156. Sinus sagittalis inferior, 12,13
157. Sinus sagittalis superior, 12,13
158. Sinus sphenoidalis, 4,5,6,7,11,12,13,14
159. Spina iliaca anterior superior, 1,2,7,8,14
    Spleen: see 52
    Splen: see 52
160. Sternum, 1,2,8,9
    Stomach: see 196
161. Tentorium cerebelli, 11,14
    Tongue: see 60
162. Testis, 5
163. Trachea, 5,6,14
164. Truncus brachiocephalicus, 5,14
165. Truncus coeliacus, 5,10,12,14
166. Ureter, 5,6,13,14
167. Uterus, 14
168. Vagina, 14
169. Vasa epigastrica inferior, 5,8,9
170. Vasa gastrica, 11
171. Vasa gastro-omentalis, 10
172. Vasa lienalis (vasa splenica), 12,13
173. Vasa mesenterica inferior, 12,13
174. Vasa mesenterica superior, 5,12,13
175. Vasa ovarica, 14
    Vasa splenica: see 172
176. Vasa testicularis, 5,6
177. Vasa thoracicae internae, 9,10
178. V. axillaris, 3,10,11
179. V. comitans a. brachialis, 3,8,10,11
180. V. brachiocephalica, 3,4,10,11
181. V. cava inferior, 5,6,11,14
182. V. cava superior, 4,5,10,11
183. V. cephalica, 3,4,8,9,11,12,13,14
184. V. femoralis, 5,6,14
185. V. iliaca communis, 5,6,14
186. V. iliaca externa, 5,6,14
187. V. iliaca interna, 5,6,14
188. V. jugularis interna, 3,4,5,10
189. V. mesenterica inferior, 13
190. V. mesenterica superior, 5
191. V. portae hepatis, 5,11,12,13
192. V. pulmonalis, 11,14
193. V. renalis, 6,14
194. V. saphena magna, 8,9
195. V. subclavia, 3,4,10,11
196. Ventriculus (gaster; stomach), 3,4,10,11
197. Ventriculus dexter, 5,10,11
198. Ventriculus sinister, 5,10,11
199. Vertebra, 6,7,11,14
200. Vesica biliaris (vesica fellea; gall bladder), 3,4,10,11
201. Vesica urinaria, 3,4,5,6,12,13
202. Vesicula seminalis, 6

    1. The glands and tissues making up the system and their secretions

      a. The thyroid

      b. The adrenal glands

      c. The pituitary

      d. Hypothalamus

      e. Pancreatic islets

      f. Parathyroid glands

      g. Gastrointestinal mucosa

      h. Thymus, pineal body, kidneys, and other possible endocrine organs or hormones

    2. The effects of the endocrine system upon sex-oriented processes

      a. Glands affected by endocrine secretions: the testes, the ovaries, the placenta

      b. Female processes under endocrine control: the menstrual cycle, gestation, parturition, the secretion of milk, and the termination of menstrual life

F. The structures and functions of the reproductive system

    1. The male reproductive system

    2. The female reproductive system

G. The structures and functions of the excretory system

    1. The structures: kidneys, ureters, urinary bladder, urethra

    2. The excretory process

H. The structures and functions of the supportive-protective system

    1. The composition and properties of bone

    2. The connective tissues

    3. The joints

    4. The bursae

    5. The sinuses

    6. The muscular system

    7. The structure and properties of muscle

      a. Striated, skeletal, or voluntary muscle

      b. Nonstriated, smooth, or involuntary muscle

      c. Cardiac muscle

      d. The contraction of muscle fibres
        [see 323.D.]

    8. The integument and derivatives: skin, hair, and nails

I. The body cavities and their membranes: the thoracic cavity, the abdominal cavity

J. The structure and functions of the nervous system

    1. The central nervous system: the brain and spinal cord, the cerebrospinal fluid

    2. The peripheral nervous system: cranial nerves, spinal nerves, and that part of the autonomic system that is outside the brain and spinal cord

    3. The autonomic nervous system: the sympathetic and parasympathetic systems

    4. The eye and the process of vision

    5. The ear and the process of audition

    6. Other sensory receptors

      a. Cutaneous (skin) senses: touch, heat, cold, and pain

      b. Kinesthetic (motion) sense

      c. Vestibular sense (equilibrium): acceleration, rotation, orientation, and balance

    d. Taste (gustatory) sense

    e. Smell (olfactory) sense

K. The composition and properties of body fluids and tissues
[see 332.D.]

Suggested reading in the *Encyclopædia Britannica*:

MACROPAEDIA: Major articles dealing with the structures and functions of the human body

Biochemical Components of Organisms	Digestion and Digestive Systems	Muscles and Muscle Systems	Respiration and Respiratory Systems
Blood	Endocrine Systems	Nerves and Nervous Systems	Sensory Reception
Circulation and Circulatory Systems	Excretion and Excretory Systems	Nutrition	Supportive and Connective Tissues
	Integumentary Systems	Reproduction and Reproductive Systems	Tissues and Fluids

MICROPAEDIA: Selected entries of reference information

General subjects

bones and skeletal system:
bone
bone marrow
cancellous bone
cartilage
compact bone
joint
osteoblast
osteoclast
osteocyte
osteon
periosteum
skeleton
cardiovascular system—blood:
  ABO blood group system
agglutinin
blood
blood cell formation
blood typing
coagulation
complement
erythrocyte
hemoglobin
hemolysis
leukocyte
lymphocyte
platelet
Rh blood group system
serum albumin
cardiovascular system—blood vessels:
aorta
artery
capillary
vein
vena cava

cardiovascular system—heart:
atrium
cardiac output
coronary circulation
diastole
heart
heart sound
heart valve
heartbeat
systole
ventricle
cardiovascular system—other:
blood pressure
cardiovascular system
pulmonary circulation
systemic circulation
cavities and membranes:
abdominal cavity
peritoneum
pleura
sinus
thoracic cavity
connective tissues:
collagen
connective tissue
elastic fibre
ligament
mast cell
reticular fibre
tendon
digestive system:
anal canal
anus
appetite
argentaffin cell

bile
bilirubin
cecum
chewing
chyme
colon
defecation
digestion
digestive nerve plexus
esophagus
feces
gallbladder
gastric gland
intestinal gas
large intestine
liver
pancreas
Paneth cell
peristalsis
pharynx
plica circularis
pylorus
rectum
satiety
small intestine
stomach
swallowing
vermiform appendix
villus
endocrine system:
adrenal gland
adrenaline and noradrenaline
adrenocorticotropic hormone
androgen
calcitonin
corticoid
endocrine system
enterogastrone
estrogen

follicle-stimulating hormones
gastrin
glucagon
hormone
insulin
Langerhans, islets of
luteinizing hormone
neurohormone
ovary
parathyroid gland
pineal gland
pituitary gland
progesterone
prolactin
relaxin
renin
steroid hormone
testis
testosterone
thymus
thyroid gland
excretory system:
excretion
kidney
loop of Henle
renal artery
renal capsule
renal collecting tubule
renal pelvis
renal pyramid
urinary bladder
urination
urine
integument and its derivatives:
dermis
epidermis
hair

mammary gland
perspiration
sweat gland
lymphatic system:
  lymph
  lymph node
  lymph nodule
  lymphoid tissue
  Peyer's patch
  spleen
  thymus
  tonsil
*mouth, teeth, and
  gums:*
  canine tooth
  cementum
  dentine
  enamel
  gum
  incisor
  molar
  palate
  periodontal
    membrane
  permanent tooth
  premolar
  primary tooth
  saliva
  salivary gland
  tongue
  tooth
muscles:
  abdominal muscle
  abductor muscle
  adductor muscle
  biceps muscle
  extensor muscle
  flexor muscle
  gluteus muscle
  iliocostalis muscle

latissimus dorsi
levator muscle
muscle
pectoralis muscle
sphincter muscle
*nervous system—
  autonomic:*
  adrenergic nerve
    fibre
  autonomic nervous
    system
  cranial nerve
  facial nerve
  ganglion
  spinal nerve
  vagus nerve
*nervous system—
  central:*
  brain
  cerebral
    dominance
  cerebral fissure
  cerebrospinal fluid
  laterality
  meninges
  spinal cord
*nervous system—ear
  and hearing:*
  auricle
  bone conduction
  ear
  eustachean tube
  external auditory
    canal
  inner ear
  sound reception
  tympanic
    membrane
  vestibulocochlear
    nerve

*nervous system—eye
  and vision:*
  aqueous humour
  cone
  eye
  eyelid
  focusing
  iris
  lens
  macula lutea
  optic nerve
  retina
  rhodopsin
  rod
  tear duct and
    gland
*nervous system—
  other:*
  nervous system
  neuron
  neurotransmitter
  proprioception
  smell
  taste
*reproductive
  system—female:*
  fallopian tube
  menopause
  menstruation
  oogenesis
  ovary
  ovulation
  ovum
  uterine cervix
  uterus
  vagina
  vulva

*reproductive
  system—male:*
  bulbourethral
    gland
  ductus deferens
  ejaculation
  epididyme
  erection
  penis
  prostate gland
  scrotum
  semen
  seminal vesicle
  sperm
  spermatic cord
  spermatogenesis
  testis
*reproductive
  system—other:*
  orgasm
  placenta
  sexual intercourse
  umbilical cord
respiratory system:
  diaphragm
  larynx
  lung
  nose
  pulmonary
    alveolus
  respiration
  trachea
other:
  bursa
  human body
  mucus
  reticuloendothelial
    system

<u>Biographies</u>
See Section 10/34 of Part Ten

INDEX: See entries under all of the terms above

Section 422.   **Human Health**

A. Stages in the human life cycle

1. Fertilization: the beginning of life
[see also 311 and 331.E.]

2. Prenatal development
[see also 338.B.]

3. Birth

4. Postnatal development
[see also 338.B.]

5. Reproduction
[see also 337]

6. Aging

7. Dying and death

B. Definitions and ranges of normality in human health

C. Bodily mechanisms for the maintenance of human health during stress

1. The maintenance of the internal environment and the adaptation of cells to severe stress

2. Defenses against disease

a. Maintenance of integrity of skin and mucosal linings

b. Role of the phagocytic cells of the body
[see 421.A.3., B., and C.]

c. Inflammation: the response to biological insult

d. The immune response

3. Role of the blood in the prevention of hemorrhage

4. Healing: the processes of regeneration and organization in the repair of tissues

5. The alarm reaction: preparation through the effects of certain hormones for either flight or resistance
[see 421.E.1.b.]

D. Other regimes affecting standard values in human health

1. Nutrition and diet

a. Functions of food

b. Classes of food

c. Recommended intakes of nutrients to meet standards of physiological and metabolic requirements

d. Feeding behaviour

e. Therapeutic diets

2. Exercise and physical conditioning

a. Exercise needs: maintenance of health, avoidance of exercise injuries, and assessment of exercise adequacy

b. Physiological responses to exercise and the effects of physical conditioning

3. The state of sleep and its effects

a. The nature of sleep: criteria for and problems in defining sleep

b. Psychophysiological variations in sleep; *e.g.,* REM, NREM, light and deep sleep, dreaming

c. Effects of general and selective sleep deprivation

Suggested reading in the *Encyclopædia Britannica:*

MACROPAEDIA: Major articles dealing with human health

Death
Exercise and Physical Conditioning
Nutrition

MICROPAEDIA: Selected entries of reference information

General subjects

baths and spas:	*life cycle—birth:*	aging	interferon
bath	natural childbirth	death	interleukin
furo	parturition	middle age	phagocytosis
sauna	presentation	old age	*other:*
spa	*life cycle—prenatal:*	*protective*	health
Turkish bath	embryo	*mechanisms of the*	immunization
exercise:	fertilization	*body:*	nutrition
aerobics	fetus	antibody	preventive
exercise	implantation	coagulation	medicine
jogging	pregnancy	homeostasis	sleep
physical	*life cycle—other:*	immunity	vegetarianism
education	adolescence	inflammation	

Biographies
See Section 10/35 of Part Ten

INDEX: See entries under all of the terms above

Section 423.   Human Diseases

A. Characteristics, causes, and classifications of human disease

B. The detection and diagnosis of disease

C. The treatment of disease: therapeutics

   1. Aspects of medical treatment: factors for consideration in the formulation of a therapeutic regimen

   2. Major therapeutic techniques

      a. Surgical treatment
         [see 10/35.B.1.b.]

      b. Biological therapy

      c. Pharmacodynamic therapy

      d. Chemotherapy

      e. Substitution therapy

      f. Radiation therapy

      g. Physical therapy

      h. Occupational therapy

      i. Shock therapy

      j. Burn treatment

      k. Organ and tissue transplants

      l. Psychological therapy
         [see 436.D.]

D. The symptoms, diagnosis, and treatment of diseases of the body as a whole

   1. Physiological shock

2. Metabolic diseases and disorders

3. Nutritional diseases: disorders related to nutritional deficiencies and excesses

4. Diseases and disorders of fluid and electrolyte balance

5. Infectious or contagious diseases: the impairment of health by living invaders of the body

6. Diseases and disorders present at the time of birth

7. Childhood diseases

8. Disorders and injuries caused by physical agents: electrical shock; exposure to extremes of temperature, radiation, and pressure; motion sickness; wounds

9. Dehydration and associated disorders

10. Poisoning
    [see 10/35.B.2.g.]

11. Allergenic diseases and anaphylactic shock

E. The symptoms, diagnosis, and treatment of diseases affecting any organ or tissue of the body: tumours, hyperplasia, atrophy

F. Diseases of particular bodily systems

1. The cardiovascular system

   a. The heart and the great vessels

   b. The blood vessels

   c. Blood circulation

   d. The blood and blood-forming tissues

2. The lymphatic system

   a. Disorders of lymphatic vessels and their drainage

   b. Disorders of lymphoid tissue

3. The respiratory system

   a. Infectious diseases of the respiratory system

   b. Allergic lung diseases

   c. Bronchopulmonary diseases

   d. Diseases of the nonpulmonary structures

   e. Disorders in the dynamics of respiration

4. The digestive system

   a. The mouth, pharynx, and associated structures

   b. The esophagus

   c. The stomach and duodenum

   d. The small intestine and appendix

   e. The large intestine

   f. The digestive glands

   g. Disorders in the digestion and absorption of foods

5. The endocrine system

   a. The pituitary

   b. The thyroid

   c. The parathyroids

   d. The adrenals

   e. The gonads and placenta

   f. Female sex-oriented process under endocrine control: menstrual disorders, abnormal changes in pregnancy
   [see 10/35.B.1.c.]

g. The pancreas

h. Other endocrine glands: pineal gland, thymus

6. The reproductive system

a. Genetic and congenital abnormalities

b. Functional genital disorders

c. Infections

d. Structural changes of unknown causes: tumours and injuries

e. Diseases of the mammary glands

7. The excretory system
[see 10/35.B.1.d.]

a. Functional aspects: disorders of urine production and micturition

b. The kidneys and tubules

c. The urinary tract: ureters, bladder, and urethra

8. The supportive-protective system

a. The skeletal system and bone

b. Connective tissue: bone and periosteum, cartilage, tendon, and ligament

c. The joints

d. The bursae

e. The sinuses and the body cavities and their membranes

f. Muscle

g. The skin

9. The nervous system
[see 10/35.B.1.f.]

a. Neurological manifestations secondary to other diseases, neurochemical disorders, and development defects

b. Disorders of the peripheral nerves

c. Disorders of the spinal cord and autonomic nervous system

d. Disorders of the central nervous system

e. Other disorders of the general nervous system

f. Disorders of the eye and vision
[see 10/35.B.1.e.]

g. Disorders of the ear and hearing
[see 10/35.B.1.e.]

h. Disorders of other sensory receptors

i. Disorders of speech

j. Headache

Suggested reading in the *Encyclopædia Britannica:*

MACROPAEDIA: Major articles dealing with human diseases

Blood	Digestion and	Integumentary	Respiration and
Burns	Digestive Systems	Systems	Respiratory
Cancer	Disease	Metabolism	Systems
Childhood	Endocrine Systems	Muscles and	Sensory Reception
Diseases and	Excretion and	Muscle Systems	Supportive and
Disorders	Excretory	Nerves and	Connective
Circulation and	Systems	Nervous Systems	Tissues
Circulatory	Immunity	Nutrition	Transplants, Organ
Systems	Infectious Diseases	Poisons and	and Tissue
Diagnosis and		Poisoning	
Therapeutics			

MICROPAEDIA: Selected entries of reference information

General subjects

*diagnosis—laboratory
  tests:*
  basal metabolic
    rate
  blood analysis
  blood count
  Bromsulphalein
    test
  cardiac
    catheterization
  electrocardiography
  electroencephalography
  electromyography
  endoscopy
  enzyme analysis
  epinephrine
    tolerance test
  glucose tolerance
    test
  inulin clearance
  kidney function
    test
  liver function test
  Papanicolaou's
    stain
  protein-bound
    iodine test
  pulmonary
    function test
  Rubin's test
  serological test
  skin test
  thyroid function
    test
  tuberculin test
  urinalysis
*diagnosis—
  radiography and
  ultrasound:*
  angiocardiography
  angiography
  brain scanning
  cholecystography
  contrast medium
  diagnostic
    radiology
  echocardiography
  echoencephalography
  myelography
  phonocardiography
  pneumoencepha-
    lography
  radiology
  tomography
  urography
diagnosis—other:
  autopsy
  diagnosis
  gynecological
    examination

knee-jerk reflex
lumbar puncture
multiphasic health
  screening
sphygmomanometer
stethoscope
*disorders—allergic
  and immunological:*
  acquired immune
    deficiency
    syndrome
  allergy
  anaphylaxis
  angioedema
  asthma
  autoallergic disease
  autoantibody
  autoimmunity
  drug allergy
  hay fever
  hypersensitivity
  reagin
  serum sickness
*disorders—blood
  diseases:*
  agranulocytosis
  anemia
  aplastic anemia
  erythroblastosis
    fetalis
  folic-acid-deficiency
    anemia
  hemoglobinopathy
  hemophilia
  hereditary
    spherocytosis
  hypoprothrombinemia
  iron-deficiency
    anemia
  leukemia
  leukocytosis
  leukopenia
  methemoglobinemia
  pernicious anemia
  polycythemia
  purpura
  septicemia
  sickle-cell anemia
  thalassemia
  thrombocytopathy
  uremia
disorders—cancers:
  breast cancer
  cancer
  carcinogen
  carcinoma
  Ewing's tumour of
    bone
  Hodgkin's disease
  laryngeal cancer

leukemia
multiple myeloma
nephroblastoma
osteosarcoma
renal carcinoma
sarcoma
thyroid tumour
tumour
*disorders—
  cardiovascular:*
  air embolism
  aneurysm
  angioma
  aorta, coarctation
    of the
  aortic insufficiency
  aortic stenosis
  arteriosclerosis
  arteriovenous
    fistula
  arteritis
  atrial fibrillation
  coronary heart
    disease
  embolism
  endocarditis
  heart block
  heart failure
  heart
    malformation
  hypertension
  hypotension
  infarction
  milk leg
  mitral insufficiency
  mitral stenosis
  myocardial
    infarction
  patent ductus
    arteriosus
  pericarditis
  pulmonary heart
    disease
  pulmonary stenosis
  Raynaud's disease
  rheumatic fever
  shock
  stroke syndrome
  syncope
  thrombophlebitis
  varicose vein
  ventricular
    fibrillation
  ventricular septal
    defect
  Wegener's
    granulomatosis
*disorders—cavity and
  membrane:*
  mediastinitis

peritonitis
pleurisy
polyp
pyothorax
sinus squeeze
*disorders—congenital
  and hereditary
  metabolic diseases:*
  acatalasia
  alkaptonuria
  Andersen's disease
  cystathioninuria
  cystic fibrosis
  cystinosis
  cystinuria
  de Toni-Franconi
    syndrome
  Fabry's disease
  Forbes' disease
  galactosemia
  Gaucher's disease
  glucose-6-phosphate
    dehydrogenase
    deficiency
  glycogen storage
    disease
  gout
  Hartnup disease
  Hers' disease
  homocystinuria
  Hunter's syndrome
  Hurler's syndrome
  hyperammonemia
  iminoglycinuria
  lipid storage
    disease
  maple-syrup urine
    disease
  Maroteaux-Lamy
    syndrome
  McArdle's disease
  metachromatic
    leukodystrophy
  methemoglobinemia
  Niemann-Pick
    disease
  phenylketonuria
  Pompe's disease
  porphyria
  Sanfilippo's
    syndrome
  Scheie's syndrome
  Tay-Sachs disease
  tyrosinemia
  von Gierke's
    disease
  Wilson's disease

disorders—other
congenital and
hereditary:
  achondroplasia
  acrocephalosyndactyly
  agenesis
  albinism
  Albright's
    syndrome
  angioma
  atresia and stenosis
  cerebral palsy
  chromosomal
    disorder
  cleft palate
  cleidocranial
    dysostosis
  congenital disorder
  craniosynostosis
  cretinism
  cryptorchidism
  cutis laxa
  D1-trisomy
  digit malformation
  Down's syndrome
  Dupuytren's
    contracture
  dwarfism
  dysplasia
  E-trisomy
  erythroblastosis
    fetalis
  harelip
  heart
    malformation
  hemophilia
  hereditary
    spherocytosis
  hermaphroditism
  hypophosphatasia
  intussusception
  Klinefelter's
    syndrome
  mandibulofacial
    dysostosis
  Marfan's syndrome
  microcephaly
  Morquio's
    syndrome
  muscular
    dystrophy
  nervous system
    malformation
  neurofibromatosis
  osteochondroma
  osteogenesis
    imperfecta
  patent ductus
    arteriosus
  pectus excavatum
  peromelia
  pseudohermaphroditism
  respiratory distress
    syndrome

Siamese twin
sickle cell anemia
teratology
thalassemia
Turner's syndrome
urogenital
  malformation
vitiligo
von Willebrand's
  disease
disorders—connective
tissue:
  amyloidosis
  Dupuytren's
    contracture
  herniated disk
  lupus
    erythematosus
  tendinitis
disorders—ear and
hearing:
  deafness
  ear squeeze
  earwax impaction
  labyrinthitis
  Ménière's disease
  otitis media
  presbycusis
  stirrup fixation
disorders—endocrine:
  acromegaly
  Addison's disease
  adrenogenital
    syndrome
  Albright's
    syndrome
  chromophobe
    adenoma
  cretinism
  cryptorchidism
  Cushing's
    syndrome
  diabetes insipidus
  diabetes mellitus
  dwarfism
  endemic goitre
  Fröhlich's
    syndrome
  gigantism
  granulomatous
    thyroiditis
  Graves' disease
  Hashimoto's
    disease
  hyperaldosteronism
  hyperparathyroidism
  hypothyroidism
  myxedema
  parathyroid
    adenoma
  pheochromocytoma
  Plummer's disease
  Riedel thyroiditis
  Sheehan's
    syndrome

Stein–Leventhal
  syndrome
thyroid tumour
thyroiditis
disorders—excretory
system:
  Bright's disease
  cystitis
  enuresis
  hematuria
  kidney failure
  kidney stone
  nephroblastoma
  nephrosclerosis
  nephrotic
    syndrome
  pyelonephritis
  renal carcinoma
  renal cyst
  renal
    osteodystrophy
  uremia
  urethritis
  urinary tract
    obstruction
disorders—eye and
vision:
  amblyopia
  astigmatism
  blepharitis
  blindness
  cataract
  colour blindness
  conjunctivitis
  detached retina
  double vision
  exophthalmos
  glaucoma
  hyperopia
  iris
  keratitis
  lens dislocation
  myopia
  night blindness
  nystagmus
  optic atrophy
  optic neuritis
  presbyopia
  ptosis
  retinitis
    pigmentosa
  retrolental
    fibroplasia
  scleritis
  strabismus
  sty
  trachoma
  uveitis
  visual-field defect
disorders—
gastrointestinal:
  appendicitis
  cestodiasis
  cholera

coccidiosis
colic
colitis
constipation
diarrhea
dysentery
enteritis
fasciolopsiasis
gastritis
hookworm disease
ileus
indigestion
intestinal
  diverticulum
intestinal
  obstruction
intestinal squeeze
intussusception
myiasis
nausea
pancreatitis
peptic ulcer
salmonellosis
trichinosis
trichomoniasis
vomiting
disorders—hepatic
and biliary:
  cholecystitis
  cirrhosis
  clonorchiasis
  fatty liver
  gallstone
  hepatitis
  jaundice
disorders—infectious
diseases caused
by bacteria
and related
organisms:
  anthrax
  bartonellosis
  bejel
  boutonneuse fever
  brucellosis
  chancroid
  chlamydia
  cholera
  diphtheria
  dysentery
  glanders
  gonorrhea
  granuloma
    inguinale
  impetigo
  Legionnaires'
    disease
  leprosy
  leptospirosis
  listeriosis
  lymphogranuloma
    venereum
  mastitis
  melioidosis

osteomyelitis
paresis
plague
psittacosis
puerperal fever
pyelonephritis
Q fever
rat-bite fever
rheumatic fever
Rocky Mountain
  spotted fever
salmonellosis
scarlet fever
septicemia
streptobacillary
  fever
sty
syphilis
tetanus
toxic shock
  syndrome
trachoma
trench fever
tuberculosis
tularemia
typhoid
typhus
whooping cough
yaws
disorders—infectious
diseases caused by
fungi:
  actinomycosis
  aspergillosis
  blastomycosis
  candidiasis
  coccidioidomycosis
  cryptococcosis
  histoplasmosis
  Madura foot
  mycosis
  nocardiosis
  ringworm
  sporotrichosis
  thrush
disorders—infectious
diseases caused by
parasites:
  ascariasis
  cestodiasis
  Chagas' disease
  clonorchiasis
  coccidiosis
  dysentery
  echinococcosis
  fasciolopsiasis
  filariasis
  hookworm
  kala-azar
  malaria
  paragonimiasis
  schistosomiasis
  sleeping sickness
  toxoplasmosis

trichinosis
trichomoniasis
disorders—infectious
diseases caused by
various agents:
  conjunctivitis
  endocarditis
  infection
  meningitis
  otitis media
  pharyngitis
  pneumonia
  septic arthritis
  splenitis
  tonsillitis
  venereal disease
  zoonosis
disorders—infectious
diseases caused by
viruses:
  acquired immune
    deficiency
    syndrome
  adenovirus
    infection
  chicken pox
  Colorado tick fever
  common cold
  dengue
  encephalitis
  herpes simplex
  herpes zoster
  infectious
    mononucleosis
  influenza
  kuru
  measles
  mumps
  pappataci fever
  poliomyelitis
  pox disease
  rabies
  Rift Valley fever
  roseola infantum
  rubella
  smallpox
  wart
  yellow fever
disorders—lymphatic
system:
  Hodgkin's disease
  lymphedema
  lymphogranuloma
    venereum
  sporotrichosis
  tonsillitis
disorders—muscle:
  cramp
  dermatomyositis
  lumbago
  muscle tumour
  muscular
    dystrophy

myasthenia gravis
myositis
myotonia
tetanus
tetany
trichinosis
disorders—nervous
system:
  Alzheimer's disease
  amyotrophic
    lateral
    sclerosis
  analgesia
  aphasia
  apraxia
  ataxia
  cerebral palsy
  chorea
  coma
  convulsion
  encephalitis
  epilepsy
  focal seizure
  grand mal
  herpes zoster
  hydrocephalus
  hyperactivity
    syndrome
  kernicterus
  kuru
  listerosis
  meningitis
  microcephaly
  multiple sclerosis
  nervous system
    malformation
  neuralgia
  neuritis
  paralysis
  paresis
  Parkinson's disease
  petit mal
  Pick's disease
  poliomyelitis
  psychomotor
    seizure
  rabies
  sciatica
  senile brain disease
  sleeping sickness
  syringomyelia
  tic
  vertigo
disorders—nutritional
diseases:
  anorexia
  anorexia nervosa
  beriberi
  bulimia
  calcium deficiency
  celiac disease
  chlorine deficiency
  cobalt deficiency

copper deficiency
fluorine deficiency
iodine deficiency
kwashiorkor
magnesium
  deficiency
malnutrition
manganese
  deficiency
obesity
osteomalacia
pellagra
phosphorus
  deficiency
rickets
scurvy
tropical sprue
vitamin A
  deficiency
vitamin A excess
vitamin B2
  deficiency
vitamin B12
  deficiency
vitamin D excess
vitamin E
  deficiency
vitamin K
  deficiency
disorders—oral:
  caries
  gingivitis
  tooth squeeze
  thrush
disorders—poisoning:
  antimony
    poisoning
  arsenic poisoning
  botulism
  cadmium
    poisoning
  cyanide poisoning
  fish poisoning
  food poisoning
  lead poisoning
  medicinal
    poisoning
  mercury poisoning
  mushroom
    poisoning
  poison
  shellfish poisoning
  venom
disorders—pregnancy
related:
  abortion
  ectopic pregnancy
  hydatidiform mole
  miscarriage
  placenta accreta
  placenta praevia
  placentae abruptio

placental infarction
premature birth
disorders—pressure
injuries and other
disorders caused by
physical agents:
  acceleration stress
  acoustic trauma
  air embolism
  altitude sickness
  barotrauma
  bends
  blast injury
  burn
  crush injury
  deceleration injury
  decompression
   sickness
  ear squeeze
  ebullism
  electrical shock
  frostbite
  heatstroke
  hypothermia
  intestinal squeeze
  ionizing radiation
   injury
  mediastinal
   emphysema
  motion sickness
  nitrogen narcosis
  rotational stress
  sinus squeeze
  skin squeeze
  snakebite
  spatial
   disorientation
  subcutaneous
   emphysema
  taravana syndrome
  temperature stress
  thoracic squeeze
  tooth squeeze
  vibration injury
  wound
disorders—
 reproductive:
  amenorrhea
  cervical erosion
  cervicitis
  chlamydia
  cryptorchidism
  dysmenorrhea
  dyspareunia
  endometriosis
  galactorrhea
  gynecomastia
  hermaphroditism
  hydrocele
  impotence
  leukorrhea
  oligomenorrhea
  orchitis

premenstrual
 syndrome
priapism
prostatic disorder
pseudohermaphroditism
puerperal fever
Stein–Leventhal
 syndrome
uterine bleeding
vesiculitis
vulvitis
disorders—
 respiratory system:
  adenovirus
   infection
  alveolar proteinosis
  anthracosis
  asbestosis
  atelectasis
  berylliosis
  bronchiectasis
  bronchitis
  byssinosis
  common cold
  cough
  emphysema
  hyperventilation
  hypoxia
  influenza
  laryngeal cancer
  laryngitis
  Legionnaires'
   disease
  lung congestion
  lung infarction
  nasal polyp
  nasal tumour
  paragonimiasis
  pharyngitis
  pickwickian
   syndrome
  pneumoconiosis
  pneumonia
  psittacosis
  respiratory distress
   syndrome
  silicosis
  tracheitis
  tuberculosis
  whooping cough
disorders—skeletal:
  achondroplasia
  acromegaly
  ankylosing
   spondylitis
  bone lesion
  callus
  cleidocranial
   dysostosis
  craniosynostosis
  dislocation
  dysplasia
  dwarfism

Ewing's tumour of
 bone
flatfoot
fluorosis
fracture
gigantism
hamartoma
hypophosphatasia
listeriosis
mastoiditis
metatarsalgia
Morquio's
 syndrome
multiple myeloma
neurogenic
 anthropathy
osteoarthritis
osteochondroma
osteogenesis
 imperfecta
osteomyelitis
osteoporosis
osteosarcoma
Paget's disease of
 bone
parathyroid
 adenoma
Pott's disease
rheumatoid
 arthritis
septic arthritis
spondylolisthesis
disorders—skin:
  acne
  baldness
  bedsore
  boil
  cutis laxa
  erythema
  exfoliative
   dermatitis
  hemangioma
  herpes simplex
  herpes zoster
  hives
  hyperhidrosis
  ichthyosis
  impetigo
  insect bite and
   sting
  keratosis
  mole
  nevus
  pemphigus
  pinta
  pseudoxanthoma
   elasticum
  psoriasis
  ringworm
  scleroderma
  seborrheic
   dermatitis
  vitiligo
  wart

disorders—venereal
 diseases:
  chancroid
  chlamydia
  gonorrhea
  granuloma
   inguinale
  herpes simplex
  lymphogranuloma
   venereum
  syphilis
  venereal disease
disorders—other:
  asthenia
  atrophy
  childhood diseases
   and disorders
  cyst
  dehydration
  disease
  fever
  gangrene
  hamartoma
  headache
  hernia
  potassium
   deficiency
  progeria
  Reye's Syndrome
  sarcoidosis
  Sjögren's syndrome
  sodium deficiency
  splenitis
  splenomegaly
  sudden infant
   death syndrome
  tumour
infectious agents:
  bacteria
  prion
  virus
treatments—
 prosthetic devices:
  artificial organ
  contact lenses
  denture
  eyeglasses
  hearing aid
  pacemaker
  prosthesis
treatments—surgery:
  abortion
  amputation
  cesarean section
  coronary bypass
  cryosurgery
  heart transplant
  hysterectomy
  kidney transplant
  microsurgery
  skin graft
  surgery
  transplant
  vasectomy

treatments—	artificial	hydrotherapy	physical therapy
therapeutics:	respiration	hyperbaric	pseudolaryngeal
acupuncture	blood transfusion	chamber	speech
adjuvant	chemotherapy	massage	radiation therapy
antidepressant	desensitization	moxa treatment	respiratory therapy
drug	diathermy	occupational	therapeutics
	hydropathy	therapy	

Biographies

See Section 10/35 of Part Ten

INDEX: See entries under all of the terms above

Section 424.   The Practice of Medicine and the Care of Health

A. Medical education

B. Fields of specialized medical research; the related disciplines of osteopathy, dentistry, and nursing
[see 10/35.C.]

C. The practice of medicine

1. The kinds of medical practice in various countries

a. General practice and first-contact care: the general practitioner versus the specialist, clinic and health centre practice

b. Hospital and specialist practice: general surgery, pediatrics, anesthetics, pathology, teaching practice

c. Governmental practice: public health service, military practice, space medicine

d. Research

2. Maintenance of professional standards

a. The ethical basis of medical practice; *e.g.,* the Hippocratic oath, problems relating to euthanasia and abortion

b. Licensure requirements for practice: the wide variation among countries

c. Legal restrictions on practice

d. Professional organizations and the maintenance of standards

D. Public health services and administration

E. Hospital services and facilities

F. Environmental sanitation and health: the control of air, water, and soil pollution
[see 737.C.]

G. Efforts directed toward the prevention of malnutrition: the recognition and attempted solution of problems relating to nutrient requirements, world food supply, and world population

H. The prevention and control of infection

1. Vaccination and immunization

2. The quarantine and isolation of infected victims

3. Destruction of infectious agent or carrier; *e.g.,* aseptic and antiseptic precautions, control of disease carriers, disinfection

4. The use of therapeutic agents and prophylactic medication

5. The prevention and control of epidemics

I. Industrial and social medicine

1. The scope of industrial and occupational medicine

2. Health and safety laws: the regulation of working hours; restrictions on female and child labour; the elimination of health, safety, and fire hazards; the control of foods and drugs; pollution control
[see 552.D.]

J. The economics of health and disease

Suggested reading in the *Encyclopædia Britannica*:

MACROPAEDIA: Major articles dealing with the practice of medicine and the care of health

Birth Control
Medicine
Occupational Diseases and Disorders

MICROPAEDIA: Selected entries of reference information

General subjects

agencies and programs:	*health-care fields:*	pharmacy	quarantine
Food and Drug	aerospace medicine	plastic surgery	*other:*
Administration	chiropractic	psychiatry	blood bank
International Fund	dental auxiliary	surgery	birth control
for Agricultural	dentistry	*medical ethics:*	contraception
Development	epidemiology	abortion	flying doctor
Medicare	hematology	euthanasia	service
National Health	industrial medicine	Hippocratic oath	health maintenance
Service	midwifery	medical	organization
World Food	nursing	jurisprudence	hospice
Programme	optometry	*preventive medicine:*	Rospital
World Health	osteopathy	immunization	medical association
Organization	paramedical	preventive	public health
	personnel	medicine	social security

Biographies

See Section 10/35 of Part Ten

INDEX: See entries under all of the terms above

Division III. Human Behaviour and Experience
[For Part Four headnote see page 143.]

The outlines in the six sections of Division III set forth the discoveries and theories in the psychological sciences concerning human capacities, human behaviour, and human experience.

Section 431 is concerned with the questions of the definition and origins of human behaviour and experience. It also indicates the stages in the development of a person's behaviour and experience.

The outline in Section 432 deals with the capacities by which humans receive, organize, and interpret information about the current environment that influences behaviour. It treats the following subjects: attention; sensation; perception; the perception of time, of space, and of movement; perceptual illusions and hallucinations; and parapsychological phenomena.

Section 433 is concerned with current internal states that affect behaviour and conscious experience. It treats the determinants and manifestations of activation level; motivational states; emotional states; and transient states affecting behaviour and experience, such as sleep, dreams, hypnosis, fatigue, and intoxication.

Section 434 is concerned with persisting capacities that influence human behaviour and conscious experience. The outline treats the nature and assessment of human abilities and attitudes; sensorimotor abilities; intellectual abilities; and the distribution of intelligence.

Section 435 is concerned with the development of a person's potentials by learning and thinking. The outline treats diverse general theories of learning; deals separately with psychomotor, perceptual, and conceptual learning; and then treats memory and forgetting and the theories about and the types of the higher thought processes.

The outline in Section 436 sets forth those parts of psychology, psychopathology, and psychotherapy that consider the functioning, the integration, and the disintegration of the person as a whole. It treats diverse definitions and theories of personality and the self; theories of personality adjustment and maladjustment; and the diagnosis and kinds of psychiatric treatment of psychoses and psychoneuroses.

Section 431. Human Nature and Experience: General Considerations

A. The relative contribution of opposing factors in human behaviour and conscious experience, the degree to which these factors interact to produce human behaviour and conscious experience

1. Mankind as radically distinct from nature and mankind as homogeneous and continuous with the rest of nature

   a. Behavioral capacities and performances that humans have in common with other primates and higher mammals

   b. Behavioral capacities and performances held to be distinctive of humans; *e.g.*, propositional language, cumulative transmission of culture

   c. The explanation of allegedly distinctive human traits in accordance with the principle of phylogenetic continuity: the evolutionary development of mankind
   [see also 341 and 411]

2. The relative weights of genetic and environmental factors: the nature–nurture controversy

   a. Elements of genetic endowment; *e.g.*, physiological and psychological characteristics, reflexes and instincts

   b. Environmental conditions; *e.g.*, ecological factors, cultural conditioning, personal socialization experiences

3. Cognitive, conative, and affective dimensions of behaviour and experience

   a. The cognitive dimension: sensation and perception; memory and imagination; concept formation, ideation, and reasoning

   b. The conative dimension: desires, needs, cravings, drives; motivation and purpose; the voluntary and the involuntary

   c. The affective dimension: the emotions, the pleasant and the unpleasant; the sentiments

4. The observed elements of behaviour and the inferred dispositional tendencies: actions and powers; habits, inclinations, and capacities

5. Emergent problems in the study of human behaviour and experience: the data and hypotheses of parapsychology; the comparison of human and artificial, machine-created intelligence

B. Stages in the development of human behaviour

1. General aspects of human development

2. Prenatal growth and development

3. Birth: effects of the birth experience on the person's subsequent history

4. Infancy: the first 18 months

5. Early childhood and childhood: one to 12 years

6. Adolescence: puberty to adulthood

7. Young adulthood and maturity

8. Old age and death
[see also 338.E.]

Suggested reading in the *Encyclopædia Britannica*:

MACROPAEDIA: Major articles dealing with human nature and experience: general considerations

Behaviour, Innate Factors in Human
Behaviour, The Development of Human
Psychology

MICROPAEDIA: Selected entries of reference information

General subjects

adjustment	creativity	insight	psychological
adolescence	emotion	instinct	development
attitude	etiquette	intelligence	reflex
behaviour genetics	habit	memory	sibling rivalry
child development	human behaviour	middle age	thanatology
culture	imitation	old age	thought

Biographies

See Sections 10/35 and 10/36 of Part Ten

INDEX: See entries under all of the terms above

Section 432.   Influence of the Current Environment on a Person's Behaviour and Conscious Experience: Attention, Sensation, and Perception

A. Attention to the environment: awareness of internal and external events
[see 341]

1. The problem of defining attention

2. The development of theories of attention: the influence of stimulus–response and behaviourist studies

3. Classification of attentive phenomena: the influence of adaptive processes on modes and degrees of attention

4. Determinants of attention: temperament, health, social suggestion, novelty, interests, and unconscious influences

5. Physiological mechanisms of attention

6. Analysis of attentive phenomena in terms of information theory

B. Sensation: the reception of information about the environment

1. The senses in general
[see 421.J. and 423.F.9.]

2. Vision

   a. The work of the retina

   b. The transduction process: the conversion of the retinal image into a set of messages in the brain

   c. Perceptual processes of vision

   d. Responses of the cerebral cortex to visual stimuli

3. Audition

   a. The mechanisms of the external, middle, and inner ear: functions and processes involved in the transmission of sound and its conversion into neural messages

   b. The work of the auditory nerve and the auditory pathways of the central nervous system: encoding, processing, and discrimination of pitch, loudness, localization, and duration of sound

   c. The measurement of auditory phenomena: diagnosis and correction of hearing disorders

   d. The function of the semicircular canals in maintaining equilibrium: the vestibular systems
   [see B.6., below]

4. Cutaneous senses: the punctate nature and discriminatory capacity of skin to respond to pressure, pain, heat, and cold

   a. The variety of nerve terminals exhibiting a broad range of sensitivity to different stimuli

   b. Localization of skin sensations: the nature of dermatomes

   c. The concept of adequate stimulation and paradoxical cold: adaptation to pressure and thermal situations; itch, tickle, and vibration

    d. The sensory experience of pain: its cause and function; external signs and qualities, theories of pain, modes of treatment

  5. Kinesthesis: the function and types of sensory structures and the role of kinesthetic feedback in movement control and orientation

  6. Vestibular senses: the role of the vestibular receptors and the semicircular canals of the inner ear in maintaining equilibrium

  7. The taste sense: the form and location of taste buds, the neural pathways, types of taste receptors, factors affecting taste

  8. The olfactory sense: the form, location, and nerve supply of olfactory receptors; olfactory qualities; odour-inducing factors; factors affecting odour sensitivity; effects on behaviour

C. Perception: the process of translating sensory stimulation into organized experience

  1. Contemporary theories and new concerns: the influence of Gestalt and behaviourist theories

  2. Central problems of continuing concern

  3. Principles of perceptual organization

    a. The Gestalt principle of *Prägnanz,* or good form, and the laws of grouping under it: closure, good continuation, similarity, proximity, and common fate; the significance of the phi phenomenon

    b. Context effects: the influence of surrounding stimuli and of previously experienced stimuli on the observer

    c. Perceptual constancy: the tendency of objects to appear stable in size, shape, brightness, or colour despite changing conditions of stimulation

  4. Differences in perceptual functioning among individuals, among classes of individuals, and within individuals

D. The perception of time

  1. Sequential activities related to time perception

  2. Perception of sequence and duration

  3. Factors affecting time perception; *e.g.,* type of activity, level of motivation, personality traits, drugs, sensory deprivation, hypnosis

E. The perception of space

  1. The nature of space perception: orientation to the environment

  2. Perception of depth and distance: gross tactual-kinesthetic, eye muscle, visual, and auditory cues

  3. Interrelations among the senses

  4. Social and interpersonal aspects of space perception: territorial behaviour, reason in perception, and nativistic and empiricistic considerations

F. The perception of movement

  1. Visual cues for perceiving self-motion and motion of objects

  2. Nonvisual cues: auditory, kinesthetic, and vestibular cues

G. Perceptual illusions and hallucinations

  1. Types of illusory experience

  2. Hallucinations

    a. Neurological factors in hallucinations

    b. Types of hallucinatory experience

H. Theories of parapsychological phenomena

  1. Extrasensory perception: telepathy, clairvoyance, precognition, and prophecy

  2. Parapsychological phenomena of a nonperceptual nature: psychokinesis

  3. Theories of perceptual and of nonperceptual parapsychological phenomena: physical theories, field theories, and theories of the collective unconscious; projection hypothesis

Suggested reading in the *Encyclopædia Britannica*:

MACROPAEDIA: Major articles dealing with the influence of the current environment on a person's behaviour and conscious experience: attention, sensation, and perception

> Attention
> Perception, Human
> Psychology

MICROPAEDIA: Selected entries of reference information

General subjects

parapsychological	consciousness	synesthesia	sensation
phenomena:	delirium	time perception	sense
extrasensory	eidetic image	*sensation:*	smell
perception	hallucination	chemoreception	sound reception
parapsychological	illusion	flavour	thermoreception
phenomenon	movement	mechanoreception	*other:*
precognition	perception	pain	attention
telepathy	pain	photoreception	circadian rhythm
perception:	perception	proprioception	stress
autokinetic effect	space perception	receptor	human behaviour

Biographies

> See Sections 10/35 and 10/36 of Part Ten

INDEX: See entries under all of the terms above

Section 433.   **Current Internal States Affecting a Person's Behaviour and Conscious Experience**

A. Motivational states: needs and desires that channel a person's behaviour and experience

1. Diverse theories of motivation: psychoanalytic, drive, arousal, incentive, and hedonic theories

2. Specific human needs and motives, *with special attention to* achievement, anxiety, aggression, and sexual behaviour and deviations

3. Situational and interactional factors: stresses in stimulus field, cognitive evaluation, balance and congruity, and cognitive dissonance

4. Recent developments and practical applications of motivation theory: emphasis on reinforcement and instinct, the use of token systems

B. Emotional states: bodily conditions and feelings accompanying motivation and arousal conditions

1. The nature of emotion

2. Diverse conceptions of emotion: the roles of the nervous system

3. Expression of emotions: the startle response; facial, vocal, and postural manifestations

C. Transient states affecting behaviour and experience

1. Sleep

2. Dreams

3. Hypnosis and related states of altered consciousness

4. Fatigue

5. Transient states caused by altered body chemistry

Suggested reading in the *Encyclopædia Britannica*:

MACROPAEDIA: Major articles dealing with the current internal states affecting a person's behaviour and conscious experience

> Emotion and Motivation, Human
> Psychology
> Sex and Sexuality
> Sleep and Dreams

MICROPAEDIA: Selected entries of reference information

General subjects

emotional states:
  anxiety
  emotion
  empathy
  feeling
  frustration
  temperament
motivational states:
  agonism
  conflict
  drive
  libido
  motivation
  scatologia
  sexual motivation
  sex

sexual behaviours
  and problems:
  dyspareunia
  exhibitionism
  frigidity
  homosexuality
  impotence
  masochism
  masturbation
  pedophilia
  rape
  sadism
  sexual dysfunction
  sodomy
  transsexualism
  transvestism

voyeurism
zoophilia
transient states—
  chemically induced:
  alcoholism
  antidepressant
  drug
  chemical
    dependency
  drug abuse
  hallucinogen
  narcotic
  sedative-hypnotic
    drug
  stimulant
  tranquillizer

transient states—
  sleep and sleep
  disorders:
  dream
  insomnia
  narcolepsy
  sleep
transient states—
  other:
  autohypnosis
  combat fatigue
  fatigue
  hypnosis
other:
  consciousness
  introspection
  unconscious

Biographies

See Sections 10/35 and 10/36 of Part Ten

INDEX: See entries under all of the terms above

Section 434. Persisting Capacities and Inclinations That Influence Human Behaviour and Conscious Experience

A. The nature of human capacities
[see 435.A.]

B. The assessment of human abilities: psychological measurement

  1. Types of testing instruments and methods

  2. Development of standardized tests

  3. Assessment of test results

C. Sensorimotor abilities: bodily skills and mechanical abilities

D. Intellectual abilities: theories of intelligence

E. The distribution of intelligence

  1. Problems concerning the establishment of intelligence standards and intelligence distribution

  2. Retardation

  3. The gifted

  4. Group differences in intelligence: the measurement and interpretation of differences in age, socioeconomic class, race, sex, and other factors

F. Personal propensities and idiosyncrasies affecting behaviour and experience

G. Attitudes

  1. The nature of attitudes

  2. The functions of attitudes

  3. The development of attitudes

  4. The measurement of attitudes: the use and validity of questionnaires, interviews, sampling techniques, opinionnaires, and content analysis

H. Persuasion and change of attitude

Suggested reading in the *Encyclopædia Britannica:*

MACROPAEDIA: Major articles dealing with the persisting capacities and inclinations that influence human behaviour and conscious experience

Intelligence, Theories and Distribution of
Psychological Tests and Measurement
Psychology

MICROPAEDIA: Selected entries of reference information

General subjects

aptitude test	genius	intelligence test	psychological
creativity	gifted child	mental age	testing
differential	human behaviour	mental retardation	sensorimotor skill
psychology	intelligence	prodigy	

Biographies

See Sections 10/35 and 10/36 of Part Ten

INDEX: See entries under all of the terms above

Section 435.   **Development of a Person's Potentials: Learning and Thinking**

A. Diverse theories of human learning

　1. Modern learning theories

　2. Major issues in learning theories

　3. Transfer of training

B. Psychomotor learning

C. Perceptual learning

D. Conceptual learning and concept formation

E. Memory: retention and forgetting of learned habits and content

F. Abnormalities of memory: amnesia, paramnesia and confabulation, hypermnesia—enhancement of memory

G. The higher thought processes

　1. The psychology of higher thought processes

　2. The role of language in the higher thought processes

　3. Meaning

　4. Types of thinking: realistic and autistic

Suggested reading in the *Encyclopædia Britannica:*

MACROPAEDIA: Major articles dealing with the development of a person's potentials: learning and thinking

Learning and Cognition, Human
Memory
Psychology
Thought and Thought Processes

MICROPAEDIA: Selected entries of reference information

General subjects

amnesia	conditioning	memory	recognition
association	discrimination	mnemonic	social learning
attitude	generalization	perceptual learning	suggestion
brainwashing	imitation	persuasion	thought
cognition	insight	psychomotor	training, transfer of
concept formation	learning	learning	

Biographies

See Sections 10/35 and 10/36 of Part Ten

INDEX: See entries under all of the terms above

Section 436. Personality and the Self: Integration and Disintegration of the Person as a Whole

A. Definitions of personality

1. Physiological theories of personality: theories based on body humours, somatotypes, physiognomy, and phrenology

2. Psychoanalytic theories of personality: the importance of id, ego, superego, life and death instincts, and the collective unconscious

3. Social analytic theories of personality: the importance of drive to power, need achievement, and functional autonomy

4. Eclectic theories of personality: role theories, factor analysis of personality traits

B. Measurement of personality

1. Methods of assessment

2. Evaluating assessment techniques

C. Personality functioning and adjustment

1. The subjective aspect of personality: development of awareness of self

2. Strains and challenges put on adequate personality functioning: physical, psychological, and social stresses; *e.g.,* frustration, conflict, personal inadequacy, deprivation of accustomed gratification

3. Responses to environmental strains on personality functioning: reactions, defense mechanisms, and adjustment dynamisms for coping with environmental demands

D. Persisting disturbances of personality integration: psychiatric disturbance

1. The psychoses: schizophrenia, affective psychoses, involutional psychoses, paranoia, senile psychoses, arteriosclerotic psychoses, general paresis, alcoholic psychoses, psychosis associated with Huntington's chorea, psychosis associated with epilepsy

2. The psychoneuroses: anxiety reactions; dissociative reactions—amnesia, somnambulism, depersonalization, fugue states; phobic reactions; obsessive-compulsive reactions; depressive reactions; character reactions; fatigue reactions—neurasthenia; hypochondriacal reactions; conversion reactions—hysteria; traumatic, soterial, and military reactions; transient reactions and special syndromes; sexual deviations

3. Prevalence of psychiatric disturbance: epidemiology

4. Psychiatric treatment

5. Prevention of psychiatric disturbance: mental hygiene

Suggested reading in the *Encyclopædia Britannica:*

MACROPAEDIA: Major articles and a biography dealing with personality and the self: integration and disintegration of the person as a whole

Freud
Mental Disorders and
  Their Treatment
Personality
Psychology

MICROPAEDIA: Selected entries of reference information

General subjects

personality—tests:	self	obsessive–	nondirective
association test	superego	compulsive	psychotherapy
projective test	*psychiatric*	disorder	psychoanalysis
Rorschach Test	*disturbances:*	paranoia	psychodrama
personality—theories:	affective disorder	personality disorder	psychopharma-
anal stage	anxiety	phobia	cology
analytic psychology	autism	psychoneurosis	psychosurgery
defense mechanism	delusion	psychosomatic	psychotherapy
ego	depression	disorder	sensitivity training
extrovert	fetishism	psychosis	shock therapy
humour	hypochondriasis	schizophrenia	*other:*
id	hysteria	*therapies:*	Bedlam
inferiority complex	lycanthropy	aversion therapy	counselling
introvert	manic-depressive	behaviour therapy	human behaviour
Oedipus complex	psychosis	biofeedback	mental hygiene
oral stage	mental disorder	child psychiatry	sibling rivalry
personality	multiple	group therapy	stress
physiognomy	personality		

Biographies

See Sections 10/35 and 10/36 of Part Ten

INDEX: See entries under all of the terms above

Introduction to Part Five:
Man the Social Animal

by Harold D. Lasswell

We are part of society when we share in comprehensive arrangements for living with one another and for managing the environment. The simplest societies are the primitive bands who to this day live in jungles and deserts, and on isolated mountains and beaches around the globe. The most complex technological societies bind the world's cities together as part of an evolution that, barring catastrophe, is forming a planetary society of mankind.

Whether primitive or civilized, all societies must cope with the parallel problems that are generated by the urgencies of human nature and the necessities of a common life. Arrangements are made for kinship and procreation; for safety, health, and comfort; for producing and consuming commodities and services. Arrangements also develop latent talent into skills of communication, body movement, and environmental management. Institutions specialize in the gathering and dissemination of news and images of the natural and social environment. Some institutions give respect or disrespect to individuals and groups on a temporary or permanent basis, and distinguish between what is considered to be responsible or irresponsible conduct. Government, law, and politics seek to resolve the conflicting demands that arise within or among communities.

At first glance we are less likely to be impressed by the parallels than by the differences among societies. The differences are conspicuous, if we consider, say, a horde of big-city commuters as compared with a band of technologically handicapped people who are continually in search of the next meal. An anthropologist who lived with such a band a few years ago in the rain forests of eastern Bolivia reported that apart from the hammocks they slept in, three-foot digging sticks, and cumbersome long bows and arrows, these naked seminomads carried no material objects with them. Modern urban dwellers usually feel some contempt for these bearers of an Old Stone Age culture and speculate on a possible weakness of the brain to account for their lack of technological progress. Such speculations are dismissed by modern anthropologists as without foundation. As we get acquainted with primitive societies it dawns upon us that they have met some of the same problems that we have by adopting solutions whose ingenuity equals or even excels our own. This may apply, for instance, to arrangements for transmitting political authority from one generation to the next, or for preventing violently aggressive behaviour.

Societies do indeed differ from one another in the degree that they encourage specialization. In the simplest societies everybody does everything, with exceptions that are closely linked to differences of sex and age. On the other hand, many tribes use professional specialists, such as warriors, medicine men, blacksmiths, potters, weavers, musicians, and carvers. The world that we call civilized appeared with the invention of writing. Literacy provides a means of storing and retrieving information without relying exclusively on the memory of the old. Records and education multiply the number of learned professions. Urban civilization marks the emergence of such institutions as the territorial state, formal legislative codes of law, regular taxes, bureaucratized civil and military services, monumental public works, complex systems of taxation, and official records.

One way to bring out the degrees of likeness and difference among societies, whether primitive or civilized, is to compare the priorities that are given to institutions of the same kind. No one doubts that every society must concern itself to some extent with food. It is only in bands of the kind mentioned above that near-total preoccupation with hunger deemphasizes, although without abolishing, all other interests. Where existence is less hard the accumulation of wealth may become the principal value sought, as among some merchant cities and trading tribes. War and preparation for war may take top priority as it did for millennia among the shepherds of Inner Asia and the river-valley agriculturalists who were conquered by herdsmen-warriors. Some agricultural societies emphasize worship and encourage forms of knowledge, like astronomy, that enhance religion. In some societies, notably in East India, the accent is on ritual purity or impurity, and every kin group is assigned a position in the respect system of caste and class.

While priorities may remain stable for generations in a given society, this is not necessarily the case. At one time the peoples of Scandinavia were warriors and brigands. Today we perceive them as among those who are most involved with the values of civil society. In the United States, the early colonizers of New England were heavily oriented toward religion, morality, and political freedom. More recently, the most general trend has been toward secular activities, especially those connected with wealth. Throughout the contemporary world, "development" often carries the connotations of economic modernization, political independence, scientific education and research, personal freedom, and social justice.

Besides allocating priorities, every society strikes a temporary or durable balance between the accumulation and the immediate enjoyment of every value. The modes of accumulation depend on the value in question. Investment in wealth production, for instance, may involve adding fertilizers to the soil, or building an infrastructure of roads and bridges, or inculcating the values of saving and investment. Expanded educational opportunity implies that more per capita hours of teaching and learning, and more physical equipment, are made available, and that the importance of education is successfully communicated. If health opportunities are to be multiplied, it is necessary to add facilities and to spread the practice of personal hygiene. A society cultivates public enlightenment with installations for scientific and scholarly purposes, and for mass communication. Human relations improve as the roles of love, friendship, and loyalty expand in "an era of good feeling," and as social discrimination wanes. Levels of responsible conduct typically rise as opportunities become more available for worship and more people join in formulating and applying moral standards. During a given period the institutions of government, law, and politics sometimes accumulate more support.

The examples mentioned above refer to the "positive" accumulation of a valued outcome. Accumulations may be "negative," as when disasters destroy property, spread epidemics, or interfere with education.

All societies necessarily make arrangements for the sharing of wealth, power, and other values. Among individuals and groups these arrangements exhibit all degrees of equality and inequality. Wealth and income are sometimes widely distributed. By contrast, they may be monopolized in the hands of a few. Political participation may be dispersed or concentrated. Opportunities may be equalized or monopolized for health, education, and information; or for respect, affection, and responsible conduct.

Characteristic of every society is the attempt to maintain itself by controlling the minds of young and old. People not only hunt or plow, trade or fight. They are also likely to believe in what they do and how they do it. It is not necessarily true that in a system of inequality those who occupy any particular station, however exalted or lowly, entertain any doubts about the justification of the system. A stable society carries on within the framework of a common map of perception, belief, and identity. In such a setting the individual learns from earliest infancy to think, feel, and act in ways that bring positive rather than negative consequences from the social and natural environment. Socialization is the process by which private motivations are channeled into acceptable public acts.

In civilized societies reliance on the results of early education is heavily supplemented by government, law, and politics. The legal system is made up of several sets of authoritative and controlling prescriptions. One set is constitutive. It prescribes "who decides what and how." It centralizes or decentralizes formal and effective power, and it separates power among agencies and groups. Structures may be differentiated to plan, to promote, to legislate, to execute, or to review and appraise. Regulation defines the degree of protection given to the fundamental institutions of every sector of society. Tradition alleges that a legal order is blind to values and practices that lie outside the established beliefs, faiths, and loyalties ("ideologies") of the society with which it is involved. In consequence, legal systems may defend widely different balances between value accumulation and enjoyment, and sharply contrasting patterns of equality and inequality in the sharing of political power, wealth, respect, or any other value. The legal order may protect economic systems whose structures are capitalistic, socialistic, or cooperative; family systems that permit one or more members of the sexes to marry and raise children; religious faiths that exalt monotheism and polytheism; and so on through the infinite variety of human practices.

One set of prescriptive norms is supervisory. Individuals and groups may be given wide latitude to make private

contractual agreements or to seek redress of private wrongs. Nonetheless, the decision makers of the community are prepared to play a supervisory role by enforcing common norms if an unsettled private controversy is brought to their notice by the parties. Prescriptions also lay down the principles and procedures to be followed if the body politic organizes and administers a continuing enterprise, of which services of transportation, communication, banking, insurance, and housing are examples. A legal system includes correctional or sanctioning measures to obtain compliance with prescribed norms. Value deprivations are imposed on those who have failed or are expected to fail to comply. Deprivations range in severity from capital punishment, confiscation of property, or life imprisonment, to a light fine or reprimand.

A legal system is stabilized when the effective elements in society perceive themselves as relatively better off by continuing the system than by adopting alternative arrangements. To some extent a legal order may exhibit cyclical fluctuations, as when deviations are tolerated within limits which, if exceeded, generate reform activities that restore the former situation with little change. In a capitalist economy "creeping monopoly" may invade trade unions, employers' associations, or natural resource and industrial enterprises. In a socialist economy "black markets" may introduce "creeping competition." In either case, cyclical movements may restore the original relationship before they have quietly stabilized a structural innovation, or prepared the way for violent revolutionary change.

If the view is correct that worldwide interdependence is increasing, the traditional blindfold of legal systems must be put aside long enough to give explicit consideration to competing value goals and practices around the globe. Interdependence implies that whether they like it or not, the members of an emerging planetary society must take one another into account. Being taken into account implies that beliefs, faiths, and loyalties, as well as overt behaviours, are examined by public and private decision makers. The demand to be better informed about the social environment creates an enormous opportunity and responsibility for those who study society.

We expect anthropologists to provide us with knowledge of primitive societies and other specialists to focus on the processes and institutions of civilized society. Political scientists and legal scholars concentrate on government, law, and politics. Economists specialize in the production and distribution of wealth. The role of educators is relatively clear. So, too, is the role of sociologists who concern themselves with a sector of society, such as the family, social class and caste, professions and occupations, communication, public health, or comparative morals and religion.

Social scientists are continually under pressure to provide a map of the past and probable future impact of the forces that shape society. They are asked, for instance, to explain the causes of war and other forms of violence, and to suggest strategies that lead to "victory" in a specific conflict or to show how war itself may be eliminated as an instrument of public policy. Social scientists are asked for explanations of why an economy experiences inflation, or how it generates changing levels of employment and unemployment. Specialists are expected to discover the sources of alienation that separate young and old or threaten the unity of a family, a school, a church, a political party, or a national state. These examples suggest the wide-ranging demands that confirm the importance of adding to our knowledge of society.

We recognize the existence of a problem when we perceive that our goals are inconsistent with one another or when there are discrepancies between what we want and what we have or expect. In public policymaking, the first step is to answer the question, "Whose values are to be realized?" The social scientist who participates in tackling or solving a policy problem has an option: he may adopt the criteria of a "client" or he may rely on his own values.

The study of social institutions is sometimes affected by diverging norms of professional responsibility. No conflict need arise if a social scientist is personally committed to a line of research that happens to be popular with influential members of the body politic. No anxiety or guilt is felt if the findings are applied by current decision makers. A frequent example is the study of administrative agencies according to their "dollar efficiency" or according to the accuracy and speed of communication between central offices and field stations.

In contrast to this harmonious relationship is the inner and perhaps visible turmoil of social scientists whose research interests are unacceptable to many members of the current establishment. The researchers may want to study the effect of military expenditures on society. The problem may be to find how a given level of military outlay modifies the structure of the civilian economy and influences both the production and delivery of services specialized for health, education, public information, family welfare, and other social outcomes. If the information gathered in the course of a given project is classified as secret, no scientist can lawfully report his findings. Perhaps the investigator will violate the letter of the law in the hope of mobilizing an effective demand for change. But it may be that such a strategy will backfire. Instead of arousing community protest against authority, the revelations may result in established leaders successfully taking advantage of an alleged "breach of security" to suppress inquiry and discussion.

Another complication affecting the social investigator is the degree of genuine consent that he must obtain from those whom he proposes to study. Physicians, surgeons, and biologists confront similar questions when they plan to give a test, run an experiment, administer a drug, or perform an operation. Is it always necessary to explain to a prospective subject the risks he will run? Is the investigator professionally or legally bound to make sure that the language of explanation can be understood by the individual concerned? If a social scientist plans to study the facts of life in a prison or a mental hospital, should he reveal his purpose, even when it would be easier to gain confidence by posing as a fellow prisoner or a fellow patient? Similar issues rise in connection with field studies of primitive tribes, of peasant communities, of foreign societies, and of many other social settings.

In recent times, professional opinion has emphasized the importance of obtaining "shared participation" in the pursuit of knowledge. Many investigators willingly accept the challenge of cultivating group demand for a project and for a hand in data gathering and analysis. At every stage, arrangements are made for laymen to work side by side with professional sociologists, social psychologists, political scientists, and other investigators. As a result, some communities have learned to study themselves, assessing the degree to which they are involved in ethnic and other forms of discrimination. Unusual groups have joined in self-study. For instance, murderers and persons who have survived as targets of murderous assault have cooperated in scientific research on the causes and consequences of murder, and on possible strategies of prevention. Instead of resenting the role of "guinea pig" in science, it is typical for those who choose to participate in programs of self-observation to improve their individual insight while contributing to the enhancement of society's stock of knowledge.

Whether the client or the investigator is the source of the value criteria adopted for a policy problem, questions of value priority are bound to arise. The relative importance of political, economic, and other aims cannot be satisfactorily settled in programs of national or regional development unless the full range of possible goals is considered. It is essential to take timing into account. When a new nation-state first secedes from an empire, political power has top priority. The "ex-colony" tries to ensure its independence of external control, to obtain support from outside powers, and to unify its people. Economic development occupies a high priority position. Other targets, such as health, education, the expressive arts, and environmental protection, seem to be less urgent. The allocation of manpower and facilities to various institutions depends on the priority of the specific outcomes in which these institutions specialize.

Social scientists have an indirect influence on priorities by asking questions about them, and also by presenting a factual map of past trends, causes, and future contingencies. Scientists often devise small-scale pretests in order to try out solutions that may eventually be applied on a larger scale.

In adapting to the needs of this interdependent world, the scientists of society require of themselves that they measure the direction and intensity of the value demands of political, economic, ethnic, and all other identifiable groups anywhere on the globe. Acknowledging the perils of a divided and militant world, the most compelling task is to discern and make public the conditions under which a world public order of government and law could become a more perfect instrument of human dignity, security, and welfare. Many small-scale programs show how to reduce the human cost of transforming today's inadequate institutions into more effective systems of communication and organization.

For the first time in history it can be truly asserted that the scientists of society have been provided with technological instruments of sufficient sophistication to assist in meeting the demands that are made upon them. Retrieval and dissemination make it possible to map past, present, and future events. Social analysts know that the key question for the future is to resolve whether or not the spectacularly changing technology of knowledge, and especially knowledge of society, will be in the hands of a limited class or caste that seeks to serve its own advantage. The alternative is to share the control of information widely among all territorial and pluralistic groups. Unless individuals and groups are able to obtain access to comprehensive stocks of information, they will be blind judges of public policy. Without adequate access, their criticism will be dismissed as exercises in ignorance and bias. Critics will be in no position to develop realistic alternatives to the plans of governmental or private monopolists of knowledge. "Knowledge is power"; if there is to be self-control, there must be prompt and total access to information.

The chief novelty about the computer and other technically advanced means of processing and transmitting information is that, in principle, everyone can be given prompt access to a selective "map of the whole." An image of the total deployment of man in space or of the total activities of a corporate enterprise can be made available to everyone from the highest official to the humblest worker. The salient facts can be made vivid, concise, and substantially accurate in images that may be supplemented in whatever detail is desired. The range of possible expenditures for any political, economic, or social program can be summarized and related to its potential impact on society.

Human society has attained an unparalleled height of danger and opportunity. The study of society shares in both. The unprecedented accumulation of knowledge enables us to recognize that the scale of our problems is also without precedent.

Part Five. Human Society

All studies of mankind take account of the effect of the social nature of humans. This is true of the treatment in Part Four of human evolution, health, and general nature and behaviour. It is also true of the treatments, in subsequent parts, of art, technology, religion, history, and the sciences and philosophy.

A special set of interrelated sciences, however, takes society and social behaviour as its direct subject of inquiry. The outlines in the six divisions and the twenty-five sections of Part Five are concerned with the complementary work of these social sciences.

The social sciences have themselves been the object of historical and analytical study. These studies are presented in the articles referred to in Section 10/36 of Part Ten. The outline in that section covers the history of the social sciences generally, and the nature, scope, methods, and interrelations of anthropology, sociology, economics, and political science.

The social sciences have become increasingly interdependent and interpenetrating, and no regulative agreement exists about how their distinction should be understood. Nevertheless, the diverse domains are, in practice, distinguishable. The breakdown of Part Five into six divisions reflects the currently operative distinction between cultural and social anthropology, the several branches of sociology, economics, political science, jurisprudence and law, and educational philosophy and science.

Division I. Social Groups: Peoples and Cultures

The outlines in the four sections of Division I set forth anthropological accounts of the development and the variety of sociocultural forms.

Section 511. Peoples and Cultures of the World

A. In the Arctic

  1. In the eastern Arctic

  2. In the western Arctic

B. In North America

  1. In the sub-Arctic

  2. On the Northwest Coast

  3. In California

  4. On the Plateau

  5. In the Great Basin

  6. In the Southwest

  7. On the Plains

  8. In the eastern woodlands

  9. In the Southeast

C. In Middle America

    1. In northern Mexico

    2. In Meso-America

    3. In Central America and the northern Andes

    4. In the Caribbean

D. In South America

    1. In the central and southern Andes

    2. In the tropical forest

    3. Among the South American nomads

E. In Europe

    1. On the Atlantic fringe

    2. On the plain

    3. Along the Mediterranean

    4. On the Alpine climax

F. In the Middle East and North Africa

    1. In the Maghrib: northwestern Africa

    2. In the Mashriq: northeastern Africa and southwest Asia

    3. In Iran

    4. In Turkey

G. In Asia

    1. In Siberia

    2. In Central Asia

    3. In East Asia

    4. In South Asia

    5. In Southeast Asia

H. In sub-Saharan Africa

    1. In the western Sudan

    2. In the eastern Sudan

    3. On the Guinea coast

    4. In the Congo

    5. In central and lower East Africa

    6. In the East African Horn

    7. Among the Khoisan peoples: Hottentots and Bushmen

I. In Oceania

    1. In Australia

    2. In Melanesia

    3. In Polynesia

    4. In Micronesia

Suggested reading in the *Encyclopædia Britannica*:

MACROPAEDIA: Major articles dealing with the peoples and cultures of the world

Africa
American Indians
Arctic, The
Asia
Australia
Central Africa
Culture, The Concept and Components of
East Indies, The
Eastern Africa
Europe

Iran
Mediterranean Sea
North Africa
Pacific Islands
Sudan
Turkey and Ancient Anatolia
Union of Soviet Socialist Republics
West Indies
Western Africa

MICROPAEDIA: Selected entries of reference information

General subjects

Africa—Congo:
　Ambo
　Azande
　Bemba
　Bulu
　Chokwe
　Duala
　Fang
　Ila
　Kaonde
　Kongo
　Kuba
　Lozi
　Luba
　Lunda
　Mangbetu
　Maravi
　Mbundu
　Mbuti
　Mongo
　Ovimbundu
　Pygmy
　Tabwa
　Yaka
　Yao
　Yaunde
*Africa—Ethiopian
　and Somalian:*
　Afar
　Amhara and Tigre
　Galla
　Gurage
　Konso
　Saho
　Sidamo
　Somali
　Tigre
*Africa—Guinea
　Coast:*
　Adangme
　Akan
　Anyi
　Ashanti
　Baga

Baule
Dan
Edo
Efik
Ekoi
Ewe
Fanti
Fon
Ga
Guro
Ibibio
Idoma
Igbira
Igbo
Ijaw
Isoko
Itsekiri
Kissi
Kpelle
Kru
Lamba
Mamprusi
Mbembe
Mende
Nupe
Temne
Tiv
Urhobo
Yakö
Yoruba
Africa—Malagasy:
Antaimoro
Antandroy
Bara
Betsileo
Merina
Sakalava
Tanala
Tsimihety
*Africa—southern and
　lower eastern:*
Acholi
Anuak
Bantu peoples

Baster
Bergdama
Chaga
Chewa
Fipa
Ganda
Gogo
Gusii
Ha
Haya
Hehe
Herero
Hutu
Kamba
Karamojong
Khoikhoin
Kikuyu
Kipsikis
Lango
Lovedu
Luguru
Luhya
Luo
Luvale
Makonde
Manyika
Masai
Mfengu
Mpondo
Nandi
Ndebele
Ngoni
Nguni
Nkole
Nsenga
Nyakyusa
Nyamwezi
Nyika
Nyoro
Okiek
Pedi
San
Sandawe
Shona

Soga
Sotho
Swazi
Tembu
Tonga
Toro
Tsonga
Tswana
Turkana
Tutsi
Venda
Xhosa
Zaramo
Zulu
Africa—Sudan:
Baga
Bagirmi
Bambara
Bamileke
Bamum
Banda
Baqqārah
Bari
Baya
Bobo
Bongo
Dagomba
Dinka
Dogon
Fali
Fulani
Fur
Grusi
Guang
Hausa
Igala
Kabābīsh
Kanuri
Lala
Lotuko
Lugbara
Madi
Malinke
Mande

Mossi
Ngbandi
Nilotes
Nuba
Nuer
Sara
Senufo
Serer
Songhai
Tuareg
Tukulor
Wolof
Arctic:
Aleut
Chukchi
Dolgan
Eskimo
Even
Evenk
Gilyak
Kamchadal
Ket
Komi
Koryak
Lapp
Nenets
Ostyak and Vogul
Yakut
Yukaghir
Asia—Central and
East:
Ainu
Ami
Buryat
Chahar
Chuang
Daghur
Hani
Hui
Kalmyk
Kazakh
Khalkha
Kirgiz
Oyrat
Pai
Puyi
Sanka
Tadzhik
Tibetan peoples
Tung
Turkic peoples
Turkmen
Tuvinian
Uighur
Uzbek
Yao
Yi
Asia—South:
Afrīdī
Andamanese
Baḍaga
Baluchi

Bhīl
Bhutia
Brahui
Chakma
Chenchu
Chin
Dafla
Durrānī
Ghilzay
Gond
Gurung
Ḥazāra
Ho
Jāṭ
Khāsi
Khond
Koch
Koli
Korku
Kota
Kuki
Kurumba
Lepchā
Limbu
Magar
Magh
Mina
Mishmi
Mīzo
Munda peoples
Nāga
Newar
Nūristāni
Pahāṛī
Pashtun
Rai
Sansi
Santāl
Savara
Sinhalese
Tamang
Tamil
Tharu
Toda
Vedda
Asia—South
Siberian:
Buryat
Khakass
Nenets
Ostyak and Vogul
Oyrat
Soyot
Tofalar
Tuvinian
Uighur
Yakut
Asia—Southeast:
Achinese
Atoni
Balinese
Batak

Bisaya
Buginese
Cebuano
Cham
Dayak
Dusun
Ifugao
Igorot
Ilocano
Jakun
Javanese
Kachin
Karen
Kayan
Kenyah
Kubu
Lampong
Madurese
Magindanao
Malay
Manggarai
Maranao
Miao
Minahasan
Minangkabau
Mon
Montagnard
Muong
Murut
Ngada
Palaung
Pangasinan
Rejang
Samal
Sasak
Semang
Senoi
Sikanese
Solorese
Sundanese
Tagalog
Tai
Tasaday
Tau Sug
Tenggerese
Tetum
Toradja
Wa
Europe:
Balt
Bashkir
Basque
Bulgarian
Caucasian peoples
Chuvash
Circassian
Finnic peoples
Fleming and
 Walloon
Gypsy
Hungarian
Lapp

Mari
Mordvin
Slav
Szekler
Tatar
Vlach
See also
 Section 514
Middle America and
northern Andes:
Achagua
Amuzgo
Arawak
Arhuaco
Bribrí
Cakchiquel
Caquetío
Cayapa
Cenú
Chatino
Chinantec
Chocho
Chocó
Chol
Chontal
Chortí
Ciboney
Colorado
Cuicatec
Cumanagoto
Cuna
Goajiro
Guaymí
Huastec
Huichol and Cora
Ixcatec
Jicaque
Kekchí
Lacandon
Lenca
Maya
Mazatec
Miskito
Mixe-Zoquean
Mixtec
Nahua
Otomí
Paéz
Palenque
Patángoro
Pijao
Pocomam
Popoloca
Puruhá
Quiché
Sumo
Taino
Tairona
Tarasco
Tepehuan
Tojolabal
Totonac

Tzeltal
Tzotzil
Tzutujil
Yucatec Maya
Zapotec
Middle East and
North Africa:
  Arab
  Armenian
  Bakhtyārī
  Baluchi
  Baqqārah
  Bedouin
  Beja
  Berber
  Cuman
  Druze
  Ḥarāṭīn
  Kabābīsh
  Kabyle
  Kurd
  Lur
  Rif
  Shawia
  Teda
  Tuareg
  Turkmen
North America—
Californian:
  Cahuilla
  Chumash
  Diegueño
  Juaneño
  Luiseño
  Maidu
  Mission Indians
  Miwok
  Pomo
  Serrano
  Shastan
  Wintun
  Yana
  Yokuts
  Yuki
North America—
Eastern Woodland:
  Abnaki
  Cayuga
  Conoy
  Delaware
  Erie
  Fox
  Huron
  Illinois
  Kickapoo
  Mahican
  Malecite
  Massachuset
  Menominee
  Miami
  Mohawk

Mohegan
Montauk
Nanticoke
Narraganset
Nauset
Neutral
Nipmuc
Ojibwa
Oneida
Ottawa
Pamlico
Passamaquoddy
Pennacook
Penobscot
Pequot
Pocomtuc
Potawatomi
Powhatan
Sauk
Seneca
Shawnee
Susquehanna
Tionontati
Tuscarora
Wampanoag
Wappinger
Wendat
Wenrohronon
Winnebago
North America—
Great Basin:
  Bannock
  Mono
  Paiute
  Shoshoni
  Ute
  Washo
North America—
Northwest
Coast:
  Bella Coola
  Chinook
  Coast Salish
  Haida
  Hupa
  Kwakiutl
  Nootka
  Tlingit
  Tsimshian
  Wiyot
  Yurok
North America—
Plains:
  Arapaho
  Arikara
  Assiniboin
  Atsina
  Blackfoot
  Cheyenne
  Comanche
  Crow

Dakota
Hidatsa
Kansa
Kiowa
Mandan
Omaha
Osage
Oto
Ponca
Quapaw
Sarcee
Tonkawa
Wichita
North America—
Plateau:
  Flathead
  Kutenai
  Modoc and
    Klamath
  Nez Percé
  Sahaptin
  Salish
  Yakima
North America—
Southeast:
  Apalachee
  Caddo
  Calusa
  Catawba
  Cherokee
  Chickasaw
  Chitimacha
  Choctaw
  Creek
  Natchez
  Seminole
  Timucua
North America—
Southwest:
  Apache
  Chiricahua
  Hopi
  Jicarilla Apache
  Karankawa
  Mescalero
  Mojave
  Navajo
  Papago
  Pima
  Pueblo Indians
  Yuman
  Zuni
North America—
Sub-Arctic:
  Algonkin
  Beaver
  Beothuk
  Carrier
  Chipewyan
  Cree
  Dogrib

Ingalik
Kutchin
Micmac
Montagnais and
  Naskapi
Sekani
Slave
Tahltan
Tanaina
Tanana
Yellowknife
Oceania:
  Aranda
  Australian
    aborigine
  Chamorro
  Hawaiian
  Kariera
  Maori
  Trobriander
South America—
central and southern
Andean:
  Araucanian
  Atacama
  Aymara
  Chavín
  Chimú
  Diaguita
  Huarpe
  Inca
  Mapuche
  Quechua
South America—
nomadic:
  Abipón
  Alacaluf
  Charrúa
  Chono
  Guató
  Guayakí
  Makú
  Mataco
  Mbayá
  Ona
  Puelche
  Purí and Coroado
  Querandí
  Sirionó
  Tehuelche
  Warrau
  Yámana
  Yaruro
South America—
tropical forest:
  Apapocuva
  Bororo
  Botocudo
  Canelo
  Carajá
  Chiriguano

Ge	Maxakali	Shavante	Tupian
Guaraní	Mundurukú	Sherente	Tupinambá
Jívaro	Mura	Shipibo	Witoto
Kawaíb	Nambicuara	Tucuna	Yanoamö

Biographies
   See Section 10/36 of Part Ten

INDEX: See entries under all of the terms above

Section 512.   The Development of Human Culture

A. Diverse theories of culture: conceptions involved in the analysis of culture

   1. Definitions of culture

   2. Culture and personality

   3. Cultural comparisons: ethnocentrism, cultural relativism

   4. Cultural adaptation and change

   5. Cultural patterns

   6. Cultural institutions
      [see 513]

B. Types of cultures

   1. Cultures of primitive and nonurban societies

      a. Cultures of nomadic and settled hunters and gatherers

      b. Horticultural societies: societies in which primitive agriculture is supplemental to hunting and gathering

      c. Cultures of pastoralists and herdsmen: distribution and characteristics

      d. Cultures of peasants and settled agriculturists

   2. Cultures of civilized societies: theories of their origin and evolution

   3. The development of modern industrial civilization: mass society

C. Processes of cultural change
   [see Division II, below]

Suggested reading in the *Encyclopædia Britannica*:

MACROPAEDIA: Major articles dealing with the development of human culture

Culture, The Concept and Components of	Social Sciences, The
Modernization and Urbanization	Social Structure and Change
Social Differentiation	

MICROPAEDIA: Selected entries of reference information

General subjects

acculturation	culture area	hydraulic	peasantry
age–area	environmentalism	civilization	primitive culture
hypothesis	folk society	Kulturkreis	region
cultural evolution	Gemeinschaft and	Mesolithic Period	social Darwinism
culture	Gesellschaft	modernization	survival
culture-and-	hunting and	Neolithic Period	transhumance
personality	gathering society	nomadism	urban revolution
studies		Paleolithic Period	

Biographies
   See Section 10/36 of Part Ten

INDEX: See entries under all of the terms above

Section 513.   **Major Cultural Components and Institutions of Human Societies**

A. Systems of relationship based upon marriage and descent: kinship

1. General aspects of kinship

2. Laws and customs regarding mate selection, sexual behaviour, marriage and divorce, legitimacy
[see also 553.B.]

3. Rules of residence; *e.g.,* virilocal, uxorilocal, neolocal

4. Descent systems: unilineal, cognatic, and variant forms

5. Control of resources, inheritance, and succession: the family as a centre for transmission of economic, religious, political, and other powers and goods

6. Kinship and social change: kinship as an evolving social institution

B. Other social structures

1. The varieties of groups and other associations within societies

2. Organization by status: class systems, caste systems, systems characterized by slavery or serfdom

C. Types of economic systems

1. The economic systems of primitive or nonurban peoples

a. Production, division of labour, role differentiation

b. Exchange of goods, distribution of wealth

c. Property and property rights

2. The economic systems of developed nations
[see Division III, below]

D. Other elements common to all cultures but differing in expression or practice between cultures

1. Education and socialization: formal and informal enculturation

2. Religious belief, folklore
[see 811]

3. Legal systems
[see 551.B.]

4. Artistic expression: literature, visual arts, performing arts; crafts
[see 611, 612, and 613]

5. Linguistic systems
[see 514, below]

6. Recreation, sports and games

Suggested reading in the *Encyclopædia Britannica:*

MACROPAEDIA: Major articles dealing with major cultural components and institutions of human societies

Culture, The Concept and Components of
Family and Kinship
Social Differentiation
Social Sciences, The
Sports, Major Team and Individual
Sports and Games, The History of

MICROPAEDIA: Selected entries of reference information

General subjects

kinship:	blood brotherhood	gens	lineage
avoidance	clan	joint family	matriarchy
relationship	cross-cousin	kin	nuclear family
avunculate	extended family	kinship	patriarchy
band	family	kinship terminology	phratry

Biographies

See Section 10/36 of Part Ten

INDEX: See entries under all of the terms above

Section 514.   Language and Communication

A. Communication as a foundation of human culture and as the essential element in social and cultural interaction, the role of communication in the modification of human behaviour

B. Nonverbal communication

1. Communication by means of bodily gestures and posture, by facial expression

2. Laughter and nonword sounds as communication

3. The use of signals, signs, symbols, icons, and cultural artifacts

4. Cybernetic communication: computer languages, human language-computer interfaces, and artificial intelligence and expert systems

5. Parapsychological forms of communication: telepathy
[see 432.H.]

C. The nature of language

1. Definitions of language

2. Ways of studying language: phonetics, grammar, semantics

3. Language variants: dialects, slang, and specialized variants (*e.g.,* jargon, pidgins, creoles)

4. Speech: the psychological and physiological bases

5. Meaning and style in language: structural and lexical meanings; semantic flexibility; language and conceptualization; style

6. Language and culture: transmission of language; language and social differentiation; control of language for cultural ends; language learning and literacy; written language and spoken language

7. Linguistic change and language typology

8. Cryptology: codes, ciphers, and other means of encrypting language

D. The structure of speech and language

1. The phonetics of speech (articulatory, acoustic, linguistic); phonetic transcription; experimental phonetics

2. The physiology of speech: regulators (respiratory and brain functions); the larynx; voice production (including synthetic voice production)

3. Speech disorders

E. Written language: systems of notation

1. The nature, origin, and evolution of writing: from pictures to the alphabet

2. The typology of writing: semasiography, phonography, metagraphy

3. Systems of writing: alphabetic, hieroglyphic, cuneiform, ideographic

4. Adjuncts to writing: punctuation, shorthand

5. Calligraphy and the art of handwriting: Greek, Latin, early Semitic, Arabic, Indic, East Asian

F. Linguistics: the scientific study of language and language development
[see also 10/36 G.]

1. The development of linguistic theory

2. Synchronic linguistics: structural, transformational-generative grammar, tagmemics, stratificational grammar, the Prague school

3. Diachronic linguistics: linguistic change, comparative method, language classification

4. Dialectology and the study of linguistic geography

5. Semantics: the study of language and meaning

6. The study of writing

G. Language and society

1. Attitudes toward language: taboos in language use, myths about the origin of language, the relation of language and thought

2. The connection of language with history, the role of language in the transmission of culture

3. The role of language in cross-cultural relations

4. The use of language as a political instrument

5. The role of language in unifying social and occupational groups

H. Languages of the world

1. The classification of language

2. Languages spoken in Europe and areas of European colonization

   a. Indo-European languages

      i. Indo-Iranian languages
[see H.3.a.i., below]

     ii. Celtic languages

    iii. Italic languages
[see H.6.c., below]

    iv. Romance languages

     v. Greek language

    vi. Baltic languages

   vii. Slavic languages

  viii. Germanic languages

    ix. English language

     x. Albanian language

    xi. Armenian language

   xii. Tocharian language
[see H.6.e., below]

   b. Non-Indo-European languages

      i. Uralic languages

     ii. Basque language

3. Languages of Asia and Oceania

   a. Languages of Asia

      i. Indo-Iranian languages

      ii. Dravidian languages

     iii. Austro-Asiatic languages

     iv. Sino-Tibetan languages

      v. Tai languages

     vi. Japanese language

    vii. Korean language

   viii. Altaic languages

     ix. Uralic languages
[see H.2.b.i., above]

      x. Paleosiberian languages

     xi. Caucasian languages

  b. Languages of Oceania

      i. Austronesian languages

     ii. Australian Aboriginal languages

    iii. Papuan languages

4. Languages of Africa and the Middle East

  a. African languages

      i. Niger-Congo languages

     ii. Chari-Nile and Nilo-Saharan languages

    iii. Khoisan languages

  b. Hamito-Semitic languages

      i. Semitic languages

     ii. Egyptian language

    iii. Berber languages

    iv. Cushitic languages

     v. Chadic languages

5. Indian languages of the Americas

  a. Eskimo-Aleut languages

  b. North American Indian languages

  c. Mexican and Central American Indian languages

  d. South American and Caribbean Indian languages

6. Extinct languages of the world

  a. Anatolian languages

  b. Etruscan language

  c. Italic (non-Romance) languages

  d. Sumerian language

  e. Tocharian language

  f. Sources of other ancient languages: ancient epigraphic remains

7. Constructed languages

  a. Special international or universal languages, including Esperanto and Interlingua; Basic English

  b. Machine languages: Fortran, Algol
[see 735.D.3.]

Suggested reading in the *Encyclopædia Britannica*:

MACROPAEDIA: Major articles dealing with language and communication

Communication
Cryptology
Humour and Wit
Language
Languages of the World

Linguistics
Names
Speech
Writing

MICROPAEDIA: Selected entries of reference information

General subjects

*alphabets and other
writing systems:*
alphabet
Arabic alphabet
Aramaic alphabet
Armenian alphabet
Brāhmī
Braille
Canaanite
  inscriptions
Chinese writing
  system
cuneiform writing
Cypriot syllabary
Cyrillic alphabet
demotic script
Devanāgarī
Eggjum Stone
Ethiopic alphabet
Etruscan alphabet
Glagolitic alphabet
Gothic alphabet
Grantha alphabet
Greek alphabet
Gregg shorthand
Gupta script
Gurmukhi
  alphabet
Hebrew alphabet
hieroglyph
Hittite hieroglyphic
  writing
Iguvine Tables
Indic writing
  systems
kana
Kensington Stone
Kharoṣṭī
Kök Turki
  alphabet
Korean writing
Latin alphabet
Linear B

Mayan
  hieroglyphic
  writing
Myazedi
  inscription
Nabataean
  alphabet
North Semitic
  alphabet
ogham writing
Pahlavi alphabet
Palmyrenian
  alphabet
Phoenician
  alphabet
pictography
Pitman shorthand
Rosetta Stone
runic alphabet
Sarada script
shorthand
Sinaitic
  inscriptions
South Semitic
  alphabet
Speedwriting
stenotypy
syllabary
Syriac alphabet
Ugaritic alphabet
  writing
*grammar, syntax,
  and vocabulary:*
abbreviation
agglutination
auxiliary
gender
grammar
honorific
mood
morpheme
name
patronymic

punctuation
slang
speculative
  grammar
surname
syntax
tense
voice
languages—African:
African languages
Bantu languages
Central Sudanic
  languages
Eastern Sudanic
  languages
Khoikhoin
  language
Khoisan language
Kwa languages
Meroitic language
Niger-Congo
  languages
Nilotic languages
Nubian languages
San languages
Swahili language
West Atlantic
  languages
Xhosa language
Zulu language
languages—Altaic:
Altaic languages
Chuvash language
Kazakh language
Kirgiz language
Mongol language
Mongolian
  languages
Tatar language
Turkic languages
Turkish language
Turkmen language
Uighur language

Ural-Altaic
  languages
Uzbek language
*languages—
  Austro-Asiatic:*
Austro-Asiatic
  languages
Khmer language
Mon-Khmer
  languages
Munda languages
Nicobarese
  languages
Vietnamese
  language
*languages—
  Austronesian:*
Austronesian
  languages
Cebuano
Javanese language
Malay language
Melanesian
  languages
Micronesian
  languages
Oceanic languages
Polynesian
  languages
Tagalog language
*languages—
  Caucasian:*
Avar-Ando-Dido
  languages
Caucasian
  languages
Georgian language
Kartvelian
  languages
Laz language
Mingrelian
  language
Nakh languages

languages—
Dravidian:
  Dravidian
    languages
  Kannada language
  Malayalam
    language
  Tamil language
  Telugu language
languages—
Hamito-Semitic:
  Akkadian language
  Amharic language
  Arabic language
  Aramaic language
  Berber languages
  Chadic languages
  Coptic language
  Cushitic languages
  Eblaite language
  Egyptian language
  Geʿez language
  Hamito-Semitic
    languages
  Hausa language
  Hebrew language
  Phoenician
    language
  Semitic languages
  South Arabic
    language
  Syriac language
languages—Indo-
European (Baltic):
  Baltic languages
  Latvian language
  Lithuanian
    language
  Old Prussian
    language
languages—
Indo-European
(Celtic):
  Breton language
  Brythonic
    languages
  Celtic languages
  Cornish language
  Goidelic languages
  Irish language
  Pictish language
  Scottish Gaelic
    language
  Welsh language
languages—
Indo-European
(Germanic):
  Afrikaans language

Danish language
English language
Faeroese language
Frisian language
German language
Germanic
  languages
Gothic language
Icelandic language
Middle English
  language
Netherlandic
  language
Norwegian
  language
Old English
  language
Old Norse
  language
Old Saxon
  language
Scandinavian
  languages
Swedish language
Swiss German
  language
Yiddish
languages—
Indo-European
(Greek):
  Demotic Greek
    language
  Greek language
  Katharevusa Greek
    language
  Koine
languages—
Indo-European
(Indo-Iranian):
  Apabhraṃsa
    language
  Assamese language
  Avestan language
  Bengali language
  Bihari languages
  Burushaski
    language
  Dardic languages
  Gujarati language
  Hindi language
  Hindustani
    language
  Indian languages
  Indo-Aryan
    languages
  Indo-Iranian
    languages
  Iranian languages

Kashmiri language
Marathi language
Oriya language
Ossetic language
Pahari languages
Pahlavi language
Pāli language
Parthian language
Pashto language
Persian language
Prākrit languages
Punjabi language
Romany language
Sanskrit language
Sindhi language
Sinhalese language
Urdu language
languages—
Indo-European
(Romance and
Italic):
  Catalan language
  Franco-Provençal
    dialect
  French language
  Italian language
  Italic language
  Ladino language
  Latin language
  Mozarabic
    language
  Occitan language
  Oscan language
  Osco-Umbrian
    language
  Portuguese
    language
  Rhaetian dialects
  Romance
    languages
  Romanian
    language
  Sabellic dialects
  Sardinian language
  Spanish language
  Umbrian language
  Vulgar Latin
languages—
Indo-European
(Slavic):
  Belorussian
    language
  Bulgarian language
  Czech language
  Lekhitic languages
  Macedonian
    language

Old Church
  Slavonic language
Polish language
Russian language
Serbo-Croatian
  language
Slavic languages
Slovak language
Slovene language
Sorbian languages
Ukrainian
  language
languages—
Indo-European
(other):
  Albanian language
  Anatolian
    languages
  Armenian
    language
  Hittite language
  Indo-European
    languages
  Indo-Hittite
    languages
  Luwian language
  Lydian language
  Raetian language
  Tocharian
    language
languages—
international and
artificial:
  Basic English
  Esperanto
  Ido
  Interlingua
  Novial
  Volapük
languages—
Meso-American
Indian:
  American Indian
    languages
  Cakchiquel
    language
  Maya languages
  Mixe-Zoque
    languages
  Nahua language
  Oto-Manguean
    languages
  Quiché language
  Uto-Aztecan
    languages
  Yucatec language

INDEX: See entries under all of the terms above

Division II. **Social Organization and Social Change**
[For Part Five headnote see page 173.]

The outlines in the four sections of Division II present general sociological theories of social order and social change, and sociological studies of basic social institutions, social processes, and social problems.

Section 521. **Social Structure and Change**

A. The structure of society: diverse theories of social structure and organization, various types of social structure

B. The social effects of bureaucratic and industrial specialization

  1. The social effects of industrialization and modernization

  2. The social effects of organizational specialization: bureaucracy

  3. The social effects of industrial specialization and automation
  [see 712.C.]

C. Social control

  1. The process of socialization: the transmission of patterns of normative behaviour by family, peer groups, and education

  2. Theories of alienation: definitions, causes, manifestations, and proposed solutions

  3. The regulation of behaviour that departs from social norms

    a. By punishment, rehabilitation, and reform of criminals

    b. By psychological therapy

    c. By persuasion

D. Factors operative in social change

  1. The role of ideology in social change

  2. Contact with other cultures as a factor in social change

  3. The influence of environment as a factor in social change

  4. The role of demographic factors in social change

  5. The role of art in social change: art as an ideological instrument

  6. Religion as a factor for and against social change

  7. The role of intellectual factors in social change

  8. The relationship of economic factors to social stability

  9. Technological factors in social change

  10. The role of collective behaviour in social change

  11. The role of public opinion in social behaviour

E. Social movements and social change

  1. Characteristics of social movements

  2. Selected types of social movements

    a. Movements centred on religious concepts or personalities

    b. Humanitarian and reform movements

    c. Interest group movements

    d. Revolutionary movements

    e. Nationalist movements
    [see also 541.C.3.b.vii.]

Suggested reading in the *Encyclopædia Britannica:*

MACROPAEDIA: Major articles dealing with social structure and change

    Collective Behaviour
    Crime and Punishment
    Public Opinion
    Social Sciences, The
    Social Structure and Change
    Work and Employment

MICROPAEDIA: Selected entries of reference information

General subjects

punishment and rehabilitation:
amnesty
Auburn system
Baumes Laws
Borstal system
commutation
deportation
Elmira system
exile and banishment
indeterminate sentence

Irish system
mark system
ostracism
panopticon
parole
penal colony
Pennsylvania system
prison
probation
recidivism
reformatory
workhouse

social change:
civil disobedience
revitalization movement
sanction
satyāgraha
sit-in
social change
social Darwinism
social movement
temperance movement

social norms and associated phenomena:
assimilation
collective behaviour
folkway
norm
public opinion
role
social structure

Biographies

    See Section 10/36 of Part Ten

INDEX: See entries under all of the terms above

Section 522.   **The Group Structure of Society**

  A. The various types of groups: patterns of group relations

    1. Classifications of groups

    2. The modern family: its organization and functions

    3. Special-interest groups
       [see also 541.B.3.]

    4. Minorities and ethnic groups

  B. The social effects of racial and ethnic prejudice

  C. Special social concerns

    1. The adolescent

    2. The aged

    3. Women

    4. Cultural minorities
       [see A.4., above]

    5. The poor

    6. Criminals and delinquents

    7. Sexual deviants

    8. Prostitutes

    9. Drug and alcohol users

    10. Suicidal persons

D. Social service: organized public and private activities to alleviate human wants and needs

1. The background of social and welfare services: modern and historical influences

2. Fields of service

a. Family welfare

b. Child welfare

c. Youth welfare

d. Group welfare

e. Disaster relief

f. Community development

g. Medical and psychiatric social services

h. School social services
[see also 561.C.4.]

i. Correctional services: probation, parole, and delinquency control

---

Suggested reading in the *Encyclopædia Britannica*:

MACROPAEDIA: Major articles dealing with the group structure of society

Alcohol and Drug Consumption	Social Differentiation
Crime and Punishment	Social Sciences, The
Family and Kinship	Social Welfare
Sex and Sexuality	

MICROPAEDIA: Selected entries of reference information

General subjects

family and marriage:
  adoption
  betrothal
  bride-price
  consensual union
  divorce
  dowry
  exchange marriage
  exogamy and
    endogamy
  family
  group marriage
  henogamy
  joint family
  levirate
  marriage
  nuclear family
  parent
  polyandry
  polygamy

  surrogate
  motherhood
interest groups and
  social movements:
  black nationalism
  Civil Rights
    Movement
  ethnic group
  interest group
  lobbying
  minority
  social group
  temperance
    movement
  women's liberation
    movement
social legislation and
  social services:
  affirmative action
  almoner

  almshouse
  child welfare
  philanthropic
    foundation
  prohibition
  service club
  social service
  social settlement
  social welfare
    program
  woman suffrage
social problems:
  alcoholism
  child abuse
  crime
  delinquency
  drug abuse
  habitual offender
  incest
  old age

  organized crime
  poverty
  prostitution
  racial segregation
  racism
  rape
  suicide
  white-collar crime
other:
  assimilation
  charisma
  Gemeinschaft and
    Gesellschaft

Biographies

See Section 10/36 of Part Ten

Section 523.   **Social Status**

A. Social differentiation and stratification

1. The concepts of differentiation and stratification: distinctions and interrelationships

2. Factors producing social, economic, and cultural differences: sex differentiation, age differentiation, racial differentiation, intellectual differentiation, social and cultural factors [see 521.D.]

3. The process of stratification: its relationship to differentiation

a. Economic differentiation: the basis of stratification

b. Class, status, and power as forms of stratification

c. The relation of the individual to society: the effects of differentiation and stratification

B. Varieties of social stratification and social mobility

1. The relation of social class to caste, status, elites, and other concepts

2. Theories of social class: divergent conceptions of the importance of classes in social structures and of the nature of class relationships

3. Types and characteristics of and comparisons among modern social classes: upper class, working class, and middle class; the special case of the peasant class

4. Social mobility

5. The idea of a classless society: approximations to an equality of conditions

6. Social immobility: slavery, serfdom, and forced labour

Suggested reading in the *Encyclopædia Britannica*:

MACROPAEDIA: Major articles dealing with social status

> Servitude
> Social Differentiation
> Social Sciences, The

MICROPAEDIA: Selected entries of reference information

General subjects

labour and servitude:	serfdom	apartheid	minority
contract labour	slavery	caste	racial segregation
forced labour	statute labour	clan	social class
freedman	*social differentiation,*	ethnic group	social mobility
labour, division of	*stratification, and*	family	social status
migrant labour	*segregation:*	ghetto	
peonage	age set	kinship	

Biographies

> See Section 10/36 of Part Ten

INDEX: See entries under all of the terms above

Section 524.   **Human Populations: Urban and Rural Communities**

 A. The composition and change of human populations

  1. Determinants of population

   a. Human fertility and its control

   b. Mortality: death rates and longevity

   c. Migration and refugee movements

  2. Historical changes in population

  3. Theories of population

   a. Premodern beliefs: pronatalism versus birth control

   b. Mercantilist theory

   c. Laissez-faire theory

   d. Malthusian theory

   e. Marxist theory

   f. Modern theories of population; *e.g.,* optimum population size, optimum rate of population growth, relationship between population and demographic movements

   g. Ecological theories concerning the relationship between human population growth and the conservation of natural resources

  4. Governmental policies influencing population growth and composition

  5. The future of the world's population: population projections and problems of the population explosion

 B. Development of modern cities

  1. Characteristics of urbanization

  2. History of urbanization

  3. Patterns of urban planning

   a. Methods and materials of urban planning and redevelopment

   b. Social aspects of urban planning and redevelopment

  4. Trends in urbanization

   a. Megalopolis: the coalescence of several metropolitan areas into a contiguous agglomeration of people and activity

   b. Suburbanization: the growth of politically separate but economically dependent residential communities surrounding large cities

   c. Regional integration: levels of economic and cultural interaction between the city and its hinterland

   d. The role of technology in extending the dominance and influence of urban concentrations

   e. Problems of urban growth and population control

   f. Problems of environmental change: pollution, climatic change

 C. Development of modern rural societies

Suggested reading in the *Encyclopædia Britannica:*

Macropaedia: Major articles dealing with human populations: urban and rural communities

  Birth Control
  Cities
  Climate and Weather
  Modernization and Urbanization

  Population
  Rural Society and Agriculture, Modern
  Social Sciences, The

MICROPAEDIA: Selected entries of reference information

General subjects

age distribution	human fertility	new town	urban climate
birth control	and fecundity	pollution	urban planning
census	human migration	population	urbanization
city	human mortality	refugee	vital rates
contraception	metropolitan area	rural society	zoning
demography			

Biographies

See Section 10/36 of Part Ten

INDEX: See entries under all of the terms above

Division III.   **The Production, Distribution, and Utilization of Wealth**
[For Part Five headnote see page 173.]

The outlines in the seven sections of Division III deal with the economic order in human society.

Section 531.   **Economic Concepts, Issues, and Systems**

A. Some basic concepts of economics

1. The concept of economic activity as a process of choosing among scarce resources

2. The concept of division of labour

3. The concepts of diminishing returns and optimization

4. The concept of marginality

5. The concept of capital

6. The concept of competition

7. The concept of comparative advantage

8. The concepts of growth and development

B. Levels of economic analysis

1. Microeconomics: the economic decisions of individuals, households, and firms

2. Sectoral economics: the economic arrangements of industries, groups, and regions

3. Macroeconomics: the economy as a whole

C. The comparison of different economic systems

1. Archetypal economic systems

a. The pure private enterprise economy: a theoretical model

b. The centrally planned economy: the pure socialist model

c. The mixed economy with various degrees of economic planning

2. Western-type market economies

3. Soviet- and socialist-type economic systems

4. Mixed economies in developing countries

5. Other economic systems

   a. Primitive economic systems

   b. Feudal economic systems

Suggested reading in the *Encyclopædia Britannica:*

MACROPAEDIA: Major articles dealing with economic concepts, issues, and systems

  Economic Systems
  Economic Theory
  Government Finance
  International Trade

MICROPAEDIA: Selected entries of reference information

General subjects

economic concepts:	margin	command	kula
capital	marginal utility	economy	potlatch
diminishing	microeconomics	communism	silent trade
returns, law of	spillover	economic system	*other:*
distribution theory	supply and	socialism	bourgeoisie
labour, division of	demand	*primitive economic*	Gosplan
laissez-faire	*economic systems:*	*activities:*	labour, hours of
macroeconomics	capitalism	barter	mercantilism
		gift exchange	proletariat

Biographies

  See Section 10/36 of Part Ten

INDEX: See entries under all of the terms above

Section 532.   **The Consumer and the Market: Pricing and the Mechanisms for Distributing Goods**

  A. Scarcity, utility, and value: their roles in pricing, their relationship to the consumer

  B. The satisfaction of material wants: the behaviour of consumers

   1. National consumption levels in the private sector: trends in expenditures for goods and services

   2. Factors influencing consumers' tastes and spending

   3. The protection of consumer interests

  C. Markets as an economic institution in a mixed economy

   1. Markets classified by reference to competition and monopoly

    a. Purely competitive markets as distinguished from markets of imperfect competition: monopoly, oligopoly, and monopolistic competition

    b. Influences affecting the behaviour of sellers under various competitive conditions

    c. The concept of workable competition

    d. Government regulation of monopolistic practices

   2. Major types of markets

    a. Markets for primary commodities

    b. Markets for manufactured goods

    c. Markets for money and capital: the market for short-term loans, the securities market

    d. The market for labour and services
     [see 533.C.1.]

   3. The counterpart of the market under full-scale economic planning: markets under socialism

   4. The historical development of markets: the market in economic theory, the relationship of the market to social welfare and politics

   5. Markets in international trade
    [see 533.F.]

6. The function of the market in the establishment of equilibrium between supply and effective demand

D. The price system in capitalist economies

1. The price system as a means of organizing economic activity: the determination of what is to be produced, how goods are to be produced, and who gets the product

2. Limitations on and failures of the price system: areas in which the price system does not function

   a. Control of prices by business: price-fixing
   [see C.1.a., above]

   b. Government-established price controls and subsidies: regulations concerning public utilities and bank interest rates
   [see 534.B.4.b., and 534.B.6.b.]

   c. Economic relationships not susceptible to control by prices: "externalities," such as air pollution and highway congestion
   [see 737.C.1.]

   d. Imperfect knowledge on the part of buyers as to alternative uses of their buying power
   [see 532.B.2.]

3. The role of the public sector in the distribution of goods and services: government budgets
   [see 534.B.1. and 535.B.1.]

Suggested reading in the *Encyclopædia Britannica*:

MACROPAEDIA: Major articles dealing with the consumer and the market: pricing and the mechanisms for distributing goods

Economic Theory
Government Finance
International Trade
Markets
Social Sciences, The

MICROPAEDIA: Selected entries of reference information

General subjects

consumer protection:	credit card	cartel	marketing board
antitrust law	demand curve	cobweb cycle	monopolistic
Better Business	indifference curve	commodity	competition
Bureau	marginal utility	exchange	monopoly
consumerism	supply and	commodity	price
fair-trade law	demand	trade	price
consumption:	*market organization*	futures	discrimination
consumer's surplus	*and pricing:*	hedging	price maintenance
consumption	auction	marginal-cost	rebate
consumption	bazaar	pricing	
function	black market	market	

Biographies

See Section 10/36 of Part Ten

INDEX: See entries under all of the terms above

Section 533. **The Organization of Production and Distribution**

A. The organization of the production of goods

1. Analysis of costs and output in the short run: the production function, substitution, the relationship of marginal cost to market price, marginal product

2. Analysis of costs and output in the long run for profit maximization and cost minimization

B. The organization of the distribution of goods

1. The relation between the productive process and the incomes derived from it
[see also 534.A.2. and A.3.b.]

2. The earnings of land, labour, and capital employed in the productive process

C. The inputs of the productive process

1. Labour as an input in the productive process

a. The labour force: size, quality, and deployment of work force

b. Methods of fixing rates of pay

c. The structure of pay: differences in the earnings of various occupations

d. Changes in the general level of pay

e. Employment and unemployment

f. The inferior economic and social status of temporary, seasonal migrant labourers

g. The organization of unions

h. The influence of the union on the supply of labour, wages, and output

i. Capital elements in labour: education and training

j. The economic role of managers and entrepreneurs

2. Land and raw materials as inputs
[see also 724]

3. Energy as an input

4. Capital as an input in the productive process

D. Institutional arrangements that facilitate production and output

1. The nature and characteristics of money

a. The basic functions of money

b. The various forms of money

c. The quantity theory of money: views of classical and neoclassical monetary theorists, views of Keynesian income theorists

2. The monetary functions of commercial banks and central banks

a. Historical development of banking systems

b. The structure of modern national banking systems

c. Principles and functions of commercial banking systems

d. Principles and functions of central banking systems

e. The money market: various national and international markets for short-term funds

f. International monetary institutions: proposals for future monetary cooperation and an international currency unit

g. The market for long-term funds: savings institutions, the stock and bond market, credit unions, mortgage institutions, farm cooperative banks, insurance institutions, mutual funds, pension funds

h. The nature and functions of government credit agencies

3. The use of economic statistics in the determination of production and output

a. National income statistics

b. Price statistics: the use and construction of indexes of retail and wholesale prices

c. Economic forecasting

4. The structure of business corporations

E. Agricultural economics

1. The relationship between agricultural and economic development

2. Efforts to control prices and production in agriculture: government price supports, subsidies, and acreage limitations

3. The behaviour of farm prices and the consequences for the incomes of farmers

4. The effect of technology on world agriculture: the increase in acreage and in crop yields

5. The organization of farming: types of farms

F. The geographical distribution of resources and markets: international trade

1. Classical and contemporary theories of international and interregional trade

2. National and regional factors influencing trade

a. Tariffs, embargoes, and quotas imposed to obtain revenue, protect domestic industry, and secure a favourable balance of payments

b. Changes in the conditions of production: costs, labour, and technology

c. Price movements

d. National domestic taxes and subsidies
[see also 534.B.4.]

3. International trade arrangements

G. The role of government in production and distribution

1. The theory of public expenditures: the role of taxation in the budgetary process and problems of effective tax administration

2. The justification of the government's claim to share in resource use: problems of balancing resource consumption between the public and private sectors

3. The growth in government spending in the 19th and 20th centuries: the rise in military and social welfare expenditures

4. Government operation of basic industries

H. Methods of business organization

1. The keeping of accounts

a. Accounting as an information system

b. Various types of company financial statements; *e.g.,* the balance sheet, the income statement

c. Principles of accounting measurement: asset and cost measurement

d. Cost accounting: formulation of budgetary plans, performance reports, profit analyses

2. The management of business funds

a. Short-term and intermediate-term financial operations: planning and control, the cash budget, accounts receivable, inventories

b. Long-term financial operations: the design of capital structure and the issuance of securities

c. Consolidations and mergers

3. The management of human resources: personnel administration

a. Personnel departments: their functions and services

b. Manpower planning, recruitment, and placement

c. Employee training and development

d. Methods of maintaining employee incentive and commitment

4. The administration and control of production

a. The flow channels of information and materials

        b. The control function: maintaining conformity between operations and the plan

        c. Production scheduling

        d. Inventory adjustment

    5. The distribution of goods

        a. The functions of a marketing department in a large firm

        b. Retailing

        c. Wholesaling

        d. Marketing goods to industry, marketing farm products

        e. The application of market research techniques to merchandising

I. Advertising

J. The distribution of risk

    1. The nature of insurance

    2. Fire and marine insurance

    3. Casualty and surety insurance: liability insurance, theft insurance, aviation insurance, workmen's compensation or industrial injury insurance, credit insurance, title insurance, suretyship

    4. Private life and health insurance

    5. Government-sponsored and/or government-administered health insurance
       [see 534.B.4.c.]

    6. Underwriting of risks: rate making

    7. Legal aspects of insurance

K. Consumer credit

    1. Types of consumer credit: installment loans and noninstallment, or single-payment, loans

    2. Historical development of consumer credit in industrialized countries

        a. Lending institutions and the question of interest rates

        b. Costs and hazards of consumer credit

    3. Efforts to protect the consumer: the dimensions of consumer credit

---

Suggested reading in the *Encyclopædia Britannica:*

Section 534.   **The Distribution of Income and Wealth**

A. The distribution of wealth and income by categories of the population

  1. The nature and measurement of wealth and income

  2. Methods of classifying the distribution of wealth and income

   a. Distribution by factor shares: wages, profits, interest, and rent

   b. Distribution according to the number of persons in various classes of wealth and income

  3. Patterns of wealth and income distribution among various countries and among persons within a country

   a. Frequency distributions: the Lorenz diagram, the Gini and Pareto coefficients

   b. Comparisons among wealth and income groups

B. The routes by which government affects the distribution of wealth and income

  1. The national budget as the program of the government's revenues and expenditures

  2. The nature and purposes of taxation

   a. Principles of taxation; *e.g.,* adequacy, adaptability, universality, ability to pay

   b. The effect of taxes on the distribution of income: progressive and regressive taxes

   c. The burden of taxation: the problem of shifting and incidence

   d. Characteristics of national tax systems: comparisons of tax burdens

  3. Kinds of taxes

   a. Taxes on real and personal property

   b. Sales and excise taxes

   c. Tariffs and export taxes

   d. Taxes on personal income and capital gains

   e. Taxes on corporation income and excess profits

   f. Death and gift taxes

   g. Social security and payroll taxes

  4. Transfers and subsidies

   a. Interest payments on the public debt
   [see B.5., below]

   b. Subsidies and tax concessions

   c. Government-sponsored and government-administered welfare programs

  5. The financing of budgetary deficits and surpluses

  6. Direct controls over the private sector

   a. Price, wage, and profit control

   b. Control of restrictive practices: antitrust legislation, regulations imposed upon public utilities, labour legislation imposed on unions
   [see also 532.C.1.d.]

   c. Economic mobilization for war

  7. Land reform: the redistribution of land tenure

Suggested reading in the *Encyclopædia Britannica*:

MACROPAEDIA: Major articles dealing with the distribution of income and wealth

MICROPAEDIA: Selected entries of reference information

General subjects

Biographies

See Section 10/36 of Part Ten

INDEX: See entries under all of the terms above

Section 535.   Macroeconomics

A. National income and employment theory

    1. The concern of income and employment theory with changes in aggregate output, employment, and prices

        a. The classical law of markets contrasted with the Keynesian theory of effective demand

        b. The classical and Keynesian theories of unemployment

    2. The circular flow of income and expenditure: national product as goods and as earnings

    3. Analyses of fluctuations in national income

B. International economic and financial equilibrium and disequilibrium

    1. Foreign exchange markets: problems of alternative monetary standards and fixed and fluctuating exchange rates

        a. Equilibrating movements in the balance of payments and the mechanisms of adjustment: arbitrage, short-term movements, interest rates, and forward exchange

        b. Disequilibrating movements as a response to currency devaluation: covering, hedging, and speculation

        c. Balance of payments accounting

        d. Methods for adjusting to fundamental disequilibrium: fiscal and monetary policy, incomes policy, devaluation and revaluation, and restrictions on capital movements

    2. International monetary and financial institutions: the International Monetary Fund, the Group of Ten, and other attempts at international cooperation

a. Problems of maintaining adequate gold and currency reserves: gold crises, special drawing rights

b. The aftermath of major wars: economic and financial crises, economic nationalism

C. Business cycles

1. The statistical study of cycles: the identification and measurement of business cycles, various cyclical theories

2. Theories of the business cycle and business cycle models

3. Countercyclical monetary and fiscal policy

D. Inflation and deflation

Suggested reading in the *Encyclopædia Britannica:*

MACROPAEDIA: Major articles dealing with macroeconomics

Economic Theory
Government Finance
International Trade
Social Sciences, The

MICROPAEDIA: Selected entries of reference information

General subjects

economic cycles:
business cycle
depression
inflation
Keynesian
  economics
panic
recession
fiscal and monetary
  policy:
bimetallism
bullionism
deficit financing
economic stabilizer
fiscal policy
fractional reserve
  system
full employment
gold-exchange
  standard
gold standard
Gresham's law

incomes policy
monetarism
national income
  accounting
nationalization
open-market
  operation
parity
regional
  development
  program
silver standard
sterling area
two-tier gold
  system
*international
  monetary and
  financial institutions:*
International
  Bank for
  Reconstruction
  and Development

International
  Development
  Association
International
  Finance
  Corporation
International
  Monetary Fund
United Nations
  Capital
  Development
  Fund
trade:
customs union
embargo
exchange rate
free port
free trade
General
  Agreement on
  Tariffs and Trade
imperial preference

international
  exchange
international
  payment
international trade
most-favoured-
  nation treatment
payments,
  balance of
protectionism
quota
reciprocity
tariff
trade, balance of
trade, terms of
trade agreement

Biographies
See Section 10/36 of Part Ten

INDEX: See entries under all of the terms above

Section 536.   **Economic Growth and Planning**

A. The nature and causes of economic growth

1. Various factors influencing economic growth; *e.g.,* technology, markets, the supply of capital, the labour force, governmental fiscal policies

2. The theory of economic growth and models of growth

a. Various models of economic growth: supply-determined models, demand-determined models, and target-instrument models

b. The practical functions of growth theory and mathematical growth models

3. Social costs and benefits of economic growth

4. Economic growth in developing countries

a. The relationship between economic underdevelopment and low per capita income: the rate of increase of gross domestic product (GDP) as compared to population growth

b. Various theories of national economic development and economic retardation

5. Changes in economic efficiency as measured by changes in output per unit of input: economic productivity

B. Planning for economic growth and stability

1. The nature of economic planning

2. Economic planning in Communist countries

3. Economic planning in developed non-Communist countries

4. Economic planning in developing countries

Suggested reading in the *Encyclopædia Britannica:*

MACROPAEDIA: Major articles dealing with economic growth and planning

Economic Growth and Planning
Economic Theory
Government Finance
International Trade
Social Sciences, The

MICROPAEDIA: Selected entries of reference information

General subjects

| economic | economic growth | Gosplan | international trade |
| development | economic planning | government budget | productivity |

Biographies

See Section 10/36 of Part Ten

INDEX: See entries under all of the terms above

Division IV. **Politics and Government**
[For Part Five headnote see page 173.]

The outlines in the four sections of Division IV treat general theories of the state and of government; the structure, branches, and offices of government; the functioning of government; and international relations in peace and war.

Section 541. **Political Theory**

A. The national state as viewed in political theory

   1. Properties of statehood: sovereignty

   2. The state and the individual

   3. The national state in the international community
      [see also 552.B.]

   4. Various conceptions of the bases of legitimacy and authority of government

     a. Continuing consent of the governed: popular sovereignty

     b. The social contract

     c. Venerable sanction: hereditary monarchy, constitutional succession

     d. Divine right: God as the source of political authority

   5. Theories of constitutionalism, modern constitutional governments
      [see also 551.B.4.]

     a. Origins and theories of constitutional government

     b. Features of constitutional government

     c. Methods of constitutional growth: evolution and substantive replacement

B. Patterns of political action as viewed in political theory

   1. Political action within small groups, villages, or communities

   2. Political action by organized parties

   3. Political action by special-interest groups

   4. The political influence of public opinion

C. Political concepts, ideologies, and problems

   1. The concept of political power

   2. The concept of human rights

   3. Modern ideologies

     a. The importance of ideology to a political system or movement: the relationship between ideological and civil politics

     b. Current political ideologies and tendencies

        i. Anarchism

       ii. Communism

      iii. Conservatism

      iv. Fascism

       v. Liberalism

      vi. Marxism

      vii. Nationalism

     viii. Socialism

4. Contemporary political issues and problems

    a. The problem of church and state: its background and contemporary form

    b. The urban problem: the administration of cities and metropolitan areas
[see also 524.B. and 542.A.1.c.]

    c. The problem of international cooperation and integration
[see also 544.A.]

    d. The issue of centralization of power versus decentralization

    e. The problem of adapting traditional political forms to changing conditions

    f. Bureaucracy: the issue of responsive government
[see 542.C.]

Suggested reading in the *Encyclopædia Britannica*:

MACROPAEDIA: Major articles dealing with political theory

Constitution and Constitutional Government	Political Parties and Interest Groups
Human Rights	Social Sciences, The
Ideology	Socio-Economic Doctrines
Marxism, Marx and	and Reform Movements, Modern

MICROPAEDIA: Selected entries of reference information

General subjects

charters and documents:
  Communist Manifesto, The
  Constitution of the United States of America
  Kapital, Das
  Magna Carta
  Rights, Bill of
  Rights of Man and of the Citizen, Declaration of the
  Universal Declaration of Human Rights
concepts of sovereignty:
  church and state
  divine rights of kings

established church powers, separation of
representation
self-determination
social contract
sovereignty
political ideologies:
  anarchism
  Christian Socialism
  collectivism
  Communism
  conservatism
  corporatism
  democracy
  dialectical Materialism
  Eurocommunism
  fascism
  Fourierism
  Guild Socialism

Idéologie
ideology
individualism
jingoism
Leninism
liberalism
Maoism
Marxism
National Communism
National Socialism
nationalism
nihilism
pluralism
radical
revisionism
social democracy
socialism
Stalinism
Syndicalism
totalitarianism

Trotskyism
utopia
political organizations:
  commonwealth
  interest group
  political machine
  political party
  popular front
  soviet
  state
status of the individual:
  alien
  bourgeoisie
  citizenship
  freedman
  nationality
  naturalization
  proletariat
  refugee

Biographies

Bakunin, Mikhail Aleksandrovich
Bebel, August
Bentley, Arthur F.
Bernstein, Eduard
Blanc, Louis
Brecht, Arnold
Burke, Edmund
Engels, Friedrich

Herzen, Aleksandr
Jefferson, Thomas
Kropotkin, Peter
Laski, Harold J.
Lasswell, Harold D.
Lenin, Vladimir Ilich
Lippman, Walter

Mao Zedong
Marx, Karl
Plekhanov, Georgy Valentinovich
Proudhon, Pierre-Joseph
Rousseau, Jean-Jacques

Tocqueville, Alexis de
Trotsky, Leon
Webb, Sidney and Beatrice
See also Section 10/36 of Part Ten

INDEX: See entries under all of the terms above

Section 542.   **Political Institutions: the Structure, Branches, and Offices of Government**

A. Political systems

1. Levels and structures of various systems of government

a. Supranational political systems: empires; leagues, confederations, and commonwealths; regional federations; world congresses
[see 544.A.]

b. National political systems: the unitary nation-state system, the federal state system

c. Urban governments

d. Other subnational political systems: tribal community governments, rural community governments, regional community governments
[see 521.A.]

2. Types and models of political systems

B. The branches of government

1. The concentration of legislative and executive functions: parliamentary rule

2. The legislature

3. The executive

4. The judiciary
[see also 552.F.1.]

C. Public administration: the planning, organization, and coordination of governmental bureaucratic operations; civil service

---

Suggested reading in the *Encyclopædia Britannica:*

MACROPAEDIA: Major articles dealing with political institutions: the structure, branches and offices of government

Cities
Government, The Forms of
Political Systems
Public Administration
Social Sciences, The

MICROPAEDIA: Selected entries of reference information

General subjects

administrative units:	dictatorship	*municipal*	*titles and offices:*
borough	federalism	*government:*	chancellor
canton	government	alderman	count
city	military	burgomaster	duke
city-state	government	city manager	emperor
commonwealth	monarchy	commission system	grand duke
commune	oligarchy	mayor	king
county	two-party system	pao chia	landgrave
municipality	*legislative bodies:*	town meeting	lord
state	Commons,	*public administration:*	prime minister
shire	House of	administrative law	prince
township	Congress of the	bureaucracy	tsar
courts and judiciary:	United States	cabinet	*other:*
See Section 552	Diet	civil service	assembly
governmental forms	Knesset	ombudsman	local option
and systems:	Lords, House of	public	states' rights
absolutism	Parliament	administration	tenure
aristocracy	Representatives,	regulatory agency	
bicameral system	House of	spoils system	
democracy	Senate		

Biographies
   See Section 541

INDEX: See entries under all of the terms above

Section 543.   **The Functioning of Government: the Dynamics of the Political Process**

A. The ways in which political power is exercised

  1. Internal and external security functions of government

  2. The conduct of foreign relations: the function of government in relation to other sovereign states, its own dependencies, and international organizations
   [see 544.A. and 544.E.]

  3. Supervisory functions of government: the resolution of conflicts through mediation and the adjudication of suits
   [see also 552.F.1. and 3.]

  4. Regulatory functions of government: the establishment and active enforcement of standards

  5. Law enforcement and the corrective functions of government: sanctions, inducements, and penalties
   [see also 522.C.6. and D.2.i.]

  6. Enterprising functions of government
   [see 355.D., 424.D., 522.D., 533.G.4., 534.B.4.c. and 6.b., 561, 724.A.2.a., and 732.I.]

B. Government's role in production and consumption

C. Methods of changing the form of government

  1. Peaceful changes: by electoral process (plebiscite), by constitutional mandate

  2. Violent changes: revolution, civil war, conquest by a foreign power

---

Suggested reading in the *Encyclopædia Britannica*:

MACROPAEDIA: Major articles dealing with the functioning of government: the dynamics of the political process

  Censorship
  Crime and Punishment
  Police
  Political Parties and Interest Groups
  Political Systems
  Social Sciences, The

MICROPAEDIA: Selected entries of reference information

General subjects

censorship:	*electoral process:*	*law enforcement:*	sheriff
banning	absentee voting	capital punishment	*legislative procedure:*
censor	Australian Ballot	constable	cloture
censorship	election	criminal	filibuster
obscenity	electoral college	investigation	legislative
pornography	plebiscite	Federal Bureau of	investigative
electoral	plurality system	Investigation	powers
constituencies:	political	Interpol	parliamentary
constituency	convention	KGB	procedure
gerrymandering	political party	police	rules of order
legislative	primary election	posse comitatus	*other:*
apportionment	referendum and	punishment	revolution
pocket borough	initiative	ranger	sabotage
proportional	suffrage	Royal Canadian	terrorism
representation		Mounted Police	

Biographies

See Section 541

INDEX: See entries under all of the terms above

Section 544. International Relations: Peace and War

A. The politics of international relations

B. International treaties and agreements
[see also 533.F.3.]

C. Foreign policy and diplomacy

D. The use of intelligence and counterintelligence activities in the preservation of national security and the conduct of international affairs

E. War among states

1. Degrees and kinds of war: limited war; total war; ethnic or tribal wars; religious wars; national, regional, and worldwide wars; civil wars and insurrections

2. The conduct of war

   a. Military strategy

   b. Military tactics

   c. Military logistics

   d. Effects of psychological warfare on troops and civilians during wartime

   e. International law relating to the treatment of persons during wartime
   [see also 552.B.4.]

Suggested reading in the *Encyclopædia Britannica:*

MACROPAEDIA: Major articles dealing with international relations: peace and war

Intelligence and Counterintelligence
Social Sciences, The
United Nations
War, The Theory and Conduct of

MICROPAEDIA: Selected entries of reference information

General subjects

aggression and warfare:	terrorism	international organization	National Security Agency
aggression	total war	legate	Ultra
amphibious warfare	visit and search	mediation	*military organization and personnel:*
annexation	war	neutralism	
belligerency	*diplomacy and international agreements:*	power, balance of	admiral
blitzkrieg		treaty	aide-de-camp
blockade	alliance	United Nations	air force
civil defense	ambassador	*intelligence gathering:*	armed force
conquest	armistice	BND	army
convoy	arms control	Central Intelligence Agency	battalion
economic warfare	collective security	counterespionage	brevet
embargo	consul	espionage	captain
infiltration	executive agreement	intelligence	cavalry
mobilization	foreign service	KGB	chasseur
sabotage	geopolitics	MI-5	coast guard
safe-conduct	international agreement	MI-6	
ship-of-the-line warfare		Mossad	

commandant
company
division
dragoon
frogman
general
general staff
grenadier
guerrilla
hussar
infantry
legion
lieutenant
marine
marshal

mercenary
military police
militia
navy
phalanx
platoon
privateer
quartermaster
ranger
regiment
streltsy

military science:
air power
deterrence

fail-safe
just war
logistics
military science
sea power
strategy
tactics

sovereignty:
colonialism
dominion
extraterritoriality
home rule
imperialism
influence,
   sphere of

protectorate
sovereignty
territorial waters

other:
concentration
   camp
conscientious
   objector
conscription
fifth column
impressment
martial law
military, naval,
   and air academies

Biographies

*diplomats and
statesmen:*
Adenauer, Konrad
Ben-Gurion, David
Bismarck,
   Otto von
Bunche, Ralph
Chamberlain,
   Neville
Chou En-lai
Churchill, Winston
Clemenceau,
   Georges
Curzon, George
   Nathaniel
Curzon,
   Marquesse
Disraeli, Benjamin
Dulles, John
   Foster
Eisenhower,
   Dwight D.
Gandhi, Mohandas
   Karamchand
Gaulle, Charles de

Gladstone,
   William Ewart
Goebbels, Joseph
Gromyko, Andrey
   Andreyevich
Hammarskjöld,
   Dag
Hitler, Adolf
Ho Chi Minh
Kennedy, John F.
Khrushchev,
   Nikita S.
Kissinger,
   Henry A.
Lie, Trygve
Marshall,
   George C.
Metternich,
   Klemens,
   Fürst von
Mussolini, Benito
Nasser, Gamal
   Abdel
Nehru, Jawaharlal

Roosevelt,
   Franklin D.
Stalin, Joseph
Stevenson,
   Adlai E.
Sun Yat-sen
Thant, U
Weizmann, Chaim
Wilson, Woodrow

*intelligence agents
and officers:*
Baker, Lafayette
   Curry
Bancroft, Edward
Boyd, Belle
Burgess, Guy; and
   Maclean, Donald
Donovan,
   William J.
Hiss, Alger
Mata Hari
Redl, Alfred
Schulmeister, Karl
Van Deman,
   Ralph H.

Winterbotham,
   Fredrick William
Yardley, Herbert
   Osborne

military theorists:
Clausewitz,
   Carl von
Douhet, Giulio
Jomini, Henri,
   baron de
Liddell Hart, Sir
   Basil
Mahan, Alfred
   Thayer
Montalembert,
   Marc-René,
   marquis de
Montecuccoli,
   Raimonde
Scharnhorst,
   Gerhard Johann
   David von
Vauban, Sébastien
   le Prestre de

INDEX: See entries under all of the terms above

Division V.   **Law**

[For Part Five headnote see page 173.]

The outlines in the three sections of Division V treat philosophies and systems of law; the profession and practice of law; the branches of public law; and the branches of private law.

Section 551.   **Philosophies and Systems of Law; the Practice of Law**

A. Western and non-Western philosophies of law

  1. Western philosophy of law

    a. The scope of the Western philosophy of law and its relationship to other branches of philosophy

    b. Problems of the philosophy of law, various approaches to a theory of law or jurisprudence

    c. The relationship between law and morality: the influence of the principles of natural law

    d. Historical survey of legal theories from the ancient world to the 20th century

  2. Non-Western philosophies of law: Islāmic, Chinese, and other non-Western philosophies of law

B. Ancient and modern legal systems

  1. Primitive law: the legal systems of nonliterate peoples

  2. Ancient systems of law

    a. Egyptian law

    b. Cuneiform law

    c. Chinese law

    d. Greek law

    e. Hellenistic law

    f. Roman law

    g. Germanic law

  3. Medieval European law

    a. Origins and development of medieval European law

    b. Sources and institutions of medieval constitutional law

    c. Institutions of private law in medieval Europe

    d. Development of canon law

  4. Modern systems of law

    a. Anglo-American common law

    b. Continental civil law

    c. Soviet and socialist law

C. The study of the distinctions and parallels among diverse legal systems

D. The profession and practice of law

  1. The profession of law

  2. Legal ethics

  3. Educational requirements for the legal profession

Suggested reading in the *Encyclopædia Britannica*:

MACROPAEDIA: Major articles dealing with the philosophies and systems of law; the practice of law

Law, The Profession and Practice of
Legal Systems, The Evolution of Modern Western

MICROPAEDIA: Selected entries of reference information

General subjects

ancient legal codes, principles and institutions:
aedile
archon
Basilica
censor
civitas
clientship
comitia
concubinage
cuneiform law
decemviri
delator
delict
dicastry
Egyptian law
emphyteusis and
  superficies
Greek law
Hammurabi,
  Code of
hypothec
interdict
jus gentium
jus Latii
Justinian, Code of
manus
nomos
Pandects
patria potestas
proscription
Roman law
Roman legal
  procedure
stipulatio
talion
Twelve Tables,
  Law of the
ecclesiastical law:
canon law
Codex Juris
  Canonici
Corpus Juris
  Canonici

decretal
dispensation
ecclesiastical court
excommunication
False Decretals
Gratian's
  Decretum
Ḥadīth
Halakha
Mishna
penitential book
Sharī'ah
Talmud
Torah
legal practitioners:
advocate
assessor
attorney general
barrister
lawyer
notary
solicitor
*medieval European
law—codes and
systems:*
Anglo-Saxon law
Brehon law
capitulary
Germanic law
Jérusalem,
  Assises de
Sachsenspiegel
Salic Law
Salic Law of
  Succession
Scandinavian law
Welsh law
Westminster,
  Statutes of
*medieval European
law—institutions
and officers:*
audiencia
Augmentations,
  Court of

Chambre des
  Comptes
Chambre des
  Enquêts
Chambre des
  Requêts
Clarendon,
  Assize of
court baron
Court Leet
curia regis
fehmic court
High Commission,
  Court of
High Court of
  Admirality
law merchant
legal glossator
manorial court
Parlement
piepoudre court
prerogative court
prévôt
Privy Council
Reichskammergericht
Requests, Court of
Star Chamber,
  Court of
*medieval European
law—principles:*
blood money
clergy, benefit of
composition
compurgation
copyhold
demesne
entail
feudal land tenure
feudalism
fief
frankpledge
freehold
heriot
homage and fealty
liege

peine forte et dure
right, petition of
seisin
serjeanty
socage
tallage
usury
wardship and
  marriage
wergild
*modern legal codes
and systems:*
adat
Chinese law
German Civil
  Code
Indian law
Israeli law
Japanese Civil
  Code
Japanese law
Napoleonic Code
Prussian Civil
  Code
Roman–
  Dutch law
Scottish law
Soviet law
Swiss Civil Code
other:
assize
bar association
civil law
common law
custom
disbarment
duel
equity
feud
law
law code
movable and
  immovable
natural law
sumptuary law

Biographies

Austin, John
Blackstone, Sir
  William
Brandeis, Louis
Brennan, William
  J., Jr.

Brougham and
  Vaux, Henry
  Peter Brougham,
  1st Baron
Burger, Warren E.

Cardozo, Benjamin
  Nathan
Cockburn, Sir
  Alexander James
  Edmund
Coke, Sir Edward

Darrow, Clarence
Draco
Erskine, Thomas
  Erskine, 1st
  Baron

Field, Stephen
J(ohnson)
Fortas, Abe
Frankfurter, Felix
Grotius, Hugo
Hale, Sir Matthew
Hand, Learned
Harlan, John
Marshall

Holmes, Oliver
Wendell, Jr.
Jackson, Robert H.
Johnson, William
Mansfield (of Caen
Wood), William
Murray, 1st
earl of
Marshall, John

Matthews, Stanley
Miller, Samuel
Freeman
Pufendorf, Samuel,
Freiherr von
Savigny, Friedrich
Karl von
Solon
Stone, Harlan Fiske

Story, Joseph
Taney, Roger
Brooke
Waite, Morrison
Remick
Warren, Earl
White, Edward
Douglass

INDEX: See entries under all of the terms above

Section 552.   **Branches of Public Law, Substantive and Procedural**

A. Laws defining and implementing the authority and power of the state

   1. Basic laws governing the organization and functions of the state: constitutional law

   2. Laws governing public administration: regulation of the organization, powers, duties, and functions of public administrative authorities

B. Laws governing relations among sovereign states

   1. Sources and concepts of international law

   2. The attempt to create a supranational legislative and executive authority: the United Nations

   3. The attempt to create a supranational judicial authority

   4. The attempt to impose rules of warfare

   5. The attempt to limit and punish war crimes and crimes against peace and humanity

   6. The attempt to preserve the peaceful uses and exploration of outer space

C. Laws governing acts viewed as crimes

   1. Principles and doctrines of criminal law: comparisons between common law and civil law systems
      [see also 543.A.5.]

   2. Laws governing offenses committed by military forces and other persons subject to military discipline

D. Laws promoting the public welfare
   [see 424.I.2.]

   1. Laws providing for general social security and welfare

   2. Laws promoting public health and safety

   3. Laws regulating the health, safety, and welfare of workers

E. Laws governing taxation
   [see also 534.B.2. and 3.]

F. Laws of judicial procedure

   1. The organization and administration of the legal system: the courts and the judiciary

   2. Methods and procedures of the law

      a. Criminal procedure

      b. Civil procedure
         [see 553.E.]

      c. Administrative procedure

   3. Methods of adjudicating litigious disputes: the jury system, systems of arbitration

Suggested reading in the *Encyclopædia Britannica*:

MACROPAEDIA: Major articles dealing with branches of public law, substantive and procedural

Constitutional Law
Criminal Law
International Law
Judicial and Arbitrational Systems

Public Administration
Taxation
United Nations
War, The Theory and Conduct of

MICROPAEDIA: Selected entries of reference information

General subjects

constitutional law:
advisory opinion
attainder
commerce clause
constitution
due process
equal protection
ex post facto law
interstate
  commerce
judicial review
police power
powers,
  delegation of
privacy, rights of
standing to sue
states' rights
*courts, court officials,
and juries:*
amicus curiae
Appeal, Court of
assigned counsel
attorney general
bailiff
Chancery, Court of
Common Pleas,
  Court of
comrades' court
coroner
Counseil d'État
Cour de 'Cassation
court
court-martial
Crown Court
family court
Federal
  Constitutional
  Court
grand jury
High Court of
  Justice
juge d'instruction
jury
justice of the peace
juvenile court
lord chancellor
lord chief justice
lord high steward
lord steward
magistrates' court

ministère public
petit jury
prosecutor
public defender
Queen's Bench,
  Court of
rapporteur
Supreme Court of
  Japan
Supreme Court of
  the United States
Tax Court
United States
  Court of Claims
United States
  Court of Military
  Appeals
criminal law:
accomplice
arson
assault and battery
bribery
child abuse
confidence game
conspiracy
contempt
counterfeiting
crime, délit, and
  contravention
criminal law
delinquency
diminished
  responsibility
disorderly conduct
disturbing the
  peace
embezzlement
entrapment
extortion
felony and
  misdemeanour
forgery
fraud
hijacking
homicide
infamy
insanity
kidnapping
lynching
mayhem

mens rea
mutiny
obscenity
pardon
perjury
poaching
rape
riot
sedition
seduction
self-defense
smuggling
solicitation
theft
treason
unlawful assembly
usury
vagrancy
criminal procedure:
accused, rights of
acquittal
arraignment
arrest
bail
clergy, benefit of
commutation
confession
double jeopardy
exclusionary rule
extenuating
  circumstances
extradition
habeas corpus
impeachment
indictment
inquest
interrogation
outlawry
preventive
  detention
probation
recognizance
search and seizure
self-incrimination
sentence
warrant
*general procedural
law:*
adversary
  procedure

appeal
assize
brief
certiorari
circumstantial
  evidence
competence and
  jurisdiction
complaint
demurrer
domicile
equity
evidence
examination
interlocutory
  decree
judgment
law report
legal fiction
legal maxim
limitation,
  statute of
mistrial
nolle prosequi
pleading
privileged
  communication
procedural law
stare decisis
summary
  jurisdiction
venue
international law:
aggression
air law
armistice
asylum
Berne Convention
Calvo Doctrine
continuous voyage
contraband
genocide
Hague Convention
high seas
international law
laws, conflict of
mutiny

Section 553.   Branches of Private Law, Substantive and Procedural

A. Law of property

1. Historical development of property rights

2. Methods of acquiring property rights

3. Types of property rights classified by types of ownership

4. Laws concerning tangible property: the distinctions between real and personal property

5. Laws protecting intangible or incorporeal property rights

   a. Easements and servitudes: profits and mineral rights

   b. Rights to the exclusive exploitation of literary, dramatic, musical, and other artistic works

   c. Rights to the exclusive exploitation of inventions and other discoveries of useful processes and materials

   d. Rights to the exclusive exploitation of symbols and other devices used to identify the origin or ownership of business products

6. Laws concerning the temporal division of property rights

   a. Common law land ownership: freehold and leasehold estates

   b. Civil law land ownership: dominium (absolute ownership) and usufruct (life estate)

7. Laws concerning trusts: ownership for the benefit of others

   a. The elements of a trust: settlor, trust property, trustee, beneficiary, trust instrument

   b. Types of trusts: express, implied, constructive, statutory, and public and private trusts

   c. Trusts established for the benefit of families, social and philanthropic organizations, and business corporations

   d. The status of the trust in civil law systems: a comparison of the trust and the fidei commissum

8. Law of mortgages

9. Laws concerning bankruptcy

B. Family law

1. Laws governing the institution of the family and the relationships among its members
   [see also 513.A.2.]

   a. Laws concerning the marriage contract: civil effects of marriage, the legal status of married women

   b. Laws concerning children: legitimacy, adoption, and guardianship; parental obligations and rights

   c. Laws concerning the termination of marriage: divorce and other forms of marital dissolution

2. Laws concerning the devolution of property by means of inheritance

C. Law of torts

1. The doctrine of strict liability as compared with negligence liability: recent changes in tort liability burden

2. Intentional personal injuries: battery and assault, false imprisonment, mental anguish

3. Intentional injuries to property: trespass to land and chattels, nuisance, unlawful appropriation and conversion of property

4. Injuries resulting from negligent acts

    a. Injuries resulting from failure to comply with required standards of care: the proximate cause doctrine, effects of contributory negligence and third-party intervention

    b. The employer's liability and the master–servant relationship

    c. The manufacturer's liability to the consumer

5. Injuries to personality and personal relationships: physical, mental, and economic injuries

    a. Defamation: libel and slander, other invasions of privacy and interference with familial relationships

    b. Interference with economic relationships: deceptive practices, unfair competition, infringement

D. Laws governing economic transactions

1. Law of contracts

2. Law of commercial transactions

    a. Principal elements of commercial law: commercial transactions as contracts

        i. Sales of goods and requirements for delivery

        ii. Transfer of negotiable instruments; *e.g.,* promissory notes, checks, drafts or bills of exchange

        iii. Issuance of documents of title; *e.g.,* bills of lading, warehouse receipts

        iv. Issuance of letters of credit

        v. The use of security interests (liens and pledges) as collateral for loans of money

    b. Laws governing the relationship between agent and principal in the transaction of commercial and other legal affairs

3. Law of business associations

    a. Principal forms of business associations

        i. Partnerships

        ii. Corporate companies or corporations

        iii. Cooperative and mutual organizations

        iv. State and municipal corporations, quasi-public enterprises and utilities
        [see also 534.G.4. and 535.B.6.b.]

    b. Laws governing the management and control of business entities

    c. The structure of corporate finance

        i. Common and preferred shares of stock: rights and interests of owners of equity capital

        ii. Borrowed capital: rights acquired by holders of bonds and debentures

        iii. Reinvestment of company earnings

    d. Trends in laws governing mergers and consolidations: employee participation
    [see also 533.H.2.c.]

    e. Laws governing the liquidation of insolvent business and nonbusiness estates: the law of bankruptcy

4. Labour law

5. Laws governing commercial transportation

    a. Laws regulating the carriage of goods

    b. Maritime law

    c. Air law

E. Civil procedural law

1. Elements of civil procedure

    a. National or territorial jurisdiction and venue of courts: the competence of a court to handle a case

b. Jurisdiction or venue in private international law: the source and nature of the conflict of laws, foreign judgments and choice of law

c. Definitions and limitations of parties to a suit: class actions and amicus curiae

d. Provisional remedies sought prior to trial; *e.g.,* writs of attachment, injunctions, and other restraining orders

e. The commencement of civil action: summons, pleadings, appearance, pretrial motions, discovery procedures, and pretrial conference

2. The conduct of civil trials: the law of evidence

3. The rendering of judgment in civil cases: assessment of damages, res judicata, collateral estoppel

4. Post-trial appeals and other methods of review

Suggested reading in the *Encyclopædia Britannica:*

MACROPAEDIA: Major articles dealing with branches of private law, substantive and procedural

Business Law	Property Law
Family Law	Torts
Inheritance and Succession	Transportation Law
Procedural Law	

MICROPAEDIA: Selected entries of reference information

General subjects

business law:
affreightment
agency
air law
antitrust law
average
bankruptcy
business law
caveat emptor
cessio bonorum
composition
consideration
contract
copyright
debtor and creditor
guaranty and
 suretyship
hypothec
insolvency
labour law
lading, bill of
liquidation
maritime law
patent
performance
receivership
right-to-work law
salvage
trademark
civil procedure:
abatement
arbitration
astreinte
attachment

attorney,
 power of
damages
declaratory
 judgment
escrow
foreclosure
garnishment
injunction
joinder and
 impleader
liability
lien
mandamus, writ of
replevin
settlement
writ
estate law:
executor
gift
heir
inheritance
intestate succession
legacy
probate
will
family law:
adoption
alimony
annulment
common-law
 marriage
community
 property

concubinage
consensual union
divorce
guardian
illegitimacy
marriage law
minor
morganatic
 marriage
separation
property law:
abandonment
adverse possession
ancient lights
bailment
beneficiary
condominium
deforcement
domain
easement
ejectment
eminent domain
emphyteusis and
 superficies
entail
escheat
landlord and
 tenant
mortgage
mortmain
movable and
 immovable
ownership
possession

preemption
prescription
property
real and personal
 property
remainder
restrictive covenant
reversion
riparian contract
servitude
treasure trove
trust
use
usufruct
tort law:
assault and battery
contributory
 negligence
conversion
damages
defamation
delict
fraud
manufacturer's
 liability
misrepresentation
negligence
nuisance
tort
trespass
trover

Biographies

See Section 551

INDEX: See entries under all of the terms above

Division VI. **Education**
[For Part Five headnote see page 173.]

The outlines in the two sections of Division VI treat the subjects of education and the world's educational systems.

Section 561. **The Aims and Organization of Education**

A. Philosophies of education
[see also 435.A.]

B. The learning process and the teaching art

  1. Processes of learning and thinking: experimental findings and theories
[see 435]

  2. Pedagogy: the art and science of teaching

    a. Components of the teaching situation

    b. General theories concerning the role of the teacher in the learning process

    c. The organization of instruction: contemporary practices and techniques

    d. Instructional media: speaking–listening facilities, visual and observational aids, computer-based instruction

C. The organization of education

  1. Phases or levels of education

    a. Preschool education

    b. Elementary and secondary education

    c. Higher education: colleges, universities, and professional schools

    d. Special education: education of exceptional children

    e. Education of the adult population

    f. Vocational training: apprenticeship and employee training

  2. The preparation and performance of teachers

    a. The education of teachers

    b. The teaching profession

  3. The economics of education

  4. Social aspects of education

Suggested reading in the *Encyclopædia Britannica:*

MACROPAEDIA: Major articles dealing with the aims and organization of education

Education, Higher
Education, Social and Economic Aspects of
Education, Special
Philosophies of the Branches of Knowledge
Teaching

MICROPAEDIA: Selected entries of reference information
General subjects

adult education:	lyceum movement	elementary	Grundschule
adult education	*elementary and*	education	Gymnasium
chautauqua	*secondary education:*	eleven-plus	Hauptschule
movement	comprehensive	graded school	high school
folk high school	school	grammar school	informal school

Biographies
    See Section 562

INDEX: See entries under all of the terms above

Section 562.   **Education Around the World**

A. Systems of education

  1. The formation of educational policy

  2. Administrative functions and procedures

  3. Types of educational systems and their characteristics

    a. Centralized systems: systems in which control is exercised through a national administrative agency

    b. Decentralized systems: systems in which control is exercised at the regional or local level

    c. Joint national and local systems

    d. Systems controlled by political parties

    e. Sectarian systems: national and regional sectarian systems, sectarian education as an alternative system to public education

B. History of education: philosophies, practices, and institutions

  1. Education in ancient cultures

    a. Ancient Indian education

    b. Ancient Chinese education

    c. Ancient Hebrew education

    d. Ancient Greek education

    e. Ancient Roman education

  2. Education in the Persian, Byzantine, early Russian, and Islāmic civilizations

    a. Ancient Persian education: influences of Zoroastrian and Sāsānid cultures

    b. Byzantine education: influences of Greek Christian and humanistic culture; development of primary, secondary, and higher educational institutions

    c. Kiev and Muscovy: Russian education to the period of the early Romanovs

    d. Islāmic education

  3. Education in the European Middle Ages

    a. Christian education to the 8th century: early schools; development of monastic schools in England, Ireland, Italy, and Spain

    b. The cultural revival under Charlemagne and his successors

    c. The 12th-century renaissance: reform of monastic schools and the rise of secular urban schools, development of universities and grammar schools, courtly education

4. Education in Asian civilizations from *c.* 700 to the eve of Western influence

    a. Indian education from *c.* 700 to 1707

    b. Chinese education from 618 to 1911

    c. Japanese education from ancient times to 1867

5. European education during the Renaissance and Reformation

    a. Development of Renaissance education: Arabic and secular influences on Humanism

    b. The humanistic tradition in Italy

    c. The humanistic tradition in northern and western Europe

    d. Education during the Reformation and Counter-Reformation

6. European education in the 17th and 18th centuries

    a. The social and historical setting

    b. Educational theories and practices

    c. European influences in New World educational development

7. Western education in the 19th century

    a. The social and historical setting: nationalism, industrialism, urbanization, political revolution and reform

    b. The early reform movements: the new pedagogy and psychology

    c. Development of national systems of education

    d. Spread of Western educational practices to Asian countries

8. Education in the 20th century

    a. Political, social, economic, and intellectual trends

    b. Traditional and experimental educational movements in the West

    c. The modernization of education in Asia and Africa

    d. Education in colonies and newly-emerging nations in Africa, Asia, and Latin America

C. International educational activities

Suggested reading in the *Encyclopædia Britannica*:

MACROPAEDIA: Major articles dealing with education around the world

    Education, Systems of
    Education, History of
    Religious Education
    Teaching

MICROPAEDIA: Selected entries of reference information

General subjects

educational systems:	progressive	hornbook	Winnetka Plan
coeducation	education	land-grant college	*other:*
correspondence	*history of education:*	lyceum movement	academy
education	cathedral school	mechanics'	Nobel Prize
educational system	charity school	institute	Pugwash
liberal arts	chautauqua	nation	Conference
minority education	movement	normal school	
monitorial system	Dalton Plan	philanthropinum	
parochial education	Froebelism	Quincy Plan	

Biographies

Adler, Mortimer J.	Cygnaeus, Uno	Hopkins, Johns	Richards, Ellen
Alcuin	Dewey, John	Hutchins,	Swallow
Bagley, William	Eaton, John	Robert M.	Sadler, Sir Michael
Chandler	Froebel, Friedrich	Lancaster, Joseph	Ernest
Basedow, Johann	Griswold, Alfred	Mann, Horace	Stowe, Calvin E.
Bernhard	Whitney	Montessori, Maria	
Comenius, John	Herbart, Johann	Pestalozzi, Johann	
Amos	Friedrich	Heinrich	

INDEX: See entries under all of the terms above

Introduction to Part Six:
The World of Art

by Mark Van Doren

Let us imagine if we can a world entirely without art: without story, image, edifice, or significant sound. If we can, for perhaps it is impossible. Such a world might well be invisible, inaudible, ineffable, and intangible. Even if we could see it, hear it, feel it, we would not know we did, at least as men know things. Without the earliest of all arts, language, we would scarcely know of what we were deprived: the privilege, namely, of expressing our satisfaction or dissatisfaction with what had taken place before our eyes. Without the arts of speaking, listening, thinking, counting, and measuring—without the intellectual arts—we could not assess or repossess the experience we had undergone. Without the useful arts we could make nothing, build nothing worthy to contain and shelter our bodies, to be a home wherein our thought might rest. And then without the fine arts—the arts that serve only themselves, that are ends, not means, that justify themselves when they give us nothing but pleasure—we would be shallow and poor of mind, with little or no sense of the world's depth and colour, or of ourselves as creatures for whom the present moment is also past and future. We call these arts fine not because they are better than the others but because they are different, as beauty is different from use—beauty that is its own excuse for being.

None of them is more intimately ours than story. The art of literature is the art of story; there are songs and there are essays long and short, there are histories, there are biographies, there are treatises, sermons, and discussions of everything under the sun, but story is our first and last entertainment—when we are children and when we are too old to care any more what truth is unless it comes in the past tense, with persons reflecting in their lives the peculiar radiance that attends the accidents of time and character. Stories may vary in length from the anecdote to the epic, from the fairy tale to the novel, the imaginary biography, the romance. And they may reach us in many forms: in the theatre, for instance, where they may employ flesh-and-blood actors to convey their meaning or where they may be only flickers of light and shade upon a screen that has no depth save what we give it in our imaginations; where, in other words, they call themselves plays or motion pictures or where, if music also sounds and dancers whirl and pose, they call themselves ballets.

Nature does not tell stories; only artists do, and in the process they work transformations that measure the distance between matter and mind. In nature, so far as we can know it, there are no beginnings and no ends in the sense familiar to both writers and readers of fiction and drama, or for that matter history, which likewise imposes form upon a welter of events. No matter how simple a tale is, or how complex, how few the words in it or how many, it is a human construction that no animal or plant, and of course no stone, would find in the least degree interesting;

whereas human beings hold their breaths until an end is reached. Ends are intelligible as the raw materials of life seem not to be; if life itself does not become intelligible through story, it becomes in some mysterious way both beautiful and clear, and for the time being that suffices.

Each of the fine arts flourishes both in large and in little forms. Just as story has a choice between the brevity of folk tales and the elaboration of epics and romances, so statements about life may be as compendious as a proverb—the wisdom of many and the wit of one—or as bulky as the longest book in numberless volumes. So music—the sound of other worlds—reaches our ears either as simple song or as opera and symphony and other complex forms. There are those who say that the song, like the anonymous fable or tale, is more lasting and important than compositions of great complexity can ever be; and they also say that the lyric poem, at least when it is perfect, as in truth it seldom is, has more to tell us, or at least deeper ways of touching us, than the most tremendous tragedy in five acts or the subtlest comic novel in a thousand pages. When a memorable melody attaches itself to a lyric or a ballad, something indeed does come into existence and hang there as if for perpetuity. Music is the most ineffable of all the arts. It has its own language and it listens to itself; we do not so much hear it as overhear it, nor can we speak very sensibly about what we have overheard. Successful music, powerful music, has an effect upon us that many have tried in vain to describe; it takes us out of ourselves, they say, and perhaps they need to say no more than that. Even then they may be speaking only of the music that is native to them; Eastern music sounds like mere noise to untrained Western ears, and Western music has a monotony, say the Chinese, that Europeans of course deny is there. The same thing is true, though in lesser measure, of all the arts. East and West have different eyes as well as ears, and different thoughts.

The arts of drawing and painting, of etching and lithography, of engraving and decorative design, have covered many surfaces—canvas, plaster, parchment, paper—which no longer show where the artist's hand once worked; for the materials of these arts are perishable, as the marble of sculptors has been, as the bronze, as the wood. Much remains, but more does not. Even the cave paintings of prehistoric France and Africa, hailed by modern man when he discovered them as miracles of survival, may not survive the visits that living people rushed to pay them. Ancient Greek music has failed to survive for a further reason: we do not know how it was written or how it sounded; we are told that it had almost magical powers over those who heard it in its time, but that time is gone, along with the time when paintings adorned the walls and columns of Greek temples and houses. Painting has been for centuries the queen of the arts in Europe. Belgium,

The Netherlands, France, Germany, Spain, Italy, and England—each of them in its turn, and sometimes in more than one turn, has enriched the world with shapes and colours that only genius could have foretold, only passion could have brought into being. And that is but half the story; in China long before, in India, in Persia, in Japan, in Russia, the brushes of painters, sometimes tipped with gold, beautified and glorified the palaces of emperors, the tombs of princes, and the dwelling places of great gods. In Egypt for millennia the order of the world was registered in stone and gold, and the written word itself was pictures.

Sculpture, that once was solid and now is full of spaces— or may be—left open by the ingenuity of workers in metal, has changed as architecture has changed. Both arts now cultivate openness: buildings are closed, but the exterior is glass, so that space plays games with itself inside, and the effect is of a lightness that winds might blow away, except of course that the buildings look lean and strong enough to remain just where they are. It has always been true that architects desired the effect of lightness, as all art does, heaviness being a quality that no mind admires; any building weighs tons, but we are not supposed to think of that; rather indeed we are expected to imagine that brick and stone for once have learned to lie lightly on the earth, which they do not seem to press at all. So with Classical sculpture, from Greek days on; the charm of it was its poise, its grace, its management of idea in marble. So too with Classical architecture; the Parthenon is both massive and weightless, like a ship that might sail yet does not. And always in China and Japan there have been those curled and tapered roofs that still look as if at this very instant in time they are taking wing. The open revolution, then, was only a restatement of what had long been understood though some of its secrets were forgotten.

Abstraction in all the arts, for there is no art from which it is absent, is again a restatement of what has always been true, however feebly it was recognized by schools of artists who had lost contact with reality. Great painting, great music, great poetry, great architecture—great landscape architecture too—have never been strangers to abstraction, just as they have never been slaves to an incomplete understanding of what is meant when we say that art is imitation. It *is* imitation, but of what? Of essences, not accidents; of the truth that is hard to see; of beauty that is basic; of shapes that will not change; of colours that will not fade. And if, say, the great painters of the past, comprehending this, still "copied nature," they did not do so inanely. They did so, on the contrary, with huge effort aimed at the verities that underlie verisimilitude, so that in one sense they were not copying at all; they were extracting essences, they were reducing appearances to the ideas that informed them; they were, in a word, abstracting truth from vessels that contained it. But they did not say they were doing this. They said they were copying nature. And when later on they were taken at their word by painters with inadequate aspiration, the result was woeful insipidity, was mediocrity and flatness. The heroic remedy was warfare against representation as such, was a shortcut to abstraction that could have its weakness too, was a loss, in all but the great revolutionaries, of the contact with Earth

which no art ever can be without. Abstract painting at its best—and the worst does not matter—imitates nature at nature's best; is "like" nature after all, for nature is brilliant and strong, and abstract painting convinces us of this even though it dispenses with the particulars with which we used to be fascinated and of which we were quite properly fond.

A world entirely without art would be worse than invisible, inaudible, ineffable, and intangible. It would be a world without temporal dimension, it would be a world that human minds could not remember. Human memory is unique in its capacity not only to recall but also to utilize the past, and to apply it; and better still, to re-create it so that it becomes a part of the present moment, which is more like eternity than anything else we shall ever experience. Human memory is nothing less than the origin of human art.

"The Greeks fabled not unwisely," said Sir Thomas Browne, "in making Memory the mother of the Muses." The memory of man is indeed a wonderful thing, and his richest possession. Not only is it the source of all our arts, it is their record too, stored in the mind of the beholder, the listener. Plato even asked us to conceive "in the mind of man a block of wax, the gift of Memory, and when we wish to remember anything which we have seen, or heard, or thought in our own minds, we hold the wax to the perceptions and thoughts, and in that material receive the impression of them as from the seal of a ring; and we remember and know what is imprinted as long as the image lasts." An artist whose poems or pictures or musical ideas have great power is certainly, we feel, the possessor of a memory that is always at his command, bringing to him at any moment whatever detail he needs, and reminding him too of the knowledge he has, and never forgets, of the way the world is put together, so that he does not misrepresent things as they are. The human race itself can be said to be such an artist, for it has its myths which it keeps alive, its stories that are "so true," someone has said, "that they couldn't have happened." There is such a thing as folk memory, the mother perhaps of all our thoughts and feelings, and the guardian of such wisdom as we have.

A story that cannot be remembered, a song that fades out of the mind, a hero whose name escapes us, a sentence we thought we would never forget but somehow do—such works of art must be defective at the core. But there are others that we could not forget if we tried, and it is those we live with in the company of friends who remember them too. Perhaps the final justification of art is the two-fold pleasure it gives: the pleasure of remembering great and beautiful things that we cannot lose, and the pleasure of sharing them with others who possess them in the same fashion.

There is a limited number of such things, of these greatest of human works of art; by definition there can be no superfluous masterpieces. The ones we have are numerous after all, and no single person can claim to have done justice to every one of them, or can claim to know what further ones are still unborn, Mnemosyne, goddess of Memory and Mother of the Muses, will have the deciding vote as to which ones, now or in the future, will survive the ravages of time.

Part Six. Art

The outlines in the twelve sections of Part Six are concerned with mankind's creation, experience, and evaluation of works made primarily for aesthetic enjoyment and contemplation. The arts of making things primarily for practical use are treated in Part Seven, on technology.

Division I. **Art in General**

The outlines in the three sections of Division I treat the theory and classification of the arts; the experience and criticism of works of art; and the nonaesthetic contexts of art.

Section 611. **Theory and Classification of the Arts**

A. The philosophy of art

  1. Diverse conceptions of the scope of art

  2. Diverse theories concerning the nature, functions, and effects of art: mimetic theories, expressive theories, formalist theories, pragmatic theories

  3. The making of works of art: the creative process

B. Classification of the arts

  1. Major distinctions among the kinds of art

    a. By reference to the intention of the maker or the recipient of the work of art: useful art, fine art, arts that are both useful and fine

    b. By reference to the manipulation of physical matter: the production of artistic works that are physical objects

    c. By reference to performers as interpreters or creators of works of art

    d. By reference to the use of notational devices; *e.g.,* literature, music, dance

  2. Other distinctions among the kinds of art; *e.g.,* space and time arts, primary and auxiliary arts

  3. The characterization of works of art by reference to the cultural or social circumstances of their production or the extent and character of their audience: the primitive, folk, and popular arts

  4. Style in the arts

    a. The nature of style

    b. The varieties of style; *e.g.,* personal, school, ethnic, regional, and period styles

    c. The dynamics of style: the historical development, diffusion, change, and duration of style in the arts

---

Suggested reading in the *Encyclopædia Britannica:*

MACROPAEDIA: Major articles dealing with the theory and classification of the arts

Arts, Classification of the
Arts, Style in the
Philosophies of the Branches of Knowledge

MICROPAEDIA: Selected entries of reference information

| art | folk art | mimesis | race, milieu, and |
| fine art | inspiration | popular art | moment |

INDEX: See entries under all of the terms above

Section 612.   Experience and Criticism of Works of Art; the Nonaesthetic Contexts of Art

A. The aesthetic experience: the apprehension, interpretation, and appreciation of works of art

  1. Influences affecting the apprehension of works of art: individual temperament, social and cultural conditioning, acquired attitudes and values

  2. The interpretation of works of art

    a. Meaning in art

    b. Symbol and myth in the arts
       [see Division II, below]

  3. The appreciation of works of art

  4. Special problems of appreciation and apprehension

    a. In the sphere of literature
       [see 621]

    b. In the sphere of the theatrical arts
       [see 622, 623, and 625]

    c. In the sphere of music
       [see 624]

    d. In the sphere of the visual arts
       [see 626, 627, 628, and 629]

B. The criticism of works of art

  1. Diverse criteria of evaluation: aesthetic criteria; criteria related to the union of form and content; criteria related to meaning; criteria related to social, moral, or religious significance; criteria related to technique; criteria related to the intention of the artist

  2. The practice of criticism

    a. The functions of the critic in relation to the artist, to his work, and to its public reception

    b. Critical methods: analytical, interpretative, and descriptive types of criticism

    c. Critical styles: journalistic criticism, scholarly criticism, annotative and referential criticism

    d. Critical approaches to the arts

    e. Factors affecting the excellence of criticism

C. Scholarship in the arts

  1. Resources and methods of scholarship in the field of the arts

  2. The relation of scholarship in the arts to other humanistic disciplines; *e.g.*, to linguistic studies, to history, to archaeology

D. The interaction of the arts with social, economic, and cultural institutions

  1. Social uses of art
     [see 521.D.5.]

  2. Social control of art: censorship and related forms of regulation

3. The arts and religion
   [see 811.E.1.]

4. Technology, science, and the arts
   [see 711.B.4.]

5. The arts in education: aesthetic education

E. The economics of art

1. Factors affecting the economic value of a work of art

2. Systems of financing artistic activities

3. The art market

4. Remuneration of artists and protection of their rights

5. Fraudulence in the arts: forgery, piracy, plagiarism

F. The training and work of the artist

1. The preparation of the artist: methods of training

2. Art as a vocation: conditions of work in the arts

3. Professionalism and amateurism in the arts

G. The preservation and dissemination of works of art

1. The role of institutions: libraries and archives; museums and galleries; producing associations—the preservation of works of art by performance

2. The role of writing and notation

3. The role of industry and commerce

4. The role of mechanical and electronic media

5. The role of oral tradition

6. The role of imitative tradition

7. The role of fairs, festivals, exhibitions, expositions, and related phenomena

---

Suggested reading in the *Encyclopædia Britannica:*

MACROPAEDIA: Major articles dealing with the experience and criticism of works of art; the nonaesthetic contexts of art

    Art Conservation and Restoration
    Arts, Criticism of the
    Arts, Practice and Profession of the
    Libraries
    Museums

MICROPAEDIA: Selected entries of reference information

General subjects

Actors Studio	copyright	Public Works of	Treasury Section
antique	Degenerate Art	Art Project	of Painting and
Armory Show	forgery	Royal Academy of	Sculpture
art conservation	library	Dramatic Art	Universal
art criticism	little magazine	Salon	Copyright
art history	MacDowell Colony	Salon des	Convention
Beaux-Arts,	maniera	Indépendants	WPA Federal Art
École des	Mbari Mbayo Club	Stanislavsky	Project
Berne Convention	museum	method	World Intellectual
censorship	propagandistic art	Treasury Relief Art	Property
		Project	Organization

Biographies

Baumgarten, Alexander Gottlieb	Fenollosa, Ernest F.	Ruskin, John	Vasari, Giorgio
Cotton, Sir Robert Bruce, 1st Baronet	Fry, Roger	Santayana, George	Winckelmann, Johann
	Read, Sir Herbert	Thou, Jacques-Auguste de	
	Rossetti, William		

INDEX: See entries under all of the terms above

Section 613.   Characteristics of the Arts in Particular Cultures

A. Arts of the Stone Age peoples

B. Arts of the Western tradition

    1. In antiquity: the arts of ancient Egypt and the Near East, ancient Greek and Hellenistic arts, ancient Roman and Early Christian arts

    2. Arts of the Middle Ages

    3. Arts from the Renaissance to the present in Europe and America

C. Arts of Asian peoples

    1. In the Far East: China, Japan, Korea

    2. In Central Asia: Turkey, Afghanistan, Turkistan, Mongolia, and Siberia; Tibet and other Himalayan countries; the arts of the nomadic peoples

    3. In South Asia: India, Sri Lanka, Kashmir, Pakistan, Bangladesh

    4. In Southeast Asia: Burma, Cambodia, Indonesia, Malaysia, Thailand, Vietnam, the Philippines

D. Arts of the Middle East and of the Islāmic peoples

    1. Arts of the Jewish peoples

    2. Arts of North Africa and of the Arab world

E. Arts of the African peoples

    1. Arts of Sudanic cultures

    2. Arts of Central African cultures

    3. Arts of East African cultures

    4. Arts of South African cultures

    5. Arts of West African cultures

F. Arts of the Oceanian peoples

    1. Arts of Melanesia

    2. Arts of Micronesia

    3. Arts of Polynesia

    4. Arts of the Australian aboriginal peoples

G. Arts of the American Indian peoples

    1. Arts of the Eskimo and North American Indian peoples

    2. Arts of Meso-American peoples

    3. Arts of South American peoples

H. Primitive, folk, and popular arts
[see also 611.B.3.]

Suggested reading in the *Encyclopædia Britannica:*

MACROPAEDIA: Major articles dealing with the characteristics of the arts in particular cultures; historical development of the arts

African Arts	East Asian Arts	Islāmic Arts	South Asian Arts
American	Egyptian Arts	Oceanic Arts	Southeast
Indians	and Architecture,	Popular Arts	Asian Arts
Central Asian	Ancient	Prehistoric Peoples	
Arts	Folk Arts	and Cultures	

MICROPAEDIA: Selected entries of reference information

arts in particular	Baroque period	Impressionism	Régence style
cultures:	Bohemian school	Jacobean age	Regency style
African arts	Byzantine art	Louis XIII style	Renaissance art
Central Asian arts	Carolingian art	Louis XIV style	Rococo art
East Asian arts	Classicism and	Louis XV style	Romanesque art
Egyptian art	Neoclassicism	Louis XVI style	Romanticism
Islāmic arts	Constructivism	Mannerism	Stijl, de
Oceanic arts	Cubism	Merovingian art	Stuart style
Paleolithic Period	Dada	minimalism	Surrealism
South Asian arts	Early Christian art	modern art	Symbolist
Southeast Asian	Early	Mozarabic art	movement
arts	Netherlandish art	naïve art	Visigothic art
historical periods,	Empire style	Naturalism	
styles, schools, and	Expressionism	Novembergruppe	
movements:	formalism	Op art	
Aestheticism	Futurism	Ottonian art	
Anglo-Saxon art	Georgian style	Pop art	
Art Deco	Gothic art	Queen Anne style	
Art Nouveau	Henry IV style	Realism	

INDEX: See entries under all of the terms above

Division II.	**The Particular Arts**

[For Part Six headnote see page 221.]

Division I deals generally with the theory and classification of the arts, the experience and criticism of works of art, and the interaction of the arts with social, cultural, and economic institutions.

The outlines in the nine sections of Division II treat the particular arts: literature; theatre; motion pictures; music; dance; architecture, garden and landscape design, and urban design; sculpture; drawing, painting, printmaking, and photography; and the arts of decoration and functional design.

Section 621.	**Literature**

A. The art of literature

1. The nature and scope of literature: the distinction between literature and other forms of writing

2. Literary composition

3. The content of literature: its subject matter

    4. Literature and its audience

    5. The integration of literature with other arts

    6. Literary genres: diverse systems of classifying literary works

    7. Writings on literature: theoretical treatises, scholarly research and writing, critical writing

B. Techniques of literature

    1. Rhetoric: the art of discourse

        a. Elements of rhetoric: figures of speech; *e.g.*, metaphor, simile, personification, hyperbole, allegory, parallelism

        b. The relation of rhetoric to grammar and syntax, to literary diction and style, and to prosody

    2. Prosody: the manipulation of the elements of language that contribute to acoustic and rhythmic effects in literature

        a. Elements of prosody

            i. Rhythmic elements; *e.g.*, accent, beat, cadence, the foot, the stanza, metre

            ii. Acoustic elements; *e.g.*, rhyme, assonance, alliteration

        b. Prosodic style: the uses of prosody in verse, prose, drama, and oratory

C. Kinds of literary composition

    1. Poetry: distinctions between poetry and prose

    2. Narrative imaginative literature

        a. Epic; *e.g.*, the "literary" epic, the beast epic, the mock epic, the romantic epic

        b. Saga: the king's sagas, legendary sagas, the sagas of Icelanders, and related forms

        c. Romance: the romance of love, chivalry, and adventure; *e.g.*, Arthurian romance, the pastoral romance, the Gothic romance, the historical romance

        d. The novel

        e. The short story and its antecedents; *e.g.*, the tale, the sketch

        f. Fable, parable, allegory, and related forms

        g. Ballad, lay, idyll

    3. Dramatic or theatrical literature

        a. Tragedy

        b. Comedy

        c. Tragicomedy

        d. Farce and related forms

        e. Melodrama

        f. Religious drama and ritual

        g. Radio, motion-picture, and television scripts

    4. Lyric literature

        a. Music-based lyrics; *e.g.*, ballad, hymn, madrigal

        b. Language-based lyrics; *e.g.*, sonnet, ode, elegy, pastoral

    5. Satiric literature: satire, parody, lampoon

    6. Nonfictional prose literature

        a. The essay

        b. History as literature

        c. Criticism as literature

        d. Doctrinal and religious literature

        e. Philosophical literature

        f. Political literature

        g. Polemical literature

    h. Scientific literature

    i. Reportage: journalism

    j. Aphorism, epigram, adage, maxim, and related short forms

    k. The dialogue: philosophical and literary dialogues

    l. Travel literature

    m. Epistolary literature: the letter as literature

    n. The oration, the speech, and related forms

    o. Biographical and autobiographical literature; *e.g.*, character sketch, critical biography, popular biography, interpretive biography, letter, diary, journal, memoir

  7. Children's literature

  8. Primitive, folk, and popular literature
[see 613]

D. The history of literature

  1. Literature of Western peoples

  2. Literatures of non-Western peoples
[see 613]

Suggested reading in the *Encyclopædia Britannica:*

MACROPAEDIA: Major articles and biographies dealing with literature

General subjects

African Arts	Dutch Literature	Latin-American	Russian Literature
American Indians	English Literature	Literature	Scandinavian
American	French Literature	Latin Literature	Literature
Literature	German Literature	Literature, The	South Asian Arts
Australia and	Greek Literature	Art of	Southeast Asian
New Zealand,	Hebrew Literature	Literature, The	Arts
Literatures of	Homeric	History of	Spanish Literature
Belgian Literature	Epics, The	Western	Yiddish Literature
Canadian	Hungarian	Oceanic Arts	Yugoslav
Literature	Literature	Polish Literature	Literature
Celtic Literature	Islāmic Arts	Popular Arts	
Central Asian Arts	Italian Literature	Portuguese	
Chinese Literature	Japanese Literature	Literature	
Czechoslovak	Korean Literature	Rhetoric	
Literature			

Biographies

Cervantes	Dostoyevsky	Johnson, Samuel	Shakespeare
Chaucer	Goethe	Milton	Tolstoy
Dante	Greek Dramatists,	Molière	Virgil
Dickens	The Classical	Montaigne	Voltaire

MICROPAEDIA: Selected entries of reference information

General subjects

dramatic literature:	comedy	humours,	revenge tragedy
Absurd, Theatre	dialogue	comedy of	Senecan tragedy
of the	domestic tragedy	intrigue,	sentimental
anagnorisis	dramatic literature	comedy of	comedy
catharsis	fabula Atellana	manners,	slapstick
chronicle play	fabula palliata	comedy of	sotie
climax	farce	melodrama	tragedy
cloak and sword	hamartia	New Comedy	tragicomedy
drama	Hocktide play	Old Comedy	unities
comédie	hubris	prologue and	Wakefield plays
larmoyante		epilogue	

well-made play
York plays
elements of prosody:
  accent
  alliteration
  anapest
  assonance
  caesura
  cynghanedd
  dactyl
  euphony and
    cacophony
  foot
  hexameter
  iamb
  metre
  pentameter
  prosody
  refrain
  rhyme
  rhythm
  spondee
  sprung rhythm
  stanza
  trochee
elements of rhetoric:
  conceit
  hyperbole
  metaphor
  metonymy
  parallelism
  personification
  rhetoric
  simile
epics:
  beast epic
  bylina
  chanson de geste
  cycle
  epic
  epyllion
  Heike monogatari
  Heldenlieder
  heroic poetry
  mock-epic
  skaldic poetry
fable, parable,
  allegory, and
  related forms:
  allegory
  bestiary
  dream allegory
  fable
  parable
  proverb
  riddle
folk literature and
  folklore:
  ballad revival

dilemma tale
fairy tale
folklore
gaucho literature
good-night
legend
praise song
Raven cycle
romancero
tall tale
trickster tale
literary criticism:
  affective fallacy
  Cambridge critics
  Chicago critic
  Formalism
  Freudian criticism
  literary criticism
  mimesis
  New Criticism
  New Humanism
  organic unity
  race, milieu, and
    moment
  sublime
literary devices:
  anachronism
  anaphora
  consciousness,
    stream of
  flashback
  in medias res
  interior monologue
  irony
  malapropism
  palindrome
  paradox
  pathetic fallacy
  plot
literary groups and
  schools:
  Acmeist
  arcádia
  Arzamas society
  Black Mountain
    poet
  Bloomsbury group
  Cavalier poet
  cénacle
  Confederation
    group
  crepuscolarismo
  Decadent
  fleshly school of
    poetry
  Göttinger Hain
  graveyard school
  Gruppe 47
  Hartford wit

Heidelberg
  Romantics
Imagist
Jena Romantics
Kailyard school
Knickerbocker
  school
Lost Generation
makar
Metaphysical poet
Montreal group
neōteros
'98, Generation of
Northeastern
  school
Parnassian
Philosophe
rhetoriqueur
Sicilian school
University wit
lyric poetry:
  alcaic
  alexandrine
  alliterative verse
  alphabet rhyme
  blank verse
  bouts-rimés
  Breton lay
  broadside ballad
  clerihew
  couplet
  cywydd
  dithyramb
  doggerel
  dramatic
    monologue
  eclogue
  elegy
  epigram
  epinicion
  epithalamium
  fabliau
  Fescennine verse
  flyting
  free verse
  fu
  haiku
  ghazal
  gnomic poetry
  Horatian ode
  idyll
  jōruri
  Klephtic ballad
  lauda
  light verse
  limerick
  lyric
  macaronic
  muwashshah

nonsense verse
nursery rhyme
ode
ottava rima
pattern poetry
Pindaric ode
poetry
praise song
rhyme royal
sestina
sonnet
Spenserian stanza
terza rima
triolet
vers de société
vers libre
villanelle
waka
yüeh-fu
movements and
  periods:
  American
    Renaissance
  Arabic literary
    renaissance
  Augustan Age
  Beat movement
  Ciceronian period
  Creacionismo
  decadentismo
  Elizabethan
    literature
  Gaelic revival
  Gilded Age
  Golden Age
  Harlem
    Renaissance
  Hermeticism
  Imaginism
  Irish literary
    renaissance
  Midwestern
    Regionalism
  moderne
  gennembrud, det
  Modernismo
  Negritude
  Restoration
    literature
  scapigliatura
  Scottish
    renaissance
  Socialist Realism
  Sturm und Drang
  Swedish
    Enlightenment
  Transcendentalism
  Ultraísmo
  Unanimisme

verismo
Victorian literature
Young Germany
Young Poland
  movement
national literatures:
  African arts
  ´American
    literature
  Anglo-Norman
    literature
  Arabic literature
  Armenian
    literature
  Australian
    literature
  Belgian literature
  Breton literature
  Bulgarian literature
  Burmese literature
  Canadian literature
  Caribbean
    literature
  Celtic literature
  Central Asian arts
  Chinese literature
  Coptic literature
  Czechoslovak
    literature
  Danish literature
  Dutch literature
  English literature
  Estonian literature
  Ethiopian
    literature
  Finnish literature
  French literature
  Georgian literature
  German literature
  Greek literature
  Hebrew literature
  Hungarian
    literature
  Icelandic literature
  Indian literature
  Indonesian
    literatures
  Irish literature
  Italian literature
  Japanese literature
  Korean literature
  Latin literature
  Latin-American
    literature
  Latvian literature
  Lithuanian
    literature
  New Zealand
    literature

Norwegian
  literature
Oceanic arts
Polish literature
Portuguese
  literature
Provençal
  literature
Romanian
  literature
Russian literature
Sanskrit literature
Scandinavian
  literature
Scottish literature
South African
  literature
Southeast Asian
  arts
Spanish literature
Swahili literature
Swedish literature
Swiss literature
Syriac literature
Thai literature
Tibetan literature
Turkish literature
Ukrainian
  literature
Urdu literature
Walloon literature
Welsh literature
Yiddish literature
Yugoslav literature
popular literature:
  best-seller
  detective story
  hard-boiled fiction
  mystery story
  Onitsha market
    literature
  science fiction
  work song
prose forms:
  antinovel
  apology
  Bildungsroman
  biography
  confession
  diary
  epistolary novel
  essay
  frame story
  Gothic novel
  historical novel
  Künstlerroman
  Indianista novel
  literary sketch
  manners, novel of

maqāmah
memoir
nonfiction novel
novel
novella
picaresque novel
problem novel
psychological novel
roman à clef
roman-fleuve
sentimental novel
short story
tradición
romances:
  Alexander
    romance
  Arthurian legend
  Hellenistic
    romance
  rímur
  romance
*sagas and related
  heroic prose:*
  Edda
  Fenian cycle
  fornaldar saga
  heroic prose
  Icelanders' sagas
  lygi sagas
  Ossianic ballads
  saga
  scél
  Ulster cycle
satire:
  burlesque
  fool's literature
  Juvenalian satire
  parody
  pasquinade
  satire
  travesty
themes and types:
  ancients and
    moderns
  archetype
  Beatrice
  Bluebeard
  courtly love
  Deirdre
  Dietrich von Bern
  Don Juan
  Excalibur
  Faust
  Galahad
  Grail
  Guinevere
  Hagan
  hero
  Isengrim

Lancelot
Lohengrin
Mephistopheles
Merlin
Morgan le Fay
noble savage
Perceval
poèt maudit
Round Table
superfluous man
type name
other:
  anthology
  bard
  black humour
  Bluestocking
  cancioneiro
  cànkam literature
  Chandos portrait
  chapbook
  character writer
  children's
    literature
  classical literature
  conceptismo
  costumbrismo
  culteranismo
  dolce stil nuovo
  emblem book
  fellow traveller
  five-year-plan
    literature
  frontier humour
  goliard
  Hindi literature
  jongleur
  journalism
  literature
  local colour
  Marinism
  pastoral literature
  poet laureate
  préciosité
  rāwī
  saudade
  Spielmann
  troubadour
  trouvère
  Utopian literature
  Weltschmerz
  yellow journalism
  Zhdanovshchina

Biographies

African writers:
Achebe, Chinua
Beti, Mongo
Bosman, Herman
Charles
Boudjedra, Rachid
Clark, John Pepper
Cordeiro da Matta,
Joaquim Dias
Dib, Mohammed
Ekwensi, Cyprian
Ferreira, Manuel
Kezilahabi,
Euphrase
Khatibi,
Abdelkebir
Laye, Camara
Mutswairo,
Solomon M.
Ngugi, James
Okara, Gabriel
Ousmane,
Sembène
Oyono, Ferdinand
Leopold
Rabéarivelo,
Jean-Joseph
Soromenho,
Fernando
Monteiro de
Castro
Soyinka, Wole
Tutuola, Amos
Yacine, Kateb

American writers:
Adams, Henry
Alger, Horatio
Anderson,
Sherwood
Asch, Sholem
Baldwin, James
Bellow, Saul
Berryman, John
Bradstreet, Anne
Bryant, William
Cullen
Burroughs,
William
Caldwell, Erskine
Capote, Truman
Cather, Willa
Chapman,
John Jay
Cooper, James
Fenimore
Crane, Hart
Crane, Stephen
Dickinson, Emily
Donnelly, Ignatius

Dos Passos, John
Dreiser, Theodore
Emerson, Ralph
Waldo
Faulkner, William
Fitzgerald, F. Scott
Frost, Robert
Green, Julien
Harte, Bret
Hawthorne,
Nathaniel
Hearn, Lafcadio
Hecht, Ben
Hemingway,
Ernest
Henry, O.
Hughes, Langston
Inge, William
Irving, Washington
James, Henry
Lanier, Sidney
Lewis, Sinclair
Locke, Alain
London, Jack
Longfellow, Henry
Wadsworth
Lowell, Robert, Jr.
Mailer, Norman
Melville, Herman
Miller, Arthur
Miller, Henry
Nabokov, Vladimir
Nevins, Allan
O'Neill, Eugene
Parker, Dorothy
Poe, Edgar Allan
Pound, Ezra
Salinger, J.D.
Sandburg, Carl
Saroyan, William
Shepard, Sam
Sherwood,
Robert E.
Simms, William
Gilmore
Sinclair, Upton
Stein, Gertrude
Steinbeck, John
Stevens, Wallace
Stowe, Harriet
Beecher
Thoreau, Henry
David
Thurber, James
Twain, Mark
Van Doren, Mark
Vidal, Gore
Warren, Robert
Penn

Whitman, Walt
Whittier, John
Greenleaf
Wiesel, Elie
Williams,
Tennessee
Wolfe, Thomas
Wright, Richard

Australian writers:
Boldrewood, Rolf
Clarke, Marcus
FitzGerald, Robert
David
Lawson, Henry
McAuley, James
Phillip
Paterson, A.B.
Richardson, Henry
Handel
Stewart, Douglas
White, Patrick

*British and Irish
writers:*
Addison, Joseph
Akenside, Mark
Arden, John
Auden, W.H.
Austen, Jane
Beaumont, Francis
Behan, Brendan
Belloc, Hilaire
Bennett, Arnold
Blake, William
Boswell, James
Brontë, Charlotte
Brontë, Emily
Browne, Sir
Thomas
Browning,
Elizabeth Barrett
Browning, Robert
Bunyan, John
Burns, Robert
Butler, Samuel
Byron, George
Gordon Byron,
6th Baron
Carlyle, Thomas
Carroll, Lewis
Cary, Joyce
Chatterton,
Thomas
Chaucer, Geoffrey
Chesterton, G.K.
Coleridge, Samuel
Taylor
Collins, William
Congreve, William
Conrad, Joseph

Cowper, William
Crabbe, George
Crichton, James
De Quincey,
Thomas
Defoe, Daniel
Dickens, Charles
Donne, John
Douglas, Gawin
Dowson, Ernest
Dryden, John
Dunbar, William
Durrell, Lawrence
Edgeworth, Maria
Eliot, George
Eliot, T.S.
Evelyn, John
Farquhar, George
Fielding, Henry
Fletcher, John
Forster, E.M.
Foxe, John
Galsworthy, John
Gascoigne, George
Gaskell, Elizabeth
Cleghorn
Gay, John
Glyn, Elinor
Graves, Robert
Greene, Graham
Greene, Robert
Hardy, Thomas
Hazlitt, William
Herrick, Robert
Heywood, John
Hopkins, Gerard
Manley
Housman, A.E.
Hudson, W.H.
Hunt, Leigh
Isherwood,
Christopher
Johnson, Samuel
Jonson, Ben
Joyce, James
Keats, John
Kipling, Rudyard
Kyd, Thomas
Lawrence, D.H.
Lewis, Wyndham
Lyndsay, Sir David
Lytton of
Knebworth,
Edward
George Earle
Bulwer-Lytton,
1st Baron
Mandeville, Sir
John

Marlowe,
  Christopher
Meredith, George
Middleton,
  Thomas
Milton, John
Moore, George
O'Casey, Sean
Orwell, George
Otway, Thomas
Pinter, Harold
Pope, Alexander
Ramsay, Allan
Richardson,
  Samuel
Rossetti, Dante
  Gabriel
Ruskin, John
Scott, Sir Walter,
  1st Baronet
Shakespeare,
  William
Shaw, George
  Bernard
Shelley, Percy
  Bysshe
Sheridan, Richard
  Brinsley
Sidney, Sir Philip
Skelton, John
Smollett, Tobias
Southey, Robert
Spenser, Edmund
Steele, Sir Richard
Sterne, Laurence
Stevenson, Robert
  Louis
Swift, Jonathan
Swinburne,
  Algernon Charles
Synge, John
  Millington
Tennyson, Alfred
  Tennyson,
  1st Baron
Thackeray,
  William
  Makepeace
Thomas, Dylan
Trollope, Anthony
Udall, Nicholas
Walpole, Horace,
  4th earl of Orford
Waugh, Evelyn
Wells, H.G.
Wilde, Oscar
Wither, George
Woolf, Virginia
Wordsworth,
  William

Yeats, William
  Butler
Canadian writers:
Callaghan, Morley
Davies, Robertson
de la Roche, Mazo
Grove, Frederick
  Philip
Hémon, Louis
Johnson, Pauline
Lampman,
  Archibald
Layton, Irving
Leacock, Stephen
MacLennan, Hugh
Moodie, Susanna
  Strickland
Pratt, E.J.
Richardson, John
Richler, Mordecai
Roberts, Sir
  Charles George
  Douglas
Scott, Duncan
  Campbell
Scott, F.R.
Service, Robert W.
Smith, A.J.M.
Early Greek and
Roman writers:
Aeschylus
Aristophanes
Bacchylides
Catullus, Gaius
  Valerius
Cicero, Marcus
  Tullius
Ennius, Quintus
Euripides
Hesiod
Homer
Horace
Juvenal
Lucan
Lucian
Lucretius
Martial
Menander
Ovid
Petronius Arbiter,
  Gaius
Pindar
Plautus
Pliny the Elder
Pliny the Younger
Pollio, Gaius
  Asinius
Propertius, Sextus
Sappho

Seneca, Lucius
  Annaeus
Sophocles
Statius
Suetonius
Tacitus
Terence
Theocritus
Tibullus, Albius
Varro, Marcus
  Terentius
Virgil
Xenophon
East Asian writers:
Akutagawa
  Ryūnosuke
Bashō
Buson
Cheng Chen-to
Chikamatsu
  Monzaemon
Chou Tso-jen
Ding Ling
Fujiwara Sadaie
Futabatei Shimei
Ihara Saikaku
Kakinomoto
  Hitomaro
Kawabata
  Yasunari
Kuo Mo-jo
Lao She
Li Po
Lu Hsün
Mao Dun
Mori Ōgai
Mishima Yukio
Murasaki Shikibu
Natsume Sōseki
Ōe Kenzaburō
Ou-yang Hsiu
Shiga Naoya
Tu Fu
Wang An-shih
Zeami Motokiyo
French writers:
Adamov, Arthur
Anouilh, Jean
Apollinaire,
  Guillaume
Artaud, Antonin
Balzac, Honoré de
Baudelaire, Charles
Beauvoir,
  Simone de
Beckett, Samuel
Camus, Albert
Chateaubriand,
  François-Auguste-
  René, vicomte de

Chenier, André de
Chrétien de Troyes
Claudel, Paul
Cocteau, Jean
Colette
Constant,
  Benjamin
Corneille, Pierre
Diderot, Denis
Dumas, Alexandre
Duras, Marguerite
Flaubert, Gustave
France, Anatole
Gautier, Théophile
Genet, Jean
Gide, André
Giraudoux, Jean
Hugo, Victor
Huysmans,
  Joris-Karl
Ionesco, Eugène
Jarry, Alfred
La Fontaine,
  Jean de
Laforgue, Jules
Lamartine,
  Alphonse de
Machaut,
  Guillaume de
Mallarmé,
  Stéphane
Marivaux, Pierre
Marot, Clément
Maupassant,
  Guy de
Mauriac, François
Mérimée, Prosper
Mistral, Frederic
Molière
Nerval, Gérard de
Proust, Marcel
Rabelais, François
Racine, Jean
Rimbaud, Arthur
Sade, Marquis de
Sand, George
Sartre, Jean-Paul
Scarron, Paul
Staël-Holstein,
  Anne-Louise-
  Germaine
  Necker,
  baronne de
Stendhal
Valéry, Paul
Verlaine, Paul
Vigny,
  Alfred-Victor,
  comte de
Villon, François

Voltaire
Zola, Émile
German writers:
Alexis, Willibald
Arndt, Ernst
Moritz
Arnim,
Bettina von
Böll, Heinrich
Brecht, Bertolt
Broch, Hermann
Büchner, Georg
Chamisso,
Adelbert von
Dürrenmatt,
Friedrich
Fontane, Theodor
Freiligrath,
Ferdinand
Freytag, Gustav
Frisch, Max
George, Stefan
Goethe, Johann
Wolfgang von
Görres, Joseph von
Gottfried von
Strassburg
Grass, Günter
Grillparzer, Franz
Grimm, Jacob
Ludwig Carl and
Wilhelm Carl
Grimmelshausen,
Hans Jacob
Christoph von
Haller,
Albrecht von
Hartmann
von Aue
Hauptmann,
Gerhart
Hebbel, Friedrich
Heine, Heinrich
Herder, Johann
Gottfried von
Hesse, Hermann
Hoffmann, E.T.A.
Hoffmannsthal,
Hugo von
Hölderlin,
Friedrich
Immermann, Karl
Leberecht
Jean Paul
Johnson, Uwe
Kafka, Franz
Kaiser, Georg
Kaschnitz, Marie
Luise
Keller, Gottfried

Kleist,
Heinrich von
Mann, Thomas
Meyer, Conrad
Ferdinand
Morgenstern,
Christian
Mörike, Eduard
Friedrich
Novalis
Opitz, Martin
Rilke, Rainer
Maria
Schiller,
Friedrich von
Schnitzler, Arthur
Sternheim, Carl
Stifter, Adalbert
Storm, Theodor
Woldsen
Sudermann,
Hermann
Tieck, Ludwig
Trakl, George
Walafrid Strabo
Walther von der
Vogelweide
Wedekind, Frank
Werfel, Franz
Wieland,
Christoph Martin
Wolfram von
Eschenbach
Zuckmayer, Carl
Zweig, Stefan
Hebrew writers:
Agnon, Shmuel
Yosef
Berdichevsky,
Micah Joseph
Bialik, Ḥayyim
Naḥman
Ḥisdai ibn Shaprut
ibn Ezra, Moses
Ibn Gabirol
Judah ha-Levi
Zunz, Leopold
Hungarian writers:
Ady, Endre
Arany, János
Eötvös, József
Báró
Kazinczy, Ferenc
Petöfi, Sándor
Indian writers:
Chatterjee, Bankim
Chandra
Harishchandra
Iqbāl, Sir
Muḥammad

Kālidāsa
Tagore,
Rabindranath
Tulsīdās
Italian writers:
Alfieri, Vittorio,
Conte
Amicis,
Edmondo De
Angiolieri, Cecco
Aretino, Pietro
Ariosto, Ludovico
Bacchelli, Riccardo
Bandello, Matteo
Basile,
Giambattista
Belli, Giuseppe
Gioacchino
Betti, Ugo
Boccaccio,
Giovanni
Boiardo, Matteo
María
Buzzati, Dino
Calvino, Italo
Campanella,
Tommaso
Carducci, Giosuè
Casa, Giovanni
Della
Castiglione,
Baldassare
Cavalcanti, Guido
Chiabrera, Grazia
D'Annunzio,
Gabriele
Dante Alighieri
Folengo, Teofilo
Foscolo, Ugo
Gadda, Carlo
Emilio
Giraldi,
Giambattista
Goldoni, Carlo
Gozzi, Carlo,
Conte
Leopardi,
Giacomo
Levi, Carlo
Machiavelli,
Niccolò
Maffei, Francesco
Scipione
Malaparte, Curzio
Manzoni,
Alessandro
Marinetti, Filippo
Tommaso
Marino,
Giambattista

Metastasio, Pietro
Montale, Eugenio
Moravia, Alberto
Parini, Giuseppe
Pascoli, Giovanni
Pavese, Cesare
Petrarch
Pirandello, Luigi
Politian
Pratolini, Vasco
Pulci, Luigi
Quasimodo,
Salvatore
Sannazzaro,
Jacopo
Silone, Ignazio
Svevo, Italo
Tasso, Torquato
Tassoni,
Alessandro
Ungaretti,
Giuseppe
Verga, Giovanni
Vittorini, Elio
Latin-American
writers:
Agustini, Delmira
Alegría, Ciro
Alencar, José de
Amado, Jorge
Asturias, Miguel
Angel
Azuela, Mariano
Bandeira, Manuel
Bello, Andrés
Benedetti, Mario
Bioy Casares,
Adolfo
Blest Gana,
Alberto
Borges, Jorge Luis
Cardenal, Ernesto
Carpentier, Alejo
Cruz, Sor Juana
Inés de la
Cunha, Euclides de
Darío, Rubén
Durão, José de
Santa Rita
Echeverría,
Esteban
Ercilla y Zúñiga,
Alonso de
Fernández de
Lizardi, José
Joaquín
Freyre, Gilberto de
Mello
Fuentes, Carlos
Gallegos, Rómulo

Gama, José
Basílio da
García Márquez,
Gabriel
Gonçalves Dias,
Antônio
Gonzaga, Thomaz
Antônio
Graça Aranha,
Jośe Pereira da
Guillén, Nicolas
Guimarães Rosa,
João
Güiraldes, Ricardo
Hernández, José
Herrera y Reissig,
Julio
Huidobro, Vicente
García
Ibarbourou,
Juana de
Icaza, Jorge
Isaacs, Jorge
Lins do Rego, José
López y Fuentes,
Gregorio
Lugones, Leopoldo
Lynch, Benito
Machado de Assis,
Joaquim María
Mallea, Eduardo
Mármol, José
Martí, José Julián
Matto de Turner,
Clorinda
Mera, Juan León
Mistral, Gabriela
Neruda, Pablo
Nervo, Amado
Olmedo, José
Joaquín
Onetti, Juan
Carlos
Palma, Ricardo
Paz, Octavio
Quiroga, Horacio
Ramos, Graciliano
Reyes, Alfonso
Riviera, José
Eustacio
Roa Bastos,
Augusto
Sabato, Ernesto
Sarmiento,
Domingo
Faustino
Silva, José
Asunción
Storni, Alfonsina
Torres Bodet,
Jaime

Vallejo, César
Vargas Llosa,
Mario
Vega, Garcilaso de
la: el Inca
Veríssimo, Enrico
Lopes
Zorrilla de San
Martín, Juan
Middle Eastern
writers:
Cevdet Paşa,
Ahmed
Ferdowsī
Gökalp, Ziya
Ḥāfeẓ
Ibn Baṭṭūṭah
Ibn Ḥazm
Jāḥiẓ, al-
Kemal, Namık
Maʿarrī, al-
Mutanabbī, al-
Omar Khayyam
Saʿdī
Taha Hussein
New Zealand writers:
Baxter, James K.
Mansfield,
Katherine
Sargeson, Frank
Sinclair, Keith
Portuguese writers:
Camões, Luís de
Castelo Branco,
Camilo
Deus, João de
Eça de Queirós,
José Maria de
Herculano
de Carvalho
e Araújo,
Alexandre
Quental, Antero
Tarquínio de
Sá de Miranda,
Francisco de
Vicente, Gil
Vieira, António
Scandinavian writers:
Almqvist, Carl
Jonas Love
Andersen, Hans
Christian
Asbjørnsen, Peter
Christen; and
Moe, Jørgen
Engebretsen
Bergman, Hjalmar
Fredrik Elgérus
Bjørnson,
Bjørnst-jerne
Martinius

Dinesen, Isak
Ewald, Johannes
Fröding, Gustaf
Hamsun, Knut
Holberg, Ludvig,
Friherre Holberg
Ibsen, Henrik
Jensen,
Johannes V.
Lagerkvist, Pär
Lagerlöf, Selma
Laxness, Halldór
Pontoppidan,
Henrik
Rydberg, Viktor
Snorri Sturluson
Strindberg, August
Undset, Sigrid
Wergeland, Henrik
Arnold
Slavic writers:
Akhmatova, Anna
Aksakov, Sergey
Timofeyevich
Andrić, Ivo
Babel, Isaak
Emmanuilovich
Bely, Andrey
Bezruč, Petr
Blok, Aleksandr
Aleksandrovich
Březina, Otakar
Bulgakov, Mikhail
Afanasyevich
Čapek, Karel
Chekhov, Anton
Dostoyevsky,
Fyodor
Ehrenburg, Ilya
Grigoryevich
Fredro, Aleksander
Gogol, Nikolay
Gorky, Maksim
Ilf, Ilya; and
Petrov, Yevgeny
Ivanov, Vsevolod
Vyacheslavovich
Jirásek, Alois
Katayev, Valentin
Khomyakov,
Aleksey
Stepanovich
Krleža, Miroslav
Kundera, Milan
Lermontov,
Mikhail
Lomonosov,
Mikhail
Vasilyevich
Mandelstam, Osip
Emilyevich

Mayakovsky,
Vladimir
Vladimirovich
Modrzewki,
Andrzej
Pasternak, Boris
Pilnyak, Boris
Potocki, Wacław
Pushkin,
Aleksandr
Rozanov, Vasily
Vasilyevich
Saltykov, Mikhail
Yevgrafovich,
Graf
Seifert, Jaroslav
Sienkiewicz,
Henryle
Sinyavsky, Andrey
Donatovich
Slowacki, Juliusz
Solzhenitsyn,
Aleksandr
Tikhonov, Nikolay
Semyonovich
Tolstoy, Leo
Tsvetayeva,
Marina Ivanovna
Turgenev, Ivan
Voznesensky,
Andrey
Andreyevich
Yesenin, Sergey
Aleksandrovich
Yevtushenko,
Yevgeny
Aleksandrovich
Zamyatin,
Yevgeny
Ivanovich
Spanish writers:
Alarcón y Ariza,
Pedro Antonio de
Aleixandre,
Vicente
Azorín
Baroja, Pío
Bécquer, Gustavo
Adolfo
Benavente y
Martínez, Jacinto
Blasco Ibáñez,
Vicente
Buero Vallejo,
Antonio
Calderón de la
Barca, Pedro
Cervantes
Saavedra,
Miguel de

INDEX: See entries under all of the terms above

Section 622. **Theatre**

A. The art of theatre

  1. The nature and origins of theatre as an art

  2. Functions of theatre and theatrical production; *e.g.*, theatre as social, moral, or religious expression; theatre as entertainment

  3. Problems of theatre and theatrical production

  4. Interrelation of theatrical performance and audience

  5. The arts of design in the theatre: staging and the design of stages, sets, lights, costumes, and makeup
[see C.2., below]

  6. Directing

  7. Acting

  8. The roles of other arts in the theatre: literature, music, dance, painting, and architecture
[see C., below]

B. Kinds and methods of theatrical production

  1. Diverse kinds of theatrical production

    a. Kinds defined by the nature of the production itself

      i. The traditional dramatic forms or genres; *e.g.*, tragedy, comedy
[for these forms as literature, see 621.C.3.]

      ii. Dramatic improvisation: commedia dell'arte and related forms

      iii. Mime and pantomime

      iv. Puppet, marionette, and shadow plays and related forms

      v. Nondramatic theatrical production
[see B.1.f., below]

b. Kinds defined by their special purpose or audience; *e.g.*, religious theatre, civic theatre, educational theatre, court theatre

c. Kinds defined by their system of production; *e.g.*, single-performance productions, repertory systems, stock companies, touring companies

d. Kinds defined by the controlling artist; *e.g.*, actor-dominated productions, dramatist-controlled productions, productions controlled by a nonperforming director

e. Kinds defined by their style: general aesthetic style; styles of particular countries, historical periods, and playwrights

f. Kinds defined by the lack of a unified dramatic structure

    i. Circuses and carnivals

    ii. Pageants, parades, and related forms

    iii. Popular entertainments: music hall, variety, and burlesque productions; nightclub shows; cabaret; musical comedy and revue

g. Kinds defined by the cultural character of their audience: primitive, folk, and popular theatre
[see 611.B.3.]

2. Methods of theatrical production

C. Elements of theatrical production

1. The production area: theatre buildings, stages, auditoriums

a. Theatre as place: kinds and uses of theatre buildings, stages, and auditoriums

b. The historical development of theatres in Western and non-Western cultures

2. Staging and stage design: the arrangement of words, dance, music, costumes, makeup, lighting, sound, and properties for theatrical effect

D. The history of theatre

1. Western theatre

2. Non-Western theatre
[see 613]

Suggested reading in the *Encyclopædia Britannica*:

MACROPAEDIA: Major articles dealing with the theatre

African Arts	Pageantry and	Theatre, The Art	Theatrical
American Indians	Spectacle	of the	Production
Central Asian Arts	Popular Arts	Theatre, The	
East Asian Arts	South Asian Arts	History of	
Folk Arts	Southeast Asian	Western	
Oceanic Arts	Arts		

MICROPAEDIA: Selected entries of reference information

General subjects

dramatic conventions and techniques:	directing	*movements and tendencies:*	*popular dramatic entertainment:*
agon	hanamichi	Absurd, Theatre	burlesque show
alienation effect	open stage	of the	cabaret
lazzo	proscenium	biomechanics	carnival
soliloquy	régisseur	Cruelty, Theatre of	circus
elements of theatrical production:	repertory theatre	environmental	conjuring
	skene	theatre	Fasching
acting	Stanislavsky	Fact, Theatre of	ice show
actor-manager	method	little theatre	masque
system	stock company	Living Newspaper	mime and
chorus	summer theatre	Open Theatre	pantomime
courtyard	theatre	theatricalism	minstrel show
theatre	theatre-in-the-round		music hall and
			variety

pageant
revue
shell game
son et lumière
vaudeville
Wild West show
*staging and stage
design:*
cyclorama
deus ex machina
ekkyklema
footlights
limelight
Linnebach lantern
mansion
multiple setting
pageant wagon
perspective scenery
scene shifting
sound effects
spotlight
stage design
stage machinery
trap
stock characters:
Brighella

Capitano
Columbine
Dottore
Guignol
Harlequin
Kasperle
Miles Gloriosus
Pantaloon
Pedrolino
Punch
Scaramouche
soubrette
zanni
*types of theatrical
production:*
afterpiece
auto sacramental
black theatre
bunraku
ching-hsi
Comédie-Française
Comédie-Italienne
commedia dell'arte
commedia erudita
drame bourgeois
droll

epic theatre
farce
Fastnachtsspiel
heroic tragedy
interlude
Jesuit drama
Kabuki theatre
Karagög
liturgical drama
ludi scaenici
melodrama
miracle play
morality play
mumming play
mystery play
Nō theatre
ombres chinoises
Passion play
sacra
rappresentazione
Satyr play
wayang
Yiddish drama
other:
benefit
performance

children's
company
choragus
civic theatre
claque
clown
East Asian arts
Enfants san Souci
Englische
Komödianten
improvisation
Islāmic arts
juggler
Misrule, Lord of
Oceanic arts
peep show
South Asian arts
Southeast Asian
arts
toy theatre
ventriloquism

Biographies

actors and actresses:
Ashcroft, Dame
Peggy
Barrymore, Lionel
Bernhardt, Sarah
Booth, Edwin
Cooper, Dame
Gladys
Duse, Eleonora
Gwyn, Nell
Irving, Sir Henry
Kean, Edmund
Kemble, John
Philip
Kendal, Dame
Margaret; and
William Hunter

Kortner, Fritz
Lenya, Lotte
Lunt, Alfred; and
Fontanne, Lynn
Mathews, Charles
Murdoch, James
Edward
Neuber, Caroline
Olivier, Laurence
Paxinou, Katina
Siddons, Sarah
Taylor, Laurette
Terry, Ellen
Worth, Irene
directors:
Barrault,
Jean-Louis
Burian, Emil

Craig, Edward
Gordon
Guthrie,
Tyrone
Littlewood,
Joan
Popov, Alexey
Dmitriyevich
Reinhardt, Max
Stanislavsky,
Konstantin
Zavadsky, Yury
Alexandrovich
producers:
Belasco, David
Meyerhold,
Vsevolod
Yemilyevich

Richardson, Tony
Shubert brothers
other:
Barnum, P.T.
Henslowe, Philip
Lupino family
Macready, William
Charles

INDEX: See entries under all of the terms above

Section 623.   Motion Pictures

A. The art of motion pictures

   1. The nature of motion-picture art: the question of the legitimacy of motion pictures as art, the classification of motion pictures

   2. The component arts of motion pictures

      a. The role of the writer of the script or screenplay
        [see 621.C.3.g.]

      b. Motion-picture acting: characteristics that distinguish it from acting in the theatre; *e.g.*, nonconsecutive filming

      c. The role of the director

      d. The role of the film editor

      e. The use of technology in the creative process: the camera, sound, animation, and other special effects

   3. Motion-picture production: scenic design, costumes and make-up, lighting, shooting, editing, film processing

B. The interrelation of other arts in motion pictures: literature, music, dance, painting and drawing, architecture

C. The nonaesthetic contexts of motion pictures

   1. The motion-picture industry

   2. Functions of motion pictures: their use as media of education and propaganda

   3. The study and appreciation of motion pictures

D. The history of motion pictures

Suggested reading in the *Encyclopædia Britannica*:

MACROPAEDIA: Major article dealing with motion pictures

   Motion Pictures

MICROPAEDIA: Selected entries of reference information

General subjects

animation	documentary film	musical film	street film
auteur theory	dubbing	New Wave	Technicolor
ciné-club	film festival	newsreel	3-D
cinéma vérité	horror film	reel	underground film
CinemaScope	montage	scenario	
Cinerama	motion picture	script	

Biographies

actors and actresses:	Pickford, Mary	Fellini, Federico	Rossellini, Roberto
Bergman, Ingrid	Strasberg, Lee	Godard, Jean-Luc	Sennett, Mack
Bogart, Humphrey	Sydow, Max von	Griffith, D.W.	Sternberg,
Brando, Marlon	Tracy, Spencer	Hitchcock, Sir	Josef von
Chaplin, Charlie	Welles, Orson	Alfred	Stroheim,
Garbo, Greta	*directors:*	Kazan, Elia	Erich von
Gielgud, Sir John	Anderson, Lindsay	Kurosawa Akira	Truffaut, François
Gish, Lillian	Antonioni,	Lubitsch, Ernst	Vertov, Dziga
Guinness, Sir Alec	Michelangelo	Malle, Louis	*producers:*
Hepburn,	Bergman, Ingmar	Ousmane,	de Mille, Cecil B.
Katharine	Bertolucci,	Sembène	Disney, Walt
Lloyd, Harold	Bernardo	Pabst, G.W.	Korda, Sir
March, Fredric	Buñuel, Luis	Pagnol, Marcel	Alexander
Mastroianni,	Cavalcanti, Alberto	Paul	*other:*
Marcello	Clair, René	Ray, Satyajit	Muybridge,
Mifune Toshiro	Dreyer, Carl	Renoir, Jean	Eadweard
Muni, Paul	Theodor	Resnais, Alain	Westmore family
Olivier, Laurence	Eisenstein, Sergey	Rohmer, Eric	

Section 624.   Music

    A. The art of music

        1. Diverse conceptions of music as an art

        2. Problems of musical meaning

        3. Problems of musical interpretation

        4. The relation of music to other human activities

        5. Writings about music

    B. The sources of musical sound

        1. The physical aspects of musical sound: tone, movement, pitch, timbre
           [see 128.E.6.]

        2. The human voice: techniques, styles, and historical developments of the art of singing in Western and non-Western cultures
           [see also 421.C.1. and 3.]

        3. Musical instruments: the history, technology, and technique of classes and specific types of instruments

           a. Idiophonic and membranophonic instruments: instruments that produce sound by means of percussion

           b. Aerophonic instruments: instruments that produce sound by the vibration of a column of air

           c. Chordophonic instruments: instruments that produce sound by the vibration of struck, plucked, or bowed strings

           d. Electrophonic instruments: instruments that produce sound by electrical, electromechanical, or electronic means; *e.g.*, electronic organs, tape recorders, synthesizers, computers

    C. The elements of music: their patterning and modes of organization in composition

        1. Pitch

           a. Interval: the difference in pitch between two tones

           b. Scale: a pattern of pitch relationships expressed as a series of intervals dividing an octave

           c. Tuning and temperament: the organization and modification of systems of pitch relationships

           d. Motive and theme

           e. Mode, melody type, tune family

         2. Duration (time)

           a. Pulse and metre

           b. Rhythm

           c. Tempo

        3. Timbre

        4. Harmony

        5. Counterpoint

        6. Texture: monophonic, homophonic, heterophonic, polyphonic

        7. Orchestration and instrumentation

        8. Musical forms and variations

    D. Musical notation

    E. Forms of musical composition

        1. Instrumental forms

           a. Sonata

           b. Symphony

c. Chamber music: music for small ensemble; *e.g.*, duet, trio, quartet, quintet

d. Concerto

e. Variation forms; *e.g.*, chaconne, passacaglia, variation set

f. Fugue

g. Forms for electrophonic instruments: *e.g.*, tape music, computer music

2. Vocal forms

   a. Solo vocal forms

      i. Liturgical chant

      ii. Secular song; *e.g.*, chanson, canzone

      iii. "Art song"; *e.g.*, lied, concert aria

   b. Choral forms

      i. Sacred choral forms; *e.g.*, mass, motet, anthem, cantata, oratorio

      ii. Secular choral forms; *e.g.*, secular cantata, symphonic choral music

      iii. Occasional choral music: choral forms composed to commemorate an occasion of state; *e.g.*, a royal marriage

   c. Vocal forms for solo or choral performance

      i. Madrigal

      ii. Lied, chanson, glee

F. Musical performance

G. Music for the theatre
[see 622.A.8.]

1. General considerations about theatrical music; *e.g.*, its nature and elements, its role as distinct from the role of concert music, its relation to other elements of theatre

2. Types of theatrical music

   a. Opera

   b. Music for theatrical dance; *e.g.*, ballet, modern dance
   [see 625]

   c. Music theatre; *e.g.*, musical comedy, operetta, zarzuela, Nō theatre
   [see 622.B.1.]

   d. Incidental and background music; *e.g.*, for the theatre, for motion pictures and television

H. Jazz

1. General considerations about jazz: its differentiation from and relation to folk music, popular music, and "art" music; its emphasis on the performer as creator; the importance of improvisation; its reflection of social and cultural forces

2. Development of jazz styles

I. Primitive, folk, and popular music
[see 613]

J. Recording and reproduction of music

1. Types of music reproduction: mechanical, acoustical, electrical
[see 735.F.]

2. Techniques of music recording: the role of the producer

3. Effects of music recording: on composition, on teaching, on criticism, on performance, on musicology

4. Development of music recording

K. The history of music

1. Western music

2. The music of non-Western peoples
[see 613]

Suggested reading in the *Encyclopædia Britannica:*

General subjects

tune family
tuning and
  temperament
white noise
whole-tone scale
ensembles—
  instrumental:
  band
  orchestra
  quartet
  quintet
  trio
ensembles—vocal:
  antiphonal singing
  choir
  quartet
  responsorial
    singing
  trio
forms—general:
  aleatory music
  aria
  Bar form
  barcarole
  berceuse
  binary form
  caccia
  cantilena
  capriccio
  carol
  character piece
  clausula
  conductus
  cyclic form
  finale
  fuging tune
  lai
  minuet
  nocturne
  quodlibet
  recitative
  serenade
  ternary form
harmonic elements:
  appoggiatura
  atonality
  cadence
  chord
  chromaticism
  drone
  enharmonic
  harmony
  interval
  inversion
  key
  modulation
  monody
  organum
  pedal point
  polytonality
  thorough bass

tonality
tritone
idiophones:
  bell
  bell chime
  carillon
  castanets
  celesta
  clapper
  claves
  crotal
  cymbal
  glass harmonica
  glockenspiel
  gong
  handbell
  Jew's harp
  jingling Johnny
  marimba
  mbira
  music box
  rattle
  scraper
  sistrum
  slit drum
  steel drum
  stone chimes
  triangle
  tubular bells
  vibraharp
  wind-bell
  xylophone
instrumental forms:
  canzona
  chaconne
  chamber music
  chorale prelude
  concerto
  concerto grosso
  courante
  divertimento
  estampie
  étude
  fanfare
  fantasia
  gigue
  impromptu
  invention
  Konzertstück
  march
  musique concrète
  overture
  passacaglia
  prelude
  quartet
  quintet
  ricercare
  rondo
  scherzo
  sinfonia
  sonata
  sonatina

suite
symphonic poem
symphony
toccata
trio
trio sonata
vocal-instrumental
  concerto
instruments—
  classifications:
  aerophone
  brass instrument
  chordophone
  electronic
    instrument
  electrophone
  idiophone
  keyboard
    instrument
  membranophone
  percussion
    instrument
  reed instrument
  stringed
    instrument
  transposing
    musical
    instrument
  wind instrument
  woodwind
instruments—
  components:
  crook
  keyboard
  pipe
  stop
  tracker action
  valve
jazz styles:
  bebop
  Chicago style
  cool jazz
  Dixieland
  free jazz
  jazz
  jazz-rock
  Kansas City style
  New Orleans style
  scat
  swing
medieval musicians:
  meistersinger
  minnesinger
  minstrel
  troubadour
  trouvère
  wait
membranophones:
  bass drum
  drum
  dùndún pressure
    drum

friction drum
kettledrum
snare drum
ṭablāh
tambourine
timpani
tsuzumi
music history, theory,
  and training:
  affections, doctrine
    of the
  Ars Antiqua
  Ars Nova
  colour music
  conservatory,
    musical
  ethnomusicology
  musical societies
    and institutions
  musicology
  program music
  Roman de Fauvel
  schola cantorum
  solfeggio
musical schools and
  styles:
  Burgundian school
  concertato style
  empfindsamer Stil
  Franco-Netherlandish
    school
  Gebrauchsmusik
  gymel
  Mannheim school
  Notre-Dame
    school
  Postromantic
    music
  serialism
  Tin Pan Alley
musical textures:
  heterophony
  homophony
  monophony
  polyphony
non-Western music:
  ālāpa
  Carnatic music
  Chinese music
  colotomic structure
  dastgah
  gagaku
  gamelan
  Hindustani music
  Japanese music
  Korean music
  maqām
  nagauta
  raga
  tāla
  taqsīm

Turkish music
Vedic chant
notation:
  accidental
  clef
  mensural notation
  musical notation
  neume
  note
  score
  shape-note hymnal
  staff
  tablature
  time signature
performance
  technique:
  bel canto
  improvisation
  musical expression
  singing
popular forms:
  bluegrass
  blues
  boogie-woogie
  bossa nova
  calypso
  country and
    western
  folk song
  gospel music
  highlife
  kivela
  ragtime
  reggae
  rhythm and blues
  rock
  shanty
  spiritual
rhythmic elements:
  accent
  aksak

beat
eurhythmics
īqā'āt
isorhythm
metre
polyrhythm
rhythm
rhythmic mode
rubato
syncopation
theatre music:
  ballad opera
  cabaletta
  Camerata
  cavatina
  drinking song
  incidental music
  intermezzo
  libretto
  music drama
  musical comedy
  Nigerian theatre
  opera
  opera buffa
  opéra-comique
  opera seria
  operetta
  Singspiel
  verismo
  zarzuela
vocal forms—sacred:
  Ambrosian chant
  Anglican chant
  anthem
  antiphon
  Armenian chant
  Byzantine chant
  canonical hours
  cantata
  canticle
  chorale

Coptic chant
Ethiopian chant
Gallican chant
Gregorian chant
hymn
kontakion
liturgical music
mass
Mi-Sinai tune
motet
Mozarabic chant
Old Roman chant
oratorio
Passion music
plainchant
psalm tone
psalmody
requiem mass
responsory
Russian chant
Sarum chant
sequence
Syrian chant
Te Deum
  Laudamus
troparion
trope
vocal forms—secular:
  air de cour
  ayre
  ballade
  balletto
  cantiga
  cantillation
  canzonetta
  carnival song
  catch
  chanson
  frottola
  glee
  goliard songs

lied
madrigal
madrigal comedy
mélodie
musique mesurée
nigun
rondeau
serenata
song
villancico
villanella
villota
virelai
yodel
vocal registers:
  alto
  baritone
  bass
  castrato
  countertenor
  falsetto
  soprano
  tenor
other:
  bull-roarer
  cantor
  change ringing
  computer music
  conducting
  Greek music
  metronome
  music
  musical
    composition
  national anthem

Biographies

composers—Ars Nova
  period:
  Adam de la Halle
  Landini, Francesco
  Machaut,
    Guillaume de
  Sachs, Hans
composers—Baroque:
  Bach, Johann
    Sebastian
  Buxtehude,
    Dietrich
  Corelli, Arcangelo
  Couperin, François
  Couperin, Louis
  Dittersdorf, Karl
    Ditters von
  Frescobaldi,
    Girolamo
  Handel, George
    Frideric

Purcell, Henry
Rameau,
  Jean-Philipp
Scarlatti,
  Domenico
Schein, Johann
  Hermann
Schütz, Heinrich
Telemann, Georg
  Philipp
Vivaldi, Antonio
composers—Classical
  period:
  Arne, Thomas
  Bach, Carl Philipp
    Emanuel
  Beethoven,
    Ludwig van
  Boccherini, Luigi
  Boyce, William
  Cherubini, Luigi

Clementi, Muzio
Gluck, Christoph
Haydn, Joseph
Mozart, Wolfgang
  Amadeus
Pleyel, Ignace
  Joseph
composers—modern:
  Barber, Samuel
  Bartók, Béla
  Berg, Alban
  Bernstein, Leonard
  Boulez, Pierre
  Cage, John
  Carter, Elliott, Jr.
  Copland, Aaron
  Cowell, Henry
  Debussy, Claude
  Hindemith, Paul
  Honegger, Arthur
  Ives, Charles

Janáček, Leoš
Krenek, Ernst
Messiaen, Olivier
Milhaud, Darius
Penderecki,
  Krzysztof
Poulenc, Francis
Prokofiev, Sergey
Ravel, Maurice
Roussel, Albert
Satie, Erik
Schoenberg,
  Arnold
Scriabin,
  Aleksandr
Shostakovich,
  Dmitry
Stockhausen,
  Karlheinz
Strauss, Richard
Stravinsky, Igor

Villa-Lobos, Heitor
Webern,
  Anton von
Weill, Kurt
Xenakis, Iannis
composers—opera:
Bellini, Vincenzo
Bizet, Georges
Britten, Benjamin,
  Baron Britten of
  Aldeburgh
Cimarosa,
  Domenico
Donizetti, Gaetano
Gounod, Charles
Henze, Hans
  Werner
Lully,
  Jean-Baptiste
Massenet, Jules
Menotti, Gian
  Carlo
Meyerbeer,
  Giacomo
Offenbach, Jacques
Paisiello, Giovanni
Puccini, Giacomo
Rossini,
  Gioacchino
Scarlatti,
  Alessandro
Sullivan, Sir
  Arthur
Verdi, Giuseppe
Wagner, Richard
composers—popular:
Arlen, Harold
Billings, William
Comden, Betty;
  and Green, Adolf
Duke, Vernon
Foster, Stephen
Gershwin, George
Lerner, Alan Jay
Loewe, Frederick
Mercer, Johnny
Porter, Cole
Rodgers, Richard
Sondheim, Stephen
Warren, Harry
composers—
  Renaissance:
Blow, John
Byrd, William
Cabezón,
  Antonio de
Dowland, John
Dufay, Guillaume
Gabrieli, Andrea
Gabrieli, Giovanni
Gibbons, Orlando
Isaac, Heinrich
Josquin des Prez

Lasso, Orlando di
Monteverdi,
  Claudio
Morley, Thomas
Ockeghem, Jean d'
Palestrina,
  Giovanni
  Pierluigi da
Tallis, Thomas
Weelkes, Thomas
Wilbye, John
Zarlino, Gioseffo
composers—
  Romantic period:
Balakirev, Mily
Berlioz, Hector
Borodin,
  Aleksandr
Brahms, Johannes
Bruckner, Anton
Chabrier,
  Emmanuel
Chopin, Frédéric
Delius, Frederick
Dukas, Paul
Dvořák, Antonín
Elgar, Sir Edward
Fauré, Gabriel
Franck, César
Glière, Reinhold
Glinka, Mikhail
Grieg, Edvard
Holst, Gustav
Indy, Vincent d'
Liszt, Franz
MacDowell,
  Edward
Mahler, Gustav
Mendelssohn, Felix
Mussorgsky,
  Modest
Paderewski, Ignacy
Paganini, Niccolò
Rachmaninoff,
  Sergey
Respighi, Ottorino
Rimsky-Korsakov,
  Nikolay
Rubinstein, Anton
  Grigoryevich
Saint-Saëns,
  Camille
Schubert, Franz
Schumann, Robert
Sibelius, Jean
Smetana, Bedřich
Tchaikovsky, Peter
  Ilich
Vaughan Williams,
  Ralph
Weber, Carl
  Maria von
Wolf, Hugo

conductors:
Ansermet, Ernest
Beecham, Sir
  Thomas
Beinum,
  Eduard van
Bernstein, Leonard
Damrosch, Walter
  Johannes
Furtwängler,
  Wilhelm
Goossens, Sir
  Eugene
Karajan,
  Herbert von
Klemperer, Otto
Koussevitzky,
  Serge
Mengelberg,
  Willem
Monteux, Pierre
Munch, Charles
Nikisch, Arthur
Ormandy, Eugene
Reiner, Fritz
Solti, Sir George
Stokowski,
  Leopold
Szell, George
Thomas, Theodore
Toscanini, Arturo
Walter, Bruno
Weingartner, Felix
instrument makers:
Amati family
Bohn, Theodor
Cavaille-Coll,
  Aristide
Cristofori,
  Bartolomeo
Guarneri family
Hammond,
  Laurens
Stein, Johann
  Andreas
Steinway, Henry
  Engelhard
Stradivari, Antonio
Willis, Henry
Wurlitzer family
musicians—blues,
  country, gospel, pop,
  rock:
Acuff, Roy
Baez, Joan
Beatles, the
Carter family
Charles, Ray
Crosby, Bing
Franklin, Aretha
Guthrie, Woody
Hendrix, Jimi
Jackson, Mahalia

Jolson, Al
Lauder, Sir Harry
Monroe, Bill
Presley, Elvis
Rainey, Ma
Seeger, Pete
Sinatra, Frank
Smith, Bessie
musicians—ragtime,
  jazz, swing, bebop:
Armstrong, Louis
Basie, Count
Coltrane, John
Davis, Miles
Dorsey, Jimmy
  and Tommy
Ellington, Duke
Gillespie, Dizzy
Goodman, Benny
Hines, Earl
Holiday, Billie
Joplin, Scott
Kenton, Stan
Miller, Glenn
Parker, Charlie
Shaw, Artie
Silver, Horace
Whiteman, Paul
musicologists:
Adler, Guido
Burney, Charles
Chrysander, Karl
  Franz Friedrich
Guido of Arezzo
Hornbostel, Erich
  Moritz von
Sachs, Curt
Sharp, Cecil
pianists:
Bülow, Hans,
  Freiherr von
Busoni, Ferruccio
Cortot,
  Alfred-Denis
Gieseking, Walter
Godowsky,
  Leopold
Hess, Dame Myra
Horowitz,
  Vladimir
Paderewski,
  Ignacy Jan
Rubinstein, Anton
  Grigoryevich
Schnabel, Artur
singers—baritones
  and basses:
Chaliapin, Fyodor
  Ivanovich
Fischer, Johann
  Ignaz Ludwig
Fischer-Dieskau,
  Dietrich

Section 625. **Dance**

A. The art of dance

1. The nature of dance as art: its origins and functions

2. Choreography and dance notation

3. Diverse classifications of kinds of dance

4. Theoretical, critical, and descriptive writing about dance

5. The integration of dance with other arts: dance in the theatre, in motion pictures
   [see 622.A.8. and 623.B.]

B. Ballet

1. The nature of ballet as an art

2. The integration of ballet with other arts; *e.g.*, with opera, drama, motion pictures, television

3. Major kinds of ballet: traditional, classical, modern, abstract, expressive

4. The history of ballet

C. Modern dance

1. Principles underlying modern dance: expression and communication of feeling

2. The relation of modern dance to other arts; *e.g.*, with musical theatre, drama, motion pictures, television

3. Development of modern dance: kinds, theories, techniques, and methods of modern dance

D. Primitive, folk, and popular dance
   [see 613]

E. The history of dance

1. The dance of Western peoples

2. The dance of non-Western peoples
   [see 613]

Suggested reading in the *Encyclopædia Britannica*:

MACROPAEDIA: Major articles dealing with dance

African Arts
American Indians
Central Asian Arts
Dance, The Art of
Dance, The
  History of
  Western

East Asian Arts
Folk Arts
Oceanic Arts
Popular Arts
South Asian Arts
Southeast Asian
  Arts

MICROPAEDIA: Selected entries of reference information

General subjects

ballet:
  assemblé
  ballet
  Ballet comique de
    la reine
  ballet movement
  ballet position
  battement
  brisé
  classical ballet
  costume, ballet
  entrechat
  fouetté en tournant
  International Ballet
    Competitions
  pirouette
folk dance:
  bourrée
  capoeira
  carole
  clog dance
  conchero
  country dance
  csárdás
  fandango

farandole
flamenco
hora
hornpipe
huayño
hula
jarabe
jig
jota
juba
kolo
ländler
maypole dance
mazurka
Morris dance
polka
polska
reel
rigaudon
sarabande
seguidilla
square dance
sword dance
syrtos
Virginia reel

voladores, juego
  de los
*Indian classical
  dance:*
  bhārata-nātya
  garabā
  kathak
  kathākali
  manipuri
  orissi
popular dance:
  allemande
  basse danse
  bergamasca
  branle
  cakewalk
  chaconne
  Charleston
  contredanse
  courante
  estampie
  fox-trot
  galliard
  gavotte
  gigue

jazz dance
jitterbug
mambo
minuet
passacaglia
passepied
pavane
quadrille
rumba
samba
tango
twist
volta, la
waltz
other:
  bugaku
  choreography
  dance
  dance notation
  eurhythmics
  Labanotation
  modern dance
  tap dance

Biographies

Balanchine,
  George
Baryshnikov,
  Mikhail
Bournonville,
  August
Cunningham,
  Merce
deMille, Agnes

Diaghilev, Sergey
Dolin, Anton
Duncan, Isadora
Fokine, Michel
Fonteyn, Dame
  Margot
Graham, Martha
Helpmann, Sir
  Robert

Humphrey, Doris
Jooss, Kurt
Laban, Rudolf
Lifar, Serge
Massine, Léonide
Nijinsky, Vaslav
Nikolais, Alwin
Nureyev, Rudolf
Pavlova, Anna

Petit, Roland
Rambert, Dame
  Marie
Saint Denis, Ruth
Tamiris, Helen
Taylor, Paul
Weidman, Charles

INDEX: See entries under all of the terms above

Section 626.   **Architecture, Garden and Landscape Design, and Urban Design**

    A. The art of architecture

        1. Elements of design and principles of composition

        2. Aesthetic aspects of building materials and constructional systems used in architecture
           [for technological aspects, see 733]

           a. Building materials; *e.g.*, stone, brick, wood, iron and steel, concrete

           b. Constructional systems; *e.g.*, load-bearing wall and nonload-bearing wall, post and lintel, arch, vault, dome, truss, framed structures

        3. Diverse structural elements and details of buildings; *e.g.*, floors, walls, ceilings, roofs, windows, doors, stairways

        4. Architectural ornamentation: mimetic ornament, applied ornament, organic ornament

        5. Diverse kinds of architecture and building types determined by their functions

           a. Domestic, or residential, architecture; *e.g.*, houses, apartments, castles, hotels

           b. Religious and commemorative architecture; *e.g.*, temples, churches, synagogues, mosques, tombs, shrines, memorials, monuments

           c. Governmental architecture; *e.g.*, town halls, capitols, courthouses, post offices

           d. Recreational architecture; *e.g.*, theatres, auditoriums, athletic facilities, museums, libraries

           e. Educational and public welfare architecture; *e.g.*, schools and universities, hospitals, prisons, aqueducts

           f. Commercial and industrial architecture; *e.g.*, office buildings, banks, stores, factories, refineries

           g. Agricultural architecture; *e.g.*, barns, stables, silos

           h. Military architecture; *e.g.*, forts, castles, armouries
              [see also 736]

        6. Primitive and folk architecture
           [see 613]

        7. The history of architecture

           a. Western architecture

           b. The architecture of non-Western peoples
              [see 613]

    B. Garden and landscape design

    C. Urban design: the artistic aspects of city planning
       [for the sociological, political, economic, and psychological aspects of urban design, see 524.B.; for the technological aspects, see 737.C.2.]

Suggested reading in the *Encyclopædia Britannica*:

MACROPAEDIA: Major articles dealing with architecture, garden and landscape design, and urban design

African Arts	Folk Arts
American Indians	Garden and Landscape Design
Architecture, The Art of	Oceanic Arts
Architecture, The History of Western	Popular Arts
Central Asian Arts	South Asian Arts
East Asian Arts	Southeast Asian Arts
Egyptian Arts and Architecture, Ancient	

MICROPAEDIA: Selected entries of reference information

<u>General subjects</u>

architecture—	*architecture—*	fortification	acroterion
building materials	*military:*	kremlin	anthemion
and techniques:	alcázar	*architecture—*	brattishing
See Section 733 of	castle	*ornamentation:*	bucranium
Part Seven		acanthus	

candelabrum
coffer
diaper
finial
fluting and reeding
fret
frieze
gingerbread
hoodmold
nailhead
ornament
pinnacle
pulvinated frieze
reticulated work
rinceau
running-dog
  pattern
rustication
scrollwork
stalactite work
strapwork
stringcourse
stuccowork
swag
architecture—
  recreational:
  amphitheatre
  auditorium
  furo
  Islāmic bath
  odeum
  stadium
  thermae
  Turkish bath
architecture—
  religious:
  abbey
  aisle
  ambo
  ambulatory
  apse
  baldachin
  baptistery
  basilica
  campanile
  chancel
  chantry
  chapel
  chapter house
  chevet
  choir
  choragic
    monument
  church
  cloister
  confessional
  crypt
  gopura
  hagioscope
  hall church
  iconostasis
  jinja

Lady chapel
lantern of the dead
lych-gate
minaret
mosque
narthex
nave
obelisk
pagoda
presbytery
pulpit
rood screen
sacristy
sedilia
śikhara
slype
stave church
stūpa
temple
torii
transept
triforium
ziggurat
architecture—
  residential:
  apartment house
  bungalow
  chalet
  château
  cliff dwelling
  cottage
  desert palace
  domus
  hogan
  igloo
  inn
  insula
  lodge
  log cabin
  longhouse
  manor house
  palace
  pueblo
  ranch house
  residential
    architecture
  saltbox
  tent
  tepee
  villa
  yurt
architecture—
  structural elements
  and building details:
  alcove
  anta
  arcade
  arch
  atlas
  atrium
  balcony
  balustrade

bay window
beam
belvedere
bema
bond
bracket
brise-soleil
buttress
canopy
cantilever
capital
carrel
caryatid
casement window
chigai-dana
chimneypiece
clerestory
colonnade
column
console
corbel
corbel table
cornerstone
cupola
cusp
dome
door
dormer
entablature
exedra
fenestration
footing
foyer
framed building
gable
gallery
gargoyle
geodesic dome
hip roof
hypocaust
intercolumniation
lantern
loft
loggia
louver
lunette
mansard roof
megaron
moucharaby
newel
oriel
Palladian window
patio
pedestal
pediment
pendant
pendentive
penthouse
piano nobile
pilaster
podium
porch

porte-cochère
portico
quoin
retaining wall
roof
rose window
rotunda
salomónica
setback
spandrel
spire
squinch
staircase
term
thermal window
tracery
truss
tympanum
vault
wall
window
architecture—
  styles, schools, and
  movements:
  African arts
  Akbar period
    architecture
  Art Deco
  Art Nouveau
  Baroque period
  Bauhaus
  Burgundian
    Romanesque style
  Byzantine art
  Carolingian arts
  Carpenter Gothic
  Central Asian arts
  Chicago School
  Churrigueresque
  chusimp'o style
  Cistercian style
  Classicism and
    Neoclassicism
  Composite order
  Constructivism
  Corinthian order
  Doric order
  Early Christian art
  Egyptian Art
  Empire style
  Federal style
  Functionalism
  Futurism
  Gothic art
  Gothic Revival
  Greek Revival
  Henry IV style
  International Style
  Ionic order
  Isabelline
  Islāmic arts
  Kara-yo

Biographies

INDEX: See entries under all of the terms above

Section 627.   **Sculpture**

A. The art of sculpture

   1. Elements of design and principles of composition

   2. The iconography of sculpture

   3. Materials of sculpture; *e.g.*, stone, wood, metal, clay, ivory, plaster, concrete, glass fibre, wax, paper

   4. Tools, methods, and techniques of sculpture; *e.g.*, carving, modeling, casting and molding, surface finishing

B. The diverse kinds of sculpture

   1. Kinds of sculpture distinguished by their spatial context; *e.g.*, sculpture in the round, relief sculpture, kinetic sculpture, environmental sculpture

   2. Kinds of sculpture distinguished by subject matter

      a. Representational sculpture; *e.g.*, human figures, devotional images and objects, portraits, still lifes, animal figures

      b. Nonrepresentational sculpture

      c. Decorative sculpture

   3. Kinds of sculpture distinguished by their special uses or functions

      a. Ceremonial and ritualistic objects

      b. Coins and medals

      c. Commemorative sculpture; *e.g.*, monuments, tombs, tombstones, stelae
         [see 626.A.5.b.]

      d. Masks

   4. Primitive and folk sculpture
      [see 613]

C. The history of sculpture

   1. Western sculpture

   2. The sculpture of non-Western peoples
      [see 613]

Suggested reading in the *Encyclopædia Britannica*:

MACROPAEDIA: Major articles dealing with sculpture

   Masks
   Popular Arts
   Sculpture, The Art of
   Sculpture, The History of Western

MICROPAEDIA: Selected entries of reference information

General subjects

styles:			*types:*
Amarāvati sculpture	Futurism	Rococo art	Airport art
Baroque art	Gandhāra art	Romanesque art	bieri
beak style	Jōgan style	Sānchi sculpture	bird stone
Bhārhut sculpture	korwar style	South Indian bronze	colossus
Classicism and Neoclassicism	Kushān art	Sukhothai style	cylinder seal
Cubism	malanggan style	Tami style	Daedalic sculpture
Eastern Indian bronze	Mannerism	Tempyō style	death mask
Fujiwara style	Massim style	Tori style	environmental sculpture
	Mathurā art	U Thong style	figurehead
	Northern Wei sculpture	Western Indian bronze	gigaku mask
	Renaissance		

gisant	mobile	*other:*	Oceanic arts
kachina	relief sculpture	African arts	sculpture
kinetic sculpture	segoni-kun	armature	South Asian arts
kore	stabile	Central Asian arts	Southeastern
kouros	Tanagra figurine	contrapposto	Asian arts
mbulu-ngulu	telum figure	Gothic art	
minimalism	terra-cotta	lost-wax process	
moai figure	uli figure	modelling	

Biographies

Ammannati, Bartolommeo	Donatello	Houdon, Jean-Antoine	Pisano, Nicola
Bernini, Gian Lorenzo	Epstein, Sir Jacob	Lehmbruck, Wilhelm	Praxiteles
Berruguete, Alonso	Flaxman, John	Lipchitz, Jacques	Puget, Pierre
Brancusi, Constantin	Gabo, Naum	Lysippus	Rodin, Auguste
Brunelleschi, Filippo	Ghiberti, Lorenzo	Maillol, Aristide	Saint-Gaudens, Augustus
Calder, Alexander	Giacometti, Alberto	Michelangelo	Sluter, Claus
Canova, Antonio	Giambologna	Milles, Carl	Smith, David
Cellini, Benvenuto	Gill, Eric	Moore, Henry	Thorvaldsen, Bertel
Della Robbia, Luca	Girardon, François	Myron	Tinguely, Jean
	Hepworth, Dame Barbara	Oldenburg, Claes	Verrocchio, Andrea del
	Hildebrand, Adolf von	Phidias	
		Pisano, Giovanni	

INDEX: See entries under all of the terms above

Section 628.   Drawing, Painting, Printmaking, and Photography

A. Drawing

  1. Elements of design and principles of composition

  2. Drawing media; *e.g.*, chalk, charcoal, crayon, ink, pastel, pencil, scratchboard, silverpoint, wash

  3. Diverse kinds of drawing

    a. Kinds of drawing determined by subject matter; *e.g.*, portraits, landscapes, figure compositions, still lifes

    b. Kinds of drawing determined by special uses
      [for aspects of drawing related to writing, see 629.C.4.]

      i. Animation

      ii. Caricature, cartoon, comic strip

      iii. Cartography and mapping

      iv. Drafting

  4. The history of drawing

B. The art of painting

  1. Elements of design and principles of composition

  2. The iconography of painting

  3. Painting media; *e.g.*, acrylic, casein, encaustic, fresco, gouache, ink, oil, tempera, watercolour

  4. Related media and techniques

    a. Calligraphy
      [see 629.C.4.a.]

    b. Drawing
      [see A., above]

    c. Mosaic

    d. Photography
      [see D., below]

e. Printmaking
[see C., below]

f. Stained glass

g. Tapestry

5. The kinds of painting

    a. Kinds of painting determined by the type of form of the physical object on which the picture is painted

        i. Fixed objects; *e.g.*, cave painting, mural painting

        ii. Movable objects: easel painting, fan painting, manuscript illumination, miniature painting, screen painting, scroll painting

    b. Kinds of painting determined by subject matter

        i. Representational painting; *e.g.*, devotional painting, genre painting, landscape painting, narrative painting, portrait painting

        ii. Nonrepresentational painting

    c. Kinds of painting determined by the maker or by the audience: primitive and folk painting
[see 613]

6. The history of painting

    a. Western painting

    b. The paintings of non-Western peoples
[see 613]

C. Printmaking

1. Printmaking as an art: its characteristics and problems; *e.g.*, the problem of originality versus reproduction

2. Printmaking media

    a. Relief or cameo media; *e.g.*, woodcuts and linoleum cuts, wood engraving

    b. Intaglio media; *e.g.*, aquatint, drypoint, etching, lift-ground prints, line engraving, mezzotint, soft-ground prints, stipple, engraving

    c. Surface media: lithography, monoprint, serigraphy

3. Printmaking tools and techniques
[see 735.E.4.]

D. Photography as an art

1. The nature and problems of photography as an art

2. Photographic equipment and techniques: lenses; cameras; exposure, processing, and printing
[for technological aspects, see 735.G.]

3. The kinds of photography

    a. Major kinds of photography determined by subject matter; *e.g.*, portraits, landscapes

    b. Kinds of functional photography; *e.g.*, photojournalism and photo reportage, holography, astronomical photography, aerial photography, radiography

---

Suggested reading in the *Encyclopædia Britannica*:

MACROPAEDIA: Major articles and biographies dealing with drawing, painting, printmaking, and photography

General subjects

Caricature, Cartoon, and Comic Strip	Painting, The History of Western
Drafting	Photography
Drawing	Popular Arts
Folk Arts	Printmaking
Painting, The Art of	

Biographies

Leonardo da Vinci	Picasso	Titian
Michelangelo	Rembrandt	Velázquez

MICROPAEDIA: Selected entries of reference information

General subjects

drawing:	Group f.64	p'o-mo	Action painting
aerial perspective	Linked Ring	scroll painting	Ada group
anamorphosis	Photo-Secession	Six Masters of	Antwerp
animation	Group	the early Ch'ing	Mannerists
blot drawing	photomontage	period	art brut
brush drawing	tintype	ts'un	Automatism
caricature	vortograph	wen-jen-hua	Avignon school
cartoon	*prehistoric painting:*	Wu school	Bambocciati
chalk drawing	Altamira	*styles of painting—*	Barbizon school
charcoal drawing	Font-de-Gaume	*Indian:*	Biedermeier style
chiaroscuro	Franco-Cantabrian	Basohli painting	Blaue Reiter, Der
comic strip	school	Būndi painting	Bolognese school
crayon	Gargas	Company school	Brücke, Die
drapery	Laseaux, Grotte de	Deccani painting	Camden Town
drawing	macaroni	Eastern Indian	group
écorché figure	Tassili-n-Ajjer	painting	Cobra
foreshortening	Trois Frères, Les	Kālīghāṭ painting	Cubism
isometric drawing	X-ray style	Kishangarh	Dada
line-and-wash	*printing:*	painting	Danube school
drawing	aquatint	Mālwa painting	Düsseldorf school
metal point	bookplate	Mewār painting	Eight, The
pastel	cliché-verre	Mughal painting	English school
pen drawing	decalcomania	Pahari painting	Fauvism
pencil drawing	drypoint	Rājasthanī	fête champêtre
perspective	embossing	painting	Flemish art
sanguine	engraving	South Asian arts	Fontainebleau,
scratchboard	etching	Western Indian	school of
sgraffito	ink	painting	fore-edge painting
silhouette	intaglio	*styles of painting—*	Fronte Nuova delle
sketch	linocut	*Islāmic:*	Arti
squaring	lithography	Baghdad school	Futurism
wash drawing	mezzotint	Herāt school	genre painting
painting:	monotype	Isfahan school	Geometric style
aerial perspective	printmaking	Islāmic arts	Ghent-Bruges
anamorphosis	relief printing	Jalāyirid school	school
bark painting	rubbing	Mosul school	Haarlem school
casein painting	stencilling	Shīrāz school	Hiberno-Saxon
drapery	wood engraving	Tabriz school	style
encaustic painting	woodcut	*styles of painting—*	Hudson River
gesso	*styles of painting—*	*Japanese:*	school
gouache	*Chinese:*	chinsō	Impressionism
grisaille	Ch'an painting	Kanō school	Intimism
oil painting	Che school	Nan-ga	Italianate painters
painting	Eight Eccentrics of	nise-e	Jack of Diamonds
panel painting	Yang-chou	scroll painting	Japanism
perspective	Eight Masters of	Shijō school	London group
sand painting	Nanking	suiboku-ga	Luminism
sizing	Four Masters of	Tosa school	Macchiaioli
tempera painting	Anhwei	Ukiyo-e	Metaphysical
watercolour	Four Masters	Yamato-e	painting
photography:	of the Yüan	*styles of painting—*	minimalism
albumen paper	Dynasty	*Western:*	Moscow school
carte-de-visite	kung-pi	Abstract	Nabis
Fotoform	Ma-hsia school	Expressionism	Nazarene
gelatin process		Abstraction-Création	Neo-Expressionism

Neo-Impressionism
Neue
   Künstlervereinigung
Neue Sachlichkeit
New York school
Norwich school
Novgorod school
Op art
Orphism
Peredvizhniki
plein air painting
Pont-Aven school
Pop art
Postimpressionism
Pre-Raphaelite
   Brotherhood

Precisionism
Pskov school
Purism
Rayonism
Romanticism
singerie
Social Realism
still-life painting
Stroganov school
Suprematism
Surrealism
Symbolist
   movement
Synchromism
Synthetism
Tachism

tondo
trompe l'oeil
Utrecht school
vanitas
veduta
Venetian school
Vingt, Les
Vladimir-Suzdal
   school
Winchester school
Worpswede school
styles of painting—
other:
   African arts
   Amarna style
   Central Asian arts

Egyptian art
Sogdian art
Southeastern
   Asian arts
wondjina style
other:
collage
design
diorama
folk art
limner
mural
panorama
popular art
Poussinist
Rubenist

Biographies

illustrators:
Beardsley, Aubrey
Beerbohm,
   Sir Max
Crane, Walter
Daumier, Honoré
Gibson, Charles
   Dana
Leech, John
Nast, Thomas
Pyle, Howard
Rockwell, Norman
Thurber, James
painters—British:
Burne-Jones, Sir
   Edward Coley
Constable, John
Gainsborough,
   Thomas
Hogarth, William
Lawrence, Sir
   Thomas
Lewis, Wyndham
Millais, Sir John
   Everett, 1st
   Baronet
Palmer, Samuel
Reynolds, Sir
   Joshua
Rossetti, Dante
   Gabriel
Stubbs, George
Turner, J.M.W.
Wilson, Richard
painters—Dutch:
Bosch,
   Hiëronymus
Bouts, Dirck
Cuyp, Aelbert
   Jacobsz
Gogh, Vincent van
Hals, Frans
Mondrian, Piet

Rembrandt
   Harmenszoon
   van Rijn
Ruisdael,
   Jacob van
Scorel, Jan van
Steen, Jan
Terborch, Gerard
Vermeer, Jan
painters—East Asian:
Hasegawa, Tōhaku
Hiroshige
Hokusai
Hsia Kuei
Ma Yüan
Ogata Kōrin
Sesshū
Shiba Kōkan
Tomioka Tessai
Tung Ch'i-ch'ang
painters—Flemish:
Bruegel, Pieter, the
   Elder
Campin, Robert
David, Gerard
Eyck, Jan van
Goes, Hugo
   van der
Mabuse, Jan
Massys, Quentin
Memling, Hans
Rubens, Peter Paul
Van Dyck, Sir
   Anthony
Weyden, Rogier
   van der
painters—French:
Bonnard, Pierre
Bourdon, Sébastien
Braque, Georges
Cézanne, Paul
Chardin,
   Jean-Baptiste-Siméon
Claude Lorrain

Corot, Camille
Courbet, Gustave
David,
   Jacques-Louis
Degas, Edgar
Delacroix, Eugène
Duchamp, Marcel
Fouquet, Jean
Fragonard,
   Jean-Honoré
Gauguin, Paul
Géricault,
   Théodore
Gros,
   Antoine-Jean,
   Baron
Ingres,
   Jean-Auguste-
   Dominique
Le Brun, Charles
Léger, Fernand
Manet, Édouard
Matisse, Henri
Monet, Claude
Pissarro, Camille
Poussin, Nicolas
Renoir,
   Pierre-Auguste
Rouault, Georges
Rousseau, Henri
Seurat, Georges
Toulouse-Lautrec,
   Henri de
Vuillard, Édouard
Watteau, Antoine
painters—German:
Cranach, Lucas,
   the Elder
Dürer, Albrecht
Ernst, Max
Grünewald,
   Matthias
Holbein, Hans, the
   Elder

Holbein, Hans, the
   Younger
Kirchner, Ernst
   Ludwig
Lochner, Stefan
Marc, Franz
Nolde, Emil
Pacher, Michael
painters—Italian:
Andrea del Sarto
Angelico, Fra
Antonello da
   Messina
Bassano, Jacopo
Bellini, Gentile
Bellini, Giovanni
Bellini, Jacopo
Boccioni, Umberto
Botticelli, Sandro
Bramantino
Canaletto
Caravaggio
Carracci family
Castagno,
   Andrea del
Cavallini, Pietro
Cimabue
Correggio
Crespi, Giovanni
   Battista
Crivelli, Carlo
Duccio di
   Buoninsegna
Gaddi, Taddeo
Gentileschi, Orazio
Ghirlandajo,
   Domenico
Giorgione
Giotto de Bondone
Giovanni di Paolo
Giulio Romano
Leonardo da Vinci
Lippi, Fra Filippo
Lorenzetti, Pietro

Lotto, Lorenzo
Mantegna, Andrea
Martini, Simone
Masaccio
Masolino
Michelangelo
Modigliani,
    Amedeo
Orcagna, Andrea
Parmigianino
Perugino
Piazzetta,
    Giovanni Battista
Piero della
    Francesca
Piero di Cosimo
Pisanello, Il
Primaticcio,
    Francesco, Il
Raphael
Roberti,
    Ercole de'
Signorelli, Luca
Tiepolo, Giovanni
    Battista
Tintoretto
Titian
Uccello, Paolo
Veronese, Paolo
Vitale da Bologna
painters—Spanish:
Dalí, Salvador
Goya, Francisco de
Greco, El
Miró, Joan

Murillo, Bartolomé
    Esteban
Picasso, Pablo
Ribera, José de
Velázquez de
    Cuéllar, Diego
Zurbarán,
    Francisco de
*painters—United
    States:*
Allston,
    Washington
Beckmann, Max
Benton, Thomas
    Hart
Bingham, George
    Caleb
Cassatt, Mary
Cole, Thomas
Curry, John
    Steuart
Davis, Stuart
de Kooning,
    Willem
Eakins, Thomas
Frankenthaler,
    Helen
Gorky, Arshile
Homer, Winslow
Hopper, Edward
Hurd, Peter
Inness, George
Motherwell,
    Robert
O'Keeffe, Georgia

Peale, Charles
    Willson
Pollock, Jackson
Rothko, Mark
Sargent, John
    Singer
Shahn, Ben
Warhol, Andy
Whistler, James
    McNeill
Wood, Grant
Wyeth, Andrew
painters—other:
Behzad
Chagall, Marc
Clouet, Jean
Kandinksy,
    Wassily
Klee, Paul
Kokoschka, Oskar
Loutherbourg,
    Philip James de
Munch, Edvard
Orozco, José
    Clemente
Rivera, Diego
photographers:
Abbott, Berenice
Adams, Ansel
Atget, Eugène
Bourke-White,
    Margaret
Brady, Mathew B.
Brandt, Bill
Brassaï

Cartier-Bresson,
    Henri
Hine, Lewis
    Wickes
Nadar
Ray, Man
Robinson, Henry
    Peach
Siskind, Aaron
Smith, W. Eugene
Steichen, Edward
Stieglitz, Alfred
Strand, Paul
Weston, Edward
White, Minor
*printmakers and
    engravers:*
Bewick, Thomas
Blake, William
Bresdin, Rodolphe
Callot, Jacques
Currier, Nathaniel;
    and Ives, James
Duvet, Jean
Klinger, Max
Kollwitz, Käthe
Lucas van Leyden
Méryon, Charles
Raimondi,
    Marcantonio
Schongauer,
    Martin
Villon, Jaques

INDEX: See entries under all of the terms above

Section 629.   Arts of Decoration and Functional Design

A. The nature and scope of the arts of decoration and functional design

B. The kinds of decorative arts and types of decorative objects classified by the materials and methods used to produce or decorate them, or both

1. Clay

2. Fabrics

3. Gems

4. Glass

5. Metals

6. Paper; *e.g.*, papier-mâché, wallpaper

7. Stone

8. Wood

9. Other kinds of inorganic materials
    with special attention to

    a. Plaster, cement, and concrete

    b. Plastics and other synthetic materials

10. Other kinds of organic materials
with special attention to

    a. Flowers, foliage, and related botanical materials; *e.g.*, bouquets, garlands, wreaths
[for garden and landscape design, see 626.B.]

    b. Plant fibres, reeds, branches, and related materials; *e.g.*, baskets, mats

    c. Skins, furs, and related materials

    d. Shell, horn, bone, ivory, and related materials

    e. Wax

11. Special decorative finishing materials, processes, and techniques

    a. Enamelwork; *e.g.*, cloisonné, champlevé, painted enamels

    b. Lacquerwork; *e.g.*, carved lacquer, inlaid lacquer, laque burgauté

    c. Inlay work; *e.g.*, veneering, intarsia, marquetry

C. The arts of functional design: kinds and types of artistic object classified by their function

1. Dress design and body decoration

    a. Dress and dress accessories
[for the technological aspects of garment making, see 732.B.3.]

    b. Jewelry

    c. Body decoration: cosmetics; hairdressing and hair adornment; physical modification; perfumes, scents, and fragrances

2. Industrial design

    a. Industrial design as an art

    b. Diverse kinds of industrial design classified by function; *e.g.*, design of commercial equipment, design of communications equipment, design of household appliances, design of transportation equipment

3. Interior design

    a. Interior design as an art

    b. The integration of interior design and decoration with architecture: the design and decoration of interior architectural elements

        i. Ceilings

        ii. Floors

        iii. Floor coverings; *e.g.*, rugs, carpets, mats

        iv. Walls; *e.g.*, molding, paneling, wallpaper

        v. Windows and doors

        vi. Other interior architectural elements; *e.g.*, heating units, stairs and staircases

    c. Objects used for interior decoration: furniture and accessory furnishings
[for technological aspects, see 732.B.4.]

4. The design of materials and objects for communication and identification

    a. Handwriting systems and styles: calligraphy, lettering, illuminating
[for forms of writing, see 514.E.]

    b. Printing arts: typography and printing design, illustration, bookbinding
[for printmaking, see 628.C.]

    c. Advertising art and design

    d. The design of signs and symbols used primarily for identification; *e.g.*, heraldic design

    e. The design of exhibitions and displays; *e.g.*, museum and gallery display

5. The design and decoration of diverse kinds of specialized functional objects

    a. The design of coins and currency and of medals

    b. The design and decoration of play materials

    c. Automata: the design of decorative mechanical objects

    d. The design and decoration of arms
[for the technological aspects of arms, see 736]

Suggested reading in the *Encyclopædia Britannica*:

MACROPAEDIA: Major articles dealing with the arts of decoration and functional design

African Arts	East Asian Arts	Popular Arts	Southeast Asian
Central Asian Arts	Folk Arts	Printing,	Arts
Decorative Arts	Heraldry	Typography, and	Writing
and Furnishings	Marketing and	Photoengraving	
Dress and	Merchandising	South Asian Arts	
Adornment	Oceanic Arts		

MICROPAEDIA: Selected entries of reference information

General subjects

body decoration:
barber
body modifications
and mutilations
hairdressing
mustache
tattoo
toupee
wig
calligraphy:
black letter
bokuseki
calligraphy
cancellaresca
Carolingian
minuscule
chia-ku-wen
chrysography
hsiao-chuan
Insular script
italic script
ku-wen
Kūfic script
li-shu
majuscule
Merovingian script
minuscule
naskhī script
palimpsest
rubrication
ta-chuan
ta'liq script
testegiatta
ts'ao-shu
uncial
*decorative art styles
and motifs:*
African arts
arabesque
Art Deco
Art Nouveau
Arts and Crafts
Movement
auricular style
Biedermeier style
Central Asian arts
chinoiserie
curvilinear style

Directoire style
Empire style
Gates of Paradise
ghaṭa-pallava
Indian goods
Islāmic arts
istoriato style
Koguryō style
Louis XIII style
Louis XIV style
Louis XV style
Louis XVI style
Mosan school
Mosul school
Oceanic arts
patralata
Proto-Geometric
style
Queen Anne style
Régence style
Regency style
rocaille
Scythian art
South Asian arts
Southeastern
Asian arts
streamlining
Turkish style
William and Mary
style
vyāla
Yi style
dress and adornment:
aigrette
buckle
bustle
button
Chilkat weaving
chiton
cockade
codpiece
commode
corset
crinoline
dhoti
doublet
dress
fan

farthingale
glove
hat
Highland dress
hoopskirt
hosiery
inrō
Kashmir shawl
kimono
loincloth
moccasin
pajamas
p'ao
paṭolā
peplos
petticoat
Phrygian cap
poke bonnet
redingote
ruff
sandal
sari
shawl
shoe
skirt
sokutai
stomacher
suit
surcoat
sweater
swimsuit
tippet
toga
trousers
tunic
turban
yashmak
*enameling and
enamelware:*
Battersea
enamelware
Birmingham
enamelware
Canton enamel
champlevé
cloisonné
en résille
enamel miniature

enamelwork
Limoges painted
enamel
Schwarzlot
*floral and foliage
decorations:*
corsage
floral decoration
garland
ikebana
Ikenobō
Ko
lei
moribana
nageire
nosegay
Ohara
rikka
shōka
wreath
zen'ei ikebana
*furniture and
accessories:*
Act of Parliament
clock
armoire
banjo clock
basket chair
bath chair
bed
bedspread
bench
bentwood furniture
bonheur du jour
bookcase
bureau
cabinet
cabriole leg
campaign furniture
cane furniture
Carlton House
table
cassone
cellarette
chair
chest
chest of drawers
cheval glass

Chippendale
coffer
commode
console
corner furniture
cottage furniture
couch
country furniture
court cupboard
cradle
cupboard
davenport
desk
dresser
dressing table
drop-leaf table
drum table
Early American
  furniture
escutcheon
fold stool
furniture
gateleg table
girandole
highboy
klismos
ladder-back chair
love seat
marquetry
ming ch'i
ogee clock
ottoman
Parsons table
Pembroke table
pew
pillar and scroll
  shelf clock
prie-dieu
scissors chair
secretary
settee
settle
Shaker furniture
sideboard
stool
table
taboret
throne
tilt-top table
treen
tripod
trundle bed
upholstery
vargueno
veneer
wainscot chair
wardrobe
washhand stand
whatnot
wickerwork
Windsor chair
glassware:
  Altare glass

amberina glass
Amelung glass
Baccarat glass
Blaschka glass
Bohemian glass
Burmese glass
cameo glass
crown glass
crystallo ceramie
cut glass
engraved glass
etched glass
façon de Venise
flint glass
Hedwig glass
Humpen glass
lustred glass
Mary Gregory
  glass
millefiori glass
mosaic glass
Mughal glass
opaline glass
perfume bottle
Portland Vase
pressed glass
Römer
ruby glass
Sandwich glass
satin glass
Venetian glass
verre églomisé
Waterford glass
witch ball
Zwischengoldgläser
heraldry, arms, and
insignia:
armorial ensign
arms, coat of
chevron
ecclesiastical
  heraldry
fasces
flag
fleur-de-lis
herald
heraldic memorial
heraldry
labarum
monogram
orb
sceptre
tartan
interior design
accessories:
chandelier
Coromandel
  screen
curtain
doorstop
mirror
molding
niche

panelling
sconce
toko-no-ma
wainscot
wallpaper
jewelry and
gemstones:
agate
almandine
amethyst
andradite
armlet
aventurine
baroque pearl
bead
beryl
birthstone
brooch
cameo
carat
carnelian
cat's-eye
chatelaine
Chinese jade
choker
chrysoberyl
citrine
coronet
crown
crown jewels
cultured pearl
diamond
diamond cutting
emerald
fibula
filigree
Florentine
  diamond
garnet
gemstone
granulation
hei tiki
jadeite
jewelry
lapis lazuli
lip ring, lip plug,
  and lip plate
magatama
nephrite
netsuke
nose ring
onyx
opal
parure
pearl
pendant
periodot
peristerite
phenakite
ring
ruby
ruby spinel
sapphire

sard and sardonyx
topaz
torque
ts'ung
turquoise
variscite
watch fob
lacquerwork and
related techniques:
chinkin-bori
decoupage
fundamiji
gilding
hiramaki-e
hirameji
japanning
Kamakura-bori
kanshitsu
lacquerwork
laque burgauté
maki-e
nashiji
raden
rō-iro
togidashi maki-e
metalwork and
metalware:
Bīdrī ware
britannia metal
bronze work
caudle cup
chasing
chia
chien
chüeh
chung
copper work
cruse lamp
damascening
dinanderie
dōtaku
fang-i
fu
golden rose
goldwork
hallmark
Häufebecher
ho
hollow ware
horse brass
hu
incense burner
ironwork
Jungfrauenbecher
karat
kovsh
kuang
kuei
leadwork
li
Luristan Bronze
medal
metalwork

nef
niello
ormolu
p'an
pierced work
po-shan hsiang-lu
pomander
Pontypool ware
pyx
saltcellar
samovar
sauceboat
Sheffield plate
silverwork
snuffer
steeple cup
sterling
tankard
tea and coffee
  service
tinware
toleware
touchstone
trivet
yu
*mosaics and stained
glass:*
  commesso
  Cosmati work
  emblēma
  gemmail
  mosaic
  opus sectile
  opus tassellatum
  opus vermiculatum
  pebble mosaic
  pietra dura
  stained glass
  tessara
  tessellated
    pavement
*pottery—earthenware
and stoneware:*
  Abstbessingen
    faience
  agateware
  albarello
  Alcora faience
  amphora
  Aprey faience
  Astbury ware
  Bartmannkrug
  basaltes ware
  bianco sopra
    bianco
  Bizen ware
  black-figure
    pottery
  bucchero ware
  Caffaggiolo
    maiolica
  Castel Durante
    ware

Castelli ware
cauliflower ware
celadon
Cistercian ware
comb pottery
creamware
Deruta ware
Doulton ware
Dutch ware
earthenware
Enghalskrug
Faenza maiolica
faience
faience fine
Greek pottery
Hafner ware
Haji ware
Hausmalerei
Hispano-Moresque
  ware
ironstone china
jasperware
Kreussen
  stoneware
Liverpool delft
Lunéville faience
Lung-ch'üan ware
lustreware
Lyon faience
maiolica
Marseille faience
mezza maiolica
Minton ware
Moustiers faience
Nevers faience
Niderviller ware
Norwich ware
Orvieto ware
Pan-shan ware
Paris ware
Paterna ware
pottery
Pueblo pottery
punch'ŏng pottery
raku ware
red-figure pottery
Rockingham ware
Rörstrand faience
Rouen ware
Saint-Amand-les-
  Eaux ware
Saint-Porchaire
  faience
Savona faience
Schleswig faience
Siena pottery
Southwark and
  Lambeth
  delftware
Staffordshire figure
Stockelsdorf
  faience
stoneware

Strålsund faience
Strasbourg ware
temmoku ware
terra-cotta
terra sigillata ware
tin-glazed
  earthenware
ting
Ting ware
tortoiseshell ware
Turin faience
Tz'u-chou ware
Urbino maiolica
Venice maiolica
Vincennes ware
Wedgwood ware
Westerwald
  stoneware
Zürich ware
pottery—porcelain:
  Affenkapelle ware
  Belleek ware
  Berlin ware
  bone china
  Bow porcelain
  Bristol ware
  Buen Retiro ware
  caddy
  Capodimonte
    porcelain
  carrack porcelain
  Caughley ware
  Chantilly porcelain
  Chelsea porcelain
  Coalport porcelain
  Derby ware
  deutsche Blumen
  Doccia porcelain
  Doulton ware
  Dutch ware
  eggshell porcelain
  flambé glaze
  Hausmalerei
  Imari ware
  Jesuit ware
  Kakiemon ware
  Karatsu ware
  Ki Seto ware
  Kutani ware
  Kyō-yaki
  Limoges ware
  ling lung ware
  lithophane
  Liverpool
    porcelain
  Longton Hall
    porcelain
  Lowestoft
    porcelain
  Medici porcelain
  Meissen porcelain
  Mikawachi
    porcelain

Minton ware
Nanking porcelain
Niderviller ware
Nymphenburg
  porcelain
Oribe ware
Paris ware
Petit porcelain
Pinxton porcelain
Plymouth
  porcelain
porcelain
Rockingham ware
Rouen ware
Royal Copenhagen
  porcelain
Saint-Amand-les-Eaux
  ware
Saint-Cloud
  porcelain
Saint Petersburg
  porcelain
Seto ware
Sèvres porcelain
Shino ware
Spode porcelain
Strasbourg
  porcelain
Te-hua porcelain
Tournai porcelain
Vienna porcelain
Vincennes ware
Worcester
  porcelain
ying-ch'ing ware
Zürich ware
pottery—other:
  alabastron
  potter's mark
  pottery
  slipware
  transfer painting
printing arts:
  black letter
  block book
  bookbinding
  italic
  Romain du Roi
  roman
  sans serif
  typography
textile arts—lace:
  Alençon lace
  blonde lace
  bobbin lace
  Brussels lace
  Buckinghamshire
    lace
  Genoese lace
  lace
  lace pattern book
  needle lace
  Spanish lace

Valenciennes lace
Venetian needle
  lace
textile arts—
  needlework:
  bargello work
  beadwork
  Berlin woolwork
  broderie anglaise
  chikan work
  crewel work
  embroidered
    pictures
  embroidery
  needlepoint
  opus anglicanum
  petit point
  quillwork
  raised work
  sampler
  Turkey work
  whitework
textile arts—rugs and
  carpets:
  Admiral carpet
  Afghan carpet
  Alcaraz carpet
  Ardabīl Carpet
  Arraiolos rug
  Aubusson carpet
  Axminster carpet
  Baku rug
  Baluchi rug
  Bergama carpet
  Bījār carpet
  bird rug
  Bokhara rug
  Brussels carpet
  Cairene rug
  Chichi rug
  Chodor carpet
  Cuenca carpet

Dagestan rug
Damascus rug
Dragon rug
Ersari carpet
Ferahan carpet
Garden carpet
Gendje carpet
Ghiordes carpet
Hamadan rug
Hatchlu rug
Herāt carpet
Hereke carpet
Heriz carpet
Indo-Isfahan carpet
Isfahan carpet
Joshagan rug
Karabagh rug
Kāshān carpet
Kazakh rug
Kermān carpet
Khorāsān carpet
Khotan rug
kilim
Kirshehr rug
Konya carpet
Kuba carpet
Kula carpet
Kurdish rug
Lâdik carpet
Lotto carpet
medallion carpet
Mekri carpet
Melas carpet
Mughal carpet
Mujur rug
Ottoman carpet
palas
Panderma rug
Polish carpet
prayer rug
Qashqā'ī rug
rug and carpet

rya rug
Salor rug
Sarūk carpet
Savonnerie carpet
Senna rug
Seraband rug
Shīrāz rug
Shirvan rug
Silé rug
Smyrna carpet
Soumak
Spring of Khosrow
  Carpet
Tabrīz carpet
Tekke carpet
Transylvanian rug
Ushak carpet
Vase carpet
Verné rug
Yomut carpet
Yürük rug
textile arts—other:
  bāndhanī work
  crochet
  jāmdānī
  kimkhwāb
  knitting
  Navajo weaving
  paisley
  qalamkārī textile
  quilting
  tapestry
  tatting
  textile
  toile de Jouy
  verdure tapestry
  weaving
other:
  altarpiece
  aryballos
  automaton
  azulejo

basketry
Bauhaus
billboard
cha-shitsu
Christmas tree
decorative art
Deutscher
  Werkbund
effigy mound
featherwork
frame design
interior design
kirikane
knife case
krater
mazer
paper folding
papier-mâché
parfleche
patch box
pichhwāi
pilgrim bottle
piqué work
poster
retable
sandwich board
sign
snuffbox
t'ao-t'ieh
tatami
tea ceremony
tester
tortoiseshell
totem pole
trencher
yurt

Biographies

Aalto, Alvar
Asam, Cosmas
  Damian and Egid
  Quirin
Astbury, John
Boulle,
  André-Charles
Breuer, Marcel
Chippendale,
  Thomas
Cressent, Charles
Deskey, Donald

Didot family
Eames, Charles
Exekias
Gallé, Émile
Germain, Thomas
Gill, Eric
Goddard family
Hepplewhite,
  George
Klint, Kaare
Majorelle, Louis

Mardersteig,
  Giovanni
Mi Fei
Morison, Stanley
Morris, William
Northwood, John
Palissy, Bernard
Phyfe, Duncan
Pisanello, Il
Poggio Bracciolini,
  Gian Francesco

Roentgen, David
Saarinen, Eero
Sheraton, Thomas
Sōtatsu
Tassie, James
Thonet, Michael
Tiffany, Louis
  Comfort
Townsend family
Wedgwood, Josiah
Wood family

INDEX: See entries under all of the terms above

Introduction to Part Seven:
Knowing How and Knowing Why

by Lord Ritchie-Calder

Benjamin Franklin defined man as "the tool-making animal." If he had added the phrase "with foresight," he would have adequately described *Homo faber,* man the technologist.

Inventiveness was the indispensable condition for the survival of the human species. Without fur or feather, carapace or scale, ancestral man stood naked to the elements; and without fang or claw or tusk to fight his predators, without speed to elude them, without camouflage to deceive them or the ability to take to the trees like his cousin, the ape, he was physically at a hopeless disadvantage. What he developed to deal with his deficiencies was the capacity to invent. He possessed not only sensory perceptions (though these were less acute than those of many of his fellow creatures), he also possessed imagination and finger-skills. He did not just improvise to meet an emergency as an ape might in using a broken branch as a weapon; he also saw the need for keeping a club handy—he planned ahead. Other creatures had their inherited instincts, their built-in experience. Some, like the beaver or the weaverbird, with their biological tools, could contrive quite elaborate structures; others, like the bees or the ants, could evolve efficient organizations; others, like the squirrel, were provident in the sense of laying in stores. With nimbleness of brain and hand, a combination of gray matter and motor-cells, man could scheme to outreach, with club, or spear or sling, his natural enemies; he could manage nature and escape from the restraints of his environment. He clothed himself in pelts and moved to inhospitable climes, he mastered fire and dared to bring it into his dwelling for heating and cooking, he learned to cultivate and plant the soil, he domesticated animals, and he devised specialized tools like the hoe and the ax to improve the efficiency of his labour.

From earliest time and beginning with the simplest contrivances, every discovery and invention has depended on the fact that the human being is not only a perceptual but also a conceptual creature capable of observing, memorizing, and juxtaposing images. He can make a mental design, a techno-poetic fantasy, even when the means of actually producing it are not available. Seven hundred years ago Roger Bacon could imagine a power-driven ship, a horseless carriage, an airplane, the miniaturized servo-motor, "but one finger in length and one in width," and the bathysphere. The vision cannot materialize, however, unless man has the method. This is the process by which he makes an observation (perceptual); forms a hypothesis (conceptual); experiments to test this "hunch"; formulates a theory to justify his insights; and by further proofs produces "laws" according to which anyone can go on repeating the results. With spoken language, he can transfer experience, father to son, master to apprentice, generation to generation. With written language, he can produce the textbooks that are the ready-reckoners for other innovators who thereby do not

have to rediscover Newton's laws or the laws of thermodynamics every few years. This systematic treatment of the arts and crafts is the simplest expression of the meaning of "technology," from the Greek roots *techne,* arts, and *logia,* words. The ancient Greeks had no such combined term because their philosophers divorced manual skills from intellectual pursuits. Plato berated Eudoxus and Archytas when by experiments and recourse to instruments they solved problems that the theorists considered insoluble. He accused them of "making use of matter which requires manual labour and is the object of servile trades."

This intellectual condescension still persists, although individual technologists have won recognition from scientific societies and learned academies. The prejudice is suggested by the acceptance of the term "science *and* technology." Yet both science and technology use the scientific method. Was Leonardo da Vinci, apart from being an artist, a scientist or a technologist? In terms of discovering and testing new knowledge he was a man of science, but his designs for practical innovations outnumbered those of Thomas Alva Edison. Edison, 400 years later, patented over 1,000 inventions. They included major ones, for which he is remembered, but also hundreds of bits of useful hardware, important in their way. He made only one scientific discovery, the Edison effect, which he patented but did not pursue. The rest were derived from scientific knowledge and developments. He saw the profitable relevancies that lesser men missed; he fitted the mental nut to the mental bolt and created things.

Customarily, science, or the scientific hierarchy, is divided into four categories:

Pure, or academic, research is the pursuit of knowledge for its own sake. It is mainly the work of an individual, or the group he leads. The pure scientist has to justify himself only before a jury of his peers. He is judged not by the usefulness but by the integrity of his work. He is the Maker Possible.

Oriented fundamental research is still basic science; that is to say, the scientist is still questioning nature, seeking to extend knowledge and understanding, but he is not a free agent indulging his curiosity. He is restrained within a frame of reference. For instance, in studying chemical reactions at high pressures he is not assuming that he is going to discover polyethylene, or if he is studying gases at high temperatures he is not necessarily thinking of jet engines or rockets; but he is compiling data that will be important in a general field and likely to have some foreseen applications. In the big corporations, this is called "speculative research." Such a scientist is likely to have adequate research facilities, endowments, or contracts. He is the Maker Probable.

Applied research is programmed research. The target is specified, and results are expected. The predicted yield is the measure of the support. The scientist is held accountable in the annual report. He is the Maker to Happen.

Development is really technology, but coupling it with research (R and D) keeps it in the scientific hierarchy and away from the "rude mechanicals." It is the transfer of laboratory results, through the pilot plant, to the production line. R and D is far and away the most expensive scientific bracket because large-scale trial and error ("back to the drawing board") involves multimillions of dollars. The R and D scientist is the Maker to Work.

Through the craft guilds and their "mysteries" and their conversion to factory methods, technology had an evolutionary history in many cultures and many lands. Alfred North Whitehead claimed that "the greatest invention of the nineteenth century was the invention of the method of invention." Nowhere was this better demonstrated than at Edison's "invention factory" at Menlo Park, New Jersey, where, starting in 1876, Edison organized the first industrial research laboratory. In folklore, he is regarded as a "loner," who invented by intuition. In fact, he systematized the process of invention, coordinating and applying relevant knowledge through a hard-worked team that included mathematicians, physicists, chemists, and skilled mechanics. Invention was no longer the private indulgence of the gifted amateur or the rare professional; a techno-methodology had been created to guarantee commercial success. In Edison's case the result was often a "package deal"—not just the incandescent lamp, but the generating plant and the transmission system. In the case of Henry Ford, it was not just the Model T, but the assembly line, which he enlarged to a factory that was one-fifth of a mile long, with a conveyor-belt system that synchronized each stage of construction with the delivery of each part to the operator. He embodied scientific management, with its time-and-motion studies and production engineering.

The feedback system between the know-why (academic science) and the know-how (technology) is recalibrating the time-function of change. A new scientific discovery (explanation of a phenomenon) is seized by the technologists and put to work. In turn the technologists provide the instruments that, with greater refinements and speed, enable the scientists to make further discoveries. An outstanding example is cybernetics. The pencil-and-paper mathematicians had long known the principles of the computer, but they had to wait for the post-World War II electronic engineers to produce the "hardware." Now with instant responses, or nearly so, and vast computer capacities and prodigious "memories," with means not only for numerical calculation but for logical simulation, with feedback (like a burned finger signaling to the brain and the brain withdrawing the finger from the hot plate), scientists are not only able to do calculations so complex that they would not previously have attempted them, but they are also learning, from the engineers, about the nature of systems, including the systems of nature itself. Cybernetics deals with the information-processing aspects, as distinguished from the energy-transforming aspects, of all systems regardless of their physical nature. This has facilitated the development of automatic control, telecommunications, and computing; it is applicable also to systems engineering, economics, and neurophysiology.

Though we acknowledge the truth of Whitehead's apho-

rism, his essentially engineering approach to technology is too restrictive. Every advance in the practical arts from hunting to food-gathering to cultivation, to animal husbandry, to irrigation, to mining, and on through construction, transportation, food-processing, heating, power generation, lighting, communications, military engineering, and clinical medicine has produced social and cultural changes. The Neolithic Revolution was as climacteric as the Industrial Revolution. Moreover, the preoccupation with Western technology ignores the cultural origins of many major innovations and forgets that, historically, the European Dark Ages (not so dark as is often supposed) coincided with Golden Ages of material advances in China, India, and pre-Columbian America. Only in recent years have historians (Singer, Crombie, Lynn White, Hall, Needham, Forbes, and others) given serious attention to these facts. The anthropologists, looking at cultural influences, have been similarly remiss. Economists have been preoccupied with the "production function" and sociologists with the social effects of innovation (from television to freeways) and with work-force redundancy. The present distortions, produced by rapid technological change, obscure the fact that civilization itself derived from excess production and redundancy. When agriculture surpassed subsistence, fewer tillers were required to support the cities, with their artisans (specializing in other forms of production), their priesthoods, their scholars, their soldiery and warrior-kings, their tithe-gatherers, their merchants, and their money-changers. Technological displacement today, whether it is called unemployment, underemployment, leisure, or nonwork, similarly calls for social readjustments to find nonmanufacturing expressions of human capacities.

No explanation of the intrinsic or historic attributes of technology can convey the love-hate overtones that the term has acquired. In the ogre sense of the word, it has become a threat to lives and livelihoods and to the total environment. In the efficiency sense, it is hailed as the methodological solution of all our problems from government administration to the production of miracle grains to abolish hunger. Some, like Jacques Ellul and B.F. Skinner, claim that we are already the hostages of our man-made environment: the first maintaining that technology has taken over all of man's activities and not just his productive activities; the second, that autonomous man, with free will and freedom and dignity, is now an anachronism and has to be intentionally controlled by the "technology of behaviour."

Obviously this usage is stretching the meaning of "technology" beyond the foregoing derivations and descriptions—the etymology; the cultural origins; the scientific precedents; the nuts-and-bolts and something popularly promoted to capital letters as "The Machine." This usage expands even Harold Lasswell's accommodating version: "The ensemble of practices by which one uses available resources to achieve values." It is more consistent with the French *la technique,* which refers to any complex of standardized means for attaining predetermined ends. Thus it would apply to organization, government institutions, systems of politics or religions, or anything which reduces spontaneous or impulsive behaviour to a rationale. As was said of *la technique* of wartime operational research, "it ran the war by numerical thinking instead of gusts of emotion."

In adventurously exploring the three divisions and fifteen sections of the encyclopaedia's treatment of technology of which this introduction is, hopefully, the appetizer, the reader will find other interpretations and probably produce his own. In common usage, however, the preoccupation is with "The Machine" and the effects of its products on our lives.

Resentment against the replacement of men by machines goes back beyond Ned Ludd and the machine-wreckers of the Industrial Revolution, but present-day attitudes are of a different order of magnitude. They derive from the speed and scale of change. Hahn and Strassmann's laboratory discovery of uranium fission in 1938 was transformed into a nuclear bomb in 1945. If there is no nuclear war, history will consider the Manhattan Project, which produced the bomb, as important as the bomb it produced. It is the archetype of the crash program in which men, materials, and methods are mobilized to attain an objective in a given time. Man on the Moon by 1970 was another example, with the time-target beaten by six months. The time-lapse between a fundamental scientific discovery and its practical application has been reduced from centuries to decades to years to months. Since World War II, we have had the Atomic Age, the Cybernetic Age, the Space Age, and now the Bioengineering Age, in which not only by organ transplants but also by the deliberate manipulation of genes it may be possible to engineer the nature of man himself. Thus in the growing up of the postwar generation there have been four major epochs nearly as significant as the Stone Age, the Iron Age, the Renaissance, and the Industrial Revolution. At the same time there has come the shocked awareness of the effects on the environment of the wastes of technology. Again this is a matter of scale and lack of prescience. (The ore miners and metal workers of Cyprus and Asia Minor were polluting the Mediterranean with heavy metals 5,000 years ago, but the effects were insignificant compared with volcanic debris.) When people complain, however, of "interference with the environment" they should be mindful that such interference has been the *sine qua non* of the survival of *Homo sapiens.* Moreover, when we try to get rid of our guilt-sense about the effects of misused technology and reject the gadgeting we ashamedly enjoy, we should not go too far and "throw out the baby with the bathwater." We cannot go back to the apes nor even to Arcadia.

The great problem is how to force ebullient technology and its transnational expansion to produce human well-being, not just in the quantity of artifacts but in improving the quality of life, including redressing of the mischief in the environment. This requires an enlightened and informed society that knows what it wants and is not cult-ridden or crash-programmed into accepting what it does not want or need. This cannot be achieved through programmed learning nor the technology of behaviour nor systems engineering. We are back with the know-why as the initiator and the monitor of the know-how.

Part Seven. Technology

Several points should be noted about the relations of this part to other parts. Technology involves applications of the knowledge of nature dealt with in Parts One, Two, and Three and in turn has an influence on the development of that knowledge. It has a major role in relation to human communication and an influence on the cultural, social, economic, political, legal, and educational life of mankind, dealt with in Part Five; and a conditioning effect on the development of the fine arts, dealt with in Part Six. To a degree, technological developments affect developments in the religious life of humans, dealt with in Part Eight. Technology is a major dimension in the history of mankind, the subject of Part Nine.

The branches of technology and of engineering have themselves become the subject of historical and analytical studies. Those studies are presented in Section 10/37 of Part Ten.

Division I.   **The Nature and Development of Technology**

The outlines in the two sections of Division I treat the scope and history of technology, and the organization of human work.

Section 711.   **Technology: Its Scope and History**

A. General conceptions or definitions of technology

B. Relations between technology and other spheres of contemporary life

    1. Technology and wealth

    2. Technology and war

    3. Technology and education

    4. Technology and art
      [see also 612.D.4.]

    5. Technology and social institutions
      [see also 512.B.3.]

    6. Technology and the underdeveloped regions: the export of Western technology
      [see also 512.B.3.]

    7. Effects of technology on the environment

C. History of technology: sociocultural consequences of technological changes
  [see also 512.B.]

    1. Technology in the ancient world

      a. The beginnings of technology (to *c.* 3000 BC): emergence of the earliest communities, use of stone tools and weapons, beginnings of mining and agriculture

      b. The urban revolution (*c.* 3000–500 BC): early civilization in the valleys of the Nile and Tigris–Euphrates, waterworks for irrigation, urban manufacturing

      c. Technological achievements of Greece and Rome (500 BC–AD 500): mastery of iron, invention of mechanical contrivances, architectural and constructional works

2. Technology from the Middle Ages to 1750

   a. Medieval advances (AD 500–1500): harnessing of wind power and waterpower; construction of canals, tunnels, and bridges; construction of full-rigged ships; invention of printing

   b. The emergence of Western technology (1500–1750): invention of early scientific instruments and tools, birth of steam power, development of agricultural and constructional techniques

3. The Industrial Revolution (1750–1900)

   a. Advances in power technology: development of steam power, internal-combustion engine, and electric power; exploitation of mineral and fossil fuels

   b. Development of industries: iron and steel, textiles, chemicals, transportation, communications

4. Technology in the 20th century

   a. Early developments: exploitation of hydroelectric power; synthesizing of fibres, plastics, rubber, dyes, and drugs; rationalization of production

   b. Space Age technology: atomic power, automation and the computer, rocketry and space exploration, advances in agricultural technology, advances in transportation and communication

   c. Effects of technology on the environment

Suggested reading in the *Encyclopædia Britannica*:

MACROPAEDIA: Major articles and a biography dealing with technology: its scope and history

   Edison
   Technology, The History of

MICROPAEDIA: Selected entries of reference information

General subjects

industrial engineering	manufacturing	safety engineering	service industries
Industrial Revolution	research and development	security and protection system	technology
	safety		

Biographies

   See Section 10/37 of Part Ten

INDEX: See entries under all of the terms above

Section 712.   The Organization of Human Work

A. The organization of work

   1. The organization of work in the prehistoric world
      [see also 512.B.1.]

      a. Origin of division of labour based on age and sex differences, initial absence of class divisions

      b. Communal organization: specialization required by the development of pottery, textiles, agriculture, and metallurgy

   2. The organization of work in the ancient world

      a. Theories of civilization's development: explanations of the origin of hierarchical organization

      b. Effect of social classes on the organization of labour

      c. Organization of agricultural labour

      d. Organization of industrial labour by craft

      e. Organization of labour for large-scale construction

   3. The organization of work in the medieval world: the manor system, the craft guilds, organization of free labour for large-scale construction

4. Changes in production techniques from the 16th to the 18th century: foundations of modern industrial production

5. Mass production: the organization of labour by product rather than by process

6. The use of machines as replacements for labour

B. The application of scientific methods to managerial functions

1. Operations research: the application of scientific method to the management of organized systems

2. Systems engineering: the utilization of scientific and technological knowledge in planning and designing complex systems

3. Systems-design techniques, tools, and procedures

   a. Techniques: use of flow charts and other symbolic models, precise formulation of suitable objectives

   b. Tools: optimization theory, communication theory, queuing theory, game theory
   [see also 10/23.E. and F.]

   c. Procedures: exploratory planning, development planning

C. The relation between man and machine in industrial production

1. The effects on mankind of the rationalization of work: psychological and social aspects of mass production and automation

2. The human-factors approach: the design of machines, tools, and work environments with consideration for the capabilities and limitations of humans

---

Suggested reading in the *Encyclopædia Britannica:*

MACROPAEDIA: Major articles dealing with the organization of human work

Automation
Industrial Engineering and Production Management
Work and Employment

MICROPAEDIA: Selected entries of reference information

General subjects

assembly line	game theory	mathematical	systems engineering
automation	Hawthorne	programming	time-and-motion
critical path	research	operations research	study
analysis	human-factors	queuing theory	trade organization
domestic service	engineering	robot	work
domestic system	mass production	standardization	

Biographies

See Section 10/37 of Part Ten

INDEX: See entries under all of the terms above

Division II. **Elements of Technology**
[For Part Seven headnote see page 265.]

Division I is concerned with the nature and effects of technology as a whole. The outlines in the five sections of Division II deal with technical processes not specific to any of the major fields of technology. The technologies of the major fields are dealt with in Division III.

Section 721. **Technology of Energy Conversion and Utilization**

A. Major types of energy useful to mankind

  1. Primary energy sources: thermonuclear reaction, nuclear fission, radioactivity

  2. Recurring energy sources: solar energy, natural thermal energy, wind and water energy

  3. Nonrenewable energy sources: coal, gas, petroleum

B. Devices and techniques for the utilization of energy

  1. Devices for utilizing muscle energy: pulley, lever, block and tackle, treadmill
  [see 722.B.2.]

  2. Devices for utilizing wind and water energy: sails and sailboats, windmills, waterwheels, turbines

  3. Devices for utilizing gravitational energy: pendulums, counterweight mechanisms

  4. Devices for utilizing strain and compression energy

    a. Steam engines and steam power plants

    b. Steam turbines
    [see B.2., above]

    c. Compressed-air and compressed-gas tools and machines

    d. Hydraulic devices

  5. Devices for utilizing magnetic and electrical energy

    a. Magnets, electromagnets

    b. Electric motors: induction motors, synchronous motors, commutator motors utilizing ac and dc

  6. Devices for utilizing rotational energy: centrifuges, gyroscopes

  7. Devices for utilizing heat energy: heat exchangers, refrigeration equipment

  8. Devices for utilizing chemical energy

    a. Internal-combustion engines: gasoline and gas turbine engines; diesel engines; jet, turbojet, fan-jet, and turboprop engines; rocket engines

    b. Chemical explosives: black powder, nitroglycerin, dynamites, nitrocellulosic explosives, military explosives, other modern high explosives

  9. Devices and materials for utilizing nuclear energy: nuclear reactors, radioactive isotopes
  [see also 112.B.]

C. Devices for energy conversion

  1. Thermoelectric devices

  2. Thermionic devices

  3. Magnetohydrodynamic and electrogasdynamic devices

  4. Batteries and fuel cells

  5. Lamps and other lighting devices

6. X-ray tubes
[see also 111.D.1.]

7. Devices for electric power generation: turbine-driven generators, engine-driven generators, nuclear-powered generators, hydraulic-turbine-driven generators, thermoelectric generators, dynamos

D. Devices for energy concentration and control

1. Electron tubes

2. Semiconductor devices

3. Other solid-state devices

E. Devices for unlimited production of free energy: attempts to design perpetual motion machines

---

Suggested reading in the *Encyclopædia Britannica*:

MACROPAEDIA: Major articles dealing with the technology of energy conversion and utilization

Electronics
Energy Conversion
Energy, The Concept of

Industries, Chemical Process
Industries, Extraction and Processing
Refrigeration

MICROPAEDIA: Selected entries of reference information

General subjects

chemical explosives:
    blasting
    blasting cap
    dynamite
    explosive
    firework
    gunpowder
    nitrocellulose
    RDX
*compression energy
and its devices:*
    bellows
    cogeneration
    compressor
    piston and cylinder
    pneumatic device
    propellant
    steam engine
electrical devices:
    battery
    cell
    electric generator
    electric motor
    electrolytic cell
    electromagnet
    fuel cell
    fuse
    linear motor
    magneto

motor–
    generator set
    voltage regulator
electronic devices:
    amplifier
    antenna
    antenna array
    band-pass filter
    diode
    electric circuit
    electric switch
    electron tube
    electronics
    ferrite
    grid
    ignitron
    integrated circuit
    klystron
    memory tube
    photoelectric cell
    photomultiplier
        tube
    printed circuit
*heat exchange and
    related devices:*
    boiler
    cogeneration
    condenser
    cooling system
    evaporator

heat exchanger
heat pipe
refrigeration
*internal-combustion
engines:*
    carburetor
    choke
    diesel engine
    fuel injection
    gasoline engine
    ignition system
    internal-combustion
        engine
    jet engine
    knocking
    ramjet
    rotary engine
    spark plug
    supercharger
    turbojet
    turboprop
major types of energy:
    electric power
    energy
    fire
    fossil fuel
    geothermal energy
    hydraulic power
    hydroelectric power
    solar energy

tidal power
waterpower
moving-fluid devices:
    centrifugal pump
    hydraulic
        transmission
    pump
    turbine
    waterwheel
    windmill
nuclear reactors:
    breeder reactor
    fusion reactor
    nuclear reactor
rockets:
    Atlas rocket
    Delta
    launch vehicle
    rocket
    Saturn
    Thor rocket
    V-2 rocket
other:
    blowpipe
    magnetohydro-
        dynamic device
    perpetual motion
    thermionic device
    transducer

Biographies

Braun, Wernher von
De Forest, Lee
Diesel, Rudolf
Evans, Oliver

Goddard, Robert
    Hutchings
Nobel, Alfred
    Bernhard

Sperry, Elmer
    Ambrose
Stevens, John
Tesla, Nikola

Watt, James
Westinghouse,
    George

See also Section 10/37 of Part Ten

INDEX: See entries under all of the terms above

Section 722.   **Technology of Tools and Machines**

A. Hand tools

   1. Early history of hand tools: Paleolithic and Neolithic stone tools, development of metal tools

   2. Basic types of hand tools

      a. Percussive tools: hammers, axes

      b. Cutting, drilling, and abrading tools: knives, saws, files

      c. Screw-based tools: screwdrivers, wrenches

      d. Measuring and defining tools: levels, dividers, rules

      e. Tool auxiliaries: workbench, vise

   3. Power-driven hand tools: electric drills and circular saws, pneumatic hammers and riveters

B. Machines and machine components

   1. Simple machines: lever, wedge, wheel and axle, pulley, and screw

   2. Machine mechanisms: devices that transmit motion by means of flexible connectors, rigid connecting links, or direct contact

   3. Machine components

      a. Gears

      b. Cams

      c. Linkages

      d. Flywheels

      e. Belt and chain drives

      f. Couplings

      g. Clutches

      h. Brakes

      i. Bearings

      j. Shafts and shaft accessories

      k. Screws

      l. Springs

   4. Friction accommodation and reduction

      a. Bearings
         [see B.3.i., above]

      b. Lubricants and their functions, types, and properties

C. Machine tools: stationary power-driven machines for shaping and forming parts made of metal or other materials

   1. History and characteristics of machine tools

   2. Operation of metal-cutting tools

   3. Basic machine tools: turning machines, shapers and planers, drilling machines, milling machines, grinding machines, power saws, and presses

   4. Modifications of basic machines; *e.g.,* turret lathes, production millers

   5. Special-purpose machines; *e.g.,* gear-cutting machines, broaching machines

D. Computer-aided machining

   1. Computer numerical control

   2. Computer-aided design and computer-aided manufacturing (CADCAM)

   3. Robots

   4. Computer-integrated manufacturing

E. Nonconventional methods of machining

1. Electrical methods: electron-beam machining, electrical-discharge machining, electrochemical machining, ion beam machining, laser machining, plasma arc machining

2. Other methods: ultrasonic machining, chemical machining, photochemical machining, water-jet machining

---

Suggested reading in the *Encyclopædia Britannica*:

MACROPAEDIA: Major article dealing with the technology of tools and machines

Tools

MICROPAEDIA: Selected entries of reference information

General subjects

basic machine tools:	router	flywheel	toggle mechanism
auger	saw	gear	transmission
boring machine	screwdriver	Geneva	washer
drill press	vise	mechanism	*simple machines:*
grinding machine	wrench	governor	capstan
lathe	*machine components:*	Harmonic Drive	crank
milling machine	air brake	linkage	inclined plane
planer	air spring	machine	lever
punch press	automatic	mandrel	pulley
reamer	transmission	mechanism	wheel
router	ball bearing	nut	wheel and axle
sander	bearing	pin fastener	*other:*
sawing machine	belt drive	rack and pinion	block and tackle
shaper	bolt	ratchet	divider
hand tools:	brake	Rolamite	jack
adz	cam	roller bearing	level
ax	clutch	screw	lubrication
brace and bit	differential gear	shaft coupling	pantograph
chisel	eccentric-and-rod	shaft seal	square
drill	mechanism	slider-crank	tool
file	escapement	mechanism	tool and die
hammer	flexible shaft	spring	making
pliers			

Biographies

See Section 10/37 of Part Ten

INDEX: See entries under all of the terms above

Section 723.   Technology of Measurement, Observation, and Control

A. Theory of measurement
[see 10/31.B.3.b.]

B. Units and standards of measurement

1. Systems of weights and measures: standards for the measurement of mass and length

2. Standards and techniques for measurement of time

C. Principles and processes by which instruments of measurement operate

D. Common types of measuring instruments

1. Instruments for measuring basic dimensions

a. Devices for measuring length: rules, calipers, micrometers

b. Devices for measuring mass and weight: scales, balances

c. Devices for measuring time: mechanical, electric, and atomic clocks

d. Devices for measuring temperature: gas, liquid, and electrical resistance thermometers

   e. Devices for measuring electric current and other electrical properties: galvanometers, ammeters, voltmeters

   f. Devices for measuring light intensity: photometers, light meters, exposure meters

  2. Instruments for measuring physical properties and relationships derived from basic dimensions

   a. Instruments for measuring pressure: barometers, manometers

   b. Instruments for measuring rate of flow: flowmeters, water meters, gas meters

   c. Instruments for measuring position by angulation and direction finding

    i. Compasses: magnetic compasses, gyrocompasses
     [see also 212.B.]

    ii. Surveying instruments: levels, transits, sextants

   d. Instruments for measuring gravity: gravimeters

   e. Instruments for making optical measurements: polarimeters, refractometers

   f. Instruments for measuring ionizing radiation: Geiger counters, scintillation counters

   g. Instruments for measuring volumetric and mechanical properties of materials, including density, viscosity, and mechanical strength

E. Instruments used for observing and recording

  1. Instruments for observing phenomena

   a. Microscopes: optical and electron microscopes

   b. Telescopes: optical, radio, and airborne telescopes

   c. Spectroscopes and spectrographs

   d. Interferometers

  2. Instruments for recording phenomena: cameras
   [see 735 G.]

F. Special instruments and apparatus used in scientific research

  1. General laboratory equipment: filters, mixers, centrifuges

  2. Research reactors

  3. Particle accelerators: betatrons, cyclotrons, linear resonance accelerators, synchrotrons

  4. Mass spectrometers

  5. Chromatographs

  6. Seismographs
   [see also 213.B.]

  7. Particle detectors: bubble chambers, scintillation counters

G. Major systems of measurement and observation

  1. Surveying
   [see D.2.c.ii., above, and 733.A.2.]

  2. Mapping and cartography

  3. Hydrographic charting

  4. Oceanographic measurement
   [see also 222.B., E., F., and G. and 738.B.]

  5. Meteorological measurement
   [see also 221 and 223]

  6. Astronomical observations

  7. Navigational techniques and devices

  8. Radiological techniques and devices

H. Instrumentation and control systems

  1. Instrumentation systems: systems that operate or actuate control devices or record measurements automatically

  2. Control systems

  3. Telemetry systems: remote monitoring and control

Suggested reading in the *Encyclopædia Britannica*:

MACROPAEDIA: Major articles dealing with technology of measurement, observation, and control

Analysis and Measurement,
  Physical and Chemical
Calendar
Climate and Weather
Mapping and Surveying

Measurement and Observation
Navigation
Particle Accelerators
Time

MICROPAEDIA: Selected entries of reference information

General subjects

astronomical devices:
  astrolabe
  astronomical
    observatory
  Cassegrain reflector
  coronagraph
  Keplerian telescope
  Mills cross
  radio
    interferometer
  radio telescope
  Schmidt telescope
  telescope
  X-ray telescope
calendars:
  Aztec calendar
  Chinese calendar
  Dionysian period
  Egyptian calendar
  French republican
    calendar
  Greek calendar
  Gregorian calendar
  international date
    line
  Jewish calendar
  Julian calendar
  leap year
  lunar calendar
  Mayan calendar
  Muslim calendar
  perpetual calendar
  Roman republican
    calendar
  solar calendar
  Tibetan calendar
*instruments for
  measuring distance:*
  altimeter
  caliper
  depth finder
  gauge
  range finder
  strain gauge
  vernier caliper
*instruments for
  measuring force:*
  balance
  gravimeter

Roberval balance
spring balance
torsion balance
*instruments for
measuring electrical
and magnetic
quantities:*
  ammeter
  bridge
  cathode-ray
    oscilloscope
  electrometer
  electroscope
  galvanometer
  magnetometer
  ohmmeter
  oscillograph
  signal generator
  voltmeter
  watt-hour meter
*instruments for
measuring motion
and fluid flow:*
  accelerometer
  airspeed indicator
  anemometer
  gas meter
  speedometer
  tachometer
  venturi tube
*instruments and
techniques for
measuring
properties of liquids:*
  hydrometer
  Jolly balance
  pH meter
  polarimetry
  viscometer
*instruments and
techniques for
measuring
radiation:*
  actinometer
  bolometer
  cloud chamber
  coincidence
    counting
  densitometer

dosimeter
frequency meter
ionization chamber
photometer
radiometer
scintillation
  counter
solid-state detector
spark chamber
wavemeter
*mapping and
surveying:*
  aerial photography
  cartography
  contour mapping
  hydrographic
    charting
  isobar
  isotherm
  itinerarium
  map
  metes and bounds
  photogrammetry
  projection
  surveying
  theodolite
  topographic map
  triangulation
  trilateration
  weather map
meteorology:
  anemometer
  barometer
  ceilometer
  hygrometry
  isentropic chart
  isobar
  isotherm
  psychrometry
  radiosonde
  temperature-humidity
    index
  weather bureau
  wind rose
  World Weather
    Watch
*navigational
techniques and
devices:*
  celestial navigation

compass
consol
dead reckoning
direction finder
great circle route
inertial guidance
  system
loran
loxodrome
navigation
navigation chart
portolan chart
radio direction
  finder
radio range
sextant
shoran
solar compass
particle accelerators:
  betatron
  cyclotron
  particle accelerator
  synchrotron
*pressure
  measurement:*
  barometer
  pressure gauge
  reversing
    thermometers
*radiological dating
  techniques:*
  carbon-14 dating
  common-lead
    dating
  fission-track dating
  helium dating
  ionium–thorium
    dating
  lead-210 dating
  potassium–argon
    dating
  protactinium-231–
    thorium-230
    dating
  radiation-damage
    dating

INDEX: See entries under all of the terms above

Section 724.   Extraction and Conversion of Industrial Raw Materials

A. The world's physical and biological resources

1. The identification and distribution of natural resources

2. The management of resources

a. Conservation of natural resources

b. Salvage operations

B. Technology of the extraction industries

1. Mining and quarrying
[see also 214.A.4.c.]

a. Processes: underground mining, surface mining and quarrying

b. Products: coal, salt, stone, metal ores, sulfur, phosphates

2. Techniques of extracting petroleum and gas
[see also 214.D.]

C. Primary conversion of raw materials

1. Petroleum refining
[see also 214.D.2. and 3.]

2. Coal processing: production of coke, coal tar, light oil, gas, and chemicals
[see also 214.D.1.]

3. Production and processing of metal ores and metals
[see also 214.A.4.c.]

    a. Aluminum

    b. Calcium

    c. Chromium

    d. Cobalt

    e. Copper

    f. Gold

    g. Iron

    h. Lead

    i. Magnesium

    j. Mercury

    k. Nickel

    l. Platinum

    m. Silver

    n. Sodium and potassium

    o. Steel and steel alloys

    p. Tin

    q. Titanium

    r. Tungsten

    s. Uranium

    t. Zinc

    u. Rare-earth metals
[see 121.B.12.]

    v. Metal alloys

4. Production of synthetic gemstones and industrial crystals

5. Processing of stone, sand, clay, and gravel

    a. Manufacture of conventional and special types of glass and glass products

    b. Manufacture of cement, gypsum plasters, and plastic cements

    c. Manufacture of industrial ceramics

    d. Manufacture of bricks and tiles

6. Processing of water to obtain salt, magnesium, oxygen, hydrogen, and other elements

7. Processing of air to obtain oxygen, nitrogen, noble gases, and other gases

8. Processing of plant and animal products

    a. To obtain paper and pulp

    b. To obtain roundwood, sawn wood, veneer, plywood and laminated constructions, particle board, and fibreboard

    c. To obtain tobacco and other nonfood products

    d. To obtain leather and hides

    e. To obtain furs

    f. To obtain natural fibres

    g. To obtain pharmaceuticals

    h. To obtain oils, fats, and waxes

    i. To obtain resins and other products

Suggested reading in the *Encyclopædia Britannica:*

MACROPAEDIA: Major articles dealing with the extraction and conversion of industrial raw materials

Conservation of Natural Resources
Industrial Glass and Ceramics
Industries, Extraction and Processing

MICROPAEDIA: Selected entries of reference information

General subjects

alloys:
 alloy
 aluminum bronze
 amalgam
 brass
 bronze
 calamine brass
 cupronickel
 Duralumin
 electrum
 ferroalloy
 misch metal
 pewter
 solder
 stainless steel
 steel
animal fibres, furs,
 and hides:
 alpaca
 camel hair
 cashmere
 fur
 horsehair
 leather
 llama fibre
 mohair
 rabbit hair
 silk
 specialty hair fibre
 wool
ceramics:
 adobe
 brick
 cement
 firebrick
 kiln
 mullite
 porcelain
  enamelling
 Portland cement
 pottery
 refractory
 tile
coal and its
 processing:
 coal
 coal tar
 coke
 lignite
forest products—
 lumber:
 balsa

ebony
fir
greenheart
hardwood
lancewood
logging
mahogany
narra
oak
pine
rosewood
seasoning
spruce
teak
wood
forest products—oils
 and resins:
 balsam
 copal
 dammar
 dragon's blood
 drying oil
 gamboge
 gum
 lac
 mastic
 myrrh
 naval stores
 pine oil
 resin
 rosin
 tall oil
 turpentine oil
 wood tar
forest products—
 rubber:
 balata
 chicle
 guttapercha
 latex
 rubber
forest products—
 other:
 cork
 lignin
 paper pulp
 tannin
glassmaking:
 Bakewell glass
 blow molding
 fibreglass
 flint glass

glassblowing
Jena glass
mirror
Orrefors glass
Pitkin glass
Pittsburgh glass
plate glass
Pyrex
safety glass
silvering
soda-lime glass
South Jersey glass
metals of major
 economic
 importance:
 aluminum
 calcium
 cast iron
 chromium
 cobalt
 copper
 gold
 iron
 lead
 magnesium
 mercury
 nickel
 platinum
 potassium
 silver
 sodium
 tin
 titanium
 tungsten
 uranium
 wrought iron
 zinc
mineral sources of
 nonmetals:
 asbestos
 barite
 chrysotile
 feldspar
 fluorite
 gilsonite
 graphite
 gypsum
 kaolin
 kimberlite
 limestone
 mica
 phosphorite

pumice
quartz
shale
soapstone
spodumene
sulfur
tremolite
mining and
 quarrying:
 Frasch process
 mining
 placer mining
 quarry
 stoping
 surface mining
oils, fats, and
 waxes—edible:
 See Section 731
oils, fats, and
 waxes—inedible:
 castor oil
 Chinese wax
 drying oil
 essential oil
 fat
 fish oil
 grease
 lanolin
 lavender
 linseed
 oil
 oil cake
 oil extraction
 oil palm
 oil plant
 perilla oil
 pine oil
 sperm oil
 spermaceti
 tall oil
 turpentine
 turpentine oil
 wax
 whale oil
ore processing:
 basic oxygen
  process
 Bessemer process
 blast furnace
 Cowper stove
 crucible process
 cupola furnace

Biographies
See Section 732

INDEX: See entries under all of the terms above

Section 725. Technology of Industrial Production Processes

A. Materials processing: the operations that are used to transform industrial materials from a raw-material state into finished parts or products

  1. Preliminary processing of raw materials

    a. Mechanical processing; *e.g.,* crushing, mixing, blending, separating, grading

    b. Chemical processing; *e.g.,* leaching, smelting, coagulation, polymerization

  2. Forming: processes in which parts are produced by casting or molding liquid materials or by applying pressure to solid materials

    a. Processing liquid materials

      i. Casting metals; *e.g.,* sand casting, die casting

      ii. Casting and molding nonmetals; *e.g.,* slip casting, injection molding

    b. Processing solid materials; *e.g.,* rolling, forging, stamping, pressing

  3. Material removal: processes for shaping parts by removing portions of a solid piece of material

  4. Joining: processes for bonding materials to each other

    a. Thermal joining: welding, brazing, and soldering
      [see B.5., below]

  b. Adhesive bonding: natural and synthetic adhesives and their uses

 5. Property modification: alteration or improvement of the properties of materials

  a. Thermal processing

   i. Basic heat-treating operations: annealing, stress relieving, and hardening

   ii. Radio-frequency heating: induction and dielectric heating

   iii. Zone melting: zone refining and other techniques

   iv. Exposure to cryogenic temperatures

  b. Processing of materials by exposure to physical conditions other than heat or cold

   i. Processing of materials in a vacuum

   ii. Use of ultrasonic and infrasonic waves

   iii. Other processes; *e.g.,* exposure to radiation

  c. Mechanical and chemical processing

 6. Finishing processes: modification of the surfaces of materials

  a. Mechanical and chemical processes; *e.g.,* cleaning, polishing, embossing, coating

  b. Electrochemical processes: electroplating

B. Metallurgy

 1. Mineral dressing: crushing and grinding, concentration or mineral preparation

 2. Process metallurgy

  a. Pyrometallurgy: metallurgical processes that involve the use of heat

   i. Gas–solid reactions; *e.g.,* roasting

   ii. Distillation: processes for refining metals by condensing metal vapours

   iii. Ferrous metallurgical processes: techniques for making iron and steel

   iv. Nonferrous metallurgical processes: techniques for producing copper, lead, zinc, and other metals

   v. Melting, alloying, casting, and ingot solidification

  b. Electrometallurgy: metallurgical processes that involve electrochemical reactions

   i. Electrowinning, electrorefining

   ii. Electroplating
    [see A.6.b., above]

  c. Hydrometallurgy

 3. Metal processing

  a. Cold and hot working; *e.g.,* forging, rolling, drawing

  b. Foundry processes; *e.g.,* sand casting, die casting

  c. Surface treatments; *e.g.,* hot dipping, metal cladding

  d. Powder metallurgy: powder manufacture, processes, and products

  e. Nuclear engineering metallurgy: production, fabrication, and application of uranium and other metals of importance in nuclear engineering

  f. Heat treatment: precipitation, allotropic transformation, and decomposition reactions

  g. Special products; *e.g.,* coins, medals, tokens

 4. Physical metallurgy

  a. Metallography
   [see also 125.D.1.]

  b. Corrosion

  c. Inspection and testing: mechanical and nondestructive testing

 5. Welding, brazing, and soldering

  a. Basic principles: the metallurgy of metal joining

  b. Welding processes; *e.g.,* forge welding, arc welding, resistance welding, brazing, soldering

    c. Types of joints; *e.g.,* fillet welds, brazed joints

    d. Weldability of metals

    e. Testing and inspection of welds: nondestructive and destructive methods

    f. Applications; *e.g.,* construction of bridges, storage tanks, and ships

    g. Recent developments; *e.g.,* plasma welding, laser welding, ultrasonic welding

C. Materials handling in the production process

    1. Types of materials-handling systems by process

    2. Materials-handling equipment; *e.g.,* wheeled carts, power trucks, trailer trains, racks, bins, conveyors

    3. Transportation of materials
      [see also 734]

    4. Technology of storage and warehousing

D. Technology of packaging

Suggested reading in the *Encyclopædia Britannica:*

MACROPAEDIA: Major articles dealing with the technology of the industrial production processes

    Adhesives
    Handling, Packaging, and Storage
    Industries, Extraction and Processing

MICROPAEDIA: Selected entries of reference information

<u>General subjects</u>

adhesives, fasteners, and joining processes:	conveyor	powder metallurgy	terneplate
	hose	rolling	tinplate
	industrial truck	sintering	*packaging:*
adhesive	materials handling	wire	aerosol container
bolt	pipeline	*metal treating and finishing:*	barrel
brazing	stoker		bottle
cement	storage	annealing	containerization
joint	*metal forming:*	anodizing	drum
mortar	anvil	electroless plating	packaging
rivet	die-casting	electroplating	*thermal processing:*
screw	forging	galvanizing	cryogenics
soldering	founding	plating	dielectric heating
water glass	goldbeating	porcelain	induction heating
welding	grinding machine	enamelling	radio-frequency
materials handling:	investment casting	surface hardening	heating
Archimedes screw	mint	tempering	zone melting

<u>Biographies</u>

    See Section 732

INDEX: See entries under all of the terms above

Division III.   **Major Fields of Technology**
[For Part Seven headnote see page 265.]

Division I of Part Seven is concerned with the nature and effects of technology as a whole. Division II deals with technical processes not specific to any of the major fields of technology. The outlines in the eight sections of Division III deal with the major fields of technology, differentiated by the various needs, purposes, products, and services that have elicited technological development.

Section 731.   **Agriculture and Food Production**

A. The history of agriculture

B. Farm management

  1. Basic management problems and practices

  2. Farm labour, draft animals, and farm machinery

  3. Farm buildings

  4. Farming in relation to other disciplines; *e.g.,* weather, pollution control

C. Crop farming

  1. Soil preparation and care

  2. Plant propagation, seeding and cultivation

  3. Harvesting and crop processing

  4. Specialized crop farming techniques: dryland farming, tropical farming, hydroponic farming, greenhouse farming

  5. Control of pests and disease organisms

  6. Major crops

   a. Horticultural crops: vegetables and legumes, fruits and nuts, flowers

   b. Cereals

   c. Forest crops: trees, rubber

   d. Production of other major field crops; *e.g.,* coffee, tea, cocoa, sugar, tobacco

D. Livestock farming

  1. Animal breeding

  2. Major flock and stock animals

   a. Cattle

   b. Swine

   c. Sheep and goats

   d. Horses

   e. Poultry

   f. Bees

   g. Other livestock; *e.g.,* buffalo, asses and mules, camels

  3. Disease control

E. Technology of hunting and fishing, whaling

F. Food processing

  1. Fruit and vegetable processing

  2. Cereals, cereal products, and other starch products

  3. Bakery products: basic ingredients, types of products and production methods, market preparation, quality maintenance and testing

  4. Confectionery and candy production

  5. Meat and meat products

  6. Fish and marine products

  7. Dairying and dairy products

    a. Milk production and handling techniques

    b. Dairy products: fluid and concentrated milk, dried milk, ice cream, butter, and cheese

  8. Beverage production

    a. Technology of brewing

    b. Technology of wine making

    c. Technology of producing distilled liquor

    d. Technology of producing nonalcoholic beverages: soft drinks, coffee, tea

  9. Spices, herbs, and flavourings

 10. Cane sugar, beet sugar, and other sweeteners

 11. Oils, fats, and waxes

 12. Eggs and egg products

 13. Cocoa and chocolate products

G. Food preservation

  1. Methods of preservation

    a. Low-temperature preservation: refrigeration and freezing

    b. Preservation by drying and by smoking

    c. High-temperature preservation: canning and pasteurization

    d. Fermentation and pickling

    e. Chemical preservation

    f. Preservation by heat radiation and by ionizing radiation

  2. Food storage and packaging

H. Techniques for controlling the quality of food

  1. Evaluation of food quality: sensory evaluation; objective evaluation by chemical, instrumental, and microbiological methods

  2. Control of food quality

  3. Regulation of food quality by legislation, grading, and inspection

I. Food sources and new product development

  1. History and development of new foods and new food products

  2. Utilization of new food sources; *e.g.,* oilseeds, leaves, grasses, single-cell protein

  3. Development of new market forms

  4. Development of special foods; *e.g.,* for space exploration

Suggested reading in the *Encyclopædia Britannica*:

MACROPAEDIA: Major articles dealing with agriculture and food production

Agriculture, The History of
Agricultural Sciences
Beverage Production
Farming and Agricultural Technology
Fishing and Marine Products, Commercial
Food Processing

Forestry and Wood Production
Gardening and Horticulture
Gastronomy
Industries, Extraction and Processing
Public Works

MICROPAEDIA: Selected entries of reference information

General subjects

beekeeping:
beekeeping
beeswax
honey
nectar
royal jelly
beverages:
absinthe
alcoholic beverage
aquavit
beer
brandy
champagne
coffee
cognac
distilled liquor
gin
liqueur
maté
proof
pulque
rum
sake
soft drink
tea
tequila
vodka
whiskey
wine
cereal crops:
barley
buckwheat
cereal
corn
millet
oats
popcorn
rice
rye
sorghum
wheat
cereal grain products:
bran
breakfast cereal
couscous
dumpling
hominy
noodle

paella
pasta
tamale
cooking:
baking
boiling
braising
broiling
cookbook
frying
leavening agent
pressure cooker
sauce
shortening
tandoori cookery
wok
egg and dairy products:
butter
butterfat
buttermilk
candling
cheese
churn
cream
dairying
egg
ice cream
milk
yogurt
farm equipment and buildings:
barbed wire
barn
binder
cellar
combine
corn harvester
cotton gin
cotton harvester
cream separator
crib
crop duster
cultivator
farm machinery
fence
grain drill
grain elevator

harrow
hog house
laying house
millstone
plow
reaper
sakia
scarecrow
silo
sprayer
thresher
tractor
windrower
farming techniques:
chinampa
contour farming
crop rotation
drainage
dry farming
fertilizer
hacienda
hydroponics
irrigation
Norfolk
  four-course
  system
open-field system
organic farming
paddy
plantation
ranch
tenant farming
terrace cultivation
three-field system
till-less agriculture
fishing and sea products:
agar
ambergris
aquaculture
baleen whale
bêche-de-mer
caviar
commercial fishing
factory ship
fishery
lobster pot
net

roe
seafood
sponge
tuna
whale catcher
whaling
food preservation:
dehydration
fermentation
food preservation
freezing
pasteurization
preservative
refrigeration
smoking
horticulture:
graft
horticulture
pruning
transplant
livestock and feeds:
cattle
feed
goat
hay
livestock
pig
sheep
silage
meat products:
aspic
bacon
beef
frankfurter
game
gelatin
ham
hamburger
lamb
meat
pork
sausage
veal
venison
oils, fats, and waxes—edible:
babassu palm
beeswax

Biographies

Burbank, Luther
Carver, George Washington
See also Section 10/34 of Part Ten

Knipling, Edward Fred
McCormick, Cyrus Hall

INDEX: See entries under all of the terms above

Section 732.   **Technology of the Major Industries**

A. Principles of organization of work and production
[see 712]

B. Major manufacturing industries

 1. The aerospace industry

 2. The automotive industry

 3. The clothing and footwear industry

 4. The furniture industry

C. The major fabrication industries

 1. The textile industry

 2. The steel industry
[see also 725.B.]

 3. The leather and hide industry

 4. The fur industry

 5. The floor-covering industry

 6. The electronics industry

 7. The tool and die industry

 8. The lumber industry

 9. The cutlery industry

 10. The abrasives industry

D. The major process industries

 1. The chemical industry

 2. The petroleum industry
[see also 724.B.2.]

 3. The paper industry

 4. The pharmaceuticals industry
[see also 10/35.C.4.]

 5. The plastics industry

6. The rubber industry

7. The surface-coating industry

8. The dye and pigment industry
[see also 122.G.1.t.]

9. The man-made fibre industry

10. Production of industrial and residential gases

11. The cosmetics and personal care industry

E. The construction industries
[see 733]

F. The service industries

1. Hotels and motels

2. Restaurants

3. Food service systems

4. Book, newspaper, and magazine publishing

5. The transportation industry
[see 734]

6. Security and protection systems

G. The utilities industries: the power, gas, telephone, and telegraph industries

H. The merchandising and marketing of consumer goods
[see 533.H.5.]

I. Industrial research and development

J. Technology of industrial safety

Suggested reading in the *Encyclopædia Britannica*:

MACROPAEDIA: Major articles and a biography dealing with the technology of the major industries

Dress and Adornment	Industries, Extraction and Processing
Ford, Henry	Industries, Manufacturing
Forestry and Wood Production	Industries, Textile
Industrial Glass and Ceramics	Publishing
Industries, Chemical Process	

MICROPAEDIA: Selected entries of reference information

General subjects

abrasives:	blimp	turbojet	*chemical processing:*
abrasive	Delta	turboprop	ammonia–soda
corundum	flight simulator	V-1 missile	process
emery	fuselage	V-2 rocket	autoclave
silicon carbide	glider	wind tunnel	contact process
synthetic diamond	helicopter	Zeppelin	detergent
aerospace:	instrument landing	*automotive:*	drug
air-cushion	system	automobile	dye
machine	jet engine	bus	fertilizer
airframe	launch vehicle	diesel engine	Haber–Bosch
airplane	monoplane	electric automobile	process
airport	ramjet	gasoline engine	Leblanc process
airship	rocket	motorcycle	man-made fibre
Atlas rocket	Saturn	tire	paper
autogiro	seaplane	tractor	pigment
automatic pilot	STOL airplane	truck	pitch
balloon	supersonic flight	vehicular safety	reactor
biplane	Thor rocket	devices	retort

rubber
soap
surface-active
  agent
clothing and
  footwear industry:
  button
  fur
  glove
  hat
  hosiery
  leather
  needle
  sewing machine
  shoe
  zipper
cosmetics and
  personal care:
  ambergris
  attar of roses
  cologne
  cosmetic
  emollient
  lavender
  musk
  myrrh
  perfume
cutlery:
  cleaver
  cutlery
  flatware
  razor
  scissors
  sword
dyes and pigments:
  acid dye
  anthraquinone
  anthraquinone dye
  azo dye
  carmine
  catechu
  cochineal
  Congo red
  direct red
  dye
  India ink
  indigo
  lithopone
  naphthol
  pigment
  quercitron bark
  reactive dye
  sulfur dye
  vat dye
electronics:
  See Section 721
floor coverings:
  See Section 629 of
    Part Six
food service and
  lodging:
  cafe

cafeteria
fast-food restaurant
hotel
inn
motel
public house
tavern
youth hostel
furniture:
  bed
  cabinet
  chair
  chest of drawers
  couch
  cupboard
  davenport
  desk
  home appliance
  settee
  stool
  table
gases, industrial and
  domestic:
  argon
  carbon dioxide
  carbon monoxide
  chlorine
  fluorine
  helium
  hydrogen
  liquefied
    natural gas
  liquefied
    petroleum gas
  natural gas
  nitrogen
  oxygen
  sulfur dioxide
industrial safety:
  fire prevention and
    control
  flash point
  safety
  safety engineering
  sprinkler system
lumber:
  chipboard
  ebony
  fibreboard
  fir
  greenheart
  hardwood
  lancewood
  mahogany
  narra
  oak
  particle board
  pine
  plywood
  rosewood
  softwood
  spruce

teak
wood
man-made fibres and
  films:
  azlon
  cellophane
  cellulose acetate
  metallic fibre
  modacrylic
  nylon
  polyacrylonitrile
  polyester
  polyolefin
  polyurethane
  rayon
  spinneret
papermaking:
  Fourdrinier
    machine
  kraft process
  paper
  paper pulp
  parchment
  sulfite process
petroleum:
  See Section 724
plastics:
  Bakelite
  celluloid
  foamed plastic
  Formica
  Lucite
  melamine
  nylon
  plastic
  polyacrylonitrile
  polychlorotri-
    fluoroethylene
  polyolefin
  polystyrene
  polysulfone
  polytetrafluoroethylene
  polyurethane
  polyvinyl alcohol
  resin
  silicone
  urea-formaldehyde
    resin
publishing:
  book
  codex
  gazette
  journalism
  little magazine
  news agency
  newsletter
  newspaper
  newspaper
    syndicate
  pamphlet
  publishing

royalty
yellow journalism
rubber:
  accelerator
  foam rubber
  hose
  tire
  vulcanization
security and
  protection:
  barbed wire
  cipher
  code
  cryptology
  fence
  key
  lock
  police
  security and
    protection
    systems
steel:
  basic oxygen
    process
  Bessemer process
  blast furnace
  Cowper stove
  crucible process
  cupola furnace
  ingot
  open-hearth
    process
  ore dressing
  smelting
  steel
  stainless steel
surface coatings:
  black varnish
  Brunswick black
  drying oil
  Formica
  paint
  porcelain
    enamelling
  shellac
  varnish
textile industry:
  batik
  bleach
  braiding
  dye
  felting
  knitting
  loom
  mercerization
  plain weave
  resist printing
  sizing

spinning
spinning wheel
textile
twisting
weaving
yarn
textiles:
  bombazine
  calico
  cambric

canvas
cheviot
corduroy
crash
crepe
crepe de Chine
damask
duck
flannel
fustian

gabardine
gauze
gingham
khaki
muslin
pile
taffeta
tweed
tool and die industry:
  See Section 722

transportation:
  See Section 734
utilities:
  broadcasting
  electric power
  postal systems
  public enterprise
  public utility
  regulatory agency

Biographies

Bagehot, Walter
Beach, Alfred Ely
Beaverbrook, Max
  Aitken, 1st Baron
Bessemer, Sir
  Henry
Burnham, Edward
  Levy-Lawson, 1st
  Baron
Carnegie, Andrew
Caxton, William
Chandler family
Cotta family
Cowles family
Dana, Charles A.
Drake, Edwin
  Laurentine
du Pont family
Ford, Henry

Girardin, Émile de
Gollancz, Sir Victor
Greeley, Horace
Guggenheim, Meyer
  and Daniel
Haley, Sir William
Halliburton,
  Richard
Harper brothers
Hearst, William
  Randolph
Hughes, Howard
Hunt, H.L.
Kelly, William
Knopf, Alfred A.
Lippmann, Walter
Luce, Henry R.
Macmillan, Daniel
  and Alexander

Manutius, Aldus,
  the Elder
Murdoch, Rupert
Nelson, William
  Rockhill
Northcliffe (of
  the Isle of
  Thanet), Alfred
  Charles William
  Harmsworth,
  Viscount
Nuffield (of
  Nuffield), William
  Richard Morris,
  Viscount
Ochs, Adolph
  Simon
Page, Walter Hines
Pearson, Drew

Pew, J. Howard and
  Joseph N., Jr.
Pulitzer, Joseph
Rockefeller, John D.
Schwab, Charles M.
Siemens,
  Werner von
Siemens, Sir
  William
Squibb, E.R.
Stone, I.F.
Thyssen family
Wallace, De Witt
  and Lila Bell
  Acheson
Yerkes, Charles
  Tyson

INDEX: See entries under all of the terms above

Section 733.   Construction Technology

A. General building construction

  1. Preconstruction planning: design programming, drafting

  2. Surveying procedures: techniques for laying out building foundations
     [see also 723.D.2.c.ii.]

  3. Building materials

     a. Earth, clay, and sod

     b. Lumber

     c. Bricks and tiles: other fired clay and ceramics
        [see 724.C.5.d.]

     d. Stone

     e. Mortar, cement, portland cement, and plaster
        [see 724.C.5.b.]

     f. Metals; *e.g.,* iron, steel, aluminum, copper
        [see 724.C.3.]

     g. Glass
        [see 724.C.5.a.]

     h. Concrete, reinforced concrete, and prestressed concrete

     i. Composition materials, plastics

  4. Testing of building materials

  5. Construction machinery

     a. Transport machinery

     b. Lifting machinery; *e.g.,* cranes, cables, ropes

6. Construction techniques

    a. Carpentry

    b. Masonry construction

    c. Steel construction

    d. Concrete construction

7. Building components

    a. Foundations and footings

    b. The structural frame

    c. Floor systems

    d. Roof systems

    e. Space-enclosure systems

    f. Finish hardware; *e.g.,* locks, hinges, doorknobs

    g. Auxiliary systems

        i. Plumbing systems

        ii. Heating, ventiliating, and air-conditioning systems

        iii. Electrical wiring

        iv. Systems for illumination: interior and exterior lighting

        v. Vertical transport systems; *e.g.,* elevators, moving stairways

        vi. Chimneys and flues

8. Acoustics and sound-control techniques

B. Construction of civil engineering works

1. Dams

2. Aqueducts

3. Bridges

4. Underground construction

5. Harbour and hydraulic works

6. Lighthouses and lightships

7. Stadiums

C. Prefabrication and shop fabrication

Suggested reading in the *Encyclopædia Britannica:*

MACROPAEDIA: Major articles dealing with construction technology

    Analysis and Measurement, Physical and Chemical
    Building Construction
    Drafting
    Lighting and Lighting Devices

MICROPAEDIA: Selected entries of reference information

General subjects

bridges:	box frame	post-and-lintel	settling
bridge	construction	system	shoring
covered bridge	cantilever	scaffold	soil mechanics
military bridge	carpentry	skyscraper	*building materials:*
movable bridge	Chicago School	truss	aggregate
pontoon bridge	drywall	wall	brick
suspension	construction	wattle and daub	cement
bridge	framed building	*building foundations:*	clapboard
viaduct	half-timber work	cofferdam	concrete
building construction:	hypostyle hall	pier	lath
beam	log cabin	retaining wall	mortar

Section 734. Transportation Technology

A. History of transportation

1. Primitive transportation; *e.g.,* travois, slide car, sledge, pack animal, dugout

2. The wheel and the road: development of the vehicle wheel, roads of the ancient world, beginnings of the modern road

3. Sails and oars: beginnings of shipping and shipbuilding, growth of inland waterways

4. Steam transportation

   a. The railroad: the first locomotives, the spread of railways, the construction of railroad bridges and tunnels

   b. Steam navigation: the first steamships, introduction of iron ships, decline of sailing fleets

5. Development of modern transportation

   a. Construction of road vehicles, roads, bridges, and tunnels

   b. Development of mass urban transport and traffic networks

   c. Development of the air transport industry

B. Roads and highways and their construction

C. Vehicles and devices for transportation across country and on roads and highways

1. Nonwheeled transportation devices; *e.g.,* bridles, saddles, harnesses, stirrups

2. Animal-drawn wheeled vehicles: wagons, coaches, and carriages

3. Bicycles

4. Automobiles

5. Trucks and buses

D. Rail transportation

E. Stationary conveyance systems; *e.g.,* pipelines, conveyor belts
[see 725.C.2.]

F. Water transportation

1. Types of ships and other waterborne vessels

2. Ship design and construction

   a. Ship design: hydrodynamic and hydrostatic factors that influence ship stability and maneuverability, structural strength and safety considerations

   b. Shipbuilding, shipyard layout and construction; planning, fabrication, and assembly; launching, outfitting, and trials

   c. Power units for propulsion: steam generators, internal-combustion engines, gas turbines, and nuclear reactors

3. Canals and inland waterways

4. Harbour works: docks and quays, bulk terminals
   [see 733.B.5.]

G. Air transportation

1. Aircraft: configurations, flight characteristics, missions, and special uses

   a. Lighter-than-air craft: balloons, airships

   b. Heavier-than-air craft: fixed-wing aircraft, rotary-wing aircraft, experimental and research aircraft

   c. Air-cushion machines

2. Airports

3. Air transport industry

4. Space travel
   [see 738.C.]

5. Aeronautical and space research

H. Traffic control: history, problems associated with traffic, government regulations, conventional and computerized techniques of control

---

Suggested reading in the *Encyclopædia Britannica:*

MACROPAEDIA: Major article dealing with transportation technology

   Transportation

MICROPAEDIA: Selected entries of reference information

General subjects

air transport:	STOL airplane	harness	boulevard
air-cushion	supersonic flight	horse collar	bus
machine	Zeppelin	horsecar	electric automobile
airframe	*animal-powered*	landau	expressway
airplane	*transport:*	one-horse shay	motorcycle
airport	bridle	phaeton	road
airship	brougham	post chaise	tire
autogiro	buggy	ricksha	tractor
automatic pilot	carriage	rockaway	truck
balloon	cart	saddle	*rail transport:*
biplane	chaise	sedan	coach
blimp	chariot	stage wagon	freight car
glider	coach	stagecoach	locomotive
helicopter	Concord coach	sulky	marshalling yard
instrument landing	Conestoga wagon	troika	railroad
system	curricle	wagon	sleeping car
monoplane	gig	*highway transport:*	
seaplane	hansom cab	automobile	

turbo train	lifeboat	seamanship	litter
water transport:	lighthouse	ship	livery company
anchor	lightship	shipyard	pipeline
buoy	lock	square sail	Roman road
canal	longship	steamboat	system
canoe	motorboat	tanker	shipping route
castle	ocean liner	trawler	Silk Road
clipper ship	paddle wheel	tugboat	tonnage
fog signal	raft	umiak	traffic control
gondola	rigging	*other:*	transportation
harbour	road at sea, rules	aqueduct	velocipede
hydrofoil	of the	bicycle	
jib	rowboat	containerization	
kayak	rudder	elevator	
lateen sail	sail	escalator	

Biographies

Cooper, Peter	MacCready, Paul	Piccard, Auguste	Tupolev, Andrey
Ford, Henry	Beattie	Sage, Russell	Nikolayevich
Fulton, Robert	Montgolfier,	Sikorsky, Igor Ivan	Wright, Orville
Gibbs, William	Joseph-Michel	Stephenson,	and Wilbur
Francis	and	George	
Langley, Samuel P.	Jacques-Étienne	Trevithick,	
Lear, William P.	Oberth, Hermann	Richard	
Lindbergh,	Julius		
Charles A.			

INDEX: See entries under all of the terms above

Section 735.   **Technology of Information Processing and of Communications Systems**

A. Communication and information theory
[see 10/23.F.]

B. Calculating devices: the abacus, tally sticks, mechanical and electromechanical calculators
[see C.2., below]

C. Office machines

1. Writing and reproducing machines: typewriters, dictating and transcribing machines, word processors, duplicating machines and processes, copying machines and processes

2. Calculating and accounting machines

3. Miscellaneous office machines

D. Computers
[see also 10/23.A.6. and 7.]

1. Types of computers: analogue and digital computers, hybrid computer systems

2. Programming systems: the encoding and entering of instructions into computer memory, the concept of software, the systems approach to writing computer programs

3. Computer languages

4. Computer applications

E. General information-recording devices

1. Simple recording implements and devices; *e.g.,* writing implements, slates, chalkboards

2. Typewriters and word processors

3. Printing machines and processes

4. Production of printing plates: engraving and other techniques

   a. Mechanical techniques: woodcut, mechanical engraving, etching, lithography

   b. Photomechanical techniques: photoengraving

F. Sound recording and reproducing devices
[see also 128.E.]

   1. Mechanical systems: phonographs

   2. Magnetic systems: tape recorders

   3. Optical systems: motion-picture sound tracks

   4. Auxiliary equipment: microphones, amplifiers, speaker systems

   5. High fidelity concepts and systems

G. The technology of photography

   1. Still photography
[see also 628.D.]

   2. Motion-picture and television photography
[see also 623]

   3. Holography: laser photography
[see also 128.B.4.]

H. Information systems and processing

   1. Types of information systems

      a. Accounting systems
[see 10/36.D.3.]

      b. Abstracts, bibliographies, reviews

      c. Medical information systems

      d. Libraries as information systems: library science

      e. Dictionaries and lexicons

      f. Encyclopaedias

      g. Atlases and map collections

   2. Storage and retrieval: indexes and indexing; files; information centres; microform recording; cassette, disk, and other forms of computer storage

   3. The use of information-processing systems: the application of modern data-processing technology to the problems of information storage and retrieval

I. Major systems of communication

   1. Book, newspaper, and magazine publishing

   2. Postal systems and equipment

   3. Telegraph systems and equipment

   4. Telephone and telecommunications systems and equipment

   5. Radio communications systems and equipment

   6. Television communications systems and equipment

   7. Communications satellite systems and equipment

   8. Electronic networks

   9. Encryption and decryption techniques and devices: signal security and message authentication, history of cryptology

J. Major systems of detection and remote sensing

   1. Radar systems and equipment

   2. Sonar systems and equipment

K. Electronic components and techniques used in communications

   1. Components

      a. Active components: vacuum and gas-filled tubes, semiconductor devices

      b. Passive components: resistors, capacitors, and inductors; ferrites; other solid-state devices; antennas and wave guides

      c. Integrated circuits: miniature arrays of interconnected active or passive circuit elements

2. Sensing devices and transducers: piezoelectric devices, microphones and other pickups for sound and vibration, sensors

3. Circuitry

Suggested reading in the *Encyclopædia Britannica:*

MACROPAEDIA: Major articles dealing with the technology of information processing and of communications systems

Broadcasting
Computers
Cryptology
Electronics
Encyclopaedias and Dictionaries
Information Processing
Libraries

Motion Pictures
Photography
Postal Systems
Printing, Typography, and
Photoengraving
Telecommunications Systems

MICROPAEDIA: Selected entries of reference information

General subjects

computers:
abacus
analogue computer
artificial
intelligence
computer
computer-aided
engineering
computer-assisted
instruction
computer program
computer
programming
languages
computer science
differential
analyzer
differentiator
digital computer
harmonic analyzer
input/output
device
integrator
microcomputer
microprocessor
time-sharing
word processing
*electronic
communication
systems and devices:*
amateur radio
broadcasting
cable television
citizen's band
radio
Comsat
Echo
facsimile
transmission
Intelsat
loading
minicam
modem
modulation

multiplexing
Morse Code
radio
satellite
communication
shortwave radio
superheterodyne
reception
telecommunications
system
telegraph
telephone
teleprinter
television
Telex
Telstar
UHF
undersea cable
VHF
video telephone
videodisk
videotape recorder
*libraries and their
organization:*
archives
Bliss Classification
bookmobile
Colon
Classification
Dewey Decimal
Classification
library
classification
Library of
Congress
Classification
library science
Universal Decimal
Classification
office machines:
accounting
machine
calculator
cash register

dictating machine
duplicating
machine
hectograph
photocopying
machine
stencil duplicator
typewriter
*photography and
cameras:*
animation
camera
camera lucida
camera obscura
CinemaScope
Cinématographe
Cinerama
collotype
dye-transfer
process
electrophotography
enlarger
exposure meter
filter
fluorescence
photography
holography
Kinetoscope
microform
minicam
motion picture
negative
photography
shutter
speed
Technicolor
viewfinder
wet collodion
process
postal systems:
airmail
Penny Post
postal system
special delivery

Thurn and Taxis
postal system
ZIP Code
*printing and printing
materials:*
colour printing
computerized
typesetting
embossing
engraving
etching
flatbed press
gravure printing
incunabula
ink
intaglio
letterpress printing
Linotype
lithography
mezzotint
Monotype
offset printing
photocomposition
photoengraving
printing
proofreading
rotary press
typesetting
machine
*sound recording and
sound devices:*
cassette
digital sound
recording
flutter and wow
high-fidelity sound
system
loudspeaker
magnetic recording
microphone
phonograph
sound recording
sound track

stereophonic sound	eraser	pen	quill
system	information	pencil	stylus
other:	processing	public-address	
dictionary	information	system	
encyclopaedia	science	qalam	

Biographies

Alembert, Jean Le	Fessenden,	Morse, Samuel	Thomas, Lowell
Rond d'	Reginald Aubrey	F.B.	Vincent of
Armstrong,	Gutenberg,	Muybridge,	Beauvais
Edwin H.	Johannes	Eadweard	Webster, Noah
Bell, Alexander	Josephson,	Niépce, Nicéphore	Winchell, Walter
Graham	Brian D.	Popov, Aleksandr	Zworykin,
Benton, William	Land, Edwin	Stepanovich	Vladimir Kosma
Diderot, Denis	Herbert	Sarnoff, David	
Dimbleby, Richard	Lumière, Auguste	Siemens,	
Disney, Walt	and Louis	Werner von	
Ferrié,	Marconi,	Siemens, Sir	
Gustave-Auguste	Guglielmo	William	

INDEX: See entries under all of the terms above

Section 736. Military Technology

A. Offensive and defensive delivery and payload systems

    1. Development of early weaponry

        a. Primitive and ancient weapons and delivery systems

            i. Shock weapons; *e.g.,* clubs, stone axes, swords

            ii. Missile weapons and delivery systems; *e.g.,* spears, javelins, slings, crossbows

            iii. Siege weapons and methods; *e.g.,* catapults

            iv. Weapons and supply carriers; *e.g.,* horses, elephants, camels

        b. Gunpowder weapons; *e.g.,* artillery, matchlocks, muskets, rifles, rockets

    2. Development of modern weaponry

        a. Modern advances in artillery and gunlike weapons; *e.g.,* recoilless rifles, mortars, breechloaders, explosive shells

        b. Modern advances in military small arms: machine guns, automatic rifles, pistols, submachine guns, and support weapons

        c. Ammunition; *e.g.,* smokeless powder, propellants, high explosives, projectiles, fuses, complete rounds

        d. Mines, grenades, and chemicals

        e. Rockets and missiles

        f. Modern land weapons carriers: tanks, armoured vehicles

        g. Naval ships and craft: naval delivery systems

        h. Aircraft delivery systems

        i. Nuclear warheads and missile systems

        j. Nonballistic weapons: chemical, biological, and psychological warfare

B. Logistics systems, military engineering

C. Purely defensive equipment and systems

    1. Individual protective gear: body armour, helmets

    2. Fortifications

        a. Early fortifications: forts, fortresses, towers, palisades, garrison camps, entrenchments

        b. Modern fortifications: pillboxes, bunkers, bomb shelters, trenches, coastal batteries

3. Warning and detection systems

4. Antimissile missiles: deployment techniques and launch systems

---

Suggested reading in the *Encyclopædia Britannica*:

MACROPAEDIA: Major articles dealing with military technology

War, The Technology of
War, The Theory and Conduct of

MICROPAEDIA: Selected entries of reference information

General subjects

explosives and
incendiaries:
  atomic bomb
  bomb
  grenade
  missile
  napalm
  neutron bomb
  nitroglycerin
  nuclear weapon
  PETN
  shell
  smart bomb
  thermonuclear
   bomb
  torpedo
launch vehicles and
rockets:
  Atlas rocket
  cruise missile
  Nike missile
  Polaris missile
  Poseidon missile
  rocket
  Thor rocket
  V-1 missile
  V-2 rocket
mechanized ground
warfare:
  armoured vehicle
  panzer division
  tank
military aircraft:
  attack aircraft
  AWACS
  B-17
  B-24
  B-29
  B-52
  bomber

F-4
F-16
F-100
F-104
fighter aircraft
Harrier
Hurricane
Ilyushin IL-76
ME-109
MiG
Mirage
Mosquito
P-38
P-47
P-51
Spitfire
Stuka
torpedo plane
trainer
TU-16
V-2
Zero
personal protective
equipment:
  armour
  chain mail
  gas mask
  helmet
warships:
  aircraft carrier
  battleship
  cruiser
  destroyer
  frigate
  galleon
  galley
  ironclad
  minesweeper
  monitor
  submarine

U-boat
weapons:
  AK-47
  antiaircraft gun
  antitank weapon
  Armalite rifle
  artillery
  automatic pistol
  automatic rifle
  bayonet
  bazooka
  Big Bertha
  bow and arrow
  Bren machine gun
  Browning
   automatic rifle
  cannon
  carbine
  catapult
  coastal artillery
  crossbow
  dagger
  field artillery
  flame thrower
  flintlock
  Garand rifle
  Gatling gun
  Greek fire
  gun
  lance
  Lee-Enfield rifle
  Luger pistol
  machine gun
  MAG
   machine gun
  matchlock
  Mauser rifle
  MG42
  musket

pistol
repeating rifle
revolver
rifle
sling
spear
Spencer carbine
Springfield rifle
Sten gun
submachine gun
sword
Thompson
  submachine gun
Uzi
  submachine gun
weapon
other:
Agent Orange
alcázar
ammunition
biological warfare
camouflage
chemical warfare
fortification
military bridge
military
  engineering
naval base
proximity fuze
ram
sapper
shrapnel
snorkel
Strategic Defense
  Initiative
strategic weapons
  system
tactical weapons
  system

Biographies

Braun,
  Wernher von
Fermi,
  Enrico

Goddard, Robert
  Hutchings
Krupp von Bohlen
  und Halbach,
  Alfried

Krupp von Bohlen
  und Halbach,
  Gustav
Krupp, Alfred

Oppenheimer, J.
  Robert
Teller, Edward

See also Section 544 of Part Five

INDEX: See entries under all of the terms above

Section 737.   **Technology of the Urban Community**

A. Basic engineering services of the city

   1. Water-supply systems

   2. Sanitation systems

      a. Development and operation of sewage disposal systems

      b. Construction and operation of street clearance and refuse disposal systems

   3. Urban transportation systems

   4. Interurban transportation systems
      [see 734]

   5. Technology of electric power
      [see 721.C.7.]

   6. Fire prevention and control

B. Technology of the basic social services of the city

   1. Police technology

      a. Traffic control technology
         [see 734.H.]

      b. Crime control technology

   2. Design, construction, and maintenance of recreational facilities; *e.g.,* parks, stadiums, racetracks, planetariums, aquariums

C. Technological responses to new urban problems

   1. Control of air, water, land, and other pollution

   2. The planning of cities and urban environments: the systems approach to urban design and construction, the development of new towns

---

Suggested reading in the *Encyclopædia Britannica:*

MACROPAEDIA: Major articles dealing with technology of the urban community

   Conservation of Natural Resources
   Fire Prevention and Control
   Police
   Public Works

MICROPAEDIA: Selected entries of reference information

General subjects

fire prevention and control:	*police technology:*	muffler	incinerator
fire alarm	criminal	pollution	refuse disposal
fire engine	investigation	smog	system
fire escape	electronic	urban dust	sedimentation tank
fire extinguisher	eavesdropping	*urban transport:*	sewage system
fire fighting	fingerprint	elevated transit	sludge
fire prevention and	handcuffs	line	*water-supply systems:*
control	lie detector	monorail	conduit
fireboat	*pollution control:*	streetcar	desalination
halon	acid rain	subway	qanat
smoke detector	electrostatic	taxicab	reservoir
sprinkler	precipitation	trolleybus	water purification
system	emission-control	*waste disposal:*	water softener
	system	activated-sludge	water-supply
		system	system

Biographies

   See Section 10/37 of Part Ten

INDEX: See entries under all of the terms above

Section 738. **Technology of Earth and Space Exploration**

A. Techniques and equipment of surface and underground exploration

1. Types and purposes of exploration

   a. Scientific exploration: the determination of the properties of the Earth's interior

   b. Resource exploration: the discovery of sources of ores, building materials, fuels, water, and geothermal reserves

   c. Exploration for construction: the planning of tunnels, foundations, and other works

2. Methods of exploration

   a. Indirect methods: geophysical and geochemical methods

   b. Direct methods: on-site testing by means of excavation, boring, and sampling of soil and rock

B. Techniques and equipment of undersea exploration

1. Platforms for exploratory work

   a. Surface vessels; *e.g.,* deep-sea drilling ships and twin-hull vessels

   b. Submersibles

   c. Aircraft and satellites: application of remote sensing and satellite telemetry

   d. Buoys and other unmanned units; *e.g.,* the Self-Propelled Underwater Research Vehicle (SPURV)

2. Navigational methods and systems for establishing the precise location of discoveries

3. Developments in oceanographic sampling and measurement techniques; *e.g.,* acoustic methods and solid-state microelectronic ocean-current measuring devices

C. Techniques and equipment of space exploration

1. History of space flight prior to Sputnik I: early speculations and fictional accounts, development of space flight theory and technology during the 20th century

2. Space programs since 1957

   a. Space launch vehicles: rockets designed to provide orbital or escape velocity for manned or unmanned spacecraft

   b. Unmanned space probes

      i. The use of sounding rockets to explore the upper atmosphere of Earth

      ii. The use of orbiting satellites for scientific purposes; *e.g.,* to measure the natural phenomena of space; to study the relationship between Sun, Earth, and space; to test instrumentation and communication techniques

      iii. The use of unmanned spacecraft to probe the Moon and planets

   c. Manned space programs: the Mercury, Gemini, Apollo, and Space Shuttle programs of the U.S.; the Vostok, Voskhod, and Soyuz/Salyut programs of the U.S.S.R.

   d. The use of Earth-oriented satellites: communications, Earth survey, and navigation satellites

3. Elements of space flight

   a. The environment of space: the definition of space, characteristics affecting space flight

   b. Technology of spacecraft subsystems

   c. Launch principles and techniques: gravitational forces, staging techniques, and acceleration rates

   d. Mechanics and techniques of space flight

      i. Types of trajectories: suborbital, Earth orbital, Earth escape, and interplanetary

      ii. Navigation in space

      iii. Rendezvous and docking

      iv. Re-entry and recovery

4. Contributions of space exploration to advances in the physical sciences

D. Techniques of life-support systems for exploration

    1. Systems used in undersea exploration

    2. Systems used in space exploration

Suggested reading in the *Encyclopædia Britannica*:

MACROPAEDIA: Major articles dealing with the technology of earth and space exploration

    Exploration
    Public Works

MICROPAEDIA: Selected entries of reference information

General subjects

launch vehicles:	Surveyor	*unmanned Earth*	Transit
Delta	Zond	*satellites:*	Vanguard
launch vehicle	*ocean and seafloor*	Aryabhata	Vela
Saturn	*exploration:*	Biosatellite	*other:*
man in space:	bathymetry	Cosmos	Hohmann orbit
Apollo program	bathyscaphe	Discoverer	interplanetary
astronaut	bathysphere	Earth satellite	exploration
Gemini	Challenger	ERTS	National
life-support system	Expedition	Orbiting	Aeronautics
Mercury	diving bell	Astronomical	and Space
Skylab Program	Glomar Challenger	Observatory	Administration
Soyuz	mesoscaphe	Orbiting	prospecting
space shuttle	*translunar probes:*	Geophysical	seismic survey
space station	Helios	Observatory	sounding rocket
Voskhod	Mariner	Pegasus	space exploration
Vostok	Pioneer	satellite	spacecraft
moon probes:	Venera	observatory	unidentified flying
Apollo program	Viking	Seasat	object
Luna	Voyager	Sputnik	
Moon exploration	Zond	TIROS	

Biographies

    Armstrong, Neil
    Oberth, Hermann Julius
    Scott, David R.
    See also Section 721

INDEX: See entries under all of the terms above

Introduction to Part Eight:
Religion as Symbolism

by Wilfred Cantwell Smith

There is more to human life than meets the eye. More to oneself; more to one's neighbour; more to the world that surrounds us. There is more to the past out of which we come; and especially, it would seem, more to the present moment, maybe even infinitely more. There is more to the interrelationships that bind us together as persons. And the further we probe, men have always found, the deeper the mystery, or the reward, or the involvement. It is this "more," perhaps, that provides at least one of the bases for human religion. We men have seldom been content to be "superficial," to remain on the surface, to imagine that reality does not transcend our finite grasp; and throughout most of our history on this planet we have ordered our lives, both personal and cultural, in terms of that transcendence.

Yet how is one to point to what one does not visually see? How to resort to a milieu beyond all space? How to talk or to think about what transcends not only words but the reach of the mind? How even to feel about what one does not touch? Man's inherent and characteristic capacity to do these things finds expression through his special relation to symbols. These have proven over the centuries sometimes more, sometimes less, adequate to such a task, but in any case indispensable, and ubiquitous. Such symbols, it turns out, have the power not merely to express men's otherwise inchoate awareness of the richness of what lies under the surface, but also to nurture and to communicate and to elicit it. They have an activating as well as a representational quality, and an ability to organize the emotions and the unconscious as well as the conscious mind, so that into them men may pour the deepest range of their humanity and from them derive an enhancement of the personality. Without the use of symbols, including religious symbols, man would be radically less than human.

Quite diverse types of things have served the purpose: a beaver, the sky, a ceremonial procedure, silence; erotic love, or austere asceticism; the Qur'ān; a historical figure; reason. The variety has been immense, different groups having chosen different things to serve them as symbols, not all equally successful. Virtually universal, however, is that men have found it possible to designate some item from within the visible world and to sacralize it in such a way that it becomes then for them the symbol or locus of the invisible, the transcendent. In Japan, a simple open gateway (*torii*) marks off the shrine precincts: one passes through it, leaving behind psychologically, symbolically, the humdrum ordinary world to enter the sacred space of the temple; and after worship, one again moves through the gate in the other direction, to reenter now the realm of everyday life, but as a renewed person. Virtually all peoples have set aside some portion of what outsiders would regard as ordinary terrain to serve for them as sacred space, erecting in it temple, church, or shrine whereby is then represented for them, often with great force, quite another dimension of reality.

Similarly with time: the Jew, for instance, sets apart one day in seven, whereby the other six days symbolize the mundane world with its bitter imperfections, perhaps its devastating pain, and at best its transient successes, while the Sabbath creatively represents the inviolate splendour of transcendence—with which therefore the other six days, however bleak, cannot keep him out of touch. Every people has its festivals, weekly or seasonal or occasional, its sacred times when life in its empirical and work-a-day aspects is transcended and life in its timeless dimension is reaffirmed, reactivated: moments when truth, significance, worth are recognized and cultivated—and carried back then into the ordinary world.

Men are somehow aware, if only through imaginative vision or sensibility or our special capacity for hope, not only of what is but also of what ought to be. They have sensed that the *status quo* (nowadays, the *fluxus quo*) is not the final truth about man or the world. They have felt, to take one example, that social justice and concord, personal righteousness, health, joy, stand over against the current observable condition of strife, loneliness, wickedness, poverty, and sorrow not as fancy against truth, wishful and irrational dreaming against reality, but in some fashion *vice versa*—as a norm by which the present imperfect world is judged, in some sense a truth in relation to which empirical actuality is in some sense an error. This too has been affirmed symbolically. One rather common way of doing so has been by representing a more perfect world elsewhere. Some have located their utopias chronologically in the past ("Once upon a time"; or Golden Age theories, as in Greece and India); or in the future (millennialisms, a coming just ruler, secular ideas of progress, a life after death); or geographically, somewhere else (the medieval Irish "Isle of the Blessed" in the then inaccessible Western Sea); or high above the sky (heaven, the heaven of heavens); or in a domain beyond time (Paradise); or in another realm than this universe (a metaphysical order, idealist realities).

However it be symbolized and articulated, a moral dimension to human life has been perceived and affirmed. Man has been aware not only of the profitable and the disadvantageous but also of the better and the worse, and has been inspired by some power to pursue the better; he has known that some actions are right, some wrong, and that it matters. At most times and most places, morality has been an integral part of the religious complex (although situations have on occasion arisen when the two have become historically dislocated—when a given form of religion has seemed not good; or to put it another way, when man's sense of what is worthwhile, and the inherited symbols by which worth used to be formulated, have no longer converged).

If the panorama of man's religious life is, in its outward form, selected mundane data symbolizing the more than mundane, then the task of the student of religion is to know those data but to consider them not in themselves but in their role in men's lives. Our concern is not primarily the doctrines and scriptures and prayers and rites and institutions; but rather, what these do to a man. Not the tribal dance, so much as what happens to the African dancing; not the caste system, so much as what kind of person the Hindu becomes within it, or without it; not the events at Sinai, so much as what role the recounting of these events has played in both Jewish and Christian life over the centuries since; not the Qur'ān so much as what the Qur'ān means to a Muslim.

In illustration, let us consider as an example a statue of the Buddha, and take note specifically of one small part of it, the pose of the right hand. Among several such stylized poses used throughout the Buddhist world, we may choose just one, the *abhaya mudra* ("fearlessness pose"), in which the right arm is somewhat raised, that hand held straight up, palm facing out. Over and above the more universal significance of such a gesture (power, authority, benediction), in the Buddhist case this represents also an incident from the life of the Buddha, in which reputedly a wild elephant charging him and his group was stopped in its tracks when the Teacher raised his hand so, and became tame. The gesture gives artistic expression, then, to the Buddha's fearlessness in the face of the threat, and also to his conferring of fearlessness, and of grounds for fearlessness, on his disciples: his serene triumph over danger.

To say that this particular feature of sculpture symbolizes for Buddhists the overcoming of fear is to indicate not merely that it depicts an event in someone else's life, but also that it effects a change in one's own—since, to repeat, symbols not only represent but activate. The animal in its fury in the remembered anecdote may itself be taken as symbolic, representative of the pressures and assaults of life, which faith in the Buddha gives one the inner resources to withstand: the passions, for instance, to which such faith bestows on one the power quietly to say "no." To understand this particular item in the religious life of Buddhists, accordingly, is to know the history of how a Japanese emperor or a Thai merchant or a Chinese peasant through contemplating it in some nearby temple has had his life transformed, his fear removed, his personality healed. A parallel may be observed of the role in the lives of Christians, over the centuries, of the story of Christ's stilling of the tempest. His words, "Peace, be still!" read in the Lesson, and the portrayal of the scene in stained-glass windows, have served to symbolize, for men of faith, on the one hand Christ's power over the elements in his own life, and on the other hand the power that their faith in Him has in their lives, they have then found, to confer peace, to quell storms.

A special sort of symbolization, developed characteristically in, for instance, the Western world but by no means only there, has been the conceptual. A few recent philosophers have itched to legislate that concepts must be used to refer only to the sensible or phenomenal world; that it is illegitimate to use them symbolically to refer to a transcendent order. It would be manifestly stultifying to apply so austere a restriction to art or to most other human pursuits, apart from the natural sciences (from which these men have learned it). Such an orientation has seemed to work rather well with the "objective" world—better, with the objective facets of the world (at least, until one raises moral questions about atomic bombs or ecology); but it appears stubbornly to misunderstand life in its distinctively human form.

One of the most powerful symbols in human history has, without question, been the *concept* "God." This concept, like other religious and other human symbols, has demonstrably meant different things to different persons and groups and ages; yet it is hardly too drastic an oversimplification to suggest that the concept has on the whole at least subsumed, integrated, deepened, and made operationally effective in the lives of many hundreds of millions of persons and in the life and social cohesion of many thousands of communities their awareness and their potential awareness of the entire range of transcendence with which they are surrounded or endued—of grandeur, order, meaning, aspiration, awe, hope, virtue, responsibility, rapport, integrity, worth, renewal. The highest, deepest, most comprehensive that they were capable of attaining, individually and socially, was organized, focused, and nurtured in and through this concept. (Given the distinction, observed by all believing theorists, between God and men's ideas of God, such theorists may themselves make this same point by saying that God has used the idea of God to enter men's lives; that the concept has served as a sacrament. More recent developments, with the concept "God" no longer serving so effectively, as a symbol, for many, will be touched on below.)

Although correlative conceptualizations are virtually worldwide and history-long, this particular concept was developed in its most powerful and characteristic form in the Near East and has permeated, at times dominated, the civilizations that have emerged from there to cover almost half the planet, especially the Islāmic and the Judeo-Christian. The Indian counterpart has been in many respects closely similar; in many, subtly different. China and Japan, although also employing symbolic concepts richly, have tended toward other religious and cultural patterns than this particular one.

Even so major a symbol, however, as the concept "God," however all-embracing it may seem, is in the end significant not in isolation but within a whole system of ideas, practices, values, and the like, forming a pattern of which it is no doubt the keystone but not the totality. Certainly minor symbols like the pose of the right hand in a piece of sculpture or medium ones like the ceremonial holiness of the Sabbath, however significant they have been in the lives of many millions of persons, derive their meaning and their power from each being one item within a large pattern of symbolic structures, such as the Buddhist complex or the Christian.

And even these great complexes, each of which has an elaborate and ever-changing history, constitute systems to be understood not in themselves, as structures to be looked at, but rather in terms of the ambience that they make available for men and women to live within. "In order to understand Buddhists, one must look not at something called Buddhism, but at the universe, so far as possible through Buddhist eyes." It is not the symbols themselves that one must grasp, so much as the orientation that they induce: how the whole complex of symbols enables those who live in terms of it to see a sunset, a broken marriage, prosperity, the onset of cancer, one's election to public office.

The religious history of the Hindu community is a history, in part, of traditional ceremonial and ideological and sociological patterns. Yet in more significant part it is a history, however difficult this may be to discern, of fortitude and of quiet humaneness, of a conviction that life is worth living and death worth dying, that goals are worth striving for, that the immediate is caught up in the eternal. The Buddhist metaphors have served to kindle in the mind and heart of the Buddhist the perhaps unconscious awareness that one's own fortune is not a reason for gloating, or one's neighbour's fortune, for envy; that knowledge is more important than wealth, and wisdom than knowledge; that the world is to be appreciated and not merely exploited; that one's fellow is to be treated as an end, not merely as a means; that sorrow is not a reason for despair. Islāmic law, theology, architecture, and the rest have been symbols that at their best have crystallized and nurtured, for Muslims, the courage and serenity, the sense of order and the aspiration to justice, the forbearance, the humility, the participation in community, that the Islāmic system traditionally inspired. Christian symbols have given both form and actuality, among Christians, to many things, including for instance the ability of human suffering to become redemptive.

Of course, religious symbols and sets of symbols have been used also for mean and destructive purposes. Man's wickedness, and not only his capacity for virtue, has been expressed and even encouraged by his symbol systems, at times. Through them he has found his freedom, his transcendence of the immediately given, his ability to move beyond being merely an organism reacting to its environment; but sometimes he has used these destructively, or has become a victim of their inherent ambiguities. Nothing has turned a society into a community so effectively as religious faith: to share common symbols is about the most powerful of social cohesions. And yet few gulfs have been greater than those that separate differing religious communities, few hostilities so fierce as those between groups whose symbols differ.

Religious symbols do not raise man above the human level; only to it.

A final word about history. The history of religion has at times been mistaken for the history of its symbols; but this is superficial. The same symbols have discernibly changed their meanings over time, and indeed from person to person, and even within one person's life; also,

persisting or widespread orientations and perceptions have been expressed in strikingly different symbolizations. The true history of religion is more deeply personalist—not in the sense of individualist: the personal is also the social, and especially so in the religious realm. The true history of religion, not yet written, is the history of the depth or shallowness, richness or poverty, genuineness or insincerity, splendid wisdom or inane folly, with which men and women and their societies have responded to such symbols as were around them. It is also, however, the tale, and to some degree this can be told, of when and in what fashion they have forged new symbols, or neglected or found themselves unable to respond to old. And nowadays it is also the story of how they deal or fail to deal with a plurality of symbolisms.

A man's faith is in some sense the meaning that his religious symbols have for him; but more profoundly, it is the meaning that life has for him, and that the universe has, in the light of those symbols. For religious symbols do not "have" meanings of their own; they crystallize in various ways the meaning of the world, of human life. There is a history of their varying ability to do this, at various times and places (or of men's varying ability to have them do it). How new symbols or patterns of symbols emerge is too complex or controversial a question to be summarized here; but how they develop once launched, how they are reinterpreted (sometimes radically) over the centuries, how their success in pointing beyond themselves often gives way to a rigidity and narrowness in which they or their institutions are prized or defended simply in themselves; how iconoclastic movements arise, to shatter the symbols (literally, smashing idols; or figuratively, attacking concepts and mores), whether in the name of something higher or out of misunderstanding, and often both; saddest of all, how a time may arrive when the symbols no longer serve a community, no longer communicate a transcendent vision, and then a profound malaise settles on the society and life comes to seem without meaning, and men become alienated from each other and even from themselves and from the world in which they live—all this the historian can trace.

In recent Western history an aberrational tendency has arisen to imagine that human life is fundamentally or naturally "secular," and that religion has been an added extra, tacked on here and there to the standardly human. This view now appears to be false. Rather, the various religious systems have expressed varying ways of being human. The unbiased historian cannot but report that it has been characteristic of man to find that life has meaning and to formulate that meaning in symbolic ways, whether grostesque or sublime.

Part Eight. Religion

The outlines in the eleven sections of Part Eight set forth studies of religion in general and studies of the particular religions. The ways in which religion is related to studies of human society, the fine arts, the history of civilizations, and science and philosophy are dealt with in Parts Five, Six, Nine, and Ten.

Division I.   Religion in General

The outlines in the two sections of Division I deal with diverse views of the nature, purpose, validity, and value of religion, and with the problems, methods, and results of the empirical, comparative, and phenomenological study of religions and of religious experience.

Section 811.   Knowledge and Understanding of Religion

A. The philosophy of religion: diverse views of the nature and characteristics of religion

 1. Basic questions and problems

  a. The existence of the divine or sacred (God)

  b. The attributes of the divine or sacred

  c. The extent to which mankind can have knowledge of the divine or sacred

  d. The special problems of free will, evil and suffering, and immortality

 2. Questions about the nature and character of the divine or sacred

  a. Whether the divine or sacred is personal or impersonal

  b. Whether the divine or sacred is one or more unique beings or powers

B. Theology as an attempt to understand and state the rationale of religious belief

 1. Theology in relation to divine revelation

  a. The role of Sacred Scriptures

  b. Doctrine and dogma

  c. Articles of faith: religious creeds

 2. Mystical theology: immediate experience of the divine or sacred

 3. Doctrines concerning God or the gods

  a. Polytheism

  b. Religious dualism

  c. Monotheism

   i. Theism

   ii. Deism

   iii. Pantheism and panentheism

  d. Atheism and agnosticism

4. Doctrines of creation

5. Angelology

6. Doctrines of divine government and providence

7. Eschatological theories

8. Doctrines of grace and salvation

9. Sacramental doctrines

10. The doctrine of the Covenant

11. Miracles

C. The study and classification of religions

D. Other systems of belief

1. Myth and mythology

2. Magic

3. Witchcraft

4. Shamanism

5. Astrology and alchemy

6. Ancestor worship

7. Hero worship

8. Nature worship

E. Religion in relation to other aspects of human experience

1. Religion and art
   [see also Part Six]

2. Religion and science

3. Religion and society
   [see also 521.D.6.]

4. Religion and morality
   [see also 10/52.B.6.]

5. Religion and philosophy
   [see also Part Ten, Division V]

Suggested reading in the *Encyclopædia Britannica:*

MACROPAEDIA: Major articles dealing with the knowledge and understanding of religion

Doctrines and Dogmas, Religious
Myth and Mythology
Philosophies of the Branches of Knowledge
Religion, Social Aspects of

Religions, The Study and Classification of
Religious and Spiritual Belief, Systems of
Theology

MICROPAEDIA: Selected entries of reference information

General subjects

basic concerns and phenomena of religion:	miracle	superstition	fideism
covenant	moral theology	theodicy	High God
creation myth	mysticism	theology	monotheism
creed	myth	theophany	Neo-Paganism
eschatology	paradise	*conceptions of the divine or sacred:*	pantheism
evil, problem of	prayer	agnosticism	polytheism
faith	prophet	animism	religious
first cause	revelation	anthropomorphism	syncretism
free will	sacrament	atheism	secularism
heaven	sacrifice	Deism	supernaturalism
hell	salvation	deus otiosus	theism
immortality	scripture	dualism	
	sin	extrinsicism	
	soul		

Biographies

Campbell, Joseph	Frazer, Sir James	Malinowski,	Tiele, Cornelius
Durkheim, Émile	George	Bronisław	Petrus
Eliade, Mircea	James, William	Müller,	Tylor, Sir Edward
Evans-Pritchard, Sir	Jung, Carl (Gustav)	(Friedrich) Max	Burnett
Edward (Evan)	Lang, Andrew	Otto, Rudolf	Wach, Joachim
Frankfort, Henri	Lévi-Strauss, Claude	Söderblom, Nathan	Weber, Max

INDEX: See entries under all of the terms above

Section 812. **The Religious Life: Institutions and Practices**

A. Religious rites and customs

  1. Rituals of worship

    a. Prayer

    b. Confession

    c. Pilgrimage

    d. Sacrifice

  2. Passage and purification rites: birth, puberty, marriage, death

  3. Religious regulation of personal and social behaviour

    a. Religious law
      [see 551.B.3.d. and 827.F.6.]

    b. Dietary customs

    c. Monasticism

    d. Celibacy

    e. Asceticism

    f. Prophecy and divination

  4. Religious feasts and festivals

B. Religious leaders and institutions

  1. The religious state: theocracies, sacred kingships

  2. Forms of religious organization: church, temple, congregation, sect, council; the priesthood

  3. Sainthood

  4. Institutions of religious education

C. Material manifestations of religious beliefs

  1. Sacred writings

  2. Art and architecture, religious symbolism and iconography

  3. Ceremonial and religious objects, the sacraments

  4. Religious dress and vestments

Suggested reading in the *Encyclopædia Britannica:*

MACROPAEDIA: Major articles dealing with the religious life: institutions and practices

Doctrines and Dogmas, Religious
Religious Education
Religious Experience
Religious Symbolism and Iconography
Rites and Ceremonies, Sacred
Sacred Offices and Orders

MICROPAEDIA: Selected entries of reference information

General subjects

disciplines and
practices:
  asceticism
  celibacy
  fasting
  feast
  human sacrifice
  meditation
  pilgrimage
  prayer
  sacrament
  sacrifice
  tonsure

places of worship:
  altar
  church
  high place
  mosque
  synagogue
religious offices,
orders, and
personages:
  abbot
  canonization
  hagiology
  hermit

martyr
monasticism
priesthood
prophet
sacred kingship
saint
shaman
rites of passage and
associated practices:
  anointment
  Baptism
  burial
  circumcision

cremation
embalming
marriage
passage rite
purification
other:
  amen
  aniconism
  confession of faith
  creed
  idolatry
  relic
  scripture

Biographies

See Section 811

INDEX: See entries under all of the terms above

Division II.   **The Particular Religions**
[For Part Eight headnote see page 303.]

The outlines in the nine sections of Division II treat the particular religions of mankind, in different historical eras and world areas.

Section 821.   **Prehistoric Religion and Primitive Religion**

A. Prehistoric religion

  1. The study of prehistoric religion: nature, scope, methods of interpretation, problems special to the subject
     [see also 10/41.B.]

  2. Inferred prehistoric religious beliefs and practices

     a. Burial customs and cults of the dead

     b. Cannibalism

     c. Sacrifices: human, animal, and other offerings

     d. Hunting rites and animal cults

     e. Female fertility deities

     f. Shamanism, sorcery, and magic

  3. Religions attributed to various prehistoric cultural stages and regions

B. Primitive religion

   1. The nature and significance of primitive religion

   2. Primitive views of reality

      a. The distinction between the sacred and the profane

      b. Dynamistic, daemonistic, and theistic views of the sacred: the concept of mana

      c. Animism: external reality viewed as living presence

      d. Sacred time and times, sacred space and places, and man's nature, origin, and destiny: primitive cosmogonies, cosmologies, eschatologies

   3. The nature and function of myth and symbol in primitive religion: their role in ritual, the iconographic character of primitive art

   4. Primitive religious practices and institutions

      a. Sacrifice, purification, passage rites

      b. Worship or veneration centred on natural objects or forces

      c. Totemism: the socioreligious system in which men are intimately related to plants, animals, or other natural phenomena

      d. Worship of ancestors, kings, and heroes

      e. The roles of asceticism, shamanism, divination, and spiritualistic practices

   5. The primitive religions of the major world areas

Suggested reading in the *Encyclopædia Britannica:*

MACROPAEDIA: Major articles dealing with prehistoric religion and primitive religion

    Doctrines and Dogmas, Religious
    Prehistoric Peoples and Cultures

MICROPAEDIA: Selected entries of reference information

General subjects

amulet	devarāja	moon worship	soul loss
animal worship	Dreaming, the	mother goddess	Stonehenge
animals, master	Earth Mother	phallicism	Sun Dance
of the	fire walking	rain dance	sun worship
animism	headhunting	reindeer sacrifice	taboo
Blessingway rite	hieros gamos	Rice Mother	thunder cult
bull cult	High God	sacred clown	tjurunga
burial mound	mana	sacred pipe	totemism
cannibalism	medicine society	shaman	vision quest
Corn Mother	megalith	skull cult	world tree

Biographies

  See Section 811

INDEX: See entries under all of the terms above

Section 822.   **Religions of Ancient Peoples**

    A. Religions of the ancient Near Eastern peoples

        1. Characteristics of the ancient Near Eastern religions

        2. Mesopotamian religions

        3. Egyptian religion

            a. Historical developments from the late Neolithic Period to the Hellenistic Age

            b. Religious literature and mythology

            c. Beliefs and doctrines: the Egyptian pantheon

            d. Major forms of Egyptian religion

            e. Religious symbolism and iconography

        4. Religions of the ancient peoples of Asia Minor

        5. Syrian and Palestinian religions

        6. Religions in the Arabian Peninsula

    B. Religions of the Iranian peoples

        1. General characteristics of the Iranian religions

        2. Early Indo-Iranian religion: nature-polytheism
           [see also 823.A.1.]

        3. Religion of the Scythians, Sarmatians, and Alani
           [see F., below]

        4. The cult of Ahura Mazdā (Ormazd): its influence on the preaching of Zoroaster and the priestly institutions of the Magi

        5. Mithraism

        6. Zurvanism

        7. Manichaeism
           [see E.3., below]

    C. Greek religion

        1. Historical development

        2. Greek mythology and other religious literature

        3. Religious beliefs and speculation: the Greek pantheon

        4. Worship, practices, institutions

        5. Religious art and iconography

    D. Roman religion

        1. Historical development

        2. Roman gods, goddesses, numina, and genii and their place in family and civic religion

        3. Worship, practices, institutions

        4. Religious art: sculpture, metalwork, painting, mosaic

    E. Religions of the Hellenistic world

        1. Mystery religions

        2. Gnosticism

        3. Manichaeism

        4. Hellenistic religious philosophies: neoplatonism, stoicism, epicureanism
           [see also 10/51.A.1.c.]

        5. Quasi-scientific and magical cults; *e.g.*, numerology, astrology

        6. Judaism
           [see 826]

7. Christianity
[see 827]

F. Religions of the early peoples of eastern and central Europe

1. Scythian religion

2. Religions of the Sarmatians and associated peoples

3. Religion of the pre-Christian Slavic peoples

G. Religions of the ancient Celtic and Germanic peoples

1. Religion of the Celts

2. Religion of the Germanic peoples

H. Religions of the early peoples of northeastern Europe

1. Religion of the Baltic peoples

2. Religion of the Finno-Ugric peoples

I. Religions of pre-Columbian American civilizations

1. Inca religion

2. Mayan religion

3. Aztec religion

Suggested reading in the *Encyclopædia Britannica:*

MACROPAEDIA: Major articles dealing with religions of ancient peoples

Doctrines and Dogmas, Religious
European Religions, Ancient
Middle Eastern Religions, Ancient
Mystery Religions
Pre-Columbian Civilizations

MICROPAEDIA: Selected entries of reference information

General subjects

*Anatolian and Asia
Minor religions:*
  Hebat
  huwasi stone
  Kubaba
  Tarhun
  Teshub
*Arabian religion
(pre-Islāmic):*
  ḥanīf
  Ilumquh
  Lāt, al-
Aztec religion:
  Chicomecóatl
  Coatlicue
  Huitzilopochtli
  nagual
  Ometecuhtli
  Quetzalcóatl
  Tezcatlipoca
  Tlaloc
  Tlazoltéotl
  Tonatiuh
  Xipe Totec
  Xiuhtecuhtli
Baltic religion:
  Dievs

gabija
Kalvis
Laima
lauma
Mēness
Pērkons
Saule
Zemes māte
Celtic religion:
  Belenus
  Brân
  Brigit
  Celtic religion
  Cernunnos
  Danu
  Dôn
  Druid
  Esus
  Goibniu
  Llyr
  Lugus
  Medb
  Ogmios
  Pwyll
  Sucellus
  Teutates
  Tuatha Dé Danann

Egyptian pantheon:
  Amon
  Anubis
  Apepi
  Apis
  Aton
  Atum
  Bast
  Bes
  Buto
  Geb
  Hathor
  Horus
  Hu, Sia, and Heh
  Isis
  Ma'at
  Mut
  Nekhbet
  Nu
  Nut
  Opet
  Osiris
  Ptah
  Re
  Sarapis
  Sebek
  Seth

Shu
Taurt
Thoth
*Egyptian worship,
practices, and
institutions:*
  Book of the Dead
  Canopic jar
  Egyptian religion
  Heb-Sed festival
  Hermetic writings
  mortuary temple
  reanimation rite
  scarab
Finno-Ugric religion:
  äppäräs
  haltia
  Ilmarinen
  Kekri
  kobdas
  kuala
  lud
  maa-alused
  Madderakka
  Manala
  mudor šuan
  noiade

Panathenaea
Pyanopsia
Scirophoria
Thargelia
Thesmophoria
Inca religion:
  Chosen Women
  huaca
  Inti
  Pachacamac
  Viracocha
Iranian religion
  (*pre-Islāmic*):
  millet
  Mithra
  Mithraism
  Yima
Mayan religion:
  Ah Kin
  Bacab
  Chac
  Cizin
  Dresden Codex
  Itzamná
  Madrid Codex
  Paris Codex
  Popol Vuh
Mesopotamian
  pantheon:
  Adad
  Anu
  Ashur
  Bel
  Belit
  Damu
  Dumuzi-Amau-
    shumgalana
  Ea
  Ereshkigal
  Ishkur
  Ishtar
  Lamashtu
  Marduk
  Meslamtaea
  Mesopotamian
    religion

Nabu
Nergal
Ningishzida
Ninhursag
Ninsun
Ninurta
Shamash
Sin
Tammuz
Mesopotamian
  religious literature
  and mythology:
  Adapa
  Enmerkar
  Eridu Genesis
  Etana Epic
  Gilgamesh
  Inanna and Bilulu
  Lahmu and
    Lahamu
  Lament for the
    Destruction of Ur
  Mesopotamian
    mythology
mystery religions:
  Andania Mysteries
  Attis
  Cabeiri
  Corybantes
  Eleusinian
    Mysteries
  Eumolpus
  galli
  Great Mother of
    the Gods
  hierophantēs
  Iacchus
  Jupiter Dolichenus
  mystery religion
  Orpheus
  Taurobolium
Roman pantheon:
  Aeneas
  Ascanius
  Asclepius
  Bona Dea

Cacus and Caca
Camilla
Ceres
Cupid
Diana
Dioscuri
Faunus
Fides
Fortuna
Fury
Janus
Juno
Jupiter
Lar
Liber and Libera
Libitina
Mars
Mercury
Minerva
Neptune
Penates
Picus
Psyche
Quirinus
Salus
Saturn
Silvanus
Sol
Venus
Vesta
Roman worship,
  practices, and
  institutions:
  fetial
  flamen
  genius
  Haruspices
  lectisternium
  Lupercalia
  Matronalia
  Parilia
  pontifex
  Roman religion
  Salii
  supplicatio
  Vestal Virgin

Slavic religion:
  domovoy
  leshy
  mer
  Perun
  rusalka
Syrian and
  Palestinian
  pantheon:
  Anath
  Asherah
  Astarte
  Atargatis
  Baal
  Dagon
  El
  Kothar
  Melqart
  Resheph
  Shadrafa
  Tanit
  Yamm
Zoroastrianism:
  Ahriman
  Ahura Mazdā
  amesha spenta
  Avesta
  fravashi
  Gabar
  Gahanbar
  Gayōmart
  haoma
  magus
  Nōrūz
  Parsi
  Rashnu
  Saoshyans
  Sraosha
  Verethraghna
  Vohu Manah
  yazata
  Zoroastrianism
  Zurvanism

Biographies

  Akhenaton
  Anquetil-Duperron, A(braham)- H(yacinthe)
  Basilides
  Imhotep

  Kartēr
  Mani
  Valentinus
  Zoroaster

INDEX: See entries under all of the terms above

Section 823.   **Hinduism and Other Religions of India**

A. History of Hinduism

1. The origins of Hinduism: Indo-European roots and other influences

2. The prehistoric and protohistoric periods, through the 2nd millennium BC: the religions of the indigenous prehistoric peoples and of the Indus Valley civilization

3. The Vedic period (2nd millennium–7th century BC)

    a. The religion of the Ṛgveda

    b. The religion of the later Vedas and *Brāhmaṇa*s

    c. The religion of the *Upaniṣad*s

4. The heterodox period (7th–2nd century BC): challenges to Brahmanism by reformers and ascetic groups
   [see also D.l., below, and 824]

5. The early Hindu period (2nd century BC–4th century AD): the rise of the major sects and other developments

6. The Purāṇic period (4th–8th century)

7. The rise of devotional Hinduism (8th–11th century): the Tamil hymnists, the *Bhāgavata-Purāṇa* after Hinduism

8. The age of *bhakti* (11th–19th century)

9. The modern period (19th–20th century)

10. Hinduism today

B. Intellectual, spiritual, and imaginative expressions of Hinduism
   [see also C.4., below]

1. Hindu sacred literature

    a. Primary scriptures regarded as eternal revelations: the Veda

    b. Post-Vedic Sanskrit literature; *e.g.,* epics, *Purāṇa*s, *Tantra*s

    c. Sacred literature in Indian regional languages

2. Hindu mythology: varieties of myths, modes of representation and themes

3. Hindu philosophy: the integral relation of philosophy and religion in Hinduism

4. Hindu mysticism: its general characteristics, varieties, goals, and methods

C. Beliefs, practices, and institutions of Hinduism

1. Common characteristics of Hindu belief

    a. Views about God or the sacred

    b. Views about the universe

    c. Views about mankind

       i. *Ahiṃsā,* the obligation to respect all living beings

       ii. The doctrines of *karman, saṃsāra,* and transmigration

       iii. The three *mārga*s: the paths of duties, of knowledge, and of devotion

2. The forms of Hinduism

    a. Vedism and Brahmanism

    b. Vaiṣṇavism

    c. Śaivism

    d. Tantrism and Śāktism

    e. Folk Hinduism

    f. Ethical, social, and nationalist movements in modern Hinduism

3. Rituals, social practices, and institutions

   a. Sacrifice and worship

   b. Sacred times and places

   c. The class hierarchy: the caste system

   d. Religious orders, holy men, the four stages of life

4. Cultural expressions of Hindu values and ideas

   a. The traditional religious functions of Indian art: symbols and images

      i. Types of symbols: *yantra*s, *maṇḍala*s, *liṅga*s, *yoni*s

      ii. Icons: their role in expressing theological elements of Hinduism

   b. The religious expression of particular arts

D. Other religions of India

   1. Jainism

      a. History of Jainism

         i. Early background: traditional accounts of Mahāvīra's predecessors

         ii. The life, work, and teachings of Vardhamāna Mahāvīra

         iii. Later developments (6th century BC–20th century AD)

      b. Myths about Jaina "great souls": Tirthaṅkaras, ascetic and monastic figures, and lesser deities

      c. Beliefs, practices, and institutions of Jainism

   2. Sikhism

      a. History of Sikhism

         i. Islāmic and Hindu background (11th–15th century)
            [see also A., above, and 828.A.]

         ii. The origin of Sikhism in the life and work of Nānak, first of the ten Gurūs (15th–16th century)

         iii. The establishment and growth of Sikhism under the nine succeeding Gurūs, the establishment of Sikh militarism (16th–18th century)

         iv. The condition of Sikhism during the Sikh empire (18th–19th century)

         v. The condition of Sikhism under British rule (19th–20th century)

         vi. Sikhism in independent India and Pakistan

      b. Sikh religious literature

      c. Beliefs, practices, and institutions of Sikhism

   3. Parsiism: Zoroastrianism in India
      [see 822.B.4.]

      a. History of Parsiism

      b. Sources of beliefs and doctrines in Zoroastrian literature

      c. Beliefs, practices, and institutions of the Parsis

Suggested reading in the *Encyclopædia Britannica*:

MACROPAEDIA: Major articles dealing with Hinduism and other religions of India

Hinduism
Indian Philosophy
Jainism
Sikhism

MICROPAEDIA: Selected entries of reference information

General subjects

Hinduism—
caste system:
Agarwālā
Bania
bhāīband
Brāhmaṇa
Camār
caste
Christian caste
Dāsa
Devadāsī
Ḍom
dvija
gotra
Islāmic caste
jajmānī system
jāti
Kṣatriya
kul
Mahar
Marāthā
Nambūdiri
Nāyar
outcaste
pañcāyat
pollution and
  purification
sabhā
Śūdra
untouchable
Vaiśya
varṇa
Hinduism—deities
and mythology:
Aditi
Agni
Ardhanārīśvara
Balarāma
Brahmā
Brahman
Caṇḍī
churning of the
  milky ocean
Dharma-Ṭhakur
Durgā
Gaṇeśa
Garuḍa
grāmadevatā
Hanumān
Harihara
Indra
Jagannātha
Kālī
Kalkin
Kāma
Krishna
Kubera
Kūrma
Lakṣmī

Manasā
Manu
Matsya
Meru, Mount
Murugaṇ
nāga
Nandi
Narasimha
Naṭarāja
Paraśurāma
Pārvatī
Prajāpati
Rādhā
rākṣasa
Rāma
Rāvaṇa
Saptamātṛkā
Sarasvati
Sītā
Śiva
Skanda
Sūrya
vāhana
Vāmana
Varāha
Varuṇa
Vāsudeva
Vishnu
yakṣa
Yama
yuga
Hinduism—forms,
sects, movements,
and orders:
Ajīvika
Arya Samaj
Bhāgavata
bhakti
Brahmo Samaj
Caitanya
  movement
Dādūpanthī
daśnāmī sannyāsin
Gāṇapatya
Kānphaṭa Yogi
Kāpālika and
  Kālāmukha
Kashmir Śaivism
Liṅgāyat
Nātha
Pāñcarātra
Pāśupata
Prarthana Samaj
Rādhā Soāmi
  Satsang
sādhu and swāmī
Śaiva-siddhānta
Śaivism
Śāktism

sampradāya
sannyasi
Satnāmī sect
Saura sect
Smārta sect
Śrīvaiṣṇava
Swāmī-Nārāyāṇī
Tantric Hinduism
Teṅkalai
Vaḍakalai
Vaikhānasa
Vaiṣṇava
vairāgin
Vaiṣṇava-
  Sahajiyā
Vaiṣṇavism
Vallabhācārya
Hinduism—
philosophy and
doctrine:
Advaita
ahaṃkāra
ānanda
anumāna
artha
āsana
āstika
ātman
avatar
Bhedābheda
cakra
Cārvāka
cow, sanctity
  of the
deva
dharma
Dvaita
Haṭha Yoga
indriya
jñāna
karman
kuṇḍālinī
mārga
māyā
Mīmāṃsā
nirguṇa
Nyāya
prakṛti
pramāṇa
prāṇa
prāṇāyāma
pratyakṣa
puruṣa
śabda
samādhi
Sāṃkhya
saṃsāra
sat
tat tvam asi

upādhi
Vaiśeṣika
Vedānta
Viśiṣṭādvaita
yama
Yoga
Hinduism—ritual
and practice:
antyeṣṭi
ārtī
ashram
aśvamedha
darshan
dikṣā
Dīwālī
guru
Holī
Janmāṣṭamī
kīrtana
Kumbha Melā
liṅga
Mahā-śivarātrī
Navarātrī
Om
Poṅgal
pradakṣiṇa
prasāda
pūjā
Rathayātrā
saṃskāra
soma
śrāddha
Śrī-Nāthajī
suttee
tapas
tilaka
tīrtha
upanayana
Vedic sacrifice
yajña
Hinduism—
sacred and secular
literature:
Āgama
Aranyakas
Artha-śāstra
Aṣṭchāp
Bhagavadgītā
Bhāgavata-Purāṇa
Brāhmaṇa
Dharma-śāstra
Gītagovinda
Gṛhya-sūtra
Kalpa-sūtra
Mahābhārata
maṅgal-kāvya
Manu-smṛti
Nāyaṇar
Purāṇa

Rāmāyaṇa	Bāhubali	Pārśvanātha	gurdwārā
Smṛti	Digambara	Paryuṣaṇa	Gurū
Śrauta-sūtra	dravya	Ṛṣabhanātha	Harimandir
Śruti	gaccha	siddha	Khālsā
sūtra	guṇasthāna	Sthānakavāsī	Nāmdhārī
Tantra	Jaina canon	Śvetāmbara	Niraṅkārī
Upanishad	Jaina vrata	syādvāda	Rām Rāiyā
Veda	Jainism	Tīrthaṅkara	Sikhism
Jainism:	jīva	*Sikhism:*	Singh Sabhā
ahiṃsā	Kālakācāryakathā	Ādi Granth	Udāsī
ajīva	Kalpa-sūtra	Akāl Takht	*other:*
Ariṣṭanemi	leśyā	Akālī	Parsi
aṣṭamaṅgala	nirjarā	Dasam Granth	

Biographies

Aurobindo, Śrī	Keshab	Mīrā Bāī	Rāmānuja
Caitanya	Chunder Sen	Nānak	Ray, Rammohan
Dayananda	Madhva	Ram Singh	Śaṅkara
Sarasvati	Mahāvīra	Ramakrishna	Tara Singh
Fateh Singh, Sant	Meher Baba	Ramana Maharshi	Vivekananda
Gobind Singh			

INDEX: See entries under all of the terms above

Section 824.   Buddhism

A. History of Buddhism

1. The cultural context: its background in Hinduism; its geographical, ethnic, and cultural base
   [see also 823]

2. The founding of Buddhism: the life, work, and teachings of Siddhārtha Gautama (6th–5th century BC)

3. Developments in India (6th century BC–12th century AD)

4. Buddhism in Central Asia and China
   [see also 825.A.]

5. Buddhism in Korea and Japan
   [see also 825.D. and E.]

6. Buddhism in Tibet and the Himalayan kingdoms

7. Buddhism in Ceylon (Sri Lanka) and Southeast Asia to the mid-19th century

8. Buddhism in the late 19th and 20th centuries

B. Intellectual, spiritual, and imaginative expressions of Buddhism
   [see also C.4., below]

1. Buddhist sacred literature

2. Buddhist mythology: basic types, contents, and functions of myths

3. Buddhist philosophy: the role and contribution of systematic reflective thought

4. Buddhist mysticism: universal characteristics; regional and historical variations; goals, techniques, and approaches

C. Beliefs, practices, and institutions of Buddhism

1. Traditional beliefs and doctrines

   a. Views of the nature of reality; *e.g.,* the impermanence of all existence, the absence of self, the underlying state of suffering and its causes

   b. The Eightfold Path to salvation or release

   c. The goal of the Eightfold Path: Nirvāṇa

   d. The Threefold Refuge—in the Buddha, the doctrine, and the community

e. Views of the gods, spirits, and demons: the role of miraculous powers

2. The main forms of Buddhism

a. The Theravāda school and other ancient schools

    i. Views of the nature of things: cosmology, the classification of *dharma*s

    ii. The emphasis on self-cultivation and self-salvation: the stages leading to *arhat*ship, the levels of meditation

    iii. Doctrines concerning Buddha and Buddhahood

    iv. Characteristics of the individual ancient and transitional schools

b. The Mahāyāna version

    i. Views of the nature of absolute reality: the ultimate realization of the meditative quest

    ii. Views of the transcendence of the Buddha: the three aspects of the Buddha, the *bodhisattva* ideal

    iii. Characteristics of the individual Mahāyāna schools; *e.g.,* Mādhyamika, Yogācāra, Avataṃsaka, Zen, devotional schools

c. Esoteric Buddhism: Tantrism, Tibetan Buddhism, Shingon

3. Practices and institutions

a. Universal or prevalent ethical and religious practices

b. Monastic institutions: the characteristics and role of the *saṅgha*

c. Ceremonies and festivals: the religious year, popular traditions, passage rites

d. Regional variations in practices

4. The religious and cultural role of Buddhist art

a. Symbolism and iconography

b. Religious expression in the arts

5. The relationship of Buddhism to nationalist movements: its contemporary situation, its prospects

---

Suggested reading in the *Encyclopædia Britannica:*

MACROPAEDIA: Major article dealing with Buddhism

    Buddhism, The Buddha and

MICROPAEDIA: Selected entries of reference information

General subjects

deities and mythology:	Ni-ō	Nichiren	*offices and personages:*
Amitābha	Saṃvara	Buddhism	bhikku
Avalokiteśvara	Shih Wang	Pure Land	bodhisattva
Bhaiṣajyaguru	Tārā	Buddhism	cakravartin
brahma-loka	Ti-ts'ang	Reiyū-kai	Dalai Lama
dharmapāla	Vairocana	Rinzai	lama
Dhyāni-Buddha	Vajrapāṇi	Risshō-Kōsei-kai	mahāsiddha
Five Great Kings	Vajrayoginī	Ritsu	Nechung oracle
Hārītī	yi-dam	Rnying-ma-pa	Panchen Lama
Hevajra	*forms, sects, schools, and orders:*	Sammatīya	pratyeka-buddha
Kṣitigarbha	Bka'-brgyud-pa	Sarvāstivāda	upāsaka
lokapāla	Dge-lugs-pa	Sautrāntika	*philosophy and doctrine:*
Lumbinī	eighteen schools	Shingon	Abhidharmakośa
Mahā Māyā	Hīnayāna	Sōka-gakkai	abhijñā
mahāpuruṣa	Jōjitsu	Sōtō	akriyāvāda
Maitreya	Kegon	Theravāda	ālaya-vijñāna
Mañjuśrī	Kusha	Tibetan Buddhism	anattā
Māra	Mādhyamika	T'ien-t'ai	arhat
Myō-ō	Mahāsaṅghika	Vajrayāna	ariya-puggala
nāman	Mahāyāna	Yogācāra	Zen

arūpa-loka
āsrāva
bhava-cakra
bhūmi
bodhi
brahma-loka
brahmacarya
brahmavihāra
dharma
dukkha
Eightfold Path
Four Noble Truths
kammaṭṭhāna
karman
Kegon
Kusha
Mādhyamika
mahāmudrā
Nirvāṇa
pāramitā
prajñapti
Pramāṇa-vārttika
pratītya-samutpāda
pratyaya
puñña
saddhā
saṃsāra
saṃvṛti-satya
Sarvāstivāda
Satori
sīla
skandha
smṛtyupasthāna
śūnyatā
tri-ratna
tri-svabhāva
practices and
institutions:
  abhiṣeka

Buddhist
  meditation
dhāranī
gcod
gtor-ma
kōan
kyūdō
maṇḍala
mantra
mudrā
nang-mchod
pabbajjā
pāramitā
pātimokkha
phyi-mchod
sādhana
saṅgha
Smon-lam
  chen-mo
upasaṃpadā
uposatha
vassa
vihāra
zazen
sacred and secular
literature:
Abhidhamma
  Piṭaka
Abhidhammattha-
  saṅgaha
Abhidhammāvatāra
Abhidharmakośa
Abhisamayālaṅ-
  kārāloka
Amitāyur-dhyāna-sūtra
aṅgā
aṭṭhakathā
Avadāna
Avataṃsaka-sūtra

Bhadracaryā-
  praṇidhāna
bhāṇavāra
Bka'-'gyur
Bstan-'gyur
Buddhacarita
Dhammapada
Diamond Sūtra
gsung-'bum
Guhyasamāja
  Tantra
Heart Sūtra
Jātaka
Khuddaka Nikāya
Lalitavistara
Laṅkāvatāra-sūtra
Lotus Sūtra
Mahāvairocana-
  sūtra
Mahāvastu
Mahāyāna-śrad-
  dhotpāda-śāstra
Milinda-pañha
Mūlamadhyama-
  kakārikā
Prajñāpāramitā
Pramāṇa-vārttika
Pure Land Sūtra
Satyasiddhi-śāstra
  sūtra
Sutta Piṭaka
Suttanipāta
Ta-ts'ang Ching
Tipiṭaka
Vinaya Piṭaka
symbolism,
iconography, and
ritual objects:
Borobuḍur

butsudan
caitya
Gandhāra art
Jōgan style
kapāla
Kara-yo
Mai-chi-shan
maṇḍala
Mathurā art
mudrā
Northern Wei
  sculpture
pagoda
prayer wheel
Sānchi sculpture
stūpa
Sukhothai style
Tempyō style
Tenjiku
thang-ka
thread cross
T'ien-lung Shan
Tōdai-ji
U Thong style
vajra
yab-yum
Yün-kang caves
other:
Abhayagiri
Bon
Buddhist council
Mahāvihāra
mappō
rock edicts

Biographies

Asaṅga
Aśoka
Bodhidharma
Dōgen

Fa-hsien
Hasegawa Tōhaku
Hōnen
Hsüan-tsang

Hui-neng
Kūkai
Nāgārjuna
Nichiren

Padmasambhava
Shinran

INDEX: See entries under all of the terms above

Section 825.   **Indigenous Religions of East Asia: Religions of China, Korea, and Japan**

A. Characteristics and development of Chinese religion

   1. The distinction and relationship between the folk religions and the literate religions in China

   2. History of religion in China

      a. The emergence of Chinese religion: ancestor worship, early cosmological beliefs

      b. The formulation of the Great Tradition: the development of the Confucian and Taoist ways (6th–1st century BC)

      c. The dominance of the Buddhist Way and the rise of Taoist-inspired cults (1st–16th century)

      d. The modern period: the effects of Western religions and of nationalism and secularism on familial and social systems

3. Traditional concepts in Chinese religious thought: the relation of the individual to the cosmos and to society

4. Ritual practices and institutions

5. Chinese religious symbolism

6. Chinese mythology

B. Confucianism

1. History of Confucianism

a. Background in the institutions of the predynastic sage-emperors and the founders of the first three dynasties

b. Origin in the life and teachings of Confucius (551–479 BC), the first Sage

c. The Confucian school and its various forms: the teachings of Mencius, the second Sage, and of Hsün-tzu (*c.* 5th–3rd century BC)

d. Establishment of Confucianism as the state orthodoxy of the Han Empire: eclectic tendencies, skeptical and rationalistic reactions (2nd century BC–3rd century AD)

e. Introduction of Confucianism into Korea and Japan (lst and 4th centuries AD)
[see D. and E., below]

f. Confucianism during the time of Buddhist ascendancy: its continued role in the family system, the government bureaucracy, and the examination system; textual studies

g. The emergence and development of Neo-Confucianism (11th–20th century): metaphysical and humanistic emphases, the teaching of Chu Hsi, the development of Neo-Confucian schools

h. Varied responses to intellectual and material challenges of the West and to other developments: reformist and conservative movements, the effect of political developments on Confucian ideology and scholarship

i. Confucianism today: its current demographic and social aspects

2. Confucian literature

3. Confucianism as a religion and as a philosophy

C. Taoism

1. History of Taoism

a. Origin and early developments: the first evidence of the teachings of Lao-tzu and Chuang-tzu (*c.* 4th–3rd century BC)

b. Developments during the Ch'in and Han periods (3rd century BC–3rd century AD): esoteric traditions, the Huang–Lao tradition, revolutionary messianism, developments in philosophy

c. Developments from the 2nd to the 6th century: brief recognition of Taoism as the state religion; interaction with Buddhism; ceremonial, alchemical, and scriptural traditions

d. Developments under the T'ang, Sung, and later dynasties: internal developments, the role of alchemy, syncretistic tendencies

e. The later development of philosophical and religious Taoism from the 14th century to the present time

2. Taoist literature

3. Taoism as a religion and as a philosophy

D. The religions of Korea

1. History of Korean religion from prehistoric times to the present: the influence of Chinese, Japanese, and Western religions

2. Religious literature and mythology

3. Beliefs and doctrines

4. Practices and institutions

E. The religions of Japan

1. History of Japanese religion

a. Early clan religion before the 6th century AD

b. Early historic and medieval periods (6th–16th century): the introduction of Buddhism, the impact of Chinese influences on Shintō, other developments

c. The Tokugawa era (1603–1867): Neo-Confucian Shintō, Sect Shintō, other developments

d. The Meiji era and after (1868 to the present): new religious movements

2. Shintō: the Way of the Gods

a. History of Shintō
   [see E.1., above]

b. Characteristics of primitive Shintō: the role of guardian shrines and shamans

c. Shintō literature and mythology: the form and content of the *Koji-ki, Nihon-gi,* and other writings

d. Basic beliefs and doctrines: concepts of mankind, the sacred and related precepts and principles

e. Ritual practices and institutions

3. Japanese religious art and symbolism

4. Japanese mythology

Suggested reading in the *Encyclopædia Britannica:*

MACROPAEDIA: Major articles dealing with indigenous religions of East Asia: religions of China, Korea, and Japan

Chinese Literature
Confucianism, Confucius and
Japanese Literature
Shintō
Taoism

MICROPAEDIA: Selected entries of reference information

General subjects

Chinese deities and mythology:	shen	Shu Ching	tengu
Chang Kuo-lao	Shen Nung	Ssu shu	uji-gami
Ch'ang O	Shou Hsing	Ta hsüeh	Ukemochi no
Ch'eng Huang	Shun	Tso chuan	kami
ch'i-lin	Ta Yü	Wu Ching	Yama-no-kami
Chih Nü	T'ien	*Japanese deities and*	Yorimitsu
Chung-li Ch'üan	Ts'ai Shen	*mythology:*	*Japanese religious*
feng-huang	Tsao Chün	Amaterasu	*movements:*
Fu Hsi	Ts'ao Kuo-chiu	Amenouzume	Hito-no-michi
Fu Shen	Tsao Shen	Benten	Hōtoku
Han Hsiang	T'u-ti	Daikoku	Kirishitan
Ho Hsien-ku	Wen Ti	Ebisu	Kokugaku
Hou Chi	Wu hsing	Fukurokuju	Konkō-kyō
Hou I	Yao	goryō	Kurozumi-kyō
Hou T'u	Yü Ti	Hachiman	Neo-Confucianism
Hsi Wang Mu	*Confucianism—*	hitogami	Ōmoto
Huang Ti	*philosophy:*	Ho-musubi	PL Kyōdan
Kuan Ti	Confucianism	Inari	Shinbutsu shūgō
K'uei Hsing	hsiao	Izanagi and	Tenshō Kōtai
Lei Kung	jen	Izanami	Jingū-kyō
Li T'ieh-kuai	li	Jimmu	*Korean religion:*
Lu Hsing	T'ien Ming	kami	changsŭng
Lü Tung-pin	*Confucianism—*	kappa	Ch'ŏndogyo
lung	*sacred literature:*	Kusanagi	mudang
Men Shen	Chou li	Ninigi	P'alkwanhoe
Nü Kua	Ch'un-ch'iu	Ōkuninushi	Poch'ŏngyo
Pa Hsien	Chung yung	Sarudahiko	p'ungsuchirisol
P'an Ku	I Ching	Shichi-fuku-jin	Sansin
p'an-t'ao	Li chi	Sugawara	*Shintō—precept and*
San Kuan	Lun yü	Michizane	*practice:*
She Chi	Mencius	Sukunahikona	harai
	Shih ching	Susanoo	jinja

kami	shōzoku	Shrine Shintō	hsin-shu
kamidana	tamaya	Shugen-dō	hsü
Kojiki	torii	State Shintō	Huai-nan-tzu
matsuri	ujigami	Tajong-gyo	Lieh-tzu
musubi	*Shintō—sects and*	Tangun	p'o
Nihon shoki	*schools:*	Tenri-kyō	p'u
norito	Fukkom Shintō	*Taoism:*	Tao
Shichi-go-san	Ise Shintō	Chuang-tzu	Tao-te Ching
shinsen	Kyōha Shintō	Dōkyō	te
shinshoku	Ryōbu Shintō	Five Pecks of Rice	tzu-jan
shintai	Sannō Ichijitsu	hsien	wu-wei
shinten	Shintō		

Biographies

Ch'eng Hao and	Hayashi Razan	Lieh-tzu	Tung Chung-shu
Ch'eng I	Hsün-tzu	Mencius	Wang Ch'ung
Chu Hsi	Lao-tzu	Motoori Norinaga	Wang Yang-ming
Chuang-tzu	Liang Shu-ming	Shao Yung	Yen Yüan

INDEX: See entries under all of the terms above

Section 826.   **Judaism**

A. History of Judaism

  1. The biblical era

  2. The Hellenistic era
     [see also 822.E.]

  3. The Talmudic era in Palestine and Babylonia: the foundations of rabbinic Judaism
     [see also B.3., below]

  4. The medieval era: the European and Islāmic phases of rabbinic Judaism (7th–18th century)

  5. The modern era from *c.* mid-18th century: developments in modern Judaism

  6. Judaism today: its current demographic and social aspects

B. Intellectual, spiritual, and imaginative expressions of Judaism
   [see also C.4., below]

  1. Biblical literature

    a. Canons, texts, and vernacular versions of the Bible; *e.g.,* Septuagint, Targum

    b. TaNaKh, the Hebrew Bible: Torah, Nevi'im, Ketuvim

    c. Noncanonical literature: Apocrypha, pseudepigrapha

  2. Qumrān literature (Dead Sea Scrolls)

  3. Talmud and Midrash

  4. Judaic exegesis and hermeneutics

  5. Mystical and devotional writings

  6. Jewish philosophical writings

  7. Jewish myth and legend

C. Beliefs, practices, and institutions of Judaism

  1. Basic beliefs and doctrines

    a. Doctrines concerning God

    b. Doctrines concerning the Jewish people: the concept of Covenant
       [see also 811.B.10.]

    c. Doctrines concerning mankind

    d. Doctrines concerning the universe

e. Eschatology: views about the future age of mankind and the world, the King-Messiah and his reign
[see also 811.B.7., 827.F.1.d., and 829.A.]

2. Basic practices and institutions

a. Individual and familial practices

b. Synagogue practices and other public institutions: the role of the rabbi, chief rabbinates, and general councils and conferences

c. Sacred times: the sabbath, the Jewish holidays

d. Sacred places: the land of Israel and Jerusalem

e. The sacred language: Hebrew

3. Present-day forms of Judaism

a. Orthodox Judaism

b. Reform, or Liberal, Judaism

c. Conservative Judaism

d. Other variations in belief and practices: Reconstructionism, Ḥasidism, regional or ethnic groups

4. Art and iconography

a. The anti-iconic principle: the influence of the biblical prohibition against idolatry

b. Uses of the visual arts in ceremony and ritual: ceremonial objects, synagogue architecture, paintings, manuscript illumination

c. Music: Jewish liturgical modes, the influence of folk traditions, vocal and instrumental music

d. Literature: traditional legends and poetic exegesis, later religious poetry and tales

---

Suggested reading in the *Encyclopædia Britannica*:

MACROPAEDIA: Major articles and a biography dealing with Judaism

Doctrines and Dogmas, Religious
Judaism
Moses

MICROPAEDIA: Selected entries of reference information

General subjects

beliefs and doctrines:	Daniel, Book of	Joel, Book of	Septuagint
'aguna	Dead Sea Scrolls	Jonah, Book of	Solomon, Song of
'avera	Deuteronomy	Joshua, Book of	Ten
chosen people	Ecclesiastes	Judges, Book of	Commandments
Derekh Eretz	Eden, Garden of	Ketuvim	Torah
eschatology	Esther, Book of	Kings, books of	Zechariah, Book of
Gehenna	Exodus	Lamentations of	Zephaniah,
gemilut ḥesed	Ezekiel, Book of	Jeremiah	Book of
Halakha	Ezra and	Leviticus	*forms, sects, and*
Hebraic law	Nehemiah,	Malachi, Book of	*movements:*
Israeli law	books of	Masoretic text	Ashkenazi
messiah	Genesis	Micah, Book of	Bene-Israel
minhag	Habakkuk,	Nahum, Book of	Conservative
mitzvah	Book of	Nevi'im	Judaism
mitzwot ma'asiyyot	Haggai, Book of	Noahide laws	Falasha
'olam ha-ba	Hexapla	Numbers	Ḥasidism
Shekhina	Holiness, Code of	Obadiah, Book of	Oriental Jew
Bible:	Hosea, Book of	Old Testament	Orthodox Judaism
Amos, Book of	Isaiah, Book of	Proverbs	Reconstructionism
Babel, Tower of	Israel, Kingdom of	Psalms	Reform Judaism
Chronicles, books	Jeremiah, Book of	Ruth, Book of	Samaritan
of the	Job, Book of	Samuel, books of	Sephardi

	Jewish philosophers:	Baeck, Leo	Josephus, Flavius
Hirsch, Samson Raphael	Buber, Martin	Dubnow, Simon M.	Kohler, Kaufmann
Ishmael ben Elisha	Israeli, Isaac ben Solomon	Ezra	Maccabees
Johanan ben Zakkai	Maimon, Salomon	Frank, Jacob	Magnes, Judah Leon
Judah ben Samuel	Maimonides, Moses	Günzburg, Horace, Baron	Manasseh ben Israel
Judah ha-Nasi	Mendelssohn, Moses	Günzburg, Joseph (Yozel)	Shabbetai Tzevi
Karo, Joseph ben Ephraim	Philo Judaeus	Hertz, Joseph Herman	Wise, Isaac Mayer
Luria, Isaac ben Solomon	Rosenzweig, Franz	Herzl, Theodor	Zuckerman, Itzhak
Moses de León	*other:*	ibn Tibbon, Judah ben Saul	
Rashi	Anielewicz, Mordecai		
Sa'adia ben Joseph			

INDEX: See entries under all of the terms above

Section 827.   Christianity

A. History of Christianity before the schism of 1054

   1. The development of the Christian Church from the time of Jesus to the reign of Constantine

      a. The origins and growth of the primitive church (*c.* AD 30–70)

      b. Post-apostolic developments in the early Christian Church (*c.* AD 70–325)

   2. The early Christian Church from the reign of Constantine to the pontificate of Gregory I the Great (*c.* 4th–6th century)

      a. The establishment of Christianity as the state religion of the Roman Empire: the problem of the alliance between church and empire, the increasingly important role played by the bishop of Rome as pope

      b. Doctrinal controversies that occasioned the further development of Christian theology

      c. The relation of the Christian religion to the culture of the late empire

   3. The growing division between Eastern and Western Christianity

      a. The political and religious bases of increasing tensions between Rome and Constantinople

      b. The relation of Christianity to the Western and Byzantine cultures (7th–11th century)

      c. Developments affecting institutions and practices in the East and the West: the expansion of Christianity in the West, the rise of the independent churches in the East

      d. The Photian schism and the beginnings of the great East–West schism

B. History of Eastern Orthodoxy from the schism of 1054 to the present

   1. The church of imperial Byzantium

   2. Developments from the fall of Constantinople (1453) to the early 19th century

   3. The Orthodox churches in the 19th century: developments in various areas

   4. The Orthodox Church since World War I

   5. The Eastern Church today

C. History of the Roman Catholic Church from the schism of 1054 to the present

   1. The medieval and Renaissance eras (*c.* 11th–16th century)
[see 923.A.1.c. and A.2.a.i.]

      a. Development of the papacy as the chief spiritual and temporal power in the West

      b. Religious and cultural characteristics of Latin Christianity
[see also F.6.a., below, 10/51.A.2., and 10/53.A.1.j.]

   2. The era of the Reformations and the wars of religion: from Luther's reform to the Peace of Westphalia (16th–17th century)

      a. Background of the Protestant Reformation in late medieval and Renaissance Catholicism
[see D.1.a., below]

b. The Protestant Reformation
[see D.1., below]

c. The Catholic Reformation and Counter-Reformation

d. The wars of religion
[see D.1.h., below]

e. Missionary endeavours in other areas: the role of the church in the explorations and colonial policies of the European powers

3. The transition era: from the Peace of Westphalia to the French Revolution (17th–18th century)

4. The modern age: from the French Revolution to World War I (18th–20th century)

5. Developments in the 20th century
[see also I., below]

6. Roman Catholicism today: its current demographic and social aspects

D. History of Protestantism

1. The Protestant Reformation and its aftermath, to the Peace of Westphalia (16th–17th century)
[see also 961.A.]

a. Its background in European Roman Catholic Christendom

b. Luther and the German Reformation

c. The Reformation in Switzerland, France, and the Low Countries
[see 961.A.5.e., g., and h.]

d. The English, Scottish, and Irish reformations
[see 961.A.5.d.]

e. Expansion of the Reformation to Scandinavia, the Baltic states, and eastern, central, and southern Europe

f. Radical reform movements

g. The Catholic Reformation and Counter-Reformation
[see C.2., above]

h. The wars of religion: church–state relations and the gradual development of the concept of religious liberty during the 16th and 17th centuries

2. The transition era: from the Peace of Westphalia to the French Revolution (17th–18th century)

a. Political developments affecting the continental Protestant churches

b. Developments in German Protestantism

c. The challenge of Rationalism, Deism, and the Enlightenment: the Protestant response

d. Developments in English Protestantism

e. Developments in American Protestantism during the Colonial period

f. Developments in the Dutch Reformed churches

g. Developments in other continental European churches

3. The modern age: from the American and French revolutions to World War I (18th–20th century)

4. Developments in Protestantism after World War I
[see also I., below]

5. Protestantism today: its current demographic and social aspects

E. Intellectual, spiritual, and imaginative expressions of Christianity
[see also F.7., below)

1. Biblical literature: the Old Testament, the New Testament, the Apocrypha

2. Biblical exegesis and hermeneutics

3. Patristic literature

4. Formal, official statements of beliefs and doctrines: creeds, dogmas, confessions of faith

5. Writings of the post-patristic theologians, reformers, and church leaders

6. Writings of the great mystics

7. The relation of philosophy to Christian thought and statement: Christian philosophy and anti-philosophy

8. Myth and legend: biblical folk and nonbiblical literature, the role of myth in Christianity, "demythologization"

F. Beliefs, practices, and institutions of Christianity

1. Doctrines concerning the nature and activity of God

   a. The nature of God: the oneness of God, the transcendence of God, God as Father

   b. The self-revelation of God: the understanding of God as Creator, Sustainer, and Judge

   c. Christology: teachings concerning the person of Jesus Christ

   d. Eschatology: political and apocalyptic messianic concepts, expectation of the Kingdom of God
   [see also 826.C.1.e.]

   e. The role of the Holy Spirit in the church: the tensions between continuity and revolution, institutional authority and charismatic activity, and order and freedom

   f. The doctrine of the Holy Trinity

2. Doctrines concerning intermediary beings, powers, or principles; *e.g.,* the angels, Satan
   [see also 811.B.5.]

3. Doctrines concerning the physical world

4. Doctrines concerning mankind

5. Doctrines concerning the church: Scripture, tradition, creeds, and confessions as normative expressions of Christian belief; the nature and role of doctrine and dogma

6. Practices and institutions common or predominant among the various traditional forms of Christianity

   a. The structure of church institutions: canon law and church polity

   b. The role and characteristics of the liturgy: the church as a worshiping community, the church year

   c. Forms of Christian life: monasticism, the saintly life

7. Art and iconography

   a. Major eras, regions, and schools of Christian art

   b. The expression of Christian faith and themes in the arts

G. The major traditional forms of Christianity

1. Eastern Orthodoxy
   [see also J.l., below]

2. Roman Catholicism: Latin and Eastern rite churches

3. Protestantism

H. Major forms of Protestantism

1. Lutheran churches

2. Reformed and Presbyterian churches: Calvinism

3. The Anglican Communion

4. The Free churches

   a. Baptists

   b. Disciples of Christ

   c. Congregationalists

   d. Methodists

   e. Friends

   f. Unitarians and Universalists

I. Ecumenical, interdenominational, and intradenominational associations

J. Variations of the traditional forms of Christianity and special new forms

1. In Eastern Christianity

   a. Syrian Orthodox Church of Antioch

   b. East Syrian Church

   c. Armenian Church

   d. Coptic Church

   e. Ethiopian Church

2. In Roman Catholicism

   a. Ritual and other variations within the jurisdiction of the Roman Catholic Church
   [see G.2., above]

   b. Old Catholic churches

3. In Protestantism

   a. Holiness churches

   b. Pentecostal churches

   c. Millenarian churches

      i. Adventists

      ii. Jehovah's Witnesses

   d. Old-line Protestant sects and their derivations

      i. Mennonites, including Amish and Hutterites

      ii. The Moravian Church

      iii. Brethren

   e. Other independent churches: various Fundamentalist, evangelical, and other sectarian groups

   f. The Negro churches

4. Special forms tangentially related to traditional Christianity

   a. New Thought: Unity and other groups

   b. Christian Science

   c. Mormonism

Suggested reading in the *Encyclopædia Britannica:*

MACROPAEDIA: Major articles and biographies dealing with Christianity

Biblical Literature and Its Critical
   Interpretation
Calvinism, Calvin and
   Christianity
Doctrines and Dogmas, Religious
Eastern Orthodoxy

Jesus: The Christ and Christology
Luther
Paul, The Apostle
Protestantism
Roman Catholicism

MICROPAEDIA: Selected entries of reference information

General subjects

belief, doctrine, and dogma:			
absolution	Ascension	concordat	Holy Spirit
adiaphorism	Assumption	confession	hope
agapē	atonement	consubstantiation	Immaculate
Alpha and Omega	benefice	deadly sin	Conception
anathema	blasphemy	Erastianism	imprimatur
angel	bull	eschatology	Incarnation
Annunciation	catechism	evangelical church	indulgence
Antichrist	catechumen	faith	Inner light
apostasy	catholic	God, Kingdom of	justification
apostolic	charity	grace	kerygma and
succession	cherub	heaven	catechesis
	Christ, two	hell	Last Judgment
	natures of	heresy	limbo

logos
Mariology
martyr
millennium
miracle
Monophysite
moral theology
mystical body of
  Christ
nomocanon
original sin
orthodox
predestination
purgatory
resurrection
Sacred Heart
saint
saints, communion
  of the
Satan
Second Coming
seraph
sin
soul
stigmata
Theotokos
tongues, gift of
transubstantiation
Trinity
Turin, Shroud of
Virgin Birth
Visitation
canon law:
  annates
  benefice
  canon law
  Codex Juris
    Canonici
  conclave
  concordat
  consistory
  Corpus Juris
    Canonici
  decretals
  dispensation
  ecclesiastical court
  encyclical
  excommunication
  False Decretals
  Gratian's
    Decretum
  legate
  nomocanon
  nuncio
  ordination
  papal infallibility
  penitential book
  simony
church polity and
  ecclesiastical
  hierarchy:
  almoner

archbishop
archdeacon
autocephalous
  church
bishop
Bishops, Synod of
cardinal
cathedral
chaplain
church
churchwarden
clergy
collegiality
conciliarism
congé d'élire
congregation
council
deacon
diocese
elder
episcopacy
episcopus vagans
free church
holy order
metropolitan
ministry
papacy
parish
patriarch
pope
prelate
presbyter
presbyterian
presbytery
priest
primate
Roman Curia
schism
secular institute
synod
vicar
churches—Eastern
  Independent:
  Armenian
    Apostolic Church
  Christians of Saint
    Thomas
  Coptic Church
  Ethiopian
    Orthodox Church
  Nestorian
  Syrian Jacobite
    Church
churches—Eastern
  Orthodox:
  Bulgarian
    Orthodox Church
  Cyprus, Church of
  Greece, Church of
  Ecumenical
    Patriarchate of
    Constantinople

Georgian
  Orthodox Church
Greek Orthodox
  Patriarchate of
  Alexandria
Greek Orthodox
  Patriarchate of
  Antioch and All
  the East
Greek Orthodox
  Patriarchate of
  Jerusalem
Japanese Orthodox
  Church
Jerusalem,
  Synod of
Old Believer
Orthodox Church
  in America
Orthodox Church
  of Czechoslovakia
Orthodox Church
  of Finland
Orthodox Church
  of Poland
Renovated Church
Romanian
  Orthodox Church
Russian Orthodox
  Church
Serbian Orthodox
  Church
churches—
  Protestant (Anglican
  Communion):
  Anglican Church
    of Australia
  Anglican
    Communion
  Anglican
    Evangelical
  Anglican
    religious
    community
  Anglo-Catholicism
  Broad Church
  Canada, Anglican
    Church of
  Canterbury
    and York,
    Convocations of
  Canterbury,
    archbishop of
  Church Army
  Church
    Commissioners
  Church Missionary
    Society
  England,
    Church of
  Episcopal Church
    in Scotland

Ireland, Church of
Lambeth
  Conference
New Zealand,
  Church of the
  Province of
Nonjuror
Oxford Movement
Protestant
  Episcopal Church
South Africa,
  Church of the
  Province of
Wales, Church in
churches—Protestant
  (Baptist):
  All-Union Council
    of Evangelical
    Christians and
    Baptists
  American Baptist
    Association
  American Baptist
    Churches in the
    U.S.A.
  Baptist Federation
    of Canada
  Baptist General
    Conference
  Baptist Missionary
    Association of
    America
  Baptist Union of
    Great Britain and
    Ireland
  National
    Association of
    Free Will Baptists
  Primitive Baptist
  Southern Baptist
    Convention
churches—Protestant
  (Congregationalist):
  Congregational
    Church of
    England and
    Wales
  Congregational
    Council for
    World Mission
  Congregationalism
churches—Protestant
  (Disciples of Christ):
  Disciples of Christ
  World Convention
    of Churches of
    Christ
churches—Protestant
  (Friends):
  Friends, Society of
  Friends General
    Conference

Friends United
Meeting
Friends World
Committee for
Consultation
churches—Protestant
(Holiness):
Christian and
Missionary
Alliance
Free Methodist
Church of North
America
God (Anderson,
Ind.), Church of
Holiness
movement
Nazarene, Church
of the
Pillar of Fire
United House of
Prayer for All
People
Wesleyan Church
churches—Protestant
(Lutheran):
American
Evangelical
Lutheran Church
American
Lutheran Church
Augustana
Evangelical
Lutheran Church
Batak Protestant
Christian Church
Evangelical Church
in Germany, The
Evangelical Church
of Czech Brethren
Evangelical
Lutheran Church
Evangelical
Lutheran Church
in Tanzania
Evangelical
Lutheran Church
of Denmark
Finland, Church of
Lutheran Church
in America
Lutheran Church
in Württemberg
Lutheran
Church—
Missouri Synod
Lutheran Church
of Oldenburg
Lutheran Council
in the United
States of America

Lutheran
Synodical
Conference
Lutheran World
Federation
Lutheranism
National Church
of Iceland
Norway, Church of
Sweden, Church of
United Evangelical
Lutheran Church
United Evangelical
Lutheran Church
of Germany
Wisconsin
Evangelical
Lutheran Synod
churches—Protestant
(Methodist):
Evangelical United
Brethren Church
Methodism
United Methodist
Church
World Methodist
Council
churches—Protestant
(millenarian):
Adventist
Christadelphian
Christian Catholic
Church
Jehovah's Witness
Plymouth
Brethren
Shaker
churches—Protestant
(Negro):
African Methodist
Episcopal Church
African Methodist
Episcopal Zion
Church
Christian
Methodist
Episcopal Church
National Baptist
Convention,
U.S.A., Inc.
National Baptist
Convention of
America
National
Primitive Baptist
Convention, Inc.
churches—Protestant
(old-line):
Amish
Brethren

Bohemian
Confession
ecclesiola in
ecclesia
Ephrata
Community
Hussite
Hutterite
Mennonite
Moravian Church
Taborite
Ultraquist
Unitas Fratrum
churches—Protestant
(Pentecostal):
Assemblies of God
God, Church of
God in Christ,
Church of
International
Church of the
Foursquare
Gospel
Jesus Only
Latter Rain revival
Pentecostal
Assemblies of the
World, Inc.
Pentecostal
Church of God of
America, Inc.
Pentecostal
Holiness Church,
Inc.
Pentecostalism
churches—Protestant
(Reformed and
Presbyterian):
Christian
Reformed Church
in North America
Cumberland
Presbyterian
Church
Dutch Reformed
Church
Dutch Reformed
Church in Africa
Dutch Reformed
Mission Church
in South Africa
Evangelical Church
in Germany, The
Evangelical Church
of Czech Brethren
Free Church of
Scotland
Iona Community
Netherlands
Reformed
Church, The

Presbyterian
Church (U.S.A.)
Presbyterian
Church in
Ireland
Presbyterian
Church of
England
Presbyterian
Church of
Wales
Presbyterian
churches
Reformed church
Reformed Church
in America
Reformed Church
of France
Reformed Church
of Hungary
Reformed
Churches in The
Netherlands
Scotland,
Church of
United Church of
Canada
United Free
Church of
Scotland
United
Presbyterian
Church
United Reformed
Church in
England and
Wales
churches—Protestant
(Unitarian and
Universalists):
Unitarian
Universalist
Association
Unitarianism
Universalism
churches—Protestant
(United Church of
Christ):
American Board of
Commissioners
for Foreign
Missions
Evangelical and
Reformed Church
General Council
of Congregational
Christian
Churches
United Church of
Christ

churches—Protestant
(*other*):
  Christ, Church of
  Conservative
    Baptist
    Association of
    America
  Evangelical
    Alliance
  Evangelical Free
    Church of
    America
  General
    Association of
    Regular Baptist
    Churches
  Independent
    Fundamental
    Churches of
    America
  National
    Association of
    Congregational
    Christian
    Churches
  National
    Association of
    Evangelicals
  New Church
  Undenominational
    Fellowship
    of Christian
    Churches and
    Churches of
    Christ
churches—Roman
  and Eastern
  Catholic:
  Armenian Catholic
    Church
  Belorussian
    Catholic Church
  Bulgarian Catholic
    Church
  Chaldean Catholic
    Church
  Coptic Catholic
    Church
  Eastern rite church
  Italo-Albanian
    Church
  Malabarese
    Catholic Church
  Malankarese
    Catholic Church
  Maronite Church
  Old Catholic
    Church
  Old Catholic
    Church of the
    Netherlands

Polish National
  Catholic Church
  of America
Roman Catholic
  Church of
  Romania
Russian Catholic
  Church
Ruthenian
  Catholic Church
Syrian Catholic
  Church
Ukrainian Catholic
  Church
churches—other:
  Christian Science
  Family of Love
  Mormon
  New Apostolic
    Church
  New Church
  Peace Mission
  Reorganized
    Church of
    Jesus Christ of
    Latter-day Saints
  Unity School of
    Christianity
heresies:
  Adoptionism
  Albigenses
  Anomoean
  Aphthartodocetism
  Arianism
  Cathari
  Macedonianism
  Monarchianism
  Montanism
  Pelagianism
  Pneumatomachian
  Sabellianism
  Semi-Arianism
history:
  Acacian Schism
  Anabaptist
  anticlericalism
  antinomianism
  Antioch,
    Council of
  antipope
  Apology of
    the Augsburg
    Confession
  Apostle
  Ariminum,
    Council of
  Arles, Council of
  Arminianism
  Augsburg,
    Peace of

Augsburg
  Confession
Augsburg Interim
auto-da-fé
Avignon papacy
Barmen, Synod of
Basel, Council of
Belgic Confession
Brest-Litovsk,
  Union of
caesaropapism
Cambrai,
  League of
Cameronian
camp meeting
Chalcedon,
  Council of
Children's Crusade
Chinese Rites
  controversy
Christian Socialism
circuit rider
Clergy Reserves
collegia pietatis
Confessing Church
Constance,
  Council of
Constantine,
  Donation of
Constantinople,
  councils of
covenant theology
Covenanter
Counter-Reformation
crusade
Dead Sea Scrolls
Death of God
  movement
Desert Fathers
devotio moderna
Diamper, Synod of
Donatist
Dort, Synod of
Douai-Reims Bible
Dukhobor
Eastern Orthodoxy
Ebionite
ecumenism
Eight Saints, War
  of the
Elvira, Council of
Ephesus,
  councils of
Familist
Ferrara-Florence,
  Council of
Fundamentalism
Gallican
  Confession
Gallicanism

Geneva Bible
Geneva Catechism
German Christian
Great Awakening
Guarantees,
  Law of
Half-Way
  Covenant
Hampton Court
  Conference
Helvetic
  Confession
Holiness
  movement
Holy League
Homoean
homoousian
Hsi-an monument
Huguenot
Iconoclastic
  Controversy
Independent
Inquisition
Institutes of
  the Christian
  Religion
Investiture
  Controversy
Jerusalem,
  Council of
Jesuit Estates
  controversy
Lambeth
  Quadrilateral
Lateran Council
Lateran Treaty
Lollard
Lutheranism
Lyon, councils of
Marburg,
  Colloquy of
Marprelate
  Controversy
Melchite
Milan, Edict of
mission
Modernism
Monothelite
Moral
  Re-Armament
Neoorthodoxy
Nicaea, councils of
Ninety-Five
  Theses
Nisibis, School of
Oneida
  Community

Manual of
Discipline
Moses,
Assumption of
Prophets, The
Lives of the
Solomon,
Psalms of
Solomon,
Wisdom of
Tobit, Book of
Twelve Patriarchs,
Testaments of the
War of the Sons
of Light Against
the Sons of
Darkness, The
literature—patristic:
Ambrosiaster
Apologist
Apostolic
Constitutions
Apostolic Father
Barnabas, Letter of
Clement, First
Letter of
Clementine
literature
Didachē
Diognetus,
Letter to
Hippolytus,
Canons of Saint
Martyrdom of
Polycarp
patristic literature
Peregrinatio
Etheriae
Shepherd of
Hermas
Testamentum
Domini
literature—other:
apocalyptic
literature
apocrypha
biblical criticism
biblical source
biblical translation
demythologization
Douai-Reims Bible
exegesis
Geneva Bible
hermeneutics
logia
Mormon, Book of
Peshitta
Philokalia
polyglot Bible
Targum
Vulgate

liturgical year:
Advent
All Saints' Day
All Souls' Day
Ascension of the
Lord, Feast of the
Ash Wednesday
Candlemas
Christmas
church year
Corpus Christi,
Feast of
Easter
Ember Days and
Ember Weeks
Epiphany
Good Friday
holy days of
obligation
Holy Family, Feast
of the
Holy Innocents,
Feast of the
Holy Saturday
Holy Week
Jubilee, Year of
Lent
Maundy Thursday
Michaelmas
Palm Sunday
Pentecost
Reformation Day
Rogation Days
Shrove Tuesday
Sunday
Transfiguration,
Feast of the
*religious communities
and orders:*
Anglican religious
community
Augustinian
Basilian
Benedictine
Bridgettine
Camaldolese
Capuchin
Carmelite
Carthusian
Charity of Saint
Vincent de Paul,
Daughters of
Christian Brother
Cistercian
Common Life,
Brethren of the
Divine Word
Missionary
Dominican
Franciscan
Good Shepherd
Sister

Grandchamp
and Taizé
communities
Hesychasm
Holy Ghost Father
Hospitaler
Jesuit
Little Brothers of
Jesus and Little
Sisters of Jesus
Marianist
Marist Brother
Marist Father
Mary Immaculate,
Oblates of
Maurist
Mechitarist
mendicant
Mercedarian
Mercy, Sisters of
Minim
monasticism
Oratorian
Passionist
Premonstratensian
Redemptorist
Sacred Heart,
Society of the
Salesian
Servite
Spiritual
Templar
Teutonic Order
Trappist
Trinitarian
Ursuline
Vincentian
Visitandine
White Father
Zoe
*worship, liturgy,
ritual, and
iconography:*
acolyte
Agnus Dei
Alexandrian rite
anointment
Antiochene rite
Apostles' Creed
Armenian rite
Athanasian Creed
Baptism
Basil, Liturgy of
Saint
bell, book, and
candle
benediction
breviary
Byzantine rite
cantor
Chaldean rite
chalice
chrismation

Common Order,
Book of
Common Prayer,
The Book of
Concord, The
Book of
confession
confessional
Confessions,
Book of
confirmation
creed
cross
cross, sign of the
Cross, Stations
of the
crucifixion
Dies Irae
divine office
doxology
Ecce Homo
epiclesis
Eucharist
exorcism
feet, washing of
godparent
Hail Mary
hands, laying on of
Heidelberg
Catechism
Holy Family
Holy Sepulchre
holy water
icon
iconostasis
Imitation of Christ
James, Liturgy of
Saint
Jesus prayer
kanōn
Last Supper
Lord's Prayer
lector
Liturgical
Movement
Madonna
Magnificat
mass
missal
monstrance
Nativity
Nicene Creed
orant
Pietà
prayer
Preconsecrated
Offerings, Liturgy
of the
procession
pyx
rosary
Sabbatarianism

sacrament
shepherds,
   adoration of the
thurible
tithe
troparion

True Cross
vespers
Westminster
   Catechism
Westminster
   Confession

See Section 624 of
   Part Six for
   sacred music
other:
   Christianity
   Eastern
      Orthodoxy

liberation theology
Protestantism
Roman
   Catholicism
World Council of
   Churches

Biographies

*early Christian
figures—to 1054:*
   Ambrose, Saint
   Anastasius Sinaita,
      Saint
   Anastasius the
      Librarian
   Ansgar, Saint
   Anthony of Egypt,
      Saint
   Aphraates
   Aristedes
   Arsenius the Great
   Athanasius, Saint
   Athenagoras
   Augustine, Saint
   Augustine of
      Canterbury, Saint
   Basil the Great,
      Saint
   Bede the
      Venerable, Saint
   Benedict Biscop,
      Saint
   Benedict of Nursia,
      Saint
   Berengar of Tours
   Chad, Saint
   Chrysostom, Saint
      John
   Clement I, Saint
   Clement of
      Alexandria, Saint
   Colman of
      Lindisfarne, Saint
   Cuthbert, Saint
   Cyprian, Saint
   Cyril and
      Methodius, Saints
   Cyril of
      Alexandria, Saint
   Damasus I, Saint
   Diadochus of
      Photice
   Dionysius of
      Alexandria, Saint
   Dustan of
      Canterbury, Saint
   Ennodius, Magnus
      Felix
   Ephraem Syrus,
      Saint
   Erigena, Johannes
      Scotus

Eusebius of
   Caesarea
Eusebius of
   Nicomedia
Euthymius I
Euthymius the
   Great, Saint
Evagrius Ponticus
Fursey, Saint
Gennadius of
   Marseilles
Germanus I, Saint
Germanus of
   Auxerre, Saint
Gregory I, Saint
Gregory VII, Saint
Gregory of
   Nazianzus, Saint
Gregory of Nyssa,
   Saint
Gregory of Tours,
   Saint
Gregory
   Thaumaturgus,
   Saint
Hesychius of
   Jerusalem
Hilarion, Saint
Hincmar of Reims
Hippolytus of
   Rome, Saint
Honorius I
Humbert of Silva
   Candida
Ignatius of
   Antioch, Saint
Irenaeus, Saint
Isaac the Great,
   Saint
Isidore of Seville,
   Saint
Jerome, Saint
Joan, Pope
John of Damascus,
   Saint
John of Jerusalem
Justin Martyr,
   Saint
Kenneth, Saint
Leo I, Saint
Leo III, Saint
Leo IX, Saint
Liberius
Lucifer

Macarius the
   Egyptian
Mark the Hermit
Martin of Tours,
   Saint
Nemesius of
   Emesa
Nestorius
Nicephorus I, Saint
Nicetas of
   Remesiana
Nicholas, Saint
Nicholas I
Nicholas I, Saint
Nilus of Ancyra,
   Saint
Ninian, Saint
Novatian
Origen
Oswald of York,
   Saint
Palladius
Paschal I, Saint
Paschasius
   Radbertus, Saint
Patrick, Saint
Pelagius I
Pelagius II
Philoponus, John
Philostorgius
Philoxenus of
   Mabbug
Photius
Polycarp, Saint
Priscillian
Rabanus Marus
Sergius I, Saint
Severian of Gabala
Severus of Antioch
Simplicius, Saint
Sophronius
Stephen VI
Sulpicius Severus
Symmachus, Saint
Tertullian
Theodore Ascidas
Theodore of
   Canterbury, Saint
Theodore of
   Cyrrhus
Theodosius of
   Alexandria
Theōdūrus Abū
   Qurrah

Theophilus of
   Alexandria, Saint
Ulfilas
Vigilius
Vincent of Lérins,
   Saint
Wilfrid, Saint
Willibrord, Saint
Zosimus, Saint
*Christian figures—
medieval and
Renaissance:*
   Aelred of Rievaulx,
      Saint
   Ailly, Pierre d'
   Alexander III
   Alexander VI
   Arnold of Brescia
   Benedict (XIII)
   Bernard of
      Clairvaux, Saint
   Bonaventure, Saint
   Boniface VIII
   Borgia, Cesare, duc
      de Valentinois
   Catherine of Siena,
      Saint
   Celestine V, Saint
   Clare of Assisi,
      Saint
   Clement V
   Clement VI
   Dominic, Saint
   Duns Scotus, John
   Eckehart, Meister
   Edmund of
      Abington, Saint
   Francis of Assisi,
      Saint
   Gerson, Jean
      Charlier de
   Gilbert of
      Sempringham,
      Saint
   Gregory VII, Saint
   Gregory IX
   Gregory of Rimini
   Honorius III
   Hus, John
   Innocent II
   Innocent III
   Innocent IV
   Isaac of Stella
   Jerome of Prague

Joachim of Fiore
John XXII
John (XXIII)
John of Avila,
  Saint
John of Matha,
  Saint
John of Mirecourt
John of Salisbury
Julius II
Malachy, Saint
Martin V
Milíč of Kroměříž
Nicholas III
Nicholas IV
Nicholas V
Nicholas of
  Clémanges
Nicholas of Cusa
Nicholas of
  Hereford
Paschal II
Paul II
Peter Lombard
Petrus Aureoli
Pius II
Prester John
Rokycana, Jan
Savonarola,
  Girolamo
Seven Holy
  Founders
Sixtus IV
Suso, Heinrich
Thomas Aquinas
Urban II
Urban VI
William de la
  Mare
William of
  Auvergne
William of
  Auxerre
William of
  Champeaux
William of Hirsau
William of
  Saint-Amour
William of
  Saint-Thierry
Wycliffe, John
*Eastern Orthodox
figures—from 1054:*
  Akindynos,
    Gregorios
  Anthony of Kiev
  Antony
    Khrapovitshy
  Bulgakov,
    Macarius
  Cydones,
    Demetrius

Eugenikos,
  Markos
Euthymius of
  Tŭrnovo
Gemistus Plethon,
  George
Gennadios II
  Scholarios
Gregory of Sinai
Isidore of Kiev
Jeremias II
John XI Becchus
Joseph of
  Volokolamsk
Maximus the
  Greek
Mogila, Peter
Nicephorus
  Callistus
  Xanthopoulos
Nikon
Palamas, Saint
  Gregory
Planudes,
  Maximus
Prokopovich,
  Feofan
Sergius
Theophylactus of
  Orchida
Tikhon
*New Testament
figures:*
  Anne and
    Joachim, Saints
  James, Saint
  John the Apostle,
    Saint
  John the Baptist,
    Saint
  Joseph, Saint
  Judas Iscariot
  Luke, Saint
  Mark, Saint
  Mary
  Mary Magdalene,
    Saint
  Peter the Apostle,
    Saint
  Pilate, Pontius
  Stephen, Saint
  Thomas, Saint
*Old Testament
figures:*
  Abraham
  Amos
  David
  Deborah
  Ezekiel
  Isaiah
  Jacob
  Jeremiah

Jezebel
Jonah
Jonathan
Joseph
Melchizedek
Moses
Noah
Samson
Samuel
Saul
Solomon
Protestant figures:
  Agricola, Johann
  Arminius, Jacobus
  Ballou, Hosea
  Baxter, Richard
  Beecher, Henry
    Ward
  Beza, Theodore
  Biddle, John
  Bonhoeffer,
    Dietrich
  Bucer, Martin
  Bultmann, Rudolf
  Bunyan, John
  Bushnell, Horace
  Carey, William
  Chalmers, Thomas
  Channing, William
    Ellery
  Clauberg, Johann
  Cranmer, Thomas
  Dávid, Ferenc
  Eddy, Mary Baker
  Edwards, Jonathan
  Erastus, Thomas
  Farel, Guillaume
  Flacius Illyricus,
    Matthias
  Fox, George
  Franck, Sebastian
  Harnack,
    Adolf von
  Hembyze, Jan van
  Henderson,
    Alexander
  Hooker, Richard
  Huntingdon,
    Selina Hastings,
    countess of
  Jewel, John
  Joris, David
  Judson, Adoniram
  Karlstadt,
    Andreas Rudolf
    Bodenstein von
  Keble, John
  Knox, John
  Kuyper, Abraham
  Labadie, Jean de
  Lefèvre d'Étaples,
    Jacques

Leighton, Robert
McPherson, Aimee
  Semple
Mather, Cotton
Mather, Increase
Mather, Richard
Maurice, Frederick
  Denison
Melanchthon,
  Philipp
Melville, Andrew
Menno Simons
Müntzer, Thomas
Niebuhr, Reinhold
Ochino,
  Bernardino
Oecolampadius,
  John
Penn, William
Ritschl, Albrecht
Robinson, John
Rogers, John
Schaff, Philip
Schleiermacher,
  Friedrich
Schwenckfeld,
  Kaspar
Servetus, Michael
Smith, Joseph
Socinus, Faustus
Spalatin, Georg
Spener, Philipp
  Jakob
Strauss, David
  Friedrich
Swedenborg,
  Emanuel
Tait, Archibald
  Campbell
Tillich, Paul
Vermigli, Peter
  Martyr
Wesley, Charles
Wesley, John
Whitman, Marcus
Williams, Roger
Young, Brigham
Zinzendorf,
  Nikolaus Ludwig,
  Graf von
Zwingli, Huldrych
*Roman Catholic
figures—
post-Reformation:*
  Arnauld, Antoine
  Arnauld family
  Bellarmine, Saint
    Robert
  Benson, Edward
    White

Bérulle, Pierre de
Borromeo, Saint
  Charles
Bossuet,
  Jacques-Bénigne
Cajetan
Calasanz, Saint
  Joseph
Carroll, John
Clement VII
Clement XI
Clement XIII
Coindre, André
Döllinger, Johann
  Joseph Ignaz von
Drexel, Katharine
Erasmus,
  Desiderius
Innocent XI,
  Blessed
Jansen, Cornelius
  Otto

John XXIII
John of Saint
  Thomas
John of the Cross,
  Saint
John Paul II
Lacordaire, Henri
Lamennais,
  Félicité
Laval, François de
  Montmorency
Leo X
Leo XII
Leo XIII
Loyola, Saint
  Ignatius of
Maritain, Jacques
Newman, John
  Henry
Paul II
Paul III
Paul IV

Paul VI
Pius IV
Pius V, Saint
Pius VI
Pius VII
Pius IX
Pius X, Saint
Pius XI
Pius XII
Ricci, Matteo
Sarpi, Paolo
Sixtus V
Smet,
  Pierre-Jean de
Stein, Edith
Teilhard de
  Chardin, Pierre
Teresa, Mother
Teresa of Ávila
Tyrrell, George
Uganda,
  Martyrs of

Urban VIII
Ussher, James
Victoria,
  Francisco de
Wiseman, Nicholas
Xavier, Saint
  Francis

INDEX: See entries under all of the terms above

Section 828.   **Islām**

A. History of Islām

  1. The pre-Islāmic setting in Arabia
     [see also 822.A.6.]

  2. The origin of Islām in the life and teachings of the Prophet Muḥammad, the Messenger of Allāh (6th–7th century AD)

  3. The foundations of the Islāmic community and the early expansion of Islām beyond Arabia (7th and 8th centuries)

  4. The development of Islāmic religion, culture, and society during the first centuries of the caliphate of the ʿAbbāsids (8th–11th century)

  5. The Middle Ages of Islām: developments in theology, law, and culture (11th–18th century)

  6. Islām in the modern world (18th–20th century)

  7. Islām today

B. Intellectual, spiritual, and imaginative expressions of Islām
   [see also C.4., below]

  1. The Qurʾān: its form and contents, views about its origin, interpretations or translations

  2. The Ḥadīth: the oral tradition

  3. Islāmic law: Sharīʿah, *fiqh*

  4. Islāmic theology and philosophy: philosophic and antiphilosophic trends in Islām, the major schools of Islāmic philosophy

  5. The mystical path: Ṣūfism

  6. Mythical elements and elaborations of Islāmic beliefs and doctrines

C. Beliefs, practices, and institutions of Islām

  1. Beliefs and doctrines

     a. Doctrines concerning God

     b. Doctrines concerning the universe

     c. Doctrines concerning mankind

    d. Doctrines concerning Satan and other intermediate beings, powers, or principles [see also 811.B.5.]

    e. Doctrines concerning Muḥammad and the nature of prophecy

    f. Eschatological doctrines

    g. Social and ethical doctrines

2. The forms of Islām: the orthodox community and its variations

    a. Khārijism: the doctrines of the Khārijīs and Ibāḍīs

    b. Muʿtazilism

    c. Sunnism

    d. Shīʿism and its subsects: the Ismāʿīlīs and other Ismāʿīlī sects

    e. Religious groups of Islāmic origin, now considered non-Islāmic; *e.g.*, Druzes, Bahāʾī faith [see 829.E.]

    f. Variations among the urban and rustic Ṣūfī orders

3. Practices and institutions

    a. The Five Pillars of Islām: the profession of faith, the five daily prayers, the obligatory tax (*zabāt*), fasting, the pilgrimage to Mecca

    b. Sacred places and days: the mosque and festivals in public worship

    c. The family: Islāmic teaching regarding marriage, divorce, chastity, and inheritance

    d. The Sharīʿah: law and jurisprudence, the schools of law

4. Art and iconography

    a. Major eras, regions, and schools of Islāmic art

    b. The expression of Islāmic faith and themes in the arts

    c. The religious and cultural context of Islāmic art and iconography: the effect of the anti-iconic principle on representational art

5. Modern reform movements

Suggested reading in the *Encyclopædia Britannica*:

MACROPAEDIA: Major articles dealing with Islām

    Islām, Muḥammad and the Religion of
    Islāmic World, The

MICROPAEDIA: Selected entries of reference information

General subjects

belief, law, and philosophy:	isnād	tawḥīd	miḥnah
ʿādah	istiḥsān	uṣūl al-fiqh	Murjiʾah
ahl al-Kitāb	istiṣlāḥ	*history:*	Qarāmiṭah
Allāh	jihād	Almohads	rāshidūn, ar-
ʿaqil	kalām	Almoravids	Sālimīyah
ʿārīyah	kasb	Badr, Battle of	*myth, legend,*
bidʿah	kiswah	Bāṭinīyah	*eschatology:*
Dahrīyah	Mālikīyah	caliph	Barṣīṣā
diyah	millet	Caliphate	Burāq
fayḍ	muftī	Companions of the Prophet	Dajjāl, ad-
ghaybah	Muʿtazilah	Dīn-i Ilāhī	Dhū al-faqār
Ḥadīth	Qadarīyah	Ditch, Battle of the	ghūl
Ḥanābilah	qāḍī	Hāshimīyah	Hārūt and Mārūt
Ḥanafīyah	qiyās	hijrah	hātif
ʿiddah	raḍāʿ	Ḥudaybiyah, Pact of al-	ḥawrāʾ
ijmāʿ	rahbānīyah	Ikhwān aṣ-Ṣafāʾ	Iblīs
ijtihād	Shāfiʿīyah	imām	Idrīs
ikhtilāf	Sharīʿah	jizyah	ʿifrīt
ʿilm al-ḥadīth	shirk	kharāj	isrāʾ
imām	taqlīd		Isrāfīl
	tashbīh		ʿIzrāʾīl

jahannam
Jibrīl
jinnī
Khiḍr, al-
mahdī
Mīkāl
miʿrāj
shaitan
Sheba, Queen of
Yājūj and Mājūj
offices and orders:
  caliph
  imām
  marabout
  qurrāʾ
  Shādhilīyah
Qurʾānic literature:
  basmalah
  fātiḥah
  fawātiḥ
  Qurʾān
  surah
ritual, practice,
observance:
  adhān
  ʿĀshūrāʾ
  Black Stone of
    Mecca
  crescent
  ghusl
  hajj

hijrah
ʿīd
iḥrām
jihād
jumʿah
Kaʿbah
khitān
khuṭbah
mawlā
mawlid
minaret
minbar
mosque
muezzin
mutʿah
qiblah
rajm
Ramaḍān
ṣalāt
ṣawm
sayyid
sharīf
subḥah
sunna
tafsīr
tahajjud
talbīyah
taqīyah
taʿziyah
ʿumrah
zakāt

zāwiyah
ziyārah
zuhd
sects, schools,
branches:
  Bohrā
  Deoband school
  Dönme
  Druze
  Ismāʿīlīyah
  Ithnā ʿAsharīyah
  Khawārij
  Mahdist
  Māturīdīyah
  Muʿtazilah
  Rāfiḍah
  Shīʿah
  Ṣūfism
  Sunnite
  Wahhābīyah
  Yazīdī
Ṣūfism:
  Aḥmadīyah
  Bektāshīyah
  Chishtīyah
  dervish
  dhikr
  fakir
  fanāʾ
  ḥāl
  ḥaqīqah

kashf
khirqah
Malāmatīyah
maqām
Mawlawīyah
mujāhadah
mushāhadah
Naqshbandīyah
Qādirīyah
Qalandarīyah
Rifāʿīyah
samāʿ
shaṭḥ
Shaṭṭārīyah
Subud
Ṣūfism
Suhrawardīyah
ṭarīqah
other:
  Ahl-e Ḥaqq
  American Muslim
    Mission
  Islām
  Khōjā
  Muhammadiyah
  Mʾzabite
  sheikh
  ʿulamāʾ

Biographies

leaders and teachers:
  ʿAbd Allāh
  Abū Bakr
  Ahmad Khan, Sir
    Sayyid
  Aḥsāʾī, al-
  ʿAlī
  Ghaznavid
    Dynasty
  Ḥallāj, al-
  Jaʾfar ibn
    Muḥammad

Jalāl ad-Dīn
  ar-Rūmī
Jamāl ad-Dīn
  al-Afghānī
Junayd, Shaykh
Mahdī, al-
Muḥammad
Rashīd Riḍā
Shaʿrānī, ash-
ʿUmar I
ʿUmar II
ʿUmar Tal

theologians and
philosophers:
  ʿAbduh,
    Muḥammad
  Abū Ḥanīfah
  Aḥmad ibn
    Ḥanbal
  Ashʿarī, Abū
    al-Ḥasan al-
  Averroës
  Avicenna
  Fakhr ad-Dīn
    ar-Rāzī

Ghazālī, al-
Ḥasan
  al-Baṣrī, al-
Ibn al-ʿArabī
Ibn ʿAqīl
Ibn Ḥazm
Ibn Taymīyah
Muḥāsibī, al-
Sirhindī, Shaykh
  Aḥmad
Suhrawardī, as-
Ṭabarī, aṭ-

Section 829.   Other Religions and Religious Movements in the Modern World

    A. New religious movements reflecting the impact of dominant cultures and religions

    B. Negro cults in Western cultures

        1. The Nation of Islām, or Black Muslims
        [see E.3., below]

        2. Black Jewish cults: the Church of God; the Commandment Keepers, or Black Jews; the Church of God and Saints of Christ

    C. Theosophical groups

    D. Spiritualist groups

    E. Religions and religious movements of Islāmic origin or influenced by Islām

        1. The Bahā'ī faith

        2. The Druze religion

        3. The Nation of Islām, or Black Muslims

    F. Residues or revivals of ancient and primitive religious beliefs and practices in modern civilizations

        1. Witchcraft, black magic, Satanism
        [see also 811.D.3.]

        2. Prophecy, divination, astrology

        3. Healing cults or practices

        4. Pharmacological cults or practices

Suggested reading in the *Encyclopædia Britannica:*

MACROPAEDIA: Major article dealing with other religions and religious movements in the modern world

      Doctrines and Dogmas, Religious

MICROPAEDIA: Selected entries of reference information

General subjects

African Greek	Ghost Dance	Kuga Sorta	Ringatu
Orthodox Church	Handsome Lake	Macumba	Rizalist cult
Aiyetoro	cult	Maria Legio	Rosicrucian
Aladura	Hare Krishna	mashriq al-adhkār	Scientology
American Muslim	Harris movement	Moorish Science	spiritual assembly
Mission	Hauhau	Temple of	Telakhon
anthroposophy	healing cult	America	theosophy
Azalī	ḥudūd	Native American	Unification
Bahā'ī faith	I Am movement	Church	Church
Braid movement	Iglesia ni	New Thought	'uqqāl
Cao Dai	Kristo	Peace Mission	Voodoo
cargo cult	Indian Shaker	Psychiana	Zionist church
Druze	Church	Rastafarian	
Ethiopianism	Kimbanguist	Ratana Church	
faith healing	Church of Zaire	Religious Science	

Biographies

Bāb, the	Blavatsky, Helena	Gurdjieff, Georges	Muhammad,
Bhaktivedanta,	Petrovna	Ivanovitch	Elijah
A(bhay)	Divine, Father	Mahesh Yogi,	Smohalla
C(haranaravinda)	Fard, Wallace D.	Maharishi	Steiner, Rudolf
		Moon, Sun Myung	

INDEX: See entries under all of the terms above

Introduction to Part Nine:
The Point and Pleasure of Reading History
by Jacques Barzun

Everything that we call the arts and the humanities comes out of some natural desire and acquires value by satisfying it. Painting and music and literature are important not because there are museums and concert halls and libraries to be kept supplied but because human beings want to draw and sing and tell stories as well as enjoy seeing others fulfill these native and universal impulses.

Among the humanities, history holds a special place in that its origin within each of us is not even dependent on impulse. A person may lack altogether the wish to sing or the knack of telling a story, but everybody without exception finds occasion to say: "I was there; I saw it; I remember it very well." In saying (or even thinking) these words, every man is a historian. History is inescapably a part of consciousness. The Greeks expressed this truth by describing Clio, the muse of history, as the daughter of memory.

Without going into the subtleties of how we are able to remember and what the contents of memory actually are, it is clear that as soon as we take thought about our experiences, whether the farthest back or the nearest and most immediate, we are dealing with what is past. The so-called present vanishes in the very act of reflecting upon it, and the future is all surmise and imagination. Hence the greater our interest in the facts and truths of human existence— our own existence included—the greater, necessarily, is our concern with the past. "To live in the past" ought not, therefore, to be the phrase of reproach that it commonly is. The larger part of the thoughtful life that one leads during the intervals of action cannot be anything but some form of living in the past. If this part of our lives is to be criticized, it should be in words different from the cliché. One should ask, *How* does he or she live in the past? *What past* does he or she recall, prefer, imagine?

It is at this point that history as the organized story of the whole human past comes in to contribute its pleasures and its illumination to the thoughtful life. A person who remembered only his own past would be pretty poor indeed—living on a starvation diet. Actually, it is a question whether such a life is not an impossible supposition. Everybody remembers pieces of other people's pasts; everybody, whether he means to or not, finds that he has learned about his country, his town, his street, his business office, or his factory many things that came to pass well before his time. To possess that information, if it is accurate, is in essence a knowledge of history. It differs in extent but not in kind from a knowledge of how Rome rose and fell. And this relation tells us what reading history affords in the first instance. Just as knowing about our neighbours' and friends' histories adds to our sense of reality, so does reading history: it gives us vicarious experience.

If we add to the habitual, unconscious intake of personal and local history the daily filling of the mind by news reports—which is contemporary history and which usually brings with it fragments of a remoter past—we begin to see that every man who lives in a modern, communicative society is forced to become in some sense a conscious historian. His interest begins with himself and his environment, but it is soon stretched out, haphazardly, into such domains of history as chance or special interests have developed. And special interests need not mean explicitly intellectual ones; baseball and chess, model trains and furniture, pottery and boat-building have their heroes and revolutions too, and whoever cares about these activities or artifacts for themselves inevitably becomes engrossed in their histories.

It is of course true that when we ordinarily speak of someone having an interest in history we mean the political, social, or cultural history of great civilizations; and for a long time history was arbitrarily taken to mean the sequence that leads from the ancient civilizations of the eastern Mediterranean to the modern ones of the West. It is a tremendous spectacle, even though concentrated on a relatively small territory. But now that certain dynamic elements of Western civilization have aroused the rest of the world to both imitation and resistance, it has become imperative to widen the panorama and see behind the vast and confused modern scene the several histories of the great Eastern civilizations as well as the traditions and vicissitudes of the African societies.

Two questions readily occur at the mere thought of so much to know. Can a reader who is not a professional historian find his way in this huge maze of names, dates, and facts? And if he can, why should he? The answer to the first question is the old reply of the mathematician to the nervous student: "What one fool can do, another can." A real compliment is concealed in this gruff retort, for what it implies is that given an interest, a motive, any man can inform himself about any part of world history through secondary accounts such as are digested in an encyclopaedia. There is no obligation to master every detail, to dispute or criticize sources—in a word, to ape the professional, who, for the best of reasons, limits himself to a small segment of the whole. A *reader* of history is one who follows with his mind the steps another took on his voyage of discovery; and this is easier in history than in mathematics, for history is told in plain words and deals with ordinary human relationships.

So the main difficulty lies in the second question: Why embark on the journey? The answers are numerous and varied, for temperaments differ, as do "special interests" in the sense referred to above. But there is one answer that covers the rest; it is the answer suggested by what was said earlier about every man's unconscious absorption of haphazard fragments of history. The best motive for reading history deliberately is curiosity about the portions missing from one's own picture of the past. Curiosity: How did things come to be as they are? How was it when they were different? Is it true that once upon a time men did thus and so? History deals with particulars, and most recorded particulars contain puzzles, contradictions, enormities, all of them spurs to curiosity: the Hudson River in the state of New York was named after the navigator often called Hendrik Hudson, who first sailed up the stream. But why Hendrik and not Henry? Well, Henry was his baptismal name; how did he acquire the other and why? The full answer leads really to a comprehensive view of exploration and colonization by the national states at the dawn of the modern age—the aims, drives, desires, errors, follies, cruelties, and incalculable consequences of a great movement that occupies two and a half centuries and that has continued in different forms down to the landings on the Moon.

The most striking feature of history is its fusion of purposeful direction and unexpected drift. For example, read about Plato, Aristotle, and the ancient mathematicians, and you will discover how their speculations and discoveries have been transformed and amplified into the methods and systems that we still work with. But you will also be told how at various times these same streams of thought or belief generated entirely new and remote, strange and absurd consequences. Again, ancient astrology led to the science of astronomy, and science (as we think) replaces superstition. Yet astrology fills columns in 20th-century newspapers and the minds of their millions of readers. What is the explanation? We lack the pythoness of Delphi, in whom Socrates believed or affected to believe, and we have no official college of augurs to scan the entrails of birds as a guide to future political action, but fortune-tellers are never out of business and we do have Gallup polls. Truly, the wonders of cultural history are infinite.

To conjure up these beliefs and institutions in this comparative fashion is not to equate them with one another or across the centuries; it is rather to stress the identity in diversity that is the principle of human affairs and that makes human history accessible to any willing reader. In different times and places, men are the same and also different. The differences are due to the varying emphases given by one people at one time to some element of life and feeling or to some form of its expression. This is most easily seen in the plastic arts. Think of the representations of the human body in Egypt, Greece, medieval Europe, the west coast of Africa, pre-Columbian America, and the art galleries of world capitals in the second half of the 20th century: is it the same human body or different? The question is really idle, for it is both and neither. In paint or marble there is strictly no human body, only a view of it, a feeling about it. Similarly, what we see in history is not so much Man distorted in one way or another as *men* who existed *only as we see them;* that is, in their society and culture, under their skies and gods, never staying put for more than a short time, never to be reduplicated elsewhere or at a later time, even when the effort to imitate is strong and shrewd—as in the Italian Renaissance, which tried to restore the ancient culture of Greece and Rome.

Despite this irreducible plasticity, diversity, and restlessness, we draw historical parallels, we make comparisons. That we can do so is what persuades us of the unity and continuity of history. When we find the Celtic druids and

the Aztecs making human sacrifices to their gods we say we recognize a human tendency, though we profess to abhor it. Yet some future reader of history might be tempted to compare with those ancient peoples our contemporary revolutionists, who sacrifice 400,000 kulaks (or some other hapless group) for the good of the tribe and its eternal prosperity. But we also notice a strange difference: we know that fanatical faith presides over each type of human sacrifice, ancient and modern, but even as we condemn we think we understand the modern more readily: we know its background, have heard its advocates. It is one of the illuminations of history, not merely to know abstractly, but, by learning the local shape of things, to feel how the reality of each time and place differs; how the faiths diverge in contents and origins and thus in persuasiveness. We may now lump together the Celts and the Aztecs, but they were far apart in thought and character: in short, nothing is truly comparable; in history everything is *sui generis.*

The wise reader of history keeps his equilibrium between these two extremes of likeness and difference. He tries to see the unfamiliar in the familiar, and vice versa. He stands away from his own prejudices and satisfies his curiosity by trying to sympathize with what is farthest away or most alien. This is very hard to do when what is before us is a bloody sacrifice, a massacre, a piece of treachery or cynical greed that violates our sensibilities as well as our moral principles. But to sympathize is not to condone or approve, it is only to acknowledge in oneself the ever-present possibility of the same feeling or action. Certainly the enlightened 20th century has no warrant for looking down on times and places where treachery and massacre were commonplace. And it is a sobering observation to find in both past and present the evidence that inhumanities have been and are being committed by the brutish and civilized alike, the ignorant and the educated, the cynical and the devout, the selfish and the heroic.

A principal good derived from history is thus an increase in self-knowledge, through a fellow-feeling with men singly and in groups as history tells about them. That self-knowledge in turn makes the reader of history less ready to find "monsters of error" in his own time and place. Let it be said again, he need not condone or accept with indifference, but he is spared one of the very errors that perpetuates man's inhumanity to man—fanatical self-righteousness.

On the constructive side, what history tells is the long series of efforts to overcome the constraints of nature and the difficulties of living in society. Those efforts we call civilizations. They start small. In the West they first take the form of city-states. They clash, with one another or with the barbarians "outside." Trade and war, war and trade expand the scope of power, government, and law. Great men introduce broader conceptions of citizenship, morals, and religions. Others invent practical devices of administration, manufacture, and—again—war. Still others discover the workings of nature, create mathematics or art or systems of philosophy. A concentration of such activities over a given territory is what is meant by a high civilization—Egypt, Greece, the Hellenistic Age, Rome, the Saracens, the High Middle Ages, the Renaissance. And also China, Japan, the Khmers, India, the Mayas, the Incas, and so on.

Along this hazardous and always violent course, innumerable characters rise and play their parts. Their fates provide stories within the story. Visibly, biographies are the bricks of which history is made, for the story of mankind can only be the stories of men. But by a paradox of man's social existence, the life of communities is not a simple sum of individual lives. The reader of history must therefore imagine from the printed page characteristic acts, moods, errors, disasters, achievements that are nobody's doing and everybody's doing. This imagining is another important good bestowed by historical reading, for it dispels the illusion that H.G. Wells called the "governess view" of history: They (the bad people) are doing this terrible thing to Us (the good people). The fallacy in it is to suppose that any large group acts as with one mind, clear in purpose and aware of consequences. Such a projection of the single ego upon whole masses is a form of provincialism that is encountered in most political discussions and certainly in all social prejudices: "If the President would only act . . . if those people would only see reason. . . ." A reader of history is cured of this simple-mindedness by developing a new sense—the historical sense—of how mankind in the mass behaves, neither free nor fatally pushed, and in its clearest actions mysterious even to itself.

It is this peculiarity that, while marking the difference between history and biography (where acts can be deemed individual and responsible), has led many minds to postulate a meaning in history, a meaning discoverable but obscured by the multiplicity and confusion of facts. A famous passage in Cardinal Newman's *Apologia* records in admirable prose the feelings that lead to the elaboration of philosophies of history; for Newman it is of course the traditional Christian interpretation that unifies the multiplicity and resolves the confusion:

> To consider the world in its length and breadth, its various history, the many races of man, their starts, their fortunes, their mutual alienation, their conflicts; and then their ways, habits, governments, forms of worship; their enterprises, their aimless courses, their random achievements and acquirements, the impotent conclusion of long-standing facts, the tokens so faint and broken, of a superintending design, the blind evolution of what turn out to be great powers or truths, the progress of things, as if from unreasoning elements, not towards final causes, the greatness and littleness of man, his far-reaching aims, his short duration, the curtain hung over his futurity, the disappointments of life, the defeat of good, the success of evil, physical pain, mental anguish, the prevalence and intensity of sin, the pervading idolatries, the corruptions, the dreary hopeless irreligion, that condition of the whole race, so fearfully yet exactly described in the Apostle's words, "having no hope and without God in the world,"—all this is a vision to dizzy and appal; and inflicts upon the mind the sense of a profound mystery, which is absolutely beyond human solution.

Other famous philosophies, from Vico's and Hegel's to Marx's and Spengler's, discover a direction in history, or a principle of action, and often a goal or terminus (as in Marx), after which history as we know it shall cease and a kind of second Eden be restored.

To the practical writer or reader of history these philosophies appeal mainly by their suggestiveness; they are valued for their scattered insights and analogies. As systems they negate the very spirit of history, which seeks the concrete and particular, the opposite of system and abstraction. True, there have been historians who took a middle course and attempted to find empirical regularities in history— again with occasionally suggestive results—but very soon their methods begin to do violence to the facts in order to group them and count them and treat them like identities in physical science. When the physical world itself has not yet been fully systematized, to assume or "find" a system in history without the means and the liberties that science uses is to think like neither a scientist nor a historian. It is in fact an attempt to remove the difficulty of history at the cost of destroying its unique merit and interest.

By the "liberties" that science takes is meant the experimenter's elimination of all but a very few components in a given trial, so as to ascertain precisely the nature and amount of a given effect. When this is done, the result is usually stated in causal terms—so much of this, under such and such conditions, will produce so much of that. Hardly anyone needs to be told that history defies a similar treatment. Its elements cannot be exactly measured, and although each historical situation presents to the discerning eye a variety of clear conditions or factors, the isolating of *a* cause for what happens is beyond reach.

That is but another way of saying that history is and must remain a story. And a story, if properly told, is a whole, to be understood as a whole—synthetically, not analytically. History in this regard resembles the arts. We say we "analyze" a work of art, but that is to speak metaphorically. We can enjoy and understand the products of art only as wholes. In history, the artful story is offered as a true story, and great pains are taken to see that it is true. But except in the broadest sense, the historical wholes are not given as such in the record; they are devised by the historian, to make the welter of facts intelligible and hence able to be remembered. Clio was not only the muse of history but also of eloquence, by which the Greeks meant good, intelligible prose, to be spoken before an audience unused to books. The same requirements still hold; written history must be readable with pleasure, or Clio is defeated.

But, it will be said, from many diverse writers will come divergent stories, rival interpretations. That is true, for only a divine mind could know "how it actually happened." But this limitation of history is also a merit, for it can thereby be written and read over and over again in as many versions as are plausible or accessible. There is and will be no final statement; the perspective forever changes, and with it the interest of history renews itself into infinity. As the philosopher William James once remarked, "What has been concluded that we should conclude about it?"

Part Nine. The History of Mankind

The outlines in the thirty-nine sections, in seven divisions, of Part Nine deal with the history of the peoples and civilizations of the world.

Certain points should be noted about Part Nine.

History, like philosophy, has developed methods applicable to the subject matter of other disciplines. The results of these applications are set forth in other parts. Each of the nine sections of Division II of Part Six includes a historical treatment of each of the arts. Similarly, each of the nine sections of Division II of Part Eight includes a historical treatment of each of the particular religions dealt with. Certain sections of the five divisions of Part Ten set forth the history of logic and mathematics; the history of science generally; the history of each of the natural and social sciences; the history of medicine; the history of technology; the history of philosophy; the history of humanistic scholarship; and the history of historiography and of the study of history itself.

It should also be noted that here and in the other portions of the Outline of Knowledge that treat historical matters, the level of detail is greater than that elsewhere. This reflects the editors' belief that an outline of history imposed upon a geographical or chronological base requires a high degree of particularization.

The topical breakdown of the history of mankind into seven divisions and thirty-nine sections reflects more or less traditional judgments—judgments regarding the regional divisions of world history; the identification of peoples and civilizations; the temporal periodization in historical accounts of particular civilizations; and the periods of relative isolation and of relative confluence of different civilizations.

The titles of the seven divisions in this part indicate the regional and temporal divisions used. Introductory headnotes for each of the seven divisions indicate the temporal periodizations used in the accounts of particular civilizations.

Division I.   **Peoples and Civilizations of Ancient Southwest Asia, North Africa, and Europe**

The outline in Section 911 first treats of the geography of the regions covered in the section, the sources for the history of the peoples in these regions, and the character and achievements of ancient Near Eastern, Aegean, and North African civilizations. It then deals separately with the history of each of the peoples in these regions in ancient times.

The outline in Section 912 begins with the history of the peoples of non-Classical ancient Europe. It then deals with the whole course of the Classical Greco-Roman civilization, extending from the emergence of Classical Greece from Archaic Greece, through the Hellenistic Age and the history of republican Rome, to the history of the Roman Empire up to AD 395.

Section 911. **Early Peoples and Civilizations of Southwest Asia and Egypt, the Aegean, and North Africa**

A. The character and achievements of ancient Near Eastern, Aegean, and North African civilizations; the geography of these regions; archaeological and documentary historical sources; historiographic problems

B. Mesopotamia and Iran to *c.* 1600 BC

   1. Development of river valley civilization in Mesopotamia

      a. The Late Neolithic, Chalcolithic, and protohistoric (pre-urban) periods

      b. The Sumerians from their origins to the end of the Early Dynastic Period (*c.* 2350 BC)

         i. Their conjectured origins: literary and other historical sources (king lists and invention of cuneiform writing), early kings and legendary figures (Gilgamesh)

         ii. Foundation of city-states (*e.g.,* Kish, Ur, Uruk, Lagash, Mari, Umma): rivalry among the cities, the temple city and theocracy, social and economic organization, contacts with Egyptian and Indus Valley civilizations, Sumerian culture

      c. Sumer and Akkad from *c.* 2350 to 2000 BC

         i. The ascendancy of the Semitic Akkadians under Sargon I of Akkad and his successors, invasions and the fall of the dynasty

         ii. The unification of Sumer, Akkad, and Elam under the 3rd dynasty of Ur (*c.* 2112–2004 BC): administration and composition of the empire, Ur in decline

      d. The Old Babylonian Period and the early history of Assyria

         i. Isin and Larsa: rivalry and political fragmentation, literary texts, decentralization

         ii. Early Assyria: Ashur, Nineveh, and Urbilum; Akkadian inscriptions and language; the economy; the reign of Shamshi-Adad I (*c.* 1813–1781 BC)

         iii. Establishment of the Old Babylonian Empire under the dynasty of Hammurabi (*c.* 1792–1750 BC): law, society, and literature

      e. Hurrian expansion to *c.* 1600 BC and the decline of the Old Babylonian Empire after *c.* 1750 BC

   2. Early Elam (Iran): cultural ties and political and military interaction with Mesopotamia

C. Emergence of river valley civilization in Egypt (to *c.* 1600 BC)

   1. The Predynastic Period (to *c.* 3100 BC) and the Early Dynastic Period (1st and 2nd dynasties, *c.* 3100–*c.* 2686 BC): unification of Upper and Lower Egypt under King Menes (Narmer), capital at Memphis

   2. The Old Kingdom (*c.* 2686–2160 BC) and the First Intermediate Period (*c.* 2160–*c.* 2040 BC)

      a. The Old Kingdom (3rd–6th dynasties, *c.* 2686–*c.* 2181 BC): divine kingship; the building of the great pyramids near Memphis; centralized government; class structure; agriculture, manufactures, and foreign trade; hieroglyphic writing, science, and technology; the arts

      b. The First Intermediate Period (7th–11th dynasties, *c.* 2181–1991 BC): governmental decentralization; collapse of the Old Kingdom and ensuing disunity and foreign raids; reunification by Mentuhotep II under the 11th dynasty, ruling from Thebes

   3. The Middle Kingdom (*c.* 2040–1786 BC) and the Second Intermediate Period (1786–1567 BC)

      a. The Middle Kingdom (12th dynasty, 1991–1786 BC): the cult of Amon; developments in the monarchical institutions; the conquest of Nubia, trade, and exploration; the arts

      b. The Second Intermediate Period (13th–17th dynasties, 1786–1567 BC): internal decentralization and the Asiatic Hyksos occupation

D. Early civilizations in Syria and Palestine, Anatolia, and the Aegean to *c.* 1600 BC

   1. Emergence of civilization in Syria and Palestine

      a. The Stone Age cultures and their transition from the Neolithic to the Early Bronze Age until *c.* 2300 BC, agricultural and technological developments, Proto-Urban settlements, Jericho

         i. Paleolithic and Mesolithic periods: development of horticulture and the domestication of animals

      ii. Pre-Pottery Neolithic areas, grouped houses and town walls, arrival of new peoples and their rectangular architecture, Pottery Neolithic areas, molded plaster vessels, dark-faced burnished ware and the spread of its associated culture

      iii. The Chalcolithic Period and the Early Bronze Age: migrations and spread of Ḥalafian culture, development of trade, beginnings of urbanization, Early Bronze Age cities

  b. The Intermediate Period (*c.* 2300–*c.* 1900 BC) and the Middle Bronze Age (*c.* 1900–*c.* 1525 BC): revival of trade and connecting link between the greater states; *e.g.,* Aleppo, Byblos, Alalakh in Syria

      i. The Amorite invasion: breakup of settled areas by nomadic peoples, bronze weapons and votive objects

      ii. Reappearance of urban civilization in the Middle Bronze Age: hieroglyphics, clay tablets, development of new pottery in Canaan

2. Emergence of civilizations in Anatolia, Cyprus, and the Aegean

  a. Anatolia: the Neolithic, Chalcolithic, and Bronze ages; settlement by the Hittites

      i. Neolithic farming communities: house styles, tools and weapons, pottery, foodstuffs

      ii. Appearance of painted pottery in the Chalcolithic Period, uses of metal

      iii. Bronze Age culture; *e.g.,* Troy, Alaca Hüyük: jewelry, pottery, burial customs, metalworking, weaponry, migrations

      iv. The Hittite occupation of Anatolia and establishment of the Old Hittite Kingdom (*c.* 1700–*c.* 1500 BC): expansion into northern Mesopotamia and Syria under Hattusilis and Mursilis, the Hurrian invasions, the Middle Kingdom

  b. The Late Neolithic, Chalcolithic, and Bronze ages in Cyprus

  c. The early Aegean civilizations (to *c.* 1450 BC)

      i. The Paleolithic, Neolithic, and Chalcolithic ages in Greece, Crete, and the Aegean islands; the pre-Greek (Early Bronze or Helladic) population of Greece from *c.* 3000 BC; the Early Bronze or Cycladic Age in the Aegean islands; the shaft grave period on the mainland

      ii. The Minoan civilization on Crete: the period of the Early Palaces (*c.* 2200–1700 BC), cultural efflorescence, Kamáres ware, commerce, Knossos, Middle Cycladic culture, period of the Later Palaces (*c.* 1700–*c.* 1450 BC) on Crete, the arts, Linear A tablets

E. The era of the Egyptian and Hittite empires (*c.* 1600–1050 BC): the expansion of the Indo-Europeans

1. The New Kingdom of Egypt (18th–20th dynasties, 1567–1085 BC)

  a. The 18th dynasty (1567–1320 BC): the emergence of strong centralized administration, territorial expansion, religious and cultural developments

      i. Expulsion of the Hyksos from Egypt under Ahmose (1570–1546 BC): cult of Amon-Re, expansion into Syria and Palestine, contacts with the Aegean and its arts

      ii. Egyptian culture and prosperity in the reigns of Amenhotep III (1417–1379 BC) and Akhenaton (Amenhotep IV): domination over Nubia, erection of new temples at Thebes, cult of the god Aton, subsequent eclipse of the dynasty

  b. The 19th and 20th dynasties (1320–1085 BC): political shift to the north, new construction, foreign policies

      i. Reassertion of Egyptian power: campaigns against the Hittites and Libyans, succession disputes

      ii. The reign of Ramses III (1198–1166 BC) and subsequent decline of the 20th dynasty, campaigns against the Sea Peoples, growth of influence of the priests of Amon-Re

  c. Society and culture in the New Kingdom: the king as the embodiment of the state; the civil service; the military; the priesthood; the artisans, common people, and slaves; trade and commerce

2. The Hittite Empire and its conflict with Egypt; Syria and Palestine under Egyptian and Hittite domination; the period of the migrations of new peoples

  a. The Hittite Empire (*c.* 1525–1190 BC)

      i. Expansion of the Hittite Empire under Suppiluliumas I into Syria (*c.* 1365 BC): reduction of the Mitannian state, ensuing conflicts and treaties with Egypt, relations with neighbouring states

ii. The capital of the Hittite Empire at Hattusa (Boğazköy): geographical position, architecture, invasions from the West, fall of the empire and destruction of the capital (*c.* 1190 BC), emergence of the Indo-European Phrygians as the chief Anatolian power

b. Syria and Palestine under Egyptian, Mitannian, and Hittite domination, and the period of the migrations of new peoples (*c.* 1550–1200 BC)

i. The development of Levantine seafaring trade: the Levantine city-states (*e.g.,* Ugarit), political organization, economy, culture, development of the linear alphabet by the Canaanites and the spread of its use

ii. The origins of the Hebrews in the patriarchal age and their sojourn in and Exodus from Egypt in the 13th century BC, their conquest of Palestine, the Sea Peoples and the Philistine conquest of the Palestinian littoral

iii. The Syro-Hittite states and the migration of the Semitic Aramaeans into Syria and Palestine *c.* 1100 BC and their foundation of states in Syria: spread of the Aramaic language, trends in religion and the arts

3. Mesopotamia from *c.* 1600 to *c.* 900 BC

a. The Kassites in Babylonia (*c.* 1595–*c.* 1155 BC): their conjectured origins, their adoption of Mesopotamian culture, Elamite and Assyrian invasions after *c.* 1250, the fall of the Kassites

b. The kingdom of the Hurrians and the Mitanni (*c.* 1500–1360 BC) in northern Mesopotamia, its displacement by Assyria

c. The rise of Assyria (*c.* 1360–1076 BC): expansion under Ashur-uballit I (*c.* 1365–*c.* 1330 BC), conquest of Babylon, continued expansion to Tiglath-pileser I (*c.* 1115–*c.* 1077 BC), temporary eclipse of Assyria (to *c.* 900 BC)

4. The Elamite kingdom and its struggle with Babylonia in the 13th and 12th centuries BC

5. Mycenaean (Achaean, Late Helladic) civilization in Greece (*c.* 1450–1100 BC): the eruption of Thera (*c.* 1500 BC), the conquest of Minoan Crete (*c.* 1450 BC), and the arrival of the Greeks

a. The overthrow of the existing social order, introduction of new artistic styles, conquest of the Cyclades, the evidence of the Linear B tablets, destruction of the palace at Knossos and period of the Mycenaean Empire

b. The end of the Bronze Age in the Aegean: destruction of Mycenaean centres, invasion from the north and the coming of the Greeks

c. The people of the Bronze Age Aegean: physical types, dress, society, economy, warfare, religion, and arts

F. The era of the new states of Southwest Asia: the beginning of the Iron Age (*c.* 1050–700 BC)

1. Egypt and Babylonia in decline, further Assyrian expansion

a. Egypt under the 21st–25th dynasties (1085–656 BC): loss of influence in Syria, disunity and the diminution of royal power, Libyan domination, civil war and Kushite (Ethiopian) rule, the Assyrian conquest (671–664 BC)

b. Babylonia (*c.* 1050–750 BC): the brief resurgence of Babylonian power under Nebuchadrezzar I (1124–1103 BC); the cult of Marduk; Aramaean, Assyrian, and Chaldean invasions from the 11th to the 9th century BC

c. Emergence of Assyria as the dominant Mesopotamian state after *c.* 900 BC: internal dissension and the challenge of Urartu in the 8th century BC

2. Palestine, Syria, Anatolia, and Iran

a. Development of Canaanite–Phoenician commercial city-states from *c.* 1100 to *c.* 700 BC (*e.g.,* Tyre, Sidon): trade and colonization, Phoenician civilization

b. The Hebrew kingdom (*c.* 1020–*c.* 700 BC): subjection of the Philistines, territorial expansion in Syria and Palestine

i. The reigns of David and Solomon in the 10th century, growth of separate kingdoms of Judah (south) and Israel (north, conquered by Assyria in 722 BC)

ii. The cult of Yahweh and biblical literature, social and political structure, arts

c. The neo-Hittite states of southeastern Anatolia: Carchemish, Milid (Malatya), Tabal, and Que (*c.* 1180–700 BC); conquest by the Aramaeans and Assyrians

d. Foundation of Urartu in about the 13th century BC, rise of the Urartian kingdom (*c.* 840–*c.* 744 BC), Assyrian influences, the Cimmerian invasion (*c.* 714 BC) and destruction of the kingdom (*c.* 609 BC), influence of the Urartian state, the Armenian Empire under the Artaxiads

     e. Phrygia in central and western Anatolia (*c.* 1180–*c.* 700 BC): capital at Gordium, relations with Assyrians and Luwians, the Cimmerian invasions in the beginning of the 7th century, the cult of Cybele

     f. The Aramaean kingdoms (*e.g.,* Damascus) and their cultural and commercial role: conquest by Assyria

     g. The Neo-Elamite period: the occupation of Iran by the Indo-European Medes and Persians by the 9th century BC

G. The era of the Assyrian and Neo-Babylonian empires and the Achaemenid Persian Empire (746–250 BC)

  1. The first imperial unification of the ancient Near East under the Assyrian Empire (746–609 BC)

     a. Assyrian culture in the context of the Mesopotamian tradition: the great cities; *e.g.,* Nineveh

     b. Expansion of the empire under Tiglath-pileser III (744–727 BC), Sargon II (721–705 BC), and Sennacherib (704–681 BC); decline from the reign of Ashurbanipal (668–627 BC); conquest by the Medes (625–609 BC)

  2. The interval between Assyrian and Achaemenid hegemony (610–539 BC)

     a. The Neo-Babylonian Empire (636–539 BC): conquests, treatment of Jews, decline of the empire

        i. The reign of Nebuchadrezzar II (604–562 BC): subjection of Syria and Palestine, the Babylonian Exile of the Jews and the post-Exile period, building activities

        ii. The last kings of Babylonia: internal dissension and early relations with Persia, surrender to Cyrus II the Great (539 BC)

     b. The Anatolian kingdom of Lydia (*c.* 700–*c.* 547 BC): early relations with Assyria, the Cimmerian invasions, suzerainty over the Greeks in Anatolia, Greco-Lydian culture, growth of independent Cilicia in the late 7th century, conquest by Persia

     c. Saite Egypt (26th dynasty, 664–525 BC) and its reassertion of independence after Assyrian rule; revival of traditional Egyptian culture, subjection to Persia

     d. The Kingdom of the Medes in Iran (*c.* 700–550 BC) and the establishment of the Achaemenid Persian Empire

        i. Conjectured origins of the Median state, expulsion of the Scythians, extension of control over the other Iranian peoples and into Armenia and eastern Anatolia after the downfall of Assyria

        ii. Cyrus II the Great's (550–529 BC) establishment of his rule from Anatolia to east of Iran, relative generosity toward subject peoples

  3. The Achaemenid Persian Empire (529–330 BC) under the successors of Cyrus II the Great, Greek rule to *c.* 250 BC

     a. The empire under Cambyses II, Darius I, and Xerxes I (529–465 BC): the subjugation of Egypt, establishment of peace in the empire, penetration of the Balkan Peninsula and the unsuccessful attempts to conquer mainland Greece

     b. Xerxes' weak successors: continued involvement in Greek affairs; internal disunity in the 4th century, resulting in conquest by Alexander III the Great (330 BC)

     c. Achaemenid society and culture: Zoroastrianism, Persepolis and other capitals, social structure and economy

     d. Seleucid rule to *c.* 250 BC, movement of Iranian peoples, revolt of the high satrapies

H. The Parthian and Sāsānian empires (*c.* 250 BC–AD 651), Armenia

  1. The revival of Iranian power with the establishment of the Parthian Empire by Arsaces, formation of the Arsacid Parthian state

     a. The "Philhellenistic Period" (*c.* 171 BC–*c.* AD 10): eastern and western expansion until the mid-1st century BC, wars with Rome until the settlement of 20 BC

     b. The "Anti-Hellenistic Period" (AD 2–162): Parthian government under Artabanus III (AD 12–38), dissolution of the Parthian state

     c. Roman invasions and the end of the Parthian Empire (AD 162–226)

  2. Extension of Iranian power under the Sāsānian Empire

     a. Foundation of the empire: the rise of Ardashīr I in the early 3rd century BC, the wars of Shāpūr I (AD 241–272), organization of the empire

    b. Religious developments: Zoroastrianism, Christianity, Manichaeism; art and literature

    c. Foreign policy: conflicts with the Romans, Byzantines, and Turks under Khosrow I (AD 531–579) and Khosrow II (AD 590/591–628); subsequent decline and extinction of the empire with the Arab conquest (AD 636/637–651)

  3. Armenia: client status under the Iranian empires of Rome in the period dominated by the Arsacids

I. The Nilotic Sudan, South Arabia, and Ethiopia until *c.* AD 600; North Africa until the Roman conquest (from 146 BC)

  1. Emergence of civilization in the Nilotic Sudan (Nubia): the origins of Nubian culture

  2. Egyptianization and the Kingdom of Kush (*c.* 1786–751 BC), conquest of Egypt (*c.* 730 BC) and later expulsion by the Assyrians (by 654 BC), conquest by Aksum (AD 350)

  3. Pre-Islāmic South Arabia: the kingdoms of Maʿīn, Sabaʾ, Qatabān, Ḥaḍramawt, and the tribes of central and northern Arabia; economic activities; religion; foreign relations

  4. Ethiopia to *c.* AD 650

    a. Remotest antiquity: the land of Punt, the Sabaean period

    b. The Aksumite Empire (2nd century AD): the Abyssinian peoples, maritime trade, Ezana's rule (4th century AD), reign of Ella-Asbeha (6th century AD) and relations with Persia

  5. North Africa until the Roman conquest

    a. Emergence of civilization in North Africa: the Early Neolithic culture in the Maghrib and Libya, the Berbers, the influence of Egypt, the advent of the mercantile Phoenicians and their foundation of Carthage *c.* 814 BC (Utica, 1101 BC?), the Greeks in Cyrenaica from *c.* 630 BC

    b. Emergence of Carthage as the leading western Mediterranean power: conflicts with the Greeks in the western Mediterranean, extension of Carthaginian power into Spain and the clash with Rome in the Punic Wars resulting in the destruction of Carthage (146 BC)

    c. Roman penetration into North Africa: the native kingdoms of Numidia and Mauretania and their eventual incorporation into the Roman Empire

---

Suggested reading in the *Encyclopædia Britannica:*

MACROPAEDIA: Major articles dealing with early peoples and civilizations of Southwest Asia and Egypt, the Aegean, and North Africa

Afghanistan	Iran	Palestine
Arabia	Iraq	Prehistoric Peoples
Egypt	Israel	and Cultures
Greco-Roman	Jordan	Syria
Civilization,	Lebanon	Turkey and
Classical	North Africa	Ancient Anatolia

MICROPAEDIA: Selected entries of reference information

General subjects

Anatolia, Crete, and Cyprus:	Harran	Paphlagonia	Ḥimyar
	Hittite	Perga	Kindah
Ahhiyawa	Karatepe	Phocaea	Nabataean
Alaca Hüyük	Kaska	Phrygia	Sabaʾ
Alişar Hüyük	Kizzuwadna	Pisidia	Ṣāliḥ
Amathus	Knossos	Sakcagöz	Tanūkh
Anatolia	Kültepe	Salamis	Thamūd
Armenia	Luwian	Sardis	*Egypt:*
Arzawa	Lycaonia	Soli	Abū Jirāb
Aspendus	Lycia	Tarsus	Abū Ruwaysh
Bithynia	Lydia	Troas	Abu Simbel
Boğazköy	Milid	Troy	Amarna, Tell el-
Çatalhüyük	Minoan	Xanthus	Amratian culture
Chalcedon	civilization	Yazılıkaya	Badarian culture
Cilicia	Muṣaṣir	Zincirli Hüyük	Beni Hasan
Citium	Mysia	*Arabia:*	Canopus
Gordium	Pamphylia	Arabia Felix	

Dahshūr
Dayr al-Baḥrī
Dayr al-Madīnah
Elephantine
Gerzean culture
Giza, Pyramids of
Hermopolis Magna
Hierakonpolis
Hyksos
Kadesh, Battle of
Kahun
Karnak
Kawa
Kings, Valley
 of the
Lāhūn, al-
Luxor
Ma'ādī, al-
Madīnat Habu
Maydūm
Memphis
Naukratis
nome
Oxyrhynchus
Palermo Stone
Pelusium
Per Ramessu
pharaoh
Ramesseum
Sais
Ṣaqqārah
Sarapeum
Tanis
Tasian culture
Thebes
Turin Papyrus

*Mesopotamia and
Iran:*
 Adab
 Akhlame
 Akkad
 Amorite
 Anbar
 Anshan
 Ashur
 Assyria

Babylon
Babylonia
Birāk, Tall
Borsippa
Calah
Chaldea
Ctesiphon
Cunaxa, Battle of
Dur Sharrukin
Elam
Elymais
Erech
Eridu
Eshnunna
Fertile Crescent
Gaugamela,
 Battle of
Granicus, Battle
 of the
Guti
Hammurabi,
 Code of
Hasanlu
Hassuna
Hatra
Ḥīrah, al-
Hurrian
Isin
Jazīrah, al-
Kassite
Khwārezm
Kish
kudurru
Lagash
Larsa
Lullubi
Mannai
Media
Mesene
Mesopotamia
Mitanni
Nineveh
Nippur
Nisa
Nuzu
Osroëne

Parni
Parthia
Pasargadae
Persepolis
Persis
Satrap
Shahr-e Sokhta
Shuruppak
Sippar
Sumer
Susa
Teishebaini
Ten Thousand
 Immortals
Tepe Gawra
Tepe Yahya
Toprakkale
'Ubayd, Tall al-
Ur
Urartu

North Africa:
 Capsian industry
 Carthage
 Cyrenaica
 Fezzan
 Gaetulia
 Hadrumetum
 Hippo
 Lambessa
 Leptis
 Mauretania
 Numidia
 Ptolemais
 Sabratha
 Thugga
 Tripolitania
 Utica
 Volubilis

Palestine and Syria:
 Ai
 'Ajjul, Tall al-
 Alalakh
 Aleppo
 Bashan
 Beth Yerah
 Canaan

Carchemish
Dibon
Ebla
Edom
Far'ah, Tall al-
Fāri'ah, Tall al-
Galilee
Gath
Gezer
Ghassulian culture
Gibeon
Gilead
Ḥalaf, Tall
Ḥasi, Tel
Hierapolis
Jericho
Jezreel
Judaea
Judah
Kadesh
Kadesh, Battle of
Karkar
Katna
Kiriath-sepher
Mari
Megiddo
Nora
Palestine
Palmyra
Philistine
Phoenicia
Samaria
Ugarit

other:
 Aksum,
  Kingdom of
 Meroe
 Mycenae
 Napata
 Nubia
 Ophir
 Pelasgi
 Punt
 Sea People
 tell

Biographies

Egypt:
 Akhenaton
 Amenhotep III
 Ankhesenamen
 Hatshepsut
 Mentuhotep II
 Merneptah
 Ramses II
 Ramses III
 Ramses IV
 Saite dynasty
 Sesostris I
 Sesostris III
 Snefru

Thutmose I
Thutmose III
Thutmose IV
Tutankhamen
Israel:
 Abraham
 David
 Moses
 Solomon
*Mesopotamia
(Akkad, Assyria,
Babylonia):*
 Ashurbanipal
 Ashurnarsipal II

Esarhaddon
Hammurabi
Merodach-Baladan II
Nebuchadrezzar II
Sargon
Sargon II
Sennacherib
Tiglath-pileser III
Persia (Iran):
 Achaemenian
  dynasty
 Arsacid dynasty
 Artaxerxes II
 Cambyses II

Cyrus II
Darius II
Khosrow I
Khosrow II
Sāsānian dynasty
Shāpūr II
Xerxes I
other:
 Suppululiumas I
 Tigranes II the
  Great

INDEX: See entries under all of the terms above

Section 912. **Peoples of Ancient Europe and the Classical Civilizations of the Ancient Mediterranean World to AD 395**

A. Non-Classical ancient Europe

    1. The geography and ethnography of Europe, archaeological and documentary historical sources, historiographic problems

    2. Europe before the Iron Age

        a. Spread of Neolithic farming communities throughout all of Europe by *c.* 2000 BC

        b. Spread of Bronze Age industry throughout Europe by *c.* 1500 BC: population movements into southeastern Europe and southwestern Asia in the 2nd millennium BC, the Indo-Europeans

    3. Non-Classical Europe in the Iron Age (*c.* 650 BC–*c.* AD 100)

        a. The Etruscans and other Italic peoples, the non-Greek peoples of the Balkan Peninsula

            i. Conjectured Etruscan origins; Etruscan language and writing; cities; government and society; art and religion; maritime expansion; foreign relations with the Greeks, Carthaginians, and other Italic peoples; decline after *c.* 500 BC and eventual Roman conquest in the mid-3rd century

            ii. Other Italic peoples: the Umbro-Sabellians, Oscans, Apulians, Latins, Siculi, Ligurians, Veneti, and Piceni; their cultures; their relations with the Greeks, Etruscans, and Carthaginians; eventual absorption by Rome

            iii. Non-Greek peoples of the Balkan Peninsula; *e.g.,* Illyrians, Thracians: their culture and relationship to Classical civilizations

        b. Trans-Alpine Europe and the Iberian Peninsula

            i. The Celts: the Halstatt Period (7th–6th centuries BC); Celtic occupation of Europe from the Danube to the Iberian Peninsula and the British Isles by *c.* 500 BC; Celtic penetration of Italy, the Balkan Peninsula, and Anatolia during the La Tène period (after *c.* 500 BC); subjugation in Gaul by Rome by 50 BC and later by the Germans by the 5th century AD; Celtic art, religion, and social and political organization

            ii. The Germans: their acquisition of Iron Age culture, migration into the Elbe–Rhine region by *c.* 500 BC, pressure on the Celts and Rome, inundation of the western half of the Roman Empire by the 5th century AD, Germanic social and political organization, religion and mythology

        c. Ancient peoples of the European steppe

            i. The Cimmerians: conjectured origins; southward migration, under Scythian pressure, from north of the Caucasus into Southwest Asia in the 8th and 7th centuries BC

            ii. The Scythians (Sakas): westward migration from the 8th century BC and eventual establishment in India and southern Russia after *c.* 600 BC; the Kingdom of the Royal Scyths in southern Russia from *c.* 600 BC to *c.* AD 100; relations with the Greeks and with Achaemenid Persia; government, society, and military tactics; art and religion

            iii. The Sarmatian migration into southern Russia in the 4th century BC and gradual displacement of the Scythians by *c.* AD 100; conflict with Rome; conquest by the Goths and Huns in the 3rd and 4th centuries AD; society, art, and religion

B. Archaic Greece and the development of Classical Greek civilization (*c.* 1200–323 BC)

    1. The Early Archaic and Archaic periods (*c.* 1200–*c.* 500 BC)

        a. The Dorian invasions, the Greek migrations to Anatolia, and their results (Proto-Geometric Period, *c.* 1100–*c.* 900 BC)

        b. The Geometric Period (*c.* 900–*c.* 750 BC): the world of Homer and Hesiod, the beginning of writing and of the *polis,* mythology and religious developments, the panhellenic centres (*e.g.,* Olympia, Delphi), social and political organization

        c. The Archaic Period (*c.* 750–*c.* 500 BC)

            i. General trends in the *poleis:* displacement of monarchy by aristocracy, development of a money economy, socioeconomic crises and the rise and fall of tyranny, the colonization movement, relations among the *poleis* (*e.g.,* leagues, wars)

      ii. The *poleis* of mainland Greece: the emergence of Spartan dominance over the Peloponnese and of a military-oriented polity and repression; aristocracy and tyranny at Athens, the reforms of Solon, and the institution of democracy under Cleisthenes; tyranny, aristocracy, and economic expansion at Corinth; the other *poleis* of the Peloponnese, the Isthmus, Euboea, and Boeotia

      iii. The Greeks in Asia Minor (Anatolia): Dorian and Aeolian cities; Miletus, Ephesus, and other Ionian cities; their commercial and cultural efflorescence

      iv. The Greek islands: the Cyclades, Sporades, Crete, Cyprus, and the Ionian Islands

      v. The Greek colonies and emporia in the West and Africa: southern Italy and Sicily (*e.g.,* Cumae, Syracuse), Gaul and the Iberian Peninsula (*e.g.,* Massilia), Cyrene and Naukratis

      vi. The Greeks in the North: Chalcidice, Thrace, Propontis (*e.g.,* Byzantium, Abydos, Lampsacus), and Pontus (*e.g.,* Black Sea region, Sinope, and Trapezus)

      vii. The arts in the Archaic Period; rationalism and irrationalism and the beginnings of philosophy and science, Orphism and the cult of Dionysus

      viii. The Greco-Persian Wars: the Persian (Achaemenid) conquest of Asia Minor and Thrace and the Ionian revolt (499 BC), Darius' (490 BC) and Xerxes' (480 BC) invasions of Greece and eventual Greek victory, the Greek offensive (479 BC), results of the wars, Herodotus' account of the conflict

2. The Classical period (*c.* 500–323 BC)

  a. Athens in the age of Pericles

     i. The Delian League and the Athenian Empire

     ii. Temporary retardation and final development of the democracy, society and economy

     iii. Cultural efflorescence; *e.g.,* the rebuilding of the Acropolis, drama, the pre-Socratic philosophers

  b. The Peloponnesian League and the other Greek states in the 5th century BC: relations among the Greek states from 479 to 431 BC

  c. The Peloponnesian War (431–404 BC): the war to the Peace of Nicias (421), renewal of the war and the defeat of Athens, intellectual and political changes at Athens (*e.g.,* oligarchic revolution, the Sophists and Socrates), Thucydides' account of the war

  d. The era of the Spartan and Theban hegemonies in Greece: Spartan policies toward the Greek states, relations with Persia, Athens and Thebes against Sparta, the Second Athenian League and the restoration of democracy, Theban expansion and containment, peace and the balance of power in Greece

  e. The northern kingdoms: Epirus, the rise of Macedonia and the conquest of Greece under Philip II

  f. The western Greeks: conflict with Carthage, the rise of Syracuse under Dionysius the Elder

  g. Greek culture in the 4th century BC: developments in philosophy and the arts

  h. The empire of Alexander III the Great: relations with the Greeks; the conquest of the Persian Empire (334–330 BC), Bactria, and the Indus Valley (330–323 BC); the ideals and governing practices of Alexander and the diversity of his empire

C. The Hellenistic Age (323–27 BC)

1. Establishment of the Hellenistic kingdoms and monarchies

  a. The regency and warfare among rival generals after Alexander's death (323–276 BC)

  b. Macedonian and Ptolemaic Egypt (323–30 BC)

     i. The Ptolemaic dynasty: dynastic strife and the end of the dynasty with the death of Cleopatra (30 BC)

     ii. Government and civilization of Hellenistic Egypt

  c. The Seleucid Kingdom in Asia: the dynasty, government, society, culture, and economy in its diverse regions; Jewish resistance; territorial losses in the 3rd century

  d. Greek rule in Bactria and India

  e. The Attalid kingdom of Pergamum and the native states in Asia Minor: Bithynia, Pontus, Cappadocia, Galatia, and Rhodes

  f. The Antigonid kingdom of Macedonia: government and foreign policy

g. Greece: social and political changes in the *polis,* the Achaean and Aetolian leagues, Athens and the other Greek states

h. The western Greeks, Epirus, Sicily under Agathocles (317–289 BC) and Hieron II (*c.* 270–216/215 BC) until its absorption by Rome

2. Relations among the Hellenistic states and other peoples from *c.* 275 to 27 BC

a. Expansionist policies of the Ptolemies in the Aegean and Asia Minor and Syria and their conflicts with the Seleucids

b. Conflicts between the Greek leagues and the Antigonids in the 3rd century BC

c. The Celtic migrations: expansion into the Iberian Peninsula, the British Isles, and Rome and southern Italy; later expansion into central Europe, the Carpathians, and the Balkans

d. The vigorous policies of Antiochus III and Philip V; the breakup of the Seleucid Empire; the entrance of Rome into the affairs of the Hellenistic states, resulting in their eventual incorporation into the Roman Empire

3. Hellenistic political, social, economic, and cultural institutions

a. Hellenistic monarchy and royal administration

b. Cultural developments: developments in philosophy, science, the arts, education, and religion

D. The rise of Rome

1. The character and achievements of the Romans, the archaeological and documentary historical sources (*e.g.,* Pompeii and Herculaneum), historiographic problems

2. Early (regal) Rome to the 6th century BC

a. Myths of origins and the early monarchy

b. The Etruscan hegemony and formative influence over Rome

c. Development of Roman social, religious, political, and military institutions; Roman virtues

3. The early Roman Republic (6th century–264 BC)

a. Overthrow of the monarchy and establishment of the republic and its institutions: the magistracies, judicial institutions, the Senate, plebeian institutions

b. Expansion of Rome in Italy: Rome and its Latin neighbours, the Gallic invasion and further conquests, Roman mastery of Italy

4. The middle republic: the emergence of Rome as the leading Mediterranean power (264–133 BC)

a. The First and Second Punic Wars

i. The First Punic War (264–241 BC) and its aftermath: the emergence of Roman naval power and acquisition of Sicily (241 BC), later annexation of Corsica and Sardinia (238 BC)

ii. Roman expansion into Cisalpine Gaul and entry into Greek affairs

iii. The Second Punic War (218–201 BC): Hannibal's invasion of Italy, his initial victories, and the war of attrition in Italy; Roman defeat of the Carthaginians at the Battle of the Metaurus (207 BC); the First Macedonian War (214–205 BC) and the conflict in Spain; Roman counteroffensive and victory in Africa (202 BC); Roman pacification of conquered territories

b. Establishment of Roman hegemony in the Hellenistic world

i. Establishment of a Roman protectorate over Greece after the Second Macedonian War (200–196 BC), the conquest of Macedonia and Illyricum (168 BC), the reduction of Rhodes, Roman exclusion of Seleucid power from the Aegean

ii. The Third Punic War (149–146 BC): the destruction of Carthage, subjugation of Macedonia and Greece

iii. Beginning of Roman provincial administration, abuses, Romanization of the empire

c. Roman government and economy in the middle republic: consuls, the Senate, and popular assemblies; development of large business interests, grazing estates, and urban immigration

d. Roman culture in the middle republic: Hellenizing influences

5. The late Roman Republic (133–31 BC)

a. Social and economic ills in Italy and the reform movement of the Gracchi (133–121 BC) and its results: the rise of middle-class equites

   b. Roman wars against the Celts and the conquest of Gallia Narbonensis (121 BC), wars against Jugurtha of Numidia (112–105 BC) and the Germans (105–101 BC), Marius' career and military reforms

   c. Events in Asia and the first war with Mithradates VI Eupator (88–84 BC): Italian allies (*socii*) against Rome in the Social War (90–89 BC) and their subsequent enfranchisement, the dictatorship and constitution of Sulla (82–80 BC)

   d. The Roman state in the two decades after Sulla

      i. Pompey's early career, revolts against Roman rule, Pompey's alliance with Crassus and repeal of the Sullan system, his extraordinary commands

      ii. Growing political suspicion and the outbreak of violence in the mid-1st century BC: the conspiracies of Catiline, Cicero's decline, the rise of Caesar and Pompey

   e. The alliance of Caesar, Pompey, and Crassus (59–44 BC): Caesar's conquest of Gaul; political maneuvers and the outbreak of the Civil War; Caesar's triumph, dictatorship, and assassination

   f. The initial cooperation of Octavian and Mark Antony in the Triumvirate and Octavian's achievement of sole power (43–31 BC): the annexation of Egypt and its administration

   g. Roman law during the late republic: the development of new procedures, the role of magistrates, the law of succession

   h. Culture in the late republic: oratory and philosophy, the arts

E. The Roman Empire (31 BC–AD 395)

   1. Consolidation of the empire under the Julio-Claudians (31 BC–AD 68)

      a. Augustus' establishment of the principate (27 BC–AD 14): the role of the *princeps;* the imperial administration, fiscal and military reforms, and the founding of new colonies; social and religious legislation; economic growth

      b. The Roman Empire at the time of Augustus: provincial administration, the imperial frontiers, the western provinces, the eastern provinces, the economic unification of the Mediterranean

      c. Foreign policy: Roman relations with Parthia and the other states in the East; the southern, western, and northern frontiers

      d. The culture of the Augustan Age: contributions of Livy, Virgil, and Horace; religion; the visual arts

      e. The empire under Tiberius (AD 14–37), Gaius (AD 37–41), Claudius I (AD 41–54), and Nero (AD 54–68): internal and frontier policies, the annexation of Britain, Tacitus' accounts, civil war and revolt in "the year of the four Emperors" (AD 69)

   2. Growth of the empire under the Flavians and Antonines (AD 69–192)

      a. The Flavian emperors (AD 69–96): Vespasian's fiscal and provincial reorganization, military and frontier policies, Titus and the suppression of the Jewish revolt, Domitian's despotism, military development and frontiers

      b. The Antonine emperors (AD 96–192): the reigns of Nerva, Trajan, Hadrian, Antoninus Pius, Marcus Aurelius, and Commodus; the beginning of imperial decline after AD 180

   3. The zenith of the Roman Empire in the late 1st and 2nd centuries AD

      a. The city of Rome and the empire: methods of Roman imperialism; the cities, culture, society, politics, and economy of the western and eastern provinces; the legions and frontier defenses

      b. Greco-Roman culture of the late 1st and 2nd centuries AD: developments in philosophy, religion, technology, and the arts

   4. Changes and crises in the Roman Empire in the 3rd and 4th centuries AD

      a. Civil wars, conflict with Parthia, the growth of bureaucracy, and militarization of government under the Severan dynasty (AD 193–235)

      b. Religious and cultural life: the public religions under the empire, the rise and spread of Christianity and other Eastern religions, official persecution of Christianity

      c. The transformation of Greco-Roman culture in late antiquity (3rd and 4th centuries AD), Greek revival and growth of Christian theology

      d. Military anarchy and disintegration of the Roman Empire (AD 235–270): the Gordians, the beginning of Germanic invasions, loss of eastern provinces, economic and social crisis

e. The recovery of the Roman Empire and the establishment of the dominate (AD 270–337): the recovery measures of Aurelian and his immediate successors

    i. Diocletian's (284–305) fundamental political and economic measures: persecution of Christians, struggle for power

    ii. Constantine the Great (307–337) and his conversion to Christianity, administration, and founding of Constantinople

f. The Roman Empire under the 4th-century successors of Constantine to Theodosius I (AD 379–395)

    i. The rule of Constantine's sons (337–361): renewed wars with Sāsānid Persia and increased penetration of the empire by the Germans

    ii. Julian's reign (361–363): the attempt to restore the old empire

    iii. Establishment of Christianity as the sole state religion; social, economic, and urban decline; remnants of pagan culture

g. The provinces under the later empire and the eclipse of the empire in the West: Germanic hegemony and the invasions by other peoples

---

Suggested reading in the *Encyclopædia Britannica:*

MACROPAEDIA: Major articles and biographies dealing with peoples of ancient Europe and the Classical civilizations of the ancient Mediterranean world to AD 395

Alexander the Great	Caesar	France	Greece
Athens	Constantine the Great	Greco-Roman Civilization,	Italy
Augustus	Europe	Classical	Mediterranean Sea
			Rome

MICROPAEDIA: Selected entries of reference information

General subjects

ancient Europe—	Boii	Lucania	Sarmatian
Balkans:	Carnuntum	Mamertini	Scythian
Dacia	Chatti	Marsi	Side
Getae	Cimbri	Paeligni	Soli
Illyria	Gepidae	Piceni	Steppe, The
Paeonia	Hallstatt	Populonia	*Greece—Archaic*
Triballi	Heuneburg	Praeneste	*period:*
ancient Europe—	Lingones	Sabine	Acarnania
Britain:	Marcomanni	Samnite	Achaean
Caledonia	Reinheim	Segesta	Aetolia
Creswell Crags	*ancient Europe—*	Siculi	agora
Kent's Cavern	*Iberia:*	Stabiae	amphictyony
Pict	Arevaci	Umbri	Amphipolis
Silures	Celtiberia	Veii	Apamea Cibotus
Skara Brae	Iberian	Veneti	apella
ancient Europe—	Lusitani	Villanovan culture	Archaic period
Gaul:	Numantia	Volsci	archon
Aedui	*ancient Europe—*	Volsinii	Areopagus
Arausio,	*Italy:*	Vulci	Assus
Battle of	Alba Fucens	*ancient western Asia:*	Boeotian League
Belgae	Ardea	Alani	Bosporus,
Gaul	Ateste	Anazarbus	Kingdom of the
Helvetii	Aurunci	Antioch	boule
La Tène	Boii	Bactria	Calydon
Morini	Caere	Cappadocia	Caulonia
Senones	Este	Caria	Chersonese, Tauric
Sequani	Etruscan	Cimmerian	Chersonese,
Veneti	Felsina	Commagene	Thracian
ancient Europe—	Golasecca	Doura-Europus	Clazomenae
Germany:	Hernici	Galatia	Cnidus
Agri Decumates	Hirpini	Hierapolis	Colchis
Alemanni	Latium	Isauria	Colophon
Arevaci	Lavinium	Pontus	Corinth

Cumae
Cyrene
Cyzicus
deme
Dorian
Ecclesia
Eleusis
Elis
ephebus
Ephesus
ephor
Eretria
Erythrae
eupatrid
geōmoroi
Gortyn
Greco-Persian
  Wars
Halicarnassus
helot
Himera
hoplite
Ionia
Lampsacus
Lelantine War
Leontini
Magna Graecia
Magnesia ad
  Maeandrum
Mantineia
Marathon,
  Battle of
metic
Miletus
Mouseion
Olynthus
Orchomenus
Paestum
Parian Chronicle
Parthenon
Pella
Pergamum
Phaestus
Phigalia
phyle
Plataea
polis
Priene
prytaneum
Selinus
Sicyon
sortition
strategus
Tegea
Thermopylae
Theseum

Thespiae
Tiryns
Trojan War
trophy
tyrant
Greece—Classical
  period:
  Anabasis
  Aornos, Siege of
  Artemis,
    Temple of
  Chalcidian League
  cleruchy
  Corinth, League of
  Delian League
  Gaugamela,
    Battle of
  Granicus, Battle
    of the
  Hydaspes, Battle
    of the
  Leuctra, Battle of
  Macedonia,
    Kingdom of
  paideia
  Peloponnesian War
  Philippi
  tetrarch
Hellenistic Age:
  Achaean League
  Aetolian League
  Antioch
  Bastarnae
  Cynoscephalae
  Hellenistic Age
  Ipsus, Battle of
  Issus, Battle of
  Lamian War
  Petra
  Seleucia on the
    Tigris
  Seleucid Kingdom
  Syrian Wars
Roman Empire:
  Adrianople,
    Battle of
  Aelia Capitolina
  Althiburos
  Antinoöpolis
  Antonine Wall
  Capernaum
  Carrhae, Battle of
  dominus
  emperor
  fasces
  fiscus

Five Good
  Emperors
foedus
Hadrian's Wall
Herculaneum
indiction
itinerarium
labarum
Monumentum
  Ancyranum
Mursa, Battle of
Notitia Dignitatum
Ostia
Pompeii
princeps
procurator
Thugga
tribune
Tusculum
Roman provinces:
  Africa, Roman
    province of
  Alps
  Arabia
  Asia
  Belgica
  Dacia
  Gallia Comata
  Illyria
  Lugdunensis
  Mauretania
  Moesia
  Narbonensis
  Numidia
  Pannonia
  Paphlagonia
  Raetia
  Transalpine Gaul
Roman Republic:
  Acta
  Actium, Battle of
  aedile
  aerarium
  angaria
  Cannae, Battle of
  Capua
  Cagliari
  censor
  civitas
  clientship
  colony
  comitia
  consul
  curia
  Decapolis
  decemviri

decurio
delator
dictator
eques
fasti
gladiator
Ilerda,
  Campaign of
Ilipa, Battle of
imperium
interrex
Italy
Jewish Revolt
latifundium
Latin League
legate
lictor
limes
Macedonian
  Wars
Munda, Battle of
municipium
Optimates and
  Populares
pater patriae
patrician
Pharsalus, Battle of
plebeian
Pollentia
praetor
Praetorian Guard
prefect
proconsul
proscription
province
publican
Punic Wars
Pydna, Battle of
quaestor
Roman Republic
  and Empire
Rubicon
Secular Games
Senate
Social War
Thapsus, Battle of
tribe
triumph
triumvirate
other:
  Beaker folk
  Lake Dwellings
  shell mound
  Urnfield

Biographies

Greece and
  Macedonia:
  Agesilaus II
  Alcibiades
  Argead dynasty

Cimon
Cleisthenes of
  Athens
Demosthenes
Dionysius the Elder

Epaminondas
Lycurgus
Miltiades the
  Younger
Peisistratus

Pericles
Philip II
Philip V
Pyrrhus
Solon

Themistocles	Ptolemy IV	Cato, Marcus	Maecenas, Gaius
Theramenes	Philopator	Porcius	Marcus Aurelius
Hellenistic states:	Ptolemy V	Cicero, Marcus	Marius, Gaius
Antigonus I	Epiphanes	Tullius	Nero
Monophthalmus	Ptolemy VI	Claudius	Pilate, Pontius
Antigonus II	Philometor	Claudius Caecus,	Pompey the Great
Gonatas	Ptolemy IX	Appius	Romulus and
Antiochus I Soter	Soter II	Constantine I	Remus
Antiochus III	Ptolemy XII	Diocletian	Seneca, Lucius
Antiochus IV	Auletes	Domitian	Annaeus
Epiphanes	Ptolemy XIII	Gallienus, Publius	Severus, Septimius
Arsinoe II	Theos Philopator	Licinius Egnatius	Severus Alexander
Cleopatra VII	Seleucus I Nicator	Germanicus Caesar	Scipio Aemilianus
Thea Philopator	*Rome:*	Gracchus, Gaius	Scipio Africanus
Mithradates VI	Agrippa, Marcus	Sempronius	Major
Eupator	Vipsanius	Gracchus, Tiberius	Sulla, Lucius
Ptolemy I Soter	Antony, Mark	Sempronius	Cornelius
Ptolemy II	Aurelian	Hadrian	Theodosius I
Philadelphus	Caesar, Julius	Herod	Tiberius
Ptolemy III	Caligula	Herod Agrippa I	Trajan
Euergetes	Caracalla	Herod Antipas	Valentinian I
		Julian	Vespasian

INDEX: See entries under all of the terms above

Division II.   **Peoples and Civilizations of Medieval Europe, North Africa, and Southwest Asia**
[For Part Nine headnote see page 343.]

The outlines in the four sections of Division II deal with the civilizations directly descendant from those of the ancient Near East and of Classical antiquity, which are treated in the two sections of Division I. The general period covered in Division II is the Middle Ages, beginning with the death of Theodosius I in AD 395, conventionally taken as marking the permanent division of the Roman Empire into East and West, and extending to *c.* 1500, conventionally taken as the starting point of modern history.

The sectional organization of this division and the outlines in its four sections reflect significant cultural and political interaction between the Eastern Christian, Western Christian, and Islāmic spheres, and also involve some breaking points in the history of each sphere.

Section 921.   **Western Europe, the Byzantine (Eastern Roman) Empire, and the States of Eastern Europe from AD 395 to *c.* 1050**

    A. The study of medieval and Byzantine history: the historical sources, historiographic problems, chronological outline

    B. The eclipse of the Roman Empire in the West and the development and Christianization of Germanic successor states (AD 395–*c.* 750)

        1. The end of the Western Roman Empire and the Germanic Völkerwanderung (AD 395–*c.* 500)

            a. The general decline of government, economy, society, and culture; the Visigothic invasions in the 5th century and settlement in Provence and Spain

            b. Establishment of the Germanic hegemony: the invasions of Vandals; the invasions of Angles, Saxons, and Jutes (Britain); the Frankish conquest of Gaul (*c.* 481/482–511) and the Burgundian flight to the south; the Huns; abolition of the Western Empire and Ostrogothic rule in Italy (493–553); other Germanic tribes—the issue of Arianism versus Catholic Christianity; Germanic law and society

2. The Germanic successor states and the remnants of the Roman Empire in the West from *c.* 500 to 750

   a. Byzantine conquests and later diminution of Byzantium's western possessions (540–751), the Exarchate of Ravenna, Lombard conquests in Italy, beginning of the political role of the Roman papacy

   b. Early development of the Germanic kingdoms: the Visigothic kingdom to 711, origins of early feudalism

      i. The Anglo-Saxon kingdoms in England and the Celtic kingdoms in Ireland

      ii. The Franks under the Merovingians and early Carolingians: the successors of Clovis, rise and establishment of the Carolingians under Charles Martel and Pepin III the Short (714–768), Carolingian relations with the papacy and entry into Italian affairs

   c. Effects of the rise of Islām on western Europe

3. Religion, the arts, and society in the early Middle Ages: the amalgamation of late Classical and Germanic cultures and Christianity

   a. Conversion of the Celts and the Germans to Catholic Christianity: religious and cultural functions of monasticism and the Western Church

   b. The arts, intellectual life, and education in the early Middle Ages

   c. Social and economic life in the early Middle Ages

C. The early Byzantine Empire (AD 395–717)

   1. Origins of Byzantium in the late Roman Empire: the reforms of Diocletian and Constantine

   2. Persistence of Greco-Roman society in the East in the 5th century: the empire from the death of Theodosius I to the accession of Heraclius (610)

      a. Economic and social policies: agriculture, coinage, relations with the barbarians (*e.g.,* Huns, Goths, Isaurians, Avars, Slavs)

      b. Ecclesiastical controversies, Syrian and Egyptian disaffection, and the beginning of conflict with the Western Church

      c. The empire at the end of the 5th century: internal tensions, political and economic policies under Anastasius I

      d. The reign of Justinian I (527–565): realignment with the Roman Church, Code of Justinian, military campaigns in the West, effects of the plague, later campaigns

      e. Early Byzantine culture: Christianity, the arts, and intellectual life

      f. Justinian's successors (565–610): relations with the barbarians and with the Persians, revolt of the army

   3. Rehabilitation of the empire under the dynasty of Heraclius (610–685)

      a. Heraclius' reorganization of the empire along military lines: wars with Persia; the loss of Syria, Palestine, Armenia, and Egypt to the Arabs and continued Arab pressures; recognition of Byzantine overlordship in the Balkans

      b. Decline of the dynasty (685–711): renewed wars with the Slavs; settlement with the Arabs; fiscal, agricultural, and defensive policies; military anarchy (711–717)

D. Western Christendom and Scandinavia from the Carolingian era to the general European revival (*c.* 750–*c.* 1050)

   1. The Carolingian Empire and its later dissolution (*c.* 750–887), France in the 10th century

      a. The reign of Charlemagne (king, 768–814; emperor from 800): further military expansion of the Frankish kingdom; legislation, administration, and defense; ecclesiastical policies; patronage of arts and learning

      b. Decline and dissolution of the Carolingian Empire under the successors of Charlemagne: the society, government, and culture of the Frankish world

         i. Louis the Pious; partitioning of the empire by the Treaty of Verdun (843) between Louis's sons (Lothair, Charles the Bald, and Louis the German); Muslim, Norman, and Magyar invasions and the debilitation of central authority

         ii. The Frankish world: society, institutions, economic life, the church, literature and the arts

      c. The East Frankish kingdom (Germany): the last Carolingians (to 911), the emergence of the four stem duchies (Saxony, Franconia, Swabia, and Bavaria)

      d. The West Frankish kingdom (France): dynastic rivalry between Carolingians and Robertians (to 987) and the ascendancy of the feudal magnates

      e. The Middle Frankish kingdom (Lotharingia): Burgundy, Provence, and Italy

  2. The British Isles and Scandinavia (*c.* 800–1066)

      a. England: the decline of Mercia and the rise of Wessex; the 9th-century Danish invasions; King Alfred's legal, administrative, and ecclesiastical policies and patronage of the arts; Anglo-Saxon political unification and monastic revival in the 10th century; the conquest of the Danes and their rule over the Anglo-Danish state; the reign of Edward the Confessor and the Norman Conquest

      b. Development of the Kingdom of Scotland, the Welsh, Ireland during the Norse invasions

         i. Roman penetration in Scotland: Christianity, Norse influence

        ii. Early Christianity in Wales: relations with the Anglo-Saxons, Welsh society

       iii. Ireland: conversion to Christianity, monasticism, the Norse invasions

      c. The Viking Age in Scandinavia: the Vikings and Varangians, widespread raids and conquests (*c.* 800–*c.* 1050), social and political organization, arts, paganism and conversion to Christianity from *c.* 850

  3. Germany, Burgundy, and Italy: development of the Holy Roman (German) Empire (911–1056)

      a. Revival of central authority in Germany and intervention in Italy by the Saxon dynasty: Conrad (911–918), rise of the nobility, early opposition from Arnulf of Bavaria, drive against Magyars and Slavs, Germanic kingship

      b. Promotion of the German church under Otto I (936–973): his conquest of Italy and establishment of the Holy Roman Empire (962), early Salian kings (1024–56)

      c. Development of medieval Italy: political, economic, and social developments on the peninsula and in Sicily

         i. Origins of the Papal States and growth in power of the papacy; early years of the commercial cities of Venice in the north and Gaeta, Naples, Sorrento, and Amalfi in Campania; the Arabs in Sicily

        ii. Cities and countryside: persistence of an urban tradition despite the exodus to rural areas, the role of bishops in urban life, economy and society

  4. The Kingdom of France under the early Capetians (987–1180): the relative weakness of the monarchy vis-à-vis the great feudatories (Normandy and Anjou), Capetian attempts to expand the royal domain

  5. Growth of the Christian states in northern Spain (Asturias–Leon–Castile, Navarre, Aragon–Catalonia): their relations with one another and with the Muslims in Spain, the first phase of the Reconquista to the fall of Toledo (1085)

  6. The sociopolitical and economic structure of early medieval Europe: origins, development, and spread of feudalism; its elements and structure; the manorial economy and mainly localized commerce to *c.* 1050

E. Peoples and states of eastern Europe to *c.* 1050: early empires and later development of Christianized states

  1. The Slavic peoples: origins, early society and culture, movement into Pannonia and south Russia, plundering expeditions and eventual settlement in the Balkans

  2. The eastern European states and peoples within the Byzantine orbit

      a. The Bulgarian domains to 1018: origins, migration into the Balkans (*c.* AD 650) and mixture with the local Slavic populations, early contacts and wars with Byzantium, adoption of Christianity (870), the First Bulgarian Empire (893–1014) and subsequent conquest by Byzantium

      b. The Balkans: the migration of the Croats and Serbs into the Balkans and their subsequent relations with the Bulgars and Byzantium to *c.* 1050

      c. Exploration and the rise of the Rus raids on Constantinople, development of trade routes, Khazar state north of the Black Sea

      d. The state of Kievan Rus (*c.* 980–1054): Slavic-Varangian (Scandinavian) origins, economic decline, social and political institutions

  3. Eastern European states within the orbit of Western Christendom

a. Developments in Moravia and Bohemia to 1055: the Celtic and Germanic tribes supplanted by Slavic peoples in the 6th century, Czech dominance in the 8th century, unification under the Přemysl rulers

    i. Unification of Greater Moravia under Mojmír (814): religious conflicts with Frankish clergy and temporary adherence to the Eastern rite, political expansion

    ii. The early Přemysl rulers of Bohemia: capital at Prague, ties with Bavaria and the Saxon dynasty, Boleslav I (929–967), Boleslav II (967–999), annexation of Moravia under Břetislav (1034–55)

b. The Avar Empire and the early Magyar (Hungarian) kingdom to *c.* 1050: alliance with the Carolingian ruler Arnulf, establishment of the Árpád dynasty, settlement of the central plain, conversion to Christianity, reign of Stephen I (997–1038)

c. Development of the Kingdom of Poland in the 10th century and Polish conversion to Western Christianity, civil strife and later restoration under Casimir I (1039–58)

F. The zenith and incipient decline of the Byzantine Empire (717–1081), the growth of Venice

1. The age of Iconoclasm (717–867): the reforms of Leo III the Isaurian, repulse of the Arabs, Bulgar incursions and continued religious dissension under Leo's successors

2. The Macedonian era (867–1025): territorial expansion, foreign relations, continued strength and prosperity under its rulers until 1025

    a. Military revival, relations with Slavs and Bulgars, estrangement from the West

    b. Culture and administration: legal reforms under Basil I and Leo VI

    c. Social and economic change: reforms of Basil II

3. Byzantine decline and subjection to Western influences: 11th-century weakness, arrival of new enemies, the schism with Rome (1054)

4. Venice: the development of its institutions, commerce, and naval power in the early Middle Ages

---

Suggested reading in the *Encyclopædia Britannica:*

MACROPAEDIA: Major articles and a biography dealing with Western Europe, the Byzantine (Eastern Roman) Empire, and the states of eastern Europe from AD 395 to *c.* 1050

Bulgaria	Greco-Roman	Istanbul	United Kingdom
Byzantine Empire,	Civilization,	Italy	Venice
The History	Classical	Poland	
of the	Holy Roman	Rome	
Charlemagne	Empire, The	Spain	
Europe	History of the	Steppe, The	
France	Hungary	History of the	
Germany	Ireland	Eurasian	

MICROPAEDIA: Selected entries of reference information

General subjects

barbarian invaders	Suebi	logothete	feudalism
and successor	Vandal	Manzikert,	fief
kingdoms:	Visigoth	Battle of	homage and fealty
Alani	*Byzantine and*	Mardaïte	knight
Alemanni	*Western Roman*	Mons Lactarius,	knight service
Angle	*empires:*	Battle of	liege
Antae	Byzantine Empire	Myra	manorialism
Avar	Carthage,	Nicaea, empire of	Middle Ages
Frank	Exarchate of	Poson, Battle of	serfdom
Goth	Ecloga	pronoia system	serjeanty
Hun	Epanagoge	Ravenna	vassal
Jute	eparch	Rhodian Sea Law	wardship and
Lombard	Farmer's Law	Taginae, Battle of	marriage
Ostrogoth	Ghassān	theme	*Merovingian and*
Pecheneg	Iconoclastic	*early medieval society*	*Carolingian era:*
Saxon	Controversy	*and culture:*	Aquitaine
	Justinian, Code of	feudal land tenure	Austrasia

Biographies

*national
development—
British Isles:*
 Aethelberht I
  (Kent)
 Agricola
 Alfred
 Athelstan
 Augustine of
  Canterbury, Saint
 Bede the
  Venerable, Saint
 Boudicca
 Brian
 Canute
 Conn Cetchathach
 Dunstan of
  Canterbury, Saint
 Edgar
 Edmund I
 Edmund II
 Edward (the Elder)
 Edward (the
  Martyr)
 Edward (the
  Confessor)
 Edwin
 Egbert
 Godwine
 Hardecanute
 Harold I
 Harold II
 Kenneth I
 Kenneth II
 Kenneth III
 Macbeth
 Malcolm II
 Malcolm III
 Offa
 Olaf Guthfrithson
 Olaf Sihtricson
 Oswald, Saint
 Patrick, Saint
 Sweyn
 Theodore of
  Canterbury,
  Saint

Tostig
*national
development—
eastern European
states:*
 Arpad
 Boleslav I
 Boleslav II
 Boleslaw I
 Boris I (Bulgaria)
 Bratislav I
 Mieszko I
 Mieszko II
 Oleg
 Rurik
 Rurik dynasty
 Samuel (Bulgaria)
 Stephen I
  (Bulgaria)
 Svyatoslav I
 Vladimir I
 Yaroslav I
*national
development—
France:*
 Adalbero of
  Ardennes
 Charles III
  (France)
 Eudes
 Geoffrey II
  (Anjou)
 Henry I (France)
 Hugh Capet
 Hugh the Great
 Lothair (France)
 Louis III (France)
 Louis IV (France)
 Louis V (France)
 Richard I
  (Normandy)
 Richard II
  (Normandy)
 Robert I (France)
 Robert II (France)
 Robert I
  (Normandy)

Robert the Strong
Rollo
Rudolf (France)
William I
 (Normandy)
*national
development—
Germany,
Burgundy,
and Italy:*
 Arnulf
 Arnulf I
 Berengar
  (Germany/Holy
  Roman Empire)
 Berengar II (Italy)
 Boso
 Charles III
  (Germany/Holy
  Roman Empire)
 Charles (Provence)
 Conrad I
  (Germany/Holy
  Roman Empire)
 Conrad II
  (Germany/Holy
  Roman Empire)
 Henry I
  (Germany/Holy
  Roman Empire)
 Henry II
  (Germany/Holy
  Roman Empire)
 Henry III
  (Germany/Holy
  Roman Empire)
 Leo IX (pope)
 Louis III
  (Germany/Holy
  Roman Empire)
 Otto I (Germany/
  Holy Roman
  Empire)
 Otto II (Germany/
  Holy Roman
  Empire)

Otto III
 (Germany/Holy
 Roman Empire)
Rudolf (Germany/
 Holy Roman
 Empire)
Sylvester II (pope)
*national
development—
Iberia:*
 'Abd ar-Raḥmān I
 'Abd ar-Raḥmān II
 'Abd
  ar-Raḥmān III
 Alfonso I
  (Asturias/Leon)
 Ferdinand I
  (Castile)
 Manṣūr, Abū
  'Amir al-
 Pelayo
 Sancho III
  (Navarre)
 Ṭāriq ibn Ziyād
*national
development—
Scandinavia:*
 Canute
 Erik I (Norway)
 Erik the Red
 Haakon I
 Harald I
  (Denmark)
 Harald I (Norway)
 Harald II (Norway)
 Harald III
  (Norway)
 Hardecanute
 Leif Eriksson
 Olaf I (Norway)
 Olaf II (Norway)
 Ragnar Lothbrok
 Rollo
 Sweyn I
  (Denmark)
 Sweyn II
  (Denmark)

INDEX: See entries under all of the terms above

Section 922.   **The Empire of the Caliphate and Its Successor States to *c*. AD 1055**

A. The study of Islāmic history: the historical sources, historiographic problems

B. The rise and spread of Islām and the Arab Empire to the end of the Umayyad dynasty (AD 622–750)

1. Islām and Arab expansion in the 7th century

   a. The life and career of Muḥammad and the rise of Islām, the doctrine of the *jihād* (holy war)

   b. Muslim expansion outside Arabia under the four Patriarchal Caliphs (632–661)

      i. Abū Bakr (632–634) and 'Umar I (634–644): the tribe of Quraysh; divisions among the followers of Muḥammad; the conquest of Iraq and the Sāsānid (Persian) Empire and the Byzantine territories of Jordan, Palestine, Syria, and Egypt

      ii. 'Uthmān (644–656) and 'Alī (656–661): expeditions into North Africa, Armenia, and Persia; social and religious grievances; civil unrest; the origins of Shī'ism

2. The Umayyad caliphate (661–750)

   a. The consolidation of the caliphate (661–684) under Mu'āwiyah I and his successors: westward orientation of the caliphate and its capital at Damascus, growing opposition to the Umayyads

   b. The zenith of Umayyad power with the advent of the Marwānids: 'Abd al-Malik (685–705) and al-Walīd (705–715), suppression of revolts, new conquests

   c. The later Umayyads (715–750): conciliation of state policies with religion, peace and prosperity under Hishām (724–743), disintegration of the empire under his successors and the 'Abbāsid revolt

   d. Umayyad government and society

      i. Administration of the Arab lands: utilization of local officials, the position and functions of the caliph, Islāmization and Arabization, social classes

      ii. Cultural life under the Umayyads: spread of the Arabic language, literary revival, fragmentation into religious sects, accomplishment in the arts

C. The 'Abbāsid Empire and its successor states (750–*c*. 1055)

1. The 'Abbāsid caliphate from 750 to 945

   a. Establishment of the new dynasty and its advance under Abū al-'Abbās as-Saffāḥ (749–754), al-Manṣūr (754–775), and al-Mahdī (775–785); the 'Abbāsids at their zenith (786–861)

   b. Decline of the caliphate after the death of al-Mutawakkil (861): growth of provincial autonomy

   c. Economic and social life under the 'Abbāsids: manufactures and trade

   d. Cultural life under the 'Abbāsid caliphate

      i. Religion: theology and philosophy, Islāmic mysticism

      ii. The arts and sciences: Greek and Persian influences, the aniconic principle in the arts

2. Eclipse of the 'Abbāsids and the growth of provincial dynasties from *c*. 755 to 1055

   a. The Umayyad amirate and caliphate in Spain (756–1031) and its capital at Córdoba

      i. Foundation of the independent amirate by 'Abd ar-Raḥmān I (756–788): defeat of the Franks at Roncevalles (778), political and cultural splendour in the reign of 'Abd ar-Raḥmān II, defeat of the *muwallad*s

      ii. The Umayyad caliphate under 'Abd ar-Raḥmān an-Nāṣir III: relations with Arabs, Berbers, and the Christian states in Spain; conquest of Morocco by his successors; the *ṭā'ifa*s and internal disorders

      iii. Social and economic life in Muslim Spain: the culture of Muslim Spain, developments in literature and the sciences

   b. The Fāṭimid state of North Africa and Syria from 909 to *c*. 1055: the foundation of the Fāṭimid caliphate in Tunisia and Algeria, its conquest of Morocco (926) and Egypt (969), and expansion into Syria

   c. Other dynasties in North Africa and Syria: the Shī'ite Idrīsids of Morocco (789–926); the Rustamid kingdom in the central Maghrib (787–911); the Aghlabid state in Tunisia, Algeria, and Sicily (800–909); minor dynasties

d. The Sāmānid dynasty of Khorāsān (875–999) and its role in the Islāmization of the Turkic peoples: patronage of art and learning

e. The Būyid dynasty in Iran and Iraq (932–1055): Shī'ism and the Iranian revival, Isfahan

f. Other eastern states: the Qarmaṭians in eastern Arabia (c. 900–1078), the Turkish Qarakhanid dynasty of Mā Warā 'an-Nahr (Transoxania) and eastern Turkistan (922–c. 1050), the Turkish Ghaznavids of Afghanistan and northwestern India (998–1050), minor states and dynasties

---

Suggested reading in the *Encyclopædia Britannica*:

MACROPAEDIA: Major articles dealing with the Empire of the Caliphate and its successor states to c. AD 1055

Arabia
Islāmic World, The
Mecca and Medina

MICROPAEDIA: Selected entries of reference information

General subjects

amīr	Hāshimīyah	Nahāvand,	Ṣaqālibah
caliph	iqṭā'	Battle of	Ṣiffīn, Battle of
Caliphate	jizyah	Poitiers, Battle of	taifa
dīwān	Karbalā', Battle of	(732)	Wāsiṭ
fitnah	kharāj	rāshidūn, ar-	Zanj rebellion
Fusṭāṭ, al-	Khorram-dīnān	riddah	
ghanīmah	Kūfah	Rustamid	
ḥājib	Mozarab	Kingdom	

Biographies

'Abbāsid dynasty	Būyid dynasty	Ma'mūn, al-	Sāmānid dynasty
'Abd al-Malik	Fāṭimid dynasty	Manṣūr, al-	Sīmjūrid dynasty
'Abd ar-Raḥmān III	Ghaznavid dynasty	Mazyadid dynasty	Umayyad dynasty
Abū Muslim	Ḥamdānid dynasty	Mosāferīd dynasty	'Uthmān ibn 'Affān
'Alī	Hārūn ar-Rashīd	Mu'āwiyah I	Zeyārid dynasty
Barmakids	Hūdid dynasty	Mu'tamid, al-	
Bāvand dynasty	Kā'ūsīyeh dynasty	Najāḥid dynasty	
	Mahmūd	Ṣaffārid dynasty	

INDEX: See entries under all of the terms above

Section 923.   Western Christendom in the High and Later Middle Ages (*c.* 1050–*c.* 1500)

A. The medieval western European revival and the economy, society, and culture of Western Christendom in the High Middle Ages

1. Society, economy, and culture

a. Western European society in the High Middle Ages: the feudal nobility, the clergy, the bourgeoisie, the peasantry (serfs), the status of women

b. Growth of agricultural productivity and population: revival of a money economy, manufacturing, and the commercial effects of the Crusades; revival of towns and population movements

c. The church in medieval society: growth of papal hegemony, reform movements affecting the church (the friars of St. Francis), use of the Inquisition from 1233, role of religion in medieval society

d. The culture of the High Middle Ages

i. Establishment of schools and universities

ii. The intellectual revival of the 11th and 12th centuries, Scholasticism, developments in philosophy and theology

        iii. The arts: Latin and vernacular literature, Romanesque and Gothic visual arts, music, theatre, the decorative arts

    e. The status of Jews in medieval society and their economic role, persecutions, and migrations

  2. The Holy Roman Empire, the papacy, and Italy from *c.* 1050 to *c.* 1300

    a. The empire, the papacy, and Italy in the era of the Investiture Controversy

        i. Church reform in the 10th and 11th centuries and the clash between the papacy and the emperors over lay investiture (at its height between the emperor Henry IV and Pope Gregory VII): the resulting incipient decline of German monarchical authority under the Salian emperors

        ii. The Norman conquest of southern Italy and Sicily and establishment of a strong monarchy: relations with the papacy, Venice, and the Byzantine Empire

        iii. The growth of communes in northern Italy, the status of German imperial power, the political role of the papacy in Italy, the commercial expansion of Italian cities (*e.g.,* Genoa, Pisa), continued growth of Venetian maritime power

    b. The empire under the Hohenstaufen dynasty and after its extinction to *c.* 1300, the papacy and Italy

        i. Steady inroads of the German princes into German monarchical authority: colonization of Slavic territory, development of commercial centres (*e.g.,* Lübeck), the reign of Frederick I Barbarossa and Frederick II, extinction of the Hohenstaufen dynasty and the Great Interregnum (1250–73), the election and reign of Rudolf of Habsburg

        ii. The Kingdom of Sicily: centralized government, ethnic mixture, Palermo, control by the Hohenstaufens (1194–1266), the Angevin conquest and expulsion (1282), the advent of Aragonese control

        iii. The decline of German imperial control in northern Italy and the continued development of the communes (*e.g.,* Milan, Pisa, Florence, Siena): their internal and external conflicts

        iv. Continued commercial expansion of Italian cities: Venetian expansion in the Levant and aid to the Normans in the conquest of Byzantium (1204), commercial inroads into the Levantine trade by Genoa and Pisa

  3. The growth of the Kingdom of France under the later Capetian dynasty (1180–1328), the Low Countries

    a. Growth of the power of the French kings and extension of the territory under their control

        i. Philip II Augustus (1180–1223): acquisition of territory and consolidation of the realm, royal administration, feudal policies

        ii. Louis VIII (1223–26) and Louis IX (1226–70): institution of the granting of appanages to nobility, the Albigensian Crusade, rise of bureaucracy, attitudes toward the clergy and the lay nobility

        iii. The later Capetians: Philip IV the Fair (1285–1314), claims of the monarchy, beginnings of the States General, conflict with Boniface VIII

        iv. Foreign relations: conflict with the Holy Roman Empire under Philip II, the religious crusades of Louis IX, the wars of Philip IV

        v. Economy, society, and culture in the 13th century: increase in population, growth of towns and urban prosperity, rural life, religion, culture and learning

    b. The Low Countries: development of the territorial principalities and the rise of towns; *e.g.,* Ghent, Bruges

        i. Secular and spiritual principalities

        ii. Struggle for independence, French and British influence

        iii. Social and economic structure

  4. The Spanish Christian kingdoms of Castile and Leon, Aragon (including Barcelona), Portugal, and Navarre (1035–*c.* 1260): their expansion into Muslim territory, their mutual rivalries, their ethnic-cultural mixtures, and their internal political development; the role of the church

    a. The medieval empire (1035–1157): the division of the kingdoms and the emergence of Portugal as an independent state

    b. The rise of Castile and Aragon and the expulsion of the Muslims, led especially by the rulers of Aragon (James I, 1213–76) and Castile (Ferdinand III, 1217–52)

    c. Society, economy, and culture: administration of the Spanish kingdoms; development of feudalism, growth of towns, and appearance of trade and industry; establishment of the Cortes; foundation of the universities of Valencia and Salamanca

5. The Kingdom of England and its continental dependencies from the Norman Conquest to the death of Edward I; Scotland, Wales, and Ireland (1066–1307)

    a. The Norman Conquest: introduction of feudalism and the development of royal administration under William I the Conqueror (1066–87) and his immediate successors

        i. Church–state relations and the place of the clergy in the feudal structure, the Domesday survey

        ii. Strengthening of central government under William's successors: relations with the church in their reigns

        iii. The period of the Anarchy (1135–54): Matilda and Stephen, civil war

    b. The early Plantagenets

        i. The reign of Henry II (1154–89): military and administrative reforms, Henry's conflict with the church and the struggle with Becket, the rebellions of Henry's sons

        ii. Richard I (1189–99): administration in Richard's absence, the Saladin Tithe, attempts to establish a standing army

        iii. The reign of John (1199–1216): loss of French possessions, John's conflict with Innocent III, the revolt of the barons and Magna Carta

        iv. Henry III (1216–72) and Edward I (1272–1307): Simon de Montfort and the Barons' War; Edward's restoration of royal power and his legal, administrative, and military policies

    c. Scotland, Wales, and Ireland: relations between the Kingdom of Scotland and the English crown, the extent of English control in Wales and Ireland

        i. The unification of Scotland and the development of the monarchy

        ii. Norman infiltration in Wales, the three kingdoms, internal conflicts and the Edwardian settlement

        iii. Ireland: the Anglo-Norman invasion and its effects, establishment of the Irish Parliament

6. Scandinavia (*c.* 1050–*c.* 1300): establishment of the kingdoms of Denmark, Norway, and Sweden

    a. The trend toward unity and strong monarchy: political developments in the three kingdoms

    b. Expansion into Finland, Iceland, and Greenland: introduction of feudalism, economic developments and influence of the Hanseatic League, society

7. The Slavic and Magyar states of Western Christendom (*c.* 1050–*c.* 1300)

    a. Poland: the reigns of Bolesław II (1058–79) and Bolesław III (1102–38), the division of Poland between Bolesław III's sons, the seniority system, territorial losses, the early role of the Teutonic Order in eastern Europe, internal developments

    b. Bohemia under the later Přemysl rulers (1055–1306): struggles within the ruling family, privileges secured from the Holy Roman emperor, territorial expansion, losses to Rudolf of Habsburg

        i. German interference in Bohemia: attacks upon the position of the Prague princes by Frederick I Barbarossa, the Golden Bull of Sicily (1212)

        ii. Political and economic growth: German immigration, founding of urban communities, expansion under Otakar II (1253–78) into Austria, silver mining and coinage

    c. Hungary: the early kings, expansion into Transylvania and Dalmatia, the nobility, Golden Bull (1222), Mongol invasion (1241), extinction of the Árpád dynasty in 1301

B. The decline of medieval European political institutions, economy, and culture and the incipient transition to the modern age (*c.* 1300–*c.* 1500)

1. The culture of the late Middle Ages in western Europe

    a. The early Renaissance in Italy: historiographic problems, the contribution of the city-states, developments in literature and the fine arts

        i. Revival of Greek studies and the formation of Classical libraries in Italy: Humanism, relationship of Humanism to Christianity

      ii. New concepts and techniques in painting, sculpture, and architecture: patronage of the arts by the papacy

   b. The late Gothic style in northern Europe

   c. Late medieval intellectual developments: political theory, law, and the decline of ideals of imperial unity and papal supremacy; the rising power of national monarchies; decline of Scholasticism; science; witchcraft

2. Late medieval society and economy

   a. The exaggeration of chivalry and declining importance of the feudal nobility in the face of changing military technology and organization: growing influence of the bourgeoisie, growth of royal government

   b. Gradual inflation and continued development of capitalism: peasant revolts; economic, social, and political effects of the Black Death (1347–50); gradual disappearance of serfdom in western Europe; decline in prosperity and population; the guild system; the Hanseatic League

3. The church in the later Middle Ages: papal monarchy and taxation, the Avignon papacy (1309–77) and the Great Schism (1378–1417), the conciliar movement and other reform movements with regard to the church, mysticism

4. Germany, Bohemia, and the Swiss Confederation (*c.* 1300–*c.* 1500)

   a. Limitations on the imperial office and the continued ascendancy of the princes in Germany: internal strife between the cities and the princes, the Habsburg and Luxemburg emperors, the division of the Habsburg lands and the enhancement of Habsburg power and influence in Europe by 1500

      i. Development of the individual states

      ii. Society, economy, and culture in the 14th and 15th centuries

   b. Bohemia in the later Middle Ages: political and religious developments

      i. The Luxemburg dynasty (1310–1437): territorial expansion under Charles I, growth of the city of Prague, Wenceslas IV

      ii. Beginning of the religious reform movement (*c.* 1360): the Chapel Bethlehem's preachers, the activities of Jan Hus and his execution at the Council of Constance (1415)

      iii. The struggle between Sigismund and the Hussites: the Four Articles of Prague, Žižka's leadership of the Hussites, the Hussite preponderance (1437–71), George of Poděbrady

      iv. The Jagiellon kings (1471–1526): the decline of royal authority, growth of power of the first two estates

   c. Early Swiss history, development of the Swiss Confederation after 1291, struggle against the Habsburgs, the French invasion and the Peace of Constance (1446)

5. Italy in the late Middle Ages and the Renaissance

   a. Social and political developments in the period 1300–1400: withdrawal of imperial and papal authority, Italian society, the crises of the 14th century (*e.g.,* the Black Death, economic decline, urban unrest)

   b. The Italian states in the 14th century: forms of rule, use of mercenaries, cultural developments

      i. Milan: the Visconti family, rule at home, expansion in northern Italy, Visconti attitudes toward the state

      ii. Florence: republicanism, the cloth industry, banking, movement into the city from the countryside, plots against the republic

      iii. Venice: republican institutions, economic prosperity and commercial empire

      iv. The Papal States: their locations and proprietors, breakdown of papal control during the Avignon papacy and the Great Schism (1378–1417)

      v. Naples, Sicily, and the other Italian states (*e.g.,* Angevin rule in Naples until its union with Sicily in 1442 under Alfonso V of Aragon); Savoy; Genoa; Verona

   c. The Italian states in the 15th century: expansion of the major Italian powers, Italy as a political system, cultural developments

      i. The crisis of Florentine republicanism: the threat from Gian Galeazzo Visconti of Milan and his successors, Florentine historiography, rule by the Medici

      ii. The Papal States: papal policy to strengthen its position, reliance of the popes on their relatives to control the domains

      iii. Despotisms: Alfonso I (Alfonso V of Aragon) in Naples and Sicily and division of the territory on his death in 1458, the Sforza in Milan

      iv. Venice: the stability of Venetian life, increased interests in activities on the Italian peninsula

6. France and the Low Countries (*c.* 1300–*c.* 1500)

    a. The period of the Hundred Years' War: the stages of the war, the role of the French kings in the conflict, the war's significance

      i. Remote and proximate causes of the war: the problem of English lands in France, the problem of the French succession, the Flemish revolt

      ii. From the outbreak of the war (1337) to the Treaty of Brétigny (1360): the reign of Philip VI (1328–50), the Crécy campaign and its aftermath (1346–54), negotiations during John II the Good's captivity (1356–60), burgeoning power of the estates and revolt of the peasants

      iii. From the Treaty of Brétigny (1360) to the accession of Henry V of England (1413): Charles V (1364–80), the dispute over Flanders, temporary peace, Charles VI (1380–1422), struggle between Burgundians and Armagnacs

      iv. From the accession of Henry V (1413) to the siege of Orléans (1428–29): Charles VII (1422–61); France divided between the dauphin Charles, Philip the Good of Burgundy, and Henry V of England

      v. Recovery and reunification (1429–83) and the expulsion of the English: Joan of Arc and the stirring of French national feeling, reconquest of Maine and Normandy, conquest of Guyenne (1453), final settlement at Picquigny (1475)

    b. Administrative and military reforms and the strengthening of royal power vis-à-vis the nobility and towns under Charles VII (1422–61) and Louis XI (1461–83): foreign, fiscal, and ecclesiastical policies; social and cultural developments

    c. The Low Countries: continued growth of towns, industry, and commerce, with attendant class conflicts and interference by the French monarchy; unification under the House of Burgundy; Burgundian administration

7. England, Wales, Scotland, and Ireland (*c.* 1307–*c.* 1500)

    a. Royal decline under the later Plantagenets and the struggle for the crown between the Lancastrians and Yorkists

      i. Royal decline under Edward II (1307–27) and its restoration under Edward III (1327–77): the Hundred Years' War, domestic achievements, the crises of Edward III's later reign

      ii. Richard II (1377–99): the Peasants' Revolt (1381), the influence of John Wycliffe, later political struggles and Richard's deposition

      iii. Henry IV (1399–1413), Henry V (1413–22), and Henry VI (1422–61 and 1470–71): rebellions under Henry IV and his relations with Parliament, domestic rivalries and the loss of France under Henry VI, Cade's rebellion and the Wars of the Roses

      iv. The reigns of Edward IV (1461–70 and 1471–83) and Richard III (1483–85): England in the late Middle Ages

    b. Scotland: the wars of independence, relations with the English crown, Bruces and Stewarts, Scotland in the 15th century

    c. Establishment of English suzerainty over Wales, fluctuating English influence in Ireland and the rise to power of the earls of Kildare

8. Spain and Portugal (*c.* 1300–*c.* 1500)

    a. Castile and Leon: continued pressure on the Muslims under Alfonso XI (1312–50), increasing power of the Cortes, development of the woolen industry, literary achievements

    b. The Aragon Confederation (Aragon, Catalonia, and Valencia): acquisition of Sicily (1282) and growth of Aragon as a Mediterranean power; the Cortes, law, and administration; acquisition of the Kingdom of Naples (1442) under Alfonso V (1416–58)

    c. Creation of a united Spain and expansion of Spanish dominance in the early Age of Discovery

      i. The union of Aragon and Castile–Leon under Ferdinand and Isabella: strengthening of their positions vis-à-vis the nobility, the Inquisition and the treatment of Jews, conquest of Granada (1492) and acquisition of Naples (1503)

> ii. Spanish explorations and territorial acquisitions: colonial policy in the New World, the Atlantic trade

> d. Portugal: development of the monarchy under the House of Avis (1383–1580); alliance with England; consolidation of the monarchy and establishment of its overseas empire under John I (1385–1433), Prince Henry the Navigator, and Manuel I (1495–1521)

9. The Scandinavian kingdoms (c. 1300–c. 1500)

> a. Developments in the 14th century leading to the formation of the Kalmar Union (1397–1523), Scandinavia under the union

> b. Developments in Denmark, Norway, and Sweden during the union: decline of Norway and rise of Sweden

10. Hungary, Poland–Lithuania, and the Teutonic Order

> a. Hungary under foreign kings: foreign affairs, economy, and society under the Angevins and Sigismund; the reign of Matthias Corvinus (1458–90)

> b. Poland–Lithuania, the Teutonic Order, and the Baltic peoples

>> i. The Mongol invasions (1241–42) and reestablishment of the Kingdom of Poland (1253–1382): Władysław I and the struggle with the Teutonic Order; Casimir III and Louis I of Hungary; social classes, the church, and policies toward the Jews

>> ii. The Jagiellon dynasty (1382–1492): the union of Poland and Lithuania (1385–86), extension of the empire, growth in power of the nobility and growth of parliamentarianism

---

Suggested reading in the *Encyclopædia Britannica:*

MACROPAEDIA: Major articles dealing with western Christendom in the High and later Middle Ages (c. 1050–c. 1500)

Amsterdam	Germany	Lisbon	Portugal
Antwerp	Habsburg, The	London	Prague
Austria	House of	Low	Rome
Crusades, The	Holy Roman	Countries, The	Spain
Czechoslovakia	Empire, The	Madrid	Sweden
Denmark	History of the	Milan	Switzerland
Europe	Hungary	Naples	United Kingdom
Finland	Iceland	Norway	Venice
Florence	Ireland	Paris	Vienna
France	Italy	Poland	

MICROPAEDIA: Selected entries of reference information

General subjects

European politics and polity:	Templar	Dupplin Moor,	*national affairs—east central Europe:*
Agincourt,	Teutonic Order	Battle of	Cuman
Battle of	Western Schism	Hastings, Battle of	Golden Bull of
Avignon papacy	Worms,	Lollard	1222
Bouvines, Battle of	Concordat of	Magna Carta	Koszyce, Pact of
Castillon, Battle of	*national affairs—*	Norman Conquest	Mazovia
Crécy, Battle of	*Britain and Angevin*	Northampton,	Moravia
crusade	*Empire:*	Assize of	*national affairs—*
Holy Roman	Angevin Empire	Ordainer	*France:*
Empire	Bannockburn,	Oxford,	Albigenses
Hundred	Battle of	Provisions of	Aquitaine
Years' War	Barnet, Battle of	Paston Letters	Brittany
Inquisition	Barons' War	Peasants Revolt	Burgundy
Investiture	Bosworth Field,	Roses, War of the	Hundred
Controversy	Battle of	tanistry	Years' War
Norman	Clarendon,	Tewkesbury,	Jacquerie
Orléans, Siege of	Assize of	Battle of	Normandy
Poitiers,	Clarendon,	Towton, Battle of	Praguerie
Battle of	Constitutions of	Westminster,	Provence
	Domesday Book	Statutes of (1275–90)	

Stephen
Tudor, House of
Tyler, Wat
Wallace, Sir
  William
Warwick, Richard
  Beauchamp, 1st
  earl of
Warwick, Richard
  Neville, earl of
William I
  (England)
William II
  (England)
William I
  (Scotland)
William the
  Aetheling
Wycliffe, John
York, House of
York, Richard
  Plantagenet, 3rd
  duke of
east central Europe:
Andrew II
  (Hungary)
Árpád dynasty
Béla III (Hungary)
Béla IV (Hungary)
Bolesław II
  (Poland)
Bolesław III
  (Poland)
Břetislav I
  (Bohemia)
Casimir I (Poland)
Casimir II (Poland)
Casimir III
  (Poland)
Casimir IV
  (Poland)
Charles I
  (Hungary)
George (Bohemia)
Hunyadi, János
Jadwiga
Jagiełłon dynasty
John (Bohemia)
John I Albert
  (Poland)
Ladislas I
  (Hungary)
Ladislas IV
  (Hungary)
Ladislas V
  (Hungary)
Louis I (Hungary)
Matthias I
  (Hungary)
Olesnicki,
  Zbigniew
Otakar I
  (Bohemia)

Otakar II
  (Bohemia)
Piast dynasty
Stanislaus of
  Kraków, Saint
Stephen V
  (Hungary)
Vladislas II
  (Bohemia)
Wenceslas I
  (Bohemia)
Władysław I
  (Poland)
Władysław II
  Jagiełło (Poland)
Władysław III
  Warnenczyk
  (Poland)
France:
Berry, Jean de
  France, duc de
Blanche of Castille
Caboche, Simon
Capetian dynasty
Charles (Burgundy)
Charles IV
  (France)
Charles V (France)
Charles VI
  (France)
Charles VII
  (France)
Charles VIII
  (France)
Coeur, Jacques
Gondi family
Guesclin,
  Bernard du
Henry I (France)
Joan of Arc, Saint
John (IV)
  (Brittany)
John IV (or V)
  (Brittany)
John (Burgundy)
John II (France)
La Trémoille,
  Georges de
Louis VII (France)
Louis VIII
  (France)
Louis IX (France)
Louis X (France)
Louis XI (France)
Lusignan family
Marcel, Étienne
Montfort family
Philip II
  (Burgundy)
Philip III
  (Burgundy)
Philip I (France)
Philip II (France)

Philip III (France)
Philip IV (France)
Philip V (France)
Philip VI (France)
Rais, Gilles de
René I (Anjou)
Richemont,
  Arthur,
  constable de
Suger
Valois dynasty
Germany and the
Low Countries:
Adalbert
Adolf (German
  king)
Albert I
  (Brandenburg)
Albert III Achilles
  (Brandenburg)
Albert I (German
  king)
Albert II (German
  king)
Artevelde,
  Jacob van
Charles IV
  (emperor)
Conrad III
  (German king)
Conrad IV
  (German king)
Frederick I
  (Brandenburg)
Frederick I
  (emperor)
Frederick II
  (emperor)
Guy (Flanders)
Habsburg,
  House of
Henry II
  Jasomirgott
  (Austria)
Henry X
  (Bavaria)
Henry III
  (emperor)
Henry IV
  (emperor)
Henry V (emperor)
Henry VI
  (emperor)
Henry VII
  (emperor)
Henry (VII)
  (German king)
Henry III
  (Saxony)
Henry Raspe
Hermann von
  Salza

Hohenstaufen
  dynasty
Jacoba
Lothair II (or III)
  (emperor)
Louis II
  (Flanders)
Louis IV
  (emperor)
Otto IV
  (emperor)
Philip (emperor)
Richard (German
  king)
Rudolf I
  (German king)
Rupert (German
  king)
Sigismund
  (emperor)
Welf dynasty
Wenceslas
  (German king)
Wettin dynasty
Wittelsbach,
  House of
Iberian peninsula:
Afonso I
  (Portugal)
Afonso II
  (Portugal)
Afonso V
  (Portugal)
Alfonso I
  (Aragon)
Alfonso II
  (Aragon)
Alfonso III
  (Aragon)
Alfonso IV
  (Aragon)
Alfonso V
  (Aragon)
Alfonso VI
  (Castile/Leon)
Alfonso VII
  (Castile/Leon)
Alfonso IX
  (Castile/Leon)
Alfonso X
  (Castile/Leon)
Alfonso XI
  (Castile/Leon)
Charles II
  (Navarre)
Cid, the
Edward (Portugal)
Ferdinand II
  (Aragon)
Ferdinand I
  (Castile/Leon)
Ferdinand II
  (Castile/Leon)

Ferdinand III
(Castile/Leon)
Ferdinand IV
(Castile/Leon)
García V (Navarre)
Henry II (Castile/
Leon)
Henry III (Castile/
Leon)
Henry IV (Castile/
Leon)
Isabella I
James I (Aragon)
James II (Aragon)
John I (Aragon)
John II (Aragon)
John II (Castile/
Leon)
John I (Portugal)
John II (Portugal)
Muḥammad XI
(Granada)
Peter II (Aragon)
Peter III (Aragon)
Peter IV (Aragon)
Peter I (Castile/
Leon)
Ramón
Berenguer I
Ramón
Berenguer II
Ramón
Berenguer III
Ramón
Berenguer IV
Sancho III Garcés
(Navarre)
Urraca
Italy and the papacy:
Adorno family
Alberti family
Alexander III
(pope)
Amadeus VI
(Savoy)
Amadeus VII
(Savoy)
Amadeus VIII
(Savoy)
Bardi family
Bentivoglio family
Boccanegra family
Bonacolsi family

Boniface VIII
(pope)
Borgia family
Carrara family
Castracani,
Castruccio
Charles I (Naples)
Charles II (Naples)
Charles III
(Naples)
Charles I (Sicily)
Cola di Rienzo
Colonna family
Contarini family
Corsini family
Dandolo, Enrico
Dandolo,
Vincenzo
Dandolo family
della Scala family
Drogo de
Hauteville
Este, House of
Ezzelino III da
Romano
Fieschi family
Gherardesca family
Gonzaga dynasty
Gregory VII (pope)
Gregory IX (pope)
Gregory X (pope)
Grimaldi family
Innocent III (pope)
Joan I (Naples)
Joan II (Naples)
Ladislas (Naples)
Lauria,
Ruggiero di
Leo IX (pope)
Louis (Naples)
Malaspina family
Malatesta family
Martin I (Sicily)
Medici,
Cosimo de'
Medici,
Lorenzo de'
Medici, Piero di
Cosimo de'
Medici, Piero di
Lorenzo de'
Medici family
Mocenigo family
Montefeltro family

Morosini family
Ordelaffi family
Orsini family
Paschal II (pope)
Pepoli family
Peruzzi family
Piccinino, Niccolò
Piccolomini family
Polenta family
Polo, Marco
Robert (Apulia)
Robert (Naples)
Roger (Apulia)
Roger I (Sicily)
Roger II (Sicily)
Sambuccio
d'Alando
Savonarola,
Girolamo
Sforza, Francesco
Sforza, Ludovico
Sforza family
Spinola family
Uguccione della
Fagginola
Urban II (pope)
Visconti family
Visconti, Gian
Galeazzo
Visconti, Matteo I
William I (Sicily)
William II (Sicily)
William de
Hauteville
*Scandinavia and the
Baltic States:*
Absalon
Algirdas
Canute IV
(Denmark)
Christian I
(Denmark)
Christopher I
(Denmark)
Christopher III
(Denmark)
Erik V
(Denmark)
Erik VI
(Denmark)
Erik VII
(Denmark)
Erik XIII
(Sweden)

Eskil
Gediminas
Haakon I
Haakon IV
Haakon V
Haakon VI
Inge I
John (Denmark)
Kestutis
Magnus I
(Norway)
Magnus III
(Norway)
Magnus IV
(Norway)
Magnus V
(Norway)
Magnus VI
(Norway)
Magnus I
(Sweden)
Magnus II
(Sweden)
Margaret I
(Denmark)
Mindaugas
Olaf II (Norway)
Olaf III (Norway)
Olaf (Sweden)
Sigurd I
Sverrir Sigurdsson
Sweyn II
(Denmark)
Valdemar II
(Denmark)
Valdemar IV
(Denmark)
Valdemar
(Sweden)
Vytautas
the Great
Władysław II
Jagiełło
Switzerland:
Brun, Rudolf
Bubenberg,
Adrian von
Diesbach,
Niklaus von
Nicholas of Flüe,
Saint
Stüssi, Rudolf
Waldman, Hans

INDEX: See entries under all of the terms above

Section 924. **The Crusading Movement, the Islāmic States of Southwest Asia, North Africa, and Europe, and the States of Eastern Christendom from *c.* 1050 to *c.* 1480**

A. The expansion of western Europe in the crusading movement and the Muslim response, the states of Eastern Christendom and the crusader states from *c.* 1050 to *c.* 1480

1. The crusading era and the states of Eastern Christendom (*c.* 1050–*c.* 1480)

  a. The First Crusade (1096–99) and the establishment of the Latin states

    i. Background of the First Crusade: religious renewal in Europe, disruption of the pilgrimage routes by the Muslims, role of papal leadership at the Council of Clermont (1095), preparations for the Crusade and its participants

    ii. The sieges of Antioch (1097–98) and Jerusalem (1099): establishment of the crusader states

  b. The Second (1147–48) and Third (1188–92) crusades: the crusader states to 1187, the institutions of the First Kingdom, the magnates of the Third Crusade

  c. The Byzantine Empire from 1081 to 1204, policies aimed at revival implemented by Comnenus dynasty

    i. Alexius I Comnenus and the First Crusade: pressures from the Seljuqs and Pechenegs

    ii. The later Comneni and fluctuating relations with the Venetians, Normans, and crusaders

    iii. The Fourth Crusade (1202–04) and the establishment of the Latin empire

  d. The later crusades: decline of the crusading movement and of the Latin enclaves, results of the crusades

    i. The Latin East after the Third Crusade: the Fifth (1218–21) and Sixth (1227–29) crusades

    ii. The crusades of Louis IX of France (1248–50, 1270), final loss of the crusader states, Kingdom of Cyprus

  e. Russia (1054–1300): the lands of Rus and the rise of new centres (*e.g.,* Novgorod, Vladimir, Galicia), the Mongol invasion (1223) and Tatar rule

  f. The Second Bulgarian Empire under the Asenid dynasty from *c.* 1185, decline after 1241

2. The Slavic states of Eastern Christendom from *c.* 1300 to *c.* 1500

  a. Russia: the rise of the Muscovite state under the suzerainty of the Golden Horde and its later successful revolt (1380), expansion and establishment of Moscow as the leading Russian power under Tsar Ivan III (1462–1505), foreign policy

  b. The Balkans: growing strength of Serbia vis-à-vis the Byzantine and Bulgarian empires; subjugation of Albania, Macedonia, and Bulgaria under Stefan Dušan in the 14th century; Romania; subjection to the Ottoman Turks by 1453

3. Restoration of the Byzantine Empire under the Palaeologus dynasty (1261), efforts to restore Byzantine power in the Balkans, foreign relations, cultural life

  a. Michael VIII (1261–82) and attempts to revive the empire, threats from the West, relations with the papacy

  b. The successors of Michael VIII: cultural revival, civil wars

  c. Turkish expansion, limited recovery by the Byzantine Empire before the final Turkish assault, the fall of Constantinople (1453)

B. The Islāmic states of Southwest Asia, North Africa, and Europe (*c.* 1050–*c.* 1480): Turkish and Kurdish dynasties, the Mongol invasions, and the rise of the Ottoman Empire

1. Southwest Asia before the Mongol invasions

  a. The Great Seljuq Empire in Syria, Iraq, and Iran (*c.* 1050–*c.* 1190)

    i. Origins and conversion of the Seljuqs to Islām and their establishment in Khorāsān (*c.* 1000) under Maḥmūd of Ghazna, the foundation of the Seljuq state under Toghrïl Beg (1038–63), his conquest of Iran and Iraq and establishment of a protectorate over the ʿAbbāsid caliphate

    ii. Extension of Seljuq hegemony into Syria and Palestine and victory over the Byzantines, partition and partial breakup of the empire after 1092, Seljuq restoration of Sunnī supremacy and patronage of the Iranian cultural revival

  b. Great Seljuq successor states (*c.* 1100–*c.* 1250): the Zangīd *atabeg*s in Syria and northern Iraq, the Ismāʿīlī Assassins in Iran and Syria (*c.* 1090–*c.* 1250), the Khwārazm shahs of Iran and Central Asia (1097–1234), other dynasties

  c. The foundation of the independent sultanate of Rum from territory conquered from Byzantium in Anatolia (from 1071), commercial prosperity and territorial expansion in the 13th century, the Turkish Dānishmendid state in northern Anatolia (*c.* 1071–1177) and its absorption by the Seljuqs

2. The Mongolian invasions of eastern Europe and Southwest Asia in the 13th century

3. Southwest Asia and eastern Europe after the Mongolian invasions

  a. Mongol successor states (*c.* 1250–*c.* 1480)

    i. The Mongolian Il Khans in Iraq and Iran (*c.* 1250–1353): trade, administration, and eventual conversion to Islām; the Timurids and other Il Khan successor states

    ii. The khanate of the Golden Horde in southern Russia (from 1240): adoption of Islām, gradual absorption of the Mongols into the Turkish *ulus* to form the Tatar people, the zenith of the empire in the early 14th century, Timur's invasion (1395) and its later partition

  b. Turkish Anatolia and the rise of the Ottoman Empire to 1481

    i. Origins and expansion of the Ottoman state (*c.* 1300–1402): its expansion in Anatolia and conquest of Serbia and Bulgaria in the 14th century, defeat by Timur (1402), restoration of the empire and beginning of the Ottoman challenge to the European states by the invasion of Hungary (1434), conquest of Constantinople (1453) and conquest of Anatolia

    ii. Development of Ottoman administrative and military institutions

4. North Africa and Muslim Spain (*c.* 1050–*c.* 1490)

  a. The decline of the Fāṭimids (*c.* 1050–1171) in the face of Seljuq and crusader invasions

  b. The Ayyūbids and Mamlūks in Egypt and Syria (1171–*c.* 1500)

    i. Establishment of the Ayyūbid dynasty in Egypt and expansion of its control over Muslim Syria under Saladin (1171–93): conflict with the crusader states, pacific policies of his successors

    ii. Displacement of the Ayyūbids by the Turkish Mamlūks in 1250, the Bahri Mamlūks' resistance to the Mongols and extension of European power in Syria under Quṭuz and Baybars I (1260–77), their displacement by the Burjī Mamlūks in 1382, Mamlūk administration and military institutions, the continued maintenance of Sunnī orthodoxy

  c. The Berber Almoravid and Almohad empires in northwest Africa and Spain (1056–1269)

    i. Almoravid origins as a religious reform federation in the western Sudan, conquest of Morocco and western Algeria under Abū Bakr and Yūsuf ibn Tāshufīn (1062–92), the latter's intervention in Spain against the expanding Christian states, Almoravid conquest of Muslim Spain (1090–91), weakness and decline in the face of the renewal of the Reconquista and the Almohad revolt in North Africa (*c.* 1123)

    ii. The Almohad religious reform movement under the Berber Muḥammad ibn Tūmart (d. 1130) and the extension of Almohad control over Muslim Spain (capital at Seville) and the Maghrib (1145–72), initial containment of the Reconquista and later disintegration of the empire in Spain after 1212, subsequent eclipse in the Maghrib, Almohad patronage of philosophy and the arts

  d. The east medieval dynasties of North Africa (13th–15th century): political and cultural developments

    i. The Ḥafṣids in Tunisia, the ʿAbd al-Wādid kingdom of Tilimsān, the Marīnids in eastern Morocco and their problems with the Arabs, political life, the Naṣrid kingdom of Granada

    ii. Religious, intellectual, and artistic life: Ṣūfism, literary and artistic influences from Muslim Spain

Suggested reading in the *Encyclopædia Britannica:*

MACROPAEDIA: Major articles dealing with the crusading movement, the Islāmic states of Southwest Asia, North Africa, and Europe, and the states of Eastern Christendom from *c.* 1050 to *c.* 1480

Albania	Crusades, The	Jerusalem	Syria
Balkans	Egypt	North Africa	Turkey and
Bulgaria	Islāmic	Romania	Ancient Anatolia
Byzantine Empire, The History of the	World, The	Spain	

MICROPAEDIA: Selected entries of reference information

General subjects

Balkans:
Bogomil
Croatia
Epirus,
 Despotate of
Kosovo, Battle of
 (1389)
Kosovo, Battle of
 (1448)
Maritsa River,
 Battle of the
Moldavia
Morea,
 Despotate of
Serbia
Thrace
Vlach
Walachia
Zara, Siege of
*Iberia and
 northwestern Africa:*
Almohads
Almoravids

Barghawāṭah
Granada
Moor
Morisco
Mozarab
Navas de Tolosa,
 Battle of Las
Reconquista
Valencia
*Middle East—
Crusades:*
Antioch,
 Principality of
Arsūf, Battle of
Children's
 Crusade
crusade
Ḥaṭṭin, Battle of
Holy Lance
Jérusalem,
 Assises de
Jerusalem,
 Kingdom of

Nicopolis, Battle of
Saracen
Middle East—other:
Ak Koyunlu
Anatolia
Ankara, Battle of
Assassin
'ayyār
Kara Koyunlu
Little Armenia
Mamlūk
Myriocephalon,
 Battle of
Nicaea, empire of
Seljuq
Russia:
Crimea, Khanate
 of the
Golden Horde
Kipchak
Kulikovo, Battle of
Moscow, Grand
 Principality of

Neva, Battle of the
Novgorod,
 Treaty of
Pechenegs
Peipus, Battle of
 Lake
Rus
Suzdal,
 Principality of
Tver,
 Principality of
Ugra, Battle of the
veche
Vladimir
Volhynia
other:
Bari, Siege of
bashi-bazouk
Jalāyirid
pronoia system

Biographies

*Christians—Balkans
 and Russia:*
Alexander Nevsky,
 Saint
Ivan III
Ivan Asen I
Ivan Asen II
Kotromanić
 dynasty
Rurik dynasty
Stefan Dušan
Vasily I
*Christians—
 Byzantine Empire:*
Alexius I
 Comnenus
Isaac II Angelus

John III Ducas
 Vatatzes
Manuel I
 Comnenus
Manuel II
 Palaeologus
Metochites,
 Theodore
Michael VIII
 Palaeologus
*Christians—Crusader
 states:*
Bohemond I
John
 (Constantinople)
Lusignan family
Mézières,
 Philippe de

Raymond
 (Antioch)
Reginald of
 Châtillon
*Muslims—Iberia and
 northwestern Africa:*
'Abd al-Mu'min
Aftasid dynasty
Ḥafṣid dynasty
Hammūdid
 dynasty
Hūdid dynasty
Zīrid dynasty
*Muslims—Middle
 East:*
Alp-Arslan
Artuqid dynasty

Baybars I
Dānishmend
 dynasty
Eldegüzid dynasty
Ghāzān, Maḥmūd
Khwārezm-Shāh
 dynasty
Mehmed II
Murad I
Murad II
Niẓām al-Mulk
Saladin
Salghurid dynasty
Sanjar
Toghrïl Beg
Zangid dynasty

INDEX: See entries under all of the terms above

Division III.   **Peoples and Traditional Civilizations of East, Central, South, and Southeast Asia**
[For Part Nine headnote see page 343.]

For each nation or group of peoples covered in this division, the outline treats first of the geography and ethnography and then moves into the chronology of the respective civilization: Sections 931 and 932 outline the Chinese dynasties from the Ch'in through the late Ch'ing (mid-19th century).

Section 933 deals with the peoples of inner Asia and the steppe and covers the early histories of Manchuria, Turkistan, and Afghanistan; of the Mongol Empire and its successor states; and of Tibet and Nepal.

Section 934 outlines the character and achievements of the Japanese and Korean civilizations from their beginnings until the Meiji Restoration of 1868 and the Japanese annexation of Korea in 1910.

Sections 935 and 936 treat of the civilizations of the Indian subcontinent, of the early political units of India and Ceylon, the period of Muslim hegemony, the Mughal and Marāthā empires, and, for Ceylon, the arrival of the Portuguese in 1505.

Section 937 deals with the peoples and civilizations of Southeast Asia, including the histories of Burma, Siam, Cambodia, Vietnam, and Malaya, as well as the islands of the Indonesian Archipelago, until *c.* 1600.

Section 931.   **China to the Beginning of the Late T'ang (AD 755)**

A. The character and achievements of Chinese civilization, the geography and ethnography of China, archaeological and documentary historical sources, historiographic problems

B. The emergence of traditional Chinese civilization

1. The prehistoric period

  a. The Paleolithic and Mesolithic stages in North China: industries in the Ordos region, microlithic tools

  b. The Neolithic stage: pebble tools and domesticated animals, "Mongolian Neolithic"

  c. The Yang-shao Painted Pottery culture

      i. Stratigraphy: villages of Hsi-yin-ts'un and Yang-shao-ts'un, pottery styles

      ii. Painted pottery styles, sites in Kansu, ornamental designs, stone implements

  d. The Lung-shan Black Pottery complex and western limits of Black Pottery culture, the Late Neolithic Period in South China and the Early Bronze Age in North China, bronze objects in the Ordos region

2. The beginnings of the Chinese civilization: the early dynasties

  a. Origins of the Chinese people and culture: legends and cultural centres, the Hsia dynasty (*c.* 2205–*c.* 1766 BC)

  b. The Shang, or Yin, period (*c.* 1766–*c.* 1122 BC): Chengchow site as early capital and cultural centre at Anyang, social system, early calendar, warfare, industry and commerce, script

  c. The Western (early) Chou (1122–771 BC): the conquest of Shang under Wen Wang and Wu Wang (1111 BC), Chou feudal system

  d. The Eastern (later) Chou (771–481 BC), also called the Chun Ch'iu period; internal chaos; period of the Warring States (481–221 BC)

      i. Breakdown of the Chou feudal system: capital at Loyang, rivalry among Chou states, various Chou successor states in the Warring States period (481–221 BC)

      ii. Social, political, and cultural changes: decline of feudalism, urbanization and assimilation, rise of monarchy under Wen Kung, economic development

  e. The Classical period of Chinese literature and philosophy: Chinese religion and cosmology, Confucianism and Taoism, the "hundred schools" (the Naturalists, the Dialecticians, Mo-tzu, Meng-tzu [Mencius], Chuang-tzu, the Legalists)

C. The unification of China under the Ch'in and Han dynasties (221 BC–AD 220)

1. Establishment of the Ch'in empire (221–206 BC): development of central government, fall of the dynasty after death of Shih Huang Ti

   a. Early successes of the Ch'in under Mu Kung, reforms of Hsiao Kung and Shang Yang

   b. Ch'in strategy, unification of China by the Ch'in (221 BC), abolition of feudal system, highway building and construction of the Great Wall in the reign of Shih Huang Ti, the minister Li Ssu, political repression

2. The Han dynasty

   a. Western (Former or Earlier) Han (206 BC–AD 8) and the Wang Mang usurpation (AD 9–23)

      i. Establishment of the dynasty by Liu Pang (Han Kao Tsu): the capital at Ch'ang-an, reign of Liu Heng (Han Wen Ti) from 179 to 157 BC, consolidation of Imperial power

      ii. Expansion under Han Wu Ti (140–87 BC) into southern China and Central Asia, dynastic crisis (91–87 BC), ascendancy of the Wang family and Wang Mang's usurpation of throne (AD 9–23)

   b. The Eastern (Later) Han: restoration of the dynasty by Liu Hsiu (Han Kuang Wu Ti) (AD 25–57), capital at Loyang, domestic and foreign policy, decline of government after AD 125

   c. Political developments, foreign relations, and cultural attainments in the Han period

      i. The Han political system: the structure and the practice of government

      ii. Relations with other peoples: the Hsiung-nu of Central Asia, Pan Ch'ao's campaigns in Central Asia

      iii. Han cultural life: educational developments, invention of paper, prose writing, developments in music and the visual arts, introduction of Buddhism

D. The breakdown and revival of the empire

1. The Six Dynasties period (AD 220–589)

   a. The division of the empire into the Three Kingdoms of Wei (North China), Shu Han (Szechwan), and Wu (South China): era of barbarian invasions and rule, the period of the Sixteen Kingdoms (304–589)

   b. Intellectual and religious trends: decline in Confucianism, Taoist resurgence, spread of Buddhism

2. The reunification of China under the Sui and early T'ang dynasties

   a. The Sui (581–618): Sui founder Yang Chien (Sui Wen Ti), institutional reforms

   b. The reign of Yang Ti (605–618): integration of the South, foreign affairs, military reverses and collapse of the dynasty

   c. The early T'ang (618–624) and the period of T'ang power (626–755)

      i. Li Yüan's (618–626) establishment of the dynasty: resistance to T'ang conquest, administration of the state, fiscal and legal system

      ii. The era of good government in the reign of T'ai Tsung (626–649): educational and administrative reforms, conquest of eastern Turks, Kao Tsung (649–683) and influence of Empress Wu, conquest of Oxus Valley and later military reverses

      iii. Prosperity and progress in the reign of Hsüan Tsung (712–756): internal reforms, military reorganization

---

Suggested reading in the *Encyclopædia Britannica*:

MACROPAEDIA: Major articles dealing with China to the beginning of the late T'ang (AD 755)

   Asia
   China
   Nanking

MICROPAEDIA: Selected entries of reference information

General subjects

ancient cultures and historic sites:	Ch'in tomb	Hsiung-nu	Sha-ch'ing
Ch'i-chia culture	Great Wall of China	Lung-shan culture	*dynastic capitals:*
		Pan-p'o-ts'un	An-yang

Section 932.   **China from the Late T'ang (AD 755) to the Late Ch'ing (c. 1839)**

A. The late T'ang dynasty, the Ten Kingdoms, the Five Dynasties, and the Sung dynasty

1. The late T'ang and the Northern Sung

   a. The late T'ang (755–907): the rebellion of An Lu-shan (755–757) and its effects, provincial separatism, attempts to restore central authority, growth in power of provincial warlords

   b. T'ang cultural life: the growing influences of Buddhism, developments in music and the visual arts

   c. Social and economic developments: the decline of the aristocracy and social mobility, agricultural advances and expansion of trade

   d. The period of the Five Dynasties and the Ten Kingdoms (907–960)

      i. The short-lived Five Dynasties in North China: the Liang dynasty, advance of talented bureaucrats in government posts

      ii. The more permanent Ten Kingdoms: the Tanguts; the Khitan, or Liao, empire; the kingdoms of Wu, the Southern T'ang, the Southern P'ing, the Ch'u, the Earlier and Later Shu, the Min, the Southern Han, and the Wu-yüeh

   e. The Northern Sung (960–1126): foundation of the dynasty and its expansion under T'ai Tsu and T'ai Tsung and their successors

      i. Unification and centralization of the empire: development of the Imperial civil service in Chao K'uang-yin's (T'ai Tsu's) reign (960–976), further consolidation under Tseng Tsung (998–1022)

      ii. Reforms in the reign of Shen Tsung (1068–85): leadership of Wang An-Shih, criticism of the reforms leading to the decline and fall of the dynasty

2. The Southern Sung (1126–1279): survival and consolidation, defeat by the Juchens and removal of the Sung to South China under Kao Tsung

3. Sung cultural and economic developments; *e.g.,* resurgence of Neo-Confucianism, visual arts and music, scholarship, historiography, invention of printing, manufacturing advances

B. Mongol–Chinese rule under the Yüan dynasty (1279–1368)

1. The Mongol conquest of China: imposition of Mongol government and policies

   a. Genghis Khan's conquest of the Chin (1211–34), invasion of the Sung and the establishment of the Yüan dynasty under Kublai Khan

   b. Mongol government and administration: transfer of the capital to Ta-tu (Peking), nonassimilation with the Chinese, expansion of trade

   2. Religious and intellectual life, relations with the West, decline of Mongol rule

      a. Religious toleration and patronage of Buddhism, the status of the Confucian scholar, developments in the arts

      b. Yüan China and the West: commercial and cultural contacts, arrival of Catholic missionaries

C. The Ming and Ch'ing dynasties to *c.* 1839: the tribute system, relative stability, ethnocentrism, and emphasis on cultural unity

   1. The Ming dynasty (1368–1644)

      a. Foundation of the Ming and its political and social structure

         i. Peasant uprisings and the foundation of the dynasty (1368) by Chu Yüàn-chang (Hung-wu): pattern of dynastic succession, gradual degeneration of Ming government

         ii. Government and administration: local and central government, later innovations to coordinate central government and regional administration

      b. Developments in foreign relations and economic policy

      c. Cultural life in the Ming period: philosophy and religion, developments in the visual arts, music, literature, and scholarship

   2. The Ch'ing (Manchu) dynasty to *c.* 1839

      a. The Manchu rise to power (1644): preservation of the Ming administration under joint Manchu–Chinese supervision

         i. Manchu entrance in Peking and territorial conquest ending with the seizure of Taiwan (1683): early Ch'ing institutions

         ii. Early foreign relations in Asia, contacts with the West

      b. Mid-Ch'ing social and economic developments: the role of religious associations, expansion of industry, social unrest, intellectual and cultural advances

         i. Advances in agriculture through increased rice cultivation and introduction of new crops, expansion of crafts and industries, commerce and finance

         ii. Population growth and immigration, religious associations, the White Lotus Rebellion (1796–1804)

         iii. Cultural developments; *e.g.,* government interference in scholarship; introduction of Western sciences; advances in music, literature, and the visual arts

      c. Dynastic degeneration and widespread governmental corruption beginning in the 1760s; economic decline, famine, and social unrest in the early 1800s

---

Suggested reading in the *Encyclopædia Britannica*:

MACROPAEDIA: Major articles and a biography dealing with China from the late T'ang (AD 755) to the late Ch'ing (*c.* 1839)

Asia	Genghis Khan
Canton	Nanking
China	Peking
Chungking	

MICROPAEDIA: Selected entries of reference information

General subjects

capital cities:	Yang-chou	Sung dynasty	kowtow
Canton	*dynasties, kingdoms,*	T'ang dynasty	pao-chia
Ch'ang-sha	*and states:*	Ten Kingdoms	Tung-lin
Ch'eng-tu	Chin dynasty	Yüan dynasty	*other:*
Chungking	(Juchen)	*government and*	Cathay
Hang-chou	Ch'ing dynasty	*society:*	Hakka
Lo-yang	Five Dynasties	Banner System	Nerchinsk,
Nanking	Hsi Hsia	Canton System	Treaty of
Peking	Liao dynasty	Chinese civil	White Lotus
Sian	Ming dynasty	service	Rebellion

Biographies

emperors:

Cheng-te	T'ai Tsu (Sung)	Cheng	Wu San-kuei
Chia-ch'ing	T'ai Tsung (Sung)	Ch'eng-kung	Yüeh Fei
Ch'ien-lung	Yung-cheng	Cheng Ho	*Westerners:*
(Ch'ing)	(Ch'ing)	Dorgon	Polo, Marco
Hung-wu	Yung-lo (Ming)	Hsü Kuang-ch'i	Ricci, Matteo
K'ang-hsi (Ch'ing)	*statesmen and*	Huang Tsung-hsi	
Kublai Khan	*military leaders:*	Nurhachi	
Shen Tsung (Sung)	An Lu-shan	Ou-yang Hsiu	
		Wang An-shih	

INDEX: See entries under all of the terms above

Section 933.   **Inner (Central and Northeast) Asia to *c.* 1750**

A. The peoples of the steppes, their cultures, and their interactions with neighbouring civilizations; the geography and ethnography of Inner Asia; archaeological and documentary historical sources; historiographic problems

B. The peoples and states of Inner Asia to *c.* AD 1200

   1. The Hsiung-nu tribal confederation dominating Mongolia, southern Siberia, and eastern Turkistan from *c.* 400 BC to *c.* AD 50; pressure on it and its destruction by Han China

   2. The Manchurian tribes: attempts at unification, fluctuating relations with the Chinese until the advent of the Mongols

      a. The Tung-hu tribes and Chinese presence in Manchuria to the 3rd century BC, ascendancy of the Hsien-pei and establishment of the Yin kingdom by Mu-jung Hui (AD 352), the Parhae (P'o-hai) kingdom (AD 712)

      b. The Khitan and Juchen empires: penetration into China, Korea, and Mongolia; Juchen conquest of Chinese Sung territory; capital at Yen-ching (Peking); conquest by Mongols in 1234

   3. Development of West and East Turkistan to *c.* 1750

      a. West Turkistan: the early empires, Muslim rule, the Chagatai khans and Timurids, the Uzbek and Kazakh khanates

      b. East Turkistan (Kashgaria): Kirgiz, Uighur tribes, Qarakhanid rule in the 10th century, Mongol conquest and rule in the 13th century, conquest by Manchus (1758–59)

   4. The Mongolian and Tungusic states from the 10th to the 13th century: the Liao (Khitan) empire and the later Chin (Juchen) state in North China and Manchuria (947–1125), the Western Liao (Kara khitai) of Turkistan (1124–1211)

   5. The development of Afghanistan to *c.* 1700: rule by Achaemenians and Greeks to *c.* 1st century AD, various nomadic rulers, advent of Muslim control in the 7th century, Mongol conquest (1221), later rule by Timurids and Mughals

C. The Mongol Empire and its successor states

   1. The establishment of a united Mongol Empire in Central, eastern, and western Asia by Genghis Khan and his successors (1206–60)

      a. The rise of Genghis Khan and his military and political organization, tactics, and conquests

      b. The division of his empire among his sons: further expansion under Ögödei Khan, Mangu (Möngke) Khan's friendly relations with Western Christendom

   2. The Mongol successor states

      a. The completion of the conquest of China (1260–79) and the foundation of the Yüan dynasty by Kublai Khan

      b. The Chagatai khanate (*ulus*) of Turkistan in the 13th and 14th centuries

      c. Timur's (Tamerlane's) establishment of the Timurid dynasty (1370–1506): his capital at Samarkand; his conquests; Turkistan, Afghanistan, and Transoxania under his successors

      d. The Iranian Il Khans (1258–1335): the Golden Horde (later Kipchak empire) in southern Russia and its successor states (1240–1783)

e. Mongolia from the 13th to the 18th century: internecine strife, the revival of Buddhism, subjection to Yüan China and later autonomy and disunity until the ascendancy of the Manchus (Ch'ing China) in the 18th century

D. Tibet and Nepal to *c.* 1750

1. Tibet to *c.* 1750

a. The legendary origins of the Tibetan people, consolidation of Tibet under Gnam-ri srong-btsan (*c.* AD 570–619), later rulers to the 9th century, introduction of Buddhism, cultural developments

b. Tibetan disunity from the 9th to the 14th century: eclipse and resurgence of Buddhism, conquest by Mongols, developments in literature and the visual arts

c. Rule by the Dge-lugs-pa (Yellow Hat) monastic order, unification of Tibet (1642), Tibet under Chinese overlordship (1720)

2. Nepal to *c.* 1750: rule by Indian princely families, influence of Hinduism, relations with China and Tibet

E. The waning of nomad power from the 16th to the 18th century: the Manchu conquest of China and parts of Inner Asia, the Afghans as the last nomad power in Inner Asia, Russian expansion into Siberia and western Turkistan

---

Suggested reading in the *Encyclopædia Britannica*:

MACROPAEDIA: Major articles and a biography dealing with inner (Central and Northeast) Asia to *c.* 1750

Asia
China
Genghis Khan
Mongolia
Nepal

MICROPAEDIA: Selected entries of reference information

General subjects

dynasties and empires:	Uzbek dynasty	Oyrat	Samarkand
	Yüan dynasty	Yüeh-chih	Sogdiana
Chin dynasty	*peoples:*	*other:*	Turkistan
(Juchen)	Chahar	Karakorum	
Golden Horde	Hsiung-nu	Parhae	
Gtsang dynasty	Juan-juan	Qarluq	
Liao dynasty	Mongol	confederation	

Biographies

Abahai	Möngke	Phag-mo-gru	Timur
Batu	Moẓaffarid dynasty	family	Timurid dynasty
Il-Khanid dynasty	Nurhachi	Qarakhanid	Willem van
Kublai Khan	Ögödei	dynasty	Ruysbroeck

INDEX: See entries under all of the terms above

Section 934.   Japan to the Meiji Restoration (1868), and Korea to 1910

A. Introduction: the character and achievements of Japanese and Korean civilizations, the geography and ethnography of Japan and Korea, archaeological and documentary historical sources, historiographic problems

B. Early Japan

  1. Prehistoric cultures: nonceramic cultures in the Paleolithic Period, Jōmon (5th or 4th millennium to *c.* 250 BC) and Yayoi (*c.* 250 BC–AD 250) Neolithic pottery cultures, agriculture and the influx of Chinese culture

  2. The ancient period: unification of Japan under the Yamato court and subsequent governments (*c.* 250–710)

     a. The rise and fall of the Yamato court: relations with Korea, internal power struggles, introduction of Buddhism

     b. The governmental reforms of Shōtoku Taishi of the Soga family: theories of ideal government, the 12 court rank and the "Seventeen Article Constitution," relations with China, spread of Buddhism

     c. The Taika reforms (645), elimination of the Soga family, land reform, intervention in Korea, the *ritsu-ryō* system of social and land reform

  3. The Imperial state from 710 to 1185

     a. Government-directed religious and cultural developments in the Nara period (710–784): flowering of Buddhism; Chinese and Indian influences on literature, music, and the visual arts

     b. The Heian period (794–1185): changes in the *ritsu-ryō* system, ascendancy of the Fujiwara family and growing importance of the aristocracy

          i. Failure of Taika land reforms, power struggles among the nobility, growth of Fujiwara control over government, rise of Japanese literature and rejection of Chinese culture

         ii. Government by "cloistered" emperors: decline of Fujiwara power and rise of the samurai class, the Hōgen (1156) and Heiji (1159) uprisings, introduction of feudalism

C. Feudal Japan

  1. The Kamakura period (1192–1333)

     a. Minamoto Yoritomo and the founding of the *bakufu* (shogunate) at Kamakura (1192), the samurai *shugo* as feudal lords

     b. The rise of the Hōjō family from 1199: the Jōkyū Disturbance (1221), Hōjō Yasutoki's (1224–42) administrative reforms, the Jōei law code

     c. Resistance to the Mongol invasions of Japan (1274 and 1281), the Kamakura *bakufu* and feudal administration of farming regions

     d. Buddhist culture during the Kamakura period (*e.g.,* growth of Zen) and Neo-Confucianism; literature, philosophy, and the visual arts

     e. Decline of Kamakura society: economic problems leading to the rise of daimyo (domain lord) class and decline of *bakufu*

  2. The second feudal era: the Muromachi, or Ashikaga, period (1338–1573)

     a. The Kemmu Restoration (1333) and return to direct Imperial rule: the emperor Go-Daigo, the Kemmu legal code, Ashikaga Takauji and the dual dynasties (1336–92)

     b. Yoshimitsu's establishment of the Muromachi *bakufu* (1378) and unification of the dual dynasties (1392): taxation and strong military governors, feudal warfare after 1428

     c. Increased trade with China: piracy, the Ōnin War (1467–77), provincial self-government and growing influence of farmers

  3. The period of the "warring country" and the beginning of unification under the Oda regime

     a. Unification under *sengoku* (civil war) daimyo league leaders: development of commerce and guilds

     b. Arrival of the Portuguese (1543) and Spanish (1549): opening of trade, Catholic Jesuit missionary activity (1549)

   c. Cultural development in the 15th and 16th centuries: the influence of Zen Buddhism on philosophy, drama, literature, and the visual arts

   d. The Azuchi-Momoyama period (1574–1600): unification under Oda Nobunaga (1550–82) and Toyotomi Hideyoshi (1582–98)

4. The Tokugawa period (1603–1867): military–bureaucratic rule

   a. Establishment (1603) and consolidation of the Tokugawa (Edo) *bakufu* by Tokugawa Ieyasu: Japanese policy of national seclusion (1630s) from Christian missionaries and most European traders

   b. The Tokugawa postfeudal military–bureaucratic system: class structure and *bakuhan* system

   c. Industrial and commercial developments, advances in literature and the visual arts

   d. The weakening of the *bakuhan* system and its eventual collapse

      i. Economic crises: impoverishment of small farmers and commercial problems, political reform, opening of Japan to Western influences (1840s)

      ii. Cultural developments in the 18th and 19th centuries: Confucianism and the Shintō revival, Buddhism, literature and the visual arts

      iii. The Tempō reform and downfall of the *bakuhan*: economic and administrative measures, pressure from Europe and the U.S.

D. Korea to 1910

   1. The prehistoric origins of the Korean people, the use of ironware and emergence of tribal states in the Bronze Age

   2. The Three Kingdoms of Korea (Koguryŏ, Paekche, and Silla) and their interactions (*c.* 57 BC–AD 668), introduction of Buddhism, literature and the visual arts

   3. The unification of Korea under Silla control (668–918): adoption of Chinese governmental organization and land tenure system, emergence of provincial magnates, cultural developments

   4. The Koryŏ dynasty (918–1392): social and cultural developments, military rule, land reform and social change after the Mongol invasions (1231–*c.* 1261)

   5. The Yi state of Chosen (1392–1910)

      a. The establishment of a Confucian state: royal bureaucratic government, decline of Buddhism and emergence of Confucian culture, introduction of printing

      b. Invasions by Japan (1592–98) and China (1619–27): Korea as a Ch'ing (Manchu) vassal, Silhak scholarship and cultural development, introduction of Roman Catholicism

      c. Relations with foreign countries: growth of Japanese influence, the Tonghak Revolt (1894) and government reform, Japanese supremacy in Korea (1910)

Suggested reading in the *Encyclopædia Britannica*:

MACROPAEDIA: Major articles dealing with Japan to the Meiji Restoration (1868), and Korea to 1910

   Asia
   Japan
   Korea
   Kyōto
   Ōsaka–Kōbe Metropolitan Area
   Tokyo–Yokohama Metropolitan Area

MICROPAEDIA: Selected entries of reference information

General subjects

Jàpan—government and society:	han	shugo	Hōgen Disturbance
be	kabane	tennō	Jinshin-no-ran
Bushidō	kampaku	uji	Ōnin War
chōnin	kebiishi	wakō	Sekigahara,
daimyo	rangaku	za	Battle of
Dajōkan	rōnin	*Japan—historic*	Shimabara
equal-field system	samurai	*events:*	Rebellion
	shogunate	Gempei War	

Japan—historic
periods:
  Asuka period
  Azuchi-Momoyama
    period
  Bunka-Bunsei
    period
  Genroku period
  Heian period
  Jōmon culture
  Kamakura period
  Muromachi period

Nara period
Tokugawa period
Tumulus period
Yayoi culture
Japan—laws and
treaties:
  Harris Treaty
  Kanagawa,
    Treaty of
  Kansei reforms
  Seventeen Article
    Constitution

Taihō code
Taika era reforms
Korea—government
and society:
  Hwarangdo
  kolp'um
  Koryŏ dynasty
  Silhak
  Sŏhak
  sŏwŏn
  Unified Silla
    dynasty

yangban
Yi dynasty
Korea—states:
  Kaya
  Koguryŏ
  Nangnang
  Paekche
  Parhae
  Silla

Biographies

Japan—emperors:
  Antoku
  Daigo, Go-
  Himiko
  Kammu
  Sanjo, Go-
  Shirakawa
  Shirakawa, Go-
  Shōmu
  Tenji
  Toba, Go-
  Uda
Japan—shoguns:
  Ashikaga
    Tadayoshi
  Ashikaga Takauji
  Ashikaga
    Yoshimasa
  Ashikaga
    Yoshimitsu
  Minamoto
    Yoritomo

Tokugawa
  Hidetada
Tokugawa Iemitsu
Tokugawa Ieyasu
Tokugawa
  Yoshimune
Japan—warriors and
statesmen:
  Abe Masahiro
  Arai Hakuseki
  Fujiwara family
  Fujiwara
    Kamatari
  Fujiwara
    Michinaga
  Fujiwara Tokihira
  Hayashi Shihei
  Hōjō family
  Hōjō Tokimasa
  Hōjō Tokimune
  Hōjō Yasutoki
  Hōjō Yoshitoki

Ii Naosuke
Kusunoki
  Masashige
Maeda family
Matsudaira
  Sadanobu
Minamoto
  Yoshitsune
Mōri family
Nitta Yoshisada
Oda Nobunaga
Sakuma Zōzan
Shimazu family
Shimazu Nariaki
Shōtoku, Taishi
Soga Umaku
Taira family
Taira Kiyomori
Takasugi Shinsaku
Tanuma Okitsugu
Toyotomi
  Hideyoshi

Japan—other:
  Dōkyō
  Honda Toshiaki
  Nichiren
  Tokugawa
    Mitsukuni
  Yamaga Sokō
Korea:
  Chajang Yulsa
  Ch'oe Che-u
  Ch'oe Si-hyŏng
  Han Yong-an
  Kojong
  Sejong
  Son Pyŏng-hi
other:
  Harris, Townsend
  Perry, Matthew C.
  Valignano,
    Alessandro
  Xavier, Saint
    Francis

INDEX: See entries under all of the terms above

Section 935.   The Indian Subcontinent and Ceylon to *c.* AD 1200

A. The character and achievements of traditional Indian civilizations and their influence on Ceylonese and Southeast Asian civilizations, the geography and ethnography of the Indian subcontinent and Ceylon, archaeological and documentary historical sources, historiographic problems

B. India from the prehistoric period to AD 300: the emergence of civilization in the Indus River Valley, the growth of kingdoms and the great empires

  1. Late Stone Age hunters and Neolithic settlement in Baluchistan and the Indus Valley, first settlements east of the Indus

  2. Indus civilization (*c.* 2300–*c.* 1750 BC): social, economic, and cultural developments

    a. Development of urban centres; *e.g.,* Mohenjo-daro, Harappā, Kalibangan, Lothal

    b. Developments in agriculture, animal husbandry, metalwork and pottery, transportation, and trade

    c. Developments in languages, religion, and the visual arts

  3. The development of the Indo-Aryan states (*c.* 1500–600 BC): urbanization at Kāśī (Vārānasi) and elsewhere in the Ganges Valley, other cultures in the Indian subcontinent

    a. Early Ganges cultures to *c.* 1200 BC: social organization and religious development

    b. Later Ganges cultures to *c.* 600 BC: development of the caste system and emergence of Brahmin, Kṣatriya, Vaiśya, and Śūdra castes

    4. Pre-Mauryan states (*c.* 600–150 BC): development of political and economic systems, Taxila as a cultural centre

        a. The early development of Buddhism and Jainism, growth of Magadhan ascendancy

        b. Invasion of Alexander the Great (327 BC) and establishment of Greek settlements

    5. Development of the Mauryan Empire (*c.* 321–185 BC): the capital at Pāṭaliputra (Patna)

        a. Establishment of the empire by Candragupta Maurya (*c.* 321–*c.* 297 BC) and consolidation by Aśoka (*c.* 265–238 BC)

        b. Mauryan economic, social, and administrative developments, evolution of the concept of the state

    6. The rise of small kingdoms in the north (150 BC–AD 300): Indo-Greek and Asian rulers, various local republics and kingdoms (Śuṅga, Kaliṅga, Andhra)

    7. South Indian civilizations to AD 300

        a. Development of guilds, banking systems, and extensive maritime trade with the West

        b. Cultural and religious development; *e.g.,* patronage of religious art and literature, growth of sects in Hinduism and Jainism, assimilation of foreigners into caste society

C. North India, the Deccan, and South India (AD 300–750)

    1. The Guptas of North India (AD 320–540): expansion and administration of territory, invasions by the Hūṇas (*c.* mid-5th century), successor states to the Guptas

    2. Various kingdoms of the Deccan: the Vākāṭaka dynasty, the Viṣṇukuṇḍins, the Cālukyas, and the Rāṣṭrakūṭas

    3. The Pallavas in South India: developments in religious art and architecture, literature, and science

D. North India (750–1200), the Deccan, and South India (750–*c.* 1330): new dynasties and centres of power

    1. The tripartite struggle in North India, the Rājput kingdoms, Turkish control in Ghazna from 998

    2. The decline of the Cālukyas in the Deccan and the rise of the Cōlas in the 10th century, later Hoysaḷas and Pāṇḍyas control, relations with the south

    3. Social, economic, and cultural developments; *e.g.,* feudalism and economic decentralization, partial social mobility, growth of Tantrism, literature and the visual arts

E. Ceylon from the prehistoric period to the end of the Classical Age (AD 1200)

    1. Prehistoric settlements in Ceylon, colonization by Indo-Aryan tribes in the 5th century BC, conversion to Buddhism (*c.* 3rd century BC)

    2. Ceylon in the Classical Age (*c.* 200 BC–AD 1200): the Polonnaruva dynasties, growth of Sinhalese political institutions, social and agricultural developments

---

Suggested reading in the *Encyclopædia Britannica*:

MACROPAEDIA: Major articles dealing with the Indian subcontinent and Ceylon to *c.* AD 1200

    Asia
    India
    Indian Ocean Islands
    Nepal
    Sri Lanka

MICROPAEDIA: Selected entries of reference information

General subjects

historic regions and sites:			*kingdoms and states:*
Bhārhut	Gedrosia	Patna	Anuradhapura,
Brahmarṣi-désa	Halebīd	Śrāvastī	kingdom of
Gandhara	Kalibangan	Taxila	Avanti
Gauḍa	Kaliṅga	Vaiśālī	Kosala
	Mālwa	Valabhī	Magadha
	Nālandā	Vārānasi	

Mauryan Empire	Indus Valley	Rājput	*other:*
peoples and society:	Civilization	Sūdra	Dīpavamsa
Brahman	Kulinism	Vaiśya	Rājataraṅgiṇī
Chandelā	Licchavi	Varṇa	Serendib
Hephthalite	Mallas	Yavana	Tarāorī, Battles of

Biographies

Aśoka	Gaṅga dynasty	Mahendra	Śaiśunāga dynasty
Buddha	Gurjara-Pratihāra	Maitraka dynasty	Śaka satrap
Cālukya dynasty	dynasty	Menader	Samudra Gupta
Candra Gupta	Harṣa	Nanda dynasty	Sātavāhana
Candra Gupta I	Hoysaḷa dynasty	Pāla dynasty	dynasty
Candra Gupta II	Īśānavarman	Pallava dynasty	Sena dynasty
Cōla dynasty	Kalacuri dynasty	Pāṇḍya dynasty	Śuṅga dynasty
Duṭṭhagāmaṇī	Kaniṣka	Parākramabāhu I	Vākāṭaka dynasty
Gāhaḍavāla	Kauṭilya	Rāṣṭrakūṭa	Yādava dynasty
dynasty	Kushān	dynasty	

INDEX: See entries under all of the terms above

Section 936.   **The Indian Subcontinent from *c.* 1200 to 1761, and Ceylon from *c.* 1200 to 1505**

A. North India under Muslim hegemony (*c.* 1200–1526)

   1. The completion of the Ghurid conquest; the Delhi sultanate (1206–1526): the military and administrative policies of the five dynasties

     a. The consolidation of the conquest of North India by the Slave dynasty (1206–90)

     b. The revival of efficient administration by the Khaljī dynasty (1290–1320)

     c. The Tughluq dynasty (1320–1413): administrative reforms by Muḥammad ibn Tughluq (1325–51), Mughal invasion (1398) and decline of Tughluq control

     d. Tenuous control by the Sayyid dynasty (1414–51), expansion and decline of Lodī dynasty (1451–1526)

     e. Cultural and religious developments during the Delhi sultanate; *e.g.,* Islāmic and Hindu movements and education

   2. The 14th-century rise of regional kingdoms in the north: Bengal, Mālwa, Gujarāt, Jaunpur, and Kashmir

B. The Deccan (*c.* 1320–1627) and South India (1336–1646)

   1. The Deccan (*c.* 1320–1627): the Bahmanī dynasty and the five Deccan sultanates

     a. The Bahmanī dynasty (1347–*c.* 1527): introduction of Muslims into the Deccan and their relations with the Hindus

     b. The rise (*c.* 1500) of the five sultanates of Ahmadnagar, Berār, Bīdar, Bijāpur, and Golconda; Muslim–Hindu relations; Mughal conquests in the Deccan in the 16th century

   2. The Hindu Vijayanagar Empire (1336–1646) in South India

     a. Foundation of the state (1336) and its expansion in South India: conflicts with Muslim dynasties in the Deccan, decentralization and decline of state

     b. Administrative and social organization of the empire, cultural and religious development

C. The beginning of the political and administrative unification of the subcontinent under the Mughal Empire (1526–1761)

   1. The origins of the Mughals: the conquest of North India under Bābur, the Mughals' use of firearms

   2. Extension and consolidation of empire by Akbar (1556–1605)

     a. Subjection of neighbouring territories: the conquest and annexation of Bihār, Bengal, Afghanistan, and Kashmir

     b. Akbar's administrative, fiscal, military, judicial, and religious policies

3. The empire under Jahāngīr (1605–27), Shāh Jahān (1628–58), and Aurangzeb (1659–1707): developments in the arts and agriculture

4. Mughal decline in the 18th century: dynastic disputes and weakness after 1707 culminating in foreign invasions (1731–61)

D. The emergence of the Marāthā Empire in Mahārāshtra: rise to power and decline after 1761

1. The foundation (1674–80) of the dynasty by Śivajī: his challenge to Mughal authority in the Deccan, the Marāthā war of independence

2. The Marāthās as the major power in India in the early 18th century: the contribution of the peshwas (prime ministers) to Marāthā success, struggle with the Portuguese, establishment of the Marāthā Confederacy

E. Ceylon from c. 1200 to the arrival of the Portuguese (1505)

1. Political and economic changes in the Sinhalese state: collapse of central authority, foreign invasions, growth of foreign trade

2. Developments in culture and the Buddhist religion

Suggested reading in the *Encyclopædia Britannica*:

MACROPAEDIA: Major articles dealing with the Indian subcontinent from c. 1200 to 1761, and Ceylon from c. 1200 to 1505

Asia
India
Indian Ocean Islands
Nepal
Sri Lanka

MICROPAEDIA: Selected entries of reference information

General subjects

government and society:
Ashta Pradhan
Cūlavaṃsa
Faṣlīera
Ḥabshī
jāgīrdār
Mahāvaṃsa
manṣabdār
peshwa
Pindari
rājākariya

Biographies

Mughal emperors:
Akbar
Aurangzeb
Bābur
Humāyūn
Jahāngīr
Shah Jahan
ruling families:
'Adil Shāhī dynasty

Rājāvaliya
historic events:
Barāri Ghāt, Battle of
Gogūnda, Battle of
Jājau, Battle of
Karnāl, Battle of
Pānīpat, Battles of
Tālikota, Battle of
historic regions and sites:
Asīrgarh

Āravīdu dynasty
Gaṅga dynasty
Hoysaḷa dynasty
Khaljī dynasty
Lodī dynasty
Mughal dynasty
Slave dynasty
others:
Gobind Singh

Bengal
Bharatpur
Bijāpur
Chandragiri
Gokonda
Gulbarga
Kāmarūpa
Karnātaka
Mahāvihāra
Mālwa
Serendib
Vijayanagar

Ḥusayan Shāh
'Ala' ad-Dīn
Hyder Ali
Iltutmish
Muḥammad ibn Tughluq
Mu'izz-ud-Dīn
Muḥammad ibn Sām

kingdoms and states:
Bahmanī sultanate
Bundelā
Delhi Sultanate
Hyderābad
Jaffna
Kōṭṭe kingdom
Marāthā confederacy

Quṭb-ud-Dīn Aybak
Prithvi Nārāyaṇ Shah
Shēr Shāh of Sūr
Sirāj-ud-Dawlah
Śivājī

INDEX: See entries under all of the terms above

Section 937.   The Peoples and Civilizations of Southeast Asia to *c.* 1600

A. The character and achievements of traditional Southeast Asian civilizations, South and East Asian influences, the geography and ethnography of Southeast Asia, archaeological and documentary historical sources, historiographic problems

B. Mainland Southeast Asia to *c.* 1600

1. Burma from the Anyathian culture (5000 BC–AD 1600)

    a. Origins of civilization in Burma: the Anyathian Stone Age culture, the Mons of Lower Burma (*c.* 3rd century BC–11th century AD), Indian trade and cultural influences

    b. The Tibeto-Burmese invasions of the Upper Irrawaddy Valley (*c.* 500 BC) and the establishment of the Pyu state of Upper Burma (*c.* AD 50)

    c. The city kingdom of Pagan (849–1287): the influence of Theravāda Buddhism, Pagan as a cultural centre, destruction by the Mongols (1287)

    d. Burma from *c.* 1300 to *c.* 1600: reunification and expansion

2. The Thai people and the kingdom of Siam to *c.* 1500

    a. The origins and settlement of the Thais: the kingdom of Nanchao in Yunnan (8th century AD)

    b. Establishment of Thai power at Sukhothai (*c.* 1220): social and cultural developments

    c. Establishment of the Thai state of Ayutthaya (1350): organization of administrative, social, and legal systems; wars with Cambodia during the reign of King Trailok (1448–88)

    d. Laos to *c.* 1600: the Lao as a branch of the Thai people, establishment of the Lan Xang kingdom by Fa Ngum (1353–71), later rulers to 1571, successful Burmese invasion (1574)

3. Cambodia from the prehistoric period to *c.* 1500

    a. Prehistoric peoples in Cambodia, mythological origins of kingdom of Funan (*c.* AD 100) and the influence of Indian culture

    b. Emergence of the state of Chenla and its dominance (*c.* 598) over Funan

    c. Establishment of the state of Angkor (*c.* 800) by the Khmer dynasty, Javanese influences on religion and the concept of kingship, social and administrative structures, expansion (*c.* 1113) and decline (1177) of state

    d. Jayavarman VII (1181–*c.* 1218) and the reestablishment and extension of Khmer authority

    e. Decline of the Angkor kingdom after 1220, introduction of Theravāda Buddhism, Thai invasions (1369 and 1389) and fall of city of Angkor (1444)

4. Vietnam from the prehistoric period to *c.* 1615

    a. The legendary and historical origins of the Vietnamese people, the influence of Chinese rule (from 111 BC) on Vietnamese society

    b. The states of Funan (*c.* 1st–6th century AD) and Champa (AD 192–1471) in southern Vietnam, annexation by Nam Viet in northern Vietnam (1471)

    c. Chinese political and cultural domination of Nam Viet from 111 BC to AD 939; independence under Ly, Tran, and Le dynasties (939–1600); political unification of Nam Viet and Champa (1471); government and society in precolonial Vietnam

5. Malaya to the 16th century AD

    a. Rise of Indianized states and their role in the formation of Malaya: the advent of Islām and the rise of the sultanate of Malacca (*c.* 1400–1511)

    b. Early European intrusions: the Portuguese conquest of Malacca (1511), Chinese aggressions in the 16th century

C. Islands of the Indonesian Archipelago to *c.* 1600

1. The settlement of the Indonesian Archipelago: the introduction of Hinduism by Indian Brahmins

2. The Malay kingdom of Śrivijaya in southeast Java: the influence of Buddhism, the importance of the maritime trade with China from the 7th to the 12th century

3. Central Java in the 8th and 9th centuries: cultural, religious, and economic development during the Shailendra dynasty; the concept of divine kingship

4. Eastern Java and the rest of the archipelago from 1019 to 1292: political and cultural developments, the Singhasāri empire of Kertanagara and the royal cult

5. The Majapahit empire in eastern Java (1319–89): religious and cultural developments

6. The spread of Islām in Indonesia: the rise of Muslim states in Sumatra and Java (c. late 13th century), conflicts between Islām and older Indonesian cultures

Suggested reading in the *Encyclopædia Britannica:*

MACROPAEDIA: Major articles dealing with the peoples and civilizations of Southeast Asia to c. 1600

Asia
East Indies, The
Southeast Asia, Mainland

MICROPAEDIA: Selected entries of reference information

General subjects

Burma, Malaya, and Siam:	Ngasaunggyan, Battle of	Champa	Demak Sultanate
Dvaravati	Nong Sa Rai,	Dong Son culture	Kaḍiri,
Hlutdaw	Battle of	Funan	Kingdom of
Mon kingdom	Pagan	Lovek	Majapahit Empire
Mrohaung,	Sadki Na grades	Nam Viet	priyayi
Arakanese	Śrivijaya Empire	Vyadhapura	Singhasāri,
Kingdom of	*Indochina:*	*Indonesian*	Kingdom of
Nanchao	Angkor	*Archipelago:*	Tarumanegara
		Buginese	

Biographies

Burma, Malaya, and Siam:	Ramathibodi I	Le Loi	Trung Sisters
Anwarahta	Ramkhamhaeng	Le Thanh Tong	*Indonesian*
Bayinnaung	Toungoo dynasty	Ly Bon	*Archipelago:*
Mahmud Shah	Trailok	Ngo Quyen	Erlangga
Malacca,	*Indochina:*	Nguyen dynasty	Gajah Mada
sultanate of	Chan	Setthathirat I	Hayam Wuruk
Mangrai	Dinh Bo Lin	Suryavarman I	Kertanagara
Narameikhla	Fa Ngum	Suryavarman II	Shailendra dynasty
Naresuan	Jayavarman VII	Tran dynasty	
	Later Ly dynasty	Tran Hung Dao	

INDEX: See entries under all of the terms above

Division IV. **Peoples and Civilizations of Sub-Saharan Africa to 1885**
[For Part Nine headnote see page 343.]

The history of North Africa, because of its early involvement with Europe and Islām, is dealt with up to c. 1480 in Sections 911 and 924; and it is carried to the 19th century in Section 962. The history of Nilotic Sudan to c. AD 550 and of Ethiopia to c. AD 650 is dealt with in Section 911.

With those exceptions, the five sections of Division IV deal first with the geography and ethnology and then with the histories of the peoples and civilizations of the African continent to c. 1885.

Section 941.   West Africa to *c.* 1885

A. The geography and ethnography of West Africa, definition of the region, the archaeological and documentary historical sources and historiographic problems, the character and achievements of civilizations in West Africa

B. West Africa until the advent of the Europeans (*c.* AD 1500)

    1. Development of the West African monarchies of Ghana and Kanem to *c.* AD 1000

    2. Development of the western Sudan empires

        a. Emergence of the Keita dynasty of the Mali empire (*c.* 1235): Timbuktu as the cultural and commercial centre of Mali, fall of the Mali empire (*c.* late 15th century) and rise of the Songhai empire of Gao

        b. The migrations of the Fulani people, migrations and military conquests of the Mande-speaking peoples, development of trade routes by the Dyula

C. The precolonial period of European activity (*c.* 1400–*c.* 1885): exploration, development of the slave trade, and eventual collapse of indigenous states

    1. Portuguese trade with the Guinea states from *c.* 1460

    2. The rise and expansion of the Atlantic slave trade (*c.* 1600–*c.* 1860): the pattern and development of European slave trade routes, the African slave merchant class

    3. The Islāmic revolutions in the western Sudan: spiritual and military leadership of Sīdī Mukhtār (d. 1811) and Usman dan Fodio (d. 1817), the Fulani and Hausa *jihād*s (holy wars) and conquests

    4. West Africa from 1800 to *c.* 1885

        a. The Guinea coastlands and the European antislavery movements

        b. British colonial settlements from *c.* 1800: the colonies of Sierra Leone, the Gold Coast, Lagos, and Ashanti

        c. 19th-century British and French exploration of the West African interior, establishment of colonies, and exploitation of trade

---

Suggested reading in the *Encyclopædia Britannica*:

MACROPAEDIA: Major articles dealing with West Africa to *c.* 1885

    Africa
    Western Africa

MICROPAEDIA: Selected entries of reference information

General subjects

Akan states	British West Africa	Fulani empire	Royal Niger
Akwamu	Dahomey,	Hausa states	Company
Ashanti empire	Kingdom of	Kanem-Bornu	Songhai empire
Audaghost	Djénné	Kumbi	Tukulor empire
Bambara states	Fanti confederacy	Mali empire	Wolof empire
Benin, Kingdom of	French West Africa	Mossi states	Yoruba states
Bono		Oyo empire	

Biographies

Agaja	Mūsā	Sonni 'Alī
Beecroft, John	Osei Tutu	Sumanguru
Faidherbe, Louis	Park, Mungo	Sundiata
Muhammad I	Rābiḥ az-Zubayr	'Umar Tal
Askia	Samory	Usman dan Fodio

INDEX: See entries under all of the terms above

Section 942. **The Nilotic Sudan and Ethiopia from** *c.* AD 550 to 1885

A. The Nilotic Sudan from *c.* 550 to 1885

1. The medieval Christian kingdoms of Nobatia, Maqurrah, and 'Alwah; the Beja people

2. The spread of Muslim domination from *c.* 639: Mamlūk attacks in the 13th and 14th centuries, invasion of nomadic Arabs in the 15th century and intermarriage with Nubians, Kingdom of 'Alwah as the last Christian barrier until its conquest (*c.* 1500)

3. The rise of the Funj (*c.* 1500), the spread of Islām

4. The Egyptian occupation from 1820 to 1885: the administration of Muḥammad 'Alī and his successors, Ismā'īl Pasha and the growth of British influence

B. Ethiopia and Eritrea from *c.* AD 650 to 1855

1. The decline of the Christian Aksum empire (*c.* 600–*c.* 976): cordial relations with Islāmic states to the 8th century, conflicts with neighbouring peoples in the 9th century

2. The Zague dynasty (*c.* 11th century), the Solomonid restoration (1270), the influence of the Coptic Church on culture and religion

3. Contacts with the Portuguese (1520–1632) and Turkish attacks on Ethiopia (1523–43, 1578, and 1589), brief conciliation with the Roman Catholic Church (1595–1610)

4. Gonder Ethiopia (1632–1855): alliance with Egyptian Coptic Church, friendly relations with Muslims, rivalry between the Gallas and Tigreans

---

Suggested reading in the *Encyclopædia Britannica:*

MACROPAEDIA: Major articles dealing with the Nilotic Sudan and Ethiopia from *c.* AD 550 to *c.* 1885

    Africa
    Eastern Africa
    Sudan

MICROPAEDIA: Selected entries of reference information

General subjects

Adal	Darfur	Kordofan
Aksum,	Ethiopia	Sudan, The
Kingdom of	Ifat	

Biographies

Aḥmad Grāñ	Funj dynasty	Mahdī, al-	Sahle Selassie
Amda Tseyon	Gordon, Charles	Menelik II	Yohannes IV
Covilhã, Pêro da	George	Mikael Sehul	Zague dynasty

INDEX: See entries under all of the terms above

Section 943.   **East Africa and Madagascar to *c.* 1885**

A. The geography and ethnography of East Africa and Madagascar: definition of the region, the archaeological and documentary historical sources and historiographic problems, the character and achievements of civilizations in East Africa

B. East Africa to *c.* 1856 and Madagascar to *c.* 1810

1. The development of the coastal regions and of Madagascar and other offshore islands

   a. Medieval commercial contacts of Azania with Arabia, India, and the Mediterranean: the development of coastal trading cities

   b. The Shirazi dynasty (*c.* late 12th–15th century): the spread of Islām and growth of towns

   c. The Portuguese invasions and occupation from 1502: gradual expulsion of the Portuguese (1631–98), the Omani influence (*c.* 1700–1856)

   d. Madagascar from *c.* AD 1000 to 1810: early Indonesian settlement, later Muslim and African influx, kingdoms of Sakalava and Merina (1500–1810)

2. The peoples and states of the East African interior to *c.* 1800

   a. The Stone Age origins of the East African interior peoples in the Rift Valley (now Kenya, Tanzania, and Uganda)

   b. The Iron Age settlements in the Rift Valley, the Bantu migrations and the Chwezi peoples

   c. The Somali and Galla invasions (*c.* 10th–15th century), migrations of Nilotic and Kushitic peoples (*c.* 16th–18th century)

C. East Africa from 1856 to *c.* 1900 and Madagascar from 1810 to 1896

1. Internal developments in East Africa

   a. Development of political institutions and military kingships as defenses against Ngoni raids and Masai raiders: expansion of Rwanda and Buganda

   b. The rise of Zanzibar as the leading East African coastal power: the slave trade

   c. European exploratory and missionary activities

2. Formation of the Kingdom of Madagascar (1810–61), English and French influences in the late 19th century

---

Suggested reading in the *Encyclopædia Britannica*:

MACROPAEDIA: Major articles dealing with East Africa and Madagascar to *c.* 1885

   Africa
   Eastern Africa
   Indian Ocean Islands

MICROPAEDIA: Selected entries of reference information

General subjects

Boina	Bunyoro	Merina	Somaliland
Buganda	Menabé	Sakalava	Zanzibar

Biographies

Barghash	Livingstone, David	Mutesa I	Zwangendaba
Kirk, Sir John	Mirambo	Saʿīd ibn Sulṭān	

INDEX: See entries under all of the terms above

Section 944.   **Central Africa to *c.* 1885**

A. The geography and ethnography of Central Africa, definition of the region, the archaeological and documentary historical sources and historiographic problems, the character and achievements of civilizations in Central Africa

B. Central Africa to *c.* 1885

1. The origins of Central African cultures in the Stone Age, emergence and expansion of the Bantu-speaking peoples

2. The development of the Bantu states from *c.* AD 1400: the Luba and Lunda kingdoms, the Mongo people, the Kongo (Congo) kingdom

3. Development of Portuguese hegemony over Central Africa from 1491: trade and missionary activity, military support of the Kongo kingdom, control of the slave trade, influence on Central African unity

Suggested reading in the *Encyclopædia Britannica:*

MACROPAEDIA: Major articles dealing with Central Africa to *c.* 1885

Africa
Central Africa

MICROPAEDIA: Selected entries of reference information
General subjects

Anziku, Kingdom of Association Internationale Africaine	Berlin West Africa Conference Congo Free State Kakongo,	Kongo Kingdom Kuba, Kingdom of Loango, Kingdom of	Ngoy, Kingdom of Rwanda, Kingdom of Wadai,
Bagirmi, Kingdom of	Kingdom of Kazembe	Luba-Lunda states Lunda Empire	Kingdom of

Biographies

Afonso I	Livingstone, David
Brazza, Pierre- Paul-François- Camille Savorgnan de	Msiri Stanley, Sir Henry Morton Tippu Tib

INDEX: See entries under all of the terms above

Section 945.   **Southern Africa to *c.* 1885**

A. The geography and ethnography of southern Africa: definition of the region, the archaeological and documentary historical sources and historiographic problems, the character and achievements of civilizations in southern Africa

B. Southern Africa before *c.* 1500

1. Origins of mankind and development of culture in the Stone Age and Iron Age, the migrations of Bantu-speaking peoples in southern Africa from *c.* AD 200–400

2. The southeast coast trade in the Late Iron Age and interior trade routes to Great Zimbabwe (southwestern Rhodesia), Ingombe Ilede (Zambia), and Mapungubwe (northern Transvaal)

C. Southern Africa from *c.* 1500 to *c.* 1885

1. Portuguese expansion (1530s) into the Zambezi Valley and defeat of the Mwene Mutapa's empire in 1629: Portuguese defeats (1694) by the Rozwi empire

2. The Portuguese in west central Africa: conquests over the Kongo kingdom (1681) and Ndongo kingdom (early 17th century), control of the slave trade

3. The Dutch settlement at the Cape of Good Hope from 1652: expansion toward the Orange River and relations with the Khoisans

4. Early 19th-century African migrations and rise of the Zulu Empire (1816) under Shaka, later black migrations into Rhodesia

5. The slave and ivory trade north of the Zambezi in the 19th century: decline of the slave trade in some areas and increased commerce in ivory, Yao migration into present-day Malawi, influence of missionaries

6. The Cape eastern frontier: Boer and Xhosa resistance to the British, the Boer Great Trek (1835–54) into the interior, continued friction with the British

   a. Relations between Boers and the black population in the Transvaal

   b. Establishment of the Orange Free State, the British colonies of Natal and Cape Colony

7. The era of mineral discoveries and confederation: diamonds and gold, Transvaal–Pedi and Zulu wars

8. Portuguese loss of control in Angola and Mozambique in the mid-19th century, Portuguese reemergence of control in the early 20th century, German annexation of South West Africa (1884)

Suggested reading in the *Encyclopædia Britannica:*

MACROPAEDIA: Major articles dealing with Southern Africa to *c.* 1885

   Africa
   South Africa
   Southern Africa

MICROPAEDIA: Selected entries of reference information

General subjects

Afrikaner Bond	Gun War	Maravi	Rozwi
Blood River,	Imbangala	Confederacy	Sand River and
Battle of	Isandhlwana and	Matamba	Bloemfontein
Cape Frontier	Rorke's Drift,	Mfecane	conventions
Wars	Battles of	Mozambique	uitlanders
Gaza	Kaffraria	Conventions	Zimbabwe
Great Trek	Kasanje	Mwene Matapa	Zulu War
Griqua	Lunda Empire	Ndongo	Zululand

Biographies

Brand, Sir	Gungunhana	Mswati	Rhodes, Cecil
Johannes	Joubert, Petrus	Mzilikazi	Robinson, Sir
Henricus	Jacobus	Philip, John	Hercules
Burgers, Thomas	Kruger, Paul	Potgieter, Hendrik	Sebetwane
François	Livingstone, David	Pretorius, Andries	Shaka
Cetshwayo	Lobengula	Pretorius,	Shepstone, Sir
D'Urban, Sir	Mackenzie, John	Marthinus Wessel	Theophilus
Benjamin	Mshweshwe	Retief, Piet	Sobhuza I

INDEX: See entries under all of the terms above

Division V.   **Peoples and Civilizations of Pre-Columbian America**
[For Part Nine headnote see page 343.]

The subject in Section 951 is Andean civilization to *c.* 1540. The outline begins with the character and achievements of Andean civilization, with the ethnography and geography of the Andean region, and with archaeological and documentary historical sources. It goes on to the history of the pre-Inca cultures and states in the Andean region. It then deals with the empire of the Incas to the time of the Spanish conquest (1532–40).

The subject in Section 952 is Meso-American civilization to *c.* 1540. The outline begins with the geography and ethnography of Meso-America and with the character and achievements of Meso-American civilization. It goes on to the history of Meso-American civilizations until their conquest and destruction by the Spanish.

Section 951.   **Andean Civilization to *c.* AD 1540**

A. The character and achievements of Andean civilization, the geography and ethnography of the Andean region, archaeological and documentary historical sources, historiographic problems

B. Pre-Inca cultures and states

   1. Late Preceramic (*c.* 3500–*c.* 1800 BC) cultures: development of agriculture

   2. Initial (*c.* 1800–*c.* 1000 BC) and Early Horizon, or Chavín and Paracas (*c.* 1000–*c.* 200 BC), cultures in Peru: development of textiles, pottery, and ceremonial architecture

   3. Early Intermediate (Florescent, or Classic) Period (*c.* 200 BC–*c.* AD 600): metallurgy, pottery, and textile production in the Nazca and Moche cultures

   4. Middle Horizon Period (*c.* AD 600–*c.* 1000): the Huari and Tiahuanaco cultures, urban settlements, cultural decline after *c.* AD 800

   5. Late Intermediate Period (*c.* AD 1000–*c.* 1400): pottery and the introduction of bronze, the Chimu Empire (*c.* 1300–*c.* 1460) located at Chan Chan, spread of urban settlements

C. The empire of the Incas (*c.* 1400–*c.* 1540)

   1. The origins and development of the Inca Empire

      a. The autochthonic mythical origins of the Inca dynasty, establishment of the Cuzco Valley settlement (*c.* 1400)

      b. The reigns of Capac Yupanqui, Inca Roca, Yahuar Huacac, and Viracocha Inca: Inca expansion into the Urubamba Valley and Titicaca Basin, the Chancas invasion (1438)

      c. Inca victory over the Chancas (1438), Incan civil war between Cuzco and Calca factions, Cuzco victory and reign of Pachacuti Inca Yupanqui (1438–*c.* 1471), renewed battles with Chancas (*c.* 1445), further conquest of Titicaca Basin region, victory over Chimú Empire

      d. Inca conquests during the reign of Topa Inca Yupanqui (*c.* 1471–*c.* 1493): annexation of highland Bolivia, northern Chile, northwestern Argentina, and southern Peru

      e. Reign of Huayna Capac (*c.* 1493–*c.* 1525): conquest of northeastern Peru and northern Ecuador, Atahuallpa's victory (1532) over Huascar in civil war

      f. The Spanish conquest of the Incas (1532–40): Pizarro's execution of Atahuallpa and support of Topa Huallpa (1533), later support of Manco Inca (1533–35); Manco's rebellion and defeat (1536), Spanish consolidation of power

   2. Incan government, society, and culture

      a. Divine monarchy and the royal corporations, administrative hierarchy, taxation, the census and the quipu system of numerical records

      b. The settlement of people loyal to the Incas in newly conquered territories, the spy system, religious practices, military policy and organization, technology, agriculture, transportation system, calendar, oral narratives

Suggested reading in the *Encyclopædia Britannica*:

MACROPAEDIA: Major articles dealing with Andean civilization to *c.* AD 1540

Argentina

Bolivia

Chile

Colombia

Ecuador

Latin America, The History of

Lima

Peru

Pre-Columbian Civilizations

MICROPAEDIA: Selected entries of reference information

General subjects

Araucanian

Atacama

Chan Chan

Chavín

Chimú

El Paraíso

Huari

Inca

Machu Picchu

Mochica

Nazca

Pachacamac

Paracas

Quechua

Tiahuanaco

Biographies

Almagro, Diego de

Atahualpa

Huascar

Pizarro, Francisco

Pizarro, Gonzalo

INDEX: See entries under all of the terms above

Section 952.   Meso-American Civilization to *c.* AD 1540

A. The character and achievements of Meso-American civilization, the geography and ethnography of Meso-America, archaeological and documentary historical sources, historiographic problems

B. Meso-America in the Pre-Classic and Classic periods

1. The development of Meso-American civilization in the Pre-Classic periods

a. Late Pleistocene and Early Hunter (*c.* 21,000–*c.* 6500 BC) peoples of Meso-America, development of agriculture (*c.* 6500–*c.* 1500 BC)

b. Early Formative Period (*c.* 1500–*c.* 900 BC): the Ocós and Caudros settlements, the Olmec civilization at San Lorenzo (*c.* 1150–*c.* 900 BC) and development of its stone monuments

c. Middle Formative Period (*c.* 900–*c.* 300 BC): the Olmecs at La Venta (*c.* 800–*c.* 400 BC); ceremonial architecture, pottery, and writing system; colonization and trade; pre-Maya villages in Guatemala

d. Late Formative Period (*c.* 300 BC–*c.* AD 100): regionalism and cultural integration, the Cuicuilco-Tilcomán cultures in the Valley of Mexico, the Zapotecs of Oaxaca, the Izapan civilization, Mayas of the Chicanel in northern Petén

2. Maya and non-Maya Meso-America in the Classic Period (*c.* AD 100–*c.* 900)

a. Early Classic Period (*c.* AD 100–*c.* 600)

i. Teotihuacán cultural and urban development, ceremonial architecture and pottery, the Zapotecs at Monte Albán

ii. The Cotzumalhuapo culture in the Maya highlands, Tzakol and Tepeu cultures in lowland Maya civilization (*c.* AD 300–*c.* 900)

b. Late Classic non-Maya Meso-America (*c.* AD 600–*c.* 900): decline of Teotihuacán political and cultural influence, rise of Xochicalco culture, the Mixtecs of northern Oaxaca

c. Late Classic lowland Maya culture (*c.* AD 600–*c.* 900)

i. Urban settlements, temple-pyramids and palaces, Maya art, the calendar and writing system

ii. Maya religion, social and political life, the collapse of the Maya civilization (*c.* AD 900)

C. Post-Classic Period in the Valley of Mexico and the Yucatán Peninsula (*c.* 900–*c.* 1519)

1. The rise and decline of the Toltec state in southern Mexico and the Yucatán Peninsula (*c.* 900–*c.* 1200): secular and religious institutions, art and architecture, the legend of Quetzalcóatl, Toltec–Maya culture of Tollan (Tula) and Chichén-Itzá

2. The development of the Aztec state and extension of Aztec rule over the Valley of Mexico (*c.* 1325–1519): military campaigns of Itzcoatl, Montezuma I, and Ahuitzotl; administrative techniques under Montezuma II (1502–20)

3. Aztec culture and society up to the time of the Spanish conquest; *e.g.,* agriculture and technology, political organization, governmental structure, militarism, economy, religion, art and architecture

D. The Spanish conquest of the Aztec state and the Yucatán Peninsula (1519–*c.* 1540): destruction of Aztec government and culture, imposition of Spanish colonial policies and religion

---

Suggested reading in the *Encyclopædia Britannica:*

MACROPAEDIA: Major articles dealing with Meso-American civilization to *c.* AD 1540

Latin America, The History of
Mexico
Mexico City
Pre-Columbian Civilizations

MICROPAEDIA: Selected entries of reference information

General subjects

cultural centres:		*peoples:*	
Chapultepec	Palenque		Yucatec Maya
Chichén Itzá	Teotihuacán	Chichimec	Zapotec
Kaminaljuyú	Texcoco	Chol	*other:*
Mayapán	Tikal	Lacandón	Aztec calendar
Mitla	Tula	Maya	Mayan calendar
Monte Albán	Uxmal	Olmec	Quetzalcóatl
	Xochicalco	Toltec	

Biographies

Alvarado, Pedro de   Cuauhtémoc
Cortés, Hernán,   Griljalba, Juan
   marqués del Valle   Marina
   de Oaxaca   Montezuma II

INDEX: See entries under all of the terms above

Division VI.   The Modern World to 1920

[For Part Nine headnote see page 343.]

The theme of western expansion, imperialism, and colonialism pervades Division VI. The separation of the history of the modern world (*c.* 1500–*c.* 1920) into eleven sections reflects conventional regional analyses of modern history, and, within each of those sections, conventional judgments regarding turning-point dates of the regional histories.

Section 961.   **Western Europe from *c.* 1500 to *c.* 1789**

A. The effects of religious and cultural change: the emergence of the nation-state system, the predominance and decline of Habsburg power centred in Spain (*c.* 1500–1648)

1. The later Renaissance in Italy and northern Europe

   a. The influence of Italian statecraft and political theory: Machiavelli and the principle of *raison d'état*

   b. Cultural and intellectual life in the later Renaissance

2. The Scientific Revolution: the emergence of modern science and technology in the 16th and 17th centuries

3. The emergence of a religiously divided Europe in the 16th century

   a. The Protestant Reformation and its political and social consequences

   b. The Catholic Reformation and Counter-Reformation

4. International diplomacy and warfare (1494–1648)

   a. The Italian Wars (1494–1516) and the concept of balance of power: French and Austro-Spanish expansionism in Italy

   b. French and Austrian struggles for supremacy in Europe (1515–59): French anti-Habsburg alliances with England, German Lutheran princes, and the Turks

   c. Conflicts between Catholic and Protestant powers after *c.* 1555: religious wars in France and the Low Countries, conflict with the Ottoman Empire

   d. The Thirty Years' War (1618–48) and the Peace of Westphalia: the end of religious struggles and resecularization of international affairs

5. National and dynastic states (*c.* 1500–1648)

   a. Italy in the 16th and 17th centuries: political, economic, social, and cultural developments

      i. The French invasion (1494) and conquests of Naples (1495) and Milan (1499), the influence of Savonarola, the anti-French League of Venice and the Spanish defeat of France (1525)

      ii. Italy under Spanish domination: Catholic religious reforms; Spanish Habsburg rule in Naples, Sicily, Sardinia, and Milan

      iii. Relations between Spain and the independent states of Italy: Savoy, Genoa, Tuscany, Venice, and the Papal States

   b. Spain from 1516 to 1665

      i. Establishment of the Habsburg dynasty (1516) by Charles I (Holy Roman Emperor Charles V), Spanish hegemony in Europe and the Americas, domestic and foreign policies of Philip II (1556–98), the Armada (1588), cultural developments in Spain's Golden Age

      ii. Political and economic decline during the reigns of Philip III (1598–1621) and Philip IV (1621–65): expulsion of the Moriscos (1609), Olivares' administration, loss of Portugal (1640)

   c. Portugal from *c.* 1500 to 1648: domination of East Indian trade, union with Spain (1580), independence under House of Bragança (1640)

   d. The British Isles (*c.* 1485–1649)

      i. Henry VII (1485–1509): dynastic unity in England after the Wars of the Roses; political, judicial, social, and economic developments

      ii. Henry VIII (1509–47): foreign and domestic policies; the divorce question, the English Reformation, and the establishment of the Church of England; Edward VI (1547–53) and Mary I (1553–58)

      iii. Elizabeth I (1558–1603): social and cultural developments; domestic policies; dynastic challenge of Mary, Queen of Scots; struggle with Spain

      iv. James I (1603–25) of England (James VI of Scotland) and establishment of the Stuart dynasty: developments in religious doctrine, foreign relations, economic policy, and the arts; conflicts between crown and Parliament

     v. Charles I (1625–49) and the English Civil War (1642–51): economic and political disputes between crown and Parliament; royal personal rule (1629–40); persecution of Puritans; the Long Parliament, Oliver Cromwell, and the Civil War; execution of Charles I (1649)

     vi. Scotland in the 16th and 17th centuries: reigns of James IV and James V; Mary, Queen of Scots (1542–67), and the Scottish Reformation; John Knox and Calvinism; James VI (1567–1625) of Scotland (James I of England, 1603–25) and personal union of the two crowns

     vii. Ireland in the 16th and 17th centuries: subjugation of Ireland by Henry VIII and Elizabeth I, the Irish revolt of 1641, Cromwell's invasion and anti-Catholic policies during the Commonwealth

   e. France from 1483 to 1643

     i. Development of a standing army and a professional bureaucracy in the reigns of Charles VIII (1483–98), Louis XII (1498–1515), Francis I (1515–47), and Henry II (1547–59)

     ii. The Protestant Reformation and the French Wars of Religion (1562–98): the reigns of Catherine de Médicis (1560–74) and Henry III (1574–89), religious compromise and restoration of strong monarchy under Henry IV of Bourbon (1589–1610)

     iii. The reign of Louis XIII (1610–43) and Cardinal de Richelieu: suppression of the Huguenots and the nobles, French success in the Thirty Years' War

   f. Germany and the Holy Roman Empire from *c.* 1500 to 1648: the Reformation, Counter-Reformation, and Thirty Years' War

     i. Maximilian I (1493–1519), Martin Luther, and the origins of Lutheranism; Charles V and the Diet and Edict of Worms (1521); the Peasants' Revolt (1524–25); diets of Speyer (1526 and 1529) and Augsburg (1530); the Schmalkaldic League and ensuing wars; abdication of Charles V (1555) and Peace of Augsburg

     ii. Ferdinand I (1556–64) and Maximilian II (1564–76), internal disunity under their successors, the Thirty Years' War (1618–48), political and religious settlements of the Peace of Westphalia (1648)

   g. The Swiss Confederation from 1474 to 1648

     i. Swiss victory over Charles the Bold in the Burgundian War (1474–77), military prestige of the confederation, victory over Maximilian I (1499), the Italian campaigns (1499–1516)

     ii. The Swiss Reformation: Zwingli and Calvin, the Counter-Reformation and emergence of Catholic and Protestant cantons, neutrality in the Thirty Years' War (1618–48), European recognition by the Peace of Westphalia (1648)

   h. The Low Countries from 1494 to 1648

     i. Habsburg unification of the Low Countries (1494); further consolidation under the future emperor Charles V (1506–55); economic, cultural, and religious developments; revolt of the provinces (1567–79)

     ii. Establishment of the United Provinces of the Netherlands (the Dutch Republic) in 1579: leadership of the House of Orange, continued war against Spanish Habsburg power

     iii. Commercial supremacy of the Dutch Republic, intermittent wars with Spain (1621–48)

     iv. Cultural, social, religious, and economic developments in the Dutch Republic

   i. Scandinavia from 1523 to 1648: separation of Sweden from Denmark–Norway (1523) and Dano-Swedish conflicts; Christian III of Denmark (1534–59), Gustav I Vasa (1523–60), and Gustavus II Adolphus (1611–32) of Sweden; participation in Thirty Years' War (1618–48)

B. European overseas expansion and commercial development from *c.* 1400 to 1763

  1. The beginning of European imperialism: rapid expansion of European trade with and control over the non-European world after *c.* 1450

   a. Advances in geographical knowledge and technological improvements; *e.g.,* ship design, navigational instruments, cartography

   b. Voyages of discovery and exploration: establishment of colonial empires

     i. Discovery, exploration, and early settlement of the Americas

      ii. Discovery, exploration, and early settlement of the coastal regions of Africa, Australia, India, and the East Indies

2. The decline of the feudal system and growth of commercial activity

    a. The changing relationship between tenant and landlord, agricultural developments, evolving role of the guilds, decline of Hanseatic League, demographic movements

    b. The decline in Mediterranean trade and growth of Antwerp and Amsterdam as international trade centres, the growth of a landed merchant class

3. Technological advances and pre-Industrial Revolution manufacturing systems: development of "putting-out" system and decline of guild power

4. The impact of colonial expansion on Europe

    a. Economic effects

      i. Development of new business organizations to direct colonial exploitation: joint-stock and chartered companies

      ii. The "price revolution": the relationship between the influx of precious metals from the Americas to Europe and the price rise in the 16th century

      iii. Growth of mercantilism: theories and policies of economic nationalism developed by European powers, the concept of the balance of trade

      iv. Increase in volume of world trade: the growth of the luxury trade (silks, spices, precious metals), the agricultural trade (tobacco, sugar, and coffee), the raw materials trade

      v. Development and importance of the slave trade

    b. Political effects: the relationship between Spain's status as an international power and its colonial possessions in the 16th century, colonial rivalries among European powers in the 17th and 18th centuries

C. France and Great Britain as the dominant powers in Europe, the emergence of Prussia and Austria as European powers

1. International wars and diplomacy (*c.* 1649–*c.* 1790)

    a. The Age of Louis XIV (1661–1715): French successes in the War of Devolution (1667–68) and the Dutch War (1672–79), defeat in the War of the League of Augsburg (1689–97) and the War of the Spanish Succession (1701–14)

    b. Development of the alliance system: the balance of power

      i. The Quadruple Alliance: the emergence of Prussia and Austria as European powers, the War of the Austrian Succession (1740–48)

      ii. The Seven Years' War (1756–63) and France's defeat and loss of colonial territory in the Americas

      iii. French recovery and Franco-Spanish cooperation (1778–81) against Britain in the U.S. War of Independence, Russian-Prussian partition of Poland (1772)

2. The European states (*c.* 1648–*c.* 1790)

    a. Great Britain from 1649 to *c.* 1790

      i. Oliver Cromwell, the Commonwealth, and the Protectorate (1649–60); the Stuart Restoration (1660) under Charles II (1660–85) and James II (1685–88); the Glorious Revolution of 1688 and end of crown rule without Parliament

      ii. Limited monarchy under William III (1689–1702) and Mary II (1689–94) and Anne (1702–14); growth of Whig and Tory political parties (1689–1714); the Hanoverian succession and emergence of the cabinet system under George I and George II; Whig supremacy and political stability to 1760; ministries of Walpole, Pelham, and Pitt

      iii. Early years of George III's reign (1760–1820) to *c.* 1790: eclipse of Whig power and political instability (1760–70), failure of colonial policies and U.S. War of Independence, beginning of parliamentary and reform movements

      iv. Economic, cultural, and social developments: agricultural innovations, population growth, origins of the Industrial Revolution and factory system, influence of Methodism

      v. Formal union of England and Scotland (1707), Edinburgh's status as an intellectual centre, Protestant Ascendancy in Ireland and growth of Irish patriotism among the Anglo-Irish, Wales in the 18th century

    b. France from *c.* 1650 to *c.* 1790

     i. The Frondes, Louis XIV's minority (1643–61), and Mazarin's control of government to 1661

     ii. The Age of Louis XIV (1661–1715): development of the central government, the Versailles court, military policies, mercantilist policies of Colbert

     iii. Louis's religious and political policies: revocation (1685) of the Edict of Nantes and the Huguenot emigration, political influence of Jansenism, royal absolutism

     iv. French cultural development in the 17th century

     v. The *ancien régime* (1715–89): the close relationship between society and the state, the new urban class, the decline of the monarchy under Louis XV (1715–74) and Louis XVI (1774–92), power of the *parlements,* agricultural and industrial growth, domestic and colonial trade

     vi. The reform movement: the influences of nationalism and individualism; attacks on political, social, and economic policies of the *ancien régime;* conflict between the nobility and bourgeoisie; the financial crisis and attempts at reform by Necker and Turgot; the States General and the beginning of the Revolution (1789)

  c. The lands ruled by the Austrian Habsburgs (1648–1790)

     i. Austrian consolidation and expansion under Leopold I (1658–1705), Joseph I (1705–11), and Charles VI (1711–40): conquest of Hungary and penetration of the Balkans in the Austro-Turkish wars (1683–99 and 1716–18), War of the Spanish Succession (1701–14) and acquisition of the Spanish Netherlands (1713)

     ii. The Pragmatic Sanction and the accession of Maria Theresa (1740); War of the Austrian Succession (1740–48) and loss of Silesia to Prussia (1741); military, administrative, and educational reforms of Maria Theresa; acquisition of Polish Galicia (1772); failure of Joseph II's (1765–90) foreign policies and his enlightened domestic reforms (1780–90)

  d. Germany and the rise of Prussia (*c.* 1640–*c.* 1790)

     i. Frederick William, the Great Elector (1640–88): strengthening of Hohenzollern power in Brandenburg and Prussia, end of Polish suzerainty over Prussia, War of the Spanish Succession (1701–14), Austro-Prussian rivalry in the 18th century, Frederick I (1701–13) and Frederick William I (1713–40) of Prussia

     ii. Frederick II the Great (1740–86): War of the Austrian Succession (1740–48), Seven Years' War (1756–63), partitions of Poland (1772–95), development of Idealism (Goethe and Schiller), enlightened reform and benevolent despotism

     iii. The influence of Pietism, the German cultural revival in the second half of the 18th century

  e. Spain and Portugal

     i. Spain from 1665 to *c.* 1790: continued decline under Charles II (1665–1700); War of the Spanish Succession (1701–14) and establishment of the Bourbon dynasty; pro-French foreign policy under Philip V, Ferdinand VI, and Charles III; administrative and economic reforms of Charles III

     ii. Portugal from 1640 to *c.* 1777: increasing economic and diplomatic ties to England under John IV (1640–56), Afonso VI (1656–83), Pedro II (1683–1706), and John V (1706–50); economic, religious, and administrative reforms under Pombal and Joseph I (1750–77)

  f. Italy in the 18th century

     i. Government reforms and the rule of Joseph II (1765–90) in Lombardy, reigns of Francis of Lorraine (1738–65) and Peter Leopold (1765–90) in Tuscany

     ii. The viceroyalty of Naples and the kingdom of Sicily: economic and social unrest, rule of Charles VI in Sicily, transfer of Naples and Sicily to Charles III in 1734, the Bourbon regime

  g. The United Provinces of the Netherlands from 1648 to 1789; economic and political stagnation; the first (1650–72) and second (1702–47) stadholderless periods; the patriotic movement; social, religious, and cultural development

  h. Scandinavia from *c.* 1648 to *c.* 1792

     i. Swedish wars of conquest against Poland and Denmark–Norway under Charles X Gustav (1654–60) and Charles XI (1672–97), war with Russia under Charles XII (1697–1718) and displacement of Sweden by Russia as the chief Baltic power after the Great Northern War (1700–21)

ii. Social and economic conditions in the Scandinavian countries

iii. Denmark–Norway losses in the First Northern War with Sweden (1655–60); economic stagnation (1720–66), "Enlightened" reforms under Christian VII (1766–1808), Struensee, and Bernstorff; revival of settlement in Greenland (1714)

iv. Growth of parliamentary government in Sweden: Frederick I (1720–51) and Adolf Frederick (1751–71), the "Hats" and "Nightcaps" political parties, absolutism reestablished by Gustav III (1771–92)

i. The Swiss Confederation (c. 1650–1790): Villmergen wars (1656–1712), the influence of the Enlightenment

3. The age of the Enlightenment

a. Origins in the 17th century: Scientific achievements, developments in political and religious philosophies, developments in the arts

b. Expansion in the 18th century: the spread of religious, political, economic, and scientific theories in western Europe; cultural developments

---

Suggested reading in the *Encyclopædia Britannica*:

MACROPAEDIA: Major articles and biographies dealing with Western Europe from *c.* 1500 to *c.* 1789

Albania	Denmark	Greece	Malta
Amsterdam	Dublin	Habsburg, The	Manchester
Antwerp	Edinburgh	House of	Marseille
Athens	Elizabeth I of	Hamburg	Mediterranean Sea
Austria	England	Holy Roman	Milan
Bacon, Francis	Europe	Empire, The	Naples
Balkans	European Overseas	History of the	Norway
Barcelona	Exploration and	Hungary	Paris
Berlin	Empires, The	Iceland	Portugal
Bourbon, The	History of	Ireland	Rome
House of	Finland	Italy	Spain
Brussels	Florence	Lisbon	Sweden
Cologne	France	London	Switzerland
Columbus	Frederick the Great	Low	United Kingdom
Cromwell, Oliver	Geneva	Countries, The	Venice
Czechoslovakia	Germany	Madrid	Vienna

MICROPAEDIA: Selected entries of reference information

General subjects

cultural and	Belgrade, Treaty of	Nordlingen,	Stolbovo, Treaty of
economic:	Blenheim, Battle of	Battle of	Thirty Years' War
Baroque period	Breda, Treaty of	Northern War,	Utrecht, treaties of
bullionism	Cambrai,	First	Vienna, Siege of
Classicism and	League of	Northern War,	Westphalia,
Neoclassicism	Carlowitz,	Second	Peace of
Enlightenment	Treaty of	Oudenaarde,	Wittstock, Battle of
mercantilism	Cateau-Cambresis,	Battle of	*national affairs—*
Physiocrat	Peace of	Pavia, Battle of	*Britain:*
Renaissance	Devolution,	Poland,	Armada
international	War of	Partition of	Bishops' Wars
relations:	Dutch War	Pragmatic Sanction	Boyne, Battle
Åbo, Treaty of	Fontenoy, Battle of	of Charles VI	of the
Aix-la-Chapelle,	Grand Alliance,	Pyrenees, Peace	cabal
Treaty of	War of the	of the	Clarendon Code
Altranstädt,	Lepanto, Battle of	Ramillies, Battle of	Cloth of Gold,
treaties of	Lützen, Battle of	Rocroi, Battle of	Field of
Anglo-Dutch War	Madrid, Treaty of	Russo-Turkish	Culloden,
Austrian	Marignano,	Wars	Battle of
Succession, War	Battle of	Seven Years' War	Darnel's case
of the	Medina del	Silesian Wars	Declaratory Act
Bavarian	Campo, Treaty of	Spanish	Dover, Treaty of
Succession,	Mohács, Battle of	Succession, War	English Civil
War of the	Neva, Battle of the	of the	Wars

Biographies

Cranmer,
  Thomas
Cromwell,
  Oliver
Cromwell,
  Richard
Cromwell,
  Thomas, earl
  of Essex
Darnley,
  Henry Stewart,
  Lord
Davison,
  William
Digby,
  Sir Kenelm
Drake,
  Sir Francis
Edward VI
Eliot, Sir John
Elizabeth I
Essex, Robert
  Devereux, 2nd
  earl of
Fairfax of
  Cameron,
  Thomas Fairfax,
  3rd Baron
Fawkes, Guy
Fisher, Saint John
Flood, Henry
Fox, Charles James
Gage, Thomas
Gardiner, Stephen
George I
George II
George III
Gilbert, Sir
  Humphrey
Godolphin, Sidney
  Godolphin,
  earl of
Gowrie, John
  Ruthven, 3rd
  earl of
Grafton, Augustus
  Henry Fitzroy,
  3rd duke of
Grattan, Henry
Grenville, George
Grey, Lady Jane
Gwyn, Nell
Hakluyt, Richard
Hamilton, John
  Hamilton, 1st
  marquess of
Hampdon, John
Hastings, Warren
Hawkins, Sir John
Henderson,
  Alexander
Henrietta Maria

Henry VII
Henry VIII
Howe, Richard
  Howe, earl
Hudson, Henry
Huntly, George
  Gordon, 1st
  marquess and 6th
  earl of
Hutchinson,
  Thomas
James I (Britain)
James II (Britain)
James IV
  (Scotland)
James V (Scotland)
Jane Seymour
Jeffreys (of Wem),
  George Jeffreys,
  1st baron
Knox, John
Lambert, John
Latimer, Hugh
Laud, William
Leeds, Thomas
  Osborne, 1st
  duke of
Leicester, Robert
  Dudley, earl of
Leven, Alexander
  Leslie, 1st earl of
Lilburne, John
Lovat, Simon
  Fraser, 11th Lord
Maitland (of
  Lethington),
  William
Marlborough, John
  Churchill, 1st
  duke of
Marlborough,
  Sarah Jennings,
  duchess of
Mary (Queen of
  Scots)
Mary I
Mary II
Masham, Abigail,
  Lady Masham
Monck, George,
  1st duke of
  Albemarle
Monmouth, James
  Scott, duke of
Montagu, Ralph
  Montagu, 1st
  duke of
Moray, James
  Stewart, 1st
  earl of
More, Sir Thomas

Morton, James
  Douglas, 4th
  earl of
Newcastle, William
  Cavendish, 1st
  duke of
Norfolk, Thomas
  Howard, 3rd
  duke of
Norfolk, Thomas
  Howard, 4th
  duke of
Northampton,
  Henry Howard,
  earl of
Northumberland,
  John Dudley,
  duke of
Oates, Titus
O'Donnell, Manus
O'Neill, Owen Roe
O'Neill, Shane
Ormonde, James
  Butler, 12th earl
  and 1st duke of
Oxford, Robert
  Harley, 1st earl of
Pitt, William, the
  Elder
Pole, Reginald
Pole, Richard de la
Portsmouth,
  Louise-Renée
  de Kéroualle,
  duchess of
Prynne, William
Pym, John
Raffles, Sir
  Stamford
Raleigh, Sir Walter
Riccio, David
Rupert, Prince
Sackville (of
  Drayton Manor),
  George Sackville
  Germain, 1st
  viscount
Saint John, Oliver
Salisbury, Robert
  Cecil, 1st earl of
Sandwich, Edward
  Montagu, 1st
  earl of
Saye and Sele,
  William Fiennes,
  1st viscount
Schomberg,
  Frederick
  Herman, duke of
Seymour (of
  Sudley), Thomas
  Seymour, Baron

Shaftesbury,
  Anthony Ashley
  Cooper, 1st
  earl of
Shrewsbury,
  Charles Talbot,
  duke and 12th
  earl of
Somerset, Edward
  Seymour, 1st
  duke of
Stanhope, James
  Stanhope, 1st earl
Stirling, William
  Alexander, 1st
  earl of
Strafford, Thomas
  Wentworth, 1st
  earl of
Stuart, House of
Sussex, Thomas
  Radcliffe, 3rd
  earl of
Tudor, House of
Tyrconnell, Rory
  O'Donnell, 1st
  earl of
Tyrone, Conn
  O'Neill,
  1st earl of
Tyrone, Hugh
  O'Neill, 2nd
  earl of
Vane, Sir Henry,
  the Younger
Walpole, Robert,
  1st earl
  of Orford
Walsingham, Sir
  Francis
Wildman,
  Sir John
Wilkes, John
William III
Winthrop,
  John
Wolsey, Thomas,
  Cardinal
Wyat, Sir
  Thomas, the
  Younger
France:
Anne of
  Austria
Beaufort, François
  de Vendôme,
  duc de
Bernis, François-
  Joachim de
  Pierre de
Bourbon, Charles
  III, 8e duc de

Doria family
Este, House of
Farnese family
Ferdinand I
  (Tuscany)
Ferdinand II
  (Tuscany)
Fieschi family
Fieschi,
  Gian Luigi
Francis (I)
  (Tuscany)
Gonzaga dynasty
Guicciardini,
  Francesco
Julius II (pope)
Leo X (pope)
Machiavelli,
  Niccolò
Medici family
Medici,
  Giovanni de'
Medici,
  Lorenzino de'
Morosimi family
Savoy, House of
Sforza family
Sixtus V (pope)
Low Countries:
Coen, Jan
  Pieterszoon
Diemen,
  Anthony van
Egmond,
  Lamoraal,
  graaf van
Farnese,
  Alessandro,
  duca di Parma e
  Piacenza
Frederick Henry,
  prince of Orange
Hembyze, Jan van
Heyn, Piet
Hoorne, Filips van
Montmorency,
  graaf van

John Maurice of
  Nassau
John William Friso
Louis of Nassau
Margaret of
  Austria
Maurice
Oldenbarnevelt,
  Johan van
Orange, House of
Ruyter, Michiel
  Adriaanszoon de
Tasman, Abel
  Janszoon
Tromp, Maarten
William I
William II
William III
William IV
William V
Witt, Johan de
Portugal:
Albuquerque,
  Afonso de, the
  Great
Cabral, Pedro
  Álvares
Covilhã, Pêro da
Dias, Bartolomeu
Gama, Vasco da,
  1er conde da
  Vidigueira
Henry the
  Navigator
Magellan,
  Ferdinand
Pombal, Sebastião
  de Carvalho,
  marquês de
Scandinavia:
Adolf Frederick
  (Sweden)
Armfelt, Gustaf
  Mauritz
Charles IX
  (Sweden)

Charles X Gustav
  (Sweden)
Charles XI
  (Sweden)
Charles XII
  (Sweden)
Christian II
  (Denmark)
Christian III
  (Denmark)
Christian IV
  (Denmark)
Christina
De la Gardie,
  Jacob Pontusson,
  Greve
Frederick I
  (Sweden)
Frederick I
  (Denmark)
Frederick II
  (Denmark)
Frederick III
  (Denmark)
Gustav I Vasa
  (Sweden)
Gustav II Adolf
  (Sweden)
Gustav III
  (Sweden)
John III (Sweden)
Oxenstierna (af
  Södermöre), Axel,
  Greve
Oxenstierna, Bengt
  Gabrielsson,
  Greve
Spain:
Alba, Fernando
  Álvarez de
  Toledo y
  Pimentel, 3er
  duque de
Alberoni, Giulio
Balboa, Vasco
  Núñez de
Bonaparte, Joseph

Charles I
Charles II
Charles III
Farnese,
  Alessandro,
  duca di Parma e
  Piacenza
Ferdinand V
Ferdinand VI
Floridablanca,
  José Moñino
  y Redondo,
  conde de
Juan de Austria
Juan José de
  Austria
Margaret of
  Angoulême
Margaret
  of Austria
Olivares, Gaspar
  de Guzmán
  y Pimental,
  conde-duque de
Orry, Jean
Pérez, Antonio
Philip I
Philip II
Philip III
Philip IV
Philip V
Riperdá, Juan
  Guillermo
Riperdá,
  duque de
Santa Cruz,
  Alvaro de
  Bazán,
  marqués de
Soto,
  Hernando de
Vespucci,
  Amerigo

INDEX: See entries under all of the terms above

Section 962. **Eastern Europe, Southwest Asia, and North Africa from *c.* 1480 to *c.* 1800**

A. The Christian states of eastern Europe

1. Poland–Lithuania (1492–1795): gradual weakening of the monarchy, decline and dismemberment of the state

   a. The Golden Age of the Polish–Lithuanian empire (1492–1572)

      i. Foreign relations: Ottoman invasions, Russian invasion of Lithuania, alliance with Turks (1533) and reestablishment of Polish security, renewed Russian aggression

      ii. Domestic developments: population movements, constitutional reform, prosperous foreign trade, exploitation of the peasantry and their reduction to serfdom, effects of the Renaissance and the Reformation

   b. Establishment of the royal republic (1572–1648)

      i. The Interregnum (1572–75) and reform of the monarchy: Stephen Bathory (1575–86) and Sigismund III Vasa (1587–1632), indecisive wars with Sweden for possession of the Baltic region

      ii. Władysław IV Vasa (1632–48): the Cossack revolt, economic prosperity, increased power of the nobility, effect of the Counter-Reformation

   c. The period of wars and disintegration (1648–97): the Cossack–Russian and Swedish invasions in the reign of John II Casimir (1648–68), loss of Ducal Prussia to Brandenburg (1657), Michael Wiśniowiecki (1669–73), John III Sobieski's (1674–96) victories over the Turks

   d. The Saxonian era, the Russian Protectorate, and the partitions of Poland among Russia, Prussia, and Austria

      i. The reigns of Augustus II (1697–1733) and Augustus III (1733–63): participation in the Great Northern War, relations with Prussia, the Seven Years' War (1756–63)

      ii. The reign of Stanisław II August Poniatowski (1764–95): the Confederation of Bar, reform, the partitions of Poland (1772, 1793, and 1795)

2. Hungary: the Jagiellon kings (1490–1526) and the partition period (1526–1699)

   a. The peasant revolt (1514), defeat by the Ottoman Turks at Battle of Mohács (1526)

   b. Division into Ottoman and Habsburg sectors in the 16th century, the spread of Protestantism, the Fifteen Years' War, the rise of Transylvania, defeat of the Turks (1686) and subjection of all Hungary to the Habsburgs in 1699

3. Emergence of the Russian Empire (*c.* 1500–1796)

   a. Extension of Muscovite control over Russia under Vasily III (1505–33), Ivan IV the Terrible (1533–84), and Boris Godunov (1598–1605); civil revolt in the Time of Troubles (1598–1613)

   b. The Romanov Muscovy: election of Michael Romanov as tsar (1613) and continued autocracy under his successors, expansion into the Ukraine, 17th-century cultural and religious life

   c. The beginning of westernization and further expansion under Peter I the Great (1689–1725): the Petrine state

      i. The Table of Ranks and the new nobility: reform of the clerical hierarchy, urban legislation, building of St. Petersburg, conquest of the Baltic provinces

      ii. Development of Russia's status as a European power in Peter's reign: westernization of its culture

      iii. Peter I's weak successors: Anna (1730–40) and Elizabeth (1741–62)

   d. Further westernization and expansion under Catherine II the Great (1762–96): partitions of Poland and successful wars against the Ottoman Empire

   e. Education and social change in the 18th century: the impact of the Enlightenment

B. The Islāmic states of eastern Europe, Southwest Asia, and North Africa

1. The Ottoman Empire from 1481 to 1807, Morocco from 1459 to 1830

   a. The Ottoman Empire as the dominant power of Southwest Asia and southeastern Europe (1481–1566)

    i. Consolidation of the empire in the reign of Bayezid II (1481–1512), Selim I's (1512–20) successes against Iran and seizure of Syria and Egypt, Süleyman I's (1520–66) conflicts with the Habsburgs in Hungary and annexation of Iraq

    ii. Classical Ottoman society and administration: the class structure, the *mukata'a,* religious and civil law

  b. Decline of the Ottoman Empire (1566–1807): corruption and nepotism

    i. Foreign relations: conflicts with the Russians, Austrians, and Iranians

    ii. Attempts at reform in government administration; defeats by Poles, Habsburgs, and Russians

  c. Imperial disintegration in the 18th and early 19th centuries: westernization and rise of local rulers

  d. Morocco: disunity after the fall of the Marīnid dynasty, the anti-Portuguese policy of the Sa'dī of Marrakesh, increasing isolation under the 'Alawī dynasty (1659–1830)

2. Iran and Afghanistan

  a. Iran from *c.* 1500 to 1779

    i. The rise of the Shī'ite Ṣafavid dynasty: conflict with the Turks, possession of western Afghanistan, disintegration and later restoration of the state by 'Abbās I (1587–1629), relations with European powers, decline and foreign invasions in the later 17th century, the arts under the Ṣafavids

    ii. The expulsion (1730–32) of the Afghans, Russians, and Turks by Nāder Shah; invasions of India and Turkistan (1738–39); attempts to unite Shī'ite and Sunnī Muslims; establishment of Zand and Qājār dynasties

  b. Afghanistan from *c.* 1500 to 1812: national awakening and rise of Afghan power in the early 18th century, subjection by Nāder Shah (1732), establishment of the Durrānī dynasty (1747), intrusions in India and involvement in British affairs

---

Suggested reading in the *Encyclopædia Britannica:*

MACROPAEDIA: Major articles and biographies dealing with Eastern Europe, Southwest Asia, and North Africa from *c.* 1480 to *c.* 1800

Afghanistan	Cyprus	Jordan	Steppe, The
Africa	Czechoslovakia	Lebanon	History of the
Alexandria	Damascus	Leningrad	Eurasian
Arabia	Egypt	Moscow	Syria
Asia	Europe	North Africa	Turkey
Austria	Hungary	Palestine	Union of Soviet
Baghdad	Iran	Peter I the Great,	Socialist
Beirut	Iraq	of Russia	Republics
Budapest	Israel	Poland	Warsaw
Bulgaria	Istanbul	Prague	Yugoslavia
Cairo	Jerusalem	Romania	

MICROPAEDIA: Selected entries of reference information

General subjects

international:	Lepanto, Battle of	Three Kings,	nizam-ı cedid
Åbo, Treaty of	Livonian War	Battle of the	Ottoman Empire
Altranstädt,	Mohács, Battle of	Transylvania	pasha
treaties of	Northern War,	Vienna, Siege of	Phanariote
Andrusovo,	First	Zenta, Battle of	Rumelia
Truce of	Northern War,	*Ottoman Empire:*	Sublime Porte
Baltic states	Second	aga	vizier
Belgrade, Treaty of	Podolia	Aleppo	*Poland:*
Bereszteczko,	Poland,	'ayn	Bar,
Battle of	Partitions of	bey	Confederation of
Capitulation	Polish Succession,	derebey	Galicia
Çeşme, Battle of	War of the	dey	Henrician Articles
Chāldirān,	Russo-Turkish wars	Janissary	Warsaw,
Battle of	Silesia	Jelālī Revolts	Compact of
Deulino, Truce of	Stolbovo, Treaty of	kanun	

Section 963.   Europe from 1789 to c. 1920

      i. The War of the First Coalition (1792–97): French support for revolution in neighbouring lands and annexation of Nice, Savoy, Austrian Netherlands, the Rhineland, and the Batavian Republic; Napoleon's Italian Campaign; the Treaty of Campo Formio (1797)

      ii. The French expedition to Egypt and Syria (1798–1802): Continental campaigns of the Second Coalition (1798–1802), French occupation of Rome and Naples, Marengo and Hohenlinden, Peace of Lunéville (1801) and Treaty of Amiens (1802), Napoleon's reorganization of the German states and the formal end of the Holy Roman Empire (1806)

      iii. The Third Coalition (1805–07) and the battles of Trafalgar, Austerlitz, Jena, and Friedland: the subjugation of Prussia, Treaty of Tilsit (1807) and the peak of Napoleon's power, the Continental System and its failure

      iv. The Franco-Austrian War (1809), the Spanish uprising and the Peninsular War (1808–14), Napoleon's defeat in the Russian campaign (1812) and the campaign of the Fourth Coalition, downfall (1814) and exile of Napoleon

      v. The Hundred Days and Napoleon's final defeat at Waterloo (1815), the Congress of Vienna and Metternich's attempt to restore the old order in Europe

  d. Political, economic, and social effects of French occupation in Germany, Italy, Switzerland, and the Low Countries

  e. Great Britain from 1789 to 1815

      i. The influence of the French Revolution on the growth of English radicalism: governmental hostility to reform, Pitt's ministries and the war with France, Canning and Castlereagh, British gains in the peace settlements

      ii. Suppression of the Irish Rebellion of 1798 and union of Great Britain and Ireland (1801): Irish social, economic, and cultural life in the 17th and 18th centuries

  f. Russia in the reigns of Paul I (1796–1801) and Alexander I (1801–25): Russian participation in the Napoleonic Wars, the initial liberal reforms of Alexander I

  g. Prussia (1786–1815)

      i. Military decline following the death of Frederick II the Great: participation in the French Revolutionary Wars, defeat by Napoleon in 1806

      ii. The Stein reforms: Prussian leadership of Germany in the wars of liberation (1813–14), territorial acquisitions in the Vienna peace settlement (1815)

  h. Austria (1790–1815): the reigns of Leopold II (1790–92) and Francis II (1792–1806; as emperor of Austria, Francis I, 1804–35); participation in the coalitions against Napoleon, shift to compliance with him, and eventual intervention in the wars of liberation

  i. The smaller German states under French influence: the Confederation of the Rhine

  j. Spain and Portugal

      i. Spain in the reign of Charles IV (1788–1808), French occupation (1808) and British aid in the War of Independence (Peninsular War), restoration of the Bourbons

      ii. Portugal: alliance with Britain in the struggle against France

  k. Scandinavia from 1789 to 1815

      i. Denmark: defeat by the British (1801), alliance with France after 1807, the loss of Norway to Sweden (1814)

      ii. Sweden: Gustav IV and Charles XIII, the loss of Finland to Russia (1809), installation of Bernadotte as crown prince (1810), his anti-Napoleonic policy and the acquisition of Norway

  l. Italy during the French Revolution: support of revolutionary goals, French invasion and establishment of the republics, the French Consulate and the Napoleonic Empire

2. Pan-European developments in the first half of the 19th century: economic, intellectual, cultural, and social movements

  a. The Industrial Revolution

      i. British commercial, agricultural, and military growth: the factory system and advances in textile and machine technology, development of railroads

      ii. Conditions on the Continent and the spread of the factory system to Belgium, France, and Germany

    iii. The social consequences of the Industrial Revolution: division between capitalist and worker, wages and living and working conditions, new abundance of manufactured goods

b. The legacy of the French Revolution: cultural nationalism, populism, influence of Napoleon

c. The Romantic movement: individualism and concern for nature and "folk" in contrast with the Enlightenment

d. New facilities for scientific study in France and other Continental countries: effects of technological developments and scientific thought on society, principle of evolution

e. Philosophy: the role of Immanuel Kant and his disciples (Fichte, Hegel, and Schopenhauer), German Idealism

f. Religion and its alternatives: Catholic and Protestant revivals, Jewish emancipation, scientific positivism and the cult of art

g. The beginning of "scientific history" and modern philology

h. International war and diplomacy in the age of Metternich

    i. Congress of Europe: the Quadruple and Holy alliances for maintenance of the Vienna settlement, French intervention in Spain (1823), Austrian intervention in Italy (1821 and 1830), changes in the Congress system with the Revolution of 1830 in France and Belgium

    ii. General European unrest: the revolutions of 1848 and their suppression, Austrian intervention in Italy, Russian intervention in Hungary

i. Great Britain and Ireland (1815–50)

    i. Economic depression and social unrest following the Napoleonic Wars: repression by the government

    ii. Political and social reform measures (1822–48); *e.g.,* penal reforms, Catholic Emancipation (1828), First Reform Bill (1832), abolition of slavery in British colonies (1833), new Poor Law (1834), repeal of the Corn Laws (1846), Navigation Acts, the Chartist movement, the growth of trade unionism and the Factory Act (1847), Public Health Act (1848)

    iii. Developments in Ireland: the Great Famine of the 1840s, Roman Catholic unrest, O'Connell and the Young Ireland movement

j. France from 1814 to 1852

    i. The Restoration (1814, 1815–30): moderate constitutionalism under Louis XVIII, reaction and clericalism under Charles X

    ii. The Revolution of 1830, Louis-Philippe and the July monarchy, the preservation of the status quo under Guizot, growing dissatisfaction with the regime in the 1840s

    iii. The Revolution of 1848: Socialist thought and the establishment of the Second Republic, suppression of Socialist experiments, presidency of Louis-Napoléon

k. Germany from 1815 to *c.* 1850

    i. The German Confederation: Austrian domination under Metternich, the student national unity movement and its repression by the Carlsbad Decrees (1819), beginning of industrialization and the Zollverein

    ii. The revolutions of 1848–49: the Frankfurt National Assembly and its failure to unite Germany

    iii. Frederick William IV: restoration of the German Confederation, return to conservative policies, continued industrialization

l. The Austrian Empire from 1815 to 1850

    i. Development of national consciousness among the peoples of the empire: cultural revival among Magyars, Croats, Serbians, Poles, Romanians, Czechs, Slovaks, and Slovenes; German and Italian nationalism

    ii. Metternich's hostility to liberalism: Austria as a symbol of reaction in Italy

    iii. The revolutions of 1848 and 1849 in Vienna, Prague, and Budapest

m. The Italian states from 1815 to 1850

    i. The Vienna settlement: the Austrian Habsburgs in Lombardy–Venetia, the Bourbons in the Two Sicilies, Victor Emmanuel in Savoy, the Carbonari

    ii. Abortive revolutions in Naples and Piedmont (1820); economic slump and revival; rebellions in Modena, Parma, the Romagna, the Marches, and Umbria (1831)

    iii. The *Risorgimento:* Mazzini, Young Italy, and Young Europe; the early liberalism of Pope Pius IX

    iv. The revolutions of 1848: the first phase of the Italian War of Independence, defeat of Piedmont by Austria (1848–49)

n. Switzerland from 1815 to 1860: conservative constitution of 1815, the Sonderbund War (1847), the new federal state established (1848–60), policy of neutrality

o. Russia from 1815 to *c.* 1850: later conservatism of Alexander I, the Decembrist revolt (1825), Nicholas I's (1825–55) conservative policies

    i. Rule by bureaucracy, social classes, intellectual life, the empire and its various nationalities

    ii. Foreign policy: conflict with Poland, relations with Turkey

p. The Low Countries from 1814 to 1848: union of The Netherlands, Luxembourg, and Belgium (1814); Belgian Revolution (1830) and establishment as a separate monarchy under Leopold I (1831–65); constitutional reform (1848) in The Netherlands

q. Spain and Portugal from 1815 to 1850

    i. Spain under Ferdinand VII, revolution and abortive liberal government (1820–23), loss of South American empire (1820s), Isabella II and the succession dispute, First Carlist War (1833–39) and the "Spanish marriages" controversy

    ii. Portuguese loss of Brazil (1822), civil war between constitutionalists and absolutists (1832–34), British intervention (1826–34), Maria II (1834–53) and civil strife between Septembrists and Saldanha

r. Scandinavia from 1815 to 1850

    i. Denmark in the reigns of Frederick VI (1808–39) and Christian VIII (1839–48): beginning of economic problems, tendencies toward constitutional government culminating in the constitution of 1849, war over Schleswig-Holstein (1848–51)

    ii. Developments in Sweden–Norway: conservative era under Charles XIV John (1818–44), liberal reforms after 1840 and under Oscar I (1844–59), Norway's struggle to assert independence from Sweden

    iii. Finland and Iceland: Finnish political organization and Russian influence, the position of Iceland after the Treaty of Kiel (1814)

s. The Balkan states from *c.* 1804 to 1850

    i. Serbian uprising (1804–13) and the rise of the principality, restoration of Ottoman power in Serbia (1813–15), Serbian autonomy (1830) under Ottoman Empire, Miloš Obrenović recognized as prince of Serbia (1833–39) and government of Alexander Karageorge (1842–58)

    ii. Greek revolution (1821–30) and establishment of independence, internal strife under Otho I (1832–62), constitutional government introduced in 1843

B. Realism and materialism, nationalism, the reorganization of Europe, imperialist expansion (1850–*c.* 1920)

  1. European cultural and economic life from 1850 to 1920

    a. Philosophy and political and social thought: the prevalence of Determinism and Materialism

    b. Developments in the arts, philosophy, and religion

    c. Scientific theory and practice: Einsteinian relativity, the social effects of medical advances, development of the behavioral sciences, new views of the universe

    d. Economic life: the course of industrialization (1870–1914)

      i. Industrial proliferation: expansion into new areas such as the U.S., eastern Europe, and Japan

      ii. Changing balance of economic power in Europe: emergence of Germany as the leading industrial power, decline of British industrial strength

      iii. The revolution in transportation and communications: steam navigation and the beginning of air travel; the internal-combustion engine; the telegraph, telephone, and radio; industrialization on the eve of World War I

2. International war and diplomacy from 1850 to *c.* 1920: *Realpolitik* and European diplomatic realignments

   a. The era of Italian and German unification

      i. Final dissolution of the Congress of Vienna alliance system: the Crimean War (1853–56) and its aftermath

      ii. The Italian War of Independence: French intervention against Austria in Italy, the establishment of the Kingdom of Italy (1861)

      iii. Bismarck and the creation of the German Empire: victories over Denmark (1864), Austria (1866), and France (1870–71)

   b. The first period of German predominance

      i. Bismarck's system of alliances: the Dreikaiserbund and the isolation of France, the Russo-Turkish War (1877–78) and the Congress of Berlin (1878–79), the Triple Alliance (1882)

      ii. The Franco-Russian alliance (from 1893) and the Entente Cordiale (1904): Russia's defeat in the Far East (1904–05) and the formation of the Triple Entente (1907)

      iii. Prelude to World War I: the Moroccan and Bosnian crises, the Balkan Wars (1912–13), the outbreak of war between the great powers (1914)

   c. The resurgence of European imperialism (*c.* 1875–1914)

      i. Renewed interest in overseas expansion by the European powers in the late 19th century: new acquisitions and new colonial powers, development of new theories of imperialism

      ii. The European penetration of Asia and the partitioning of Africa: Russian expansion, economic penetration of China, rise of Japan, scramble for Africa

   d. World War I (1914–18) and the Treaty of Versailles (1919)

      i. The Serbian crisis and general mobilization: the opening German offensive in the east and west (August 1914), stabilization of the Western Front, trench warfare, new military technology (air power, tanks, and poison gas), the Battle of Verdun, renewed stalemate

      ii. The entrance of Italy, Turkey, Japan, and other nations into the war: campaigns in the Balkans and the Middle East

      iii. German submarine warfare and the U.S. entry into the war (1917); the Russian Revolution (1917), military collapse, and the Treaty of Brest-Litovsk (1918); the last Allied offensive and the armistice (1918)

      iv. Total war and the mobilization of whole populations; the dissolution of the Austro-Hungarian, Russian, and Ottoman empires

      v. The leadership, industrial strength, strategic plans and goals, and tactical and logistical procedures of the belligerents

      vi. The Paris Peace Conference (1919–20) and the peace treaty: Wilson's influence; German reparations, restrictions, and territorial losses; reorganization of central Europe and the Middle East by the Allies; the mandates and the League of Nations

3. The European states from 1850 to *c.* 1920

   a. Great Britain and Ireland and expansion of overseas empire (1850–1920)

      i. Mid-Victorian politics and economics: liberalism and free trade, the Great Exhibition (1851), Russell's and Palmerston's foreign policies regarding the Crimean War and the Indian Mutiny, Second Reform Bill (1867)

      ii. Mid-Victorian society and religion: Victorian social attitudes (duty, thrift, hard work, and character), liberalism and the High Church movement, revival of Scottish Calvinism

      iii. Gladstone's liberalism and "Tory Democracy" and imperialism under Disraeli; Third Reform Bill (1884); the Irish Question and the rise of Fenianism, Parnell, and the Home Rule movement; Chamberlain and the split in the Liberal Party; Fabian socialism and growth of the Labour movement; South African War (1899–1902)

      iv. The return of the Liberals (1905–14): Lloyd George's people's budget and National Insurance Act (1911), Parliament Act of 1911, continuing struggle over Ireland and Unionism in Ulster

     v. British participation in World War I: Lloyd George's Coalition government, the Easter Rising of 1916 in Ireland

b. France from 1852 to 1920: the Second Empire and the Third Republic

     i. Napoleon III's authoritarian policies and reassertion of France's role in Europe (the Crimea and Italy): partnership with Britain (1852–60), the liberal years (1859–70), foreign policy failures and defeat by Germany (1871)

     ii. The siege of Paris, the Commune, and the establishment of the Third Republic (1870); attempts at restoration; the "Republican Republic"; opportunist control under Gambetta; the Boulangists; colonial expansion; the Dreyfus affair; separation of church and state (1905)

     iii. The prewar years: conflicts between French rightists and Socialists, alignment with Russia and Britain before World War I, nationalism and revanchism

     iv. World War I (1914–18): German occupation of northeastern France, the crisis of 1917, the Clemenceau government, French human and material losses in the war

c. The unification of Germany and Prussia (1850–1920)

     i. William I and tentative reform: clashes with the liberals, Bismarck and reform of the Prussian Army, parliamentary subservience to the crown

     ii. Prussian and Austrian differences over the subjugation of Schleswig-Holstein (1864–66), the exclusion of Austria and the union of north and south Germany in the German Empire after the defeat of France (1871)

     iii. Bismarck as imperial chancellor (1871–90): *Kulturkampf* and the breach with the National Liberals, anti-Socialist measures and social legislation, Bismarck's consolidation of German power and formation of the Triple Alliance (1882)

     iv. The accession of Emperor William II (1888) and the fall of Bismarck; chancellorships of Caprivi, Hohenlohe, and Bülow (1890–1909); estrangement from Russia and rivalry with Britain; colonial expansion; militarists and Social Democrats in the period before World War I

     v. World War I (1914–18) and increasing influence of the army: German military defeat (1918), establishment of the German Republic (1919)

d. The Austrian and Austro-Hungarian Empire from 1850 to 1920

     i. Constitutional experiments: the Kremsier and Stadion constitutions; the "Bach System," the October Diploma (1860), and the February Patent (1861); federalism and centralism (1850–67); the role of Emperor Francis Joseph (1848–1916); exclusion from Italy (1859) and Germany (1866); the *Ausgleich* (Compromise) and the establishment of the Dual Monarchy (1867)

     ii. Austria: the liberal ascendancy under the Auersperg ministry (1871–78) and the coalition of clericals, German aristocrats, and Slavs under Taaffe (1879–93); relations between Austrians and Slavic minorities in the empire; the introduction of universal male suffrage (1907); foreign policy (1878–1908); annexation of Bosnia and Hercegovina and the crises in the Balkans

     iii. Hungary: the Andrássy government, internal conflict between the opponents and advocates of the Compromise of 1867, social reforms and economic progress, Magyar supremacy maintained under Tisza (1875–90)

     iv. Adherence to the Triple Alliance, increasing governmental paralysis and subordination to Germany during World War I, the dissolution of the Habsburg monarchy (1918) and the dismemberment of the empire

e. The Russian Empire from *c.* 1850 to 1917

     i. Defeat in the Crimean War (1853–56), abolition of serfdom (1861) and local government reforms under Alexander II (1855–81), Polish rebellion of 1863 and the spread of revolutionary sentiment, the assassination of the Tsar (1881)

     ii. Reversal of the reform movement under Alexander III (1881–94), the *zemstvos*, government hostility to non-Russian minorities, Nicholas II (1894–1917), anti-reform policies, foundation of the Social Democrats and Social Revolutionaries

     iii. Economic, cultural, and social developments: Russification policies, foreign policies

     iv. Disorders following defeat in the Russo-Japanese War (1904–05), the Dumas, World War I and the abolition of the monarchy (1917)

f. Italy from 1850 to 1920

i. Cavour and the unification of Italy under Victor Emmanuel of Piedmont: alliance with France and domestic liberalism, papal opposition, Austrian defeat and territorial cessions in northern Italy in the war of 1859, Garibaldi and the conquest of the south, the annexation of Venetia from Austria (1866) and acquisition of Rome (1870)

ii. The Kingdom of Italy: Minghetti, Depretis, and Crispi; Italian adherence to the Triple Alliance; growth of Socialism, labour movements, and militant nationalism; the Giolitti era; participation in World War I

g. Switzerland from 1850 to 1920: domestic policies, neutrality in World War I

h. Spain and Portugal

i. Continued civil strife in Spain: control by the military; Carlists, *moderados, progressistas,* and republicans; the First Republic (1873–74); constitutional monarchy in 1876; further colonial losses in the Spanish-American War (1898)

ii. The reaction against liberalism following Spain's defeat, Spanish involvement in Morocco, civil tensions and neutrality in World War I

iii. Alternating progressive and conservative governments in Portugal under Pedro V (1853–61) and Luís I (1861–89), dispute with Great Britain over colonial policies, financial difficulties, dictatorship in 1906, the Portuguese Republic (1910) and Portugal's adherence to the British alliance in World War I

i. Scandinavia from 1850 to 1920

i. Denmark: the Schleswig-Holstein question, defeat by Prussia and Austria (1864) and loss of the duchies, social and economic change under the Conservative regime

ii. Sweden–Norway: parliamentary reforms in Sweden under Charles XV (1859–72), foreign policy, attitudes in Sweden and in Norway toward the Swedish–Norwegian union

iii. Finland and Iceland: the language problem and political reforms in Finland, its relations with Russia, Iceland's demands for self-government

j. The Low Countries from 1848 to 1920

i. The Netherlands: liberalization after 1848, the establishment of the independence of Luxembourg (1890), Queen Wilhelmina and World War I

ii. Belgian Liberal government (1857–84), rise of Catholic and Belgian Workers' (Socialist) parties, the education controversy and Catholic party rule (1884–1914), universal male suffrage and child labour laws, Leopold II's establishment of Congo Free State (1885) and annexation as Belgian Congo (1908), Flemish resistance to the French-speaking elite

iii. World War I: Dutch neutrality and the German conquest of Belgium

k. The Balkan States from 1850 to 1920: power conflicts resulting in the Balkan Wars (1912–13) and World War I

i. Greece: the overthrow of Otho I (1862), the constitution of 1864, acquisition of the Ionian Islands (1864) and Thessaly (1881), Cretan union with Greece (1908), Venizélos' policies, eventual adherence to the Triple Entente in World War I

ii. Serbia: restoration of Miloš Obrenović in 1858, defeat by Turkey (1876), the Kingdom of Serbia (1882), the pro-Austrian policy of the Obrenović dynasty, restoration of the Karageorgević dynasty and pro-Russian orientation, conflict with Austria-Hungary, conquest by the Central Powers in World War I

iii. Bulgaria: "great Bulgaria" established by the Treaty of San Stefano (1878), Prince Alexander I and Russian influence (1879–86), Ferdinand I (1887–1918) and Stambolov's formation of a government, revolt of the Macedonian minority (1903), separation from Turkey (1908), adherence to the Central Powers in World War I

iv. Romania: union of Moldavia and Walachia under Alexandru Cuza (1861), Carol I (1866–1914; king after 1881), independence from Turkey (1878), alignment with the Triple Entente and conquest by the Central Powers in World War I

Suggested reading in the *Encyclopædia Britannica:*

MACROPAEDIA: Major articles and biographies dealing with Europe from 1789 to *c.* 1920

Albania	Austria	Berlin	Bulgaria
Amsterdam	Balkans	Bismarck	Cologne
Athens	Barcelona	Budapest	Czechoslovakia

Denmark
Dublin
Edinburgh
Europe
Finland
Florence
France
Geneva
Germany
Greece
Hamburg
Hungary
Iceland

International
  Relations,
  20th-Century
Ireland
Italy
Lisbon
London
Low
  Countries, The
Madrid
Malta
Manchester
Marseille

Mediterranean Sea
Milan
Moscow
Naples
Napoleon
Norway
Paris
Poland
Portugal
Prague
Romania
Rome
Spain

Sweden
Switzerland
Union of Soviet
  Socialist
  Republics
United Kingdom
Venice
Victoria and the
  Victorian Age
Vienna
Warsaw
Wellington
Yugoslavia

MICROPAEDIA: Selected entries of reference information

General subjects

culture:
  capitalism
  Classicism and
    Neoclassicism
  Industrial
    Revolution
  laissez-faire
  Marxism
  nationalism
  Romanticism
  Socialism
*international
  relations—French
  Revolutionary
  period and
  aftermath:*
    Aix-la-Chapelle,
      Congress of
    Amiens, Treaty of
    Batavian Republic
    Borodino, Battle of
    Campo Formio,
      Treaty of
    Çanak, Treaty of
    Dresden, Battle of
    Europe, Concert of
    Eylau, Battle of
    First of June,
      Battle of the
    Fleurus, Battle of
    French
      Revolutionary
      and Napoleonic
      wars
    Friedland, Battle of
    Holy Alliance
    Jassy, Treaty of
    Jena, Battle of
    Laibach,
      Congress of
    Leipzig, Battle of
    Lodi, Battle of
    Mantua, Siege of
    Marengo, Battle of
    Peninsular War

Pressburg,
  Treaty of
Pyramids, Battle
  of the
Quadruple
  Alliance (1813)
Schönbrunn,
  Treaty of
Tilsit, Treaties of
Toulon, Siege of
Trafalgar, Battle of
Troppau,
  Congress of
Ulm, Battle of
Verona,
  Congress of
Vienna,
  Congress of
Wagram, Battle of
Waterloo, Battle of
*international
  relations—
  nationalism and
  balance of powers:*
    Algeciras
      Conference
    Akkerman,
      Convention of
    Alma, Battle of the
    Balaklava,
      Battle of
    Balkan League
    Balkan Wars
    Berlin, Congress of
    Bosnian Crisis of
      1908
    Bulgarian Horrors
    Crimean War
    Dreikaiserbund
    Dual Alliance
    Eastern Question
    Edirne, Treaty of
    1830,
      Revolutions of
    1848,
      Revolutions of

Entente Cordiale
Europe, Concert of
Franco-German War
Greco-Turkish
  wars
Hague Convention
Italo-Turkish War
Königgrätz,
  Battle of
Moroccan crises
Neuchâtel crisis
Novara, Battle of
Pan-Slavism
Pig War
power, balance of
Quadruple
  Alliance (1834)
Règlement
  Organique
Reinsurance
  Treaty
Russo-Japanese War
Russo-Turkish
  wars
San Stefano,
  Treaty of
Schleswig-Holstein
  question
Sedan, Battle of
Serbo-Bulgarian War
Serbo-Turkish War
Sevastopol,
  Siege of
Solferino, Battle of
Straits Question
Triple Alliance
Villafranca,
  Conference of
Vlorë
  proclamation
*international
  relations—
  World War I and
  aftermath:*
    Allied Powers

Brest-Litovsk,
  treaties of
Constantinople
  Agreement
Corfu Declaration
Dardanelles
  Campaign
Fourteen Points
Isonzo, Battles
  of the
June Offensive
Jutland, Battle of
Lusitania
Marne, First Battle
  of the
Marne, Second
  Battle of the
Meuse-Argonne,
  battles of
Mudros,
  Armistice of
Paris Peace
  Conference
Saint-Jean-de-
  Maurienne,
  Agreement of
San Remo,
  Conference of
Somme, First
  Battle of the
Somme, Second
  Battle of the
Sykes-Picot
  Agreement
Verdun, Battle of
Versailles,
  Treaty of
World War I
*national affairs—
  Britain and Ireland:*
    Catholic
      Emancipation
    Chartism
    Clapham Sect
    Combination Acts
    Conservative Party
    Corn Laws

Don Pacifico
Affair
Easter Rising
Fabian Society
Fenian
Guild Socialism
Home Rule
Irish Rebellion
Labour Party
Land League
Liberal Party
London Dock
Strike
Luddite
Oxford Movement
Parliament Act of
1911
Peterloo Massacre
Phoenix Park
murders
pocket borough
Reform Bill
Taff Vale Case
test act
Tolpuddle Martyrs
Union, Act of
(Britain-Ireland)
United Irishmen,
Society of
national affairs—
France:
Action Française
Alsace-Lorraine
anticlericalism
assignat
Bastille
Batavian Republic
Bonapartist
Brumaire, Coup of
18–19
Chouan
Cisalpine Republic
Civil Constitution
of the Clergy
Continental
System
Corps Législatif
Directory
1801, Concordat of
émigré
Enragé
Entente Cordiale
Feuillants, Club
of the
Fourierism
French Revolution
Gauches,
Cartel des
Girondin
guillotine
Hébertist
Helvetic Republic
Hundred Days

Jacobin Club
July Revolution
Montagnard
Napoleonic Code
National Assembly
National
Convention
Orléanist
Paris,
Commune of
Peninsular War
Plain, The
Public Safety,
Committee of
Revolutionary
Tribunal
Rights of Man and
of the Citizen,
Declaration of the
Roman Republic
sansculotte
September
Massacres
Tennis Court Oath
Terror, Reign of
Thermidorian
Reaction
Vendée, Wars
of the
Ventôse Decrees
national affairs—
Germany and
Austria:
Agrarian League
Austria-Hungary
Burschenschaft
Carlsbad Decrees
Centre Party
Croato-Hungarian
Compromise of
1868
Deutschlandlied
1848,
Revolutions of
Ems telegram
Erfurt Union
Parliament
Frankfurt National
Assembly
Freikorps
German
Confederation
Heimwehr
Junker
Kulturkampf
March laws
Olmütz,
Punctation of
Pan-Germanism
Prussia
Rhine,
Confederation
of the

Schleswig-Holstein
question
Seven Weeks' War
Social Democratic
Party of Germany
Spartacus League
Zollverein
national affairs—
Italy:
Carbonaro
Cisalpine Republic
Cispadine
Republic
Custoza, Battles of
fascio siciliano
Fiume question
Guarantees,
Law of
Irredentist
Italo-Turkish War
Ligurian Republic
Parthenopean
Republic
Popolare
Risorgimento
Roman Republic
Solferino, Battle of
Statuto Albertino
Thousand,
Expedition of the
Villafranca,
Conference of
Young Italy
national affairs—
Poland:
Congress Kingdom
of Poland
Cracow,
Republic of
January
Insurrection
liberum veto
November
Insurrection
Poland,
Partitions of
Warsaw, Duchy of
national affairs—
Russia:
Black Hundreds
Bloody Sunday
Bolshevik
Brest-Litovsk,
treaties of
Bund
Communist Party
of the Soviet
Union
Decembrist
Duma
Emancipation
Manifesto
intelligentsia

January
Insurrection
Kadet
Labour,
Liberation of
Leninism
Liberation,
Union of
Menshevik
mir
Narodnik
November
Insurrection
October Manifesto
Octobrist
Orthodoxy,
Autocracy, and
Nationality
Pan-Slavism
Progressive Bloc
Russian Civil War
Russian
Revolution of
1905
Russian
Revolution of
1917
Russian
Social-Democratic
Workers' Party
Russo-JapaneseWar
Russo-Polish War
Russo-Turkish
wars
Russification
Slavophile
Socialist
Revolutionary
Party
Stolypin land
reform
Third Department
Zemlya i Volya
zemstvo
national affairs—
Scandinavia:
Bodø Affair
Eider Program
Fennoman
movement
Kiel, Treaty of
Pan-Scandinavianism
Riksdag
national affairs—
Spain and Portugal:
Carlism
Oranges, War
of the
Peninsular War
Pragmatic
Sanction of King
Ferdinand VII
Spanish–
American War

Spanish Marriages,
Affair of the
Verona, Congress of
*national affairs—
other:*
Flemish Movement
Greek
Independence,
War of
Guarantees, Law of

Moldavia
Sonderbund
Wallachia
*overseas empires and
commerce:*
Algeciras
Conference
Berlin, Congress of
Bowring Treaty
British East Africa

British Empire
British South
Africa Company
British West Africa
Clayton-Bulwer
Treaty
East India
Company
Fashoda Incident

French Equatorial
Africa
French Morocco
French West Africa
German East Africa
German South West
Africa
influence, sphere of
Open Door policy
protectorate

Biographies

*Austrian Empire and
Austria-Hungary:*
Andrássy, Gyula,
Gróf
Berchtold,
Leopold,
Graf von
Beust, Friedrich
Ferdinand,
Graf von
Beneš, Edvard
Charles, Archduke
Cobenzl, Ludwig,
Graf von
Conrad von
Hötzendorf,
Franz, Graf
Deák, Ferenc
Francis II
(Germany/Holy
Roman Empire)
Francis Ferdinand,
Archduke of
Austria-Este
Francis Joseph
Gentz, Friedrich
Habsburg,
House of
Károlyi, Mihály,
Gróf
Kaunitz, Wenzel
Anton von
Kossuth, Lajos
Kun, Béla
Leopold II
(Germany/Holy
Roman Empire)
Mazaryk, Tomáš
Metternich,
Klemens,
Fürst von
Radetzky, Joseph,
Graf
Rudolf, Archduke
and Crown
Prince of Austria
Schwarzenberg,
Felix, Fürst zu
Schwarzenberg,
Karl Philipp,
Fürst zu

Stadion, Johann
Philipp, Graf von
Balkans:
Carol I
Dhiliyiánnis,
Theódoros
Ferdinand I
(Bulgaria)
Ferdinand I
(Romania)
Garašanin, Ilija
Kapodístrias,
Ioánnis Antónios,
Komis
Karageorge
Mavrokordátos,
Aléxandros
Milan IV (or II)
Miloš
Nicholas I
(Montenegro)
Otto (Greece)
Pašić, Nikola
Peter I
(Montenegro)
Peter I (Serbia)
Stamboliyski,
Aleksandŭr
Venizélos,
Eleuthérios
Britain and Ireland:
Aberdeen, George
Hamilton-Gordon,
4th earl of
Albert, Prince
Consort of Great
Britain and
Ireland
Asquith, H.H.
Balfour, Arthur
James Balfour,
1st earl of
Bentinck, Lord
William
Bright, John
Brougham and
Vaux, Henry
Peter Brougham,
1st Baron
Campbell-Bannerman,
Sir Henry

Canning, Charles
John Canning,
Earl
Canning, George
Cardigan,
James Thomas
Brudenell, 7th
earl of
Carson, Edward
Henry Carson,
Baron
Casement, Sir
Roger
Castlereagh,
Robert Stewart,
Viscount
Chamberlain,
Joseph
Churchill, Lord
Randolph Henry
Spencer
Churchill, Sir
Winston
Clare, John
Fitzgibbon, 1st
earl of
Cobbett, William
Cobden, Richard
Cockburn, Sir
Alexander James
Edmund
Collingwood,
Cuthbert
Collingwood, 1st
Baron
Collins, Michael
Cornwallis, Charles
Cornwallis, 1st
Marquess and
2nd Earl
Cromer, Evelyn
Baring, 1st earl of
Curzon, George
Nathaniel
Curzon,
Marquess
Dalhousie,
James Andrew
Broun Ramsay,
marquess and
10th earl of

Derby, Edward
Stanley, 14th
earl of
Devonshire,
Spencer Compton
Cavendish, 8th
duke of
Dillon, John
Disraeli, Benjamin
Dundonald,
Thomas
Cochrane, 10th
earl of
Edward VII
Fisher, John
Arbuthnot Fisher,
1st Baron
Forster, William
Edward
Fox, Charles James
French, John
George III
George IV
George V
Gladstone,
William Ewart
Goldie, Sir George
Grenville, William
Wyndham
Grenville, Baron
Grey, Charles
Grey, 2nd Earl
Grey, Sir Edward
Griffith, Arthur
Haig, Douglas
Haig, 1st Earl
Haldane, Richard
Burdon
Hardie, J. Keir
Howe, Richard
Howe, Earl
Hyndman, Henry
Mayers
Jellicoe, John
Rushworth
Jellicoe, 1st Earl
Kitchener, Herbert
Lansdowne, Henry
Charles Keith
Petty-Fitzmaurice,
5th marquess of

Frederick
William II
Frederick
William III
Frederick
William IV
Gneisenau,
August, Graf
Neidhardt von
Hardenberg, Karl
August, Fürst von
Hindenburg,
Paul von
Hohenlohe-
Schillingsfürst,
Chlodwig Karl
Viktor, Fürst zu
Hohenzollern
dynasty
Holstein,
Friedrich von
Kiderlen-Wächter,
Alfred von
Louis I (Bavaria)
Louis II (Bavaria)
Ludendorff, Erich
Marx, Karl
Maximilian I
(Bavaria)
Maximilian II
(Bavaria)
Moltke,
Helmuth von
Radowitz, Joseph
Maria von
Roon, Albrecht
Theodor Emil,
Graf von
Scharnhorst,
Gerhard Johann
David von
Schlieffen, Alfred,
Graf von
Stein, Karl,
Reichsfreiherr
vom und zum
Tirpitz, Alfred von
William I (German
Empire)
William II
(German Empire)

Italy:
Bandiera, Attilio
and Emilio
Bonaparte, Joseph
Bourbon, House of
Cavour, Camillo
Benso, conte di
Charles Albert
Charles Felix
Consalvi, Ercole

Crispi, Francesco
D'Annunzio,
Gabriele
Depretis, Agostino
Farini, Luigi Carlo
Ferdinand I
(Naples)
Ferdinand II
(Naples)
Francis I (Naples)
Francis II (Naples)
Garibaldi,
Giuseppe
Gioberti, Vincenzo
Giolitti, Giovanni
Mazzini, Giuseppe
Murat, Joachim
Orlando, Vittorio
Emanuele
Pelloux, Luigi
Savoy, House of
Umberto I
Victor
Emmanuel I
Victor
Emmanuel II
Victor
Emmanuel III
Visconti-Venosta,
Emilio, Marchese

Low Countries:
Albert (Belgium)
Bonaparte, Louis
Leopold I
(Belgium)
Leopold II
(Belgium)
William I
(Netherlands:
king)
William II
(Netherlands:
king)
William III
(Netherlands:
king)

Portugal:
Beresford, William
Carr Beresford,
Viscount
Charles
John VI
Maria I
Maria II
Michael
Pedro I (Brazil)

Russia:
Alexander I
Alexander II
Alexander III
Alexandra

Arakcheyev,
Aleksey
Andreyevich,
Graf
Bennigsen, Leonty
Leontyevich,
Graf von
Catherine II
Chernyayev,
Mikhayl
Grigoryevich
Gorchakov,
Mikhail
Dmitriyevich,
Knyaz
Guchkov,
Aleksandr
Ivanovich
Ignatyev, Nikolay
Pavlovich, Graf
Kerensky,
Aleksandr
Fyodorovich
Kornilov, Lavr
Georgiyevich
Kutuzov, Mikhail
Illarionovich,
Knyaz
Lenin, Vladimir
Ilich
Lobanov-Rostovsky,
Aleksey
Borisovich,
Knyaz
Lvov, Georgy
Yevgenyevich,
Knyaz
Milyukov, Pavel
Nikolayevich
Milyutin, Dmitry
Alekseyevich,
Graf
Nesselrode, Karl
Vasilyevich, Graf
Nicholas I
Nicholas II
Orlov, Aleksey
Fyodorovich,
Knyaz
Paskevich, Ivan
Fyodorovich
Paul
Pobedonostsev,
Konstantin
Petrovich
Pozzo di Borgo,
Charles-André,
comte
Rasputin, Grigory
Yefimovich

Rostopchin,
Fyodor
Vasilyevich, Graf
Savinkov, Boris
Viktorovich
Shāmil
Skobelev, Mikhail
Dmitriyevich
Speransky, Mikhail
Mikhaylovich,
Graf
Stolypin, Pyotr
Arkadyevich
Witte, Sergey
Yulyevich, Graf

Scandinavia:
Branting, Karl
Hjalmar
Charles XIII
(Sweden)
Charles XV
(Sweden)
Christian VIII
Christian IX
Christian X
Frederick VI
(Denmark)
Frederick VII
(Denmark)
Frederick VIII
(Denmark)
Gustav IV Adolf
Gustav V
Haakon VII
Oscar I
Oscar II

Spain:
Alfonso XII
Alfonso XIII
Bonaparte, Joseph
Cánovas del
Castillo, Antonio
Carlos Luís de
Borbón
Carlos María de
los Dolores de
Borbón
Carlos María
Isidro de Borbón
Castelar y Ripoll,
Emilio
Charles IV
Ferdinand VII
Godoy, Manuel de
Isabella II
María Cristina I
María Cristina II
Serrano y
Domínguez,
Francisco

INDEX: See entries under all of the terms above

Section 964.   European Colonies in the Americas from 1492 to *c.* 1790

A. The geography and ethnography of the Americas

B. Spanish and Portuguese colonies in the Americas, other European powers in South America and the Caribbean to *c.* 1790

1. Spanish discovery, exploration, and conquest of the Caribbean islands, Mexico, Central America, Peru, Venezuela, Colombia, and Río de la Plata (1492–*c.* 1550)

2. Spain's colonial empire

a. Colonial administration: the Council of the Indies, viceroys and other provincial officials, *audiencias,* legal restrictions on public officials

b. Indian policy: slavery and peonage under the *encomienda* and *repartimiento,* the missionary role of the Roman Catholic Church, decline of the Indian population, introduction of black slaves

c. Colonial economy: expansion of agriculture; gold and silver mining; cattle industry; mercantilism, smuggling, and piracy

3. The exploration and colonization of Brazil by the Portuguese (from 1500)

a. Colonial economic policies: introduction of black slavery, gold and diamond mining, agricultural and commercial development

b. Colonial administration: establishment of captaincies (1533), centralized royal control (1549), role of the Roman Catholic Church, the Brazilian racial mixture

4. Administrative reforms of the Spanish Bourbon kings (1700–88): decentralization of the governments of Peru, Venezuela, and Chile; encouragement of trade and agriculture

5. Spanish colonial expansion into North America (*c.* 1600–1790): settlements and religious missions

6. English, French, and Dutch territorial and economic expansion (from *c.* 1600) into areas of Spanish and Portuguese colonization in Latin America and the Caribbean

C. Norse, English, Dutch, and Swedish discoveries, explorations, and settlements in North America (*c.* 1000–1763)

1. Norse voyages to Greenland and North America (*c.* 1000)

2. Early English exploration and attempted settlement (1497–*c.* 1600), Dutch and Swedish settlement and later expulsion by the English

3. Development of the English colonies in North America

a. The founding of the 13 Colonies: economic, political, and religious reasons for settlement

b. Economic, political, and social development

i. British economic policies: mercantilism and the Navigation Acts

ii. Colonial administration: loose royal control prior to 1763, self-government and local political activity

iii. Social mobility and the rise of economic classes: immigration and the introduction of slavery, agricultural and commercial development

c. Colonial cultural and scientific achievements; *e.g.,* the American Philosophical Society, newspapers and almanacs, the beginning of public education, the "Great Awakening"

d. Conflicts with the French and Indians and expulsion of French power from North America (1763)

D. French discoveries, explorations, and settlements in North America: New France and Louisiana (1524–1763)

1. The settlement of New France: missionaries, Indian relations, and the fur trade; royal administration and joint-stock companies

2. Expansion and eventual conflict with the English, resulting in the eclipse of French power in North America (1763)

Suggested reading in the *Encyclopædia Britannica*:

MACROPAEDIA: Major articles and a biography dealing with European colonies in the Americas from 1492 to *c.* 1790

Boston	New Orleans
Canada	New York City
Columbus	North America
Latin America, The History of	Philadelphia
Montreal	South America

MICROPAEDIA: Selected entries of reference information

General subjects

English and French colonization of North America:
Acadia
Albany Congress
Culpeper's Rebellion
French and Indian War
French Shore
Hat Act
Hudson's Bay Company
Iron Act
Iroquois League
Jamestown
King George's War
King Philip's War
King William's War
London Company
Lost Colony
Massachusetts Bay Colony
Mayflower
Mayflower Compact
Molasses Act

Monongahela, Battle of the
New England, Council for
New England Confederation
New France
New Hampshire Grants
Nootka Sound controversy
Nova Scotia, baronetage of
Paxton Boys Uprising
Pilgrim Fathers
Plymouth Company
Powhatan War
proprietary colony
Quebec, Battle of
Queen Anne's War
Salem witch trials
1763, Proclamation of
Sovereign Council

Sugar Act
Walking Purchase
Yamasee War
Spanish and Portuguese colonization of the Americas:
alcalde
asiento de negros
audiencia
bandeira
cabildo
caciquismo
Cibola, Seven Golden Cities of
conquistador
Contratación, Casa de
corregidor
donatário
Eldorado
encomienda
fazenda
Indies, Laws of the
mameluco
New Granada, Viceroyalty of

New Spain, Viceroyalty of
Palmares, Republic of
peninsular
Peru, Viceroyalty of
Plata, Viceroyalty of la
Pueblo Rebellion
Real Cuerpo de Minería
reducción
repartimiento
residencia
Santo Domingo
Spanish treasure fleet
Strangford Treaty
other:
Middle Passage
New Sweden
Vinland

Biographies

English explorers and colonizers:
Cabot, John
Cabot, Sebastian
Cook, James
Hudson, Henry
Johnson, Sir William, 1st Baronet
Mather, Cotton
Mather, Increase
Penn, William
Pocahontas
Smith, John
Stirling, William Alexander, 1st earl of

Williams, Roger
Winthrop, John
French explorers and colonizers:
Bienville, Jean-Baptiste Le Moyne, sieur de
Cartier, Jacques
Champlain, Samuel de
Frontenac, Louis de Buade, comte de Palluau et de
La Salle, René-Robert Cavalier, sieur de

La Vérendrye, Pierre Gaultier de Varennes, sieur de
Laval, François de Montmorency
Spanish and Portuguese explorers and colonizers:
Balboa, Vasco Núñez de
Cabral, Pedro Álvares
Columbus, Christopher
Coronado, Francisco Vázquez de

Díaz de Solís, Juan
Las Casas, Bartolomé de
Narváez, Panfilo de
Soto, Hernando de
Velázquez, Diego
Vespucci, Amerigo
other:
Bering, Vitus
Chirikov, Aleksey Ilich
John Maurice of Nassau

INDEX: See entries under all of the terms above

Section 965.   **Development of the United States and Canada from 1763 to 1920**

A. The United States to 1865: national formation and territorial expansion, conflict between North and South

1. Establishment and consolidation of the United States (1763–1816)

  a. The American Revolutionary period (1763–87)

    i. Political and economic opposition to Britain's taxation policies culminating in the Declaration of Independence (1776)

    ii. The U.S. War of Independence (1775–83): land and sea campaigns, military leadership, French military support, peace treaty (1783)

    iii. The government of the Articles of Confederation (1781–87) and evolution of a western lands policy

  b. The strengthening of the national government (1787–1816)

    i. The Constitutional Convention, the federal Constitution, and the struggle for ratification (1787–89)

    ii. Development of national policies and formation of political parties: Hamilton's economic policies, foreign relations during the administrations of Washington and John Adams, Federalists and Democratic-Republicans

    iii. Jefferson's administration and the Louisiana Purchase (1803), Madison's administration and the War of 1812, role of the Supreme Court

2. The United States from 1816 to 1850: nationalism, expansionism, extension of the franchise, and industrialization

  a. Strengthening of national feelings: administrations of Monroe and John Quincy Adams, Supreme Court under Marshall

    i. "The Era of Good Feelings" (1816–24): nationalism and sectionalism, the Missouri Compromise (1820)

    ii. Developments in commerce and finance: industrialization and early labour movements, transportation and internal improvements, cotton and slavery

    iii. Social development: German and Irish immigration (1830–50), urbanization and social mobility

  b. Jacksonian democracy (1829–41): extension of the franchise; development of Democratic, Whig, and minor party politics; bank war; nullification; Indian removal policy

  c. The "Age of Reform" (1830–50): the Abolitionist movement and other reform activities, diverse religious attitudes

  d. Westward expansionism: annexation of Texas, acquisition of Oregon, the Mexican War (1846–48) and the annexation of California and New Mexico, the Compromise of 1850

  e. Cultural development to 1850: the growth of the novel, poetry, music, the visual arts, historical writings, the Transcendentalist movement

3. The United States from 1850 to 1865: sectionalism, secession, and Civil War

  a. Sectionalism and slavery: economic and psychological bases of slavery, the failure of popular sovereignty, the Abolitionist movement, literature of the period

  b. Political and geographical polarization: disruption of the Democratic and Whig parties, emergence of the Republican Party, and Lincoln's election (1860)

  c. Secession of the Southern states and the Civil War (1861–65)

    i. Relative military strengths: strategies and tactics of North and South

    ii. The land and sea war (1861–65): initial Confederate victories, Union success in the West and final victory over the South

    iii. Foreign affairs of the Union and the Confederacy, moves toward emancipation during the war

B. The United States from 1865 to 1920: Reconstruction, industrialization, increased immigration, development of the West, and emergence as a world power

1. Radical Reconstruction (1866–77) and the New South (1877–1900)

a. Lincoln's plan for Reconstruction and congressional opposition (1864–65), conflicts between the Radical Republican-controlled Congress and Andrew Johnson, state "Black Codes" and federal civil rights legislation

b. Reconstruction (1866–77): freedmen, sharecropping, and "Black Reconstruction"; Grant's administrations and the decline of Republican control in the South

c. The New South (1877–1900): conservative Democrats in control and erosion of black rights, Populist resurgence in the 1890s, white supremacy and Jim Crow legislation, the black response

2. The transformation of American society: the United States from 1865 to 1900

    a. Urbanization and immigration: southern and eastern European immigrants and growth of slums, problems of prejudice, rise of city machine politics, development of public education

    b. The development of the West (1865–1900)

        i. The quest for gold and silver: boom and bust in mining towns

        ii. Cattlemen and the open range: the cattle industry (1866–88), the cowboy and cattle drives, conflicts with settlers

        iii. Westward expansion of the railroads: early government subsidies, relationship of the transcontinental carriers to the national economy

        iv. Violation of the Indian treaties: settlers' encroachments on Indian lands, Indian wars, corruption among agents of the Bureau of Indian Affairs

    c. The industrialization of the American economy: the manufacturing boom

        i. Technological advances in the iron and steel industry; exploitation of oil, ores, lumber, and other natural resources

        ii. Development of trusts and holding companies: development of a legal climate favourable to big business

    d. U.S. foreign trade and commerce: growth of exports and imports

    e. Emergence of national labour union organizations: strikes and boycotts, collective bargaining, antilabour stance of government, the Haymarket Riot (1886)

    f. National politics (1877–1900): general ascendancy of Congress and decline of the presidency

        i. Aftermath of the disputed election of 1876: the Compromise of 1877, the end of Southern Reconstruction, and Hayes's administration (1877–81); inflation and the silver issue

        ii. The election of 1880 and the presidency of Garfield: Garfield's assassination (1881), Arthur's administration (1881–85), establishment of the Civil Service Commission (1883)

        iii. The election of 1884 and Cleveland's first administration (1885–89): the reemergence of presidential leadership, the Treasury surplus and tariff issues, the Interstate Commerce Act (1887) and federal regulation of railroads

        iv. The election of 1888 and Benjamin Harrison's administration (1889–93): congressional leadership, the Sherman Anti-Trust and Sherman Silver Purchase acts, and the McKinley Tariff Act (1890)

        v. Depressed agricultural conditions (1887–97): the Farmers' Alliances and the establishment of the Populist Party (1891), farmers' defection from Republican Party

        vi. The election of 1892 and Cleveland's second administration (1893–97): gold reserves and the Panic of 1893, repeal of the Sherman Silver Purchase Act (1893), lowering of the tariff

        vii. The election of 1896 and McKinley's administration (1897–1901): the raising of the tariff (1897) and the Gold Standard Act (1900), gradual economic recovery

3. Imperialism, the Progressive Era, and the rise to world power (1896–1920)

    a. The emergence of the U.S. as an imperial power

        i. The Spanish–American War and U.S. suzerainty over Cuba; acquisition of the Philippines, the Hawaiian Islands, and Puerto Rico (1898)

        ii. The "Open Door" policy and armed intervention in China (1900)

        iii. Acquisition of the Panama Canal Zone (1903) and the Roosevelt Corollary to the Monroe Doctrine: intervention in Haiti, the Dominican Republic, Cuba, and Nicaragua

b. The Progressive Movement (*c.* 1896–1920)

    i. Scholars, social workers, and "muckrakers" as leaders of the Progressive Movement; social and political urban reforms by state government

    ii. Theodore Roosevelt's administrations (1901–09) and expansion of presidential power and regulatory legislation, Taft's administration (1909–13) and the defection of Progressive Republicans in the 1912 election

    iii. Wilson's first administration (1913–17): tariff, currency, credit, tax, and labour reforms; intervention in Mexican affairs

c. The role of the U.S. in World War I

    i. Initial U.S. neutrality: loans and supplies to the Allies, submarine warfare and the break with Germany

    ii. U.S. entry into the war: mobilization of manpower and the economy, decisive effect of U.S. military forces on the Western Front (1918)

    iii. Wilson's policies at the Paris Peace Conference (1919) and the U.S. Senate rejection of the Treaty of Versailles (1920), the election of 1920 and the return to isolationism

4. Cultural developments from 1865 to 1920

    a. Advances in fiction, poetry, drama, music, and the visual arts

    b. Developments in education and historical writings, growth of American philosophy

C. Canada under British colonial rule from 1763 to 1867, the Dominion of Canada from 1867 to 1920

1. British colonial administration: the Quebec Acts of 1763 and 1774, immigration of United Empire Loyalists after U.S. War of Independence, establishment of French- and English-speaking provinces

2. Social, political, and economic development from 1790 to 1850

    a. Immigration, westward expansion, and the fur trade; participation in the War of 1812

    b. Dissension between French and English settlers: the rebellions of 1837, the Union of Upper and Lower Canada (1841), self-government for domestic affairs (1848)

3. The Dominion of Canada from 1867 to 1920

    a. The Confederation movement and the establishment of the Dominion (1867)

    b. Westward expansion and internal disunity

        i. Louis Riel and the first Métis-Indian rebellion (1870), establishment of the provinces of Manitoba and British Columbia

        ii. The transcontinental railroad, suppression of the second Métis-Indian rebellion (1885), economic depression and downfall of the Conservative government (1896)

    c. Liberal governments under Laurier and economic prosperity (1896–1911)

        i. The Klondike gold rush (1897) and the settlement of the Northwest Territories, creation of the provinces of Alberta and Saskatchewan (1905)

        ii. Involvement in Britain's imperialist policies: participation in South African War (1899), border disputes with the United States

    d. Economic nationalism and the Conservative government (1911–17): participation in World War I, recognition of Canadian autonomy (1917)

Suggested reading in the *Encyclopædia Britannica:*

MICROPAEDIA: Selected entries of reference information

General subjects

Canada:

Aroostook War
Assiniboia
Bering Sea Dispute
British North
America Act
Canada Company
Canada East
Canada West
Canadian Pacific
Railway
Carnarvon Terms
Charlottetown
Conference
Clear Grits
Clergy Reserves
Hunters' Lodges
Jesuit Estates
controversy
Liberal Party of
Canada
Métis
North West
Company
Pacific Scandal
Parti Rouge
Progressive
Conservative
Party of Canada
Quebec, Battle of
Quebec Act
Red River
Settlement
Reform Party
Rush–Bagot
Agreement
Seven Oaks
Massacre

United States—
Revolutionary
period:

Bennington,
Battle of
Bonhomme
Richard
and Serapis,
engagement
between
Boston, Siege of
Boston Tea Party
Brandywine, Battle
of the
Bunker Hill,
Battle of
Camden, Battle of
Carlisle
Commission
Cherokee wars and
treaties

Cherry Valley
Raid
Continental
Congress
Correspondence,
Committees of
Cowpens, Battle of
Declaratory Act
Democratic Party
Embargo Act
Essex Junto
Fallen Timbers,
Battle of
Federalist, The
Federalist Party
Franco-American
Alliance
Germantown,
Battle of
Gnadenhütten
Massacre
Green Mountain
Boys
Guilford Court
House, Battle of
Independence,
Declaration of
Intolerable Acts
Kings Mountain,
Battle of
Lexington and
Concord,
Battles of
Long Island,
Battle of
Loyalist
minuteman
Monmouth Court
House, Battle of
Moore's Creek
Bridge, Battle of
Nonimportation
Agreements
Oriskany, Battle of
Pinckney's Treaty
Purple Heart
Quartering Act
Quebec, Battle of
Regulators of
North Carolina
Republican Party
Saintes, Battle
of the
Saratoga,
Battles of
Stamp Act
Stars and Stripes
Suffolk Resolves
Tea Act

Townshend Acts
Trenton and
Princeton,
battles of
Tripolitan War
United States War
of Independence
Valley Forge
Virginia Capes,
Battle of
Virginia
Declaration of
Rights
White Plains,
Battle of
Wyoming
Massacre
XYZ Affair
Yorktown,
Siege of

United States—early
years:

Alien and Sedition
Acts
American Fur
Company
Annapolis
Convention
Anti-Federalists
Châteauguay,
Battle of
Chippewa,
Battle of
Confederation,
Articles of
Constitution of the
United States
Constitutional
Convention, U.S.
Creek War
Democratic Party
1812, War of
Embargo Act
Essex Decision
Fallen Timbers,
Battle of
Federalist, The
Federalist Party
Fries's Rebellion
Ghent, Treaty of
Hartford
Convention
Jay Treaty
Lake Erie,
Battle of
Lewis and Clark
Expedition
Locofoco Party
Louisiana Party

Lundy's Lane,
Battle of
Marbury v.
Madison
Monroe Doctrine
National
Republican Party
New Orleans,
Battle of
Northwest
Ordinances
Northwest
Territory
nullification
Pinckney's Treaty
Republican Party
Rights, Bill of
Saint Clair's Defeat
Shay's Rebellion
Star-Spangled
Banner, The
Thames, Battle
of the
Tippecanoe,
Battle of
Uncle Sam
Virginia and
Kentucky
Resolutions
War Hawk
West Florida
Controversy
Western Reserve
Whig Party
Whiskey
Rebellion
Workingmen's
Party

United States—
nationalism and
westward
expansion:

Alamo
Alaska Purchase
American frontier
Bear Flag Revolt
Buena Vista,
Battle of
Cerro Gordo,
Battle of
Chisholm Trail
Clayton–Bulwer
Treaty
Comstock Lode
Contreras,
Battle of
cowboy
Gadsden
Purchase

Bank War
Bering Sea
 Dispute
Black Friday
Brook Farm
Brownsville Affair
Chicago Race
 Riot of 1919

Crédit Mobilier
 Scandal
Dawes General
 Allotment Act
East Saint Louis
 Race Riot
 of 1917

Niagara
 Movement
Nonpartisan
 League
Prohibition Party
Resumption Act
 of 1875
slave rebellions

Stalwart
Talented Tenth
Tammany Hall
Universal Negro
 Improvement
 Association
Wounded Knee

Biographies

American Indian
 leaders:
 Brant, Joseph
 Cochise
 Crazy Horse
 Dull Knife
 Geronimo
 Joseph, Chief
 McGillivry,
  Alexander
 Pontiac
 Red Jacket
 Sitting Bull
 Tecumseh
 Washakie
Canadians:
 Baldwin, Robert
 Borden, Sir Robert
 Brown, George
 Durham, John
  George Lambton,
  1st earl of
 Galt, Sir
  Alexander
  Tilloch
 Lansdowne, Henry
  Charles Keith
  Petty-Fitzmaurice,
  5th marquess of
 Laurier, Sir
  Wilfrid
 Macdonald, Sir
  John
 Mackenzie,
  William Lyon
 Papineau, Louis
  Joseph
 Riel, Louis
U.S. Abolitionists:
 Brown, John
 Delany, Martin R.
 Douglass,
  Frederick
 Garrison, William
  Lloyd
 Julian, George W.
 Tappan, Arthur
U.S. diplomats:
 Blaine, James
 Harris, Townsend
 House, Edward M.
 Page, Walter
  Hines

Randolph, John
U.S. explorers and
 frontiersmen:
 Boone, Daniel
 Carson,
  Christopher
 Clark, George
  Rogers
 Cody, William F.
 Crockett, Davy
 Frémont, John C.
 Peary, Robert
  Edwin
 Whitman, Marcus
U.S. industrialists:
 Hanna, Mark
 Hewitt, Abram
 Martin, Luther
 Rockefeller,
  John D.
 Vanderbilt family
 See also Section
  732 of Part Seven
U.S. military
 leaders—Civil War:
 Beauregard, Pierre
  Gustave Toutant
 Breckinridge,
  John C.
 Butler,
  Benjamin F.
 Early, Jubal A.
 Farragut, David
 Forrest, Nathan
  Bedford
 Grant, Ulysses S.
 Jackson, Thomas
  Jonathan
 Johnston,
  Joseph E.
 Lee, Robert E.
 McClellan,
  George B.
 Meade, George G.
 Morgan, John
  Hunt
 Mosley, John
  Singleton
 Pinchback,
  Pinckney Brenton
  Stewart
 Pope, John
 Schurz, Carl

Sheridan, Philip H.
Sherman, William
 Tecumseh
Sickles, Daniel E.
Stuart, J.E.B.
U.S. military
 leaders—Mexican
 War:
 Gorgas, Josiah
 Kearney, Stephen
  Watts
 Scott, Winfield
 Taylor, Zachary
 Thomas, George
  Henry
U.S. military
 leaders—
 Revolutionary War:
 Arnold, Benedict
 Greene, Nathanael
 Hale, Nathan
 Hampton, Wade
 Jones, John Paul
 Kościuszko,
  Tadeusz
 Lafayette,
  Marie-Joseph-
  Paul-Yves-
  Roch-Gilbert
  du Motier,
  marquis de
 Washington,
  George
U.S. military
 leaders—other:
 Custer, George
  Armstrong
 Jackson, Andrew
 Mitchell, William
 Perry, Matthew C.
 Pershing, John J.
U.S. presidents:
 Adams, John
 Adams, John
  Quincy
 Arthur, Chester A.
 Buchanan, James
 Cleveland, Grover
 Fillmore, Millard
 Garfield, James A.
 Grant, Ulysses S.
 Harrison,
  Benjamin

Harrison, William
 Henry
Hayes,
 Rutherford B.
Jackson, Andrew
Jefferson, Thomas
Johnson, Andrew
Lincoln, Abraham
McKinley,
 William
Madison, James
Monroe, James
Pierce, Franklin
Polk, James K.
Roosevelt,
 Theodore
Taft, William
 Howard
Taylor, Zachary
Tyler, John
Van Buren,
 Martin
Washington,
 George
Wilson, Woodrow
U.S. social reformers
 and religious
 leaders:
 Garvey, Marcus
 Grimké, Sarah and
  Angelina
 La Follette,
  Robert M.
 Noyes, John
  Humphrey
 Truth, Sojourner
 Washington,
  Booker T.
 Woodhull,
  Victoria
 Wright, Frances
 Young, Brigham
U.S. statesmen and
 political figures—
 Civil War and
 Reconstruction:
 Bates, Edward
 Blair, Francis
  Preston, Jr.
 Boutwell, George
  Sewall
 Brownlow,
  William G.

Chase, Salmon P.
Clay, Henry
Crittenden,
   John J.
Davis, Henry
   Winter
Davis, Jefferson
Douglas,
   Stephen A.
Mason, James
   Murray
Owen,
   Robert Dale
Revels, Hiram R.
Seward,
   William H.
Sherman, John
Stanton, Edwin M.
Stevens, Thaddeus
Sumner, Charles
Vallandigham,
   Clement L.

Vance, Zebulon B.
Welles, Gideon
U.S. statesmen and
   political figures—
   Federalist period:
Burr, Aaron
Clinton, Dewitt
Dayton, Jonathan
Hamilton,
   Alexander
Pinckney, Charles
U.S. statesmen and
   political figures—
   Revolutionary War:
Adams, John
Adams, Samuel
Franklin,
   Benjamin
Henry, Patrick
Mason, George
Otis, James

Paine, Thomas
Pendleton,
   Edmund
Revere, Paul
Rush, Benjamin
Wilkinson, James
U.S. statesmen and
   political figures—
   other:
Altgeld, John Peter
Benton, Thomas
   Hart
Bryan, William
   Jennings
Hay, John
Houston, Sam
Lansing, Robert
Lodge, Henry
   Cabot
Root, Elihu
Webster, Daniel

U.S. Supreme Court
justices:
Brandeis, Louis
Field, Stephen J.
Harlan, John
   Marshall
Holmes, Oliver
   Wendell
Jay, John
Marshall, John
Matthews, Stanley
Miller, Samuel
   Freeman
Story, Joseph
Taney, Roger
   Brooke
Waite, Morrison
   Remick
White, Edward
   Douglas

INDEX: See entries under all of the terms above

Section 966.   **Development of the Latin-American and Caribbean Nations to *c.* 1920**

A. The Latin-American independence movement (1790–1825)

   1. Background of the Latin-American wars of independence

      a. Discontent among Indians, Creoles, and mestizos: the influence of the Enlightenment, the U.S. War of Independence, and the French Revolution

      b. Influence of Toussaint-Louverture's successful slave revolt (1791–94): war with the French (1802–03) and the establishment of Haiti (1804)

      c. Spanish involvement in European wars: the Peninsular War in Spain (1808–14), Napoleon's seizure of the Spanish throne and Creole support of Ferdinand VII

   2. The Spanish South American War of Independence (1810–25), the establishment of the independent Empire of Brazil (1822)

      a. The struggle for independence in New Granada

         i. Initial phases of the revolt under Miranda and Bolívar (1811–14), military setbacks (1815)

         ii. Final expulsion of the Spanish from Venezuela, Colombia, Ecuador, and Panama (1821); establishment of the Republic of Gran Colombia (1821–29)

      b. Establishment of the United Provinces of the Río de la Plata (1813) at Buenos Aires; division of provinces into states of Paraguay, Buenos Aires, and Uruguay (1828)

      c. San Martín's military support of the Chilean independence movement under O'Higgins (1817–18), the liberation of Peru (1821)

      d. San Martín's withdrawal and assumption of control by Simón Bolívar, final defeat of Spanish troops (1824), Upper Peru's emergence as independent state of Bolivia (1825) under Sucre

      e. The Portuguese government in exile in Brazil (1808–22): reforms of King John VI (1816–22), establishment of the independent Empire of Brazil under Pedro I (1822)

   3. The Mexican War of Independence (1810–21): Hidalgo's revolt (1810–11), social and economic reforms under Morelos (1811–15), Iturbide's leadership (1820–21)

B. Mexico from independence (1821) through the end of the Revolution (1917)

   1. Mexico from 1821 to 1855

a. The independent Mexican Empire under Iturbide (1821–23), Santa Anna and the establishment of the Mexican Republic (1824), the constitution of 1824, Centralist–Federalist struggles

b. Santa Anna's military career and intermittent terms as president (1833 to 1855): the Alamo (1836); war with U.S. (1846–48) over Texas, New Mexico, and California

2. Mexico from 1855 to 1876

a. Juárez and La Reforma: social and economic reforms of the 1857 constitution, anticlericalism, the civil war (1857–60)

b. French intervention (1862) and Emperor Maximilian's puppet rule (1864–67): attempted liberal reforms; loss of conservative support; French withdrawal, defeat of imperial forces, and Maximilian's execution (1867)

c. Restoration of the republic under Juárez' leadership (1867–72), educational and economic reforms, Lerdo's presidency (1872–76), further separation of church and state

3. The Porfirio Díaz dictatorship (1876–1911)

a. Díaz' economic and social policies: maintenance of public order and suppression of dissent, economic development through foreign investment, reconciliation with church, middle-class control of land

b. Emergence of radical and liberal political clubs (c. 1900): internal unrest; labour strikes; Madero's unsuccessful challenge to Díaz' reelection (1909); armed revolt, Díaz' resignation, and Madero's election (1911)

4. The Mexican Revolutionary period (1910–17): Huerta's coup and Madero's execution (1913); Carranza's loose alliance with Pancho Villa, Zapata, and Obregón; civil war; the constitution of 1917; Carranza's election (1917)

C. Central America and the Caribbean to c. 1920

1. The Central American republics to c. 1920

a. Independence from Spain (1821), participation in Mexican Empire (1822–23), federation of United Provinces of Central America (1823), armed conflict between Conservatives and Liberals, collapse of the federation (1838)

b. Guatemala from 1838 to 1920: Carrera's Conservative dictatorship (1838–65), social and economic reforms of Barrios (1873–85) and subsequent Liberal regimes to 1898, Estrada Cabrera's administration (1898–1920)

c. Honduras from 1838 to 1920: Conservative domination to the 1870s, Aurelio Soto's Liberal regime (1876), return of Conservative control (1885), U.S. investments and military intervention (1912)

d. El Salvador to 1930: establishment of the republic (1841), Liberal–Conservative conflicts to 1885, coffee economy, political stability (1899–1930)

e. Nicaragua from 1838 to 1920: Liberal–Conservative conflicts, foreign intervention in the 1850s, stable Conservative governments (1857–93), economic growth, Zelaya's Liberal regime (1893–1909), U.S. military intervention from 1910

f. Costa Rica from 1838 to 1920: the coffee economy and social stability, Guardia dictatorship (1870–82) and the 1871 constitution, orderly presidential succession after 1890, Río San Juan dispute with Nicaragua

g. Panama to 1920: union with Gran Colombia (1821–1903), civil war, U.S. intervention and establishment of Republic of Panama (1903), building of Panama Canal (1904–14), U.S. control of Canal Zone

h. British colonial and U.S. economic interests in, and conflicts over, the Central American region; *e.g.,* in British Honduras

2. The island states of the Caribbean (c. 1800–1930)

a. Haiti to 1934: independence in 1804, civil war between the blacks and mulattoes, black hegemony under Christophe (later Henri I, 1806–20), ascendancy of mulattoes under Boyer (1820–43), political instability (1843–1915), U.S. military occupation (1915–34)

b. The Dominican Republic to 1930: the struggle for independence (to 1844), despotic regimes (1844–1916), U.S. armed intervention (1916–30)

c. Cuba from 1790 to 1934

i. 19th-century social and economic developments: growth of the sugar industry, the abolition of slavery (1886)

   ii. Spanish suppression of Cuban liberation movement in the Ten Years' War (1868–78), economic relations with United States, the Cuban War of Independence from Spain (1895–98)

   iii. Cuba as a U.S. protectorate until 1934: military occupation (1899–1901), Republic of Cuba (1902), later U.S. occupation (1906–09), dictatorships and the sugar industry

  d. The remaining European insular and mainland possessions in the Caribbean region from *c.* 1810 to *c.* 1920

D. The successor states of Gran Colombia to *c.* 1930

 1. Venezuela from 1810 to 1935

  a. Venezuelan independence movement (1810–30), national development under Páez (1830–48), Conservative Party rule

  b. Monagas family regime (1848–58) and turmoil between Liberal and Conservative parties to 1870, regime of Guzmán Blanco (1870–88)

  c. Political instability to 1892, Crespo's regime (1892–96), the Castro (1899–1908) and Gómez (1908–35) dictatorships

 2. Colombia from 1819 to 1930

  a. Independence (1819), participation in Gran Colombia to 1830, power struggle between Conservative and Liberal parties (1840–80), social reforms, anticlericalism

  b. Political instability and civil wars (1880s and 1899–1903), loss of Panama (1903), development of coffee industry (1909–28)

E. The Indian nations of the Andes to *c.* 1930

 1. Ecuador from 1822 to 1925

  a. Participation in Gran Colombia (1822–30), independent republic (1830), dictatorial regimes to 1845, political instability (1845–60)

  b. Clericalism in García Moreno's dictatorship (1860–75), Liberal ascendancy after 1875, Alfaro's administrations (1897–1911), social problems, depression in the 1920s

 2. Peru from 1824 to 1930

  a. Establishment of republic (1824), power struggle among caudillos (1824–41), temporary union with Bolivia (1836–39), orderly government under Castilla (1845–51 and 1855–62)

  b. Spanish military invasion (1864–69), Pardo's civilian government (1872–76) and economic crises, War of the Pacific (1879–84) and loss of territory to Chile, establishment of Peruvian Corporation (1889)

  c. Economic and social reforms of Piérola's administration (1895–1908), conflict between Democratic and Civilian parties, Leguía's administrations (1908–12 and 1919–30) and economic development, formation of the Aprista Movement

 3. Bolivia from 1809 to 1930

  a. Participation in Latin American wars of independence (1810–25), Bolivian independence (1825), Sucre's presidency (1826–28), economic decline

  b. Dictatorship of Santa Cruz (1829–39), temporary union with Peru (1836–39), silver-mining boom, War of the Pacific (1879–84) and territorial loss to Chile

  c. Conservative Party rule (1880–99), economic growth, the Federal Revolution (1899), Montes' leadership in Liberal Party rule (1899–1920), growth of tin-mining industry, Republican Party coup (1920), economic decline

F. Chile from 1810 to 1920

 1. Chile from the 1810 establishment of the republic to 1860

  a. The provisional government (1810–12), return of Spanish rule (1812), defeat of Spanish troops by combined Chilean–Argentinian army (1817)

  b. Bernardo O'Higgins as head of state (1817–23): liberal reforms and conservative opposition, O'Higgins' abdication (1823), political instability (1823–30)

  c. The conservative hegemony (1830–61): the 1833 constitution; political stability and conservative governments under Portales, Ovalle, Prieto, Bulnes, and Montt; economic prosperity; growth of liberal faction

2. The widening of liberal influence and the growth of political splinter groups (1861–91)

    a. The "Liberal Republic" under Pérez (1861–71) and the liberal–conservative alliance: cultural and economic ties with Great Britain, political conflict over church–state relations (1872)

    b. The War of the Pacific (1879–84) and threatened European intervention: annexation of saltpetre-mining provinces from Peru and Bolivia, civil war and Balmaceda's abdication (1891)

3. The parliamentary republic (1891–1920): era of legislative supremacy; growth of middle and lower classes; formation of Democratic (1887), Radical (1888), and Socialist (1901 and 1912) parties

G. The successor states of the Río de la Plata (excluding Bolivia) to *c.* 1920

    1. Argentina to 1930

        a. Efforts toward reconstruction (1820–29), confederation under Rosas and ascendancy of Buenos Aires (1829–52)

            i. Dominance of Buenos Aires: interprovincial rivalries, presidency of Rivadavia (1826–27)

            ii. The Rosas government (1829–52): domestic politics and foreign policies

        b. Period of national consolidation (1852–80), conservative regimes (1880–1916)

            i. The constitution of 1853 and civil wars (1853–60), government under Mitre (1862–68) and his successors

            ii. Economic development during Roca's administration (1880–86), economic crisis of 1890

            iii. The rise of radicalism: growth of social unrest, electoral reform of 1912

        c. The Radical regimes (1916–30): Irigoyen's presidency (1916–22), continued Radical rule in the 1920s, growth of foreign influence in the economy, military coup (1930)

    2. The Uruguayan struggle for independence and national unity (1811–1929)

        a. Independence from Spain (1811) and participation in United Provinces of the Río de la Plata (1813–28), establishment of independent Uruguay (1828)

        b. Civil war (1839–51) between Colorado and Blanco political parties, participation in war against Paraguay (1865–70), military rule (1875–90)

        c. Civilian rule and continued political crises and insurrections (1890–1904), Peace of Acequá (1904) and return to orderly government, social and economic reforms, economic boom during World War I

    3. Paraguay from 1810 to 1924

        a. Independence from Spain (1811), struggle with Buenos Aires for autonomy, establishment of independent Paraguay (1813)

        b. Isolationism during Rodríguez Francia's dictatorship (1814–40), encouragement of foreign trade during Carlos Antonio López' dictatorship (1841–62)

        c. Francisco Solano López' regime (1862–70): loss of territory after war with Brazil and Argentina (1864–70), political instability after 1870

H. Brazil from the establishment of the empire to the fall of the First Republic (1822–1930)

    1. The independent Empire of Brazil (1822–89)

        a. The empire under Pedro I (1822–31): the constitution of 1824, Pedro's abdication (1831), internal disunity during the regency (1831–40)

        b. The empire under Pedro II (1840–89): intervention in Uruguayan affairs and war with Paraguay (1864–70); cessation of slave trade (1853), gradual emancipation, and abolition of slavery (1888)

    2. Brazil during the First Republic (1889–1930)

        a. The constitution of 1891 and social reforms, military dictatorships (1891–94), civilian governments (1894–1914)

        b. Brazilian participation in World War I, postwar prosperity to 1922, economic problems during the 1920s, increasing political role of the military, civil disorders leading to the revolution of 1930

Suggested reading in the *Encyclopædia Britannica*:

MACROPAEDIA: Major articles dealing with the development of the Latin-American and Caribbean nations to *c.* 1920

Argentina	Colombia	Mexico	South America
Bolivia	Ecuador	Mexico City	Uruguay
Brazil	Guianas, The	North America	Venezuela
Buenos Aires	Havana	Paraguay	West Indies
Caracas	Latin America,	Peru	
Central America	The History of	Rio de Janeiro	
Chile	Lima	São Paulo	

MICROPAEDIA: Selected entries of reference information

General subjects

Central America and the Caribbean:	Chapultepec	San Jacinto,	Itata and
Canal Zone	Chilpancingo,	Battle of	Baltimore
Cuban	Congress of	*South America:*	incidents
Independence	científico	Acto Adicional	mazorca
Movement	Contreras,	of 1834	Pacific, War of the
Hay-Bunau-Varilla	Battle of	Ayacucho,	Paraguayan War
Treaty	Escocés and	Battle of	Pavón, Battle of
Maine, destruction	Yorkino	Bidlack Treaty	Peruvian-Bolivian
of the	Gadsden Purchase	Boyacá, Battle of	Confederation
Platt Amendment	Grito de Dolores	Bryan–Chamorro	Pipiolo and
Santiago, Battle of	Guadalupe	Treaty	Pelucón
Spanish–	Hidalgo,	Carabobo,	Rio Branco Law
American War	Treaty of	Battle of	Talambo affair
United Provinces	Iguala, Plan de	Cepeda, battles of	Tenentismo
of Central	Indigenismo	Chacabuco,	Thousand Days,
America	Mexican	Battle of	War of a
Mexico:	Revolution	Civilista	Tucumán,
Buena Vista,	Mexican War	estancia	Congress of
Battle of	Palo Alto, Battle of	gaucho	Water Witch
Celaya, Battle of	Pastry War	Gran Colombia	incident
Cerro Gordo,	Puebla, Battle of	Guayaquil	
Battle of	Reforma, La	Conference	
	Rurales		

Biographies

Central America and the Caribbean:	Díaz, Porfirio	Artigas, José	O'Higgins,
	Guerrero, Vicente	Gervasio	Bernardo
Barrios, Justo	Hidalgo y Costilla,	Batlle y Ordóñez,	Pedro I
Rufino	Miguel	José	Pedro II
Dessalines,	Huerta, Victoriano	Bolívar, Simón	Reyes, Rafael
Jean-Jacques	Iturbide,	Carrera, José	Rivadavia,
Estrada Cabrera,	Agustín de	Miguel	Bernardino
Manuel	Juárez, Benito	Fonseca, Manuel	Rosas, Juan
Estrada Palma,	Madero, Francisco	Deodoro da	Manuel de
Tomás	Maximilian	Guzmán Blanco,	San Martín,
Martí (y Pérez),	Morelos (y Pavón),	Antonio	José de
José Julián	José María	Haya de la Torre,	Silva Xavier,
Morazán,	Santa Anna,	Víctor Raúl	Joaquim José da
Francisco	Antonio López de	López, Francisco	Sucre, Antonio
Toussaint-Louverture	Villa, Pancho	Solano	José de
Zelaya, José Santos	Zapata, Emiliano	Miranda,	Uriburu,
Mexico:	*South America:*	Francisco de	José Félix
Carranza,	Andrada e Silva,	Mitre, Bartolomé	Urquiza, Justo
Venustiano	José Bonifácio de	Moreno, Mariano	José de

INDEX: See entries under all of the terms above

Section 967. **Australia and Oceania to *c.* 1920**

A. The character and historical development of the diverse peoples of Oceania and the effects of colonization

 1. The historical sources and historiographic problems

 2. Geography, ethnography, and prehistory of Australia, Melanesia, Micronesia, and Polynesia (including New Zealand)

 3. European exploration and colonial settlement: missionaries, trading societies, and colonial government

B. Australia to 1920

 1. Early European exploration by sea and land

 2. British colonization of New South Wales in 1788, expansion and development of self-government (1830–60), economic growth and the federation movement (1860–1901), the establishment of the commonwealth in 1901, social tensions, cultural developments

 3. Early years of the commonwealth: establishment of a White Australia immigration policy, Labor Party reforms, industrial growth, cooperation with Britain in World War I

 4. Relations with the Aboriginal population

C. New Zealand to 1928

 1. The extension of British control over, and annexation of, North and South Islands (1838–41)

 2. Relations between the indigenous Maori people and the British: encroachments and ensuing conflicts

 3. Establishment of self-government (1852): economic development and immigration

 4. Politics and foreign relations (1890–1928): Liberal and Reform Party governments, radical politics, the Labour Party, cooperation with Britain in World War I

Suggested reading in the *Encyclopædia Britannica:*

MACROPAEDIA: Major articles dealing with Australia and Oceania to *c.* 1920

 Australia
 Melbourne
 New Zealand
 Pacific Islands
 Sydney
 United States of America: *Hawaii*

MICROPAEDIA: Selected entries of reference information

General subjects

Australia:	Immigration	United Australia	New Zealand
ANZAC	Restriction Act	Party	Labour Party
Australian	Kanaka	Van Diemen's	New Zealand
Colonies	Lambing Flat	Land	Political Reform
Government Act	Riots	White Australia	League
Australian Labor	larrikin	Policy	Waitangi,
Party	Liberal Party of	*New Zealand:*	Treaty of
Australian	Australia	ANZAC	Young Maori
Patriotic	National Party	Hauhau	Party
Association	New South Wales	Maori King	*other:*
Black War	Corps	Movement	Melanesia
blackbirding	Port Phillip	Maori	Micronesia
bushranger	Association	Representation	Polynesia
Castle Hill Rising	Port Phillip	Act	
Emancipist	District	Maori Wars	
Eureka Stockade	Rum Rebellion	New Zealand	
Exclusive	squatter	Company	

Biographies

Australia:
Arthur, Sir George,
  1st Baronet
Barton, Sir
  Edmund
Deakin, Alfred
Forrest, Sir John
Hughes, William
  Morris
Macarthur, John
Parkes, Sir Henry

Sturt, Charles
Torrens, Sir
  Robert Richard
Wentworth, W.C.
New Zealand:
Kingi, Wiremu
Massey, William
  Ferguson
Pomare, Sir Maui
Seddon, Richard
  John

other:
Bougainville,
  Louis-Antoine de
Clunies-Ross
  family
Cook, James
Dumont d'Urville,
  Jules-Sébastien-César
Flinders, Matthew
Kamehameha I
Kamehameha IV

Mitchell, Sir
  Thomas
Livingstone
Oxley, John
Tasman, Abel
  Janszoon
Wakefield,
  Edward Gibbon
Weld, Sir
  Frederick
  Aloysius

Section 968.   **South Asia Under the Influence of European Imperialism from *c.* 1500 to *c.* 1920**

A. European activity in India (1498–*c.* 1760)

1. Portuguese commercial relations with India from 1498: establishment of the colony of Goa, decline of Portuguese hegemony and rise of British and Dutch influence

2. Dutch trading posts and conflicts with the British

3. The British and French in India

   a. Establishment and growth of British settlements and trading posts (1600–1740): the East India Company, relations with indigenous peoples

   b. Development of French trading companies from 1674: Anglo-French rivalry (1740–63) and establishment of British hegemony

   c. The British seizure of Calcutta (1757) and Clive's establishment of British control over the local Bengal ruler (1757–60)

B. Extension of British power (1760–1858)

1. Growth of the political power of the British East India Company and attempts by the British crown to regulate its affairs

   a. Securing of British supremacy in Bengal

   b. Warren Hastings (1774–85) and the transition of the status of the company from revenue farmer to a ruling power in India

   c. Wars with the Marāthās and Mysore at the end of the 18th century

   d. Expansion and consolidation of British control over various Indian states during administrations of Lord Wellesley (1798–1805), Lord Minto (1807–13), and Lord Hastings (1813–23)

   e. The organization and determination of administrative policy: Cornwallis and the transition toward British administrative procedures

   f. Completion of British annexation of, or domination over, the Afghan, Sikh, and Lower Burmese kingdoms in the 1840s and 1850s

2. The political, legal, economic, social, and cultural effects of the first century of British influence

3. The cause, outbreak, suppression, and effects of the Indian Mutiny (1857): the British crown's assumption of total responsibility for the government of India

C. British imperial power (1858–1920)

1. Climax of the raj: social and economic policies, government organization, the influence of the viceroys

2. British foreign policy in India: conflicts with Russia over the northwest frontier, the incorporation of Burma (1886), the Second Afghan War (1878–80) and the creation of the North-West Frontier Province (1901), the Third Afghan War (1919)

3. Beginning of Indian nationalism in the late 19th century and the British response: formation of the Indian National Congress (1885), policies of Lord Curzon (1899–1905), partition of Bengal, founding of the nationalist Muslim League, the Indian Councils Act of 1909

4. World War I and its aftermath: India's contribution to the war effort, anti-British activity, the Amritsar massacre, the Government of India Act (1919), Hindu–Muslim relations, the emergence of Mahatma Gandhi and the adoption of his noncooperation policy

D. Ceylon under foreign rulers from *c.* 1505 to 1920

1. Portuguese political and commercial activities in Ceylon (1505–1658): conflict with the Kandyan kingdom

2. Dutch rule in Ceylon (1658–1796) and its influence on the political, economic, judicial, and administrative systems; commercial enterprises and missionary attempts

3. The British in Ceylon from 1796: unification and early administration, the reforms of 1833, the transition from a subsistence to a commercial economy, the beginnings of constitutional government, nationalist unrest during World War I

E. Tibet and Nepal from *c.* 1750 to *c.* 1920

1. Decline of Chinese influence in Tibet: administration and culture under the Manchus

2. Nepal's territorial expansion under the Shah rulers, decline of Shah family and rise of Thapa and Rana families, accommodation with the British to preserve Nepal's independence

---

Suggested reading in the *Encyclopædia Britannica:*

MACROPAEDIA: Major articles dealing with South Asia under the influence of European imperialism from *c.* 1500 to *c.* 1920

Asia
Calcutta
India
Indian Ocean Islands
Nepal
Sri Lanka

MICROPAEDIA: Selected entries of reference information

General subjects

colonial administration and policy:
Afrīdī
Bengal, Partition of
Colebrook–Cameron Commission
Cornwallis Code
dastak
Defence of India Act
Durand Line
East India Company
forward policy
Government of India Act
Ilbert Bill
lapse, doctrine of
McMahon Line
maḥalwārī system
Rowlett Acts
Sadr Dīwānī ʿAdlāt
Scott-Moncrieff Commission
Thesavalamai
tombo
zamindar

historic events:
Amritsar, Massacre of
Baksar, Battle of
Barrackpore Mutiny
Black Hole of Calcutta
Carnatic Wars
Fīroz Shāh, Battle of
Gujrat, Battle of
Indian Mutiny
Marāthā Wars
Miāni, Battle of
Mysore Wars
Rohilla War
Sikh Wars
Sobraon, Battle of
Vellore Mutiny
Wandīwāsh, Battle of

historic states and sites:
Cis-Sutlej states
Kandy, kingdom of
Saint David, Fort
Saint George, Fort
William, Fort

nationalist groups and movements:
Ghadr
Indian Association
Indian National Congress
Khilafat Movement
Muslim League
Non-cooperation Movement
Servants of India Society

treaties:
Alingar, Treaty of
Amritsar, Treaty of
Banaras, Treaties of
Bassein, Treaty of
Deogaon, Treaty of
Kandyan Convention
Lucknow Pact
Malvana, Convention of
Purandhar, Treaty of
Surji-arjungaon, Treaty of
Wadgaon, Convention of

Section 969. **Southeast Asia Under the Influence of European Imperialism to *c.* 1920**

A. The states and European colonies of mainland Southeast Asia from *c.* 1600 to *c.* 1920

1. Burma and Malaya from *c.* 1600 to *c.* 1920: the advent of British rule

a. Burma from *c.* 1600 to *c.* 1920

i. Renewed expansionism and wars with the Mons, Thais, and Chinese under the Alaungpaya dynasty from 1752: the First and Second Anglo-Burmese Wars (1824–26, 1852), traditional Burmese administration

ii. The Third Anglo-Burmese War (1885) and union with British India (1886): effects of British colonialism

b. Malaya from *c.* 1630 to *c.* 1920: loss of autonomy through Dutch and British intrusions

i. Dutch intervention in the Malay states (1633), immigration (*c.* 1650) of Minangkabau and Bugis people from Sumatra

ii. British invasions in Malaya (1795), clashes between Malays and Chinese immigrants (1874), British intervention and assumption of power from sultanates of Malaya

2. Indochina and the development of French rule from *c.* 1615

a. Portuguese and French missionary involvement in Vietnam and Vietnamese reaction (1615–1858), French intervention in Indochina and territorial acquisition of Cochinchina and Cambodia (1858–63)

b. Period of colonization (1873–93); establishment of French protectorates in Annam, Tongking, and Laos; French administration in Indochina

3. Siam from *c.* 1620 to *c.* 1910

a. Trade relations with China and other Asian countries, influence of Theravāda Buddhism, Dutch and French intrusions and establishment of trade in the 1660s

b. Burmese invasion (1767) and end of Ayutthayan kingdom domination; political reunification and establishment of Chakkri dynasty (1782); social, cultural, and legal development in the early 19th century; Chinese immigration; expansion of trade with the U.S. and with European countries; reign of Mongkut (1851–68)

c. Political, social, and economic reforms in the reign of Chulalongkorn (1868–1910): Anglo-French activity in Southeast Asia and acquisition of Siamese territory (1893–1909)

4. Laos from *c.* 1600: establishment of separate kingdoms of Luang Prabang and Vientiane in 1707, Siamese domination from 1778, establishment of French protectorate in 1893

B. The states and European colonies of the Indonesian Archipelago and the Philippines from *c.* 1500 to *c.* 1920

1. The Portuguese and the Spanish in Southeast Asia

a. Portuguese naval and commercial activities, domination of the Strait of Malacca, and rivalry with the Spanish in the Spice Islands; collapse of Portuguese commercial empire with the defeat by the Dutch (1641)

b. The Philippines to *c.* 1920

i. The people and culture of the Philippines prior to the arrival of the Spanish

ii. Spanish control of the Philippines (1571–1898): government administration and influence of the Roman Catholic Church, land policy and overseas trade, rise of nationalism in the 19th century

iii. The Philippine Revolution of 1896–98, U.S. support in ousting the Spanish, subsequent U.S. takeover and administration to *c.* 1920

2. The Dutch and other European powers in Indonesia from *c.* 1600 to *c.* 1920

a. The Dutch East India Company (1602–1799): Coen's establishment of Dutch commercial supremacy, company rule in Java, decline and abolition of the company

b. The French and British in Java (1806–15), Dutch rule in the 19th century

i. The Culture System (Cultuur-stelsel) and its deleterious effects on Java (1830–70): the Liberal Policy

ii. The Ethical Policy and the rise of nationalism: social and economic benefits, formation of nationalist organizations

---

Suggested reading in the *Encyclopædia Britannica*:

MACROPAEDIA: Major articles dealing with Southeast Asia under the influence of European Imperialism to *c.* 1920

Asia
Burma
East Indies, The
Philippines
Southeast Asia, Mainland

MICROPAEDIA: Selected entries of reference information

General subjects

Indonesian	Muhammadiyah	Annam	Pangkor
Archipelago:	Padri War	Barrackpore	Engagement
Achinese War	Peranakan	Mutiny	Perak War
Amboina	Perhimpunan	Bowring Treaty	Phaulkon-Tachand
Massacre	Indonesia	Chinese	conspiracy
Budi Utomo	Preanger System	Engagement	Saigon, Treaty of
Buginese	priyayi	Cochinchina	Selangor Civil War
Culture System	Sarekat Islām	Ghee Hin	Sino-French War
Dutch East Indies	Volksraad	Hai San	Straits Settlements
Ethical Policy	*mainland Southeast*	Hlutdaw	Tonkin
Gianti Agreement	*Asia:*	Indochina	*Philippine Islands:*
Mataram	Anglo-Burmese	Naning War	barangay
	Wars	Pahang Civil War	

INDEX: See entries under all of the terms above

Section 96/10. China from 1839 Until the Onset of Revolution (to *c.* 1911), and Japan from the Meiji Restoration to *c.* 1910

A. China under the late Ch'ing: the challenges of rebellion and Western penetration

1. The Western challenge (1839–60) and the collapse of the tributary system: rebellion and the reestablishment of the Ch'ing government

 a. Problems created by the opium trade: British demands for trade advantages and diplomatic parity culminating in the Opium War (1839–42)

  i. The Opium War and its aftermath: granting of commercial privileges to Western powers

  ii. Reactions to foreign trade gains: anti-foreign movements concentrated at Canton

 b. Popular uprisings of the Taiping and Nien and rebellions in western China, the effects of the rebellions

2. Contending forces of westernization and Chinese tradition from *c.* 1850

 a. The "self-strengthening" movement: its effect on foreign relations and on domestic life

  i. Western attempts at treaty revision and the chilling of Sino-Russian relations, hostility toward Christian missionaries

  ii. Industrialization for self-strengthening: mining and the weapons industry, malpractice and corruption in business

 b. Increasing foreign encroachments (1870–95): loss of Central Asian territories, problems resulting from Chinese hesitancy to engage in regular diplomatic relations, Korea and the Sino-Japanese War (1894–95)

c. The reform movement of K'ang Yu-wei, the conservative reaction, and the Boxer Rebellion (1900) as expressions of anti-foreign feelings: Western seizure of Peking (1900) and further Ch'ing concessions, U.S. Open Door Policy

d. Reformist and revolutionist movements at the end of the dynasty: Ch'ing reforms after 1901, the Republican movement and the 1911 Revolution

    i. Sun Yat-sen and the United League: constitutional movements after 1905

    ii. Peasant uprisings and the 1911 Revolution

B. The modernization of Japan and its emergence as a world power (1868–c. 1910)

1. The Meiji Restoration and the process of modernization

a. The fall of the Tokugawa, leadership and initial policies of the new government, samurai opposition and government countermeasures

b. Beginning of Japanese modernization: abolition of feudalism; fiscal and economic policies; growth of *zaibatsu* (cartels); development of national loyalties; religious, educational, and cultural policies

c. Politics in Meiji Japan: creation of political parties, oligarchic control and gradual development of representative institutions

2. Foreign relations in Imperial Japan: dispute with China over Korea, success in the Russo-Japanese War (1904–05), annexation of Korea (1910), economic expansion in China

---

Suggested reading in the *Encyclopædia Britannica*:

MACROPAEDIA: Major articles dealing with China from 1839 until the onset of revolution (to *c.* 1911), and Japan from the Meiji Restoration to *c.* 1910

Asia	Japan	Shanghai	Tokyo-Yokohama
Canton	Korea	Taiwan	Metropolitan
China	Nanking	Tientsin	Area
Hong Kong	Peking		

MICROPAEDIA: Selected entries of reference information

General subjects

China—domestic affairs:	*China—international relations:*	kazoku	Root–Takahira Agreement
Chinese Revolution	Boxer Rebellion	Meiji Restoration	Russo-Japanese War
Ch'ing dynasty	Chinese Eastern Railway	Paulownia Sun, Order of the	Tsushima, Battle of
Ch'ing-liu tang	Ili crisis	Rising Sun, Order of the	*other:*
cohong	Kuldja, Treaty of	zaibatsu	Sino-Japanese
Five-Power Constitution	Lay–Osborn flotilla	*Japan—international relations:*	War (1894–95)
Hundred Days of Reform	Open Door policy	Anglo-Japanese Alliance	Shimonoseki, Treaty of
Kiangnan Arsenal	Opium Wars	Gentlemen's Agreement	South Manchurian
likin	Sino-French War	Lansing–Ishii	Railway
Nien Rebellion	Tientsin Massacre	Agreement	treaty port
Taiping Rebellion	*Japan—domestic affairs:*	Portsmouth, Treaty of	Unequal Treaty
Three Principles of the People	Charter Oath		
T'ung-wen kuan	genrō		
	Kaishintō		

Biographies

China:	Li Hung-chang	Tso Tsung t'ang	Fukuzawa Yukichi
Chang Chih-tung	Liang Ch'i-ch'ao	Tuan ch'i-jui	Gotō Shōjirō,
Chang Ping-lin	Lin Tse-hsü	T'ung-chih	Hakushaku
Ch'i-ying	Sheng Hsüan-huai	Tz'u-hsi	Inoue Kaoru,
Huang Hsing	Soong family	Yang Hsiu-ch'ing	Kōshaku
Hung Hsiu-ch'üan	Sun Yat-sen	*Japan:*	Itagaki Taisuke,
K'ang Yu-wei	Sung Chiao-jen	Abe Isoo	Hakushaku
Kuang-hsü	Ts'ai Yüan-p'ei	Etō Shimpei	Itō Hirobumi,
Kung Ch'in-wang	Tseng Kuo-fan	Fujita Tōko	Kōshaku

Section 96/11. **Southwest Asia and North Africa (*c.* 1800–1920), and Sub-Saharan Africa (1885–*c.* 1920) Under the Influence of European Imperialism: the Early Colonial Period**

A. The Ottoman Empire from 1807 to 1920: European intervention and the continuation of westernization

    1. The empire under Mahmud II: internal reforms and centralization, the Greek revolt (1821–32), the Egyptian revolt (1831–41), Russian intrusions in Turkey

    2. Reaction, revolt, and further disintegration until World War I

        a. The era of the Tanzimat reforms (1839–76)

        b. Crisis of 1875–78 and the loss of Romania, Serbia, Montenegro, and most of Bulgaria; the constitution of 1876

        c. The growth of Turkish nationalism in the reign of Abdülhamid II (1876–1909) and dissolution of the empire, domination by Germany in World War I

B. Egypt, the Maghrib, and the Arabian Peninsula: the development of Arab nationalism and Zionism

    1. The emergence of modern Egypt (1798–1922)

        a. Egypt under French (1798–1801) and British (1801–03) occupation, centralized administration of Muḥammad ʿAlī and his successors (1805–82), construction of Suez Canal (1858–69), European financial and military intervention

        b. Egypt under British rule (1882–1922): reforms by Baring's (later 1st Earl Cromer) administration (1883–1907), revival of nationalism, World War I and independence (1922)

    2. The Maghrib from 1830 to *c.* 1930: European penetration into Algeria, Tunisia, Libya, and Morocco

        a. Algeria from 1830 to 1920: the French conquest (1830–71) and colonial settlements, national resistance movement under Abdelkader, suppression of the Muslim population

        b. Tunisia from 1830 to *c.* 1930: French influence to 1881 and status as a French protectorate from 1881

        c. Morocco from 1830 to 1920: growth of French, Spanish, and British influence and decline of the traditional government; establishment of French and Spanish zones and protectorates (1912)

        d. Libya (Tripolitania and Cyrenaica) from *c.* 1834 to 1920: subjection to direct Turkish rule (1835), growth of Italian influence resulting in conquest (1911–12)

    3. Arab nationalism from *c.* 1850 to 1920, emergence of Zionism as a factor in Middle Eastern affairs

        a. Origins, growth, and early accomplishments of Arab nationalism; British encouragement in World War I; the postwar settlement

        b. Origins of the Zionist movement and Jewish immigration to Palestine after 1880, World War I developments and the beginning of conflict between Zionists and Arab nationalists

C. Iran under the Qājār dynasty from 1779 to 1925, Afghanistan from 1809 to 1921

   1. Iran: the reign of Āghā Moḥammad Khān and the subsequent European penetration of Iran by the British and Russians, overthrow of the Qājār dynasty (1925)

   2. Afghanistan: the Barakzai dynasty, conflicts with the British government of India, British recognition of Afghan independence (1921)

D. Sub-Saharan Africa from *c.* 1885 to *c.* 1920

   1. The decline in the slave trade; European commercial, missionary, and exploratory activities in the 19th century; the imperialistic scramble for African colonies; the Berlin West Africa Conference (1884–85) and the European partition of Africa

   2. The establishment of European colonies in West Africa in the late 19th century

     a. French, British, and German rivalry: takeover of the Gold Coast, Senegal, Togo, the Cameroons, Dahomey, and the Ivory Coast

     b. Problems in establishing effective colonial regimes: military problems, control of the territories, reliance on Africans and development of indirect rule

   3. Northeast Africa: foreign influences and national movements

     a. The Mahdist movement in the Sudan (1881–98) and the Anglo-Egyptian condominium from 1899

     b. The consolidation of central governmental power in Ethiopia: Tewodros II (1855–68), Yohannes IV (1872–89), and Menelek II (1889–1913); struggles against Egypt, the Sudan, and Italy

   4. East Africa and Madagascar: German, British, French, and Italian conquests and establishment of colonies; relations with indigenous peoples

   5. European penetration into Central Africa during the 19th century and establishment of permanent colonies

     a. British explorations under Livingstone and Stanley: attempts to explore the interior

     b. King Leopold II's colonial enterprise in the Congo: establishment of the Belgian Congo (Congo Free State) and Belgium's Congo policies until World War I

     c. The French colonies and colonial administration until World War II

   6. The scramble for southern Africa, the British–Boer conflict and the establishment of the Union of South Africa (1910), curtailment of economic and political rights of Africans and Asians, the Botha (1910–19) and Smuts (1919–24) governments and Nationalist Party opposition under Hertzog

---

Suggested reading in the *Encyclopædia Britannica*:

MACROPAEDIA: Major articles dealing with Southwest Asia and North Africa (*c.* 1800–1920), and sub-Saharan Africa (1885–*c.* 1920) under the influence of European Imperialism: the early colonial period

Afghanistan	Eastern Africa	Lebanon	Sudan
Africa	Egypt	North Africa	Syria
Arabia	Indian Ocean	Palestine	Turkey and
Asia	Islands	South Africa	Ancient Anatolia
Central Africa	Iran	Southern Africa	Western Africa

MICROPAEDIA: Selected entries of reference information

General subjects

Arabian peninsula:	*Egypt and the Nilotic*	Wafd	*Ottoman Empire:*
'Abdali Sultanate	*Sudan:*	*North Africa:*	Akkerman,
Āl Bū Sa'īd	Anglo-Egyptian	Algeciras	Convention of
Dynasty	Condominium	Conference	Armenian
Dir'iyah, Battle	Fashoda Incident	Ḥusaynid Dynasty	massacres
of ad-	Khartoum,	Italo-Turkish War	Bulgarian Horrors
Mulaydah, Battle	Siege of	Moroccan Crises	Çanak, Treaty of
of al-	Mahdist	Tripolitan War	Capitulation
Qu'aiti Sultanate	Omdurman,	Young Tunisians	Constantinople
Wahhābīyah	Battle of		Agreement

Defense of Rights,
Associations
for the
Edirne, Treaty of
Greco-Turkish
wars
Greek
Independence,
War of
Halepa, Pact of
Hünkâr İskelesi,
Treaty of
Italo-Turkish War
Macedonian
question
Mudros,
Armistice of
Navarino, Battle of
Ottoman Empire
Pan-Turanianism

Pan-Turkism
Plevna, Siege of
Rumelia
Saint-Jean-de-
Maurienne,
Agreement of
San Stefano,
Treaty of
Serbo-Turkish War
Sèvres, Treaty of
Straits question
Tanzimat
Young Ottomans
Young Turks
sub-Saharan Africa:
Adowa, Battle of
Afrikaner Bond
Belgian Congo
Berlin West Africa
Conference

British East Africa
British South
Africa Company
British West Africa
Buganda
Congo Free State
German East
Africa
Moyen-Congo
Mozambique
Conventions
National Party of
South Africa
Rwanda,
Kingdom of
Royal Niger
Company
Somaliland
South Africa Act
South African War

Togoland
Tukulor Empire
Ucciali, Treaty of
uitlander
Vereeniging,
Peace of
Wadai,
Kingdom of
Zanzibar Treaty
other:
Durrand Line
King-Crane
Commission
Mizrahi
Persian Cossack
Brigade
Zionism

Biographies

Afghanistan:
'Abdor Raḥmān
Khān
Dōst Moḥammad
Khān
Ḥabībollāh Khān
Shāh Shojā'
Shīr 'Alī Khān
Egypt:
Cromer, Evelyn
Baring, 1st earl of
Ismā'īl Pasha
Kāmil, Muṣṭafā
Muḥammad 'Alī
Nubar Pasha
Sa'īd Pasha
'Urābī Pasha
Iran:
Khaz'al Khan
Mīrzā Taqī Khān
Nāṣer od-Dīn
Qājār Dynasty
Ottoman Empire:
Abdulhamid II
Abdülmecid I
Enver Paşa

Mahmud II
Mehmed V
Mehmed VI
Midhat Paşa
Reşid Paşa,
Mustafā
Selim III
Şevket Paşa,
Mahmud
sub-Saharan Africa:
Botha, Louis
Brazza,
Pierre-Paul-
François-Camille
Savorgnan de
Chilembwe, John
De la Rey,
Jacobus Hercules
Goldie,
Sir George
Gungunhana
Hofmeyr, Jan
Jameson, Sir
Leander Starr,
Baronet

Kagwa,
Sir Apolo
Kruger, Paul
Loch of Drylaw,
Hengy
Brougham
Loch,
1st Baron
Lugard (of
Abinger),
Frederick John
Dealtry Lugard,
Baron
Menelik II
Milner (of Saint
James's and Cape
Town), Alfred
Milner, Viscount
Msiri
Mwanga
Rābih as-Zubayr
Rhodes, Cecil
Roberts, Joseph
Jenkins
Robinson, Sir
Hercules

Samory
Smuts, Jan
Christian
Stanley, Sir Henry
Morton
Steyn, Marthinus
Theunis
Tippu Tib
Wet, Christiaan
Rudolf de
Yohannes IV
Sudan:
'Abd Allāh
Gordon, Charles
George
Kitchener, Herbert
Kitchener, 1st
Earl
Mahdī, al-
Osman Dinga
other:
Abdelkader
Ibrahim Pasha
Jamāl ad-Dīn
al-Afghānī
Lawrence, T.E.

INDEX: See entries under all of the terms above

Division VII. **The World Since 1920**
[For Part Nine headnote see page 343.]

The first of the eight sections in Division VII, reflecting the increasing internationalization since 1920, broadly treats major developments in contemporary world history. The remaining seven sections deal separately with the histories, since 1920, of the several regions of the world.

Section 971. **International Movements, Diplomacy, and War Since 1920**

A. The period between the World Wars (1920–39)

1. Immediate postwar problems (1920–24)

a. Failure of attempts to establish Socialist and new democratic governments in Europe: dictatorships in the new nations of central and eastern Europe

b. Diplomacy after the Paris Peace Conference (1919–20): establishment of the League of Nations; U.S., Soviet Russian, and German diplomatic isolation; crises concerning enforcement of the peace settlement

2. The temporary amelioration of international relations by the Locarno (1925) and Kellogg–Briand (1928) agreements, European recovery and the rapprochement with Germany

3. International affairs in the 1930s

a. The upsurge of strife in Asia: civil conflict in China and the Japanese seizure of Manchuria (1931–32), rise of the militarists in Japan and the Greater East Asia Coprosperity Sphere

b. The Popular Front and the Spanish Civil War (1936–39): unchecked Italian aggression against Ethiopia (1935–36), failure of the League of Nations and other diplomatic attempts (*e.g.,* the Munich Conference) to avert war

c. The European colonial empires and client states: increased demands for self-determination among subject peoples, realignment of colonial powers

4. Economic developments in the postwar period (1920–39)

a. Increased government control (1920–29): reconstruction, social welfare, and inflation

b. Economic and political impact of the Great Depression (1929): collapse of the world market and responses by various governments

c. The establishment of Nazi Germany and economic recovery based on rearmament, Germany's alignment with Italy and Japan, the New Deal policy in the U.S., War Communism and the New Economic Policy in Soviet Russia

B. World War II (1939–45)

1. German conquest of Poland (1939) and France (1940); the German–Soviet pact (1939) and subsequent German invasion of the Soviet Union (1941); the Battle of Britain (1940) and the war in North Africa (1940–42)

2. The war in Asia and the Pacific (1937–45)

a. Further Japanese aggression in China from 1937: the clash between U.S. and Japanese interests in the Pacific, the attack on Pearl Harbor (1941) and U.S. entry into the war

b. Japanese conquests in the western Pacific and Southeast Asia (1941–42); the Allied counteroffensive from 1942, resulting in Japanese defeat (1945)

3. The war in Europe and North Africa (1942–45)

a. Beginning of U.S. active participation (1942), Allied progress against the Axis Powers in North Africa and Europe

b. Collapse of the German Eastern Front (1943) and Soviet conquest of eastern Europe (1943–44), Allied invasions of Italy (1943) and France (1944) and the defeat of Germany (1945)

4. The leadership, industrial strength, strategic plans and goals, and tactical and logistical procedures of the Axis Powers

5. Allied wartime leadership and diplomacy: the Atlantic Charter; industrial strength, strategic plans and goals, and tactical and logistical procedures

6. The burgeoning of military technology; *e.g.,* developments in communications devices, naval ships and aircraft, ground weapons and missiles, atomic bombs

C. International relations

1. International relations before and during World War II

a. The Eurocentric world and its collapse

b. Ideologies in World War II

i. The Nazi–Soviet pact

ii. Roosevelt, Churchill, and the Atlantic Charter

iii. Soviet expansion, Stalin and the Nazis, annexations

2. The postwar years (1945–57)

a. The end of the war and the early United Nations (UN)

i. The atomic bombs

ii. Truman's fundamental principles

iii. The UN as a Western organization

b. Reconstruction and European political instability

c. The beginnings of the Cold War

i. Consolidation of Soviet power in eastern Europe: the "iron curtain"

ii. The Cold War as *Realpolitik* and as ideology

iii. The confrontation in Germany: the Berlin blockade

iv. The formation of the North Atlantic Treaty Organization (NATO)

d. East, South, and Southeast Asia, 1945–57

i. The colonial territories of Asia

ii. Civil war in China and Communist rule

iii. The Korean War: its meaning, course, and consequences

iv. The transformation of the American role in Southeast Asia

e. The Middle East (1945–57)

i. The U.S. in the Middle East

ii. The Iranian and Turkish cases

iii. Palestine: Israel and the Arabs

iv. Nasser and the Suez crisis

f. The continuing Cold War

i. The U.S. policy of containment

ii. The late Truman administration

iii. The Eisenhower years and McCarthyism

iv. De-Stalinization in the Soviet Union

v. Unrest among the satellites

vi. NATO and European economic recovery

vii. Soviet responses

viii. The problem of nuclear energy: the balance of terror, France as a nuclear power

ix. The Austrian treaty and the German problem

3. The period since 1957

a. The Great Powers and the world

i. Postwar economic growth: U.S. economic dominance

ii. Decolonization

iii. The Soviet Union and "national liberation"

iv. The new states: nonalignment and domestic problems, aid programs

v. The Third World as a zone of conflict in the Cold War

vi. Latin America in the Cold War: Fidel Castro

vii. The Berlin Wall and the Cuban Missile Crisis: consequences

viii. Sino-Soviet relations: the consequences of their rift

ix. Peaceful coexistence and détente

x. Resolution of the German problem, the two Germanys

xi. The Helsinki conference (1973)

xii. Arms buildup and deterioration of superpower relations

b. The lesser powers

i. Peace in postwar Europe

ii. Integration movements in western Europe, Gaullism

iii. The new Europe: regional separatism

iv. Eastern Europe: the Soviet variety of imperialism

c. Areas of conflict

i. Southeast Asia: the Indochina War

ii. The Middle East: the Arab–Israeli wars, the new role of petroleum, the Iranian revolution

iii. East–West involvement in Africa south of the Sahara

D. Economic developments from 1940

Suggested reading in the *Encyclopædia Britannica:*

MACROPAEDIA: Major articles dealing with international affairs since 1920

Europe
International Relations, 20th-Century

MICROPAEDIA: Selected entries of reference information

General subjects

between the World Wars:	Lausanne Conference (1923)	Russo-Polish War	Arab–Israeli wars
Anschluss		San Remo, Conference of	Arab League
Anti-Comintern Pact	Lausanne Conference (1932)	Spanish Civil War	Bandung Conference
Dawes Plan	Little Entente	Sudetenland	Berlin blockade and airlift
Fiume question	Locarno, Pact of	Vilnius dispute	
Genoa, Conference of	London Naval Conference	Washington, treaties of	Central Treaty Organization
German-Soviet Nonaggression Pact	mandate	Young Plan	Colombo Plan
	Maginot Line	*since 1945:*	Cuban Missile Crisis
Great Depression	Memel dispute	African Unity, Organization of	Economic Cooperation and Development, Organisation for
Italo-Ethiopian War	Mukden Incident	Alliance for Progress	
Kellogg–Briand Pact	Munich agreement	American States, Organization of	Eisenhower Doctrine
	Nations, League of Polish Corridor	Antarctic Treaty	

Eurocommunism
Europe, Council of
European Coal and
  Steel Community
European
  Communities
European Defense
  Community
European
  Economic
  Community
European Free
  Trade Association
European
  Parliament
General
  Agreement on
  Tariffs and Trade
Geneva Accords
Helsinki Accords
Indochina wars
International Bank
  for Economic
  Cooperation
International
  Finance
  Corporation
International
  Investment Bank
International
  Monetary Fund
iron curtain
Korean War
Maoism
Marshall Plan
Mutual Economic
  Assistance,
  Council for

North Atlantic
  Treaty
  Organization
Nuclear Test-Ban
  Treaty
Nürnberg Trials
Outer Space Treaty
Palestine
  Liberation
  Organization
Petroleum
  Exporting
  Countries,
  Organization of
San Francisco
  Conference
Security and
  Cooperation
  in Europe,
  Conference on
Southeast
  Asia Treaty
  Organization
Stalinism
Strategic Arms
  Limitation Talks
terrorism
Truman Doctrine
U-2 Affair
United Nations
Vietnam War
Warsaw Treaty
  Organization
Western European
  Union
World War II:
  Alamein, battles
  of el-

Atlantic, Battle
  of the
Atlantic Charter
Bataan Death
  March
Bretton Woods
  Conference
Britain, Battle of
Bulge, Battle of the
Cairo conferences
Casablanca
  Conference
Coral Sea, Battle
  of the
Dumbarton Oaks
  Conference
Free French
Guadalcanal,
  Battle of
Holocaust
lend–lease
Leningrad, Siege of
Leyte Gulf,
  Battle of
Manhattan Project
Midway, Battle of
Normandy
  Invasion
Pearl Harbor
  attack
Philippine Sea,
  Battle of the
Potsdam
  Conference
Quebec
  Conferences
Resistance

Stalingrad,
  Battle of
Tehrān
  Conference
Ultra
Wake Island,
  Battle of
Warsaw Ghetto
  Uprising
Warsaw Uprising
World War II
Yalta Conference

Biographies

Adenauer, Konrad
Ben-Gurion, David
Brezhnev, Leonid
  Ilich
Chamberlain,
  Neville
Chou En-lai
Churchill, Sir
  Winston
Dulles, John
  Foster

Eisenhower,
  Dwight D.
Franco, Francisco
Gandhi, Mohandas
  Karamchand
Gaulle, Charles de
Gromyko, Andrey
  Andreyevich
Hammarskjöld, Dag
Hitler, Adolf
Ho Chi Minh
Kennedy, John F.

Khrushchev,
  Nikita
Marshall,
  George C.
Montgomery,
  Bernard Law
  Montgomery, 1st
  Viscount
Mussolini,
  Benito
Nasser, Gamal
  Abdel

Nehru, Jawaharlal
Perón, Juan
Roosevelt,
  Franklin D.
Schuman, Robert
Spaak, Paul-Henri
Stalin, Joseph
Sun Yat-sen
Truman, Harry S.
Wilson, Woodrow

INDEX: See entries under all of the terms above

Section 972. **Europe Since *c.* 1920**

A. The nations of western Europe since *c.* 1920

  1. Great Britain and Ireland

    a. Developments in Great Britain

      i. Economic depression, labour unrest, and domestic politics in the interwar period: formation of the first Labour government under MacDonald (1923), Baldwin's government (1924–29) and the General Strike of 1926, the National Government (1931–39)

      ii. British colonial and Commonwealth relations (1920–39): division of Ireland into the Irish Free State (after 1937 named Eire) and Northern Ireland (1922), the Indian problem

      iii. Interwar foreign policy (1931–39), Churchill's government (1940–45) and Britain's stand against the Axis Powers in World War II

      iv. The Labour government (1945–51) and the welfare state, role in NATO and relationship to the European Economic Community (Common Market), the Conservative government (1951–64), disintegration of the British Empire, Labour government (1964–70), Conservative government (1970–74), Labour government (1974–79), entrance into the Common Market (1973), Thatcher government (from 1979), Falklands war with Argentina (1982), European Communities budget controversy

    b. Developments in Ireland since *c.* 1920

      i. Division of Ireland and establishment of the Irish Free State and Northern Ireland (1922), the Cosgrave and De Valera governments, entrance into the Common Market (1973), death of De Valera (1975), Jack Lynch as prime minister (1966–73 and 1977–79), the Haughey and FitzGerald governments

      ii. Northern Ireland since 1922: growing antagonism between Roman Catholics and Protestants, economic stagnation, continuing violence

  2. France since 1920

    a. From 1920 to the end of World War II

      i. Developments in the interwar period: internal financial crises and German reparations, collective security, the Great Depression, political instability and conflicts between right and left in the 1930s

      ii. Social, cultural, and economic developments under the Third Republic

      iii. World War II: defeat by Germany (1940) and the Vichy government; de Gaulle, the Free French, and Resistance movements; French participation in the Allied victory (1944–45)

    b. The postwar period

      i. The Fourth Republic (1946–58): constitution of the Fourth Republic; the realignment of parties; colonial independence movements; the French Indochina War, the Algerian War, and the crisis of 1958; de Gaulle's return to power

      ii. The Fifth Republic: settlement of the Algerian question, independence of the French African colonies, Common Market, the student revolt of 1968, de Gaulle's retirement and continued rule by the Gaullist coalition, government of Valéry Giscard d'Estaing, election of François Mitterrand and Socialist government in 1981

  3. Germany since 1920

    a. From 1920 to the end of World War II

      i. The German Republic (1919–33): the Weimar Constitution, reaction to the Treaty of Versailles and reparations payments, opposition from the left and the right, attempts to stabilize the republic and reestablish Germany's international position, the rise to power of National Socialists (Nazis) and the end of the republic

      ii. The Third Reich (1933–45): the Nazi revolution and establishment (1934–39) of the totalitarian police state by Hitler; persecution of the Jews; rearmament, expansion in eastern Europe, and formation of Axis alliance; World War II conquests throughout Europe; defeat by Allies (1945)

b. The postwar period

    i. Germany after World War II (1945–49): occupation by the Allies, partition between west and east zones

    ii. The formation of the Federal Republic of Germany and the leadership of Konrad Adenauer, role in NATO, economic recovery, continued Christian Democratic Union rule under Erhard and Kiesinger, Social Democratic chancellors Willy Brandt and Helmut Schmidt, success of *Ostpolitik*, Euromissiles controversy, return to power of Christian Democrats under Helmut Kohl (1982)

    iii. The German Democratic Republic: the Ulbricht government, the Berlin Wall, economic recovery and the beginning of rapprochement with the West, collective leadership under Erich Honecker (1971), formal relations between two Germanys, admission to UN (1973), growth of trade with the Federal Republic

4. Italy since 1920

  a. The Fascist era

    i. The postwar cabinets, foreign relations and the Fiume affair, the Fascist Party's rise to power (1922), Mussolini and the Fascist dictatorship

    ii. Rapprochement with Germany, conquest of Ethiopia, effects of the Great Depression, Italian participation in World War II, the fall of Mussolini

  b. Postwar Italy: the politics of the republic, the De Gasperi era (1947–53), ministerial instability, economic recovery, struggle against terrorism in the late 1970s and early 1980s, parliamentary shift to the centre-left, declining strength of the Christian Democrats, first Socialist premier (1983)

5. Spain and Portugal

  a. Spain since 1920

    i. The military government of Primo de Rivera and establishment of the republic: the Civil War, German and Italian intervention, and Franco's victory; Spain's neutralism in World War II

    ii. Rapprochement with the NATO powers in the postwar era: the Franco regime

    iii. Last years of the Franco regime, government under King Juan Carlos, constitution of 1978, Basque separatism, moves toward regional self-government (1979)

  b. Portugal: military revolt (1926), the Salazar regime (1928–68), the constitution of 1933, neutralism in World War II, the effort to maintain the Portuguese colonial empire in the 1950s and 1960s, revolution of 1974, end of colonial involvement, constitution of 1976, minority and coalition governments

6. Scandinavia since *c.* 1900

  a. Denmark since *c.* 1900

    i. Foreign policy, World War I, and economic effects of the war; the Great Depression; German occupation

    ii. The postwar period: 1953 constitution; military, economic, and social policies; coalition governments

  b. Sweden since *c.* 1900

    i. Political reforms and defense policies prior to World War I, neutrality during the war

    ii. Politics in the interwar period: economic reforms and foreign policy, neutrality in World War II

    iii. Social and political reforms and establishment of the welfare state, neutralist foreign policy, new constitution (1975), defeat (1976) and return to power (1982) of the Social Democrats

  c. Norway since *c.* 1900

    i. Separation from Sweden (1905); World War I, the Great Depression, and gradual economic recovery; foreign policy and German occupation during World War II

    ii. Political and social developments in the postwar period, foreign policy, economic effects of North Sea petroleum discoveries

  d. Finland and Iceland since *c.* 1900

    i. Finland: liberation from Russia (1918), parliamentary government, agrarian reform, growth of political parties, language problems, foreign policy and activities during World War II, domestic and foreign policies in the postwar period, presidency of Urho Kekkonen (1956–81), neutrality and relations with the Soviet Union

    ii. Iceland: political developments (in union with Denmark) in the interwar period, aid to the Allies in World War II, establishment as an independent republic (1944), foreign relations, economic dependence on fishing, "cod wars" with Britain (1975–76)

7. The Low Countries since 1920: Belgium, The Netherlands, and Luxembourg in the interwar period; German occupation in World War II; postwar loss of colonial possessions and integration in the European Economic Community; Benelux membership in NATO; Dutch industrialization and development of North Sea gas; Walloon–Fleming division in Belgium; attempts to resolve communal disputes

8. Switzerland since 1920: Swiss neutrality in World War II, immigration and economic policies, dependence on alien workers and resulting tension, postwar neutrality policy

B. Eastern and central Europe

1. The Soviet Union from the establishment of the Communist state

  a. From 1917 to the end of World War II

    i. The governments of 1917; the October Revolution and establishment of the Soviet government; Civil War, War Communism, and the New Economic Policy; the struggle for succession after Lenin's death (1924) and the rise of Stalin

    ii. Foreign policy, society, and culture under the New Economic Policy: purges and consolidation of Stalinism, Soviet foreign policy in the 1930s

    iii. World War II: consolidation in eastern Europe, the German offensive (1941) and the Battle of Stalingrad, Soviet advance into Europe, resurgent nationalism and strengthening of the regime, Soviet military and political position in 1945

  b. The postwar period

    i. Soviet economic recovery after the war: Stalin's monopoly of power until his death (1953), Cold War relations with the U.S. and other countries, deterioration of relations with the People's Republic of China

    ii. De-Stalinization and the Khrushchev era (1957–64): ideological disputes with China, economic problems

    iii. The Brezhnev–Kosygin era (1964–82) and collective leadership: agricultural problems and achievements in industrial production, foreign policy and space exploration, continued censorship and discontent among intellectuals

    iv. Short rule of Andropov (1982–84) and Chernenko (1984–85), efforts to alleviate economic stagnation, deterioration of relations with the U.S., succession of Gorbachev

2. The states of central Europe

  a. Austria since 1918

    i. Establishment of the First Republic (1918), economic reconstruction and political strife, association with Italy, authoritarian rule of the Dollfuss and Schuschnigg governments, the *Anschluss* (annexation by Germany) and participation in World War II

    ii. The Second Republic: independence in 1945, Allied occupation to 1955, restoration of sovereignty and establishment as a neutral state (1955), Kreisky's Socialist government (1970–83), coalition government under Sinowatz

  b. Hungary since 1918

    i. Establishment of the republic (1918); Béla Kun's "soviet republic"; loss of Transylvania, Slovakia, and Croatia by the Treaty of Trianon (1920); the Horthy regency (1920–45); financial crisis and the rise of the radical right; reacquisition of Slovakian territory in partnership with Germany; World War II; restoration of the Trianon frontiers (1947)

    ii. The postwar People's Republic: the reaction against Soviet domination in the Revolution of 1956, suppression of the revolt, the Kádár regime, introduction of the New Economic Mechanism

  c. Czechoslovakia since 1914

    i. The struggle for independence under Tomáš Masaryk, establishment of the republic (1918), consolidation of internal affairs

      ii. Discontent among Sudeten German and Slovak minorities: attempts at rapprochement with Germany, the Munich agreement (1938) and German takeover of Czechoslovakia, participation in World War II

      iii. The restoration of Czechoslovakia in 1945, the dominant role of the Communists, Jan Masaryk, Communist rule from 1948

      iv. Developments since 1948: the People's Democracy (1948–60), collectivization of land and adjustments to the Soviet pattern, attempts at liberalization and reform, "Prague Spring" under Dubček (1968), invasion by five Warsaw Pact countries and partial return to the Soviet line since 1968, emergence of the dissident Charter 77 movement in 1977

    d. Poland since 1918

      i. Establishment of the Second Polish Republic (1918), the "Polish Corridor," Polish–Soviet War of 1920–21, the Piłsudski regime, social and economic problems, German invasion and joint German–Soviet partition (1939), permanent loss of territory to the Soviet Union and annexation of German territory (1945)

      ii. Postwar developments: relations with the Roman Catholic Church, agricultural and industrial growth, the 1956 uprising, the Gomułka and Gierek governments, labour unrest and the formation of Solidarity, the Kania and Jaruzelski governments, imposition of martial law (1981–82) and suppression of Solidarity, relations with the Roman Catholic Church under John Paul II

    e. The establishment (1918) of Latvia, Estonia, and Lithuania as independent states following the breakup of the Russian Empire; political and economic development in the interwar period; incorporation into the Soviet Union (1940); German occupation (1941–44); collectivization and industrialization in the postwar period

  3. The Balkans: Greece, Yugoslavia, Bulgaria, Romania, and Albania since *c.* 1919

    a. Settlement of the borders of Balkan states (1919–26): continued dislocation of nationality groups, growth of peasant political parties and Communism

    b. Government reactions to civil unrest in the interwar period: land reform and industrialization, police repression, foreign relations, the Great Depression, political instability

    c. German invasion and Axis occupation (1940–45): resistance movements and Communist leadership of the partisans

    d. Postwar developments: establishment of Communist governments in Yugoslavia, Albania, Romania, and Bulgaria; Yugoslav break with the Soviet Union (1948); establishment of collective presidency after the death of Tito (1980); Greek military dictatorship (1967–74); return to civilian rule and repudiation of the monarchy (1974); leftist government under Papandreou from 1980; entry into the European Economic Community (1981); Albanian alignment with China (1961–78); increasing international isolation; Romanian nationalism and independence in foreign policy

C. The arts and intellectual life in Europe since 1920: increasing concern with the problems of alienation and despair, the importance of popular culture

---

Suggested reading in the *Encyclopædia Britannica:*

MACROPAEDIA: Major articles and biographies dealing with Europe since *c.* 1920

Albania	Denmark	International	Manchester
Amsterdam	Dublin	Relations,	Marseille
Antwerp	Edinburgh	20th-Century	Mediterranean Sea
Athens	Europe	Ireland	Milan
Austria	Finland	Italy	Moscow
Balkans	Florence	Kiev	Naples
Barcelona	France	Lenin	Norway
Berlin	Geneva	Leningrad	Paris
Brussels	Germany	Lisbon	Poland
Budapest	Greece	London	Portugal
Bulgaria	Hamburg	Low	Prague
Churchill	Hitler	Countries, The	Romania
Cologne	Hungary	Madrid	Rome
Czechoslovakia	Iceland	Malta	Spain

Stalin
Sweden
Switzerland

Union of Soviet
Socialist
Republics

United Kingdom
Venice
Vienna

Warsaw
Yugoslavia

MICROPAEDIA: Selected entries of reference information

General subjects

France:
Action Française
Bloc National
Foreign Legion
Free French
French
  Communist Party
Gauches,
  Cartel des
Maginot Line
National Centre of
  Independents and
  Peasants
Popular
  Republican
  Movement
Radical–Socialist
  Party
Rally for the
  Republic
Republican Party
Stavisky affair
Vichy France
Germany:
Anschluss
Baby Yar
Beer Hall Putsch
Berlin blockade
  and airlift
Christian
  Democratic
  Union
Christian Social
  Union
concentration
  camp
Dawes Plan
Drang nach Osten
East Prussia
extermination
  camp
Free Democratic
  Party
Freikorps
Führer
German
  Democratic
  Republic
German National
  People's Party
German-Soviet
  Nonaggression
  Pact
Germany, Federal
  Republic of

Gestapo
Hitler Youth
Holocaust
IG Farben
July Plot
Kristallnacht
Lausanne
  Conference
  (1932)
Mein Kampf
Memel dispute
Munich agreement
National
  Democratic Party
  of Germany
National Socialism
Nazi Party
Nürnberg Rally
Nürnberg trials
Oder–Neisse Line
Odessa
Polish Corridor
Red Army Faction
Reichstag fire
SA
Social Democratic
  Party of Germany
SS
Sudetenland
Wannsee
  Conference
Young Plan
Ireland:
Black and Tan
Fianna Fáil
Fine Gael
Home Rule
Irish Republican
  Army
Labour Party
Sinn Féin
Italy:
Blackshirt
Christian
  Democracy
Fiume question
Italian Communist
  Party
Italian Socialist
  Party
Italo-Ethiopian War
Lateran Treaty
Rome, March on
Poland:
Auschwitz

Curzon Line
Katyn Massacre
Korfanty Line
Oder–Neisse Line
Polish Corridor
Poznań Riots
Russo-Polish War
Solidarity
Vilnius dispute
Warsaw Ghetto
  Uprising
Warsaw Uprising
Spain:
Civil Guard
ETA
Falange
International
  Brigades
Rif War
Spanish Civil War
U.S.S.R.:
Basmachi
  Revolt
collectivization
Cominform
Communist Party
  of the Soviet
  Union
de-Stalinization
Democratic
  Centralist
Doctors' Plot
Far Eastern
  Republic
German-Soviet
  Nonaggression
  Pact
Gosplan
Gulag
Karakhan
  Manifesto
KGB
kolkhoz
Kronshtadt
  Rebellion
kulak
Leningrad
  Affair
Leninism
Lenin's Testament
Moscow, Treaty of
purge trials
Russian Civil War
Russo-Polish War
samizdat

secret speech
soviet
sovkhoz
Stalinism
Sun–Joffe
  Manifesto
Trotskyism
Twentieth
  Congress of the
  Communist Party
  of the Soviet
  Union
Warsaw Pact
Workers'
  Opposition
United Kingdom:
Britain, Battle of
Conservative
  Party
general strike
Labour Party
Liberal Party
Munich agreement
Plaid Cymru
Scottish National
  Party
Social Democratic
  Party
Ulster Defence
  Association
Ulster Volunteer
  Force
Westminster,
  Statute of (1931)
Yugoslavia:
Anti-Fascist
  Council of
  National
  Liberation of
  Yugoslavia
Chetnik
National
  Communism
Serbs, Croats,
  and Slovenes,
  Kingdom of
other:
Arrow Cross Party
Baltic states
Bulgarian Agrarian
  Union
EAM-ELAS
EDES
Iron Guard
Zveno Group

Biographies

Balkans:
Alexander II (Yugoslavia)
Boris III (Bulgaria)
Constantine II (Greece)
George II (Greece)
Hoxha, Enver
Metaxas, Ioannis
Papagos, Alexandros
Papandreou, Andreas
Papandreou, Georgios
Tito, Josip Broz
Zhivkov, Todor
Zog I

Czechoslovakia:
Beneš, Edvard
Dubček, Alexander
Gottwald, Klemens
Hácha, Emil
Masaryk, Jan
Masaryk, Tomáš
Zapotocky, Antonín

France:
Beaufre, André
Bidault, Georges
Blum, Léon
Briand, Aristide
Chaban-Delmas, Jacques
Coty, René
Couve de Murville, Maurice
Daladier, Édouard
Debré, Michel
Decoux, Jean
Doumergue, Gaston
Faure, Edgar
Gaulle, Charles de
Giscard d'Estaing, Valéry
Lattre de Tassigny, Jean de
Laval, Pierre
Mendès-France, Pierre
Millerand, Alexandre
Mitterrand, François
Mollet, Guy
Monnet, Jean
Painlevé, Paul
Pétain, Philippe
Pleven, René

Poincaré, Raymond
Pompidou, Georges
Poujade, Pierre
Reynard, Paul
Salan, Raoul
Schuman, Robert
Soustelle, Jacques
Tardieu, André
Thorez, Maurice

Germany and Austria:
Adenauer, Konrad
Brandt, Willy
Brüning, Heinrich
Dollfuss, Engelbert
Ebert, Friedrich
Erhard, Ludwig
Eichmann, Adolf
Goebbels, Joseph
Göring, Hermann
Guderian, Heinz
Hess, Rudolf
Himmler, Heinrich
Hindenburg, Paul von
Hitler, Adolf
Honecker, Erich
Hugenberg, Alfred
Kapp, Wolfgang
Kesselring, Albert
Kiesinger, Kurt Georg
Kohl, Helmut
Ludendorff, Erich
Papen, Franz von
Rathenau, Walther
Ribbentrop, Joachim von
Roehm, Ernst
Rommel, Erwin
Rosenberg, Alfred
Rundstedt, Gerd von
Schacht, Hjalmar
Schleicher, Kurt von
Schmidt, Helmut
Schuschnigg, Kurt von
Seyss-Inquart, Arthur
Speer, Albert
Strasser, Gregor and Otto
Strauss, Franz Joseph
Stresemann, Gustav

Ulbricht, Walter
Hungary:
Bethlen, István Gróf
Horthy de Nagybánya, Miklós
Kádár, János
Nagy, Imre
Rákosi, Matyás
Ireland:
Cosgrave, Liam
Cosgrave, William Thomas
Costello, John A.
De Valera, Eamon
Fitzgerald, Garret
Griffith, Arthur
Haughey, Charles James
Lemass, Sean F.
Lynch, John
Italy:
Andreotti, Giulio
Bagdoglio, Pietro
Berlinguer, Enrico
Ciano, Galeazzo
De Gasperi, Alcide
Moro, Aldo
Mussolini, Benito
Togliatti, Palmiro
Umberto II
Victor Emmanuel III
Low Countries:
Baudouin I
Bernhard, Prince of The Netherlands
Juliana
Leopold III (Belgium)
Spaak, Paul-Henri
Wilhelmina
Poland:
Gierek, Edward
Gomułka, Władysław
Jaruzelski, Wojciech
Piłsudski, Józef Klemens
Sikosski, Władysław
Wałęsa, Lech
Scandinavia and Baltic states:
Bernadotte, Folke, Greve
Erlander, Tage

Hammarskjöld, Dag
Hansson, Per Albin
Kekkonen, Urho Kaleva
Palme, Olof
Quisling, Vidkun
Smetona, Antanas
Ulmanis, Kārlis
Wallenberg, Raoul

Spain and Portugal:
Alfonso XIII
Azaña y Díaz, Manuel
Franco, Francisco
Gil Robles, José María
Juan Carlos
Primo de Rivera, Miguel
Salazar, Antonio de Oliveira

United Kingdom:
Attlee, Clement
Baldwin, Stanley
Beaverbrook, Max Aitken, 1st Baron
Benn, Tony
Bevan, Aneurin
Bevin, Ernest
Birkenhead, Frederick Edwin Smith, 1st earl of
Callaghan, James
Chamberlain, Neville
Charles, Prince of Wales
Churchill, Sir Winston
Curzon, George Nathaniel
Curzon, Marquess
Douglas-Home, Sir Alec
Eden, Anthony
Edward VIII
Elizabeth II
George V
George VI
Halifax, Edward Frederick Lindley Wood, 1st earl of
Heath, Edward
Henderson, Arthur
Hoare, Sir Samuel
Kinnock, Neil

Law, Bonar
Linlithgow, Victor
  Alexander John
  Hope, 2nd
  marquess of
Lloyd George,
  David
MacDonald,
  Ramsay
Macmillan, Harold
Montgomery,
  Bernard Law
Montgomery, 1st
  Viscount
Mountbatten,
  Louis
Mountbatten, 1st
  Earl
Nicolson, Sir
  Harold
Samuel, Herbert
  Louis Samuel, 1st
  Viscount
Strachey, John
Thatcher,
  Margaret

Wilson, Harold
U.S.S.R.:
  Andropov, Yury
    Vladimirovich
  Beria, Lavrenty
    Pavlovich
  Brezhnev, Leonid
    Ilich
  Bukharin, Nikolay
    Ivanovich
  Bulganin, Nikolay
    Aleksandrovich
  Chernenko,
    Konstantin
    Ustinovich
  Dzerzhinsky,
    Feliks
    Edmundovich
  Gorbachev,
    Mikhail
    Sergeyevich
  Gromyko, Andrey
    Andreyevich
  Kaganovich, Lazar
    Moiseyevich

Kamenev, Lev
  Borisovich
Khrushchev,
  Nikita
Kosygin, Aleksey
  Nikolayevich
Lenin, Vladimir
  Ilich
Litvinov, Maksim
  Maksimovich
Mikoyan, Anastas
  Ivanovich
Molotov,
  Vyacheslav
  Mikhaylovich
Ordzhonikidze,
  Grigory
  Konstantinovich
Radek, Karl
Rakovsky,
  Khristian
  Georgiyevich
Rykov, Aleksey
  Ivanovich
Savinkov, Boris
  Viktorovich

Stalin, Joseph
Suslov, Mikhail
  Andreyevich
Trotsky, Leon
Vyshinsky, Andrey
  Yanuaryevich
Voroshilov,
  Kliment
  Yefremovich
Yezhov, Nikolay
  Ivanovich
Zhukov, Georgy
  Konstantinovich
Zinovyev, Grigory
  Yevseyevich

INDEX: See entries under all of the terms above

Section 973. **The United States and Canada Since 1920**

A. The United States since 1920

1. The post-World War I Republican administrations

   a. Politics and economics under Harding and Coolidge (1921–29): favouritism toward big business, restriction of immigration, "Coolidge prosperity"

   b. Social conditions in the 1920s: prohibition, growth of organized crime, and the jazz age

   c. Hoover's administration (1929–33) and the Great Depression: the stock market crash, domestic and international repercussions, Hoover's attempts to effect economic recovery

2. The effects of the New Deal and World War II: the presidency of Franklin D. Roosevelt (1933–45)

   a. Comprehensive New Deal measures for economic recovery, relief, and reform

   b. Reform measures of the second New Deal and the election of 1936

      i. Judicial invalidation of New Deal legislation: power struggle between Supreme Court and President

      ii. Labour legislation and union activity: strengthening of the Democratic coalition

   c. Foreign policy between the World Wars: isolationism and neutrality, opposition to Japanese expansionism in Asia and economic sanctions against Japan, lend-lease aid to Britain (1940–41), the "good neighbor" policy in Latin America

   d. The U.S. in World War II: wartime mobilization, regulation of production and manpower, the role of U.S. forces in defeating the Axis powers in Europe and the Pacific, U.S. military occupation of Japan and participation with the Allies in occupation of Germany

3. The U.S. after World War II: the era of the Cold War

   a. The Truman administration (1945–53)

      i. Foreign policy aimed at the containment of Communism: the Truman Doctrine and the Marshall Plan (1947), the Point Four Program (1949), the creation of NATO, U.S. support of Nationalist China

      ii. Programs of the Fair Deal: the conversion to a peacetime economy, labour disputes and inflation, the Taft–Hartley Act (1947), the Social Security Act (1950)

     iii. McCarthyism and the emergence of the radical right

     iv. The Korean War (1950–53): wartime mobilization of the U.S. economy, peace and bilateral security treaties with Japan (1951), the election of 1952

      v. Maintenance of a large postwar military establishment: collaboration of science and industry

   b. The Eisenhower administrations (1953–61)

       i. Intensification of the civil rights movement and innovative decisions of the Warren Court, passage of the Civil Rights acts of 1957 and 1960

      ii. Foreign policy during the Eisenhower years: John Foster Dulles and the Suez crisis (1956), the U.S. in the space race (1958), intervention in Lebanon (1958), continued support of Nationalist China, the U-2 affair

     iii. Social and economic problems: recessions (1953–54 and 1957–58), growing racial unrest, unemployment, labour strikes and the Landrum–Griffin Act (1959)

4. Intensification of government activity and social tensions in the 1960s and 1970s

   a. The election of 1960 and the Kennedy administration (1961–63): the Cuban missile crisis (1962), the Nuclear Test-Ban Treaty (1963), military aid to South Vietnam, the assassination of John F. Kennedy (1963)

   b. The Lyndon B. Johnson administrations (1963–69)

       i. Civil Rights acts of 1964 and 1968, the 1964 election, Medicare and other social welfare legislation, inflation and increased governmental economic activity

      ii. Increasing alienation among the youth and minority groups: protests in cities and on campuses, the assassinations of Robert F. Kennedy and Martin Luther King, Jr. (1968), the anti-Vietnam War movement, the election of 1968

     iii. Johnson's foreign policy: expansion of U.S. involvement in the Vietnam War from 1965, commencement of Paris peace talks (1968), U.S. military and economic aid to Middle Eastern and Latin-American countries

   c. The Nixon administrations (1969–74)

       i. Nixon's foreign policy: the continuing Vietnam War and the Paris peace talks, the Cambodian invasion (1970), rapprochement with the People's Republic of China, Vietnam War cease-fire agreement (1973)

      ii. Inflation, high unemployment, and temporary price and wage controls; cabinet reorganization; anti-war demonstrations; the election of 1972

     iii. The Watergate scandal, the resignation (1973) of Vice Pres. Spiro T. Agnew and appointment of Gerald R. Ford, the resignation (1974) of Nixon

   d. The Ford administration (1974–77)

       i. Continuance of foreign policy under Secretary of State Henry A. Kissinger: détente with the Soviet Union, conclusion of the Vietnam War, continuing Strategic Arms Limitation Talks (SALT)

      ii. Presidential pardon of Nixon, continuing inflation and unemployment, financial crisis in New York City, scandal centred on intelligence-gathering agencies

     iii. Celebration of the bicentennial of the Declaration of Independence (1976), the election of 1976

   e. The Carter administration (1977–81)

       i. Carter's foreign policy: human rights and conduct of foreign affairs, Panama Canal treaties (1977–78)

      ii. Presidential pardon of Vietnam draft evaders; presentation to Congress of programs on energy and on reform of the federal bureaucracy and of electoral, federal welfare, and Social Security systems; continuing inflation and unemployment

   f. The Reagan administrations (1981–   )

       i. Economic program, recession and recovery

      ii. Anti-Communist foreign-policy stance and deteriorating relations with the Soviet Union, involvement in the Central American–Caribbean region and the Middle East

g. Scientific advances in the 1960s, 1970s, and 1980s: nuclear weapons technology, space exploration and development of the space shuttle, the computer revolution

5. Cultural developments since the 1920s: the influence of the mass media on popular arts; developments in literature, philosophy, and the visual arts—the weakening of the legacy of European culture and traditions

B. Canada since 1920

1. Canada between the World Wars

a. The Liberal government under King (1921–30): Commonwealth relations, nationalism and the return to isolationism

b. The Great Depression and relief measures of the Conservative government (1930–35): return of the Liberal government (1935); foreign trade, welfare legislation, financial reforms, minor political parties

2. Canadian participation in World War II: mobilization of manpower and production, development of armed forces

3. Canada since 1945

a. Postwar foreign policy: North American continentalism and collective security: participation in NATO, the UN, and the Korean War; U.S.–Canadian economic relations

b. Involvement in British Commonwealth affairs: relations with Third World nations

c. Franco-Canadian relations and French separatism in Quebec: conflicts between French- and English-speaking Canadians

d. Postwar prosperity: expansion of manufacturing and mining industries; economic nationalism; relations with Indians, Eskimo, and Métis

e. Internal politics since 1945: Liberal Party control (1945–57), the Progressive Conservative coalition (1957–63), Liberal government after 1963 and the Trudeau years (1968–79, 1980–84), Canada's constitution (1982), Progressive Conservative government from 1984

Suggested reading in the *Encyclopædia Britannica*:

MACROPAEDIA: Major articles and a biography dealing with the United States and Canada since 1920

Canada
North America
Roosevelt, Franklin D.
United States of America

MICROPAEDIA: Selected entries of reference information; see also Sections 965 and 971

General subjects

Canada:
  Canada Act
  Co-operative
    Commonwealth
    Federation
  Liberal Party of
    Canada
  New Democratic
    Party
  Parti Québecois
  Progressive
    Conservative
    Party
  Social Credit Party
U.S. domestic
affairs and social
programs:
  Adkins v.
    Children's
    Hospital

Agricultural
  Adjustment
  Administration
American Civil
  Liberties Union
black nationalism
Black Panther
  Party
Bonus Army
bootlegging
Brain Trust
Brown v. Board
  of Education of
  Topeka
Christian Front
Civil Rights Act
Civil Rights
  Movement
Civilian
  Conservation
  Corps

Democratic Party
Dixiecrat
Fair Deal
Farmer–Labor
  Party
Great Society
Hoover
  Commission
Indian
  Reorganization
  Act
Liberal Party
National Recovery
  Administration
New Deal
Nisei
Ohio Gang
Peace Corps
Progressive Party
Public Works
  Administration

Republican Party
Sacco–Vanzetti
  case
Scopes Trial
Scottsboro case
Social Security Act
Taft–Hartley Act
Teapot Dome
  Scandal
Tennessee Valley
  Authority
Warren
  Commission
Watergate Scandal
Works Progress
  Administration
U.S. foreign relations:
  America First
    Committee
  Bay of Pigs
    invasion

Cuban Missile Crisis
Eisenhower Doctrine
Good Neighbor Policy
Gulf of Tonkin Resolution

Korean War
lend-lease
Marshall Plan
Nuclear Test-Ban Treaty
Pueblo Incident
Strategic Arms Limitation Talks

Truman Doctrine
Vietnam War
other:
German-American Bund
John Birch Society
Manhattan Project

National Security Act

Biographies

Canadians:
Bennett, Richard Bedford, Viscount Bennett
Diefenbaker, John G.
King, W.L. Mackenzie
Lesage, Jean
Mulrony, Martin Brian
Saint Laurent, Louis
Trudeau, Pierre Elliott

U.S. government and diplomatic figures:
Acheson, Dean
Borah, William E.
Bundy, McGeorge
Byrnes, James F.
Curley, James M.
Daugherty, Harry Micajah
Dawes, Charles G.
Dirksen, Everett McKinley
Dulles, John Foster
Farley, James A.
Foster, William Z.
Fulbright, James William
Garner, John Nance
Hobby, Oveta Culp
Hoover, J. Edgar
Hopkins, Harry L.
Hull, Cordell
Humphrey, Hubert H.
Hurley, Patrick J.
Ickes, Harold L.
Jones, Jesse H.
Kellogg, Frank B.
Kennan, George F.
Kennedy, Robert F.

Kissinger, Henry A.
Knowland, William Fife
Long, Huey
McCarthy, Eugene J.
McCarthy, Joseph R.
McGovern, George S.
McNamara, Robert Strange
Mansfield, Michael J.
Moley, Raymond
Morganthau, Henry, Jr.
Moses, Robert
Norris, George W.
Perkins, Frances
Rayburn, Sam
Rockefeller, Nelson Aldrich
Smith, Alfred E.
Stevenson, Adlai E.
Stimson, Henry L.
Taft, Robert A.
Vance, Cyrus
Vandenberg, Arthur H.
Wagner, Robert F.
Walker, James J.
Wallace, George C.
Wallace, Henry A.
Weaver, Robert C.
Willkie, Wendell L.

U.S. jurists and lawyers:
Black, Hugo
Brandeis, Louis
Brennan, William J., Jr.
Burger, Warren E.
Cardozo, Benjamin Nathan
Darrow, Clarence

Dewey, Thomas E.
Douglas, William O.
Fortas, Abe
Frankfurter, Felix
Goldberg, Arthur J.
Hand, Learned
Holmes, Oliver Wendell, Jr.
Hughes, Charles Evans
Marshall, Thurgood
O'Connor, Sandra Day
Stone, Harlan Fiske
Vinson, Fred M.
Warren, Earl

U.S. military leaders:
Bradley, Omar N.
Buckner, Simon Bolivar, Jr.
Carlson, Evans
Clark, Mark
Clay, Lucius D.
Doolittle, James H.
Eichelberger, Robert L.
Halsey, William F., Jr.
Leahy, William D.
LeMay, Curtis E.
MacArthur, Douglas
McAuliffe, Anthony C.
Marshall, George C.
Mitchell, William
Mitscher, Marc A.
Nimitz, Chester W.
Patton, George S.
Rickover, Hyman G.
Ridgway, Matthew B.

Smith, Walter Bedell
Spaatz, Carl
Stilwell, Joseph W.
Taylor, Maxwell D.
Wainright, Jonathan M.

U.S. presidents:
Carter, Jimmy
Coolidge, Calvin
Eisenhower, Dwight D.
Ford, Gerald R.
Harding, Warren G.
Hoover, Herbert
Johnson, Lyndon B.
Kennedy, John F.
Nixon, Richard M.
Reagan, Ronald W.
Roosevelt, Franklin D.
Truman, Harry S.

U.S. social and religious figures:
Addams, Jane
Dix, Dorothea
Du Bois, W.E.B.
King, Martin Luther, Jr.
Malcolm X
Rankin, Jeanette
Roosevelt, Eleanor
Sanger, Margaret
Thomas, Norman
other:
Hiss, Alger
Oswald, Lee Harvey
Rosenberg, Julius and Ethel

INDEX: See entries under all of the terms above

Section 974.   **Latin-American and Caribbean Nations Since *c.* 1920**

A. Mexico since 1920

   1. Obregón's coup and Carranza's execution (1920), land reforms during Obregón's (1920–24) and Calles' (1924–28) regimes, rule by Calles' National Revolutionary Party (1928–34)

   2. Cárdenas' Six-Year Plan (1934–40): social and economic reforms, reorganization of the National Revolutionary Party, expropriation of foreign industry (1938), election of Avila Camacho (1940)

   3. Mexico during World War II: economic and military cooperation with the United States, wartime industrialization

   4. Mexico since 1945

      a. Economic and social development: the Institutional Revolutionary Party and peaceful presidential successions, female suffrage (1958), foreign trade and industrialization, emergence as a major oil and gas producer, oil boom and financial crisis of the early 1980s, nationalization of the banks (1982)

      b. Urbanization and educational advancements, relations with the U.S. and other countries, tensions over illegal immigration to the U.S., influx of Central American refugees and efforts at peacemaking in the region, social and economic planning in the 1970s and 1980s

B. Central America and the Caribbean since *c.* 1920

   1. The Central American republics since *c.* 1920

      a. Guatemala since 1920

         i. Successive presidential governments in the 1920s, Ubico's dictatorship (1931–44), social reforms of Arévalo's regime (1945–50)

         ii. Growth of Communist influence during Arbenz' regime (1951–54), military coup (1954), anti-Communist activity in Castillo Armas' regime (1954–57), domination by the armed forces from 1970, increased guerrilla and terrorist activity from 1980

      b. Honduras since 1920: political unrest in the 1920s; Carías Andino's dictatorship (1932–49); administrations of Gálvez (1949–54), Lozano Díaz (1954–56), Villeda Morales (1957–63), and successive military governments; return to civilian rule in 1982; involvement in regional conflicts

      c. El Salvador since 1920: military dictatorships to 1944, governments of Castaneda Castro (1945–48), junta rule and PRUD domination (1948–60), continued authoritarian military governments thereafter, war with Honduras (1969–70), civil war of the 1970s and early 1980s and U.S. involvement, election of Duarte as civilian president (1984)

      d. Nicaragua since 1920: continued U.S. military intervention until 1933, Sacasa's regime (1933–36), Somoza family's dominance (1937–79), Sandinista rule, counterrevolutionary movements and U.S. involvement

      e. Costa Rica since 1920: border disputes with Panama until 1941, orderly presidential succession, industrialization and urbanization, economic problems of the early 1980s

      f. Panama since 1920: unstable local politics and U.S. intervention, economic development, National Guard rule under Omar Torrijos (1968–78), the Panama Canal treaties with the U.S. (1978)

      g. Belize since 1920: progress toward independence, government of George Price (1961–84), achievement of independence in 1981

   2. The island states of the Caribbean since the end of U.S. occupation

      a. Haiti since 1934: internal struggle for power (1934–57), presidency of François Duvalier (1957–71) and succession by his son in 1971, relations with Dominican Republic, social and economic problems, exodus of illegal immigrants to the U.S. from the late 1970s

      b. Dominican Republic since 1930: Trujillo's dictatorship (1930–61), economic and social services development, later repression ending with Trujillo's assassination, alternating elected governments and military juntas, the 1965 revolution and U.S. intervention, relative political stability from the mid-1970s

      c. Cuba since 1934

         i. Fulgencio Batista's first (1933–44) and second (1952–59) dictatorships, growth of the military and middle classes, the sugar industry

         ii. The Cuban Revolution of 1959: Fidel Castro's program for Cuban Socialism

iii. Cuba under Castro: nationalization of foreign-owned property, Cuban emigration, alignment with the Soviet bloc, the 1962 missile crisis, the effort to form a Socialist society, second wave of emigration in 1980, military involvement in Africa

d. The new nations of the Caribbean region: Antigua and Barbuda, The Bahamas, Barbados, Dominica, Grenada, Jamaica, St. Christopher and Nevis, St. Lucia, St. Vincent and the Grenadines, Trinidad and Tobago; efforts toward development and regional cooperation; U.S. involvement in the region; military intervention in Grenada (1983)

e. U.S. and European territories and possessions in the Caribbean region: Puerto Rico and the Virgin Islands, Bermuda and other British insular possessions, French Guiana and French insular possessions, Netherlands Antilles

C. Venezuela and Colombia since *c.* 1930

1. Venezuela since 1935

a. Abortive attempts at democratic government amid renewed military dictatorships (1935–58), constitution of 1961, the Acción Democrática party's economic reforms, political stabilization under Acción Democrática and Social Christian (COPEI) governments

b. Social and economic development from 1959, growing economic importance of petroleum, nationalization of the petroleum industry (1976), efforts toward development and industrial diversification

2. Colombia since 1930

a. Liberal Party rule (1930–46): social and land reforms during López' administrations (1934–38 and 1942–45)

b. Reemergence of Conservative rule under Ospina Pérez (1946–50), civil unrest and political repression (1948–53), military dictatorships to 1958, coalition of Conservatives and Liberals in National Front government

c. Economic problems in the 1960s and 1970s, return to stable government under Lleras Restrepo (1966–70) and Pastrana Borrero (1970–74), formal end of National Front arrangement in 1974 and subsequent elections, increasing activity by left-wing guerrillas and right-wing paramilitary groups, Betancur Cuartas' amnesty offer to guerrillas (1982), growth of drug trafficking and associated corruption

D. Ecuador, Peru, and Bolivia since *c.* 1930

1. Ecuador since 1925

a. Economic development and participation in World War II, loss of territory to Peru (1942)

b. Various administrations of Velasco Ibarra and other presidents and military coups after 1945, constitution of 1979 and return to civilian rule, economic and social effects of the exploitation of petroleum after 1972

2. Peru since 1930

a. The overthrow of Leguía (1930); Sánchez Cerro's administration (1931–33); the Aprista uprising and Sánchez Cerro's assassination; Benavides' administration (1933–39), social reforms, and the outlawing of the Apristas

b. Prado's first administration (1939–45); wartime cooperation with the U.S. and economic prosperity, legalization and re-outlawing of the Apristas during Bustamante's administration (1945–48), Odría's military dictatorship (1948–56) and suppression of Apristas

c. Re-legalization of Apristas and economic prosperity during Prado's second term (1956–62), military seizure of power (1962), social reforms of Belaúnde Terry's administration (1963–68), military takeover in 1968, restoration of civilian rule (1980) and return of Belaúnde as president, economic difficulties of the early 1980s, rise of Sendero Luminoso guerrillas, accession of left-of-centre government under Gárcia Pérez (1985)

3. Bolivia since 1930

a. The revolt of 1930, Salamanca's presidency (1930–36), the effect of the Great Depression on the mining industry, the Chaco War (1932–35) and loss of territory to Paraguay

b. Military coup (1936), rise of MNR and PIR political parties, 1943 military coup and the Villaroel dictatorship (1943–46), political instability to 1951, military junta (1951–52)

c. The Bolivian National Revolution (1952), nationalization of the tin industry, electoral and land reforms, Paz Estenssoro's administrations (1952–56 and 1960–64), U.S. economic aid, civil disorders, alternating military and civilian governments in the 1960s and 1970s, return to civilian rule under Siles Zuazo (1982), foreign debt and other economic problems, effects of drug trafficking, return of Paz Estenssoro as president (1985)

E. Chile since 1920

   1. Chile from 1920 to 1938

      a. The presidency of Alessandri Palma (1920–24, 1925), military coup (1924), return to civilian rule (1925), constitution of 1925 and reduction of legislative power, political instability, military dictatorship under Ibáñez del Campo (1927–31)

      b. Economic crises during the 1930s: brief return to civilian rule under Montero Rodríguez, military coup and 100-day rule of Socialist Republic, Alessandri Palma's second administration (1932–38)

   2. Chile from 1938 to 1952: the era of the Radical Party presidencies

      a. The administrations of Cerda (1938–41) and Ríos (1942–46): agrarian reforms, Chilean neutrality until 1942, economic prosperity

      b. González Videla's administration (1946–52): strengthened economic ties with the U.S., return of Conservative Party influence

   3. Chilean politics since 1952

      a. Ibáñez del Campo's administration (1952–58) and strong presidential leadership, administration of Alessandri Rodríguez (1958–64), social and economic problems, proliferation of leftist political parties and realignment of conservative parties

      b. Frei's administration (1964–70) and nationalization of the economy, Allende's Marxist administration (1970–73), military coup (1973) and military rule under Pinochet Ugarte, political repression, economic experimentation and difficulties

F. Argentina, Uruguay, and Paraguay since *c.* 1930

   1. Argentina since 1930

      a. The conservative restoration (1930–43): economic ties with Great Britain, electoral fraud and violence in the 1930s, neutrality in World War II

      b. The Perón era (1943–55): his rise to and fall from power, economic policies

      c. Argentina since 1955: attempts to restore constitutionalism, military dictatorships, civil wars and Peronista resurgence, return (1973) and death (1974) of Perón, military coup (1976), excesses and economic failures of military rule, invasion of the Falklands/Malvinas and defeat by Britain (1982), return to civilian rule under Alfonsín (1983), foreign debt problems

   2. Uruguay since 1929

      a. The Great Depression, dictatorship of Gabriel Terra (1933–38), election of Alfredo Baldomir (1938), Uruguayan neutrality until 1945, economic boom and social reforms

      b. Post-World War II developments: the constitution of 1951 and the plural executive, recession (1954–58), 1958 election of Nationalists (Blancos), return of Colorado Party and restoration of presidential powers (1966), Tupamaro insurgency, dismissal of Congress (1973) and assumption of effective control by the military, severe recession of the early 1980s, restoration of civilian government (1985)

   3. Paraguay since 1924

      a. The Great Depression, victory over Bolivia in Chaco War (1932–35), Allied alignment in World War II

      b. Political instability and economic retardation: Stroessner's dictatorship since 1954

G. Brazil since 1930: the Second Republic

   1. The Getúlio Vargas dictatorship (1930–45): the revolution of 1930, the constitutions of 1934 and 1937, Vargas' consolidation of power (1937), social and economic legislation, Allied participation in World War II, Vargas' forced resignation (1945)

   2. Political, social, and economic developments in Brazil since 1945

      a. Election of Eurico Gaspar Dutra (1945) and the constitution of 1946: restoration of civil and personal liberties and representative government, outlawing of Communist Party (1947)

      b. Re-election of Vargas (1950), economic crises and governmental corruption, Vargas' forced resignation and suicide (1954)

      c. Interim presidency of João Café Filho (1954), election of Juscelino Kubitschek as president and João Goulart as vice president (1955), economic development and inflation

    d. Election of Jânio Quadros as president and Goulart's re-election as vice president (1960), Quadros' resignation (1961), governmental opposition to Goulart, parliamentary experiment with figurehead president and prime minister as head of state, 1963 plebiscite giving Goulart full presidential powers

    e. Social and economic unrest: re-emergence of Communist Party, nationalization of oil refineries, revolution and exile of Goulart (1964), Pascoal Ranieri Mazzilli as interim president and beginning of military rule

    f. Castelo Branco's presidency (1964–67): the First, Second, and Third Institutional acts; suspension of existing political parties; creation of artificial two-party system; constitution of 1967

    g. The presidencies of Costa e Silva, Médici, Geisel, and Figueiredo after 1967: economic growth and reduction of inflation; the constitution of 1967; moves toward democratization; end of controlled two-party system (1979) and formation of new parties; gains by the opposition party in the election of 1982; increased concentration of authority in central government (1983); recession, resurgent inflation, and foreign debt problems of the early 1980s, return to civilian government (1985)

    h. Social developments since 1945: urbanization and education, increased electorate, role of the church and the military in national politics

H. Development of Latin-American literature, music, and visual arts in the 20th century: the intermingling of European, Indian, and African cultures

---

Suggested reading in the *Encyclopædia Britannica:*

MACROPAEDIA: Major articles dealing with Latin-American and Caribbean nations since *c.* 1920

Argentina	Colombia	Lima	São Paulo
Bolivia	Ecuador	Mexico	South America
Brazil	Guianas, The	Mexico City	Uruguay
Buenos Aires	Havana	Paraguay	Venezuela
Central America	Latin America,	Peru	West Indies
Chile	The History of	Rio de Janeiro	

MICROPAEDIA: Selected entries of reference information

General subjects

Central America and the Caribbean:	Communist Party of Cuba	*Mexico:* Indigenismo	descamisado Estado Novo
Bay of Pigs invasion	Cuban missile crisis	Institutional	Peronista
Canal Zone	Sandinista	Revolutionary	Rio de Janeiro,
Central American	26th of July	Party	Protocol of
Common	Movement	Sinarquismo	Shining Path
Market	West Indies	*South America:*	Tupamaro
	Associated States	Chaco War	

Biographies

Central America and the Caribbean:	Torrijos (Herrera), Omar	Echeverría (Álvarez), Luis	Frei (Montalva), Eduardo
Batista, Fulgencio	Trujillo (Molina),	López Mateos,	Haya de la Torre,
Bosch, Juan	Rafael (Leónidas)	Adolfo	Víctor Raúl
Castro, Fidel	Ubico (Castañeda),	Obregón, Alvaro	Ibáñez del Campo,
Duvalier, François	Jorge	*South America:*	Carlos
Guevara, Che	*Mexico:*	Allende (Gossens),	Perón, Eva
Guzmán	Alemán,	Salvador	Perón, Juan
Fernández,	Miguel	Belaúnde Terry,	Rojas, Pinilla
Silvestre Antonio	Calles, Plutarco	Fernando	Gustavo
Somoza Debayle,	Elías	Câmara, Helder	Vargas, Getúlio
Anastasio	Cárdenas, Lázaro	Pessoa	

INDEX: See entries under all of the terms above

Section 975. **East Asia: China in Revolution, the Era of Japanese Hegemony, and the Influence of the United States in the 20th Century**

A. China since 1912

    1. The development of the republic (1912–20)

        a. Early power struggles: Chinese involvement in World War I

            i. Japanese gains in the early part of the war: Yüan Shih-k'ai's attempts to become emperor

            ii. Conflict over entry into the war, formation of a rival southern government, changes brought about by the war

        b. Modernization and the growth of nationalism: emergence of a new intelligentsia, riots and protests

    2. The interwar years (1920–37)

        a. The beginnings of a national revolution: the Kuomintang, the Chinese Communist Party, cooperation between the two parties

        b. Reactions to warlords and foreigners: militarism in China, the continued presence of foreign interests, reorganization of the Kuomintang

        c. Struggles within the two-party coalition: influence of Soviet Russia

            i. Outbreak of clashes with foreigners: Kuomintang opposition to the radicals

            ii. The Northern Expedition: peasant uprisings leading to the expulsion of the Communists from the Kuomintang, Communist movement into the hills and plains of central China

        d. The Nationalist government from 1928 to 1937: Chiang Kai-shek's attempts to eliminate the Communists

            i. Attempts at economic reform and failure in agriculture, educational reform, economic competition with the Japanese in Manchuria

            ii. Renewal of Japanese aggression: war between the Communists and Nationalists, the Long March, formation of the United Front against Japan

    3. The war against Japan (1937–45)

        a. Communist–Nationalist cooperation in the early stages of the war, renewed conflict between the two groups

        b. International alliance against Japan: U.S. military aid, internal conflicts, the crisis of 1944 and Nationalist deterioration, Communist growth and international efforts to prevent civil war

    4. The development of Kuomintang and Chinese Communist ideologies

        a. Origins and background of modern ideologies: social and political conditions, China's ideological heritage

        b. The political ideas of Sun Yat-sen: nationalism, democracy, and livelihood

        c. The political ideas of Chiang Kai-shek: idealization of Chinese tradition

        d. The development of Maoist ideology: the role of peasants, the "people's war," the border regions

    5. Emergence of the People's Republic of China

        a. The Civil War (1945–49): the race for territory, Communist successes and ultimate victory

        b. Economic reforms and reforms in the traditional Chinese social structure (1949–57)

            i. Reconstruction and consolidation of power (1949–52): participation in the Korean War, agrarian reform

            ii. The transition to socialism (1953–57): rural collectivization, urban nationalization

        c. The period of the Great Leap Forward and the transition to the Cultural Revolution

            i. New directions in national policy (1958–61): literature and arts for the masses, rural communes

            ii. Readjustment and reaction (1961–65): restoration of order, China as a nuclear power

        iii. The Great Proletarian Cultural Revolution (1966–76): attacks on cultural leaders and party members, resistance to Peking

        iv. Mao's "Reconstruction" (1969–71): the Chinese challenge to Soviet Communism, the Ninth Congress of the Chinese Communist Party (April 1969)

    d. International relations: UN representation (1971), rapprochement with the U.S. and Japan (1972), continuing friction with the Soviet Union, U.S. diplomatic relations with China (1979), increased cultural and economic contacts overseas, signing of Hong Kong agreement with Great Britain (1984)

    e. Internal affairs: the 10th Congress of the CCP (August 1973) and the fourth National People's Congress and new national constitution (January 1975), death of Zhou Enlai (January 1976) and factional strife, death of Mao Zedong (September 1976), ascendancy of Deng Xiaoping disgrace and conviction of Maoist Gang of Four, new party and national constitutions (1982), changes in economic structure and introduction of economic incentives

  6. The Nationalist government in Taiwan since 1949: initial repression and consolidation; leadership of Chiang Kai-shek until his death; alliance with the U.S. and economic growth; loss of UN representation (1971); Taiwanese separatism; loss of diplomatic support from most nations, including U.S. (1979); economic prosperity

B. Japan since *c.* 1910

  1. Japan's political, economic, and social developments in the early 20th century

    a. Constitutional government: party politics, participation by bureaucrats and business elites

    b. Social and economic changes: attempts to organize labour, cultural trends, growth of educated classes

  2. The rise and fall of Imperial Japan (*c.* 1920–45)

    a. The rise of the militarists, growth of antigovernment sentiment

    b. Antigovernment acts: the seizure of initiative in foreign policy by the military, the outbreak of war with China (1937), Axis leanings

    c. Japan's proclamation of the Greater East Asia Co-prosperity Sphere (1938), official alignment with the Axis powers (1940), and deterioration of relations with the other Western powers: Tōjō's cabinet and outbreak of war with the U.S. (1941)

    d. Initial Japanese successes in Southeast Asia and the South Pacific, the Allied counterattack culminating in the fire and atomic bombing of Japanese cities, Japan's unconditional surrender (1945)

    e. Postwar Japan: political reform, economic and social changes, international relations and cultural developments

        i. Japan under U.S. military occupation (1945–52): democratization of Japanese society; constitutional, land, and labour reforms; increased rights for women

        ii. International relations and politics; loss of Korea and other territories, relations with China and the U.S., growth of radical political movements in the 1960s, politics of moderation

        iii. Restoration of Japanese independence (1952): great economic growth, admission to the UN (1956), return of the Bonins and Ryukyus, Japan as a major world trader, economic tensions with U.S. and the European Communities, rapprochement with China (1978), overtures toward Southeast Asia and Korea, long dominance of Liberal-Democratic Party and intra-party factionalism

C. Korea since 1910

  1. Japanese rule (1910–45): military control, the March 1st independence movement and formation of a provisional Korean government in exile (1919), resistance movements and the end of Japanese rule

  2. Korea since 1945

    a. Division into South and North Korea (1948): U.S. and Soviet military aid to and disputes over the two Korean republics

    b. North Korean invasion (1950) of South Korea and the Korean War (1950–53): U.S. and UN intervention, Chinese participation, armistice (1953)

    c. South Korea since the armistice: the regimes of Syngman Rhee (1948–60) and Park Chung Hee (1961–79), the assassination of Park and its consequences, economic growth

d. North Korea since the armistice: consolidation of Communist government power under Kim Il-sung, relations with the Soviet Union and the People's Republic of China, military and industrial growth

---

Suggested reading in the *Encyclopædia Britannica*:

MACROPAEDIA: Major articles and a biography dealing with East Asia: China in revolution, the era of Japanese hegemony, and the influence of the United States in the 20th century

Asia	Japan	Nanking	Tientsin
Canton	Korea	Peking	Tokyo–Yokohama
China	Mao Zedong	Shanghai	Metropolitan
Hong Kong	Mongolia	Taiwan	Area

MICROPAEDIA: Selected entries of reference information; see also Sections 96/10 and 971

General subjects

China:
Chinese
  Communist
  Party
Cultural
  Revolution
Eighth Route
  Army
Gang of Four
Great Leap
  Forward
Karakhan
  Manifesto
Kiangsi Soviet
Long March
Maoism
May Fourth
  Movement

May Thirtieth
  Incident
Nationalist Party
Open Door policy
Red Guards
Sian Incident
Sun–Joffe
  Manifesto
Three Principles of
  the People
warlord
Japan:
Clean Government
  Party
Democratic
  Socialist Party
Japan Communist
  Party

Japan Socialist
  Party
kamikaze
Liberal-Democratic
  Party
Minseitō
Rikken Seiyūkai
State Shintō
Twenty-one
  Demands
zaibatsu
Korea:
Korean Provisional
  Government
Korean War
March First
  Movement
Nationalist Party

Pueblo Incident
Singanhoe
38th parallel
*Sino-Japanese
  relations:*
Lytton
  Commission
Marco Polo Bridge
  Incident
Mukden Incident
Shantung question
Sino-Japanese
  War (1937–45)
Twenty-One
  Demands
United Front

Biographies

China:
Chang Kuo-t'ao
Chang Ping-lin
Chen Boda
Ch'en Tu-hsiu
Chiang Ching-kuo
Chiang Kai-shek
Chiang K'ang-hu
Ch'ü Ch'iu-pai
Deng Xiaoping
Feng Yü-hsiang
Guo Moruo
Hu Han-min
Hu Shih
Hu Yaobang
Hua Guofeng
Jiang Qing
Kang Sheng
Kuo T'ai-ch'i
Li Ta-chao
Lin Biao
Liu Shaoqi

Soong
  Ch'ing-ling
Soong, T.V.
Soong family
Sun Yat-sen
Ts'ai Yüan-p'ei
Tuan Ch'i-jui
Wang Ching-wei
Yüan Shih-k'ai
Zhao Ziyang
Zhou Enlai
Zhu De
Japan:
Araki Sadao
D'Aquino, Iva
  Toguri
Hamaguchi Osachi
Hatoyama Ichirō
Hirohito
Ikeda Hayato
Inukai Tsuyoshi
Ishibashi Tanzan
Katō Takaaki

Kawakami Hajime
Kishi Nobusuke
Konoe Fumimaro,
  Kōshaku
Miki Kiyoshi
Miki Takeo
Minobe Tatsukichi
Nagano Osami
Nosaka Sanzō
Okawa Shūmei
Ōkuma Shigenobu,
  Kōshaku
Satō Eisaku
Shidehara Kijūrō
Taishō
Tanaka Giichi
Tanaka Kakue
Tōjō Hideki
Ugaki
  Kazushige
Yamagata
  Aritomo,
  Kōshaku

Yamamoto
  Gonnohyōe
Yamamoto
  Isoroku
Yoshida Shigeru
Yoshino Sakuzō
Korea:
Chun Doo Hwan
Kim Chong Il
Kim Dae Jung
Kim Il-sung
Kim Young Sam
Park Chung Hee
Rhee, Syngman
other:
Hurley, Patrick J.
MacArthur,
  Douglas
Reischauer,
  Edwin O.
Stilwell, Joseph W.

INDEX: See entries under all of the terms above

Section 976.   **South and Southeast Asia: the Late Colonial Period and the Emergence of New Nations Since 1920**

A. India, Pakistan, Bangladesh, Ceylon, Tibet, and Nepal since 1920

   1. India since *c.* 1920: nationalism and the decline of the raj

      a. Dyarchy and the conflict between British policy and the aims of Indian nationalism: the Congress and Gandhi's technique of active, nonviolent revolution; Round Table Conferences

      b. The Government of India Act (1935), the political and economic effects of World War II, partition and independence (1947), Hindu–Muslim polarization

   2. India since 1947

      a. Domestic policies: the constitution and the reorganization of the states under Nehru and the Congress Party (1947–64); administrations of Shastri (1964–66), Indira Gandhi (1966–77 and 1980–84), and Morarji Desai (1977–79), continued communal unrest, massacres in Assam (1983), suppression of Sikh extremists in Punjab (1984), assassination of Indira Gandhi (1984), election of Rajiv Gandhi (1984)

      b. Foreign policy: conflicts with Pakistan over Kashmir (1948–49 and 1965–66) and over East Pakistan (Bangladesh) in 1971, hostile relations with the People's Republic of China and Chinese incursion (1962), neutralist position

   3. Pakistan (1947–71); Pakistan and Bangladesh since 1971

      a. National consolidation (1947–51) under Jinnah and Liaquat Ali Khan: economic and political instability

      b. Military government of Ayub Khan (1958–69); economic and political reforms; relations with India and the Western and Socialist powers; administration of Yahya Khan (1969–71); civil war between East and West Pakistan and secession of East Pakistan (Bangladesh, since 1971); administrations of Zulfikar Ali Bhutto (1971–77) and Mohammad Zia ul-Haq; Pakistan under martial law; unrest in North-West Frontier Province, Baluchistan, and Sind; repercussions of Soviet invasion of Afghanistan (1979)

   4. Bangladesh since 1971: emergence of nation; administrations of Mujibur Rahman (1971–75), Zia ur-Rahman (1975–81), and Hossain Mohammad Ershad; Bangladesh under martial law

   5. Ceylon since 1920 (Sri Lanka after 1972)

      a. Nationalism and the demand for constitutional reform (1920–31), the 1931 constitution, effect of World War II

      b. Dominion status (1947) and rule by United National Party government (1948–56, 1965–70, and after 1977); Sri Lanka Freedom Party leadership and administrations of S.W.R.D. Bandaranaike (1956–59), Sirimavo Bandaranaike (1960–65, 1970–77), and J.R. Jayawardene; the constitutions of 1972 and 1978; Sinhalese-Tamil tensions; anti-Tamil riots (1983) and continuing unrest

   6. Tibet since *c.* 1911: Tibetan independence (1911), relations with Britain and China, Chinese invasion (1949) and hegemony re-established, complete Chinese governmental control after 1959

   7. Nepal: British withdrawal (1947) and revival of Nepalese royal control under Tribhuvan (1951–55), Mahendra (1955–72), and Birendra; domestic politics

B. Mainland Southeast Asia since 1920

   1. Burma since 1920

      a. Emergence of Burmese nationalism and the British response (1920–37), limited constitutional government (1937–42), the Japanese occupation (1942–45)

      b. Postwar independence (1948) under U Nu, adoption of leftist–neutralist position, internal conflict and military government under U Ne Win after 1962, continued economic problems, socialist state and new constitution (1974), minority insurgencies, U Ne Win's retirement from government (1981)

   2. Malaya and Singapore since 1920

      a. British economic policies in Malaya, Japanese occupation (1941–45), British return to power (1945) and progress toward self-government

b. Suppression of Communist insurgents (1948–60), creation of Federation of Malaya (1957) and reestablishment as Malaysia (1963), Singapore's withdrawal (1965) from Malaysia and creation of independent Republic of Singapore, dominance of National Front in Malaysia, regime of Lee Kuan Yew in Singapore (from 1965), industrialization and growing prosperity

3. Thailand since 1920

   a. Post-World War I escape from unequal treaties, problems of kingship and repression, the coup d'etat of 1932 and the establishment of constitutional monarchy, militaristic and pro-Japanese nationalism, the Japanese occupation during World War II

   b. Loss of wartime gains and political instability, military domination (1947–68, 1971–73, and since 1976), border incursions from Cambodia and influx of refugees

4. Indochina since 1920: emergence of independent states and continued strife

   a. French direct administration of Vietnam and indirect administration of Cambodia and Laos: growth of Vietnamese nationalistic movements and Ho Chi Minh's formation of the Indochina Communist Party (1930), French administration during Japanese occupation in World War II, postwar French administration in southern Vietnam and Cambodia

   b. Ho Chi Minh's government in northern Vietnam and the French attempt to reconquer the north (1946–54), the Geneva Agreements and legal "temporary" division of Vietnam (1954), French withdrawal and U.S. limited intervention

   c. Vietnam from 1955 to 1975

      i. North Vietnam: industrialization, relations with other Communist and other Asian countries, war with South Vietnam, U.S. military intervention, cease-fire agreement (1973), conquest of South Vietnam (1975)

      ii. South Vietnam: civil war and formation of National Liberation Front (1960), U.S. military intervention, cease-fire agreement (1973), end of regime of Nguyen Van Thieu, conquest by North Vietnam (1975)

   d. Socialist Republic of Vietnam: establishment of united Vietnamese government (July 2, 1976), political and economic problems, invasion (1978) and occupation of Cambodia, exodus of ethnic Chinese refugees and border war with China (1979)

   e. Laos since 1950: civil war to 1954, Geneva Conference (1954) and creation of Laos as a neutral state, domestic instability and continued civil war between Pathet Lao and rightists, military involvement of the U.S. and North Vietnam, Pathet Lao victory and the Lao People's Democratic Republic (from 1975), domination by Vietnam

   f. Cambodia since independence (1953): Sihanouk's domestic politics and severing of relations with the U.S. (1965); deposition of Sihanouk (1970) and Lon Nol and pro-Western realignment; return, and then resignation, of Sihanouk (1975); new constitution of Democratic Kampuchea (1976); ruthless administration and designation of the Communist Party of Kampuchea as the governing body (1977); capture of Phnom Penh by Vietnamese forces (1979) and establishment of Vietnamese-dominated regime; formation of coalition government-in-exile supported by Association of Southeast Asian Nations (1982)

C. Indonesia and the Philippines

   1. Indonesia since 1920

      a. Dutch administration of Indonesia from 1920 to independence in 1949

         i. Dutch administrative suppression of nationalist and Communist revolts in the 1920s and 1930s, accommodation with moderate nationalist parties, Japanese occupation in World War II

         ii. Sukarno's proclamation of Indonesian independence (1945), Dutch attempt to regain control and UN intervention, formal granting of independence in 1949

      b. Constitutional democracy (1950) and Guided Democracy (1957–65) under Sukarno; military coup (1965), purge of Communists, and Sukarno's loss of influence; administration of Suharto (from 1966); takeover of East Timor (1976); economic effects of the oil boom

   2. The Philippines since 1920

      a. Economic and social policies of U.S. administration in the 1920s and 1930s, growth of nationalist political parties, establishment as a commonwealth (1935), Japanese occupation (1941–45), return of U.S. control and commonwealth status

      b. Establishment of the Republic of the Philippines (1946), political developments under successive presidents, U.S.–Philippine relations, administration of Ferdinand E. Marcos (from 1965), Communist and Muslim insurgencies, rule under martial law (1972–81), assassination of opposition leader Benigno Aquino (1983) and resulting unrest

---

Suggested reading in the *Encyclopædia Britannica*:

MACROPAEDIA: Major articles and a biography dealing with South and Southeast Asia: the late colonial period and the emergence of new nations since 1920

Asia	East Indies, The	Indian Ocean	Philippines
Bangladesh	Gandhi	Islands	Southeast Asia,
Burma	Hong Kong	Nepal	Mainland
Delhi	India	Pakistan	Sri Lanka

MICROPAEDIA: Selected entries of reference information; see also Sections 968, 969, and 971

General subjects

Indian subcontinent:	Servants of India	seventeenth	Hare–Hawes–
Delhi Pact	Society	parallel	Cutting Act
Donoughmore	Simon	Viet Cong	Hukbalahap
Commission	Commission	Viet Minh	Rebellion
dyarchy	Sinhala Maha	Viet Nam Quoc	Mandium Affair
Government of	Sabha	Dan Dang	Sakdal Uprising
India Acts	Sinhala Only Bill	*Indonesia:*	Tydings–
hartal	Soulbury	Hague Agreement	McDuffie Act
Indian National	Commission	Linggadjati	Woods–Forbes
Congress	Tashkent	Agreement	Mission
Lee Commission	Agreement	Pancasila	*other:*
Muslim League	*Indochina:*	Peranakan	Burma Road
Non-cooperation	Dien Bien Phu,	Renville	Malayan People's
Movement	Battle of	Agreement	Anti-Japanese
Poona Pact	Hoa Hao	Sarekat Islām	Army
Red Shirt	Indochina	Sutardjo Petition	Promoters
Movement	Khmer Rouge	Volksraad council	Revolution
Round Table	National	*Philippines:*	Stilwell Road
Conference	Liberation Front	Bell Trade Act	Straits Settlements
Rowlatt Acts	Pathet Lao		

Biographies

Burma and Thailand:	Bandaranaike,	Menon, V.K.	Chu Van Tan
Aung San	S.W.R.D.	Krishna	Cuong De
Ba Maw	Bhutto,	Naidu, Sarojini	Ho Chi Minh
Khuang	Zulfikar Ali	Narayan, Jaya	Huyanh Tan Phat
Aphaiwong	Bose, Subhas	Prakash	Katay Don
Ne Win, U	Chandra	Nehru, Jawaharlal	Sasorith
Nu, U	Desai, Morarji	Nehru, Motilal	Ngo Dinh Diem
Phibunsongkhram,	Fateh Singh, Sant	Osman Ali	Nguyen Cao Ky
Luang	Gandhi, Indira	Pandit, Vijaya	Nguyen Huu Tho
Pridi Phanomyong	Gandhi, Mohandas	Lakshmi	Nguyen Van Thieu
San, Saya	Karamchand	Patel, Vallabhbhai	Norodom
Sarit Thanarat	Gandhi, Rajiv	Jhaverbhai	Sihanouk, Prince
Saw, U	Ghaffar Khan,	Prasad, Rajendra	Phan Boi Chau
Thanom	Abdul	Sankaran Nair, Sir	Phetsarath
Kittikachorn	Giri, Varahagiri	Chettur	Ratanavongsa,
Thant, U	Venkata	Sastri, Srinivasa	Prince
Indian subcontinent:	Jinnah,	Tara Singh	Pol Pot
Abdullah, Sheikh	Mohammed Ali	Yahya Khan, Agha	Souphanouvong
Muhammad	Kamaraj,	Mohammad	Souvanna Phouma
Ayub Khan,	Kumaraswami	*Indochina:*	Truong Chinh
Mohammad	Liaquat, Ali Kahn	Bao Dai	Vo Nguyen Giap

Indonesia:
- Agus Salim, Hadji
- Hatta, Mohammad
- Malik, Adam
- Sjahrir, Sutan
- Suharto
- Sukarno
- Tan Malaka,
  - Ibrahim Datuk

Philippines:
- Aguinaldo, Emilio
- Aquino, Benigno Simon, Jr.

Garcia, Carlos Polestico
Macapagal, Diosdado
Magsaysay, Ramon
Marcos, Ferdinand E.
Quezon, Manuel
Quirino, Elpidio
Recto, Claro Mayo
Roxas, Manuel

other:
- Brooke Raj
- Decoux, Jean
- Lee Kuan Yew
- Linlithgow, Victor Alexander John Hope, 2nd marquess of
- Nūr al-Hilmī, Burhanuddin bin Muhammad
- Tan Cheng Lock

INDEX: See entries under all of the terms above

Section 977. **Australia and Oceania Since 1920**

A. International developments in the Pacific and the disposition of the dependent territories in Oceania since 1920

1. The post-World War I situation of the occupying powers in Oceania: the League of Nations mandate system

2. World War II in the Pacific: the rise and fall of Japanese power, effects of the war on indigenous peoples

3. Post-World War II reorganization: economic and social effects of UN trusteeship administrations, movements toward autonomy among the indigenous peoples, independent island states

B. Australia since 1920

1. Developments to 1945: decline of the Labor Party and the Nationalist–Country coalition, industrial and rural development, the Great Depression, formation of the United Australia Party and Lyons' administrations (1931–39), Allied participation in World War II

2. Social, economic, and political development since 1945: European immigration, Labor Party government to 1949 and Liberal–Country alternation with Labor thereafter, lessening of ties with Britain and greater emphasis on Asia, affluent society and laissez-faire attitude, cultural contributions

C. New Zealand since c. 1920

1. Developments to 1945: United (Liberal)–Reform coalition governments, the Great Depression, Labour Party victory (1935) and social welfare programs, participation with Allies in World War II

2. New Zealand since 1945: National and Labour governments, increased participation in Pacific and Asian affairs, Maori nationalism

---

Suggested reading in the *Encyclopædia Britannica*:

MACROPAEDIA: Major articles dealing with Australia and Oceania since 1920

- Australia
- Melbourne
- New Zealand
- Pacific Islands
- Sydney
- United States of America: Hawaii

MICROPAEDIA: Selected entries of reference information; see also Section 967

General subjects

Australian Democratic Labor Party
Australian Democrats
New Zealand National Party

Biographies

Australia:		*New Zealand:*	
Bruce, Stanley	Gorton, Sir John	Forbes, George	Lange, David
Melbourne Bruce,	Grey	William	Muldoon, Robert
Viscount	Lyons, Joseph	Fraser, Peter	Nash, Sir Walter
Chifley, Joseph	Aloysius	Holland, Sir	Ngata, Sir Apirana
Benedict	Menzies, Sir	Sidney	Turupa
Curtin, John	Robert Gordon	Holyoake, Sir	Savage, Michael
Fraser, Malcolm	Page, Sir Earle	Keith Jacka	Joseph
	Whitlam, Gough		

INDEX: See entries under all of the terms above

Section 978. **Southwest Asia and Africa: the Late Colonial Period and the Emergence of New Nations in the 20th Century**

A. Turkey since 1919 and Cyprus since 1920

    1. The War of Independence (1919–23) and the development of the Turkish nation under the leadership of Mustafa Kemal Atatürk

    2. Atatürk's one-party government: secularization, social and economic reforms

    3. Turkey since 1938: World War II and the postwar period, the republic since 1961

        a. Wartime neutrality until alignment (1945) with the Allies: postwar problems with the Soviet Union, political developments

        b. Turkey under the Democrats (1950–60): economic growth and political repression, the army coup (1960)

        c. New constitution (1961) and government under the Republican People's and Justice parties, crisis (1971) and recovery, military coup (1980), formation of civilian government (1983), urbanization and industrialization and great economic growth, mixed relations with East and West and with the Arab world

    4. Cyprus since 1920: British administration to 1960, the Republic of Cyprus, political disunity over the *énosis* question, Turkish invasion (1974) and division of island, unilateral declaration of Turkish Republic of Northern Cyprus (1983)

B. Development of the Arab states and Israel in Southwest Asia and Egypt

    1. The Arab lands of Southwest Asia under the mandate system

        a. Lebanon and Syria under the French mandate (1920–41): Arab demands for independence, the Druze revolt in Syria (1925–27), establishment of the Lebanese Republic (1926) and internal crises resulting in suspension of the constitution (1932), the Franco-Syrian Treaty (1936), Allied occupation in World War II, Syrian and Lebanese independence (1945)

        b. Iraq from 1918 to 1945: British occupation and mandate, independence (1932), political unrest and the role of the military, World War II and British intervention (1939–45)

        c. Palestine and Transjordan under British mandate (1920–48): the Balfour Declaration and the acceleration of Jewish settlement and conflicts with the Arabs; the Palestine Revolt (1936–39) and the Peel Commission; the Biltmore Resolution (1942); the partition of Palestine, the Palestine War, and the emergence of Israel (1948) and Jordan (1946)

    2. Egypt from 1922 to 1945: Wafd-led opposition to the continued British presence, politics in the early Farouk regime, participation in World War II

    3. The Arab states in the Fertile Crescent, Egypt, and Israel since 1945

        a. Lebanon: the multireligious political system, the Khuri regime (1943–52), the presidency of Chamoun and the 1958 crisis, later regimes and the civil war of 1974–76, the Israeli invasion of 1982, renewed civil war, de facto division into spheres of influence, government of national unity (1984), continuing civil disorder

   b. Syria: political instability in the postwar decade, temporary union with Egypt (1958–61), the secessionist regime (1961–63), Ba'thist Syria after 1963, conflicts with Israel, role in the Lebanese civil wars, relations with Palestine Liberation Organization, domestic unrest, suppression of Muslim Brotherhood uprising in Hamah (1982)

   c. The League of Arab States (1945), the partition of Palestine, and the establishment of the State of Israel (1948) and the Hashimite Kingdom of Jordan (1950)

      i. The establishment of Israel (1948) and resultant conflicts with the Arabs: immigration and politics, foreign aid and economic development, renewed hostilities with the Arab states in the Suez War (1956), the Six-Day War (1967) and the diplomatic stalemate, the war of October 1973, role in the 1974–76 Lebanese civil war, treaty with Egypt (1979), invasion of Lebanon (1982), expansion of Jewish settlements in occupied territory

      ii. Economic and political problems in Jordan under King Hussein: ambivalent foreign policy, Israeli annexations (1967) and the Palestine Liberation Movement, Black September (1970) for the Palestinians

   d. Iraq: postwar reconstruction and social upheavals (1945–58), the revolution of 1958, politics under the republic, military coups (1963–68), oil and the economy, the Ba'th regime since 1968, the Kurdish question, invasion of Iran (1980) and stalemated war

   e. Egyptian politics in the last years of Farouk's regime, the Egyptian revolution (1952) and Nasser's rise to power, the Suez crises (1956), the Six-Day War (1967), Sadat's presidency (1970–81), Mubarak's presidency

4. The Arabian Peninsula since *c.* 1920: the political, economic, and social effects of the discovery of oil and the resultant influx of wealth; British and other great power influences

   a. Emergence of the Kingdom of Saudi Arabia under Ibn Sa'ūd (1924); oil discoveries and exploitation; the government under Faisal (1964–75), Khalid (1975–82), and Fahd; foreign relations; rise as a dominant Arab power

   b. The other Arabian states: Bahrain and Qatar, Kuwait, Oman, the United Arab Emirates, Yemen (Aden), Yemen (Ṣanʿāʾ); Yemeni wars and union negotiations; formation of Gulf Cooperation Council (1981)

C. Iran and Afghanistan since *c.* 1920

1. Iran since 1925

   a. The regime of Reza Shah (1925–41): economic and social reforms, relations with Germany and invasion by Allies during World War II

   b. The regime of Mohammad Reza Pahlavi (1941–79), nationalization of oil resources (1951), land reform (from 1962), expansion of economy from petroleum revenues

   c. The Islāmic Republic: revolution of 1978–79, the republican regime, support of Muslim fundamentalist movements, Iraqi invasion (1980) and stalemated war

2. Afghanistan since independence (1921): civil disorders, attempts at reform, and economic improvements; constitutional revisions; relations with other countries; the republic from 1973; Soviet invasion of 1979 and guerrilla resistance

D. North Africa since 1920

1. The final decades of European rule

   a. French colonial policies, the French protectorate and the Spanish zone in Morocco, the administration of Algeria and the Algerian War, the beginning of nationalist movements in Tunisia

   b. Libya under the domination of the Fascist Italian government (1922–43)

2. Establishment of independent states in the Maghrib

   a. Postwar British and French occupation of Libya, independence (1951), the republic (from 1969), emergence of Qaddafi (1970), disruptive role in world affairs

   b. The emergence of independent Tunisia (1956): formation of republic (1957), Tunisia under Bourguiba

   c. The emergence of independent Morocco (1956): government under Mohammed V (d. 1961) and Hassan II, the Spanish Zone and its reduction to Ceuta and Melilla, dispute over Spanish (Western) Sahara

   d. The Algerian War (1954–62), French evacuation, and the emergence of independent Algeria (1962): government under Ben Bella (overthrown 1965), Boumedienne (1965–78), and Bendjedid; adoption of socialist and Islāmic National Charter (1976)

e. Mauritania and the Spanish (Western) Sahara: independent Mauritania (from 1960), Polisario revolt in Western Sahara, division of Western Sahara between Mauritania and Morocco and Moroccan takeover of Mauritanian zone (1979)

E. The maturation of the European colonial system and the nationalist movements in sub-Saharan Africa since 1920

1. Completion of effective occupation by the European powers: the post-World War I division of former German colonies among other colonial powers, the mandate system

2. Administrative policies and attitudes of each colonial power: economic development, effects of colonialism on the societies and institutions of the African peoples

3. World War II and postwar changes in colonial policies: decline of the colonial system and rise of African nationalist parties, establishment of independent African countries from 1957, the Organization of African Unity, the assertiveness of white-settled Africa

4. West Africa since *c.* 1920

   a. Colonial rule from *c.* 1920 until independence, independent Liberia's economic ties to the U.S.

      i. Economic developments in French West Africa: Senegal, French Sudan, Upper Volta, Niger

      ii. Economic developments in British colonies: The Gambia, Sierra Leone, Gold Coast, Nigeria

   b. Decolonization and independence

      i. Emergence of African leaders: rise of a new class of educated Africans

      ii. Formation of African independence movements, independence for all the former colonies between 1957 and 1975, the countries of West Africa after independence, problems of economic development, political instability, military coups and emergence of one-party states

5. Ethiopia and the Nilotic Sudan since *c.* 1917

   a. Ethiopia and Eritrea since 1917: internal division and the rise of Haile Selassie, the Italian conquest (1936), Eritrea under Italian rule, federation (1952) and union (1962) with Ethiopia, establishment of the military government (1974), abolition of the monarchy and death of Haile Selassie (1975), Eritrean revolt and Somali invasion of the Ogaden, development of Socialist state under Mengistu

   b. The Anglo-Egyptian Sudan: growth of national consciousness and creation of the independent republic (1956), military coup (1958) and the Abbud government (1958–64), revolt in the southern provinces, return to civilian rule, government of Ja'afar an-Numayri (1969–85) and temporary resolution of the southern problem, renewed tension in the south following introduction of Islāmic law (1983) and administrative decentralization, military coup (1985)

6. East Africa and Madagascar since *c.* 1920

   a. The European colonies in East Africa from *c.* 1920 to the beginning of independence (1960)

      i. The colonial economics: growth of export trade (cotton, cloves, coffee), extension of the railroads

      ii. Somalia as an Italian trust territory (1950), problems in British Somaliland

      iii. Crises of colonial rule in the 1950s: Mau Mau resistance in Kenya; independence movements in Uganda, Tanganyika, and Zanzibar

   b. Developments since independence

      i. Somalia: independence (1960), internal tensions and territorial disputes, conflict with Ethiopia, military takeover (1969) and regime of Siyad Barre, break with the Soviet Union (1977), war with Ethiopia (1977–78) and continued unrest in the Ogaden, influx of refugees

      ii. Economic cooperation among the formerly British East African nations: the East African Community and its end (1977)

      iii. Tanzania (formerly Tanganyika and Zanzibar): revolt against Arab control in Zanzibar (1964), Nyerere and introduction of *ujamaa* socialism, tension with Uganda and invasion in support of revolt against Amin (1978), economic difficulties

      iv. Uganda: independence (1962) and economic growth, the Obote and Amin governments, reign of terror and economic decline, deposition of Amin (1979), reinstatement (1980) and overthrow (1985) of Obote

    v. Kenya: independence (1963) and subsequent domestic politics and foreign relations under Kenyatta's leadership, death of Kenyatta (1978) and succession of Daniel arap Moi, establishment of one-party state (1982)

  c. Madagascar: the French administration, independence (1960) and subsequent domestic politics and foreign relations

7. Central Africa after World War II: the intensification of nationalist movements and the acquisition of independence by the former European colonies

  a. The emergence of French and Belgian colonies as republics: internal divisions and the fate of the republics

    i. The Democratic Republic of the Congo (Republic of Zaire since 1971): the Congolese nationalist movement and independence (1960), secession of Katanga province and UN intervention (1960–64), regime of Mobutu Sese Seko

    ii. Central African Republic: independence (1960), subsequent domestic politics and foreign relations, establishment and overthrow (1979) of Central African Empire under Bokassa I

    iii. The People's Republic of the Congo: independence (1960), ethnic rivalries, domestic politics and foreign relations

    iv. Gabon Republic: independence (1960), subsequent domestic politics and foreign relations

    v. Burundi and Rwanda: independence (1962), overthrow of Ntare V of Burundi (1966), warfare between Tutsi and Hutu (early 1970s)

  b. Republic of Equatorial Guinea: the Spanish administration, independence (1968), repressive regime of Macías Nguema, military coup (1979)

8. Southern Africa since *c.* 1920

  a. Southern Africa from *c.* 1920 to *c.* 1945

    i. Political and economic developments in white-settler-controlled Union of South Africa: the Hertzog administration (1924–33) and the Hertzog–Smuts coalition (1933–39), political disunity and Allied participation in World War II

    ii. White-settler control of Southern Rhodesia: relations with Northern Rhodesia and Nyasaland; colonial government economic, social, and political discrimination against black Africans; Portuguese rule in Angola and Mozambique

    iii. Indian, Coloured, and black African responses to colonial government-sanctioned discrimination: growth of local political organizations, separatist church movements, and mass nationalist movements

  b. Southern Africa since 1945: political developments in white-controlled colonies and nations, emergence of black nations

    i. Republic of South Africa (formerly the Union of South Africa): Afrikaner National Party administrations since 1948, government-sanctioned apartheid, independence as republic (1960), anti-apartheid movements and growing international isolation, Soweto riots (1976), establishment of black homelands, new constitution (1983), increasing black resistance

    ii. South West Africa/Namibia: international and internal resistance to incorporation into South Africa, revocation of UN mandate (1966), international efforts toward independence

    iii. Botswana, Lesotho, and Swaziland: British administration of the High Commission Territories, independence (1966, 1968), subsequent relations with South Africa

    iv. British Central Africa: postwar conditions in Northern Rhodesia, Southern Rhodesia, and Nyasaland; the Federation of Rhodesia and Nyasaland (1953–63); rise of black nationalist movements; independence of Zambia and Malawi (1964)

    v. Zimbabwe (formerly Southern Rhodesia): Rhodesia's unilateral declaration of independence (UDI, 1965), civil war, establishment of Zimbabwe (1980)

    vi. Developments in the Portuguese colonies of Angola and Mozambique: economic advances, nationalist movements, and independence in the mid-1970s; continued guerrilla activity; arrival of Cuban troops in Angola; border war between Angola and South Africa; Mozambique–South Africa nonaggression pact (1984)

Suggested reading in the *Encyclopædia Britannica*:

MACROPAEDIA: Major articles and a biography dealing with Southwest Asia and Africa: the late colonial period and the emergence of new nations in the 20th century

Afghanistan	Cyprus	Jordan	Sudan
Africa	Eastern Africa	Lebanon	Syria
Arabia	Egypt	North Africa	Turkey and
Asia	Iran	Palestine	Ancient Anatolia
Atatürk	Iraq	South Africa	Western Africa
Central Africa	Israel	Southern Africa	

MICROPAEDIA: Selected entries of reference information; see also Section 96/11

General subjects

central Africa:
Belgian Congo
Moyen-Congo
Ruanda-Urundi
Rwanda,
Kingdom of
eastern Africa:
Buganda
German East
Africa
Italian East Africa
Mau Mau
Somaliland
Ethiopia and the Nilotic Sudan:
Anglo-Egyptian
Condominium
Italian East Africa
Italo-Ethiopian War
Mahdist
Middle East:
Anglo-Egyptian
Treaty
Arab Legion
Balfour
Declaration
Ba'th Party

Druze revolt
Fatah, al-
Gaza
Gaza strip
Haganah
Hashimite
Ikhwān
Iranian–Iraqi War
Irgun Zvai Leumi
Israel Labour Party
Jewish Agency
Likud
Mapam
Muslim
Brotherhood
Palestine
Palestine
Liberation
Organization
Peel Commission
Stern Gang
Suez Crisis
United Arab
Republic
Wafd
Zionism

North Africa:
Algerian Reformist
Ulamas,
Association of
Cyrenaica
Destour
Destourian
Socialist Party
National Action
Bloc
National
Liberation Front
Rif War
Tripolitania
Ottoman Empire and Turkey:
Ankara, Treaty of
Greco-Turkish
Wars
Lausanne
Conference
Moscow, Treaty of
southern Africa:
African National
Congress
apartheid
banning

National Party of
South Africa
New Republic
Party
Pan-African
Congress
Progressive Federal
Party
Rhodesia and
Nyasaland,
Federation of
South African
Party
South West
Africa People's
Organization
United Party
western Africa:
Biafra
British West Africa
French West
Africa
Mali Federation
Togoland
other:
EOKA

Biographies

central Africa:
Boganda,
Barthélemy
Bokassa, Eddine
Ahmed
Éboué, Felix
Kasavubu, Joseph
Lumumba, Patrice
M'ba-Derlinon
Mobutu Sese Seko
Mutesa II
Nyerere, Julius
Obote, Milton
Tshombe, Moise

eastern Africa:
Amin, Idi
Haile Selassie
Kenyatta, Jomo
Mboya, Tom
Odinga, Oginga
Iran:
Khomeini,
Ruhollah
Mohammad Reza
Shah Pahlavi
Mosaddeq,
Mohammad
Reza Shah Pahlavi

Middle East—Egypt:
Farouk I
Fu'ād I
Luṭfī as-Sayyid,
Ahmad
Māhir Pasha, 'Alī
Mubārak, Hosnī
Naguib,
Muhammad
Nahhās Pasha,
Muṣṭafā an-
Nasser, Gamal
Abdel
Sādāt, Anwar el-

Zaghlūl, Sa'd
Middle East—Israel and Zionism:
Ahad Ha'am
Begin, Menachem
Ben-Gurion, David
Ben-Zvi, Itzhak
Dayan, Moshe
Herzl, Theodor
Jabotinsky,
Vladimir
Meir, Golda
Peres, Shimon
Shamir, Yitzhak

Sharon, Ariel
Weizman, Chaim
Middle East—other Arab:
  'Aflaq, Michel
  'Arafāt, Yāsir
  Assad, Hafiz al-
  Chamoun, Camille
  Chehab, Fuad
  Fayṣal I
  Gemayel family
  Hawrani,
    Akram al-
  Ḥusaynī, Amīn al-
  Hussein (ibn Talal)
  Hussein, Saddim
    at-Takrītī
  Ibn Saʻūd
  Kassem, Abdul
    Karim
  Nuri as-Said
North Africa:
  Abbas, Ferhat
  Abd el-Krim
  Ben Bella, Ahmed

Boumedienne,
  Houari
Bourguiba, Habib
Idris I
Muhammad V
Qaddafi,
  Muammar al-
southern Africa:
  Banda, H.
    Kamuzu
  Biko, Stephen
  Hertzog, J.B.M.
  Kaunda, Kenneth
  Lutuli, Albert
  Malan, Daniel F.
  Mandela, Nelson
    Rohihlahia
  Mugabe, Robert
  Neto, Agostinho
  Nkomo, Joshua
  Smith, Ian
  Smuts, Jan
    Christian
  Sobhuza II

Strijdom, Johannes
  Gerhardus
Tutu, Desmond
Verwoerd, Hendrik
  Frensch
Vorster, John
Welensky, Sir Roy
Turkey:
  Atatürk, Kemal
  Bayar, Celâl
  Çakmak, Fevzi
  Demirel, Süleyman
  Ecevit, Bülent
  İnönü, İsmet
  Menderes, Adnan
western Africa:
  Akintola, Samuel
    Ladake
  Awolowo, Obafemi
  Azikiwe, Nnamdi
  Balewa, Sir
    Abubaker Tafawa
  Daddah, Moktar
    Ould
  Danquah, J.B.

Diori, Hamani
Gowon, Yakubu
Guèye, Lamine
Houphouët-Boigny,
  Félix
Keita, Modibo
Maga, Hubert
Margai, Sir Milton
Nkrumah, Kwame
Ojukwu,
  Odumegwu
Olympio, Sylvanus
Rawlings, Jerry J.
Senghor, Léopold
Touré, Sékou
Tubman, William
  V.S.
Zinsour, Émile
  Derlin
other:
  Amānollāh Khān
  Makarios III
  Zahir Shah,
    Mohammad

INDEX: See entries under all of the terms above

Introduction to Part Ten:
Knowledge Become Self-conscious

by Mortimer J. Adler

The words *universe* and *encyclopaedia* have an obvious similarity of meaning. Both come from words—in the one case, Latin, in the other, Greek—that mean a totality or all-inclusive whole. Whether the universe is finite or infinite, and however it is constituted or organized, it embraces everything that is. Nothing lies outside it; everything that happens occurs within it. Can one say, with equal assurance, that the encyclopaedia is a similar totality or whole? Perhaps we cannot say that of any actual, historic encyclopaedia. But that is the ideal which all encyclopaedias attempt to embody.

It is not just the similarity of the universe and the encyclopaedia as totalities or wholes that interests us, but also how these two wholes are related to each other. One of them, the universe, embraces not only everything that is, but also everything that is knowable. The other, the encyclopaedia, sets for itself the goal of reporting everything that is and can be known about the universe. The one is mirrored or reflected in the other—the macrocosm in the microcosm.

The universe includes man—man a moving body, man a living organism, man a social animal, and man not only as a doer and seeker but also as a maker and knower of things. Among the things that man seeks to know and understand is his own knowledge—his abilities, efforts, and achievements in the sphere of knowing itself. Whether or not Aristotle was correct in saying that the highest form of intellectual activity is thinking about thinking itself, it is certainly true that "knowledge become self-conscious" is a distinctive characteristic of the human enterprise of knowing. We not only seek to know whatever can be known, but we also, reflexively, turn our knowing back upon itself when we pay attention to how we know what we know, the various ways in which we know, and the divisions or branches of our knowledge.

The organization of the encyclopaedia—the way in which the branches of knowledge have been distinguished from one another and related to one another—has changed remarkably from age to age. In antiquity, before there were any real encyclopaedias, learned men envisaged the whole of human knowledge as having a certain structure of related parts or subdivisions. The organization of knowledge in medieval encyclopaedias exhibited quite a different pattern. Later encyclopaedias introduced still other changes in the picture; and that picture has changed in important respects during the last century and is undergoing further changes today.

The new *Britannica* presents us with an outline of knowledge that is radically different in its fundamental framework and its organizational scheme from the outlines that might have been constructed for an ancient encyclopaedia—if there had been any such thing—or a medieval one. The Outline of Knowledge set forth in this

Propædia volume is divided into ten parts, each of which is broken down into divisions and sections. Division by division, from Part One through Part Nine, the outline covers what we know about the universe with the help of such sciences as physics, chemistry, astronomy, geology, meteorology, biology, medicine, psychology, anthropology, sociology, political science, economics, and technology. It also covers what we know as a result of systematic study and scholarship in such fields as education, law, the arts, religion, and history.

The knowledge of the universe that we possess by means of the disciplines mentioned above is outlined in Parts One through Nine and expounded in the articles to which the outline refers. What about Part Ten—the part to which this essay is an introduction? Where and how does that fit into the picture?

To some extent the answer has already been given. Here in Part Ten we are concerned with "knowledge become self-conscious"—with knowledge about knowledge—with our knowing turned, reflexively, back upon itself. Here it is not the knowable universe we are considering. It is, instead, the world of knowledge itself: its diverse disciplines, modes of inquiry, fields of scholarship or systematic study—in short, as the title of Part Ten indicates, the branches of knowledge. Whereas the other nine parts of the Outline of Knowledge cover *what we know* about the knowable universe, the outline of Part Ten covers what we know about the sciences or other disciplines *whereby we know* that which we know.

The answer just given is not the whole answer to the question provoked by the special character of Part Ten. What we know about the various sciences and the diverse disciplines that comprise the world of knowledge almost always includes an account of the methods of inquiry, verification or demonstration, and argument employed by scientists or scholars in a particular field of knowledge. While interest in such matters does not exhaustively represent the concerns of logic, the science of logic does provide the underpinnings for our study of the methodology of the other learned disciplines, including history and philosophy as well as the various sciences. What we know about logic itself as a science—its history and, as it were, the philosophy of it—therefore properly belongs in the outline of Part Ten, together with an indication of the scope and content of the science itself.

For a somewhat different reason mathematics is also treated here in the same way as logic. The knowledge attained by the mathematician has extraordinarily wide and diverse applicability in other spheres of inquiry and branches of knowledge—in most, if not all, of the natural sciences and in many of the social sciences. Like logic, mathematics belongs here not only for its usefulness in other sciences, but also for its own sake as a science. We are concerned with its content as well as with its method, history, and philosophy.

In addition to logic and mathematics, two other disciplines occupy a special place in any consideration of the branches of knowledge. One is history; the other, philosophy.

History as a field of study includes more than the history of peoples, of nations, of cultures, and of social institutions. It includes the history of human learning itself, of all the branches of knowledge. It includes not only the history of the natural and social sciences, but also the history of logic, of mathematics, of philosophy, and of history itself as one of the learned disciplines. And, in addition to there being a history of the study of history (*i.e.,* historiography), there is also a logic of history (its methodology) and a philosophy of history.

Like history, philosophy is operative in the study of all the other disciplines as well as of itself. Philosophy become self-conscious is concerned with questions about the nature and scope of philosophy, about whether it has a method or methods and a subject matter or subject matters peculiarly its own. Philosophy is also concerned about its own historical development and, in that history, about its changing relationship to other disciplines, especially to religion and to the sciences. As there is a history and a philosophy of history, so there is a philosophy of philosophy and a history of philosophy—a statement which probably cannot be made about any other two disciplines in the entire range of the branches of knowledge.

In addition, as each of the other disciplines has a history, so there is a philosophy of each of the other disciplines. We have already noted that there is a philosophy of logic and of mathematics. So, too, there is a philosophy of science in general and of the different sciences in particular; and also a philosophy of education, of law, of art, and of religion.

All of this, however, does not exhaust the content of philosophy, any more than the history of all the branches of knowledge exhausts the content of history, or any more than the application of logic and mathematics to other disciplines exhausts their content as disciplines with knowledge to offer. But in the case of philosophy, as not in the case of logic and mathematics, it is sometimes questioned whether it can rightly claim to offer us knowledge of the universe as well as knowledge about knowledge itself and an understanding of the various branches of knowledge. That question, together with the question of how the knowledge that philosophers claim to have stands in relation to other forms of knowledge, constitutes what is, perhaps, the most fundamental problem dealt with by philosophers when they philosophize about philosophy itself. Whether or not the knowledge they claim to have is comparable in its validity to the knowledge achieved in other spheres of inquiry, philosophy, like science, covers a wide range of subject matters and involves a large number of distinct subdivisions, each with its own problems and controversies (*e.g.,* metaphysics, philosophy of nature, epistemology, philosophy of mind, philosophy of man, ethics, political philosophy, and aesthetics).

Concerning the whole range of disciplines that are represented in an exhaustive inventory of the branches of knowledge, three questions stand out as the most challenging. Of these, the first two have been debated over and over again—in earlier epochs as well as in our own century, and in the context of organizations of knowledge quite different from that which prevails or is acceptable today.

One is the question about whether the various branches of knowledge can or should be arranged in a hierarchical order, in an ascending scale from lower to higher, or from less to more fundamental. In antiquity they were so arranged; as, for example, in Aristotle's ordering of the speculative sciences, beginning with physics and rising through mathematics to metaphysics as the science of first principles and ultimate causes; and in his characterization of politics as the architectonic or controlling discipline in the sphere of practical knowledge, directive of human action. So, too, in the Middle Ages, a hierarchical organization prevailed, in which theology was regarded as queen of the sciences, philosophy as its handmaiden, with all the other disciplines contributing their portions of knowledge for the greater glory of God and for the better understanding of man's destiny under Divine Providence. If, in accordance with the prevailing view today, a hierarchical order is rejected, is there any other order to replace it, and in terms of what criteria or principles can such an alternative be constructed? Is there, as the introductory essay in this volume suggests, a circle of learning instead of a hierarchy of the branches of knowledge—a circle in which no point is either a beginning or an end, and lines can be drawn from any point to any other?

The second question, to which different answers have been given at different times and to which conflicting answers are still being given today, asks about the coherence of the world of knowledge as a whole. Do all its constituent parts—its various component disciplines or branches of knowledge—adhere together harmoniously, each somehow complementing the other? Or, on the contrary, is the world of knowledge torn asunder by irremediable conflicts—by territorial disputes, by conflicting claims to sovereignty, by assertions and denials of legitimacy? Underlying whatever answers may be given to these questions, a deeper difference of opinion may exist concerning the unity of truth itself. If, for example, there is some truth in science and some truth in philosophy or in religion, must these diverse approximations of whatever truth man can possess be consistent with one another? Or, on the contrary, can there be some truth in science and some in philosophy or in religion, even though the truth of the one stands in sharp conflict to the truth of the other? Can there be, in short, a multiplicity of truths, each of which deserves that name, but each of which must be kept out of contact with the others, by being isolated in logic-tight compartments?

Unlike the two preceding questions, the third is one that has come to the forefront only recently. It concerns what many contemporary commentators regard as an unfortunate rift in the realm of knowledge—the chasm between the sciences, on the one hand, and the humanities, on the other. In the long history of the latter term, different disciplines have been grouped together on the side of the humanities and in contradistinction to the sciences. Today, the humanities group is generally thought to include language and literature, the fine arts, history, philosophy, and religion.

It is assumed that there are fundamental differences, in method or approach and in criteria of validity, between the humanistic disciplines, on the one hand, and the sciences, both natural and social, on the other. Of course there are, but they are not entirely clear. By reference to methodology or to criteria of validity, certain of the disciplines called humanistic closely resemble those called scientific. For example, mathematicians and logicians do their work by sitting still and thinking, not by undertaking experiments or by going out into the field to collect data or do research. Philosophy is like them in this respect; but mathematics and logic are usually regarded as sciences, whereas philosophy is grouped with the humanities. Furthermore, the criteria of validity thought to be applicable to philosophy do not operate as criteria for judging the excellence of literature or of other fine arts, yet all three are classified as humanities.

Supposing that some line can be clearly drawn to divide the humanities from the sciences, the problem that agitates those who contemplate the world of learning is whether it is one world or two—whether the rift or chasm that separates the sciences from the humanities involves an iron curtain that prevents communication between them. It is not within the purpose or the province of this essay to provide an answer to that question. Nevertheless, an answer would appear to be suggested by the conception of the encyclopaedia as a totality, as an organized whole. That conception would seem to favour the view that, in the circle of learning, there are no impenetrable barriers to communication or unbridgeable breaks in continuity. Underlying it is the faith that the whole world of knowledge is a single universe of discourse.

Part Ten. The Branches of Knowledge

Several points should be noted about the relations of this part to the preceding parts. The results of investigations in the natural and social sciences, and in medicine and technology—their content or knowledge—are set forth in Parts One through Five, and in Part Seven. Accordingly, the outlines in the seven sections of Division III in this part are confined to questions about the history of these disciplines, and about their nature, scope, structure, methods, and principal problems or tasks. Direct historical accounts of the peoples and civilizations of the world are set forth in Part Nine, whereas Section 10/41 in Division IV of this part is confined to historical and analytical studies of the discipline of history itself, treating the history of historical writing, the methods of modern historical investigation and research, speculative philosophies of history, and philosophical analyses of the specific character of historical knowledge.

The case is different with Divisions I, II, and V—on logic, mathematics, and philosophy. The results of these disciplines have not been dealt with in previous parts. In the history of each of these disciplines, substantive developments have persistently involved, and issued from, positions taken not only *within them,* but also from positions taken *about them.* Accordingly, the outlines in the sections of Divisions I, II, and V treat the substantive results of logical, mathematical, and philosophical inquiry, on the one hand, and the historical and analytical studies of the nature, scope, branches, methods, and principal problems of logic, mathematics, and philosophy, on the other.

In Part Six on the arts and Part Eight on religion, the outlines include historical and analytic studies of knowledge and inquiry concerning the arts and religion. Such studies, then, are not included separately in Part Ten. They are, however, treated in Section 10/42 of this part, insofar as the study of the arts and of religion are, together with the study of language, history, and philosophy, component disciplines of the humanities—a group of disciplines traditionally distinguished from the natural and social sciences, and traditionally considered to have, taken together, a special educational and cultural role. Section 10/42 sets forth a historical review of the changing conceptions of the humanities and of humanistic scholarship, and treats issues about the definition and scope of the humanities, about their distinction from the sciences, and about their role in education and culture.

Division I.   **Logic**

The outlines in the two sections of Division I deal with the history and philosophy of logic and with the content of the disciplines of formal logic, metalogic, and applied logic.

The outline in Section 10/11 first treats the history of logic in the West and the history of Indian and Chinese logic; and then treats differing conceptions of the field and scope of logic, problems in the philosophy of logic concerning meaning, truth, and ontology, and the place of logic among the sciences and disciplines.

Section 10/12 deals first with formal logic, treating the propositional calculus, the predicate calculus, the theory of the syllogism, modal logic, and set theory and natural-number arithmetic. It goes on to the nature and elements of metalogic, which studies the syntax and semantics of formal languages, formal systems, and logical calculi. Finally, it deals with the applications of logic in different domains of inquiry and discourse.

Section 10/11.   History and Philosophy of Logic

A. History of logic

1. Ancient logic

a. Precursors of ancient logic: contributions of the Sophists, Socrates, and Plato to theories of language and the axiomatic method

b. Aristotle and the logic of predicates: theories of the structure of language, theories of opposition and conversion, development of syllogistic and modal logic

c. Later developments in the logic of predicates: contributions of Theophrastus and Galen

d. Founding of the logic of propositions: contributions of Theophrastus and the Megarians, Stoic logic

2. Medieval logic

a. Development of medieval logic: Arabic contributions, disputes between the "old logic" and the "new logic" after the translation of Aristotle's *Organon*, summations by William of Sherwood and Peter of Spain

b. Medieval theories of language and their relation to the development of logic: the theory of categorematic and syncategorematic terms, the theory of supposition

c. Medieval developments in formal logic: the logic of predicates, of propositions, and of modal expressions; logical fallacies and paradoxes

3. Modern logic from the Renaissance to the 20th century

a. Logic in the Renaissance: the influence of Neoplatonism and of the rise of the natural sciences, the logics of Petrus Ramus and of Port-Royal

b. The rise of mathematical logic during the Enlightenment: contributions of Leibniz (*e.g.,* his general calculus of reasoning and general methodology), the search for clarity and the use of diagrams

c. Development of mathematical logic in the 19th century: expansions of syllogistic, Boole's algebra of logic, refinements of the calculus, the study by Frege and Cantor of the relation between logic and the foundations of mathematics

4. Logic in the 20th century

a. The conflict of Logicism, the view that mathematics is a continuation of logic, with Intuitionism and Formalism: Russell's Logicism and the theory of types, Brouwer's Intuitionism, Hilbert's Formalism

b. Developments in the logic of propositions and in the logic of predicates

c. Metalogical studies: the study of the properties of axiomatized systems; syntax and semantics as metalogical disciplines

5. Logic in the East

a. Indian logic: its origins in the commentaries on the scriptural texts called *sūtra*s, special problems in grammar and special types of inference, interest in the logical implications of the notion of negation

b. Chinese logic: its origins in reflections on the characteristics of controversies between the major philosophies of Confucianism, Taoism, and Moism; its neglect after the establishment of Neo-Confucianism in the 11th century AD

B. Philosophy of logic

1. The organization of logic as a discipline

a. The nature and varieties of logic: differing conceptions of its field and scope, varieties of logical symbolism

b. Features and problems of logic: concerns with logical semantics or model theory, questions of the limitations of logic, Gödel's incompleteness theorems, the question of logic and computability

2. Issues and developments in the philosophy of logic

a. Problems in meaning and truth: logical semantics of modal concepts, logic and informativeness

    b. Problems of ontology: problems concerning individuation and existence

    c. Alternative logics: modal logics, intuitionistic logic

  3. The place of logic among the sciences and disciplines

Suggested reading in the *Encyclopædia Britannica:*

MACROPAEDIA: Major articles dealing with the history and philosophy of logic

    Logic, The History and Kinds of
    Philosophies of the Branches of Knowledge

MICROPAEDIA: Selected entries of reference information

General subjects

abstraction	axiom	fallacy	types, theory of
analogy	De Morgan laws	possibility	universal
analytic	dialectic	thought, laws of	
proposition	ekthesis		

Biographies

Boole, George	Leibniz, Gottfried	Peirce, Charles	Socrates
Carnap, Rudolf	Wilhelm	Sanders	Whitehead, Alfred
Frege, Gottlob	Leśniewski,	Ramus, Petrus	North
Gödel, Kurt	Stanislaw	Russell, Bertrand	

    See also Sections 10/51, 10/52, and 10/53

INDEX: See entries under all of the terms above

Section 10/12. Formal Logic, Metalogic, and Applied Logic

  A. Formal logic

    1. The propositional calculus: the logic of unanalyzed sentences in combination

      a. General features of the propositional calculus: symbols employed for propositional connectives or operators (*i.e.,* "not," "and," "or," "if . . . then," "is equivalent to"), propositional variables

      b. Special systems of the propositional calculus

    2. The predicate calculus: the logic of quantified functions of terms

      a. General features of the predicate calculus: individual variables and predicate variables, universal and existential quantifiers (*i.e.,* "any" or "all," "some" or "one")

      b. The lower predicate calculus: the logic of individual variables

      c. Higher order predicate calculi: the logics of classes of variables

    3. Syllogistic: the theory of the syllogism

    4. Modal logic: the logic of necessity, possibility, and contingency; systems of and validity in modal logic

    5. Set theory and natural-number arithmetic

  B. Metalogic: the study of the syntax and the semantics of formal languages, formal systems, and logical calculi

    1. The nature and elements of metalogic

    2. The nature of a formal system and of a formal language

    3. Discoveries about formal mathematical systems: completeness and consistency, decidability and undecidability

    4. Discoveries about logical calculi

    5. Model theory: the study of the interpretations, or models, that satisfy the axioms of a given formal system

C. Applied logic

1. The critique of forms of reasoning

   a. Theory of argumentation: the new rhetoric

   b. Analysis of logical fallacies: material, verbal, and formal fallacies

2. Epistemic logic: logic dealing with the concepts of belief, knowledge, assertion, doubt, and question

3. Practical logic: logic dealing with the concepts of choosing, planning, commanding, and permitting

4. Logics of physical application

5. Hypothetical reasoning and counterfactual conditionals: logic involving consequents whose antecedents are known to be false

---

Suggested reading in the *Encyclopædia Britannica:*

MACROPAEDIA: Major articles dealing with formal logic, metalogic, and applied logic

Logic, The History and Kinds of
Rhetoric

MICROPAEDIA: Selected entries of reference information

General subjects

analytic proposition	deduction	modus ponens and modus tollens	rhetoric
axiom	dichotomy	mood	set theory
axiomatic method	dilemma	predicate calculus	syllogistic
categorical proposition	enthymeme	predication	
condition	formal system	propositional calculus	
conjunction	logic	recursive function	
conversion	metalogic	reduction	
	modal logic		
	modality		

Biographies

Antiphon	Lewis, C.I.	Quintilian
Isocrates	Peano, Giuseppe	Zeno of Elea

See also Sections 10/51, 10/52, and 10/53

INDEX: See entries under all of the terms above

Division II.   **Mathematics**
[For Part Ten headnote see page 479.]

The outlines in the three sections of Division II treat the history and foundations of mathematics, the branches of mathematics, and the applications of mathematics.

Section 10/21 deals first with the general history of mathematics, with the development of representative non-probabilistic areas of mathematics, and with the historical development of probabilistic areas. The treatment of the foundations of mathematics covers the axiomatic method, the genetic method, 20th-century rival formulations of the foundations of mathematics, and current investigations of the foundations of mathematics.

Section 10/22, the branches of mathematics, first treats set theory, arithmetic, elementary multivariate algebra, linear and multilinear algebra, and algebraic structures, including the subjects of homological algebra and universal algebra. It goes on to deal with Euclidean and non-Euclidean geometry, projective geometry, analytic and trigonometric geometry, differential geometry, and algebraic geometry. It then deals with the subdivisions of mathematical analysis: real analysis, complex analysis, differential equations, functional analysis, Fourier analysis, the theory of probability, and vector and tensor analysis. The outline next deals with combinatorics and combinatorial geometry, and with number theory. Finally, it treats topology: general topology, topological groups and differential topology, and algebraic topology.

Section 10/23, applications of mathematics, first treats mathematics as a calculatory science and then goes on to deal with statistics, numerical analysis, definitions and examples of automata and the development of automata theory, the mathematical theory of optimization, information theory, and the mathematical aspects of physical theories.

Section 10/21.   **History and Foundations of Mathematics**

A. History of mathematics

   1. The development of mathematics in general, through ancient, medieval, and modern times

      a. Ancient and medieval periods

         i. Ideas and methods originating or developing in Mesopotamia and Egypt

         ii. Greek and Hellenistic mathematics

         iii. The Middle Ages: Islāmic mathematics and its transmission to the West

      b. The modern period

         i. The 17th century: discovery of logarithms and analytic geometry, development of calculus by Newton and Leibniz

         ii. The 18th century: advances in geometry, algebra, and analysis; contributions of the Bernoulli family, Euler, Lagrange, Laplace, and others

         iii. The 19th and 20th centuries: development of non-Euclidean geometry by Bolyai, Lobachevsky, and others; contributions to the theories of groups, functions, and complex variables; development of algebraic geometry; influence of physical science on analysis; study of the foundations of mathematics

   2. Historical development of representative nonprobabilistic areas of mathematics

      a. Numerals and numeral systems
         [see also 10/23.A.1.]

         i. Simple grouping systems: ancient Egyptian, Babylonian, Greek, and Roman numerals

         ii. Development of multiplicative, ciphered, and positional numeral systems

      b. Introduction of symbolic notations to represent mathematical quantities, operations, and relationships

      c. Calculatory science
         [see also 10/23.A.]

         i. The history of mathematical tables, including tables of logarithms

         ii. The evolution of analogue devices: origins of harmonic analyzers, differential analyzers, and the slide rule

        iii. The evolution of digital devices: development of computational aids from the abacus to the modern electronic digital computer
[see 10/23.A.7.]

    d. Geometry
[see also 10/22.C.]

        i. Egyptian, Babylonian, and Greek geometry

        ii. The algebraic approach: development of analytic geometry

        iii. Development of projective geometry

        iv. Development of non-Euclidean geometry

        v. Philosophical aspects of geometry

        vi. Modern ideas and topics in geometry: the axiomatic method; geometrical transformations; the concept of space, differential geometry, and topology

    e. Algebra
[see also 10/22.B.]

        i. Babylonian, Egyptian, and Greek contributions

        ii. Contributions from the Orient, India, and the Islāmic world

        iii. Medieval and modern European developments

        iv. Evolution of the theory of algebraic equations of one variable: solutions prior to and after Galois

3. Historical development of probabilistic areas of mathematics
[see also 10/22.D.6.]

    a. Development of the mathematical theory of probability

        i. The abstract calculus of probability: the common structure of theories of probability

        ii. Alternative views of probability: the frequency theory of probability, the range theory of probability and the principle of indifference, the belief theory of probability, subjective and objective notions of probability

        iii. Bernoulli's theorem, inverse probability, and asymptotic probabilities

    b. Development of mathematical statistics: the history of the theory of stochastic processes, origins of control theory

B. Foundations of mathematics

    1. The axiomatic method: mathematical analysis based upon a set of axioms, or unproved statements

        a. Euclidean geometry
[see also 10/22.C.1.]

        b. Non-Euclidean geometry
[see also 10/22.C.2.]

        c. The formal axiomatic method

    2. The genetic method: mathematical analysis based upon the orderly construction or generation of objects with unknown properties from objects with known properties

        a. Arithmetic and analysis
[see also 10/22.B.1.]

        b. The concept of cardinal number and the theory of sets
[see also 10/22.A.2.]

    3. The crisis in the foundations of mathematics after 1900: reformulations in terms of the three alternative philosophical positions of Intuitionism, Logicism, and Formalism

        a. The paradoxes

        b. Intuitionism

        c. Logicism, Formalism, and the metamathematical method

    4. Current directions in investigations of the foundations of mathematics

        a. Intuitionistic studies of the foundations of mathematics: application of formalistic procedures to Intuitionism

        b. Non-Intuitionistic studies of the foundations of mathematics: trends in recursion theory, proof theory, model theory, and set theory

Suggested reading in the *Encyclopædia Britannica*:

MACROPAEDIA: Major articles and biographies dealing with the history and foundations of mathematics

MICROPAEDIA: Selected entries of reference information

General subjects

Biographies

INDEX: See entries under all of the terms above

Section 10/22.   Branches of Mathematics

A. Set theory

   1. Origins of set theory and the definitions of a set and a set element, or member

   2. Introduction to set theory

     a. Fundamental set concepts

     b. Essential features of Cantorian set theory

   3. Axiomatic set theory: formal analyses of set theory based upon certain fundamental assumptions or undefined notions called axioms
[see also 10/21.B.3.a.]

     a. Postulates of axiomatic set theory: the Zermelo–Fraenkel axioms, the von Neumann–Bernays–Gödel axioms

     b. Limitations of axiomatic set theory: failure of attempts to prove the consistency of axiomatic set theory, Gödel's theorem

     c. The present status of axiomatic set theory: profound changes in axiomatic set theory as a result of recent discoveries

B. Algebra

1. Arithmetic

a. Fundamental definitions and laws: the concepts of natural number and integer; the binary operations of addition and multiplication; the commutative and associative laws of addition; the commutative, associative, and distributive laws of multiplication

b. Theory of divisors: extension of natural number concepts to non-integers, fractions resulting from the binary operation of division

c. Number systems and notation: use of the positional principle and the symbol zero to specify magnitude in sequences of digits; number systems having different bases—*e.g.,* binary, decimal, and sexagesimal systems
[see also 10/23.A.1.]

d. Arithmetic calculation with decimals: binary operations with decimals; divisibility rules; calculation of square, cube, and higher roots

e. Logarithms: formal definition of logarithms, use of logarithms to reduce the operations of multiplication and division to the simpler operations of addition and subtraction
[see also 10/23.A.4.b.]

2. Elementary and multivariate algebra

a. Algebra as an extension and generalization of arithmetic

b. Basic algebraic properties of numbers

c. Polynomials and rational functions

d. Solution of equations: the principal problem of elementary algebra

3. Linear and multilinear algebra

a. Linear algebra

i. Vector spaces

ii. Matrices

iii. Linear transformations and linear operators

iv. Linear functionals and their relation to linear transformations

v. Inner products and inner product spaces: self-conjugate, or Hermitian, matrices; unitary and orthogonal matrices

vi. Linear operators in an inner product space: self-adjoint, or Hermitian, operators; unitary and orthogonal operators; the spectral theorem for normal operators

b. Multilinear algebra

4. Algebraic structures

a. Lattices

b. Groups

c. Fields

d. Rings

e. Categories

f. Homological algebra

g. Universal algebra

C. Geometry

1. Euclidean geometry

a. Geometry as an abstract doctrine: the axiomatization of the foundations of geometry; axioms of order, incidence, congruence, parallels, and continuity and results derived from them

b. The measure of polygons and polyhedra: the theories of equivalence and measure and their relation, Euclid's contribution and its modern extension and generalization

c. Transformation geometry: reflection, rotation, and translation of geometric figures; homotheties and similitudes

d. Geometric constructions: the equivalence between Euclidean constructions and existence theorems, gauge constructions, ruler and compass constructions, construction with compass only

e. Geometry of more than three dimensions: the generalization of Euclidean geometry

f. The concept of convexity and convex sets

2. Non-Euclidean geometry
[see also 10/21.B.1.b.]

a. Distinction between Euclidean and non-Euclidean geometry: hyperbolic geometry and elliptic geometry

b. Geometric representations of the hyperbolic plane and hyperbolic space

c. Coordinates in spherical and elliptical space: interpretations of four-dimensional Euclidean space

d. Coordinates in the hyperbolic plane and hyperbolic trigonometry

e. Transformations: hyperbolic geometry as characterized by its group of reflections

3. Projective geometry

a. The procedure of projection as the foundation of projective geometry

b. Homogeneous coordinates: location of points in space

c. Complex geometry: introduction of complex numbers as homogeneous coordinates

d. Abstract geometries: extension and generalization of projective geometry to space of any number of dimensions

4. Analytic and trigonometric geometry

a. Plane analytic geometry: fundamental procedures and concepts

b. Trigonometry

c. Coordinates and transformation of coordinates

d. Projective and solid analytic geometry: extensions of analytic geometry to the projective plane and to three or more dimensions

e. Special curves: named curves that have been studied with regard to problems in mathematics or the physical sciences; *e.g.,* the folium of Descartes, the lemniscate of Bernoulli, the cardioid, the cycloid, the catenary, the brachistochrone

5. Combinatorial geometry
[see E.1.c., below]

6. Differential geometry
[see also F.2.e., below]

7. Algebraic geometry
[see also F.3., below]

D. Analysis

1. Real analysis

a. Origins and concepts of real analysis

b. Number systems and their properties

c. Functions and differential calculus

d. Measure and integral calculus

2. Complex analysis

a. Theory of analytic functions of one complex variable

b. Theory of analytic functions of several complex variables

c. Potential theory

3. Differential equations

a. Ordinary differential equations

b. Partial differential equations

c. Special functions that arise as solutions to differential equations; *e.g.,* the hypergeometric function, Legendre polynomials, spherical harmonics, Bessel functions

d. Dynamical systems on manifolds

4. Functional analysis

    a. General features of functional analysis

    b. Calculus of variations

    c. Generalized functions: the theory of distributions

5. Fourier analysis

    a. The theory of series

    b. Fourier series

    c. Harmonic analysis and integral transforms

    d. Representations of groups and algebras: Fourier analysis on non-Abelian groups

6. Theory of probability

    a. Heuristic introduction to probability: the need for a mathematically precise definition of probability

    b. Probability on finite dimensional spaces

    c. Probability on infinite dimensional spaces

7. Vector and tensor analysis

    a. Scalars, vectors, tensors, and the physical quantities that give rise to them

    b. Vector algebra and analysis

    c. Tensor algebra and analysis

E. Combinatorics and number theory

  1. Combinatorics and combinatorial geometry

    a. The nature and scope of combinatorics: the definition of combinatorics as the branch of mathematics concerned with arrangements, operations, and selections within a finite or a discrete system

    b. Methods, results, and unsolved problems of combinatorial theory, exclusive of geometric considerations

    c. Combinatorial geometry

  2. Number theory

    a. Elementary number theory: properties of the whole numbers, or integers
      [see B.1.a., above]

    b. Algebraic number theory: properties of algebraic numbers

    c. Analytic number theory

    d. Geometric number theory

    e. Probabilistic number theory

F. Topology

  1. General topology

    a. Definition and basic concepts of topology; the subject matter and applications of topology as exemplified by certain simple topological problems and their solutions

    b. Topological spaces: methods for constructing topological spaces; Euclidean n-dimensional space, Hilbert space, Cartesian-product space, and other examples of topological spaces

    c. Topological properties

    d. Topological problems of current interest; *e.g.,* the planar fixed-point problem, the polyhedral Schoenflies problem

  2. Topological groups and differential topology

    a. Interaction between analysis and topology

    b. The theorems of Tikhonov and Ascoli: embedding of a topological space as a subspace of a compact space

    c. Continuous groups

    d. Analysis on manifolds: topological implications of problems in global analysis

    e. Differential topology
      [see also C.6., above]

3. Algebraic topology
[see also C.7., above]

   a. The nature and scope of algebraic topology and its context within general topology, the basic concepts of topological spaces and maps

   b. Invariants: unchanging quantities that play a central role in the classification of spaces and maps

   c. Homotopy theory: homotopy classes and the concept of homotopy-equivalent spaces

   d. Homology and cohomology theory: definition of a simplex, axiomatic homology theory

   e. Homotopy groups: stability and suspension

   f. Definition and properties of fibres, fibre bundles, and fibrings

   g. Sheaf cohomology

   h. Spectral sequences: Serre, Rothenberg–Steenrod, and Eilenberg–Moore spectral sequences

   i. Further developments in homotopy theory: Eilenberg–MacLane spaces, the methods of killing homotopy groups, Serre's C-theory

   j. Generalized homology and cohomology theory: K-theory, the spectral sequence of G.W. Whitehead–Atiyah–Hirzebruch

   k. Recent advances in algebraic topology

Suggested reading in the *Encyclopædia Britannica*:

Section 10/23.   Applications of Mathematics

A. Mathematics as a calculatory science

1. Numerical notations

a. Aggregations, or units used to assist counting or grouping of objects

b. Ancient numerical notations

c. Decimal notation and modern notational developments

2. Geometrical aids

a. Early applications of geometry

b. Instruments for observation and navigation

c. Mapping

d. Applications of geometry to celestial measurement

e. Optical instruments

f. Drawing instruments

3. Mathematical models: physical constructions used to aid the visualization of mathematical ideas or relationships

4. Calculatory aspects of algebra

a. Algebraic notation

b. Logarithms

c. Slide rules

5. Calculation using tables and graphs

a. Mathematical tables

b. Graphs and graphical procedures

6. Analogue computation
[see also 735.D.]

a. Types of problems solvable by analogue computation

b. Analogue computers

7. Digital computation
[see also 735.D.]

a. Digital calculators

b. Punched cards

c. Programmed machines (digital computers)

B. Statistics

1. The basic principles of statistical inference: application of the concepts and techniques of probability theory to the analysis of data

a. The concept of a statistical experiment: mathematical description of experiments in terms of random variables

b. Distribution functions and their properties: the median, mean, variance, and standard deviation of a distribution; the Gaussian or normal distribution

2. Estimation: techniques for approximating the parameters of families of distributions of random variables

3. Hypothesis testing: techniques for determining the correctness of alternative hypotheses concerning given data and an assumed probability model

4. Structure in data: use of regression analysis to discover systematic patterns

C. Numerical analysis

1. Introduction: definition, origins, and basic concepts of numerical analysis

2. Finite differences

a. Types of differences and their application to the problem of interpolation

b. Analysis with finite differences: numerical differentiation, numerical integration, summation of series

c. Difference and differential-difference equations

3. Applications of numerical analysis

D. Automata theory
[see also 712.A.6.]

1. Introduction: definition and examples of automata, development of the basic concepts of automata theory, the analogy between automata and the nervous systems of living organisms

2. Neural nets and automata

3. Probabilistic questions: random effects in the operation of automata

4. Classification of automata

E. Mathematical theory of optimization

1. The theory of games: analysis of the strategic features of conflict situations

2. Linear and nonlinear programming (mathematical programming)

3. Cybernetics

4. Control theory

F. Information theory
[see 735.A.]

1. Origins and definitions of information theory

2. Central problems of information theory

3. Principles of information theory

4. Applications of information theory to cryptography, linguistics, and other fields

G. Mathematical aspects of physical theories

1. Mechanics of particles and systems
[see also 126.A.]

2. Fluid mechanics
[see also 126.E.]

3. Mechanics of solids
[see also 126.C.]

4. Statistical mechanics
[see also 124.A.9.]

5. Electromagnetic theory
[see also 127.E.]

6. Relativity theory: space and time as a four-dimensional continuum
[see also 131.D.]

7. Riemannian geometry
[see also 10/22.C.6.]

8. Quantum mechanics
[see also 111.A.4.c.]

9. Dimensional analysis

Suggested reading in the *Encyclopædia Britannica:*

MACROPAEDIA: Major articles dealing with applications of mathematics

Automata Theory
Computers
Game Theory
Information Processing
Information Science
Numerical Analysis
Optimization, The Mathematical Theory of
Statistics

MICROPAEDIA: Selected entries of reference information

General subjects

computers and other mathematical devices:
abacus
analogue computer
calculator
central processing unit
computer programs
computer programming language
differential analyzer
differentiator
digital computer

harmonic analyzer
input/output device
integrator
microprocessor
planimeter
quipu
slide rule
time-sharing
Turing machine
numerical analysis:
difference equation
interpolation
numerical analysis
optimization:
control theory
cybernetics

game theory
linear programming
mathematical programming
optimization
queuing theory
statistics:
decision theory
distribution function
estimation
freedom, degree of
inference
mean
normal distribution

point estimation
sampling
statistics
Student's t-test`
other:
algorithm
automata theory
distortion
dimensional analysis
eigenvalue
gamma function
graph
graph theory
information theory
mathematical model
pi theorem

Biographies

Babbage, Charles
Boole, George
Napier, John

Neumann, John von
Pascal, Blaise

Turing, Alan Mathison
Weyl, Herman

Wiener, Norbert

INDEX: See entries under all of the terms above

Division III. **Science**
[For Part Ten headnote see page 479.]

The results of investigations in the natural, social, and medical sciences and the achievements of technology are dealt with in Parts One through Five and in Part Seven. The outlines in the seven sections of Division III are concerned with inquiries that have viewed those sciences and technology as the objects of historical and analytical studies.

Section 10/31 deals with science taken generally. It first presents a synoptic history of Western and Eastern science. It then deals with the nature and scope of the philosophy of science, and with analyses of the empirical procedures and formal structures of science, of science's modes of discovery, and of validating concepts and theories.

Section 10/32 is on the physical sciences. The outline first deals with the historical evolution of astronomy and astrophysics, of physics, and of chemistry. Then, for each of them, it treats issues about the nature, scope, component disciplines, methods, and principal problems of the discipline.

Similarly, Section 10/33 first deals with the history of the several complementary Earth sciences, and then with studies of the nature, scope, methods, and principal problems of the geological, hydrologic, and atmospheric sciences.

Section 10/34 is first concerned with the historical development of the biological sciences and with issues about the methodology, scope, and conceptual structure of biology as a whole. It then sets forth the work done at four levels of biological research: the molecular, cellular, organismic, and population levels. Finally, it treats issues in the philosophy of biology: issues about the nature of biological systems, issues concerning evolution and evolutionary theory, and biological issues with ethical implications.

Section 10/35 treats the history of medicine; the many specialized fields of medical practice and research; and such affiliated disciplines as dentistry, osteopathy, nursing, and pharmacy.

Section 10/36 is on the social sciences and psychology. It first deals with the general historical development of the social sciences. It then separately treats the development, nature, scope, and methods of the particular social sciences: anthropology, sociology, economics, and political science. Finally, it deals with the history, scope, and methods of psychology.

Section 10/37 treats the history of the technological sciences; the academic and professional aspects of engineering; the nature and scope of agricultural sciences; and the nature and scope of such recently developed interdisciplinary fields as bionics, systems engineering, and cybernetics.

Section 10/31. History and Philosophy of Science

A. History of science

1. Introduction: problems and difficulties of tracing the development of science

2. Science in ancient and medieval Western civilization

   a. Science in Greek civilization

      i. Protoscience in Greece before the age of Pericles: empirical versus religious or mythological explanations of natural phenomena

      ii. Development of scientific attitudes: the beginning of disciplined observation, inference, definition, and classification; the Platonic versus the Aristotelian view of nature

      iii. Science during the Hellenistic Age: the emergence of Alexandria as the foremost centre of scientific research

   b. Science in Rome: the contrast between Roman success in law and technology and Roman failure in science

   c. Medieval science

3. Science in other civilizations: Islāmic science; science in India, China, and Japan

4. European science in the early modern period

   a. The rebirth of science in the Renaissance

      i. The state of science in Europe in the early 15th century

      ii. The influence of advances in printing, mining, metallurgy, and other areas of technology: the demands placed upon science by increases in trade and exploration

      iii. The coexistence of new scientific discoveries and old philosophical views

   b. The revolution in natural philosophy

      i. The radical reformulation of the objects, methods, and functions of natural knowledge: the work of Bacon, Descartes, and Galileo
      [see also 10/42.A.3.]

      ii. Results of the new philosophy: establishment of scientific societies, progress in particular fields of science

   c. Characteristics of European science

5. Science in the age of modern revolutions

   a. Science during the Industrial Revolution

   b. Intellectual origins of revolution: the spirit of the Enlightenment

   c. The institutional organization of science under the French Revolution

   d. Romantic reaction and science: the proponents of *Naturphilosophie*

6. Science in the 19th century: difference in styles of research; progress in physics, chemistry, and biology

7. Science in the early 20th century: the social organization and style of science, the common pattern of advance in scientific research

8. Contemporary problems and prospects: the moral, political, and environmental difficulties facing science

B. Philosophy of science
[see also 10/52.B.2.]

1. The nature and scope of the philosophy of science and its relation to other disciplines: the diverse concerns of and methods of approach to the philosophy of science

2. Historical development of the philosophy of science

   a. Classical and medieval periods: the alternative viewpoints of the Stoics and Epicureans and of the Platonists and Aristotelians

   b. The 17th century: the debate about scientific methodology, Bacon's inductive approach and Descartes's deductive approach

   c. The 18th century: Empiricist, Rationalist, and Kantian interpretations of Newtonian physics

   d. From the beginning of the 19th century through World War I: the influence of Kant's belief in the unique rationality of the classical synthesis of Euclid and Newton

   e. The 20th-century debate: responses to relativity, quantum mechanics, and other profound changes in the natural sciences; Logical Positivism versus Neo-Kantianism

3. Elements of the scientific enterprise

   a. Empirical, conceptual, and formal elements and their theoretical interpretation: diverse views of the relative importance of observation, theory, and mathematical formulation

   b. Empirical procedures of science: measurement, design of experiments, classification

   c. The formal structures of science: the problem of constructing a purely formal analysis of scientific inference, the distinction between scientific laws and empirical generalizations

   d. Conceptual change and the development of science: historical problems concerning the changing theoretical organization of science

4. Movements of scientific thought: the basic procedures of intellectual development in science

   a. Scientific discovery: the extreme positions of formalism, which emphasizes the rational elements of scientific discovery, and of irrationalism, which emphasizes the role of intuition, guesswork, and chance

   b. Validation and justification of new concepts and theories: the view that prediction is the crucial test of scientific validity; the view that coherence, consistency, and comprehensiveness are the essential requirements of a scientific theory

   c. Unification of the theories and concepts of separate sciences: attempts to construct an axiomatic system for all of natural science, the reductionist problem of achieving a consistent conceptual basis for two or more sciences

5. The philosophical status of scientific theory

   a. The status of scientific propositions and concepts of entities: diverse views of the epistemological status of scientific propositions and of the ontological status of scientific concepts

   b. The relationship between philosophical analysis and scientific practice: the application of different philosophical doctrines and approaches to different sciences

6. The relevance of scientific knowledge to other spheres of human experience and concern: the social significance of science and of scientific attitudes, limitations on the scientific endeavour

7. The relation between science and the humanities: questions of differences between scientific and humanistic methodologies
   [see 10/42.B.3.]

Suggested reading in the *Encyclopædia Britannica:*

MACROPAEDIA: Major articles and biographies dealing with the history and philosophy of science

Classification	Kelvin	Newton	Science, The
Theory	Locke	Philosophies of	History of
Franklin	Measurement	the Branches of	
Galileo	Theory	Knowledge	

MICROPAEDIA: Selected entries of reference information

General subjects

Baconian method	scientific theory
hypothetico-deductive method	typology
nature, law of	

Biographies

Albertus Magnus, Saint	Bacon, Roger	Empedocles
Anaxagoras	Bruno, Giordano	Oresme, Nicholas
Anaximenes of Miletus	Buffon, Georges-Louis Leclerc, comte de	Poincaré, Henri

INDEX: See entries under all of the terms above

Section 10/32. The Physical Sciences

A. History of the physical sciences: the evolution of astronomy, physics, and chemistry

1. History of astronomy

a. Ancient astronomy

    i. Time reckoning and astronomical prediction: development of lunar and solar calendars, prediction of eclipses and of first appearances of the New Moon

    ii. Early cosmologies

    iii. Ancient astronomical records, treatises, and star catalogs

b. Medieval astronomy: European and Islāmic contributions

c. Astronomy in the 16th and 17th centuries

    i. The geocentric and heliocentric world systems

    ii. The discovery of the laws of planetary motion

    iii. The invention and use of the telescope

    iv. The theory of universal gravitation
      [see 2.c., below]

d. Astronomy in the 18th century

    i. Development of celestial mechanics: the calculation of orbits, the three-body problem, the dynamical stability of gravitational systems

    ii. Improvements in telescope design and increased accuracy of measurements: the discovery of the aberration of light

    iii. Speculations concerning the origin of the solar system, the nature of nebulae, and the structure of the universe

e. Astronomy in the 19th century

    i. The discovery of Neptune and the asteroids, the search for a planet within the orbit of Mercury

    ii. Improved determinations of stellar positions and magnitudes; the first measurements of stellar parallax; the compilation of catalogs of nebulae, stars, and star clusters

    iii. Improvements in telescope design and the development of new astronomical tools

f. Astronomy in the 20th century

    i. Improvements in optical instruments

    ii. The beginnings of statistical studies of stars, nebulae, and galaxies

    iii. Theories of stellar structure: new theories of the sources of stellar energy

    iv. Astronomical tests of general relativity: the gravitational red shift, the deflection of light, the precession of the perihelion of Mercury, the cosmological red shift

    v. Detection of radio emissions from the Sun and the Milky Way: development of radio telescopes; radio signals from stars and galaxies, quasi-stellar radio sources, and pulsars; black holes

    vi. Refinements in spectroscopic methods

g. Recent developments and emerging trends; *e.g.,* use of satellites and space probes, development of X-ray and infrared astronomy

2. History of physics

a. Greek physics: speculations concerning the nature of space, matter, and motion

b. Medieval physics: the influence of Aristotle

c. Physics in the 16th and 17th centuries: discoveries and theories in mechanics and optics

d. Physics in the 18th and 19th centuries

    i. Development of theories of light: the wave theory versus the corpuscular theory, the search for the ether

    ii. Development of the theories of electricity, magnetism, and electromagnetic waves

    iii. Developments in thermodynamics: theories of heat, the laws of thermodynamics, the impossibility of perpetual motion, the kinetic theory of gases

    iv. Development of the atomic theory of matter: the discovery of the electron, the discovery of radioactivity and X-rays, the discovery of spectral regularities

e. Physics in the 20th century

    i. Development of the theory of relativity

    ii. Development of the quantum theory, wave mechanics, statistical mechanics, and related theories

    iii. Development of theories and laws concerning atomic structure, nuclear interactions, and elementary particles

    iv. Development of plasma physics

    v. Development of electronics and related fields of study

    vi. Modern developments in physics: atomic beams, nuclear magnetic resonance, and electron spin resonance methods; development of nonlinear optics; the development of lasers and masers

3. History of chemistry

a. Chemistry before 1700

    i. The rise of alchemy: the goal of the alchemists—to prolong life and to transmute base metals to gold

    ii. The influence of the new mechanical philosophy on chemistry: the work of Boyle

b. Chemistry in the 18th century

    i. Studies of combustion and respiration: the phlogiston theory, the work of Lavoisier and Cavendish

    ii. Laboratory discoveries: isolation and identification of gases; discoveries of new elements, compounds, and chemical reactions

c. Chemistry in the 19th century

    i. Development of the periodic table of the elements: the work of Mendeleyev and Meyer

    ii. Discoveries of new elements, isotopes, and radioactive elements

    iii. Development of more accurate methods of analysis

    iv. Development of theories of molecular structure and chemical reaction

    v. Development of organic chemistry: introduction of the concept of valence, the study of aromatic compounds, development of the structural theory

    vi. Development of electrochemistry: the theory of chemical affinity in electrical terms

    vii. Development of industrial chemistry: the application of chemical principles and reactions to industrial processes

d. Chemistry in the 20th century

    i. Development of instrumental methods of chemical analysis

    ii. Explanation of chemical phenomena by principles of atomic and molecular structures

    iii. Application of quantum mechanics to chemical bonding

B. The nature and scope of astronomy and astrophysics: the major subject matters and principal problems
[see also Part One, Division III]

1. The nature of astronomy and methods of study

2. Component disciplines of astronomy and their relationship to other sciences: planetary and lunar sciences; meteoritics; the study of comets, minor planets, and the origin of the solar system

3. Investigaton of the scale of the universe and of the distribution of objects within it: the determination of positions, the measurement of distances

4. Orbit theory: its role in astronomy

5. Astrophysics: the study of stars, galaxies, and the universe; cosmology and cosmogony

C. The nature and scope of physics: its major subject matters, methods, and problems
[see also Part I, Divisions I and II]

1. The nature of physics: its concern with matter and energy and their interactions

2. Component disciplines of physics: mechanics, thermodynamics, heat, electricity, magnetism, sound, optics, quantum mechanics, states of matter, nuclear and atomic physics

3. The experimental and theoretical methods of physics

4. The relationship of physics to other disciplines

5. Interdisciplinary fields of physics: astrophysics, biophysics, geophysics

6. Philosophical problems in physics: at the formal level, quantum level, macrophysical level, and cosmological level

D. The nature and scope of chemistry: its major subject matters and problems
[see also 121, 122, and 123]

1. The nature of chemistry: its concern with the composition, properties, and changes of matter

2. The subdivisions of chemistry: inorganic, organic, analytical, and physical chemistry

3. The methods of chemistry

4. The study of chemical transformations

5. Interdisciplinary fields of chemistry: biochemistry, geochemistry, chemical engineering

---

**Suggested reading in the *Encyclopædia Britannica:*

MACROPAEDIA: Major articles and biographies dealing with the physical sciences

Bohr	Heisenberg	Newton	Physical
Copernicus	Helmholtz	Pascal	Sciences, The
Einstein	Kepler	Philosophies of	Planck
Faraday	Lavoisier	the Branches of	Rutherford
Galileo	Maxwell	Knowledge	

MICROPAEDIA: Selected entries of reference information

General subjects

major fields and	quantum	bubble chamber	radio
component	mechanics	centrifuge	interferometer
disciplines:	radio and radar	chromatography	radio telescope
aerodynamics	astronomy	cloud chamber	satellite
astronomy	statistical	digital computer	observatory
biochemistry	mechanics	laser	sounding rocket
celestial mechanics	thermodynamics	mass spectrometry	spacecraft
chemistry	ultraviolet	microscope	spectrochemical
cosmology	astronomy	molecular beam	analysis
fluid mechanics	x-ray astronomy	nuclear magnetic	star catalog
infrared astronomy	*methodology and*	resonance	telescope
mechanics	*instrumentation:*	particle	
optics	astronomical	accelerator	
physics	observatory	photometry	

Biographies

astronomers:

Ambartsumian, Viktor Amazaspovich
Banneker, Benjamin
Bessel, Friedrich Wilhelm
Bradley, James
Brahe, Tycho
Cannon, Annie Jump
Cassini, Gian Domenico
Eddington, Sir Arthur Stanley
Eudoxus of Cnidus
Gamow, George
Halley, Edmund
Herschel, Sir John
Herschel, Sir William
Hipparchus
Hubble, Edwin Powell
Kuiper, Gerard Peter
Laplace, Pierre-Simon, marquis de
Le Verrier, Urbain-Jean-Joseph
Lovell, Sir Bernard
Messier, Charles
Newcomb, Simon
Ptolemy
Russell, Henry Norris
Schwarzchild, Karl
Struve, Otto

chemists:

Arrhenius, Svante
Berthelot, Marcellin
Berthollet, Claude-Louis, Comte
Berzelius, Jöns Jacob
Boyle, Robert
Bunsen, Robert Wilhelm
Cannizzaro, Stanislao
Cori, Carl and Gerty
Crookes, Sir William
Curie, Marie
Curie, Pierre
Dalton, John
Davy, Sir Humphry
Debye, Peter
Gay-Lussac, Joseph-Louis
Haber, Fritz
Hahn, Otto
Hodgkin, Dorothy Mary
Joliot-Curie, Frédéric and Irène
Kendrew, Sir John Cowdery
Langmuir, Irving
Libby, Willard F.
Liebig, Justus, Freiherr von
Mendeleyev, Dmitry Ivanovich
Mulliken, Robert Sanderson
Pasteur, Louis
Pauling, Linus
Priestley, Joseph
Ramsay, Sir William
Rose family
Sanger, Frederick
Scheele, Carl Wilhelm
Seaborg, Glenn T.
Soddy, Frederick
Stahl, Georg Ernst
Woodward, R.B.
Wöhler, Friedrich

physicists:

Alvarez, Luis Walter
Arago, François
Bardeen, John
Becquerel, Henri
Bethe, Hans Albrecht
Bragg, Sir Lawrence
Bragg, Sir William
Bridgman, P.W.
Broglie, Louis-Victor, 7e duc de
Cavendish, Henry
Dirac, P.A.M.
Fermi, Enrico
Feynman, Richard Phillips
Gell-Mann, Murray
Gibbs, J. Willard
Henry, Joseph
Hertz, Heinrich
Hooke, Robert
Huygens, Christiaan
Kapitsa, Pyotr Leonidovich
Kirchhoff, Gustav Robert
Landau, Lev Davidovich
Lee, Tsung-Dao
Lorentz, Hendrik Antoon
Mach, Ernst
Mayer, Maria Goeppert
Meitner, Lise
Michelson, A.A.
Mössbauer, Rudolf Ludwig
Oppenheimer, J. Robert
Pauli, Wolfgang
Plücker, Julius
Purcell, E.M.
Raman, Sir Chandrasekhara Venkata
Rayleigh, John William Strutt, 3rd Baron
Rutherford, Ernest
Schrödinger, Erwin
Stokes, Sir George Gabriel
Thompson, Sir Benjamin
Thomson, Sir Joseph John
Tomonaga Shin'ichirō
Yang, Chen Ning
Young, Thomas
Yukawa Hideki

Section 10/33.   The Earth Sciences

    A. The history of the Earth sciences

        1. The origins of the Earth sciences in prehistoric times

        2. The Earth sciences from antiquity to the 16th century

          a. Geological sciences

              i. Speculations about earthquakes and volcanic eruptions

             ii. Speculations about fossils

            iii. Study of landforms and land–sea relations

          b. Hydrologic and atmospheric sciences

              i. Theories of groundwater circulation and precipitation

             ii. The origin of the Nile and the cause of its floods

            iii. Study of the tides

        3. The Earth sciences in the 16th, 17th, and 18th centuries

          a. Geological sciences

              i. The beginnings of mineralogy: the study of ore deposits

             ii. The development of paleontology and stratigraphy

            iii. The controversy between the Neptunists and Plutonists: Earth history according to Werner and Hutton

          b. Hydrologic sciences

               i. Theories of spring discharge

             ii. The earliest quantitative investigations of the global water balances

          c. Atmospheric sciences

               i. The study of water vapour in the atmosphere

             ii. The study of atmospheric pressure, temperature, and circulation

        4. The Earth sciences in the 19th century

          a. Geological sciences

              i. The development of crystallography and the classification of minerals and rocks

             ii. The concept of faunal succession and organic evolution: contributions of William Smith, Charles Darwin, and others

            iii. The concept of uniformitarianism: contributions of Charles Lyell and others

            iv. Evidence for an Ice Age: the work of Louis Agassiz

             v. The concept of geological time and estimates of the age of the Earth

            vi. Concepts of landform evolution

            vii. The study of gravity, isostasy, and the Earth's figure

          b. Hydrologic sciences

               i. The study of groundwater flow and surface water discharge: Darcy's law

             ii. The beginnings of oceanography as a discipline

          c. Atmospheric sciences

               i. The study of the composition of the atmosphere

             ii. The study of clouds, fog, dew, and storms

            iii. The study of weather and climate: the origin of synoptic meteorology

        5. The Earth sciences in the 20th century

          a. Geological sciences

              i. Development of radiometric dating

             ii. The experimental study of rocks: experimental petrology

iii. Development of seismology: the study of the internal structure of the Earth

iv. Astrogeological research: the application of the Earth sciences to the investigation of the planets and their satellites

v. Advances in paleontology: the development of paleoecology and micropaleontology, the study of Precambrian life

vi. The theory of plate tectonics: an outgrowth of the ideas of continental drift and seafloor spreading

b. Hydrologic sciences

i. The study of water resources and seawater chemistry

ii. The exploitation of oceanic resources: desalinization, tidal power, and minerals from the sea

iii. The charting of the ocean floors: progress in bathymetry

iv. The study of ocean circulation, currents, and waves

v. The study of glacier motion and high-latitude ice sheets

c. Atmospheric sciences

i. The application of modern technology to meteorology: ground-based remote-sensing instruments, orbiting satellites, computer models simulating atmospheric features

ii. Advances in weather forecasting and cloud physics

iii. The study of the properties and structure of the atmosphere

iv. The development of weather modification methods

v. The classification of climate

B. The nature, scope, and methods of the particular Earth sciences
[see also Part Two]

1. Physical geography: the study of the distribution and spatial patterns of soils, water, climate, landforms, and other Earth features

2. The geological sciences: mineralogy, petrology, economic geology, and geochemistry; geodesy, geophysics, structural geology, and volcanology; geomorphology; glacial geology; engineering, environmental, and urban geology; historical geology, paleontology, stratigraphy, and astrogeology

3. The hydrologic sciences: hydrology, limnology, glaciology, oceanography

4. The atmospheric sciences: meteorology, climatology, aeronomy; the study of the atmospheres of other planets
[see 223 and 723.G.5.]

Suggested reading in the *Encyclopædia Britannica*:

MACROPAEDIA: Major articles dealing with the Earth sciences

Earth Sciences, The
Geography

MICROPAEDIA: Selected entries of reference information

General subjects

component	geochronology	paleogeography	barometer
disciplines:	geohydrology	paleogeology	bathymetry
astrogeology	geology	palynology	bathyscaphe
bioclimatology	geomorphology	pedology	bathythermograph
biogeochemistry	geophysics	petrology	dating
chemical	hydrology	sedimentology	digital computer
hydrology	hydrometeorology	seismology	gravimeter
climatology	marine geology	structural geology	ionization chamber
dendrochronology	marine geophysics	tectonics	magnetometer
economic geology	meteorology	volcanology	radiosonde
environmental	mineralogy	*methodology and*	Richter scale
geology	oceanography	*instrumentation:*	seismograph
geochemistry	paleoclimatology	aerial photography	weather map

other:

International
Geophysical Year

<u>Biographies</u>

Agassiz, Louis	Ekman, V. Walfrid	Leonardi, Piero	Runcorn, Stanley
Agricola, Georgius	Gilbert,	Lyell, Sir Charles	Keith
Bjerknes, Vilhelm	Grove Karl	Maury, Matthew	Simpson, George
F.K.	Goldschmidt,	Fontaine	Gaylord
Buch, Leopold,	Victor Moritz	Mohorovičić,	Smith, William
Freiherr von	Hess, H.H.	Andrija	Suess, Eduard
Cuvier, Georges,	Holmes, Arthur	Powell, John	Van Hise, Charles
Baron	Humboldt,	Wesley	Richard
Dana, James D.	Alexander von	Press, Frank	Werner, Abraham
Daubré,	Hutton, James	Romer, Alfred	Gottlob
Gabriel-Auguste	Köppen, Wladimir	Sherwood	

Section 10/34. The Biological Sciences

A. History of the biological sciences

1. Origin and early development of biological ideas

   a. Views of life and living things in ancient Eastern and Middle Eastern civilizations

   b. Biology in the Greco-Roman world: theories about mankind and the origin of life; Aristotelian concepts of classification, reproduction, heredity, and descent; botanical investigations; initial anatomical discoveries

   c. Biology in the Middle Ages: the influence of Arabian biologists, the development of botany and zoology as separate disciplines, further discoveries in anatomy

   d. Biology in the Renaissance: the influence of the craft of printing and artists' illustrations on the dissemination of botanical knowledge, the beginning of the scientific study of anatomy through the use of dissection

2. Developments in the biological sciences in the 17th, 18th, and 19th centuries

   a. Biology in the 17th and 18th centuries

      i. The discovery of the circulation of blood

      ii. The establishment of scientific societies

      iii. The development of the microscope: the classical microscopists

      iv. The rise of modern taxonomy: the systematic classification of plants and animals

      v. The emergence of comparative biological studies

      vi. Experimental approaches to the origin of life: the theory of spontaneous generation

   b. Biology in the 19th century

      i. The effect of geographical explorations on the development of the biological sciences

      ii. The development of cell theory: the establishment of cellular biology

      iii. The theory of evolution: the impact of the concept of natural selection

      iv. The rise of embryology: discoveries concerning reproduction and development of organisms

      v. The emergence of genetics: the study of heredity and its mechanisms

3. Biology in the 20th century

   a. The establishment of molecular biology

      i. The one-gene, one-enzyme theory and its effects

      ii. The discovery of the genetic significance of DNA and RNA: deciphering the genetic code

   b. The emergence of intradisciplinary specialties; *e.g.,* cell physiology, cytochemistry, ecology, population biology

    c. The application to biology of the concepts and techniques of other sciences: the development of biochemistry and biophysics, the importance of biological discoveries to medicine and agriculture

B. The nature, scope, and methodology of the biological sciences
[see also Part Three]

    1. Molecular biology: biochemistry, biophysics, genetics

    2. Cell biology: cancer research, microbiology, radiation biology, tissue culture, transplantation biology

    3. Organismic biology: botany, ecology, embryology, ethology, eugenics, genetics, gnotobiology, morphology, paleontology, physiology, zoology

    4. Population biology: biogeography, comparative psychology, ecology, population genetics, taxonomy

C. Philosophy of biology

    1. The range of topics in biophilosophy; *e.g.,* old questions investigated anew in the light of biological advances and new standards of philosophical rigour

    2. Issues concerning the nature of biological systems

    3. Issues concerning evolution

    4. Issues with ethical implications

Suggested reading in the *Encyclopædia Britannica:*

MACROPAEDIA: Major articles and biographies dealing with the biological sciences

    Biological Sciences, The
    Darwin
    Genetics and Heredity, The Principles of
    Harvey
    Pasteur
    Philosophies of the Branches of Knowledge

MICROPAEDIA: Selected entries of reference information

General subjects

component	ethology	paleontology	chromatography
disciplines:	eugenics	palynology	classification
agrostology	exobiology	parasitology	electrophoresis
anatomy	genetic engineering	physiology	fluoroscope
biogeography	genetics	protozoology	microscope
biology	herpetology	synecology	nuclear magnetic
biophysics	human ecology	taxonomy	resonance
botany	ichthyology	teratology	radioactive isotope
cytology	mammalogy	zoology	spectroscopy
ecology	microbiology	*methodology and*	testcross
embryology	morphology	*instrumentation:*	
entomology	ornithology	centrifuge	

Biographies

anatomists:	Huxley, T.H.	*botanists:*	Hooker, Sir
Müller, Johannes	Lamarck,	Bentham, George	William Jackson
Peter	Jean-Bapiste	Brown, Robert	Linnaeus, Carolus
Sabin, Florence	de Monet,	Candolle,	Nägeli, Karl
Rena	chevalier de	Augustin	Wilhelm von
Vesalius, Andreas	Loeb, Jacques	Pyrame de	Ray, John
biologists:	Lysenko, Trofim	Cohn, Ferdinand	Sprengel, Christian
Bateson, William	Denisovich	Dodge, Bernard	Konrad
Carson, Rachael	Malpighi, Marcello	Ogilvie	Stakman, Elvin
Ehrenberg,	*biophysicists:*	Gray, Asa	Charles
Christian	Crick, Francis	Hoagland, Dennis	*embryologists:*
Gottfried	Harry Compton	Robert	Baer, Karl Ernst,
Elton, Charles	Watson, James	Hooker, Sir Joseph	Ritter von
Huxley, Sir Julian	Dewey	Dalton	Spemann, Hans

geneticists:
  Beadle, George
    Wells
  Dobzhansky,
    Theodosius
  Mendel, Gregor
  Morgan, Thomas
    Hunt
  Weismann, August
  Wright, Sewall
microbiologists:
  Dubos, René
  Hérelle, Félix d'
  Merchnikoff, Élie
  Waksman, Selman
    Abraham

physiologists:
  Bayliss, Sir
    William Maddock
  Bernard, Claude
  Einthoven, Willem
  Galen of
    Pergamum
  Haller,
    Albrecht von
  Macleod, J.J.R.
  Müller, Johannes
    Peter
  Pavlov, Ivan
    Petrovich
  Sherrington, Sir
    Charles Scott

Spallanzani,
  Lazzaro
Starling, Ernest
  Henry
zoologists:
  Cuvier, Georges,
    Baron
  de Beer, Sir Gavin
  Haeckel, Ernst
  Lorenz, Konrad
  Rafinesque,
    Constantine
    Samuel
other:
  Galton, Sir Francis
  Galvani, Luigi

Geoffroy,
  Saint-Hilaire,
  Étienne
Gesner, Conrad
Leeuwenhoek,
  Antoine van
Owen, Sir Richard
Swammerdam, Jan
Wallace, Alfred
  Russel

INDEX: See entries under all of the terms above

Section 10/35. Medicine and Affiliated Disciplines

A. History of medicine and surgery

1. Early medicine: Western medicine before 1800, Oriental medicine before *c.* 1900

    a. The medicine of prehistoric peoples

    b. The practice of medicine among the Babylonians, the ancient Egyptians, and the Hebrews

    c. Medicine and surgery in the Orient: the beginning of systematized medicine

        i. Medicine in India: the Vedic and Brahmanistic heritage, the influence of religious and magical beliefs, surgical practices

        ii. Medicine in China: the influence of the cosmic theory of Yin and Yang; the use of herbals, drugs, and acupuncture

        iii. Medicine in Japan: assimilation of Chinese and European practices

    d. The beginning of systematic medicine in the Greco-Roman world

        i. Early influences: mythological beliefs, the investigations and theories of early philosophers

        ii. The work of Hippocrates: theories on the nature and treatment of disease, the charter of medical conduct

        iii. The spread of Greek teachings to Rome: the acceptance of Galen as a medical authority

    e. Medicine from the fall of Rome through the Middle Ages

        i. Reservoirs of medical learning: the role of medieval monasteries in preserving the medical heritage of Greece and Rome, contributions of Arabian medicine

        ii. Establishment of the first organized medical school at Salerno

    f. Medicine in the Renaissance

        i. Improvements in anatomical theory and surgery

        ii. The control of medical practice in Britain

        iii. The work of Paracelsus and Fracastoro

    g. Medicine in the 17th century

        i. Discoveries concerning the circulation of the blood: use of the experimental method, importance of the microscope to medical studies

        ii. The iatrochemical and iatrophysical theories: the view of life as a series of chemical processes versus the view of life as a mechanism governed by physical laws

    h. Medicine in the 18th century

      i. Genesis of the medical school and the hospital

     ii. The beginning of medical specialties: emergence of surgery, obstetrics, and pathology as separate disciplines

    iii. Improvement in techniques of vaccination and in the treatment of disease: the rise and decline of systems of animism and mesmerism

2. The rise of scientific medicine in the 19th century

   a. New doctrines, laws, and concepts; *e.g.,* the cell and cellular pathology, natural selection, homeostasis, pathogenesis, the Mendelian laws

   b. Further advances in physiology

   c. Establishment of bacteriology: verification of the germ theory, the identification of disease-producing organisms, the introduction of antisepsis

   d. The discovery and use of anesthesia

   e. Other advances: the discovery of the transmission of disease by insects, initial measures to control typhoid, the discovery of X-rays, the development of the ophthalmoscope and the stethoscope

3. Medicine in the 20th century

   a. Advances in chemotherapy: the discovery, development, and use of antibiotics and synthetic drugs in the treatment of bacterial diseases

   b. Advances in immunology

      i. Improvements in vaccines that control bacterial diseases; *e.g.,* typhoid, diphtheria, tetanus, tuberculosis

     ii. The introduction and use of vaccines to control viral diseases; *e.g.,* yellow fever, influenza, poliomyelitis, measles

   c. Developments in endocrinology: the discovery of insulin and the control of diabetes, the use of cortisone as an anti-inflammatory agent, the study and use of sex hormones

   d. Advances in other fields

      i. Nutrition: the treatment of deficiency diseases through the discovery and identification of vitamins

     ii. Cancer research: the treatment of malignant disease through the application of radiation therapy

    iii. Tropical medicine: the treatment of yellow fever, malaria, and leprosy through the discovery and application of synthetic organic compounds derived from quinine and other sources; the application of insecticides to control malaria and yellow fever

    iv. Medical technology and biomedical instrumentation: the use of electronic devices to monitor physiological processes, to conduct automatic laboratory analyses, and to perform other diagnostic and therapeutic procedures

4. Surgery in the 20th century

   a. The state of surgery prior to 1900: the importance of antisepsis, asepsis, and anesthesia to the development of modern surgery

   b. The emergence of surgical specialties: the development of new surgical and diagnostic techniques

   c. Improvements in the treatment of wounds; *e.g.,* the development of plastic surgery, postsurgical rehabilitation

   d. The use of blood transfusions and other intravenous techniques to reduce shock, treat fluid loss, and restore electrolyte balance

   e. The introduction of inhalation anesthetic procedures; *e.g.,* improvements in thoracic surgery

B. Fields of specialized medical practice or research

1. Hospital residency specialties

   a. Radiology

   b. Surgery
     [see 423.C.2.a.]

   c. Obstetrics and gynecology
     [see 423.F.5.f.]

d. Urology
[see 423.F.7.]

e. Ophthalmology and otolaryngology
[see 423.F.9.f. and g.]

f. Neurology
[see 423.F.9.]

g. Psychiatry

h. Other hospital specialties; *e.g.,* anesthesiology, pathology

2. Other clinical specialties

a. Aerospace medicine

b. Medical jurisprudence

c. Occupational medicine

d. Public health

e. Endocrinology

f. Immunology

g. Toxicology

h. Tropical medicine

3. Nonclinical specialties and the basic medical sciences: medical physiology and pathological physiology, nutrition, pharmacology and experimental therapeutics, gerontology

4. Ancillary medical disciplines: cytotechnology, medical records, medical technology, X-ray technology

C. Disciplines affiliated with medicine
[see 424.B.]

1. History and practice of dentistry

2. History and practice of osteopathy

3. History and practice of nursing

4. History and practice of pharmacy

Suggested reading in the *Encyclopædia Britannica:*

MACROPAEDIA: Major article dealing with medicine and affiliated disciplines

Medicine

MICROPAEDIA: Selected entries of reference information

General subjects

aerospace medicine	gerontology and	ophthalmology	pharmacy
anesthesiology	geriatrics	oral surgery	plastic surgery
cardiology	hematology	orthodontics	prosthodontics
dentistry	homeopathy	orthopedics	psychiatry
dermatology	immunology	osteopathy	public health
emergency	internal medicine	otolaryngology	radiology
medicine	nephrology	pathology	sports medicine
endocrinology	neurology	pediatrics	surgery
endodontics	nursing	pedodontics	toxicology
epidemiology	obstetrics and	peridontics	tropical medicine
forensic medicine	gynecology	pharmacology	urology
gastroenterology			

Biographies

Alexander, Franz	Bekhterev,	Carrel, Alexis	Fleming, Sir
Avicenna	Vladimir	Cohn, Ferdinand	Alexander
Barnard,	Mikhaylovich	De Bakey, Michael	Fracastoro,
Christiaan	Blackwell,	Ellis	Girolamo
Barnard, Claude	Elizabeth	Ehrlich, Paul	Freud, Sigmund
	Blalock, Alfred		Galvani, Luigi

Section 10/36.   The Social Sciences and Psychology and Linguistics

A. History of the social sciences

   1. Origins of the social sciences

      a. Precursors of the social sciences in the Middle Ages and the Renaissance

      b. Heritage of the Enlightenment: social reforms and revolution

   2. 19th-century developments in the social sciences

      a. The influence of new concepts in social, political, economic, and scientific theories

      b. Development of the separate disciplines; *e.g.,* economics, political science, anthropology, sociology, social statistics, social geography

   3. 20th-century developments in the social sciences

      a. The influence of social upheaval in the non-Western world: the revolution of rising expectations

      b. The influence of Marxism

      c. The influence of Freudian ideas

      d. The changing character of the disciplines

           i. Specialization and cross-disciplinary approaches

          ii. The increasing professionalism of social scientists as consultants and decision makers in government and business

         iii. The introduction of mathematical and other quantitative methods: the use of computers

          iv. The influence of empiricism: the collection of data, the use of surveys and polls, the testing of theories

      e. Major theoretical influences: developmentalism, the social-systems approach, structuralism and functionalism

B. The nature of anthropology
   [see also Part Five, Division I]

   1. The background of anthropology

   2. The scope and methods of anthropology: the division between cultural and physical anthropology

C. The nature of sociology
   [see also Part Five, Division II]

   1. The background of contemporary sociology

   2. The methodology of contemporary sociology

   3. The status of contemporary sociology

   4. Emergent trends in sociology

   5. Cognate disciplines: criminology, penology, social psychology, demography, human geography

D. The nature of economics
   [see also Part Five, Division III]

   1. Development of theories of economics

2. The scope and methods of the study of economics: microeconomics, macroeconomics

3. Cognate disciplines: mathematical economics, econometrics, accounting

E. The nature of political science
[see also Part Five, Division IV]

1. The history of political science

2. The scope and methods of contemporary political science

3. Cognate disciplines: the study of public opinion, public law, public administration, political systems, and international relations

F. History and methods of psychology
[see also Part Four, Division III]

1. The history of psychology

2. The nature and scope of psychology

3. Special branches and cognate disciplines of psychology: physiological psychology, social psychology

G. The nature of linguistics
[see also Part Five, Division I]

1. The history of linguistics

2. The nature and scope of linguistics

3. Linguistics and other disciplines: psycholinguistics, sociolinguistics, linguistic anthropology, linguistic geography, computational linguistics, mathematical and statistical linguistics, stylistics, and semantics

---

Suggested reading in the *Encyclopædia Britannica*:

MACROPAEDIA: Major articles and biographies dealing with the social sciences and psychology

Freud	Smith, Adam
Geography	Psychology
Marxism, Marx and	Social Sciences, The

MICROPAEDIA: Selected entries of reference information

General subjects

anthropology and allied disciplines:
anthropological linguistics
anthropology
ethnography
neoevolutionism
particularism
structuralism
economics:
Austrian school of economics
classical economics
econometrics
economics
historical school of economics
institutional economics

Keynesian economics
macroeconomics
managerial economics
welfare economics
linguistics:
anthropological linguistics
comparative linguistics
computational linguistics
dialectology
ethnolinguistics
historical linguistics
linguistics
neurolinguistics
semiotics

sociolinguistics
structural linguistics
synchronic linguistics
political science:
geopolitics
political science
psychology:
analytic psychology
applied psychology
behaviourism
clinical psychology
comparative psychology
developmental psychology
educational psychology

experimental psychology
functionalism
Gestalt psychology
humanistic psychology
individual psychology
industrial psychology
physiological psychology
psychology
social psychology
sociology and allied disciplines:
criminology
demography
futurology
penology

Biographies

anthropologists:
Benedict, Ruth
Boas, Franz
Dart, Raymond Arthur

Frazer, Sir James George
Hale, Horatio Emmons

Kroeber, Alfred Louis
Leakey, L.S.B.
Leakey, Richard

Lévi-Strauss, Claude
Malinowski, Bronisław

Section 10/37. The Technological Sciences

A. History of the technological sciences

B. Nature and scope of engineering

  1. Engineering as a profession

  2. Branches of engineering: civil engineering, aeronautical engineering, chemical engineering, electrical and electronics engineering, mechanical engineering, optical engineering

C. The nature and scope of agricultural sciences
   [see also 731.B., C., and D.]

  1. History of the agricultural sciences
     [see A., above]

  2. Subdivisions of the agricultural sciences: soil science, plant production, animal production, agricultural economics and management, agricultural engineering

D. The nature and scope of recently developed interscience disciplines

  1. Bionics

    a. Mimicry of nature as the basis for bionics; *e.g.,* design of torpedoes with surface layers similar to a dolphin's skin, construction of vehicles with articulated legs

    b. The use of natural models to understand and solve engineering problems; *e.g.,* natural neural networks as models for electronic circuits, the human brain as a model for computers and information-processing devices

  2. Systems engineering and operations research
     [see 712.B.]

  3. Cybernetics, control theory, and information science
     [see 10/23]

Suggested reading in the *Encyclopædia Britannica:*

MACROPAEDIA: Major articles dealing with the technological sciences

Engineering
Optics, Principles of

MICROPAEDIA: Selected entries of reference information

General subjects

acoustical engineering	chemical engineering	industrial engineering	petroleum engineering
aeronautical engineering	civil engineering	mechanical engineering	
bioengineering	electrical and electronics engineering	nuclear engineering	
bionics			

Biographies

Beach, Alfred Ely	Eads, James Buchanan	Mauchly, John W.	Steinmetz, Charles Proteus
Brunel, Isambard Kingdom	Eckert, John P.	Pierce, George Washington	Taylor, Frederick Winslow
Brunel, Sir Marc Isambard	Edison, Thomas Alva	Roebling, John Augustus	Tsiolkovsky, Konstantin Eduardovich
Burbank, Luther	Hollerith, Herman	Sikorsky, Igor	Whitney, Eli
Carver, George Washington	McCormick, Cyrus Hall	Stakman, Elvin Charles	

INDEX: See entries under all of the terms above

Division IV.   **History and the Humanities**
[For Part Ten headnote see page 479.]

The outlines in the two sections of Division IV deal with historiography and the study of history, and with the humanities and humanistic scholarship.

Section 10/41 first treats the history of historical writing in the major cultures of both East and West, and the disciplines and methods involved in modern historical investigation and research. It then treats the speculative philosophies of history that have appeared in the West and the East, and philosophical analyses of the specific character of historical knowledge.

Section 10/42 first sets forth a historical review of changing conceptions of the humanities and of humanistic scholarship, covering all the major periods and mutations, from the Greek ideal of *paideia* to contemporary developments. It then treats issues about the nature and scope of the humanities; about the relation of the component disciplines to one another; and about their distinction from the sciences, their validity as ways of knowing, and their role in education.

Section 10/41. Historiography and the Study of History 509
          10/42. The Humanities and Humanistic Scholarship 511

Section 10/41.   **Historiography and the Study of History**

A. Historiography: the types of historical writing

   1. Development of historiography: the history of historical writing

      a. In the ancient world

         i. Near Eastern historiography

         ii. Classical historiography: Greek and Roman

         iii. Early Christian historiography

      b. In the Middle Ages

         i. Western Christian historiography

         ii. Byzantine historiography

    c. From the Renaissance to the present

        i. Renaissance historiography

        ii. Early modern historiography

        iii. Enlightenment historiography: the 18th century

        iv. 19th- and 20th-century historiography

    d. Non-Western historiographical traditions

        i. Islāmic historiography

        ii. East Asian historiography

  2. Types of historical writing: diverse ways of distinguishing or classifying kinds of historical writing by method or function

  3. Factors involved in the writing of history: the background of the author and his vantage point, method of work, and purpose

B. Modern historical investigation and research: sources and methods

  1. Sources for historical writing: material remains, written materials, folklore, place-names

  2. Auxiliary disciplines for ascertaining and interpreting the sources

    a. Anthropology

    b. Archaeology

    c. Bibliography

    d. Chronology

    e. Diplomatics

    f. Epigraphy

    g. Genealogy

    h. Geography

    i. Heraldry

    j. Iconography and iconology

    k. Linguistics

    l. Paleography

    m. Psychoanalysis

    n. Sigillography

    o. Textual criticism

C. Philosophy of history: speculations about the historical process, philosophical analysis of the writing of histories

  1. Conceptions of the philosophy of history

  2. Speculative philosophy of history: diverse explanations of the pattern of historical events

  3. Critical or analytical philosophy of history: the analysis of history as a discipline

---

Suggested reading in the *Encyclopædia Britannica:*

MACROPAEDIA: Major articles dealing with historiography and the study of history

    History, The Study of
    Philosophies of the Branches of Knowledge

MICROPAEDIA: Selected entries of reference information

General subjects

archaeology	genealogy	iconography	sigillography
bibliography	geography	linguistics	textual criticism
diplomatics	historiography	paleography	
epigraphy	history	papyrology	

Biographies

archaeologists:
Bede the
Venerable, Saint
Bingham, Hiram
Biondo, Flavio
Clarendon, Edward
Hyde, 1st earl of
Evans, Sir Arthur
Garstang, John
Geoffrey of
Monmouth
Gibbon, Edward
Giovanni da Pian
del Carpini
Guicciardini,
Francesco
Herodotus
Ibn Khaldūn
Liutprand of
Cremona
Livy
Mariette, Auguste
Mas'ūdī, al-
Petrie, Sir Flinders
Rassam, Hormuzd
Sayce,
Archibald H.
Schliemann,
Heinrich
Squier, E.G.

Stein, Sir Aurel
Stephens, John
Lloyd
Woolley, Sir
Leonard
geographers:
Kropotkin, Peter
Mackinder, Sir
Halford John
Strabo
historians:
Acton of
Aldenham, John
Emerich Edward
Dalberg Acton,
1st Baron
Adams, Brooks
Aulard,
François-Alphonse
Bancroft, George
Barros Arana,
Diego
Beard, Charles A.
Becker, Carl
Bernstein, Edward
Burckhardt, Jacob
Bury, J.B.
Collingwood, R.G.
Froude, James
Anthony

Geyl, Pieter
Lamprecht, Karl
Gottfried
Macaulay of
Rothley, Thomas
Babington
Macaulay, Baron
McMaster, John
Bach
Michelet, Jules
Niebuhr, Barthold
Georg
Pan Ku
Parkman, Francis
Prescott,
William H.
Polybius
Procopius
Ranke,
Leopold von
Robinson, James
Harvey
Sallust
Schlesinger,
Arthur M.
Ssu-ma Ch'ien
Ssu-ma Kuang
Tacitus
Tawney, Richard
Henry

Thucydides
Tocqueville,
Alexis de
Toynbee, Arnold
Tuchman,
Barbara
Turner, Frederick
Jackson
Tyler, Moses Coit
Webb, Sidney and
Beatrice
Woodson,
Carter G.
historiographers:
Braudel, Fernand
Meinecke,
Friedrich
Muratori,
Lodovico
Antonio
Pasquier, Étienne
Thou, Jacques-
Auguste de
other:
Dugdale, Sir
William
Pirenne, Henri

INDEX: See entries under all of the terms above

Section 10/42. The Humanities and Humanistic Scholarship

A. History of humanistic scholarship

1. The beginnings of learning: the ideal of *paideia*

   a. Homeric education: the ideal of the hero

   b. The Sophists and Socrates: the turn to *logos*, the beginnings of rhetoric

   c. Plato and the Academy: the relation of theology to mythology, mathematics in the service of philosophy

   d. Aristotle and the Lyceum: the invention of logic, the division and organization of the sciences

   e. Hellenistic scholarship: the development of literary and textual criticism, Alexandria and Pergamum as cultural centres

   f. The Roman ideal of *humanitas*: the training of the orator

   g. The conflict of cultural ideals: the battle among rhetoric, philosophy, and science

2. Christian learning in antiquity and the Middle Ages

   a. The Christianization of pagan culture: the reconciliation of classical humanism with Christian revelation

   b. The codification of the liberal arts: the trivium and the quadrivium

   c. The founding of the universities

   d. The Scholastic method: logic and the genres of theological exposition

   e. Faith and reason: the distinction of philosophy from sacred theology

3. The development of humane letters from the Renaissance to the present

    a. The idea of Renaissance: the ideal of the classical, the rise of the vernacular, the concept of the dignity of the free individual

    b. Humanism and the new learning

    c. The search for a universal method

    d. The separation of science from philosophy: the rise and development of empirical science

    e. The quarrel between ancients and moderns: the problem of progress in learning

    f. The growth of modern humanistic scholarship: the transition from the ideal of belles lettres to the scientific investigation of antiquity through archaeology and philology

    g. The rise and development of the liberal arts college and the graduate school
      [see 562.B.]

    h. The growth and proliferation of special disciplines: the knowledge explosion

    i. The development of the conflict between the humanities and the sciences

    j. The organization of the contemporary university: questions of its social responsibility, the profession of learning
      [see 561.C.c.]

4. The Jewish tradition of humanistic scholarship: its nature, methods, and development; its relation to classical and Christian learning

5. The Islāmic tradition of humanistic scholarship: its nature, methods, and development; its relation to classical and Christian learning

6. The humanities and humanistic scholarship in the East: in India, in China, in Japan

B. The humanities

1. Diverse views of the definition and scope of the humanities

2. The humanities as an educational program: the question of the humanities as a unified field of study

3. Theories of the humanities as a fundamental division of knowledge: the question of the distinction of the humanities from the sciences

4. Problems about the humanities

Suggested reading in the *Encyclopædia Britannica:*

MACROPAEDIA: Major articles and biographies dealing with the humanities and humanistic scholarship

    Bacon, Francis
    Erasmus
    Humanism
    Scholarship, Classical

MICROPAEDIA: Selected entries of reference information

General subjects

humanism	paideia	Renaissance	scholasticism
humanities	reason	Renaissance man	

Biographies

Adams, Henry	Estienne, Henri II	Melanchthon,	Valla, Lorenzo
Alberti, Leon	George of	Philipp	Wang Wei
Battista	Trebizond	Scaliger, Julius	
Alcuin	Lefèvre d'Étaples,	Caesar	
Bentley, Richard	Jacques	Taine, Hippolyte	

INDEX: See entries under all of the terms above

Division V. **Philosophy**
[For Part Ten headnote see page 479.]

The outlines in the three sections of Division V treat the history of philosophy; the nature and the divisions of philosophy; and philosophical schools and doctrines.

Section 10/51 first deals with theories about philosophy as a whole: theories about its nature, scope, methods, forms of exposition, and about the criteria of meaning and truth in philosophical thought. It then treats the traditional component disciplines of philosophy: metaphysics, the philosophy of nature, epistemology, the philosophy of mind, the philosophy of mankind, ethics, political philosophy, and aesthetics. In the case of each of these eight disciplines, the outline treats its historical development; its nature and scope; its relations to other branches of philosophy and other intellectual disciplines; and its principal problems. At the end, the outline of this section indicates other sections that treat disciplines involving philosophical studies of other subjects: language, logic, mathematics, art, science, religion, law, education, and history.

The outline in Section 10/52 presents a synoptic history of philosophy, taken generally. The outline treats problems involved in the writing of the history of philosophy, the history of Western philosophy, the history of non-Western philosophies, and philosophies associated with religions.

Section 10/53 begins by listing 25 major philosophical schools in the West. The section then deals with doctrinal differences between these schools on major philosophical issues, treating differences in theories about Being and existence; about thought, knowledge, and the faculties of the mind; and about human conduct.

Section 10/51. History of Philosophy

A. History of Western philosophy

1. Ancient Greek and Roman philosophy

a. The beginnings of philosophy in Greece: the Pre-Socratic philosophers

i. Cosmology and the metaphysics of matter: theories of the origin and nature of the physical world, monistic and pluralistic cosmologies

ii. The rise of problems in the theory of knowledge: problems about the real and phenomenal worlds

iii. The metaphysics of number: Pythagorean speculations about number and the nature of reality, advances toward the foundation of quantitative science

iv. Anthropology and relativism: the Sophists' criticism of cosmological and metaphysical speculations, man as the measure of all things, the positions of the Sophists about the conventionality of law and justice

b. The maturity of Greek philosophy

i. The ethical concerns and positions of Socrates: the Socratic method of teaching, the influence of Socrates

ii. The philosophy of Plato: his dialogues on issues in politics, ethics, metaphysics, epistemology, and cosmology; his emphasis on the relations of mathematics to philosophy

iii. The philosophy of Aristotle: his criticisms of Platonic metaphysics and theory of knowledge; the corpus of his works on logic; his teleological positions in biology, ethics, and politics; his empirical researches in the natural sciences and on laws and political institutions

c. Hellenistic and Roman philosophy: developments from the time of Alexander III the Great to the closing of the philosophical schools in Athens

i. The philosophy of the Stoics: the teaching of Zeno of Citium concerning the basis of human happiness, the further elaboration of Stoic thought by Cleanthes and Chrysippus, the role of Stoicism during the late Roman Republic and the empire

ii. The philosophy of the Epicureans: the teaching of Epicurus concerning the universe, the role of pleasure, and man's relationship to the gods

iii. The philosophy of the Skeptics: the teaching of Pyrrhon of Elis concerning man's lack of certainty in knowing, the role of the Skeptics in preserving the doctrines of ancient philosophers

iv. The philosophy of the Neo-Pythagoreans and of the Neoplatonists: the teaching of Plotinus concerning the various levels of being, Neo-Pythagorean schools in Asia Minor

v. Jewish and Christian philosophy during the Hellenistic Age: diverse attempts to relate the teachings of the Hellenistic and Roman schools to Jewish and Christian theology

2. Philosophy in the Middle Ages

a. Early medieval philosophy

i. The patristic period: Augustine's use of Neoplatonist thought in his theology and his doctrine of man, the role of Boethius' translations and commentaries, Anselm's proofs of the existence of God, the methodology of Abelard

ii. Philosophy and the liberal arts in the schools of the Christian West from the 9th to the 11th century

b. The contribution of Arabic and Jewish philosophy: the role of the Islāmic philosophers in increasing the influence of Aristotle in the West, the teaching of Solomon ibn Gabirol and Maimonides

c. The age of the Schoolmen: the attempt to reconcile philosophy and theology, the teaching of Bonaventure and Albertus Magnus, Thomas Aquinas' synthesis of Aristotelianism and Christian theology

d. Philosophy in the late Middle Ages: new styles of philosophy and theology that vied with Thomism, the criticism of Aristotelian thought by Duns Scotus and Ockham, the speculative mysticism of Eckehart, Nicholas of Cusa's doctrine of the "coincidence of opposites"

3. Modern philosophy

a. Philosophy in the Renaissance

i. Political theory: the views of Machiavelli, Bodin, Hobbes, Grotius, and others on the nature and moral status of political power

ii. Humanism: the influence of the writings of Plato on moral theory and literary endeavour; renewed interest in Atomistic Materialism, ancient Skepticism, and Stoicism
[for humanistic scholarship in the Renaissance, see also 10/42.A.3.]

iii. Philosophy of nature: the pluralistic, machinelike, and mathematically ordered character ascribed to the natural world; the influence of discoveries in anatomy, physics, and astronomy on philosophy

b. The early modern period: the rise of Empiricism and Rationalism

i. Developments in the Empiricist tradition: Bacon's attempt to formulate a new scientific method, Hobbes's theory of knowledge

ii. Developments in the Rationalist tradition: the antiempirical character of Descartes's metaphysics and the dualism of his doctrine of man and the world, the speculative systems of philosophy provided by the writings of Spinoza and Leibniz

c. Philosophy in the period of the Enlightenment, or the Age of Reason

i. Epistemological issues: the attempt of Locke and Berkeley to inquire into the origin and nature of reason, Hume's science of man, Kant's critical examination of reason

ii. Developments in the philosophy of science: Materialist views, the effect of scientific discoveries on philosophical thought

iii. Social and political philosophy: the concern of Locke and Rousseau with the freedom and equality of citizens, developments in religious philosophy

d. Philosophy in the 19th century

i. The resurgence of the metaphysical spirit: the Idealism of Fichte, Schelling, and Hegel

ii. Developments in the empirical and scientific tradition: Comte's Positivism and its subsequent influence on the philosophy of science, J.S. Mill's theory of knowledge and ethics, the dialectical Materialism of Marx and Engels

iii. The reaction against Rationalism: Kierkegaard's preoccupation with the states of consciousness, Schopenhauer's doctrine of cosmic will, the writings of Nietzsche

e. Philosophy in the 20th century

   i. Independent speculative and social philosophies: Bergson's intuitionism, Whitehead's speculative philosophy, William James's and Dewey's Pragmatism

   ii. Developments in Marxist thought: Lenin's metaphysical Materialism and his theory of knowledge, the continuing attempt to make theory serve practice

B. Non-Western philosophy

1. Indian philosophy

   a. Early Indian philosophical thought: the role of Hindu and Buddhist sacred literature in presystematic philosophy, the concepts of Brahman and *ātman* in Hindu thought and of selflessness and Nirvāṇa in early Buddhist writings

   b. The beginning of system building in Indian philosophy: the role of the *sūtra*, metaphysical and epistemological concerns, ethical and political thought, the teaching of the Ājīvikas and Cārvākas

   c. The further developments of systematic thought in India: Realism and Idealism in metaphysical and epistemological thought, the relation of pluralistic and monistic views to various linguistic philosophies

   d. The schools of Vedānta: the contribution of Śaṅkara and Rāmānuja and their followers; the schools of Nimbārka, Vallabha, and Caitanya

   e. The Vaiṣṇava and Śaiva schools: philosophical systems based on the literature of Vaiṣṇavism and Śaivism

   f. Later Indian philosophical thought: the influence of Islāmic thought and European philosophy, recent trends

2. Chinese philosophy

   a. The classical Chinese philosophical schools; *e.g.*, Confucianism, Taoism, Yin-Yang, Moism, Dialecticians, the Legalist school

   b. Neo-Taoist and Buddhist thought

   c. Neo-Confucianism: the development of the concept of principle

   d. 20th-century Chinese philosophy: the effects of Western thought and of Maoism

3. Japanese philosophy

   a. Early Japanese philosophical thought: the introduction of Buddhism and Confucianism, the Six Schools of Nara, Tendai and Shingon philosophy

   b. Developments during the Kamakura and Muromachi periods: the origins and concerns of the Zen, Jōdo (Pure Land), and Nichiren sects; tendencies in Shintō and Confucian thought

C. Philosophies associated with religion

1. Hindu philosophy
   [see 823.B.3.]

2. Buddhist philosophy
   [see 824.B.3.]

3. Confucian philosophy
   [see 825.B.3.]

4. Taoist philosophy
   [see 825.C.3.]

5. Jewish philosophy
   [see 826.B.6.]

6. Islāmic philosophy
   [see 828.B.4.]

7. Christian philosophy
   [see 827.E.7.]

Suggested reading in the *Encyclopædia Britannica:*

MACROPAEDIA: Major articles and biographies dealing with the history of philosophy

Aristotelianism,	Hegelianism,	Mill, John Stuart	Smith, Adam
Aristotle and	Hegel and	Nietzsche	Socrates
Augustine	Hume	Philosophy,	Taoism
Cartesianism,	Indian Philosophy	The History of	Thomism,
Descartes and	Kantianism,	Western	Thomas
Christianity	Kant and	Platonism,	Aquinas and
Chu Hsi	Locke	Plato and	
Confucianism,	Marxism,	Rousseau,	
Confucius and	Marx and	Jean-Jacques	

MICROPAEDIA: Selected entries of reference information

General subjects

Arabic philosophy:
  ahl al-Kitāb
  Bāṭinīyah
  Dahrīyah
  fayḍ
  ghaybah
  ikhtilāf
  kalām
  kasb
  Māturīdīyah
  Murji'ah
  Mu'tazilah
  Qadarīyah
  Rāfiḍah
  rahbānīyah
  rajm
  Sālimīyah
  shirk
  tahajjud
  talbīyah
  taqīyah
  tashbīh
  tawḥīd
  ziyārah
Chinese philosophy:
  ch'i
  Chinese
    philosophy
  hsien
  hsu
  jen
  Legalism
  Moism
  p'u
  T'ai Chi
  Tao
  te
  T'ien Ming
  tzu-jan
  wu-wei
  yin-yang
Greek philosophy:
  apathy
  cosmopolitanism
  emanationism
  entelechy

epochē
first cause
form
hylomorphism
logos
man, the
  measure of
microcosm
Not-Being,
  denial of
opposites, table of
paradoxes of Zeno
sensationalism
virtue,
  teachability of
Indian philosophy:
  Abhidharmakośa
  abhijñā
  Advaita
  ahaṃkāra
  ajīva
  Ājīvika
  akriyāvāda
  ālaya-vijñāna
  ānanda
  anumāna
  Artha-śāstra
  āsana
  asrāva
  āstika
  ātman
  Bhedābheda
  Brahman
  brahmavihāra
  cakra
  Cārvāka
  dravya
  Dvaita
  Haṭha Yoga
  indriya
  jīva
  jñāna
  kammaṭṭhāna
  karma
  Kashmir Śaivism
  kuṇḍālinī

Mādhyamika
māyā
Mīmāṃsā
nirguṇa
Nyāya
pāramitā
prajñapti
prakṛti
pramāṇa
prāṇa
prāṇāyāma
pratītya-samutpāda
pratyakṣa
pratyaya
puruṣa
śabda
Śaiva-siddhānta
samādhi
Sāṃkhya
samsāra
saṃvṛti-satya
sat
skandha
smṛtyupasthāna
syādvāda
tat tvam asi
tri-svabhāva
upādhi
Vaiśeṣika
Vedānta
Viśiṣṭādvaita
yama
Yoga
Yogācāra
Japanese philosophy:
  Japanese
    philosophy
  Jōjitsu
  Kegon
  Nichiren
    Buddhism
  Pure Land
    Buddhism
  Ritsu
  Shingon
  Zen

*medieval Western
  philosophy:*
  fideism
  intention
  Ockham's razor
  Scholasticism
  tabula rasa
*modern Western
  philosophy:*
  a priori knowledge
  antinomy
  as if, philosophy of
  axiology
  categorical
    imperative
  cogito, ergo sum
  common sense,
    philosophy of
  concept
  constitution theory
  deontological
    ethics
  deus otiosus
  dialectical
    Materialism
  eudaemonism
  good-reason theory
  humanism
  ideal language
  identity theory
  innate idea
  interactionism
  irrationalism
  I–Thou
  leap of faith
  mathematician
  meta-ethics
  metalanguage
  methodic doubt
  mind–body dualism
  monad
  natural law
  normative ethics
  noumenon
  occasionalism

panpsychism	preestablished	secularism	synthesis
phenomenalism	harmony	social contract	teleological ethics
phenomenon	protocol sentence	solipsism	theodicy
physicalistic	radical empiricism	sufficient reason,	transcendental
Materialism	reductionism	principle of	Idealism
	revisionism	superman	unified science

Biographies

Anaximenes of	Inoue Tetsujirō	Maimonides,	Spinoza,
Miletus	Israeli, Isaac ben	Moses	Benedict de
Averroës	Solomon	Nārājunga	
Avicenna	Justin Martyr,	Nishida Kitarō	
Buber, Martin	Saint	Schopenhauer,	
Chuang-tzu	Lao-tzu	Arthur	

See also Sections 10/52 and 10/53

INDEX: See entries under all of the terms above

Section 10/52. The Nature and the Divisions of Philosophy

A. The nature, scope, and methods of philosophy
[for the major philosophical schools in the West, see 10/53; for the development of non-Western philosophy, see 10/51.B.]

   1. Diverse conceptions of philosophy

   2. Diverse views of the methods of philosophy

   3. The forms of philosophical exposition; *e.g.*, dialogues, commentaries, histories, systematically ordered treatises

   4. Criteria of meaning and truth in philosophical thought

B. The divisions of philosophy

   1. Metaphysics, or speculative philosophy in general

      a. The history, nature, and scope of metaphysics
      [for schools of thought in metaphysics, see 10/53.B.1.]

      b. The relation of metaphysics to other parts of philosophy; *e.g.*, ethics, logic, natural theology

      c. Problems in metaphysics

   2. The philosophy of nature: the philosophical problems concerning the phenomena, laws, and theories of the natural sciences
   [see also 10/31.B.]

      a. The history, status, and scope of the philosophy of nature

      b. The relation of the philosophy of nature to science, the philosophy of science, and metaphysics

      c. The basic aspects of the natural order

      d. The philosophy of physics

      e. The philosophy of biology

   3. Epistemology, or theory of knowledge

      a. The history, nature, and scope of epistemology
      [for schools of thought in epistemology, see 10/53.C.]

      b. The relation of epistemology to metaphysics, philosophy of mind, logic, and other disciplines

      c. Problems in epistemology

   4. The philosophy of mind, or philosophical psychology

      a. The history, nature, and scope of the philosophy of mind

      b. The relation of the philosophy of mind to the empirical and mathematical sciences and to other philosophical disciplines

      c. Problems in the philosophy of mind

    5. The philosophy of man, or philosophical anthropology

      a. The history, nature, and scope of philosophical anthropology
        [for schools of thought in philosophical anthropology, see 10/53.B.3.]

      b. The relation of philosophical anthropology to physical and cultural anthropology and to other disciplines in philosophy and the social sciences

      c. Problems in philosophical anthropology

    6. Ethics, or moral philosophy

      a. The history, nature, and types of ethics: the distinction between metaethics and normative ethics

      b. The relation of ethics to other philosophical disciplines or to other branches of knowledge or experience

      c. Problems in ethics

    7. Political philosophy

      a. The nature and scope of political philosophy: its relation to political science

      b. The form of political statements and arguments

      c. The history of political philosophy

    8. Aesthetics

      a. The nature and scope of aesthetics as a discipline

      b. The development of aesthetics: approaches to the study of the aesthetic experience

      c. Problems in aesthetics

      d. The relation of aesthetics to other disciplines

    9. The philosophy of language

  10. The philosophy of logic
      [see 10/11.B.]

  11. The philosophy of mathematics
      [see 10/21.B.]

  12. The philosophy of art
      [see 611.A.]

  13. The philosophy of science
      [see 10/31.B.]

  14. The philosophy of religion
      [see 811.A.]

  15. The philosophy of law
      [see 551.A.]

  16. The philosophy of education
      [see 561.A.]

  17. The philosophy of history
      [see 10/41.C.]

Suggested reading in the *Encyclopædia Britannica:*

MACROPAEDIA: Major articles and biographies dealing with the nature and the divisions of philosophy

Aesthetics	Philosophical	Political	Rousseau,
Epistemology	Anthropology	Philosophy,	Jean-Jacques
Ethics	Philosophies of	The History of	Smith, Adam
Metaphysics	the Branches of	Western	Time
Mind, The	Knowledge		
Philosophy of			

MICROPAEDIA: Selected entries of reference information

General subjects

aesthetics:
aesthetics
primitivism
epistemology:
a priori knowledge
dualism
epistemology
Idéalogie
psychologism
ethics:
altruism
axiology
categorical
imperative
comparative ethics
conscience
egoism
ethical relativism
ethics
eudaemonism
good-reasons
theory

metaethics
moral theology
normative ethics
probabilism
teleological ethics
virtue
metaphysics:
appearance
dualism
creative evolution
form
Great Chain of
Being
intuition
irrationalism
metaphysics
microcosm
naturalism
ontology
phenomenon
pluralism and
monism

reason
supernaturalism
voluntarism
philosophy of mind:
belief
choice
free will
identity theory
immortality
intentionality
interactionism
mind
mind–body
dualism
other minds
psychophysical
parallelism
political philosophy:
divine right of
kings
general will
human rights

nomos
political
philosophy
powers,
separation of
social contract
other:
emergence
hylozoism
philosophical
anthropology
philosophy
spiritualism
teleology
time

Biographies

aesthetics:
Baumgarten,
Alexander
Gottlieb
Bosanquet,
Bernard
Croce, Benedetto
Gilson, Étienne
Santayana, George
epistemology:
Cassirer, Ernst
Dühring, Eugen
Locke, John
Mill, John Stuart
ethics:
Abelard, Peter
Cudworth, Ralph
Cumberland,
Richard
Hutcheson, Francis
Moore, G.E.
Scheler, Max
Whewell, William
metaphysics:
Aurobindo, Śrī
Berdyayev,
Nikolay
Aleksandrovich

Berkeley, George
Bradley, F.H.
Campanella,
Tommaso
Clauberg, Johann
Descartes, René
Feuerbach, Ludwig
Fichte, Johann
Gottlieb
Geulincx, Arnold
Green, T.H.
Hegel, Georg
Wilhelm
Friedrich
Heidegger, Martin
Husserl, Edmund
Jacobi, Friedrich
Wilhelm
Jaspers, Karl
Kant, Immanuel
Kierkegaard, Søren
Leibniz, Gottfried
Wilhelm
Lewes, George
Henry
Malebranche,
Nicolas
Marcel, Gabriel

Meinong, Alexius
Nietzsche,
Friedrich
Norris, John
Schelling, Friedrich
Wilhelm
Joseph von
Schopenhauer,
Arthur
Spinoza,
Benedict de
Whitehead, Alfred
North
political philosophy:
Bentham, Jeremy
Berlin, Sir Isaiah
Burke, Edmund
Engels, Friedrich
Han-Lei-tzu
Herzen, Aleksandr
Hobbes, Thomas
Mill, James
Machiavelli,
Niccolò
Montesquieu,
Charles-Louis de
Secondat, baron
de La Bréde et de

Paine, Thomas
other:
Adler, Mortimer J.
Alembert, Jean Le
Rond d'
Aron, Raymond
Bayle, Pierre
Condillac, Étienne
Bonnot de
Cousin, Victor
Dilthey, Wilhelm
Gioberti, Vincenzo
Helvétius,
Claude-Adrien
Hoffer, Eric
Rodó, José
Enrique
Spencer, Herbert
Strauss, David
Friedrich
Swedenborg,
Emanuel
Teilhard de
Chardin, Pierre
Vico, Giambattista
Weil, Simone
Wittgenstein,
Ludwig

See also Sections 10/51 and 10/53

INDEX: See entries under all of the terms above

Section 10/53.   Philosophical Schools and Doctrines

A. Major philosophical schools in the West

   1. Philosophical schools in antiquity and in the Middle Ages

      a. Pythagoreanism

      b. The Sophists

      c. Eleaticism

      d. Atomism

      e. Platonism

      f. Aristotelianism

      g. Stoicism

      h. Epicureanism

      i. Skepticism

      j. Scholasticism

   2. Philosophical schools in the modern period

      a. Cartesianism

      b. Empiricism
[for Empiricist tendencies in earlier philosophy, see A.1.b. and i., above; for contemporary Logical Empiricism, see A.2.i., below]

      c. Rationalism
[for Rationalist tendencies in ancient and medieval philosophy, see A.1.a., c., e., and j., above]

      d. Materialism
[for dialectical Materialism, see A.2.j., below]

      e. Kantianism

      f. Idealism

      g. Hegelianism

      h. Utilitarianism

      i. Positivism and Logical Empiricism
[for metalogical studies, see 10/12.B.; for studies in the foundations of mathematics, see 10/21.B.]

      j. Marxism

      k. Realism

      l. Pragmatism

     m. Phenomenology

      n. Existentialism

      o. Analytic and Linguistic philosophy

B. Theories of Being and existence

   1. Different types of metaphysical theory: Platonism; Aristotelianism; Thomism; Cartesianism; Idealism; Materialism—dialectical Materialism, Atomism, and Naturalism; Pythagoreanism; Organismic dynamism

   2. Different views concerning the existence, attributes, and knowledge of God: agnosticism, atheism, Deism, fideism, humanism, pantheism, theism

   3. Different conceptions of man as knower, doer, and maker: Existentialism, humanism, Phenomenology, Pragmatism, Rationalism, irrationalism

   4. Different views concerning the existence of the mind and its relation to the body: Materialism, dualism, immaterialism

C. Theories of thought, knowledge, and faculties of mind

   1. Different conceptions of the object of knowledge: sense-datum theory, Phenomenalism, Idealism, Realism

2. Different conceptions of the validity of knowledge: Kantianism, Positivism, Pragmatism, Skepticism

3. Different views of the sources or foundations of knowledge: Rationalism, Empiricism

4. Different views of the status of the universal: Realism, Conceptualism, Nominalism

5. Different views of the epistemic status of scientific theories; *e.g.*, Realism, conventionalism, and operationalism; the Unity of Science principle; reductionism

D. Theories of conduct

1. Metaethical theories: intuitionism, Naturalism, Noncognitivism, good reasons theories

2. Deontological theories: Rationalism, intuitionism, Existentialism

3. Teleological theories: Eudaemonism, Utilitarianism

Suggested reading in the *Encyclopædia Britannica*:

MACROPAEDIA: Major articles dealing with Western philosophical schools and doctrines

Aristotelianism, Aristotle and	Marxism, Marx and	Religious and Spiritual Belief,
Cartesianism, Descartes and	Philosophical Schools and	Systems of Thomism, Thomas
Hegelianism, Hegel and	Doctrines, Western	Aquinas and
Kantianism, Kant and	Platonism, Plato and	

MICROPAEDIA: Selected entries of reference information

General subjects

absolute Idealism	eclecticism	Neo-Hegelianism	Skepticism
Academy, Greek	Eleaticism	Nominalism	solipsism
Alexandrist	Empiricism	Personalism	Sophist
Analytic philosophy	Epicureanism	Phenomenology	Stoicism
Atomism	Ethical Culture	Positivism	theism
Cambridge Platonists	Existentialism	Pragmatism	transcendental Idealism
Cynic	Idealism	process philosophy	Utilitarianism
Cyrenaic	Latin Averroism	Pythagoreanism	Vienna Circle
Deism	Logical Positivism	Rationalism	
determinism	Materialism	realism	
	Megarian school	Scholasticism	
	naturalism	sensationalism	

Biographies

Albertus Magnus, Saint	Carnap, Rudolf	Hume, David	Pico della Mirandola,
Apuleius, Lucius	Cohen, Hermann	Husserl, Edmund	Giovanni, Conte
Athenagoras	Comte, Auguste	James, William	di Concordia
Berdyayev, Nikolay Aleksandrovich	Cousin, Victor	Jaspers, Karl	Plotinus
	Dewey, John	Kierkegaard, Søren	Royce, Josiah
	Dühring, Eugen	Lewes, George Henry	Sartre, Jean-Paul
Bernard de Chartres	Duns Scotus, John	Maine de Biran, Marie-François-Pierre	Scheler, Max
Boethius, Anicias Manlius Severinus	Fichte, Johann Gottlieb	Malebranche, Nicolas	Schlick, Moritz
	Francis of Meyronnes	Marcel, Gabriel	Unamuno, Miguel de
Bosanquet, Bernard	Gentile, Giovanni	Maritain, Jacques	William de la Mare
Bradley, F.H.	Godfrey of Fontaines	More, Henry	
Buridan, Jean	Green, T.H.	Ockham, William of	
	Heidegger, Martin		

See also Sections 10/51 and 10/52

INDEX: See entries under all of the terms above

ERIC P. HAMP. *Robert Maynard Hutchins Distinguished Service Professor of Linguistics and of Behavioral Sciences; Director, Center for Balkan and Slavic Studies, University of Chicago.*

SHIGEKI HIJINO. Secretary of the University Advisory Committee of Japan. *Managing Editor,* Newsweek Japan, *TBS-Britannica Company, Ltd., Tokyo.*

YOSHIO HIYAMA. *Emeritus Professor of Marine Biology, University of Tokyo.*

TAKEMOCHI ISHII. *Professor of Engineering, University of Tokyo.*

PETER KENNEDY. *Professor of Economics, Simon Fraser University, Burnaby, British Columbia.*

JOSEPH M. KITAGAWA. *Emeritus Professor of the History of Religions and of Far Eastern Languages and Civilizations, University of Chicago; Dean, Divinity School, 1970–80.*

UWE W. KITZINGER. *President, Templeton College; Emeritus Fellow of Nuffield College, University of Oxford.*

JACQUES LE GOFF. *Professor of History, School of Higher Studies in Social Sciences, Paris.*

KURT LIPSTEIN. *Emeritus Professor of Law, University of Cambridge; Fellow of Clare College, Cambridge.*

H. CHRISTOPHER LONGUET-HIGGINS. *Royal Society Research Professor of Experimental Psychology, University of Sussex, Brighton, England.*

JOHN LYONS. *Master of Trinity Hall, University of Cambridge.*

ISABEL McBRYDE. *Professor of Prehistory, The Faculties, Australian National University, Canberra.*

FREDERICK R.W. McCOURT. *Professor of Chemistry and of Applied Mathematics, University of Waterloo, Ontario.*

SAUNDERS Mac LANE. *Max Mason Distinguished Service Professor Emeritus of Mathematics, University of Chicago.*

DONALD GUNN MacRAE. *Martin White Professor of Sociology, London School of Economics and Political Science, University of London.*

EDWARD McWHINNEY. *Queen's Counsel. Professor of International Law and Relations, Simon Fraser University, Burnaby, British Columbia. Member, Permanent Court of Arbitration, The Hague, and Institute of International Law, Geneva.*

OTFRIED MADELUNG. *Professor of Theoretical Physics, University of Marburg, West Germany.*

A.W. MARTIN. *Senior Fellow in History, Research School of Social Sciences, Australian National University, Canberra.*

DAVID ALFRED MARTIN. *Professor of Sociology, London School of Economics and Political Science, University of London. Elizabeth Scurlock Professor of Human Values, Southern Methodist University, Dallas, Texas.*

RUSSELL L. MATHEWS. *Emeritus Professor of Economics, Australian National University, Canberra.*

AKIRA MATSUMURA. *Emeritus Professor of Japanese Language, University of Tokyo.*

BEDE MORRIS. *Professor and Head, Department of Immunology, John Curtin School of Medical Research, Australian National University, Canberra.*

MICHIO NAGAI. *Special Adviser to the Rector of United Nations University, Tokyo. Former Professor of Education, Tokyo Institute of Technology. Minister of Education of Japan, 1974–76.*

HAJIME NAKAMURA. Chairman of the University Advisory Committee of Japan. *Founder-Director, Eastern Institute, Inc., Tokyo. Emeritus Professor of Indian and Buddhist Philosophy, University of Tokyo.*

DONALD M. NICOL. *Koraës Professor of Byzantine and Modern Greek History, Language, and Literature, King's College, University of London.*

BARRY W. NINHAM. Chairman of the Australian National University Advisory Committee. *Professor and Head, Department of Applied Mathematics, Research School of Physical Sciences, Australian National University, Canberra.*

WENDY DONIGER O'FLAHERTY. *Professor and Chair of the History of Religions; Professor of Indian Studies, University of Chicago.*

SIR BRIAN PIPPARD. Chairman of the British Universities Advisory Committee. *Cavendish Professor Emeritus of Physics, University of Cambridge.*

JOHN CHARLES POLANYI. *University Professor and Professor of Chemistry and of Physics, University of Toronto.*

P. NØRREGAARD RASMUSSEN. *Professor of Economics, University of Copenhagen.*

A. EDWARD SAFARIAN. Co-Chairman of the Canadian Universities Advisory Committee. *Professor of Economics; Fellow of Trinity College and Massey College, University of Toronto.*

PEDRO SCHWARTZ. *Professor of the History of Economic Doctrines, Complutensian University of Madrid.*

SIR RICHARD SOUTHERN. Emeritus Chairman of the British Universities Advisory Committee. *President, St. John's College, Oxford, 1969–81; Chichele Professor of Modern History, University of Oxford, 1961–69.*

IAN G. STEWART. *Professor of Economics, University of Edinburgh.*

C. ANTHONY STORR. *Emeritus Fellow, Green College, Oxford; Clinical Lecturer in Psychiatry, University of Oxford, 1974–84. Consultant Psychotherapist, Oxford Health Authority, 1974–84.*

GRANT STRATE. *Professor of Dance; Director, Centre for the Arts, Simon Fraser University, Burnaby, British Columbia.*

HITOSHI TAKEUCHI. *Editor in Chief,* Newton Magazine. *Emeritus Professor of Earth Science, University of Tokyo.*

KEITH THOMAS. *President, Corpus Christi College, University of Oxford.*

A. DOUGLAS TUSHINGHAM. *Emeritus Professor of Near Eastern Studies, University of Toronto. Chief Archaeologist, Royal Ontario Museum, Toronto, 1964–79.*

DONALD WALKER. *Professor of Biogeography, Research School of Pacific Studies, Australian National University, Canberra.*

DONOVAN W.M. WATERS. *Professor of Law, University of Victoria, British Columbia.*

GÜNTHER WILKE. *Professor of Chemistry, University of the Ruhr, Bochum. Director, Max Planck Institute for Coal Research, Mülheim an der Ruhr, West Germany.*

C. BARRIE WILSON. *Professor of Architectural Science, University of Edinburgh.*

TATSURO YAMAMOTO. *Emeritus Professor of Oriental History, University of Tokyo.*

ITSUJI YOSHIKAWA. *Director, Yamato Bunkakan Museum, Nara, Japan. Emeritus Professor of Art History, University of Tokyo.*

Library Advisory Committee

ALICE S. BASOMS. *Humanities Librarian, New Trier High School, Illinois.*

THOMAS M. BROWN. *Library Director and Associate Professor of Library Science, Concord College, Athens, West Virginia.*

THELMA FREIDES. *Head, Readers' Services, State University of New York College at Purchase.*

JUDITH H. HIGGINS. *Director, Learning Resource Center, Valhalla High School, New York.*

PATRICIA HOGAN. *Librarian, Itasca Community Library, Illinois.*

TZE-CHUNG LI. *Dean, Graduate School of Library and Information Science, Rosary College, River Forest, Illinois.*

MONA McCORMICK. *Reference Librarian, University of California, Los Angeles.*

GERALD R. SHIELDS. *Assistant Dean, State University of New York at Buffalo.*

PATRICIA K. SWANSON. *Head of Reference Services, University of Chicago Library.*

Outline of Knowledge

Staff

MORTIMER J. ADLER. Editor.

CHARLES VAN DOREN. Associate Editor. *Vice President, Editorial, Encyclopædia Britannica, Inc., 1973–82.*

WILLIAM J. GORMAN (d. 1982). Associate Editor. *Senior Fellow, Institute for Philosophical Research.*

• *Indicates persons who served as contributors to or consultants on the* Outline of Knowledge.

Part One. Matter and Energy

•A.G.W. CAMERON. *Professor of Astronomy, Harvard University.*

EDWARD U. CONDON (d. 1974). *Professor of Physics, University of Colorado, Boulder, 1963–70.*

•ALBERT V. CREWE. *William E. Wrather Distinguished Service Professor of Physics and Biophysics, University of Chicago.*

•FARRINGTON DANIELS (d. 1972). *Professor of Chemistry, University of Wisconsin, Madison, 1928–59.*

RAYNOR L. DUNCOMBE. *Professor of Aerospace Sciences, University of Texas at Austin.*

UGO FANO. *Emeritus Professor of Physics, University of Chicago.*

•HELLMUT FRITZSCHE. *Professor and Chairman, Department of Physics; Professor, James Franck Institute, University of Chicago.*

JACK HALPERN. *Louis Block Distinguished Service Professor of Chemistry, University of Chicago.*

•MORTON HAMERMESH. *Professor of Physics, University of Minnesota, Minneapolis.*

JOSEPH J. KATZ. *Senior Chemist, Argonne National Laboratory, Argonne, Illinois.*

MALCOLM H. MacFARLANE. *Professor of Physics, Indiana University, Bloomington.*

NORMAN HARRY NACHTRIEB. *Emeritus Professor of Chemistry, University of Chicago.*

EUGENE N. PARKER. *Distinguished Service Professor of Physics and of Astronomy and Astrophysics, University of Chicago.*

•VINCENT E. PARKER. *Emeritus Professor of Physics, California State Polytechnic University, Pomona; Dean, School of Science, 1967–77.*

SIR BRIAN PIPPARD. *Cavendish Professor Emeritus of Physics, University of Cambridge.*

STUART ALAN RICE. *Dean, Division of Physical Sciences; Frank P. Hixon Distinguished Service Professor of Chemistry, University of Chicago.*

LOCKHART B. ROGERS. *Graham Perdue Professor of Chemistry, University of Georgia, Athens.*

ROBERT G. SACHS. *Director, Enrico Fermi Institute; Professor of Physics, University of Chicago.*

RUPERT WILDT (d. 1976). *Professor of Astrophysics, Yale University, 1957–73.*

•MARK W. ZEMANSKY (d. 1981). *Professor of Physics, City College, City University of New York.*

Part Two. The Earth

J HARLEN BRETZ (d. 1981). *Professor of Geology, University of Chicago, 1926–47.*

HORACE ROBERT BYERS. *Emeritus Professor of Meteorology, Texas A&M University, College Station.*

•R.J. CHORLEY. *Professor of Geography, University of Cambridge; Fellow of Sidney Sussex College, Cambridge.*

JULIAN R. GOLDSMITH. *Charles E. Merriam Distinguished Service Professor of Geophysical Sciences, University of Chicago.*

BERNHARD KUMMEL (d. 1980). *Professor of Geology, Harvard University, 1962–80.*

WALTER LANGBEIN (d. 1982). *Senior Scientist, Geological Survey, United States Department of the Interior, Washington, D.C., 1936–75.*

PAUL EDWIN POTTER. *Professor of Geology, University of Cincinnati, Ohio.*

•WILLIAM STELLING VON ARX. *Senior Scientist, Woods Hole Oceanographic Institution, Massachusetts, 1968–78.*

BRIAN F. WINDLEY. *Professor and Head, Department of Geology, University of Leicester, England.*

•PETER J. WYLLIE. *Professor of Geology and Chairman, Division of Geological and Planetary Sciences, California Institute of Technology, Pasadena.*

Part Three. Life on Earth

•N.J. BERRILL. *Strathcona Professor of Zoology, McGill University, Montreal, 1946–65.*

JOHN TYLER BONNER. *George M. Moffett Professor of Biology, Princeton University.*

•V.G. DETHIER. *Gilbert Woodside Professor of Zoology, University of Massachusetts, Amherst.*

PETER W. FRANK. *Professor of Biology, University of Oregon, Eugene.*

•HAROLD J.F. GALL. *Emeritus Professor of Biology, University of Chicago.*

CARL GANS. *Professor of Zoology, University of Michigan, Ann Arbor.*

ERNEST M. GIFFORD, JR. *Professor of Botany, University of California, Davis.*

•LOUIS S. GOODMAN, M.D. *Distinguished Professor of Pharmacology, University of Utah, Salt Lake City.*

•GARRETT HARDIN. *Emeritus Professor of Human Ecology, University of California, Santa Barbara.*

EMANUEL MARGOLIASH. *Professor of Biochemistry and Molecular Biology, Northwestern University, Evanston, Illinois.*

•ERNST WALTER MAYR. *Alexander Agassiz Professor Emeritus of Zoology, Harvard University.*

•JOHN ALEXANDER MOORE. *Emeritus Professor of Biology, University of California, Riverside.*

THOMAS PARK. *Emeritus Professor of Biology, University of Chicago.*

•THEODORE T. PUCK. *Professor of Biochemistry, Biophysics, and Genetics, University of Colorado Health Sciences Center, Denver; Director, Eleanor Roosevelt Institute for Cancer Research.*

G. LEDYARD STEBBINS. *Emeritus Professor of Genetics, University of California, Davis.*

JOHN W. THIERET. *Professor of Botany, Northern Kentucky University, Highland Heights; Chairman, Department of Biological Sciences, 1973–80.*

●BIRGIT VENNESLAND. *Head, Vennesland Research Laboratory, Max Planck Society, 1970–81; Director, Max Planck Institute for Cell Physiology, Berlin, 1968–70.*

●PAUL B. WEISZ. *Professor of Biology, Brown University, Providence, Rhode Island.*

RUPERT L. WENZEL. *Emeritus Curator of Insects, Field Museum of Natural History, Chicago; Chairman, Department of Zoology, 1970–77.*

●RALPH H. WETMORE. *Emeritus Professor of Botany, Harvard University.*

●EMIL H. WHITE. *D. Mead Johnson Professor of Chemistry, Johns Hopkins University, Baltimore, Maryland.*

Part Four. Human Life

●EMMET BLACKBURN BAY, M.D. (d. 1973). *Professor of Medicine, University of Chicago.*

WILLIAM CAMERON BOWMAN. *Deputy Principal; Professor of Pharmacology, University of Strathclyde, Glasgow.*

●SIR WILFRID EDWARD LE GROS CLARK (d. 1971). *Professor of Anatomy, University of Oxford.*

MIHALY CSIKSZENTMIHALYI. *Professor of Human Development and of Education and Chairman, Department of Behavioral Sciences, University of Chicago.*

PETER P.H. DE BRUYN, M.D. *Emeritus Professor of Anatomy, University of Chicago.*

HARVEY J. DWORKEN, M.D. *Professor of Medicine, Case Western Reserve University, Cleveland, Ohio.*

●RUSSELL S. FISHER, M.D. *Chief Medical Examiner, State of Maryland, Baltimore. Professor of Forensic Pathology, University of Maryland Medical School, Baltimore.*

CECIL A. GIBB. *Visiting Fellow, Office for Research in Academic Methods; Emeritus Professor of Psychology, School of General Studies, Australian National University, Canberra.*

ROY R. GRINKER, SR., M.D. *Emeritus Professor of Psychiatry, University of Chicago. Director, Institute for Psychosomatic and Psychiatric Research and Training, Michael Reese Hospital and Medical Center, Chicago, 1951–76.*

●F. CLARK HOWELL. *Professor of Anthropology, University of California, Berkeley.*

WILLIAM WHITE HOWELLS. *Emeritus Professor of Anthropology, Harvard University.*

HOWARD F. HUNT. *Professor of Psychology in Psychiatry, New York Hospital—Cornell University Medical Center, White Plains, New York.*

WILLIAM KESSEN. *Eugene Higgins Professor of Psychology; Professor of Pediatrics, Yale University.*

●GREGORY A. KIMBLE. *Professor of Psychology, Duke University, Durham, North Carolina.*

●JOSEPH BARNETT KIRSNER, M.D. *Louis Block Distinguished Service Professor of Medicine, University of Chicago.*

●ERICH KLINGHAMMER. *Associate Professor of Psychology, Purdue University, West Lafayette, Indiana.*

LOUIS LASAGNA, M.D. *Dean, Sackler School of Graduate Biomedical Sciences; Dean for Academic Affairs, School of Medicine, Tufts University, Medford, Massachusetts.*

●WARREN STURGIS McCULLOCH, M.D. (d. 1969). *Neurophysiologist, cyberneticist. Staff Member, Research Laboratory of Electronics, Massachusetts Institute of Technology, Cambridge, 1952–69.*

●WILLIAM J. McGUIRE. *Professor of Psychology, Yale University.*

●SIR PETER MEDAWAR. *President, Royal Postgraduate Medical School, University of London. Jodrell Professor of Zoology and Comparative Anatomy, University College, London, 1951–62. Director, National Institute, Mill Hill, London, 1962–71. Nobel Prize for Physiology or Medicine, 1960.*

DRUMMOND RENNIE, M.D. *Chairman of Medicine, West Suburban Hospital, Oak Park, Illinois. Professor of Medicine, Rush Medical College, Chicago.*

JOHN TALBOT ROBINSON. *Emeritus Professor of Anthropology and of Zoology, University of Wisconsin, Madison.*

IRVING SARNOFF. *Professor of Psychology, New York University, New York City.*

JAMES A. SHANNON, M.D. *Professor of Biomedical Sciences, Rockefeller University, New York City, 1970–75. Director, National Institutes of Health, Bethesda, Maryland, 1955–68.*

WILFRED SIRCUS, M.D. *Senior Consultant Physician, Gastrointestinal Unit; former Reader in Medicine, University of Edinburgh.*

WILLIAM H. TALIAFERRO (d. 1973). *Eliakim Hastings Moore Distinguished Service Professor of Microbiology, University of Chicago, 1954–60. Senior Immunologist, Division of Biological and Medical Research, Argonne National Laboratory, Argonne, Illinois, 1960–69.*

ILZA VEITH. *Emeritus Professor of Psychiatry and the History of Health Sciences, University of California, San Francisco.*

MAXWELL M. WINTROBE, M.D. *Distinguished Professor of Internal Medicine, University of Utah, Salt Lake City.*

Part Five. Human Society

ROBERT McC. ADAMS. *Secretary, Smithsonian Institution, Washington, D.C. Provost, University of Chicago, 1982–84; Harold H. Swift Distinguished Service Professor of Anthropology, 1975–84; Director, Oriental Institute, 1962–68 and 1981–82.*

FRANCIS A. ALLEN. *Edson R. Sunderland Professor of Law, University of Michigan, Ann Arbor.*

CLEVELAND AMORY. *Author and lecturer. President of The Fund for Animals.*

●WILLIAM J. BAUMOL. *Professor of Economics, Princeton University and New York University, New York City.*

●DANIEL BELL. *Henry Ford II Professor of Social Science, Harvard University.*

●GIULIANO H. BONFANTE. *Former Professor of Linguistics, University of Turin, Italy.*

●KENNETH E. BOULDING. *Distinguished Professor Emeritus of Economics, University of Colorado, Boulder.*

ROBERT J. BRAIDWOOD. *Emeritus Professor of Old World Prehistory, Oriental Institute, University of Chicago.*

●LEWIS A. COSER. *Distinguished Professor of Sociology, State University of New York at Stony Brook.*

MAURICE CRANSTON. *Emeritus Professor of Political Science, London School of Economics and Political Science, University of London.*

●SIGMUND DIAMOND. *Giddings Professor of Sociology, Columbia University.*

ALLISON DUNHAM. *Arnold I. Shure Professor Emeritus of Urban Law, University of Chicago.*

FRED R. EGGAN. *Harold H. Swift Distinguished Service Professor Emeritus of Anthropology, University of Chicago.*

●CARL J. FRIEDRICH (d. 1984). *Eaton Professor of the Science of Government, Harvard University, 1955–71.*

DAVID A. GOSLIN. *Executive Director, Commission on Behavioral and Social Sciences and Education, National Research Council, National Academy of Sciences, Washington, D.C.*

ANDREW HACKER. *Professor of Political Science, Queens College, City University of New York, Flushing.*

JOHN HACKETT. *Director for Financial, Fiscal, and Enterprise Affairs, Organization for Economic Cooperation and Development, Paris.*

ERIC P. HAMP. *Robert Maynard Hutchins Distinguished Service Professor of Linguistics and of Behavioral Sciences; Director, Center for Balkan and Slavic Studies, University of Chicago.*

CHARLES M. HARDIN. *Emeritus Professor of Political Science, University of California, Davis.*

PHILIP M. HAUSER. *Lucy Flower Professor Emeritus of Urban Sociology; Emeritus Director, Population Research Center, University of Chicago.*

•ROBERT J. HAVIGHURST. *Emeritus Professor of Education and of Human Development, University of Chicago.*

JEROME HOLTZMAN. *Author and journalist. Baseball Columnist,* Chicago Tribune.

•HARRY KALVEN, JR. (d. 1974). *Professor of Law, University of Chicago, 1953–74.*

EDMUND JAMES KING. *Emeritus Professor of Education, King's College, University of London.*

GEORGE FREDERICK KNELLER. *Emeritus Professor of Education, University of California, Los Angeles.*

JOHN RICHARD KRUEGER. *Former Professor of Uralic and Altaic Studies, Indiana University, Bloomington.*

JOHN LYONS. *Master of Trinity Hall, University of Cambridge.*

•RAVEN I. McDAVID, JR. (d. 1984). *Professor of English and of Linguistics, University of Chicago, 1964–77.*

DONALD GUNN MacRAE. *Martin White Professor of Sociology, London School of Economics and Political Science, University of London.*

RUSSELL L. MATHEWS. *Emeritus Professor of Economics, Australian National University, Canberra.*

JEANNETTE R. MIRSKY. *Visiting Fellow, Department of East Asian Studies, Princeton University, 1970–74.*

HANS J. MORGENTHAU (d. 1980). *Leonard Davis Distinguished Professor of Political Science, City College, City University of New York, 1968–74. Albert A. Michelson Distinguished Service Professor of Political Science and Modern History, University of Chicago, 1963–68.*

•PAUL MUNDY. *Professor of Sociology; Chairman, Department of Criminal Justice, Loyola University, Chicago.*

HLA MYINT. *Professor of Economics, London School of Economics and Political Science, University of London.*

ALEXANDER NOVE. *Emeritus Professor of Economics, University of Glasgow.*

•KENYON POOLE. *Emeritus Professor of Economics, Northwestern University, Evanston, Illinois.*

•C. HERMAN PRITCHETT. *Emeritus Professor of Political Science, University of California, Santa Barbara, and University of Chicago.*

ALBERT J. REISS, JR. *William Graham Sumner Professor of Sociology; Lecturer in Law, Yale University.*

•MAX RHEINSTEIN (d. 1977). *Max Pam Professor of Comparative Law, University of Chicago, 1942–68.*

CHARLES SZLADITS (d. 1986). *Adjunct Professor of Comparative Law, Columbia University.*

•SOL TAX. *Emeritus Professor of Anthropology, University of Chicago. Director, Center for the Study of Man, Smithsonian Institution, Washington, D.C., 1968–76.*

•CHARLES RAYMOND WHITTLESEY. *Emeritus Professor of Finance and Economics, University of Pennsylvania, Philadelphia.*

AARON B. WILDAVSKY. *Professor of Political Science, University of California, Berkeley.*

TURRELL V. WYLIE (d. 1984). *Professor of Tibetan Studies, University of Washington, Seattle, 1972–84.*

Part Six. Art

•RUDOLF ARNHEIM. *Emeritus Professor of Psychology of Art, Carpenter Center for the Visual Arts, Harvard University.*

WALTER BLAIR. *Emeritus Professor of English, University of Chicago.*

JOHN ELY BURCHARD (d. 1975). *Professor of Humanities and Dean, School of Humanities and Social Science, Massachusetts Institute of Technology, Cambridge, 1948–64.*

ALBERT BUSH-BROWN. *Chancellor, Long Island University, Greenvale, New York.*

•ROBERT JESSE CHARLESTON. *Keeper, Department of Ceramics, Victoria and Albert Museum, London, 1963–76.*

CHARLES GRANT ELLIS. *Research Associate, The Textile Museum, Washington, D.C.*

•CLIFTON FADIMAN. *Author and editor. Member, Board of Editors,* Encyclopædia Britannica.

•FRANCIS FERGUSSON. *Professor of Comparative Literature, Princeton University, 1973–81. Professor of Comparative Literature, Rutgers University, New Brunswick, New Jersey, 1953–69.*

HELMUT GERNSHEIM. *Photo-historian and author. Founder of the Gernsheim Collection.*

•JOHN GLOAG (d. 1981). *Novelist and writer on architecture and industrial design.*

OLEG GRABAR. *Aga Khan Professor of Islāmic Art, Harvard University.*

•RICHARD GRIFFITH (d. 1969). *Lecturer on Motion Pictures, Wesleyan University, Middletown, Connecticut, 1967–69. Curator, Museum of Modern Art Film Library, New York City, 1951–65.*

•RICHARD HOGGART. *Warden, Goldsmiths' College, University of London, 1976–84. Professor of English, University of Birmingham, England, 1962–73.*

HANS HUTH (d. 1977). *Curator of Painting, 1944–57; Curator of Decorative Arts, 1958–63, Art Institute of Chicago.*

DONALD KEENE. *Professor of Japanese, Columbia University.*

ARTHUR KNIGHT. *Professor of Cinema, University of Southern California, Los Angeles.*

•EDWARD LOCKSPEISER (d. 1973). *Officier d'Académie, Paris. Writer and broadcaster on music.*

•ROY McMULLEN (d. 1984). *Author, critic, and art historian.*

WILLIAM W. MELNITZ. *Emeritus Dean, College of Fine Arts; Emeritus Professor of Theater Arts, University of California, Los Angeles. Professor of Theater; Associate Director, Max Reinhardt Archive, State University of New York, Binghamton, 1969–73.*

•LEONARD B. MEYER. *Benjamin Franklin Professor of Music and Humanities, University of Pennsylvania, Philadelphia.*

•MICHAEL MORROW. *Former Music Editor,* Encyclopædia Britannica. *Director, Musica Reservatus, London.*

RAY NASH (d. 1982). *Professor of Art, Dartmouth College, Hanover, New Hampshire, 1949–70.*

BRUNO NETTL. *Professor of Music and of Anthropology, University of Illinois, Urbana.*

● BEAUMONT NEWHALL. *Visiting Professor of Art, University of New Mexico, Albuquerque. Director, George Eastman House, Rochester, New York, 1958–71.*

DOROTHY MARGARET PARTINGTON. *Literary critic and historian.*

● SIR HERBERT READ (d. 1968). *Poet and critic. Watson Gordon Professor of Fine Art, University of Edinburgh, 1931–33. Editor,* The Burlington Magazine, *1933–39. Charles Eliot Norton Professor of Poetry, Harvard University, 1953–54.*

● RICHARD ROUD. *Film critic. Program Director, London and New York Film Festivals.*

● GEORGE SAVAGE (d. 1982). *Art consultant. Author of* Porcelain Through the Ages; Pottery Through the Ages; *and others.*

NICOLAS SLONIMSKY. *Conductor, composer, writer, and editor. Lecturer in Music, University of California, Los Angeles, 1964–67.*

● WOLFGANG STECHOW (d. 1974). *Professor of Fine Arts, Oberlin College, Oberlin, Ohio, 1940–63.*

● JOSHUA C. TAYLOR (d. 1981). *Director, National Collection of Fine Arts, Smithsonian Institution, Washington, D.C., 1970–81. William Rainey Harper Professor of Humanities and Professor of Art, University of Chicago, 1963–74.*

WALTER TERRY (d. 1982). *Dance critic and editor,* Saturday Review *magazine;* New York Herald Tribune; *and others.*

● EVERARD M. UPJOHN (d. 1978). *Professor of Fine Arts, Columbia University, 1951–70.*

● PIERRE VERLET. *Chief Curator of Art Objects from the Middle Ages to the Modern Period, Louvre Museum, Paris, 1945–65. Chief Curator, National Museum of Sèvres Porcelain, Sèvres, France, 1945–65. Chief Curator, Cluny Museum, Paris, 1945–65.*

EDWARD WASIOLEK. *Avalon Foundation Distinguished Service Professor of Slavic, English, and Comparative Literature, University of Chicago.*

● RENÉ WELLEK. *Sterling Professor Emeritus of Comparative Literature, Yale University.*

● GLYNNE WILLIAM GLADSTONE WICKHAM. *Emeritus Professor of Drama, University of Bristol, England; Dean, Faculty of Arts, 1970–72.*

● RAYMOND (HENRY) WILLIAMS. *Professor of Drama, University of Cambridge, 1974–83; Fellow of Jesus College, Cambridge.*

C. BARRIE WILSON. *Professor of Architectural Science, University of Edinburgh.*

● PAUL S. WINGERT (d. 1974). *Professor of Art History and Archaeology, Columbia University.*

● BRUNO ZEVI. *Professor of Architectural History, University of Rome, 1963–79.*

Part Seven. Technology

BRIAN D.O. ANDERSON. *Professor and Head, Department of Systems Engineering, Research School of Physical Sciences, Australian National University, Canberra.*

ALLEN V. ASTIN (d. 1984). *Director, National Bureau of Standards, Washington, D.C., 1952–69.*

D.A. BROWN. *Emeritus Professor of Library Administration, University of Illinois, Urbana; Agricultural Librarian, 1948–72.*

GRACE ROGERS COOPER. *Museum consultant. Curator, Division of Textiles, National Museum of History and Technology, Smithsonian Institution, Washington, D.C., 1946–76.*

● CONSTANTINE APOSTOLOS DOXIADIS (d. 1975). *Chairman, Doxiadis Associates International, Athens; Chairman, Board of Directors, Doxiadis Associates, Inc., Washington, D.C. Chairman, Board of Directors, Athens Technological Organization. President, Athens Center of Ekistics.*

● EUGENE S. FERGUSON. *Professor of History, University of Delaware, Newark, 1969–79. Curator of Technology, Hagley Museum, Greenville, Delaware, 1969–79.*

NEAL FITZSIMONS. *Principal, Engineering Counsel, Kensington, Maryland.*

S. PAUL JOHNSTON (d. 1985). *Director, National Air and Space Museum, Smithsonian Institution, Washington, D.C., 1964–69.*

● MELVIN KRANZBERG. *Callaway Professor of the History of Science and Technology, Georgia Institute of Technology, Atlanta.*

WARREN PERRY MASON. *Senior Research Associate, Henry Krumb School of Mines, Columbia University, 1969–77. Head of Mechanics Research, Bell Telephone Laboratories, Murray Hill, New Jersey, 1948–65.*

● HARVEY G. MEHLHOUSE. *Chairman of the Board, Western Electric Company, New York City, 1971–72; President, 1969–71; Vice President, 1965–69.*

REID T. MILNER. *Emeritus Professor of Food Science, University of Illinois, Urbana.*

HARRY F. OLSON (d. 1982). *Staff Vice President, RCA Laboratories, Princeton, New Jersey, 1966–67; Director, Acoustical and Electromechanical Laboratory, 1942–66.*

● ROBERT SMITH WOODBURY (d. 1983). *Professor of the History of Technology, Massachusetts Institute of Technology, Cambridge.*

Part Eight. Religion

CHARLES JOSEPH ADAMS. *Professor of Islāmic Studies, McGill University, Montreal.*

SALO WITTMAYER BARON. *Emeritus Professor of Jewish History, Literature, and Institutions, Columbia University; Director, Center of Israel and Jewish Studies, 1950–68.*

THE REV. COLMAN J. BARRY, O.S.B. *Regents Professor of History, Saint John's University, Collegeville, Minnesota; Director, Institute for Spirituality, 1977–83.*

● ARTHUR LLEWELLYN BASHAM (d. 1986). *Professor of Asian Civilizations, Australian National University, Canberra.*

J.A.B. ᴠᴀɴ BUITENEN (d. 1979). *Distinguished Service Professor of Sanskrit and Indic Studies, University of Chicago, 1974–79.*

● THE REV. JAMES T. BURTCHAELL. *Professor of Theology, University of Notre Dame, Indiana; Provost, 1970–77.*

P. JOSEPH CAHILL, S.J. *Professor of Religious Studies, University of Alberta, Edmonton.*

● THE REV. J.V. LANGMEAD CASSERLEY (d. 1978). *Professor of Apologetics, Seabury-Western Theological Seminary, Evanston, Illinois, 1959–77.*

EDWARD J.D. CONZE (d. 1979). *Visiting Professor of Religious Studies, University of Lancaster, England, 1973–75.*

H. BYRON EARHART. *Professor of Religion, Western Michigan University, Kalamazoo.*

MIRCEA ELIADE (d. 1986). *Sewell L. Avery Distinguished Service Professor, Divinity School; Professor, Committee on Social Thought, University of Chicago.*

GEORGE WOLFGANG FORELL. *Carver Professor of Religion, University of Iowa, Iowa City.*

B.A. GERRISH. *John Nuveen Professor of Historical Theology, Divinity School, University of Chicago.*

JUDAH GOLDIN. *Professor of Oriental Studies and Post-Biblical Hebrew Literature, University of Pennsylvania, Philadelphia.*

•ROBERT M. GRANT. *Carl Darling Buck Professor of Humanities; Professor of Early Christian History, Divinity School, University of Chicago.*

HERBERT V. GUENTHER. *Emeritus Professor of Far Eastern Studies, University of Saskatchewan, Saskatoon.*

•ICHIRO HORI (d. 1974). *Professor of the History of Religions, Seijo University and Kokugakuin University, Tokyo.*

THORKILD JACOBSEN. *Emeritus Professor of Assyriology, Harvard University.*

•JOSEPH M. KITAGAWA. *Emeritus Professor of the History of Religions and of Far Eastern Languages and Civilizations, University of Chicago; Dean, Divinity School, 1970–80.*

CHARLES H. LONG. *William Rand Kenan, Jr., Professor of the History of Religion, University of North Carolina at Chapel Hill. Professor of the History of Religions, Duke University, Durham, North Carolina.*

THE REV. GEORGE W. MacRAE, S.J. (d. 1985). *Stillman Professor of Roman Catholic Theological Studies, Divinity School, Harvard University, 1973–85.*

MARTIN E. MARTY. *Fairfax M. Cone Distinguished Service Professor, Divinity School, University of Chicago. Associate Editor,* The Christian Century.

THE REV. JOHN MEYENDORFF. *Dean, St. Vladimir's Orthodox Theological Seminary, Tuckahoe, New York. Professor of Byzantine and East European History, Fordham University, New York City.*

HAJIME NAKAMURA. *Founder-Director, Eastern Institute, Inc., Tokyo. Emeritus Professor of Indian and Buddhist Philosophy, University of Tokyo.*

•JAROSLAV JAN PELIKAN. *Sterling Professor of History, Yale University.*

•RABBI JAKOB JOSEF PETUCHOWSKI. *Research Professor of Judeo-Christian Studies, Hebrew Union College—Jewish Institute of Religion, Cincinnati, Ohio.*

EDWIN G. PULLEYBLANK. *Professor of Chinese, University of British Columbia, Vancouver.*

•FAZLUR RAHMAN. *Professor of Islāmic Philosophy, University of Chicago.*

J. COERT RYLAARSDAM. *Emeritus Professor of Old Testament Theology, Divinity School, University of Chicago. Emeritus Professor of Theology, Marquette University, Milwaukee, Wisconsin.*

THE REV. D. HOWARD SMITH. *Lecturer in Comparative Religions, University of Manchester, 1953–66.*

JONATHAN ZITTELL SMITH. *Robert O. Anderson Distinguished Service Professor of the Humanities, University of Chicago.*

WILFRED CANTWELL SMITH. *Emeritus Professor of the Comparative History of Religion, Harvard University.*

R.J. ZWI WERBLOWSKY. *Professor of Comparative Religion, Hebrew University of Jerusalem.*

Part Nine. The History of Mankind

•FREDERICK B. ARTZ (d. 1983). *Professor of History, Oberlin College, Ohio, 1934–62.*

•JACQUES BARZUN. *University Professor Emeritus, Columbia University; Dean of Faculties and Provost, 1958–67.*

JOHN A. BRINKMAN. *Charles H. Swift Distinguished Service Professor of Mesopotamian History, University of Chicago.*

JOHN F. CADY. *Distinguished Professor Emeritus of History, Ohio University, Athens.*

AINSLIE T. EMBREE. *Professor of History, Columbia University.*

JOSEPH FLETCHER (d. 1984). *Professor of Chinese and Central Asian History, Harvard University, 1972–84.*

WALTER EMIL KAEGI, JR. *Professor of Byzantine and Roman History, University of Chicago.*

HERBERT S. KLEIN. *Professor of History, Columbia University.*

•LEONARD KRIEGER. *University Professor of History, University of Chicago.*

PHILIP A. KUHN. *Professor of History; Director, John King Fairbank Center for East Asian Research, Harvard University.*

DONALD P. LITTLE. *Professor and Director, Institute of Islāmic Studies, McGill University, Montreal.*

DONALD M. LOWE. *Professor of History, San Francisco State University.*

JAMES G. LYDON. *Professor of History, Duquesne University, Pittsburgh.*

PAUL T. MASON. *Professor of History, Duquesne University, Pittsburgh.*

HERBERT GEORGE NICHOLAS. *Rhodes Professor Emeritus of American History and Institutions, University of Oxford; Fellow of New College, Oxford, 1951–78.*

DONALD MacGILLIVRAY NICOL. *Koraës Professor of Byzantine and Modern Greek History, Language, and Literature, King's College, University of London.*

STEWART IRVIN OOST (d. 1981). *Professor of Ancient History, University of Chicago, 1965–81.*

RICHARD E. PIPES. *Frank B. Baird, Jr., Professor of History, Harvard University.*

JAN M. VANSINA. *Vilas Professor of History, University of Wisconsin, Madison.*

GORDON RANDOLPH WILLEY. *Senior Professor of Anthropology; Bowditch Professor Emeritus of Mexican and Central American Archaeology, Harvard University.*

GEORGE MACKLIN WILSON. *Professor of History and of East Asian Languages and Cultures, Indiana University, Bloomington.*

Part Ten. The Branches of Knowledge

MONROE C. BEARDSLEY. *Professor of Philosophy, Temple University, Philadelphia.*

•OTTO ALLEN BIRD. *Emeritus Professor of Arts and Letters, University of Notre Dame, Indiana.*

•WING-TSIT CHAN. *Anna R.D. Gillespie Professor Emeritus of Philosophy, Chatham College, Pittsburgh. Emeritus Professor of Chinese Philosophy and Culture, Dartmouth College, Hanover.*

RODERICK M. CHISHOLM. *Andrew Mellon Professor of the Humanities and Professor of Philosophy, Brown University, Providence, Rhode Island.*

JAMES DANIEL COLLINS (d. 1985). *Professor of Philosophy, St. Louis University, Missouri.*

ALAN DONAGAN. *Professor of Philosophy, California Institute of Technology, Pasadena.*

•WILLIAM H. DRAY. *Professor of Philosophy and of History, University of Ottawa.*

ELDON DYER. *Distinguished Professor of Mathematics, Graduate School, City University of New York.*

•NORWOOD HANSON (d. 1967). *Professor of Philosophy, Yale University, 1963–67.*

•J.H. HEXTER. *Distinguished Historian in Residence, Washington University, St. Louis, Missouri. Charles L. Stillé Professor of History, Yale University, 1967–78.*

MORRIS KLINE. *Emeritus Professor of Mathematics, New York University, New York City.*

EDWARD HERMAN LEZAK. *Actuary, Continental Assurance Company, Chicago.*

•RICHARD P. McKEON (d. 1985). *Charles F. Grey Distinguished Service Professor of Philosophy and of Greek, University of Chicago, 1947–76.*

•THE REV. ERNAN V. McMULLIN. *Professor of Philosophy, University of Notre Dame, Indiana.*

•KARL MENGER (d. 1985). *Professor of Mathematics, Illinois Institute of Technology, Chicago, 1946–71.*

•ARTHUR NORMAN PRIOR (d. 1969). *Fellow, Balliol College, University of Oxford. Professor of Philosophy, Manchester University, 1959–66.*

•NICHOLAS RESCHER. *University Professor of Philosophy, University of Pittsburgh. Editor,* American Philosophical Quarterly.

PAUL ARTHUR SCHILPP. *Emeritus Professor of Philosophy, Northwestern University, Evanston, Illinois. Distinguished Professor, Southern Illinois University, Carbondale, 1965–77.*

•SEYMOUR SCHUSTER. *Professor of Mathematics, Carleton College, Northfield, Minnesota.*

HENRY BABCOCK VEATCH. *Emeritus Professor of Philosophy, Georgetown University, Washington, D.C.*

JULIUS R. WEINBERG (d. 1971). *Vilas Professor of Philosophy, University of Wisconsin, Madison.*

IZAAK WIRSZUP. *Emeritus Professor of Mathematics, University of Chicago.*

Geography

NATHANIEL O. ABELSON. *Former Map Librarian, Dag Hammarskjöld Library, United Nations, New York City.*

IBRAHIM A. ABU-LUGHOD. *Professor of Political Science, Northwestern University, Evanston, Illinois.*

GEORGE I. BLANKSTEN. *Professor of Political Science, Northwestern University, Evanston, Illinois.*

NORTON S. GINSBURG. *Director, Environment and Policy Institute, East-West Center, Honolulu.*

HELVI A. KALMAN. *Writer and Editor, Department of Public Information, United Nations, New York City, 1958–79.*

HANS E. PANOFSKY. *Curator of Africana, Northwestern University Library, Evanston, Illinois.*

G. ETZEL PEARCY (d. 1980). *Professor of Geography, California State University, Los Angeles, 1969–73.*

IVOR G. WILKS. *Melville J. Herskovits Professor of African Studies, Northwestern University, Evanston, Illinois.*

Authors of Propædia Essays

Part One

NIGEL CALDER. *Physicist and science writer. Science Correspondent,* New Statesman, *1966–71. Editor,* New Scientist, *1962–66. Author of* Robots; Technopolis: Social Control of the Uses of Science; *and others.*

Part Two

PETER J. WYLLIE. *Petrologist, educator, and author. Professor of Geology and Chairman, Division of Geological and Planetary Sciences, California Institute of Technology, Pasadena. Author of* Ultramafic and Related Rocks; The Dynamic Earth; *and others.*

Part Three

RENÉ DUBOS (d. 1982). *Microbiologist, pathologist, and author. Professor of Pathology, Rockefeller University, New York City, 1957–71. Author of* So Human an Animal; Mirage of Health; A God Within; *and others.*

Part Four

LOREN EISELEY (d. 1977). *Anthropologist, poet, and essayist. Benjamin Franklin Professor of Anthropology and the History of Science, University of Pennsylvania, 1961–77; Curator of Early Man, University of Pennsylvania Museum, 1948–77. Author of* The Immense Journey; The Invisible Pyramid; *and others.*

Part Five

HAROLD D. LASSWELL (d. 1978). *Political scientist and author. Professor of Law, 1946–70, and of Political Science, 1952–70, Yale University. Author of* Psychopathology and Politics; Politics: Who Gets What, When, How; A Pre-View of Policy Sciences; *and others.*

Part Six

MARK VAN DOREN (d. 1972). *Poet, critic, and teacher. Professor of English, Columbia University, 1920–59. Author of lyric and narrative poems, novels, stories, plays, and works of criticism and biography.*

Part Seven

PETER RITCHIE RITCHIE-CALDER, BARON RITCHIE-CALDER (d. 1982). *Author, journalist, and educator. Senior Fellow, Center for the Study of Democratic Institutions, Santa Barbara, California, 1972–75. Montague Burton Professor of International Relations, University of Edinburgh, 1961–67. Author of* Birth of the Future; Medicine and Man; The Evolution of the Machine; *and others.*

Part Eight

WILFRED CANTWELL SMITH. *Educator and author. Emeritus Professor of the Comparative History of Religion, Harvard University. Author of* Islam in Modern History; The Meaning and End of Religion; Questions of Religious Truth; *and others.*

Part Nine

JACQUES BARZUN. *Historian, educator, and author. University Professor Emeritus, Columbia University; Dean of Faculties and Provost, 1958–67. Author of* Berlioz and the Romantic Century; Darwin, Marx, and Wagner; The House of Intellect; On Writing, Publishing, and Editing; *and others.*

Part Ten

MORTIMER J. ADLER. *Philosopher and editor. Director of the Institute for Philosophical Research. Editor of the* Syntopicon *of* Great Books of the Western World; *Chairman, Board of Editors,* Encyclopædia Britannica; *Director of Planning, Fifteenth Edition. Author of* The Idea of Freedom; The Conditions of Philosophy; The Common Sense of Politics; *and others.*

Initials of
Contributors

Listed are the initials signed to articles in the MACROPAEDIA and MICROPAEDIA, the names of the persons identified by the initials, a brief description of the persons so identified, and the titles of the articles with which they were involved.

A.   Morys George Lyndhurst Bruce, 4th Baron Aberdare. *Chairman of Committees, House of Lords, United Kingdom. Author of* The Story of Tennis; Willis Faber Book of Tennis and Rackets.
SPORTS, MAJOR TEAM AND INDIVIDUAL (*in part*)

A.Ad.   Anthony Adamovich. *Vice President, Byelorussian Institute of Arts and Sciences, Inc., Bronx, New York. Senior Editor, Radio Liberty. Author of* Opposition to Sovietization in Belorussian Literature.
UNION OF SOVIET SOCIALIST REPUBLICS (*in part*)

A.A.F.   Arnold A. Friedmann. *Professor of Design, University of Massachusetts, Amherst. Coauthor of* Interior Design.
DECORATIVE ARTS AND FURNISHINGS (*in part*)

A.A.G.P.   António Armando Gonçalves Pereira. *Professor of Commercial and Maritime Law, Technical University of Lisbon.*
SOUTHERN AFRICA (*in part*)

A.Ai.   Ayinipalli Aiyappan. *Special Officer, Tribal Research and Training Centre, Chevayur, Calicut, India. Editor of* Social Revolution in a Kerala Village.
INDIA (*in part*)

A.A.Ke.   Arno Artur Keerna. *Former Director, Institute of Economics, Estonian S.S.R. Academy of Sciences, Tallinn. Author of papers on the Estonian S.S.R.*
UNION OF SOVIET SOCIALIST REPUBLICS (*in part*)

A.Al-Sh.   Ahmed S. Al-Shahi. *Lecturer in Social Anthropology, University of Newcastle upon Tyne, England.*
SUDAN (*in part*)

A.A.M.   Aleksey Aleksandrovich Mints. *Chief, Department of Economic Geography, Institute of Geography, Academy of Sciences of the U.S.S.R., Moscow. Author of books on Transcaucasia.*
UNION OF SOVIET SOCIALIST REPUBLICS (*in part*)

A.A.Ma.   The Rev. Armand Maurer, C.S.B. *Professor of Philosophy, Pontifical Institute of Mediaeval Studies, University of Toronto. Author of* Medieval Philosophy.
PHILOSOPHY, THE HISTORY OF WESTERN (*in part*)

A.A.P.   Alexander A. Parker. *Emeritus Professor of Spanish Literature, University of Texas at Austin. Author of* The Allegorical Drama of Calderón *and others.*
CALDERÓN DE LA BARCA, PEDRO (Micropædia)

A.A.Ps.   Adamantios A. Pepelasis. *Former Professor of Economics, Virginia Polytechnic Institute and State University, Blacksburg.*
TAXATION (*in part*)

A.As.   Arthur C.V.D. Aspinall (d. 1972). *Professor of Modern History, University of Reading, England, 1947–65. Author of* The Cabinet Council, 1783–1835 *and others.*
CANNING, GEORGE (Micropædia)
FOX, CHARLES JAMES (Micropædia)
PITT, WILLIAM, THE YOUNGER (*in part*) (Micropædia)

A.A.S.   Arthur A. Siebens, M.D. *Darnall Professor of Rehabilitation Medicine and Surgery; Chief, Division of Rehabilitation Medicine, Johns Hopkins University, Baltimore. Author of* "The Mechanics of Breathing" *in* The Physiological Basis of Medical Practice.
RESPIRATION AND RESPIRATORY SYSTEMS (*in part*)

A.A.Si.   Andrew Annandale Sinclair. *Historian and filmmaker. Author of* Guevara *and others.*
GUEVARA, CHE (*in part*) (Micropædia)

A.B.   Alan Bullock, Baron Bullock. *Founding Master of St. Catherine's College, Oxford, 1960–1980; Vice Chancellor, University of Oxford, 1969–73. Author of* Hitler: A Study in Tyranny *and others.*
HITLER (*in part*)

A.B.-B.   Albert Bush-Brown. *Chancellor, Long Island University, Greenvale, New York. Author of* Louis Sullivan; *coauthor of* The Architecture of America.
ARCHITECTURE, THE HISTORY OF WESTERN (*in part*)

A.B.C.   Andrew Barnett Christie, M.D. *Honorary Physician, Fazakerly Hospital, Liverpool. Former Head, Department of Infectious Diseases, University of Liverpool. Author of* Infectious Diseases: Epidemiology and Clinical Practice.
INFECTIOUS DISEASES (*in part*)

A.Be.   André Beaufre (d. 1975). *General, French Army. Director, French Institute of Strategic Studies, Paris. Author of* Introduction à la stratégie *and others.*
WAR, THE THEORY AND CONDUCT OF (*in part*)

A.B.F.   Albert B. Friedman. *William Starke Rosecrans Professor of English Literature, Claremont Graduate School, Claremont, California. Author of* The Ballad Revival; *Editor of* Ywain and Gawain.
LITERATURE, THE ART OF (*in part*)

A.B.Fo.   Arthur B. Ford. *Geologist, Branch of Alaskan Geology, Geological Survey, U.S. Department of the Interior, Menlo Park, California. Author of* "Review of Antarctic Geology" *in* American Geophysical Union Transactions.
ANTARCTICA

A.B.G.   Ashley B. Gurney. *Research Entomologist, Systematic Entomology Laboratory, U.S. Department of Agriculture, Washington, D.C., 1955–75. Author of numerous articles on classification and distribution of insects.*
INSECTS (*in part*)

A.B.Ga.   Alfred B. Garrett. *Emeritus Professor of Chemistry, Ohio State University, Columbus.*
DALTON, JOHN (Micropædia)

A.B.Gr.   Alfred Byrd Graf. *President, Roehrs Company (horticultural publishers); Vice President, Roehrs Exotic Nurseries, Farmingdale, New Jersey. Author of* Exotica.
GARDENING AND HORTICULTURE (*in part*)

A.Bh.   Agehananda Bharati. *Professor and Chairman, Department of Anthropology, Syracuse University, New York. Author of* The Tantric Tradition.
SACRED OFFICES AND ORDERS (*in part*)

A.B.J.   Abeodu Bowen Jones. *Permanent Representative of Liberia to the United Nations. Author of* Grand Cape Mount County; *coeditor of* The Official Papers of William V.S. Tubman, President of the Republic of Liberia.
WESTERN AFRICA (*in part*)

A.B.K.   Alexander B. Klots. *Research Associate, Department of Entomology, American Museum of Natural History, New York City. Emeritus Professor of Biology, City University of New York. Author of* Field Guide to the Butterflies

of North America *and others.*
INSECTS *(in part)*

A.Bo.   Alfonso Bosellini. *Professor of Geology, University of Ferrara, Italy.*
MINERALS AND ROCKS *(in part)*

A.Br.   Adam Bromke. *Professor of Political Science, McMaster University, Hamilton, Ontario. Author of* Poland's Politics: Idealism vs. Realism.
GOMUŁKA, WŁADYSŁAW (Micropædia)

A.B.R.   Andreas B. Rechnitzer. *Special Deputy for International and Interagency Affairs, Office of the Oceanographer of the Navy, Alexandria, Virginia.*
EXPLORATION *(in part)*

A.Bu.   Allison Butts (d. 1977). *Professor of Metallurgy and Materials Science, Lehigh University, Bethlehem, Pennsylvania, Editor of* Copper: The Science and Technology of the Metal, Its Alloys and Compounds.
INDUSTRIES, EXTRACTION AND
   PROCESSING *(in part)*

A.B.W.   The Rev. Allan Bernard Wolter, O.F.M. *Professor of Philosophy, Catholic University of America, Washington, D.C. Author of* The Transcendentals and Their Function in the Metaphysics of Duns Scotus.
DUNS SCOTUS, JOHN (Micropædia)

A.By.   André Berry. *Author of* Florilège des troubadours; Anthologie de la poésie occitane; *and others.*
PROVENÇAL LITERATURE (Micropædia)

A.C.   Angela Codazzi. *Professor of Geography and Director, Institute of Geography, University of Milan, 1945–60.*
ITALY *(in part)*

A.C.B.   A. Craig Baird (d. 1979). *Professor of Speech, University of Iowa, Iowa City, 1928–52. Author and editor of* American Public Addresses; *coauthor of* Speech Criticism; General Speech; Communication.
ORATORY (Micropædia)

A.C.Bi.   Alan Curtis Birnholz. *Associate Professor of Art History, State University of New York at Buffalo.*
TOULOUSE-LAUTREC, HENRI DE
   (Micropædia)

A.C.Bk.   Alfred C. Beck, M.D. *Emeritus Professor of Obstetrics and Gynecology, State University of New York Downstate Medical Center at Brooklyn. Author of* Obstetrical Practice.
REPRODUCTION AND REPRODUCTIVE
   SYSTEMS *(in part)*

A.C.Br.   Armin C. Braun. (d. 1986). *Professor of Bacteriology, The Rockefeller University, New York City, 1959–81; Head, Laboratory of Plant Biology, 1955–81. Editor of* Plant Tumor Research.
GROWTH AND DEVELOPMENT,
   BIOLOGICAL *(in part)*

A.C.Bs.   Sir Alan Cuthbert Burns (d. 1980). *Permanent Representative of the United Kingdom on the United Nations*

Trusteeship Council, 1947–56. Governor and Commander-in-Chief, Gold Coast, 1941–47.
WESTERN AFRICA *(in part)*

A.C.C.   The Rev. Arthur C. Cochrane. *Emeritus Professor of Systematic Theology, Dubuque Theological Seminary, Iowa. Author of* The Existentialists and God *and others.*
BARTH, KARL (Micropædia)

A.C.G.   A.C. Grayling. *Visiting Lecturer, King's College, University of London. Author of* An Introduction to Philosophical Logic.
METAPHYSICS *(in part)*

A.C.G.B.   Alan C.G. Best. *Associate Professor of Geography, Boston University. Coauthor of* African Survey.
SOUTHERN AFRICA *(in part)*

A.C.H.   Alan Crawford Howie. *Lecturer in Music, Victoria University of Manchester.*
BRUCKNER, ANTON (Micropædia)

A.C.Ha.   Sir Alister C. Hardy (d. 1985). *Linacre Professor of Zoology, University of Oxford, 1946–61. Author of* "Charles Elton's Influence in Ecology" in Journal of Animal Ecology.
ELTON, CHARLES (Micropædia)

A.C.Hy.   Arthur C. Hardy (d. 1977). *Professor of Optics and Photography, Massachusetts Institute of Technology, Cambridge, 1933–61. Author of* Handbook of Colorimetry *and others.*
COLOUR *(in part)*

A.C.M.   Adolfo C. Mascarenhas. *Director, Institute of Resource Assessment, University of Dar es Salaam, Tanzania.*
EASTERN AFRICA *(in part)*

A.Co.   Alexander Cowie. *Emeritus Professor of Mechanical and Aerospace Engineering, Illinois Institute of Technology, Chicago. Associate Editor, Technology,* Encyclopædia Britannica, Chicago, 1967–72. Author of Kinematics and Design of Mechanisms.
MECHANICS *(in part)*

A.C.O.   Albert Cook Outler. *Emeritus Professor of Theology, Southern Methodist University, Dallas, Texas. Author of* Who Trusts in God *and others.*
DOCTRINES AND DOGMAS, RELIGIOUS
   (in part)

A.Cr.   Arthur Cronquist. *Senior Scientist, New York Botanical Garden, Bronx. Author of* An Integrated System of Classification of Flowering Plants *and others.*
ANGIOSPERMS *(in part)*

A.D.   Allison Danzig. *Sportswriter,* The New York Times, 1923–68. *Author of* The History of American Football; The Racquet Game; *and others.*
SPORTS, MAJOR TEAM AND INDIVIDUAL
   (in part)

A.Da.   Adrien Dansette (d. 1976). *Member of the Academy of Moral and*

Political Sciences, Paris. *Author of* Les Affaires de Panama.
LESSEPS, FERDINAND, VICOMTE DE
   (Micropædia)

A.D.B.   Alexander D. Baxter. *Engineering Consultant. Professor of Aircraft Propulsion, College of Aeronautics, Cranfield, England, 1950–57. Author of* Design of Liquid Propellant Rocket Motors.
ENERGY CONVERSION *(in part)*

A.De.   Aleksandar R. Despić. *Professor of Physical Chemistry, University of Belgrade. Author of chapter 4 in* Modern Aspects of Electrochemistry, *vol. 7.*
CHEMICAL REACTIONS *(in part)*

A. de A.-M.   Alamiro de Avila-Martel. *Professor of Roman Law and History of Law; Director of the Central Library, University of Chile, Santiago.*
COINS AND COINAGE *(in part)*

A. De C.   Alexander De Conde. *Professor of History, University of California, Santa Barbara. Author of* The Quasi-War: The Politics and Diplomacy of the Undeclared War with France, 1797–1801 *and others.*
HAMILTON, ALEXANDER *(in part)*
   (Micropædia)

A.Dem.   Abraham Demoz. *Professor of Linguistics; Director, Program of African Studies, Northwestern University, Evanston, Illinois.*
EASTERN AFRICA *(in part)*

A.D.G.   Andrew Dewar Gibb (d. 1974). *Regius Professor of Law, University of Glasgow, 1934–58. Coauthor of* Scottish Judicial Dictionary *and others.*
LEGAL SYSTEMS, THE EVOLUTION OF
   MODERN WESTERN *(in part)*

A.D.H.B.   Adrian David Hugh Bivar. *Lecturer in Iranian and Central Asian Art and Archaeology, School of Oriental and African Studies, University of London.*
IRAN *(in part)*

A.D.H.C.   Antony Dacres Hippisley Coxe. *Author of* A Seat at the Circus.
PAGEANTRY AND SPECTACLE *(in part)*

A.D.M.   Arthur D. Murphy. *Adjunct Professor of Cinema, University of Southern California, Los Angeles.*
MOTION PICTURES *(in part)*

A.D.Mo.   Arnaldo Dante Momigliano. *Alexander White Visiting Professor, University of Chicago. Professor of Ancient History, University College, University of London, 1951–75. Author of* Claudius, The Emperor and His Achievement *and others.*
CLAUDIUS I (Micropædia)

A.D.N.   Arne D. Naess. *Emeritus Professor of Philosophy, University of Oslo. Author of* Four Modern Philosophers *and others.*
HEIDEGGER, MARTIN (Micropædia)

A.Do.   Andreas Dorpalen (d. 1982). *Professor of History, Ohio State University, Columbus, 1958–78. Author*

of Hindenburg and the Weimar Republic.
HINDENBURG, PAUL VON (Micropædia)

Ad.S. **Adele Smith Simmons.**
*President, Hampshire College, Amherst,
Massachusetts. Member, Board of
Editors, Encyclopædia Britannica, Inc.,
Chicago. Author of* Modern Mauritius.
INDIAN OCEAN ISLANDS (*in part*)

A.Du. **The Rev. Avery Dulles, S.J.**
*Professor of Systematic Theology,
Catholic University of America,
Washington, D.C. Author of* Models of
Revelation *and others.*
DOCTRINES AND DOGMAS, RELIGIOUS
(*in part*)

A.E.A. **Alfred E. Alford.** *Managing
Director, Media & Marketing
Ltd., Belize.*
CENTRAL AMERICA (*in part*)

A.E.Ar. **Annette Elizabeth Armstrong.**
*Former Fellow and Tutor in Modern
Languages, Somerville College, Oxford;
former Lecturer in French Literature,
University of Oxford. Author of* Ronsard
and the Age of Gold; Robert Estienne,
Royal Printer.
RONSARD, PIERRE DE (Micropædia)

A.Eb. **Arimichi Ebisawa.** *Guest
Professor of History, International
Christian University, Tokyo. President,
Society of Historical Studies of
Christianity, Japan.*
ODA NOBUNAGA (Micropædia)

A.E.Cn. **Aksel E. Christensen** (d.
1981). *Professor of History, University of
Copenhagen, 1948–76.*
DENMARK (*in part*)

A.E.D. **Augustus E. DeMaggio.**
*Professor of Biology, Dartmouth College,
Hanover, New Hampshire.*
TISSUES AND FLUIDS (*in part*)

A.E.El. **Albert Edward Elsen.** *Haas
Professor of Art History, Stanford
University, California. Author of* Origins
of Modern Sculpture *and others.*
SCULPTURE, THE HISTORY OF WESTERN
(*in part*)

A.E.M. **Adolphe Erich Meyer.**
*Emeritus Professor of Educational
History, New York University, New York
City. Author of* An Educational History
of the American People *and others.*
EDUCATION, HISTORY OF (*in part*)

A.E.R. **Alfred Edward Ringwood.**
*Professor of Geochemistry; Director,
Research School of Earth Sciences,
Australian National University,
Canberra. Designer of models of
development of the Earth's interior
through geochemical research. Author of*
Petrology of the Earth's Mantle.
EARTH, THE (*in part*)

A.E.S. **Alan Edouard Samuel.** *Professor
of Greek and Roman History, University
College, University of Toronto. Author of*
Ptolemaic Chronology *and others.*
EGYPT (*in part*)

A.E.Sc. **Alfred Eric Scott.** *Former
Editor in Chief, Editorial and*

Publications Section, Commonwealth
Scientific and Industrial Research
Organization. Melbourne.
AUSTRALIA (*in part*)

A.E.Si **Akiba Ernst Simon.** *Emeritus
Professor of Education, Hebrew
University of Jerusalem. Author of*
Martin Bubers lebendiges Erbe *and
others.*
BUBER, MARTIN (Micropædia)

A.E.Sm. **Arthur Eltringham Smailes**
(d. 1984). *Professor of Geography, Queen
Mary College, University of London,
1955–73.*
EUROPE (*in part*)

A.E.Ta. **Alfred Edward Taylor** (d.
1945). *Professor of Moral Philosophy,
University of Edinburgh, 1924–41.
Author of* Plato; Socrates; *and others.*
PHILOSOPHICAL SCHOOLS AND
DOCTRINES, WESTERN (*in part*)
SOCRATES

A.E.W. **Albert E. Wood.** *Emeritus
Professor of Biology, Amherst College,
Massachusetts.*
MAMMALS (*in part*)

A.F. **Anne Foner.** *Professor of
Sociology, Rutgers University, New
Brunswick, New Jersey. Coauthor of*
Aging and Retirement *and others.*
SOCIAL DIFFERENTIATION (*in part*)

A.F.A.H. **Andreas F.A. Heldrich.**
*Professor of Civil Law, University
of Munich, West Germany. Author
of* Internationale Zuständigkeit und
anwendbares Recht.
TORTS

A.F.A.M. **Alice F.A. Mutton** (d. 1979).
*Reader in Geography, Queen Mary
College, University of London. Author of*
Central Europe; Western Europe.
EUROPE (*in part*)

A.F.B. **The Hon. Alastair Francis
Buchan** (d. 1976). *Montague Burton
Professor of International Relations,
University of Oxford, 1972–76. Founder
and Director, International Institute for
Strategic Studies, London, 1958–69.
Author of* The Spare Chancellor: The
Life of Walter Bagehot.
BAGEHOT, WALTER (Micropædia)

A.Fe. **Albert Feuerwerker.** *Professor
of History, University of Michigan,
Ann Arbor. Author of* China's Early
Industrialization.
CHINA (*in part*)

A.F.H. **Alfred F. Havighurst.** *Emeritus
Professor of History, Amherst College,
Massachusetts. Author of* Twentieth
Century Britain *and others.*
UNITED KINGDOM (*in part*)

A.F.Ho. **Arthur F. Holmes.** *Professor
of Philosophy, Wheaton College, Illinois.
Author of* Christian Philosophy in the
Twentieth Century *and others.*
CHRISTIANITY (*in part*)

A.Fi. **Andrew Field.** *Professor of
Comparative Literature, Griffith
University, Brisbane, Australia. Author of*

Nabokov: His Life in Art; Nabokov: His
Life in Part.
NABOKOV, VLADIMIR (Micropædia)

A.Fr. **Lady Antonia Fraser.** *Writer.
Author of* Mary, Queen of Scots
and others.
MARY (SCOTLAND) (Micropædia)

A.F.R. **Anne F. Rockwell.** *Free-lance
writer and illustrator. Author of* Glass,
Stones and Crown: The Abbé Suger and
the Building of St. Denis *and others.*
SUGER (Micropædia)

A.F.Sh. **Arthur Frank Shore.** *Brunner
Professor of Egyptology, University of
Liverpool, England. Author of* Portrait
Painting from Roman Egypt.
PAINTING, THE HISTORY OF WESTERN
(*in part*)
SCULPTURE, THE HISTORY OF WESTERN
(*in part*)

A.F.St. **Adolf F. Sturmthal** (d. 1986).
*Professor of Labor and Industrial
Relations, University of Illinois, Urbana.
Author of* Left of Center: European
Labor since World War II *and others.*
WORK AND EMPLOYMENT (*in part*)

A.Fu. **André Fu-Kiau kia Bunseki-L.**
*Director, Centre of Development
and Scientific Research in African
Languages, Kumba, Zaire.*
CENTRAL AFRICA (*in part*)

A.F.W. **Arthur F.Wright** (d. 1976).
*Charles Seymour Professor of History,
Yale University, 1961–76. Author of*
"The Formation of Sui Ideology" in
Chinese Thought and Institutions.
WEN TI (SUI DYNASTY) (Micropædia)

A.F.We. **Arthur Frederick Wells** (d.
1966). *Praelector in Classics, University
College, University of Oxford.*
LUCRETIUS (Micropædia)

A.G.B.H. **Åke Gunnar Birger
Hultkrantz.** *Professor and Chairman,
Department of Comparative Religion,
University of Stockholm. Author of* The
Study of American Indian Religions.
AMERICAN INDIANS (*in part*)

A.G.Bo. **Allan G. Bogue.** *Frederick
Jackson Turner Professor of History,
University of Wisconsin, Madison.*
NORTH AMERICA (*in part*)

A.Ge. **Arthur Gelb.** *Deputy Managing
Editor,* The New York Times. *Coauthor
of* O'Neill.
O'NEILL, EUGENE (*in part*) (Micropædia)

A.G.H. **A. Gordon Hammer.** *Emeritus
Professor of Psychology, Macquarie
University, North Ryde, Australia.
Author of* Elementary Matrix Algebra
for Psychologists and Social Scientists.
HYPNOSIS (*in part*) (Micropædia)

A.G.Ha. **The Rev. Adalbert G.
Hamman.** *Professor at Patristic Institute,
Rome. Editor,* Patrologiae Latinae
Supplementum. *Author of* La Prière
and others.
RITES AND CEREMONIES, SACRED
(*in part*)

A.Gi. Alexander Gillies (d. 1977). *Professor of German Language and Literature, University of Leeds, England, 1945–72. Author of* Goethe's Faust: An Interpretation *and many other books on German writers and literature.*
GERMAN LITERATURE (*in part*)

A.G.J. Adriaan G. Jongkees. *Professor of Medieval History, State University of Groningen, The Netherlands. Author of* Het koninkrijk Friesland in de vijftiende eeuw *and others.*
WILLIAM I (NETHERLANDS STADHOLDER) (*in part*) (Micropædia)

A.G.L. Andrew George Lehmann. *Professor, School of European Studies, University of Buckingham, England. Author of* Sainte-Beuve: A Portrait of the Critic *and others.*
SAINTE-BEUVE, CHARLES-AUGUSTIN (Micropædia)

A.G.Ly. A. Gordon Lyne. *Honorary Research Associate, Queen Victoria Museum, Launceston, Australia. Former Senior Principal Research Scientist, Division of Wildlife Research, Commonwealth Scientific and Industrial Research Organization, Blacktown, Australia. Author of* Marsupials and Monotremes of Australia.
MAMMALS (*in part*)

Ag.M. Agnes Mongan. *Emeritus Curator of Drawings, Fogg Art Museum, Harvard University. Coauthor of* Ingres Centennial Exhibition, 1867–1967; Drawings in the Fogg Museum.
INGRES, JEAN-AUGUSTE-DOMINIQUE (Micropædia)

A.G.M. Alan Gibbs Massey. *Reader in Inorganic Chemistry, Loughborough University of Technology, England. Coauthor of* Inorganic Chemistry in Non-aqueous Solvents.
CHEMICAL ELEMENTS (*in part*)

A.G.Ma. Alla Genrikhovna Massevitch. *Vice President, Astronomical Council, Academy of Sciences of the U.S.S.R., Moscow. Author of* Life of the Sun.
AMBARTSUMIAN, VIKTOR AMAZASPOVICH (Micropædia)

A.G.M.v.M. Andrew G.M. van Melsen. *Professor of Philosophy, Catholic University of Nijmegen, The Netherlands. Author of* From Atomos to Atom *and others.*
PHILOSOPHICAL SCHOOLS AND DOCTRINES, WESTERN (*in part*)

A.Gn. Alfonz Gspan (d. 1977). *Scientific Adviser, Slovene Academy of Sciences and Arts, Ljubljana. Editor,* Slovenski biografski leksikon. *Coauthor of* Incunabule v Sloveniji *and others.*
YUGOSLAV LITERATURE (*in part*)

A.G.N.F. Antony Garrard Newton Flew. *Professor of Philosophy, University of Reading, England. Author of* God and Philosophy; The Presumption of Atheism.

RELIGIOUS AND SPIRITUAL BELIEF, SYSTEMS OF (*in part*)

A.G.P. Alexis G. Pincus. *Visiting Professor of Ceramics, Rutgers University, New Brunswick, New Jersey. Coauthor of* Utilization of Ceramics in Microelectronics.
INDUSTRIAL GLASS AND CERAMICS (*in part*)

A.G.W. A. Geoffrey Woodhead. *Fellow of Corpus Christi College, Cambridge; Emeritus Lecturer in Classics, University of Cambridge. Adjunct Professor of Classics, Ohio State University, Columbus. Author of* The Greeks in the West *and others.*
HISTORY, THE STUDY OF (*in part*)

A.G. y B. Antonio García y Bellido (d. 1972). *Professor of Archaeology, University of Madrid, Spain. Director, Spanish Institute of Archaeology. Member, Royal Academy of History. Author of* Las Colonizaciones Púnica y Griega en la península ibérica.
SPAIN (*in part*)

A.H.A. A. Hilary Armstrong. *Gladstone Professor Emeritus of Greek, University of Liverpool. Editor of* The Cambridge History of Later Greek and Early Mediaeval Philosophy; *translator of Plotinus.*
PLATONISM, PLATO AND (*in part*)
PLOTINUS (Micropædia)

A.H.Ao. Anselm H. Amadio. *Chaplain; Instructor in Philosophy, Illinois Institute of Technology, Chicago. Staff Writer, Philosophy and Religion,* Encyclopædia Britannica, *Chicago, 1970–73.*
ARISTOTELIANISM, ARISTOTLE AND (*in part*)
PALAMAS, SAINT GREGORY (Micropædia)

A.H.C. Arthur Herbert Cook. *Director, Brewing Industry Research Foundation, Nutfield, England, 1958–71. Editor of* Barley and Malt: Biology, Biochemistry, Technology.
BEVERAGE PRODUCTION (*in part*)

A.H.Ca. Arthur H. Cash. *Professor of English, State University of New York, College at New Paltz. Author of* Laurence Sterne: The Early and Middle Years *and others.*
STERNE, LAURENCE (Micropædia)

A.H.D. Andrew Hutchinson Dawson. *Lecturer in Geography and Modern Russian Studies, University of St. Andrews, Scotland. Author of many papers on the geography of Poland.*
POLAND (*in part*)
WARSAW (*in part*)

A.H.E. Archie H. Easton. *Emeritus Professor of Mechanical Engineering, University of Wisconsin, Madison. Honorary Chairman of the Board, Safety Engineering Associates, Inc. (consulting engineers), Madison.*
TRANSPORTATION (*in part*)

A.H.F. Rabbi Albert H. Friedlander. *Dean of Rabbinic Studies, Leo Baeck*

College, London. Minister, Westminster Synagogue, London. Author of Leo Baeck: Teacher of Theresienstadt *and others.*
BAECK, LEO (Micropædia)

A.H.Gt. Ann Hutchinson Guest. *Director, Language of Dance Centre, London. Notation Teacher, Royal Academy of Dancing, London. Author of* Labanotation *and others.*
DANCE, THE ART OF (*in part*)

A.H.H. A.H. Hanson (d. 1971). *Professor of Politics, University of Leeds, England, Author of* Public Enterprise and Economic Development.
PUBLIC ENTERPRISES (*in part*)

A.H.Ho. Albert Habib Hourani. *Former Reader in the Modern History of the Middle East, University of Oxford. Author of* Arabic Thought in the Liberal Age, 1798–1939.
SYRIA (*in part*)

A.H.K. Andrew H. Knoll. *Associate Professor of Biology, Harvard University. Author of numerous papers on Precambrian paleontology and paleobotany.*
GEOCHRONOLOGY (*in part*)

A.H.McD. Alexander Hugh McDonald (d. 1979). *Lecturer in Ancient History, University of Cambridge, 1952–73. Author of* Republican Rome.
TACITUS (Micropædia)

A.H.M.J. Arnold Hugh Martin Jones (d. 1970). *Professor of Ancient History, University of Cambridge, 1951–70.*
PALESTINE (*in part*)

A.H.P. Arnold H. Price. *Bibliographer, American Historical Association, Washington, D.C. Former Area Specialist for Central Europe, Library of Congress, Washington, D.C.*
CLAUSEWITZ, CARL VON (Micropædia)

A.H.Ro. Arthur H. Rosenfeld. *Professor of Physics, University of California, Berkeley. Coauthor of* Nuclear Physics.
SUBATOMIC PARTICLES (*in part*)

A.H.S. Anna Hester Smith. *Former Head Librarian, Johannesburg Public Library. Former Director, Africana Museum, Johannesburg.*
JOHANNESBURG

A.H.St. Alan Howard Stratford. *Chairman, Alan Stratford and Associates (air transport consultants), Lymington, England. Author of* Air Transport Economics in the Supersonic Era *and others.*
TRANSPORTATION (*in part*)

A.I.I. Aleksandr Ilyich Imshenetsky. *Senior Research Associate, Scientific Council on the Location of U.S.S.R. Productive Forces, Academy of Sciences of the U.S.S.R., Moscow.*
UNION OF SOVIET SOCIALIST REPUBLICS (*in part*)

A.I.M. Albert I. Mendeloff, M.D. *Emeritus Physician in Chief, Sinai*

Hospital, Baltimore. *Professor of Medicine, Johns Hopkins University, Baltimore. Coauthor of* Digestive Diseases.
DIGESTION AND DIGESTIVE SYSTEMS (*in part*)

Ai.S.   Aidan William Southall. *Professor of Anthropology, University of Wisconsin, Madison. Editor of* Social Change in Modern Africa; *coeditor of* Madagascar: Society and History.
INDIAN OCEAN ISLANDS (*in part*)

A.J.Bo.   Arthur James Boucot. *Professor of Geology, Oregon State University, Corvallis. Authority on Silurian paleontology and stratigraphy.*
GEOCHRONOLOGY (*in part*)

A.J.Ca.   A.J. Cain. *Derby Professor of Zoology, University of Liverpool. Editor of* Function and Taxonomic Importance.
BIOLOGICAL SCIENCES, THE (*in part*)

A.J.E.   Armand J. Eardley (d. 1972). *Professor of Geology, University of Utah, Salt Lake City, 1965–70; Dean, College of Mines and Mineral Industries, 1954–65. Author of* Structural Geology of North America.
NORTH AMERICA (*in part*)

A.J.H.   Arlen J. Hansen. *Professor of English, University of the Pacific, Stockton, California.*
LITERATURE, THE ART OF (*in part*)

A.J.Ha.   Anna J. Harrison. *Professor of Chemistry, Mount Holyoke College, South Hadley, Massachusetts.*
PHYSICAL SCIENCES, THE (*in part*)

A.J.I.   Aaron J. Ihde. *Professor of Chemistry and History of Science, University of Wisconsin, Madison. Author of* The Development of Modern Chemistry.
PAULING, LINUS (Micropædia)

A.J.K.   Anthony John Kirby. *University Lecturer in Chemistry, University of Cambridge. Coauthor of* Organic Chemistry of Phosphorus.
CHEMICAL COMPOUNDS (*in part*)

A.J.P.   Anthony J. Podlecki. *Professor and Head, Department of Classics, University of British Columbia, Vancouver. Author of* The Political Background of Aeschylean Tragedy.
GREEK DRAMATISTS, THE CLASSICAL (*in part*)

A.J.P.T.   A.J.P. Taylor. *Lecturer in International History, University of Oxford, 1953–63; Fellow of Magdalen College, Oxford, 1938–76. Author of* Bismarck; The Struggle for Mastery in Europe, 1848–1918; *and others.*
BISMARCK (*in part*)
GERMANY (*in part*)

A.J.Sc.   Alvin J. Schumacher. *Author of* Thunder on Capitol Hill: The Life of Chief Justice Roger B. Taney.
TANEY, ROGER BROOKE (Micropædia)

A.J.Sh.   Aaron J. Sharp. *Alumni Distinguished Service Professor Emeritus of Botany, University of Tennessee,*

Knoxville. *Associate Editor,* Journal of the Hattori Botanical Laboratory, *devoted to bryology.*
BRYOPHYTES AND PRIMITIVE VASCULAR PLANTS (*in part*)

A.J.So.   Alan James Southward. *Zoologist and Senior Principal Scientific Officer, Marine Biological Association of the United Kingdom, Plymouth. Author of* Life on the Sea-Shore.
ECOSYSTEMS (*in part*)

A.J.T.   Arnold Joseph Toynbee (d. 1975). *Director of Studies, Royal Institute of International Affairs, London, 1925–55. Research Professor of International History, University of London, 1925–55. Author of* A Study of History *and many others.*
CAESAR (*in part*)
TIME (*in part*)

A.J.V.   Alan John Villiers (d. 1982). *Free-lance writer. President, Society for Nautical Research, London. Author of* Captain James Cook; The Way of a Ship; *and many others.*
COOK, JAMES (Micropædia)

A.Ka.   Adrienne L. Kaeppler. *Curator of Oceanic Ethnology, National Museum of Natural History, Smithsonian Institution, Washington, D.C. Lecturer in Music, University of Hawaii, Honolulu. Author of several publications on Polynesian dance.*
OCEANIC ARTS (*in part*)

A.K.C.   The Rt. Rev. Albert Kenneth Cragg. *Assistant Bishop, Diocese of Oxford. Reader in Religious Studies, University of Sussex, Brighton, England, 1973–78. Author of* Counsels in Contemporary Islam *and others.*
ISLĀM, MUḤAMMAD AND THE RELIGION OF (*in part*)

A.K.Ca.   Alan K. Campbell. *Vice Chairman of the Board and Executive Vice President, Management and Public Affairs, ARA Services, Inc., Philadelphia. Dean, Maxwell Graduate School of Citizenship and Public Affairs, Syracuse University, New York, 1969–76. Author of* The States and the Urban Crisis.
UNITED STATES OF AMERICA (*in part*)

A.K.Ch.   Abdel Kader Chanderli. *Senior Adviser, the Arab Fund, Kuwait. President and General Manager, C.A.M.E.L. Petroleum Company, Algiers, 1969–75. Ambassador of Algeria to the United Nations, 1962.*
NORTH AFRICA (*in part*)

A.Ke.   Annajane Kennard. *Former Librarian,* Straits Times Press, *Malaysia.*
EAST INDIES, THE (*in part*)
SOUTHEAST ASIA, MAINLAND (*in part*)

A.K.H.   A. Kent Hieatt. *Professor of English, University of Western Ontario, London. Author of* Chaucer, Spenser, Milton: Mythopoeic Continuities and Transformations; *coeditor of* Spenser's Selected Poetry.
SPENSER, EDMUND (*in part*)
(Micropædia)

A.K.McC.   Arthur Kilgore McComb (deceased). *Author of* The Baroque Painters of Italy *and others.*
SCULPTURE, THE HISTORY OF WESTERN (*in part*)

A.Kn.   Arthur Knight. *Professor of Cinema, University of Southern California, Los Angeles. Film Critic,* The Hollywood Reporter. *Author of* The Liveliest Art; The Hollywood Style.
CHAPLIN, CHARLIE (Micropædia)

A.Ko.   Arthur Koestler (d. 1983). *Author of* The Act of Creation; Darkness at Noon; *and many others.*
HUMOUR AND WIT

A.K.O.   Anders Kristian Orvin. *Director, Norwegian Polar Research Institute, Oslo, 1958–61.*
ARCTIC, THE (*in part*)

A.K.P.   A. Keith Pierce. *Astronomer, Solar Division, Kitt Peak National Observatory, Tucson, Arizona.*
SOLAR SYSTEM, THE (*in part*)

A.K.Pa.   Andrew K. Pawley. *Associate Professor of Linguistics, University of Auckland, New Zealand. Author of "Samoan Phrase Structure: The Morphology-Syntax of a Western Polynesian Language" in* Anthropological Linguistics *and other articles on the languages of Oceania.*
LANGUAGES OF THE WORLD (*in part*)

A.K.R.   A.K. Ramanujan. *Professor, Departments of South Asian Languages and Civilizations and of Linguistics and Committee on Social Thought, University of Chicago. Author of* Speaking of Śiva *and others.*
SOUTH ASIAN ARTS (*in part*)

A.K.S.   Arthur K. Solomon. *Professor of Biophysics, Medical School, Harvard University. Author of numerous scientific papers and of* Why Smash Atoms?
BIOLOGICAL SCIENCES, THE (*in part*)

A.K.Se.   Anna K. Seidel. *Member, French School of the Far East, Kyōto. Author of* La divinisation de Lao tseu dans le taoisme des Han.
TAOISM (*in part*)

Ak.W.   Akira Watanabe (deceased). *Chairman, Department of Geography, Ochanomizu Women's University, Tokyo. Editor of* Gazetteer of Japan.
JAPAN (*in part*)

A.Ky.   Ado Kyrou. *Writer and motion-picture and television director. Author of* Le Surréealisme au cinéma; Luis Buñuel; *and others.*
BUÑUEL, LUIS (Micropædia)

A.L.   Alberto Lecco. *Novelist, poet, essayist, and reviewer. Author of* Anteguerra *and others.*
MILAN

A.L. al-S.M.   Afaf Lutfi al-Sayyid Marsot. *Professor of History, University of California, Los Angeles. Author of* Egypt and Cromer.

CROMER, EVELYN BARING, 1ST EARL OF (Micropædia)

Al.B.   Alfredo Bosisio. *Professor of Medieval History, University of Pavia, Italy. Author of* Storia di Milano *and others.*

SFORZA, LUDOVICO (Micropædia)

A.L.B.   Arthur Llewellyn Basham (d. 1986). *Professor of Asian Civilizations, Australian National University, Canberra. Author of* History and Doctrines of the Ājīvikas *and others.*

HINDUISM (*in part*)

Al.Be.   Alfons Becker. *Professor of Medieval History, Johannes Gutenberg University of Mainz, West Germany. Author of* Papst Urban II (1088–1099) *and others.*

URBAN II (Micropædia)

Al.Bo.   Alan Bowness. *Director, Tate Gallery, London. Author of* Modern European Art; Recent British Painting.

COROT, CAMILLE (Micropædia)
MOORE, HENRY (*in part*) (Micropædia)

Al.C.   Alphonse Chapanis. *Professor of Psychology, Johns Hopkins University, Baltimore. Author of* Research Techniques in Human Engineering.

INDUSTRIAL ENGINEERING AND
   PRODUCTION MANAGEMENT (*in part*)

A.L.C.   Arthur L. Cohen. *Emeritus Professor of Botany and of Biological Sciences, Washington State University, Pullman; Director, Electron Microscope Center, 1962–79.*

PROTOPHYTES (*in part*)

A.Le.   Aureliano Leite (d. 1976). *President of the São Paulo Historical and Geographical Institute. Member of the São Paulo Academy of Letters. Member of the Brazilian Historical and Geographical Institute. Author of* História da Civilização Paulista.

SÃO PAULO (*in part*)

Al.G.   Albert Goodwin. *Emeritus Professor of Modern History, Victoria University of Manchester. Author of* The French Revolution *and others.*

LOUIS XVI (FRANCE) (Micropædia)
NECKER, JACQUES (Micropædia)

Al.Go.   Alan Gowans. *Professor of History in Art, University of Victoria, British Columbia. Author of* Building Canada, An Architectural History of Canadian Life; The Unchanging Arts; Images of American Living; *and others.*

ARCHITECTURE, THE ART OF (*in part*)

Al.Gr.   Alan Gregg, M.D. (d. 1957). *Vice President, Rockefeller Foundation, 1951–56; Director of Medical Sciences, 1930–51.*

MEDICINE (*in part*)

A.L.H.   Arnold Lionel Haskell (d. 1980). *Director, 1946–65, and Governor, 1966–77, Royal Ballet School; Governor, Royal Ballet, London, 1957–80. Author of* Ballet: A Complete Guide to Appreciation *and others.*

DANCE, THE ART OF (*in part*)

A.L.-Ho.   Alexander Marie Norbert Lernet-Holenia (d. 1976). *Novelist and playwright. Author of* Prinz Eugen *and others.*

EUGENE OF SAVOY (Micropædia)

A.Li.   Assar Lindbeck. *Professor of International Economics; Director, Institute for International Economics Studies, University of Stockholm. Author of* A Study in Monetary Analysis *and others.*

GOVERNMENT FINANCE (*in part*)

A.Lip.   Adolf Lippold. *Professor of History, University of Regensburg, West Germany. Author of* Theodosius der Grosse und seine Zeit *and others.*

THEODOSIUS I (ROMAN AND BYZANTINE
   EMPIRE) (Micropædia)

A.L.L.   Arthur L. Lange. *Vice President, Mincomp Corporation, Denver, Colorado. Former Editor of* Cave Studies. *Investigator of cavern development through experimental and theoretical studies.*

CONTINENTAL LANDFORMS (*in part*)

A.L.La.   Arthur Lon Labanauskas. *Research Editor, Science, Encyclopædia Britannica, Chicago, 1969–73.*

EARTH, THE (*in part*)

A.L.Ll.   Albert Lancaster Lloyd (d. 1982). *Ethnomusicologist. Member, Editorial Board, English Folk Dance and Song Society, London. Member, International Folk Music Council. Author of* Folk Song in England *and others.*

POPULAR ARTS (*in part*)

A.L.M.   Akinlawon Ladipo Mabogunje. *Former Professor and Head, Department of Geography, University of Ibadan, Nigeria. Vice President, International Geographical Union. Author of* Urbanization in Nigeria.

AFRICA (*in part*)

Al.N.   Allan Nevins (d. 1971). *Historian. Senior Research Associate, Henry E. Huntington Library and Art Gallery, San Marino, California, 1958–69. Dewitt Clinton Professor of History, Columbia University, 1931–58. Author of* The American States During and After the Revolution; The Emergence of Modern America; *and many biographies.*

WASHINGTON, GEORGE (*in part*)

Al.R.   Alfredo Riva. *Assistant Professor of Industrial Chemistry, University of Bologna, Italy.*

MALPIGHI, MARCELLO (*in part*)
   (Micropædia)

A.L.R.   Alexander L. Ringer. *Professor of Musicology, University of Illinois, Urbana. Author of* The Hunt as a Musical Topic: A Brief History of the Chasse.

MUSIC, THE ART OF (*in part*)

A.L.Ra.   Arthur Lionel Rawlings (d. 1959). *Chief Research Engineer, Bulova Research and Development Laboratories, Woodside, New York.*

NAVIGATION (*in part*)

Al.Re.   Albert Resis. *Associate Professor of History, Northern Illinois University, DeKalb. Author of articles on Russian and Soviet history.*

LENIN

Al.S.   Albert M. Soboul (d. 1982). *Professor of the History of the French Revolution, University of Paris I. Author of* Précis d'histoire de la révolution française *and others.*

CARNOT, LAZARE (Micropædia)
DANTON, GEORGES (Micropædia)
FRANCE (*in part*)

A.L.S.   A.L. Srivastava. *Emeritus Professor of History, Āgra College, Āgra University, India. Author of* The Mughal Empire *and others.*

INDIA (*in part*)

A.L.T.   Sir A. Landsborough Thomson (d. 1977). *President, British Ornithologists' Union, 1948–55. President, Zoological Society of London, 1954–60. Chairman of Trustees, British Museum (Natural History), London, 1967–69. Author of* Problems of Bird Migration.

BIRDS (*in part*)

A.L.Tu.   Anthony Leonid Turkevich. *James Franck Distinguished Service Professor of Chemistry, Enrico Fermi Institute and Department of Chemistry, University of Chicago. Author of papers on reactions of energetic particles with atomic nuclei.*

ATOMS (*in part*)

A.Lu.   Ante Lui. *Former Professor of Biology, University of Zagreb, Yugoslavia.*

BALKANS (*in part*)

A.L.W.   A.L. Waddams. *Manager, Market Research and Information Division, BP Chemicals (UK) Ltd., London. Author of* Chemicals from Petroleum *and others.*

INDUSTRIES, EXTRACTION AND
   PROCESSING (*in part*)

A.M.   Abdou Moumouni. *Director, Office of Solar Energy, Niamey, Niger. Author of* L'Education en Afrique.

EDUCATION, HISTORY OF (*in part*)

A.Ma.   Andrew Henry Robert Martindale. *Professor of Visual Arts, University of East Anglia, Norwich, England. Author of* Gothic Art.

ARCHITECTURE, THE HISTORY OF
   WESTERN (*in part*)
PAINTING, THE HISTORY OF WESTERN
   (*in part*)
SCULPTURE, THE HISTORY OF WESTERN
   (*in part*)

A.M.B.   Alfred M. Beeton. *Professor of Natural Resources and Atmospheric and Oceanic Science; Director, Great Lakes and Marine Waters Center, University of Michigan, Ann Arbor. Author of numerous scientific articles on the Great Lakes.*

NORTH AMERICA (*in part*)

A.M.-C.   Arturo Morales-Carrión. *Executive Director, Puerto Rican*

Endowment for the Humanities, San Juan. Author of Puerto Rico: A Political and Cultural History *and others.*

WEST INDIES, THE (*in part*)

A.M.C.L. Agnes M.C. Latham. *Former Reader in English, Bedford College, University of London. Editor of* The Poems of Sir Walter Ralegh *and others.*

RALEIGH, SIR WALTER (Micropædia)

A.M.D. A.M. Dauer. *Chairman, Department of Afro-American Studies, College of Music and Dramatic Arts, Graz, Austria. Author of* Studien zur Ethnogenese bei den Mangbetu.

AFRICAN ARTS (*in part*)

A.M.G. Alan M. Gaines. *Program Director for Experimental and Theoretical Geochemistry, National Science Foundation, Washington, D.C.*

MINERALS AND ROCKS (*in part*)

A.M.Ga. Aleksandr Mikhaylovich Gavrilov. *Senior Scientist, Leningrad Hydrological Institute.*

EUROPE (*in part*)

A.M.G.-G. Angel M. García-Gómez. *Head, Department of Spanish and Latin-American Studies, University College, University of London. Author of* The Legend of the Laughing Philosopher and Its Presence in Spanish Literature, 1500–1700.

SPANISH LITERATURE (*in part*)

A.Mi. Arthur Mizener. *Mellon Foundation Professor Emeritus of Humanities, Cornell University, Ithaca, New York. Author of* The Far Side of Paradise: A Biography of F. Scott Fitzgerald *and others.*

FITZGERALD, F. SCOTT (Micropædia)

A.M.J. The Rev. A.M. Jones. *Lecturer in African Music, School of Oriental and African Studies, University of London, 1952–66. Author of* Studies in African Music *and others.*

AFRICAN ARTS (*in part*)

A.M.N. Alois M. Nagler. *Henry McCormick Professor Emeritus of Dramatic History and Criticism, Yale University. Author of* Sources of Theatrical History *and others.*

BERNHARDT, SARAH (Micropædia)
DUSE, ELEONORA (Micropædia)

A.Mo. Alberto Monroy, M.D. *Former Director, Zoological Station, Naples. Author of* Chemistry and Physiology of Fertilization.

REPRODUCTION AND REPRODUCTIVE SYSTEMS (*in part*)

A.Moz. Asokendu Mozumder. *Associate Faculty Fellow, Radiation Laboratory and Department of Chemistry, University of Notre Dame, Indiana. Coauthor of* Advances in Radiation Chemistry.

RADIATION (*in part*)

A.M.P. Andrew M. Pullen. *Computer graphics researcher. Coauthor of* Creative Computer Graphics.

COMPUTERS (*in part*)

A.M.Q. Anthony M. Quinton, Baron Quinton. *President, Trinity College, Oxford; former Lecturer in Philosophy, University of Oxford. Chairman, British Library Board. Author of* The Nature of Things *and others.*

BACON, FRANCIS (*in part*)
PHILOSOPHICAL SCHOOLS AND
    DOCTRINES, WESTERN (*in part*)

A.M.Sl. Axel Mose Sløk. *Managing Director and Editor, Confederation of Danish Agricultural Employers' Associations, Copenhagen. Coauthor and editor of* The Danish Legislation 1968–71.

DENMARK (*in part*)

A.M.W. A.M. Winchester. *Emeritus Professor of Biology, University of Northern Colorado, Greeley. Author of* Genetics *and others.*

BIOLOGICAL SCIENCES, THE (*in part*)
GENETICS AND HEREDITY, THE
    PRINCIPLES OF (*in part*)

A.N. Alvin Novick. *Associate Professor of Biology, Yale University. Researcher on the biology of bats. Coauthor of* The World of Bats.

MAMMALS (*in part*)

A.Na. Arata Naka. *Former Professor of Japanese History of Education, University of Tokyo. Author of* The Formation of the Modern Textbook System.

EDUCATION, HISTORY OF (*in part*)

An.A.A. Anwar Abdel Aleem. *Professor of Biological Oceanography; Chairman, Department of Oceanography, University of Alexandria, Egypt.*

ASIA (*in part*)

An.B. Anthony Burgess. *Novelist and critic. Author of* A Clockwork Orange; The Novel Now; Urgent Copy.

LITERATURE, THE ART OF (*in part*)

An.Br. André Brincourt. *Director of Cultural Services,* Le Figaro, *Paris. Author of* André Malraux ou le temps du silence.

MALRAUX, ANDRÉ (Micropædia)

An.C.B. Andrew C. Brix. *Second Secretary, International Bureau of the Universal Postal Union, Berne, Switzerland.*

POSTAL SYSTEMS (*in part*)

A.Ne. Andries Nel. *Professor of Geography, University of Stellenbosch, South Africa. Author of* Stad en dorp; Die warm Reënstreke.

SOUTH AFRICA (*in part*)

A.Ni. Arnold Niederer. *Former Professor of European Ethnology, University of Zürich, Switzerland. Coauthor of* Atlas der schweizerischen Volkskunde.

EUROPE (*in part*)

A.N.J. Alexander Norman Jeffares. *Professor of English, University of Stirling, Scotland. Author of* W.B. Yeats:

Man and Poet; A New Commentary on the Poems of W.B. Yeats. *Editor of* Selected Poems and Prose: Whitman.

WHITMAN, WALT (Micropædia)

A.N.K. Aleksey Nilovich Kosarev. *Senior Scientist in Oceanography, Department of Geography, Moscow M.V. Lomonosov State University.*

ASIA (*in part*)

An.L. Antonino Lombardo. *Inspector General of National Archives, Rome. Professor of the Study of Archives, University of Rome. Coauthor of* Documenti del commercio veneziano nei secoli XI-XIII.

DANDOLO, ENRICO (Micropædia)

A.N.L.W. Arthur N.L. Wina. *Member of Parliament, 1962–68 and 1973– ; Minister of Finance, 1963–67; Minister of Education, 1967–68, Government of Northern Rhodesia, renamed Zambia in 1964.*

AFRICA (*in part*)

A.No. Alexander Nove. *Emeritus Professor of Economics, University of Glasgow, Scotland. Author of* An Economic History of the U.S.S.R.

ECONOMIC GROWTH AND PLANNING
    (*in part*)

An.Pa. Angel Palerm (d. 1980). *Director, Institute of Social Sciences, Universidad Iberoamericana, Mexico City.*

MEXICO (*in part*)

A.N.R.N. Alastair N.R. Niven. *Honorary Fellow, Institute of Commonwealth Studies, University of London. Special Assistant to the Secretary General, Association of Commonwealth Universities. Author of* D.H. Lawrence: The Novels *and others; editor of* The Commonwealth Writer Overseas.

AUSTRALIA AND NEW ZEALAND,
    LITERATURES OF (*in part*)

A.N.R.R. Arthur Napoleon Raymond Robinson. *Chairman, Tobago House of Assembly. Author of* The Mechanics of Independence: Patterns of Political and Economic Transformation in Trinidad and Tobago.

WEST INDIES, THE (*in part*)

An.S. Ailon Shiloh. *Professor and Director of Graduate Studies, Department of Anthropology, University of South Florida, Tampa. Editor of* Peoples and Cultures of the Middle East.

ASIA (*in part*)

An.Sc. Annemarie Schimmel. *Professor of Indo-Muslim Culture, Harvard University. Author of* Gabriel's Wing; Islamic Calligraphy; Mystical Dimensions of Islam; *and others.*

ISLĀM, MUḤAMMAD AND THE RELIGION
    OF (*in part*)
ISLĀMIC ARTS (*in part*)
JALĀL AD-DIN AR-RŪMI (Micropædia)

An.Sh. Ann Sheehy. *Research Associate, Central Asian Research Centre, London.*

UNION OF SOVIET SOCIALIST REPUBLICS
(in part)

A.N.W.   Alfred North Whitehead (d. 1947). *Professor of Philosophy, Harvard University, 1924–36. Author of* Process and Reality *and many others.*

PHILOSOPHIES OF THE BRANCHES OF
KNOWLEDGE (in part)

A.N.Y.   A.N. Yiannopoulos. *W.R. Irby Professor of Law, Tulane University, New Orleans. Author of* Civil Law Property *and others.*

PROPERTY LAW (in part)
TRANSPORTATION LAW (in part)

A.O.J.C.   A.O.J. Cockshut. *G.M. Young Lecturer in 19th-century English Literature, University of Oxford; Fellow of Hertford College, Oxford. Author of* The Achievement of Walter Scott; Anglican Attitudes: A Study of Victorian Religious Controversies; *and others.*

CARLYLE, THOMAS (Micropædia)
SCOTT, SIR WALTER, 1ST BARONET
(in part) (Micropædia)

A.Pa.   André Parrot (d. 1980). *Archaeologist. Director of the Louvre, Paris, 1968–72. Member of the Institute of France. Author of* Abraham and His Times *and others.*

ABRAHAM (Micropædia)

A.P.D.   Anatoly Petrovich Domanitsky. *Senior Scientist, Leningrad Hydrological Institute.*

EUROPE (in part)

A.P.E.   Adolphus Peter Elkin (d. 1979). *Professor of Anthropology, University of Sydney, 1934–56. Editor of* Archaeology and Physical Anthropology in Oceania.

AUSTRALIA (in part)

A.P.G.   Alberto Passos Guimarães. *Geography Editor,* Enciclopédia Mirador Internacional, *Rio de Janeiro.*

RIO DE JANEIRO

A.P.L.   Aleksandr Petrovich Lisitsin. *Head, Laboratory of Physical Methods of Research, Institute of Oceanology, Academy of Sciences of the U.S.S.R., Moscow. Author of* Processes of Recent Sedimentation in the Bering Sea; Sedimentation in the World Ocean; *and others.*

NORTH AMERICA (in part)

A.P.M.   Aleksandr Pavlovich Muranov. *Senior Scientist, Leningrad Hydrological Institute. Author of* Velichayshiye reki mira.

ASIA (in part)

A.P.Ma.   Arthur Paul Mattuck. *Professor of Mathematics, Massachusetts Institute of Technology, Cambridge.*

MATHEMATICS, THE HISTORY OF
(in part)

A.Q.Y.   Angel Quintana Yoingco. *Executive Director, National Tax Research Center, Manila, Philippines. Consultant, Graduate School, Lyceum of the Philippines, Manila. Coauthor of* Fiscal Systems and Practices in Selected

Asian Countries *and others.*

TAXATION (in part)

A.R.   Alan Ryalls. *Former Editor,* Camping and Caravanning *magazine, Camping Club of Great Britain and Ireland. Author of* Modern Camping.

CAMPING (Micropædia)

A.Ra.   Agatha Ramm. *Former Fellow of Somerville College, Oxford; former Lecturer in Modern History, University of Oxford.*

GERMANY (in part)

Ar.B.   Arnaldo Bruschi. *Professor of the History of Architecture, University of Rome. Author of* Bramante architetto.

BRAMANTE, DONATO (Micropædia)

A.R.B.   A. Richard Baldwin. *Vice President and Executive Director of Research, Cargill, Inc., Minneapolis, Minnesota, 1964–73. Editor,* Journal of the American Oil Chemists' Society.

FOOD PROCESSING (in part)

Ar.Br.   Sir Arthur Bryant (d. 1985). *Author of* Samuel Pepys *and many others.*

PEPYS, SAMUEL (Micropædia)

A.R.Bu.   Andrew Robert Burn. *Visiting Professor, A College Year in Athens, Inc., 1969–72. Reader in Ancient History, University of Glasgow, 1965–69. Author of* Persia and the Greeks *and others.*

THEMISTOCLES (Micropædia)

A.R.C.   A. Robert Caponigri (d. 1983). *Professor of Philosophy, University of Notre Dame, Indiana. Author of* History and Liberty: The Historical Writings of Benedetto Croce.

CROCE, BENEDETTO (Micropædia)

Ar.D.   Arthur J.M. Doucy. *Professor of Social Economics; former Director, Institute of Sociology, Free University of Brussels. Author of* Traité d'économie sociale.

LOW COUNTRIES, THE (in part)

A.Re.   Alan Reed (deceased). *Head, Department of Architecture, Faculty of Construction Technology and Design, Polytechnic of the South Bank, London. Fellow of the Royal Institute of British Architects.*

BUILDING CONSTRUCTION (in part)

Ar.H.   Rabbi Arthur Hertzberg. *Adjunct Professor of History, Columbia University. Author of* Being Jewish in America *and others. Editor of* The Zionist Idea.

JUDAISM (in part)

A.-R.H.   Abdul-Rahman Hamidé. *Professor of Geography, Damascus University. Author of* La Région d'Alep.

SYRIA (in part)

Ar.Hü.   Arthur Hübscher. *Former Director, Schopenhauer Archives, Frankfurt. Senior President, International Schopenhauer Society, Frankfurt. Author of many books on Schopenhauer. Editor of* Schopenhauer's Works.

SCHOPENHAUER, ARTHUR (Micropædia)

A.Ri.   Alan Rich. *Music Critic,* Newsweek *magazine. Author of* Music: Mirror of the Arts *and others.*

MUSIC, THE ART OF (in part)

A.R.J.   Alan R. Jefferson. *Light Orchestral Manager, British Broadcasting Corporation, London, 1968–73. Professor of Vocal Interpretation, Guildhall School of Music and Drama, London, 1967–74. Author of* The Lieder of Strauss *and others.*

STRAUSS, RICHARD (Micropædia)

A.R.K.   Alan Roy Katritzky. *Kenan Professor of Organic Chemistry, University of Florida, Gainesville. Coauthor of* Principles of Heterocyclic Chemistry.

CHEMICAL COMPOUNDS (in part)

A.R.Ki.   Albert Roland Kiralfy. *Emeritus Professor of Law, King's College, University of London. Author of* The English Legal System.

LEGAL SYSTEMS, THE EVOLUTION OF
MODERN WESTERN (in part)

Ar.Kn.   Arthur Kelman. *L.R. Jones Professor of Plant Pathology, University of Wisconsin, Madison. Editor of* Sourcebook of Exercises in Plant Pathology.

DISEASE (in part)

Ar.L.S.   Arthur L. Schawlow. *Professor of Physics, Stanford University, California. Co-winner, Nobel Prize for Physics, 1981, for the development of laser spectroscopy.*

LASER (in part) (Micropædia)
MASER (in part) (Micropædia)

Ar.M.   Arthur Mitzman. *Professor of History, University of Amsterdam. Author of* The Iron Cage: An Historical Interpretation of Max Weber.

WEBER, MAX (in part) (Micropædia)

A.R.M.   Alexander Reginald Myers (d. 1980). *Professor of Medieval History, University of Liverpool, 1967–80. Author of* The Household of Edward IV.

EDWARD IV (ENGLAND AND GREAT
BRITAIN) (Micropædia)
HENRY VII (ENGLAND) (in part)
(Micropædia)

A.R.McB.   Alexander R. McBirney. *Professor of Geology, Center for Volcanology, University of Oregon, Eugene. Author of* Igneous Petrology.

MINERALS AND ROCKS (in part)

A.R.Mi.   Andrew Ronald Mitchell. *Professor of Numerical Analysis, University of Dundee, Scotland. Author of* Computational Methods in Partial Differential Equations.

NUMERICAL ANALYSIS (in part)

A.Ro.   Arnold Rood. *Professor of Dramatic Art, Dowling College, Oakdale, New York. Author of* Edward Gordon Craig, Artist of the Theatre, 1872–1966; *coauthor of* Edward Gordon Craig: A Bibliography; *editor of* Gordon Craig on

Movement and Dance.
CRAIG, EDWARD GORDON
(Micropædia)

A.R.P. Allison R. Palmer. *Centennial Science Program Coordinator, Geological Society of America, Boulder, Colorado. Professor of Paleontology, State University of New York at Stony Brook, 1966–80. Coauthor of* Cambrian of the New World.
GEOCHRONOLOGY (*in part*)

Ar.R. Arthur Robinson, M.D. *Professor of Biochemistry, Biophysics, and Genetics and of Pediatrics, University of Colorado, Denver. Director, Cytogenetics Laboratory, National Jewish Hospital and Research Center—National Asthma Center, Denver.*
GENETICS AND HEREDITY, THE
PRINCIPLES OF (*in part*)

A.R.R. Allien R. Russon. *Emeritus Professor of Management, College of Business, University of Utah, Salt Lake City. Author of* Methods of Teaching Shorthand.
WRITING (*in part*)

A.R.S. Alarich R. Schultz. *Professor of Botany, Federal University of Rio Grande do Sul, Pôrto Alegre, Brazil. Author of* Estudo Prático da Botânica Geral.
SOUTH AMERICA (*in part*)

Ar.Sp. Arnold Spekke (d. 1972). *Author of* History of Latvia *and others.*
UNION OF SOVIET SOCIALIST REPUBLICS
(*in part*)

A.R.W. Almon Robert Wright. *Senior Historian, U.S. Department of State, Washington, D.C., 1958–66. Coeditor of* Foreign Relations: The American Republics, 1941–48.
CENTRAL AMERICA (*in part*)

A.S. Alvin Seiff. *Senior Staff Scientist, Space Science Division, Ames Research Center, National Aeronautics and Space Administration, Moffett Field, California. Author of scientific papers on the atmospheres of Mars and Venus.*
SOLAR SYSTEM, THE (*in part*)

A.S.A. Ass'ad Sulaiman Abdo. *Lecturer in Geography; President of the Saudi Geographical Society, University of Riyadh, Saudi Arabia. Author of* Land and Air Transport in Saudi Arabia.
MECCA AND MEDINA (*in part*)

As.B. Asa Briggs, Baron Briggs. *Provost of Worcester College, University of Oxford. Author of* The Age of Improvement, 1783–1867 *and others.*
COBDEN, RICHARD (Micropædia)
UNITED KINGDOM (*in part*)

A.Sc. Aaron Scharf. *Professor of Art History, Open University, Milton Keynes, England, 1969–82. Author of* Art and Photography; Pioneers of Photography.
CARTIER-BRESSON, HENRI (Micropædia)

A.S.Cu. Alan S. Curtis. *Professor of Music, University of California, Berkeley. Author of* Sweelinck's

Keyboard Music.
RAMEAU, JEAN-PHILIPPE (Micropædia)

A.S.D. A.S. Davidsohn. *Consulting Chemist. Coauthor of* Soap Manufacture; Synthetic Detergents.
INDUSTRIES, CHEMICAL PROCESS (*in part*)

A.Se. Amulya Chandra Sen. *Former Editor,* The Indo-Asian Culture. *Author of* Asoka's Edicts *and others.*
AŚOKA (Micropædia)

As.F. Astrid Friis (d. 1966). *Professor of History, University of Copenhagen.*
DENMARK (*in part*)

A.S.F. Angus Stewart Fletcher. *Distinguished Professor of English and Comparative Literature, City University of New York. Author of* Allegory: The Theory of a Symbolic Mode *and others.*
LITERATURE, THE ART OF (*in part*)

A.Sg. Alfred Steinberg. *Free-lance writer. Author of* Man from Missouri: The Life and Times of Harry S. Truman *and others.*
TRUMAN, HARRY S. (Micropædia)

A.S.G. Arthur S. Gelston, Jr. *Former Assistant in History, University of California, Berkeley.*
BRAZIL (*in part*)

A.Sh. Amnon Shiloah. *Professor of Musicology, Hebrew University of Jerusalem. Author of* The Theory of Music in Arabic Writings *and others.*
ISLĀMIC ARTS (*in part*)

A.Si. Alfredo Siragusa. *Former Director, School of Geographical Sciences, University of Salvador, Buenos Aires. Author of* Geomorfología de la provincia de Buenos Aires *and others.*
ARGENTINA (*in part*)

A.S.K. Arvid S. Kapelrud. *Professor of Old Testament, University of Oslo. Author of* Israel.
AARON (Micropædia)

A.S.K.-F. Alexander Sydney Kanya-Forstner. *Professor of History, York University, Downsview, Ontario. Author of* The Conquest of the Western Sudan.
FAIDHERBE, LOUIS (Micropædia)

A.S.L. Arthur Stanley Link. *George H. Davis '86 Professor of American History; Director of the Woodrow Wilson Papers, Princeton University. Author of* Wilson. *Editor of* The Papers of Woodrow Wilson.
UNITED STATES OF AMERICA
(*in part*)

A.S.M. Arve Sverre Moen (d. 1976). *Cultural Editor,* Arbeiderbladet *(newspaper), Oslo. Member of the Board, Edvard Munch Museum, Oslo. Author of* Edvard Munch *and others.*
MUNCH, EDVARD (Micropædia)

A.So. Angelo Solmi. *Film critic,* Oggi *(weekly literary periodical). Former Managing Editor, Rizzoli Editore, Milan. Author of* Storia di Federico Fellini *and others.*

FELLINI, FEDERICO (*in part*)
(Micropædia)

A.Sp. Athelstan Spilhaus. *Special Assistant to the Administrator, National Oceanic and Atmospheric Administration, U.S. Department of Commerce, Washington, D.C. 1974– 80. Author of* Waste Management and Control.
CONSERVATION OF NATURAL
RESOURCES (*in part*)

A.S.Pa. Ante S. Pavelić. *Writer. Author of* Dr. Ante Trumbić: Problemi hrvatsko-srpskih odnosa *and others.*
YUGOSLAVIA (*in part*)

A.S.R. Alfred S. Romer (d. 1973). *Alexander Agassiz Professor of Zoology, Harvard University, 1947–65.*
SIMPSON, GEORGE GAYLORD
(Micropædia)

A.St. Anthony Standen. *Executive Editor,* Kirk-Othmer Encyclopedia of Chemical Technology, *New York City, 1963–70. Author of* Science Is a Sacred Cow.
INDUSTRIES, CHEMICAL PROCESS
(*in part*)

A.S.Wi. Arthur Strong Wightman. *Thomas D. Jones Professor of Mathematical Physics, Princeton University.*
SUBATOMIC PARTICLES (*in part*)

A.T. Armen Leonovich Takhtajan. *Director; Chief, Department of Higher Plants, Komarov Botanical Institute, Academy of Sciences of the U.S.S.R., Leningrad. Author of* Flowering Plants: Origin and Dispersal.
ANGIOSPERMS (*in part*)

A.Ta. Allen Tate (d. 1979). *Poet and critic. Regents' Professor of English, University of Minnesota, Minneapolis, 1966–68. Editor of* T.S. Eliot: The Man and His Work, A Critical Evaluation by Twenty-six Distinguished Writers *and others.*
ELIOT, T.S. (Micropædia)

A.Te. Ahmet Temir. *Emeritus Professor of Turcology and Mongolian Language, University of Ankara.*
TURKEY AND ANCIENT ANATOLIA
(*in part*)

A.T.L. Anthony Thornton Luttrell. *Former Assistant Director, British School at Rome.*
ITALY (*in part*)

A.T.v.M. Arthur Taylor von Mehren. *Story Professor of Law, Harvard University. Author of* The Civil Law System.
BUSINESS LAW (*in part*)

A.Ty. Andrew Tracey. *Director, International Library of African Music, Rhodes University, Grahamstown, South Africa. Editor,* African Music *(journal of the African Music Society).*
AFRICAN ARTS (*in part*)

A.U. Arne Unhjem. *Professor of Philosophy, Wagner College, Staten*

Island, New York. Author of Dynamics of Doubt: A Preface to Tillich.
TILLICH, PAUL (Micropædia)

Au.G.   Aubrey Gorbman. *Professor of Zoology, University of Washington, Seattle. Coauthor of* Textbook of Comparative Endocrinology; *editor of* General and Comparative Endocrinology.
ENDOCRINE SYSTEMS (*in part*)

Au.L.R.   Austin L. Rand (d. 1982). *Research Associate, Archbold Biological Station, Lake Placid, Florida. Chief Curator of Zoology, Field Museum of Natural History, Chicago, 1955–70. Author of* Ornithology: An Introduction; *coauthor of* Birds of New Guinea.
BIRDS (*in part*)

Au.T.   Auguste Toussaint. *Director of Mauritius Archives, Port Louis, 1945–70. Author of* History of the Indian Ocean *and others.*
INDIAN OCEAN ISLANDS (*in part*)

A.Va.   Amry Vandenbosch. *Emeritus Professor of Political Science, University of Kentucky, Lexington. Coauthor of* The United Nations.
UNITED NATIONS (*in part*)

A.v.B.   Andres R.F.T. von Brandt. *Emeritus Professor of Fish Catching Techniques, University of Hamburg. Director, Institute for Fish Catching Techniques, Ministry for Food and Agriculture, Hamburg, 1936–71. Author of* Fish Catching Methods of the World.
FISHING AND MARINE PRODUCTS, COMMERCIAL (*in part*)

A.V.B.N.   A.V.B. Norman. *Master of the Armouries, Tower of London. Author of* Arms and Armour *and others.*
WAR, THE TECHNOLOGY OF (*in part*)

A.V.D.   A. Vibert Douglas. *Emeritus Professor of Astronomy, Queen's University at Kingston, Ontario. Author of* Arthur Stanley Eddington.
EDDINGTON, SIR ARTHUR STANLEY (Micropædia)

A.Vo.   Arthur Voyce. *Historian of Russian Art and Architecture. Author of* The Art and Architecture of Medieval Russia *and others.*
ARCHITECTURE, THE HISTORY OF WESTERN (*in part*)
PAINTING, THE HISTORY OF WESTERN (*in part*)
SCULPTURE, THE HISTORY OF WESTERN (*in part*)

A.W.   Alan Walker. *Professor of Music, McMaster University, Hamilton, Ontario. Author of* An Anatomy of Musical Criticism; A Study in Musical Analysis; *and others.*
MUSIC, THE ART OF (*in part*)

A.Wa.   Andrew Warren. *Senior Lecturer in Geography, University College, University of London.*
CONTINENTAL LANDFORMS (*in part*)

A.W.C.   Alan William Cuthbert. *Sheild Professor of Pharmacology, University*

of Cambridge. Editor of Calcium and Cellular Function.
DRUGS AND DRUG ACTION (*in part*)

A.W.G.   Alan William Gentry. *Principal Scientific Officer, Department of Palaeontology, British Museum (Natural History), London. Author of numerous research papers on Old World hoofed mammals.*
MAMMALS (*in part*)

A.W.Ge.   Arnold Wycombe Gomme (d. 1959). *Professor of Greek, University of Glasgow, 1946–57. Author of* Historical Commentary on Thucydides; Greece; *and others.*
THUCYDIDES (Micropædia)

A.W.Gr.   Alic William Gray (d. 1981). *Head, Agricultural Advisory and Development Section, Electricity Council, London, 1966–70; Principal Assistant, 1948–65.*
AGRICULTURE, THE HISTORY OF (*in part*)

A.Wh.   Alwyne Wheeler. *Principal Scientific Officer, Fish Section, Zoology Department, British Museum (Natural History), London. Author of* Fishes of the World *and others.*
FISHES (*in part*)

A.W.J.   A. Walter James. *Principal, St. Catharine's, Windsor, England, 1974–82. Editor,* The Times *(London)* Educational Supplement, 1952–69. *Author of* The Christian in Politics.
ACTON OF ALDENHAM, JOHN EMERICH EDWARD DALBERG ACTON, 1ST BARON (Micropædia)

A.W.Ke.   A.W. Keuffel (deceased). *Director, Vice President, and Secretary, Keuffel and Esser Company (manufacturers of slide rules and other equipment), Morristown, New Jersey.*
MATHEMATICS, THE HISTORY OF (*in part*)

A.W.L.   Albert William Levi. *David May Distinguished University Professor Emeritus of Humanities, Washington University, St. Louis, Missouri. Author of* Philosophy and the Modern World.
PHILOSOPHY, THE HISTORY OF WESTERN (*in part*)

A.W.M.   Anne Wood Murray. *Emeritus Curator of American Costume, Division of Costume, Department of Social and Cultural History, National Museum of American History, Smithsonian Institution, Washington, D.C.*
DRESS AND ADORNMENT (*in part*)

A.Wo.   Albert Wolfson. *Professor of Biological Sciences, Northwestern University, Evanston, Illinois.*
BEHAVIOUR, ANIMAL (*in part*)

A.W.P.   Alois Wilhelm Podhajsky (d. 1973). *Director, Spanish Riding School of Vienna, 1939–64. Winner, Olympic Bronze Medal for Dressage (equestrian event), 1936. Author of* The Complete Training of Horse and Rider *and others.*
HORSES AND HORSEMANSHIP (*in part*)

A.W.R.   Alan Wescott Richards. *Development Manager, Imperial Smelting Ltd., Bristol, England. Author of articles on zinc smelting and zinc metallurgy.*
INDUSTRIES, EXTRACTION AND PROCESSING (*in part*)

A.W.Re.   Allen Walker Read. *Emeritus Professor of English, Columbia University. Author of* "Approaches to Lexicography and Semantics" *in* Current Trends in Linguistics.
ENCYCLOPAEDIAS AND DICTIONARIES (*in part*)

A.W.S.   Albert Wilbur Schlechten (d. 1984). *Director, W.J. Kroll Institute for Extractive Metallurgy, Colorado School of Mines, Golden.*
INDUSTRIES, EXTRACTION AND PROCESSING (*in part*)

A.W.T.   A.W. Tucker. *Albert Baldwin Dod Professor Emeritus of Mathematics, Princeton University. Coeditor of* Contributions to the Theory of Games.
GAME THEORY (*in part*)

A.Y.   Atsuchiko Yoshida. *Professor of Comparative Mythology, Gakushuin University, Tokyo. Author of* Origins of Japanese Myths *and others.*
LITERATURE, THE ART OF (*in part*)

Ay.Sy.   Anthony Sillery (d. 1976). *Secretary to the Curators of the Taylor Institution, University of Oxford, 1951–70. Resident Commissioner, Bechuanaland Protectorate, 1947–50.*
SOUTHERN AFRICA (*in part*)

A.Zy.   Antoni Zygmund. *Gustavus F. and Anne M. Swift Distinguished Service Professor Emeritus of Mathematics, University of Chicago. World authority on Fourier analysis. Author of* Trigonometric Series; *coauthor of* Analytic Functions.
ANALYSIS (IN MATHEMATICS) (*in part*)

B.   Robert Norman William Blake, Baron Blake. *Provost, Queen's College, University of Oxford. Author of* The Conservative Party from Peel to Churchill *and others.*
ASQUITH, H.H., 1ST EARL OF OXFORD AND ASQUITH (Micropædia)
DISRAELI, BENJAMIN, EARL OF BEACONSFIELD (*in part*) (Micropædia)
LLOYD GEORGE, DAVID (Micropædia)

B.A.   Bruno Accordi. *Former Director, Geology and Paleontology Institute, University of Rome. Author of numerous publications on geology.*
EUROPE (*in part*)

B.A.B.   Bruce A. Bolt. *Professor of Seismology, University of California, Berkeley. Author of* Earthquakes: A Primer *and others.*
EARTHQUAKES

B.A.C.   Bruce Alan Carr. *Music Administrator, Pittsburgh Symphony*

Orchestra.
MUSIC, THE ART OF (*in part*)

B.A.D. Boyce A. Drummond, Jr.
*Professor of History; Dean, School of
Liberal Arts, Henderson State University,
Arkadelphia, Arkansas. Author of*
Arkansas, Politics and Government.
UNITED STATES OF AMERICA (*in part*)

**B.A.F. Boris Aleksandrovich
Fedorovich.** *Senior Scientist, Institute of
Geography, Academy of Sciences of the
U.S.S.R., Moscow.*
ASIA (*in part*)

B.A.J. Benjamin A. Jones, Jr.
*Professor of Agricultural Engineering,
University of Illinois, Urbana. Coauthor
of* Engineering Applications in
Agriculture.
FARMING AND AGRICULTURAL
  TECHNOLOGY (*in part*)

B.A.L.C. Bryan A. L. Cranstone.
*Curator, Pitt-Rivers Museum,
Oxford, England. 1976–85. Author of*
Melanesia.
EAST INDIES, THE (*in part*)

B.Am. Barthélemy Amengual. *Editor,*
Études Cinématographiques. *Author of*
René Clair; Clés pour le cinéma.
CLAIR, RENÉ (Micropædia)

B.A.M. Boyd A. Martin. *Distinguished
Borah Professor of Political Science;
Director, Boyd and Grace Martin
Institute of Human Behavior; Director,
Bureau of Public Affairs Research,
University of Idaho, Moscow. Author of*
Idaho Voting Trends *and others.*
UNITED STATES OF AMERICA (*in part*)

B.A.R. Barbara A. Ringer. *Attorney.
Former Register of Copyrights, Copyright
Office, Library of Congress, Washington,
D.C. Coauthor of* Copyrights.
PROPERTY LAW (*in part*)

B.A.-S. Brian Abel-Smith. *Professor of
Social Administration, London School
of Economics and Political Science,
University of London. Author of* The
Poor and the Poorest *and others.*
SOCIAL WELFARE (*in part*)

B.As. Bernard Ashmole. *Lincoln
Professor of Classical Archaeology and
Art, University of Oxford, 1956–61.*
PAINTING, THE HISTORY OF WESTERN
  (*in part*)
SCULPTURE, THE HISTORY OF WESTERN
  (*in part*)

B.A.St. Barbara A. Standley.
*Free-lance editor. Former Associate
Editor,* Encyclopædia Britannica,
Chicago.
INDIA (*in part*)

B.B. Bela Balassa. *Professor of
Political Economy, Johns Hopkins
University, Baltimore, Maryland.
Consultant, International Bank for
Reconstruction and Development.
Author of* Trade Liberalization Among
Industrial Countries: Objectives and
Alternatives *and others.*
INTERNATIONAL TRADE (*in part*)

B.Be. Bernard Beckerman (d. 1985).
*Brander Matthews Professor of Dramatic
Literature, Columbia University, 1977–
85. President, American Society for
Theatre Research, 1973–79. Author of*
Shakespeare at the Globe; Dynamics of
Drama; *and others.*
THEATRICAL PRODUCTION (*in part*)

B.B.H. Bruce B. Hanshaw. *Assistant
Director for Research, Geological
Survey, U.S. Department of the Interior,
Reston, Virginia. An authority on the
geochemistry of groundwater.*
MINERALS AND ROCKS (*in part*)

B.Bl. Brand Blanshard. *Sterling
Professor Emeritus of Philosophy, Yale
University. Author of* The Nature of
Thought; Reason and Analysis.
PHILOSOPHICAL SCHOOLS AND
  DOCTRINES, WESTERN (*in part*)

B.Ble. Brebis Bleaney. *Dr. Lee's
Professor Emeritus of Experimental
Philosophy, University of Oxford.
Coauthor of* Electricity and Magnetism
and others.
ELECTRICITY AND MAGNETISM (*in part*)

B.Bo. Baruch Boxer. *Professor of
Geography and Human Ecology,
Rutgers University, New Brunswick, New
Jersey. Author of* Ocean Shipping in the
Evolution of Hong Kong.
CHINA (*in part*)
SHANGHAI
TIENTSIN

**B.Br. Barbara Buckmaster (the
Hon. Mrs. Barbara Miller)** (d. 1966).
*Writer on Balkan affairs. Member of
the Staff, Foreign Research and Press
Service, Royal Institute of International
Affairs, London.*
ROMANIA (*in part*)
UNION OF SOVIET SOCIALIST REPUBLICS
  (*in part*)

B.C. Barnaby Conrad. *Free-lance
writer. Student of bullfighting with Juan
Belmonte, 1943–46; bullfighter, 1946.
Author of* Matador; La Fiesta Brava;
Encyclopedia of Bullfighting;
and others.
BULLFIGHTING (Micropædia)

B.Ch. Brian Chapman (d. 1981).
*Professor of Government, Victoria
University of Manchester, England,
1961–81. Author of* The Profession of
Government *and others.*
PUBLIC ADMINISTRATION (*in part*)

B.C.H. Bruce C. Heezen (d. 1977).
*Associate Professor of Geology,
Lamont-Doherty Geological Observatory,
Columbia University, Palisades, New
York, 1964–77. Coauthor of* The Floors
of the Oceans.
OCEANS (*in part*)

B.Cr. Bosley Crowther (d. 1981).
*Creative consultant, Columbia Pictures,
New York City, 1968–73. Screen critic
and editor,* The New York Times, *1940–
68. Author of* The Great Films: Fifty
Golden Years of Motion Pictures.
DISNEY, WALT (Micropædia)

B.C.R. Bruce Carlisle Robertson.
*Specialist in Oriental studies. Former
Instructor in Philosophy and Religion,
Towson State College, Maryland.*
RAY, RAMMOHAN (Micropædia)

B.C.S. B. Charlotte Schreiber.
*Professor of Geology, Queens College,
City University of New York, Flushing.
Coeditor of* Sedimentology, "Earth
Science Series."
ASIA (*in part*)

B.C.So. Brian C. Southam. *Publisher,
Athlone Press, London. Author of*
Jane Austen's Literary Manuscripts;
Tennyson; *and others.*
AUSTEN, JANE (*in part*) (Micropædia)

B.D.H. Baxter D. Honeycutt. *Manager,
Exploration Support, ARCO Oil and Gas
Company, Dallas, Texas.*
ENGINEERING (*in part*)

B.Di. Bern Dibner. *Director, Burndy
Library, Norwalk, Connecticut. Author of*
Heralds of Science.
GALVANI, LUIGI (Micropædia)

B.D.N. B. Davie Napier. *Professor
of Bible, Yale University. President,
Pacific School of Religion, Berkeley,
California, 1972–78. Author of* Prophets
in Perspective *and others.*
EZEKIEL (Micropædia)

B.E. Blake Ehrlich (d. 1974).
Free-lance writer. Author of Paris on
the Seine; London on the Thames; *and
many others.*
ATHENS (*in part*)
DUBLIN
EDINBURGH
FLORENCE
ISTANBUL
LISBON
LONDON (*in part*)
MADRID (*in part*)
MARSEILLE
NAPLES
PARIS (*in part*)
ROME (*in part*)
VENICE (*in part*)
VIENNA (*in part*)

Be.J. Bernard Jaffe. *Free-lance science
writer. Chairman, Science Department,
James Madison High School, Brooklyn,
New York, 1944–58. Author of* Men of
Science in America.
FERMI, ENRICO (Micropædia)

B.E.J.P. Bernard E.J. Pagel. *Deputy
Chief Scientific Officer, Royal Greenwich
Observatory, Herstmonceux, England.
Visiting Professor of Astronomy,
University of Sussex, Brighton,
England.*
PHYSICAL SCIENCES, THE (*in part*)

Be.M. Bernd Magnus. *Professor of
Philosophy, University of California,
Riverside. Executive Secretary, North
American Nietzsche Society. Author of*
Nietzsche's Existential Imperative.
NIETZSCHE

B.E.M. Bernard E. Meland. *Emeritus
Professor of Constructive Theology,
University of Chicago. Author of* The

Realities of Faith *and others.*
OTTO, RUDOLF (Micropædia)

B.E.McK. Brian E. McKnight.
*Professor of History, University of
Hawaii, Honolulu. Author of* Village and
Bureaucracy in Southern Sung China.
CHINA (*in part*)

Be.N. Beaumont Newhall. *Visiting
Professor of Art, University of New
Mexico, Albuquerque. Director, George
Eastman House, Rochester, New York,
1958–71. Author of* The History of
Photography; Latent Image; *and others.*
PHOTOGRAPHY (*in part*)

B.E.N. Brian E. Newton. *Professor of
Linguistics, Simon Fraser University,
Burnaby, British Columbia. Author of*
The Generative Interpretation of Dialect:
A Study of Modern Greek Phonology.
LANGUAGES OF THE WORLD (*in part*)

B.F. Basil Alais Fletcher (d. 1983).
*Professor and Director, Institute of
Education, University of Leeds, England,
1961–67. Author of* A Philosophy for the
Teacher *and others.*
EDUCATION, HIGHER

B.F.S. Bradford Fuller Swan (d. 1976).
Theatre and Art Critic, The Providence
Journal and Evening Bulletin,
Rhode Island.
UNITED STATES OF AMERICA (*in part*)

B.F.W. Brian Frederick Windley.
*Professor and Head, Department
of Geology, University of Leicester,
England. Author of* The Evolving
Continents.
EARTH SCIENCES, THE (*in part*)

B.G. Branko Grünbaum. *Professor of
Mathematics, University of Washington,
Seattle. Author of* Convex Polytopes.
COMBINATORICS AND COMBINATORIAL
    GEOMETRY (*in part*)

B.Ga. Balwant Gargi. *Playwright.
Former Professor and Head, Department
of Indian Theatre, Panjab University,
Chandigarh, India. Author of* Folk
Theater of India *and others.*
SOUTH ASIAN ARTS (*in part*)

B.Ge. Barbara Gelb. *Writer. Coauthor
of* O'Neill.
O'NEILL, EUGENE (*in part*)

B.G.M. Barbara G. Mertz. *Historian
and writer. Author of* Temples, Tombs
and Hieroglyphs *and others.*
MEMPHIS (EGYPT) (Micropædia)

B.Gr. Benny Green. *Record reviewer,
British Broadcasting Corporation. Jazz
Critic,* The Observer, *London, 1958–77.
Author of* The Reluctant Art; Drums in
My Tears; *and others.*
MUSICAL FORMS AND GENRES (*in part*)

B.G.S. Bernice Giduz Schubert.
*Curator, Arnold Arboretum, Harvard
University. Coauthor of* The Begoniaceae
of Colombia.
ANGIOSPERMS (*in part*)

B.Gu. B. Gungaadash. *Head of section,
Institute of Geography and Geocryology,*

*Academy of Sciences of the Mongolian
People's Republic, Ulaanbaatar.*
MONGOLIA (*in part*)

B.H. The Rev. Basil Hall. *Fellow and
Dean, St. John's College, University
of Cambridge, 1974–79. Professor
of Ecclesiastical History, Victoria
University of Manchester,1968–74.*
CALVINISM, CALVIN AND (*in part*)

B.H.C. Ben H. Caudle. *B.J. Lancaster
Professor of Petroleum Engineering,
University of Texas at Austin. Author of*
Reservoir Engineering Fundamentals.
INDUSTRIES, EXTRACTION AND
    PROCESSING (*in part*)

B.-h.H. Bae-ho Hahn. *Professor of
Political Science, Korea University,
Seoul. Author of* Theoretical Political
Science.
KOREA (*in part*)

B.H.J. Burgess H. Jennings. *Emeritus
Professor of Mechanical Engineering,
Northwestern University, Evanston,
Illinois. Author of* Environmental
Engineering *and others.*
REFRIGERATION (*in part*)

B.H.M. Brian H. Mason. *Chairman,
Department of Mineral Sciences,
Smithsonian Institution, Washington,
D.C. An authority on the distribution of
elements in the Earth's crust. Author of*
Principles of Geochemistry.
CHEMICAL ELEMENTS (*in part*)

B.H.W. Brian H. Warmington. *Reader
in Ancient History, University of Bristol,
England. Author of* The Roman North
African Provinces *and others.*
NORTH AFRICA (*in part*)

B.H.We. Byron H. Webb. *Consultant
in dairy technology. Former Chief, Dairy
Products Laboratory, Eastern Utilization
Research and Development
Division, Agricultural Research Service,
U.S. Department of Agriculture.
Coeditor of* Fundamentals of Dairy
Chemistry.
FARMING AND AGRICULTURAL
    TECHNOLOGY (*in part*)
FOOD PROCESSING (*in part*)

B.I.B. Boris Ivan Balinsky. *Emeritus
Professor of Zoology, University of the
Witwatersrand, Johannesburg, South
Africa. Author of* An Introduction to
Embryology.
GROWTH AND DEVELOPMENT,
    BIOLOGICAL (*in part*)

Bi.C. Bin Cheng. *Professor of Air
and Space Law, University College,
University of London. Author of* The
Law of International Air Transport.
INTERNATIONAL LAW (*in part*)
TRANSPORTATION LAW (*in part*)

B.Ja. Bernard Jacobson. *Director
of Promotion, Boosey & Hawkes Ltd.
(music publisher), London; Deputy
Director of Publications, 1979–81.
Author of* The Music of Johannes
Brahms.
MUSICAL FORMS AND GENRES (*in part*)

B.J.C. Bryant J. Cratty. *Professor of
Kinesiology; Director, Perceptual-Motor
Learning Laboratory, University
of California, Los Angeles. Author
of* Movement Behavior and Motor
Learning; Perceptual and Motor
Development in Infants and Children.
LEARNING AND COGNITION, HUMAN
    (*in part*)

B.J.D.M. Bastiaan J.D. Meeuse.
*Professor of Botany, University of
Washington, Seattle. Author of* The Story
of Pollination.
REPRODUCTION AND REPRODUCTIVE
    SYSTEMS (*in part*)

B.Je. Barbara Jelavich. *Professor
of History, Indiana University,
Bloomington. Author of* History of the
Balkans *and others.*
BALKANS (*in part*)

B.J.M. Sir Basil John Mason.
*Pro-Chancellor, University of
Surrey, England. Director General,
Meteorological Office, Bracknell,
England, 1965–83. Author of* The
Physics of Clouds; Clouds, Rain and
Rainmaking.
CLIMATE AND WEATHER (*in part*)

B.Jo. Bernard Joy. *Former football
correspondent,* Evening Standard,
London. Author of Soccer Tactics.
SPORTS, MAJOR TEAM AND INDIVIDUAL
    (*in part*)

B.J.R. Brian James Roud (deceased).
Historian.
SPAIN (*in part*)

B.J.T. Brian J. Thompson. *William
F. May Professor of Engineering and
Professor of Optics; Dean, College
of Engineering and Applied Science,
University of Rochester, New York.
Author of* Physical Optics Notebook.
OPTICS, PRINCIPLES OF (*in part*)

B.J.U. Benton J. Underwood.
*Stanley G. Harris Professor Emeritus
of Social Science, Northwestern
University, Evanston, Illinois. Author of*
Experimental Psychology; *coauthor of*
Meaningfulness and Verbal Learning.
MEMORY (*in part*)

B.K. Benjamin Keen. *Emeritus
Professor of History, Northern Illinois
University, De Kalb. Editor of* Readings
in Latin American Civilization, 1492 to
the Present *and others.*
BALBOA, VASCO NÚÑEZ DE (Micropædia)
LATIN AMERICA, THE HISTORY
    OF (*in part*)

B.K.N. Basheer K. Nijim. *Professor
and Head, Department of Geography,
University of Northern Iowa, Cedar
Falls.*
ARABIA (*in part*)

B.Ku. Bernhard Kummel (d. 1980).
*Professor of Geology, Harvard
University, 1962–80. Investigator of
Mesozoic stratigraphy in the Himalayas
and Peru. Author of* History of the Earth.
GEOCHRONOLOGY (*in part*)

B.L. **Barnabas Lindars.** *Rylands Professor of Biblical Criticism and Exegesis, Victoria University of Manchester. Author of* Jesus Son of Man *and others.*
PAUL, THE APOSTLE

B.L.C. **Barbara Lovett Cline.** *Biology teacher. Author of* The Questioners: Physicists and the Quantum Theory.
BROGLIE, LOUIS-VICTOR, 7ᵉ DUC DE (Micropædia)
DIRAC, P.A.M. (Micropædia)

B.L.K. **Barry L. Karger.** *Professor of Chemistry, Northeastern University, Boston, Massachusetts. Coauthor of* Introduction to Separation Science.
ANALYSIS AND MEASUREMENT, PHYSICAL AND CHEMICAL (*in part*)

B.L.S. **Bruce Lannes Smith.** *Emeritus Professor of Political Science, Michigan State University, East Lansing. Coauthor of* Propaganda, Communication and Public Opinion.
PROPAGANDA

B.L.T. **B.L. Turner.** *Professor of Botany; Director, Plant Resources Center, University of Texas at Austin. Author of* Legumes of Texas; *coeditor of* Chemotaxonomy of the Leguminosae.
ANGIOSPERMS (*in part*)

B.L.v.d.W. **Bartel Leendert van der Waerden.** *Emeritus Professor of Mathematics, University of Zürich. Author of* Science Awakening *and others.*
EUCLID (Micropædia)

B.M. **Björn Matthíasson.** *Economist, Central Bank of Iceland, Reykjavík.*
ICELAND (*in part*)

B.Ma. **Benjamin March** (d. 1940). *Curator of Asiatic Art, Detroit Institute of Arts. Author of* The History of Chinese Painting in Outline.
DECORATIVE ARTS AND FURNISHINGS (*in part*)

B.M.H. **Bernice Margaret Hamilton.** *Associate of St. Edmund's House, University of Cambridge. Former Senior Lecturer in Politics, University of York, Heslington, England. Author of* Political Thought in 16th-Century Spain.
VITORIA, FRANCISCO DE (Micropædia)

B.M.M. **Barbara Mary Middlehurst.** *Visiting Scientist, Lunar Science Institute, Houston, Texas, 1973–74. Associate Editor, Astronomy,* Encyclopædia Britannica, *Chicago, 1968–72. Coeditor of* Moon, Meteorites and Comets.
MECHANICS (*in part*)

B.Mo. **Brita Maud Ellen Mortensen** (d. 1958). *Lecturer in Swedish, University of Cambridge, 1950–58. Coauthor of* An Introduction to Scandinavian Literature.
SCANDINAVIAN LITERATURE (*in part*)
STRINDBERG, AUGUST (Micropædia)

B.N. **Bruno Nettl.** *Professor of Music and of Anthropology, University of Illinois, Urbana. Author of* The Study of Ethnomusicology; Folk and Traditional Music of the Western Continents; *and others.*
FOLK ARTS (*in part*)

B.N.P. **Baij Nath Puri.** *Emeritus Professor of Ancient Indian History and Archaeology, University of Lucknow, India. Author of* Cities of Ancient India.
TAXILA (Micropædia).

B.N.T. **B.N. Taylor.** *Chief, Electricity Division, Center for Basic Standards, National Bureau of Standards, Washington, D.C. Coauthor of* The Fundamental Constants and Quantum Electrodynamics.
PHYSICAL PRINCIPLES AND CONCEPTS (*in part*)

B.O'G. **Brendan Anthony O'Grady.** *Professor of English, University of Prince Edward Island, Charlottetown.*
CANADA (*in part*)

B.O'K. **Bernard O'Kelly.** *Dean, College of Arts and Sciences; Professor of English, University of North Dakota, Grand Forks.*
UNITED STATES OF AMERICA (*in part*)

B.R. **Bayard Rankin.** *Associate Editor, Mathematics,* Encyclopædia Britannica, *Chicago, 1971–73. Associate Professor of Mathematics, Case Western Reserve University, Cleveland, 1960–71. Coauthor and editor of* Differential Space, Quantum Systems, and Prediction.
AUTOMATA THEORY (*in part*)

B.R.N. **B.R. Nanda.** *Former Director, Nehru Memorial Museum and Library, New Delhi. Author of* Mahatma Gandhi: A Biography *and others.*
GANDHI

B.R.S. **B. Raphael Sealey.** *Professor of History, University of California, Berkeley. Author of* A History of the Greek City States, ca. 700–338 B.C.
GRECO-ROMAN CIVILIZATION, CLASSICAL (*in part*)

B.R.W. **Bryan R. Wilson.** *Reader in Sociology, University of Oxford. Author of* Religion in Sociological Perspective *and others.*
MORMON (Micropædia)

B.S.B. **Benedikt Sigurdur Benedikz.** *Head of Special Collections, Library, University of Birmingham, England. Author of* Iceland: The Spread of Printing.
ARCTIC, THE (*in part*)
ICELAND (*in part*)
SCANDINAVIAN LITERATURE (*in part*)

B.Sc. **Bobb Schaeffer.** *Emeritus Curator of Vertebrate Paleontology, American Museum of Natural History, New York City.*
FISHES (*in part*)

B.S.-E. **Bickham A.C. Sweet-Escott.** *Group Finance Coordinator, The British Petroleum Company Ltd., 1957–72. Manager, Ionian Bank Ltd., 1950–57. Author of* Greece: A Political and Economic Survey, 1939–1953.

CYPRUS (*in part*)
GREECE (*in part*)

B.S.F. **Bernard S. Finn.** *Curator, Division of Electricity and Modern Physics, Smithsonian Institution, Washington, D.C.*
TELECOMMUNICATIONS SYSTEMS (*in part*)

B.S.L. **Bruce Sween Liley.** *Professor of Physics, University of Waikato, Hamilton, New Zealand.*
MATTER (*in part*)

B.Sv. **B. Shirendev.** *Historian. Former President, Academy of Sciences of the Mongolian People's Republic, Ulaanbaatar.*
MONGOLIA (*in part*)

B.T.D. **Bernard Thomas Donovan.** *Professor of Neuroendocrinology, Institute of Psychiatry, University of London.*
REPRODUCTION AND REPRODUCTIVE SYSTEMS (*in part*)

B.T.S. **Bradley Titus Scheer.** *Emeritus Professor of Biology, University of Oregon, Eugene. Author of* Animal Physiology.
BIOLOGICAL SCIENCES, THE (*in part*)

B.T.Sh. **Byron Thomas Shaw.** *Assistant to Administrator, Agricultural Research Service, U.S. Department of Agriculture, Washington, D.C., 1965–68.*
AGRICULTURAL SCIENCES (*in part*)

Bu.H.W. **Burns H. Weston.** *Bessie Dutton Murray Distinguished Professor of Law, University of Iowa, Iowa City. Coauthor of* International Law and World Order: An Introductory Problem-oriented Coursebook.
HUMAN RIGHTS

B.V. **Birgit Vennesland.** *Head, Vennesland Research Laboratory, Max Planck Society, 1970–81; Director, Max Planck Institute for Cell Physiology, Berlin, 1968–70.*
BIOLOGICAL SCIENCES, THE (*in part*)

B.V.Gy. **Bo Vilhelm Gyllensvärd.** *Former Director, Museum of Far Eastern Antiquities, Stockholm. Assistant Professor, Far Eastern Section, Institute of History of Art, University of Stockholm. Author of* T'ang Gold and Silver *and others.*
DECORATIVE ARTS AND FURNISHINGS (*in part*)

B.V.S. **Brian Vincent Street.** *Lecturer in Social Anthropology, University of Sussex, Brighton, England. Author of* The Savage in Literature *and others.*
TYLOR, SIR EDWARD BURNETT (Micropædia)

B.W. **Basil Willey** (d. 1978). *King Edward VII Professor of English Literature, University of Cambridge, 1946–64. Author of* Darwin and Butler: Two Versions of Evolution; Nineteenth Century Studies; *and others.*
ARNOLD, MATTHEW (*in part*) (Micropædia)

BUTLER, SAMUEL (Micropædia)
WORDSWORTH, WILLIAM (*in part*)
  (Micropædia)

B.W.A.   Bruce W. Atkinson. *Professor of Geography, Queen Mary College, University of London. Author of* The Weather Business *and others.*
CLIMATE AND WEATHER (*in part*)

B.W.B.   Bernard Winslow Beckingsale. *Former Senior Lecturer in Modern History, University of Newcastle upon Tyne, England. Author of* Burghley: Tudor Statesman *and others.*
CECIL, WILLIAM, 1ST BARON BURGHLEY
  (*in part*) (Micropædia)

B-W.C.   Byong-Wuk Chong. *Professor of Korean Literature, Seoul National University. Author of* Essays on Korean Literature; Complete Anthology of Sijo.
KOREAN LITERATURE (*in part*)

B.We.   Bruce Webster. *Senior Lecturer in History, University of Kent at Canterbury, England.*
ROBERT I (SCOTLAND) (Micropædia)

B.W.H.   Bruce W. Halstead, M.D. *Director, World Life Research Institute, Colton, California. Author of* Poisonous and Venomous Marine Animals of the World.
POISONS AND POISONING (*in part*)

B.W.M   Bernard W. Minifie. *Consultant, Knechtel Laboratories, Inc. (consultants to the candy industry), Skokie, Illinois. Author of* Science and Technology of Chocolate, Cocoa and Confectionery.
FOOD PROCESSING (*in part*)

B.W.Ma.   B.W. Mazur. *Lecturer in Polish Language and Literature, School of Slavonic and East European Studies, University of London. Author of* Colloquial Polish.
POLISH LITERATURE (*in part*)

B.Wn.   Brian Weinstein. *Professor of Political Science, Howard University, Washington, D.C. Author of* Eboué; *coauthor of* Introduction to African Politics.
CENTRAL AFRICA (*in part*)

B.Wo.   Bernard Wood. *Professor of Anatomy, Middlesex Hospital Medical School, University of London. Author of* Human Evolution; Evolution of Early Man.
EVOLUTION, HUMAN (*in part*)

B.W.W.   Bruce Withington Wilshire. *Professor of Philosophy, Rutgers University, New Brunswick, New Jersey. Author of* Metaphysics: An Introduction to Philosophy *and others.*
METAPHYSICS (*in part*)

B.Z.B.   Rabbi Ben Zion Bokser (d. 1984). *Rabbi, Forest Hills Jewish Center, Forest Hills, New York. Adjunct Professor of Political Science, Queens College, City University of New York. Author of* The Legacy of Maimonides.
MAIMONIDES, MOSES (Micropædia)

C.A.   Claude Arpigny. *Associate Professor, Institute of Astrophysics, State University of Liège, Belgium.*
SOLAR SYSTEM, THE (*in part*)

Ca.B.   Carl Bode. *Professor of English, University of Maryland, College Park. Editor of* Collected Poems of Henry Thoreau.
THOREAU, HENRY DAVID (Micropædia)

C.A.B.   Clifford A. Barnes. *Emeritus Professor of Oceanography, University of Washington, Seattle. Author of numerous articles on oceanography.*
OCEANS (*in part*)

C.A.Bl.   Conrad Alexander Blyth. *Professor of Economics, University of Auckland, New Zealand. Author of* Inflation in New Zealand *and others.*
NEW ZEALAND (*in part*)

Ca.C.   Camile Camara. *Expert in Curriculum Development, United Nations Development Program, Abidjan, Ivory Coast. Author of* Saint-Louis du Senegal.
WESTERN AFRICA (*in part*)

C.A.E.   Clive Arthur Edwards. *Senior Principal Scientific Officer, Rothamsted Experimental Station, Harpenden, England. Author of* Principles of Agricultural Entomology *and others.*
SOIL ORGANISMS

Ca.G.   Carlton Gamer. *Composer. Professor of Music, Colorado College, Colorado Springs.*
MUSICAL INSTRUMENTS (*in part*)

C.A.G.W.   C.A.G. Wiersma (d. 1979). *Professor of Biology, California Institute of Technology, Pasadena, 1947–76. Editor of* Invertebrate Nervous Systems.
SENSORY RECEPTION (*in part*)

C.A.L.   Carl Adam Lawrence (d. 1972). *Director, Bureau of Laboratories, Los Angeles County Health Department, California, 1953–70. Author of* Surface-Active Quaternary Ammonium Germicides.
ANTIMICROBIAL AGENT (*in part*)
  (Micropædia)

C.-A.La.   Charles-André Laffargue. *General, French Army (retired). Author of* Foch et la Bataille de 1918 *and others.*
FOCH, FERDINAND (Micropædia)

C.A.M.   Carlile Aylmer Macartney (d. 1978). *Research Fellow, All Souls College, University of Oxford, 1936–65. Montagu Burton Professor of International Relations, University of Edinburgh, 1951–57. Author of* Hungary: A Short History *and others.*
DEÁK, FERENC (Micropædia)
HUNGARY (*in part*)
KOSSUTH, LAJOS (Micropædia)

C.A.McC.   Charles A. McClelland. *Emeritus Professor of International Relations, University of Southern California, Los Angeles. Author of* Theory and the International System.
SOCIAL SCIENCES, THE (*in part*)

C.A.McI.   Christopher Angus McIntosh. *Editor and writer, Mitchell Beazley (publisher), London. Author of* The Swan King: Ludwig II of Bavaria *and others.*
COLOGNE (*in part*)
HAMBURG (*in part*)

C.A.M.K.   Cuchlaine Audrey Muriel King. *Emeritus Professor of Physical Geography, University of Nottingham, England. An authority on coastal geomorphology. Author of* Beaches and Coasts; An Introduction to Oceanography.
OCEANS (*in part*)

C.A.P.   Christopher A. Pallis. *Emeritus Reader in Neurology, Royal Postgraduate Medical School, University of London. Author of* The ABC of Brain Stem Death.
DEATH

C.A.R.   Colin Alistair Ronan. *Science writer and lecturer. Editor,* Journal of the British Astronomical Association. *Author of* The Cambridge Illustrated History of the World's Science *and many others.*
CALENDAR (*in part*)
COPERNICUS (*in part*)
HIPPARCHUS (*in part*) (Micropædia)
PTOLEMY (Micropædia)
RUSSELL, HENRY NORRIS (Micropædia)

C.A.Ro.   C. Ambrose Rogers. *Astor Professor of Mathematics, University College, University of London. Author of* Hausdorff Measures.
NUMBER THEORY (*in part*)

C.A.T.   Cornelius A. Tobias. *Professor of Biophysics and Medical Physics, University of California, Berkeley. Author of papers on radiation biophysics and cancer research.*
RADIATION (*in part*)

C.A.Tr.   Constantine Athanasius Trypanis. *Minister of Culture and Science, Government of Greece, 1974–77. Professor of Classical Languages and Literatures, University of Chicago, 1968–74. Author of* Medieval and Modern Greek Poetry.
GREEK LITERATURE (*in part*)

C.Au.   Charlotte Auerbach. *Emeritus Professor of Animal Genetics, University of Edinburgh. Author of* The Science of Genetics; Mutation Research: Problems, Results, and Perspectives.
GENETICS AND HEREDITY, THE
  PRINCIPLES OF (*in part*)

C.A.V.   Claude A.Villee. *Andelot Professor of Biological Chemistry, Medical School, Harvard University, Boston, Massachusetts. Author of* Biological Principles and Processes.
BIOLOGICAL SCIENCES, THE
  (*in part*)

C.A.W.   Charles A. Wert. *Professor of Metallurgy; Head, Department of Metallurgy and Mining Engineering, University of Illinois, Urbana. Coauthor of* Physics of Solids.
MATTER (*in part*)

C.B. **Colin Boocock** (d. 1973). *Director of Geological Survey, Republic of Botswana, Lobatse. Coauthor of* Notes on the Geology and Hydrogeology of the Central Kalahari Region.
AFRICA (*in part*)

C.Ba. **Clive Barker.** *Senior Lecturer in Theatre Studies, University of Warwick, England. Coeditor,* New Theatre Quarterly. *Author of* Theatre Games.
THEATRICAL PRODUCTION (*in part*)

C.B.B. **Carl B. Boyer** (d. 1976). *Professor of Mathematics, Brooklyn College, City University of New York, 1952–76. Author of* The History of the Calculus and Its Conceptual Development; History of Analytic Geometry; A History of Mathematics; *and others.*
EULER, LEONHARD (Micropædia)
FERMAT, PIERRE DE (Micropædia)

C.B.Co. **Carl B. Cone.** *Emeritus Professor of History, University of Kentucky, Lexington. Author of* Burke and the Nature of Politics; The English Jacobins.
UNITED KINGDOM (*in part*)

C.B.H. **Charles B. Hunt.** *Professor of Geology, Johns Hopkins University, Baltimore, Maryland, 1961–73. A principal investigator of the geology of the western United States. Author of* Physiography of the United States *and others.*
GEOCHRONOLOGY (*in part*)

C.B.He. **Charles B. Heiser, Jr.** *Distinguished Professor of Botany, Indiana University, Bloomington. Author of* Seed to Civilization: The Story of Food.
ANGIOSPERMS (*in part*)

C.Bi. **Cyril Bibby.** *Principal, Kingston upon Hull College of Education, University of Hull Institute of Education, England, 1959–76. Author of* Scientist Extraordinary: The Life and Scientific Work of T.H. Huxley *and others.*
HUXLEY, ALDOUS (Micropædia)
HUXLEY, SIR ANDREW FIELDING (Micropædia)
HUXLEY, SIR JULIAN (Micropædia)
HUXLEY, T.H. (Micropædia)

C.Bl. **Claude Blair.** *Keeper of Metalwork, Victoria and Albert Museum, London, 1972–82. Author of* European Armour; European and American Arms; *and others.*
DECORATIVE ARTS AND FURNISHINGS (*in part*)

C.B.MacD. **Charles B. MacDonald.** *Deputy Chief Historian, U.S. Army Center of Military History, Washington, D.C., 1967–80. Author of* The Mighty Endeavor: American Armed Forces in the European Theater in World War II.
WAR, THE TECHNOLOGY OF (*in part*)

C.B.Mo. **C.B. Monk, Jr.** *Senior Consultant, Wiss, Janney, Elstner, and Associates (consulting engineers),* Northbrook, Illinois.
BUILDING CONSTRUCTION (*in part*)

C.B.My. **Charles B. Morrey, Jr.** *Professor of Mathematics, University of California, Berkeley, 1945–73. Author of* Multiple Integrals in the Calculus of Variations.
ANALYSIS (IN MATHEMATICS) (*in part*)

C.C. **Claude Cahen.** *Emeritus Professor of Islāmic History, University of Paris. Author of* La Syrie du nord á l'époque des croisades *and others.*
ALP-ARSLAN (Micropædia)

C.C.A. **Claude C. Albritton.** *Hamilton Professor Emeritus of Geology; Vice President and Senior Scientist, Institute for the Study of Earth and Man, Southern Methodist University, Dallas, Texas. Coauthor and editor of* The Fabric of Geology; Uniformity and Simplicity.
EARTH SCIENCES, THE (*in part*)
GEOCHRONOLOGY (*in part*)

C.C.B. **Charles Calvert Bayley.** *Kingsford Professor of History, McGill University, Montreal. Author of* The Formation of the German College of Electors in the Mid-Thirteenth Century *and others.*
GERMANY (*in part*)

C.Ce. **Charles Cestre** (d. 1959). *Professor of American Literature and Civilization, University of Paris, 1917–42. Author of* Histoire de la littérature américaine *and others.*
POE, EDGAR ALLAN (*in part*) (Micropædia)

C.Ch. **Charles Chadwick.** *Carnegie Professor of French, University of Aberdeen, Scotland. Author of* Mallarmé, sa pensée dans sa poésie; Symbolism.
MALLARMÉ, STÉPHANE (Micropædia)

C.Cl. **Cecil Clutton.** *Secretary, Organs Advisory Committee, Council for Places of Worship, England. Consultant for the rebuilding of the organ, St. Paul's Cathedral, London. Fellow,* Society of Antiquaries, *London. Author of* The Organ: Its Tonal Structure and Registration; The British Organ; *and others.*
MUSICAL INSTRUMENTS (*in part*)

C.C.M. **Claudius Cornelius Müller.** *Head, East Asian Department, State Museum of Ethnology, Munich. Author of* Untersuchungen zum Erdalter she im China der Chou- und Han-Zeit.
SHIH HUANG-TI (*in part*) (Micropædia)

C.C.MacD. **C.C. MacDuffee** (d. 1961). *Professor of Mathematics, University of Wisconsin, 1943–61. President, Mathematical Association of America, 1945–46. Author of* The Theory of Matrices *and others.*
ARITHMETIC (*in part*)

C.C.O'B. **Conor Cruise O'Brien.** *Pro-Chancellor, University of Dublin. Editor in Chief,* The Observer, *London, 1978–81. Member, Seanad Eireann, Dublin, 1977–79; Dáil Eireann, 1969–77. Author of* Parnell and His Party.
PARNELL, CHARLES STEWART (Micropædia)

C.C.P. **Cuthbert Coulson Pounder.** *Marine engineering consultant. Director and Chief Technical Engineer, Harland and Wolff Ltd., Belfast, Northern Ireland, 1930–65. Coauthor of* Marine Diesel Engines.
INDUSTRIES, MANUFACTURING (*in part*)

C.C.T. **Clifford Charles Townsend.** *Principal Scientific Officer, Royal Botanic Gardens, Kew, England. Editor and coauthor of* Flora of Iraq.
ANGIOSPERMS (*in part*)

C.D. **Carlo Diano** (d. 1974). *Professor of Greek Literature, University of Padua, Italy. Author of* Lettre di Epicuro e dei suoi; *editor of* Epicuri Ethica.
EPICURUS (Micropædia)
PHILOSOPHICAL SCHOOLS AND DOCTRINES, WESTERN (*in part*)

C.D.C. **Charles D. Calnan.** *Director, Department of Occupational Dermatoses, St. John's Hospital for Diseases of the Skin, London. Editor,* Contact Dermatitis.
INTEGUMENTARY SYSTEMS (*in part*)

C.D.Cu. **Charles D. Cuttler.** *Emeritus Professor of Art History, University of Iowa, Iowa City. Author of* Northern Painting from Pucelle to Bruegel.
SLUTER, CLAUS (Micropædia)

C.De. **Charles Dédéyan.** *Emeritus Professor of Comparative Literature, University of Paris IV. Author of* Montaigne chez ses amis Anglo-Saxons.
FRANCE (*in part*)

C.D.G. **C. David Gutsche.** *Professor of Chemistry, Washington University, St. Louis, Missouri. Author of* Chemistry of Carbonyl Compounds.
CHEMICAL COMPOUNDS (*in part*)

C.D.K. **Carol D. Kiesinger.** *Arts consultant. Hiker and mountain climber. Coeditor of* The Armchair Mountaineer.
MOUNTAINEERING (*in part*) (Micropædia)

C.Do. **Clifford Dowdey** (d. 1979). *Lecturer in Creative Writing, University of Richmond, Virginia, 1958–69. Author of* Lee *and others; editor of* The Wartime Papers of Robert E. Lee.
LEE, ROBERT E. (Micropædia)

C.D.O. **Clifford David Ollier.** *Professor of Geography, University of New England, Armidale, Australia.*
ECOSYSTEMS (*in part*)

C.D.R. **C.D. Ross** (d. 1986). *Professor of Medieval History, University of Bristol, England. Author of* The Wars of the Roses *and others.*
HENRY V (ENGLAND) (Micropædia)

C.D.T. **Conrad D. Totman.** *Professor of History, Northwestern University, Evanston, Illinois. Author of* Ieyasu: Shogun *and others.*
TOKUGAWA IEYASU (Micropædia)

C.E.B.B. Charles Edmond Bradlaugh Bonner (d. 1976). *Principal Curator, Conservatory and Botanical Garden, Geneva. Author of* Index Hepaticarum.
ANGIOSPERMS (*in part*)

C.E.B.C. Charles E.B. Conybeare (d. 1982). *Reader in Geology, Australian National University, Canberra.*
INDUSTRIES, EXTRACTION AND PROCESSING (*in part*)

C.E.C. Charles Edward Casolani. *Lieutenant Colonel, British Army (retired). Amateur rider, show jumper, and trainer, 1919–56.*
HORSES (*in part*)

C.E.Ca. Concepción E. Castañeda. *Associate Professor of Spanish, Millikin University, Decatur, Illinois. Professor of Geography, University of Havana, 1960–62.*
SOUTH AMERICA (*in part*)

C.E.Co. Charles E. Cornelius. *Director, California Primate Research Center, University of California, Davis. Dean, College of Veterinary Medicine, University of Florida, Gainesville, 1971– 81. Editor of* Advances in Veterinary Science and Comparative Medicine.
DISEASE (*in part*)

C.E.E. Cyril Ernest Everard. *Senior Lecturer in Geography, Queen Mary College, University of London. Editor, Physical Geography,* Encyclopedia of Geography.
EUROPE (*in part*)

C.E.He. Charles E. Hecht. *Professor of Chemistry, Hunter College, City University of New York. Author of papers on physical and chemical processes occurring at very low temperatures.*
MATTER (*in part*)

C.E.N. Clyde Everett Noble. *Professor of Experimental Psychology, University of Georgia, Athens. Author of* Outline of Psychological Measurement; The Psychology of Cornet and Trumpet Playing; *and others.*
LEARNING AND COGNITION, HUMAN (*in part*)

C.E.No. Charles E. Nowell. *Emeritus Professor of History, University of Illinois, Urbana. Author of* The Great Discoveries and the First Colonial Empires *and others.*
EUROPEAN OVERSEAS EXPLORATION AND EMPIRES, THE HISTORY OF (*in part*)
HENRY THE NAVIGATOR (Micropædia)

C.E.R. Charles Edward Reynolds (d. 1971). *Managing Editor, Concrete Publications Ltd., London, 1960– 69. Author of* Reinforced Concrete Designer's Handbook *and others.*
BUILDING CONSTRUCTION (*in part*)

C.E.S. Courtenay Edward Stevens. *Former Fellow and Tutor in Ancient History, Magdalen College, University of Oxford.*
GERMANY (*in part*)

C.E.T. Cecil Edgar Tilley (d. 1973). *Professor of Mineralogy and Petrology, University of Cambridge, 1931–61. World authority on igneous petrology.*
BOWEN, NORMAN L. (Micropædia)
MINERALS AND ROCKS (*in part*)

C.Fa. Clifton Fadiman. *Member, Board of Editors,* Encyclopædia Britannica. *Consultant, Center for the Study of Democratic Institutions. Member, Board of Judges, Book-of-the-Month Club. Advisory Editor,* Cricket: The Children's Magazine. *Author of* The Lifetime Reading Plan *and others.*
LITERATURE, THE ART OF (*in part*)

C.F.A.S. Claude Frédéric Armand Schaeffer (d. 1982). *Professor of the Archaeology of Western Asia, College of France, Paris, 1954–69. Director of the French Archaeological Expeditions to Ras Shamra-Ugarit, Syria, and Enkomi-Alasia, Cyprus. Editor of* Ugaritica I to VII.
UGARIT (Micropædia)

C.Fe. Cyrille Felteau. *Journalist and historian. Former Editorial and News Writer,* La Presse, *Montreal.*
MONTREAL (*in part*)

C.F.F. Charles F. Fuechsel (d. 1977). *Atlantic Region Engineer, Topographic Division, Geological Survey, U.S. Department of the Interior, Washington, D.C., 1959–65. Author of numerous articles on mapping and surveys.*
MAPPING AND SURVEYING (*in part*)

C.Fi. Constantine FitzGibbon (d. 1983). *Writer. Author of* The Life of Dylan Thomas; *editor of* Selected Letters of Dylan Thomas.
THOMAS, DYLAN (Micropædia)

C.F.M. Clovis F. Maksoud. *Permanent Observer of the League of Arab States to the United Nations. Author of* The Crisis of the Arab Left *and others.*
LEBANON (*in part*)

C.F.O. Christian F. Otto. *Professor of Architecture, Cornell University, Ithaca, New York.*
BORROMINI, FRANCESCO (Micropædia)

C.F.S. Carl Fredrik Sandelin. *Novelist. Former General Manager and Editor in Chief, Finnish News Agency, Helsinki.*
FINLAND (*in part*)

C.F.Sc. Carl Frederic Schmidt, M.D. *Emeritus Professor of Pharmacology, University of Pennsylvania, Philadelphia. Clinical Professor of Pharmacology, University of South Florida, Tampa.*
NERVES AND NERVOUS SYSTEMS (*in part*)

C.F.V. Charles F. Voegelin (d. 1986). *Distinguished Professor of Anthropology and of Linguistics, Indiana University, Bloomington, 1967–76. Editor,* International Journal of American Linguistics. *Coauthor of* Classification and Index of the World's Languages *and others.*
LANGUAGES OF THE WORLD (*in part*)

C.Fy. Christopher Fyfe. *Reader in African History, University of Edinburgh. Author of* A History of Sierra Leone.
WESTERN AFRICA (*in part*)

C.G. Christiaan Glasz. *Former Professor of Public Finance, State University of Leyden, The Netherlands. Royal Commissioner, De Nederlandsche Bank.*
MARKETS (*in part*)

C.Ga. Clemente Garavito. *Vice President, Colombian Geographical Society, Bogotá. Author of numerous articles on geography.*
COLOMBIA (*in part*)

C.G.B. Carl G. Baker, M.D. *Medical Director, Ludwig Institute for Cancer Research, Zurich, 1977–82. Director, National Cancer Institute, U.S. Department of Health, Education, and Welfare, Bethesda, Maryland, 1969–72.*
CANCER (*in part*)

C.G.G. Charles Goode Gomillion. *Emeritus Professor of Sociology, Tuskegee Institute, Alabama.*
UNITED STATES OF AMERICA (*in part*)

C.G.H. Carl G. Hempel. *Stuart Professor Emeritus of Philosophy, Princeton University. University Professor of Philosophy, University of Pittsburgh, Pennsylvania. Author of* Philosophy of Natural Science.
CARNAP, RUDOLF (Micropædia)

C.G.P. Charles G. Pearson. *Chairman, Department of Journalism, Wichita State University, Kansas.*
UNITED STATES OF AMERICA (*in part*)

C.G.S. Charles Gordon Smith. *Research Fellow of Keble College, Oxford; former Lecturer in Geography, University of Oxford. Editor of* Oxford Regional Economic Atlas: The Middle East and North Africa.
ARABIA (*in part*)
SYRIA (*in part*)

C.G.Se. Claudio G. Segre. *Associate Professor of History, University of Texas at Austin. Author of* Fourth Shore: The Italian Colonization of Libya.
ITALY (*in part*)

C.G.St. Chester G. Starr. *Bentley Professor of Ancient History, University of Michigan, Ann Arbor. Author of* Rise and Fall of the Ancient World *and others.*
PEISISTRATUS (Micropædia)

C.G.T. Constantine Gennadiyevich Tikhotskiy. *Professor, Moscow M.V. Lomonosov State University. Author of numerous articles on hydrology.*
ASIA (*in part*)

C.H. Claude Harmel. *Editor,* Les Études Sociales et Syndicales, *Paris. Former Secretary, Institute for Social History, Paris. Author of* Lettre à Léon Blum sur le socialisme et la paix.
JAURÈS, JEAN (Micropædia)

C.Ha. Carl Hanson (d. 1985). *Pro-Vice-Chancellor; Professor of*

Chemical Engineering, University of Bradford, England. Editor of Recent Advances in Liquid-Liquid Extraction.
ENGINEERING (*in part*)

C.H.B.P.   Charles Henry Brian Priestley. *Professor of Meteorology, Monash University, Clayton, Australia 1978-80. Author of* Turbulent Transfer in the Lower Atmosphere.
CLIMATE AND WEATHER (*in part*)

C.H.B.R.   Christopher Hanby Baillie Reynolds. *Lecturer in Sinhalese, School of Oriental and African Studies, University of London.*
INDIAN OCEAN ISLANDS (*in part*)

C.H.C.   Charles Henry Cotter (deceased). *Senior Lecturer in Maritime Studies. University of Wales Institute of Science and Technology, Cardiff. Author of* The Physical Geography of the Oceans.
OCEANS (*in part*)

C.H.D.   Calaway H. Dodson. *Director, Marie Selby Botanical Gardens, Sarasota, Florida. Coauthor of* Orchid Flowers: Their Pollination and Evolution; The Biology of the Orchids.
ANGIOSPERMS (*in part*)

C.H.G.   Cyrus H. Gordon. *Professor of Hebraic Studies; Director, Center for Ebla Research, New York University, New York City. Emeritus Professor of Mediterranean Studies, Brandeis University, Waltham, Massachusetts. Author of* The Ancient Near East *and others.*
MIDDLE EASTERN RELIGIONS, ANCIENT (*in part*)
SOLOMON (Micropædia)

C.H.Gi.   Charles Hugh Giles. *Former Reader in Surface Chemistry and Dyeing, University of Strathclyde, Glasgow, Scotland. Author of* A Laboratory Course in Dyeing.
CHEMICAL COMPOUNDS (*in part*)

C.H.G.-S.   Charles Harvard Gibbs-Smith (d. 1981). *Research Fellow, Science Museum, London, 1976-81. Keeper, Public Relations and Education Department, Victoria and Albert Museum, London, 1947-71. Author of* Aviation: An Historical Survey; The Wright Brothers; *and others.*
WRIGHT, ORVILLE AND WILBUR (Micropædia)

C.H.H.   Charles Harold Hayward. *Free-lance writer and artist. Editor,* Woodworker, *1939-65. Author of* English Period Furniture *and others.*
INDUSTRIES, MANUFACTURING (*in part*)

C.H.Ha.   Cadet H. Hand, Jr. *Professor of Zoology, University of California, Berkeley; Director, Bodega Marine Laboratory, Bodega Bay, California.*
CNIDARIANS

C.H.Ho.   Cyrus Henry Hoy. *John B. Trevor Professor of English, University of Rochester, New York. Author of* The Hyacinth Room: An Investigation into the Nature of Comedy, Tragedy, and Tragicomedy.
LITERATURE, THE ART OF (*in part*)

C.Hi.   Christopher Hibbert. *Historian and biographer. Author of* Benito Mussolini; The Rise and Fall of Il Duce; *and others.*
MUSSOLINI, BENITO (*in part*) (Micropædia)

Ch.L.   Chao Lin. *Visiting Associate Professor of History, National Chung hsing University, Tai-chung, Taiwan. Author of* Marriage, Inheritance and Lineage Organization in Shang-Chou China.
CALENDAR (*in part*)

C.H.L.   Clarence H. Lorig (d. 1975). *Assistant Director, Battelle Memorial Institute, Columbus, Ohio, 1947-65. Author of* Copper as an Alloying Element in Steel and Cast Iron.
INDUSTRIES, EXTRACTION AND PROCESSING (*in part*)

C.H.Lo.   Charles H. Long. *William Rand Kenan, Jr., Professor of the History of Religion, University of North Carolina at Chapel Hill. Professor of the History of Religions, Duke University, Durham, North Carolina. Author of* Alpha: Myths of Creation.
DOCTRINES AND DOGMAS, RELIGIOUS (*in part*)

C.Ho.   Charles Hose (d. 1929). *Member, Sarawak State Advisory Council at Westminster, London, 1919.*
EAST INDIES, THE (*in part*)

C.H.P.   Clifford Hillhouse Pope (d. 1974). *Science writer. Curator, Division of Reptiles and Amphibians, Field Museum of Natural History, Chicago, 1941-53. Author of* The Reptile World; Turtles of the United States and Canada.
REPTILES (*in part*)

C.H.Ps.   Sir Cyril Henry Philips. *Professor of Oriental History, University of London, 1946-80; Director, School of Oriental and African Studies, 1957-76.*
ASIA (*in part*)

Ch.R.   Chaim Rabin. *Former Professor of Hebrew Language, Hebrew University of Jerusalem. Author of* Qumran Studies: A Short History of the Hebrew Language.
HEBREW LITERATURE (*in part*)

Ch.S.   Charles Süsskind. *Professor of Engineering Science, University of California, Berkeley. Editor of* The Encyclopedia of Electronics.
CAVENDISH, HENRY (*in part*) (Micropædia)

C.H.T.   Charles Henri Toupet. *Professor of Tropical Geography, University of Lyon III. Author of* Étude du milieu physique de massif de l'Assaba, Mauritanie.
WESTERN AFRICA (*in part*)

C.Hu.   Charles Y. Hu. *Former Professor of Geography, University of Maryland, College Park. Author of*
monographs on the military geography of China.
CHINA (*in part*)

C.H.V.S.   Carol Humphrey Vivian Sutherland (d. 1986). *Student of Christ Church, Oxford, 1945-75; Keeper of the Heberden Coin Room, Ashmolean Museum, University of Oxford, 1957-75. Author of* Roman Coins *and others.*
COINS AND COINAGE (*in part*)

C.H.W.   Conrad H. Waddington (d. 1975). *Buchanan Professor of Genetics, University of Edinburgh, Scotland, 1947-75. Author of* Principles of Embryology.
GROWTH AND DEVELOPMENT, BIOLOGICAL (*in part*)

C.H.Wi.   Charles Henry Wilson. *Professor of Modern History, University of Cambridge, 1965-79; Fellow of Jesus College, Cambridge. Author of* Anglo-Dutch Commerce and Finance in the Eighteenth Century *and others; coeditor of* Cambridge Economic History of Europe.
EUROPE (*in part*)
MAURICE (NETHERLANDS) (Micropædia)

C.I.   Charles Issawi. *Bayard Dodge Professor of Near Eastern Studies, Princeton University. Author of* An Arab Philosophy of History *and others.*
IBN KHALDON (Micropædia)

C.I.C.   Carleton Ivers Calkin. *Painter and restorer. Curator, Historic St. Augustine Preservation Board, Florida, 1966-73.*
SCULPTURE, THE HISTORY OF WESTERN (*in part*)

C.J.   Charles Jelavich. *Professor of History, Indiana University, Bloomington. Coauthor of* The Balkans *and others.*
BALKANS (*in part*)

C.J.A.   Charles Joseph Adams. *Professor of Islamic Studies, McGill University, Montreal. Editor of* A Reader's Guide to the Great Religions.
RELIGIONS, THE STUDY AND CLASSIFICATION OF (*in part*)

C.J.Al.   Constantine John Alexopoulos (d. 1986). *Professor of Botany, University of Texas at Austin, 1962-77. Author of* Introductory Mycology.
PROTOPHYTES (*in part*)

C.J.D.   Cornelius J. Dyck. *Professor of Anabaptist and Sixteenth-Century Studies, Mennonite Biblical Seminary, Elkhart, Indiana. Editor of* A Legacy of Faith; An Introduction to Mennonite History *and others.*
MENNO SIMONS (Micropædia)

C.J.F.D.   Charles James Frank Dowsett. *Calouste Gulbenkian Professor of Armenian Studies, University of Oxford; Fellow of Pembroke College, Oxford. Translator (with commentary) of* Movsēs Dasxuranci's The History of the Caucasian Albanians *and others.*
UNION OF SOVIET SOCIALIST REPUBLICS (*in part*)

C.J.G. **Coleman Jett Goin.** *Emeritus Professor of Biological Sciences, University of Florida, Gainesville. Coauthor of* Introduction to Herpetology; *author of numerous articles on reptiles and amphibians.*

AMPHIBIANS (*in part*)

C.J.Ga. **Cyril John Gadd** (d. 1969). *Professor of Ancient Semitic Languages and Civilizations, University of London, 1955–60. Keeper, Egyptian and Assyrian Antiquities, British Museum, London, 1948–55.*

SYRIA (*in part*)

C.J.Go. **Clarence James Goodnight.** *Professor of Biology, Western Michigan University, Kalamazoo. Coauthor of* Biology: An Introduction to the Science of Life *and others.*

ARACHNIDS (*in part*)

C.J.L.P. **Cecil John Layton Price.** *Emeritus Professor of English Language and Literature, University College of Swansea, University of Wales.*

SHERIDAN, RICHARD BRINSLEY (Micropædia)

C.J.M. **Charles John Merdinger.** *Captain, Civil Engineer Corps, U.S. Navy (retired). Deputy Director, Scripps Institution of Oceanography, University of California, San Diego, at La Jolla, 1974–80. Author of* Civil Engineering Through the Ages.

PUBLIC WORKS (*in part*)

C.J.Mo. **Cyril John Morley.** *Former Honorary Secretary, British Falconers' Club and International Association of Falconry and Conservation of Birds of Prey.*

FALCONRY (*in part*) (Micropædia)

C.Jo. **Charles Joys.** *Coauthor of* Vårt folks historie.

NORWAY (*in part*)

C.J.S. **Charles J. Sippl.** *Consultant in the computer, communications, and video fields. Coauthor of* Computer Dictionary and Handbook.

COMPUTERS (*in part*)

C.J.U **Caroline Jean Upton.** *Research Associate, Department of Social Studies, University of Newcastle upon Tyne, England.*

PACIFIC ISLANDS (*in part*)

C.K.B. **C.K. Bertram.** *President, Lucy Cavendish College, University of Cambridge, 1970–79.*

MAMMALS (*in part*)

C.-K.L. **Chi-Keung Leung.** *Reader in Geography, University of Hong Kong. Editor,* Journal of Oriental Studies *and* Asian Geographer. *Author of* China: Railway Patterns and National Goals.

CHINA (*in part*)
HONG KONG

C.K.W. **Charles Kipp Weichert** (d. 1970). *Dean, College of Arts and Sciences, University of Cincinnati, Ohio, 1958–70; Professor of Zoology, 1943–70. Author of* Anatomy of the Chordates.

ORGANS AND ORGAN SYSTEMS, PLANT AND ANIMAL (*in part*)

C.L.C. **C. Lockard Conley, M.D.** *Distinguished Service Professor Emeritus of Medicine, Johns Hopkins University and Hospital, Baltimore, Maryland; Head, Hematology Division, 1947–80. Contributor to* Medical Physiology.

BLOOD (*in part*)

C.L.Cl. **C.L. Cline.** *Ashbel H. Smith Professor Emeritus of English, University of Texas at Austin. Author of* Byron, Shelley, and Their Pisan Circle; *Editor of* The Letters of George Meredith.

MEREDITH, GEORGE (Micropædia)

C.Le. **Chan Lee.** *Professor of Geography, Seoul National University, Korea.*

KOREA (*in part*)
SEOUL

C.L.F. **Charles L. Fefferman.** *Professor of Mathematics, Princeton University.*

ANALYSIS (IN MATHEMATICS) (*in part*)

C.L.Ha. **C. Lowell Harriss.** *Emeritus Professor of Economics, Columbia University. Coauthor of* American Public Finance *and others.*

TAXATION (*in part*)

C.Li. **Chan Lien.** *Professor of Political Science, National Taiwan University, Taipei. Coauthor of* Taiwan: From Pre-history to Modern Times.

HU SHIH (Micropædia)

C.L.K. **Charlotte L. Kellner.** *Former Lecturer in Physics, Imperial College of Science and Technology, University of London. Author of* Alexander von Humboldt.

HUMBOLDT, ALEXANDER VON (Micropædia)

Cl.L. **Clifford Leech.** (d. 1977). *Professor of English, University of Toronto, 1963–74. Author of* The Dramatist's Experience with Other Essays in Critical Theory *and others; editor of* Marlowe: A Collection of Critical Essays.

JONSON, BEN (*in part*) (Micropædia)
MARLOWE, CHRISTOPHER (Micropædia)

C.L.M. **Charles L. Mantell.** *Consulting engineer. Emeritus Professor of Chemical Engineering, New Jersey Institute of Technology, Newark. Coauthor of* Calcium Metallurgy and Technology.

INDUSTRIES, EXTRACTION AND PROCESSING (*in part*)

C.L.Ma. **Clyde L. Manschreck.** *Chavanne Professor of Religious Studies, Rice University, Houston, Texas. Emeritus Professor of the History of Christianity, Chicago Theological Seminary. Editor of* Melanchthon on Christian Doctrine *and others.*

MELANCHTHON, PHILIPP (Micropædia)

C.Lo. **Constance Lowenthal.** *Assistant Museum Educator, Department of Public Education, Metropolitan Museum of Art, New York City.*

GHIBERTI, LORENZO (Micropædia)

C.L.P.P. **Charles L.P. Pellat.** *Professor of Arabic Language and Civilization, University of Paris IV, 1956–78. Author of* L'Arabe vivant *and others.*

IRAQ (*in part*)

C.L.Q. **Charles Loreaux Quittmeyer.** *Floyd Dewey Gottwald Professor of Business Administration, College of William and Mary, Williamsburg, Virginia. Author of* The Virginia Travel Trade.

UNITED STATES OF AMERICA (*in part*)

C.L.R.J. **C.L.R. James.** *Star Professor of History, University of the District of Columbia, Washington, D.C. Secretary, West Indian Federal Labor Party, 1958–62. Author of* The Black Jacobins.

WEST INDIES, THE (*in part*)

C.L.S. **Craig L. Stark.** *Technical writer and consultant. Contributing Editor,* Stereo Review *magazine. Owner, Starksonic Studio (audio testing laboratory), Montclair, New Jersey.*

SOUND (*in part*)

C.L.T. **Carol Lewis Thompson.** *Editor,* Current History, *Philadelphia.*

UNITED STATES OF AMERICA (*in part*)

C.L.W. **Carl Louis Wilson.** *Emeritus Professor of Botany, Dartmouth College, Hanover, New Hampshire. Coauthor of* Botany.

TISSUES AND FLUIDS (*in part*)

C.M. **Christopher Marriage Marsh.** *Special Engineering Adviser, British Waterways Board, 1964–66; North Western Divisional Manager, 1948–64. Author of many papers on waterways.*

PUBLIC WORKS (*in part*)

C.Ma. **Carleton Mabee.** *Professor of History, State University of New York College at New Paltz. Author of* The American Leonardo: A Life of Samuel F.B. Morse.

MORSE, SAMUEL F.B. (Micropædia)

C.M.A. **Sister Consuelo Maria Aherne.** *Professor of History, Chestnut Hill College, Philadelphia. Assistant Staff Editor for* Mediaeval Church History; *contributor to the* New Catholic Encyclopedia.

BONIFACE, SAINT (Micropædia)

C.McH. **Christine McHugh.** *Associate, Joseph D. Kaplan & Son, P.C. (law firm), Trenton, New Jersey.*

ADAMS, HENRY (Micropædia)

C.M.E. **Chester Monroe Edelmann, Jr., M.D.** *Professor of Pediatrics; Associate Dean for Clinical Affairs, Albert Einstein College of Medicine, Yeshiva University, Bronx, New York. Editor of* Pediatric Nephrology.

CHILDHOOD DISEASES AND DISORDERS (*in part*)

C.-M.H. **Chiao-Min Hsieh.** *Professor of Geography, University of Pittsburgh, Pennsylvania. Author of* China: A Geography in Perspective *and others.*

CHINA (*in part*)

C.M.K. **Cecelia M. Kenyon.** *Clarke Professor of Government, Smith College, Northampton, Massachusetts. Editor of* The Antifederalists.
JEFFERSON

C.M.N. **C.M. Naim.** *Associate Professor of Urdu, University of Chicago. Editor of* Readings in Urdu: Prose and Poetry.
SOUTH ASIAN ARTS (*in part*)

C.M.W. **Charles Morrow Wilson** (d. 1977). *Free-lance writer. Author of* Diesel: His Engine Changed the World *and others; coauthor of* Rudolf Diesel.
DIESEL, RUDOLF (Micropædia)

C.M.Wi. **C. Martin Wilbur.** *George Sansom Professor Emeritus of Chinese History, Columbia University. Author of* Sun Yat-sen: Frustrated Patriot; *coauthor of* Documents on Communism, Nationalism and Soviet Advisers in China, 1918–1927.
CHINA (*in part*)

C.M.Wo. **Christopher Montague Woodhouse.** *Member of Parliament for Oxford, 1959–66, 1970–74. Fellow of the Royal Society of London. Fellow of Trinity Hall, University of Cambridge. Coauthor of* Rhodes.
GREECE (*in part*)
RHODES, CECIL (*in part*) (Micropædia)

C.M.Y. **Sir C. Maurice Yonge.** *Regius Professor of Zoology, University of Glasgow, Scotland, 1944–64; Research Fellow in Zoology, 1965–70. Author of* Oysters.
MOLLUSKS (*in part*)

C.N. **Curtis L. Newcombe.** *Emeritus Professor of Marine Biology, San Francisco State University. Director, San Francisco Bay Marine Research Center, Richmond, California. Author of* An Experimental Study of Shock Effects on Surface and Subsurface Organisms.
ECOSYSTEMS (*in part*)

C.N.B. **Cyril Nelson Barclay** (d. 1979). *Brigadier, The Cameronians (Scottish Rifles). Editor,* The Army Quarterly and Defence Journal, *1950–66; coeditor,* Brassey's Annual: The Armed Forces Year Book, *1950–69.*
WAR, THE TECHNOLOGY OF (*in part*)
WAR, THE THEORY AND CONDUCT OF (*in part*)
MOLTKE, HELMUTH VON (Micropædia)

C.N.C. **Charles N. Cofer.** *Professor of Psychology, University of Houston, Texas, 1976–81. Coauthor of* Motivation: Theory and Research.
EMOTION AND MOTIVATION, HUMAN (*in part*)

C.N.M. **Charles Nicholas Morris.** *Deputy Director, Institute for Fiscal Studies, London. Coauthor of* The Reform of Social Security.
GOVERNMENT FINANCE (*in part*)

C.O. **Carola Oman (Lady Lenanton)** (d. 1978). *Biographer. Author of* David Garrick *and others.*
GARRICK, DAVID (Micropædia)

C.O.H. **Colin O. Hines.** *Professor of Physics (Aeronomy), University of Toronto, 1967–81. Coauthor and editor of* Physics of the Earth's Upper Atmosphere.
ATMOSPHERE (*in part*)

C.O.Hu. **Charles O. Hucker.** *Emeritus Professor of Chinese and of History, University of Michigan, Ann Arbor. Author of* The Traditional Chinese State in Ming Times *and others.*
CHINA (*in part*)
YUNG-LO (Micropædia)

Co.L. **Colin Legum.** *Associate Editor,* The Observer, *London, 1949–82; Editor,* Africa Contemporary Record, *1968–83. Author of* Pan-Africanism *and others.*
SOUTHERN AFRICA (*in part*)

Co.S.B. **Cole S. Brembeck.** *Director, Institute for International Studies in Education; Associate Dean, College of Education, Michigan State University, East Lansing. Author of* Social Foundations of Education.
EDUCATION, SOCIAL AND ECONOMIC ASPECTS OF (*in part*)

C.P. **Colin Patterson.** *Curator of Fossil Fishes, British Museum (Natural History), London. Co-editor of* Fossil Vertebrates.
FISHES (*in part*)

C.P.D. **Carlos Pablo Dubois.** *Head of Information Services, International Coffee Organization, London.*
URUGUAY (*in part*)

C.Pe. **Chaim Perelman** (d. 1984). *Professor of Logic and Ethics, Free University of Brussels. Author of* The New Rhetoric *and others.*
RHETORIC (*in part*)

C.Pf. **Carl Pfaffmann.** *Emeritus Professor of Physiological Psychology, Rockefeller University, New York City. Editor of* Olfaction and Taste, *proceedings of the Third International Symposium on Olfaction and Taste.*
SENSORY RECEPTION (*in part*)

C.P.F. **Charles Patrick FitzGerald.** *Emeritus Professor of Far Eastern History, Australian National University, Canberra. Author of* Son of Heaven (T'ang T'ai Tsung); The Empress Wu; *and others.*
T'AI TSUNG (T'ANG DYNASTY) (Micropædia)
WU HOU (Micropædia)

C.P.L. **Charles P. Loomis.** *Emeritus Professor of Sociology, University of Houston, Texas. Coauthor of* Rural Sociology, The Strategy of Change.
RURAL SOCIETY AND AGRICULTURE, MODERN (*in part*)

C.R. **Claude Robineau.** *Director of Research, Overseas Office of Scientific and Technological Research (ORSTOM), Papeete, French Polynesia, and Paris.*
PACIFIC ISLANDS (*in part*)

C.Ra. **Chakravarthi Raghavan.** *Correspondent, IPS Third World News Agency, Geneva.*
BOMBAY
INDIA (*in part*)

C.R.B. **Charles R. Bawden.** *Former Professor of Mongolian, University of London. Author of* The Modern History of Mongolia.
GENGHIS KHAN
KUBLAI KHAN (Micropædia)

C.R.G. **C. Robin Ganellin.** *Vice-President, Chemical Research, Smith Kline & French Research Limited, Welwyn, England. Coeditor of* Frontiers in Histamine Research *and others.*
DRUGS AND DRUG ACTION (*in part*)

C.R.H. **Campbell Ronald Harler** (deceased). *Adviser on tea to the Central Treaty Organization. Author of* The Culture and Marketing of Tea.
BEVERAGE PRODUCTION (*in part*)
FARMING AND AGRICULTURAL TECHNOLOGY (*in part*)

C.R.N **Charles R. Noback.** *Professor of Anatomy, College of Physicians and Surgeons, Columbia University. Author of* The Human Nervous System.
NERVES AND NERVOUS SYSTEMS (*in part*)

C.R.No. **Carl R. Noller** (d. 1980). *Professor of Chemistry, Stanford University, California. Author of* Chemistry of Organic Compounds *and others.*
CHEMICAL COMPOUNDS (*in part*)

C.Ro. **Christopher Robinson.** *Official Student in Modern Languages, Christ Church, University of Oxford. Author of* French Literature in the 19th Century *and others.*
FRENCH LITERATURE (*in part*)

C.R.R. **Charles R. Russell.** *Former Professor of Mechanical Engineering, California Polytechnic State University, San Luis Obispo. Author of* Elements of Energy Conversion.
ENERGY CONVERSION (*in part*)

C.R.T. **Charles Rowland Twidale.** *Reader in Geography, University of Adelaide, Australia. Author of* Geomorphology with Special Reference to Australia *and others.*
AUSTRALIA (*in part*)
GEOMORPHIC PROCESSES (*in part*)

C.S. **Calambur Sivaramamurti.** *Director, National Museum of India, New Delhi, 1966–69, 1971–75; Hony Adviser on Museums, Government of India, 1969–70. Author of* Indian Sculpture *and others.*
SOUTH ASIAN ARTS (*in part*)

C.Sa. **Claudio Sartori.** *Chief, Office of Research and Indexing of the Italian Musical Funds, Braidense National Library, Milan. Author of* Puccini *and others.*
PUCCINI, GIACOMO (Micropædia)

C.S.B. **Cyril S. Belshaw.** *Professor of Anthropology, University of British*

Columbia, Vancouver. Editor, Current Anthropology. *Internationally known scholar in areas of social change and economics. Author of* Traditional Exchange and Modern Markets *and others.*

ECONOMIC SYSTEMS (*in part*)

C.Sc.   Conrad Schirokauer. *Professor of History, City College, City University of New York. Author of "Chu Hsi's Political Career: A Study in Ambivalence" in* Confucian Personalities.

CHU HSI (*in part*)

C.S.C.   Carleton Stevens Coon (d. 1981). *Research Associate in Ethnology, Peabody Museum, Harvard University, 1968–81. Curator of Ethnology, University Museum, University of Pennsylvania, Philadelphia, 1948–63. Author of* The Origin of Races *and others.*

EVOLUTION, HUMAN (*in part*)

C.-S.Ch.   Cheng-Siang Chen. *Former Professor of Geography; former Director, Geographical Research Center, Chinese University of Hong Kong. Author of* Taiwan: An Economic and Social Geography *and several reports on Hong Kong.*

CHINA (*in part*)

C.Se.   Charles Seymour (d. 1963). *President, Yale University, 1937–50; Professor of History, 1918–37. Author of* The Diplomatic Background of the War; Woodrow Wilson and the World War.

WILSON, WOODROW (*in part*)
    (Micropædia)

C.S.F.   Catherine S. Fowler. *Professor of Anthropology, University of Nevada, Reno. Author of* Great Basin Anthropology: A Bibliography.

AMERICAN INDIANS (*in part*)

C.S.G.P.   Courtenay Stanley Goss Phillips. *University Lecturer in Inorganic Chemistry, University of Oxford; Fellow of Merton College, Oxford. Coauthor of* Inorganic Chemistry.

CHEMICAL ELEMENTS (*in part*)

C.S.Ha.   Craig S. Harbison. *Associate Professor of Art, University of Massachusetts, Amherst. Author of* The Last Judgment in Sixteenth Century Northern Europe *and others.*

GRÜNEWALD, MATTHIAS (Micropædia)
HOLBEIN, HANS, THE YOUNGER
    (Micropædia)

C.S.J.   Christopher Stewart Jackson. *Former Senior Lecturer in English, University of the West Indies, Cave Hill, Barbados.*

WEST INDIES, THE (*in part*)

C.Sm.   Colin Smethurst. *Marshall Professor of French, University of Glasgow, Scotland. Author of* Émile Zola, Germinal.

FRENCH LITERATURE (*in part*)

C.Sn.   Carl Sagan. *Director, Laboratory for Planetary Studies; David Duncan Professor of Astronomy, Cornell University, Ithaca, New York. Coauthor*

of Planets; Intelligent Life in the Universe.

LIFE (*in part*)
SOLAR SYSTEM, THE (*in part*)

C.S.S.   Sir Charles Scott Sherrington, M.D. (d. 1952). *Waynflete Professor of Physiology, University of Oxford, 1913–35. Co-winner, Nobel Prize for Physiology or Medicine, 1932, for discoveries regarding the function of neurons. Author of* The Integrative Action of the Nervous System.

NERVES AND NERVOUS SYSTEMS (*in part*)

C.Su.   Chusei Suzuki. *Professor of Asian History, Aichi University, Toyohashi, Japan. Author of* A Study of Mid-Ch'ing History.

CHINA (*in part*)

C.S.W.   C. Stuart Welch, M.D. (d. 1981). *Professor of Surgery, Albany Medical College, Union University, New York. Coauthor of* The Essence of Surgery.

DIAGNOSIS AND THERAPEUTICS (*in part*)

C.S.Wh.   Charles S. Whewell. *Emeritus Professor of Textile Industries, University of Leeds, England.*

INDUSTRIES, TEXTILE (*in part*)

C.S.-y.   Chuang Shang-yen. *Former Deputy Director, National Palace Museum, Taipei, Taiwan.*

MI FEI (Micropædia)

C.T.   Curt Teichert. *Adjunct Professor of Geological Sciences, University of Rochester, New York. Regents Distinguished Professor of Geology, University of Kansas, Lawrence, 1964–75. An authority on the Permian stratigraphy of the world.*

GEOCHRONOLOGY (*in part*)

C.-t.C.   Chen-tung Chang. *Senior Lecturer in Sociology, National University of Singapore. Author of* Fertility Transition in Singapore.

CHINA (*in part*)

C.T.M.Jr.   Charles T. Mason, Jr. *Professor of Plant Sciences; Curator of the Herbarium, University of Arizona, Tucson.*

ANGIOSPERMS (*in part*)

C.T.Mo.   Charles Thomas Morrissey. *Editor,* Vermont Life. *Former Chairman, Vermont Council on Humanities and Public Issues. Adjunct Professor of History, University of Vermont, Burlington, 1969–71; 1974–84.*

UNITED STATES OF AMERICA (*in part*)

C.T.R.   C.T. Ritchie. *Historian, writer, and artist. Author of* The First Canadian: The Story of Champlain *and others.*

CHAMPLAIN, SAMUEL DE (Micropædia)

C.T.W.   Cheves T. Walling. *Distinguished Professor of Chemistry, University of Utah, Salt Lake City. Author of* Free Radicals in Solution.

RADICAL (*in part*) (Micropædia)

C.V.B   Clinton V. Black. *Archivist, Jamaica Archives, Spanish Town.*

Author of The Story of Jamaica *and others.*

WEST INDIES, THE (*in part*)

C.v.d.K.   C. van de Kieft. *Professor of Medieval History, University of Amsterdam. Coauthor of* 500 Jaren Staten-Generaal in de Nederlanden.

LOW COUNTRIES, THE (*in part*)

C.V.-F.   Claudio Vita-Finzi. *Reader in Geography, University College, University of London. Author of* Recent Earth History; Archaeological Sites in Their Setting; *and others.*

GEOMORPHIC PROCESSES (*in part*)

C.V.N.   Chakravarthi V. Narasimhan. *Senior Fellow, United Nations Institute for Training and Research, New York City; Undersecretary-General of the United Nations, 1973–78. Author of* The Mahābhārata: An English Version Based on Selected Verses.

ASIA (*in part*)

C.V.W.   Dame C.V. Wedgwood. *Free-lance writer and historian. Fellow, University College, University of London. Fellow, Lady Margaret Hall, University of Oxford. Author of* Thomas Wentworth, First Earl of Strafford, 1593–1641: A Revaluation *and others.*

STRAFFORD, THOMAS WENTWORTH, 1ST
    EARL OF (Micropædia)

C.W.   Claus Westermann. *Professor of Old Testament Exegesis, University of Heidelberg. Author of* Handbook to the Old Testament.

SACRED OFFICES AND ORDERS (*in part*)

C.W.B.   Curt W. Beck. *Matthew Vassar, Jr., Professor of Chemistry, Vassar College, Poughkeepsie, New York.*

STAHL, GEORG ERNST (Micropædia)

C.W.G.   Carol W. Gelderman. *Professor of English, University of New Orleans. Author of* Henry Ford, the Wayward Capitalist.

FORD, HENRY (*in part*)

C.W.H.   Charles W. Hayford. *Associate, Department of History, Northwestern University, Evanston, Illinois, and Center for Far Eastern Studies, University of Chicago.*

LIN TSE-HSÜ (Micropædia)

C.W.H.H.   C. William H. Havard, M.D. *Consultant Physician, Royal Free Hospital and Royal Northern Hospital, London. Author of* Lectures in Medicine.

DIAGNOSIS AND THERAPEUTICS (*in part*)

C.W.Ho.   C. Warren Hollister. *Professor of History, University of California, Santa Barbara. Author of* The Impact of the Norman Conquest *and others.*

HENRY I (ENGLAND) (Micropædia)

C.W.J.   C. Wilfred Jenks (d. 1973). *Director General of the International Labour Office, Geneva, Switzerland, 1970–73. Author of* Human Rights and International Labour Standards.

BUSINESS LAW (*in part*)

C.W.M.   C.W. Minkel. *Vice Provost; Dean, Graduate School, University of Tennessee, Knoxville. Coauthor of* Latin America.

CARACAS (*in part*)
SÃO PAULO (*in part*)

C.W.Pa.   Charles William Parkin. *Fellow and Lecturer of Clare College, University of Cambridge. Author of* The Moral Basis of Burke's Political Thought.

BURKE, EDMUND (*in part*) (Micropædia)

C.W.S.   Clyde William Sanger. *Visiting Lecturer, Zimbabwe Institute of Mass Communication, 1982. Director of Information, Commonwealth Secretariat, London, 1977–79. Author of* Central African Emergency.

SOUTHERN AFRICA (*in part*)

C.W.T.   Charlton W. Tebeau. *Emeritus Professor of History, University of Miami, Coral Gables, Florida. Author of* A History of Florida.

JACKSON, THOMAS JONATHAN (Micropædia)

C.W.W.   Charles W. Wagley. *Graduate Research Professor Emeritus of Anthropology and Latin American Studies, University of Florida, Gainesville. Author of* Introduction to Brazil *and others.*

BRAZIL (*in part*)

C.Y.   Chiang Yee (d. 1977). *Painter, Professor of Chinese, Columbia University, 1968–71. Author of* Chinese Calligraphy *and others.*

WRITING (*in part*)

C.-y.C.   Chu-yuan Cheng. *Professor of Economics, Ball State University, Muncie, Indiana. Consultant, National Science Foundation, Washington, D.C. Author of* China's Economic Development: Growth and Structural Change *and others.*

CHINA (*in part*)

Cy.Do.   Cyril Domb. *Professor of Physics, Bar Ilan University, Ramat Gan, Israel. Editor of* Clerk Maxwell and Modern Science.

MAXWELL

C.-y.H.   Cho-yun Hsu. *University Professor of History and Sociology, University of Pittsburgh. Author of* Ancient China in Transition; Han Agriculture.

CHINA (*in part*)

C.Z.   Conway Zirkle (d. 1972). *Professor of Biology, University of Pennsylvania, Philadelphia, 1937–66. Author of* Death of a Science in Russia *and others.*

LYSENKO, TROFIM DENISOVICH (Micropædia)

Cz.L.   Czeslaw Lejewski. *Emeritus Professor of Philosophy, Victoria University of Manchester. Author of* "Logic and Existence," *British Journal for the Philosophy of Science, and numerous other journal articles.*

LOGIC, THE HISTORY AND KINDS OF (*in part*)

Da.Br.   David Brown. *Professor of Musicology, University of Southampton, England. Author of* Mikhail Glinka; Tchaikovsky; *and others.*

SHOSTAKOVICH, DMITRY (Micropædia)

Da.D.   David Dooling, Jr. *Science Editor, The Huntsville (Alabama) Times. Editor of* Shuttle to the Next Space Age.

EXPLORATION (*in part*)

D.A.E.S.   David A.E. Spalding. *Free-lance writer and consultant. Former Head Curator of Natural History, Provincial Museum of Alberta, Edmonton. Senior editor of* A Nature Guide to Alberta.

CANADA (*in part*)

Da.H.   David Harris (d. 1975). *Professor of History, Stanford University, California, 1941–66. Author of* A Diplomatic History of the Balkan Crisis of 1875–1878; The First Year.

EUROPE (*in part*)

D.A.H.   Donald August Holm. *Senior Geologist, Arabian American Oil Company, Dhahran, Saudi Arabia, 1946–61. Author of* "Desert Geomorphology of the Arabian Peninsula" *in* Science.

ASIA (*in part*)

D.A.He.   D. Alan Heslop. *Director, Rose Institute of State and Local Government, Claremont McKenna College, California. Editor of* Californians in Congress.

POLITICAL SYSTEMS (*in part*)

D.A.K.   David A. Kronick. *Library Director, University of Texas Health Science Center at San Antonio. Author of* A History of Scientific and Technical Periodicals.

INFORMATION PROCESSING (*in part*)

D.A.K.B.   Sir Douglas A.K. Black, M.D. *Emeritus Professor of Medicine, Victoria University of Manchester; Physician, Manchester Royal Infirmary, 1959–77. Editor of* Renal Disease.

EXCRETION AND EXCRETORY SYSTEMS (*in part*)

D.A.L.   Daniel A. Livingstone. *J.B. Duke Professor of Zoology, Duke University, Durham, North Carolina. Limnologist, Geological Survey, U.S. Department of the Interior, 1956–63.*

ECOSYSTEMS (*in part*)

D.A.Lo.   D. Anthony Low. *Smuts Professor of Commonwealth History, University of Cambridge. Author of* Buganda in Modern History.

EASTERN AFRICA (*in part*)

Da.Ma.   David Magarshack (d. 1977). *Author of* Chekhov the Dramatist; Dostoevsky; Pushkin: A Biography.

RUSSIAN LITERATURE (*in part*)

D'A.McN.   D'Arcy McNickle (d. 1977). *Professor of Anthropology, University of Saskatchewan, Regina, 1966–71. Director, American Indian Development, Inc., Boulder, Colorado, 1952–66.*

Author of The Indian Tribes of the United States *and others.*

NORTH AMERICA (*in part*)

D.An.   Donald M. Anderson. *Emeritus Professor of Art, University of Wisconsin, Madison. Author of* The Art of Written Forms.

WRITING (*in part*)

D.A.N.   David A. Norris. *Lecturer in Slavonic Studies, University of Nottingham, Eng. Translator of Edvard Kardelj's* Reminiscences.

YUGOSLAV LITERATURE (*in part*)

D.Ar.   Daniel Argov. *Former Lecturer in Modern Indian History, Institute of Asian and African Studies, Hebrew University of Jerusalem. Author of* Moderates and Extremists in the Indian Nationalist Movement, 1883–1920.

PATEL, VALLABHBHAI JHAVERBHAI (Micropædia)

D.A.S.   Donald Arnold Smith. *Principal Writer and Instructor, Frederick Electronics Corporation, Frederick, Maryland. Author of* ABC's of Vacuum Tubes *and others.*

ELECTRONICS (*in part*)

D.A.Sa.   Dawlat Ahmed Sadek. *Chairman of the Geography Department, Faculty of Arts, Ain Shams University, Cairo, Egypt.*

ARABIA (*in part*)

D.At.   Donald Attwater (d. 1977). *Author of* Penguin Dictionary of Saints; St. John Chrysostom, Pastor and Preacher.

CHRYSOSTOM, SAINT JOHN (Micropædia)

D.B.   Douglas Bush (d. 1983). *Gurney Professor of English Literature, Harvard University, 1957–66. Author of* Paradise Lost in Our Time *and others.*

MILTON (*in part*)

D.Ba.   D. Banzragch. *Scientific Secretary, Institute of Biology, Academy of Sciences of the Mongolian People's Republic, Ulaanbaatar.*

MONGOLIA (*in part*)

D.B.C.   David B. Chan. *Professor of History, California State University, Hayward. Author of* The Yung Lo Usurpation.

HUNG-WU (Micropædia)

D.B.E.   David Barnard Ericson. *Senior Research Scientist, Lamont-Doherty Geological Observatory, Columbia University. Coauthor of* The Ever Changing Sea.

OCEANS (*in part*)

D.B.-G.   David Ben-Gurion (d. 1973). *Prime Minister and Minister of Defense, Government of Israel, 1948–53, 1955–63. Author of* The Struggle *and many others.*

HERZL, THEODOR (Micropædia)

D.B.H.   Dwight B. Heath. *Professor of Anthropology, Brown University, Providence, Rhode Island. Editor of* Contemporary Cultures and Societies of

Latin America.
AMERICAN INDIANS (*in part*)

D.Bi.   David Birmingham. *Professor of Modern History, University of Kent at Canterbury, England. Author of* The Portuguese Conquest of Angola *and others.*
CENTRAL AFRICA (*in part*)
SOUTHERN AFRICA (*in part*)
WESTERN AFRICA (*in part*)

D.B.J.F.   David B. J. Frost. *Rugby Union correspondent,* The Guardian *(London). Author of* No Prisoners: Background to Rugby Touring.
SPORTS, MAJOR TEAM AND INDIVIDUAL (*in part*)

D.Bn.   David Brown. *Research Fellow, Centre of West African Studies, University of Birmingham, England.*
WESTERN AFRICA (*in part*)

D.B.O.S.   Douglas B. O. Savile. *Emeritus Research Associate, Biosystematics Research Institute, Canada Department of Agriculture, Ottawa; Principal Mycologist, 1957–75. Author of* Arctic Adaptations in Plants.
ARCTIC, THE (*in part*)

D.Br.   Doris Bry. *Writer on photography, art history, and natural science. Representative for the paintings of Georgia O'Keeffe. Author of* Alfred Stieglitz: Photographer.
STIEGLITZ, ALFRED (Micropædia)

D.B.S.   David B. Stewart. *Research Geologist, Geological Survey, U.S. Department of the Interior, Washington, D.C.*
MINERALS AND ROCKS (*in part*)

D.B.W.   David B. Wake. *Director, Museum of Vertebrate Zoology; Professor of Zoology, University of California, Berkeley.*
AMPHIBIANS (*in part*)

D.B.Wa.   Duncan Bruce Waterson. *Professor of History, Macquarie University, North Ryde, Australia.*
AUSTRALIA (*in part*)

D.C.   Douglas Cooper (d. 1984). *Art historian and critic. Author of* Toulouse Lautrec *and many other works on French artists of the late 19th and 20th century.*
GAUGUIN, PAUL (Micropædia)

D.Ca.   David Carson. *Emeritus Professor of Business Administration, Boston University. Author of* International Marketing: A Comparative Systems Approach.
MARKETING AND MERCHANDISING (in part)

D.C.A.   Dorothy C. Adkins (d. 1975). *Psychologist. Professor of Education, University of Hawaii, Honolulu, 1965–74. Author of* Test Construction.
PSYCHOLOGICAL TESTS AND MEASUREMENT (*in part*)

D.C.B.   Douglas C. Baxter. *Associate Professor of History, Ohio University, Athens.*

LOUVOIS, FRANÇOIS-MICHEL LE TELLIER, MARQUIS DE (Micropædia)

D.C.G.S.   David C.G. Sibley. *Free-lance writer and artist. Author of* With La Salle down the Mississippi *and others.*
LA SALLE, RENÉ-ROBERT CAVELIER, SIEUR DE (Micropædia)

D.C.H.   David C. Hoaglin. *Research Associate in Statistics, Harvard University. Senior Scientist, Abt Associates Inc., Cambridge, Massachusetts.*
STATISTICS (*in part*)

D.C.Hu.   David C. Hughes. *Architect.*
BUILDING CONSTRUCTION (*in part*)

D.C.J.   D. Clayton James. *Professor of History, Mississippi State University, Mississippi State. Author of* The Years of MacArthur *and others.*
MACARTHUR, DOUGLAS (Micropædia)

D.C.P.   David C. Pieri. *Member of the Technical Staff and Viking Lander Monitor Mission Project Scientist, Earth and Space Sciences Division, Jet Propulsion Laboratory, California Institute of Technology, Pasadena.*
SOLAR SYSTEM, THE (*in part*)

D.C.S.   Domingo C. Salita. *Emeritus Professor of Geology and Geography. University of the Philippines, Quezon City.*
MANILA

D.C.T.   Denis C. Twitchett. *Gordon Wu Professor of Chinese Studies, Princeton University. Author of* The Financial Administration Under the T'ang Dynasty; *editor of* Cambridge History of China.
CHINA (in part)
SSU-MA CH'IEN (Micropædia)

D.C.Th.   David Christopher Traherne Thomas. *Former Assistant Director of Art, Arts Council of Great Britain, London. Joint compiler of* The First Hundred Years of the Royal Academy, 1769–1868 *(catalog of the Royal Academy Winter Exhibition, London, 1951–52).*
DEGAS, EDGAR (Micropædia)

D.D.   David Diringer (d. 1975). *Reader in Semitic Epigraphy, University of Cambridge. 1966–68. Founder and Director, Alphabet Museum, Tel Aviv, Israel. Author of* The Alphabet *and many other works.*
WRITING (*in part*)

D.Da.   David Daiches. *Emeritus Professor of English, University of Sussex, Brighton, England. Author of* Robert Burns; Robert Burns and His World; R.L. Stevenson and His World.
BURNS, ROBERT (*in part*) (Micropædia)
STEVENSON, ROBERT LOUIS (Micropædia)

D.D.B.   Dimitry Dimitriyevich Blagoy. *Correspondent Member, Academy of Sciences of the U.S.S.R., Moscow; Member, Academy of Pedagogical Sciences of the U.S.S.R., Moscow.*

Author of Tvorchesky put Pushkina.
PUSHKIN, ALEKSANDR (*in part*) (Micropædia)

D.D.Br.   Donald Dilworth Brand (d. 1984). *Professor of Geography, University of Texas at Austin, 1949–75. Author of* Mexico: Land of Sunshine and Shadow.
NORTH AMERICA (*in part*)

D.D.F.   Don D. Fowler. *Professor of Anthropology; Director, Historic Preservation Program, University of Nevada, Reno. Coeditor of* Anthropology of the Numu, Smithsonian Contributions to Anthropology, *vol. 14.*
AMERICAN INDIANS (*in part*)

D.Dn.   D. Dashtseren. *Journalist and publicist.*
MONGOLIA (*in part*)

D.Do.   Denis Donoghue. *Henry James Professor of Letters, New York University, New York City. Author of* Yeats; *editor of* Yeats: Memoirs.
YEATS, WILLIAM BUTLER (*in part*) (Micropædia)

D.D.R.O.   D.D.R. Owen. *Professor of French, University of St. Andrews, Scotland. Author of* The Evolution of the Grail Legend *and others.*
FRENCH LITERATURE (*in part*)

D.D.T.   Donald D. Trunkey. *Professor of Surgery, University of California, San Francisco. Chief of Surgery, San Francisco General Hospital. Editor of* Current Trauma Therapy.
BURNS (*in part*)

D.E.   David A. Ede. *Associate Professor of Religion, Western Michigan University, Kalamazoo.*
ḤASAN AL-BAṢRĪ, AL- (Micropædia)

De.B.   Denis Baly. *Emeritus Professor of Religion, Kenyon College, Gambier, Ohio. Author of* The Geography of the Bible; Palestine and the Bible *and others.*
PALESTINE (*in part*)

D.E.B.   D. E. Berlyne (d. 1976). *Professor of Psychology, University of Toronto. Author of* Structure and Direction in Thinking.
THOUGHT AND THOUGHT PROCESSES (*in part*)

D.E.C.Y.   David Eryl Corbet Yale. *Reader in English Legal History, University of Cambridge; Fellow of Christ's College, Cambridge.*
HALE, SIR MATTHEW (Micropædia)

D.E.K.   Daniel E. Koshland, Jr. *Professor of Biochemistry, University of California, Berkeley. Editor of* Protein Structure and Function.
BIOCHEMICAL COMPONENTS OF ORGANISMS (*in part*)

D.E.L.   David Edward Luscombe. *Professor of Medieval History, University of Sheffield, England. Author of* The School of Peter Abelard; *editor of* Peter Abelard's Ethics.
ABELARD, PETER (Micropædia)

De.M.S. **Denis Mack Smith.** *Senior Research Fellow and Dean of Visiting Fellows, All Souls College, University of Oxford. Author of* Garibaldi; *editor of* Garibaldi.

GARIBALDI, GIUSEPPE (Micropædia)

D.E.P. **David E. Pingree.** *Professor of the History of Mathematics, Brown University, Providence, Rhode Island. Author of* Gregory Chioniades and Palaeologan Astronomy *and others.*

OCCULTISM (*in part*)

D.Er. **Donald James Erb.** *Meadows Professor of Composition, Southern Methodist University, Dallas, Texas. Composer of* "The Seventh Trumpet."

MUSIC, THE ART OF (*in part*)
MUSICAL FORMS AND GENRES (*in part*)

D.E.S. **David Eugene Smith** (d. 1944). *Professor of Mathematics, Teachers College, Columbia University, 1901–26. Author of* History of Modern Mathematics *and others.*

ARITHMETIC (*in part*)
MATHEMATICS, THE HISTORY OF
  (*in part*)

D.E.S.M. **D. E. S. Maxwell.** *Professor of English, York University, Toronto. Author of* Herman Melville; American Fiction; *and others.*

MELVILLE, HERMAN (*in part*)
  (Micropædia)

DeW.C.R. **DeWitt C. Reddick** (d. 1980). *Jesse H. Jones Professor of Journalism and Education, University of Texas at Austin, 1970–75.*

UNITED STATES OF AMERICA (*in part*)

D.E.W.W. **Donald Ernest Wilson Wormell.** *Professor of Latin, University of Dublin, 1942-78. Coauthor of* The Delphic Oracle.

PINDAR (Micropædia)

D.F. **David Foulkes.** *Research Scientist, Georgia Mental Health Institute, Atlanta. Author of* The Psychology of Sleep.

SLEEP AND DREAMS (*in part*)

D.F.B. **Donald F. Bond.** *Emeritus Professor of English, University of Chicago. Editor of* The Spectator.

ADDISON, JOSEPH (Micropædia)

D.F.Do. **Douglas F. Dowd.** *Professor of Economics, San Jose State University, California.*

OWEN, ROBERT (Micropædia)

D.Fe. **David Fellman.** *Vilas Professor Emeritus of Political Science, University of Wisconsin, Madison. Author of* The Defendant's Rights Today.

CONSTITUTIONAL LAW

D.F.G. **David Frank Gordon.** *Assistant Professor of International Relations, Michigan State University, East Lansing.*

SOUTH AFRICA (*in part*)

D.Fl. **David Flusser.** *Professor of the History of Religions, Hebrew University of Jerusalem. Author of* Jesus *and others.*

BIBLICAL LITERATURE AND ITS CRITICAL
  INTERPRETATION (*in part*)

D.G.Ch. **Donald Geoffrey Charlton.** *Professor of French; Chairman, Department of French Studies, University of Warwick, Coventry, England. Author of* Positivist Thought in France, 1852–1870 *and others.*

TAINE, HIPPOLYTE (Micropædia)

D.G.D. **Denys G. Dyer.** *University Lecturer in German, University of Oxford; Fellow of Exeter College, Oxford.*

GERMAN LITERATURE (*in part*)

D.Ge. **Deno John Geanakoplos.** *Professor of History and Religious Studies, Yale University. Author of* Emperor Michael Palaeologus and the West *and others.*

MICHAEL VIII PALAEOLOGUS
  (BYZANTINE EMPIRE) (Micropædia)

D.G.F. **Donald G. Fink.** *Emeritus Director, Institute of Electrical and Electronics Engineers, New York. Author of* Television Engineering.

BROADCASTING (*in part*)
ENGINEERING (*in part*)

D.Gi. **Douglas Stuart Gilbert** (d. 1979). *Sports columnist,* Edmonton Sun, *1978-79. Sports reporter,* Montreal Gazette, *1970-78.*

SPORTS, MAJOR TEAM AND INDIVIDUAL
  (*in part*)

D.G.J. **D. Gale Johnson.** *Eliakim Hastings Moore Distinguished Service Professor of Economics, University of Chicago. Author of* World Agriculture in Disarray *and others.*

RURAL SOCIETY AND AGRICULTURE,
  MODERN (*in part*)

D.G.J.S. **David Grenville John Sellwood.** *Principal Lecturer in Mechanical Engineering, Kingston Polytechnic, England. Author of* An Introduction to the Coinage of Parthia.

COINS AND COINAGE (*in part*)

D.G.MacR. **Donald Gunn MacRae.** *Martin White Professor of Sociology, London School of Economics and Political Science, University of London.*

MALTHUS, THOMAS ROBERT
  (Micropædia)

D.Gr. **David Greene** (d. 1981). *Senior Professor, School of Celtic Studies, Dublin Institute for Advanced Studies. Author of* The Irish Language.

LANGUAGES OF THE WORLD (*in part*)
CELTIC LITERATURE (*in part*)

D.G.R. **Donald G. Rea.** *Assistant Laboratory Director, Technology and Space Programs Development, Jet Propulsion Laboratory, California Institute of Technology, Pasadena.*

SOLAR SYSTEM, THE (*in part*)

D.G.Sc. **Dante G. Scarpelli, M.D.** *Ernest J. and Hattie H. Magerstadt Professor and Chairman, Department of Pathology, Northwestern University, Chicago.*

CANCER (*in part*)

D.G.T. **David Gordon Tucker.** *Professor and Head, Department of Electronic and Electrical Engineering, University of Birmingham, England, 1955-73.*

MEASUREMENT AND OBSERVATION,
  PRINCIPLES, METHODS AND
  INSTRUMENTS OF (*in part*)

D.H.B. **Daryle H. Busch.** *Professor of Chemistry, Ohio State University, Columbus. Coauthor of* Introduction to Qualitative Analysis; Chemistry.

CHEMICAL COMPOUNDS (*in part*)

D.H.D. **David Herbert Donald.** *Charles Warren Professor of American History and Professor of American Civilization, Harvard University. Author of* Lincoln Reconsidered *and others.*

UNITED STATES OF AMERICA (*in part*)

D.Hi. **Dorothy Hill.** *Research Professor Emeritus of Geology, University of Queensland, St. Lucia, Brisbane, Australia. Author of* Paleozoic Corals; *coauthor of* Elements of the Stratigraphy of Queensland.

OCEANS (*in part*)

D.H.J. **Douglas Henry Jones.** *Former Senior Lecturer in the History of West Africa, School of Oriental and African Studies, University of London.*

WESTERN AFRICA (*in part*)

D.H.P. **D.H. Pennington.** *Former Fellow and Tutor in History, Balliol College, Oxford; former Lecturer in Modern History, University of Oxford. Author of* Seventeenth Century Europe.

LAUD, WILLIAM (*in part*) (Micropædia)

D.H.Pe. **Douglas Henry Pike** (d. 1974). *General Editor,* Australian Dictionary of Biography, *1962-73. Author of* Australia: The Quiet Continent *and others.*

AUSTRALIA (*in part*)

D.H.R.B. **Sir Derek Harold Richard Barton.** *Director, Institute of Chemistry of Natural Substances, National Centre for Scientific Research, Gif-sur-Yvette, France. Co-winner, Nobel Prize for Chemistry, 1969, for the development of conformational analysis.*

MOLECULES (*in part*)

D.Hus. **Dyneley Hussey** (d. 1972). *Music Critic,* The Times, London, *1923-46;* The Listener, *1946-60. Author of* Verdi; Some Composers of Opera.

DONIZETTI, GAETANO (Micropædia)
VERDI, GIUSEPPE (Micropædia)

D.I. **David Irwin.** *Chairman, Department of History of Art, University of Aberdeen, Scotland. Author of* English Neoclassical Art *and others.*

CANOVA, ANTONIO, MARCHESE D'ISCHIA
  (Micropædia)
PAINTING, THE HISTORY OF WESTERN
  (*in part*)
SCULPTURE, THE HISTORY OF WESTERN
  (*in part*)

Di.B. **Dieter Brunnschweiler** (d. 1983). *Professor of Geography, Michigan State University, East Lansing. Coauthor of* Geography in Latin America: Prospect

for the Seventies.
SOUTH AMERICA (*in part*)

Di.C.   Dieter Christensen. *Professor of Music; Director, Center for Studies in Ethnomusicology, Columbia University, Author of* Die Musik der Kate und Sialum; *coauthor of* Die Musik der Ellice-Inseln.
OCEANIC ARTS (*in part*)

D.I.D.   Denis Ian Duveen. *Consultant to the cosmetics industry in Brazil. President, Duveen Soap Corporation, Brooklyn, New York, 1949–69. Coauthor of* A Bibliography of the Works of Antoine Laurent Lavoisier.
LAVOISIER

Di.L.   Dioulé Laya. *Director of the Centre for Linguistic and Historical Studies by Oral Tradition, Organization of African Unity, Niamey, Niger. Author of* "Tradition orale et recherche historique en Afrique," *Journal of World History (Unesco).*
WESTERN AFRICA (*in part*)

D.J.B.   D. Joseph Bodin. *Manager, Sales and Marketing Division, Technicolor, Inc., Chicopee, Massachusetts. Editor,* Grits & Grinds *magazine, 1967–70.*
INDUSTRIAL GLASS AND CERAMICS
   (*in part*)

D.J.Ba.   D. James Baker. *President, Joint Oceanographic Institutions Incorporated, Washington, D.C.*
EXPLORATION (*in part*)

D.J.C.   Daniel J. Crowley. *Professor of Anthropology and Art, University of California, Davis. Author of* I Could Talk Old-Story Good: Creativity in Bahamian Folklore.
WEST INDIES, THE (*in part*)

D.J.F.   Douglas John Foskett. *Director of Central Library Services and Goldsmiths' Librarian, University of London, 1978–83. Author of* Classification and Indexing in the Social Sciences *and others.*
LIBRARIES (*in part*)

D.J.G.   Douglas James Guthrie, M.D. (d. 1975). *Medical historian. Lecturer on the History of Medicine, University of Edinburgh, 1945–56. Author of* A History of Medicine *and others.*
MEDICINE (*in part*)

D.J.H.   Donald J. Hanahan. *Professor of Biochemistry, University of Texas Health Science Center at San Antonio. Author of* Lipide Chemistry.
BIOCHEMICAL COMPONENTS OF
   ORGANISMS (*in part*)

D.J.M.H.   David J.M. Higgins (d. 1975). *Associate Professor of English, Monmouth College, West Long Branch, New Jersey, 1973–75. Author of* Portrait of Emily Dickinson.
DICKINSON, EMILY (Micropædia)

D.J.R.   Donald J. Reish. *Professor of Biology, California State University, Long Beach. Author of* Marine Life of Southern California *and others.*
ANNELIDS

D.J.Ro.   David J. Robinson. *Dellplain Professor of Latin American Geography, Syracuse University, New York. Editor of* Studying Latin America.
LIMA

D.J.S.   Dirk Jan Sruik. *Emeritus Professor of Mathematics, Massachusetts Institute of Technology, Cambridge. Author of* Concise History of Mathematics *and others.*
FOURIER, JOSEPH, BARON (Micropædia)
LAGRANGE, JOSEPH-LOUIS, COMTE DE
   L'EMPIRE (Micropædia)
LOBACHEVSKY, NIKOLAY IVANOVICH
   (Micropædia)

D.J.W.   Donald John Wiseman. *Emeritus Professor of Assyriology, School of Oriental and African Studies, University of London. Author of* Chronicles of Chaldaean Kings *and others.*
ASHURBANIPAL (Micropædia)
TIGLATH-PILESER III (Micropædia)

D.K.   Delmar Karlen. *Emeritus Professor of Law, New York University, New York City. Author of* Judicial Administration: The American Experience *and others.*
JUDICIAL AND ARBITRATIONAL
   SYSTEMS (*in part*)

D.Ke.   Donald Keene. *Professor of Japanese, Columbia University. Translator into English of many of the great literary works in Japanese; and author of* World Within Walls: Japanese Literature of the Pre-Modern Era.
JAPANESE LITERATURE (*in part*)

D.La.   David Ladd. *Register of Copyrights, Copyright Office, Library of Congress, Washington, D.C.*
PROPERTY LAW (*in part*)

D.L.D.   Decima L. Douie. *Former Reader in Medieval History, University of Hull, England. Author of* The Nature and the Effect of the Heresy of the Fraticelli *and others.*
JOHN XXII (PAPACY) (Micropædia)

D.Le.   Dominica Legge. *Emeritus Professor of Anglo-Norman Studies, University of Edinburgh. Author of* Anglo-Norman Literature and Its Background *and others.*
ANGLO-NORMAN LITERATURE
   (Micropædia)

D.LeV.   David Le Vay. *Consultant Surgeon, National Health Service, U.K. Author of* Human Anatomy and Physiology.
EXCRETION AND EXCRETORY SYSTEMS
   (*in part*)

D.L.F.   Denis Llewellyn Fox (d. 1983). *Professor of Marine Biochemistry, Scripps Institution of Oceanography, University of California, La Jolla, 1948–69. Author of* Animal Biochromes and Structural Colours.
COLORATION, BIOLOGICAL (*in part*)

D.L.L.   David L. Lack (d. 1973). *Director, Edward Grey Institute of Field Ornithology, University of Oxford, 1945–73. Author of* Natural Regulation of Animal Numbers.
BIOSPHERE, THE (*in part*)

D.L.Le.   David L. Lewis. *Professor of History, Howard University, Washington, D.C. Author of* King: A Critical Biography *and others.*
KING, MARTIN LUTHER, JR.
   (Micropædia)

D.L.M.   David Livingstone Mueller. *Professor of Christian Theology, Southern Baptist Theological Seminary, Louisville, Kentucky. Author of* An Introduction to the Theology of Albrecht Ritschl *and others.*
RITSCHL, ALBRECHT (Micropædia)

D.L.N.   David Lawrence Niddrie. *Professor of Geography, University of Florida, Gainesville. Author of* Caribbean Geography *and others.*
WEST INDIES, THE (*in part*)

D.L.P.   David Leo Pawson. *Curator of Echinoderms, Smithsonian Institution, Washington, D.C. Contributor to* Physiology of Echinodermata.
ECHINODERMS

D.L.S.   David Llewelyn Snellgrove. *Emeritus Professor of Tibetan, University of London. Author of* Buddhist Himālaya *and others.*
BUDDHISM, THE BUDDHA AND (*in part*)
CENTRAL ASIAN ARTS (*in part*)

D.L.Se.   D.L. Serventy. *Principal Research Scientist, Division of Wildlife Research, Commonwealth Scientific and Industrial Research Organization, Nedlands, Australia; Officer in Charge, Western Australia Station, 1951–69. Researcher on the distribution and ecology of Australian birds. Author of* Birds of Western Australia.
BIRDS (*in part*)

D.M.   Dieter Meischner. *Professor of Geology, Georg August University of Göttingen, West Germany.*
GEOCHRONOLOGY (*in part*)

D.Ma.   The Most Rev. David Mathew (d. 1975). *Archbishop of Apamea; Assistant at the Pontifical Throne. Author of* James I.
JAMES I (GREAT BRITAIN) (Micropædia)

D.M.A.   David M. Armstrong. *Associate Professor of Natural Sciences; Museum Associate Curator, University of Colorado, Boulder.*
MAMMALS (*in part*)

D.M.Ar.   Denis Midgley Arnold (d. 1986). *Heather Professor of Music, University of Oxford, 1975–86. Author of* Monteverdi *and others.*
MONTEVERDI, CLAUDIO (*in part*)
   (Micropædia)

D.M.B.   D. Mary Benson. *Writer. Author of* Chief Albert Lutuli of South Africa *and others.*
LUTULI, ALBERT (Micropædia)

D.M.Be. Dewey M. Beegle. *Professor of Old Testament, Wesley Theological Seminary, Washington, D.C. Author of* Moses, the Servant of Yahweh *and others.*

MOSES (*in part*)

D.McI. Donald McIntyre. *Professor of Chemistry and of Polymer Science, University of Akron, Ohio. Editor of* Characterization of Macromolecular Structure.

MOLECULES (*in part*)

D.M.DeL. Dwight Moore DeLong. *Emeritus Professor of Entomology, Ohio State University, Columbus. Coauthor of* An Introduction to the Study of Insects.

INSECTS (*in part*)

D.Mé. Daniel Ménager. *Professor of French Literature, University of Paris X. Author of* Introduction à la vie littéraire du seizième siècle *and others.*

FRENCH LITERATURE (*in part*)

D.M.Ea. David Magarey Earl. *Former Professor of History, Eastern Michigan University, Ypsilanti. Author of* Emperor and Nation in Japan: Political Thinkers of the Tokugawa Period.

SAIGŌ TAKAMORI (Micropædia)

D.M.F. Donald M. Frame. *Emeritus Professor of French, Columbia University. Author of* Montaigne: A Biography; *translator of* Montaigne: The Complete Works.

MONTAIGNE

D.M.G. David M. Gates. *Professor of Botany; Director, Biological Station, University of Michigan, Ann Arbor. Author of* Energy Exchange in the Biosphere *and others.*

BIOSPHERE, THE (*in part*)

D.M.Gi. Donald M. Ginsberg. *Professor of Physics, University of Illinois, Urbana. Author of papers on electrical and magnetic properties of metals at very low temperatures.*

MATTER (*in part*)

D.M.H. Donald M. Hunten. *Professor of Planetary Sciences, University of Arizona, Tucson.*

ANALYSIS AND MEASUREMENT, PHYSICAL AND CHEMICAL (*in part*)

D.M.Ha. David M. Hayne. *Professor of French, University of Toronto. Coauthor of* Bibliographie Critique du Roman Canadien-Français, 1837–1900.

CANADIAN LITERATURE (*in part*)

D.Mi. Dorothy Middleton. *Assistant Editor, Geographical Journal, 1953–71. Author of* Baker of the Nile *and others.*

STANLEY, SIR HENRY MORTON (Micropædia)

D.M.J. Dorothy M. Johnson (d. 1984). *Free-lance writer. Author of* The Hanging Tree; A Man Called Horse; Montana.

UNITED STATES OF AMERICA (*in part*)

D.M.K. David Marcus Knight. *Senior Lecturer in History of Science, University of Durham, England. Author of* Atoms

and Elements *and others.*

ARRHENIUS, SVANTE (Micropædia)

D.M.Ke. David M. Kunzle. *Professor of Art, University of California, Los Angeles. Author of* The Early Comic Strip *and others.*

CARICATURE, CARTOON, AND COMIC STRIP (*in part*)

D.M.L. David Malcolm Lewis. *Student and Tutor in Ancient History, Christ Church, Oxford; Lecturer in Greek Epigraphy, University of Oxford. Coauthor of* A Selection of Greek Historical Inscriptions to the End of the Fifth Century B.C.

PERICLES (Micropædia)

D.M.La. David Marshall Lang. *Emeritus Professor of Caucasian Studies, University of London. Author of* A Modern History of Georgia; The Georgians; *and others.*

UNION OF SOVIET SOCIALIST REPUBLICS (*in part*)

D.M.L.-J. David Mathias Lloyd-Jones. *Musicologist and conductor; specialist in Slavic music. Artistic Director, Opera North, Leeds, England.*

DVOŘÁK, ANTONÍN (Micropædia)

D.M.Lo. David Morrice Low (d. 1972). *Classical Lecturer and Sub-dean, Arts Faculty, King's College, University of London, 1945–57. Author of* Edward Gibbon, 1737–94 *and others.*

GIBBON, EDWARD (Micropædia)

D.M.N. Donald MacGillivray Nicol. *Koraës Professor of Byzantine and Modern Greek History, Language, and Literature, King's College, University of London. Author of* The Despotate of Epiros *and others.*

BYZANTINE EMPIRE, THE HISTORY OF THE (*in part*)

D.M.P. Dorothy M. Pickles. *Writer, lecturer, and broadcaster. Author of* The Fifth French Republic; The Government and Politics of France; *and others.*

GAULLE, CHARLES DE (*in part*) (Micropædia)

D.M.Po. David Morris Potter (d. 1971). *William R. Coe Professor of American History, Stanford University, California, 1961–71.*

UNITED STATES OF AMERICA (*in part*)

D.M.S. D.M. Sen. *Vice Chancellor, University of Burdwan, West Bengal, India, 1965–69.*

INDIA (*in part*)

D.M.Sm. Dale M. Smith. *Professor of Botany, University of California, Santa Barbara. Coauthor of* The North American Sunflowers.

ANGIOSPERMS (*in part*)

D.M.W.A. Douglas M.W. Anderson. *Reader in Chemistry, University of Edinburgh. Editor of series of monographs on analysis of organic materials and functional groups.*

ANALYSIS AND MEASUREMENT, PHYSICAL AND CHEMICAL (*in part*)

D.M.Wh. D. Maxwell White. *Professor and Head, Department of Italian Language and Literature, University of Leeds, England. Author of* Zaccaria Seriman *and others.*

ITALIAN LITERATURE (*in part*)

D.N. Dika Newlin. *Composer. Professor of Music, Virginia Commonwealth University, Richmond. Author of* Bruckner-Mahler-Schoenberg; Schoenberg Remembered.

SCHOENBERG, ARNOLD (*in part*) (Micropædia)

D.N.K. David N. Keightley. *Professor of History, University of California, Berkeley. Author of* Sources of Shang History: The Oracle-Bone Inscriptions of Bronze Age China.

CHINA (*in part*)

D.N.P. Devavrat Nanubhai Pathak. *Former Vice Chancellor, Saurāshtra University, Rājkot, India. Coauthor of* Three General Elections in Gujarat.

INDIA (*in part*)

D.N.W. Donald N. Wilber. *Free-lance writer and consultant on the Middle East and Southeast Asia. Author of* Iran Past and Present *and others.*

SHĀPŪR II (PERSIA) (Micropædia)

D.O.B. Donald O. Bushman (d. 1973). *Associate Professor of Geography, University of South Carolina, Columbia, 1960–73.*

UNITED STATES OF AMERICA (*in part*)

D.O.D.W. David O.D. Wurfel. *Professor of Political Science, University of Windsor, Ontario. Coauthor of* The United States and the Philippines.

PHILIPPINES (*in part*)

D.O.E. Dietz O. Edzard. *Professor of Assyriology, Ludwig Maximilian University of Munich. Author of* Die zweite Zwischenzeit Babyloniens.

IRAQ (*in part*)

D.Ol. Daria Olivier. *Writer, translator, book reviewer, and historian. Author of* Alexandre Iᵉʳ *and others.*

ALEXANDER I (RUSSIA) (Micropædia)

D.O'N. Denis O'Neill (d. 1981). *Under Secretary, Ministry of Transport, London, 1951–68.*

TRANSPORTATION (*in part*)

Do.S. Donald Southgate. *Former Reader in Political and Constitutional History, University of Dundee, Scotland. Author of* The Most English Minister— The Policies and Politics of Palmerston *and others.*

PALMERSTON, HENRY JOHN TEMPLE, 3RD VISCOUNT (*in part*) (Micropædia)

D.P. Dimitris Pournaras. *Former Publisher and Editor of* Eleutheros *(newspaper), Athens. Former Chairman, Greek Broadcasting Corporation. Author of* Eleuthérios Venizélos *and others.*

VENIZÉLOS, ELEUTHÉRIOS (Micropædia)

D.P.C. Douglas Parodé Capper. *Commander, Royal Navy and Royal*

Navy Volunteer Reserve. Naval Historian. Author of Famous Sailing Ships of the World *and others.*

TRANSPORTATION (*in part*)

D.P.Ch.   David P. Chandler. *Research Director, Centre of Southeast Asian Studies, Monash University, Clayton, Australia. Author of* A History of Cambodia.

SOUTHEAST ASIA, MAINLAND (*in part*)

D.P.Cl.   Derek Plint Clifford. *Free-lance writer. Author of* A History of Garden Design.

GARDEN AND LANDSCAPE DESIGN (*in part*)

D.P.G.   Derek Peter Gregory. *Director, Building Services Research and Information Association, Bracknell, England.*

ENERGY CONVERSION (*in part*)

D.P.Ga.   David P. Gamble. *Professor of Anthropology, San Francisco State University. Author of* The Wolof of Senegambia.

WESTERN AFRICA (*in part*)

D.P.K.   Daniel P. Kunene. *Professor of African Languages and Literature, University of Wisconsin, Madison. Author of* The Heroic Poetry of the Basotho.

AFRICAN ARTS (*in part*)

D.P.L.   Donald P. Little. *Professor and Director, Institute of Islāmic Studies, McGill University, Montreal. Author of* An Introduction to Mamlūk Historiography *and others.*

EGYPT (*in part*)
MU'ĀWIYAH I (Micropædia)

D.P.O'C.   Daniel Patrick O'Connell (d. 1979). *Chichele Professor of International Law, University of Oxford, 1972–79. Author of* Richelieu *and others.*

RICHELIEU, ARMAND-JEAN DU PLESSIS, CARDINAL ET DUC DE (*in part*) (Micropædia)

D.P.T.   David P. Thelen. *Professor of History, University of Missouri, Columbia. Author of* Robert M. La Follette and the Insurgent Spirit.

LA FOLLETTE, ROBERT M. (Micropædia)

D.R.   Don Russell (d. 1986). *Free-lance writer. Author of* The Wild West: A History of the Wild West Shows *and others.*

RODEO (Micropædia)

D.R.C.   David R. Coffin. *Howard Crosby Butler Memorial Professor of the History of Architecture, Princeton University. Author of* Villa d'Este at Tivoli *and others.*

ARCHITECTURE, THE HISTORY OF WESTERN (*in part*)

D.R.D.   Donald Reynolds Dudley (d. 1972). *Professor of Latin, University of Birmingham, England, 1955–72. Author of* The Romans.

SENECA, LUCIUS ANNAEUS (Micropædia)

D.Re.   Donald Read. *Professor of Modern English History, University of*

Kent at Canterbury, England. Author of Cobden and Bright *and others.*

BRIGHT, JOHN (Micropædia)

D.R.G.   Denis Rolleston Gwynn (d. 1971). *Research Professor of Modern Irish History, University College, Cork, National University of Ireland, 1946–63. Author of* The History of Partition.

DE VALERA, EAMON (*in part*) (Micropædia)

D.R.H.   Delbert R. Hillers. *W.W. Spence Professor of Semitic Languages, Johns Hopkins University, Baltimore, Maryland. Author of* Treaty-Curses and Old Testament Prophets.

MIDDLE EASTERN RELIGIONS, ANCIENT (*in part*)

D.R.Ha.   David Russell Harris. *Professor of Human Environment, Institute of Archaeology, University of London.*

WEST INDIES, THE (*in part*)

D.R.I.   David Rittenhouse Inglis. *Emeritus Professor of Physics, University of Massachusetts, Amherst. Author of* Nuclear Energy: Its Physics and Its Social Challenge *and others.*

ATOMS (*in part*)

D.R.M.   Donald R. Morris. *News analyst,* The Houston (*Texas*) Post. *Author of* The Washing of the Spears: A History of the Rise of the Zulu Nation Under Shaka and Its Fall in the Zulu War of 1879.

SHAKA (Micropædia)

D.Ro.   Dov Ronen. *Associate, Center for International Affairs, Harvard University. Author of* Dahomey: Between Tradition and Modernity.

WESTERN AFRICA (*in part*)

D.R.O.-H.   Dayrell Reed Oakley-Hill. *Inspector of the Albanian Gendarmerie, 1929–38; British Liaison Officer to Albanian resistance, 1940–41; Chief of United Nations Relief and Rehabilitation Administration mission to Albania, 1945–46.*

ALBANIA (*in part*)

D.R.P.   Donald Rahl Petterson (d. 1966). *Professor of Geography, East Carolina College, Greenville, North Carolina.*

WESTERN AFRICA (*in part*)

D.R.S.   Dale R. Simpson. *Professor of Geology, Lehigh University, Bethlehem, Pennsylvania.*

MINERALS AND ROCKS (*in part*)

D.R.Sw.   Don R. Swanson. *Professor, Graduate Library School, University of Chicago. Editor of* The Role of Libraries in the Growth of Knowledge *and others.*

INFORMATION PROCESSING (*in part*)

D.S.B.   Daniel Stephen Barker. *Professor of Geology, University of Texas at Austin.*

MINERALS AND ROCKS (*in part*)

D.S.-C.   David Stafford-Clark, M.D. *Consultant Emeritus, Department of*

Psychiatry, Guy's Hospital, London, Bethlem Royal Hospital, Maudsley Hospital, and Institute of Psychiatry of the University of London. Author of Psychiatry Today *and numerous others.*

MENTAL DISORDERS AND THEIR TREATMENT (*in part*)

D.S.D.   Donald Stephen Dugdale. *Professor of Mechanical Engineering, University of Sheffield, England. Author of* Elements of Elasticity.

MECHANICS (*in part*)

D.Še.   Drago Šega. *Scientific adviser, Institute for the Slovene Literature and Literary Sciences, Slovene Academy of Sciences and Arts, Ljubljana, Yugoslavia. Editor of* Anthologie de la poésie slovène.

YUGOSLAV LITERATURE (*in part*)

D.S.H.W.N.   Davidson S.H.W. Nicol. *Under Secretary General, United Nations, and Executive Director, United Nations Institute for Training and Research, New York City, 1972–82. Permanent Representative and Ambassador for Sierra Leone to the United Nations, 1969–71. Author of* Africa: A Subjective View; *Editor of* Black Nationalism: The Writings of Africanus Horton.

AFRICA (*in part*)
WESTERN AFRICA (*in part*)

D.Si.   Denis Sinor. *Distinguished Professor of Uralic and Altaic Studies, and of History; Director, Inner Asian and Uralic Natural Resource Center, Indiana University, Bloomington. Author of* Inner Asia; History of Hungary; *and others.*

UNION OF SOVIET SOCIALIST REPUBLICS (*in part*)
HUNGARIAN LITERATURE (*in part*)

D.S.J.   David Starr Jordan, M.D. (d. 1931). *Chancellor, Stanford University, California, 1913-16; President, Indiana University, Bloomington, 1885–91; Professor of Zoology, 1879–85. Author of* A Guide to the Study of Fishes.

AGASSIZ, LOUIS (Micropædia)

D.S.L.   David S. Lifson. *Playwright and drama critic. Emeritus Professor of English, Monmouth College, West Long Branch, N.J. Author of* The Yiddish Theatre in America *and others.*

YIDDISH LITERATURE (*in part*)

D.S.La.   David S. Landes. *Coolidge Professor of History and Professor of Economics, Harvard University. Editor of* The Rise of Capitalism; *Contributor to* The Cambridge Economic History of Europe, *vol. 6.*

EUROPE (*in part*)

D.S.Lr.   David Sievert Lavender. *Historian and writer. Author of* The Great West; The Rockies; *and others.*

UNITED STATES OF AMERICA (*in part*)

D.So.   Dominique Sourdel. *Professor of Muslim Civilization, University of Paris IV. Author of* Le Vizirat 'abbāside de 749 à 936 *and others.*

MA'MŪN, AL- (Micropædia)

D.Sp. David Spring. *Professor of History, Johns Hopkins University, Baltimore. Author of* The English Landed Estate in the Nineteenth Century.
RUSSELL OF KINGSTON RUSSELL, JOHN RUSSELL, 1ST EARL (Micropædia)

D.S.R. Daniel Sommer Robinson (d. 1977). *Professor and Director, School of Philosophy, University of Southern California, Los Angeles, 1946–54. Author of* Royce and Hocking: American Idealists *and others.*
PHILOSOPHICAL SCHOOLS AND DOCTRINES, WESTERN (*in part*)

D.S.T. Derick S. Thomson. *Professor of Celtic, University of Glasgow. Author of* An Introduction to Gaelic Poetry.
CELTIC LITERATURE (*in part*)

D.Su. Denys Sutton. *Editor,* Apollo *magazine. Art Critic,* Financial Times. *Author of* Bonnard; Nocturne: The Art of James McNeill Whistler; *and others.*
BONNARD, PIERRE (Micropædia)
WHISTLER, JAMES MCNEILL (*in part*) (Micropædia)

D.T. David Turnock. *Reader in Geography, University of Leicester, England. Author of* An Economic Geography of Romania *and others.*
ROMANIA (*in part*)

D.T.E. Dudley Tate Easby, Jr. (d. 1973). *Secretary, Metropolitan Museum of Art, New York City, 1945–69; Chairman, Department of Primitive Art, 1969–71.*
DECORATIVE ARTS AND FURNISHINGS (*in part*)

D.T.F. Daniel T. Finkbeiner II. *Professor of Mathematics, Kenyon College, Gambier, Ohio. Author of* Matrices and Linear Transformations.
ANALYSIS (IN MATHEMATICS) (*in part*)

D.t.H. Dirk ter Haar. *Reader in Theoretical Physics, University of Oxford; Fellow of Magdalen College, Oxford. Author of* Elements of Thermostatistics.
LANDAU, LEV DAVIDOVICH (Micropædia)

D.T.J. The Rev. Daniel T. Jenkins. *Weyerhaeuser Professor of Systematic Theology, Princeton Theological Seminary, New Jersey, 1981–84. Author of* Christian Maturity and Christian Success *and others.*
PROTESTANTISM (*in part*)

D.Tn. David Thomson (d. 1970). *Master, Sidney Sussex College, University of Cambridge, 1957–70. Author of* Europe Since Napoleon.
EUROPE (*in part*)

D.T.R. David Talbot Rice (d. 1972). *Watson-Gordon Professor of the History of Fine Art, University of Edinburgh, 1934–72; Vice Principal, 1968–71. Author of* Byzantine Art *and others.*
ARCHITECTURE, THE HISTORY OF WESTERN (*in part*)
PAINTING, THE HISTORY OF WESTERN (*in part*)
SCULPTURE, THE HISTORY OF WESTERN (*in part*)

D.V. Dora Vallier. *Art critic. Author of* Henri Rousseau: Catalogue raisonné de l'oeuvre; Henri Rousseau; *and others.*
ROUSSEAU, HENRI (Micropædia)

D.V.B. David V. Bates, M.D. *Professor of Medicine and Physiology, University of British Columbia, Vancouver. Coauthor of* Respiratory Function in Disease.
RESPIRATION AND RESPIRATORY SYSTEMS (*in part*)

D.V.C. Dorothy V. Carrington. *Fellow, Royal Historical Society and Royal Literary Society. Author of* Granite Island: A Portrait of Corsica; This Corsica; *and others.*
FRANCE (*in part*)

D.V.Cn. Denis Victor Cowen. *Former Professor of Law, University of Chicago. Former Professor of Comparative Law, University of Cape Town.*
LEGAL SYSTEMS, THE EVOLUTION OF MODERN WESTERN (*in part*)

D.V.Co. Deryck V. Cooke (d. 1976). *Musicologist. Music Presentation Editor, British Broadcasting Corporation, London, 1965–76. Author of* Mahler, 1860–1911; *Completed Mahler's unfinished* 10th Symphony.
MAHLER, GUSTAV (Micropædia)
WAGNER, RICHARD (*in part*) (Micropædia)

D.V.D. Dimitrije V. Djordjevic. *Professor of History, University of California, Santa Barbara. Author of* Révolutions nationales des peuples balkaniques, 1804–1914 *and others.*
BALKANS (*in part*)
GREECE (*in part*)

D.V.T. Dattatraya Vishwanath Tahmankar. *London Editor,* Deccan Herald, *Bangalore, India. Author of* Lokamanya Tilak *and others.*
TILAK, BAL GANGADHAR (Micropædia)

D.W. Dorothy Whitelock (d. 1982). *Elrington and Bosworth Professor of Anglo-Saxon, University of Cambridge, 1957–69. A leading authority on Anglo-Saxon England. Author of* Beginnings of English Society; *editor of* English Historical Documents c. 500–1042.
ALFRED (Micropædia)
CANUTE (Micropædia)
UNITED KINGDOM (*in part*)

D.Wa. David Waines. *Lecturer in Arabic and Islāmic Studies, University of Lancaster, England. Author of* The Unholy War.
TABARI, AT- (Micropædia)

D.W.C. David W. Crabb. *Associate Professor of Anthropology, Princeton University. Author of* Ekoid Bantu Languages of Ogaja (Eastern Nigeria).
LANGUAGES OF THE WORLD (*in part*)

D.We. Donald Weinstein. *Professor of History, University of Arizona, Tucson. Author of* Savonarola and Florence; Ambassador from Venice.
EUROPE (*in part*)

D.W.F. Don W. Fawcett, M.D. *Professor Emeritus of Anatomy, Harvard Medical School, Harvard University. Coauthor of* Textbook of Histology.
SUPPORTIVE AND CONNECTIVE TISSUES (*in part*)

D.W.Fi. Donald W. Fiske. *Emeritus Professor of Psychology, University of Chicago. Author of* Measuring the Concepts of Personality *and others.*
PSYCHOLOGICAL TESTS AND MEASUREMENT (*in part*)

D.W.G. David W. Goodall. *Honorary Fellow, Division of Wildlife and Rangelands Research, Commonwealth Scientific and Industrial Research Organization, Perth, Australia; Senior Principal Research Scientist, Division of Land Resources Management, 1975–79.*
ECOSYSTEMS (*in part*)

D.W.I. Donald W. Insall. *Principal Architect, Donald W. Insall and Associates (architects and planning consultants), London. Commissioner, the Historic Buildings and Monuments Commission for England. Author of* The Care of Old Buildings Today *and others.*
ART CONSERVATION AND RESTORATION (*in part*)

D.W.K. Daniel Wilhelmus Kruger. *Professor of History, University of the Transkei, Umtata. Author of* Paul Kruger.
KRUGER, PAUL (Micropædia)

D.W.K.-J. Douglas W. Kent-Jones (d. 1978). *President, British Industrial Biological Research Association, Carshalton, England. Coauthor of* Modern Cereal Chemistry.
FARMING AND AGRICULTURAL TECHNOLOGY (*in part*)
FOOD PROCESSING (*in part*)
NUTRITION (*in part*)

D.W.L. Donald William Lucas (d. 1985). *P.M. Laurence Reader in Classics, University of Cambridge, 1952–69. Author of* The Greek Tragic Poets; A Commentary on Aristotle's Poetics.
GREEK LITERATURE (*in part*)

D.Wo. Douglas Woodruff (d. 1978). *Editor,* The Tablet, *London, 1936–67. Author of* Church and State in History.
PIUS IX (*in part*) (Micropædia)
PIUS V, SAINT (*in part*) (Micropædia)

D.W.O'C. Daniel William O'Connor. *Charles A. Dana Professor of Religious Studies, Saint Lawrence University, Canton, New York. Author of* Peter in Rome: The Literary, Liturgical and Archeological Evidence.
PETER THE APOSTLE, SAINT (Micropædia)

D.W.S. Denis William Stevens. *Professor of Musicology, Columbia*

University, 1964–76. Author of Tudor Church Music.

MUSICAL FORMS AND GENRES (*in part*)
PALESTRINA, GIOVANNI PIERLUIGI DA (Micropædia)

D.W.T.   Donald W. Tinkle (d. 1980). *Professor of Zoology, University of Michigan, Ann Arbor, 1965–80; Director, Museum of Zoology, 1975–80. Author of* The Life and Demography of the Side-Blotched Lizard.

EVOLUTION, THE THEORY OF (*in part*)

D.Y.-Y.H.   David Yi-Yung Hsia, M.D. (d. 1972). *Professor and Chairman, Department of Pediatrics, Stritch School of Medicine, Loyola University, Maywood, Illinois; Pediatrician in Chief, Loyola University Hospital, 1969–72. Author of* Inborn Errors of Metabolism.

METABOLISM (*in part*)

E.A.   Eric Axelson. *Emeritus Professor of History, University of Cape Town, former Assistant Principal. Author of* Portugal and the Scramble for Africa.

CAPE TOWN

E.A.A.   Edward Alter Alpers. *Professor of History, University of California, Los Angeles.*

SOUTHERN AFRICA (*in part*)

E.A.B.   Ernest Amano Boateng. *Environmental and educational consultant. Executive Chairman, Environmental Protection Council of Ghana, Accra, 1973–81. Vice Chancellor, University of Cape Coast, Ghana, 1971–73. President, Ghana Academy of Arts and Sciences, 1973–77. Author of* A Geography of Ghana.

WESTERN AFRICA (*in part*)

E.A.Bo.   Edward Allen Boyden (d. 1976). *Research Professor, Department of Biological Structure, University of Washington, Seattle, 1956–76. Professor of Anatomy, University of Minnesota, Minneapolis, 1931–54. Author of* Segmental Anatomy of the Human Lung.

RESPIRATION AND RESPIRATORY SYSTEMS (*in part*)

E.A.D.   Eugene A. Davidson. *Professor and Chairman, Department of Biological Chemistry, Milton S. Hershey Medical Center, Pennsylvania State University, Hershey. Author of* Carbohydrate Chemistry.

BIOCHEMICAL COMPONENTS OF ORGANISMS (*in part*)

E.A.Ha.   Eric Alfred Havelock. *Sterling Professor Emeritus of Classics, Yale University. Author of* The Lyric Genius of Catullus *and others.*

CATULLUS, GAIUS VALERIUS (Micropædia)

E.A.J.D.   Ernest Albert John Davies. *Publisher,* Traffic Engineering and Control; *Editor, 1960–76. Member of Parliament for Enfield East, England, 1945–59. Chairman, Labour Party Transport Committee, 1945–59. Author of* Traffic Engineering Practice.

PUBLIC WORKS (*in part*)
TRANSPORTATION (*in part*)

E.A.K.   E.A. Kracke, Jr. (d. 1976). *Professor of Chinese Literature and Institutions, University of Chicago, 1960–73. Author of* Civil Service in Early Sung China, 960–1067.

T'AI TSU (SUNG DYNASTY) (Micropædia)

Ea.L.   Earl Latham (d. 1977). *Joseph B. Eastman Professor of Political Science, Amherst College, Mass., 1948–73. Author of* The Group Basis of Politics *and others.*

SOCIAL SCIENCES, THE (*in part*)

E.Al.   Edward Allworth. *Professor of Turco-Soviet Studies; Director, Program on Soviet Nationality Problems; Executive Secretary, Center for the Study of Central Asia, Columbia University. Author of* Soviet Asia; The Soviet Asian Controversy; *and others.*

UNION OF SOVIET SOCIALIST REPUBLICS (*in part*)

E.A.M.   Edith A. Müller. *Professor of Astrophysics, University of Geneva, Switzerland.*

SOLAR SYSTEM, THE (*in part*)

E.An.   Edgar Anderson. *Professor of History, San Jose State University, California. Author of* History of Latvia, 1920–1940 *and others.*

UNION OF SOVIET SOCIALIST REPUBLICS (*in part*)

E.A.O.   Edwin A. Olson. *Professor of Earth Science, Whitworth College, Spokane, Washington. Coeditor of* Proceedings of the Sixth International Conference on Radiocarbon and Tritium Dating.

GEOCHRONOLOGY (*in part*)

E.A.P.   Edwin A. Peel. *Professor of Education, University of Birmingham, England, 1950–78. Editor,* Educational Review. *Author of* The Psychological Basis of Education.

TEACHING (*in part*)

E.Ar.   Endel Aruja. *Author of* Estonian Books and Periodicals.

UNION OF SOVIET SOCIALIST REPUBLICS (*in part*)

E.A.R.   The Rev. Edward A. Ryan, S.J. (d. 1964). *Rector, Our Lady of Martyrs Tertianship, Auriesville, New York, 1962–64. Professor of Church History, Woodstock College, Maryland, 1936–62.*

LOYOLA, SAINT IGNATIUS OF (Micropædia)

E.A.R.B.   Elizabeth A.R. Brown. *Professor of History, Brooklyn College and the Graduate Center, City University of New York.*

PHILIP IV (FRANCE) (Micropædia)

E.A.T.   E.A. Thompson. *Professor of Classics, University of Nottingham, England, 1948–79. Author of* The Early Germans; A History of Attila and the Huns; *and others.*

ATTILA (Micropædia)
EUROPE (*in part*)
STILICHO, FLAVIUS (Micropædia)
THEODORIC (ITALY) (Micropædia)

E.A.U.   E. Ashworth Underwood, M.D. (d. 1980). *Director, Wellcome Institute of the History of Medicine, London, 1946–64. Editor of* Science, Medicine and History.

HIPPOCRATES (Micropædia)
MEDICINE (*in part*)
NIGHTINGALE, FLORENCE (Micropædia)
REED, WALTER (Micropædia)
VIRCHOW, RUDOLF (Micropædia)

E.A.W.   Edwin A. Winckler. *Research Associate, East Asian Institute, Columbia University. Coeditor of* Authoritarianism and Dependency on Taiwan.

TAIWAN (*in part*)

E.B.   Edward Bridges, 1st Baron Bridges (d. 1969). *Privy Councillor. Permanent Secretary to H.M. Treasury, London, 1945–56. Author of* Portrait of a Profession.

PUBLIC ADMINISTRATION (*in part*)

E.Ba.   E. Badian. *John Moors Cabot Professor of History, Harvard University. Author of* Roman Imperialism in the Late Republic *and others.*

GRECO-ROMAN CIVILIZATION, CLASSICAL (*in part*)

E.B.D.   Edward Bronson Diethrich, M.D. *Director; Chief of Cardiovascular Surgery, Arizona Heart Institute, Phoenix.*

CIRCULATION AND CIRCULATORY SYSTEMS (*in part*)

E.Be.   Edward Kamau Brathwaite. *Poet and critic. Professor of History, University of the West Indies, Mona (Kingston), Jamaica. Author of* Rights of Passage; The Development of Creole Society in Jamaica.

CARIBBEAN LITERATURE (Micropædia)

E.B.F.   E. Bert Fowler. *Vice President, Engineering Waste Management of Illinois, Inc., Palos Heights. Author of* Application of Component Construction to Multi-story, Low-Income Housing.

BUILDING CONSTRUCTION (*in part*)

E.B.Fr.   Edmund B. Fryde. *Professor of History, University College of Wales, Aberystwyth, University of Wales. Coeditor of* Handbook of British Chronology.

HISTORY, THE STUDY OF (*in part*)

E.B.G.   Elizabeth Belmont Gasking (d. 1973). *Senior Lecturer in the History and Philosophy of Science, University of Melbourne, Australia. Author of* Investigations into Generation, 1651–1828.

SPALLANZANI, LAZZARO (Micropædia)

E.B.H.   Earl B. Hunt. *Professor of Psychology, University of Washington, Seattle, Author of* Concept Learning.

LEARNING AND COGNITION, HUMAN (*in part*)

Eb.R. **Eberhard Ruhmer.** *Former Curator in Chief, Bavarian State Painting Collection, Munich. Author of* Cosimo Tura; Grünewald; *and others.*
DÜRER, ALBRECHT (*in part*)
   (Micropædia)

E.Br. **Ernle Bradford** (d. 1986). *Author of* The Wind Commands Me: A Life of Sir Francis Drake *and others.*
DRAKE, SIR FRANCIS (Micropædia)

E.B.R. **Elwyn B. Robinson.** *University Professor Emeritus of History, University of North Dakota, Grand Forks. Author of* History of North Dakota.
NORTH AMERICA (*in part*)
UNITED STATES OF AMERICA (*in part*)

E.B.W. **E. Bright Wilson.** *Theodore William Richards Professor Emeritus of Chemistry, Harvard University. Robert A. Welch Award in Chemistry, 1978. Coauthor of* Molecular Vibrations.
ANALYSIS AND MEASUREMENT, PHYSICAL AND CHEMICAL (*in part*)

E.B.Wo. **Everett B. Woodruff.** *Consultant, A.M. Kinney, Inc., Cincinnati, Ohio. Coauthor of* Steam-Plant Operation.
ENERGY CONVERSION (*in part*)

E.Ca. **Enzo Carli.** *Director, Cathedral Museum, Siena, Italy. Author of* Duccio.
DUCCIO DI BUONINSEGNA (Micropædia)

E.C.A. **Ernst C. Abbe.** *Emeritus Professor of Botany, University of Minnesota, St. Paul.*
ANGIOSPERMS (*in part*)

E.C.D. **Edward C. Dimock, Jr.** *Professor of Bengali and Bengal Studies, University of Chicago. Author of* The Place of the Hidden Moon.
HINDUISM (*in part*)
SOUTH ASIAN ARTS (*in part*)

E.C.Du. **Elizabeth Corning Dudley.** *Research Associate, Department of Zoology, University of Maryland, College Park.*
ANGIOSPERMS (*in part*)

E.C.H. **Edgar Crawshaw Holt** (d. 1975). *Author and journalist. Author of* The Making of Italy, 1815–1870.
MAZZINI, GIUSEPPE (Micropædia)

E.Cl. **Eugene Clark.** *Professor of Economics, Washington State University, Pullman; Dean, College of Economics and Business, 1957–77.*
UNITED STATES OF AMERICA (*in part*)

E.C.LaF. **Eugene C. LaFond.** *General Manager, LaFond Oceanic Consultants, San Diego, California. Secretary General, International Association for the Physical Sciences of the Ocean. Author of* Processing Oceanographic Data.
ASIA (*in part*)

E.C.N. **E. Clifford Nelson.** *Emeritus Professor of Religion, St. Olaf College, Northfield, Minnesota. Author of* Lutheranism in North America, 1914–70 *and others.*
PROTESTANTISM (*in part*)

E.C.O. **Everett C. Olson.** *Emeritus Professor of Zoology, University of California, Los Angeles.*
ROMER, ALFRED SHERWOOD
   (Micropædia)

E.C.R. **Edward C. Riley.** *Professor of Hispanic Studies, University of Edinburgh. Author of* Cervantes's Theory of the Novel *and others.*
CERVANTES

Ed. **The Editors.**

E.D. **Edouard Delebecque.** *Emeritus Professor of Greek Language and Literature, University of Aix-Marseille I, Marseille, France. Author of* Thucydide et Alcibiade *and others.*
GRECO-ROMAN CIVILIZATION, CLASSICAL
   (*in part*)

E.D.D. **Ethel Deikman Dunn.** *Executive Secretary, Highgate Road Social Science Research Station, Inc., Berkeley, California. Coauthor of* The Peasants of Central Russia.
UNION OF SOVIET SOCIALIST REPUBLICS
   (*in part*)

Ed.G. **Edwin Gerow.** *Frank L. Sulzberger Professor of Civilizations; Professor of Sanskrit, University of Chicago. Author of* Indian Poetics.
KĀLIDĀSA (Micropædia)

E.D.G. **Ernest Dean Gardner, M.D.** (deceased). *Professor of Neurology and Anatomy, University of California, Davis. Author of* Fundamentals of Neurology *and others.*
NERVES AND NERVOUS SYSTEMS (*in part*)

E.D.H. **Earl Dorchester Hanson.** *Professor of Biology and Science in Society, Wesleyan University, Middletown, Connecticut. Author of* Animal Diversity.
BIOLOGICAL SCIENCES, THE (*in part*).

E.Di. **Erich Dimroth** (d. 1985). *Professor of Earth Sciences, University of Quebec at Chicoutimi, 1981–85.*
CONTINENTAL LANDFORMS (*in part*)

Ed.R. **Edward Rosen** (d. 1985). *Distinguished Professor of the History of Science, City University of New York. Author of* Three Imperial Mathematicians: Kepler Trapped Between Brake and Ursus *and others.*
KEPLER (*in part*)

E.D.S. **Evgeny Dmitrievich Silaev.** *Head, Department of the North and Transcaucasus, Council for Research on Productive Forces, U.S.S.R. Planning Commission, Moscow. Author of articles on Transcaucasian republics.*
UNION OF SOVIET SOCIALIST REPUBLICS
   (*in part*)

E.Du. **Enrique Dussel.** *Professor of Ethics, National Autonomous University of Mexico, Mexico City. Author of* Les Évêques hispano-américaine (1504–1620) *and others.*
LAS CASAS, BARTOLOMÉ DE
   (Micropædia)

E.E. **Eliahu Elath.** *Emeritus President, Hebrew University of Jerusalem. Chairman, Board of Governors, Afro-Asian Institute for Co-operative and Labour Studies, Tel Aviv, Israel. Ambassador of Israel to U.S., 1948–50, and to U.K., 1952–59. Author of* Israel and Her Neighbours *and others.*
ISRAEL (*in part*)

E.E.D.M.O. **E.E. David M. Oates.** *Emeritus Professor of Western Asiatic Archaeology, Institute of Archaeology, University of London. Author of* Studies in the Ancient History of Northern Iraq.
BAGHDAD

E.E.E. **E. Earle Ellis.** *Research Professor of New Testament Literature, New Brunswick Theological Seminary, New Jersey. Author of* The Gospel of Luke *and others.*
LUKE, SAINT (Micropædia)

E.Eg. **Emil Egli.** *Professor of Geography, Zürich Gymnasium. Lecturer, University of Zürich and Swiss Federal Institute of Technology, Zürich. Author of* Switzerland *and others.*
SWITZERLAND (*in part*)

E.E.L. **Edward Ernest Long** (d. 1956). *British journalist.*
EAST INDIES (*in part*)

E.E.La. **Eric Edwin Lampard.** *Professor of History, State University of New York at Stony Brook.*
CITIES (*in part*)

E.E.R. **Edgar Eugene Robinson** (d. 1977). *Margaret Byrne Professor of American History, Stanford University, California, 1931–52. Author of* Evolution of American Political Parties *and others.*
UNITED STATES OF AMERICA (*in part*)

E.E.S. **Eustace E. Suckling.** *Honorary Professor of Electrical Engineering, University of Auckland, New Zealand. Author of* Bioelectricity; The Living Battery.
ELECTRICITY AND MAGNETISM (*in part*)

E.E.Sn. **Esmond E. Snell.** *Ashbel Smith Professor of Chemistry and of Microbiology, University of Texas at Austin. Editor of* Pyridoxal Catalysis: Enzymes and Model Systems; Annual Review of Biochemistry, vol. 38–52.
NUTRITION (*in part*)

E.F. **Enno Franzius.** *Historian. Author of* History of the Byzantine Empire *and others.*
HERACLIUS (Micropædia)

E.F.B. **Edgar F. Borgatta.** *Professor of Sociology; Director, Institute on Aging, University of Washington, Seattle. Coeditor of* Handbook of Personality Theory and Research.
PERSONALITY (*in part*)

E.F.C. **Eduardo F. Catalano.** *Emeritus Professor of Architecture, Massachusetts Institute of Technology, Cambridge. Author of* Structures of Warped Surfaces.
NERVI, PIER LUIGI (Micropædia)

E.F.G.D. Emilio Fernando González Díaz. *Professor of Geomorphology, University of Buenos Aires.*
SOUTH AMERICA (*in part*)

E.F.S. Edward Fairbrother Strange (d. 1925). *Keeper of Woodwork, Victoria and Albert Museum, London. Author of* Chinese Lacquer *and others.*
DECORATIVE ARTS AND FURNISHINGS (*in part*)

E.Fu. Edmund Fuller. *Writer and editor. Book Reviewer,* Wall Street Journal. *Coeditor of* Four American Biographies *and others.*
HOLMES, OLIVER WENDELL, JR. (Micropædia)

E.F.W. Edward F. Wente. *Professor of Egyptology, Oriental Institute and Department of Near Eastern Languages and Civilizations, University of Chicago. Author of* Late Ramesside Letters.
EGYPT (*in part*)

E.G. Evel Gasparini (d. 1982). *Professor of Slavic Philology, University of Padova, Italy. Author of* Il matriarcato slavo.
EUROPEAN RELIGIONS, ANCIENT (*in part*)

E.G.Bor. Edwin Garrigues Boring (d. 1968). *Edgar Pierce Professor of Psychology, Harvard University, 1956–57; Professor of Psychology, 1928–56.*
PSYCHOLOGY (*in part*)

E.G.C. Edward Gordon Couzens (d. 1971). *Technical Director, Bexford Ltd., Manningtree, England, 1952–62. Coauthor of* Plastics in the Modern World.
INDUSTRIES, CHEMICAL PROCESS (*in part*)

E.Ge. Ettore Gelpi. *Director of life-long education activities, United Nations Educational, Scientific and Cultural Organization (Unesco), Paris. Author of* Storia dell'educazione *and others.*
EDUCATION, HISTORY OF (*in part*)

E.G.K. E. Gordon Keith. *Emeritus Professor of Finance, University of Pennsylvania, Philadelphia. Editor of* Foreign Tax Policies and Economic Growth.
TAXATION (*in part*)

E.G.P. Edwin G. Pulleyblank. *Professor of Chinese, University of British Columbia, Vancouver. Author of* The Background of the Rebellion of An Lu-shan; Chinese History and World History *and others.*
AN LU-SHAN (Micropædia)
CONFUCIANISM, CONFUCIUS AND (*in part*)

E.Gr. Endre Grastyán, M.D. *Professor of Physiology, Medical University of Pécs, Hungary. Author of* Exp. Beiträge zur Pathogenese der Commotio Cerebri.
EMOTION AND MOTIVATION, HUMAN (*in part*)

E.G.R. The Rev. Ernest Gordon Rupp. *Dixie Professor Emeritus of Ecclesiastical History, University of Cambridge. Author of* Luther's Progress to the Diet of Worms; *coauthor of* Erasmus and Luther *and others.*
ERASMUS
LUTHER

Eg.S. Egon Schaden. *Professor of Communication and Arts, University of São Paulo, Brazil. Author of* Mitologia Heróica de Tribos Indígenas do Brasil.
AMERICAN INDIANS (*in part*)

E.G.T. Sir Eric Gardner Turner (d. 1983). *Professor of Papyrology, University College, University of London, 1950–78; Director, Institute of Classical Studies, 1953–63. Author of* Greek Papyri *and many other works on papyri.*
WRITING (*in part*)

E.Ġu. Erna Gunther (d. 1982). *Professor of Anthropology, University of Washington, Seattle, 1941–67; Director, Thomas Burke Memorial Washington State Museum, 1929–67. Author of* Art in the Life of the Northwest Coast Indians *and others.*
AMERICAN INDIANS (*in part*)

E.G.W. Ernest Glen Wever. *Higgins Professor Emeritus of Psychology, Auditory Research Laboratories, Princeton University. Author of* Theory of Hearing.
SENSORY RECEPTION (*in part*)

E.H. Erich Heinz, M.D. *Emeritus Professor of Biochemistry, Johann Wolfgang Goethe University of Frankfurt, West Germany; former Chairman, Gustav Embden Center of Biological Chemistry.*
CELLS (*in part*)

E.Ha. Enriqueta Harris. *Honorary Fellow of the Warburg Institute, University of London. Author of* Goya; Velázquez; *and others.*
GOYA, FRANCISCO DE (Micropædia)
VELÁZQUEZ (*in part*)

E.H.B. Edward Howland Burtt, Jr. *Associate Professor of Zoology, Ohio Wesleyan University, Delaware, Ohio. Editor of* The Biological Significance of Color.
COLORATION, BIOLOGICAL (*in part*)

E.H.C. Edward H. Carr (d. 1982). *Wilson Professor of International Politics, University College of Wales, Aberystwyth, 1936–47. Author of* Michael Bakunin; A History of Soviet Russia; *and others.*
BAKUNIN, MIKHAIL ALEKSANDROVICH (Micropædia)

E.H.H. Eckhard H. Hess (d. 1986). *Professor of Psychology, University of Chicago, 1959–86. Author of* Imprinting.
LORENZ, KONRAD (Micropædia)

E.H.K. E.H. Kossmann. *Professor of Modern History, State University of Groningen, The Netherlands. Author of* La Fronde *and others.*
LOW COUNTRIES, THE (*in part*)

E.H.P.B. Ernest Henry Phelps Brown. *Emeritus Professor of the Economics of Labour, University of London. Author of* The Economics of Labor.
WORK AND EMPLOYMENT (*in part*)

E.H.St. Elmer H. Stotz. *Professor of Biochemistry, School of Medicine and Dentistry, University of Rochester, New York. Editor of* Comprehensive Biochemistry.
BIOLOGICAL SCIENCES, THE (*in part*)

E.H.T. Elias H. Tuma. *Professor of Economics, University of California, Davis. Author of* Twenty-six Centuries of Agrarian Reform: A Comparative Analysis *and others.*
LAND REFORM AND TENURE

E.H.T.W. E.H. Timothy Whitten. *Vice President for Academic Affairs; Professor of Geology, Michigan Technological University, Houghton. Author of* Structural Geology of Folded Rocks.
MINERALS AND ROCKS (*in part*)

E.H.W., Jr. Edmund H. Worthy, Jr. *Associate Director, Resident Associate Program, Smithsonian Institution, Washington, D.C. Founder,* Bulletin of Sung Studies.
WANG AN-SHIH (Micropædia)

E.Hy. Eric Halfpenny (d. 1979). *Editor,* The Galpin Society Journal, *1963–70.*
MUSICAL INSTRUMENTS (*in part*)

E.I.G. Estill I. Green (d. 1974). *Electrical engineer. Executive Vice President, Bell Telephone Laboratories, Inc., Murray Hill, New Jersey, 1959–60.*
SOUND (*in part*)

Ei.H. Einar Haugen. *Victor S. Thomas Professor Emeritus of Linguistics and Scandinavian, Harvard University. Author of* Norwegian Language in America; Language Conflict and Language Planning: The Case of Modern Norwegian; *and others.*
LANGUAGES OF THE WORLD (*in part*)

E.I.J.R. Erwin I.J. Rosenthal. *Emeritus Reader in Oriental Studies, University of Cambridge. Author of* Political Thought in Medieval Islam; *editor of* Averroës' Commentary on Plato's Republic.
AVERROËS (Micropædia)

E.I.U. *Economist Intelligence Unit,* The Economist, *London.*
ARGENTINA (*in part*)
AUSTRALIA (*in part*)
BRAZIL (*in part*)
CANADA (*in part*)
CHINA (*in part*)
CZECHOSLOVAKIA (*in part*)
EAST INDIES, THE (*in part*)
EGYPT (*in part*)
FRANCE (*in part*)
GERMANY (*in part*)
GREECE (*in part*)
INDIA (*in part*)
ITALY (*in part*)
JAPAN (*in part*)
MEXICO (*in part*)
POLAND (*in part*)
SOUTH AFRICA (*in part*)

SPAIN (*in part*)
SUDAN (*in part*)
TURKEY AND ANCIENT ANATOLIA
(*in part*)
UNION OF SOVIET SOCIALIST REPUBLICS
(*in part*)
UNITED KINGDOM (*in part*)
UNITED STATES OF AMERICA (*in part*)
WESTERN AFRICA (*in part*)

E.J.   Emrys Jones. *Professor of
Geography, London School of Economics
and Political Science, University of
London. Author of* Social Geography of
Belfast *and others.*
UNITED KINGDOM (*in part*)

E.J.B.   Ernest J. Briskey. *Dean, School
of Agriculture, Oregon State University,
Corvallis. Vice President, Scientific
Affairs, Campbell Soup Company,
Camden, New Jersey, 1975–79. Coeditor
of* The Physiology and Biochemistry of
Muscle as a Food.
FOOD PROCESSING (*in part*)

E.J.Bi.   E.J. Bickerman (d. 1981).
*Professor of Ancient History, Columbia
University, 1952–67. Author of*
Chronology of the Ancient World.
CALENDAR (*in part*)

E.J.C.G.   Edward J.C. Garden.
*Professor and Head, Department of
Music, University of Sheffield,
England. Author of* Tchaikovsky;
Balakirev.
TCHAIKOVSKY, PETER ILICH (*in part*)
(Micropædia)

E.Je.   Elizabeth Jenkins. *Author of*
Elizabeth the Great *and others.*
ELIZABETH I OF ENGLAND (*in part*)

E.J.E.   Eugene J. Enrico. *Professor
of Music, University of Oklahoma,
Norman. Author of* Giuseppe Torelli's
Music for Instrumental Ensemble with
Trumpet.
MUSICAL INSTRUMENTS (*in part*)

E.J.F.   Sir Edgar John Forsdyke (d.
1979). *Director and Principal Librarian,
British Museum, London, 1936–50;
Keeper of Greek and Roman Antiquities,
1932–36.*
DECORATIVE ARTS AND FURNISHINGS
(*in part*)

E.J.G.   Elmer J. Gutherz. *Division
Chief, Resource Assessment Surveys,
National Marine Fisheries Service,
National Oceanic and Atmospheric
Administration, U.S. Department of
Commerce, Pascagoula, Mississippi.
Researcher on the biology of a variety of
marine fishes.*
FISHES (*in part*)

E.J.J.   E. Jaakko Järvinen. *Chief
of Department, Finnish Institute
of Leadership, Helsinki. Editor of*
Contemporary Research in Psychology
of Perception.
PERCEPTION, HUMAN (*in part*)

E.J.Ke.   Edward John Kenney. *Kennedy
Professor Emeritus of Latin, University
of Cambridge; Fellow of Peterhouse,
Cambridge. Author of* The Classical

Text; Lucretius; *and others.*
OVID (Micropædia)
PETRONIUS ARBITER, GAIUS
(Micropædia)

E.J.M.   Elbert John Minarcik. *Former
Chief Metallurgist, Metal Division, NL
Industries, Inc., Hightstown, New Jersey.*
INDUSTRIES, EXTRACTION AND
PROCESSING (*in part*)

E.J.M.R.   Edward J.M. Rhoads.
*Associate Professor of History, University
of Texas at Austin. Author of* China's
Republican Revolution: The Case of
Kwangtung, 1895–1913.
LIN PIAO (Micropædia)

E.J.S.   Sir Edward James Salisbury (d.
1978). *Director, Royal Botanic Gardens,
Kew, England, 1943–56. Author of*
The Living Garden; The Reproductive
Capacity of Plants; *and others.*
LINNAEUS, CAROLUS (Micropædia)

E.J.Si.   Ernest J. Simmons (d.
1972). *Professor of Russian Literature;
Chairman, Department of Slavic
Languages, Columbia University, 1946–
59. Author of* Dostoyevsky: The Making
of a Novelist *and others.*
DOSTOYEVSKY (*in part*)
RUSSIAN LITERATURE (*in part*)
TOLSTOY

E.J.W.   Edwin J. Westermann.
*Emeritus Professor of History, University
of Missouri, Kansas City.*
UNITED STATES OF AMERICA (*in part*)

E.J.W.B.   Ernest J.W. Barrington.
*Emeritus Professor of Zoology,
University of Nottingham, England.
Author of* Introduction to General and
Comparative Endocrinology.
BIOCHEMICAL COMPONENTS OF
ORGANISMS (*in part*)

E.J.Wi.   E.J. Wiesenberg. *Member,
Taylor-Schechter Cairo Genizah
Research Unit, University of Cambridge
Library. Former Reader in Hebrew,
University College, University of London.
Editor and translator of* Abraham
Maimonides' Commentary on Genesis
and Exodus.
CALENDAR (*in part*)
HISTORY, THE STUDY OF (*in part*)

E.J.Wo.   Edward J. Wormley. *Products
and interior designer. Former Design
Director, Dunbar Furniture Corporation
of Indiana, New York City.*
DECORATIVE ARTS AND FURNISHINGS
(*in part*)

E.K.   Edgar Kaufmann, Jr. *Emeritus
Professor of the History of Architecture,
Columbia University. Director,
Department of Industrial Design,
Museum of Modern Art, New York
City, 1946–50. Coauthor and editor of*
The Rise of an American Architecture;
coeditor of Frank Lloyd Wright: Writings
and Buildings.
WRIGHT, FRANK LLOYD (*in part*)
(Micropædia)

E.K.B.   Eugene Kornel Balon. *Professor
of Zoology, University of Guelph,*

Ontario. Editor in Chief, Environmental
Biology of Fishes.
FISHES (*in part*)

E.Ke.   Elie Kedourie. *Professor of
Politics, London School of Economics
and Political Science, University of
London. Author of* Afghani and 'Abduh:
An Essay on Religious Unbelief and
Political Activism in Modern Islam.
JAMĀL AD-DIN AL-AFGHĀNI
(Micropædia)

E.K.H.   Earl K. Hyde. *Deputy
Director, Lawrence Berkeley Laboratory,
University of California, Berkeley.
Coauthor of* Nuclear Properties of the
Heavy Elements.
SEABORG, GLENN T. (Micropædia)

E.K.I.J.   Eino Kaarlo Ilmari Jutikkala.
*Professor of Finnish History, University
of Helsinki, 1947–50; 1954–74.*
FINLAND (*in part*)

E.K.W.   Sir Ellis K. Waterhouse
(d. 1985). *Director of Studies, Paul
Mellon Centre for Studies in British Art,
London, 1970–73. Barber Professor of
Fine Arts; Director, Barber Institute of
Fine Arts, University of Birmingham,
England, 1952–70. Author of* Italian
Baroque Painting *and others.*
CORREGGIO (Micropædia)

E.L.   Edward Lockspeiser (d. 1973).
*Writer and broadcaster on music.
Author of* Debussy: His Life and Mind
and others.
DEBUSSY, CLAUDE (Micropædia)
DIAGHILEV, SERGEY (Micropædia)
MENDELSSOHN, FELIX (Micropædia)

**E.L.H.   The Most Rev. Edward Louis
Heston, C.S.C.** (d. 1973). *Chairman,
Pontifical Social Communications
Commission, Vatican City, 1971–73.
Author of* The Holy See at Work.
PAUL VI (PAPACY) (Micropædia)

E.Li.   Edwin Lieuwen. *Professor of
Latin American History, University of
New Mexico, Albuquerque. Author of*
Venezuela *and others.*
VENEZUELA (*in part*)

E.L.K.   Edward Louis Keenan.
*Professor of History, Harvard University.
Author of* The Kurbskii-Groznyi
Apocrypha: The Seventeenth-Century
Genesis of the 'Correspondence' Between
Ivan IV and A.M. Kurbskii.
UNION OF SOVIET SOCIALIST REPUBLICS
(*in part*)

**E.Lo.   Elizabeth Pakenham, Countess
of Longford.** *Writer. Author of*
Wellington: The Years of the Sword;
Wellington: The Pillar of State;
and others.
WELLINGTON

E.L.O.M.   Ernesto La Orden Miracle.
*Diplomat. Spanish Ambassador to
Costa Rica, 1972–76, and to Nicaragua,
1966–69.*
SPAIN (*in part*)

El.R.   Elliott Rudwick (d. 1985).
Professor of Sociology and of History;

Senior Research Fellow, Center for Urban Regionalism, Kent State University, Ohio. Author of W.E.B. Du Bois: Propagandist of the Negro Protest.
DU BOIS, W.E.B. (Micropædia)

E.L.T. **Edward Lewis Turner, M.D.** *(d. 1960). Secretary, Council on Medical Education and Hospitals, American Medical Association, Chicago, 1953– 59. Professor of Medicine; Dean, School of Medicine, University of Washington, Seattle, 1945–53.*
MEDICINE (*in part*)

E.Lu. **Evan Luard.** *Fellow, St. Antony's College, University of Oxford. Member of Parliament, 1966–70; 1974–79. Author of* The United Nations: How It Works and What It Does *and others.*
UNITED NATIONS (*in part*)

E.L.Y. **Ellen Louise Young.** *Historical research specialist (manufactures).*
DECORATIVE ARTS AND FURNISHINGS (*in part*)

E.M. **Eric Mendoza.** *Professor of Science Teaching, Hebrew University of Jerusalem. Editor of Sadi Carnot's* Reflections on the Motive Power of Fire.
CARNOT, SADI (Micropædia)

E.Ma. **Erich Matthias** *(d. 1983). Professor of Contemporary History and Political Science, University of Mannheim, West Germany. Author of* Sozialdemokratie und Nation *and others.*
BEBEL, AUGUST (Micropædia)

E.McC. **Elizabeth McClintock.** *Research Associate, Department of Botany, University of California, Berkeley.*
ANGIOSPERMS (*in part*)

E.McN.E. **Ernest McNeill Eller.** *Rear Admiral, U.S. Navy (retired). Author of* The Soviet Sea Challenge *and others; coeditor of* Dictionary of American Naval Fighting Ships.
WAR, THE TECHNOLOGY OF (*in part*)

E.M.G. **Ernest M. Gifford, Jr.** *Professor of Botany, University of California, Davis. Coauthor of* Comparative Morphology of Vascular Plants.
BRYOPHYTES AND PRIMITIVE VASCULAR PLANTS (*in part*)

E.M.J.C. **Eila M.J. Campbell.** *Emeritus Professor of Geography, Birkbeck College, University of London.*
GAMA, VASCO DA, 1ER CONDE DA VIDIGUEIRA (Micropædia)
GIOVANNI DA PIAN DEL CARPINI (Micropædia)

E.M.R. **Edwin M. Ripin** *(d. 1975). Assistant Curator, Musical Instruments Department, Metropolitan Museum of Art, New York City, 1970–73. Editor of* Keyboard Instruments.
MUSICAL INSTRUMENTS (*in part*)

Em.Š. **Emil Štampar.** *Professor of Modern Serbo-Croatian Literature,*

University of Ljubljana, Yugoslavia.
YUGOSLAV LITERATURE (*in part*)

E.M.W. **Edmund Merriman Wise** *(d. 1972). Assistant to the Vice President of Research, International Nickel Company, New York City, 1955–61. Author of* Palladium: Recovery, Properties, and Uses; *editor of* Gold: Recovery, Properties, and Applications; *coeditor of* Platinum Metals and Their Alloys.
INDUSTRIES, EXTRACTION AND PROCESSING (*in part*)

E.M.Wn. **Elizabeth M. Wilkinson.** *Emeritus Professor of German, University of London. Coauthor of* Goethe: Poet and Thinker *and others.*
GOETHE (*in part*)

E.N. **Edward Norbeck.** *Professor of Anthropology, Rice University, Houston, Texas. Author of* Religion in Primitive Society *and others.*
RELIGIOUS AND SPIRITUAL BELIEF, SYSTEMS OF (*in part*)
RITES AND CEREMONIES, SACRED (*in part*)

E.N.A. **Edward Noah Abrahart.** *Former Assistant Research Manager, Clayton Aniline Co. Ltd., Manchester, England. Author of* Dyes and Their Intermediates.
INDUSTRIES, CHEMICAL PROCESS (*in part*)
INDUSTRIES, TEXTILE (*in part*)

En.S. **Enid Starkie** *(d. 1970). Reader in French Literature, University of Oxford; Fellow, Somerville College, Oxford, 1934–65. Author of* André Gide; Arthur Rimbaud; Baudelaire; *and others.*
BAUDELAIRE, CHARLES (Micropædia)
RIMBAUD, ARTHUR (*in part*) (Micropædia)

E.N.S. **Eric Norman Simons** *(d. 1983). Author of* The Queen and the Rebel: Mary Tudor and Wyatt the Younger *and others.*
MARY I (ENGLAND AND GREAT BRITAIN) (Micropædia)

E.O. **Eberhard Otto** *(d. 1974). Professor of Egyptology, Rupert Charles University of Heidelberg. Author of* Osiris und Amun; Gott und Mensch nach den ägyptischen Tempelinschriften der griechisch-römischen Zeit; *and others.*
MIDDLE EASTERN RELIGIONS, ANCIENT (*in part*)

E.O.D. **Edward O. Dodson.** *Emeritus Professor of Biology, University of Ottawa, Ontario. Author of* Evolution: Process and Product *and others.*
EVOLUTION, THE THEORY OF (*in part*)

E.O.G.T.-P. **E.O.G. Turville-Petre** *(d. 1978). Professor of Ancient Icelandic Literature and Antiquities, University of Oxford, 1953–75. Author of* Myth and Religion of the North; Origins of Icelandic Literature; *and others.*
EUROPEAN RELIGIONS, ANCIENT (*in part*)
SCANDINAVIAN LITERATURE (*in part*)

E.O.J. **The Rev. Edwin Oliver James** *(d. 1972). Chaplain of All Souls College,*

University of Oxford. Professor of the History and Philosophy of Religion, University of London. Author of Seasonal Feasts and Festivals *and numerous other works in the comparative study of religions.*
RITES AND CEREMONIES, SACRED (*in part*)
SACRED OFFICES AND ORDERS (*in part*)

E.O.W. **Edwin O. Willis.** *Associate Professor of Zoology, Paulo State University "Julio de Mesquita Filho," Rio Claro, Brazil. Author of* The Behavior of Bicolored Antbirds.
BEHAVIOUR, ANIMAL (*in part*)

E.P. **Eva Paproth.** *Director, Geological Office of Nordrhein-Westfalen, Krefeld, West Germany.*
GEOCHRONOLOGY (*in part*)

E.P.A. **E. Paul Albury, D.D.S.** *Former Senator of The Bahamas. Author of* The Story of the Bahamas.
WEST INDIES, THE (*in part*)

E.Pe. **Edward Pessen.** *Distinguished Professor of History, Baruch College and the Graduate Center, City University of New York. Author of* Jacksonian America *and others.*
UNITED STATES OF AMERICA (*in part*)

E.P.G. **Elias Panayiotis Gyftopoulos.** *Ford Professor of Engineering, Massachusetts Institute of Technology, Cambridge. Coauthor of* Thermionic Energy Conversion.
THERMODYNAMICS, PRINCIPLES OF (*in part*)

E.P.H. **Eric P. Hamp.** *Robert Maynard Hutchins Distinguished Service Professor of Linguistics and of Behavioral Sciences; Director, Center for Balkan and Slavic Studies, University of Chicago. Coeditor of* Readings in Linguistics, vol. 2.
LANGUAGES OF THE WORLD (*in part*)
LINGUISTICS (*in part*)

E.P.Ha. **Earl Parker Hanson** *(d. 1978). Consultant, Department of State, Commonwealth of Puerto Rico, 1956– 69. Professor of Geography; Chairman, Department of Geography and Geology, University of Delaware, Newark, 1949– 56. Author of* The Amazon, a New Frontier.
VENEZUELA (*in part*)

E.Po. **Ernesto Pontieri** *(deceased). Professor of Medieval and Modern History, University of Naples. Author of* Tra i Normanni nell' Italia meridionale.
ITALY (*in part*)
ROBERT (APULIA) (Micropædia)

E.P.O. **Eugene P. Odum.** *Alumni Foundation Distinguished Professor of Zoology; Director, Institute of Ecology, University of Georgia, Athens. Author of* Fundamentals of Ecology; Ecology.
ECOSYSTEMS (*in part*)

E.P.Y. **Ernest P. Young.** *Professor of History, University of Michigan, Ann Arbor. Author of* The Presidency of Yuan Shih-k'ai: Liberalism and Dictatorship in

Early Republican China.
CHINA (*in part*)

E.R.A.F.   Enid R.A. Forde. *Associate Professor of Geography, Fourah Bay College, University of Sierra Leone, Freetown.*
WESTERN AFRICA (*in part*)

E.R.C.   Eli Rush Crews, M.D. (d. 1972). *Clinical Professor of Surgery, University of Texas Medical School at San Antonio. Chief of the Burn Service, Bexar County Teaching Hospital, Texas. Author of* A Practical Manual for the Treatment of Burns.
BURNS (*in part*)

E.R.G.   Edna R. Green. *Former Head, Science Department, Philadelphia High School for Girls. Coauthor of* Biology.
BIOLOGICAL SCIENCES, THE (*in part*)

E.R.Ha.   Edward R. Hardy (d. 1981). *Lecturer in Early Church History, University of Cambridge, 1969–75. Professor of Church History, Berkeley Divinity School, New Haven, Connecticut, 1947–69. Author of* Christian Egypt: Church and People; *editor of* Christology of the Later Fathers; Faithful Witnesses; *and others.*
ATHANASIUS, SAINT (Micropædia)
BASIL THE GREAT, SAINT (Micropædia)
GREGORY OF NAZIANZUS, SAINT (Micropædia)
GREGORY OF NYSSA, SAINT (Micropædia)

Er.L.   Erik Lassen. *Director, Museum of Decorative Art, Copenhagen, 1966–82. Author of* Danish Furniture of the Classical Age *and others.*
DECORATIVE ARTS AND FURNISHINGS (*in part*)

E.R.-M.   Emir Rodríguez-Monegal. *Professor of Latin American and Comparative Literature, Yale University. Author of* Borgès par lui-même *and others.*
BORGES, JORGE LUIS (Micropædia)

E.Rn.   Edward Robinson. *Former Professor and Head, Department of Geology, University of the West Indies, Kingston, Jamaica.*
WEST INDIES, THE (*in part*)

E.R.R.   Elmar Rudolph Reiter. *Professor of Atmospheric Science, Colorado State University, Ft. Collins. Author of* Jet-Stream Meteorology *and others.*
CLIMATE AND WEATHER (*in part*)

E.R.S.   Ernest R. Sandeen (d. 1982). *Professor of History, Macalester College, St. Paul, Minnesota, 1973–82. Author of* The Roots of Fundamentalism: British and American Millenarianism 1800–1930.
DOCTRINES AND DOGMAS, RELIGIOUS (*in part*)
FUNDAMENTALISM (*in part*) (Micropædia)

E.R.Se.   Elman R. Service. *Professor of Anthropology, University of California,*

Santa Barbara. Investigator of the economic and social organization of primitive cultures. Author of* Primitive Social Organization.
CULTURE, THE CONCEPT AND COMPONENTS OF (*in part*)
PARAGUAY (*in part*)

Er.St.   Erich Steingräber. *Director General, Bavarian State Art Galleries, Munich.*
DRESS AND ADORNMENT (*in part*)

E.Ru.   Eleanor Ruggles. *Biographer. Author of* Prince of Players: Edwin Booth *and others.*
BOOTH, EDWIN (Micropædia)

E.Sa.   Emilio Sáez. *Former Professor of Medieval Spanish History, University of Barcelona, Spain. Author of* Colección diplomática de Sepúlveda.
ALFONSO V (SPAIN: ARAGON) (Micropædia)
ALFONSO VI (SPAIN: CASTILE AND LEON) (Micropædia)
JAMES I (SPAIN: ARAGON) (Micropædia)

E.S.D.   Eleanor Shipley Duckett (d. 1976). *Professor of Classical Languages and Literature, Smith College, Northampton, Massachusetts, 1928–49. Author of* The Gateway to the Middle Ages; Carolingian Portraits; *and others.*
CHARLES MARTEL (Micropædia)
PEPIN III (CAROLINGIAN DYNASTY) (Micropædia)

E.S.H.   Eric S. Higgs (d. 1976). *Director of Research, Faculty of Archaeology and Anthropology, University of Cambridge. Coeditor of* Science in Archaeology.
AGRICULTURE, THE HISTORY OF (*in part*)

E.Si.   Edith Simon. *Historian, writer, and artist. Author of* The Making of Frederick the Great *and others.*
FREDERICK THE GREAT

E.S.M.   Edmund S. Muskie. *United States Secretary of State, 1980–81. U.S. Senator from Maine, 1958–80. Author of* Journeys.
UNITED STATES OF AMERICA (*in part*)

E.S.Mi.   Earl Schenck Miers (d. 1972). *Historian, editor, and writer. Author of* The General Who Marched to Hell; The American Civil War; *and many others.*
SHERMAN, WILLIAM TECUMSEH (Micropædia)

E.Sn.   Edward Salmon (d. 1955). *Honorary Editor,* United Empire, *journal of the Royal Empire Society, 1941–46; Editor 1920–37.*
EAST INDIES, THE (*in part*)

E.S.P.   Edward S. Perkins, M.D. *Professor of Ophthalmology, University of Iowa, Iowa City. Coauthor of* Atlas of Diseases of the Eye.
SENSORY RECEPTION (*in part*)

E.S.R.   Evelyn S. Rawski. *Professor of History, University of Pittsburgh. Author of* Education and Popular Literacy in Ch'ing China.
CHINA (*in part*)

E.Sy.   Edmond Sylvain. *Attorney. Former Editor and Publisher,* La Patrie *(daily newspaper). Former Rector, State University of Haiti, Port-au-Prince.*
WEST INDIES, THE (*in part*)

E.T.   Ettore Toffoletto, M.D. *President of the Administration Council, Arts Academy, Bologna, Italy. Author of* Discorso sul Malpighi *and others.*
MALPIGHI, MARCELLO (*in part*) (Micropædia)

E.T.B.   Eric Temple Bell (d. 1960). *Professor of Mathematics, California Institute of Technology, Pasadena, 1926–60. Author of* Development of Mathematics; The Magic of Numbers.
MATHEMATICS, THE HISTORY OF (*in part*)

E.t.H.   Ernst ten Haaf. *Professor of Structural Geology, State University of Utrecht, The Netherlands.*
MINERALS AND ROCKS (*in part*)

E.Th.   Sir Eric Thompson (d. 1975). *Staff Member, Department of Archaeology, Carnegie Institution of Washington, D.C., 1935–58. Author of* The Rise and Fall of Maya Civilization *and others.*
HISTORY, THE STUDY OF (*in part*)

E.To.   Elisabeth Tooker. *Professor of Anthropology, Temple University, Philadelphia. Author of* An Ethnography of the Huron Indians, 1615–1649; The Iroquois Ceremonial of Midwinter.
AMERICAN INDIANS (*in part*)

E.T.S.   Edward Togo Salmon. *Messecar Professor Emeritus of History, McMaster University, Hamilton, Ontario. Author of* A History of the Roman World from 30 B.C. to A.D. 138 *and others.*
GRECO-ROMAN CIVILIZATION, CLASSICAL (*in part*)

E.T.Sa.   Emilie T. Sander (d. 1976). *Associate Professor of New Testament, Yale University, 1973–75. Coeditor and translator of* The Bible and the Role of Women.
BIBLICAL LITERATURE AND ITS CRITICAL INTERPRETATION (*in part*)

E.T.W.   Sir Edgar Trevor Williams. *Secretary, Rhodes Trust, 1951–80. Pro-Vice-Chancellor, University of Oxford, 1966–80; Emeritus Fellow of Balliol College, Oxford. Editor,* Dictionary of National Biography, *1940–80.*
VICTORIA AND THE VICTORIAN AGE

E.U.C.   Edward U. Condon (d. 1974). *Professor of Physics; Fellow, Joint Institute for Laboratory Astrophysics, University of Colorado, Boulder, 1963–70. Coauthor of* Handbook of Physics.
MECHANICS (*in part*)

Eu.G.   Eugen Gerstenmaier (d. 1986). *President, Bundestag (lower house of the Federal Assembly), Federal Republic of Germany, 1954–69. Author of* New Nationalism? *and others.*
ADENAUER, KONRAD (Micropædia)

Eu.M.A.   Eufronio M. Alip (deceased). *President, Philippine National Historical Society. Editor, Journal of History (quarterly). President and Manager, Alip & Sons, Inc. (publishing firm), Manila. Author of* Political and Cultural History of the Philippines *and others.*

PHILIPPINES (*in part*)

E.V.   Eugene Vanderpool. *Professor of Archaeology, American School of Classical Studies at Athens.*

ATHENS (*in part*)
OLYMPIA (*Micropædia*)

E.Va.   Ernesto Valgiglio. *Professor of Greek and Latin Grammar, University of Genoa. Author of* Silla e la crisi repubblicana.

SULLA, LUCIUS CORNELIUS (*Micropædia*)

E.V.B.B.   Eric V.B. Britter (d. 1977). *Foreign Correspondent,* The Times *(London), 1944–69.*

WEST INDIES, THE (*in part*)

E.V.G.   Elsa Vesta Goveia. *Former Professor of West Indian History, University of the West Indies, Kingston, Jamaica. Author of* Slave Society in the British Leeward Islands.

WEST INDIES, THE (*in part*)

E.v.H.   Ernst van Heerden. *Poet. Emeritus Professor of Afrikaans and Netherlands, University of the Witwatersrand, Johannesburg. Author of* Die klop *and many others.*

SOUTH AFRICAN LITERATURE (*in part*)
  (*Micropædia*)

E.Vi.   Eugène Vinaver (d. 1979). *Professor of French Language and Literature, Victoria University of Manchester, 1933–66. Author of* The Rise of Romance; *editor of* The Works of Sir Thomas Malory.

LITERATURE, THE ART OF (*in part*)

Ev.S.   Eva Schaper. *Professor of Philosophy, University of Glasgow, Scotland. Author of* Prelude to Aesthetics.

TROELTSCH, ERNST (*Micropædia*)

Ev.W.   Evert Werkman. *Columnist,* Het Parool, *Amsterdam. Author of* Amsterdam, 'n stad op palen *and others.*

AMSTERDAM (*in part*)

E.W.   Edward Weintal (d. 1973). *Diplomatic Correspondent, Chief European Correspondent, and Contributing Editor,* Newsweek *magazine, 1944–69. Coauthor of* Facing the Brink: An Intimate Study of Crisis Diplomacy.

DULLES, JOHN FOSTER (*Micropædia*)

E.W.A.   Edward W. Anderson (d. 1983). *Navigational Adviser, Aviation Division, Smiths Industries Ltd., Cheltenham, England. Author of* Principles of Navigation.

NAVIGATION (*in part*)

E.W.B.   Ernst Wilhelm Benz (d. 1978). *Professor of Church History, Philipps University of Marburg, West Germany. Author of* Evolution and Christian Hope.

CHRISTIANITY (*in part*)

E.W.G.   Eric William Gray. *Lecturer in Ancient History, University of Oxford; Official Student and Tutor in Roman History, Christ Church, Oxford, 1939–77. Editor of Greenridge and Clay's* Sources for Roman History (133–70 B.C.)

MAECENAS, GAIUS (*Micropædia*)
POMPEY THE GREAT (*in part*)
  (*Micropædia*)

E.Wi.   Edward Wichers (d. 1984). *Associate Director, National Bureau of Standards, U.S. Department of Commerce, Washington, D.C., 1958–62; Chief, Division of Chemistry, 1948–58. Author of papers on chemical reagents, pure substances, and atomic weights.*

ATOMIC WEIGHT (*in part*) (*Micropædia*)

E.Wn.   Elizabeth Wiskemann (d. 1971). *Montague Burton Professor of International Relations, University of Edinburgh, 1958–61. Tutor in Modern History, University of Sussex, England, 1961–64. Author of* Czechs and Germans *and others.*

CZECHOSLOVAKIA (*in part*)
GERMANY (*in part*)

E.W.S.   Edward W. Smykay. *Professor and Chairman, Department of Marketing, University of Baltimore. Coauthor of* Physical Distribution Management.

HANDLING, PACKAGING, AND STORAGE
  (*in part*)

E.W.W.   Eric Walter White. *Former Assistant Secretary and Literature Director, Arts Council of Great Britain, London. Author of* Stravinsky: The Composer and His Works *and others.*

STRAVINSKY, IGOR (*in part*)
  (*Micropædia*)

E.W.Z.   Ernst Walter Zeeden. *Professor of Modern and Medieval History, Eberhard Karl University of Tübingen, West Germany.*

GERMANY (*in part*)
STEIN, KARL, REICHSFREIHERR VOM
  UND ZUM (*Micropædia*)

E.Z.   Erik Zürcher. *Professor of East Asian History, State University of Leiden, The Netherlands. Author of* The Buddhist Conquest of China.

CHINA (*in part*)

E.Z.H.   E. Zudaire Huarte. *Instructor, Good Counsel Academy, Lecaroz, Spain. Author of* El conde-duque y Cataluña.

OLIVARES, GASPAR DE GUZMÁN
  Y PIMENTAL, CONDE-DUQUE DE
  (*Micropædia*)

E.Zö   Erich Zöllner. *Professor of Austrian History, University of Vienna. Author of* Geschichte sterreichs von den Anfängen bis zur Gegenwart *and others.*

AUSTRIA (*in part*)

F.A.   Frederick Alexander. *Emeritus Professor of Modern History, University of Western Australia, Nedlands. Author of* Australia Since Federation.

AUSTRALIA (*in part*)

F.A.A.   Francis A. Allen. *Edson R. Sunderland Professor of Law, University of Michigan, Ann Arbor. Author of* The Borderland of Criminal Justice.

BECCARIA, CESARE (*Micropædia*)
ERSKINE OF RESTORMEL, THOMAS
  ERSKINE, 1ST BARON (*Micropædia*)

F.A.B.   Frank A. Brown, Jr. (d. 1983). *Morrison Professor of Biology, Northwestern University, Evanston, Illinois, 1956–76. Coauthor of* Comparative Animal Physiology; The Biological Clock: Two Views.

BEHAVIOUR, ANIMAL (*in part*)
COLORATION, BIOLOGICAL (*in part*)

F.A.C.   F. Albert Cotton. *Robert A. Welch Professor of Chemistry, Texas A & M University, College Station. Author of* Chemical Applications of Group Theory.

CHEMICAL ELEMENTS (*in part*)

F.A.L.   Frank Andrew Leeming. *Senior Lecturer in Geography, University of Leeds, England.*

CHINA (*in part*)

F.A.P.   Frank A. Paine. *Secretary-General, International Association Packaging Research Institutes, England. Editor of* Fundamentals of Packaging.

HANDLING, PACKAGING, AND STORAGE
  (*in part*)

F.A.V.   Frederick Albert Valentine. *Emeritus Professor of Mathematics, University of California, Los Angeles. Author of* Convex Sets.

GEOMETRY (*in part*)

F.B.   François Bernard. *Maître des Requêtes, a judicial rank in the Council of State; Director, Civil and Military Cabinet, Ministry of Defense, Government of France, Paris.*

FRANCE (*in part*)

F.Ba.   Frank Barlow. *Emeritus Professor of History, University of Exeter, England. Author of* William I and the Norman Conquest *and others.*

WILLIAM I (ENGLAND AND GREAT
  BRITAIN) (*Micropædia*)

F.B.B.   Frank Bagnall Bessac. *Professor of Anthropology, University of Montana, Missoula. Author of* Culture Types of Northern and Western China.

ASIA (*in part*)

F.B.C.   Floyd Barton Chapman. *Ecologist, Metropolitan Park District, Columbus, Ohio. Author of* The Ruffed Grouse and Its Management in Ohio.

FALCONRY (*in part*) (*Micropædia*)

F.Be.   Fernando Benítez. *Editor,* La Cultura en México. *Professor of Journalism, National Autonomous University of Mexico, Mexico City.*

Author of Los Indios Mexicanos *and others.*
MEXICO CITY

F.B.G.   Frank B. Gibney.
Vice-Chairman, Board of Editors, Encyclopædia Britannica, Inc., Chicago. Vice-Chairman, TBS-Britannica Company Ltd., Tokyo. Author of The Khrushchev Pattern *and others.*

KHRUSHCHEV, NIKITA (Micropædia)

F.Br.   Friedrich Blendinger.
Director of Archives, Augsburg, West Germany, 1966–77. Author of Bevolkerungsgeschichte einer deutschen Reichsstadt im Zeitalter der Glaubenskämpfe.

FUGGER FAMILY (Micropædia)

F.B.S.   Frederick Bernard Singleton.
Honorary Senior Visiting Research Fellow, Postgraduate School of Yugoslav Studies, University of Bradford, England. Author of Twentieth Century Yugoslavia *and others.*

YUGOSLAVIA (*in part*)

F.C.   François Choay. *Professor of Urban Studies, University of Paris VIII. Author of* Le Corbusier; Planning in the XIXth Century; *and others.*

CORBUSIER, LE (*in part*) (Micropædia)

F.C.B.   Frederick C. Barghoorn.
Emeritus Professor of Political Science, Yale University. Author of Politics in the U.S.S.R.

UNION OF SOVIET SOCIALIST REPUBLICS
   (*in part*)

F.C.C.   Frederick C. Crews. *Professor of English, University of California, Berkeley. Author of* Out of My System: Psychoanalysis, Ideology, and Critical Method *and others.*

LITERATURE, THE ART OF (*in part*)

F.-C.Ce.   Fay-Cooper Cole (d. 1961). *Professor of Anthropology, University of Chicago, 1929–48. Research Associate, Field Museum of Natural History, Chicago. Author of* Peoples of Malaysia *and others.*

EAST INDIES, THE (*in part*)

F.C.D.III   Frederick C. Durant III.
Aerospace historian. Assistant Director, Astronautics, National Air and Space Museum, Smithsonian Institution, Washington, D.C., 1965–81.

ENERGY CONVERSION (*in part*)
EXPLORATION (*in part*)
WAR, THE TECHNOLOGY OF (*in part*)

F.C.F.   Sir Frank C. Francis. *Director and Principal Librarian, British Museum, London, 1959–68. Editor of* The Bibliographical Society, 1892–1942: Studies in Retrospect; The Treasures of the British Museum.

HISTORY, THE STUDY OF (*in part*)
LIBRARIES (*in part*)

F.C.Gi.   Frances Carney Gies.
Coauthor of Leonard of Pisa and the New Mathematics of the Middle Ages *and others.*

LEONARDO PISANO (Micropædia)

F.Ch.   Frank Chapman. *Former Senior English Master, High School for Boys, Oswestry, England. Author of "Hardy the Novelist" in* Scrutiny.

HARDY, THOMAS (Micropædia)

F.C.H.   F. Clark Howell. *Professor of Anthropology, University of California, Berkeley. Author of* Early Man.

EVOLUTION, HUMAN (*in part*)

F.C.Ke.   Fenton Crosland Kelley.
Associate Professor of Zoology, Boise State University, Idaho.

EXCRETION AND EXCRETORY SYSTEMS
   (*in part*)

F.C.M.   Frederick C. Mosher. *White Burkett Miller Professor of Public Affairs, University of Virginia, Charlottesville. Author of* Democracy and the Public Service.

PUBLIC ADMINISTRATION (*in part*)

F.C.N.   Frederick C. Nachod.
Consultant. Director of Special Projects, Sterling-Winthrop Research Institute, Rensselaer, New York, 1974–78; Chemical Liaison Staff Director, 1964–74. Coauthor of Determination of Organic Structures by Physical Methods.

MOLECULES (*in part*)

F.C.O.   Francis Christopher Oakley.
President; Professor of History, Williams College, Williamstown, Massachusetts. Author of Council Over Pope? Towards a Provisional Ecclesiology *and others.*

ROMAN CATHOLICISM (*in part*)

F.C.P.   Forrest C. Pogue. *Director, Dwight D. Eisenhower Institute for Historical Research, Smithsonian Institution, Washington, D.C. Director, George C. Marshall Research Library, Lexington, Virginia, 1964–74. Author of* George C. Marshall.

MARSHALL, GEORGE C. (Micropædia)

F.C.S.   Frank C. Shoemaker. *Professor of Physics, Princeton University. Authority on the design of apparatus for studying subatomic particles.*

PARTICLE ACCELERATORS (*in part*)

F.Ct.   François Marie-Joseph Crouzet.
Professor of the History of Northern Europe, University of Paris IV. Author of L'Economie Britannique et le Blocus Continental (1806–1813).

FRANCE (*in part*)

F.D.G.   Frank Denby Gunstone.
Professor of Chemistry, University of St. Andrews, Scotland. Author of An Introduction to the Chemistry and Biochemistry of the Fatty Acids and Their Glycerides *and others.*

CHEMICAL COMPOUNDS (*in part*)

F.D.H.   F.D. Hobbs. *Head, Environmental Modelling and Survey Unit, University of Birmingham, England. Author of* Traffic Planning and Engineering.

TRANSPORTATION (*in part*)

F.Do.   Filippo Donini. *Cultural Expert, Cultural Relations Department, Italian Ministry of Foreign Affairs, Rome, 1972–*76. *Director, Italian Institute, London, 1961–72. Author of* Vita e poesia di Sergio Corazzini.

ITALIAN LITERATURE (*in part*)

F.D.O.   Francis D. Ommanney (d. 1980). *Reader in Marine Biology, University of Hong Kong, 1957–60. Scientific staff member, Discovery Committee, 1929–39. Author of* South Latitude and North Cape *and others.*

BYRD, RICHARD E. (Micropædia)

F.D.P.   Franklin D. Parker. *Emeritus Professor of History, University of North Carolina at Greensboro. Author of* The Central American Republics *and others.*

CENTRAL AMERICA (*in part*)

F.d.Pe.   Franco della Peruta. *Professor of the History of the Risorgimento, University of Milan. Author of* I democratici e la rivoluzione italiana.

ITALY (*in part*)

F.Dr.   Franz Dölger (d. 1968). *Professor of Byzantine and Modern Greek Studies, University of Munich. Author of* Die byzantinische Dichtung in der Reinsprache.

GREEK LITERATURE (*in part*)

F.E.A.   Franz E. Anderson. *Professor of Oceanography, University of New Hampshire, Durham.*

RIVERS (*in part*)

F.E.B.   Frederick E. Bacon. *Former Metallurgical Engineer, Metals Division, Union Carbide Corporation, Niagara Falls, New York.*

INDUSTRIES, EXTRACTION AND
   PROCESSING (*in part*)

F.E.Bl.   Floyd E. Bloom, M.D.
Director, Division of Preclinical Neuroscience and Endocrinology, Scripps Clinic and Research Foundation, La Jolla, California. Coauthor of Biochemical Basis of Neuropharmacology *and others.*

DRUGS AND DRUG ACTION (*in part*)

F.E.D.   Fram E. Dinshaw. *Fellow of St. Catherine's College, University of Oxford.*

ENGLISH LITERATURE (*in part*)

F.Ek.   Frank Eyck. *Professor of History, University of Calgary, Alberta.*

GERMANY (*in part*)

F.E.K.   Frank E. Keating. *Fishing Editor,* Newsday, *Garden City, New York.*

FISHING (*in part*) (Micropædia)

F.E.Ki.   F.E. Kirby. *Professor of Music, Lake Forest College, Illinois. Author of* A Short History of Keyboard Music; An Introduction to Western Music; *and others.*

MUSICAL FORMS AND GENRES
   (*in part*)

F.E.M.   Frank Edward Manuel.
University Professor of History, Brandeis University, Waltham, Massachusetts. Author of Shapes of Philosophical History *and others.*

RELIGIOUS AND SPIRITUAL BELIEF, SYSTEMS OF (*in part*)

F.E.McE. **Frank E. McElroy.** *Director, Technical Publications, National Safety Council, Chicago. Editor in Chief of* Accident Prevention Manual for Industrial Operations.

FIRE PREVENTION AND CONTROL

F.E.R. **Frank E. Reynolds.** *Professor of Buddhist Studies and History of Religions, University of Chicago.*

ANGKOR (Micropædia)
JAYAVARMAN VII (Micropædia)

F.F. **Franco Ferracuti, M.D.** *Professor of Criminological Medicine and Forensic Psychiatry, University of Rome. Coauthor of* The Subculture of Violence.

CRIME AND PUNISHMENT (*in part*)

F.F.B. **Frederick Fyvie Bruce.** *Rylands Professor Emeritus of Biblical Criticism and Exegesis, Victoria University of Manchester. Author of* The Books and the Parchments.

BIBLICAL LITERATURE AND ITS CRITICAL INTERPRETATION (*in part*)

F.F.C. **Frederick F. Cartwright.** *Emeritus Senior Lecturer in the History of Medicine, King's College Hospital, University of London. Author of* Joseph Lister.

LISTER, JOSEPH, BARON LISTER, OF LYME REGIS (Micropædia)

F.Fe. **Fritz Fellner.** *Professor of Modern History, University of Salzburg, Austria. Author of* Schicksaljahre Österreichs.

AUSTRIA (*in part*)

F.Fo. **Frieda Fordham.** *Training analyst, Society of Analytical Psychology, London. Author of* An Introduction to Jung's Psychology *and others.*

JUNG, CARL (*in part*) (Micropædia)

F.Fr. **Frank Freidel.** *Professor of History, University of Washington, Seattle. Emeritus Professor of History, Harvard University. Author of* Franklin D. Roosevelt *and others.*

ROOSEVELT, FRANKLIN D.
UNITED STATES OF AMERICA (*in part*)

F.G.A.S. **F. Gordon A. Stone.** *Professor of Inorganic Chemistry, University of Bristol, England. Editor of* Advances in Organometallic Chemistry.

CHEMICAL COMPOUNDS (*in part*)

F.Go. **Frederick Goldbeck** (d. 1981). *Critic and musicologist. Adviser for Music, Radiotélévision Française. Author of* The Perfect Conductor *and others.*

GOUNOD, CHARLES (Micropædia)

F.Gre. **Frank Greenaway.** *Keeper, Department of Chemistry, Science Museum, London, 1967–80. Author of* John Dalton and the Atom; *editor of* Lavoisier's Essays, Physical and Chemical.

MENDELEYEV, DMITRY IVANOVICH (Micropædia)

F.Gu. **The Rev. Franco Guerello, S.J.** *Professor of Italian Literature, Social*

Institute, Turin, Italy. Editor of Lettere di Innocenzo IV dai cartolari notarili genovesi.

INNOCENT IV (Micropædia)

F.H. **François Haverschmidt.** *Ornithologist. Author of* Birds of Surinam *and numerous articles on neotropical birds.*

BIRDS (*in part*)

F.Ha. **Felix Haurowitz.** *Distinguished Professor Emeritus of Chemistry, Indiana University, Bloomington. Author of* Chemistry and Function of Proteins.

BIOCHEMICAL COMPONENTS OF ORGANISMS (*in part*)

F.H.B. **Frederick Henry Boland** (d. 1985). *Chancellor, University of Dublin, 1964–82. Representative of Ireland to the United Nations, 1956–64.*

IRELAND (*in part*)

F.Hi **Finn Hiorthøy.** *Judge of the Supreme Court of Norway, Oslo, 1955–73.*

LEGAL SYSTEMS, THE EVOLUTION OF MODERN WESTERN (*in part*)

F.H.M. **Franz H. Michael.** *Emeritus Professor of Far Eastern History and International Affairs, George Washington University, Washington, D.C. Author of* The Origin of Manchu Rule in China; The Taiping Rebellion; *and others.*

NURHACHI (Micropædia)

F.H.O. **Frederick Henry Osborn** (d. 1981). *Chairman, Executive Committee, Population Council, New York City, 1930–68; President, 1952–59. Secretary-treasurer, American Eugenics Society, 1959–70. Author of* Preface to Eugenics; *coauthor of* Dynamics of Population.

BIOLOGICAL SCIENCES, THE (*in part*)
GENETICS AND HEREDITY, THE PRINCIPLES OF (*in part*)

F.H.S. **Frank Harold Spedding** (d. 1984). *Principal Scientist, U.S. Atomic Energy Commission, Ames Laboratory, Iowa State University, Ames, 1968–74; Director, Ames Laboratory, 1947–68. Coauthor of* The Rare Earths.

CHEMICAL ELEMENTS (*in part*)

F.H.Sh. **Frank H. Shu.** *Professor and Chairman, Astronomy Department, University of Calfornia, Berkeley. Author of* The Physical Universe.

COSMOS, THE

F.Hu. **Frederick Fu Hung.** *Emeritus Professor of Geography, University of Guelph, Ontario. Author of a geography series for schools (in Chinese) and others.*

CHINA (*in part*)

F.H.W. **Fred H. Wilt.** *Professor of Zoology, University of California, Berkeley. Editor of* Methods in Developmental Biology.

GROWTH AND DEVELOPMENT, BIOLOGICAL (*in part*)

F.İ. **Fahir İz.** *Professor of Turkish Literature, Boğaziçi University, Istanbul.*

Author of Ottoman Turkish Prose; Ottoman Turkish Verse; *and others.*

CENTRAL ASIAN ARTS (*in part*)

F.J.B. **Fred J. Benson.** *Emeritus Dean, College of Engineering, Texas A & M University, College Station.*

PUBLIC WORKS (*in part*)

F.J.B.W. **Sir F.J.B. Watson.** *Director of the Wallace Collection, London, 1963–74. Surveyor of the Queen's Works of Art, 1963–72. Author of* Fragonard; Canaletto; *and others.*

FRAGONARD, JEAN-HONORÉ (Micropædia)

F.J.D. **Frederick J. Dockstader.** *Museum consultant and art historian. Director, Museum of the American Indian, Heye Foundation, New York City, 1960–75. Author of* Indian Art in North America; Indian Art in South America; *and others.*

AMERICAN INDIANS (*in part*)

F.J.E.R. **Frederic James Edward Raby** (d. 1966). *Fellow and Lecturer, Jesus College, University of Cambridge, 1948– 54. Author of* A History of Christian Latin Poetry *and others.*

LATIN LITERATURE (*in part*)

F.J.M. **Francis J. Murray.** *Professor of Mathematics, Duke University, Durham, North Carolina. Author of* Mathematical Machines.

ARITHMETIC (*in part*)

F.J.Ma. **Frank J. Malina** (d. 1981). *Trustee, International Academy of Astronautics, Paris, 1963–81; President, 1963. Founder-Editor,* Leonardo *(international journal of the contemporary artist). Editor of the first–fifth* Lunar International Laboratory Symposia.

KÁRMÁN, THEODORE VON (Micropædia)

F.J.S. **Frederick J. Streng.** *Professor of the History of Religions, Southern Methodist University, Dallas, Texas. Author of* Emptiness: A Study of Religious Meaning; Understanding Religious Life.

NĀGĀRJUNA (Micropædia)
RITES AND CEREMONIES, SACRED (*in part*)

F.-J.Se. **Franz-Josef Schmale.** *Professor of Medieval History, University of the Ruhr, Bochum, West Germany. Editor of* Quellen zur Geschichte Kaiser Heinrichs IV.

HENRY IV (GERMANY/HOLY ROMAN EMPIRE) (Micropædia)
HENRY V (GERMANY/HOLY ROMAN EMPIRE) (Micropædia)

F.J.W. **Francis James West.** *Planning Dean in Social Sciences; Professor of History and Government, Deakin University, Geelong, Australia. Author of* Political Advancement in the South Pacific *and others.*

PACIFIC ISLANDS (*in part*)

F.K. **The Most Rev. Franz Cardinal König.** *Archbishop of Vienna. Author of* Zarathustras Jenseitsvorstellungen und

das Alte Testament *and others.*
ZOROASTER (Micropædia)

F.K.A.   Franklin K. Anderson. *Senior Environmental Scientist, Ford, Bacon & Davis, Inc. (engineers), Salt Lake City, Utah. Associate Editor, Life Sciences (Botany),* Encyclopædia Britannica, *Chicago, 1970–72.*
ANGIOSPERMS *(in part)*

F.K.H.   F. Kenneth Hare. *University Professor of Geography and of Physics; Provost, Trinity College, University of Toronto. An authority on meteorology and the general circulation of the atmosphere. Author of* The Restless Atmosphere.
CLIMATE AND WEATHER *(in part)*

F.K.L.   Fang Kuei Li. *Emeritus Professor of Chinese Linguistics and Anthropology, University of Washington, Seattle. Emeritus Professor of Asian Linguistics, University of Hawaii, Honolulu. Authority on the languages of South China. Author of* The Tai Dialect of Lungchow.
LANGUAGES OF THE WORLD *(in part)*

F.L.   Fred Lukoff. *Associate Professor of Korean Language and Linguistics, University of Washington, Seattle. Author of* Spoken Korean *and others.*
LANGUAGES OF THE WORLD *(in part)*

F.La.   François Lasserre. *Emeritus Professor of Classical Greek, University of Lausanne, Switzerland. Translator and editor of* Strabon, Géographie, books *3–6, 10–12.*
STRABO (Micropædia)

F.L.J.   Frederick L. Jones (d. 1973). *Professor of English, University of Pennsylvania, Philadelphia. Coauthor of* An Examination of the Shelley Legend; *editor of* The Letters of Percy Bysshe Shelley.
SHELLEY, PERCY BYSSHE *(in part)* (Micropædia)

Fl.M.   Florence Moog. *Rebstock Professor of Biology, Washington University, St. Louis, Missouri. Author of* Structure and Development of Vertebrates.
CHORDATES *(in part)*

F.L.S.   Fred L. Spalding. *Former Associate Professor of General Engineering, University of Illinois, Urbana.*
DRAFTING

F.M.   Fosco Maraini. *Lecturer in Japanese, University of Florence. Author of* Where Four Worlds Meet *and others.*
ASIA *(in part)*
POLO, MARCO (Micropædia)

F.M.B.   Fawn McKay Brodie (d. 1981). *Professor of History, University of California, Los Angeles, 1971–77. Author of* The Devil Drives: A Life of Sir Richard Burton.
BURTON, SIR RICHARD (Micropædia)

F.McD.   Forrest McDonald. *Professor of History, University of Alabama,*

University. Author of E Pluribus Unum.
UNITED STATES OF AMERICA *(in part)*

F.M.Kg.   Felix M. Keesing (d. 1961). *Professor of Anthropology, Stanford University, California, 1942–61. Author of* Cultural Anthropology *and others.*
PREHISTORIC PEOPLES AND CULTURES *(in part)*

F.M.L.   Sir Frederick M. Lea (d. 1984). *Director of Building Research, Department of Scientific and Industrial Research, Watford, England, 1946–65. Author of* The Chemistry of Cement and Concrete.
ADHESIVES *(in part)*

F.Mo.   Francis Moran (d. 1975). *Golf writer,* The Scotsman, *Edinburgh. President, Association of Golf Writers. Author of* Golfers' Gallery.
SPORTS, MAJOR TEAM AND INDIVIDUAL *(in part)*

F.M.S.   Frank M. Shipman. *Member, Board of Directors, Brown-Forman Distillers Corporation, Louisville, Kentucky, 1951–70; Technical Director, 1940–65; Vice President, 1945–65.*
BEVERAGE PRODUCTION *(in part)*

F.M.Sw.   Frederick M. Swain. *Professor of Geology, University of Delaware, Newark. Emeritus Professor of Geology, University of Minnesota, Minneapolis. Author of* Non-Marine Organic Geochemistry.
GEOCHRONOLOGY *(in part)*

F.M.V.   Florence M. Voegelin. *Editor,* Anthropological Linguistics, *Indiana University, Bloomington; former Director, Archives of Languages of the World. Coauthor of* Classification and Index of the World's Languages *and others.*
LANGUAGES OF THE WORLD *(in part)*

F.N.   Fritz Neumark. *Emeritus Professor of Political Economy, Johann Wolfgang Goethe University of Frankfurt, Frankfurt am Main, West Germany. Author of* Grundsätze gerechter und ökonomisch rationaler Steuerpolitik.
TAXATION *(in part)*

F.N.D.   Frank N. Dauster. *Professor of Spanish, Rutgers University, New Brunswick, New Jersey. Author of* Historia del teatro hispanoamericano.
LATIN-AMERICAN LITERATURE *(in part)*

F.N.H.R.   Frank Neville H. Robinson. *Senior Research Officer, Clarendon Laboratory, University of Oxford; Fellow and Tutor in Physics, St. Catherine's College, Oxford. Author of* Noise and Fluctuations in Electronic Devices and Circuits *and others.*
ELECTRICITY AND MAGNETISM *(in part)*

F.N.M.   Fyodor Nikolayevich Milkov. *Head, Department of Physical Geography, Voronezh Lenin Komsomol State University, U.S.S.R.*
UNION OF SOVIET SOCIALIST REPUBLICS *(in part)*

F.N.S.   Fyodor Nikolayevich Sukhopara. *Head of Section, Scientific Council on the Location of the U.S.S.R. Productive Forces, Academy of Sciences of the U.S.S.R., Moscow. Coauthor of* Development of Large Economic Regions of the U.S.S.R.
UNION OF SOVIET SOCIALIST REPUBLICS *(in part)*

F.N.W.   Fred N. White. *Professor of Physiology; Director, Physiological Research Laboratory, Scripps Institution of Oceanography, University of California, San Diego, at La Jolla. Coauthor of* Animal Function: Principles and Adaptations.
RESPIRATION AND RESPIRATORY SYSTEMS *(in part)*

F.Om.   Farouk Omar. *Professor of History, College of Arts, University of Baghdad, Iraq. Author of* History of the Early 'Abbasids.
BARMAKIDS (Micropædia)

F.O.W.   Frank Osborne Wood. *Technical Director, Salt Institute, Alexandria, Virginia.*
FOOD PROCESSING *(in part)*

F.O.Wa.   Frederick O. Waage. *Emeritus Professor of the History of Art and Archaeology, Cornell University, Ithaca, New York; Chairman, Department of Fine Arts, 1942–60. Author of* Prehistoric Art *and others.*
DECORATIVE ARTS AND FURNISHINGS *(in part)*

F.P.B.   Frederick P. Bargebuhr (d. 1978). *Professor of Religion, University of Iowa, Iowa City, 1962–70. Author of* The Alhambra: A Cycle of Studies on the Eleventh Century in Moorish Spain.
IBN GABIROL (Micropædia)

F.P.K.   Frank P. Kolb. *Professor of Ancient History, Christian Albrecht University of Kiel, West Germany. Author of* Literarische Beziehungen zwischen Cassius Dio, Herodian und der Historia Augusta *and others.*
CARACALLA (Micropædia)

F.P.L.   Fritz P. Loewe (d. 1974). *Senior Lecturer in Charge, Department of Meteorology, University of Melbourne, Australia, 1938–61. A world authority on the meteorology of the Southern Hemisphere. Author of* Études de glaciologie en Terre Adélie.
CLIMATE AND WEATHER *(in part)*

F.Po.   Frederik Pohl. *Author of* Tiberius *(under the pseudonym Ernst Mason) and of many works of science fiction.*
TIBERIUS *(in part)* (Micropædia)

F.P.S.   Francis P. Shepard (d. 1985). *Professor of Marine Geology, Scripps Institution of Oceanography, University of California, La Jolla, 1948–67. World authority on marine geology and submarine canyons. Coauthor of* Submarine Canyons and Other

Sea Valleys.

OCEANS (*in part*)

F.R. **Fazlur Rahman.** *Professor of Islāmic Philosophy, University of Chicago. Author of* Islam; Islam and Modernity; *and others.*

ISLĀM, MUḤAMMAD AND THE RELIGION OF (*in part*)

F.R.A. **Francis R. Aumann.** *Emeritus Professor of Political Science, Ohio State University, Columbus. Coauthor of* The Government and Administration of Ohio.

UNITED STATES OF AMERICA (*in part*)

F.R.Al. **Frank Raymond Allchin.** *Reader in Indian Studies, University of Cambridge. Author of* "The Culture Sequence of Bactria" *in* Antiquity; *coauthor of* The Rise of Civilization in India and Pakistan.

AFGHANISTAN (*in part*)
INDIA (*in part*)

F.R.H. **F. Reed Hainsworth.** *Professor of Biology, Syracuse University, New York.*

CELLS (*in part*)

Fr.J.M. **Francis J. Terence Maloney.** *Product development executive. Author of* Glass in the Modern World.

INDUSTRIAL GLASS AND CERAMICS (*in part*)

Fr.M. **Frederick Mosteller.** *Professor of Mathematical Statistics, Harvard University. Coauthor of* Probability with Statistical Applications; Data Analysis and Regression.

STATISTICS (*in part*)

F.R.M. **Frank R. Moraes** (d. 1974). *Editor in Chief,* The Indian Express, *New Delhi, 1957–72. Author of* India Today; Jawaharlal Nehru: A Biography.

INDIA (*in part*)
NEHRU, JAWAHARLAL (*in part*) (Micropædia)

F.S. **Franklin Sherman.** *Professor of Christian Ethics; Dean of the Faculty, Lutheran School of Theology at Chicago. Coauthor of* The Place of Bonhoeffer.

BONHOEFFER, DIETRICH (Micropædia)

F.S.A. **Frederick S. Arkhurst.** *Managing Director, Ideas Ltd., Accra, Ghana. Editor of* Africa in the Seventies and Eighties: Issues in Development.

AFRICA (*in part*)

F.Sc. **Friedrich Schreyvogl** (d. 1976). *Novelist and free-lance writer. Vice Director, Vienna Burgtheater, 1954–59. Author of* Ein Jahrhundert zu früh: das Schicksal Josephs II *and others.*

JOSEPH II (GERMANY/HOLY ROMAN EMPIRE) (Micropædia)

F.So. **Friedrich Solmsen.** *Moses Slaughter Professor Emeritus of Classical Studies, University of Wisconsin, Madison. Author of* Hesiod and Aeschylus.

HESIOD (Micropædia)

F.S.P. **Francis S. Pierce.** *Editor, Congressional Budget Office,*

Washington, D.C. Associate Editor, Economics, *Encyclopædia Britannica, Chicago, 1967–73.*

INTERNATIONAL TRADE (*in part*)
VEBLEN, THORSTEIN (Micropædia)

F.T. **Frederick Tepper.** *General Manager, Instrument Division, Mine Safety Appliances Company, Pittsburgh. Coauthor of* Alkali Metal Handling and System Operating Techniques.

CHEMICAL ELEMENTS (*in part*)

F.Th. **Friedrich Thöne** (deceased). *Art historian. Author of* Lucas Cranach der Ältere *and others; coauthor of* Thieme-Becker: Künstler-Lexikon.

CRANACH, LUCAS, THE ELDER (Micropædia)

F.T.M. **Fred T. Mackenzie.** *Professor of Oceanography, University of Hawaii, Honolulu. Adjunct Professor of Geology, Northwestern University, Evanston, Illinois. Coauthor of* The Evolution of Sedimentary Rocks.

HYDROSPHERE, THE (*in part*)
OCEANS (*in part*)

F.Tr. **François Treves.** *Professor of Mathematics, Rutgers University, New Brunswick, New Jersey. Author of* Topological Vector Spaces, Distributions and Kernels; Linear Partial Differential Equations with Constant Coefficients.

ANALYSIS (IN MATHEMATICS) (*in part*)

Fu.M. **Fujimura Michio.** *Professor of History, Sophia University, Tokyo. Author of* Yamagata Aritomo *and others.*

YAMAGATA ARITOMO, KOSHAKU (Micropædia)

F.V.O'C. **Francis Valentine O'Connor.** *Director, Raphael Research Enterprises (fine arts consultants), New York City. Editor, Federal Art Patronage Notes. Author of* Federal Support for the Visual Arts: The New Deal and Now; *Coeditor of* Jackson Pollock: A Catalogue Raisonné of Paintings, Drawings, and Other Works.

DE KOONING, WILLEM (Micropædia)

F.V.Sn. **Fernand Van Steenberghen.** *Emeritus Professor of Medieval Philosophy, Catholic University of Louvain, Belgium.*

PHILOSOPHICAL SCHOOLS AND DOCTRINES, WESTERN (*in part*)

F.W.C. **Francis William Carter.** *Joint Hayter Lecturer in the Geography of Eastern Europe, University College and School of Slavonic and East European Studies, University of London. Editor of* An Historical Geography of the Balkans.

BULGARIA (*in part*)

F.W.G. **Frederick William Gibbs** (d. 1966). *Deputy Secretary and Editor, Royal Institute of Chemistry, London.*

DAVY, SIR HUMPHRY, BARONET (Micropædia)

F.Wh. **Frederick Whitehead** (d. 1971). *Reader in Old French Language and Literature, Victoria University of Manchester. Editor of* La Chanson de

Roland; La Chastelaine de Vergi.

LITERATURE, THE ART OF (*in part*)

F.Wi. **Frank Willett.** *Director and Titular Professor, Hunterian Museum and Art Gallery, University of Glasgow. Author of* African Art; Ife in the History of West African Sculpture.

AFRICAN ARTS (*in part*)

F.W.K. **Francis W. Karasek.** *Professor of Chemistry, University of Waterloo, Ontario.*

MEASUREMENT AND OBSERVATION, PRINCIPLES, METHODS, AND INSTRUMENTS OF (*in part*)

F.W.Kn. **Franklin W. Knight.** *Professor of History, Johns Hopkins University, Baltimore, Maryland. Author of* Slave Society in Cuba during the Nineteenth Century *and others.*

WEST INDIES, THE (*in part*)

F.W.McB. **F. Webster McBryde.** *Director, McBryde Center for Human Ecology, Potomac, Maryland. Author of* Cultural and Historical Geography of Southwest Guatemala *and others.*

CENTRAL AMERICA (*in part*)

F.W.W. **Frank W. Walbank.** *Rathbone Professor Emeritus of Ancient History and Classical Archaeology, University of Liverpool. Author of* A Historical Commentary on Polybius *and others.*

ALEXANDER THE GREAT (*in part*)
GRECO-ROMAN CIVILIZATION, CLASSICAL (*in part*)
PLUTARCH (*in part*) (Micropædia)
POLYBIUS (Micropædia)
YUGOSLAVIA (*in part*)

F.W.We. **Frits W. Went.** *Emeritus Professor of Botany, Desert Research Institute, University of Nevada System, Reno. Author of* The Experimental Control of Plant Growth.

ECOSYSTEMS (*in part*)

F.W.W.-S. **Francis William Wentworth-Sheilds** (d. 1969). *Artist. Principal Lecturer, Department of Printing and Graphic Design, Twickenham College of Technology, Middlesex, England, 1966–69.*

PAINTING, THE HISTORY OF WESTERN (*in part*)

F.X.M. **The Rev. Francis Xavier Murphy, C.SS.R.** *Emeritus Professor of Patristic Moral Theology, Academia Alfonsiana, Rome. Staff editor for* Patrology, *New Catholic Encyclopedia.*

ALEXANDER VI (PAPACY) (Micropædia)
PAUL III (PAPACY) (Micropædia)

G.A. **Giovanni Aquilecchia.** *Professor of Italian, University College, University of London. Author of* Giordano Bruno; *editor of Pietro Aretino's* Sei giornate.

ARIOSTO, LUDOVICO (Micropædia)
BRUNO, GIORDANO (Micropædia)
ITALIAN LITERATURE (*in part*)
TASSO, TORQUATO (Micropædia)

G.A.B. **Georg A. Borgstrom.** *Emeritus Professor of Food Science and of Geography, Michigan State University,*

East Lansing. Editor of Fish as Food.
FISHING AND MARINE PRODUCTS,
  COMMERCIAL (*in part*)

G.A.C.   G. Arthur Cooper. *Emeritus
Paleobiologist, Smithsonian Institution,
Washington, D.C. Author of* Chazyan
and Related Brachiopods.
LAMP SHELLS

G.A.C.H.   Geoffrey A.C. Herklots
(d. 1986). *Colombo Plan Botanical
Adviser to Government of Nepal, 1961–
63. Principal and Director of Research,
Imperial College of Tropical Agriculture,
Trinidad, 1953–60. Author of* Vegetables
in South-East Asia *and others.*
GARDENING AND HORTICULTURE
  (*in part*)

**G.A.F.K.   George Angus Fulton
Knight.** *President, Pacific Theological
College, Suva, Fiji, 1965–72. Author
of* A Christian Theology of the Old
Testament; Deutero-Isaiah, a Theological
Commentary; *and others.*
MACCABEES (Micropædia)

G.A.G.M.   G.A.G. Mitchell. *Professor
of Anatomy; Director, Anatomical
Laboratories, Victoria University of
Manchester, 1946–74. Author of* The
Anatomy of the Autonomic Nervous
System *and others.*
EXCRETION AND EXCRETORY SYSTEMS
  (*in part*)

G.A.H.   Geoffrey Alan Hosking.
*Professor of Russian History, School of
Slavonic and East European Studies,
University of London. Author of* Beyond
Socialist Realism: Soviet Fiction Since
Ivan Denisovich *and others.*
RUSSIAN LITERATURE (*in part*)

G.Ak.   George Akita. *Professor of
History, University of Hawaii, Honolulu.
Author of* Foundations of Constitutional
Government.
ITŌ HIROBUMI, KOSHAKU (Micropædia)

G.A.K.   Gregory A. Kimble. *Professor
of Psychology, Duke University, Durham,
North Carolina. Author of* Foundations
of Conditioning and Learning.
LEARNING AND COGNITION, HUMAN
  (*in part*)

G.A.L.   George Arthur Lindbeck. *Pitkin
Professor of Historical Theology, Yale
University. Author of* The Nature of
Doctrine: Religion and Theology in a
Post-Liberal Age *and others.*
RITES AND CEREMONIES, SACRED
  (*in part*)

G.An.   George Anastaplo. *Professor
of Law, Loyola University, Chicago.
Lecturer in the Liberal Arts, University
of Chicago. Emeritus Professor of
Political Science and of Philosophy,
Rosary College, River Forest, Illinois.
Author of* The Constitutionalist
and others.
CENSORSHIP
GREECE (*in part*)

G.A.O.   George A. Olah. *Professor
of Chemistry, University of Southern
California, Los Angeles. Coeditor of*

Carbonium Ions.
CARBONIUM ION (*in part*) (Micropædia)

Ga.P.   Gary William Poole. *Associate
Editor,* Encyclopædia Britannica,
Chicago, 1970–72.
CHAMBERLAIN, JOSEPH (Micropædia)
JOSEPHUS, FLAVIUS (Micropædia)

G.A.P.   George A. Pettitt (d. 1976).
*Assistant to the President, University of
California, Berkeley, 1936–66; Lecturer
in Anthropology, 1940–66. Author of*
Prisoners of Culture.
GESNER, CONRAD (Micropædia)

Ga.S.   Gabriel Smith. *Barrister-at-Law.
Lecturer in Industry and Finance, City
of London College. Departmental Editor,*
Journal of Business Law.
TAXATION (*in part*)

G.A.S.   George Albert Shepperson.
*William Robertson Professor of
Commonwealth and American History,
University of Edinburgh. Author of*
David Livingstone and the
Rovuma.
LIVINGSTONE, DAVID (Micropædia)

G.A.Sa.   George A. Sacher (d.
1981). *Senior Biologist, Division of
Biological and Medical Research,
Argonne National Laboratory, 1959–80.
President, Gerontological Society, 1978–
79. Coeditor of* Aging and Levels of
Biological Organization.
GROWTH AND DEVELOPMENT,
  BIOLOGICAL (*in part*)

G.A.Sm.   George Alan Smith. *Arts
consultant. Hiker and mountain
climber. Author of* Introduction to
Mountaineering; The Armchair
Mountaineer.
MOUNTAINEERING (*in part*)
  (Micropædia)

G.A.So.   G. Alan Solem. *Curator of
Invertebrates, Field Museum of Natural
History, Chicago. Author of* Land
and Freshwater Mollusca of the New
Hebrides.
MOLLUSKS (*in part*)

G.Ba.   George Barany. *Professor of
History, University of Denver, Colorado.
Author of* Stephen Szechenyi and the
Awakening of Hungarian
Nationalism.
HUNGARY (*in part*)

G.B.Cl.   George B. Clark. *Professor of
Mining Engineering; Research Associate,
Earth Mechanics Institute, Colorado
School of Mines, Golden. Coauthor of*
Elements of Mining.
INDUSTRIES, EXTRACTION AND
  PROCESSING (*in part*)

G.B.D.   George B. Dantzig. *Professor
of Operations Research and Computer
Science, Stanford University, California.
Author of* Linear Programming and
Extensions.
OPTIMIZATION, THE MATHEMATICAL
  THEORY OF (*in part*)

G.Be.   George Benneh. *Associate
Professor of Geography, University of*

Ghana, Legon.
WESTERN AFRICA (*in part*)

G.Bh.   Geoffrey Barraclough (d. 1984).
*Chichele Professor of Modern History,
University of Oxford, 1970–73.
President, The Historical Association,
1964–67.*
HOLY ROMAN EMPIRE, THE HISTORY OF
THE (*in part*)

G.Bi.   Garrett Birkhoff. *George Putnam
Professor Emeritus of Pure and Applied
Mathematics, Harvard University.
Coauthor of* Algebra.
ALGEBRA (*in part*)

G.B.K.   George Briscoe Kerferd. *Hulme
Professor Emeritus of Greek, Victoria
University of Manchester.*
PHILOSOPHICAL SCHOOLS AND
  DOCTRINES, WESTERN (*in part*)

G.Bl.   Georges Blond. *Novelist and
historian. Author of* Pétain, 1856–1951.
PÉTAIN, PHILIPPE (Micropædia)

G.B.L.   Gerhart B. Ladner. *Emeritus
Professor of History, University of
California, Los Angeles. Author of* Die
Papstbildnisse des Altertum und des
Mittelalters.
BONIFACE VIII (PAPACY) (Micropædia)
INNOCENT III (Micropædia)

G.Bo.   Gunnar Boalt. *Emeritus
Professor of Sociology, University of
Stockholm. Author of* Family and
Marriage *and others.*
FAMILY AND KINSHIP (*in part*)

G.Bor.   Günther Bornkamm. *Emeritus
Professor of New Testament Studies,
Rupert Charles University of Heidelberg.
Author of* Jesus of Nazareth.
JESUS (*in part*)

G.C.   Guido Calogero. *Former Professor
of Theoretical Philosophy, University
of Rome. Author of* Studi sull'eleatismo
and others.
PHILOSOPHICAL SCHOOLS AND
  DOCTRINES, WESTERN (*in part*)

G.Car.   Giovanni Carsaniga. *Professor
of Italian, La Trobe University,
Bundoora, Australia.*
ITALIAN LITERATURE (*in part*)

G.C.B.   Gregorio C. Borlaza. *Editorial
Consultant, Philippine Christian
University, Manila. Former President,
Philippine Normal College.*
PHILIPPINES (*in part*)

G.C.C.   George C. Cromer. *Manager,
Administrative Services, General Motors
Current Product Engineering, Warren,
Michigan.*
TRANSPORTATION (*in part*)

G.C.G.   George C. Gorman. *Professor
of Biology, University of California, Los
Angeles, 1980–82. Researcher on the
evolution, behaviour, and systematics
of lizards.*
REPTILES (*in part*)

G.C.H.   Gerald C. Hickey. *Research
Fellow, East–West Center, Honolulu.
Research Anthropologist, the RAND*

Corporation, Saigon, 1964–73. Author of
Village in Vietnam *and others.*
SOUTHEAST ASIA, MAINLAND (*in part*)

G.C.Ha. Gladys Cox Hansen. *City
Archivist, San Francisco. Author of*
San Francisco Almanac; *editor of* San
Francisco: The Bay and Its Cities.
SAN FRANCISCO (*in part*)

G.C.H.B. Göran C.H. Bauer, M.D.
*Professor and Chairman, Department
of Orthopedic Surgery, Medical School,
University of Lund, Sweden.*
SUPPORTIVE AND CONNECTIVE
TISSUES (*in part*)

G.C.I. George C. Izenour. *Emeritus
Professor of Theater Design and
Technology, Yale University.*
THEATRICAL PRODUCTION (*in part*)

G.C.K. George C. Kent, Jr. *Alumni
Professor Emeritus of Zoology,
Louisiana State University, Baton
Rouge. Author of* Comparative Anatomy
of the Vertebrates.
REPRODUCTION AND REPRODUCTIVE
SYSTEMS (*in part*)

G.C.L.B. G.C.L. Bertram. *Former
Senior Tutor, St. John's College,
University of Cambridge. Author of* In
Search of Mermaids: The Manatees of
Guiana *and others.*
MAMMALS (*in part*)

G.Cr. Gerhard Croll. *Professor of
Musicology, University of Salzburg,
Austria. General editor of* Christoph
Willibald Gluck, Complete Edition of
His Works.
GLUCK, CHRISTOPH (Micropædia)

G.C.R. George Clarence Robinson
(d. 1976). *Professor of Political
Science, University of Northern Iowa,
Cedar Falls. Editor of* Dictionary of
Presidential Disapprovals.
POLK, JAMES K. (Micropædia)

G.C.T. Gordon Conrad Thomasson.
*Assistant Professor of Anthropology,
Cuttington University College, Suakoko,
Liberia. Editor of* War, Conscription,
Conscience and Mormonism.
RELIGIOUS EDUCATION (*in part*)

G.d'A. Guido d'Agostino. *Associate
in Institutional Parliamentary History,
University of Naples.*
ITALY (*in part*)

**G.D.B. Georgy Dmitriyevich
Bessarabov.** *Head, Department of
Agrarian Resources, Government
Research Institute of Agrarian Resources,
Moscow.*
ASIA (*in part*)

G.D.C. Gerson D. Cohen. *Jacob H.
Schiff Professor of History, The Jewish
Theological Seminary of America, New
York City; Chancellor, 1972–85. Editor
and translator of Abraham ibn Daud's*
Sefer ha-Kabbala.
JUDAISM (*in part*)

G.De. George G. Dekker. *Professor of
English, Stanford University, California.
Author of* James Fenimore Cooper: The

Novelist *and others.*
COOPER, JAMES FENIMORE (Micropædia)

G. de B. Sir Gavin de Beer (d. 1972).
*Professor of Embryology, University
College, University of London, 1945–
50. Director, British Museum (Natural
History), London, 1950–60. Author of*
Charles Darwin; Atlas of Evolution;
and others.
DARWIN (*in part*)
EVOLUTION, THE THEORY OF (*in part*)
OWEN, SIR RICHARD (Micropædia)

G. de R.-C. G. de Rohan-Csermak
(deceased). *Professor of Sociology, King's
College, University of Western Ontario,
London. Founder and Editor,* Ethnologia
Europaea.
EUROPE (*in part*)

G. de S. Giorgio D. de Santillana
(d. 1974). *Professor of the History and
Philosophy of Science, Massachusetts
Institute of Technology, Cambridge.
Author of* The Crime of Galileo
and others.
GALILEO (*in part*)

G.Det. Georges Dethan. *Archivist,
French Foreign Ministry Archives,
Paris. Chief Editor,* Revue d'Histoire
Diplomatique. *Author of* Mazarin et ses
amis *and others.*
MAZARIN, JULES, CARDINAL
(Micropædia)

G.Di. Gérard Diffloth. *Associate
Professor of Linguistics, University of
Chicago.*
LANGUAGES OF THE WORLD (*in part*)

G.D.L. Geoffrey D. Lewis. *Director
of Museum Studies, University of
Leicester, England. Coeditor of* Manual
of Curatorship: A Guide to Museum
Practice.
MUSEUMS

G.D.M. George Daniel Mostow. *Henry
Ford II Professor of Mathematics, Yale
University. Editor,* American Journal of
Mathematics. *Author of* Strong Rigidity
of Locally Symmetric Spaces.
ALGEBRA (*in part*)
GEOMETRY (*in part*)

G.D.P. George Duncan Painter.
*Assistant Keeper in charge of incunabula,
Department of Printed Books, British
Library, London, 1954–74. Author of*
Proust: The Early Years; Proust: The
Later Years; *and others.*
PROUST, MARCEL (Micropædia)

G.D.W. G. Donald Whedon, M.D.
*Medical research consultant. Director,
National Institute of Arthritis,
Metabolism, and Digestive Diseases,
U.S. Department of Health and Human
Services, Bethesda, Maryland, 1962–81.*
SUPPORTIVE AND CONNECTIVE
TISSUES (*in part*)

G.Dy. George Dykhuizen. *Emeritus
Professor of Philosophy, University of
Vermont, Burlington. Author of* The Life
and Mind of John Dewey.
DEWEY, JOHN (Micropædia)

G.E. Gordon Epperson. *Professor of
Music, University of Arizona, Tucson.
Author of* The Musical Symbol: A Study
of the Philosophic Theory of Music.
MUSIC, THE ART OF (*in part*)

G.E.A. Godfrey Edward Arnold, M.D.
*Professor and Director, Division of
Otolaryngology, University of Mississippi
Medical Center, Jackson, 1963–79.
Coauthor of* Voice, Speech, Language;
Clinical Communicology.
SPEECH (*in part*)

G.E.Al. Garland Edward Allen.
*Professor of Biology, Washington
University, St. Louis, Missouri. Author
of* Thomas Hunt Morgan: The Man and
His Science.
MORGAN, THOMAS HUNT (Micropædia)

Ge.B. Gerald Bonner. *Reader in
Church History, University of Durham,
England.*
ARTS, PRACTICE AND PROFESSION OF
THE (*in part*)

Ge.C. George S. Cansdale.
*Superintendent, Zoological Society of
London, Regent's Park, 1948–53. Author
of* All the Animals of the Bible Lands
and others.
PETS (*in part*)

G.Ec. Garrett Eckbo. *Landscape
architect and consultant in urban and
environmental planning and design.
Emeritus Professor of Landscape
Architecture, University of California,
Berkeley. Author of* Landscape for Living
and others.
GARDEN AND LANDSCAPE DESIGN
(*in part*)

Ge.Ca. George Cardona. *Professor of
Linguistics, University of Pennsylvania,
Philadelphia. Author of* Studies in Indian
Grammarians *and others; coeditor of*
Indo-European and Indo-Europeans.
LANGUAGES OF THE WORLD (*in part*)

G.E.D. Glyn Edmund Daniel. *Disney
Professor Emeritus of Archaeology,
University of Cambridge; Fellow
of St. John's College, Cambridge.
Editor,* Antiquity. *Author of* The First
Civilizations; A Hundred and Fifty
Years of Archaeology; *and others.*
HISTORY, THE STUDY OF (*in part*)
SCHLIEMANN, HEINRICH (Micropædia)

Ge.E. Brother George Every, S.S.M.
(deceased). *Lecturer, Kelham Theological
College, Newark, England. Lay brother
of the Society of the Sacred Mission.
Author of* The Byzantine Patriarchate,
451–1204 *and others.*
PHOTIUS (Micropædia)

G.E.F. George Edwin Fussell. *Former
President, British Agricultural History
Society. Author of* Farming Technique
from Prehistoric to Modern Times
and others.
AGRICULTURE, THE HISTORY OF (*in part*)

**G.E.F.C. Guy Edward Farquhar
Chilver** (d. 1982). *Professor of
Classical Studies, University of Kent at
Canterbury, England, 1964–76. Author*

of "Vespasian" in Oxford Classical
Dictionary.
DOMITIAN (Micropædia)
VESPASIAN (Micropædia)

G.E.H. The Rev. G.E. Hughes.
*Professor of Philosophy, Victoria
University of Wellington, New Zealand,
1951–84. Coauthor of* The Elements of
Formal Logic.
LOGIC, THE HISTORY AND KINDS
    OF (*in part*)

G.E.H.A. Gerald E.H. Abraham.
*President, Royal Musical Association,
1970–74. Assistant Controller of Music,
British Broadcasting Corporation,
London, 1962–67. James and Constance
Alsop Professor of Music, University
of Liverpool, 1947–62. Author of* A
Hundred Years of Music; Slavonic and
Romantic Music; *and others.*
SCHUMANN, ROBERT (Micropædia)

G.E.H.F. G.E.H. Foxon (d. 1982).
*Professor of Biology, Guy's Hospital
Medical School, University of London,
1955–82. Author of "Blood and
Respiration" in* Physiology of the
Amphibia.
CIRCULATION AND CIRCULATORY
    SYSTEMS (*in part*)

Ge.M. Gerald Mast. *Professor of
English, University of Chicago. Author of*
A Short History of the Movies.
MOTION PICTURES (*in part*)

G.E.Ma. Gene E. Martin. *Professor of
Geography, California State University,
Chico. Author of* La división de la tierra
en Chile central.
SOUTH AMERICA (*in part*)

G.E.Me. George Emery Mendenhall.
*Professor of Ancient and Biblical Studies,
University of Michigan, Ann Arbor.
Author of* Law and Covenant in Israel
and the Ancient Near East
and others.
DOCTRINES AND DOGMAS, RELIGIOUS
    (*in part*)

G.E.Mi. Gordon E. Misner. *Professor
of Criminal Justice, University of
Illinois, Chicago. Coauthor of* The
Police and Society: An Environment
for Collaboration and Confrontation
and others.
POLICE (*in part*)

G.E.M.M. Gladstone E.M. Mills.
*Professor of Public Administration;
Dean, Faculty of Social Sciences,
University of the West Indies, Kingston,
Jamaica. Coeditor of* The Role of Small
Nations in a Big World.
WEST INDIES, THE (*in part*)

Ge.Mo. Gerald Moore. *Professor of
English, University of Jos, Nigeria.
Author of* Seven African Writers
and others.
AFRICAN ARTS (*in part*)

G.E.Mo. Gordon E. Moore. *Chairman
of the Board, Intel Corporation,
Santa Clara, California. Coauthor of*
Microelectronics.
ELECTRONICS (*in part*)

Ge.S. George Savage (d. 1982).
Free-lance writer. Author of Concise
History of Interior Decoration; French
Decorative Art; Porcelain Through the
Ages; *and many other works on the
decorative arts.*
DECORATIVE ARTS AND FURNISHINGS
    (*in part*)

G.Es. Gerald Eskenazi. *Sportswriter,
The New York Times. Free-lance writer.
Author of* Hockey; A Year on Ice.
SPORTS, MAJOR TEAM AND INDIVIDUAL
    (*in part*)

**G.E.S. George E. Shambaugh,
Jr., M.D.** *Emeritus Professor of
Otolaryngology, Northwestern University,
Chicago. Chief Editor,* Archives of
Otolaryngology, *1960–70. Author of*
Surgery of the Ear.
SENSORY RECEPTION (*in part*)

G.E.T. Gordon Ernest Taylor. *Senior
Scientific Officer, Royal Greenwich
Observatory, Herstmonceux, England.
President of the British Astronomical
Association, 1968–70.*
SOLAR SYSTEM, THE (*in part*)

G.Ev. Graham Evans. *Reader in
Sedimentology, Imperial College of
Science and Technology, University of
London.*
ASIA (*in part*)

G.E.W. Glen E. Woolfenden. *Professor
of Zoology, University of South
Florida, Tampa.*
BIRDS (*in part*)

G.E.Wh. Geoffrey Edleston Wheeler.
*Lieutenant Colonel, Indian Army
(retired). Director, Central Asian
Research Centre, London, 1953–68.
Author of* The Modern History of Soviet
Central Asia *and others.*
UNION OF SOVIET SOCIALIST REPUBLICS
    (*in part*)

G.F.A. Geoffrey Freeman Allen.
Editor, Jane's World Railways. *Author of*
Modern Railways *and others.*
TRANSPORTATION (*in part*)

G.F.E. George F. Ekstrom (deceased).
*Professor of Agricultural Education,
University of Missouri, Columbia.*
AGRICULTURAL SCIENCES (*in part*)

G.Fi. Gilbert Fielder. *Head, Lunar and
Planetary Unit; Reader in Environmental
Sciences, University of Lancaster,
England. Author of* Lunar Geology,
editor of Geology and Physics of
the Moon.
SOLAR SYSTEM, THE (*in part*)

G.F.K. George Frederick Kneller.
*Emeritus Professor of Education,
University of California, Los Angeles.
Author of* Movements of Thought in
Modern Education *and others.*
EDUCATION, SYSTEMS OF (*in part*)

G.Fo. Gabriel Fournier. *Professor
of Medieval History, University of
Clermont-Ferrand, France. Author of* Les
Mérovingiens *and others.*
FRANCE (*in part*)

G.F.P. Gabor F. Peterdi. *Painter and
printmaker. Professor of Printmaking,
Yale University. Author of* Printmaking;
Great Prints of the World.
PRINTMAKING

G.F.S. Gilles François Sautter.
*Professor of Geography, University of
Paris I (Panthéon-Sorbonne). Author of*
De l'Atlantique au fleuve Congo.
AFRICA (*in part*)

G.F.W. Gilbert F. White. *Gustavson
Distinguished Professor Emeritus of
Geography, University of Colorado,
Boulder. Consultant, Lower
Mekong Coordinating Committee,
1961–62. Coauthor of* The Lower
Mekong.
ASIA (*in part*)

G.G. George Gömöri. *Lecturer
in Slavonic Studies, University of
Cambridge. Author of* Polish and
Hungarian Poetry, 1945 to 1956.
HUNGARIAN LITERATURE (*in part*)

G.Ge. Gino Germani (d. 1979). *Monroe
Gutman Professor of Latin American
Studies, Harvard University. Author
of* Política y sociedad en una época de
transición.
MODERNIZATION AND URBANIZATION
    (*in part*)
SOUTH AMERICA (*in part*)

G.Gr. Guido Gregorietti. *Former
Director, Poldi Pezzoli Museum, Milan.
Author of* The Jewel Through the
Centuries.
DRESS AND ADORNMENT (*in part*)

Gg.S. Georg Schnath. *Professor of
History, Georg August University of
Göttingen, West Germany, 1949–67.*
GERMANY (*in part*)

G.G.V.D. Glyndon G. Van Deusen.
*Research Professor Emeritus of History,
University of Rochester, New York.
Author of* The Life of Henry Clay
and others.
CLAY HENRY (Micropædia)

G.G.Wd. Guido Gustav Weigend.
*Professor of Geography, Arizona State
University, Tempe.*
MEDITERRANEAN SEA (*in part*)

G.Ha. Georg Hazai. *Corresponding
Member; Deputy Director, Oriental
Studies Research Group, Hungarian
Academy of Sciences, Budapest; General
Manager, Akadémiai Kiadó és Nyomda
(publishing house of the academy).
Author of* Sovietico-Turcica.
LANGUAGES OF THE WORLD (*in part*)

G.H.B. Geoffrey H. Beale. *Royal
Society Research Professor of Genetics,
University of Edinburgh, Scotland,
1963–78. Author of* The Genetics of
Paramecium Aurelia.
WEISMANN, AUGUST (Micropædia)

G.H.D. George Harry Dury. *Emeritus
Professor of Geography and Geology,
University of Wisconsin, Madison.
World authority on fluvial processes in
geomorphology. Author of* The Face of

the Earth.
RIVERS (*in part*)

G.He. **George Hendricks** (d. 1979). *Professor of Social Sciences, Georgia Institute of Technology, Atlanta, 1962–69. Author of* Union Army Occupation of the Southern Seaboard, 1861–1865.
UNITED STATES OF AMERICA (*in part*)

G.Hi. **Gilbert Highet** (d. 1978). *Anthon Professor of Latin Language and Literature, Columbia University, 1950–72. Author of* Juvenal the Satirist; The Classical Tradition: Greek and Roman Influences on Western Literature.
JUVENAL (Micropædia)

G.H.J. **Gareth H. Jones.** *Downing Professor of the Laws of England, University of Cambridge; Fellow of Trinity College, Cambridge.*
COKE, SIR EDWARD (Micropædia)

G.H.K. **George Hall Kirby.** *Free-lance writer, editor, and translator. Author of* Looking at Germany *and others.*
GERMANY (*in part*)

G.H.S. **Genjun H. Sasaki.** *Professor of Buddhism, Otani University, Kyōto. Author of* A Study of Buddhist Psychology.
SHINRAN (Micropædia)

G.H.S.B. **Geoffrey H.S. Bushnell** (d. 1978). *Reader in New World Archaeology, University of Cambridge, 1966–70; Fellow of Corpus Christi College, Cambridge; Curator, University Museum of Archaeology and Ethnology, 1948–70. Author of* Peru *and others.*
PRE-COLUMBIAN CIVILIZATIONS (*in part*)

G.H.T.K. **George H.T. Kimble.** *Director, Survey of Tropical Africa, Twentieth Century Fund, New York City, 1953–60. Professor of Geography, Indiana University, Bloomington, 1957–66. Author of* Tropical Africa.
AFRICA (*in part*)

G.H. von W. **Georg Henrik von Wright.** *Research Professor, Academy of Finland, Helsinki. Former Chancellor, Swedish University of Åbo, Finland. Professor of Philosophy, University of Helsinki, 1946–61. Author of* A Treatise on Induction and Probability *and others.*
MATHEMATICS, THE HISTORY OF (*in part*)

G.I.B. **George I. Blanksten.** *Professor of Political Science, Northwestern University, Evanston, Illinois. Author of* Perón's Argentina; Ecuador: Constitutions and Caudillos; *and others.*
BRAZIL (*in part*)
URUGUAY (*in part*)

G.I.Bk. **George I. Back** (d. 1972). *Major General, U.S. Army.*
WAR, THE TECHNOLOGY OF (*in part*)

Gi.M. **Giovanni Macchia.** *Professor of French Language and Literature, University of Rome. Author of* L'opera completa di Watteau *and others.*
WATTEAU, ANTOINE (Micropædia)

Gi.Ma. **Giuseppe Martini.** *Former Professor of Medieval History; Director, Institute of Medieval and Modern History, University of Milan. Author of* Cattolicesimo e storicismo *and others.*
ITALY (*in part*)

Gi.T. **Giuseppe Tucci** (d. 1984). *Professor of Oriental Religion and Philosophy, University of Rome, 1933–65. Author of* Il buddhismo; Minor Buddhist Texts; *and others.*
BUDDHISM, THE BUDDHA AND (*in part*)

G.J.B. **Gilbert James Butland.** *Emeritus Professor of Geography, University of New England, Armidale, Australia.*
PARAGUAY (*in part*)
SPAIN (*in part*)

G.J.G. **George J. Goodman.** *Regents Professor Emeritus of Botany, University of Oklahoma, Norman. Author of* Spring Flora of Central Oklahoma.
ANGIOSPERMS (*in part*)

G.J.N. **Gareth Jon Nelson.** *Chairman and Curator, Department of Ichthyology, American Museum of Natural History, New York City. Author of articles on the anatomy and systematics of fishes.*
FISHES (*in part*)

G.J.P. **Gray Johnson Poole.** *Free-lance writer. Author of* Architects and Man's Skyline; *coauthor of* Men Who Dig Up History *and others.*
PETRIE, SIR FLINDERS (Micropædia)

G.J.S. **George J. Stigler.** *Charles R. Walgreen Distinguished Service Professor Emeritus of American Institutions, University of Chicago. Nobel Prize for Economics, 1982. Author of* The Theory of Price.
ECONOMIC THEORY (*in part*)

G.J.Si. **Gustavus J. Simmons.** *Manager, Applied Mathematics Department, Sandia National Laboratories, Albuquerque, New Mexico. Researcher in command and control of nuclear weapons. Author of numerous articles on cryptology and authentication.*
CRYPTOLOGY

G.J.T. **Gerald J. Toomer.** *Professor of the History of Mathematics, Brown University, Providence, Rhode Island. Author of* Diocles on Burning Mirrors.
ARCHIMEDES

G.J.W. **Gerald James Whitrow.** *Emeritus Professor of the History and Applications of Mathematics, Imperial College of Science and Technology, University of London. Author of* The Natural Philosophy of Time *and others.*
HAMILTON, SIR WILLIAM ROWAN (Micropædia)
LAPLACE, PIERRE-SIMON, MARQUIS DE (Micropædia)
POINCARÉ, HENRI (Micropædia)

G.J.Wh. **Gershon J. Wheeler.** *Free-lance writer and microwave engineer. Author of* Introduction to Microwaves; Radar Fundamentals; *and others.*

MEASUREMENT AND OBSERVATION, PRINCIPLES, METHODS, AND INSTRUMENTS OF (*in part*)

G.K. **Gerhard Kubik.** *Cultural Anthropologist, Institute of Ethnology, University of Vienna. Author of* Música Tradicional e Aculturada dos !Kung de Angola *and other works on African music.*
AFRICAN ARTS (*in part*)

G.K.E. **Geoffrey Kenyon Elliott.** *Senior Lecturer in Forestry, University College of North Wales, University of Wales, Bangor.*
ECOSYSTEMS (*in part*)

G.K.G. **G.K. Ghori.** *Visiting Professor of Geography, University of Benin, Nigeria. Former Professor of Geography, University of Mysore, India.*
INDIA (*in part*)

G.K.Ge. **Gerald K. Geerlings.** *Architect, etcher, and writer. Author of* Wrought Iron in Architecture; Metal Crafts in Architecture.
DECORATIVE ARTS AND FURNISHINGS (*in part*)

G.Kh. **George Kish.** *Professor of Geography, University of Michigan, Ann Arbor.*
ITALY (*in part*)

G.K.L. **George Knowlton Lewis.** *Professor of Geography, Boston University. Coauthor of* Boston: A Geographical Portrait.
BOSTON (*in part*)

G.K.P. **George Kerlin Park.** *Professor of Anthropology, Memorial University of Newfoundland, St. John's. Author of* The Idea of Social Structure; An Afterpiece to Peasantry.
OCCULTISM (*in part*)
RELIGIOUS AND SPIRITUAL BELIEF, SYSTEMS OF (*in part*)

G.K.S.R. **Gotthold K.S. Rhode.** *Professor of East European and Russian History; Director, Institute for East European Research, Johannes Gutenberg University of Mainz, West Germany. Author of* Kleine Geschichte Polens.
CASIMIR III (Micropædia)
CASIMIR IV (Micropædia)
JOHN III SOBIESKI (POLAND) (Micropædia)
WŁADYSŁAW II JAGIEŁŁO (Micropædia)

G.L. **George Lang.** *International hotel, restaurant, and food consultant. Columnist,* Travel & Leisure *magazine. Author of* The Cuisine of Hungary; *consulting editor of* Time-Life Foods of the World.
GASTRONOMY

G.L.C. **Gerhard L. Closs.** *A.A. Michelson Distinguished Service Professor of Chemistry, University of Chicago. Author of numerous papers on transient intermediates in chemical reactions.*
CARBANION (*in part*) (Micropædia)
CARBENE (Micropædia)

G.L.Ca.   George Law Cawkwell.
*Lecturer in Ancient History, University
of Oxford; Fellow of University
College, Oxford.*
ISOCRATES (Micropædia)

G.L.D.   Gwenda Louise Davis. *Former
Associate Professor of Botany, University
of New England, Armidale, Australia.
Author of* Systematic Embryology of the
Angiosperms.
ANGIOSPERMS (*in part*)

G.L.G.   George L. Gooberman. *Lecturer
in Electrical Engineering, National
Institute for Higher Education, Limerick,
Ireland. Author of* Ultrasonics.
SOUND (*in part*)

G.L.Go.   Gillian Lindt Gollin. *Professor
of Sociology of Religion, Columbia
University. Author of* Moravians in
Two Worlds.
ZINZENDORF, NIKOLAUS LUDWIG, GRAF
VON (Micropædia)

G.Li.   Georges Livet. *Professor of
Modern History, University of Strasbourg
II, France.*
FRANCE (*in part*)

**G.L.K.   Sir Geoffrey Langdon Keynes,
M.D.** (d. 1982). *Honorary Librarian,
Royal College of Surgeons of England.
Consulting Surgeon, St. Bartholomew's
Hospital, London. Author of* The
Life of William Harvey; A Bibliography
of the Writings of Dr. William
Harvey.
HARVEY (*in part*)

G.L.Ke.   George L. Kelling. *Professor
of Criminal Justice, Northeastern
University, Boston. Research Fellow,
John F. Kennedy School of Government,
Harvard University. Coauthor of* Newark
Foot Patrol Experiment.
POLICE (*in part*)

G.L.M.   George Leslie Miller. *Research
Manager, Murex Ltd., Rainham,
England, 1934–69.*
INDUSTRIES, EXTRACTION AND
PROCESSING (*in part*)

G.L.T.   George L. Trigg. *Editor,*
Physical Review Letters, *American
Physical Society, Ridge, New York.
Author of* Quantum Mechanics.
ATOMS (*in part*)

G.Lu.   Georg Hans Luck. *Professor
of Classics, Johns Hopkins University,
Baltimore. Author of* The Latin
Love-Elegy *and others.*
PROPERTIUS, SEXTUS (Micropædia)

G.L.V.   Gilbert L. Voss. *Professor of
Marine Science, University of Miami,
Florida. Author of* Cephalopods of the
Philippine Islands.
MOLLUSKS (*in part*)

G.M.   George Makdisi. *Professor of
Arabic and Islamic Studies; Director,
Center of Medieval Studies, University
of Pennsylvania, Philadelphia. Author
of* Ibn ʿAqīl et la resurgence de l'Islam
traditionaliste au XIᵉ siècle.
AḤMAD IBN ḤANBAL (Micropædia)

G.Ma.   Golo Mann. *Writer. Professor of
History and Political Science, Technical
University, Stuttgart, West Germany,
1960–64. Author of* Friedrich von Gentz
and others.
GENTZ, FRIEDRICH (Micropædia)

G.M.A.   Glenda M. Abramson. *Fellow,
Oxford Centre for Hebrew Studies;
Senior Research Fellow, St. Cross
College, University of Oxford. Author of*
Modern Hebrew Drama.
HEBREW LITERATURE (*in part*)

**G.M.A.R.   Gisela Marie Augusta
Richter** (d. 1972). *Curator, Greek and
Roman Department, Metropolitan
Museum of Art, New York City. Author
of* Engraved Gems of the Greeks,
Etruscans, and Romans *and others.*
DRESS AND ADORNMENT (*in part*)

G.M.B.   G. Malcolm Brown. *Director,
Institute of Geological Sciences, London.
Coauthor of* Layered Igneous Rocks.
MINERALS AND ROCKS (*in part*)

G.M.C.   Gerald M. Capers. *Emeritus
Professor of History, Tulane University,
New Orleans. Author of* John C.
Calhoun, Opportunist: A Reappraisal
and others.
CALHOUN, JOHN C. (Micropædia)

**G.McC.McB.   George McCutchen
McBride** (d. 1971). *Professor of
Geography, University of California, Los
Angeles. Visiting Professor, Carnegie
Endowment for International Peace,
South America, 1929–30; Central
America 1938. Author of* Agrarian
Indian Communities of Highland Bolivia
and others.
BOLIVIA (*in part*)

G.M.Ce.   Gerald M. Clemence (d.
1974). *Professor of Astronomy, Yale
University, 1966–74. Coauthor of*
Methods of Celestial Mechanics.
NEWCOMB, SIMON (Micropædia)

G.McK.H.   Graham McK. Hughes.
Editor, Arts Review *magazine. Former
Art Director, Worshipful Company of
Goldsmiths, London. Head of Design,
Royal Mint, London. Author of*
Modern Silver.
DECORATIVE ARTS AND FURNISHINGS
(*in part*)

G.M'C.S.   Gresham M'Cready Sykes.
*Professor of Sociology, University of
Virginia, Charlottesville. Author of* The
Society of Captives.
CRIME AND PUNISHMENT (*in part*)

G.Me.   Gustav Mensching (d. 1978).
*Professor of Comparative Religion,
Rhenish Friedrich Wilhelm University
of Bonn, West Germany. Author of*
Die Religion, Erscheinungsformen,
Strukturtypen und Lebensgesetze;
Soziologie der Religion; *and others.*
DOCTRINES AND DOGMAS, RELIGIOUS
(*in part*)

G.Mn.   Georges Mongrédien (d. 1980).
*Historian. Director of the Municipal
Council of Paris and General Council of
the Seine, 1947–67. Author of* Le Grand

Condé; Colbert; *and many others.*
CONDÉ, LOUIS II DE BOURBON, 4ᵉ PRINCE
DE (Micropædia)

G.Mo.   Gaston Monnerville. *Member,
Constitutional Council of France, 1974–
83. President, Senate of France, 1958–
68. Author of* Clemenceau *and others.*
CLEMENCEAU, GEORGES (*in part*)
(Micropædia)

**G.M.S.   The Rev. Guthrie Michael
Scott** (d. 1983). *Anglican Clergyman,
Diocese of Chichester, England.
Coauthor of* Attitude to Africa
and others.
NYERERE, JULIUS (Micropædia)

G.N.   Gerhard Neumann. *Emeritus
Professor of Earth and Planetary Science,
City College, City University of New
York. Author of* Ocean Currents.
OCEANS (*in part*)

G.Na.   Giuseppe Nangeroni. *Emeritus
Professor of Geography, Catholic
University of Milan. Author of* Geografia
e geomorfologia.
ITALY (*in part*)

G.Ne.   Graeme R. Newman. *Sociologist.
Acting Dean and Professor of Criminal
Justice, State University of New York
at Albany.*
CRIME AND PUNISHMENT (*in part*)

G.N.G.   George N. Gordon. *Professor
and Chairman, Communications
Department, Fordham University, Bronx,
New York. Author of* The Languages of
Communication; The Communications
Revolution; *and others.*
COMMUNICATION

G.N.H.   George N. Halm. *Emeritus
Professor of Economics, Tufts University,
Medford, Massachusetts. Author of*
Economic Systems: A Comparative
Analysis.
ECONOMIC SYSTEMS (*in part*)

G.N.Ha.   George N. Hatsopoulos.
*President, Thermo Electron Corporation,
Waltham, Massachusetts. Coauthor of*
Principles of General Thermodynamics.
THERMODYNAMICS, PRINCIPLES
OF (*in part*)

G.O.   George Ordish. *Editor,* Tropical
Science, *London, 1966–72. Author of*
Untaken Harvest; The Constant Pest
and others.
AGRICULTURE, THE HISTORY OF (*in part*)

G.P.   Gerhardt Preuschen. *Emeritus
Director, Max Planck Institute for
Agricultural Labour and Scientific
Farming, Bad Kreuznach, West
Germany. Author of* Die Technik im
landwirtschaftlichen Betrieb.
AGRICULTURAL SCIENCES (*in part*)

G.Pa.   Günter Passavant. *Editor,
Journals of the German Institute for
the History of Art, Florence. Author
of* Andrea del Verrocchio:
Sculptures, Paintings, and Drawings *and
others.*
VERROCCHIO, ANDREA DEL
(Micropædia)

G.Pan.   Guido Pannain (d. 1977). *Professor of the History of Music, S. Pietro a Maiella Conservatory of Music, Naples. Author of* Lineamento di storia della musica *and others.*

CORELLI, ARCANGELO (Micropædia)

G.Pe.   George Pendle (d. 1977). *Managing Director, Pendle & Rivett Ltd., London. Author of* A History of Latin America *and others.*

URUGUAY (*in part*)

G.P.G.   Georges Paul Gusdorf. *Former Professor of Philosophy, University of Strasbourg, France. Author of* Les Sciences humaines et la conscience occidentale; La Découverte de soi; Mémoire et personne.

PHILOSOPHICAL ANTHROPOLOGY (*in part*)

G.P.Gi.   Giovanni Pietro Giorgetti. *Lecturer in Italian, Birkbeck College, University of London.*

ITALIAN LITERATURE (*in part*)

G.Pi.   Sir George Pickering, M.D. (d. 1980). *Master of Pembroke College, Oxford, 1968–74; Regius Professor of Medicine, University of Oxford, 1956–68. Author of* High Blood Pressure.

OSLER, SIR WILLIAM, BARONET (Micropædia)

G.P.K.   Gertrude Prokosch Kurath. *Research Fellow, Wenner-Gren Foundation for Anthropological Research, New York City. Former Co-ordinator, Dance Research Center, Ann Arbor, Michigan. Author of* Iroquois Music and Dance *and others.*

AMERICAN INDIANS (*in part*)
FOLK ARTS (*in part*)

G.P.Ka.   Gennadi Pavlovitch Kalinin. *Former Head, Hydrological Department, Geographical Faculty, Moscow M.V. Lomonosov State University. Author of* The Problems of Global Hydrology.

HYDROSPHERE, THE (*in part*)

G.P.L.   Gilbert P. Laue. *Chief Copy Editor, Richard D. Irwin, Inc., Homewood, Illinois. Former Associate Editor, Sports, Encyclopædia Britannica, Chicago.*

SPORTS, MAJOR TEAM AND INDIVIDUAL (*in part*)

G.P.M.   George P. Majeska. *Associate Professor of History, University of Maryland, College Park.*

BALKANS (*in part*)

G.P.Ma.   The Rev. Germain P. Marc'hadour. *Professor of Philology, Catholic University of the West, Angers, France. Director,* Moreana Quarterly. *Author of* L'Univers de Thomas More *and other works on Thomas More.*

MORE, SIR THOMAS (*in part*) (Micropædia)

G.Po.   Guido Pontecorvo. *Member of research staff, Imperial Cancer Research Fund, London, 1968–75. Professor of Genetics, University of Glasgow, 1955–68. Author of* "Hermann Joseph Muller" *in* Biographical Memoirs of Fellows of the Royal Society.

MULLER, HERMANN JOSEPH (Micropædia)

G.P.R.   Gerald P. Rodnan, M.D. (d. 1983). *Professor of Medicine, University of Pittsburgh, 1967–83. Editor of* Primer on the Rheumatic Diseases.

SUPPORTIVE AND CONNECTIVE TISSUES (*in part*)

G.P.Ri.   G. Philip Rightmire. *Professor of Anthropology, State University of New York at Binghamton.*

EVOLUTION, HUMAN (*in part*)

G.P.T.   Sir George Paget Thomson (d. 1975). *Professor of Physics, University of London, 1930–52. Co-winner, Nobel Prize for Physics, 1937. Author of* J.J. Thomson and the Cavendish Laboratory.

THOMSON, SIR J.J. (Micropædia)

G.R.   Graham Reynolds. *Keeper, Departments of Prints and Drawings, 1961–74, and of Paintings, 1959–74, Victoria and Albert Museum, London. Author of* Constable, the Natural Painter *and others.*

CONSTABLE, JOHN (Micropædia)

G.R.B.   Glenn Richard Bugh. *Associate Professor of Ancient History, Virginia Polytechnic Institute and State University, Blacksburg. Author of* The Horsemen of Athens.

LEBANON (*in part*)

G.R.C.   Gerald Roe Crone. *Librarian and Map Curator, Royal Geographical Society, London, 1945–66. Author of* Maps and Their Makers *and others.*

HAKLUYT, RICHARD (Micropædia)
MACKINDER, SIR HALFORD JOHN (Micropædia)

G.R.Co.   George R. Collins. *Professor of Art History, Columbia University. Author of* Antonio Gaudí *and others; coauthor of* The Designs and Drawings of Antonio Gaudí.

GAUDÍ, ANTONIO (Micropædia)

G.Re.   George S. Rentz. *Emeritus Curator of the Middle East Collection, Hoover Institution on War, Revolution, and Peace, Stanford, California. Emeritus Lecturer in Islāmic History, Stanford University. Coauthor and editor of* Oman and the Southern Shore of the Persian Gulf.

ARABIA (*in part*)

G.R.E.   Sir Geoffrey R. Elton. *Regius Professor of Modern History, University of Cambridge. Author of* The Tudor Revolution in Government: Administrative Changes in the Reign of Henry VIII *and others.*

CRANMER, THOMAS (*in part*) (Micropædia)
CROMWELL, THOMAS, EARL OF ESSEX (Micropædia)
HENRY VIII (ENGLAND) (*in part*) (Micropædia)

G.R.F.   Gizella Rochelle Fowler. *Free-lance writer and consultant.*

DRESS AND ADORNMENT (*in part*)

G.R.G.H.   Gavin R.G. Hambly. *Professor of History, University of Texas at Dallas. Coauthor and editor of* Central Asia.

UNION OF SOVIET SOCIALIST REPUBLICS (*in part*)

G.R.H.   G.R. Hawting. *Lecturer in the History of the Near and Middle East, School of Oriental and African Studies, University of London.*

MANṢŪR, AL- (Micropædia)

G.R.M.B.   Germain René Michel Bazin. *Research Professor Emeritus of Fine Arts, York University, Toronto. Emeritus Curator, the Louvre Museum, Paris. Author of* History of World Sculpture *and others.*

RODIN, AUGUSTE (Micropædia)

G.Ro.   Gloria Robinson. *Research Affiliate in the History of Medicine, Yale University.*

HAECKEL, ERNST (Micropædia)

G.R.P.   George Richard Potter (d. 1981). *Professor of Medieval History, University of Sheffield, England. Coauthor of* A Short History of Switzerland.

SWITZERLAND (*in part*)

G.R.R.   George Richard Rumney. *Professor of Geography, University of Connecticut, Storrs. Author of* Climatology and the World's Climates.

KÖPPEN, WLADIMIR (Micropædia)

G.R.St.   George R. Stibitz. *Emeritus Professor of Physiology, Dartmouth College, Hanover, New Hampshire. Author of* Mathematics in Medicine and the Life Sciences; *coauthor of* Mathematics and Computers.

MATHEMATICS, THE HISTORY OF (*in part*)

G.R.T.   George Raynor Thompson. *Historian, U.S. Army Strategic Communications Command, 1964–72.*

WAR, THE TECHNOLOGY OF (*in part*)

G.R.W.   Gordon Randolph Willey. *Senior Professor of Anthropology; Bowditch Professor Emeritus of Mexican and Central American Archaeology, Harvard University.*

MEXICO (*in part*)
NORTH AMERICA (*in part*)

G.R.Z.   George R. Zug. *Curator, Department of Vertebrate Zoology, National Museum of Natural History, Smithsonian Institution, Washington, D.C.*

BEHAVIOUR, ANIMAL (*in part*)

G.S.   Geoffrey Sawer. *Emeritus Professor of Law, Australian National University, Canberra. Author of* Law in Society.

LAW, THE PROFESSION AND PRACTICE OF (*in part*)

G.Sa.   Gudmund Sandvik. *Professor of Legal History, University of Oslo. Author of* Det gamle veldet: Norske finansar 1760–79 *and others.*

DENMARK (*in part*)

NORWAY (*in part*)
SWEDEN (*in part*)

G.Sc.   Georg Schwarzenberger.
Emeritus Professor of International Law,
University of London. Vice President,
London Institute of World Affairs.
Author of A Manual of International
Law.
INTERNATIONAL LAW (*in part*)

G.Sh.   Gordon Shillinglaw. *Professor*
of Accounting, Columbia University.
Author of Managerial Cost Accounting
and others.
ACCOUNTING

G.S.H.   Gerald S. Hawkins. *Physicist*
and Astronomer, U.S. Information
Agency, Washington, D.C. Author of
Mindsteps to the Cosmos *and others.*
BRADLEY, JAMES (Micropædia)

G.S.Ha.   Gordon S. Haight (d. 1985).
Professor of English, Yale University
1950–68. Author of George Eliot:
A Biography; *editor of* The George
Eliot Letters.
ELIOT, GEORGE (Micropædia)

G.Si.   George Bertrand Silberbauer.
Senior Lecturer in Anthropology and
Sociology, Monash University, Clayton,
Australia. Author of Hunter and
Habitat in the Central Kalahari Desert
and others.
AFRICA (*in part*)
SOUTHERN AFRICA (*in part*)

G.S.K.   Geoffrey S. Kirk. *Regius*
Professor Emeritus of Greek, University
of Cambridge. Author of The Songs of
Homer *and others.*
HOMERIC EPICS, THE

G.S.Ke.   G. Stuart Keith. *Research*
Associate, Department of Ornithology,
American Museum of Natural History,
New York City. Author of numerous
scientific and popular articles on cranes.
BIRDS (*in part*)

G.S.L.   George S. Lane (d. 1981).
Kenan Professor of Germanic and
Comparative Linguistics, University of
North Carolina at Chapel Hill, 1950–
72. Author of Studies in Kuchean
Grammar I.
LANGUAGES OF THE WORLD (*in part*)

G.S.Lo.   George S. Losey. *Professor*
of Zoology; Associate Director, Hawaii
Institute of Marine Biology, University of
Hawaii, Honolulu.
COLORATION, BIOLOGICAL (*in part*)

G.S.O.   Glenn S. Orton. *Member of*
the Technical Staff, Earth and Space
Sciences Division, Jet Propulsion
Laboratory, California Institute of
Technology, Pasadena.
SOLAR SYSTEM, THE (*in part*)

G.S.P.F.-G.   Greville Stewart Parker
Freeman-Grenville. *Honorary Fellow,*
University of York, Heslington, England.
Former Professor of African History,
State University of New York College
at New Paltz. Author of The Medieval
History of the Coast of Tanganyika

and others.
SA'ĪD IBN SULṬĀN (Micropædia)

G.St.   George Speaight. *Former*
Editorial Director, George Rainbird Ltd.
Author of The History of the English
Puppet Theatre; Punch and Judy: A
History; *and others.*
POPULAR ARTS (*in part*)

G.S.W.   Gordon S. White, Jr. *Sports*
Reporter, The New York Times.
Coauthor of Football My Way; Big Ten
Football.
SPORTS, MAJOR TEAM AND INDIVIDUAL
(*in part*)

G.T.G.   Guy Thompson Griffith (d.
1985). *Laurence Reader in Classics,*
University of Cambridge, 1951–75;
Fellow of Gonville and Caius College,
Cambridge. Coauthor of A History of
Macedonia.
PHILIP II (MACEDONIA) (Micropædia)

G.Ts.   George Thomas Tsoumis.
Professor of Forest Utilization,
Aristotelian University of Thessaloníki,
Greece. Author of Wood as Raw
Material.
FORESTRY AND WOOD PRODUCTION
(*in part*)

G.T.S.   Glenn T. Seaborg. *University*
Professor of Chemistry; Associate
Director, Lawrence Berkeley Laboratory;
Director, Lawrence Hall of Science,
University of California, Berkeley;
Chancellor, 1958–61. Chairman,
Atomic Energy Commission, 1961–
71. Co-winner, Nobel Prize for
Chemistry, 1951. Author of Man-Made
Transuranium Elements.
CHEMICAL ELEMENTS (*in part*)

G.T.Se.   Giles Timothy Severin.
Free-lance writer. Author of Explorers of
the Mississippi.
NORTH AMERICA (*in part*)

G.Tu.   Glenn Tucker (d. 1976).
Free-lance writer and historian. Author
of Tecumseh: Vision of Glory.
TECUMSEH (Micropædia)

G.U.   George Unwin. *Reader, editor,*
and translator, George Allen & Unwin
Ltd., London. Translator of Sign,
Symbol and Script *and others.*
PUBLISHING (*in part*)

Gu.B.   Guglielmo Barblan (d. 1978).
Professor of Music History, University of
Milan. Director of the Library, G. Verdi
Conservatory of Music, Milan. Author
of Gaetano Donizetti; La musica in
Milano; *and others.*
BOCCHERINI, LUIGI (Micropædia)

Gü.P.   Günther Patzig. *Professor of*
Philosophy and Director, Philosophical
Seminar, Georg August University of
Göttingen, West Germany. Author of
Aristotle's Theory of the Syllogism.
LOGIC, THE HISTORY AND KINDS
OF (*in part*)

Gu.W.   Gunther Wolf. *Lecturer in*
History, Rupert Charles University
of Heidelberg, West Germany.

Coauthor and editor of Stupor Mundi:
Zur Geschichte Friedrichs II von
Hohenstaufen.
FREDERICK II (GERMANY/HOLY ROMAN
EMPIRE) (Micropædia)

G.V.   Georges Vajda (d. 1981). *Director*
of Studies, École pratique des Hautes
études (Institute for Advanced Research),
Paris. Author of Recherches sur la
philosophie et la Kabbale dans la pensée
juive du Moyen-Âge *and others.*
JUDAISM (*in part*)

G.v.B.   Gerhardt von Bonin, M.D. (d.
1979). *Consultant in Neuroanatomy,*
Neurological Institute, Mt. Zion
Hospital, San Francisco. Professor of
Anatomy, University of Illinois, Chicago,
1939–58. Author of Essay on the
Cerebral Cortex.
NERVES AND NERVOUS SYSTEMS (*in part*)

G.V.G.   Gerald V. Gibbs. *University*
Distinguished Professor of Mineralogy,
Virginia Polytechnic Institute and State
University, Blacksburg.
MINERALS AND ROCKS (*in part*)

G.V.K.   German Viktorovich Kopanev.
Senior Research Associate, Scientific
Council on the Location of U.S.S.R.
Productive Forces, Academy of Sciences
of the U.S.S.R., Moscow. Coauthor of
Central Asian Economic Region.
UNION OF SOVIET SOCIALIST REPUBLICS
(*in part*)

G.V.M.   Gerard V. Middleton.
Professor of Geology, McMaster
University, Hamilton, Ontario. A leading
advocate of quantitative methods in
studies of sediments.
OCEANS (*in part*)

G.V.T.M.   Geoffrey Vernon Townsend
Matthews. *Director of Research, The*
Wildfowl Trust, Slimbridge, England.
Author of Bird Navigation.
BIRDS (*in part*)

G.W.   George Woodcock. *Free-lance*
writer. Editor, Canadian Literature
(quarterly), University of British
Columbia, Vancouver, 1959–77. Author
of Anarchism; The Crystal Spirit: A
Study of George Orwell; Pierre-Joseph
Proudhon; *and others.*
ORWELL, GEORGE (Micropædia)
PROUDHON, PIERRE-JOSEPH
(Micropædia)
SOCIO-ECONOMIC DOCTRINES AND
REFORM MOVEMENTS, MODERN
(*in part*)

G.W.A.   Gösta W. Ahlström.
Professor of Old Testament and
Ancient Palestinian Studies, University
of Chicago. Author of Aspects of
Syncretism in the Israelite Religion
and others.
DOCTRINES AND DOGMAS, RELIGIOUS
(*in part*)

G.W.B.   Geoffrey W. Bromiley.
Senior Professor of Church History and
Historical Theology, Fuller Theological
Seminary, Pasadena, California. Editor
and translator of Zwingli and Bullinger

(Library of Christian Classics).
ZWINGLI, HULDRYCH (Micropædia)

G.W.Ba.   Glen W. Baxter. *Senior Lecturer on East Asian Studies, Harvard University, 1956–80; Associate Director, Harvard-Yenching Institute, 1964–80. Author of* Index to the Imperial Register of Tz'u Prosody.
PAN KU (Micropædia)

G.W.Bo.   G.W. Bowersock. *Professor of Ancient History, Institute for Advanced Study, Princeton, New Jersey. Author of* Greek Sophists in the Roman Empire; Augustus and the Greek World.
AGRIPPA, MARCUS VIPSANIUS
    (Micropædia)
GALEN OF PERGAMUM (Micropædia)
HADRIAN (*in part*) (Micropædia)

G.W.H.   Gerard Willem Huygens. *Professor of History and Dutch Literature, Rotterdam Lyceum, The Netherlands. Author of* The Dutch Writer and His Public.
DUTCH LITERATURE (*in part*)

G.Win.   Gustaf Wingren. *Emeritus Professor of Systematic Theology, University of Lund, Sweden. Author of* Man and the Incarnation: A Study in the Biblical Theology of Irenaeus *and others.*
IRENAEUS, SAINT (Micropædia)

G.W.K.   George Williams Keeton. *President, London Institute of World Affairs. Emeritus Professor of English Law, University of London. Author of* Trusts.
PROPERTY LAW (*in part*)

G.Wn.   Geo Widengren. *Emeritus Professor of the History of Religions and Psychology of Religion, University of Uppsala, Sweden. Author of several monographs on Iranian culture, history, and religion.*
MIDDLE EASTERN RELIGIONS, ANCIENT
    (*in part*)

G.W.O.   Gerrit Willem Overdijkink. *Expert on Southeast Asian affairs.*
EAST INDIES, THE (*in part*)

G.W.P.   Giles William Playfair. *Free-lance writer. Professor of Drama, Williams College, Williamstown, Massachusetts, 1956–63. Author of* Kean *and others.*
KEAN, EDMUND (Micropædia)

G.Wr.   Gordon Wright. *William H. Bonsall Professor Emeritus of History, Stanford University, California. Author of* France in Modern Times *and others.*
FRANCE (*in part*)

G.W.S.B.   Geoffrey Wallis Steuart Barrow. *Sir William Fraser Professor of Scottish History and Palaeography, University of Edinburgh. Author of* Feudal Britain *and others.*
FRANCE (*in part*)
RICHARD I (ENGLAND) (Micropædia)

G.W.W.   Goddard Williams Winterbottom. *Director of Publications, The World Bank, Washington, D.C. Associate Editor, Arts,* Encyclopædia

Britannica, *Chicago, 1967–72. Former Director of Theatre, Briarcliff College, Briarcliff Manor, New York.*
POPULAR ARTS (*in part*)

H.A.   Henri Arvon. *Professor, University of Paris X. Author of* Le Bouddhisme *and others.*
FA-HSIEN (*in part*) (Micropædia)

Ha.A.   Hans Aurenhammer. *Former Director, Austrian State Gallery, Vienna. Author of* J.B. Fischer von Erlach *and others.*
FISCHER VON ERLACH, JOHANN
    BERNHARD (Micropædia)

H.A.A.   Hamza A. Alavi. *Reader in Sociology, Victoria University of Manchester. Author of numerous articles on Pakistan; coeditor of* Rural Development in Pakistan.
PAKISTAN (*in part*)

H.A.B.R.   Helen Anne B. Rivlin. *Professor of History, State University of New York at Binghamton. Author of* The Agricultural Policy of Muḥammad ʿAlī in Egypt *and others.*
MUḤAMMAD ʿALĪ (EGYPT)
    (Micropædia)

Ha.D.   Harry Davis. *President, Systems Review Associates, Arlington, Virginia. Deputy Undersecretary of the Air Force (Systems Review), U.S. Department of Defense, Washington, D.C., 1968–73.*
WAR, THE TECHNOLOGY OF (*in part*)

H.A.D.   Harl Adams Dalstrom. *Professor of History, University of Nebraska at Omaha.*
UNITED STATES OF AMERICA (*in part*)

H.A.Da.   Hugh Alistair Davies. *Lecturer in English, University of Sussex, Brighton, England.*
ENGLISH LITERATURE (*in part*)

Ha.G.   Harvey S. Gross. *Professor of Comparative Literature, State University of New York at Stony Brook. Author of* Sound and Form in Modern Poetry *and others.*
LITERATURE, THE ART OF (*in part*)

H.Ah.   Hélène Ahrweiler. *Chancellor, University of Paris; Professor of the History of Byzantine Civilization, University of Paris I. Author of* Recherches sur l'administration de l'empire byzantin aux IXᵉ–XIᵉ siècles *and others.*
NICEPHORUS II PHOCAS (Micropædia)

Ha.He.   Hans Herzfeld (d. 1982). *Professor of Modern History, Free University of Berlin, 1950–60. Author of* Die moderne Welt, 1789–1945 *and others.*
FREDERICK WILLIAM IV (PRUSSIA)
    (Micropædia)

Ha.K.   Harold Kurtz (d. 1972). *Author of* The Trial of Marshal Ney: His Last Years and Death *and others.*
NEY, MICHEL, DUC D'ELCHINGEN
    (Micropædia)

H.A.L.   Hubert Arthur Lechevalier. *Professor of Microbiology, Rutgers*

University, New Brunswick, New Jersey. Coauthor of Three Centuries of Microbiology.
COHN, FERDINAND (Micropædia)

Ha.M.   Hans Moldenhauer. *Musicologist. Director, Moldenhauer Archives. President, Spokane Conservatory of Music and Allied Arts, Inc., Washington. Author of* Anton von Webern: A Chronicle of His Life and Work *and others.*
WEBERN, ANTON VON (Micropædia)

H.A.M.   Henry A. Millon. *Dean, Center for Advanced Study in the Visual Arts, National Gallery of Art, Washington, D.C. Author of* Baroque and Rococo Architecture *and others.*
ARCHITECTURE, THE HISTORY OF
    WESTERN (*in part*)

Ha.Ma.   Harry Magdoff. *Coeditor,* Monthly Review. *Author of* The Age of Imperialism *and others.*
EUROPEAN OVERSEAS EXPLORATION
    AND EMPIRES, THE HISTORY OF
    (*in part*)

H.A.Mi.   Hassan Ali Mirreh. *Government Civil Servant, Somalia; Secretary of State for Education, 1969–70.*
EASTERN AFRICA (*in part*)

Ha.P.   Hans H. Penner. *Dean of the Faculty; Professor of Religion, Dartmouth College, Hanover, New Hampshire. Author of articles on structuralism, myth, and ritual.*
RITES AND CEREMONIES, SACRED
    (*in part*)

H.Ar.   Hassan Arfa. *Major General, Iranian Army (retired). Author of* Under Five Shahs *and others.*
REZA SHAH PAHLAVI (Micropædia)

Ha.Ro.   Hans Roos (d. 1984). *Professor of East European History, University of the Ruhr, Bochum, West Germany. Author of* A History of Modern Poland.
POLAND (*in part*)

Ha.S.   Hans Saner. *Free-lance writer. Personal Assistant to Professor Karl Jaspers, 1962–69. Author of* Karl Jaspers.
JASPERS, KARL (Micropædia)

H.A.S.   H. Arthur Steiner. *Emeritus Professor of Political Science, University of California, Los Angeles. Editor of* Report on China; Chinese Communism in Action.
CHINA (*in part*)

Ha.Se.   Hamzah Sendut. *Vice Chancellor, University of Science, Minden, Malaysia, 1969–76.*
EAST INDIES, THE (*in part*)

H.Au.   Hermann Aubin (d. 1969). *Professor of History, University of Hamburg, 1946–54.*
EUROPE (*in part*)

H.A.W.   Herbert A. White (d. 1972). *Editor, Metals and Foundry Practice Section,* Engineering Index, *New York City.*

Initials of contributors **577**

INDUSTRIES, EXTRACTION AND
PROCESSING (*in part*)

Ha.We.   Hans Fritz Welzel
(deceased). *Professor of Penal Law
and of the Philosophy of Law, Rhenish
Friedrich Wilhelm University of
Bonn, West Germany. Author of*
Die Naturrechtslehre Samuel
Pufendorfs.

PUFENDORF, SAMUEL, FREIHERR VON
(Micropædia)

H.B.   Hans Bobek. *Emeritus Professor
of Geography, University of Vienna.
Author of* Iran: Probleme eines
unterentwickelten Landes alter Kultur.

ELBURZ MOUNTAINS (Micropædia)

H.B.A.   Harry Burrows Acton (d.
1974). *Professor of Moral Philosophy,
University of Edinburgh, 1964–74.*

CONDORCET, MARIE-JEAN-ANTOINE-
NICOLAS DE CARITAT, MARQUIS DE
(Micropædia)
SPENCER, HERBERT (Micropædia)

H.Bi.   Haralds Biezais. *Professor of
the History of Comparative Religions,
Swedish University of Åbo, Finland.
Author of* Die Gottesgestalt der lettischen
Volksreligion.

EUROPEAN RELIGIONS, ANCIENT (*in part*)

H.B.K.   Herbert B. Knechtel. *President,
Knechtel Laboratories, Inc. (consultants
to the candy industry), Skokie, Illinois.*

FOOD PROCESSING (*in part*)

H.B.-M.   Hubert Beuve-Méry. *Founder
of* Le Monde. *Author of* Le Suicide de la
IVᵉ République.

FRANCE (*in part*)

H.Bo.   Harold Borko. *Professor,
Graduate School of Library and
Information Science, University of
California, Los Angeles. Editor of*
Computer Applications in the Behavioral
Sciences.

INFORMATION PROCESSING (*in part*)

H.B.P.   Henry Bamford Parkes (d.
1972). *Professor of History, New York
University, New York City, 1949–72.
Author of* A History of Mexico.

MEXICO (*in part*)

H.Br.   Hugh Brogan. *Lecturer in
History, University of Essex, Colchester,
England. Author of* Longman History of
the United States of America.

GOVERNMENT, THE FORMS OF

H.B.Ro.   H.B. Rodgers. *Professor
of Geography, Victoria University of
Manchester. Coauthor of* Lancashire,
Cheshire and Isle of Man.

MANCHESTER

H.B.W.   Harry B. Whittington.
*Woodwardian Professor Emeritus of
Geology, Sedgwick Museum, University
of Cambridge. World authority
on trilobites and Lower Paleozoic
stratigraphy.*

GEOCHRONOLOGY (*in part*)

H.C.   The Rev. Henri Chambre, S.J.
*Associate Director of the Laboratory,
College of France, Paris. Author of* De

Karl Marx à Lénine et Mao Tsé-toung.

MARXISM, MARX AND (*in part*)

H.C.B.   Harold C. Bold. *C.L. Lundell
Professor Emeritus of Systematic Botany,
University of Texas at Austin. Author of*
Morphology of Plants *and others.*

REPRODUCTION AND REPRODUCTIVE
SYSTEMS (*in part*)

**H.C.Br.   Harold Chillingworth
Brookfield.** *Professor of Human
Geography, Australian National
University, Canberra.*

INDIAN OCEAN ISLANDS (*in part*)

H.C.G.   Howard C. Goldblatt. *Professor
of Chinese, San Francisco State
University. Author of* Hsiao Hung; *editor
of* Chinese Literature for the 1980s.

CHINESE LITERATURE (*in part*)

H.Ch.   Hoklam Chan. *Professor
of Chinese History, University of
Washington, Seattle. Coeditor of and
contributor to* Yüan Thought: Chinese
Thought and Religion Under the
Mongols.

CHINA (*in part*)

H.C.H.   H. Carl Haywood. *Professor of
Psychology and of Neurology, Vanderbilt
University, Nashville, Tennessee. Editor,*
American Journal of Mental Deficiency,
1969–79. Editor, Psychometric
Intelligence.

INTELLIGENCE, THEORIES AND
DISTRIBUTION OF (*in part*)

**H.Cha.   The Very Rev. Henry
Chadwick.** *Regius Professor Emeritus
of Divinity, University of Cambridge.
Author of* The Early Church; Origen
contra Celsum; *and others.*

CHRISTIANITY (*in part*)
JOHN THE APOSTLE, SAINT (Micropædia)
ORIGEN (Micropædia)

H.C.Ho.   Harold C. Hodge. *Emeritus
Professor of Pharmacology and
Radiation Biology, University of
Rochester, New York. Coauthor of*
Clinical Toxicology of Commercial
Products.

POISONS AND POISONING (*in part*)

H.C.R.L.   H.C. Robbins Landon.
*Free-lance writer and music historian.
Author of* Mozart *and others; coeditor of*
The Mozart Companion.

MOZART (*in part*)

H.D.   Hariprasanna Das. *Professor of
Geography, Gauhāti University, Assam,
India. Author of* Geography of Assam.

INDIA (*in part*)

H.Da.   Hugh Davson. *Honorary
Research Associate and Fellow,
Department of Physiology, University
College, University of London. Author of*
Physiology of the Eye; *editor of* The Eye.

SENSORY RECEPTION (*in part*)

H.D.F.K.   H.D.F. Kitto (d. 1982).
*Professor of Greek, University of Bristol,
England, 1944–62. Author of* Greek
Tragedy; Form and Meaning in Drama.

GREEK DRAMATISTS, THE CLASSICAL
(*in part*)

**H.-D.H.W.   Hans-Dietrich H.
Weigmann.** *Associate Director of
Research, Textile Research Institute,
Princeton, New Jersey.*

FARMING AND AGRICULTURAL
TECHNOLOGY (*in part*)

H.Di.   Heide Dienst. *Assistant, Institute
of Austrian History Research, University
of Vienna. Author of* Babenberger
Studien *and others.*

LEOPOLD I (GERMANY/HOLY ROMAN
EMPIRE) (*in part*) (Micropædia)

H.D.I.   Hans Dietrich Irmscher.
*Professor of Modern German Literary
Criticism, University of Cologne. Author
of* Probleme der Herder-Forschung.

HERDER, JOHANN GOTTFRIED VON
(Micropædia)

H.D.L.   Hywel David Lewis. *Emeritus
Professor of History and Philosophy of
Religion, King's College, University of
London. Chairman of the Council of the
Royal Institute of Philosophy. Author
of* Our Experience of God; The Elusive
Mind; *and others.*

RELIGIOUS AND SPIRITUAL BELIEF,
SYSTEMS OF (*in part*)

Hd.M.V.   Harold M. Vinacke (d.
1981). *Professor of Political Science,
University of Cincinnati, Ohio 1926–
64. Author of* History of Far East in
Modern Times.

ASIA (*in part*)

H.D.S.   Helmut Dietmar Starke.
*Free-lance writer on modern European
history.*

GERMANY (*in part*)
LUXEMBURG, ROSA (Micropædia)

H.E.   Heinz Eulau. *Professor of
Political Science, Stanford University,
California. Author of* The Politics of
Representation *and others.*

POLITICAL SYSTEMS (*in part*)

He.Ba.   Hélène J. Balfet. *Teaching
assistant, University of Aix-Marseille II,
Aix-en-Provence, France. Former staff
member for comparative technology,
Musée de l'Homme, Paris. Author of
"Basketry: A Proposed Classification" in*
Papers on Californian Archaeology.

DECORATIVE ARTS AND FURNISHINGS
(*in part*)

He.F.   Herbert Friedmann. *Emeritus
Director, Los Angeles County Museum
of Natural History. Researcher on
the evolution and ecology of brood
parasites among birds. Author of* The
Honey-Guides; The Symbolic Goldfinch.

BIRDS (*in part*)

He.Gu.   Henri Guillemin. *Emeritus
Professor of History of French
Literature, University of Geneva. Author
of* Lamartine, l'homme et l'oeuvre;
Lamartine en 1848; *and others.*

LAMARTINE, ALPHONSE DE
(Micropædia)

He.H.   Heinz Heinen. *Professor of
Ancient History, University of Trier,
West Germany. Editor,* Historia
(*journal of ancient history*). *Author of*

Untersuchungen zur hellenistischen Geschichte des 3. Jahrhunderts vor Chr. *and others.*

PTOLEMY II PHILADELPHUS (Micropædia)

H.E.H.   Hans Egon Holthusen. *Professor of German, Northwestern University, Evanston, Illinois, 1968–81. Author of* A Portrait of Rilke *and others.*

RILKE, RAINER MARIA (Micropædia)

H.E.K.   Harry Edward Korab. *Technical Director, National Soft Drink Association, Washington, D.C.*

BEVERAGE PRODUCTION (*in part*)

H.El.   Herbert Elftman. *Emeritus Professor of Anatomy, Columbia University.*

MUSCLES AND MUSCLE SYSTEMS (*in part*)

H.E.L.-H.   Hellmut E. Lehmann-Haupt. *Emeritus Professor of Bibliography and Rare Book Consultant, University of Missouri, Columbia. Author of* Gutenberg and the Master of the Playing Cards.

GUTENBERG, JOHANNES (Micropædia)

He.M.   Hershel Markovitz. *Professor of Chemistry and Polymer Science, Carnegie-Mellon University, Pittsburgh. Coauthor of* Viscometric Flows of Non-Newtonian Fluids.

MECHANICS (*in part*)

H.E.Mo.   Harold E. Moore, Jr. (d. 1980). *Professor of Botany, L.H. Bailey Hortorium, New York State College of Agriculture and Life Sciences, Cornell University, Ithaca, 1960–80. Author of several articles on the palm order.*

ANGIOSPERMS (*in part*)

H.En.   Henrik Enander. *Former Lecturer in History, University of Stockholm.*

DENMARK (*in part*)
EUROPE (*in part*)
NORWAY (*in part*)
SWEDEN (*in part*)

He.Ni.   Henri Nicolaï. *Professor of Applied Geography, Free University of Brussels.*

CENTRAL AFRICA (*in part*)

He.P.   Hermann Pálsson. *Professor of Icelandic, University of Edinburgh. Author of* Art and Ethics in Hrafnkel's Saga; *translator of* Hrafnkel's Saga *and other Icelandic stories.*

LITERATURE, THE ART OF (*in part*)

He.R.   Helmuth Rogge. *Chief Archivist, National Records Office, Potsdam, Germany, 1921–45. Author of* Friedrich von Holstein, Lebensbekenntnis in Briefen an eine Frau *and several other books on Holstein.*

HOLSTEIN, FRIEDRICH VON (Micropædia)

H.E.R.   Hugh E. Richardson. *Member, Indian Civil Service, 1930–50; Indian Trade Agent, Gyantse, and Officer in Charge, Indian Mission, Lhasa, 1936–40 and 1946–50. Author of* Tibet and Its

History *and others.*

CHINA (*in part*)

He.Ri.   Helmut Richtering. *Director, Westphalian Archive Office, Münster, for the District of Westphalia-Lippe, West Germany.*

GERMANY (*in part*)

He.S.   Henri Stern. *Director of Research, National Centre of Scientific Research, Paris. Author of* Le Calendrier de 354; L'Art byzantin.

ARCHITECTURE, THE HISTORY OF WESTERN (*in part*)
PAINTING, THE HISTORY OF WESTERN (*in part*)
SCULPTURE, THE HISTORY OF WESTERN (*in part*)

H.E.T.   Harold E. Thomas. *Research Hydrologist, Water Resources Division, Geological Survey, U.S. Department of the Interior, 1929–72. Author of* Conservation of Ground Water.

HYDROSPHERE, THE (*in part*)

He.Th.   Helmuth Thomsen (d. 1978). *Principal Curator, Museum for the History of Hamburg, 1957–71. Author of* Liebes altes Hamburg; *editor of* Hamburg.

HAMBURG (*in part*)

He.W.   Hellmut Wilhelm. *Emeritus Professor of Chinese History and Literature, University of Washington, Seattle. Author of* Change: Eight Lectures on the I Ching *and others.*

CHINESE LITERATURE (*in part*)

H.E.W.   Harold E. Wethey (d. 1984). *Professor of the History of Art, University of Michigan, Ann Arbor, 1946–72. Author of* Colonial Architecture and Sculpture in Peru; El Greco and His School; The Complete Paintings of Titian.

ARCHITECTURE, THE HISTORY OF WESTERN (*in part*)
GIORGIONE (Micropædia)
GRECO, EL (Micropædia)
TITIAN

H.Ey.   Henry Eyring (d. 1981). *Distinguished Professor of Chemistry and Professor of Metallurgy, University of Utah, Salt Lake City, 1967–81. Coauthor of* Quantum Chemistry; Theory of Rate Processes.

CHEMICAL REACTIONS (*in part*)

H.F.   Hermann Friedrich. *Former Director, Overseas Museum, Bremen, West Germany. Author of* Marine Biology.

EUROPE (*in part*)

H.F.A.   Héctor Fernando Avila. *Division Chief, International Monetary Fund Institute, Washington, D.C.*

SOUTH AMERICA (*in part*)

H.F.C.   Howard F. Cline (d. 1971). *Director, Hispanic Foundation, Library of Congress, Washington, D.C., 1952–71. Author of* Mexico: Revolution to Evolution, 1940–1960 *and others.*

MEXICO (*in part*)

H.Fe.   Herbert Feigl. *Regents' Professor Emeritus of Philosophy, University of Minnesota, Minneapolis; Director, Minnesota Center for Philosophy of Science, 1953–71. Fellow of the American Academy of Arts and Sciences. Original member of the Vienna Circle, which developed the Positivist movement. Author of "The Wiener Kreis in America" in* The Intellectual Migration: Europe and America, 1930–1960.

PHILOSOPHICAL SCHOOLS AND DOCTRINES, WESTERN (*in part*)

H.Fec.   Hans Fecher (d. 1978). *Professor of Finance; Director, Institute of Public Finance, Ludwig Maximilian University of Munich. Author of* Probleme der Zweckbindung öffentlicher Einnahmen.

TAXATION (*in part*)

H.F.J.   Herbert Felix Jolowicz (d. 1954). *Regius Professor of Civil Law, University of Oxford, 1948–54. Professor of Roman Law, University of London, 1931–48; Dean, Faculty of Law, 1937–38. Author of* Historical Introduction to the Study of Roman Law.

LEGAL SYSTEMS, THE EVOLUTION OF MODERN WESTERN (*in part*)

H.F.K.   H.F. Koeper. *Professor of Architectural History, California State Polytechnic University, Pomona. Author of* American Architecture, 1607–1976 *and others.*

AALTO, ALVAR (Micropædia)
GROPIUS, WALTER (Micropædia)
SAARINEN, EERO (Micropædia)
SULLIVAN, LOUIS (Micropædia)

H.F.M.   Herman F. Mark. *Emeritus Dean, Polytechnic Institute of New York, Brooklyn. Director, Polymer Research Institute, 1946–64. World authority on polymers and polymerization processes. Editor of* Encyclopedia of Polymer Science and Technology.

CHEMICAL COMPOUNDS (*in part*)

H.F.P.   H.F. Pearson (deceased). *Author of* A Popular History of Singapore; This Other India: A Biography of Sir Thomas Stamford Raffles.

RAFFLES, SIR STAMFORD (Micropædia)

H.Fr.   Herbert Franke. *Emeritus Professor of Far Eastern Studies, Ludwig Maximilian University of Munich. Author of* Geld und Wirtschaft in China unter der Mongolen *and others.*

CHINA (*in part*)

H.Fra.   Heinrich Fraenkel (d. 1986). *Free-lance writer. Author of* The Other Germany; *coauthor of* Hermann Göring.

GÖRING, HERMANN (*in part*) (Micropædia)

H.F.W.   Harold F. Walton. *Professor of Chemistry, University of Colorado, Boulder. Coauthor of* Ion Exchange in Analytical Chemistry.

CHEMICAL REACTIONS (*in part*)

H.F.We.   Heinz Fritz Wermuth. *Former Curator of Herpetology,*

State Museum of Natural History, Ludwigsburg, West Germany. Coauthor of Schildkröten, Krokodile, Brückenechsen.
REPTILES (*in part*)

H.G. Herbert V. Guenther. *Emeritus Professor of Far Eastern Studies, University of Saskatchewan, Saskatoon. Author of* The Life and Teaching of Nāropa; Tibetan Buddhism Without Mystification; *and others.*
BUDDHISM, THE BUDDHA AND (*in part*)

H.G.D. H. Grady Davis (d. 1975). *Former Professor of Functional Theology, Lutheran School of Theology at Chicago. Coauthor of* The Gospels in Study and Preaching.
BIBLICAL LITERATURE AND ITS CRITICAL INTERPRETATION (*in part*)

H.G.Do. Herndon G. Dowling. *Professor of Biology, New York University, New York City. Research Associate in Herpetology, American Museum of Natural History, New York City. Editor,* Yearbook of Herpetology. *Curator of Reptiles, New York Zoological Park, 1960–67.*
REPTILES (*in part*)

H.G.E. Heinrich Gustav Euler. *Professor of Modern History, University of Würzburg, West Germany. Author of* Napoleon III. in seiner Zeit, *vol. 1.*
NAPOLEON III (FRANCE) (Micropædia)

H.G.F. Henry George Forder (d. 1981). *Professor of Mathematics, University of Auckland, New Zealand, 1934–55. Author of* The Foundations of Euclidean Geometry *and others.*
GEOMETRY (*in part*)

H.G.G. Hans G. Güterbock. *Tiffany and Margaret Blake Distinguished Service Professor Emeritus of Hittitology, Oriental Institute, University of Chicago. Author of* Siegel aus Boğazköy.
BOĞAZKÖY (Micropædia)

H.G.K. Helmut Georg Koenigsberger. *Emeritus Professor of History, King's College, University of London. Author of* The Habsburgs and Europe, 1516–1660; *coauthor of* Europe in the Sixteenth Century.
ALBA, FERNANDO ALVAREZ DE TOLEDO Y PIMENTEL, 3ᵉʳ DUQUE DE (Micropædia)
JIMÉNEZ DE CISNEROS, FRANCISCO, CARDENAL (Micropædia)
PHILIP II (SPAIN) (Micropædia)
SPAIN (*in part*)

H.G.N. Herbert G. Nicholas. *Rhodes Professor Emeritus of American History and Institutions, University of Oxford. Author of* Britain and the U.S.A. *and others.*
CHURCHILL

H.Go. Hermann Goetz (d. 1976). *Director, Baroda Museum and Picture Gallery, Baroda, India, 1940–53. Curator, National Gallery of Modern Art, New Delhi, 1953–55. Author of* The Art of India *and others.*

DECORATIVE ARTS AND FURNISHINGS (*in part*)

H.G.R. Henry Godfrey Roseveare. *Reader in History, King's College, University of London. Author of* The Treasury: The Evolution of a British Institution.
CHARLES II (GREAT BRITAIN) (Micropædia)

H.Gu. Henri Guitton. *Professor of Economics, University of Paris I. Editor in Chief,* La Revue d'Économie Politique.
ECONOMIC THEORY (*in part*)

H.G.W. Harris Gaylord Warren. *Emeritus Professor of History, Miami University, Oxford, Ohio. Author of* Paraguay and the Triple Alliance: The Postwar Decade, 1869–1878.
PARAGUAY (*in part*)

H.H. Helmut Hölder. *Emeritus Professor of Paleontology, Geological-Paleontological Institute, University of Münster, West Germany.*
GEOCHRONOLOGY (*in part*)

H.Ha. Harold Hart. *Professor of Chemistry, Michigan State University, East Lansing. Coauthor of* Organic Chemistry.
CHEMICAL COMPOUNDS (*in part*)
MOLECULES (*in part*)

H.H.A. H. Harvard Arnason (d. 1986). *Art historian. Vice President for Art Administration, Solomon R. Guggenheim Foundation, New York City, 1961–69. Author of* History of Modern Art; *coauthor of two books on Alexander Calder; and others.*
CALDER, ALEXANDER (Micropædia)

H.H.A.B. Hans H.A. Bielenstein. *Professor of Chinese History, Columbia University. Author of* "The Restoration of the Han Dynasty" *in* Bulletin of the Museum of Far Eastern Antiquities.
WANG MANG (Micropædia)

H.H.B.-S. Haim Hillel Ben-Sasson (d. 1977). *Professor of Jewish Medieval History, Hebrew University of Jerusalem. Editor of* Peraqim be-toldot ha-Yehudim bi-yeme ha-benayim, *3 vol.; author of vol. 2.*
ELIJAH BEN SOLOMON (Micropædia)

H.He. Herbert Hensel (d. 1983). *Professor of Physiology; Director, Institute of Physiology, Philipps University of Marburg, West Germany. Coauthor of* Temperatur und Leben.
SENSORY RECEPTION (*in part*)

H.Hei. Helmut Heiber. *Assistant, Institute for Contemporary History, Munich. Author of* Joseph Goebbels *and others.*
GOEBBELS, JOSEPH (Micropædia)

H.-H.He. Hermann-Heino Heine. *Taxonomic Botanist, Kew Gardens, London.*
GERMANY (*in part*)

H.H.Hu. Herbert Henry Huxley. *Emeritus Professor of Classics, University of Victoria, British Columbia. Supervisor in Classics, St. John's College, University of Cambridge. Editor of Virgil's* Georgics *(Books I and IV) and others.*
MARTIAL (Micropædia)

H.Hj. Hakon Hjelmqvist. *Associate Professor of Botany, University of Lund, Sweden, 1960–71. Author of* Studies on the Floral Morphology and Phylogeny of the Amentiferae.
ANGIOSPERMS (*in part*)

H.-H.J. Hans-Heinrich Jescheck. *Emeritus Professor of Law, Albert Ludwig University of Freiburg, Freiburg im Breisgau, West Germany. Emeritus Director, Max Planck Institute for Foreign and International Criminal Law, Freiburg. Author of* Lehrbuch des Strafrechts.
CRIMINAL LAW
PROCEDURAL LAW (*in part*)

H.H.K. Howard H. Kendler. *Professor of Psychology, University of California, Santa Barbara. Author of* Psychology: A Science in Conflict *and others.*
LEARNING AND COGNITION, HUMAN (*in part*)

H.H.L. Hubert Horace Lamb. *Former Director, Climatic Research Unit, School of Environmental Sciences, University of East Anglia, Norwich, England. Investigator of climatic variation from the viewpoint of general atmospheric circulation. Author of* Climate: Present, Past and Future *and others.*
CLIMATE AND WEATHER (*in part*)

H.H.M. H. Houston Merritt, M.D. (d. 1979). *Moses Professor of Neurology, 1963–70; Dean and Vice President, Faculty of Medicine, College of Physicians and Surgeons, Columbia University, 1958–70. Consultant in Neurology, Neurological Institute, Columbia-Presbyterian Medical Center, New York City. Author of* A Textbook of Neurology *and others.*
NERVES AND NERVOUS SYSTEMS (*in part*)

H.Hn. Herbert Hoffmann. *Former Curator of Ancient Art, Museum of Art and Industry, Hamburg.*
ARCHITECTURE, THE HISTORY OF WESTERN (*in part*)

H.H.R. Harry Howe Ransom. *Professor of Political Science, Vanderbilt University, Nashville, Tennessee. Author of* The Intelligence Establishment.
INTELLIGENCE AND COUNTERINTELLIGENCE

H.H.S. Howard Hayes Scullard (d. 1983). *Professor of Ancient History, King's College, University of London, 1959–70. Author of* Roman Politics, 220–150 B.C. *and others.*
GRECO-ROMAN CIVILIZATION, CLASSICAL (*in part*)
SCIPIO AEMILIANUS (*in part*) (Micropædia)

SCIPIO AFRICANUS MAJOR (Micropædia)
SYRIA (*in part*)

H.H.W.   Hyatt H. Waggoner. *Emeritus Professor of English, Brown University, Providence, Rhode Island. Author of* Hawthorne: A Critical Study; American Poets, from the Puritans to the Present; *and others.*

HAWTHORNE, NATHANIEL (Micropædia)

H.I.   Halil Inalcik. *Professor of History, University of Chicago. Author of* "Mehmed the Conqueror (1432–1481) and His Time" *in* Speculum *and others.*

MEHMED II (Micropædia)

H.-I.M.   Henri-Irénée Marrou (d. 1977). *Professor of the History of Ancient Christianity, University of Paris, 1945–75. Author of* De la connaissance historique.

EDUCATION, HISTORY OF (*in part*)

Hi.Mo.   Hiroyuki Momo. *Emeritus Professor and former Director, Historiographical Institute, University of Tokyo.*

HISTORY, THE STUDY OF (*in part*)

H.Is.   Hildebert İsnard (d. 1983). *Professor of Geography, University of Nice, France. Professor of Geography, University of Aix-Marseille II, Aix-en-Provence, France, 1947–70. Author of* Géographie du Maghreb; Afrique tropicale; *and others.*

AFRICA (*in part*)

H.I.S.   Harold I. Sharlin. *Consultant on science policy. Former Professor of History, Iowa State University, Ames. Author of* The Making of the Electrical Age; Lord Kelvin: Dynamic Victorian.

KELVIN

STEINMETZ, CHARLES PROTEUS (Micropædia)

H.J.B.   H. John Butcher (d. 1978). *Professor of Educational Psychology, University of Sussex, Brighton, England. Author of* Human Intelligence.

INTELLIGENCE, THEORIES AND DISTRIBUTION OF (*in part*)

H.J.Bi.   Harold J. Bissell. *Emeritus Professor of Geology, Brigham Young University, Provo, Utah.*

MINERALS AND ROCKS (*in part*)

H.J.Bl.   Henry J. Blumenthal. *Reader in Greek, University of Liverpool. Coeditor of* Soul and the Structure of Being in Late Neoplatonism.

PLATONISM, PLATO AND (*in part*)

H.J.C.   Henry J. Cadbury (d. 1974). *Hollis Professor of Divinity, Harvard University, 1934–54. Chairman, American Friends Service Committee, 1928–34; 1944–60.*

FOX, GEORGE (Micropædia)

H.J.D.   Hubert Jules Deschamps (d. 1979). *Professor of Modern History of Black Africa, University of Paris, 1962–70. Colonial Administrator, Madagascar, 1926–36. Author of* History of Madagascar *and others.*

CENTRAL AFRICA (*in part*)
INDIAN OCEAN ISLANDS (*in part*)
WESTERN AFRICA (*in part*)

H.J.De.   Henri J. Delporte. *Chief Curator, Museum of National Antiquities, Saint-Germain-en-Laye, France.*

EVOLUTION, HUMAN (*in part*)

H.J. de B.   Harm J. de Blij. *Professor of Geography, University of Miami, Coral Gables, Florida. Author of* Mozambique *and others.*

SOUTHERN AFRICA (*in part*)

H.J. de V.   Herman Jean de Vleeschauwer. *Emeritus Professor of Philosophy, University of South Africa, Pretoria. Author of* L'Évolution de la pensée kantienne; *editor of* Kantstudien.

KANTIANISM, KANT AND (*in part*)

H.J.Dw.   Harvey J. Dworkin, M.D. *Professor of Medicine, Case Western Reserve University, Cleveland, Ohio. Author of* Gastroenterology: Pathophysiology and Clinical Applications *and others.*

DIGESTION AND DIGESTIVE SYSTEMS (*in part*)

H.J.Er.   Hubert Joseph Erb. *Berlin Correspondent, Associated Press.*

BERLIN (*in part*)

H.J.H.   Herbert James Hunt (d. 1973). *Professor of French Language and Literature, Royal Holloway College, University of London, 1944–66. Author of* Honoré de Balzac: A Biography.

BALZAC, HONORÉ DE (*in part*) (Micropædia)

H.-J.I.   Heinz-Jürgen Ipfling. *Professor of Educational Theory, University of Regensburg, West Germany. Author of* Jugend und Illustrierte *and others.*

EDUCATION, HISTORY OF (*in part*)

H.-J.K.   Hans-Joachim Kramm. *Professor of Economic Geography, College of Education, Potsdam, East Germany. Author of* Ökonomische Geographie der DDR.

GERMANY (*in part*)

H.J.S.   Howard James Stains. *Professor of Zoology, Southern Illinois University, Carbondale. Author of* "Carnivores and Pinnipeds" *in* Recent Mammals of the World.

MAMMALS (*in part*)

H.J.Sp.   Herbert John Spiro. *Professor of Politics, John F. Kennedy Institute for North American Studies, Free University of Berlin. U.S. Ambassador to Cameroon, 1975–77. Author of* Government by Constitution *and others.*

CONSTITUTION AND CONSTITUTIONAL GOVERNMENT

H.J.Wi.   Howard J. Wiarda. *Professor of Political Science, University of Massachusetts, Amherst. Author of* The Dominican Republic: Nation in Transition *and others.*

WEST INDIES, THE (*in part*)

H.K.   Hans Kohn (d. 1971). *Professor of History, City College, City University of New York, 1949–62. Author of* Political Ideologies of the Twentieth Century.

ISRAEL (*in part*)
SOCIO-ECONOMIC DOCTRINES AND REFORM MOVEMENTS, MODERN (*in part*)

H.Ka.   Harry Kalven, Jr. (d. 1974). *Harry A. Bigelow Professor of Law, University of Chicago, 1953–74. Coauthor of* The American Jury.

JUDICIAL AND ARBITRATIONAL SYSTEMS (*in part*)

H.K.B.   Howard Kent Birnbaum. *Professor of Physical Metallurgy, University of Illinois, Urbana. Author of numerous papers on the physics and mechanics of solids.*

MATTER (*in part*)

H.K.G.   Harry K. Girvetz (d. 1974). *Professor of Philosophy, University of California, Santa Barbara, 1951–74. Author of* The Evolution of Liberalism.

SOCIO-ECONOMIC DOCTRINES AND REFORM MOVEMENTS, MODERN (*in part*)

H.K.Gr.   Henry Kirk Greer (d. 1978). *Attorney. Coach of the U.S. Olympic Hockey team, 1948 and 1956.*

SPORTS, MAJOR TEAM AND INDIVIDUAL (*in part*)

H.Kie.   Hans Kiefner. *Professor of German Civil Law, Roman Law, and Canon Law, University of Münster, West Germany.*

SAVIGNY, FRIEDRICH KARL VON (Micropædia)

H.K.M.S.   H.K. Manmohan Singh. *Jawaharlal Nehru Professor of Economics, Punjabi University, Patiala, India.*

INDIA (*in part*)

H.Ko.   Horst Koegler. *Music Editor, Stuttgarter Zeitung. Editor,* Ballett (*annual*), 1965–83. *Author of* Concise Oxford Dictionary of Ballet.

DANCE, THE HISTORY OF WESTERN

H.Kü.   Hans Kühner. *Historian and free-lance writer. Specialist on the history of the Roman Catholic Church and the Papacy. Author of* Encyclopedia of the Papacy *and others.*

GREGORY I, SAINT (PAPACY) (Micropædia)
JULIUS II (Micropædia)

H.K.V.   Hans K. Vogt. *Emeritus Professor of General Linguistics, University of Oslo. Author of* Grammaire du géorgien moderne.

LANGUAGES OF THE WORLD (*in part*)

H.L.   Henri Laoust. *Emeritus Professor of Sociology of Islām, College of France, Paris. Editor and translator of* Le Traité de droit public d'Ibn Taimīya *and others.*

IBN TAYMĪYAH (Micropædia)

H.La.   Henri Lavondès. *Lecturer, University of Paris X, Nanterre. Former*

Director of Papeete Centre, Overseas Office of Scientific and Technological Research, Tahiti, French Polynesia.
PACIFIC ISLANDS (*in part*)

H.L.A.H.   Herbert Lionel Adolphus Hart. *Principal of Brasenose College, Oxford, 1973–78; Professor of Jurisprudence, University of Oxford, 1952–68. Author of* The Concept of Law; Law, Liberty and Morality.
AUSTIN, JOHN (Micropædia)

H.L.B.   Henry Lewis Barnett, M.D. *Emeritus Professor of Pediatrics, Albert Einstein College of Medicine, Yeshiva University, Bronx, New York. Medical Director, Children's Aid Society, New York City. Associate Editor of* Pediatrics.
CHILDHOOD DISEASES AND DISORDERS (*in part*)

H.L.C.   Hampton L. Carson. *Professor of Genetics, University of Hawaii, Honolulu. Author of* Heredity and Human Life.
GENETICS AND HEREDITY, THE PRINCIPLES OF (*in part*)

H.L.C.J.   Hans L.C. Jaffé. *Professor of Modern Art History, University of Amsterdam. Author of* Piet Mondrian; Picasso.
MONDRIAN, PIET (*in part*) (Micropædia)

H.L.E.   Herbert Leeson Edlin (d. 1976). *Publications Officer, Forestry Commission of Great Britain, London. Author of* Trees, Woods and Man *and others.*
FORESTRY AND WOOD PRODUCTION (*in part*)

H.-L.-É.T.   Henri-Louis-Étienne Terrasse (d. 1971). *Curator, Historic Monuments of Morocco, 1935–57. Director, Institute for Advanced Moroccan Studies, Rabat, Morocco, 1941–57. Chairman, Department of Islāmic Archaeology, University of Algiers, 1945–57. Director, Casa de Velázquez, Ciudad University, Madrid, 1957–65. Author of* Histoire du Maroc *and others.*
ʿABD AL-MUʾMIN (Micropædia)
NORTH AFRICA (*in part*)

H.Li.   Heinz Lieberich. *General Director, Bavarian State Archives, Munich. Author of* Ludwig der Bayer als Gesetzgeber *and others.*
LOUIS IV (GERMANY/HOLY ROMAN EMPIRE) (Micropædia)

H.L.-J.   Hugh Lloyd-Jones. *Regius Professor of Greek, University of Oxford. Author of* The Justice of Zeus *and others.*
SCHOLARSHIP, CLASSICAL

H.L.K.   Sir Hans L. Kornberg. *Sir William Dunn Professor and Head, Department of Biochemistry, University of Cambridge. Coauthor of* Energy Transformations in Living Matter; *editor of* Essays in Cell Metabolism.
METABOLISM (*in part*)

H.L.Ke.   Herbert Leon Kessler. *Professor and Chairman, Department*

of the History of Art, Johns Hopkins University, Baltimore. Author of French and Flemish Illuminated Manuscripts in Chicago Collections *and others.*
EYCK, JAN VAN (Micropædia)
WEYDEN, ROGIER VAN DER (Micropædia)

H.L.M.   Hanns Leo Mikoletzky (d. 1978). *General Director, Austrian State Archives, Vienna. Professor of History, University of Vienna. Author of* Kaiser Heinrich II und die Kirche *and others.*
HENRY III (GERMANY/HOLY ROMAN EMPIRE) (Micropædia)

H.L.Ms.   Hallam L. Movius, Jr. *Emeritus Professor of Anthropology, Harvard University; former Curator of Paleolithic Archaeology, Peabody Museum.*
PREHISTORIC PEOPLES AND CULTURES (*in part*)

H.Ln.   Helge Larsen. *Minister of Education, Danish Government, 1968–71.*
ARCTIC, THE (*in part*)

H.L.S.   The Rev. Harry Lismer Short (d. 1975). *Principal, Manchester College, University of Oxford, 1965–74. Author of* Dissent and the Community; *coauthor of* Essays in Unitarian Theology.
PROTESTANTISM (*in part*)

H.Lz.   Hans Liebeschütz (d. 1978). *Reader in Medieval History, University of Liverpool, 1955–59.*
GERMANY (*in part*)

H.M.   Hermann Mannheim (d. 1974). *Reader in Criminology, University of London, 1946–55. Author of* Comparative Criminology.
SOCIAL SCIENCES, THE (*in part*)

H.Ma.   Henry Margenau. *Eugene Higgins Professor Emeritus of Physics and Natural Philosophy, Yale University. Author of* Nature of Physical Reality; *coauthor of* Mathematics of Physics and Chemistry *and others.*
PHYSICAL PRINCIPLES AND CONCEPTS (*in part*)

H.M.A.   Harold Maurice Abrahams (d. 1978). *Broadcaster and journalist. Chairman, British Amateur Athletic Board. Olympic Gold Medalist (100-metre dash), 1924. Author of* The Olympic Games, 1896–1952.
OLYMPIC GAMES (*in part*)

H.M.K.   Horace M. Kallen (d. 1974). *Professor of Social Philosophy, New School for Social Research, New York City, 1919–52. Author of the introduction to* The Philosophy of William James, Drawn from His Own Works.
JAMES, WILLIAM (Micropædia)

H.M.L.   Henry M. Leicester. *Emeritus Professor of Biochemistry, University of the Pacific, San Francisco. Coauthor of* Source Book in Chemistry 1400–1900.
LIEBIG, JUSTUS, FREIHERR VON (Micropædia)
WÖHLER, FRIEDRICH (Micropædia)

H.M.M.   Harold M. Mayer. *Professor of Geography, University of Wisconsin, Milwaukee. Vice President, Milwaukee Harbor Commission. Author of* The Port of Chicago and the St. Lawrence Seaway; *coauthor of* Chicago, Growth of a Metropolis.
CHICAGO (*in part*)

H.M.P.   Henri M. Peyre. *Distinguished Professor Emeritus, Graduate Center, City University of New York. Sterling Professor Emeritus of French, Yale University. Author of* Literature and Sincerity *and many others; contributor to* Émile Durkheim, 1858–1917.
DURKHEIM, ÉMILE (Micropædia)
LITERATURE, THE ART OF (*in part*)

H.M.S.   Harold M. Somers. *Professor of Economics, University of California, Los Angeles; Dean, Division of Social Sciences, 1967–70. Author of* Capital Gains, Death and Gift Taxation.
TAXATION (*in part*)

H.Mu.   Hugo Munsterberg. *Professor of Oriental Art, Bard College, Annandale-on-Hudson, New York. Author of* The Arts of Japan *and others.*
OGATA KŌRIN (Micropædia)
SESSHŪ (Micropædia)
SŌTATSU (Micropædia)

H.M.V.D.   Hobart Merritt Van Deusen (d. 1976). *Archbold Assistant Curator, Department of Mammalogy, American Museum of Natural History, New York City, 1958–75. Coauthor of* "Marsupials" *in* Recent Mammals of the World.
MAMMALS (*in part*)

H.M.W.   Helen Margaret Wallis. *Map Librarian, British Library, London. Editor of* Carteret's Voyage Round the World *and others.*
TASMAN, ABEL JANSZOON (Micropædia)

H.My.   Hla Myint. *Professor of Economics, London School of Economics and Political Science, University of London. Author of* Economic Theory and the Underdeveloped Countries.
ECONOMIC GROWTH AND PLANNING (*in part*)

H.N.   Heinrich Nagel. *Professor of Civil and International Civil Procedure, Georg August University of Göttingen, West Germany. Former Presiding Judge, Hanseatic Court of Appeals, Bremen. Author of* Internationales Zivilprozessrecht *and others.*
PROCEDURAL LAW (*in part*)

H.Na.   Hajime Nakamura. *Director, Eastern Institute, Inc., Tokyo. Emeritus Professor of Indian and Buddhist Philosophy, University of Tokyo. Author of* Ways of Thinking of Eastern Peoples *and others.*
BUDDHISM, THE BUDDHA AND (*in part*)

H.Ne.   Howard Nemerov. *Poet and novelist. Edward Mallinckrodt Distinguished Professor of English, Washington University, St. Louis, Missouri. Author of* Poetry and Fiction: Essays; Reflexions on Poetry and

Poetics; *and others.*
LITERATURE, THE ART OF (*in part*)

H.N.G.   Harry Norwood Ginns (d. 1981). *Deputy Chief Engineer, Highways Engineering Division, Ministry of Transport, London, 1963–69.*
TRANSPORTATION (*in part*)

H.O.   Harold Oldroyd. *Senior Principal Scientific Officer, British Museum (Natural History), London, 1964–73. Author of* The Natural History of Flies *and others.*
INSECTS (*in part*)

Ho.B.   Howard Bay. *Stage and film designer. Emeritus Professor of Theatre Arts, Brandeis University, Waltham, Massachusetts. Author of* Stage Design.
THEATRICAL PRODUCTION (*in part*)

Ho.I.P.   Hovhanness Israel Pilikian. *Theatre director. Founder and Artistic Director of Hano-no Mask-Theatre Company. Author of* The Prince of Darkness *and others.*
REINHARDT, MAX (Micropædia)

H.O.Sc.   Hans Otto Schmitt. *Senior Adviser, International Monetary Fund, Washington, D.C.; Division Chief, 1971–80.*
ECONOMIC THEORY (*in part*)

H.P.   Heinrich Potthoff. *Contributor, Commission for the History of Parliamentarism and Political Parties, Bonn. Author of* Die deutsche Politik Beusts *and others.*
BEUST, FRIEDRICH FERDINAND, GRAF VON (Micropædia)

H.Pa.   Hans Patze. *Professor of German History; Director, Institute for Historical Research, Georg August University of Göttingen, West Germany. Author of* Die Entstehung der Landesherrschaft in Thüringen *and others.*
FREDERICK I (GERMANY/HOLY ROMAN EMPIRE) (Micropædia)

H.Pe.   Harry Perry. *Energy consultant. Senior Specialist, Congressional Research Service, Library of Congress, Washington, D.C., 1970–72.*
INDUSTRIES, EXTRACTION AND PROCESSING (*in part*)

H.P.L.   H.P. Laughlin, M.D. *Psychiatrist. Founder and First President, American College of Psychiatrists. Author of* The Neuroses; The Ego and Its Defenses; *and others.*
MENTAL DISORDERS AND THEIR TREATMENT (*in part*)

H.P.La.   Harriet Pratt Lattin. *Historian. Author of* The Peasant Boy Who Became Pope; *translator of* The Letters of Gerbert, with His Papal Privileges as Sylvester II.
SYLVESTER II (Micropædia)

H.Pr.   Helmut Preidel. *Historian. Author of* Das grossmährische Reich im Spiegel der Bodenfunde; Handel und Handwerk im frühgeschichtlichen Mitteleuropa; *and others.*

CHARLES IV (GERMANY/HOLY ROMAN EMPIRE) (Micropædia)

H.P.R.   Humphrey P. Rang. *Director, Sandoz Institute for Medical Research, University College, University of London. Coauthor of* Pharmacology.
DRUGS AND DRUG ACTION (*in part*)

H.P.Tr.   Hamilton P. Traub (d. 1983). *Editor,* Plant Life, *American Plant Life Society, La Jolla, California. Author of* The Amaryllis Manual *and others.*
ANGIOSPERMS (*in part*)

H.P.V.   Homero Pozo Vélez. *Professor of History and Geography; Dean, Faculty of Educational Science, National University of Loja, Ecuador.*
ECUADOR (*in part*)

H.R.   Helmer Ringgren. *Emeritus Professor of Old Testament Exegesis, University of Uppsala, Sweden. Author of* Israelite Religion; Messiah in the Old Testament; *and various articles on theological concepts in the Qur'ān.*
ISLĀM, MUḤAMMAD AND THE RELIGION OF (*in part*)

H.Ra.   Hassanein Muhammad Rabie. *Professor of History, University of Cairo. Author of* The Financial System of Egypt: A.H. 564–741/A.D. 1169–1341.
BAYBARS I (Micropædia)

H.Re.   Hans Reichardt. *Emeritus Professor of Mathematics, Humboldt University of Berlin. Editor of* C.F. Gauss Gedenkband anlässlich des 100. Todestages am 23. Februar 1855.
GAUSS

H.R.H.   Heribert R. Hutter. *Director, Gallery of the Academy of Fine Arts, Vienna. Author of* Drawing: History and Technique *and others.*
DRAWING (*in part*)

H.Ro.   Herbert H. Rowen. *Professor of History, Rutgers University, New Brunswick, New Jersey. Author of* John de Witt, Grand Pensionary of Holland, 1625–1672 *and others.*
LOW COUNTRIES, THE (*in part*)

H.R.O.   Horace Russell Ogden. *Former Manager, Magnesium Research Center, Battelle Memorial Institute, Columbus, Ohio.*
INDUSTRIES, EXTRACTION AND PROCESSING (*in part*)

H.R.T.   Hugh Russell Tinker. *Emeritus Professor of Politics, University of Lancaster, England. Author of* India and Pakistan: A Political Analysis; Experiment with Freedom, India and Pakistan; *and others.*
INDIA (*in part*)
PAKISTAN (*in part*)

H.R.W.   Henry R. West. *Professor of Philosophy, Macalester College, St. Paul, Minnesota. Coeditor of* Moral Philosophy: Classic Texts and Contemporary Problems.
PHILOSOPHICAL SCHOOLS AND DOCTRINES, WESTERN (*in part*)

H.S.   Helmut Sick. *Naturalist, Brazilian Academy of Sciences, Rio de Janeiro. Author of numerous papers on neotropical birds.*
BIRDS (*in part*)

H.Sa.   Heinrich Satter. *Free-lance writer. Author of* Paul Ehrlich, Begründer der Chemotherapie *and others.*
EHRLICH, PAUL (Micropædia)

H.Sc.   Heinrich Schiffers. *Lecturer in Geography, Preparatory College for Foreign Students, University of Cologne, 1965–70. Lecturer in Geography, secondary schools of Aachen and Cologne, 1930–65. Author of* Die Sahara und die Syrtenländer; The Quest for Africa.
AFRICA (*in part*)

H.Se.   Humphrey Searle (d. 1982). *Composer. Professor of Composition, Royal College of Music, London. Author of* The Music of Liszt *and others.*
LISZT, FRANZ (*in part*) (Micropædia)

H.S.H.   Helen Sawyer Hogg. *Emeritus Professor of Astronomy, University of Toronto. Astronomy columnist,* Toronto Daily Star, *1951–81.*
STARS AND STAR CLUSTERS (*in part*)

H.S.K.   Herbert S. Klein. *Professor of History, Columbia University. Author of* Bolivia: The Evolution of a Multi-ethnic Society *and others.*
BOLIVIA (*in part*)

H.S.L.   Howard S. Levie. *Colonel, U.S. Army (retired). Emeritus Professor of Law, St. Louis University, Missouri.*
WAR, THE THEORY AND CONDUCT OF (*in part*)

H.Sm.   Harlan James Smith. *Professor of Astronomy; Director, McDonald Observatory, University of Texas at Austin. Coeditor of* Planetary Atmospheres.
SOLAR SYSTEM, THE (*in part*)

H.S.M.   H.S. Morris. *Former Reader in Anthropology, London School of Economics and Political Science, University of London. Author of* Indians in Uganda.
SOCIAL DIFFERENTIATION (*in part*)

H.S.MacD.C.   H.S. MacDonald Coxeter. *Emeritus Professor of Mathematics, University of Toronto. Author of* Non-Euclidean Geometry.
GEOMETRY (*in part*)

H.S.N.   H.S. Narayana. *Former Professor of Botany, University of Rājasthān, Jaipur, India.*
ANGIOSPERMS (*in part*)

Hs.P.   Hans Plischke (d. 1972). *Professor of Ethnology, Georg August University of Göttingen, West Germany.*
GERMANY (*in part*)

H.Sp.   Herbert Spiegelberg. *Emeritus Professor of Philosophy, Washington University, St. Louis, Missouri. Author of* The Phenomenological Movement.

PHILOSOPHICAL SCHOOLS AND
DOCTRINES, WESTERN (*in part*)

H.S.P.   H. Steffen Peiser. *Chief, Office
of International Relations, National
Bureau of Standards, U.S. Department
of Commerce, Washington, D.C., 1969–
79. Author of* X-Ray Diffraction by
Polycrystalline Materials.

ATOMIC WEIGHT (*in part*)
(Micropædia)

H.Sr.   Hugo Stehkämper. *Director,
Historical Archives, Cologne.*

COLOGNE (*in part*)

H.S.R.   Hans Siegbert Reiss. *Professor
of German, University of Bristol,
England. Author of* Goethe's Novels
and others.

GERMAN LITERATURE (*in part*)

H.Ss.   Halsey Stevens. *Composer.
Emeritus Professor of Music, University
of Southern California, Los Angeles.
Author of* The Life and Music of
Béla Bartók.

BARTÓK, BÉLA (Micropædia)

H.S.Sc.   Herbert S. Schell. *Emeritus
Dean of the Graduate School, University
of South Dakota, Vermillion; former
Professor of History. Author of* South
Dakota, Its Beginning and Growth;
History of South Dakota.

UNITED STATES OF AMERICA (*in part*)

H.S.-Sm.   Sir Hubert Shirley-Smith
(d. 1981). *Consulting Engineer to
W.V. Zinn & Associates, London,
1969–78. President, Institute of Civil
Engineers, 1967. Author of* The World's
Great Bridges.

PUBLIC WORKS (*in part*)

H.St.   Hans Sturmberger. *Former
Director, Upper Austrian Provincial
Archives, Linz. Author of* Kaiser
Ferdinand II *and others.*

FERDINAND II (GERMANY/HOLY ROMAN
EMPIRE) (Micropædia)

H.S.T.   H.S. Thayer. *Professor of
Philosophy, City College, City University
of New York. Author of* Meaning
and Action: A Critical History of
Pragmatism.

PHILOSOPHICAL SCHOOLS AND
DOCTRINES, WESTERN (*in part*)

H.S.Ta.   Sir Hugh S. Taylor (d.
1974). *Professor of Chemistry, 1922–
58; Dean of the Graduate School, 1945–
58, Princeton University. Coauthor of*
Catalysis in Theory and Practice.

CHEMICAL REACTIONS (*in part*)

**H.St.J.B.P.   Harry St. John Bridger
Philby** (d. 1960). *Explorer in Arabia.
Author of* The Heart of Arabia.

ARABIA (*in part*)

H.S.-W.   Hugh Seton-Watson (d.
1984). *Professor of Russian History,
University of London, 1951–83. Author
of* The Russian Empire, 1801–1917
and others.

UNION OF SOVIET SOCIALIST REPUBLICS
(*in part*)

YUGOSLAVIA (*in part*)

H.S.Y.   Hatten Schuyler Yoder, Jr.
*Director and Petrologist, Geophysical
Laboratory, Carnegie Institution of
Washington, D.C. Investigator of
mineral and rock properties through
experimental studies.*

MINERALS AND ROCKS (*in part*)

H.T.   Holger Thesleff. *Professor of
Greek, University of Helsinki. Author
of* An Introduction to the Pythagorean
Writings of the Hellenistic Period.

PHILOSOPHICAL SCHOOLS AND
DOCTRINES, WESTERN (*in part*)

H.Ta.   Hugh Tait. *Deputy Keeper,
Department of Medieval and Later
Antiquities, British Museum, London.
Author of* Porcelain *and others.*

DECORATIVE ARTS AND FURNISHINGS
(*in part*)

H.T.C.   Hiden T. Cox. *Professor of
Biology, California State University,
Long Beach.*

ANGIOSPERMS (*in part*)

H.T.D.   Harry T. Dickinson. *Professor
of History, University of Edinburgh.
Author of* Bolingbroke *and others.*

BOLINGBROKE, HENRY SAINT JOHN, 1ST
VISCOUNT (Micropædia)

H.T.F.   Harold T. Friermood.
*Chairman, Education Council, United
States Olympic Committee. Editor of*
Handball: Official, Unified-Playing
Rules; When Volleyball Began.

HANDBALL (Micropædia)
VOLLEYBALL (Micropædia)

H.Th.   Helmut Thielicke. (d. 1986).
*Professor of Systematic Theology,
University of Hamburg, 1954–74. Author
of* Theological Ethics *and others.*

THEOLOGY

H.T.M.   Haydn T. Mason. *Professor
of French Language and Literature,
University of Bristol, England. Author of*
French Writers and their Society 1715–
1800 *and others.*

FRENCH LITERATURE (*in part*)

H.T.P.   Hugh T. Patrick. *Professor of
Far Eastern Economics, Yale University.
Author of* Monetary Policy and Central
Banking in Contemporary Japan.

MARKETS (*in part*)

H.Ty.   Hugh Tracey (d. 1977). *Founder
and Director, International Library of
African Music, Roodepoort, South Africa;
Editor,* African Music, *1954–70. Author
of* Chopi Musicians *and others.*

AFRICAN ARTS (*in part*)

H.U.   Homer Ulrich. *Emeritus
Professor of Music Literature, University
of Maryland; Head, Department of
Music, 1953–71. Editor,* American
Music Teacher. *Author of* Chamber
Music *and others.*

MUSICAL FORMS AND GENRES
(*in part*)

H.-U.H.   Hanns-Ulrich Haedeke.
*Director, German Sword Museum,
Solingen, West Germany. Author of*
Metalwork *and others.*

DECORATIVE ARTS AND FURNISHINGS
(*in part*)

Hu.M.   Hugh Sinclair Morrison (d.
1978). *Leon E. Williams Professor of
Art, Dartmouth College, Hanover, New
Hampshire, 1963–69. Author of* Early
American Architecture; Louis Sullivan.

ARCHITECTURE, THE HISTORY OF
WESTERN (*in part*)

Hu.S.   Hudson Strode (d. 1976).
*Professor of English, University of
Alabama, Tuscaloosa, 1924–63. Author
of* Jefferson Davis *and others.*

DAVIS, JEFFERSON (Micropædia)

H.U.S.   Harald Ulrik Sverdrup (d.
1957). *Director, Norwegian Polar
Institute, Oslo, 1948–57. Director,
Scripps Institution of Oceanography,
University of California, La Jolla,
1936–48. Author of* Oceanography for
Meteorologists *and others.*

NANSEN, FRIDTJOF (Micropædia)
OCEANS (*in part*)

Hu.Wa.   Hugh Wakefield (d. 1984).
*Keeper, Department of Circulation,
Victoria and Albert Museum, London,
1960–75. Author of* Nineteenth Century
British Glass; Victorian Pottery.

DECORATIVE ARTS AND FURNISHINGS
(*in part*)

H.V.   Hans Volkmann (deceased).
*Professor of Ancient History, University
of Cologne.*

ANTIGONUS I MONOPHTHALMUS
(Micropædia)
ANTIGONUS II GONATAS (Micropædia)
ANTIOCHUS III (Micropædia)
ANTIOCHUS IV EPIPHANES (Micropædia)

H. van W.   H. van Werveke (d. 1974).
*Professor of the History of Belgium,
State University of Ghent.*

ARTEVELDE, JACOB VAN
(Micropædia)

H.v.J.   Helmut von Jan. *Former
Director of the Archives and Library,
Hildesheim, West Germany.
Extraordinary Member, Palatinate
Society for the Promotion of Sciences.
Second President, Union for the Church
History of the Palatinate.*

GERMANY (*in part*)

H.V.L.   Harold V. Livermore. *Former
Professor of Spanish and Portuguese,
University of British Columbia,
Vancouver. Author of* A History of
Portugal *and others.*

ALBUQUERQUE, AFONSO DE, THE GREAT
(Micropædia)
COVILHÃ, PÊRO DA (Micropædia)
DIAS, BARTOLOMEU (Micropædia)
JOHN I (PORTUGAL) (Micropædia)
JOHN II (PORTUGAL) (Micropædia)
MANUEL I (PORTUGAL) (Micropædia)
PORTUGAL (*in part*)

H.Wa.   Hao Wang. *Professor of
Mathematical Logic, The Rockefeller
University, New York City. Author of* A
Survey of Mathematical Logic.

LOGIC, THE HISTORY AND KINDS
OF (*in part*)

H.W.B. **Hendrik W. Bode** (d. 1982). *Gordon McKay Professor of Systems Engineering, Harvard University, 1967–74. Author of* Network Analysis and Feedback Amplifier Design.

INDUSTRIAL ENGINEERING AND
 PRODUCTION MANAGEMENT (*in part*)

H.W.Br. **Harold Whitman Bradley.** *Emeritus Professor of History, Vanderbilt University, Nashville, Tennessee. Member, Tennessee House of Representatives, 1964–72. Author of* The United States, 1492–1877 *and others.*

JACKSON, ANDREW (*in part*)
 (Micropædia)
UNITED STATES OF AMERICA (*in part*)

H.We. **Herbert Weinstock** (d. 1971). *Consulting Editor, Alfred A. Knopf, Inc., New York City, 1963–71; Executive Editor, 1943–59. Author of* The Opera; Music as an Art; *and many biographies of composers.*

MUSICAL FORMS AND GENRES (*in part*)

H.W.F. **Hubert William Frings.** *David Ross Boyd Professor Emeritus of Zoology, University of Oklahoma, Norman. Coauthor of* Animal Communication.

SENSORY RECEPTION (*in part*)

H.W.F.S. **Henry W.F. Saggs.** *Emeritus Professor of Semitic Languages, University College, Cardiff, University of Wales. Author of* The Greatness That Was Babylon *and others.*

BABYLON (Micropædia)
NEBUCHADREZZAR II (Micropædia)
SENNACHERIB (Micropædia)

H.W.G. **Herman W. Goult** (d. 1977). *Editor, Cyprus Mail, Nicosia. Cyprus correspondent,* The Times *(London).*

CYPRUS (*in part*)

H.W.H. **H.W. Herbert.** *Consulting Economist, Economic Services, Brisbane, Australia.*

AUSTRALIA (*in part*)

H.Wi. **Hermann Wiesflecker.** *Professor of Austrian History, University of Graz, Austria. Author of* Maximilian I, Österreich, das Reich und Europa an der Wende zur Neuzeit *(vol. 1–3) and others.*

MAXIMILIAN I (GERMANY/HOLY ROMAN
 EMPIRE) (Micropædia)

H.W.J. **H.W. Janson** (d. 1982). *Professor of Fine Arts, Washington Square College of Arts and Science, New York University, New York City, 1949–79. Author of* The Sculpture of Donatello; History of Art; *and others.*

DONATELLO (*in part*) (Micropædia)

H.W.K. **Harold W. Kuhn.** *Professor of Mathematical Economics, Princeton University. Author of articles on linear programming and the theory of games; coeditor of* Contributions to the Theory of Games.

GAME THEORY (*in part*)

H.W.L. **Herbert W. Levi.** *Agassiz Professor of Zoology; Curator of Arachnology, Museum of Comparative Zoology, Harvard University. Coauthor of* A Guide to Spiders and Their Kin; *cotranslator and coeditor of* Invertebrate Zoology *by A. Kaestner.*

ARACHNIDS (*in part*)

H.W.M. **Horace Winchell Magoun.** *Emeritus Professor of Anatomy, University of California, Los Angeles. Author of* The Waking Brain *and others.*

NERVES AND NERVOUS SYSTEMS (*in part*)

H.W.P. **Herbert William Parke** (d. 1986). *Professor of Ancient History, Trinity College, University of Dublin, 1934–73. Author of* Greek Mercenary Soldiers.

EPAMINONDAS (Micropædia)

H.W.S. **Henry William Spiegel.** *Emeritus Professor of Economics, Catholic University of America, Washington, D.C. Author of* The Brazilian Economy.

BRAZIL (*in part*)

H.W.W. **Harold W. Wardman.** *Professor of French Studies, University of Lancaster, England. Author of* Ernest Renan: A Critical Biography; Renan Historien Philosophe.

RENAN, ERNEST (Micropædia)

Hy.K. **Hyman Kaufman.** *Professor of Mathematics, McGill University, Montreal, 1952–80. Coauthor of* Table of Laplace Transforms.

ANALYSIS (IN MATHEMATICS) (*in part*)

H.Z. **Hans Zeisel.** *Emeritus Professor of Law and Sociology, University of Chicago. Coauthor of* The American Jury.

JUDICIAL AND ARBITRATIONAL
 SYSTEMS (*in part*)

H.Z.D. **Haim Zalman Dimitrovsky.** *Lieberman Professor of Talmudic Exegesis, Jewish Theological Seminary of America, New York City. Editor and translator of* Bava metzia.

JUDAISM (*in part*)

I. **Archbishop Iakovos (James A. Coucouzes).** *Archbishop of the Greek Orthodox Church in North and South America; Exarch of the Ecumenical Patriarchate of Constantinople.*

CHRISTIANITY (*in part*)

I.A. **Isaac Asimov.** *Science writer. Professor of Biochemistry, Boston University. Author of* Asimov's Biographical Encyclopedia of Science and Technology *and many others.*

MICHELSON, A.A. (Micropædia)

I.A.A.-L. **Ibrahim A. Abu-Lughod.** *Professor of Political Science, Northwestern University, Evanston, Illinois. Author of* Arab Rediscovery of Europe: A Study in Cultural Encounters.

IRAQ (*in part*)

I.A.Y. **Ivan Alekseyevich Yerofeyev.** *Associate Professor of Economic Geography, All-Union Extra-Mural Institute of Finance and Economics, U.S.S.R. Author of* Southwestern Economic Region; *coauthor of* Kiev.

UNION OF SOVIET SOCIALIST REPUBLICS
 (*in part*)

I.B. **Ivan Barnes.** *Research Geochemist, Water Resources Division, Geological Survey, U.S. Department of the Interior. An authority on the geochemistry of freshwaters.*

HYDROSPHERE, THE (*in part*)

I.Be. **Ian D. Bent.** *Professor of Music, University of Nottingham, England. Author of numerous articles in musicological journals; Text Editor of* The New Grove Dictionary of Music and Musicians, *6th ed.*

MUSIC, THE ART OF (*in part*)

I.Bo. **Ira Bornstein.** *Nuclear Engineer, Office of the Director, Argonne National Laboratory, Illinois.*

ENGINEERING (*in part*)

I.B.S. **Isaac Bashevis Singer.** *Short-story writer and novelist. Nobel Prize for Literature, 1978. Author of* The Family Moskat *and others.*

YIDDISH LITERATURE (*in part*)

I.Bt. **Irving Brant** (d. 1976). *Member, Advisory Board, James Madison Papers, University of Chicago. Council Member, Institute of Early American History and Culture, 1959–62. Author of* James Madison *(6 vol.) and others.*

MADISON, JAMES (Micropædia)

I.C.B. **The Rev. Ignatius Charles Brady, O.F.M.** *Former Director of the theological section, College of St. Bonaventura, Grottaferrata, Italy. Coeditor and cotranslator of* Francis and Clare: The Complete Works.

FRANCIS OF ASSISI, SAINT
 (Micropædia)

I.C.C. **Ian C. Clingan.** *Former Engineer in Chief, Trinity House Lighthouse Service, London.*

PUBLIC WORKS (*in part*)

I.C.Cn. **Ivor Cecil Coffin.** *Regional Economist, Economics Department, Lloyds Bank Group, London.*

URUGUAY (*in part*)

I.C.L. **Iñigo Cavero Lataillade.** *Minister of Culture, Government of Spain, 1980–81.*

SPAIN (*in part*)

I.D'O.E. **Sir Ivo D'Oyly Elliott** (d. 1961). *Indian Civil Service, 1906–32.*

TURENNE, HENRI DE LA TOUR
 D'AUVERGNE, VICOMTE DE
 (Micropædia)

I.E. *Specialists, Institute of Economics, University of Havana.*

HAVANA (*in part*)
WEST INDIES, THE (*in part*)

I.E.-E. **Irenäus Eibl-Eibesfeldt.** *Director, Research Unit for Human Ethology, Max Planck Institute for Physiology of Behaviour, Seewiesen, West Germany. Author of* Galápagos: The Noah's Ark of the Pacific.

PACIFIC ISLANDS (*in part*)

I.F.B.   Ivor F. Burton. *Professor of Social Policy, Bedford College, University of London. Author of* The Captain-General: The Career of John Churchill, Duke of Marlborough, from 1702–1711 *and others.*

MARLBOROUGH, JOHN CHURCHILL, 1ST
   DUKE OF (Micropædia)
PIUS IX (*in part*) (Micropædia)
PIUS V, SAINT (*in part*) (Micropædia)

I.F.G.B.   Ian F.G. Baxter. *Professor of Law, University of Toronto; former Director of Family Law Study.*

FAMILY LAW

I.G.   Isabella Gordon. *Head, Crustacea Section, British Museum (Natural History), London, 1928–66. Coeditor of* Crustaceana.

CRUSTACEANS (*in part*)

I.G.S.   Irwin G. Sarason. *Professor of Psychology, University of Washington, Seattle. Author of* Personality: An Objective Approach.

PERSONALITY (*in part*)

I.G.W.   Ivor G. Wilks. *Melville J. Herskovits Professor of African Studies, Northwestern University, Evanston, Illinois.*

NKRUMAH, KWAME (Micropædia)

I.H.   Igor Hájek. *Lecturer in Czechoslovak Studies, University of Glasgow. Coauthor and coeditor of* Dictionary of Czech Writers, 1948–1979.

CZECHOSLOVAK LITERATURE (*in part*)

I.Hr.   Ivan Hrbek. *Member, Oriental Institute, Czechoslovak Academy of Sciences, Prague. Author of "The Chronology of Ibn Battute's Travels" in* Archiv Orientalni.

IBN BAṬṬŪṬAH (Micropædia)

I.Hy.B.   Isabelle Hyman. *Professor of Fine Arts, Washington Square and University College of Arts and Science, New York University, New York City.*

BRUNELLESCHI, FILIPPO (*in part*)
   (Micropædia)

I.J.   Ivar K. Johansson. *Emeritus Professor of Animal Breeding, Agricultural College of Sweden, Uppsala. Author of* Genetic Aspects of Dairy Cattle Breeding; *coauthor of* Genetics and Animal Breeding.

FARMING AND AGRICULTURAL
   TECHNOLOGY (*in part*)

I.J.G.   Ignace J. Gelb (d. 1985). *Frank P. Hixon Distinguished Service Professor, Oriental Institute and Departments of Linguistics and of Near Eastern Languages and Civilizations, University of Chicago, 1965–79. Author of* A Study of Writing *and many others.*

LANGUAGES OF THE WORLD (*in part*)
LINGUISTICS (*in part*)

I.Jo.   Inge Jonsson. *Professor of Comparative Literature, University of Stockholm. Author of* Emanuel Swedenborg *and others.*

SWEDENBORG, EMANUEL
   (Micropædia)

I.J.S.   Irving J. Stolberg. *Speaker of the House of Representatives of Connecticut. Former Assistant Professor of Geography, Southern Connecticut State College, New Haven.*

UNITED STATES OF AMERICA (*in part*)

I.K.   Irving Kaplansky. *Director, Mathematical Sciences Research Institute, Berkeley, California. Author of* Commutative Rings.

GALOIS, ÉVARISTE (Micropædia)
HILBERT, DAVID (Micropædia)
NUMBER THEORY (*in part*)

I.K.F.   Ian Keith Ferguson. *Government Botanist and Principal Scientific Officer, Royal Botanic Gardens, Kew, England. Assistant Editor of* Flora Europaea *(vol. 2–3).*

ANGIOSPERMS (*in part*)

I.K.M.   Ivan Kirillovich Myachin. *Head of Section, Mysl Publishing House, Moscow.*

MOSCOW (*in part*)

I.Ko.   Igor Kopytoff. *Professor of Anthropology, University of Pennsylvania, Philadelphia. Author of various articles on African anthropology.*

CENTRAL AFRICA (*in part*)

I.K.P.   Ismail K. Poonawala. *Professor of Arabic and Islāmic Studies, University of California, Los Angeles.*

ʿALĪ (Micropædia)

I.L.W.   Ira L. Wiggins. *Emeritus Professor of Biology, Stanford University, California. Research Associate, Department of Botany, California Academy of Sciences, San Francisco.*

GYMNOSPERMS (*in part*)

I.M.D.   Igor Mikhailovich Diakonoff. *Head, Near Eastern Department and Ancient Oriental Languages Group, Institute of Oriental Studies, Academy of Sciences of the U.S.S.R., Leningrad. Author of* Semito-Hamitic Languages.

LANGUAGES OF THE WORLD
   (*in part*)

I.M.G.   Ivan M. Goodbody. *Professor of Zoology, University of the West Indies, Mona, Kingston, Jamaica.*

CHORDATES (*in part*)

I.M.J.   Ingrid Margareta Jonsson. *Staff Research Editor,* Encyclopædia Britannica, *Chicago, 1969–73.*

OCEANS (*in part*)

I.M.L.   I.M. Lewis. *Professor and Chairman, Department of Anthropology, London School of Economics and Political Science, University of London. Author of* A Pastoral Democracy; A Modern History of Somalia from Nation to State.

EASTERN AFRICA (*in part*)

I.M.P. do A.   Ilídio Melo Peres do Amaral. *Rector and Professor of Geography, University of Lisbon. Author of numerous publications on the geography of Portugal and its former colonies.*

PORTUGAL (*in part*)

I.N.S.   Ian Naismith Sneddon. *Simson Professor of Mathematics, University of Glasgow. Author of* Elements of Partial Differential Equations *and others.*

ANALYSIS (IN MATHEMATICS) (*in part*)

I.P.   Indra Pal. *Professor and Head, Department of Geography, University of Rājasthān, Jaipur, India. Coauthor of* World in Its Natural Regions.

INDIA (*in part*)

I.P.G.   Innokentii Petrovich Gerasimov (d. 1985). *Director, Institute of Geography, Academy of Sciences of the U.S.S.R., Moscow. An authority on geomorphology and soil science.*

GEOMORPHIC PROCESSES (*in part*)

I.P.H.   Ian P. Howard. *Professor of Psychology, York University, Toronto. Coauthor of* Human Spatial Orientation.

PERCEPTION, HUMAN (*in part*)

I.P.S.   Ivan Peter Shaw. *Former Fellow and Secretary, King's College, University of London. Author of* Nationality and the Western Church Before the Reformation.

EDWARD THE BLACK PRINCE
   (Micropædia)

I.R.C.   Ian R. Christie. *Astor Professor of British History, University College, University of London. Author of* Wilkes, Wyvill and Reform *and others.*

WILKES, JOHN (Micropædia)

I.Re.   Irving Rouse. *Charles J. MaCurdy Professor Emeritus of Anthropology, Yale University.*

WEST INDIES, THE (*in part*)

Ir.W.   Irving Wallace. *Novelist and biographer. Author of* The Fabulous Showman: The Life and Times of P.T. Barnum; The Man; *and many others.*

BARNUM, P.T. (Micropædia)

I.S.   Isaac Schapera. *Emeritus Professor of Anthropology, London School of Economics and Political Science, University of London. Author of* The Tswana *and others.*

SOUTHERN AFRICA (*in part*)

I.S.C.   Ivan Stoddard Coggeshall. *Fellow, Institute of Electrical and Electronics Engineers. Assistant Vice President, Western Union Telegraph Company, New York City, 1959; Director of International Communications, 1951–58.*

TELECOMMUNICATIONS SYSTEMS
   (*in part*)

I.S. de S.   Isbelia M. Sequera de Segnini. *Director, Institute of Geography; Coordinator of Graduate Studies in Geography, Central University of Venezuela, Caracas. Author of* Dinámica de la agricultura *and others.*

VENEZUELA (*in part*)

I.S.S.   Irvin S. Snyder. *Professor and Chairman, Department of Microbiology, West Virginia University, Morgantown. Coauthor of* Bacteria and Human Disease.

DRUGS AND DRUG ACTION (*in part*)

I.T.   **Isadore Twersky.** *Littauer Professor of Hebrew Literature and Philosophy, Harvard University. Author of* Rabad of Posquières *and others.*
RASHI (Micropædia)

I.T.R.   **The Rt. Rev. Ian Thomas Ramsey** (d. 1972). *Lord Bishop of Durham, England, 1966–72. Nolloth Professor of the Philosophy of Christian Religion, University of Oxford, 1951–66. Author of* Religious Language; Christian Discourse.
PHILOSOPHIES OF THE BRANCHES OF KNOWLEDGE (*in part*)

I.V.Ko.   **Innokenty Varfolomeevich Kozlov.** *Deputy Principal Editor, Geography, Mysl Publishing House, Moscow. Author of* Sovetskiye subtropiki.
UNION OF SOVIET SOCIALIST REPUBLICS (*in part*)

I.V.N.   **Israel Vladimirovich Nestyev.** *Chief Scientist, Research Institute of History of Arts, Moscow. Author of* Prokofiev.
PROKOFIEV, SERGEY (*in part*) (Micropædia)

I.V.P.   **Igor Vladimirovich Popov.** *Senior Scientist, Leningrad Hydrological Institute. Author of* Basic Methods for the Study of Riverbed Processes.
ASIA (*in part*)

I.W.   **Immanuel Wallerstein.** *Distinguished Professor of Sociology, State University of New York at Binghamton. Author of* Africa: The Politics of Independence.
LUMUMBA, PATRICE (*in part*) (Micropædia)

I.W.H.   **Inez Whitaker Hunt** (d. 1983). *Lecturer and free-lance writer. Teacher of creative writing, University of Colorado extension, Colorado Springs, 1963–66. Coauthor of* Lightning in His Hand: The Life Story of Nikola Tesla.
TESLA, NIKOLA (Micropædia)

I.Z.   **Imre Zoltán, M.D.** *Professor of Gynecology and Obstetrics, Semmelweis Medical University, Budapest, Hungary. Coauthor of* Semmelweis élete és munkássága.
SEMMELWEIS, IGNAZ PHILIPP (Micropædia)

J.A.A.   **J.A. Andrups.** *Author of* Latvian Literature *and others.*
LATVIAN LITERATURE (Micropædia)

J.A.B.   **James Alan Bassham.** *Senior Scientist, Chemical Biodynamics Division, Lawrence Berkeley Laboratory, University of California, Berkeley. Coauthor of* Photosynthesis of Carbon Compounds; The Path of Carbon in Photosynthesis.
PHOTOSYNTHESIS

J.A.Ba.   **John A. Bailey.** *President, Transportation Systems Associates, Philadelphia. Director, Transportation Center, Northwestern University, Evanston, Illinois, 1967–75.*
TRANSPORTATION (*in part*)

Ja.Be.   **Jane Bergerol.** *Free-lance journalist based in Angola.*
SOUTHERN AFRICA (*in part*)

J.A.Bo.   **John Andrew Boyle** (d. 1978). *Professor of Persian Studies, Victoria University of Manchester, 1966–78. Editor of and contributor to* Cambridge History of Iran, *vol. 5.*
FERDOWSĪ (Micropædia)
GHĀZĀN, MAḤMŪD (Micropædia)

J.A.B.v.B.   **J.A.B. van Buitenen** (d. 1979). *Distinguished Service Professor of Sanskrit and Indic Studies, University of Chicago, 1974–79. Author of* Tales of Ancient India.
CALENDAR (*in part*)
HINDUISM (*in part*)
RĀMĀNUJA (Micropædia)
SOUTH ASIAN ARTS (*in part*)

Ja.C.   **Jan Christensen.** *Financial Editor,* Verdens Gang, *Oslo.*
NORWAY (*in part*)

J.A.Ca.   **Jorge A. Camacho.** *Free-lance writer. Staff member, British Broadcasting Corporation, 1938–69; Head of Talks and Current Affairs (Radio), 1961–69.*
BROADCASTING (*in part*)

J.A.C.B.   **J.A.C. Brown** (d. 1984). *Professor of Applied Economics, University of Oxford, 1970–84. Coauthor of* The Lognormal Distribution.
ECONOMIC THEORY (*in part*)

J.A.Cr.   **John Anthony Crook.** *Professor of Ancient History, University of Cambridge, 1979–84. Author of* Law and Life of Rome.
MARCUS AURELIUS (Micropædia)

Ja.D.   **Janusz Durko.** *Director, Historical Museum of Warsaw. Editor of* Bibliography of Warsaw.
WARSAW (*in part*)

J.Ad.   **Jean Adhémar.** *Curator of Prints, Bibliothèque Nationale, Paris. Author of* Honoré Daumier *and others.*
DAUMIER, HONORÉ (Micropædia)

Ja.F.   **James E. Faller.** *Fellow, Joint Institute for Laboratory Astrophysics, University of Colorado, Boulder.*
GRAVITATION (*in part*)

Ja.G.M.   **James Grier Miller, M.D.** *Adjunct Professor of Psychiatry, University of California, Los Angeles. President, University of Kentucky, Louisville, 1973–80.*
PSYCHOLOGY (*in part*)

J.A.H.   **John A. Haywood.** *Reader in Arabic, University of Durham, England, 1967–78. Author of* Arabic Lexicography.
FAKHR AD-DĪN AR-RĀZĪ (Micropædia)
JAʿFAR IBN MUḤAMMAD (Micropædia)
MASʿŪDĪ, AL- (Micropædia)

J.A.Ha.   **John A. Harrison.** *Emeritus Professor of History, University of Miami, Coral Gables, Florida. Editor,* The Journal of Asian Studies, *1969–72. Author of* New Light on Early and

Medieval Japanese History.
HŌJŌ FAMILY (Micropædia)

Ja.H.B.   **James H. Bready.** *Editorial writer and book columnist,* The Sun *newspapers, Baltimore.*
UNITED STATES OF AMERICA (*in part*)

J.A.Ho.   **James A. Hodges.** *Professor of History, Wooster College, Wooster, Ohio.*
UNITED STATES OF AMERICA (*in part*)

Ja.H.W.   **Jack H. Wernick.** *Manager, Materials Science Division, Central Services Organization for the regional Bell operating companies, Murray Hill, New Jersey.*
ENERGY CONVERSION (*in part*)

Ja.J.S.   **James Joseph Stilwell.** *Rear Admiral, U.S. Navy (retired). Labour arbitrator and consulting engineer.*
TRANSPORTATION (*in part*)

Ja.K.   **Jan Kazimour.** *President, Federal Statistical Office of Czechoslovakia, Prague, 1969–81.*
PRAGUE (*in part*)

J.A.K.   **Jerzy A. Kondracki.** *Emeritus Professor of Physical Geography, University of Warsaw. Author of* Geografia fizyczna Polski.
EUROPE (*in part*)
POLAND (*in part*)

J.A.Ka.   **John Anderson Kay.** *Director, Centre for Business Strategy; Professor of Industrial Policy, London Business School. Coauthor of* The British Tax System *and others.*
GOVERNMENT FINANCE (*in part*)

J.A.Ke.   **The Rev. John Arthur Kemp, S.J.** (d. 1963). *Professor of Medieval History, Loyola University, Chicago, 1959–63. Author of* History of Europe to 1500.
ANSELM OF CANTERBURY, SAINT (Micropædia)

Ja.Kn.   **Jan Knappert.** *Lecturer in Bantu, School of Oriental and African Studies, University of London. Author of* Myths and Legends of the Congo *and many others.*
AFRICAN ARTS (*in part*)

Ja.L.   **James Laver** (d. 1975). *Keeper, Departments of Engraving, Illustration and Design, and of Paintings, Victoria and Albert Museum, London, 1938–59. Author of* A Concise History of Costume.
DRESS AND ADORNMENT (*in part*)

J.Al.   **John Allan** (d. 1955). *Keeper, Department of Coins and Medals, British Museum, London, 1931–49.*
COINS AND COINAGE (*in part*)

J.A.L.   **Joseph Albert Lauwerys** (d. 1981). *Director, Atlantic Institute of Education, Halifax, Nova Scotia, 1970–76. Professor of Comparative Education, University of London, 1947–70. Coeditor,* World Year Book of Education, *1947–70.*
EDUCATION, HISTORY OF (*in part*)

Ja.La.   Janko Lavrin (d. 1986). *Professor of Russian Literature, University of Nottingham, England, 1923–53. Author of* Gogol; Russian Writers; *and others.*
GOGOL, NIKOLAY (Micropædia)

J.A.Le.   James A. Lee (d. 1981). *Consultant, Brick Institute of America, Atlanta, Georgia. Author of articles in* American Ceramic Journal *and other journals.*
INDUSTRIAL GLASS AND CERAMICS (*in part*)

Ja.L.S.   Jason Lewis Saunders. *Professor of Philosophy, City College, City University of New York. Author of* Early Stoic Philosophy.
PHILOSOPHICAL SCHOOLS AND DOCTRINES, WESTERN (*in part*)

Ja.M.   Jacques Millot (d. 1980). *Professor, National Museum of Natural History, Paris, 1943–67. Researcher on the anatomy of coelacanths and their fossil relatives.*
FISHES (*in part*)

J.A.M.   J.A. Mabbutt. *Professor of Geography, University of New South Wales, Kensington, Australia. Author of* Desert Landforms.
CONTINENTAL LANDFORMS (*in part*)

J.A.Ma.   J. Alan Mackie. *Free-lance writer.*
ALEXANDRIA (*in part*)

J.A.McG.   Joseph A. McGeough. *Regius Professor of Engineering; Head, Department of Mechanical Engineering, University of Edinburgh. Author of* Principles of Electrochemical Machining.
TOOLS (*in part*)

J.A.M.K.I.   Jozef A.M.K. IJsewijn. *Professor of Neo-Latin, Catholic University of Louvain, Belgium. Editor,* Humanistica Lovaniensia.
GROTIUS, HUGO (Micropædia)

J.A.Mn.   J. Alden Mason (d. 1967). *Curator, American Section, University Museum, University of Pennsylvania, 1926–55.*
PERU (*in part*)

J.A.Mo.   John A. Monick (d. 1981). *Research Associate, Colgate-Palmolive Company, Piscataway, New Jersey. Author of* Alcohols: Their Chemistry, Properties and Manufacture.
CHEMICAL COMPOUNDS (*in part*)

J.A.Mu.   John A. Munroe. H. *Rodney Sharp Professor Emeritus of History, University of Delaware, Newark. Editor,* Delaware History. *Author of* History of Delaware *and others.*
UNITED STATES OF AMERICA (*in part*)

J.A.O.   Juan A. Oddone. *Professor of History, Autonomous Metropolitan University, Mexico City. Author of* La formación del Uruguay moderno.
URUGUAY (*in part*)

J.A.P.   James A. Peters (d. 1972). *Curator and Supervisor, Division of* Reptiles and Amphibians, National Museum of Natural History, Smithsonian Institution, Washington, D.C., 1966–72. Specialist on the taxonomy of snakes. Author of Dictionary of Herpetology.
REPTILES (*in part*)

J.Ar.   John Armitage (d. 1980). *London Editor,* Encyclopædia Britannica, *1949–65. President, Rugby Fives Association, London, 1955–60.*
SPORTS AND GAMES, THE HISTORY OF (*in part*)

J.A.R.   James Arthur Ramsay. *Emeritus Professor of Comparative Physiology, University of Cambridge. Author of* Physiological Approach to the Lower Animals.
EXCRETION AND EXCRETORY SYSTEMS (*in part*)

Ja.S.   Jacques Soustelle. *Professor of Social Anthropology, School of Advanced Studies in the Social Sciences, Paris. Author of* La Vie quotidienne des Aztèques *and others.*
PRE-COLUMBIAN CIVILIZATIONS (*in part*)

J.A.S.   Jorge A. Suárez. *Professor of Amerindian Linguistics and of Contemporary Linguistics, National Autonomous University of Mexico, Mexico City. Coauthor of* A Description of Colloquial Guaraní.
LANGUAGES OF THE WORLD (*in part*)

J.A.S.G.   John A.S. Grenville. *Professor of Modern History, University of Birmingham, England. Author of* Lord Salisbury and Foreign Policy *and others.*
SALISBURY, ROBERT CECIL, 3RD MARQUESS OF (Micropædia)

J.A.Sh.   Jerome A. Shaffer. *Professor and Head, Department of Philosophy, University of Connecticut, Storrs. Author of* Philosophy of Mind.
MIND, THE PHILOSOPHY OF

J.A.T.   John A. Thomas. *Vice President, Corporate Research, Travenol Laboratories, Round Lake, Illinois. Coauthor of* Synopsis of Endocrine Pharmacology *and others.*
DRUGS AND DRUG ACTION (*in part*)

J.Au.   Jeannine Auboyer. *Emeritus Curator in Chief, Museum Guimet, Paris. Author of* La Vie quotidienne dans l'Inde ancienne.
RITES AND CEREMONIES, SACRED (*in part*)

Ja.W.   Jan Wojnowski. *Senior Editor, Polish Scientific Publishers, Warsaw. Editor,* Wielka Encyklopedia Powszechna, *Warsaw, 1962–70. Editor of* Literatura polska: Przewodnik encyklopedyczny.
POLISH LITERATURE (*in part*)

J.A.W.   Sir Jack Allan Westrup (d. 1975). *Professor of Music, University of Oxford, 1946–71; Fellow of Wadham College, Oxford, 1947–71. Author of* Purcell *and many others.*
MUSICAL INSTRUMENTS (*in part*)
PURCELL, HENRY (Micropædia)

J.A.Y.   Jay A. Young. *Consultant on chemical safety and health. Manager, Technical Publications, Manufacturing Chemists Association, Washington, D.C., 1976–80. Hudson Professor of Chemistry, Auburn University, Alabama, 1970–75.*
CHEMICAL REACTIONS (*in part*)

J.B.   Jonathan Barnes. *Fellow of Balliol College, University of Oxford. Author of* Aristotle; *coeditor of* Articles on Aristotle.
PLATONISM, PLATO AND (*in part*)

J.Ba.   Jacques Barzun. *University Professor Emeritus, Columbia University; Dean of Faculties and Provost, 1958–67. Author of* Berlioz and the Romantic Century; Darwin, Marx, Wagner; *and others.*
BERLIOZ, HECTOR (Micropædia)
EUROPE (*in part*)
FLAUBERT, GUSTAVE (*in part*) (Micropædia)
POE, EDGAR ALLAN (*in part*) (Micropædia)

J.B.B.   John Bernard Beer. *Fellow of Peterhouse, Cambridge; Reader in English Literature, University of Cambridge. Author of* Coleridge, the Visionary *and others.*
COLERIDGE, SAMUEL TAYLOR (*in part*) (Micropædia)
ENGLISH LITERATURE (*in part*)
FORSTER, E.M. (Micropædia)

J.-B.Ba.   Jean-Bertrand Barrère (d. 1985). *Professor of French Literature, University of Cambridge, 1954–82; Fellow of St. John's College, Cambridge. Author of* Hugo, l'homme et l'oeuvre *and other works on Victor Hugo.*
HUGO, VICTOR (*in part*) (Micropædia)

J.B.Bd.   John Brian Bird. *Professor and Chairman, Department of Geography, McGill University, Montreal.*
ARCTIC, THE (*in part*)

J.B.B.T.   John B.B. Trussell. *Chief, Division of History, Pennsylvania Historical and Museum Commission, Harrisburg.*
PHILADELPHIA (*in part*)

J.B.C.   J.B. Condliffe (d. 1981). *Senior Economist, Stanford Research Institute, Menlo Park, California, 1961–67. Professor of Economics, University of California, Berkeley, 1940–58. Author of* The Commerce of Nations.
UNITED NATIONS (*in part*)

J.B.Co.   Jerome B. Cohen. *Frank C. Engelhart Professor of Materials Science and Engineering, Northwestern University, Evanston, Illinois. Author of* Diffraction Methods in Materials Science.
MATTER (*in part*)

J.Be.   Jeremy Bernstein. *Professor of Physics, Stevens Institute of Technology, Hoboken, New Jersey. Author of* Elementary Particles and Their Currents.
SCHRÖDINGER, ERWIN (Micropædia)
YANG, CHEN NING (Micropædia)

J.B.F.   John Bailey Fernald (d. 1985). *Theatre director. Principal, Royal Academy of Dramatic Art, London, 1955–65. Professor of Dramatic Art, Oakland University, Rochester, Michigan, 1966–70. Author of* Sense of Direction.
MOTION PICTURES (*in part*)
THEATRE, THE ART OF (*in part*)

J.B.-G.   Jacqueline Beaujeu-Garnier. *Professor of Geography, University of Paris I; Director, Centre for Space Analysis Research. Author of* Géographie de la population *and others.*
FRANCE (*in part*)

J.B.Gl.   Sir John Bagot Glubb (d. 1986). *Lieutenant General; Chief of General Staff, The Arab Legion, Amman, Jordan, 1939–56. Author of* War in the Desert *and others.*
ARABIA (*in part*)
IBN SAʿŪD (Micropædia)
MECCA AND MEDINA (*in part*)

J.B.H.   John B. Heywood. *Professor of Mechanical Engineering, Massachusetts Institute of Technology, Cambridge. Coauthor of* Open-Cycle MHD Power Generation.
ENERGY CONVERSION (*in part*)

J.B.He.   James B. Hendrickson. *Professor of Chemistry, Brandeis University, Waltham, Massachusetts. Author of* The Molecules of Nature; *coauthor of* Organic Chemistry.
WOODWARD, R.B. (Micropædia)

J.B.Ho.   Joseph Bixby Hoyt. *Emeritus Professor of Geography, Southern Connecticut State College, New Haven. Author of* The Connecticut Story.
UNITED STATES OF AMERICA (*in part*)

J.B.I.   John B. Irwin. *Former Associate Professor of Astronomy, Kean College of New Jersey, Union.*
MEASUREMENT AND OBSERVATION, PRINCIPLES, METHODS, AND INSTRUMENTS OF (*in part*)

J.B.-J.   John Buettner-Janusch. *Former Professor and Chairman, Department of Anthropology, New York University, New York City. Author of* Origins of Man.
CENTRAL AMERICA (*in part*)
EVOLUTION, HUMAN (*in part*)

J.B.M.   John Barron Mays. *Former Eleanor Rathbone Professor of Sociology, University of Liverpool. Author of* The Young Pretenders: Teenage Culture in Contemporary Society *and others.*
SOCIAL DIFFERENTIATION (*in part*)

J.B.Mi.   Jean Brown Mitchell. *Fellow, Newnham College, Cambridge, 1934–68; Lecturer in Geography, University of Cambridge, 1945–68. Author of* Historical Geography.
EUROPEAN OVERSEAS EXPLORATION AND EMPIRES, THE HISTORY OF (*in part*)
GEOGRAPHY (*in part*)

J.B.P.   J. Bruce Pluckhahn. *Curator, National Bowling Hall of Fame and Museum, St. Louis, Missouri. Coauthor*
of Pins and Needlers.
SPORTS, MAJOR TEAM AND INDIVIDUAL (*in part*)

J.B.Pa.   James Bayard Parsons (d. 1985). *Professor of Chemistry, University of Chicago, 1958–61. Coauthor of* The Study of the Physical World.
INDUSTRIES, EXTRACTION AND PROCESSING (*in part*)

J.B.R.   Jean B. Richard. *Honorary Dean, Faculty of Letters and Human Sciences, University of Dijon, France. Author of* Histoire de la Bourgogne.
FRANCE (*in part*)

J.B.Ra.   John Bell Rae. *Emeritus Professor of the History of Technology, Harvey Mudd College, Claremont, California. Author of* American Automobile Manufacturers: The First Forty Years *and others.*
INDUSTRIES, MANUFACTURING (*in part*)

J.Bru.   Jean Bruhat. *Professor, Institute of Political Science; Instructor, University of Paris VIII. Author of* Les Journées de février 1848 *and others.*
BLANQUI, AUGUSTE (Micropædia)

J.B.Sm.   J(enkyn) Beverley Smith. *Reader in Welsh History, University College of Wales, Aberystwyth, University of Wales.*
UNITED KINGDOM (*in part*)

J.B.Sp.   J. Brookes Spencer. *Associate Professor of the History of Science, Oregon State University, Corvallis. Editor of* The Collected Works of Niels Bohr.
PHYSICAL SCIENCES, THE (*in part*)

J.Bu.   Joseph Buttinger. *Free-lance writer. Author of* Vietnam: A Dragon Embattled *and others.*
SOUTHEAST ASIA, MAINLAND (*in part*)

J.B.Wi.   John Bernard Wilkinson. *Former Head, Unilever Research Laboratory, Isleworth, England. Editor of* Harry's Cosmeticology.
DRESS AND ADORNMENT (*in part*)

J.C.   Jozef Cohen. *Professor of Psychology, University of Illinois, Urbana. Author of* Eyewitness Series in Psychology.
PSYCHOLOGY (*in part*)

J.C.A.   John C. Ayres (d. 1982). *D.W. Brooks Distinguished Professor of Food Science, University of Georgia, Athens. Coeditor of* Chemical and Biological Hazards in Foods *and others.*
FOOD PROCESSING (*in part*)

J.C.B.   Jon Charles Barlow. *Curator, Department of Ornithology, Royal Ontario Museum, Toronto. Professor of Zoology, University of Toronto. Researcher of the biology and taxonomy of vireos. Author of* "Xenarthrans and Pholidotes" *in* Recent Mammals of the World.
MAMMALS (*in part*)

J.C.Be.   John C. Bennett. *Emeritus President, Union Theological Seminary,*
New York City. Senior Contributing Editor, Christianity and Crisis. *Author of* Christians and the State.
NIEBUHR, REINHOLD (Micropædia)

J.C.D.   John C. Dewdney. *Reader in Geography, University of Durham, England. Author of* A Geography of the Soviet Union.
UNION OF SOVIET SOCIALIST REPUBLICS (*in part*)

J.C. de C.   Jacques Chastenet de Castaing (d. 1978). *Historian and journalist. Member of the French Academy. Author of* Léon Gambetta *and others.*
GAMBETTA, LÉON (Micropædia)

J.C. de G.-J.   John Coleman de Graft-Johnson (d. 1977). *Editor,* Economic Bulletin of Ghana. *Research Associate Professor of Economics, University of Ghana. Author of* African Glory: The Story of Vanished Negro Civilizations.
MŪSĀ (Micropædia)

J.C.F.   Jean Claude Froelich (d. 1972). *Director, Center for Advanced Studies on Modern Africa and Asia, University of Paris. Author of* Les Musulmans d'Afrique noire; *"al-Ḥādjdj ʿUmar b. Saʿīd b. ʿUthmān Tāl" in* The Encyclopedia of Islam.
ʿUMAR TALL (Micropædia)

J.C.Gi.   J. Calvin Giddings. *Professor of Chemistry, University of Utah, Salt Lake City. Author of* Dynamics of Chromatography.
ANALYSIS AND MEASUREMENT, PHYSICAL AND CHEMICAL (*in part*)

J.C.Gr.   Jerald C. Graue (d. 1982). *Associate Professor of Musicology and Music History, Eastman School of Music, University of Rochester, New York.*
MUSIC, THE ART OF (*in part*)

J.Ch.   John Cherry. *Deputy Keeper, Department of Medieval and Later Antiquities, British Museum, London.*
HISTORY, THE STUDY OF (*in part*)

J.C.H.   J.C. Holt. *Professor of Medieval History, University of Cambridge. Author of* King John *and others.*
JOHN (ENGLAND) (Micropædia)

J.C.J.   John Calhoun Jamieson (d. 1983). *Professor of Geophysics, University of Chicago, 1965–83.*
MATTER (*in part*)

J.C.J.M.   John Callan James Metford. *Emeritus Professor of Spanish, University of Bristol, England. Author of* San Martín the Liberator *and others.*
SAN MARTÍN, JOSÉ DE (Micropædia)

J.C.K.   John C. Krantz, Jr. (d. 1983). *Professor of Pharmacology, University of Maryland, Baltimore, 1935–65. Coauthor of* Pharmacologic Principles of Medical Practice.
MEDICINE (*in part*)

J.C.L.   Joseph Collins Lawrence. *Assistant Professor of History, University of British Columbia, Vancouver. Author*

of A Brief History of Sooke and District.
CANADA (*in part*)

J.C.Mi.   James Clyde Mitchell. *Official Fellow of Nuffield College, University of Oxford. Professor of Urban Sociology, Victoria University of Manchester, 1966–74.*
SOUTHERN AFRICA (*in part*)

J.Co.   Jean L. Comhaire. *Emeritus Professor of Social Anthropology, University of Juba, The Sudan. Former Sociologist, United Nations Economic Commission for Africa. Author of* Urban Administration in Africa *and others.*
WESTERN AFRICA (*in part*)

J.-C.P.   Jean-Charles Pichon. *Author of* Saint-Néron: Histoire des mythes.
NERO (Micropædia)

J.Cr.   John Cruickshank. *Professor of French, University of Sussex, Brighton, England. Author of* Albert Camus and the Literature of Revolt *and others; editor of* French Literature and Its Background.
CAMUS, ALBERT (Micropædia)

J.C.-R.   Jules-Marie Chaix-Ruy. *Professor of Philosophy, University of Nice, France, 1965–67. Author of* J.-B. Vico et l'illuminisme athée; Vie de J.-B. Vico.
VICO, GIAMBATTISTA (Micropædia)

J.C.Rd.   John Cowie Reid (d. 1972). *Professor of English, University of Auckland, New Zealand. Author of* Mind and Art of Coventry Patmore; Francis Thompson: Man and Poet; *and others.*
HOPKINS, GERARD MANLEY (Micropædia)

J.C.Re.   John C. Reilly, Jr. *Historian, Naval History Division, Office of the Chief of Naval Operations, U.S. Department of the Navy, Washington, D.C. Coauthor of* Capital Ships: A Handbook of United States Battleships and Battle Cruisers 1896–1969.
WAR, THE TECHNOLOGY OF (*in part*)

J.C.Ry.   J. Coert Rylaarsdam. *Emeritus Professor of Old Testament Theology, University of Chicago. Emeritus Professor of Theology, Marquette University, Milwaukee. Author of* Revelation in Jewish Wisdom Literature.
BIBLICAL LITERATURE AND ITS CRITICAL INTERPRETATION (*in part*)
DAVID (ISRAEL) (Micropædia)

J.C.S.   James C. Spalding. *Professor of Protestant Theology; Administrative Director, School of Religion, University of Iowa, Iowa City. Author of* The Demise of English Presbyterianism.
PROTESTANTISM (*in part*)

J.C.T.   James Chase Tyler. *Director, Biological Research Resources Program, National Science Foundation, Washington, D.C. Author of* Osteology, Phylogeny, and Higher Classification of the Fishes of the Order Plectognathi (Tetraodontiformes).
FISHES (*in part*)

J.Cul.   James Cullen. *Assistant Keeper, Royal Botanic Garden, Edinburgh. Coauthor of* The Identification of Flowering Plant Families.
ANGIOSPERMS (*in part*)

J.C.V.   J. Charles Verlinden. *Emeritus Professor of History, State University of Ghent. Director, Belgian Historical Institute, Rome. Author of* En Flandre sous Philippe II *and others.*
LOW COUNTRIES, THE (*in part*)

J.D.A.   Jean Daniel Anthony. *Professor, Laboratory of Comparative Anatomy, National Museum of Natural History, Paris. Coauthor of* Anatomie de Latimeria Chalumnae.
FISHES (*in part*)

J.D.Ad.   Jeremy D. Adler. *Lecturer in German, Westfield College, University of London.*
GERMAN LITERATURE (*in part*)

J.D.B.M.   John Donald Bruce Miller. *Professor of International Relations, Australian National University, Canberra. Author of* The Commonwealth in the World *and others.*
UNITED KINGDOM (*in part*)

J.D.C.   Jesse Dunsmore Clarkson (d. 1973). *Professor of History, Brooklyn College, City University of New York, 1945–67. Author of* A History of Russia *and others.*
SPERANSKY, MIKHAIL MIKHAYLOVICH, GRAF (Micropædia)

J.D.Co.   James Daniel Collins (d. 1985). *Professor of Philosophy, St. Louis University, Missouri. Author of* The Emergence of Philosophy of Religion *and others.*
THOMISM, THOMAS AQUINAS AND (*in part*)

J.D.C.R.   Jose Daniel Contreras R. *Head, Department of History, University of San Carlos of Guatemala. Author of* Breve historia de Guatemala.
CENTRAL AMERICA (*in part*)

J.De.   Jean Descola (d. 1981). *Historian. Director, Ibero-American Center for Study and Research, Paris. Author of* The Conquistadors *and others.*
SOTO, HERNANDO DE (Micropædia)

J. de E.   Joaquín de Entrambasaguas. *Former Professor of Spanish Literature, University of Madrid. Author of* Estudios sobre Lope de Vega.
VEGA, LOPE DE (*in part*) (Micropædia)

J. de S.   Jorge de Sena (d. 1978). *Professor of Portuguese and Comparative Literature, University of California, Santa Barbara, 1970–78. Author of* A Poesia de Camões *and others.*
CAMÕES, LUÍS DE (Micropædia)

J.D.F.   John Donnelly Fage. *Pro-Vice-Chancellor, Vice-Principal, and Professor of African History, University of Birmingham, England. Author of* A History of West Africa *and others.*
AFRICA (*in part*)

J.D.-G.   Jacques Duchesne-Guillemin. *Emeritus Professor of Indo-Iranian Studies, State University of Liège, Belgium. Author of* The Religion of Ancient Iran *and others.*
ZOROASTRIANISM AND PARSIISM

J.Di.   James Dickie. *Former Lecturer in Islāmic Studies, University of Lancaster, England. Editor of* Dīwān Ibn Shuhaid al-Andalusi.
RITES AND CEREMONIES, SACRED (*in part*)

J.D.J.H.   John David Jayne Havard, M.D. *Barrister at Law. Secretary, British Medical Association, London. Author of* Detection of Secret Homicide.
MEDICINE (*in part*)

J.D.L.   John David Legge. *Dean, Faculty of Arts, Monash University, Clayton, Australia. Author of* Central Authority and Regional Autonomy in Indonesia *and others.*
EAST INDIES, THE (*in part*)

J.D.M.   Jürgen D. Moltmann. *Professor of Systematic Theology, Eberhard Karl University of Tübingen, West Germany. Author of* Theology of Hope *and others.*
DOCTRINES AND DOGMAS, RELIGIOUS (*in part*)

J.D.Mu.   J. Derral Mulholland. *Research Scientist, McDonald Observatory and Department of Astronomy, University of Texas at Austin, and Centre for the Study and Research of Geodynamics and Astronomy, Grasse, France.*
SOLAR SYSTEM, THE (*in part*)

J.D.P.   Joseph D. Phillips. *Senior Scientist, University of Texas at Austin.*
MINERALS AND ROCKS (*in part*)

J.D.Pr.   John Douglas Pringle. *Editor, Sydney Morning Herald, 1965–70. Author of* Australian Accent.
AUSTRALIA (*in part*)
SYDNEY

J.D.Pro.   Jules David Prown. *Professor of the History of Art, Yale University. Author of* John Singleton Copley; American Painting from Its Beginnings to the Armory Show; *and others.*
EAKINS, THOMAS (Micropædia)
HOMER, WINSLOW (Micropædia)

J.D.R.   John D. Ryder. *Emeritus Professor of Electrical Engineering, Michigan State University, East Lansing. Author of* Engineering Electronics.
ENGINEERING (*in part*)

J.D.S.   James Duane Squires (d. 1981). *Professor of History, Colby–Sawyer College, New London, New Hampshire, 1933–70. Chairman, New Hampshire American Revolution Bicentennial Commission. Member, Governor's Task Force for Study of New Hampshire, 1970.*
UNITED STATES OF AMERICA (*in part*)

J.D.Sc.   John D. Schmidt. *Assistant Professor of History, Columbia*

University.
CALENDAR (*in part*)

J.D.Sm.   James Desmond Smyth.
*Emeritus Professor of Parasitology,
London School of Hygiene and Tropical
Medicine, University of London. Author
of* Physiology of Cestodes; Physiology of
Trematodes.
FLATWORMS

J.D.W.   John D. Weaver. *Free-lance
writer. Former West Coast Editor,
Travel & Leisure. Author of* Los Angeles:
The Enormous Village *and others.*
LOS ANGELES

J.E.   Jens Engberg. *Professor of
History, University of Århus, Denmark.
Author of* Det slesvigske spørgsmål
1850–1853 *and others.*
CHRISTIAN IV (DENMARK)
   (Micropædia)

Je.B.   Jean Bouvier. *Professor of
Economics, University of Paris I. Author
of* Les Rothschild *and others.*
ROTHSCHILD FAMILY (Micropædia)
TURGOT, ANNE-ROBERT-JACQUES,
   BARON DE L'AULNE (Micropædia)

J.E.B.   John Edward Bowle (d. 1985).
*Professor of Political Theory, College
of Europe, Brugge, Belgium, 1950–67.
Author of* Politics and Opinion in the
19th Century.
POLITICAL PHILOSOPHY, THE HISTORY
   OF WESTERN

J.E.Bu.   John Everett Butt (d. 1965).
*Regius Professor of Rhetoric and English
Literature, University of Edinburgh,
1959–65. Author of* Pope's Poetical
Manuscripts; *coeditor of* Letters of
Alexander Pope; *and others.*
POPE, ALEXANDER (*in part*)
   (Micropædia)

Je.C.   Jean Cousin. *Former Professor
of Latin Language and Literature,
University of Besançon, France. Author
of* Études sur Quintilien; Destin de
Rome; *and others.*
DIOCLETIAN (Micropædia)

J.E.C.   John E. Carruthers.
*Assistant General Manager, Refineries
Department, British Petroleum Company
Ltd., London, 1964–69.*
INDUSTRIES, EXTRACTION AND
   PROCESSING (*in part*)

J.E.Ca.   James Edward Canright.
*Professor of Botany, Arizona State
University, Tempe. Author of* Fossil
Plants of Indiana.
ANGIOSPERMS (*in part*)

Je.Ch.   Jerome Ch'en. *Professor of
East Asian History, York University,
Toronto. Author of* Yuan Shih-k'ai,
1859–1916.
YÜAN SHIH-K'AI (Micropædia)

J.E.C.H.   J.E. Christopher Hill.
*Master of Balliol College, University of
Oxford, 1965–78. Author of* Intellectual
Origins of the English Revolution
and others.
PYM, JOHN (Micropædia)

J.E.Co.   J.E. Coates (d. 1973).
*Professor of Chemistry, University
College of Swansea, University of Wales,
1920–48. Author of the Chemical Society
memorial lecture on Haber.*
HABER, FRITZ (Micropædia)

J.E.C.W.   J.E. Caerwyn Williams.
*Emeritus Professor of Irish, University
College of Wales, Aberystwyth,
University of Wales; Director, Centre
for Advanced Welsh and Celtic Studies,
1979–85. Editor,* Studia Celtica (*annual*);
Y Traethodydd (*quarterly*); *and*
Ysgrifau Beirniadol (*annual*). *Author of*
Traddodiad Llenyddol Iwerddon *and
others; consulting editor of* Penguin Book
of Welsh Verse.
CELTIC LITERATURE (*in part*)

Je.D.   Jean Dresch. *Emeritus Professor
of Geography, University of Paris VII.
Author of* Recherches sur l'évolution du
relief dans le Haut-Atlas *and others.*
AFRICA (*in part*)
INDIAN OCEAN ISLANDS (*in part*)
WESTERN AFRICA (*in part*)

J.E.E.   John E. Englekirk (deceased).
*Professor of Spanish and Portuguese,
University of California, Los Angeles,
1958–73. Author of* Poe in Hispanic
Literature; *coauthor of* La narrativa
uruguaya.
LATIN-AMERICAN LITERATURE (*in part*)

J.E.F.   John E. Fagg. *Emeritus
Professor of History, New York
University, New York City. Author
of* Cuba, Haiti, and the Dominican
Republic *and others.*
TOUSSAINT-LOUVERTURE (Micropædia)

J.E.Fl.   John Edgar Flint. *Professor
of Commonwealth History, Dalhousie
University, Halifax, Nova Scotia. Author
of* Nigeria and Ghana *and others.*
AFRICA (*in part*)

J.E.H.   Joseph E. Hawkins, Jr.
*Professor of Otorhinolaryngology
(Physiological Acoustics), Medical
School, University of Michigan, Ann
Arbor. Editor of* Otophysiology.
SENSORY RECEPTION (*in part*)

Je.Ho.   Jerome Holtzman. *Baseball
columnist,* Chicago Tribune. *Author of*
No Cheering in the Press Box; *editor of*
Fielder's Choice.
SPORTS, MAJOR TEAM AND INDIVIDUAL
   (*in part*)

J.E.I.   Joseph E. Illick. *Professor of
History, San Francisco State University.
Author of* William Penn the Politician
and others.
PENN, WILLIAM (Micropædia)

Je.M.   Jean Mitry. *Professor and
Director, Cinema Division, Institute of
Art and Archaeology, University of Paris
I. Author of* Esthétique et psychologie
du cinéma; Histoire du cinéma; S.M.
Eisenstein; *and others.*
EISENSTEIN, SERGEY (Micropædia)
RAY, SATYAJIT (*in part*) (Micropædia)

Jé.Ma.   José Maceda. *Professor
and Chairman, Department of Music*

*Research, University of the Philippines,
Quezon City. Author of* The Music of the
Magindanao in the Philippines.
SOUTHEAST ASIAN ARTS (*in part*)

Je.-M.B.   Jean-Marie Brugière.
*Director, Overseas Office of Scientific
and Technical Research, Centre at
Cayenne, French Guiana.*
GUIANAS, THE (*in part*)

**J.E.McM.   James Edward McMurtrey,
Jr.** *Collaborator, Tobacco and Sugar
Crops Research Branch, Agricultural
Research Service, U.S. Department of
Agriculture, Plant Science Research
Division, Beltsville, Maryland; formerly
Leader of Tobacco Investigations.*
FARMING AND AGRICULTURAL
   TECHNOLOGY (*in part*)

**J.-E.-M.-G.D.   Joseph-Edouard-Marie-
Ghislain Delmelle.** *Poet, essayist, and
critic of art and literature. Member,
International Academy of French
Culture.*
BELGIAN LITERATURE (*in part*)

J.E.Mo.   John Edward Morton.
*Professor of Zoology, University of
Auckland, New Zealand. Author of*
Molluscs *and others.*
MOLLUSKS (*in part*)

J.E.O.   Jack E. Oliver. *Irving Porter
Church Professor of Engineering,
Department of Geological Sciences;
Director, Institute for the Study of the
Continents, Cornell University, Ithaca,
New York.*
OCEANS (*in part*)
VOLCANISM (*in part*)

Je.P.   Jerzy Pruchnicki. *Associate
Professor, Technical University of
Warsaw.*
EUROPE (*in part*)

Je.-P.H.   Jean-Paul Harroy. *Emeritus
Professor of Zairian, Rwandan and
Burundian Economics, Free University
of Brussels. Author of* Afrique, terre
qui meurt.
AFRICA (*in part*)

Je.S.   Jean Selz. *Art historian and
critic. Member, International Association
of Art Critics, Paris. Author of* Modern
Sculpture: Origins and Evolution;
Matisse; *and others.*
BRANCUSI, CONSTANTIN (Micropædia)

J.E.S.   John E. Shelton. *Consultant.
Former Supervisory Physical Scientist,
Bureau of Mines, U.S. Department of the
Interior, Washington, D.C.*
INDUSTRIES, EXTRACTION AND
   PROCESSING (*in part*)

J.E.Sa.   John E. Sadler. *Head,
Education Department, City of
Birmingham College of Education,
University of Birmingham, England,
1950–67. Author of* J.A. Comenius and
the Concept of Universal Education.
COMENIUS, JOHN AMOS (Micropædia)

Je.Si.   Jerome Silbergeld. *Associate
Professor of the History of Chinese
Art, University of Washington, Seattle.*

Author of Chinese Painting Style.
CHINA (*in part*)

J.E.Sm. John Edwin Smith. *Clark Professor of Philosophy, Yale University. Author of* Experience and God.
RELIGIOUS EXPERIENCE (*in part*)

J.E.Sn. James E. Snyder. *Professor of Art History, Bryn Mawr College, Pennsylvania. Author of* Bosch in Perspective.
MEMLING, HANS (Micropædia)

Je.St. Jerry Stannard. *Professor of History of Science and Medicine, University of Kansas, Lawrence.*
PLINY THE ELDER (Micropædia)

J.E.St. John E. Stark, M.D. *Physician, Addenbrookes Hospital, Cambridge, England.*
DIAGNOSIS AND THERAPEUTICS (*in part*)

J.Ev. Joan Evans (d. 1977). *President, Society of Antiquaries, London, 1959–64. Author of* John Ruskin *and many others.*
RUSKIN, JOHN (*in part*) (Micropædia)

J.E.v.L. Johanna E. van Lohuizen. *Professor of South and South-East Asian Art, Archaeology, and Ancient History, University of Amsterdam. Author of* The "Scythian" Period *and others.*
EAST INDIES, THE (*in part*)

J.F. Jan Filip (d. 1981). *Professor of Pre-history and Proto-history; Director, Archaeological Institute, Charles University, Prague, Czechoslovakia. Author of* Celtic Civilization and Its Heritage *and others.*
EUROPE (*in part*)

J.Fa. Jean Fages. *Director of Research, Nouméa Centre, Overseas Office of Scientific and Technological Research, New Caledonia.*
PACIFIC ISLANDS (*in part*)

J.F.B. John Fleming Brock, M.D. (d. 1983). *Professor of Medicine, University of Cape Town, South Africa, 1938–70. Author of* Recent Advances in Human Nutrition, with Special Reference to Clinical Medicine.
NUTRITION (*in part*)

J.F.Br. John Fleetwood Baker, Baron Baker (d. 1985). *Professor of Mechanical Sciences, University of Cambridge, 1943–68; Fellow of Clare College, Cambridge. Author of* Differential Equations of Engineering Science *and others; coauthor of* The Analysis of Engineering Structures.
ENGINEERING (*in part*)

J.F.C. James F. Cahill. *Professor of the History of Art, University of California, Berkeley. Author of* Chinese Painting; Hills Beyond a River; *and others.*
HSIA KUEI (Micropædia)

J.F.Ca. James Ford Cairns. *Member, House of Representatives, for the Division of Lalor, Victoria, 1969–77. Lecturer in Economic History, University of Melbourne, Australia, 1946–55.*
AUSTRALIA (*in part*)

J.F.C.C. J.F.C. Conn. *Emeritus Professor of Naval Architecture, University of Glasgow.*
INDUSTRIES, MANUFACTURING (*in part*)

J.F.D. John F. Due. *Professor of Economics, University of Illinois, Urbana. Author of* Government Finance.
GOVERNMENT FINANCE (*in part*)

J.F.De. John F. Devlin. *Free-lance writer, lecturer, and consultant on Middle East affairs. Author of* Syria: Modern State in an Ancient Land *and others.*
DAMASCUS (*in part*)

J.Fe. John Ferguson. *President, Selly Oak Colleges, Birmingham, England. Professor, Dean, and Director of Studies in Arts, The Open University, Milton Keynes, England, 1969–79. Editor of* Studies in Cicero *and others.*
CICERO, MARCUS TULLIUS (*in part*) (Micropædia)

J.F.E. John F. Elliott. *Professor of Metallurgy, Massachusetts Institute of Technology, Cambridge. Coauthor of* Thermochemistry for Steelmaking.
INDUSTRIES, EXTRACTION AND PROCESSING (*in part*)

J.F.Ha. John F. Hayward (d. 1983). *Associate Director, Sotheby Parke-Bernet and Company, London and New York City. Deputy Keeper, Victoria and Albert Museum, London, 1946–65. Author of* Virtuoso Goldsmiths; Art of the Gunmaker; *and others.*
DECORATIVE ARTS AND FURNISHINGS (*in part*)

J.Fi. James Smith Findley. *Professor of Biology; Director, Museum of Southwestern Biology, University of New Mexico, Albuquerque. Author of* "Insectivores and Dermopterans" *in* Recent Mammals of the World; *numerous journal articles on mammals.*
MAMMALS (*in part*)

J.F.M. John F.M. Middleton. *Professor of Anthropology, Yale University. Author of* Lugbara Religion *and others; editor of* Magic, Witchcraft and Curing.
AFRICA (*in part*)
OCCULTISM (*in part*)

J.F.Ma. J.F. Matthews. *Lecturer in the Middle and Late Roman Empire, University of Oxford; Official Fellow of Queen's College, Oxford.*
CONSTANTINE THE GREAT (*in part*)

J.F.McD. James F. McDivitt. *Coordinator, United Nations Economic and Social Commission for Asia and the Pacific (ESCAP) Regional Mineral Resources Development Centre, Bandung, Indonesia.*
EAST INDIES, THE (*in part*)

J.F.Me. John F. Mee (d. 1985). *Mead Johnson Professor of Management, Indiana University, Bloomington. Author of* Management Thought in a Dynamic Economy.
TAYLOR, FREDERICK W. (Micropædia)

J.F.N.B. John F.N. Bradley. *Visiting Professor, University of Bordeaux I, France. Fellow, Victoria University of Manchester, England. Author of* Lidice.
CZECHOSLOVAKIA (*in part*)

J.Fo. Jean Fourastié. *Professor of Economics, National Conservatory of Arts and Crafts, Paris. Member of the Academy of Moral and Political Sciences, Institute of France. Author of* The Causes of Wealth.
WORK AND EMPLOYMENT (*in part*)

J.F.O'C. Joseph F. O'Callaghan. *Professor of Medieval History, Fordham University, New York City.*
SPAIN (*in part*)

J.F.O'G. James Francis O'Gorman. *Grace Slack McNeil Professor of American Art, Wellesley College, Massachusetts. Author of* H.H. Richardson and His Office: Selected Drawings.
RICHARDSON, HENRY HOBSON (Micropædia)

J.F.P.H. John Francis Price Hopkins. *Fellow of Corpus Christi College, Cambridge; former Lecturer in Modern Arabic, University of Cambridge.*
AFRICA (*in part*)

Jf.Pi. Josef Pieper. *Emeritus Professor of Philosophical Anthropology, University of Münster, West Germany. Author of* Scholasticism *and others.*
PHILOSOPHICAL SCHOOLS AND DOCTRINES, WESTERN (*in part*)

J.F.Q. John Francis Quinn. *Professor of Philosophy, Pontifical Institute of Mediaeval Studies, Toronto. Author of* "The Historical Constitution of St. Bonaventure's Philosophy," *in* Medieval Texts and Studies.
BONAVENTURE, SAINT (Micropædia)

J.Fr. Joseph Frankel. *Emeritus Professor of Politics, University of Southampton, England. Author of* The Making of Foreign Policy *and others.*
WAR, THE THEORY AND CONDUCT OF (*in part*)

J.F.S. Joseph Frederick Scott (d. 1971). *Vice Principal; Principal Lecturer in Mathematics, St. Mary's College, Strawberry Hill, England. Author of* A History of Mathematics.
NAPIER, JOHN (Micropædia)

J.F.W. J. Fred Weston. *Professor of Managerial Economics and Finance, University of California, Los Angeles. Author of* The Scope and Methodology of Finance *and others.*
BUSINESS ORGANIZATION (*in part*)

J.G. Joseph Gentilli. *Honorary Research Fellow, University of Western Australia, Nedlands; former Reader in Geography. Author of* Sun, Climate, Life *and others.*
CLIMATE AND WEATHER (*in part*)

J.G.B. J. Guthrie Brown (d. 1976). *Senior Consultant, Sir Alexander Gibb & Partners, Consulting Engineers.*

President, International Commission on Large Dams, 1964–67. Coauthor of Power from Water.
PUBLIC WORKS (*in part*)

J.G.C.   John Garry Cuninghame. *Principal Scientific Officer, Chemistry Division, Atomic Energy Research Establishment, Harwell, England. Author of* Chemical Aspects of the Atomic Nucleus.
ATOMS (*in part*)

J.G.Co.   James Gordon Cook. *Director, Merrow Publishing Company Ltd., Newcastle upon Tyne, England. Author of* Handbook of Textile Fibres.
INDUSTRIES, CHEMICAL PROCESS
   (*in part*)

J.G.Cr.   J.G. Crowther. *Author of* Famous American Men of Science; Science in Modern Society; *and others.*
GIBBS, J. WILLARD (Micropædia)

J.G.D.   The Rev. J. Gordon Davies. *Edward Cadbury Professor and Head, Department of Theology, University of Birmingham, England. Author of* The Early Christian Church *and others.*
NESTORIUS (Micropædia)

J.G.D.C.   John Grahame Douglas Clark. *Disney Professor Emeritus of Archaeology, University of Cambridge. Author of* Prehistoric Europe: The Economic Basis *and others.*
EUROPE (*in part*)

J.G.G.   John G. Gallaher. *Associate Professor of History, Southern Illinois University, Edwardsville. Author of "Leo X" in* New Catholic Encyclopedia.
LEO X (PAPACY) (Micropædia)

J.G.H.   John G. Hargrave (d. 1982). *Author of* The Life and Soul of Paracelsus *and others.*
PARACELSUS (Micropædia)

J.Gi.   The Rev. Joseph Gill, S.J. *Former Professor of Byzantine Greek Language and of Byzantine History, Pontifical Oriental Institute, Rome. Author of* The Council of Florence *and others.*
NICHOLAS V (PAPACY) (Micropædia)
PIUS II (Micropædia)

J.Go.   Jacques Godechot. *Emeritus Professor of Modern and Contemporary History; Honorary Dean, Faculty of Letters, University of Toulouse II, France. Author of* Les Révolutions, 1770–1799; Napoléon; *and others.*
NAPOLEON
TALLEYRAND, CHARLES-MAURICE
   DE, PRINCE DE BENEVENT (*in part*)
   (Micropædia)

J.Gol.   Judah Goldin. *Professor of Oriental Studies and Post-Biblical Hebrew Literature, University of Pennsylvania, Philadelphia. Author of* The Fathers According to Rabbi Nathan; *articles on Hillel and Johanan ben Zakkai.*
HILLEL (Micropædia)
JOHANAN BEN ZAKKAI (Micropædia)

J.G.P.   John Graham Pollard. *Deputy Director and Keeper, Department of Coins and Medals, Fitzwilliam Museum, University of Cambridge. Coeditor of* Renaissance Medals from the Samuel H. Kress Collection at the National Gallery.
COINS AND COINAGE (*in part*)

J.Gr.   Jane Gray. *Professor of Biology, University of Oregon, Eugene.*
GEOCHRONOLOGY (*in part*)

J.Gre.   J. Green. *Professor of Zoology, Westfield College, University of London. Author of* The Biology of Estuarine Animals.
CRUSTACEANS (*in part*)

J.Gt.   Jean Guiart. *Professor of Ethnology, Museum of Man, National Museum of Natural History, Paris. Author of* Oceania.
OCEANIC ARTS (*in part*)

J.G.Th.   John Gareth Thomas. *Former Registrar, University of Wales, Cardiff. Coauthor of* Wales.
UNITED KINGDOM (*in part*)

J.G.W.   J. Garth Watson. *Secretary, Institution of Civil Engineers, London, 1967–79.*
ENGINEERING (*in part*)

J.G.W. de V.   Johan G.W. de Vries. *President, Tropimex International, Inc., Miami. Former Consul General of Suriname, New York City.*
GUIANAS, THE (*in part*)

J.H.   Jakob Houtgast (d. 1981). *Associate Professor of Astronomy, Astronomical Institute, Utrecht University, The Netherlands. Coauthor of* Photometric Atlas of the Solar Spectrum.
ECLIPSE, OCCULTATION, AND TRANSIT
   (*in part*)

J.Ha.   Jack Halpern. *Louis Block Distinguished Service Professor of Chemistry, University of Chicago. Author of papers on transition metal ions and complexes.*
CHEMICAL COMPOUNDS (*in part*)

J.H.A.   John H. Adler (d. 1980). *Director, Programming and Budgeting Department, International Bank for Reconstruction and Development, Washington, D.C., 1968–76. Coauthor of* Public Finance in a Developing Country.
UNITED NATIONS (*in part*)

J.-H.B.   Jacques-Henry Bornecque. *Professor of Modern and Contemporary French Literature, University of Paris XIII. Author of* Les Années d'apprentissage d'Alphonse Daudet; Verlaine par lui-même.
DAUDET, ALPHONSE (Micropædia)

J.H.Be.   John Herbert Beynon. *Royal Society Research Professor, University College of Swansea, University of Wales. Author of* Mass Spectrometry and Its Application to Organic Chemistry.
ANALYSIS AND MEASUREMENT,
   PHYSICAL AND CHEMICAL (*in part*)

J.H.Br.   John H. Bryant, M.D. *Special Assistant to the Assistant Secretary for*

Health, U.S. Department of Health and Human Services, Bethesda, Maryland. *Author of* Health and the Developing World.
MEDICINE (*in part*)

J.He.   John Herivel. *Former Reader in the History and Philosophy of Science, Queen's University of Belfast, Northern Ireland. Author of* The Background to Newton's Principia.
HUYGENS, CHRISTIAAN (Micropædia)

J.H.-H.   John Heslop-Harrison. *Royal Society Research Professor, Welsh Plant-Breeding Station, University College of Wales, Aberystwyth, University of Wales. Author of* New Concepts in Flowering Plant Taxonomy *and numerous papers on development in plants.*
GROWTH AND DEVELOPMENT,
   BIOLOGICAL (*in part*)

J.H.Hi.   John Hugh Hill. *Emeritus Professor of Medieval History, University of Houston, Texas. Coauthor of* Raymond IV, Count of Toulouse *and others.*
BOHEMOND I (*in part*) (Micropædia)

J.H.Hy.   John H. Humphrey, M.D. *Emeritus Professor of Immunology, Royal Postgraduate Medical School, University of London. Coeditor of* Advances in Immunology.
IMMUNITY

J.H.J.   John Holmes Jellett (d. 1971). *Civil engineer. Director, Anglo Dutch Dredging Company Ltd., Beaconsfield, England. Docks engineer, Southampton, England, 1946–66.*
PUBLIC WORKS (*in part*)

J.H.K.   Joseph Henry Keenan (d. 1977). *Professor of Mechanical Engineering, Massachusetts Institute of Technology, Cambridge, 1939–66. Author of* Thermodynamics; *coauthor of* Principles of General Thermodynamics.
THERMODYNAMICS, PRINCIPLES OF
   (*in part*)

J.H.L.   J.H. Larson. *Senior Sculpture Conservator, Victoria and Albert Museum, London. Author of* Guan Yin: A Masterpiece Revealed.
ART CONSERVATION AND RESTORATION
   (*in part*)

J.Hm.   James Holderbaum. *Professor of Art, Smith College, Northampton, Massachusetts.*
SCULPTURE, THE HISTORY OF WESTERN
   (*in part*)

J.H.McM.S.   John Hearsey McMillan Salmon. *Marjorie Walter Goodhart Professor of History, Bryn Mawr College, Pennsylvania. Author of* The French Religious Wars in English Political Thought *and others.*
EUROPE (*in part*)

J.Ho.   James Houston. *Chancellor, Regent College, Vancouver, British Columbia. Author of* The Western Mediterranean World.
SPAIN (*in part*)

J.H.Py. John Horace Parry (d. 1982). *Gardiner Professor of Oceanic History and Affairs, Harvard University, 1965– 82. Author of* A Short History of the West Indies *and others.*
WEST INDIES, THE (*in part*)

J.H.R. John H. Rizley. *Consulting engineer. Former Manager, Materials Research and Process Engineering, General Dynamics Corporation, Pomona, California. Coauthor of* Metals Handbook.
INDUSTRIES, EXTRACTION AND
PROCESSING (*in part*)

J.H.Ro. Jonathan H. Robbins, M.D. *Director, Cardiology Section, Leominster Hospital, Massachusetts.*
DISEASE (*in part*)

J.H.Sh. J.H. Shennan. *Professor of European History, University of Lancaster, England. Author of* Government and Society in France, 1461–1661 *and others.*
FRANCE (*in part*)

J.H.S.L. Brigadier Joseph Harold Spence Lacey. *Former Secretary, Institution of Royal Engineers, Chatham, England; former Editor,* Royal Engineers Journal.
WAR, THE THEORY AND CONDUCT OF
(*in part*)

J.H.Sm. The Rev. James Hutchinson Smylie. *Professor of American Church History, Union Theological Seminary, Richmond, Virginia. Editor,* Journal of Presbyterian History.
ADVENTIST (Micropædia)

J.H.-s.S. The Rev. Joseph Hsing-san Shih. *Professor of Missions and Sinology, Pontifical Gregorian University, Rome, Italy. Contributor to* Studia Missionalia.
RICCI, MATTEO (Micropædia)

J.H.St. John Harris Stewart. *Research Geologist, Geological Survey, U.S. Department of the Interior, Menlo Park, California.*
CONTINENTAL LANDFORMS (*in part*)

J.Hud. Joseph Hudnut (d. 1968). *Professor of Architecture and Dean, Graduate School of Design, Harvard University, 1935–53. Author of* Modern Sculpture *and others.*
SCULPTURE, THE HISTORY OF WESTERN
(*in part*)

J.H.W. John Humphreys Whitfield. *Serena Professor Emeritus of Italian Language and Literature, University of Birmingham, England. Author of* Petrarch and the Renascence; A Short History of Italian Literature; *and others.*
PETRARCH (*in part*) (Micropædia)
PIRANDELLO, LUIGI (Micropædia)

J.H.Wa. James Hamilton Ware, Jr. *Professor of Philosophy and Religion; Chairman, Asian Studies Program, Austin College, Sherman, Texas. Author of* Chinese Religions.
CHUANG-TZU (Micropædia)

J.H.We. John H. Wellington. *Emeritus Professor of Geography, University of the Witwatersrand, Johannesburg. Author of* Southern Africa *and others.*
AFRICA (*in part*)

J.H.Wi. John Hoyt Williams. *Professor of History, Indiana State University, Terre Haute. Author of* The Rise and Fall of the Paraguayan Republic, 1800–1870.
PARAGUAY (*in part*)

J.H.Z. James Herbert Zumberge. *President, University of Southern California, Los Angeles. Author of* Elements of Geology *and others.*
CONTINENTAL LANDFORMS (*in part*)
GEOMORPHIC PROCESSES (*in part*)

J.I.D. Jorge I. Domínguez. *Professor of Government; Member, Center for International Affairs, Harvard University. Author of* Cuba: Order and Revolution.
CASTRO, FIDEL (Micropædia)

J.I.M.S. John I.M. Stewart. *Reader in English Literature, University of Oxford, 1969–73. Author of* Rudyard Kipling.
KIPLING, RUDYARD (Micropædia)

J.I.S. James Irvine Smith. *Advocate. Former Sheriff of Glasgow.*
LEGAL SYSTEMS, THE EVOLUTION OF
MODERN WESTERN (*in part*)

J.J. Jules Janick. *Professor of Horticulture, Purdue University, West Lafayette, Indiana. Author of* Horticultural Science.
GARDENING AND HORTICULTURE
(*in part*)

J.-J.C. Jean-Jacques Chevallier. *Emeritus Professor of the History of Political Thought, University of Paris. Member of the Institute of France. Author of* Mirabeau *and others.*
MIRABEAU, HONORÉ-GABRIEL RIQUETI,
COMTE DE (Micropædia)

J.J.C.S. John Jamieson Carswell Smart. *Professor of Philosophy, Institute of Advanced Studies, Australian National University, Canberra. Emeritus Professor of Philosophy, University of Adelaide, Australia. Author of* Philosophy and Scientific Realism *and others; editor of* Problems of Space and Time.
PHILOSOPHICAL SCHOOLS AND
DOCTRINES, WESTERN (*in part*)
TIME (*in part*)

J.-J.H. Jean-Jacques Hatt. *Emeritus Professor of National and Rhenish Antiquities, University of Strasbourg, France. Author of* Histoire de la Gaule romaine *and others.*
FRANCE (*in part*)

J.J.Ha. James J. Haggerty. *Free-lance writer, specializing in aviation and space technology. Editor,* Aerospace Yearbook, 1966–70. *Author of* Apollo: Lunar Landing.
INDUSTRIES, MANUFACTURING (*in part*)

J.J.Ho. John J. Honigmann (d. 1977). *Professor of Anthropology, University*

of North Carolina, 1955–77. Author of World of Man.
AMERICAN INDIANS (*in part*)

J.J.J. Joy Juanita Jackson. *Professor of History and Archivist, Southeastern Louisiana University, Hammond; Director, Center for Regional Studies. Author of* New Orleans in the Gilded Age.
NEW ORLEANS

J.J.Jo. John J. Johnson. *Emeritus Professor of History, Stanford University, California. Author of* Political Change in Latin America *and others.*
CHILE (*in part*)
MEXICO (*in part*)
LATIN AMERICA, THE HISTORY OF
(*in part*)

J.J.L. J.J. Lagowski. *Professor of Chemistry, University of Texas at Austin. Author of* The Chemical Bond.
CHEMICAL ELEMENTS (*in part*)

J.J.M. James J. Murphy. *Professor and Chairman, Department of Rhetoric, University of California, Davis. Editor of* Demosthenes' On the Crown: A Critical Case Study of a Masterpiece of Ancient Oratory.
DEMOSTHENES (Micropædia)

J.J.M.T. Jan Joseph Marie Timmers. *Former Professor of the History of Art, Jan van Eyck Academy, Maastricht, The Netherlands. Author of* Dutch Life and Art; A Handbook of Romanesque Art.
ARCHITECTURE, THE HISTORY OF
WESTERN (*in part*)
PAINTING, THE HISTORY OF WESTERN
(*in part*)
SCULPTURE, THE HISTORY OF WESTERN
(*in part*)

J.J.No. J. Jeremy Noble. *Associate Professor of Music, State University of New York at Buffalo.*
BYRD, WILLIAM (Micropædia)

J.J.P. Jan J. Poelhekke. *Emeritus Professor of Modern History, Catholic University of Nijmegen, The Netherlands. Author of* De Vrede van Munster *and others.*
FREDERICK HENRY, PRINCE OF ORANGE
(Micropædia)
OLDENBARNEVELT, JOHAN VAN
(Micropædia)

J.J.Pa. J.J. Papike. *Director, Institute for the Study of Mineral Deposits, South Dakota School of Mines and Technology, Rapid City. Editor of* Pyroxenes and Amphiboles: Crystal Chemistry and Phase Petrology.
MINERALS AND ROCKS (*in part*)

J.J.Pe. Jaroslav Jan Pelikan. *Sterling Professor of History, Yale University. Author of* The Christian Tradition: A History of the Development of Doctrine; The Riddle of Roman Catholicism; *and others.*
CHRISTIANITY (*in part*)
JESUS (*in part*)
MARY (MOTHER OF JESUS) (*in part*)
(Micropædia)

ROMAN CATHOLICISM (*in part*)

J.J.S. **John J. Stoudt.** *Professor of Philosophy, Kutztown State College, Pennsylvania, 1965–70. Free-lance writer and researcher. Author of* Jacob Boehme: His Life and Thought *and others.*

BÖHME, JAKOB (Micropædia)

J.J.Se. **Jean J. Seznec** (d. 1983). *Marshal Foch Professor of French Literature, University of Oxford, 1950–72. Author of* Marcel Proust et les dieux *and others.*

MICHELET, JULES (Micropædia)

J.J.Sp. **Joseph J. Spengler.** *James B. Duke Professor Emeritus of Economics, Duke University, Durham, North Carolina. Author of* Population Economics *and others.*

RICARDO, DAVID (Micropædia)

J.J.St. **Jane J. Stein.** *Editor,* Business and Health. *Contributing editor,* National Journal. *Author of* Making Medical Choices.

CONSERVATION OF NATURAL RESOURCES (*in part*)

J.J.Z. **J.J. Zuckerman.** *Professor of Chemistry, University of Oklahoma, Norman. Coeditor of* Determination of Organic Structures by Physical Methods.

MOLECULES (*in part*)

J.Ke. **James Kerney, Jr.** *Emeritus Editor, Trenton Times Newspapers, New Jersey.*

UNITED STATES OF AMERICA (*in part*)

J.K.-G. **Joan Kelly-Gadol** (d. 1982). *Professor of History, City College, City University of New York, 1972–82. Author of* Leon Battista Alberti.

ALBERTI, LEON BATTISTA (Micropædia)

J.Ki. **Jay Kinsbruner.** *Professor of History, Queens College, City University of New York. Author of* Bernardo O'Higgins *and others.*

O'HIGGINS, BERNARDO (Micropædia)

J.K.J. **J. Knox Jones, Jr.** *Vice President for Research and Graduate Studies, Texas Tech University, Lubbock. Researcher on the biology of a variety of mammals. Coeditor of* Orders and Families of Recent Mammals of the World.

MAMMALS (*in part*)

J.K.L. **John K. Loosli.** *Emeritus Professor of Animal Nutrition, Cornell University, Ithaca, New York. Visiting Professor of Animal Science, University of Florida, Gainesville. Coauthor of* Animal Nutrition.

FARMING AND AGRICULTURAL TECHNOLOGY (*in part*)

J.K.La. **John Kingsley Lattimer, M.D.** *Professor and Chairman, Department of Urology, Columbia University. Director, Squier Urological Clinic, Presbyterian Hospital, New York City.*

REPRODUCTION AND REPRODUCTIVE SYSTEMS (*in part*)

J.Kr. **Julian Krzyżanowski** (d. 1976). *Professor of the History of Polish Literature, University of Warsaw, 1934–66. President, Mickiewicz Literary Society. Member, Polish Academy of Sciences, Warsaw. Author of* Polish Romantic Literature *and others.*

POLISH LITERATURE (*in part*)

J.K.S. **James Kenneth Sutherland.** *Professor of Organic Chemistry, Victoria University of Manchester.*

MOLECULES (*in part*)

J.K.Sh. **John K.G. Shearman.** *Chairman, Department of Art and Archaeology, Princeton University. Author of* Andrea del Sarto *and others.*

ANDREA DEL SARTO (Micropædia)

J.Ku. **Job Kuijt.** *Professor of Botany, University of Lethbridge, Alberta. Author of* The Biology of Parasitic Flowering Plants.

ANGIOSPERMS (*in part*)

J.K.W. **James King West.** *Professor of Religion and Philosophy, Catawba College, Salisbury, North Carolina. Author of* Introduction to the Old Testament.

SAUL (Micropædia)

J.L. **Joseph Lortz** (d. 1975). *Professor of the History of Religions, Johannes Gutenberg University of Mainz, West Germany. Director, Institute for European History, Mainz. Author of* Die Reformation in Deutschland *and others.*

ROMAN CATHOLICISM (*in part*)

J.La. **Jean Lacouture.** *Former Professor, Institute for Political Studies, University of Paris. Adviser, Éditions du Seuil, Paris. Author of* Ho Chi Minh *and others.*

HO CHI MINH (Micropædia)

J.L.A.F. **Jean L.A. Filliozat** (d. 1982). *Professor of Indian Languages and Literatures, College of France, Paris. Member, Institute of France. Author of* Inde classique *and others.*

HISTORY, THE STUDY OF (*in part*)

J.L.A.-L. **Janet L. Abu-Lughod.** *Professor of Sociology and Urban Affairs, Northwestern University, Evanston, Illinois. Author of* Cairo: 1001 Years of the City Victorious.

CAIRO

J.L.C. **John L. Cornwall.** *Professor of Economics, Dalhousie University, Halifax, Nova Scotia. Author of* Modern Capitalism: Its Growth and Transformation.

ECONOMIC GROWTH AND PLANNING (*in part*)

J.-L.Ca. **Jean-Louis Caussou.** *Former Editor,* Opéra (*journal*), *Paris. Author of* Rossini.

ROSSINI, GIOACCHINO (Micropædia)

J.-L.Ch. **Jean-Léon Charles.** *Professor of Military History, Belgian Royal Military Academy, Brussels. Author of* La Ville de Saint-Trond au Moyen-Âge *and others.*

FARNESE, ALESSANDRO, DUCA DI PARMA E PIACENZA (Micropædia)

J.L.Cl. **James Lowry Clifford** (d. 1978). *Professor of English, Columbia University, 1946–69. Author of* Young Sam Johnson *and others.*

JOHNSON, SAMUEL (*in part*)

J.L.C.-T. **John Leonard Cloudsley-Thompson.** *Professor of Zoology, Birkbeck College, University of London. Author of* Spiders, Scorpions, Centipedes and Mites *and many others.*

ARTHROPODS

J.L.D. **Jack L. Dull.** *Associate Professor of History; Chairman, China Program, School of International Studies, University of Washington, Seattle. Editor of* Han Social Structure.

CHINA (*in part*)

WU TI (HAN DYNASTY) (Micropædia)

J.Le. **Jacques Levron.** *Honorary Chief Curator, Archives of France, Paris. Author of* Saint-Louis ou l'apogée du moyen-âge *and others.*

FRANCE (*in part*)

LOUIS IX (FRANCE) (Micropædia)

J.L.Fi. **John L. Fischer.** *Professor of Anthropology, Tulane University, New Orleans. Coauthor of* The Eastern Carolines.

PACIFIC ISLANDS (*in part*)

J.L.G. **Judson Linsley Gressitt** (d. 1982). *Director, Wau Ecology Institute, Papua New Guinea. Distinguished Chair of Zoology, Bernice P. Bishop Museum, Honolulu. Coauthor of* Chrysomelidae of China; Insects of Campbell Island.

INSECTS (*in part*)

J.L.H. **John Lawrance Howard.** *Head, Magnetic Division, Admiralty Compass Observatory, Slough, England. Author of several compass manuals.*

NAVIGATION (*in part*)

J.L.H.K. **John L.H. Keep.** *Professor of Russian History, University of Toronto. Author of* The Russian Revolution: A Study in Mass Mobilization.

MILYUKOV, PAVEL NIKOLAYEVICH (Micropædia)

NICHOLAS II (RUSSIA) (Micropædia)

J.-L.Hu. **Jean-Louis Huot.** *Professor of Oriental Archaeology, University of Paris I. Author of* Iran.

XERXES I (PERSIA) (Micropædia)

J.L.I.F. **John Lister Illingworth Fennell.** *Professor of Russian, University of Oxford. Author of* Ivan the Great of Moscow *and others.*

IVAN III (*in part*) (Micropædia)

J.L.K. **James L. Kaplan.** *Staff Writer,* Sports Illustrated, *New York City.*

SPORTS, MAJOR TEAM AND INDIVIDUAL (*in part*)

J.L.Ki. **John Louis King, Jr.** *Assistant Professor of History, University of the District of Columbia, Washington, D.C.*

CARVER, GEORGE WASHINGTON (Micropædia)

J.L.M.   John Lawrence Mero.
President, Ocean Resources, Inc., La Jolla, California. Author of The Mineral Resources of the Sea.
OCEANS (*in part*)

J.L.McK.   The Rev. John L. McKenzie, S.J. *Emeritus Professor of Theology, DePaul University, Chicago. Author of* The World of the Judges; Dictionary of the Bible; *and others.*
ROMAN CATHOLICISM (*in part*)
SAMUEL (Micropædia)

J.L.Me.   Julian Louis Meltzer.
Executive Vice Chairman, Yad Chaim Weizmann National Memorial, and Director, Weizmann Archives, Rehovot, Israel, 1966–75. Managing editor of Weizmann Letters and Papers.
WEIZMANN, CHAIM (Micropædia)

J.L.Ra.   John Lang Rawlinson.
Professor of History, Hofstra University, Hempstead, New York. Author of China's Struggle for Naval Development, 1839–1895.
LI HUNG-CHANG (Micropædia)

J.L.Ro.   J. Lewis Robinson. *Professor of Geography, University of British Columbia, Vancouver. Author of* Concepts and Themes in the Regional Geography of Canada *and others.*
NORTH AMERICA (*in part*)

J.L.S.   J.L. Styan. *Franklyn Bliss Snyder Professor of English Literature, Northwestern University, Evanston, Illinois. Author of* The Elements of Drama; Shakespeare's Stagecraft; Chekhov in Performance; *and others.*
LITERATURE, THE ART OF
(*in part*)

J.L.Sa.   Jeffrey L. Sammons. *Professor of German, Yale University. Author of* Heinrich Heine: A Modern Biography.
HEINE, HEINRICH (Micropædia)

J.L.Sp.   Jay L. Spaulding. *Former Visiting Professor of African History, Michigan State University, East Lansing. Coauthor of* Kingdoms of the Sudan.
SUDAN (*in part*)

J.L.T.   John L. Thomas. *Professor of History, Brown University, Providence, Rhode Island. Author of* The Liberator: William Lloyd Garrison.
GARRISON, WILLIAM LLOYD
(Micropædia)

J.L.Te.   John L. Teall (d. 1979). *Professor of History, Mount Holyoke College, South Hadley, Massachusetts, 1968–79. Coauthor of* Atlas of World History.
BYZANTINE EMPIRE, THE HISTORY OF THE (*in part*)

J.Ly.   John Lyman (d. 1977). *Professor of Oceanography; Marine Sciences Coordinator, University of North Carolina at Chapel Hill, 1968–73. Coauthor of* Ocean Sciences.
MAPPING AND SURVEYING (*in part*)

J.Lyo.   John Lyons. *Master of Trinity Hall, University of Cambridge. Professor*

of Linguistics, University of Sussex, Brighton, England, 1976–84. Author of Structural Semantics; Introduction to Theoretical Linguistics; and others.
LINGUISTICS (*in part*)

J.M.   The Rev. John Meyendorff.
Dean, St. Vladimir's Orthodox Theological Seminary, Tuckahoe, New York; Professor of Church History and Patristics, 1959–84. Professor of Byzantine and East European History, Fordham University, New York City. Author of The Orthodox Church, Its Past and Its Role in the World Today.
EASTERN ORTHODOXY

J.Ma.   Joseph Machlis. *Emeritus Professor of Music, Queens College, City University of New York. Author of* The Enjoyment of Music *and others.*
COPLAND, AARON (Micropædia)

J.MacG.   Janet MacGaffey. *Visiting Lecturer in Anthropology, Bryn Mawr College, Pennsylvania.*
KINSHASA (*in part*)

J.M.B.   John Mayston Béchervaise.
Free-lance writer. Director of Studies, Geelong Grammar School, Corio, Victoria, Australia, 1962–72. Leader, Australian National Antarctic Research Wintering Expeditions, Heard Island, 1953–54; Mawson, 1955–56 and 1959–60. Author of Australia: World of Difference *and others.*
AUSTRALIA (*in part*)

J.M.-Br.   Josef Müller-Brockmann.
Graphic designer, lecturer, and writer. IBM European Design Consultant. Author of The Graphic Artist and His Design Problems *and others.*
MARKETING AND MERCHANDISING
(*in part*)

J.M.Bu.   Julian Medforth Budden.
Former External Services Music Organizer, British Broadcasting Corporation, London. Author of The Operas of Verdi.
BEETHOVEN

J.M.C.   James Malcolm Coleman.
Director, Coastal Studies Institute, Louisiana State University, Baton Rouge.
RIVERS (*in part*)

J.M.Ca.   Janet M. Cartwright.
Chairman, Board of Trustees, Black Hawk College, Moline, Illinois.
UNITED STATES OF AMERICA (*in part*)

J.McL.   John McLaughlin. *Political Writer, Trenton Times Newspapers, New Jersey.*
UNITED STATES OF AMERICA (*in part*)

J.M.C.T.   Jocelyn M.C. Toynbee (d. 1985). *Laurence Professor of Classical Archaeology, University of Cambridge, 1951–62. Author of* The Art of the Romans.
PAINTING, THE HISTORY OF WESTERN
(*in part*)
SCULPTURE, THE HISTORY OF WESTERN
(*in part*)

J.M.-D.   Jean Martin-Demézil.
Archivist, Département of Loir-et-Cher, France, 1941–78.
FRANCE (*in part*)

J.M.F.P.   José M.F. Pastor. *Town and regional planning expert. President, Town Planning Council, Buenos Aires. Author of* Urbanismo con planeamiento *and others.*
BUENOS AIRES (*in part*)

J.M.H.   Joan Mervyn Hussey.
Emeritus Professor of History, Royal Holloway College, University of London. Author of The Byzantine World *and others; editor of* Cambridge Medieval History, *vol. 4, parts 1 and 2.*
ALEXIUS I COMNENUS (Micropædia)
BASIL I (BYZANTINE EMPIRE)
   (Micropædia)
BASIL II (BYZANTINE EMPIRE)
   (Micropædia)
GREECE (*in part*)
JUSTINIAN I (*in part*) (Micropædia)

J.M.Hi.   John M. Hills. *Emeritus Professor of Geological Sciences, University of Texas at El Paso. Author of numerous articles on the petroleum and saline deposits of the Permian basin of Texas and New Mexico.*
FOOD PROCESSING (*in part*)

J.Mi.   Jacques Miège. *Professor of Systematic Botany, University of Geneva. Former Director, Conservatory and Botanical Garden, Geneva. Editor of* Candollea and Boissiera.
ANGIOSPERMS (*in part*)

J.Mir.   Jeannette Mirsky. *Visiting Fellow, Department of East Asian Studies, Princeton University, 1970–74. Coauthor of* The World of Eli Whitney.
WHITNEY, ELI (Micropædia)

J.M.J.v.H.   Baron Jean M.J. van Houtte. *Minister of State, Government of Belgium; Minister of Finance, 1950–52, 1958–61; Prime Minister, 1952–54. Emeritus Professor of Fiscal Law, State University of Ghent. Emeritus Professor of Penal Law, State University of Liège.*
TAXATION (*in part*)

J.M.K.   Joseph M. Kitagawa. *Emeritus Professor of the History of Religions and of Far Eastern Languages and Civilizations, University of Chicago; Dean, Divinity School, 1970–80. Author of* Religions of the East *and others.*
BUDDHISM, THE BUDDHA AND (*in part*)

J.M.L.   Jacob M. Landau. *Professor of Political Sciences, Hebrew University of Jerusalem. Author of* Studies in the Arab Theatre and Cinema *and others.*
ISLĀMIC ARTS (*in part*)

J.M.Lu.   Joseph M. Lucker (d. 1980). *Editor in Chief, De Tijd, Amsterdam. Editorial Chairman of* The Netherlands Newsreel, *Polygoon. The Netherlands Delegate to* Unesco.
LOW COUNTRIES, THE (*in part*)

J.M.M.-R.   J.M. Munn-Rankin
(d. 1981). *Lecturer in Near Eastern History, University of Cambridge, 1949–*

81. Contributor to The Cambridge Ancient History.
DARIUS I (Micropædia)

J.Mo.   The Rev. Jacques Monet, S.J.
President, Regis College, Toronto School of Theology, University of Toronto. Author of The Last Cannon Shot: A Study of French-Canadian Nationalism.
LAURIER, SIR WILFRID (Micropædia)

J.M.O.   Jane M. Oppenheimer.
Emeritus Professor of the History of Science, Bryn Mawr College, Pennsylvania. Author of Essays in the History of Embryology and Biology.
BAER, KARL ERNST, RITTER VON, ELDER VON HUTHORN (Micropædia)
DRIESCH, HANS ADOLF EDUARD (Micropædia)

J.M.P.   John M. Prausnitz. *Professor of Chemical Engineering, University of California, Berkeley. Author of* Molecular Thermodynamics of Fluid-Phase Equilibria.
MATTER (*in part*)

J.M.Po.   James M. Powell. *Professor of Medieval History, Syracuse University, New York. Editor of* Innocent III: Vicar of Christ or Lord of the World?
ALEXANDER III (PAPACY) (Micropædia)
GREGORY IX (PAPACY) (Micropædia)

J.M.R.   Johannes M. Renger. *Professor of Assyriology, Free University of Berlin, West Berlin.*
HAMMURABI (Micropædia)

J.-M.-R.N.   Jacques-M.-R. Nicolle (d. 1972). *Director, Laboratory of Isomeric Biochemistry, Collège de France, Paris. Author of* Louis Pasteur, a Master of Scientific Inquiry.
PASTEUR (*in part*)

J.Ms.   Joseph Margolis. *Professor of Philosophy, Temple University, Philadelphia. Author of* Art and Philosophy *and others.*
ARTS, CRITICISM OF THE

J.M.S.   John M. Simpson. *Senior Lecturer in Scottish History, University of Edinburgh.*
UNITED KINGDOM (*in part*)

J.M.T.   James M. Tanner, M.D. *Professor of Child Health and Growth, Institute of Child Health, University of London. Author of* A History of the Study of Human Growth *and others.*
GROWTH AND DEVELOPMENT, BIOLOGICAL (*in part*)

J.Mu.   Joachim Müller. *Professor of German Literature, Friedrich Schiller University of Jena, East Germany.*
LESSING, GOTTHOLD EPHRAIM (*in part*) (Micropædia)

J.M.W.   J. Marvin Weller (d. 1976). *Professor of Invertebrate Paleontology, University of Chicago, 1945–65. One of the first to describe and analyze rhythmic deposits of the central U.S. Author of* Stratigraphic Principles and Practice.
GEOCHRONOLOGY (*in part*)

J.M.W.-H.   John Michael Wallace-Hadrill (d. 1985). *Chichele Professor of Modern History, University of Oxford, 1974–83; Fellow of All Souls College, Oxford. Author of* The Long-Haired Kings *and others.*
CLOVIS I (Micropædia)
GERMANY (*in part*)

J.M.Ws.   James M. Wells. *Former Vice President and Emeritus Custodian, John M. Wing Foundation on the History of Printing, Newberry Library, Chicago. Author of* The Scholar Printers; "Book Typography in the U.S.A." *in* Book Typography in Europe and the U.S.
PRINTING, TYPOGRAPHY, AND PHOTOENGRAVING (*in part*)

J.M.Y.   Joseph M. Yoffey, M.D. *Visiting Professor of Anatomy, Hebrew University of Jerusalem. Emeritus Professor of Anatomy, University of Bristol, England. Coauthor of* Lymphatics, Lymph and the Lymphomyeloid Complex.
CIRCULATION AND CIRCULATORY SYSTEMS (*in part*)

J.M.Yi.   J. Milton Yinger. *Professor of Sociology and Anthropology, Oberlin College, Ohio. Author of* The Scientific Study of Religion *and others.*
RELIGION, SOCIAL ASPECTS OF

J.M.Z.   J.M. Ziman. *Visiting Professor, Department of Social and Economic Studies, Imperial College of Science and Technology, University of London. Henry Overton Wills Professor of Physics, University of Bristol, England, 1976–82. Author of* Electrons and Phonons.
ATOMS (*in part*)

J.Na.   Jerome Namias. *Research Meteorologist, Scripps Institution of Oceanography, University of California at San Diego, La Jolla. Chief, Extended Forecast Division, National Weather Service, National Oceanic and Atmospheric Administration, U.S. Department of Commerce, Washington, D.C., 1941–71. Author of* "30-Day Forecasting," American Meteorological Society Monograph.
OCEANS (*in part*)

J.N.B.   John N. Burrus. *Distinguished University Professor of Sociology, University of Southern Mississippi, Hattiesburg. Author of* Life Opportunities: An Analysis of Differential Mortality in Mississippi *and others.*
UNITED STATES OF AMERICA (*in part*)

J.N.D.   James Norman Davidson (d. 1972). *Gardiner Professor of Biochemistry, University of Glasgow, 1957–72. Author of* Biochemistry of the Nucleic Acids.
BIOCHEMICAL COMPONENTS OF ORGANISMS (*in part*)

J.N.D.K.   The Rev. John N.D. Kelly. *Principal of St. Edmund Hall, Oxford, 1951–79; Lecturer in Patristic Studies, University of Oxford, 1948–76. Author of* Early Christian Creeds; Early Christian Doctrines; *and others.*
CHRISTIANITY (*in part*)

J.N.H.   John N. Hazard. *Nash Professor Emeritus of Law, Columbia University. Author of* Communists and Their Law; Managing Change in the U.S.S.R.; *and others.*
LEGAL SYSTEMS, THE EVOLUTION OF MODERN WESTERN (*in part*)

J.N.M.   Jitendra N. Mohanty. *George Lynn Cross Research Professor of Philosophy, University of Oklahoma, Norman. Author of* Gangeśa's Theory of Truth *and others.*
INDIAN PHILOSOPHY

Jn.S.   Jean Stengers. *Professor of History, Free University of Brussels.*
CENTRAL AFRICA (*in part*)

J.N.S.   Johannes Nicolaas Scheepers. *Professor and Chairman, Department of Geography, Rand Afrikaans University, Johannesburg. Author of* A Cartographic Analysis of the Man-Land Ratio: An Adventure into the Population Geography of the Transvaal.
SOUTH AFRICA (*in part*)

J.O.   The Rev. Joseph Owens, C.SS.R. *Professor of Philosophy, Pontifical Institute of Mediaeval Studies, University of Toronto. Author of* The Doctrine of Being in the Aristotelian Metaphysics.
PHILOSOPHICAL SCHOOLS AND DOCTRINES, WESTERN (*in part*)

J.O.A.   James Oladipo Adejuwon. *Professor of Geography, University of Ife, Ile-Ife, Nigeria.*
KINSHASA (*in part*)

Jo.A.B.   John Arundel Barnes. *Emeritus Professor of Sociology, University of Cambridge. Author of* Three Styles in the Study of Kinship *and others.*
FAMILY AND KINSHIP (*in part*)

Jo.A.W.   John A. Wilson (d. 1976). *Andrew MacLeish Distinguished Service Professor of Egyptology, University of Chicago, 1953–68. Author of* The Burden of Egypt *and others.*
AKHENATON (Micropædia)

Jo.B.   José Bonilla. *Town and regional planning expert. Codirector, Regional and Urban Planning Institute, Buenos Aires, 1952–82.*
BUENOS AIRES (*in part*)

Jo.Be.   John Beresford Bentley. *Managing Editor,* Air-Cushion Vehicles *(bimonthly); Editor,* Hoverfoil News.
TRANSPORTATION (*in part*)

Jo.Bo.   John Boardman. *Lincoln Professor of Classical Art and Archaeology, University of Oxford. Fellow of the British Academy. Author of* Greek Art; The Greeks Overseas; *and others.*
ARCHITECTURE, THE HISTORY OF WESTERN (*in part*)
GRECO-ROMAN CIVILIZATION, CLASSICAL (*in part*)

PAINTING, THE HISTORY OF WESTERN
  (*in part*)
SCULPTURE, THE HISTORY OF WESTERN
  (*in part*)

Jo.Br.   John Bright. *Emeritus Professor
of Hebrew and the Interpretation of
the Old Testament, Union Theological
Seminary, Richmond, Virginia. Author of*
A History of Israel *and others.*
EZRA (Micropædia)

Jo.Bu.   The Rev. John Burnaby (d.
1978). *Regius Professor of Divinity,
University of Cambridge, 1952–58.
Author of* Amor Dei: A Study in the
Religion of St. Augustine *and others.*
AUGUSTINE (*in part*)

Jo.C.   John Cogley (d. 1976). *Senior
Fellow, Center for the Study of
Democratic Institutions, Santa Barbara,
California, 1967–76; Editor,* The Center
Magazine, *1967–74. Author of* The
Layman and the Council *and others.*
JOHN XXIII (PAPACY) (Micropædia)

Jo.Ch.   Joan Chissell. *Assistant Music
Critic,* The Times, *London, 1947–
79. Author of* Chopin; Schumann;
and others.
CHOPIN, FRÉDÉRIC (*in part*)
  (Micropædia)

Jo.E.C.   John Edwards Caswell.
*Emeritus Professor of History, California
State College, Stanislaus, Turlock,
California. Author of* Arctic Frontiers:
U.S. Explorations in the Far North.
HUDSON, HENRY (Micropædia)

Jo.E.S.   Joseph E. Spencer. *Emeritus
Professor of Geography, University of
California, Los Angeles. Coauthor of*
Asia, East by South.
ASIA (*in part*)

J.O.Fl.   Joseph O. Fletcher. *Deputy
Director, Environmental Research
Laboratories, National Oceanic and
Atmospheric Administration, U.S.
Department of Commerce, Boulder,
Colorado.*
OCEANS (*in part*)

Jo.H.   Josef Haekel (deceased).
*Professor of Ethnology; Director,
Institute for Ethnology, University of
Vienna. Author of* Zum Individual- und
Geschlechtstotemismus in Australien.
RELIGIONS AND SPIRITUAL BELIEF,
  SYSTEMS OF (*in part*)

Jo.Ha.   Joseph Hashisaki. *Professor
of Mathematics, Western Washington
University, Bellingham. Coauthor of*
Theory of Arithmetic.
SET THEORY (*in part*)

Jo.Hac.   John Hackett. *Director for
Financial, Fiscal, and Enterprise Affairs,
Organization for Economic Cooperation
and Development, Paris. Author of*
Economic Planning in France.
ECONOMIC GROWTH AND PLANNING
  (*in part*)

Jo.Ho.   John Hospers. *Professor of
Philosophy, University of Southern
California, Los Angeles. Author of*

Understanding the Arts *and others.*
PHILOSOPHIES OF THE BRANCHES OF
  KNOWLEDGE (*in part*)

Jo.L.   Joan Lawson. *Specialist Teacher
of History of Ballet, Classical and
National Dance, Royal Ballet School,
London. Contributor to* The Dancing
Times, *London. Author of* European
Folk Dance *and others.*
POPULAR ARTS (*in part*)

Jo.La.   Jorgen Laessoe. *Professor of
Assyriology, University of Copenhagen.
Author of* People of Ancient Assyria
and others.
SARGON II (ASSYRIA) (Micropædia)

Jo.Ly.   John Lynch. *Professor of
Latin-American History; Director,
Institute of Latin-American Studies,
University of London. Author of* Spain
Under the Habsburgs *and others.*
CHARLES III (SPAIN) (Micropædia)

Jo.M.   John Mitchell. *Free-lance writer
and translator.*
ITALIAN LITERATURE (*in part*)

Jo.Ma.   John Marlowe. *Free-lance
writer. Author of* Anglo-Egyptian
Relations, 1800–1953; Cromer in Egypt.
ZAGHLŪL, SA'D (Micropædia)

J.O'M.B.   John O'M. Bockris.
*Distinguished Professor of Chemistry,
Texas A & M University, College
Station. Coauthor of* Fuel Cells:
Their Electrochemistry; Modern
Electrochemistry.
CHEMICAL REACTIONS (*in part*)

J.O.M.Br.   Jan O.M. Broek (d. 1974).
*Professor of Geography, University of
Minnesota, Minneapolis, 1948–70.*
EAST INDIES, THE (*in part*)

Jo.N.   John Naisbitt. *Chairman of
the Board, Center for Policy Process,
Washington, D.C. Coauthor of* Right
On!: A Documentary of Student Protest
in America.
UNITED STATES OF AMERICA (*in part*)

Jo.P.   John Edgar Prudhoe (d. 1977).
*Senior Lecturer in Drama, Victoria
University of Manchester.*
PAGEANTRY AND SPECTACLE (*in part*)

Jo.Pl.   Sir John Plumb. *Professor of
Modern English History, University of
Cambridge, 1966–74; Master of Christ's
College, Cambridge, 1978–82. Fellow of
the British Academy. Author of* England
in the Eighteenth Century; Sir Robert
Walpole; *and others.*
WALPOLE, ROBERT, 1ST EARL OF
  ORFORD (Micropædia)

Jo.Pr.   Joshua Prawer. *Professor of
History, Hebrew University of Jerusalem.
Editor in Chief, Encyclopaedia Hebraica.
Author of* The Latin Kingdom of
Jerusalem.
JERUSALEM (*in part*)

Jo.R.   John A. Rowe. *Associate
Professor of African History,
Northwestern University, Evanston,
Illinois.*
KENYATTA, JOMO (Micropædia)

J.Or.   Jean Orcibal. *Director of Studies,
Religious Sciences Division, Institute for
Advanced Research, Paris.*
PASCAL (*in part*)

J.O.R.   John O. Rasmussen, Jr.
*Professor of Chemistry, University
of California, Berkeley. Author of*
"Alpha Decay" *in* Alpha-, Beta-, and
Gamma-Ray Spectroscopy *and others.*
ATOMS (*in part*)

Jo.S.   The Rev. John Stacey. *Secretary,
Local Preachers' Office, British
Methodist Church, London; Editor,
Epworth Press. Author of* John Wyclif
and Reform *and others.*
WYCLIFFE, JOHN (Micropædia)

J.O.S.   John Oliver Stoner, Jr.
*Professor of Physics, University of
Arizona, Tucson.*
ANALYSIS AND MEASUREMENT,
  PHYSICAL AND CHEMICAL (*in part*)

Jo.S.R.   John Shipley Rowlinson. *Dr.
Lee's Professor of Chemistry, University
of Oxford. Author of* Liquids and Liquid
Mixtures.
MATTER (*in part*)

Jo.St.   John Strugnell. *Professor of
Christian Origins, Harvard University.*
JOHN THE BAPTIST, SAINT (Micropædia)

J.O'T.   James Joseph O'Toole.
*University Associates' Professor of
Management and Organization,
University of Southern California, Los
Angeles. Author of* Making America
Work.
FUTUROLOGY (*in part*) (Micropædia)

Jo.W.   John H. Wickstead. *Senior
Principal Scientific Officer, Marine
Biological Association of the United
Kingdom, Plymouth, England. Author of*
An Introduction to the Study of Tropical
Plankton *and others.*
CHORDATES (*in part*)

Jö.We.   Jörgen Weibull. *Professor of
History, Göteborg University, Sweden.
Author of* Carl Johan och Norge 1810–
1814 *and others.*
DENMARK (*in part*)
FINLAND (*in part*)
ICELAND (*in part*)
NORWAY (*in part*)
SWEDEN (*in part*)

Jo.W.H.   Sir John Wardle Houlton
(d. 1973). *President of the Swaziland
Senate, 1968–73.*
SOUTHERN AFRICA (*in part*)

Jo.W.P.   John Whitney Pickersgill.
*President, Canadian Transport
Commission, Ottawa, 1967–72. Member,
House of Commons, Parliament of
Canada, 1953–67. Coauthor of* The
Mackenzie King Record.
KING, W.L. MACKENZIE
  (Micropædia)

J.P.   Jan Pen. *Professor of Economics,
State University of Groningen, The
Netherlands. Author of* Income
Distribution *and others.*
ECONOMIC THEORY (*in part*)

J.Pa.   Juan Papadakis. *Member, Academy of Athens. Former Professor, University of Buenos Aires. Author of* Soils of the World.
SOILS

J.P.A.G.   Johannes P.A. Gruijters. *Mayor of Lelystad, The Netherlands. Minister of Housing and Physical Planning, Government of The Netherlands, 1973–77.*
LOW COUNTRIES, THE (*in part*)

J.P.D.   Jean P. Dorst. *Professor, National Museum of Natural History, Paris. Author of* The Migration of Birds *and others.*
BEHAVIOUR, ANIMAL (*in part*)
SOUTH AMERICA (*in part*)

J.P.Do.   Jean P. Doresse. *Research Master, National Centre for Scientific Research, Paris. Author of* Ethiopia *and others.*
EASTERN AFRICA (*in part*)

J.-P.E.   Jean-Pierre Erpelding (d. 1977). *President, Section of Arts and Literature, Grand-Ducal Institute, Luxembourg, 1962–68. Author of* Luxemburg 1000 Jahre.
LOW COUNTRIES, THE (*in part*)

J.P.-H.   Sir John Pope-Hennessy. *Consultative Chairman, Department of European Paintings, Metropolitan Museum of Art, New York City. Professor of Fine Arts, New York University. Author of* Italian Renaissance Sculpture; Cellini; *and others.*
CELLINI, BENVENUTO (Micropædia)

J.P.Hy.   J. Philip Hyatt (d. 1972). *Professor of Old Testament, Vanderbilt University, Nashville, Tennessee, 1944–72. Author of* Jeremiah: Prophet of Courage and Hope *and others.*
JEREMIAH (Micropædia)

J.Piv.   Jean Piveteau. *Professor of Palaeontology, University of Paris. Editor of* Oeuvres philosophiques de Buffon.
BUFFON, GEORGES-LOUIS LECLERC, COMTE DE (Micropædia)

J.P.K.   John P. Kenyon. *Professor of Modern History, University of St. Andrews, Scotland. Author of* The Stuarts.
JAMES II (GREAT BRITAIN) (Micropædia)

J.-p.L.   Jung-pang Lo (d. 1981). *Professor of History, University of California, Davis, 1969–76. Author of* K'ang Yu-wei: A Biography and a Symposium.
CHENG HO (Micropædia)
K'ANG YU-WEI (Micropædia)

J.Pl.   Jaan Puhvel. *Professor of Classics and Indo-European Studies, University of California, Los Angeles.*
HISTORY, THE STUDY OF (*in part*)

J.P.M.   John Preston Moore. *Emeritus Professor of History, Louisiana State University, Baton Rouge. Author of* The Cabildo in Peru Under the Bourbons *and others.*
PERU (*in part*)

J.P.Mo.   J. Philip Mosley. *Lecturer in Humanities, Glasgow College of Technology.*
BELGIAN LITERATURE (*in part*)

J.P.M.S.   J. Patricia Morgan Swenson. *Free-lance writer and editor. Author of* Hawaii: A Book to Begin On *and others.*
UNITED STATES OF AMERICA (*in part*)

J.P.P.   Justo Pastor Prieto (d. 1982). *Former Minister of Foreign Affairs, Paraguay, 1939; Minister of Justice and Public Education, 1931–36. Rector, National University of Asunción, 1929–31. Author of* Paraguay, la provincia gigante de las Indias *and others.*
PARAGUAY (*in part*)

J.P.Pl.   John P. Plamenatz (d. 1975). *Chichele Professor of Social and Political Theory, University of Oxford, 1967–75; Fellow of All Souls College, Oxford. Author of* The English Utilitarians.
BENTHAM, JEREMY (Micropædia)

J.Pr.   Jean Prevost. *Professor, Laboratory of Ecology and General Biology, University of Limoges, France. Researcher on the biology of Antarctic seabirds, especially penguins. Author of* Le Manchot empereur; *coeditor of* Biologie antarctique.
BIRDS (*in part*)

J.P.R.   Jean Pierre Rouch. *Director of Research, National Centre for Scientific Research, Paris. Author of* Les Songhay.
MUḤAMMAD I ASKIA (Micropædia)

J.P.Ri.   Joseph P. Riva, Jr. *Specialist in Earth Sciences (geologist), Congressional Research Service, Library of Congress, Washington, D.C. Author of* World Petroleum Resources and Reserves.
FUELS, FOSSIL (*in part*)

J.Pro.   James Alan Proudlove. *Emeritus Professor of Transport Studies, University of Liverpool. Author of* Roads.
UNITED KINGDOM (*in part*)

J.P.S.   James Patrick Saville. *Former Manager, Information Services, The Metals Society, London.*
BESSEMER, SIR HENRY (Micropædia)

J.P.-V.   Javier Pulgar-Vidal. *Emeritus Professor of Geography, National University of San Marcos, Lima. Author of* Geografía del Perú: Las ocho regiones naturales *and others.*
PERU (*in part*)

J.P.V.D.B.   John P.V. Dacre Balsdon (d. 1977). *Fellow of Exeter College, University of Oxford, 1928–69. Author of* Life and Leisure in Ancient Rome.
CICERO, MARCUS TULLIUS (*in part*) (Micropædia)
GRECO-ROMAN CIVILIZATION, CLASSICAL (*in part*)
MARIUS, GAIUS (Micropædia)

J.R.A.   John R. Abrahams. *Vice President, TelSys Consultants Group, Inc., Toronto. Author of* Information

Processing in Society; *coauthor of* Semi-Conductor Circuits; *and others.*
ELECTRONICS (*in part*)

J.R.Al.   John Richard Alden. *James B. Duke Professor Emeritus of History, Duke University, Durham, North Carolina. Author of* A History of the American Revolution.
ADAMS, SAMUEL (Micropædia)

J.R.B.   James R. Brandon. *Professor of Drama and Theatre, University of Hawaii, Honolulu. Author of* Kabuki: Five Classic Plays; Theatre in Southeast Asia; *and others.*
EAST ASIAN ARTS (*in part*)
SOUTHEAST ASIAN ARTS (*in part*)

J.R.Br.   John Russell Brown. *Professor of English, University of Sussex, Brighton, England. Author of* Shakespeare's Dramatic Style; *and others.*
SHAKESPEARE (*in part*)

J.R.C.   John R. Campbell. *Dean, College of Agriculture, University of Illinois, Urbana. Coauthor of* The Science of Animals that Serve Humanity.
AGRICULTURAL SCIENCES (*in part*)

J.R.G.   James R. Giles. *Professor of English, Northern Illinois University, De Kalb. Author of* Irwin Shaw *and others.*
AMERICAN LITERATURE (*in part*)

J.R.H.   J.R. Heirtzler. *Senior Scientist, Department of Geology and Geophysics, Woods Hole Oceanographic Institution, Massachusetts.*
MINERALS AND ROCKS (*in part*)

J.R.Ha.   John R. Hagely. *Projects Manager, Battelle-Columbus Laboratories, Columbus, Ohio.*
BUILDING CONSTRUCTION (*in part*)

J.R.J.   Jay Richard Judson. *William R. Kenan, Jr., Professor of Art History, University of North Carolina at Chapel Hill. Author of* Catalogue of Paintings: Rembrandt After Three Hundred Years *and others.*
REMBRANDT

J.R.K.   John Robert Kell (d. 1983). *Consulting engineer. Author of* Heating and Air-Conditioning of Buildings.
BUILDING CONSTRUCTION (*in part*)

J.R.Kr.   John Richard Krueger. *Former Professor of Uralic and Altaic Studies, Indiana University, Bloomington. Coauthor of* Introduction to Classical Mongolian.
CENTRAL ASIAN ARTS (*in part*)

J.R.L.H.   J.R.L. Highfield. *Fellow of Merton College, Oxford; Lecturer in Modern History, University of Oxford. Editor of* Spain in the Fifteenth Century; *coeditor of* Europe in the Middle Ages.
EDWARD III (ENGLAND AND GREAT BRITAIN) (*in part*) (Micropædia)
ISABELLA I (SPAIN) (Micropædia)

J.R.M.   John Richard Meyer. *Associate Professor of Education, University of Windsor, Ontario.*
BERNARD OF CLAIRVAUX, SAINT (Micropædia)

J.R.Me.   José Ramón Medina. *Poet and writer. Professor, Faculty of Law, Central University of Venezuela, Caracas. Former Attorney General of Venezuela. Author of* Ochenta años de literatura venezolana *and others.*
CARACAS (in part)

J.R.Mn.   J. Ronald Munson. *Professor of Philosophy, University of Missouri, St. Louis. Editor of* Man and Nature: Philosophical Issues in Biology.
PHILOSOPHIES OF THE BRANCHES OF KNOWLEDGE (in part)

J.R.M.R.   J. Roberto Moncada R. *President, MONDAI Engineers (engineering and architectural consultants), Tegucigalpa, Honduras. Director General of the National Geographic Institute, Tegucigalpa, 1969–71.*
CENTRAL AMERICA (in part)

J.R.N.   J.R. Napier. *Director, Unit of Primate Biology, Birkbeck College, University of London. Researcher on locomotion of primates. Coauthor of* A Handbook of Living Primates.
MAMMALS (in part)

J.Ro.   Joan Violet Robinson (d. 1983). *Professor of Economics, University of Cambridge, 1965–71. Author of* Theory of Imperfect Competition *and others.*
MARKETS (in part)

J.R.P.   John R. Pierce. *Emeritus Professor of Engineering, California Institute of Technology, Pasadena. Author of* The Beginnings of Satellite Communications *and others.*
TELECOMMUNICATIONS SYSTEMS (in part)

J.R.-S.   John Graham Royde-Smith. *Former Associate Editor, History, Encyclopædia Britannica, London.*
BOURBON, THE HOUSE OF (in part)
HABSBURG, THE HOUSE OF
INTERNATIONAL RELATIONS, 20TH-CENTURY (in part)

J.R.Sp.   John R. Spencer. *Professor of Art, Duke University, Durham, North Carolina. Editor of L.B. Alberti's* On Painting.
CIMABUE (Micropædia)
PAINTING, THE HISTORY OF WESTERN (in part)
SCULPTURE, THE HISTORY OF WESTERN (in part)

J.R.Su.   James R. Sutherland. *Emeritus Professor of Modern English Literature, University of London. Author of* Defoe; English Literature of the Late Seventeenth Century.
DRYDEN, JOHN (in part) (Micropædia)

J.R.T.   John Russell Taylor. *Art Critic,* The Times *(London); Film Critic, 1962–73. Professor of Cinema, University of Southern California, Los Angeles, 1972–*

78. *Author of* Cinema Eye, Cinema Ear: Some Key Film-Makers of the Sixties *and others.*
ANTONIONI, MICHELANGELO (Micropædia)
BERGMAN, INGMAR (Micropædia)

J.R.T.P.   John Richard Thornhill Pollard. *Former Senior Lecturer in Classics, University College of North Wales, University of Wales, Bangor. Author of* Birds in Greek Life and Myth; Helen of Troy; *and others.*
EUROPEAN RELIGIONS, ANCIENT (in part)

J.R.V.P.   J.R.V. Prescott. *Reader in Geography, University of Melbourne. Author of* Frontiers and Boundaries.
AUSTRALIA (in part)
MELBOURNE

J.S.   John Scarne (d. 1985). *President, John Scarne Games, Inc., North Bergen, New Jersey. Authority on gambling. Author of* Scarne's Complete Guide to Gambling; Scarne on Dice; *and others.*
ROULETTE (Micropædia)

J.S.A.   James Stephen Atherton (deceased). *Lecturer in English Literature, Wigan and District Mining and Technical College, England. Author of* The Books at the Wake.
JOYCE, JAMES (in part) (Micropædia)

J.S.Ac.   James S. Ackerman. *Arthur Kingsley Porter Professor of Fine Arts, Harvard University. Author of* The Architecture of Michelangelo; Palladio.
ARCHITECTURE, THE ART OF (in part)

J.S.B.   Joe S. Bain. *Emeritus Professor of Economics, University of California, Berkeley. Author of* Industrial Organization; Barriers to New Competition.
ECONOMIC THEORY (in part)

J.S.Bo.   John S. Bowman. *Free-lance writer and editor. Editor, "Monuments of Civilization" Series. Author of* Traveler's Guide to Crete.
GREECE (in part)

J.S.Br.   The Rev. Joseph Stanislaus Brusher, S.J. (d. 1972). *Professor of History, University of San Francisco, 1968–72. Author of* Popes Through the Ages.
GREGORY VII, SAINT (PAPACY) (Micropædia)

J.Sc.   Jefim H. Schirmann (d. 1981). *Professor of Hebrew Literature, Hebrew University of Jerusalem. Member, Israel National Academy of Sciences. Author of* The Hebrew Poetry in Spain and Provence.
JUDAH HA-LEVI (Micropædia)

J.S.D.   John S. Driscoll. *Executive Editor, Boston Globe.*
UNITED STATES OF AMERICA (in part)

J.Se.   Jakob Seibert. *Professor of Ancient History, Ludwig Maximilian University of Munich. Author of* Historische Beiträge zu den dynastischen

Verbindungen in hellenistischer Zeit *and others.*
SELEUCUS I NICATOR (Micropædia)

J.S.E.   John S. Ezell. *David Ross Boyd Professor of History; Curator, Western History Collections, University of Oklahoma, Norman. Author of* The South Since 1865.
UNITED STATES OF AMERICA (in part)

J.S.F.   Jeffrey S. Fedan. *Research Pharmacologist, National Institute for Occupational Safety and Health, Morgantown, West Virginia. Adjunct Associate Professor of Pharmacology and Toxicology, West Virginia University, Morgantown.*
DRUGS AND DRUG ACTION (in part)

J.S.G.W.   John Stuart Gladstone Wilson. *Emeritus Professor of Economics and Commerce, University of Hull, England. Author of* Banking Policy and Structure.
BANKS AND BANKING

J.Sh.   Jose Shercliff. *Lisbon Correspondent of* The Times, *(London), and the British Broadcasting Corporation.*
PORTUGAL (in part)

J.Shi.   James Shiel. *Former Reader in the History of Hellenic Thought, University of Sussex, Brighton, England. Author of* Greek Thought and the Rise of Christianity.
BOETHIUS, ANICIUS MANLIUS SEVERINUS (Micropædia)

J.Si.   Josef Silverstein. *Professor of Political Science, Rutgers University, New Brunswick, New Jersey. Author of* Burma: Military Rule and the Politics of Stagnation *and others.*
SOUTHEAST ASIA, MAINLAND (in part)

J.S.M.   John S. Mathis. *Professor of Astronomy, University of Wisconsin, Madison.*
NEBULA

J.S.Ma.   John S. Marshall (d. 1979). *Professor of Philosophy, University of the South, Sewanee, Tennessee, 1946–68. Author of* Hooker's Polity in Modern English; Hooker and the Anglican Tradition.
HOOKER, RICHARD (Micropædia)

J.S.McE.   The Rev. James Stevenson McEwen. *Professor of Church History, University of Aberdeen, Scotland, 1958–77. Author of* The Faith of John Knox.
KNOX, JOHN (in part) (Micropædia)

J.Sn.   Joshua Stern. *Lecturer in Physics, University of Maryland, College Park. Associate Editor,* Review of Scientific Instruments.
MEASUREMENT AND OBSERVATION, PRINCIPLES, METHODS, AND INSTRUMENTS OF (in part)

J.So.   Jacob Solinger. *Management consultant. Author of* Apparel Manufacturing Analysis; Apparel Manufacturing Handbook.
INDUSTRIES, MANUFACTURING (in part)

J.S.O.   Jerry S. Olson. *Senior Ecologist, Environmental Sciences Division, Oak Ridge National Laboratory, Tennessee. Professor of Botany, University of Tennessee, Knoxville. Editor of* Ecological Studies.

ECOSYSTEMS (*in part*)

J.S.R.   John S. Ryland. *Professor of Zoology, University College of Swansea, University of Wales. Author of* Bryozoans.

MOSS ANIMALS

J.S.Ro.   James Scott Robson, M.D. *Professor of Medicine, University of Edinburgh; Consultant Physician, Edinburgh Royal Infirmary. Author of numerous articles on acid-base and electrolyte metabolism and renal disorders.*

TISSUES AND FLUIDS (*in part*)

J.S.S.   John Stanley Sawyer. *Former Director of Research, Meteorological Office, Bracknell, England. Author of* The Ways of the Weather.

CLIMATE AND WEATHER (*in part*)

J.St.   James Stevenson. *Emeritus Fellow of Downing College, Cambridge; formerly University Lecturer in Divinity, University of Cambridge. Editor of* A New Eusebius; Creeds, Councils, and Controversies.

EUSEBIUS OF CAESAREA (Micropædia)

J.Ste.   Johannes Steudel (d. 1973). *Professor of the History of Medicine, Rhenish Friedrich Wilhelm University of Bonn.*

MÜLLER, JOHANNES PETER (Micropædia)

J.Su.   John Sutton. *Emeritus Professor of Geology, Royal School of Mines, Imperial College of Science and Technology, University of London.*

GEOCHRONOLOGY (*in part*)

J. Sum.   Sir John Summerson. *Curator, Sir John Soane's House and Museum, London. Author of* Inigo Jones; Sir Christopher Wren; Architecture in Britain, 1530–1830; *and others.*

JONES, INIGO (Micropædia)
WREN, SIR CHRISTOPHER (*in part*) (Micropædia)

J.S.W.   John Steven Watson. *Principal and Vice Chancellor, University of St. Andrews, Scotland. Author of* The Reign of George III.

GEORGE III (GREAT BRITAIN) (Micropædia)

J.T.B.   Joseph T. Butler. *Curator, Sleepy Hollow Restorations, Tarrytown, New York. Adjunct Associate Professor of Architecture, Columbia University. Author of* American Antiques 1800–1900 *and others.*

DECORATIVE ARTS AND FURNISHINGS (*in part*)

J.T.Bo.   John Tyler Bonner. *George M. Moffett Professor of Biology, Princeton University. Author of* Size and Cycle *and others.*

REPRODUCTION AND REPRODUCTIVE SYSTEMS (*in part*)

J.T.C.   J. Terry Copp. *Professor of History, Wilfrid Laurier University, Waterloo, Ontario. Coauthor of* Confederation: 1867 *and others.*

BORDEN, SIR ROBERT (Micropædia)

J.T.C.L.   James T.C. Liu. *Professor of History and of East Asian Studies, Princeton University. Author of* Reform in Sung China *and others.*

CHINA (*in part*)

J.T.G.O.   Jan Theodoor Gerard Overbeek. *Emeritus Professor of Physical Chemistry, Utrecht University, The Netherlands. Coauthor of* Theory of the Stability of Lyophobic Colloids.

MATTER (*in part*)

J.Th.   John Patrick Thomas. *Singer and composer. Former Assistant Professor of Music, State University of New York at Buffalo.*

MUSIC, THE ART OF (*in part*)

J.T.H.   James T. Harris. *Former Regional Representative for West Africa (Lagos, Nigeria) for the African-American Institute, New York City.*

UNITED STATES OF AMERICA (*in part*)

J.T.M.   Joe T. Marshall. *Zoologist, National Fish and Wildlife Laboratory, National Museum of Natural History, Washington, D.C. Coauthor of* Birds of Arizona.

BIRDS (*in part*)

J.Tn.   John Thompson. *Professor of Geography, University of Illinois, Urbana.*

CENTRAL AMERICA (*in part*)

J.T.Ne.   James T. Neal. *Member of the technical staff, Sandia National Laboratories, Albuquerque, New Mexico. An authority on the geology, geomorphology, and hydrology of playas.*

CONTINENTAL LANDFORMS (*in part*)

J.T.P.   James T. Peterson. *Director, Geophysical Monitoring for Climatic Change, National Oceanic and Atmospheric Administration, Boulder, Colorado.*

CLIMATE AND WEATHER (*in part*)

J.T.Pa.   John T. Paoletti. *Professor of Art History, Wesleyan University, Middletown, Connecticut.*

UCCELLO, PAOLO (Micropædia)

J.T.Sc.   Jacob T. Schwartz. *Chairman, Department of Computer Science, Courant Institute of Mathematical Sciences, New York University, New York City. Author of* Mathematical Methods in Analytical Economics; *coauthor of* Linear Operators.

ANALYSIS (IN MATHEMATICS) (*in part*)

J.T.W.   J. Tuzo Wilson. *Director General, Ontario Science Centre, Don Mills. A leading advocate of continental drift and sea floor spreading.*

OCEANS (*in part*)

J.U.   Jürgen Untermann. *Professor of Comparative Philology, University of Cologne. Author of* Die venetischen Personennamen.

LANGUAGES OF THE WORLD (*in part*)

Ju.H.   Julius S. Held. *Emeritus Professor of Art History, Barnard College, Columbia University. Author of* Flemish Painting *and others.*

VAN DYCK, SIR ANTHONY (Micropædia)

Ju.S.   Julius Stone (d. 1985). *Professor of Law, University of New South Wales, Kensington, Australia. Distinguished Professor of Jurisprudence and International Law, University of California Hastings College of Law, San Francisco. Challis Professor of Jurisprudence and International Law, University of Sydney, Australia, 1942–72. Author of* The Province and Function of Law *and others.*

PHILOSOPHIES OF THE BRANCHES OF KNOWLEDGE (*in part*)

Ju.S.B.   Julia S. Berrall. *Free-lance lecturer and writer. Author of* Flowers and Table Settings; The Garden: An Illustrated History; A History of Flower Arrangement.

DECORATIVE ARTS AND FURNISHINGS (*in part*)

J.V.   John Vaizey, Baron Vaizey (d. 1984). *Professor of Economics, Brunel University, Uxbridge, England, 1966–82. Author of* The Economics of Education *and others.*

EDUCATION, SOCIAL AND ECONOMIC ASPECTS OF (*in part*)

J.v.D.   Jacques van Doorn. *Professor of Sociology, University of Rotterdam. Editor of* Armed Forces and Society.

WAR, THE THEORY AND CONDUCT OF (*in part*)

J.v.E.   Josef van Ess. *Professor of Islamic Studies and Semitic Languages, Eberhard Karl University of Tübingen, West Germany. Author of* Die Erkenntnislehre des 'Aḍudaddīn al-Īcī.

MUḤĀSIBĪ, AL- (Micropædia)

J.V.G.   Juan Vernet Ginés. *Professor of Arabic, University of Barcelona. Author of* Los Musulmanes españoles *and others.*

SPAIN (*in part*)

J.v.H.   Jan S.F. van Hoogstraten. *Chief of Mission, Intergovernmental Committee for Migration, Bonn. Former Church World Service Director, Africa Department, National Council of the Churches of Christ in the U.S.A.*

CENTRAL AFRICA (*in part*)

J.Vi.   Jean Vidalenc. *Former Professor of Contemporary History, University of Rouen, France. Author of* Louis Blanc; La Restauration (1814–1830); *and others.*

BLANC, LOUIS (Micropædia)
MARAT, JEAN-PAUL (Micropædia)
THIERS, ADOLPHE (Micropædia)

J.V.K.   John V. Killheffer. *Associate Editor,* Science, *Encyclopædia Britannica, Chicago.*

CHEMICAL COMPOUNDS (*in part*)

INDUSTRIES, CHEMICAL PROCESS
(*in part*)

J.V.M.   John V. Murra. *Professor of Anthropology, Cornell University, Ithaca, New York. Author of* The Economic Organization of the Inka State *and others.*

AMERICAN INDIANS (*in part*)

J.V.N.   Joseph Veach Noble. *Director, Museum of the City of New York, New York City. Author of* The Techniques of Painted Attic Pottery; *coauthor of* An Inquiry into the Forgery of the Etruscan Terracotta Warriors in the Metropolitan Museum of Art.

ARTS, PRACTICE AND PROFESSION OF
THE (*in part*)

J.V.   Jack Vowles. *Lecturer in Political Studies, University of Auckland, New Zealand.*

NEW ZEALAND (*in part*)

J.V.R.   Jan L.R. Van Roey. *Honorary Archivist, City Archives, Antwerp.*

ANTWERP

J.V.S.   Joseph V. Smith. *Louis Block Professor of Physical Sciences, University of Chicago. An authority on phase equilibria in mineral systems and on crystal structure.*

MINERALS AND ROCKS (*in part*)

J.V.W.   James V. Warren, M.D. *Professor of Medicine, Ohio State University, Columbus. Contributor to* Textbook of Medicine; The Heart.

CIRCULATION AND CIRCULATORY
SYSTEMS (*in part*)

J.W.B.   Jesse W. Beams (d. 1977). *Professor of Physics, University of Virginia, Charlottesville, 1930–69. Coauthor of* Tests of the Theory of Isotope Separation by Centrifuging.

GRAVITATION (*in part*)

J.W.Ba.   John Walton Barker, Jr. *Professor of History, University of Wisconsin, Madison. Author of* Justinian and the Later Roman Empire *and others.*

BELISARIUS (Micropædia)

J.W.C.   John W. Caughey. *Emeritus Professor of American History, University of California, Los Angeles. Author of* McGillivray of the Creeks.

MCGILLIVRAY, ALEXANDER
(Micropædia)

J.W.Du.   J. Wyatt Durham. *Emeritus Professor of Paleontology; Curator of Mesozoic and Cenozoic Invertebrates, University of California, Berkeley.*

GEOCHRONOLOGY (*in part*)

J.We.   Jac Weller. *Weapons engineer, military historian, and free-lance writer. Author of* Weapons and Tactics; *coauthor of* Firearms Investigation, Identification, and Evidence; *and others.*

WAR, THE TECHNOLOGY OF (*in part*)

J.W.F.   J.W. Fiegenbaum. *Professor of Religion, Mount Holyoke College, South*

Hadley, Massachusetts.

ḤALLĀJ, AL- (Micropædia)

IBN ḤAZM (Micropædia)

J.W.Ha.   John W. Harbaugh. *Professor of Geology, Stanford University, California. Coauthor of* Computer Simulation in Geology.

EARTH SCIENCES, THE (*in part*)

J.W.Hu.   John W. Huffman, M.D. *Emeritus Professor of Obstetrics and Gynecology, Medical School, Northwestern University, Chicago. Author of* Gynecology and Obstetrics.

REPRODUCTION AND REPRODUCTIVE
SYSTEMS (*in part*)

J.Wi.   J. Williams. *Director of Nuclear Research, Atomic Energy Research Establishment, Harwell, England.*

INDUSTRIES, EXTRACTION AND
PROCESSING (*in part*)

J.W.L.   Justin W. Leonard (d. 1975). *Professor of Natural Resources and of Zoology; Research Associate, Museum of Zoology, University of Michigan, Ann Arbor, 1964–75. Coauthor of* Mayflies of Michigan Trout Streams.

INSECTS (*in part*)

J.W.Le.   John Wilson Lewis. *William Haas Professor of Chinese Politics, Stanford University, California. Author of* Leadership in Communist China *and others.*

CHINA (*in part*)

TAIWAN (*in part*)

J.W.McF.   James Walter McFarlane. *Professorial Fellow in European Literature, University of East Anglia, Norwich, England. Author of* Ibsen and the Temper of Norwegian Literature; *editor and translator of* The Oxford Ibsen.

IBSEN, HENRIK (Micropædia)

SCANDINAVIAN LITERATURE
(*in part*)

J.Wo.   John Woodward. *Former Keeper, Birmingham City Museum and Art Gallery, Birmingham, England. Author of* A Picture History of British Painting.

REYNOLDS, SIR JOSHUA (Micropædia)

J.W.O.   John W. Osborne. *Professor of History, Rutgers University, New Brunswick, New Jersey. Author of* William Cobbett: His Thoughts and His Times *and others.*

COBBETT, WILLIAM (Micropædia)

J.W.R.   James Wilmot Rowe. *Executive Director, New Zealand Employers' Federation, Wellington. Coauthor of* New Zealand.

NEW ZEALAND (*in part*)

J.W.R.T.   John W.R. Taylor. *Editor,* Jane's All the World's Aircraft. *Author of* Combat Aircraft of the World; History of Aerial Warfare; *and others.*

WAR, THE TECHNOLOGY OF (*in part*)

J.W.T.   John Walford Todd, M.D. *Former Consultant Physician, Frimley*

Park and Farnham Hospitals, Farnham, England. Author of Health and Humanity.

MEDICINE (*in part*)

J.W.Th.   John W. Thieret. *Professor of Botany, Northern Kentucky University, Highland Heights.*

ANGIOSPERMS (*in part*)

GYMNOSPERMS (*in part*)

J.W.W.   James Wreford Watson. *Emeritus Professor of Geography, University of Edinburgh. Author of* North America: Its Countries and Regions *and others.*

NORTH AMERICA (*in part*)

J.W.Wr.   John Wilfrid Wright. *Land Surveyor; free-lance writer and lecturer. Author of* Ground and Air Survey for Field Scientists.

MAPPING AND SURVEYING (*in part*)

J.Y.S.   John Y. Simon. *Professor of History, Southern Illinois University, Carbondale. Executive Director, Ulysses S. Grant Association. Editor of* The Papers of Ulysses S. Grant.

GRANT, ULYSSES S. (Micropædia)

J.Z.S.   Jonathan Zittell Smith. *Robert O. Anderson Distinguished Service Professor of the Humanities, University of Chicago.*

EUROPEAN RELIGIONS, ANCIENT (*in part*)

MYTH AND MYTHOLOGY (*in part*)

J.Z.V.   Josefina Zoraida Vázquez. *Professor of History, The College of Mexico, Mexico City. Author of* Nacionalismo y educación en México.

EDUCATION, HISTORY OF (*in part*)

K.A.B.   Kenneth A. Ballhatchet. *Professor of the History of South Asia, School of Oriental and African Studies, University of London. Author of* Race, Sex and Class under the Raj.

AKBAR (Micropædia)

DALHOUSIE, JAMES ANDREW BROUN
RAMSAY, MARQUESS AND 10TH
EARL OF (Micropædia)

K.A.H.   Keith Arnold Hitchins. *Professor of History, University of Illinois, Urbana.*

UNION OF SOVIET SOCIALIST REPUBLICS
(*in part*)

K.A.J.W.   Keith Arthur John Wise. *Entomologist, Auckland Institute and Museum, New Zealand.*

INSECTS (*in part*)

Ka.La.   Karl Lavrencic. *Journalist.*

YUGOSLAVIA (*in part*)

K.A.M.   Kazimieras Antano Meškauskas. *Member and Chief Learned Secretary of the Presidium, Lithuanian S.S.R. Academy of Sciences. Author of* Soviet Lithuania: An Economic Survey *and others.*

UNION OF SOVIET SOCIALIST REPUBLICS
(*in part*)

K.A.R.K.   Kenneth A.R. Kennedy. *Professor of Ecology, Anthropology, and Asian Studies, Cornell University, Ithaca,*

New York. Field researcher on the physical anthropology of early man in South Asia. Author of Neanderthal Man *and others.*

ASIA (*in part*)

K.A.S.   Kaj Aa. Strand. *Scientific Director, U.S. Naval Observatory, Washington, D.C., 1963–77. Editor of* Basic Astronomical Data; Vistas in Astronomy.

PARALLAX (*in part*) (Micropædia)

K.A.St.   Kaydon Al Stanzione. *Senior Engineer, Advanced Vehicle Aerodynamics, Boeing Vertol Company, Philadelphia.*

ENGINEERING (*in part*)

K.A.W.C.   Keith A.W. Crook. *Reader in Geology, Australian National University, Canberra. Coauthor of* Geological Evolution of Australia and New Zealand.

MINERALS AND ROCKS (*in part*)

K.B.   Knut Bergsland. *Emeritus Professor of Finno-Ugric Languages, University of Oslo. Scholar who proved the connection between the Eskimo and Aleut languages. Author of* "Aleut Dialects of Atka and Attu" *in* Transactions of the American Philosophical Society.

LANGUAGES OF THE WORLD (*in part*)

K.Ba.   Kurt Badt (deceased). *Art historian. Author of* Die Kunst des Nicolas Poussin; John Constable's Clouds; The Art of Cézanne; *and others.*

POUSSIN, NICOLAS (Micropædia)

K.B.D.   Kwamina Busumafi Dickson. *Vice-Chancellor, University of Cape Coast, Ghana. Author of* A Historical Geography of Ghana.

AFRICA (*in part*)

K.Be.   Karl Beckson. *Professor of English, Brooklyn College, City University of New York. Editor of* Aesthetes and Decadents of the 1890's; Oscar Wilde: The Critical Heritage.

WILDE, OSCAR (Micropædia)

K.-b.L.   Ki-baik Lee. *Professor of History, Sogang University, Seoul, Korea. Author of* Hankuksa sillon.

KOREA (*in part*)

K.C.B.   Kevin Charles Beck. *Associate Professor of Geophysical Sciences, Georgia Institute of Technology, Atlanta. Coauthor of* Clay Water Diagenesis During Burial: How Mud Becomes Gneiss.

MINERALS AND ROCKS (*in part*)

K.C.E.   Kenneth Charles Edwards (d. 1982). *Professor of Geography, University of Nottingham, England, 1948–70.*

LOW COUNTRIES, THE (*in part*)

K.-c.H.   Kung-chuan Hsiao (d. 1981). *Professor of the History of Chinese Thought, University of Washington, Seattle, 1959–68. Author of* Rural China: Imperial Control in the 19th Century.

HAN-FEI-TZU (Micropædia)

K.C.P.   Kenneth C. Parkes. *Curator of Birds, Carnegie Museum of Natural History, Pittsburgh, Pennsylvania. Author of numerous articles on the biology and systematics of birds.*

BIRDS (*in part*)

K.-D.G.   Karl-Dietrich Gundermann. *Professor of Organic Chemistry, Technical University of Clausthal, West Germany. Author of* Chemilumineszenz organischer Verbindungen.

LIGHT (*in part*)

K.E.Bo.   Kenneth E. Boulding. *Distinguished Professor Emeritus of Economics, University of Colorado, Boulder. Author of* Economics as a Science; Ecodynamics: A New Theory of Societal Evolution.

ECONOMIC THEORY (*in part*)

K.E.H.   Kenneth E. Hofer, Jr. *Vice President, L. J. Broutman and Associates, Ltd., Chicago. Former Senior Research Engineer, Materials Engineering, Illinois Institute of Technology Research Institute, Chicago.*

ANALYSIS AND MEASUREMENT, PHYSICAL AND CHEMICAL (*in part*)

K.E.N.   Kai E. Nielsen. *Professor of Philosophy, University of Calgary, Alberta. Author of* Scepticism.

RELIGIOUS AND SPIRITUAL BELIEF, SYSTEMS OF (*in part*)

K.E.P.   Kenyon Edwards Poole. *Emeritus Professor of Economics, Northwestern University, Evanston, Illinois. Author of* Public Finance and Economic Welfare.

GOVERNMENT FINANCE (*in part*)

Ke.S.   Keith Sinclair. *Professor of History, University of Auckland, New Zealand. Author of* A History of New Zealand.

NEW ZEALAND (*in part*)

K.G.   Karl Geiringer. *Emeritus Professor of Music, University of California, Santa Barbara. Coauthor of* Brahms: His Life and Work; Haydn: A Creative Life in Music.

HAYDN, JOSEPH (*in part*) (Micropædia)

K.Ga.   Kenneth Garrad. *Professor of Spanish, Flinders University of South Australia, Bedford Park (Adelaide).*

SPAIN (*in part*)

K.G.B.   Sir Kenneth (Granville) Bradley (d. 1977). *Director, Commonwealth Institute, London, 1953–69.*

SOUTHERN AFRICA (*in part*)

K.G.J.   Kingsley Garland Jayne. *Former Scholar of Wadham College, University of Oxford. Author of* Vasco da Gama and His Successors.

EAST INDIES, THE (*in part*)

K.G.L.   Kenneth G. Lieberthal. *Professor of Political Science; Research Associate, Center for Chinese Studies, University of Michigan, Ann Arbor. Author of* Central Documents and Politburo Politics in China *and others.*

CHINA (*in part*)
CULTURAL REVOLUTION (Micropædia)

K.Gr.   Kenneth I. Greisen. *Professor of Physics and Astronomy, Cornell University, Ithaca, N.Y.*

ATMOSPHERE (*in part*)

K.G.R.   Kenneth Grahame Rea. *Lecturer and Tutor in Drama, Guildhall School of Music and Drama, London. Theatre Critic and writer,* The Guardian.

THEATRE, THE HISTORY OF WESTERN

K.G.T.   Kennedy G. Tregonning. *Headmaster, Hale School, Wembley Downs, Western Australia. Raffles Professor of History, University of Singapore, 1958–66. Author of* A History of Modern Malaysia and Singapore.

SOUTHEAST ASIA, MAINLAND (*in part*)

K.Hä.   Karl H. Häuser. *Professor of Political Economy, Johann Wolfgang Goethe University of Frankfurt, Frankfurt am Main, West Germany. Coauthor of* The German Economy, 1870 to the Present.

TAXATION (*in part*)

K.H.C.   Kenneth H. Cooper. *President and Founder, The Aerobics Center, Dallas, Texas. Author of* The Aerobics Program for Total Well-being.

EXERCISE AND PHYSICAL CONDITIONING (*in part*)

K.H.D.H.   K.H.D. Haley. *Emeritus Professor of Modern History, University of Sheffield, England. Author of* The First Earl of Shaftesbury.

SHAFTESBURY, ANTHONY ASHLEY COOPER, 1ST EARL OF (Micropædia)

K.H.L.   Karl Heinz Lüling. *Former Chairman, Department of Ichthyology, Zoological Research Institute and Alexander Koenig Museum, Bonn, West Germany. Researcher on the physiology and behaviour of lungfishes.*

FISHES (*in part*)

Kh.Mo.   Khosrow Mostofi. *Professor of Political Science, University of Utah, Salt Lake City; former Director, Middle East Languages and Area Center. Author of* Aspects of Nationalism: A Sociology of Colonial Revolt.

IRAN (*in part*)

K.Ho.   Keigo Hogetsu. *Honorary Professor of Literature, University of Tokyo. Author of* Nihon shi gairon *and others.*

TAIRA FAMILY (Micropædia)

K.H.V.   Karel Hendrik Voous. *Emeritus Professor of Systematic Zoology and Zoogeography, Free University, Amsterdam, The Netherlands. Author of* Atlas of European Birds *and others.*

BIOSPHERE, THE (*in part*)

K.I.   Keith Irvine. *President, Reference Publications, Inc., Algonac, Michigan. Principal Editor, Geography, Encyclopædia Britannica, Chicago, 1969–72. Research Officer, Permanent Mission of Ghana to the United Nations,*

New York City, 1958–69. Author of The Rise of the Colored Races.
LEE KUAN YEW (Micropædia)

K.In.   Kenneth Ingham. *Professor of History, University of Bristol, England. Author of* East Africa *and others.*
AFRICA (*in part*)
EASTERN AFRICA (*in part*)
SOUTHERN AFRICA (*in part*)

K.Iw.   Kenkichi Iwasawa. *H.B. Fine Professor of Mathematics, Princeton University. Author of* Lectures on p-adic L-functions.
ANALYSIS (IN MATHEMATICS) (*in part*)

K.J.   Karl H.E. Jordan. *Emeritus Professor of Medieval and Modern History, Christian Albrecht University of Kiel, West Germany. Editor of* Die Urkunden Heinrichs des Löwen.
HENRY III (Saxony) (Micropædia)

K.J.B.   Keith J. Beven. *Lecturer in Engineering Hydrology, University of Lancaster, England.*
EARTH SCIENCES, THE (*in part*)

K.J.DeW.   Kenneth J. DeWoskin. *Associate Professor of Chinese; Associate Director, Center for Chinese Studies, University of Michigan, Ann Arbor. Author of* A Song for One or Two: Music and the Concept of Art in Early China *and others.*
CHINA (*in part*)

K.J.H.   Keith J. Hancock. *Vice-Chancellor, Flinders University of South Australia, Bedford Park.*
AUSTRALIA (*in part*)

K.J.Hi.   K. Jaakko J. Hintikka. *Professor of Philosophy, Florida State University, Tallahassee. Author of* Logic, Language-Games and Information.
PHILOSOPHIES OF THE BRANCHES OF KNOWLEDGE (*in part*)

K.J.L.   K.J. Leyser. *Fellow and Tutor in Modern History, Magdalen College, Oxford; Lecturer in Modern History, University of Oxford.*
GERMANY (*in part*)

K.J.N.   Karl J. Narr. *Professor and Director, Seminary for Prehistory and Protohistory; Director, Institute for Early Medieval Studies, University of Münster, West Germany.*
PREHISTORIC PEOPLES AND CULTURES (*in part*)

K.J.R.   Kenneth John Rea. *Professor of Economics, University of Toronto. Author of* The Political Economy of the Canadian North.
CANADA (*in part*)

K.K.   Kumar Krishna. *Research Associate, Department of Entomology, American Museum of Natural History, New York City. Professor of Biology, City College, City University of New York. Coeditor of* Biology of Termites.
INSECTS (*in part*)

K.Ku.   Karthigesapillai Kularatnam. *Former Professor and Head, Department of Geography, University of Sri Lanka,*

Colombo. Author of "Ceylon" in Developing Countries of the World.
SRI LANKA (*in part*)

K.La.   Kenneth Lamott (d. 1979). *Novelist and journalist. Author of* Anti-California *and numerous other books and magazine articles.*
SAN FRANCISCO (*in part*)

K.L.K.L.   Kai L.K. Laitinen. *Associate Professor of Finnish Literature, University of Helsinki. Author of* Suomen kirjallisuus 1917–1967; *editor of* Suomen kirjallisuuden antologia.
FINNISH LITERATURE (Micropædia)

K.L.N.   Kenneth L. Nordtvedt, Jr. *Professor of Physics, Montana State University, Bozeman.*
GRAVITATION (*in part*)

K.Lo.   Dame Kathleen Lonsdale (d. 1971). *Professor of Chemistry, University of London, 1949–68. Editor and part author of Vols. I, II, III, International Tables for X-Ray Crystallography.*
BRAGG, SIR LAWRENCE (Micropædia)
BRAGG, SIR WILLIAM (Micropædia)

K.M.   Kathy Mezei. *Associate Professor of English, Simon Fraser University, Burnaby, British Columbia. Coeditor of* The Prose of Life; Sketches from Victorian Canada.
CANADIAN LITERATURE (*in part*)

K.Ma.   Kitajima Masamoto. *Former Professor of Japanese History, Tokyo Metropolitan University. Author of* Structure of Power in the Edo Shogunate.
JAPAN (*in part*)

K.M.A.G.   Kurt Moritz Artur Goldammer. *Professor of Comparative History of Religions and of the History of Religious Art, Philipps University of Marburg, West Germany. Author of* Kultsymbolik des Protestantismus *and others.*
RELIGIOUS SYMBOLISM AND ICONOGRAPHY

K.Me.   Kenneth Mellanby *Consultant and Editor, Environmental Pollution. Director, Monks Wood Experimental Station, Huntington, England, 1961–74. Author of* Farming and Wildlife *and others.*
AGRICULTURE, THE HISTORY OF (*in part*)

K.M.G.P.   Kings Mbacazwa G. Phiri. *Senior Lecturer in History, University of Malaŵi, Zomba.*
SOUTHERN AFRICA (*in part*)

K.M.K.   Dame Kathleen Mary Kenyon (d. 1978). *Principal, St. Hugh's College, University of Oxford, 1962–73. Director, British School of Archaeology, Jerusalem, 1951–66. Author of* Archaeology in the Holy Land; Digging Up Jericho; *and others.*
PALESTINE (*in part*)

K.M.L.   Kathleen Marguerite Lea. *Emeritus Fellow of Lady Margaret Hall, University of Oxford; Vice Principal of*

Lady Margaret Hall, Oxford, 1947–71.
BACON, FRANCIS (*in part*)

K.M.S.   Kazimierz Maciej Smogorzewski. *Free-lance writer on contemporary history. London Correspondent, Kurier Polski (Warsaw), 1957–81. Founder and Editor, Free Europe, 1939–45. Author of* Joseph Pilsudski, soldat de la Pologne restaurée; Poland's Access to the Sea; *and others.*
BULGARIA (*in part*)
GERMANY (*in part*)
PIŁSUDSKI, JÓZEF (Micropædia)
POLAND (*in part*)
ROMANIA (*in part*)
UNION OF SOVIET SOCIALIST REPUBLICS (*in part*)
YUGOSLAVIA (*in part*)

K.M.W.   Karl M. Waage. *Professor of Geology; Curator of Invertebrate Paleontology, Peabody Museum of Natural History, Yale University. Coauthor of* Historical Geology.
DANA, JAMES D. (Micropædia)

K.N.   Keiji Nagahara. *Professor of History, Hitotsubashi University, Tokyo. Author of* Minamoto no Yoritomo.
MINAMOTO YORITOMO (Micropædia)

K.Na.   Kusum Nair. *Visiting Professor, Department of Economics, University of Maryland, College Park. Author of* The Lonely Furrow: Farming in the United States, Japan, and India *and others.*
AGRICULTURE, THE HISTORY OF (*in part*)

K.N.L.   Karl Nickerson Llewellyn (d. 1962). *Professor of Law, University of Chicago, 1951–62.*
MANSFIELD OF CAEN WOOD, WILLIAM MURRAY, 1ST EARL OF (Micropædia)

K.Ob.   Kalervo Oberg (d. 1973). *Professor of Anthropology, Oregon State University, Corvallis. Author of* Indian Tribes of Northern Mato Grosso, Brazil.
AMERICAN INDIANS (*in part*)

K.O.v.A.   Karl Otmar, Baron von Aretin. *Professor of Contemporary History, Technical University of Darmstadt, West Germany. Director, Institute for European History, Mainz, West Germany.*
FRANCIS JOSEPH (Micropædia)
METTERNICH, KLEMENS, FURST VON (*in part*) (Micropædia)

K.P.S.   Karl Patterson Schmidt (d. 1957). *Chief Curator of Zoology, Field Museum of Natural History, Chicago, 1941–55.*
CHINA (*in part*)
UNITED STATES OF AMERICA (*in part*)

K.R.   Klaus Ring. *Professor of Physiological Chemistry, Johann Wolfgang Goethe University of Frankfurt, West Germany.*
CELLS (*in part*)

K.Re.   Kenneth Rexroth (d. 1982). *Poet, writer, and painter. Special Lecturer, University of California, Santa Barbara. Author of* Classics Revisited *and others.*
LITERATURE, THE ART OF (*in part*)

K.-r.L. **Kwang-rin Lee.** *Professor of History, Sogang University, Seoul, Korea. Author of* History of Enlightenment in Korea.
KOREA (*in part*)

K.R.S. **Kenneth Reginald Sturley,** *Professor of Telecommunications, Ahmadu Bello University, Zaria, Nigeria, 1968–71. Chief Engineer, External Broadcasting, British Broadcasting Corporation, London, 1963–68. Author of* Radio Receiver Design *and others.*
BROADCASTING (*in part*)

K.R.St. **Karl R. Stadler.** *Professor and Head, Institute of Modern and Contemporary History, Johannes Kepler University of Linz, Austria. Author of* The Birth of the Austrian Republic.
AUSTRIA (*in part*)

K.R.V.H. **Kent R. Van Horn,** *Vice President, Research and Development, Aluminum Company of America, Pittsburgh, 1962–70; Director of Research, 1952–62; Research Metallurgist, 1929–62. Coauthor of* Aluminum in Iron and Steel; *editor of* Aluminum.
INDUSTRIES, EXTRACTION AND PROCESSING (*in part*)

K.S. **Khushwant Singh.** *Free-lance journalist. Member, Rajya Sabha* (*upper house of the Indian Parliament*)*. Author of* A History of the Sikhs *and others.*
RANJIT SINGH (Micropædia)
SIKHISM

K.S.A.J. **Kamel S. Abu Jaber.** *Professor of Political Science, University of Jordan, Amman. Author of* The Jordanians and the People of Jordan.
JORDAN (*in part*)

K.S.D. **Keith S. Donnellan.** *Professor of Philosophy, University of California, Los Angeles. Author of articles in various philosophical journals, particularly on the theory of reference.*
PHILOSOPHICAL SCHOOLS AND DOCTRINES, WESTERN (*in part*)

K.S.G. **Karl S. Guthke.** *Professor of German Literature, Harvard University. Author of* Das Leid im Werke Gerhart Hauptmanns; Gerhart Hauptmann: Weltbild im Werk.
HAUPTMANN, GERHART (Micropædia)

K.Si. **Kate Silber** (*deceased*)*. Senior Lecturer in German, University of Edinburgh, 1963–73. Author of* Pestalozzi: The Man and His Work.
PESTALOZZI, JOHANN HEINRICH (*in part*) (Micropædia)

K.S.L. **Kenneth S. Lane.** *Editorial Board Member,* Underground Space. *Consulting Engineer for dams and tunnels, and soils and rock engineering. Editor of* Proceedings of the North American Rapid Excavating and Tunneling Conference, 1972; Proceedings *of the* ASCE *symposium on* Underground Rock Chambers, 1971.
PUBLIC WORKS (*in part*)

K.S.N. **Kenneth Stafford Norris.** *Professor of Natural History, University of California, Santa Cruz. Director, Oceanic Institute, Waimanalo, Hawaii, 1968–71. Editor of* Whales, Dolphins and Porpoises.
MAMMALS (*in part*)

K.S.S. **Kamal Suleiman Salibi.** *Professor of History, American University of Beirut. Author of* The Modern History of Lebanon *and others.*
BEIRUT (*in part*)
ISRAEL (*in part*)
SYRIA (*in part*)

K.St. **The Rev. Krister Stendahl.** *Bishop of Stockholm. Andrew W. Mellon Professor of Divinity, Harvard University, 1981–84; Dean, Divinity School, 1968–79. Author of* Paul Among Jews and Gentiles *and others.*
BIBLICAL LITERATURE AND ITS CRITICAL INTERPRETATION (*in part*)

K.St.P. **Kosta Stevan Pavlowitch.** *Librarian, Department of Slavonic Studies, University of Cambridge. Yugoslav diplomat, 1928–45. Author of* The Struggle of the Serbs *and others.*
YUGOSLAVIA (*in part*)

K.S.W. **Kathrine Sorley Walker.** *Free-lance writer, editor, and dance critic. Author of* Dance and Its Creators *and others.*
BALANCHINE, GEORGE (Micropædia)
FOKINE, MICHEL (Micropædia)
PAVLOVA, ANNA (Micropædia)

K.U.K. **Khalil Ullah Kureshy.** *Professor of Geography; Director, Institute of Education and Research, University of the Punjab, Lahore, Pakistan. Editor of* Pakistan Geographical Review.
PAKISTAN (*in part*)

Ku.R. **Kurt Reindel.** *Professor of History, University of Regensburg, West Germany.*
OTTO I (GERMANY/HOLY ROMAN EMPIRE) (Micropædia)

K.v.Fr. **Kurt von Fritz** (d. 1985)*. Professor of Classical Philosophy, Ludwig Maximilian University of Munich. Author of* Die griechische Geschichtsschreibung, vol. I, *and numerous others.*
PHILOSOPHY, THE HISTORY OF WESTERN (*in part*)

K.V.J.v.F. **Kai V.J. von Fieandt.** *Emeritus Professor of Psychology, University of Helsinki. Author of* The World of Perception.
PERCEPTION, HUMAN (*in part*)

K.V.Su. **K.V. Sundaram.** *Joint Director, Planning Commission, Government of India, New Delhi.*
DELHI (*in part*)

K.V.Z. **Kamil V. Zvelebil.** *Professor of Dravidology, Utrecht University, The Netherlands. Author of* Comparative Dravidian Phonology.
LANGUAGES OF THE WORLD (*in part*)

K.W.B. **Karl W. Butzer.** *Henry Schultz Professor of Anthropology and Geography, University of Chicago. Specialist on the interrelationships among environment, prehistoric cultures, and human evolution. Author of* Environment and Archeology; *coauthor of* Desert and River in Nubia.
CLIMATE AND WEATHER (*in part*)

K.W.Bo. **Kees W. Bolle.** *Professor of History, University of California, Los Angeles. Author of* The Freedom of Man in Myth.
MYTH AND MYTHOLOGY (*in part*)

K.W.Br. **Kenneth W. Britt.** *Senior Research Associate, Empire State Paper Research Institute, State University of New York College of Environmental Science and Forestry, Syracuse. Editor of* Handbook of Pulp and Paper Technology.
INDUSTRIES, CHEMICAL PROCESS (*in part*)

K.W.C. **Kenneth Walter Cameron.** *Emeritus Associate Professor of English, Trinity College, Hartford, Connecticut. Author of* Emerson the Essayist; Young Emerson's Transcendental Vision.
EMERSON, RALPH WALDO (*in part*) (Micropædia)

K.W.K. **Kathryn Weichert Kranbuhl, M.D.** *Assistant Professor of Radiation Oncology, University of Cincinnati, Ohio.*
ORGANS AND ORGAN SYSTEMS, PLANT AND ANIMAL (*in part*)

K.W.P. **Ken W. Purdy** (d. 1972)*. Free-lance writer. Author of* Kings of the Road; Motorcars of the Golden Past.
TRANSPORTATION (*in part*)

L.A. **Lev Artsimovitch** (d. 1973)*. Head of the Plasma Physics Division, Kurchatov Institute of Atomic Energy, Moscow.*
ATOMS (*in part*)

La.B. **Larissa Bonfante.** *Professor of Classics, New York University, New York City. Author of* Etruscan Dress.
DRESS AND ADORNMENT (*in part*)

La.B.S. **Lacey Baldwin Smith.** *Peter B. Ritzma Professor of Humanities, Northwestern University, Evanston, Illinois. Author of* Tudor Prelates and Politics *and others.*
UNITED KINGDOM (*in part*)

L.A.C. **Lewis A. Coser.** *Distinguished Professor of Sociology, State University of New York at Stony Brook. Author of* The Functions of Social Conflict.
SOCIO-ECONOMIC DOCTRINES AND REFORM MOVEMENTS, MODERN (*in part*)

L.A.Cr. **Lawrence A. Cremin.** *Frederick A.P. Barnard Professor of Education, Teachers College, Columbia University. Author of* American Education: The Colonial Experience *and others.*
MANN, HORACE (Micropædia)

La.G. **Sir Lawrence Gowing.** *Slade Professor of Fine Art, University*

College, University of London. Author of Vermeer; Turner; Imagination and Reality.

PAINTING, THE HISTORY OF WESTERN (*in part*)
SCULPTURE, THE HISTORY OF WESTERN (*in part*)

La.L.   Laurence Elliot Libin. *Curator of Musical Instruments, Metropolitan Museum of Art, New York City.*

MUSICAL FORMS AND GENRES (*in part*)

L.-A.L.   Luce-Andrée Langevin. *Honorary Professor; former teacher of physical science, Lycée Fénelon, Paris. Author of* Lomonossov.

LOMONOSOV, MIKHAIL VASILYEVICH (Micropædia)

L.A.M.   Leslie A. Marchand. *Emeritus Professor of English, Rutgers University, New Brunswick, New Jersey. Author of* Byron: A Biography *and others; editor of* Byron's Letters and Journals.

BYRON, GEORGE GORDON BYRON, 6TH BARON (*in part*) (Micropædia)

L.A.Ma.   L. Andrew Mannheim. *Technical editor, writer, and consultant. Author of* Leica Way *and others; editor of* Focal Encyclopedia of Photography.

PHOTOGRAPHY (*in part*)

L.A.N.   Leonid Alekseyevich Nikiforov. *Senior Scientific Associate, Institute of History of the U.S.S.R., Academy of Sciences of the U.S.S.R., Moscow. Author of* Anglo-Russian Relations in the Reign of Peter I.

PETER I THE GREAT, OF RUSSIA (*in part*)

L.A.P.G.   L.A. Peter Gosling. *Professor of Geography, University of Michigan; Director, Center for South and Southeast Asian Studies, 1962–66.*

EAST INDIES, THE (*in part*)
SOUTHEAST ASIA, MAINLAND (*in part*)

L.A.R.   Lionel A. Rogg. *Professor of Organ, Counterpoint, Styles, and Form, Geneva Conservatory.*

MUSICAL FORMS AND GENRES (*in part*)

La.S.   Lawrence Sternstein. *Senior Lecturer in Geography, Australian National University, Canberra. Former Municipal Advisor, Bangkok Municipality, Thailand. Author of* Portrait of Bangkok *and others.*

BANGKOK

L.A.S.   Lionel Astor Sheridan. *Professor of Law, University College, University of Wales, Cardiff. Coauthor of* Equity.

LAW, THE PROFESSION AND PRACTICE OF (*in part*)

L.A.W.   Leslie A. White (d. 1975). *Professor of Anthropology, University of Michigan, Ann Arbor. Author of* The Science of Culture; The Evolution of Culture.

CULTURE, THE CONCEPT AND COMPONENTS OF (*in part*)

L.A.Wa.   Lionel A. Walford (d. 1979). *Director, Sandy Hook Marine Laboratory, Highlands, New Jersey,* 1960–71; Senior Scientist, 1971–74. *Author of* Living Resources of the Sea.

FISHES (*in part*)

L.B.   Liliana Brisby. *Editor, The World Today. Author of* Les Relations russo-bulgares, 1878–1886.

BULGARIAN LITERATURE (*in part*) (Micropædia)

L.Ba.   Lawrence Badash. *Professor of the History of Science, University of California, Santa Barbara. Author of several papers on Becquerel's work.*

BECQUEREL, HENRI (Micropædia)

L.B.A.   Leslie B. Arey. *Robert L. Rea Professor Emeritus of Anatomy, Medical School, Northwestern University, Chicago. Author of* Developmental Anatomy.

GROWTH AND DEVELOPMENT, BIOLOGICAL (*in part*)

L.B.As.   Larned B. Asprey. *Staff Member, Los Alamos National Laboratory, New Mexico. Author of numerous papers on the actinide, rare-earth, transuranium, and halogen elements.*

CHEMICAL ELEMENTS (*in part*)

L.Be.   Lyman Benson. *Emeritus Professor of Botany; Director of the Herbarium, Pomona College, Claremont, California. Author of* The Cacti of the United States and Canada *and others.*

ANGIOSPERMS (*in part*)

L.Bo.   Luis Bonilla. *Member, International Association of Literary Critics. Author of* Historia de la esclavitud *and others.*

SERVITUDE (*in part*)

L.Br.   Leon Bramson. *Assistant Director, Division of General Programs, National Endowment for the Humanities, Washington, D.C. Professor of Sociology, Swarthmore College, Pennsylvania, 1971–78. Author of* The Political Context of Sociology.

CULTURE, THE CONCEPT AND COMPONENTS OF (*in part*)

L.B.S.   Leonard Bertram Schapiro (d. 1983). *Professor of Political Science (Russian Studies), London School of Economics and Political Science, University of London, 1963–75. Author of* The Communist Party of the Soviet Union *and others.*

SOCIO-ECONOMIC DOCTRINES AND REFORM MOVEMENTS, MODERN (*in part*)

L.B.Sm.   Lyman B. Smith. *Emeritus Botanist, Smithsonian Institution, Washington, D.C. Author of* Bromeliaceae—North American Flora; Flora Neotropica.

ANGIOSPERMS (*in part*)

L.C.   Leonard W. Conversi. *Lecturer in English, Yale University.*

LITERATURE, THE ART OF (*in part*)

L.Ca.   Luigi Carluccio. *Member of the arts editorial staff,* La Gazzetta del popolo, *Turin, Italy. Author of* Giacometti: A Sketchbook of Interpretative Drawings.

CARAVAGGIO (Micropædia)

L.C.B.   Lawrence C. Bliss. *Professor and Chairman, Department of Botany, University of Washington, Seattle. Author of* Alpine Zone of the Presidential Range.

ECOSYSTEMS (*in part*)

L.C.Br.   L. Carl Brown. *Garrett Professor of Foreign Affairs; Director, Program in Near Eastern Studies, Princeton University. Author of* The Tunisia of Ahmad Bey.

NORTH AFRICA (*in part*)

L.C.D.   L.C. Dunn (d. 1974). *Professor of Zoology, 1928–62; Senior Research Associate in Biological Sciences, 1962–74, Columbia University, New York City. Author of* Heredity and Evolution in Human Populations *and others.*

GROWTH AND DEVELOPMENT, BIOLOGICAL (*in part*)
MENDEL, GREGOR (*in part*) (Micropædia)

L.C.F.   Louis C. Faron. *Professor of Anthropology, State University of New York at Stony Brook. Author of* Hawks of the Sun *and others.*

AMERICAN INDIANS (*in part*)

L.Ch.   Luciano Chiappini. *Teacher. President, Ferrarese Delegation for the History of Italy. Committeeman, Antonio Frizzi Institute for the History of Ferrara. Author of* Eleonora d'Aragona, prima duchessa di Ferrara *and others.*

ESTE, HOUSE OF (Micropædia)

L.C.H.   Lois Chapman Houghton. *Staff member, Middle East Institute, Washington, D.C.*

DAMASCUS (*in part*)

L.C.O.   Leonard C. Overton. *Country Representative, Asia Foundation, Phnom Penh, Cambodia, 1955–59, 1961–64; Saigon, South Vietnam, 1965–67.*

SOUTHEAST ASIA, MAINLAND (*in part*)

L.C.P.   Linus C. Pauling. *Research Professor, Linus Pauling Institute of Science and Medicine, Palo Alto, California. Professor of Chemistry, Stanford University, California, 1969–74. Nobel Prize for Chemistry, 1954; Nobel Prize for Peace, 1962. Author of* The Nature of the Chemical Bond *and others.*

CHEMICAL ELEMENTS (*in part*)

L.C.V.   Letterio Carlo Villari. *Director, International Institute of Volcanology, Catania, Italy.*

VOLCANISM (*in part*)

L.D.   Lovat Dickson. *Writer. Director, Macmillan & Company Ltd., London, 1941–64. Author of* H.G. Wells.

WELLS, H.G. (Micropædia)

L.De.   Ludwig Denecke. *Director, Murhard Library of the City of Kassel and State Library; Head of the Brothers Grimm Museum, Kassel, West Germany, 1959–68. Author of* Jacob Grimm und sein Bruder Wilhelm; *editor of* Brüder Grimm Gedenken.

GRIMM, JACOB LUDWIG CARL AND
   WILHELM CARL (Micropædia)

L. de R.   Leendert de Ruiter. *Professor of Comparative Animal Physiology, State University of Groningen, The Netherlands.*

BEHAVIOUR, ANIMAL (*in part*)

L. de S.R.   Luís de Sousa Rebelo. *Reader in Portuguese and Brazilian Studies, King's College, University of London. Author of* A tradicão clássica na Literatura portuguesa *and others.*

PORTUGUESE LITERATURE (*in part*)

L.D.F.   Larry D. Faller. *Associate Professor, Department of Medicine, University of California, Los Angeles. Author of papers on the application of relaxation techniques to rapid chemical processes.*

CHEMICAL REACTIONS (*in part*)

L.D.S.   Sir Laurence Dudley Stamp (d. 1966). *Professor of Social Geography, University of London, 1948–58. Author of* Asia, a Regional and Economic Geography *and others.*

EAST INDIES, THE (*in part*)

L.Du.   Louis Dupree. *Adjunct Professor of Anthropology, Pennsylvania State University, University Park. Visiting Professor, Princeton University. Field research in Afghanistan, India, Pakistan, and Bangladesh. Author of* Afghanistan.

AFGHANISTAN (*in part*)

L.Ed.   Leon Edel. *Henry James Professor Emeritus of English and American Letters, New York University, New York City. Citizens Professor Emeritus of English, University of Hawaii, Honolulu. Author of* The Life of Henry James *and others; editor of* The Complete Tales of Henry James *and others.*

JAMES, HENRY (*in part*) (Micropædia)

L.-E.H.   Louis-Edmond Hamelin. *Geographer, University of Quebec at Trois-Rivières; Rector, 1978–83. Author of* Canada.

NORTH AMERICA (*in part*)

L.El.   Lajos Elekes. *Professor of the Medieval History of Hungary, Eötvös Loránd University, Budapest. Member of the Hungarian Academy of Sciences. Author of* Hunyadi; Mátyás és kora; *and others.*

HUNYADI, JÁNOS (Micropædia)
MATTHIAS I (HUNGARY) (Micropædia)

Le.M.   Leonard Mosley. *Author of* Curzon: The End of an Epoch *and others.*

CURZON OF KEDLESTON, GEORGE
   NATHANIEL CURZON, MARQUESS
   (Micropædia)

L.E.M.   Leonard E. Mason. *Consultant in Pacific Islands affairs. Emeritus Professor of Anthropology, University of Hawaii, Honolulu. Author of* Relocation of the Bikini Marshallese.

PACIFIC ISLANDS (*in part*)

L.E.R.   Leo E. Rose. *Lecturer in Political Science, University of California, Berkeley. Editor,* Asian Survey. *Author of* Nepal: Strategy for Survival.

NEPAL (*in part*)

Le.S.   Lee Strasberg (d. 1982). *Artistic Director, Actors Studio, 1948–82. Head, Lee Strasberg Theatre Institute, New York City. Author of* Strasberg at the Actors Studio.

THEATRE, THE ART OF (*in part*)

L.F.   Linwood Fredericksen. *Undersecretary and Manager, Program Development Division, Rotary International. Associate Editor, Religion, Encyclopædia Britannica, Chicago, 1969–73. Author of* A Christian Witness in a Non-Christian Culture According to Clement of Alexandria.

BIBLICAL LITERATURE AND ITS CRITICAL
   INTERPRETATION (*in part*)
CHRISTIANITY (*in part*)
CLEMENT OF ALEXANDRIA, SAINT
   (*in part*) (Micropædia)
DOCTRINES AND DOGMAS, RELIGIOUS
   (*in part*)
RITES AND CEREMONIES, SACRED
   (*in part*)

L.F. de B.   Lieven Ferdinand de Beaufort (d. 1968). *Professor of Zoogeography, University of Amsterdam, 1929–49. Director, Zoological Museum, Amsterdam, 1922–49. Author of* Zoogeography of the Land and Inland Waters.

ASIA (*in part*)

L.F.K.W.   Lothar F.K. Wickert. *Emeritus Professor of Ancient History, University of Cologne. Author of* Theodor Mommsen: Eine Biographie; Drei Vorträge über Theodor Mommsen.

MOMMSEN, THEODOR (Micropædia)

L.Fo.   Lukas Foss. *Composer and pianist. Music Director and Conductor, Brooklyn (New York) Philharmonic. Music Director and Conductor, Milwaukee Symphony Orchestra. Composer of* Timecycle *and many other works.*

MUSIC, THE ART OF (*in part*)

L.F.S.   Leo F. Solt. *Dean, Graduate School; Professor of History, Indiana University, Bloomington. Author of* Saints in Arms: Puritanism and Democracy in Cromwell's Army.

UNITED KINGDOM (*in part*)

L.G.J.B.   Ludwig G.J. Bieler (d. 1981). *Professor of Paleography and Late Latin, University College, Dublin, National University of Ireland. Author of* Boethii Philosophiae Consolatio *and others.*

IGNATIUS OF ANTIOCH, SAINT
   (Micropædia)

L.Go.   Ludwig Goldscheider. *Art historian. Former director and designer of books for Phaidon Press Ltd., London. Author of* Kokoschka; Michelangelo; *and numerous other classic works on the art of antiquity, the Italian Renaissance, the Baroque, and the late 19th and early*

20th centuries.

KOKOSCHKA, OSKAR (Micropædia)

L.G.P.   Leslie Gilbert Pine. *Writer and lecturer. Former Editor,* Burke's Peerage. *Author of* The Genealogist's Encyclopedia; The Story of Heraldry; *and many others.*

HERALDRY
HISTORY, THE STUDY OF (*in part*)

L.G.S.   Lloyd Grenfell Stevenson, M.D. *William H. Welch Professor of the History of Medicine; Director, Institute of the History of Medicine, Johns Hopkins University, Baltimore. Author of* Sir Frederick Banting.

KOCH, ROBERT (Micropædia)

L.H.   Leslie Harris. *President and Vice-Chancellor, Memorial University of Newfoundland, St. John's. Author of* A Short History of Newfoundland and Labrador.

CANADA (*in part*)

L.H.A.   Lawrence Hugh Aller. *Emeritus Professor of Astronomy, University of California, Los Angeles. Author of* Atoms, Stars, and Nebulae *and others.*

STARS AND STAR CLUSTERS (*in part*)

L.H.B.   Leslie Hilton Brown (d. 1980). *Ornithologist, naturalist, and consultant on range management, land use, and planning. Specialist on the ecology of birds and mammals of East Africa. Author of* Africa: A Natural History; African Birds of Prey; Eagles; *coauthor of* Eagles, Hawks and Falcons of the World.

AFRICA (*in part*)
BIRDS (*in part*)

L.H.Ba.   Lawrence Howard Bannister. *Senior Lecturer in Biology and Anatomy, Guy's Hospital Medical School, University of London.*

CIRCULATION AND CIRCULATORY
   SYSTEMS (*in part*)

L.H.Bu.   Lyman H. Butterfield (d. 1982). *Editor in Chief,* The Adams Papers, *Massachusetts Historical Society, Boston, 1954–75. Editor of* Letters of Benjamin Rush.

RUSH, BENJAMIN (Micropædia)

L.H.E.   Luther Harris Evans (d. 1981). *Director, International Collections, Columbia University, 1962–71. Director General, UNESCO, 1953–58. Librarian of Congress, 1945–53. Author of* The Virgin Islands from Naval Base to New Deal.

WEST INDIES, THE (*in part*)

L.H.F.   Louis H. Feldman. *Professor of Classics, Yeshiva University, New York City. Author of* Scholarship on Philo and Josephus, 1937–1962; *editor and translator of* Josephus, *vol. 9,* Jewish Antiquities.

JUDAISM (*in part*)

L.H.H.   Ludwig Heinrich Heydenreich (d. 1978). *Director, Central Institute for the History of Art, Munich, 1947–70. Author of* Leonardo da Vinci; Leonardo architetto.

LEONARDO DA VINCI (*in part*)

L.Hi. **Lejaren Hiller.** *Birge-Cary Professor of Composition, State University of New York at Buffalo. Author of* Informationstheorie und Computermusik; *coauthor of* Experimental Music.
MUSICAL FORMS AND GENRES *(in part)*

L.H.S. **Lou Hackett Silberman.** *Hillel Professor Emeritus of Jewish Literature and Thought, Vanderbilt University, Nashville, Tennessee. Author of* American Impact; *editor of* Rabbinic Essays.
JUDAISM *(in part)*

L.H.St. **Lawrence H. Starkey.** *Designer, Concord, Inc., Fargo. Lecturer in Philosophy and Religion, North Dakota State University, Fargo, 1976–78. Associate Editor, Philosophy, Encyclopædia Britannica, Chicago, 1968–72.*
PHILOSOPHICAL SCHOOLS AND DOCTRINES, WESTERN *(in part)*

Li.L. **Libero Lenti.** *Professor of Statistics, University of Milan. Author of* Inventario dell'economia italiana.
ITALY *(in part)*

L.J. **Lucien Jerphagnon.** *Professor of Philosophy, University of Caen, France. Author of* Le Caractère de Pascal.
PASCAL *(in part)*

L.J.A. **Leonard James Arrington.** *Lemuel H. Redd Professor of Western History, Brigham Young University, Provo, Utah. Author of* Great Basin Kingdom; An Economic History of the Latter-day Saints.
UNITED STATES OF AMERICA *(in part)*

L.J.B. **Louis J. Battan.** *Professor of Atmospheric Sciences, University of Arizona, Tucson. World authority on radar meteorology and its applications. Author of* Radar Meteorology; The Nature of Violent Storms; *and others.*
CLIMATE AND WEATHER *(in part)*

L.J.Be. **Leslie John Beck** (d. 1978). *Tutor in Philosophy, Merton College, University of Oxford, 1945–54. Author of* The Method of Descartes; The Metaphysics of Descartes.
CARTESIANISM, DESCARTES AND *(in part)*

L.J.C. **Lawrence James Chisholm.** *Metric consultant. Former Special Assistant, Bureau of Product Safety, Food and Drug Administration, U.S. Department of Health, Education, and Welfare, Washington, D.C. Author of* Units of Weight and Measure.
MEASUREMENT AND OBSERVATION, PRINCIPLES, METHODS, AND INSTRUMENTS OF *(in part)*

L.J.F.Y. **Lawrence J.F. Youlten, M.D.** *Research Fellow, Department of Medicine, Guy's Hospital Medical School, University of London. Editor of* Lymphatics and Lymph Circulation.
CIRCULATION AND CIRCULATORY SYSTEMS *(in part)*

L.J.G. **Leo John Gleeson.** *Former Reader in Mathematics, Monash University, Clayton, Australia.*
SOLAR SYSTEMS, THE *(in part)*

L.J.K. **Leonie Judith Kramer.** *Professor of Australian Literature, University of Sydney. Editor of* The Oxford History of Australian Literature.
AUSTRALIA AND NEW ZEALAND, LITERATURES OF *(in part)*

L.J.S. **Lewis Judson Stannard, Jr.** *Emeritus Taxonomist, Illinois Natural History Survey, Urbana. Author of* The Phylogeny and Classification of the North American Genera of the Suborder Tubulifera (Thysanoptera).
INSECTS *(in part)*

L.J.T. **L.J. Trinterud.** *Emeritus Professor of Church History, San Francisco Theological Seminary, San Anselmo, California. Editor of* Elizabethan Puritanism.
BUCER, MARTIN (Micropædia)

L.J.W. **Louis Jolyon West, M.D.** *Professor and Chairman, Department of Psychiatry and Biobehavioral Sciences, University of California, Los Angeles; Director, Neuropsychiatric Institute; Psychiatrist in Chief, U.C.L.A. Hospital and Clinics. Author of* Hallucinations.
PERCEPTION, HUMAN *(in part)*

L.K. **Lawrence Kaplan.** *Professor of Biology, University of Massachusetts, Boston.*
GROWTH AND DEVELOPMENT, BIOLOGICAL *(in part)*

L.Kl. **Larry Klein.** *Contributing Editor,* Stereo Review *magazine; former Technical Director. Coauthor of* Electronic Test Equipment.
SOUND *(in part)*

L.K.L. **Lawrence K. Lustig.** *Former Vice President and Editor in Chief, Aretê Publishing Company, Princeton, New Jersey. Senior Editor, Earth Sciences, Encyclopædia Britannica, Chicago, 1968–73; Managing Editor, Yearbooks, 1974–77. An authority on fluvial processes in arid regions.*
CONTINENTAL LANDFORMS *(in part)*
ECOSYSTEMS *(in part)*
MINERALS AND ROCKS *(in part)*
RIVERS *(in part)*

L.K.M. **Liliya Konstantinovna Malik.** *Senior Scientist, Institute of Geography, Academy of Sciences of the U.S.S.R., Moscow. Author of* The Characteristic of the Snow Cover as One of the Factors of the Formation of High Waters in the Basin of the Ob River.
ASIA *(in part)*

L.Ko. **Lionel Kochan.** *Bearsted Reader in Jewish History, University of Warwick, England. Author of* Russia in Revolution, 1890–1918 *and others.*
WITTE, SERGEY YULYEVICH, GRAF (Micropædia)

L.Kr. **Lawrence Krader.** *Director, Ethnological Institute, Free University of Berlin. Author of* Peoples of Central Asia; Social Organization of Mongol-Turkic Pastoral Nomads; *and others.*
UNION OF SOVIET SOCIALIST REPUBLICS *(in part)*

L.Le. **Lewis Leary.** *William Rand Kenan, Jr., Professor Emeritus of English, University of North Carolina at Chapel Hill. Author of* Mark Twain; *editor of* A Casebook of Mark Twain's Wound *and others.*
TWAIN, MARK *(in part)* (Micropædia)

L.L.H. **Laurita L. Hill** (deceased). *Writer and editor. Instructor in History, University of Texas at Austin, 1963–68. Coauthor of* Raymond IV, Count of Toulouse *and others.*
BOHEMOND I *(in part)* (Micropædia)

L.Lk. **Leonhard Lenk.** *Research Historian, Institute of Bavarian History, University of Munich.*
GERMANY *(in part)*

L.L.S. **Lester L. Short.** *Chairman and Curator, Department of Ornithology, American Museum of Natural History, New York City.*
BIRDS *(in part)*

L.L.Sl. **L.L. Sloss.** *Emeritus Professor of Geology, Northwestern University, Evanston, Illinois. Coauthor of* Stratigraphy and Sedimentation.
GEOCHRONOLOGY *(in part)*

L.M. **Luis Michelena.** *Professor of Indo-European and Basque Linguistics, University of the Basque Country, Vitoria, Spain. Author of* Fonética histórica vasca; *editor of* Textos arcaicos vascos.
LANGUAGES OF THE WORLD *(in part)*

L.Ma. **Leopold Marquard** (deceased). *Publisher. President, South African Institute of Race Relations, 1957–58, 1968. Author of* The Story of South Africa *and others.*
SMUTS, JAN CHRISTIAN (Micropædia)

L.M.A. **Lewis M. Alexander.** *Professor of Geography, University of Rhode Island, Kingston. Author of* Offshore Geography of Northwestern Europe.
EUROPE *(in part)*

L.M.At. **Lewis Malcolm Atherden** (d. 1973). *Lecturer in Pharmaceutical Chemistry, University of Bath, England. Editor of* Bentley and Driver's Textbook of Pharmaceutical Chemistry.
INDUSTRIES, CHEMICAL PROCESS *(in part)*

L.M.B. **Laurie M. Brown.** *Professor of Physics and Astronomy, Northwestern University, Evanston, Illinois.*
PHYSICAL PRINCIPLES AND CONCEPTS *(in part)*

L.M.F. **Luch Mikhaylovich Fomin.** *Head, Laboratory of Sea Currents, Southern Division, Institute of Oceanography, Academy of Sciences of the U.S.S.R., Gelendzhik.*
EUROPE *(in part)*

L.M.G. **Leland Matthew Goodrich.** *James T. Shotwell Professor Emeritus* *of International Relations, Columbia University. Author of* The United Nations; *coauthor of* Charter of the United Nations: Commentary and Documents.

UNITED NATIONS (*in part*)

L.M.K. Lewis M. Killian. *Professor of Sociology, University of Massachusetts, Amherst. Author of* The Impossible Revolution; *coauthor of* Collective Behavior.

COLLECTIVE BEHAVIOUR (*in part*)

L.M.L. Ludwig M. Landgrebe. *Professor of Philosophy, University of Cologne. Director of the Husserl Archives, Cologne. Member of the International Institute of Philosophy, Paris. Author of* Phaenomenologie und Geschichte *and others.*

HUSSERL, EDMUND (Micropædia)

L.M.M. Leonard M. Marcus. *Editor in Chief,* High Fidelity *magazine and* Musical America, *1968–80.*

MUSIC, THE ART OF (*in part*)

L.Mo. Lynn Montross (d. 1961). *Historian, United States Marine Corps, 1950–61. Author of* War Through the Ages *and others.*

WAR, THE THEORY AND CONDUCT OF (*in part*)

L.M.-P. Lorenzo Minio-Paluello. *Emeritus Reader in Mediaeval Philosophy, University of Oxford; Fellow of Oriel College, Oxford, 1962–75. Director of Aristoteles Latinus, 1959–72. Editor of numerous works of Aristotle.*

ARISTOTELIANISM, ARISTOTLE AND (*in part*)

L.Ms. Luciano Martins. *Assistant Professor, Federal University of Rio de Janeiro. Research Assistant, National Centre of Scientific Research, Paris. Author of* Industrializaçᾶo, Burguesia Nacional e Desenvolvimento.

BRAZIL (*in part*)

L.M.T. Leonard Monteath Thompson. *Professor of History, Yale University; Director, Yale-Wesleyan Southern African Research Program. Author of* The Political Mythology of Apartheid.

SOUTH AFRICA (*in part*)

L.M.W. Lillian M. Weber. *Chief Horticulture Assistant to the Senior Horticulture Specialist, New York Botanical Garden, Bronx. Collaborating Editor of* New Illustrated Encyclopedia of Gardening.

TREES (*in part*)

L.N.F. Lee Nathan Feigon. *Associate Professor of History and Asian Studies, Colby College, Waterville, Maine. Staff Writer,* East Asian Affairs, Encyclopædia Britannica, *Chicago, 1970–73.*

HUNG HSIU-CH'ÜAN (Micropædia)

L.O.H. Lauri O. Honko. *Professor of Folkloristics and Comparative Religion, University of Turku, Finland. Author of* Geisterglaube in Ingermanland.

EUROPEAN RELIGIONS, ANCIENT (*in part*)

Lo.J.B. Lowell John Bean. *Professor of Anthropology, California State University, Hayward. Author of* Temalpah: An Ethnobotany of the Cahuilla Indians of Southern California; Mukat's People: An Ecological Study of the Cahuilla Indians of Southern California.

AMERICAN INDIANS (*in part*)

L.P. László Péter. *Lecturer in Hungarian History, School of Slavonic and East European Studies, University of London.*

BUDAPEST

L.P.L. Lawrence P. Lessing. *Member, Board of Editors,* Fortune *magazine, New York City, 1941–52; 1965–74. Author of* Man of High Fidelity: Edwin Howard Armstrong.

ARMSTRONG, EDWIN H. (Micropædia)

L.P.Le. Lucile P. Leone. *Chief Nurse Officer, Public Health Service, U.S. Department of Health, Education, and Welfare, Washington, D.C., 1949–66. Associate Dean, College of Nursing, Texas Women's University, 1968–71. Author of* Statewide Planning for Nursing Education.

MEDICINE (*in part*)

L.P.S. L.P. Smith. *Former President, Commission for Agricultural Meteorology, World Meteorological Organization, Geneva. Author of* Seasonable Weather.

CLIMATE AND WEATHER (*in part*)

L.P.V. Lalita P. Vidyarthi (d. 1985). *University Professor and Head, Department of Anthropology, University of Rānchī, Bihār, India, 1968–85. Author of* Socio-Cultural Implication of Industrialization in India *and others.*

ASIA (*in part*)

L.P.W. L. Pearce Williams. *John Stambaugh Professor of the History of Science; Codirector, Program in the History and Philosophy of Science and Technology, Cornell University, Ithaca, New York. Author of* Michael Faraday.

FARADAY
HELMHOLTZ
SCIENCE, THE HISTORY OF

L.P.Wi. Lancelot Patrick Wilkinson (d. 1985). *Brereton Reader in Classics, University of Cambridge, 1969–74; Fellow of King's College, Cambridge. Author of* Ovid Recalled *and others.*

LATIN LITERATURE (*in part*)

L.R.C. L. Russell Cook (d. 1978). *President, Chocolate and Confectionery Division, W.R. Grace & Company, New York City, 1965–73. Author of* Chocolate Production and Use.

FARMING AND AGRICULTURE TECHNOLOGY (*in part*)
FOOD PROCESSING (*in part*)

L.R.L. Lorna R. Levi. *Coauthor of* A Guide to Spiders and Their Kin; *cotranslator and coeditor of* Invertebrate Zoology *by A. Kaestner.*

ARACHNIDS (*in part*)

L.R.M. Laurence Reginald (Bob) Mernagh (d. 1980). *Director, Institution of the Rubber Industry, London, 1966–70. Formerly Chief Chemist and Manager of Product Engineering, Firestone Tyre and Rubber Company Ltd. Editor of* Engineering Design— Rubber.

INDUSTRIES, CHEMICAL PROCESS (*in part*)

L.R.R. Leonard R. Rogers. *Sculptor and writer. Former Head, Faculty of Three-Dimensional Design, College of Art and Design, Loughborough, England. Author of* Sculpture: Appreciation of the Arts; Relief Sculpture.

SCULPTURE, THE ART OF

L.S. Leon Sokoloff, M.D. *Professor of Pathology, State University of New York at Stony Brook. Author of* The Biology of Degenerative Joint Disease.

SUPPORTIVE AND CONNECTIVE TISSUES (*in part*)

L.S.B. Louis Stanley Berenson. *Owner and President, Berensons' Hartford Jai-Alai, Connecticut.*

JAI ALAI (Micropædia)

L.S.El.H. Laila Shukry El Hamᾱmsy. *Former Director, Social Research Center, American University in Cairo.*

EGYPT (*in part*)

L.S.F. Lewis S. Feuer. *University Professor Emeritus of Sociology and Government, University of Virginia, Charlottesville. Author of* Marx and the Intellectuals *and others.*

MARXISM, MARX AND (*in part*)

L.S.Fe. Luis Suárez Fernández. *Former Professor of History, Valladolid University, Spain.*

SPAIN (*in part*)

L.S.K. Lester S. King, M.D. *Professorial Lecturer in the History of Medicine, University of Chicago. Author of* The Growth of Medical Thought.

JENNER, EDWARD (Micropædia)

L.St. Leif Størmer (deceased). *Professor of Historical Geology, University of Oslo.*

GEOCHRONOLOGY (*in part*)

L.Sur. Leo Suryadinata. *Former Research Associate, Centre for Southeast Asian Studies, Kyōto University, Japan. Author of* The Pre-World War II Peranakan Chinese Press of Java: A Preliminary Survey.

GAJAH MADA (Micropædia)
KERTANAGARA (Micropædia)

L.S.V. Lalgudi Sivasubramanian Venkataramanan. *Director, Institute for Social and Economic Change, Bangalore, India. Author of* The Theory of Futures Trading.

MARKETS (*in part*)

L.T. Lewis Thorpe (d. 1977). *Professor of French, University of Nottingham, England, 1958–77. Editor and translator of* Two Lives of Charlemagne.

LOUIS I (GERMANY/HOLY ROMAN EMPIRE) (Micropædia)

L.T.C.R.   L.T.C. Rolt (d. 1974). *Member, Executive Committee, American Society for the History of Technology. Chairman, Talyllyn Railway Company, England, 1963–68. Author of* Great Engineers *and many others.*

TREVITHICK, RICHARD (Micropædia)

L.Th.   Laura Thompson. *Consultant in applied anthropology. Field researcher on Hopi, Pagogo, Zuni, Navaho, and Sioux reservations. Author of* Culture in Crisis: A Study of the Hopi Indians.

AMERICAN INDIANS (*in part*)

L.T.N.   Lennart T. Norman. *Archivist and historian.*

MARGARET I (DENMARK/NORWAY/ SWEDEN) (Micropædia)

SWEDEN (*in part*)

L.V.   Leo Vroman. *Physiologist, Medical Research Department, Veterans Administration Hospital, Brooklyn, New York. Author of* Blood.

TISSUES AND FLUIDS (*in part*)

L.V.A.   Lloyd Van Horn Armstrong (d. 1977). *Chief Engineer, Diesel Engine Department, Ingersoll Rand Company. Coauthor of* The Diesel Engine.

ENERGY CONVERSION (*in part*)

L.Ve.   Louis Verniers. *Honorary Secretary, General Ministry of Education, Belgium. Author of* Un millénaire d'historie de Bruxelles, des origines à 1830 *and others.*

BRUSSELS

L.v.G.   Ludwig von Gogolák. *Author of* Csehszlovákia; "T.G. Masaryks slowakische und ungarländische Politik: Ein Beitrag zur Vorgeschichte des Zerfalls Ungarns im Jahre 1918" *in* Bohemia, Jahrbuch des Collegium Carolinum; *and others.*

MASARYK, TOMÁŠ (Micropædia)

L.Vi.   Luigi Villari (deceased). *Official in the Italian Foreign Office. Author of* Italian Life in Town and Country.

ITALY (*in part*)

L.W.B.   Lewis W. Bealer. *Former Assistant Professor of History, University of Oklahoma, Norman.*

BRAZIL (*in part*)

L.We.   Leo Weaver. *Executive Director and Chief Engineer, Ohio River Valley Water Sanitation Commission, Cincinnati. Technical editor of* Municipal Refuse Disposal; Refuse Collection Practice.

PUBLIC WORKS (*in part*)

L.W.M.   Laurence Woodward Martin. *Vice Chancellor, University of Newcastle upon Tyne, England. Professor of War Studies, King's College, University of London, 1968–77. Author of* Arms and Strategy *and others.*

WAR, THE THEORY AND CONDUCT OF (*in part*)

L.Wy.   Sir Leonard Woolley (d. 1960). *Archaeologist; excavated at Ur, 1922–34,* *and many other sites. Major contributor to knowledge of the Sumerians. Author of* Digging Up the Past; Excavations at Ur; *and others.*

UR (*in part*) (Micropædia)

L.Z.   Lev Zetlin. *President, Zetlin-Argo Structural Investigations, Inc., New York City. Author of structural and civil engineering handbooks on concrete and suspension structures.*

STADIUM (Micropædia)

L.Zg.   Ladislav Zgusta. *Professor of Linguistics and of Classics; Member, Center for Advanced Studies, University of Illinois, Urbana. Author of* Kleinasiatische Personennamen; Personennamen griechischer Staedte; *and others.*

NAMES

M.A.   Marcelle Auclair (d. 1983). *Writer. Author of* Enfances et mort de Garcia Lorca; La Vie de Sainte Thérèse d'Avila; Le Livre du bonheur; *and others.*

GARCÍA LORCA, FEDERICO (Micropædia)

Ma.A.   Maurice Allais. *Professor of Economic Analysis, National College of Mines of Paris. Professor of Monetary Analysis, University of Paris. Author of* Traité d'économie pure.

INTERNATIONAL TRADE (*in part*)

M.A.A.   Maynard A. Amerine. *Emeritus Professor of Enology, University of California, Davis; Emeritus Enologist at the Agricultural Experiment Station. Author of* The Technology of Wine Making.

BEVERAGE PRODUCTION (*in part*)

Ma.A.C.   Margaret A. Carey. *Former Assistant Keeper, Department of Ethnography, British Museum, London. Author of* Myths and Legends of Africa.

AFRICAN ARTS (*in part*)

M.A.Al.   The Rev. Michel Adrien Allard, S.J. (d. 1976). *Director, Institute of Oriental Studies, St. Joseph University, Beirut, Lebanon. Author of* Le problème des attributs divins en théologie musulmane *and others.*

ASH‘ARĪ, ABU AL-ḤASAN AL- (Micropædia)

Ma.B.   Marino Berengo. *Professor of Modern History, University of Venice. Author of* La società veneta alla fine del 700 *and others.*

ITALY (*in part*)

Ma.Br.   Martin Brett. *Fellow of Robinson College, University of Cambridge. Lecturer and Senior Lecturer in Medieval History, University of Auckland, New Zealand, 1964–71. Author of* English Church under Henry I.

EUROPE (*in part*)

Ma.Bu.   Martin Butlin. *Keeper of the British Collection, Tate Gallery, London. Author of* Turner Watercolours; *coauthor of* The Paintings of J.M.W. Turner.

TURNER, J.M.W. (*in part*) (Micropædia)

Ma.C.   Malcolm Cowley. *Literary Adviser, The Viking Press. President, National Institute of Arts and Letters, New York City, 1956–59, 1961–64. Author of* The Faulkner-Cowley File; *editor of* The Portable Faulkner.

FAULKNER, WILLIAM (Micropædia)

M.A.C.   Michael Anthony Carson. *Professor of Geography, McGill University, Montreal. Coauthor of* Hillslope Form and Process.

CONTINENTAL LANDFORMS (*in part*)

M.A.Ca.   Marcello A. Carmagnani. *Professor of Latin American History, University of Turin, Italy. Author of* El salariado minero en Chile colonial.

CHILE (*in part*)

M.A.E.   M. Albert Evans. *Mining consultant. Coauthor of* Demonstration Mine Using Longwall Mining Techniques; Technical Manual on Longwall Mining Systems.

INDUSTRIES, EXTRACTION AND PROCESSING (*in part*)

Ma.E.O.   Mario E. Occhialino. *Professor of Law, University of New Mexico, Albuquerque.*

PROCEDURAL LAW (*in part*)

Ma.F.   Marvin Frankel. *Professor of Economics, University of Illinois, Urbana. Author of* British and American Manufacturing Productivity: A Comparison and Interpretation.

ECONOMIC GROWTH AND PLANNING (*in part*)

Ma.Fu.   Masutani Fumio. *Professor of the History of Religion, Taisho University, Tokyo.*

HŌNEN (Micropædia)

M.Ag.   Margarita Aguirre. *Writer. Author of* Las vidas de Pablo Neruda *and others.*

NERUDA, PABLO (Micropædia)

M.A.G.   Mahmud Ali Ghul. *Former Professor of Arabic and Semitic Languages, American University of Beirut.*

ARABIA (*in part*)

M.A.Gl.   Mary Ann Glendon. *Professor of Law, Harvard University. Author of* The New Family and the New Property.

INHERITANCE AND SUCCESSION (*in part*)
LAW, THE PRACTICE AND PROFESSION OF (*in part*)
LEGAL SYSTEMS, THE EVOLUTION OF MODERN WESTERN (*in part*)

Ma.H.   Marshall Hall, Jr. *IBM Professor Emeritus of Mathematics, California Institute of Technology, Pasadena. Author of* The Theory of Groups; Combinatorial Theory.

ALGEBRA (*in part*)

M.A.H.   Michael Anthony Hoskin. *Lecturer in History of Science, University of Cambridge. Author of* William Herschel and the Construction of the Heavens.

HERSCHEL, SIR JOHN, 1ST BARONET (Micropædia)

LOVELL, SIR BERNARD (*in part*)
(Micropædia)

Ma.Ha. **Mamie Harmon.** *Contributor to* Dictionary of Folklore, Mythology and Legend; *contributor and advisory editor to* Encyclopedia of World Art.

FOLK ARTS (*in part*)

Ma.J. **Marsden Jones.** *Professor of Arabic Studies, American University in Cairo. Editor of* Kitāb al-maghāzī lil-Wāqidī.

EGYPT (*in part*)

Ma.J.M. **Matthew James Moulton.** *Chief Editorial Writer,* The Scotsman, *Edinburgh.*

UNITED KINGDOM (*in part*)

Ma.K. **Max Kaltenmark.** *Director of Studies, École Pratique des Hautes Études (Institute for Advanced Research), Paris, 1957–78. Author of* Lao Tzu and Taoism.

LAO-TZU (Micropædia)

M.Ak. **Mustafa Akdağ** (d. 1973). *Professor of Modern History, University of Ankara. Author of* Turkiyenin iktisadi ve ictimai tarihi.

ATATÜRK

Ma.Ko. **Margaret Kohl.** *Free-lance wrter and translator. Staff member, English Department, University of Munich, 1962–68; 1978–80.*

COLOGNE (*in part*)
GERMANY (*in part*)

M.Al. **Mohammad Ali** (deceased). *Professor and Head, Department of History, Kābul University, Afghanistan. Author of* A Cultural History of Afghanistan; Afghanistan: Land of Glorious Past; *and many other works on Afghan history, culture, and economy.*

AFGHANISTAN (*in part*)
MAḤMŪD (GHAZNA) (Micropædia)

Ma.M. **Maurice Matloff.** *Adjunct Professor of History, Georgetown University, Washington, D.C. Chief Historian, Center of Military History, U.S. Department of the Army, Washington, D.C., 1973–81. Author of* Strategic Planning for Coalition Warfare, 1943–1944; *editor of* American Military History.

WAR, THE THEORY AND CONDUCT OF (*in part*)

M.A.M. **Maurice Alfred Millner.** *Former Professor of Law, University College, University of London. Author of* Negligence in Modern Law.

LEGAL SYSTEMS, THE EVOLUTION OF MODERN WESTERN (*in part*)

M.A.MacC. **Michael A. MacConaill.** *Emeritus Professor of Anatomy, University College, Cork, National University of Ireland. Coauthor of* Synovial Joints; Muscles and Movements.

SUPPORTIVE AND CONNECTIVE TISSUES (*in part*)

Ma.N. **Manning Nash.** *Professor of Anthropology, University of Chicago. Specialist on economic development and cultural change. Author of* Machine-Age Maya.

AMERICAN INDIANS (*in part*)

M.A.P. **Miodrag Al. Purković.** *Secretary, Serbian Orthodox Church of St. Sava, London.*

YUGOSLAVIA (*in part*)

Ma.R. **Mary Rowlatt** (d. 1983). *Free-lance writer on Egypt. Author of* Founders of Modern Egypt.

ALEXANDRIA (*in part*)

M.Ar. **Michael Argyle.** *Reader in Social Psychology, University of Oxford; Fellow of Wolfson College, Oxford. Author of* Social Interaction; The Psychology of Interpersonal Behaviour.

SOCIAL SCIENCES, THE (*in part*)

M.A.R. **Margaret Ann Richardson.** *Deputy Curator, Drawings Collection, Royal Institute of British Architects, London.*

PALLADIO, ANDREA (Micropædia)

M.A.Ro. **Margaret Ann Rowe.** *Lecturer in English, Palmerston North Teachers' College, New Zealand. Coauthor of* New Zealand.

NEW ZEALAND (*in part*)

M.As. **Maurice Ashley.** *Research Fellow, Loughborough University of Technology, England, 1967–70. Editor,* The Listener, *1958–67. Author of* The Greatness of Oliver Cromwell.

CHARLES I (GREAT BRITAIN) (Micropædia)
CROMWELL, OLIVER (*in part*)

M.A.S. **M.A. Screech.** *Fielden Professor of French Language and Literature, University College, University of London. Author of* Rabelais *and others.*

RABELAIS, FRANÇOIS (*in part*) (Micropædia)

M.A.Sa. **Michael Anthony Samuels.** *Vice President, International and U.S. Chamber of Commerce. Executive Director, Center for Strategic and International Studies, Georgetown University, Washington, D.C., 1977–81. U.S. Ambassador to Sierra Leone, 1974–77. Coeditor of* Portuguese Africa: A Handbook.

SOUTHERN AFRICA (*in part*)

M.A.Su. **Margaret Ann Sumner.** *Lecturer in Physiology, University of Melbourne, Australia, and University College, University of London. Author of* Thought for Food.

DRUGS AND DRUG ACTION (*in part*)

M.A.v.M. **M.A. van Meerhaeghe.** *Professor of Economics, State University of Ghent, Belgium. Author of* International Economic Institutions; International Economics.

INTERNATIONAL TRADE (*in part*)

M.B. **Minodhar Barthakur.** *Professor of Geography, Gauhāti University,*

Assam, India. Author of numerous articles on geography.

INDIA (*in part*)

M.Ba. **Michael Bar-Zohar.** *Free-lance writer. Member of the Knesset. Former Lecturer in Political Science, Haifa University, Israel. Author of* Ben-Gurion: The Armed Prophet *and others.*

BEN-GURION, DAVID (Micropædia)

M.B.C. **Malcolm Breckenridge Carpenter, M.D.** *Professor and Chairman, Department of Anatomy, Uniformed Services University of the Health Sciences, Bethesda, Maryland. Coauthor of* Human Neuroanatomy.

NERVES AND NERVOUS SYSTEMS (*in part*)

M.Be. **Manfred Bensing.** *Professor of History, Karl Marx University, Leipzig. Author of* Thomas Müntzer.

MÜNTZER, THOMAS (Micropædia)

M.B.F. **Manuel Basas Fernández.** *Former Professor, Faculty of Economic Sciences, University of Valladolid, Bilbao, Spain. Author of* Breve Historia de la ria y noble Villa de Bilbao.

SPAIN (*in part*)

M.Bg. **Mark Blaug.** *Professor of the Economics of Education, Institute of Education, University of London. Author of* Economic Theory in Retrospect.

SOCIAL SCIENCES, THE (*in part*)

M.B.G. **Manuel Ballesteros Gaibrois.** *Professor and Head, Section of American History, University of Madrid. Author of* Francisco Pizarro *and others.*

PIZARRO, FRANCISCO (Micropædia)

M.Bi. **Margarete Bieber** (d. 1978). *Associate Professor of Art History and Archaeology, Columbia University, 1937–48; Special Lecturer, School of General Studies, 1949–54. Author of* The History of the Greek and Roman Theater; The Sculpture of the Hellenistic Age.

DRESS AND ADORNMENT (*in part*)

M.B.J. **Marius B. Jansen.** *Professor of History, Princeton University. Author of* Sakamoto Ryōma and the Meiji Restoration *and others.*

JAPAN (*in part*)

M.Bl. **Miroslav Blažek.** *Professor of Human Geography and of Regional Economy, School of Economics, Prague. Author of* Economic Geography of Czechoslovakia.

CZECHOSLOVAKIA (*in part*)

M.Bn. **Maurice Burton.** *Deputy Keeper of Zoology, British Museum, London, 1925–58. Author of* Encyclopaedia of Animals *and others.*

GERMANY (*in part*)

M.Bo. **Marc Bouloiseau.** *Former Secretary, Commission for the Economic and Social History of the French Revolution. Emeritus Teaching Assistant in History of the French Revolution, University of Paris. Author of* Robespierre *and others.*

ROBESPIERRE, MAXIMILIEN-FRANÇOIS-
MARIE-ISADORE DE (Micropædia)

M.B.P.   Michel B. Pelletier. *Political
Affairs Officer, Department of Political
Affairs, Trusteeship and Decolonization,
United Nations, New York City.*
EASTERN AFRICA (*in part*)

M.B.R.   Michael B. Rowton (d. 1986).
*Professor of Near Eastern Languages
and Civilizations, Oriental Institute,
University of Chicago.*
HISTORY, THE STUDY OF (*in part*)

M.B.T.   Martin Bice Travis, Jr.
*Professor of Political Science, State
University of New York at Stony Brook.
Coeditor of and contributor to* Control of
Foreign Relations in Modern Nations.
MEXICO (*in part*)

M.Bu.   Milton Burton (d. 1985).
*Professor of Chemistry, University
of Notre Dame, Indiana, 1945–71;
Director, Radiation Laboratory, 1946–
71. Coeditor of* Advances in Radiation
Chemistry.
RADIATION (*in part*)

M.C.   Maurice Cranston. *Emeritus
Professor of Political Science, London
School of Economics and Political
Science, University of London.
Biographer of Locke and Rousseau.*
HUME (*in part*)
IDEOLOGY
ROUSSEAU, JEAN-JACQUES

M.Car.   Max Cary (d. 1958). *Reader,
then Professor of Ancient History,
University of London, 1908–46. Author
of* The Geographic Background of Greek
and Roman History.
GRECO-ROMAN CIVILIZATION, CLASSICAL
(*in part*)

M.C.G.   M. Charles Gilbert. *Professor
of Petrology and Head, Department
of Geology, Texas A&M University,
College Station.*
MINERALS AND ROCKS (*in part*)

M.Ch.   Mary Chamot. *Assistant
Keeper, Tate Gallery, London, 1950–65.
Author of* Modern Painting in England.
TURNER, J.M.W. (*in part*) (Micropædia)

M.C.J.   Marshall C. Johnston.
*Professor of Botany; Associate Director,
Plant Resources Center, University of
Texas at Austin. Coauthor of* Manual of
the Vascular Plants of Texas.
ANGIOSPERMS (*in part*)

M.Cl.   Mary Clarke. *Editor,* The
Dancing Times, *London. Author of* The
Sadler's Wells Ballet; *coauthor of* The
History of Dance *and others.*
DANCE, THE ART OF (*in part*)

Mc.M.   McKim Marriott. *Professor,
Department of Anthropology and Social
Sciences, Collegiate Division, University
of Chicago. Author of* Caste Ranking and
Community Structure in Five Regions of
India and Pakistan *and others.*
SOCIAL DIFFERENTIATION (*in part*)

M.C.M.   Michael C. Meyer. *Professor
of History; Director, Latin American*

*Area Center, University of Arizona,
Tucson. Coauthor of* The Course of
Mexican History.
MEXICO (*in part*)

M.C.Ma.   Michael C. Malin. *Associate
Professor of Geology, Arizona State
University, Tempe. Coauthor of*
Earthlike Planets.
SOLAR SYSTEM, THE (*in part*)

M.Co.   Michael Cordner. *Lecturer
in English and Related Literature,
University of York, England. Editor of*
The Plays of Sir George Etherege.
ENGLISH LITERATURE (*in part*)

M.C.R.   Marvin Chauncey Ross (d.
1977). *Curator, Hillwood (art collections
of Mrs. Merriweather Post), Washington,
D.C. Chief Curator, Los Angeles County
Museum, 1952–55.*
DECORATIVE ARTS AND FURNISHINGS
(*in part*)

M.C.S.   Malcolm C. Shurtleff.
*Professor of Plant Pathology; Extension
Plant Pathologist, University of Illinois,
Urbana. Author of* How to Control Plant
Diseases in Home and Garden.
DISEASE (*in part*)

M.D.   Myles Dillon (d. 1972). *Senior
Professor of Celtic Studies, Dublin
Institute for Advanced Studies, 1949–72.
Author of* Early Irish Society.
EUROPEAN RELIGIONS, ANCIENT (*in part*)

M.D.C.   Michael Douglas Coe.
*Professor of Anthropology, Yale
University. Author of* The Maya.
PRE-COLUMBIAN CIVILIZATIONS
(*in part*)

**M.-D.Ch.   The Rev. Marie-Dominique
Chenu, O.P.** *Professor of Theology,
University of Paris. Author of* Toward
Understanding St. Thomas.
THOMISM, THOMAS AQUINAS AND
(*in part*)

M.De.   Mary Delane. *Free-lance writer.
Women's Editor,* The Times (*London*),
1954–64. *Author of* Sardinia: The
Undefeated Island.
ITALY (*in part*)

M. de F.   Michael de Ferdinandy.
*Emeritus Professor of Humanities,
University of Puerto Rico, Río Piedras.
Author of* El emperador Carlos V:
semblanza de un hombre *and others.*
CHARLES V (GERMANY/HOLY ROMAN
EMPIRE) (Micropædia)

M. Del V.   Mario Del Viscovo.
*Professor of Economics and Politics of
Transport, University of Rome. Director,
Centre for Studies of Transportation
Systems, Rome. Author of* Il conto
nazionale dei trasporti.
ITALY (*in part*)

M.D.H.M.   Mark D.H. Miller.
*Research Associate, Syracuse University,
New York.*
SOUTH AMERICA (*in part*)

**M.D.K.   The Rev. Michael David
Knowles, O.S.B.** (d. 1974). *Regius
Professor of Modern History, University*

of Cambridge, 1954–63. Author of The
Benedictines: A Digest for Moderns; The
Evolution of Medieval Thought; Thomas
Becket; *and others.*
BECKET, SAINT THOMAS (Micropædia)
BENEDICT OF NURSIA, SAINT
(Micropædia)
HENRY II (ENGLAND) (Micropædia)
MACAULAY OF ROTHLEY, THOMAS
BABINGTON MACAULAY, BARON
(Micropædia)
ROMAN CATHOLICISM (*in part*)

M.Do.   Martin Domke (d. 1980).
*Adjunct Professor of Law, New York
University, New York City. Consultant
on Commercial and International
Arbitration. Author of* The Law and
Practice of Commercial
Arbitration.
JUDICIAL AND ARBITRATIONAL
SYSTEMS (*in part*)

M.Dr.   Moira Dunbar. *Acting Director,
Division of Earth Sciences, Defence
Research Board, Ottawa, Canada,
1975–77.*
ARCTIC, THE (*in part*)

M.Du.   Maurice Duverger. *Professor
of Comparative Political Systems,
University of Paris I. Author of* Les
Partis politiques.
POLITICAL PARTIES AND INTEREST
GROUPS (*in part*)

M. Du P.C.   Martin Du Pré Cooper (d.
1986). *Music Editor,* Daily Telegraph,
London, 1954–76. *Author of* French
Music, 1869–1924; Georges Bizet;
and others.
BIZET, GEORGES (Micropædia)
FRANCK, CÉSAR (Micropædia)

M.E.   Marcel Emerit. *Emeritus
Professor of History; Member, Academy
of Ethics and Politics, Institute of
France. Author of* L'Algérie à l'époque d'
Abd-el-Kader.
ABDELKADER (Micropædia)

M.E.Bl.   Milton E. Bliss. *Farmer
and Agricultural communications
specialist. Author of* A Handbook on
Farm Broadcasting for the Developing
Countries.
FARMING AND AGRICULTURAL
TECHNOLOGY (*in part*)

M.E.D.   M. Edward Davis, M.D.
(d. 1978). *Joseph Bolivar De Lee
Professor of Obstetrics and Gynecology,
University of Chicago, 1947–66.
Coauthor of* De Lee's Obstetrics
for Nurses.
REPRODUCTION AND REPRODUCTIVE
SYSTEMS (*in part*)

M.E.DeB.   Michael E. DeBakey, M.D.
*Chancellor, Baylor College of Medicine;
Professor and Chairman, Department
of Surgery. Director, National Heart
and Blood Vessel Research and
Demonstration Center, Methodist
Hospital, Houston, Texas. Coauthor of*
Blood Transfusion *and others.*
CIRCULATION AND CIRCULATORY
SYSTEMS (*in part*)

M.e.D.S.   Mohy el Din Sabr.
Director-General, Arab League Educational, Cultural and Scientific Organization, Cairo. Minister of Education, Republic of The Sudan, 1969–72. Author of Cultural Change and Community Development.
SUDAN (*in part*)

M.Ee.   Mircea Eliade (d. 1986). *Sewell L. Avery Distinguished Service Professor, Divinity School; Professor, Committee on Social Thought, University of Chicago.*
SACRED OFFICES AND ORDERS (*in part*)

Me.F.G.   Mercedes Fermín Gómez.
Professor of Geography, Central University of Venezuela, Caracas. Author of The Orinoco Basin.
SOUTH AMERICA (*in part*)

M.E.H.   Melvin E. Hecht. *Emeritus Professor of Geography and Regional Development, University of Arizona, Tucson.*
UNITED STATES OF AMERICA (*in part*)

M.E.M.   Martin E. Marty. *Fairfax M. Cone Distinguished Service Professor, Divinity School, University of Chicago. Associate Editor,* The Christian Century. *Author of* Righteous Empire: The Protestant Experience in America *and many other works.*
PROTESTANTISM (*in part*)
ROMAN CATHOLICISM (*in part*)

M.E.Ma.   Martin E. Malia. *Professor of History, University of California, Berkeley. Author of* Alexander Herzen and the Birth of Russian Socialism, 1812–1855.
HERZEN, ALEKSANDR (Micropædia)

M.E.Mu.   Marvin E. Mundel.
President, M. E. Mundel and Associates, Consulting Industrial Engineers, Silver Spring, Maryland.
ENGINEERING (*in part*)

M.E.O.   Milton Edgeworth Osborne.
Head, Southeast Asia—Pacific Branch, Office of National Assessments, Canberra, Australia. Author of Southeast Asia: An Introductory History.
SOUTHEAST ASIA, MAINLAND
(*in part*)

M.E.P.   Maynard E. Pirsig. *Emeritus Professor of Law, University of Minnesota, Minneapolis. Professor of Law, William Mitchell College of Law, St. Paul, Minnesota. Coauthor of* Cases and Materials on Professional Responsibility.
LAW, THE PROFESSION AND PRACTICE
OF (*in part*)

M.E.R.   Marjorie E. Reeves. *Honorary Fellow and former Vice-Principal, St. Anne's College, Oxford; former Lecturer in Modern History, University of Oxford. Author of* The Influence of Prophecy in the Later Middle Ages: A Study in Joachimism.
JOACHIM OF FIORE (Micropædia)

M.E.T.   Mary Elizabeth Tiles.
Secretary, Royal Institute of Philosophy, London. Author of Bachelard: Science

and Objectivity.
PHILOSOPHICAL ANTHROPOLOGY (*in part*)

M.E.Y.   Malcolm Edward Yapp. *Senior Lecturer in the History of the Near and Middle East, School of Oriental and African Studies, University of London.*
TURKEY AND ANCIENT ANATOLIA
(*in part*)

M.F.   Merle Fainsod (d. 1972). *Carl H. Pforzheimer Professor of Government; Director of the Library, Harvard University, 1965–72; Director, Russian Research Center, 1959–64. Author of* How Russia Is Ruled *and others.*
UNION OF SOVIET SOCIALIST REPUBLICS
(*in part*)

M.F.A.   Sir Michael Francis Atiyah.
Royal Society Research Professor, Mathematical Institute, University of Oxford. Author of K-Theory; *coauthor of* Introduction to Commutative Algebra.
GEOMETRY (*in part*)

M.F.G.   Martin F. Glaessner. *Emeritus Professor of Geology and Honorary Research Associate, University of Adelaide, Australia. Coeditor of* Geology of South Australia.
AUSTRALIA (*in part*)

M.F.Go.   Morris F. Goodman.
Associate Professor of Linguistics, Northwestern University, Evanston, Illinois. Author of several articles on African languages and A Comparative Study of Creole French Dialects.
LANGUAGES OF THE WORLD (*in part*)

M.Fl.   Marcel Florkin, M.D. (d. 1979). *Professor of Biochemistry, State University of Liège, Belgium. Author of* L'Évolution biochimique.
VESALIUS, ANDREAS (Micropædia)

M.F.M.   Mark F. Meier. *Director, Institute of Arctic and Alpine Research; Professor of Geological Sciences, University of Colorado, Boulder.*
ICE AND ICE FORMATIONS (*in part*)

M.F.Mo.   Maynard F. Moseley, Jr.
Professor of Botany, University of California, Santa Barbara. Author of a series of morphological studies on the family Nymphaeaceae.
ANGIOSPERMS (*in part*)

M.Fo.   Murray Fowler. *Emeritus Professor of Linguistics, University of Wisconsin, Madison. Coeditor of* Materials for the Study of the Etruscan Language.
LANGUAGES OF THE WORLD (*in part*)

M.Fr.   Milton Friedman. *Paul Snowden Russell Distinguished Service Professor Emeritus of Economics, University of Chicago. Senior Research Fellow, Hoover Institution, Stanford University, California. Nobel Prize for Economics, 1976. Author of* Dollars and Deficits *and others.*
MONEY

M.Fre.   Michael Freund (d. 1973). *Professor of Political Theory and History, Christian Albrecht University of*

Kiel, West Germany. Author of Deutsche Geschichte; "Friedrich Ebert" in Die grossen Deutschen; *and others.*
EBERT, FRIEDRICH (Micropædia)

M.F.R.S.   Maurice Francis Richard Shadbolt. *Short-story and travel writer; novelist. Author of* The New Zealanders *and others.*
AUSTRALIA AND NEW ZEALAND,
LITERATURES OF (*in part*)

M.F.S.   Mark F. Schwartz. *Research and Clinical Associate; Director of Educational Programs, Masters and Johnson Institute, St. Louis, Missouri.*
SEX AND SEXUALITY (*in part*)

M.G.   Marija Gimbutas. *Professor of European Archaeology, University of California, Los Angeles. Author of* The Bronze Age Cultures of Central and Eastern Europe *and others.*
BALKANS (*in part*)
PREHISTORIC PEOPLES AND CULTURES
(*in part*)
UNION OF SOVIET SOCIALIST REPUBLICS
(*in part*)

M.Ga.   Mikael Gam. *Minister for Greenland, 1960–64. Author of* Den grønlandske kvinde.
ARCTIC, THE (*in part*)

M.G.A.V.   Malcolm G.A. Vale. *Fellow and Tutor in History, St. John's College, Oxford; Lecturer in Modern History, University of Oxford. Author of* War and Chivalry *and others.*
JOAN OF ARC (*in part*)

M.G.B.   Michael Graham Balfour.
Emeritus Professor of European History, University of East Anglia, Norwich, England. Author of The Kaiser and His Times.
WILLIAM II (GERMAN EMPIRE)
(Micropædia)

M.G.G.   M. Grant Gross. *Director, Ocean Sciences Division, National Science Foundation, Washington, D.C. Author of* Oceanography.
OCEANS (*in part*)

M.Gi.   Martin Gimm. *Professor of Sinology, University of Cologne.*
DORGON (Micropædia)

M.G.L.   Mikhail Grigoriyevich Lozinsky (d. 1976). *Head, Laboratory of High-Temperature Metallography, Institute for the Study of Machines, Moscow. Author of* Industrial Applications of Induction Heating *and others.*
ENERGY CONVERSION (*in part*)

M.G.Ma.   Maxwell Gay Marwick.
Reader in Humanities (Anthropology and Sociology), Griffith University, Brisbane, Australia, 1976–81. Author of Sorcery in Its Social Setting: A Study of the Northern Rhodesian Cewa; *editor of* Witchcraft and Sorcery: Selected Readings.
OCCULTISM (*in part*)

M.Gr.   Michael Grant. *President and Vice Chancellor, Queen's University* of Belfast, Northern Ireland, 1959-66. *Author of* History of Rome; Myths of the Greeks and Romans; *and others; editor of* Latin Literature *and others.*

ANTONY, MARK (Micropædia)
AUGUSTUS
EUROPEAN RELIGIONS, ANCIENT (*in part*)
HORACE (Micropædia)

M.Gre.   Morris Greenspan. *Writer on international law. Author of* The Modern Law of Land Warfare; The Soldier's Guide to the Laws of War.

WAR, THE THEORY AND CONDUCT OF
    (*in part*)

M.G.W.   M. Gordon Wolman. *Professor and Chairman, Department of Geography and Environmental Engineering, Johns Hopkins University, Baltimore, Maryland. An authority on fluvial processes and ecological problems concerning rivers. Coauthor of* Fluvial Processes in Geomorphology.

GEOMORPHIC PROCESSES (*in part*)

M.H.   Maureen Heneghan. *Costume Designer, Stratford-on-Avon Shakespeare Company, BBC-TV, Stratford Festival, Ontario. Associate Professor of Costume Design, Brandeis University, Waltham, Massachusetts.*

THEATRICAL PRODUCTION (*in part*)

M.Ha.   Mason Hammond. *Pope Professor Emeritus of Latin Language and Literature; former Professor of Roman History, Harvard University. Author of* The Antonine Monarchy.

TRAJAN (Micropædia)

M.Has.   Margaret Hastings (d. 1979). *Professor of History, Douglass College, Rutgers University, New Brunswick, New Jersey, 1960–75. Author of* The Court of Common Pleas in Fifteenth Century England *and others.*

UNITED KINGDOM (*in part*)

M.H.Au.   Maung Htin Aung (d. 1978). *Associate Fellow, St. Antony's College, University of Oxford. Burmese Ambassador to Ceylon, 1959–63. Rector and Vice Chancellor, University of Rangoon, 1946–59. Author of* Burmese Drama; A History of Burma; *and others.*

BURMA (*in part*)
SOUTHEAST ASIAN ARTS (*in part*)

M.H.B.   M.H. Butler. *Lecturer in English, University of Leeds, England. Author of* Theatre and Crisis, 1632–1642.

ENGLISH LITERATURE (*in part*)

M.H.Bo.   Marc H. Bornstein. *Professor of Psychology and Human Development, New York University, New York City. Author of* Development in Infancy: An Introduction *and others.*

BEHAVIOR, THE DEVELOPMENT OF
    HUMAN (*in part*)

M.H.C.   Mary Heimerdinger Clench. *Adjunct Curator of Birds, Florida State Museum, University of Florida, Gainesville. Author and coauthor of numerous articles on birds.*

BIRDS (*in part*)

M.H.D.   Michael H. Day. *Professor of Anatomy, St. Thomas's Hospital Medical School, University of London. Author of* Guide to Fossil Man.

EVOLUTION, HUMAN (*in part*)

M.H.H.   Max H. Hey. *Senior Principal Scientific Officer, Department of Mineralogy, British Museum (Natural History), London, 1951–69. Author of* Catalogue of Meteorites.

SOLAR SYSTEM, THE (*in part*)

M.H.K.   Malcolm H. Kerr (d. 1984). *President, American University of Beirut, 1982–84. Professor of Political Science, University of California, Los Angeles, 1967–82. Author of* Islamic Reform: The Political and Legal Theories of Muhammad 'Abduh and Rashid Rida.

'ABDUH, MUḤAMMAD (Micropædia)

M.H.S.   The Rev. Massey H. Shepherd, Jr. *Hodges Professor Emeritus of Liturgics, Church Divinity School of the Pacific, Berkeley, California. Author of* The Worship of the Church *and others.*

CHRISTIANITY (*in part*)

M.Hu.   Mahmud Husain (d. 1975). *Vice Chancellor, University of Karāchi, Pakistan. Editor of* History of the Freedom Movement.

JINNAH, MOHAMMED ALI (Micropædia)

M.H.W.   Michael Henry Woodford. *Secretary, British Falconers' Club, London, 1956–60. Author of* A Manual of Falconry.

FALCONRY (*in part*) (Micropædia)

M.H.Z.   Martin Huldrych Zimmermann (d. 1984). *Charles Bullard Professor of Forestry, Harvard University; Director, Harvard Forest, Petersham, 1970–84. Coauthor of* Trees: Structure and Function.

TISSUES AND FLUIDS (*in part*)

Mi.B.   Michel Burdeau. *Director General, Regional Council of Bourgogne, Dijon, France. Author of numerous reports on transportation.*

FRANCE (*in part*)

M.I.B.   Michael I. Bruce. *Angas Professor of Chemistry, University of Adelaide, Australia. Coeditor of* Progress in Organometallic Chemistry.

CHEMICAL COMPOUNDS (*in part*)

M.I.C.   Dame Margaret I. Cole (d. 1980). *Honorary President, Fabian Society, England. Author of* Beatrice Webb *and others; editor of* The Webbs and Their Work.

WEBB, SIDNEY AND BEATRICE
    (Micropædia)

Mi.D.   Michael A.E. Dummett. *Wykeham Professor of Logic, University of Oxford; Fellow of New College, Oxford. Author of* Frege: Philosophy of Language *and others.*

FREGE, GOTTLOB (Micropædia)

M.I.H.   Marvin Irving Herzog. *Professor of Linguistics and Yiddish Studies; Chairman, Department of Linguistics, Columbia University. Author of* The Yiddish Language in Northern Poland; *coeditor of* The Field of Yiddish, Third and Fourth Collections.

LANGUAGES OF THE WORLD
    (*in part*)

Mi.Ma.   Michael Edward Mallett. *Professor of History, University of Warwick, England. Author of* The Borgias *and others.*

BORGIA, CESARE, DUC DE VALENTINOIS
    (Micropædia)

M.I.N.   Marion I. Newbigin (d. 1934). *Editor, Scottish Geographical Magazine Author of* Geographical Aspects of Balkan Problems *and others.*

BALKANS (*in part*)

M.I.R.   Mikhail Ivanovich Rostovtsev. *Senior Research Associate, Institute of Geography, Academy of Sciences of the U.S.S.R.; Candidate of Sciences (Geography). Coauthor of* Belorussian S.S.R.

UNION OF SOVIET SOCIALIST REPUBLICS
    (*in part*)

Mi.Ro.   Michel Rouzé. *Former producer in French broadcasting. Author of* Robert Oppenheimer and the Atomic Bomb; Robert Oppenheimer: The Man and His Theories.

OPPENHEIMER, J. ROBERT (Micropædia)

Mi.S.   Michael S. Schudson. *Associate Professor of Sociology, University of California, San Diego, at La Jolla.*

CULTURE, THE CONCEPT AND
    COMPONENTS OF (*in part*)

Mi.V.   Michele Vishny. *Art historian and critic. Author of* Mordcai Ardon; *contributor to* Arts Magazine.

PISSARRO, CAMILLE (Micropædia)

M.I.V.   Milton I. Vanger. *Professor of History, Brandeis University, Waltham, Massachusetts; Chairman of Latin American Studies, 1971–81. Author of* José Batlle y Ordoñez of Uruguay.

URUGUAY (*in part*)

M.I.W.   Matthew Immanuel Wiencke. *Professor of Classics, Dartmouth College, Hanover, New Hampshire.*

WINCKELMANN, JOHANN (Micropædia)

M.J.   Madeleine Jarry. *Principal Inspector, Mobilier National (state furniture collection); National Factories of Gobelins and Beauvais (tapestry); and of the Savonnerie (carpet factory), Ministry of Cultural Affairs, France. Author of* World Tapestry *and others.*

DECORATIVE ARTS AND FURNISHINGS
    (*in part*)

M.J.B.   Margaret J. Baigent. *Associate Professor of Nutrition, University of Toronto.*

BIOCHEMICAL COMPONENTS OF
    ORGANISMS (*in part*)

M.J.D.   Mário José Domingues. *Author of* O Marquês de Pombal *and others.*

POMBAL, SEBASTIÃO DE CARBALHO,
    MARQUÊS DE (Micropædia)

M.J.Dr.   Mark J. Dresden. *Emeritus Professor of Iranian Studies, University of Pennsylvania, Philadelphia. Editor of* Modern Persian Reader *and others.*
IRAN (*in part*)

M.J.Du.   Maxwell John Dunbar. *Emeritus Professor of Zoology, McGill University, Montreal; Chairman, Marine Sciences Center, 1963–77.*
ARCTIC, THE (*in part*)

M.J.E.   Martin J. Esslin. *Professor of Drama, Stanford University, California. Head of Radio Drama, British Broadcasting Corporation, London, 1963–77. Author of* Brecht: The Man and His Work; The Theatre of the Absurd.
BECKETT, SAMUEL (Micropædia)

M.J.E.B.   Maurice J.E. Brown (d. 1975). *Author of* Schubert: A Critical Biography; Essays on Schubert.
SCHUBERT, FRANZ (*in part*)
  (Micropædia)

M.J.K.   Martin J. Klein. *Eugene Higgins Professor of the History of Physics, Yale University.*
BOHR

M.J.Ke.   Martin J. Kemp. *Professor of Fine Arts, University of St. Andrews, Scotland.*
ARCHITECTURE, THE HISTORY OF
  WESTERN (*in part*)
PAINTING, THE HISTORY OF WESTERN
  (*in part*)
SCULPTURE, THE HISTORY OF WESTERN
  (*in part*)

M.J.L.   Margaret Jean Legum. *Free-lance journalist. Editor,* X-Ray *on Current Affairs in Southern Africa. Coauthor of* South Africa: Crisis for the West.
SOUTH AFRICA (*in part*)

M.J.Lo.   M. John Loeffler. *Professor of Geography, University of Colorado, Boulder. Author of several articles on Colorado.*
UNITED STATES OF AMERICA (*in part*)

M.J.M.   Maruice J. Meisner. *Professor of History, University of Wisconsin, Madison. Author of* Mao's China.
CHINA (*in part*)

M.J.MacL.   Murdo J. MacLeod. *Professor of History, University of Arizona, Tucson. Author of* Spanish Central America.
ECUADOR (*in part*)
WEST INDIES, THE (*in part*)

M.J.Mo.   Michel J. Mollat. *Emeritus Professor of History, University of Paris. Author of* Genèse médiévale de la France moderne; Les Affaires de Jacques Coeur.
CHARLES (BURGUNDY) (Micropædia)
COEUR, JACQUES (Micropædia)
FRANCE (*in part*)
LOUIS XI (FRANCE) (Micropædia)

M.Jo.   Matthew Josephson (d. 1978). *Author of* Edison: A Biography *and many others.*
EDISON (*in part*)

M.J.O.   Margaret J. Osler. *Associate Professor of History, University of Calgary, Alberta.*
PHYSICAL SCIENCES, THE (*in part*)

M.J.P.   Michael J. Pelczar, Jr. *Emeritus Vice President for Graduate Studies and Research; Emeritus Professor of Microbiology, University of Maryland, College Park. President, Council of Graduate Schools in the United States. Coauthor of* Microbiology; Elements of Microbiology.
BACTERIA

M.J.S.B.   Michael J.S. Belton. *Astronomer, Kitt Peak National Observatory, Tucson, Arizona.*
SOLAR SYSTEM, THE (*in part*)

M.K.   Marshall Kay (d. 1975). *Newberry Professor of Geology, Columbia University, 1967–73. Among the first to provide a synthesis of geological history in terms of geosynclines and their development. Author of* North American Geosynclines.
CONTINENTAL LANDFORMS (*in part*)

M.Ke.   Mark Keller. *Emeritus Professor, Rutgers University, New Brunswick, New Jersey; Emeritus Editor,* Journal of Studies on Alcohol. *Editor of* International Bibliography of Studies on Alcohol.
ALCOHOL AND DRUG CONSUMPTION
  (*in part*)

M.Kh.   Majid Khadduri. *Emeritus Professor of Middle East Studies, School of Advanced International Studies, Johns Hopkins University, Baltimore. Author of* Independent Iraq; Republican Iraq; Socialist Iraq.
IRAQ (*in part*)

M.Ki.   Martin Kilson. *Professor of Government, Harvard University; Research Associate, Harvard Center for International Affairs. Author of* Political Change in a West African State.
KAUNDA, KENNETH (Micropædia)

M.K.L.   Mildred K. Lehman. *Associate Administrator, Alcohol, Drug Abuse, and Mental Health Administration, U.S. Department of Health and Human Services, Rockville, Maryland.*
GODDARD, ROBERT HUTCHINGS (*in part*)
  (Micropædia)

M.K.N.   Mehdi K. Nakosteen (d. 1982). *Professor of the History and Philosophy of Education, University of Colorado, Boulder. Author of* The History and Philosophy of Education.
EDUCATION, HISTORY OF (*in part*)

M.Ko.   Mieczyslaw Kolinski (d. 1981). *Composer, ethnomusicologist, and author of many musicological and ethnomusicological articles.*
MUSIC, THE ART OF (*in part*)

M.K.P.   Macaire K. Pedanou. *Director, Office of the Commissioner for Namibia, United Nations, New York City.*
WESTERN AFRICA (*in part*)

M.Kr.   Melvin Kranzberg. *Callaway Professor of the History of Science and Technology, Georgia Institute of Technology, Atlanta. Editor in Chief,* Technology and Culture (*quarterly*), *1958–81. Coauthor of* By the Sweat of Thy Brow: Work in the Western World *and others.*
WORK AND EMPLOYMENT (*in part*)

M.Ks.   Manfred Krebs. *Former Director, Baden State Archives, Karlsruhe, West Germany.*
GERMANY (*in part*)

M.K.Sp.   Monroe K. Spears. *Moody Professor of English, Rice University, Houston, Texas. Author of* The Poetry of W.H. Auden; Dionysus and the City; *editor of* W.H. Auden: A Collection of Critical Essays.
AUDEN, W.H. (Micropædia)

M.L.   Maurits Lindström. *Professor of Geology, Geological–Paleontological Institute, Philipps University of Marburg, West Germany. Author of* Conodonts.
GEOCHRONOLOGY (*in part*)

M.L.-B.   Massimo Livi-Bacci. *Professor of Demography, University of Florence. Author of* The Demographic and Social Pattern of Emigration from the Southern European Countries.
ITALY (*in part*)

M.L.C.   Martin Lowther Clarke. *Former Professor of Latin, University College of North Wales, Bangor, University of Wales. Author of* Rhetoric at Rome; Higher Education in the Ancient World.
QUINTILIAN (Micropædia)

M.L.D.   Mikhail Leonidovich Djibladze. *Journalist.*
UNION OF SOVIET SOCIALIST REPUBLICS
  (*in part*)

M.Le.   Michel Lejeune. *Director of Research, National Center for Scientific Research, Paris. Author of* Phonétique historique du mycénien et du grec ancien *and others.*
LANGUAGES OF THE WORLD (*in part*)

M.L.Go.   Marie Louise Goodnight. *Free-lance writer and researcher. Instructor in Biological Sciences, Purdue University, West Lafayette, Indiana, 1946–65. Coauthor of* Zoology.
ARACHNIDS (*in part*)

M.Li.   Martin Lindauer. *Professor of Zoology and Comparative Physiology; Director, Zoological Institute, University of Würzburg, West Germany. Author of* Communication Among Social Bees.
INSECTS (*in part*)

Ml.J.   Michael Jaffé. *Professor of the History of Western Art; Director, Fitzwilliam Museum, University of Cambridge; Fellow of King's College, Cambridge. Author of* Rubens and Italy.
RUBENS, PETER PAUL (*in part*)
  (Micropædia)

M.Ln.   Milton Lehman (d. 1966). *Free-lance writer. Author of* This High

Man: The Life of Robert H. Goddard.
GODDARD, ROBERT HUTCHINGS (*in part*)
(Micropædia)

Ml.R.   Michael Roe. *Professor of History, University of Tasmania, Hobart, Australia. Author of* Quest for Authority in Eastern Australia, 1835–1851.
AUSTRALIA (*in part*)

M.L.R.   The Hon. Miriam Louisa Rothschild. *Coauthor of* An Illustrated Catalogue of the Rothschild Collection of Fleas (Siphonaptera) in the British Museum (Natural History) *and author of several articles on fleas.*
INSECTS (*in part*)

M.McA.   Mary McAuley. *Fellow and Tutor in Politics, St. Hilda's College, University of Oxford. Author of* Politics and the Soviet Union *and others.*
LENINGRAD (*in part*)

M.McC.   Malcolm McChesney. *Senior Lecturer in Mechanical Engineering, University of Liverpool. Coauthor of* The Dynamics of Relaxing Gases.
MATTER (*in part*)

M.Me.   Manuel Medina. *Professor of International Law and International Relations, University of Madrid.*
SPAIN (*in part*)

M.M.E.   Marc Marie Escholier (d. 1972). *Judge, Supreme Court of Appeal, Paris. Author of* Port-Royal *and others.*
JANSEN, CORNELIUS OTTO (Micropædia)

M.M.El-K.   Magdi M. El-Kammash. *Former Associate Professor of Economics, North Carolina State University at Raleigh. Author of* Economic Development and Planning in Egypt.
AFRICA (*in part*)

M.M.F.   Merrill M. Flood. *President, Merrill Flood and Associates (computer services), Santa Monica, California. Emeritus Professor of Mathematical Biology, University of Michigan, Ann Arbor. Coauthor of* Automation and the Library of Congress.
INFORMATION PROCESSING (*in part*)

M.Mi.   Mairin Mitchell. *Free-lance writer. Author of* The Odyssey of Acurio Who Sailed with Magellan *and others.*
MAGELLAN, FERDINAND (Micropædia)

M.Ml.   Michel Michel. *Assistant Master of Geography, University of Paris I.*
BRAZIL (*in part*)

M.M.M.   Maynard Malcolm Miller. *Professor of Geology; Dean, College of Mines and Earth Resources; Chief, Idaho Bureau of Mines and Geology, University of Idaho, Moscow. Director, Foundation for Glacier and Environmental Research, Pacific Science Center, Seattle, Washington. Author of numerous mongraphs and journal articles.*
UNITED STATES OF AMERICA (*in part*)

M.Mn.   Sir Max Mallowan (d. 1978). *Professor of Western Asiatic*

Archaeology, University of London, 1947–62. President, British School of Archaeology in Iraq, 1970–78. Archaeologist on staff of the British Museum Expedition to Nineveh, 1931–32; later leader of many other archaeological expeditions. Author of Nimrud and Its Remains *and others.*
NINEVEH (Micropædia)

M.M.S.   Madan Mohan Singh. *President, Engineers International, Inc., Westmont, Illinois. Manager, Soil and Rock Mechanics Section, Illinois Institute of Technology Research Institute, Chicago, 1968–74.*
BUILDING CONSTRUCTION (*in part*)

M.M.Sa.   Mostafa Moh. Salah. *Former Director, Institute of Oceanography and Fisheries, Kayed Bey, Alexandria, Egypt. Author of numerous articles on oceanography.*
MEDITERRANEAN SEA (*in part*)

M.M.W.   Maxwell M. Wintrobe, M.D. *Distinguished Professor of Internal Medicine, University of Utah, Salt Lake City. Author of* Clinical Hematology.
BLOOD (*in part*)

M.M.Wr.   Michael M. Wertheimer. *Professor of Psychology, University of Colorado, Boulder. Consultant, Veterans Administration Hospital, Denver.*
PSYCHOLOGY (*in part*)

M.N.   Marcel Nicolet. *Professor of External Geophysics, Free University of Brussels. Author of numerous articles on the atmosphere.*
ATMOSPHERE (*in part*)

M.Na.   Maurice Nadeau. *Editor,* Lettres Nouvelles *and* La Quinzaine Littéraire, *Paris. Author of* Histoire du surréalisme: *editor of the Marquis de Sade's* Oeuvres; *and others.*
SADE, MARQUIS DE (Micropædia)

M.N.B.   Marjorie Nice Boyer. *Professor of History, York College, City University of New York, Jamaica. Author of* "Medieval Suspended Carriages" *in* Speculum; *"Medieval Pivoted Axles" in* Technology and Culture.
TRANSPORTATION (*in part*)

M.N.D.   Manmath Nath Das. *Professor and Head, Department of History, Utkal University, Bhubaneswar, Orissa, India.*
INDIA (*in part*)

M.N.v.L.   Maurits N. van Loon. *Professor of Prehistory and Archaeology of Western Asia, University of Amsterdam. Research Associate in Archaeology, Oriental Institute, University of Chicago. Author of* Urartian Art.
DRESS AND ADORNMENT (*in part*)

Mo.Gr.   Moshe Greenberg. *Professor of Bible, Hebrew University of Jerusalem. Author of* The Hab/piru *and others; editor and translator of* The Religion of Israel *by Yehezkel Kaufmann.*
JUDAISM (*in part*)

M.P.   Malcolm Potts. *President, Family Health International, Research Triangle Park, North Carolina. Coauthor of* The Textbook of Contraceptive Practice *and others.*
BIRTH CONTROL

M.Pa.   Marcel Pacaut. *Professor of the History of the Middle Ages; Emeritus Director, Institute of Political Studies, University of Lyon. Author of* Louis VII et son royaume *and others.*
FRANCE (*in part*)
PHILIP II (FRANCE) (Micropædia)

M.P.B.   Michael Parker Banton. *Professor of Sociology, University of Bristol, England. Author of* The Policeman in the Community.
POLICE (*in part*)

M.P.G.   Mikell P. Groover. *Professor of Industrial Engineering, Lehigh University, Bethlehem, Pennsylvania. Author of* Automation, Production Systems, and Computer-Aided Manufacturing.
AUTOMATION (*in part*)

M.Ph.   Melba Phillips. *Emerita Professor of Physics, University of Chicago. Coauthor of* Classical Electricity and Magnetism.
ELECTROMAGNETIC RADIATION (*in part*)

M.Pl.   Maurice Platnauer (d. 1974). *Principal of Brasenose College, University of Oxford, 1956–60. Author of* Latin Elegiac Verse *and others; editor of* Aristophanes' Peace.
GREEK DRAMATISTS, THE CLASSICAL (*in part*)

M.Pm.   Dame Margery Perham (d. 1982). *Fellow of Nuffield College, Oxford, 1939–63; Reader in Colonial Administration, University of Oxford, 1939–48. Author of* Lugard; *coeditor of* The Diaries of Lord Lugard.
LUGARD OF ABINGER, FREDERICK JOHN DEALTRY LUGARD, BARON (Micropædia)

M.P.Pe.   Mikhail Platonovich Petrov. *Former Professor, Leningrad State University. Member of the Turkmen S.S.R. Academy of Sciences. Author of* Pustyni Tsentralnoy Azi *("Deserts of Central Asia").*
ASIA (*in part*)

M.Py.   E. Michael Pye. *Professor of Comparative Religion, University of Marburg, West Germany. Author of* The Study of Kanji.
RITES AND CEREMONIES, SACRED (*in part*)

M.R.   Mario Rossi. *Professor of the History of Philosophy, University of Siena, Italy. Author of* Marx e la dialettica hegeliana.
HEGELIANISM, HEGEL AND (*in part*)

M.Ra.   Marc Raeff. *Professor of History, Columbia University. Author of* Origins of the Russian Intelligentsia.
UNION OF SOVIET SOCIALIST REPUBLICS (*in part*)

M.R.D. Mary R. Dawson. *Curator, Vertebrate Fossils, Carnegie Museum of Natural History, Pittsburgh. Active in research on the biology and paleontology of rabbits.*
MAMMALS (*in part*)

M.R.Da. Milton Rockwood Daniels (deceased). Commodore, U.S. Coast Guard.
NAVIGATION (*in part*)

M.R.D.F. Michael Richard Daniell Foot. *Professor of History, Victoria University of Manchester, 1967–73. Editor of* The Gladstone Diaries.
GLADSTONE, WILLIAM EWART (*in part*)
   (Micropædia)

M.Re. Marcel Reinhard (d. 1973). *Professor of History, University of Paris. Author of* Le Grand Carnot; Paris pendant la révolution française; *and others.*
SAINT-JUST, LOUIS DE (Micropædia)

M.R.G. Mark Richard Greene. *Distinguished Professor of Insurance, University of Georgia, Athens. Author of* Risk and Insurance.
INSURANCE

M.Rh. Max Rheinstein (d. 1977). *Max Pam Professor of Comparative Law, University of Chicago, 1942–68. Coauthor of* Law of Decedents' Estates.
INHERITANCE AND SUCCESSION (*in part*)
LEGAL SYSTEMS, THE EVOLUTION OF
   MODERN WESTERN (*in part*)
PROCEDURAL LAW (*in part*)

M.R.H. Michael R. House. *Professor of Geology, University of Hull, England. Author of* Continental Drift and the Devonian System *and others.*
GEOCHRONOLGY (*in part*)

M.-R.Ho. Michel-Rostislav Hofmann. *Musicologist. Author of* Moussorgski; Histoire de la musique en Russie.
MUSSORGSKY, MODEST (Micropædia)

M.Ro. Michael Roberts. *Professor of Modern History, Queen's University of Belfast, Northern Ireland, 1954–73. Author of* Gustavus Adolphus: A History of Sweden, 1611–1632; The Early Vasas: A History of Sweden, 1523–1611; *and others.*
GUSTAV II ADOLF (Micropædia)
OXENSTIERNA (AF SODERMORE), AXEL,
   GREVE (Micropædia)

M.R.W. Marilyn R. Waldman. *Associate Professor of History; Director, Center for Comparative Studies, Ohio State University, Columbus. Author of* Toward a Theory of Historical Narrative: A Case Study in Perso-Islamicate Historiography.
ISLAMIC WORLD, THE

M.Sa. Michele Sarà. *Professor of Zoology; Director, Institute of Zoology, University of Genoa. Author of* Zoologia; Biologia generale.
SPONGES

M.S.A. Mikhail S. Arlazorov. *Staff member, Union of Cinematographers,*

Moscow. Author of Tsiolkovsky.
TSIOLKOVSKY, KONSTANTIN
   EDUARDOVICH (Micropædia)

M.Sal. Mario Salmi (d. 1980). *Professor of the History of Medieval and Modern Art, University of Rome. Author of* Il Beato Angelico *and many monographs on Italian Renaissance artists.*
ANGELICO, FRA (Micropædia)

M.S.C. Maria S. Cox. *Former Assistant Professor of Economics, University of Wisconsin, Madison.*
TAXATION (*in part*)

M.Sch. Mischa Schwartz. *Professor of Electrical Engineering, Columbia University. Author of* Information Transmission, Modulation, and Noise; *coauthor of* Communication Systems and Techniques.
TELECOMMUNICATIONS SYSTEMS
   (*in part*)

M.S.D. Margaret Stafana Drower. *Honorary Research Fellow; former Reader in Ancient History, University College, University of London. Author of* Egypt in Colour; Nubia: A Drowning Land.
THUTMOSE III (Micropædia)

M.S.F.H. M. Sinclair F. Hood. *Archaeologist. Director, British School of Archaeology, Athens, 1954–62. Author of* The Minoans: Crete in the Bronze Age *and others.*
GRECO-ROMAN CIVILIZATION, CLASSICAL
   (*in part*)

M.Sh. Minoru Shinoda. *Professor of History, University of Hawaii, Honolulu. Author of* The Founding of the Kamakura Shogunate 1180–1185.
DAIGO, GO- (Micropædia)
FUJIWARA FAMILY (Micropædia)

M.S.H. Muhammad Shamsul Huq. *President, Foundation for Research on Educational Planning and Development. Foreign Minister, 1978–82. Minister for Education and Scientific Research, Pakistan, 1969–71. Author of* Education and Manpower Development in South and Southeast Asia *and others.*
EDUCATION, HISTORY OF (*in part*)

M.S.K. Michael Scott Kranbuhl, M.D. *Staff Physician, Children's Hospital Medical Center, Cincinnati, Ohio.*
ORGANS AND ORGAN SYSTEMS, PLANT
   AND ANIMAL (*in part*)

M.S.Ki. M. Semakula M. Kiwanuka. *Former Professor and Head, Department of History, Makerere University, Kampala, Uganda. Author of* A History of Buganda.
EASTERN AFRICA (*in part*)

M.S.M. Muhsin S. Mahdi. *James Richard Jewett Professor of Arabic, Harvard University. Author of* Ibn Khaldun's Philosophy of History *and others.*
ISLĀM, MUḤAMMAD AND THE RELIGION
   OF (*in part*)

M.S.Ma. Matthew S. Magda. *Associate Historian, Division of History, Pennsylvania Historical and Museum Commission, Harrisburg.*
PHILADELPHIA (*in part*)

M.S.M.F. Michael S.M. Fordham. *Analytical psychologist. Coeditor of* The Collected Works of C.G. Jung.
JUNG, CARL (*in part*) (Micropædia)

M.Sp. Matthew Spinka (d. 1972). *Professor of Church History, Hartford Seminary Foundation, Connecticut, 1943–58. Author of* John Hus: A Biography *and others.*
HUS, JOHN (Micropædia)

M.S.S. Mark S. Slobin. *Associate Professor of Music, Wesleyan University, Middletown, Connecticut. Author of* Music in the Culture of Northern Afghanistan *and others.*
CENTRAL ASIAN ARTS
   (*in part*)

M.St. Michel Strickmann. *Associate Professor of Oriental Languages, University of California, Berkeley. Author of* Le Taoïsme du Mao Chan *and others.*
TAOISM (*in part*)

M.S.T. Michael S. Teitelbaum. *Program Officer, Alfred P. Sloan Foundation, New York City. Author of* The British Fertility Decline: Demographic Transition in the Crucible of the Industrial Revolution.
POPULATION

M.Su. Michael Sullivan. *Christensen Professor of Oriental Art, Stanford University, California. Author of* The Birth of Landscape Painting in China; The Arts of China.
MA ẎUAN (Micropædia)
EAST ASIAN ARTS (*in part*)

M.T. Morris Tanenbaum. *Executive Vice President, American Telephone and Telegraph Company, New York City. Coeditor of* Superconductors.
AUTOMATION (*in part*)
INDUSTRIAL ENGINEERING AND
   PRODUCTION MANAGEMENT (*in part*)

M.Ta. Mohamed Talbi. *Professor, Faculty of Letters and Human Sciences, University of Tunis. Author of* L'Emirat aghlabide, histoire politique 800–909.
NORTH AFRICA (*in part*)

M.T.F. Michael T. Florinsky (d. 1981). *Professor of Economics, Columbia University, 1956–63. Author of* Russia: A History and an Interpretation *and others.*
ALEXANDER III (RUSSIA) (Micropædia)

M.T.O. Martin T. Orne, M.D. *Professor of Psychiatry, University of Pennsylvania, Philadelphia; Director, Unit for Experimental Psychiatry, Institute of Pennsylvania Hospital.*
HYPNOSIS (*in part*) (Micropædia)

M.Tu. Martin Turnell (d. 1979). *Writer. Head, Programme Contracts Department, BBC, London, 1959–69.*

Author of The Art of French Fiction.
MAUPASSANT, GUY DE (Micropædia)
ZOLA, ÉMILE (Micropædia)

M.T.V.   M. Tulio Velásquez. *Director, Institute of Andean Biology, National University of San Marcos, Lima. Coauthor of* Physiological Effects of High Altitude.
SOUTH AMERICA (*in part*)

M.U.   Michitaka Uda. *Emeritus Professor, Tokyo University of Fisheries. Author of* Umi *and numerous articles on oceanography.*
ASIA (*in part*)

Mu.B.   Mukhtar Mustafa Buru. *Professor of Geography, Al-Fatah University, Tripoli, Libya. Author of* Atlas of Libyan Arab Republic.
NORTH AFRICA (*in part*)

Mu.S.   Murray Schumach. *Former Reporter,* The New York Times. *Author of* The Face on the Cutting Room Floor.
NEW YORK CITY

M.V.F.   Marion Valerie Friedmann. *Editor and translator. Author of* The Slap; *editor of* I Will Still Be Moved: Reports from South Africa.
SOUTH AFRICAN LITERATURE (*in part*) (Micropædia)

M.Vi.   Marcelle Vioux. *Free-lance writer. Author of* Francois I; Henri IV.
FRANCIS I (FRANCE) (Micropædia)

M.V.O.   Maynard V. Olson. *Assistant Professor of Genetics, Washington University, St. Louis. Author of papers on mechanisms of reactions of transition-metal compounds.*
CHEMICAL REACTIONS (*in part*)

M.W.B.   Marshall W. Baldwin (d. 1975). *Professor of History, New York University, New York City, 1954–72. Co-editor of* A History of the Crusades.
CRUSADES, THE (*in part*)

M.W.F.   Marvin W. Formo. *Manager, Oil and Protein Research, Cargill Inc., Minneapolis, Minnesota. Contributor to* Industrial Fatty Acids.
FOOD PROCESSING (*in part*)

M.W.F.T.   Michael Willmer Forbes Tweedie. *Director, Raffles Museum, Singapore, 1946–57.*
EAST INDIES, THE (*in part*)

M.Wi.   Mitchell Wilson (d. 1973). *Science writer and novelist. Author of* American Science and Invention.
MCCORMICK, CYRUS HALL (Micropædia)

M.W.L.   Maung Wai Lin. *Research Editor, Biology,* Encyclopædia Britannica, *Chicago, 1970–72.*
FISHES (*in part*)

M.W.L.K.   Michael William Lely Kitson. *Professor of the History of Art; Deputy Director, Courtauld Institute of Art, University of London. Author of* The Art of Claude Lorrain *and others.*
CLAUDE LORRAIN (Micropædia)

M.Wo.   Mary Woodall. *Director, City Museum and Art Gallery,*

Birmingham, England, 1956–64. Author of Gainsborough's Landscape Drawings; editor of The Letters of Thomas Gainsborough.
GAINSBOROUGH, THOMAS (Micropædia)

M.W.R.   Matilda White Riley. *Associate Director, Social and Behavioral Sciences Research, National Institute on Aging, National Institutes of Health, U.S. Department of Health and Human Services, Bethesda, Maryland. Coauthor of* Aging and Society (*vol. I–III*).
SOCIAL DIFFERENTIATION (*in part*)

M.W.Ri.   Michael William Richey. *Former Director, Royal Institute of Navigation, London. Coauthor of* The Geometrical Seaman.
NAVIGATION (*in part*)

Mx.M.   Max Miller (d. 1973). *Director of State Archives, Stuttgart, West Germany, 1951–66. Chairman of the Historical Commission of Baden-Württemberg.*
GERMANY (*in part*)

M.Y.S.   Margaret Yvonne Stant. *Principal Scientific Officer in Plant Anatomy, Jodrell Laboratory, Royal Botanic Gardens, Kew, England. Author of* Anatomy of the Butomaceae.
ANGIOSPERMS (*in part*)

M.Z.   Moses Zucker. *Professor of Biblical Exegesis, Jewish Theological Seminary of America, New York City. Author of* Rav Saadya Gaon's Translation of the Torah.
SA'ADIA BEN JOSEPH (Micropædia)

M.Zu.   Matinuzzaman Zuberi. *Senior Fellow and Head, Centre for International Politics and Organization, Jawaharlal Nehru University, New Delhi.*
NEPAL (*in part*)

N.   John Julius Cooper, 2nd Viscount Norwich. *Writer and broadcaster. Author of* The Normans in the South; The Kingdom in the Sun.
ROGER II (SICILY) (Micropædia)

N.A.   Nafis Ahmad. *Former Professor of Geography, University of Dacca, Bangladesh. Author of* Economic Geography of East Pakistan; *editor of* Oriental Geographer.
ASIA (*in part*)

N.Ab.   Nicola Abbagnano. *Emeritus Professor of History of Philosophy, University of Turin, Italy. Foremost Italian Existentialist philosopher. Author of* Critical Existentialism *and others.*
PHILOSOPHICAL SCHOOLS AND DOCTRINES, WESTERN (*in part*)

N.A.B.   N.A. Baloch. *Former Vice Chancellor, Islamic University, Islamabad, Pakistan; former Director, Institute of Historical and Cultural Research. Author of* Musical Instruments of the Lower Indus Valley of Sind.
PAKISTAN (*in part*)

N.A.C.   Nancy A. Curtin. *Lecturer in Physiology, Charing Cross Hospital*

Medical School, University of London.
MUSCLES AND MUSCLE SYSTEMS (*in part*)

N.A.Ct.   Nathan Altshiller Court (d. 1968). *Professor of Mathematics, University of Oklahoma, Norman, 1935–51. Author of* College Geometry; Mathematics in Fun and in Earnest.
GEOMETRY (*in part*)

N.A.F.   Nabih Amin Faris (d. 1968). *Professor of Arab History and Director, Arab Studies Programme, American University of Beirut.*
PALESTINE (*in part*)

N.A.G.   Nikolay Andreyevich Gvozdetsky. *Professor of Geography, Moscow M.V. Lomonosov State University. Author of* Kavkaz.
UNION OF SOVIET SOCIALIST REPUBLICS (*in part*)

N.A.J.   Nazir Ali Jairazbhoy. *Professor of Music, University of California, Los Angeles. Author of* The Rāgs of North Indian Music: Their Structure and Evolution.
SOUTH ASIAN ARTS (*in part*)

Na.M.   Nancy Mitford (d. 1973). *Writer. Author of* Madame de Pompadour *and others.*
POMPADOUR, JEANNE-ANTOINETTE POISSON, MARQUISE DE (Micropædia)

N.A.M.   Norman A. Malcolm. *Susan Linn Sage Professor Emeritus of Philosophy, Cornell University, Ithaca, New York. Author of* Ludwig Wittgenstein: A Memoir.
WITTGENSTEIN, LUDWIG (*in part*) (Micropædia)

Na.Mo.   Naoaki Maeno. *Emeritus Professor of Chinese Literature, University of Tokyo. Author of* Poets in the T'ang Dynasty.
LITERATURE, THE ART OF (*in part*)

N.An.   Nikolay Andreyev (d. 1982). *Reader in Russian Studies, University of Cambridge; Fellow of Clare Hall, Cambridge. Author of* Studies in Muscovy *and others.*
IVAN IV (Micropædia)

N.A.O.   Ned Allen Ostenso. *Director, Office of Sea Grant and Extramural Programs, National Oceanic and Atmospheric Administration, U.S. Department of Commerce, Rockville, Maryland. Leader or participant in several polar expeditions. Author of* Geophysical Investigations of the Arctic Ocean Basin.
ARCTIC, THE (*in part*)

N.A.R.   Nesca A. Robb (d. 1976). *Free-lance writer and lecturer. Author of* William of Orange: A Personal Portrait.
WILLIAM III (ENGLAND AND GREAT BRITAIN) (Micropædia)

N.A.Ro.   Nicholas A. Romas, M.D. *Director of Urology, St. Luke's-Roosevelt Hospital Center, New York City.*
REPRODUCTION AND REPRODUCTIVE SYSTEMS (*in part*)

N.A.W. Nixon A. Wilson. *Professor of Biology, University of Northern Iowa, Cedar Falls. Author of numerous papers on mites and ticks.*
ARACHNIDS (*in part*)

N.A.Z. Nicola Abdo Ziadeh. *Emeritus Professor of Arab History, American University of Beirut. Author of* Origins of Nationalism—Tunisia *and others.*
BOURGUIBA, HABIB (Micropædia)
CALENDAR (*in part*)
HISTORY, THE STUDY OF (*in part*)

N.B. Nevill Barbour (d. 1972). *Assistant Head, Eastern Services, British Broadcasting Corporation, 1944–56. Author of* Morocco; *editor of* A Survey of North West Africa.
NORTH AFRICA (*in part*)

N.B.P. Nicholas B. Penny. *Keeper of Western Art, Ashmolean Museum of Art and Archaeology, University of Oxford. Author of* Church Monuments in Romantic England.
SCULPTURE, THE HISTORY OF WESTERN (*in part*)

N.C. Norman Crossland. *Former Bonn correspondent,* The Economist, *London. Author of* The German Electoral System.
BERLIN (*in part*)

N.C.G. Neil C. Gustafson. *President, Anticipatory Management, Inc., Minneapolis. Former Executive Director, Commission on Minnesota's Future, Minneapolis.*
UNITED STATES OF AMERICA (*in part*)

N.C.H. Nicholas Carr Hightower, M.D. *Senior Consultant, Department of Gastroenterology, Scott and White Clinic and Scott and White Memorial Hospital, Temple, Texas. Contributor of "Digestion" in Best and Taylor,* The Physiological Basis of Medical Practice *(8th ed.).*
DIGESTION AND DIGESTIVE SYSTEMS (*in part*)

N.C.N. N. Chandrasekharan Nair. *Joint Director, Botanical Survey of India, Coimbatore. Author of* Flora of the Punjab Plains *and others.*
ANGIOSPERMS (*in part*)

N.C.P. Norman C. Polmar. *Consultant. Editor, U.S. section,* Jane's Fighting Ships, *1967–77. Author of* Atomic Submarines; The Ships and Aircraft of the U.S. Fleet; *and others.*
WAR, THE TECHNOLOGY OF (*in part*)

N.D. Norman Davies. *Professor of History, School of Slavonic and East European Studies, University of London. Author of* God's Playground: A History of Poland.
POLAND (*in part*)
WARSAW (*in part*)

N.E.N. Niels Erik Nörlund (d. 1981). *Professor of Mathematics, University of Copenhagen, 1922–56. Author of* Differenzenrechnung; Séries d'interpolation.
NUMERICAL ANALYSIS (*in part*)

N.E.S. Neil E. Salisbury. *Professor of Geography, University of Oklahoma, Norman. Coauthor of "Growth and Decline of Iowa Villages" and "The Valleys of Iowa,"* Iowa Studies in Geography.
UNITED STATES OF AMERICA (*in part*)

N.E.W. Neil E. Wiseman. *Lecturer in Computer Science, University of Cambridge. Coauthor of* Creative Computer Graphics.
COMPUTERS (*in part*)

N.F.C. Norman F. Childers. *Adjunct Professor, Department of Fruit Crops, University of Florida, Gainesville. M.A. Blake Professor Emeritus of Horticulture, Rutgers University, New Brunswick, New Jersey. Author of* Modern Fruit Science.
FARMING AND AGRICULTURAL TECHNOLOGY (*in part*)

N.G. Norman Gash. *Emeritus Professor of History, University of St. Andrews, Scotland. Author of* Sir Robert Peel *and others.*
CASTLEREAGH, ROBERT STEWART, VISCOUNT (Micropædia)
GREY, CHARLES GREY, 2ND EARL (Micropædia)
PEEL, SIR ROBERT, 2ND BARONET (Micropædia)

N.G.J. Norman Gardner Johnson (d. 1973). *Industry Manager, Explosives Department, Du Pont de Nemours and Company, Wilmington, Delaware, 1960–67; Technical Specialist, Technical Service Section, 1943–60. Author of* Safety in the Transportation, Storage, Handling and Use of Explosives.
INDUSTRIES, CHEMICAL PROCESS (*in part*)

N.G.L.H. Nicholas G.L. Hammond. *Henry Overton Wills Professor Emeritus of Greek, University of Bristol, England. Author of* A History of Greece to 322 B.C.; *editor of* Cambridge Ancient History, *3rd edition.*
GRECO-ROMAN CIVILIZATION, CLASSICAL (*in part*)
GREECE (*in part*)
XENOPHON (Micropædia)

N.Go. Noël Goodwin. *Associate Editor,* Dance and Dancers, *London. Music and Dance Critic,* London Daily Express, *1956–78. Area Editor,* The New Grove Dictionary of Music and Musicians. *Coauthor of* London Symphony: Portrait of an Orchestra.
MUSICAL FORMS AND GENRES (*in part*)

N.G.S. Neal Griffith Smith. *Biologist, Smithsonian Tropical Research Institute, Balboa, Panama.*
BEHAVIOUR, ANIMAL (*in part*)

N.H. Naofusa Hirai. *Professor of Shintō Studies, Kokugakuin University, Tokyo. Author of* Japanese Shinto.
SHINTŌ

N.H.D. Nancy Hatch Dupree. *Research Associate, Center for Afghanistan Studies, University of*
Nebraska at Omaha. Author of An Historical Guide to Afghanistan.
AFGHANISTAN (*in part*)

N.H.R. Norman H. Russell. *Professor of Biology, Central State University, Edmond, Oklahoma. Author of* An Introduction to the Plant Kingdom.
ANGIOSPERMS (*in part*)

N.I. Nobutaka Ike. *Professor of Political Science, Stanford University, California. Author of* The Beginnings of Political Democracy in Japan *and others.*
II NAOSUKE (Micropædia)

N.I.M. Nikolay Ivanovich Mikhaylov. *Professor of Geography, Moscow State University. Author of* Gory Yuzhnoy Sibiri.
ASIA (*in part*)

N.I.Mo. Nicholas Ivan Momtchiloff (d. 1964). *Economic Adviser, Industrial and Commercial Finance Corporation, London. Author of* Ten Years of Controlled Trade in South-Eastern Europe.
BULGARIA (*in part*)

N.J.B. N.J. Berrill. *Strathcona Professor of Zoology, McGill University, Montreal, 1946–65. Author of* Sex and the Nature of Things *and others.*
SEX AND SEXUALITY (*in part*)

N.J.C. Noel James Coulson (d. 1986). *Professor of Oriental Laws, University of London, 1967–86. Author of* A History of Islamic Law.
ISLĀM, MUḤAMMAD AND THE RELIGION OF (*in part*)

N.J.H. Nicholas Joseph Healy. *Adjunct Professor of Law, New York University. Attorney, Healy & Baillie, New York City. Editor,* Journal of Maritime Law and Commerce. *Coauthor of* Healy & Sharpe's Cases and Materials on Admiralty.
TRANSPORTATION LAW (*in part*)

N.J.L. Norman Jones Lamb. *Former Senior Lecturer in Portuguese and Spanish, University of Liverpool.*
PORTUGUESE LITERATURE (*in part*)

N.J.M. Nicholas John Mackintosh. *Professor of Experimental Psychology, University of Cambridge. Author of* Psychology of Animal Learning.
LEARNING, ANIMAL

N.J.P. Norman J. Padelford (d. 1982). *Professor of Political Science, Massachusetts Institute of Technology, Cambridge, 1945–71. Author of* The Panama Canal in Peace and War.
CENTRAL AMERICA (*in part*)

N.Ka. Nobuo Kanda. *Professor of East Asian History, Meiji University, Tokyo. Coauthor of* Glory of the Forbidden City in Peking.
K'ANG-HSI (Micropædia)

N.K.G. Nikolai Kallinikovich Gudzii (d. 1965). *Professor of Old Russian Language and Literature, Moscow M.V. Lomonosov State University. Member, Academy of Sciences of the U.S.S.R.*

Author of History of Early Russian Literature *and others.*

RUSSIAN LITERATURE (*in part*)

N.K.S.   N.K. Sinha (d. 1974). *Professor and Head, Department of History, University of Calcutta, 1955–68. Author of* Rise of the Sikh Power.

BOSE, SUBHAS CHANDRA (Micropædia)

CALCUTTA

N.L.G.   Nancie L. González. *Professor of Anthropology, University of Maryland, College Park. Author of* Santiago: Ethnography of a Dominican City.

WEST INDIES, THE (*in part*)

N.L.N.   Norman L. Nicholson. *Senior Professor of Geography, University of Western Ontario, London. Author of* The Boundaries of the Canadian Confederation *and others.*

CANADA (*in part*)

N.M.   Nobuhiro Matsumoto. *Emeritus Professor of Oriental History, Keio University, Tokyo. Author of* Essai sur la mythologie japonaise.

JAPANESE LITERATURE (*in part*)

N.M.C.   Nydia María Cardoze. *Professor of Geography, University of Panama, Panama City. Author of* Notas de geografía.

CENTRAL AMERICA (*in part*)

N.Mo.   Neil Morgan. *Editor,* The Tribune (*San Diego, California*). *Author of* The California Syndrome; Westward Tilt.

UNITED STATES OF AMERICA (*in part*)

N.M.Sa.   Nahum M. Sarna. *Golding Professor of Biblical Studies, Brandeis University, Waltham, Massachusetts. Author of* Understanding Genesis *and others.*

BIBLICAL LITERATURE AND ITS CRITICAL INTERPRETATION (*in part*)

N.M.Su.   N.M. Sutherland. *Reader in Early Modern History, Royal Holloway College, University of London. Author of* The Massacre of St. Bartholomew and the European Conflict, 1559–1572.

CATHERINE DE MÉDICIS (Micropædia)

N.N.G.   Nahum N. Glatzer. *Samuel Lane Professor Emeritus of Jewish History and Social Ethics, Brandeis University, Waltham, Massachusetts. University Professor, Boston University. Author of* Franz Rosenzweig: His Life and Thought *and others.*

AKIBA BEN JOSEPH (Micropædia)

ROSENZWEIG, FRANZ (Micropædia)

N.O.S.   Norman Obed Smith. *Professor of Chemistry, Fordham University, New York City. Coauthor of* The Phase Rule and Its Applications.

MATTER (*in part*)

N.P.   Norman Perrin (d. 1976). *Professor of New Testament, University of Chicago, 1969–76. Author of* The Promise of Bultmann.

BULTMANN, RUDOLF (Micropædia)

N.Pa.   Ntsomo Payanzo. *Former Assistant Professor of Sociology, National University of Zaire, Lubumbashi.*

CENTRAL AFRICA (*in part*)

N.P.A.   Nagarajan Panchapagesan Ayyar (d. 1979). *Professor of Geography, Shivaji University, Kolhāpur, India, 1977–79.*

INDIA (*in part*)

N.P.As.   N. Philip Ashmole. *Senior Lecturer in Zoology, University of Edinburgh. Author of numerous papers on the ecology of seabirds.*

BIRDS (*in part*)

N.Po.   Nicholas Polunin. *Secretary General and Editor, International Conferences on Environmental Future. Founder and Editor,* Environmental Conservation. *President, Foundation for Environmental Conservation. Author of* Circumpolar Arctic Flora *and others.*

ECOSYSTEMS (*in part*)

N.R.   Nicholas Rescher. *University Professor of Philosophy, University of Pittsburgh. Author of* Topics in Philosophical Logic.

LOGIC, THE HISTORY AND KINDS OF (*in part*)

N.Ru.   Nicolai Rubinstein. *Emeritus Professor of History, Westfield College, University of London. Author of* The Government of Florence Under the Medici, 1434–1494, *and others.*

GUICCIARDINI, FRANCESCO (Micropædia)

ITALY (*in part*)

N.R.W.   Nelson Raymond Williams. *Principal Technical Adviser to Assistant Director, U.S. Air Force Technical Applications Center, Virginia, 1961–63. Meteorologist, U.S. Weather Bureau, 1940–46. Contributor to* The Encyclopedia of Atmospheric Sciences and Astrogeology.

CLIMATE AND WEATHER (*in part*)

N.S.   Nobuo Shimahara. *Professor of the Anthropology of Education, Rutgers University, New Brunswick, New Jersey. Author of* Adaptation and Education in Japan *and others.*

EDUCATION, HISTORY OF (*in part*)

N.S.B.   Norman Spencer Brommelle. *Secretary-General, International Institute for Conservation of Historic and Artistic Works. Director, Hamilton Kerr Institute, Fitzwilliam Museum, University of Cambridge, 1978–83. Keeper, Department of Conservation, Victoria and Albert Museum, London, 1960–77.*

ART CONSERVATION AND RESTORATION (*in part*)

N.S.G.   Norton S. Ginsburg. *Director, Environment and Policy Institute, East-West Center, Honolulu. Author of* An Atlas of Economic Development; *editor of* The Pattern of Asia.

TAIWAN (*in part*)

N.Sh.   Nicholas Shrimpton. *Fellow and Tutor in English Literature, Lady Margaret Hall, University of Oxford.*

ENGLISH LITERATURE (*in part*)

N.Sl.   Nicolas Slonimsky. *Conductor, composer, writer, and editor. Lecturer in Music, University of California, Los Angeles, 1964–67. Author of* Music Since 1900; Music of Latin America; *editor of* Baker's Biographical Dictionary of Musicians.

RIMSKY-KORSAKOV, NIKOLAY (Micropædia)

N.Sm.   Ninian Smart. *Professor of Religious Studies, University of Lancaster, England, and University of California, Santa Barbara. Author of* The Religious Experience of Mankind; Philosophers and Religious Truth.

RELIGIONS, THE STUDY AND CLASSIFICATION OF (*in part*)

RELIGIOUS AND SPIRITUAL BELIEF, SYSTEMS OF (*in part*)

N.St.   Noel Stock. *Professor of English, University of Toledo, Ohio. Author of* The Life of Ezra Pound; Reading the Cantos.

POUND, EZRA (Micropædia)

N.T.   Nicholas Temperley. *Professor of Musicology, University of Illinois, Urbana. Editor of Berlioz'* Symphonie fantastique.

MUSIC, THE ART OF (*in part*)

N.V.He.   Norman V. Henfrey. *Lecturer in English, University of Bristol, England. Editor of* Selected Critical Writings of George Santayana.

SANTAYANA, GEORGE (Micropædia)

N.V.R.   Nicholas V. Riasanovsky. *Sidney Hellman Ehrman Professor of European History, University of California, Berkeley. Author of* Nicholas I and Official Nationality in Russia, 1825–1855, *and others.*

NICHOLAS I (RUSSIA) (Micropædia)

N.W.   Norman Ward. *Britnell Professor of Political Science, University of Saskatchewan, Saskatoon. Author of* The Public Purse: A Study in Canadian Democracy.

CANADA (*in part*)

N.W.D.   Norman Wilfred Desrosier. *Director of Research, National Biscuit Company, New York City. Author of* The Technology of Food Preservation.

FOOD PROCESSING (*in part*)

N.Wi.   Nico Wilterdink. *Lecturer in Sociology, University of Amsterdam. Author of* Vermogensverhoudingen in Nederland.

SOCIAL STRUCTURE AND CHANGE

N.W.S.   Nathan Wetherill Shock. *Emeritus Scientist, Gerontology Research Center, National Institute of Aging, U.S. Department of Health and Human Services, Baltimore City Hospitals. Author of* Trends in Gerontology; *editor of* Perspectives in Experimental Gerontology.

GROWTH AND DEVELOPMENT, BIOLOGICAL (*in part*)

N.Z.   Nicolas M. Zernov (d. 1980). *Spalding Lecturer in Eastern Orthodox Culture, University of Oxford, 1947–66. Author of* The Russian Religious Renaissance of the Twentieth Century *and others.*

KHOMYAKOV, ALEKSEY STEPANOVICH (Micropædia)

O.A.   Oskar Anweiler. *Professor of Education, University of the Ruhr, Bochum, West Germany. Author of* Geschichte der Schule und Pädagogik in Russland, vom Ende des Zarenreiches bis zum Beginn der Stalin-Ära.

EDUCATION, HISTORY OF (*in part*)

O.A.B.   Otto Allen Bird. *Emeritus Professor of Arts and Letters, University of Notre Dame, Indiana. Author of* Cultures in Conflict: An Essay in the Philosophy of the Humanities.

KANTIANISM, KANT AND (*in part*)
LEŚNIEWSKI, STANISŁAW (Micropædia)

O.A.O.   Oscar A. Ornati. *Professor of Manpower Management, New York University, New York City. Author of* Transportation Needs of the Poor: A Case Study of New York City.

WORK AND EMPLOYMENT (*in part*)

O.B.G.   O. Benjamin Gerig (d. 1976). *Director, Office of Dependent Area Affairs, U.S. Department of State, 1945–62.*

UNITED NATIONS (*in part*)

O.C.   Otis Cary. *Professor of American History, Doshisha University, Kyōto; Representative of Amherst College. Coauthor, and editor of* War-Wasted Asia.

KYŌTO

O.C.C.   Orville C. Cromer (d. 1980). *Professor of Mechanical Engineering, Purdue University, West Lafayette, Indiana, 1954–63. Coauthor of* Elementary Heat Power.

ENERGY CONVERSION (*in part*)
TRANSPORTATION (*in part*)

O.C.K.   Otto C. Kopp. *Professor of Geological Sciences, University of Tennessee, Knoxville. Coauthor of* Laboratory Exercises in Physical Geology.

FUELS, FOSSIL (*in part*)

O.D.   Oliver Davies. *Associate Professor of Archaeology, University of Ghana, 1952–66.*

WESTERN AFRICA (*in part*)

O.E.Z.   Oleksa Eliseyovich Zasenko. *Head, Department of the History of Ukrainian Prerevolutionary Literature, Institute of Literature, Ukrainian S.S.R. Academy of Sciences, Kiev. Coauthor of* History of Ukrainian Literature, *vol. 8.*

UKRAINIAN LITERATURE (*in part*) (Micropædia)

O.F.B.   Otto Friedrich Bollnow. *Emeritus Professor of Philosophy and Education, Eberhard Karl University of Tübingen, West Germany. Author*

of Dilthey: Eine Einführung in seine Philosophie.

DILTHEY, WILHELM (Micropædia)

O.G.   Owen Gingerich. *Professor of Astronomy and of the History of Science, Harvard University. Astrophysicist, Smithsonian Astrophysical Observatory, Cambridge, Massachusetts. Coauthor of* Solar and Planetary Longitudes for Years −2500 to +2000.

STARS AND STAR CLUSTERS (*in part*)

O.Gr.   Oleg Grabar. *Aga Khan Professor of Islamic Art, Harvard University. Author of* The Formation of Islamic Art; *coauthor of* Islamic Architecture and Its Decoration.

ISLĀMIC ARTS (*in part*)

O.J.   Oswald Jacoby (d. 1984). *Author of* Oswald Jacoby on Poker *and many other works on card playing.*

POKER (Micropædia)

O.J.B.   Ooi Jin Bee. *Professor of Geography, National University of Singapore. Editor,* Singapore Journal of Tropical Geography. *Author of* Peninsular Malaysia *and others.*

SOUTHEAST ASIA, MAINLAND (*in part*)

O.J.E.   Olin Jeuck Eggen. *Senior Astronomer, Cerro Tololo Interamerican Observatory, La Serena, Chile.*

BRAHE, TYCHO (Micropædia)
HALLEY, EDMOND (Micropædia)

O.J.H.   Oscar J. Hammen. *Emeritus Professor of History, University of Montana, Missoula. Author of* The Red '48ers: Karl Marx and Friedrich Engels.

ENGELS, FRIEDRICH (Micropædia)

O.K.   Olin Kalmbach (d. 1979). *President, Tipton and Kalmbach, Inc., Consulting Engineers, Denver.*

PUBLIC WORKS (*in part*)

O.Ke.   Oleg Kerensky. *Ballet Critic,* New Statesman, *1968–78. Author of* Ballet Scene; The World of Ballet; *and others.*

DANCE, THE ART OF (*in part*)

O.K.-J.   Ole Klindt-Jensen (d. 1980). *Professor of Prehistory, University of Århus, Denmark, 1961–80. Author of* Foreign Influences in Denmark's Early Iron Age; Denmark Before the Vikings.

PAINTING, THE HISTORY OF WESTERN (*in part*)

O.K.L.   Oleg Konstantinovich Leontiev. *Head of Geomorphology, Department of Geography, Moscow M.V. Lomonosov State University.*

ASIA (*in part*)

O.L.   Otto Leichter (d. 1973). *Correspondent for United Nations and U.S. Affairs,* Arbeiter-Zeitung, *Vienna; and* Neue Ruhr-Zeitung, *Essen, West Germany. Author of* Zwischen zwei Diktaturen.

AUSTRIA (*in part*)

O.La.   Owen Lattimore. *Emeritus Professor of Chinese Studies, University*

of Leeds, England. Foreign Member, Academy of Sciences of the Mongolian People's Republic. Author of Mongols of Manchuria; Inner Asian Frontiers of China; *and others.*

MONGOLIA (*in part*)

O.L.A.   Oliver L. Austin, Jr. *Emeritus Curator in Ornithology, Florida State Museum, University of Florida, Gainesville. Author of* Birds of the World *and of numerous papers.*

BIRDS (*in part*)

O.Li.   Otto Liess. *Former Editor,* Erdöl-Dienst, *Vienna. Author of* Albanien zwischen Ost und West *and others.*

ALBANIA (*in part*)

O.L.Z.   Oliver Louis Zangwill. *Emeritus Professor of Experimental Psychology, University of Cambridge. Author of* An Introduction to Modern Psychology; *coeditor of* Amnesia.

MEMORY (*in part*)

O.O.   Otakar Odlozilik (d. 1973). *Professor of European History, University of Pennsylvania, Philadelphia, 1955–70. Author of* Bohemia in European Affairs, 1440–1471.

CZECHOSLOVAKIA (*in part*)

O.Or.   Oystein Ore (d. 1968). *Sterling Professor of Mathematics, Yale University, 1931–68. Author of* Cardano: The Gambling Scholar *and others.*

MATHEMATICS, THE HISTORY OF (*in part*)

O.O.W.   Oscar O. Winther (d. 1970). *University Professor of History, Indiana University, Bloomington, 1965–70. Author of* The Great Northwest *and others.*

UNITED STATES OF AMERICA (*in part*)

O.P.S.   Otis P. Starkey (d. 1986). *Professor of Geography, Indiana University, Bloomington, 1946–70.*

UNITED STATES OF AMERICA (*in part*)

O.R.A.K.   Oswin R.A. Köhler. *Emeritus Professor of African Studies; former Director, Institute for African Studies, University of Cologne, West Germany. Author of* "Les Langues Khoisan" *in* Les Langues dans le monde ancien et moderne *and others.*

LANGUAGES OF THE WORLD (*in part*)

O.R.G.   Oliver Robert Gurney. *Professor of Assyriology, University of Oxford, 1965–78. Author of* The Hittites *and others.*

MIDDLE EASTERN RELIGIONS, ANCIENT (*in part*)

O.Sh.   O. Shagdarsuren. *Director, Institute of General and Experimental Biology, Academy of Sciences of the Mongolian People's Republic, Ulaanbaatar.*

MONGOLIA (*in part*)

O.T.   Oliver Taplin. *Fellow and Tutor of Magdalen College, Oxford; Lecturer in Classical Languages and Literature,*

University of Oxford. Author of Greek Tragedy in Action.

GREEK DRAMATISTS, THE CLASSICAL (*in part*)

O.W. Owen Williams. *Emeritus Professor of Geography, University of Natal, Pietermaritzburg, South Africa. Coauthor of* The Economic Framework of South Africa.

SOUTH AFRICA (*in part*)

O.W.W. O.W. Wolters. *Goldwin Smith Professor of Southeast Asian History, Cornell University, Ithaca, New York. Author of* Early Indonesian Commerce *and others.*

EAST INDIES, THE (*in part*)

P.A. Paul Avrich. *Distinguished Professor of History, Queens College, City University of New York, Flushing. Author of* The Russian Anarchists.

KROPOTKIN, PETER (Micropædia)

P.Ad. Preston Adams. *Professor of Botany, DePauw University, Greencastle, Indiana. Coauthor of* The Study of Botany.

ORGANS AND ORGAN SYSTEMS, PLANT AND ANIMAL (*in part*)

Pa.H. Pauline Heaton. *Former Acting Archivist, Bermuda.*

WEST INDIES, THE (*in part*)

P.A.H. Patrick Aidan Heelan. *Professor of Philosophy, State University of New York at Stony Brook. Author of* Quantum Mechanics and Objectivity.

HEISENBERG

Pa.M. Paul Mercier (d. 1976). *Professor of Ethnology, University of Paris V. Director of Studies, Institute for Advanced Research, Paris. Author of* Historie de l'anthropologie.

SOCIAL SCIENCES, THE (*in part*)

P.A.M. Peter A. Mackridge. *Lecturer in Modern Greek, University of Oxford. Author of* The Modern Greek Language.

GREEK LITERATURE (*in part*)

Pa.Mo. Paul Mohr. *Professor of Geology, University College Galway, National University of Ireland. An authority on the structure and evolution of the African rift system. Author of* Geology of Ethiopia.

CONTINENTAL LANDFORMS (*in part*)

Pa.N. Paul Nash. *Professor of Philosophy and Education, Boston University. Author of* Authority and Freedom in Education.

PHILOSOPHIES OF THE BRANCHES OF KNOWLEDGE (*in part*)

Pa.S. Pauline Simmons. *Associate Curator of Far Eastern Art, Metropolitan Museum of Art, New York City, 1928–58. Author of* Chinese Patterned Silks.

DRESS AND ADORNMENT (*in part*)

P.A.S. Paul A. Schwartz. *Research Associate, Rancho Grande Biological Research Station, Ministry of the*

Environment and Renewable Natural Resources, Venezuela.

BIRDS (*in part*)

P.A.S.S. Peter A.S. Smith. *Professor of Chemistry, University of Michigan, Ann Arbor. Author of* Chemistry of Open-Chain Organic Nitrogen Compounds.

CHEMICAL COMPOUNDS (*in part*)

P.Ay. Phyllis Auty. *Reader in South Slavonic History, School of Slavonic and East European Studies, University of London, 1947–74. Author of* Yugoslavia.

YUGOSLAVIA (*in part*)

P.B.Ca. Philip B. Calkins. *Former Assistant Professor of History, Duke University, Durham, North Carolina.*

INDIA (*in part*)

P.B.D. de la M. Peter B.D. de la Mare. *Emeritus Professor of Chemistry, University of Auckland, New Zealand. Author of* Electrophilic Halogenation.

CHEMICAL REACTIONS (*in part*)

P.-B.L. Pierre-Bernard Lafont. *Director of Studies, Division of Historical and Philological Sciences, École Pratique des Hautes Études (Institute for Advanced Research), Paris. Author of* Bibliographie du Laos *and others.*

SOUTHEAST ASIA, MAINLAND (*in part*)

P.C. Preston Cloud. *Emeritus Professor of Biogeology, University of California, Santa Barbara. Biogeologist, Geological Survey, U.S. Department of the Interior, 1974–79. World authority on Precambrian events and conditions in Earth history. Author of* Cosmos, Earth, and Man.

ATMOSPHERE (*in part*)

P.Ca. Pedro Calmon. *President, Brazilian Historical and Geographical Institute, Rio de Janeiro. Author of* História do Brasil.

CABRAL, PEDRO ÁLVARES (Micropædia)

P.C.-B. Peter Cannon-Brookes. *Keeper, Department of Art, National Museum of Wales, Cardiff. Coauthor of* European Sculpture; Baroque Churches.

ARCHITECTURE, THE HISTORY OF WESTERN (*in part*)
PAINTING, THE HISTORY OF WESTERN (*in part*)
SCULPTURE, THE HISTORY OF WESTERN (*in part*)

P.Ch. Pramod Chandra. *George P. Bickford Professor of Indian Art, Harvard University. Author of* Stone Sculpture in the Allahabad Museum; Bundi Painting.

SOUTH ASIAN ARTS (*in part*)

P.C.-H. Peter Crossley-Holland. *Emeritus Professor of Music, University of California, Los Angeles. Author of* Pelican History of Music, *Vol. I, part I.*

MUSIC, THE ART OF (*in part*)

P.-c.K. Ping-chia Kuo. *Emeritus Professor of History, Southern Illinois University, Carbondale. Senior Fellow,*

National Endowment for the Humanities, 1973–74. Author of China; China: New Age and New Outlook.

CANTON (*in part*)
CHINA (*in part*)
CHUNGKING (*in part*)
NANKING (*in part*)

P.Cla. Peter Classen (deceased). *Professor of Medieval and Modern History, Rupert Charles University of Heidelberg. Author of* Karl der Grosse, das Papsttum und Byzanz.

CHARLEMAGNE

P.-C.N. Pierre-Claver Nuwinkware. *Former Administrative Director, Official University of Bujumbura, Burundi. Author of* Prince Louis Rwagasore.

CENTRAL AFRICA (*in part*)

P.Co. Pierre Courthion. *Vice President, Syndicate of the French Artistic Press. Author of* Klee; Manet; Seurat; *and many other monographs on modern European artists.*

KLEE, PAUL (Micropædia)
MANET, ÉDOUARD (*in part*) (Micropædia)
SEURAT, GEORGES (Micropædia)

P.C.R. Philip C. Ritterbush. *Historian of science. Program Director, Institute for Cultural Progress, Washington, D.C. Author of* Overtures to Biology; The Speculations of Eighteenth-Century Naturalists; *and others.*

LAMARCK, JEAN-BAPTISTE DE MONTE, CHEVALIER DE (Micropædia)

P.D. P. Dayal. *Visiting Professor of Geography, North-Eastern Hill University, Shillong, India. Author of* Bihar in Maps.

INDIA (*in part*)

P.De. Pierre Descargues. *Art historian and critic. Author of* Frans Hals; Jan Vermeer; *and other monographs.*

HALS, FRANS (Micropædia)
VERMEER, JAN (Micropædia)

P. De A.C. Philip De Armond Curtin. *Professor of History, Johns Hopkins University, Baltimore. Author of* Africa Remembered *and others.*

AFRICA (*in part*)

P. de L. Pierre de Latil. *Scientific Editor,* Le Figaro, *Paris. Coauthor of* Le Professeur Auguste Piccard; Man and the Underwater World; *and others.*

PICCARD, AUGUSTE (*in part*) (Micropædia)

P.Di. Porphyrios Dikaios (d. 1971). *Professor, Archaeological Institute, Rupert Charles University of Heidelberg. Director of Antiquities, Nicosia, Cyprus, 1960–63. Author of* A Guide to the Cyprus Museum *and others.*

CYPRUS (*in part*)

P.D.O. Peter D. Owen. *Painter and printmaker. Former Senior Lecturer, Croydon College of Design and Technology, England. Author of* Painting: Appreciation of the Arts.

PAINTING, THE ART OF

P.Dr.   Philip Drucker (d. 1982). *Professor of Anthropology, University of Kentucky, Lexington, 1968–78. Author of* The Native Brotherhoods: Modern Inter-Tribal Organizations of the Northwest Coast.
AMERICAN INDIANS (*in part*)

P.Du.   Pierre Dufour. *Former Lecturer in French Literature, University of Madrid. Author of* Picasso 1950–68.
PICASSO (*in part*)

P.Du V.   Patrick Du Val. *Former Professor of Geometry, University of Istanbul. Author of* Homographies, Quaternions, and Rotations; Elliptic Functions and Elliptic Curves.
GEOMETRY (*in part*)

P.D.V.   Paul D. Vignaux. *Professor and former President, Section of Religious Sciences, École Pratique des Hautes Études (Institute for Advanced Research), Paris. Author of* Philosophy in the Middle Ages: An Introduction.
OCKHAM, WILLIAM OF (Micropædia)

P.E.   Peter Ellis. *Consultant. Former Senior Lecturer in Textiles, University of Bradford, England. Author of* The Geometry of the Plain-Square Weave *and others.*
INDUSTRIES, MANUFACTURING (*in part*)

Pe.C.   Peter Collins (d. 1981). *Professor of Architecture, McGill University, Montreal. Author of* Changing Ideals in Modern Architecture; Concrete: The Vision of a New Architecture; *and others.*
ARCHITECTURE, THE ART OF (*in part*)

Pe.G.   Peter Gray (deceased). *Andrey Avinoff Professor of Biology, University of Pittsburgh, Pennsylvania, 1964–78. Author of* Microtomist's Formulary and Guide; *editor of* Encyclopedia of Biological Sciences.
TISSUES AND FLUIDS (*in part*)

Pe.H.   Peter Heller. *Professor of German and Comparative Literature, State University of New York at Buffalo. Author of* Dialectics and Nihilism: Essays on Lessing, Nietzsche, Mann and Kafka.
KAFKA, FRANZ (Micropædia)

P.E.H.   Peter E. Herzog. *Crandall Melvin Professor of Law, Syracuse University, New York. Author of* Civil Procedure in France.
PROCEDURAL LAW (*in part*)

Pe.He.   Peter Herde. *Professor of History; Director of the Historical Institute, University of Würzburg, West Germany. Author of* Beiträge zum päpstlichen Kanzlei und Urkundenwesen im Dreizehnten Jahrhundert *and others.*
HISTORY, THE STUDY OF (*in part*)

P.E.J.   Preston E. James (d. 1986). *Maxwell Professor of Geography, Syracuse University, New York, 1964–70. Author of* All Possible Worlds: A History of Geographical Ideas; Latin America.
BRAZIL (*in part*)
URUGUAY (*in part*)

P.E.K.   Paul E. Klopsteg. *Emeritus Professor of Applied Science, Northwestern University, Evanston, Illinois. Author of* Turkish Archery and the Composite Bow.
ARCHERY (*in part*) (Micropædia)

P.E.L.   Peter Erik Lasko. *Professor of the History of Art, Courtauld Institute, University of London. Author of* Ars Sacra, 800–1200.
DECORATIVE ARTS AND FURNISHINGS (*in part*)

P.E.P.D.   Paul E. Pieris Deraniyagala (d. 1973). *Director, National Museums of Ceylon, 1939–63. Dean, Faculty of Arts, Vidyodaya University of Ceylon, 1961–64. Specialist on fossil and recent animals of the Indian subcontinent, including extinct human populations. Author of* Some Extinct Elephants, Their Relatives and the Two Living Species.
MAMMALS (*in part*)

P.Er.   Philippe Erlanger. *Plenipotentiary Minister. Former Director of Cultural Activities, Ministry of Foreign Affairs, Paris. Author of* Louis XIV *and others.*
LOUIS XIV (FRANCE) (Micropædia)

P.E.R.   Peter Edward Russell. *King Alfonso XIII Professor Emeritus of Spanish Studies, University of Oxford; Fellow of Exeter College, Oxford. Author of* The English Intervention in Spain and Portugal in the Time of Edward III and Richard II *and others.*
CID, THE (Micropædia)
SPAIN (*in part*)

Pe.S.G.   Peter Spence Gilchrist, Jr. *President, Gilchem Corporation, Charlotte, North Carolina.*
UNITED STATES OF AMERICA (*in part*)

Pe.V.   Peter Viereck. *William R. Kenan, Jr. Professor of History, Mount Holyoke College, South Hadley, Massachusetts. Author of* Conservatism Revisited *and others.*
SOCIO-ECONOMIC DOCTRINES AND REFORM MOVEMENTS, MODERN (*in part*)

P.E.W.   Paul Edward Waggoner. *Director and former Chief Climatologist, Connecticut Agricultural Experiment Station, New Haven. Author of* Agricultural Meteorology.
CLIMATE AND WEATHER (*in part*)

P.F.   Paul Fraisse. *Emeritus Professor of Experimental Psychology, University of Paris. Author of* Psychologie du temps.
PERCEPTION, HUMAN (*in part*)

P.F.B.   Paul F. Borth. *Technical Director, International Association of Photoplatemakers, South Holland, Illinois. Author of numerous articles on engraving processes.*
PRINTING, TYPOGRAPHY, AND PHOTOENGRAVING (*in part*)

P.F.L.   Peirce F. Lewis. *Professor of Geography, Pennsylvania State University, University Park. Author of* New Orleans: The Making of an Urban Landscape.
UNITED STATES OF AMERICA (*in part*)

P.F.P.   Philip F. Purrington. *Curator, Whaling Museum, New Bedford, Massachusetts. Editor of* Returns of Whaling Vessels Sailing from American Ports, 1876–1928.
FISHING AND MARINE PRODUCTS, COMMERCIAL (*in part*)

P.F.V.   Paul F. Vincent. *Senior Lecturer in Dutch, University College, University of London. Coeditor of* European Context: Studies in the History and Literature of the Netherlands.
AMSTERDAM (*in part*)
DUTCH LITERATURE (*in part*)

P.F.W.   Paul F. Watson. *Associate Professor of the History of Art, University of Pennsylvania, Philadelphia. Author of* The Garden of Love in Tuscan Art.
PIERO DELLA FRANCESCA (Micropædia)

P.G.   Paul Guichonnet. *Professor of Human Geography, University of Geneva. Author of* Genève, Reflexions sur un destin urbain; *general editor of* Histoire de Genève.
GENEVA

P.Ga.   Philippe Garigue. *Principal, Glendon College, York University, Toronto. Professor of Political Science, University of Montreal, 1957–80. Author of* La Vie familiale des Canadiens français *and others.*
CANADA (*in part*)

P.G.B.   Peter G. Bietenholz. *Professor of History, University of Saskatchewan, Saskatoon. Author of* History and Biography in the Work of Erasmus of Rotterdam *and others.*
BURCKHARDT, JACOB (Micropædia)

P.G.Be.   Peter G. Bergmann. *Professor of Physics, Syracuse University, New York, and New York University, New York City. Author of* Introduction to the Theory of Relativity.
RELATIVITY

P.G.C.   Pablo González Casanova. *Professor, Institute of Social Research, National Autonomous University of Mexico, Mexico City. Author of* La democracia en México.
MEXICO (*in part*)

P.Gd.   Pierre Grenand. *Research Assistant, Overseas Office of Scientific and Technical Research, Centre at Cayenne, French Guiana.*
GUIANAS, THE (*in part*)

P.G.   Peter Godman. *Fellow and Tutor, Pembroke College, University of Oxford. Author of* Poetry and the Carolingian Renaissance *and others.*
LATIN LITERATURE (*in part*)

P.G.P.   Peter Georgiev Pençev. *Professor of Hydrology, University of Sofia, Bulgaria. Chairman, National Committee for the International Hydrologic Program. Author of* Hydrologic Regionalization of Bulgaria.
EUROPE (*in part*)

P.Gr. Pier Groen. *Former Professor of Meteorology and Physical Oceanography, Free University, Amsterdam. Author of* The Waters of the Sea.
OCEANS (*in part*)

P.G.S. Peter G. Stein. *Regius Professor of Civil Law, University of Cambridge; Fellow of Queens' College, Cambridge. Author of* Regulæ Iuris: From Juristic Rules to Legal Maxims *and others.*
LEGAL SYSTEMS, THE EVOLUTION OF
  MODERN WESTERN (*in part*)

P.Gu. Pierre Gourou. *Honorary Professor, College of France, Paris. Emeritus Professor of Geography, Free Univerity of Brussels. Author of* L'Asie.
ASIA (*in part*)

P.G.W. Patrick Chrestien Gordon Walker, Baron Gordon-Walker (d. 1980). *Member of Parliament (Labour) for Leyton, 1966–74. Author of* The Cabinet; The Commonwealth; *and others.*
UNITED KINGDOM (*in part*)

P.H. Paul Herget (d. 1981). *Director, Cincinnati Observatory, University of Cincinnati, Ohio, 1943–78; Distinguished Service Professor of Astronomy, 1965–78. Author of* The Computation of Orbits.
SOLAR SYSTEM, THE (*in part*)

Ph.C. Philip Collins. *Emeritus Professor of English, University of Leicester, England. Author of* Dickens and Crime; Dickens and Education.
DICKENS (*in part*)

P.H.D. P.H. Davison. *Professor of English, University of Kent at Canterbury, England. Editor,* The Library (*Journal of the Bibliographical Society*), *1971–82. Author of* Popular Appeal in English Drama to 1850.
POPULAR ARTS (*in part*)

P.He. Sir Philip Hendy (d. 1980). *Adviser to the Israel Museum, Jerusalem, 1968–71. Director, National Gallery, London, 1946–67. Author of* Giovanni Bellini; Piero della Francesca and the Early Renaissance.
BELLINI, GIOVANNI (Micropædia)

P.H.G. Peter Humphry Greenwood. *Senior Principal Scientific Officer (Curator of Fishes), Department of Zoology, British Museum (Natural History), London. Author of* The Fishes of Uganda; *coauthor of the major modern classification of the bony fishes.*
FISHES (*in part*)

P.H.Ge. Paul Henry Gebhard. *Professor of Anthropology, Indiana University, Bloomington; former Director, Institute for Sex Research. Coauthor of* Pregnancy, Birth and Abortion; Sex Offenders.
SEX AND SEXUALITY (*in part*)

P.H.Gu. Pierre H. Guiguemde. *Director of Public Relations for the Parliament of Upper Volta.*
WESTERN AFRICA (*in part*)

P.H.Gul. P.H. Gulliver. *Professor of Anthropology, York University, Downsview, Ontario. Editor of* Tradition and Transition in East Africa.
EASTERN AFRICA (*in part*)

P.H.H. Perry H. Howard. *Professor of Sociology, Louisiana State University, Baton Rouge. Author of* Political Tendencies in Louisiana.
UNITED STATES OF AMERICA (*in part*)

Ph.H. J.H.t.C. Philo H.J. Houwink ten Cate. *Professor of Ancient Near Eastern History and Languages, University of Amsterdam. Author of* The Luwian Population Groups of Lycia and Cilicia Aspera during the Hellenistic Period; The Records of the Early Hittite Empire (c. 1450–1380 BC).
LANGUAGES OF THE WORLD (*in part*)
TURKEY AND ANCIENT ANATOLIA
  (*in part*)

P.Hi. Patrice Louis-René Higonnet. *Professor of History, Harvard University. Author of* Class, Ideology, and the Rights of Nobles During the French Revolution *and others.*
FRANCE (*in part*)

P.H.J.C. Peter Henry John Castle. *Reader in Zoology, Victoria University of Wellington, New Zealand. Author of numerous papers on eels.*
FISHES (*in part*)

P.H.K. Philip H. Kuenen (d. 1976). *Professor of Geology, State University of Groningen, The Netherlands, 1943–72. Authority on density currents and marine sedimentation. Author of* Marine Geology.
OCEANS (*in part*)

P.H.L. Peter H. Lee. *Professor and Chairman, Department of East Asian Languages and Literatures, University of Hawaii at Manoa, Honolulu. Author of* Songs of Flying Dragons: A Critical Reading.
KOREAN LITERATURE (*in part*)

P.H.O. Paul H. Oehser. *Editor of Scientific Publications, National Geographic Society, 1966–78. Chief, Editorial and Publications Division, Smithsonian Institution, Washington, D.C., 1950–66.*
UNITED STATES OF AMERICA (*in part*)

P.Hu. Peter J. Huizing. *Professor of Canon Law and History of Canon Law, Catholic University of Nijmegen, The Netherlands. Author of* The Sacraments in Theology and Canon Law *and others.*
CHRISTIANITY (*in part*)

P.I. Pavle Ivić. *Former Professor of Serbo-Croatian Language, History, and Dialectology, University of Belgrade. Author of* Die serbokroatischen Dialekte; *coauthor of* Accent in Serbocroatian.
LANGUAGE (*in part*)
LINGUISTICS (*in part*)

P.J.F. Pasquale J. Federico (d. 1982). *Attorney and consultant in patent law.*

Professorial Lecturer in Law, George Washington University, Washington, D.C., 1950–73. Examiner in Chief, Board of Patent Appeals, Patent Office, U.S. Department of Commerce, Washington, D.C., 1947–70. Author of Commentary on the New Patent Act *and others.*
PROPERTY LAW (*in part*)

P.J.H. Peter John Hilton. *Fellow of Battelle Research Center, Seattle, Washington. Distinguished Professor of Mathematics, State University of New York at Binghamton. Coauthor of* Homology Theory; A Course in Homological Algebra; *and others.*
ALGEBRA (*in part*)

P.J.M. P.J. Marshall. *Rhodes Professor of Imperial History, King's College, University of London. Author of* The Impeachment of Warren Hastings *and others.*
HASTINGS, WARREN (Micropædia)

P.J.Mu. Peter J. Murray. *Emeritus Professor of the History of Art, Birkbeck College, University of London. Author of* Architecture of the Italian Renaissance; *coauthor of* A Dictionary of Art and Artists.
GHIRLANDAJO, DOMENICO (Micropædia)
GIOTTO DI BONDONE (Micropædia)
PERUGINO (Micropædia)

P.J.N. Per Jonas Nordhagen. *Lecturer in Art History, University of Oslo. Coauthor of* Mosaics.
DECORATIVE ARTS AND FURNISHINGS
  (*in part*)

P.J.P. Peter J. Pollack (d. 1978). *Photographer and lecturer. Author of* The Picture History of Photography *and others.*
STEICHEN, EDWARD (Micropædia)

P.J.W. Peter John Wyllie. *Professor of Geology and Chairman, Division of Geological and Planetary Sciences, California Institute of Technology, Pasadena. Author of* The Dynamic Earth.
MINERALS AND ROCKS (*in part*)

P.K. Philip Kissam (d. 1978). *Professor of Civil Engineering, Princeton University, 1948–65. Author of* Surveying Practice.
MEASUREMENT AND OBSERVATION,
  PRINCIPLES, METHODS, AND
  INSTRUMENTS OF (*in part*)

P.K.E. Peter K. Endress. *Professor of Systematic Botany, Institute for Systematic Botany, University of Zürich.*
ANGIOSPERMS (*in part*)

P.K.K. Peter K. King. *Director, Institute of Modern Dutch Studies, University of Hull, England. Author of* Dawn Poetry in the Netherlands.
DUTCH LITERATURE (*in part*)

P.L. Philip Longworth. *Associate Professor of History, McGill University, Montreal. Author of* The Art of Victory: The Life and Achievements of Generalissimo Suvorov *and others.*

SUVOROV, ALEKSANDR VASILYEVICH, GRAF (Micropædia)

P.Le. **Pierre Leprohon.** *Writer and journalist. Author of* Jean Renoir; Charles Chaplin; Antonioni; *and others.*
RENOIR, JEAN (Micropædia)

P.L.G. **Patrick Lancaster Gardiner.** *Fellow and Tutor in Philosophy, Magdalen College, University of Oxford. Author of* The Nature of Historical Explanation *and others.*
PHILOSOPHIES OF THE BRANCHES OF KNOWLEDGE (*in part*)

P.L.Kl. **Paul Lincoln Kleinsorge.** *Emeritus Professor of Economics, University of Oregon, Eugene.*
ECONOMIC THEORY (*in part*)

P.L.v.d.B. **Pierre Louis van den Berghe.** *Professor of Sociology, University of Washington, Seattle. Author of* Race and Racism.
SOCIAL DIFFERENTIATION (*in part*)

P.Ma. **Philip Mason.** *Writer. Director, Institute of Race Relations, London, 1958–69. Indian Civil Service, 1928–47. Author of* The Founders; The Guardians; The Birth of a Dilemma; The Men Who Ruled India; *and many others.*
BENTINCK, LORD WILLIAM (Micropædia)

P.M.C. **Paul M. Cohn.** *Professor of Mathematics, University College, University of London. Author of* Universal Algebra; Free Rings.
ALGEBRA (*in part*)

P.McC. **Patrick McCarthy.** *Associate Professor of French, Haverford College, Pennsylvania. Author of* Céline; Camus.
FRENCH LITERATURE (*in part*)

P.McG.R. **Peter McGregor Ross** (d. 1974). *Professor of Engineering, University of Cambridge, 1970–74.*
ENGINEERING (*in part*)

P.McL. **Peter McLintock.** *Former Editor,* Winnipeg Free Press, *Manitoba.*
CANADA (*in part*)

P.Me. **Pierre Mertz** (d. 1982). *Chairman, Board of Editors,* Journal of the Society of Motion Picture and Television Engineers, *1954–77. Coauthor of* Communication System Engineering Handbook.
MOTION PICTURES (*in part*)

P.M.F. **Peter Marshall Fraser.** *Fellow of All Souls College, Oxford; Reader in Hellenistic History, University of Oxford.*
PALESTINE (*in part*)

P.M.H. **Philip M. Hauser.** *Lucy Flower Professor Emeritus of Urban Sociology; Emeritus Director, Population Research Center, University of Chicago. Co-editor of* The Study of Urbanization.
MODERNIZATION AND URBANIZATION (*in part*)

P.M.Ho. **Peter M. Holt.** *Emeritus Professor of the History of the Near and Middle East, University of London. Author of* Egypt and the Fertile Crescent, 1516–1922 *and others.*
EGYPT (*in part*)

P.Mi. **Peter Michelmore.** *Roving Editor,* Reader's Digest. *Author of* Einstein: Profile of the Man.
EINSTEIN
TELLER, EDWARD (*in part*) (Micropædia)

P.M.K. **Paul Murray Kendall** (d. 1973). *Professor of English, University of Kansas, Lawrence. Author of* The Art of Biography; Richard the Third; *and others.*
LITERATURE, THE ART OF (*in part*)

P.M.M. **Peter Mackenzie Millman.** *Head, Upper Atmosphere Research Section, Radio and Electrical Engineering Division, National Research Council of Canada, Ottawa, 1955–71. Author of* This Universe of Space; *editor of* Meteorite Research.
SOLAR SYSTEM, THE (*in part*)

P.Mo. **Patrick Moore.** *President, British Astronomical Association. Author of* The Unfolding Universe *and many others.*
SOLAR SYSTEM, THE (*in part*)

P.M.R. **Pierre M. Rosenberg.** *Curator, Department of Paintings, Louvre Museum, Paris. Author of* Chardin: Étude biographique et critique; Dessins français du 17ème siècle.
CHARDIN, JEAN-BAPTISTE-SIMÉON (Micropædia)

P.M.Sy. **Patrick Millington Synge** (d. 1982). *Editor, Publications of the Royal Horticultural Society, London, 1945–70. Author of* Collins Guide to Bulbs; *coauthor of* The Dictionary of Garden Plants in Colour.
GARDENING AND HORTICULTURE (*in part*)

P.Mu. **Peter Munz.** *Professor of History, Victoria University of Wellington, New Zealand. Author of* The Origin of the Carolingian Empire.
CONRAD II (GERMANY/HOLY ROMAN EMPIRE) (Micropædia)
HENRY II (SAXONY) (Micropædia)

P.M.U. **Peter Michael Urbach.** *Lecturer in Philosophy, London School of Economics and Political Science, University of London. Author of* Francis Bacon's Philosophy of Science: An Account and a Reappraisal.
BACON, FRANCIS (*in part*)

P.M.Y. **Percy Marshall Young.** *Composer. Director of Music, Wolverhampton College of Technology, England, 1944–66. Author of* A History of British Music; Handel; *and others.*
HANDEL, GEORGE FRIDERIC (*in part*) (Micropædia)

P.N.K. **Pyotr Nikolayevich Kropotkin.** *Head, Laboratory of Structural Geophysics, Institute of Geology, Academy of Sciences of the U.S.S.R., Moscow.*
ASIA (*in part*)

P.N.L. **Peter N. Ladefoged.** *Professor of Phonetics, University of California, Los Angeles. Author of* A Course in Phonetics *and others.*
SPEECH (*in part*)

P.N.P. **Philip N. Powers.** *Emeritus Professor of Nuclear Engineering, Purdue University, West Lafayette, Indiana.*
ENERGY CONVERSION (*in part*)

P.P. **Paul Petit** (d. 1981). *Professor of Ancient History, University of Grenoble II, France. Author of* Histoire général de l'Empire romaine *and others.*
GRECO-ROMAN CIVILIZATION, CLASSICAL (*in part*)

P.P.A. **Phoon Phon Asanachinta.** *Colonel, Royal Thai Army. Emeritus Professor of Geography, Chiang Mai University, Chiang Mai, Thailand.*
SOUTHEAST ASIA, MAINLAND (*in part*)

P.P.B. **Patrick Paul Billingsley.** *Professor of Mathematics and of Statistics, University of Chicago. Author of* Convergence of Probability Measures *and others.*
NUMBER THEORY (*in part*)

P.P. del C. **Pier Paolo del Campana.** *Professor of Comparative Religion, Sophia University, Tokyo. Author of* Shinran and Nichiren.
NICHIREN (Micropædia)

P.P.E. **Paul P. Ewald** (d. 1985). *Professor of Physics, Polytechnic Institute of Brooklyn, New York, 1949–59.*
BETHE, HANS ALBRECHT (Micropædia)

P.P.H. **Philip Prichard Henderson** (d. 1977). *Free-lance writer and editor. Author of* William Morris: His Life, Work and Friends; *editor of* The Letters of William Morris *and others.*
MORRIS, WILLIAM (Micropædia)

P.P.K. **P.P. Karan.** *Professor of Geography, University of Kentucky, Lexington. Author of* Nepal: A Physical and Cultural Geography; Bhutan: A Physical and Cultural Geography; *and others.*
NEPAL (*in part*)

Pp.M. **Philip Merlan** (d. 1968). *Professor of German Philosophy and Literature, Scripps College, Claremont, California, 1942–68. Author of* From Platonism to Neoplatonism *and others.*
PHILOSOPHICAL SCHOOLS AND DOCTRINES, WESTERN (*in part*)

P.P.R. **Peter P. Rohde.** *Free-lance writer. Editor, Kierkegaard's Collected Works (in progress). Author of* Søren Kierkegaard.
KIERKEGAARD, SØREN (*in part*) (Micropædia)

P.R. **Pierre Riché.** *Professor of Medieval History, University of Paris X. Author of* Education and Culture in the Barbarian West *and others.*
EDUCATION, HISTORY OF (*in part*)

P.R.A. **Pierre Robert Angel.** *Professor and Head, Department of Classical and Modern Languages, Literature* *and Civilizations, University of Tours, France. Author of* Eduard Bernstein et l'évolution du socialisme allemand *and others.*

BERNSTEIN, EDUARD (Micropædia)

P.R.C.   Peter Raymond Creevey. *Free-lance writer and journalist. Managing Editor,* The Samoa Times, *Pago Pago, American Samoa, 1963–70.*

PACIFIC ISLANDS (*in part*)

P.R.Cd.   Paul R. Clifford. *Department Head, Environmental Chemistry and Biology, Metrek Division, Mitre Corporation, McLean, Virginia. Coauthor of* Fundamentals of Organic Chemistry.

CARBONIUM ION (*in part*) (Micropædia)

P.R.G.   Peter R. Grant. *Professor of Biology, University of Michigan, Ann Arbor.*

BIOSPHERE, THE (*in part*)

P.R.Go.   Peter R. Goethals. *Writer, consultant, and research specialist on Southeast Asia. Author of* Aspects of Local Government in a Sumbawan Village.

ASIA (*in part*)

P.R.L.B.   Peter R.L. Brown. *Professor of History and Classics, University of California, Berkeley. Author of* Religion and Society in the Age of Saint Augustine.

AMBROSE, SAINT (Micropædia)

P.S.   Pierre Samuel. *Professor of Mathematics, University of Paris XI. Author of* Théorie algébrique des nombres.

ALGEBRA (*in part*)

P.S.B.   Philip S. Baker. *Former Manager, Records Management and Reproduction, Oak Ridge National Laboratory, Tennessee; Director, Isotopes Information Center, 1962–72. Author of* Radioisotopes in Industry.

ATOMS (*in part*)

P.S.Ba.   Peter S. Baker. *Assistant Professor of English, Emory University, Atlanta, Georgia. Coeditor of* The Correspondence of James Boswell with David Garrick, Edmund Burke, and Edmond Malone.

ENGLISH LITERATURE (*in part*)

P.Sc.   Peter Scott. *Emeritus Professor of Geography, University of Tasmania, Hobart.*

AUSTRALIA (*in part*)

P.S.C.   Philip S. Corbet. *Professor of Zoology, University of Dundee, Scotland. Author of* A Biology of Dragonflies.

INSECTS (*in part*)

P.Se.   Paul Seabury. *Professor of Political Science, University of California, Berkeley. Author of* Power, Freedom and Diplomacy.

INTERNATIONAL RELATIONS,
   20TH-CENTURY (*in part*)

P.S.F.   Philip S. Foner. *Independence Foundation Professor Emeritus of History, Lincoln University,*

Pennsylvania. Editor of The Complete Writings of Thomas Paine.

PAINE, THOMAS (Micropædia)

P.S.G.   Peter S. Green. *Honorary Research Associate, Royal Botanic Gardens, Kew, England; former Deputy Chief Scientific Officer. Coeditor of* Wild Flowers of the World.

ANGIOSPERMS (*in part*)

P.Si.   Peter Singer. *Professor of Philosophy; Director, Centre for Human Bioethics, Monash University, Victoria, Australia. Author of* Practical Ethics.

ETHICS

P.S.K.   Pavel Sergeyevich Kuzin. *Senior Scientist, Leningrad Hydrological Institute. Author of* Volga Zavtra.

EUROPE (*in part*)

P.S.M.   P.S. Messenger (d. 1976). *Professor of Entomology, University of California, Berkeley, 1965–76. Author of many research papers on entomology.*

BIOSPHERE, THE (*in part*)

P.S.R.   Philip S. Rawson. *Former Dean, School of Art and Design, Goldsmiths' College, London. Curator, Gulbenkian Museum of Oriental Art and Archaeology, University of Durham, England, 1960–79. Author of* The Arts of Southeast Asia *and others.*

PAGAN (Micropædia)
SOUTHEAST ASIAN ARTS (*in part*)

P.Su.   Patrick Suppes. *Lucie Stern Professor of Philosophy; Director, Institute for Mathematical Studies in the Social Sciences, Stanford University, California. Coauthor of* Foundations of Measurement.

MEASUREMENT THEORY (*in part*)

P.S.W.   Paul S. Wingert (d. 1974). *Professor of Art History and Archaeology, Columbia University. Author of* Primitive Art, Its Traditions and Styles *and others.*

MASKS

P.T.   Piero Treves. *Professor of Ancient History, University of Venice, Italy. Author of biography of Miltiades in* Oxford Classical Dictionary.

MILTIADES THE YOUNGER (Micropædia)

P.U.   Philip Soundy Unwin (d. 1981). *Free-lance editor. Senior Director, George Allen & Unwin Ltd., London. Author of* Book Publishing as a Career.

PUBLISHING (*in part*)

P.V.   Paul Veyret. *Emeritus Professor of Mountain Geography, Institute of Alpine Geography, University of Grenoble I, France. Coauthor of* Au coeur de l'Europe: Les Alpes *and others.*

EUROPE (*in part*)

P.V.G.   Pyotr Vatslavovich Gulyan. *Assistant Director, Institute of Economics, Latvian S.S.R. Academy of Sciences, Riga. Author of* Latvia in the System of the U.S.S.R. National Economy.

UNION OF SOVIET SOCIALIST REPUBLICS
   (*in part*)

P.Vi.   Paul Viallaneix. *Professor of French Literature; Director, Centre for Romantic Research, University of Clermont-Ferrand, France. Author of* Vigny par lui-même; *editor of* Vigny's Oeuvres complètes.

VIGNY, ALFRED-VICTOR, COMTE DE
   (Micropædia)

P.V.T.   Phillip Vallentine Tobias. *Professor and Head, Department of Anatomy, University of the Witwatersrand, Johannesburg. Author of* Olduvai Gorge: Cranium of Zinjanthropus.

EVOLUTION, HUMAN (*in part*)

P.W.   Paul E. Walker. *Executive Director, American Research Center in Egypt, Columbia University.*

SALADIN (Micropædia)

P.Wa.   Peggy Wagner. *Staff member, Houghton Mifflin Company, Boston. Editorial Assistant, Arts,* Encyclopædia Britannica, *Chicago, 1971–73.*

AFRICAN ARTS (*in part*)

P.W.A.   Peter William Avery. *Lecturer in Persian; Director, Middle East Centre, University of Cambridge. Author of* Modern Iran.

IRAN (*in part*)

P.W.F.   Peter W. Frank. *Professor of Biology, University of Oregon, Eugene.*

GROWTH AND DEVELOPMENT,
   BIOLOGICAL (*in part*)

P.W.H.   Paul W. Hodge. *Professor of Astronomy, University of Washington, Seattle. Author of* Galaxies *and others.*

GALAXIES

P.W.J.   Pascual W. Jordon (d. 1980). *Professor of Theoretical Physics, University of Hamburg, 1953–70. Author of* Verdrängung und Komplementarität: Eine philosophische Untersuchung.

PHILOSOPHIES OF THE BRANCHES OF
   KNOWLEDGE (*in part*)

P.W.K.   Peter W. Kingsford. *Tutor, Extra Mural Department, University of London. Author of* Engineers, Inventors, and Workers; Victorian Railwaymen; *and others.*

WATT, JAMES (Micropædia)

P.W.R.   Paul Westmacott Richards. *Emeritus Professor of Botany, University College of North Wales, University of Wales, Bangor. Author of* The Life of the Jungle *and others.*

ECOSYSTEMS (*in part*)

P.Y.   Philip Young. *Evan Pugh Professor of English, Pennsylvania State University, University Park. Author of* Ernest Hemingway; *coauthor of* The Hemingway Manuscripts.

HEMINGWAY, ERNEST (Micropædia)

P.Y.K.   Pekka Yrjö Korkala. *Former Lecturer in Psychometrics, Institute of Psychology, University of Helsinki. Coauthor of* Introduction to Psychometrics; *coeditor of* Contemporary Research in the Psychology of

Perception.
PERCEPTION, HUMAN (*in part*)

Q.W. **Quincy Wright** (d. 1970). *Professor of International Law, University of Chicago, 1931–56. Author of* Study of International Relations.
UNITED NATIONS (*in part*)

Q.Z. **Quido Záruba.** *Professor, Geological Institute, Czech Technical University in Prague. Member of the Czechoslovak Academy of Sciences. Coauthor of* Landslides and Their Control *and others.*
GEOMORPHIC PROCESSES (*in part*)

R.A. **Rosendo Arguello.** *Former President, Academy of the Geography and History of Nicaragua, Managua. Author of* Nueva Nicaragua.
CENTRAL AMERICA (*in part*)

R.Aa. **Richard I. Aaron.** *Emeritus Professor of Philosophy, University College of Wales, Aberystwyth, University of Wales. Author of* John Locke; Knowing and the Function of Reason.
EPISTEMOLOGY
LOCKE (*in part*)

R.A.A. **Ralph A. Austen.** *Associate Professor of History, University of Chicago; Chairman, Committee on African Studies, 1974–79. Author of* Northwest Tanzania Under German and British Rule.
EASTERN AFRICA (*in part*)

R.A.B. **Roland A. Budenholzer.** *John T. Rettaliata Professor Emeritus of Mechanical Engineering; Chairman, American Power Conference, Illinois Institute of Technology, Chicago.*
ENERGY CONVERSION (*in part*)

R.A.Bu. **Robert Angus Buchanan.** *Reader in the History of Technology; Director, Centre for the History of Technology, Science, and Society, University of Bath, England. Author of* Technology and Social Progress.
TECHNOLOGY, THE HISTORY OF

R.A.-C. **René Albrecht-Carrié** (d.1978). *Professor of History, Barnard College, 1945–69, and Columbia University, 1953–69. Author of* A Diplomatic History of Europe Since the Congress of Vienna.
EUROPE (*in part*)

R.A.Co. **Ralph A. Connor, D.D.S.** *Professor of Pediatric and Community Dentistry, Dalhousie University, Halifax, Nova Scotia, 1971–72. Chief, Dental Health Division, Canadian Department of National Health and Welfare, Ottawa, 1963–71.*
MEDICINE (*in part*)

R.A.E. **Robert A. East.** *Emeritus Professor of History, Brooklyn College, City University of New York. Author of* John Quincy Adams.
ADAMS, JOHN (Micropædia)

R.A.F. **Richard Antony French.** *Senior Lecturer in the Geography of the*

U.S.S.R., *University College and School of Slavonic and East European Studies, University of London. Author of* The U.S.S.R. and Eastern Europe.
KIEV (*in part*)
LENINGRAD (*in part*)
MOSCOW (*in part*)
UNION OF SOVIET SOCIALIST REPUBLICS (*in part*)

R.A.G. **Richard A. Geyer.** *Professor of Oceanography, Texas A&M University, College Station.*
NORTH AMERICA (*in part*)

R.A.Gi. **Robert Andrew Gilbert.** *Author of* The Golden Dawn: Twilight of the Magicians; *coeditor of* The Oxford Book of English Ghost Stories.
OCCULTISM (*in part*)

R.A.H. **Robert A. Hall, Jr.** *Emeritus Professor of Linguistics and Italian, Cornell University, Ithaca, New York. Author of* Pidgin and Creole Languages.
LANGUAGES OF THE WORLD (*in part*)

R.A.He. **Ronald A. Henson, M.D.** *Physician and Neurologist, London Hospital, 1949–81. Physician, National Hospital for Nervous Diseases, 1952–81.*
MUSCLES AND MUSCLE SYSTEMS (*in part*)

R.A.Hi. **Reynold Alleyne Higgins.** *Deputy Keeper of Greek and Roman Antiquities, British Museum, London, 1965–77. Author of* Minoan and Mycenaean Art *and others.*
PAINTING, THE HISTORY OF WESTERN (*in part*)
SCULPTURE, THE HISTORY OF WESTERN (*in part*)

Ra.Ho. **Ralph Holmes.** *Stage lighting designer. Senior Lighting Director, Columbia Broadcasting System, New York City.*
THEATRICAL PRODUCTION (*in part*)

R.A.Ho. **R.A. Horne.** *Senior Scientist, Energy and Environmental Engineers, Inc., Cambridge, Massachusetts. President, Free Speech Foundation, Inc., Boston. Author of* Marine Chemistry; *editor of* Water and Aqueous Solutions.
CHEMICAL COMPOUNDS (*in part*)

R.A.K. **Robert A. Kann** (d. 1981). *Professor of History, Rutgers University, New Brunswick, New Jersey, 1956–76. Author of* The Habsburg Empire.
AUSTRIA (*in part*)

R.Al. **Rex Alston.** *Broadcaster and journalist. Staff Sports Commentator and Reporter, British Broadcasting Corporation, 1942–61. Cricket Reporter,* Daily *and* Sunday Telegraph *(London), 1961–83. Author of* Watching Cricket.
SPORTS, MAJOR TEAM AND INDIVIDUAL (*in part*)

R.A.L. **Robert A. Laudise.** *Director, Physical and Inorganic Chemical Research Laboratory, Bell Laboratories, Inc., Murray Hill, New Jersey. Author of* The Growth of Single Crystals.
MATTER (*in part*)

Ra.N. **Ray Nash** (d. 1982). *Professor of Art, Dartmouth College, Hanover, New Hampshire, 1949–70. Author of* American Penmanship, 1800–1850: *editor and translator of* Calligraphy and Printing in the Sixteenth Century.
WRITING (*in part*)

R.A.N. **Robert A. Nisbet.** *Albert Schweitzer Professor Emeritus of History, Columbia University. Noted for contributions to social theory and organization. Author of* Social Change and History *and others.*
SOCIAL SCIENCES, THE (*in part*)

R.A.P. **Robert A. Pinker.** *Professor of Social Work Studies, London School of Economics and Political Science, University of London. Author of* The Idea of Welfare *and others.*
SOCIAL WELFARE (*in part*)

R.A.Pi. **Roger A. Pielke.** *Professor of Atmospheric Science, Colorado State University, Ft. Collins. Author of* Mesoscale Meteorological Modeling.
EARTH SCIENCES, THE (*in part*)

R.A.Pr. **Ralph Anthony Palmer.** *Assistant Secretary, American Society of Agricultural Engineers, 1927–69.*
AGRICULTURAL SCIENCES (*in part*)

R.A.R.T. **Ronald A.R. Tricker.** *Staff Inspector for Science, Ministry of Education, U.K., 1946–62. Author of* Bores, Breakers, Waves and Wakes; The Contributions of Faraday and Maxwell to Electrical Science; *and others.*
MECHANICS (*in part*)
OCEANS (*in part*)

R.A.S. **Richard A. Sheppard.** *Geologist, Branch of Energy Minerals, Geological Survey, U.S. Department of the Interior, Denver, Colorado.*
MINERALS AND ROCKS (*in part*)

R.Au. **Robert Austerlitz.** *Professor of Linguistics Uralic Studies, Columbia University. Coeditor of* Readings in Linguistics II; *compiler of* Finnish Reader and Glossary, *2nd ed.*
LANGUAGES OF THE WORLD (*in part*)

Ra.W. **Raymond Wolfe.** *Supervisor, Materials Research Laboratory, Bell Telephone Laboratories, Inc., Murray Hill, New Jersey. Coauthor of* Thermoelectricity.
ENERGY CONVERSION (*in part*)

R.A.W. **Richard A. Watson.** *Professor of Philosophy, Washington University, St. Louis, Missouri. Author of* The Downfall of Cartesianism.
CARTESIANISM, DESCARTES AND (*in part*)

R.A.Wa. **Robert Austin Warner.** *Emeritus Professor of Music History and Musicology; Emeritus Director, Stearns Collection of Musical Instruments, University of Michigan, Ann Arbor.*
MUSICAL INSTRUMENTS (*in part*)

R.A.We. **Richard A. Webster.** *Professor of History, University of California, Berkeley. Author of* Industrial

Imperialism in Italy, 1908–1915.
EUROPEAN OVERSEAS EXPLORATION
AND EMPIRES, THE HISTORY
OF (*in part*)

R.B.   Robert Browning. *Emeritus Professor of Classics and Ancient History, Birkbeck College, University of London. Author of* Medieval and Modern Greek *and others.*
LUCIAN (Micropædia)
GREEK LITERATURE (*in part*)

R.Ba.   Ruth Barbour. *Lecturer in Greek Palaeography, University of Oxford, 1960–67.*
WRITING (*in part*)

R.B.A.   Robert Brown Asprey. *Free-lance writer. Author of* The First Battle of the Marne; War in the Shadows; *and others.*
WAR, THE THEORY AND CONDUCT OF
(*in part*)

R.B.Ba.   Ronald B. Ballinger (d. 1981). *Professor of History, Rhode Island College, Providence. Author of* South West Africa: The Case Against the Union *and others.*
SOUTH AFRICA (*in part*)
SOUTHERN AFRICA (*in part*)

R.B.C.   Raymond Brazenor Clayton. *Professor of Biochemistry in Psychiatry, Stanford University, California. Editor of* Steriods and Terpenoids.
CHEMICAL COMPOUNDS (*in part*)

R.B.D.   Robert Bruce Davidson. *Curator of History, Provincial Museum of Alberta, Edmonton.*
CANADA (*in part*)

R.B.G.   Richard B. Goode. *Director, Fiscal Affairs Department, International Monetary Fund, Washington, D.C., 1965–81. Author of* The Corporation Income Tax.
TAXATION (*in part*)

R.B.I.   Ronald B. Inden. *Associate Professor of History, University of Chicago. Author of* Marriage and Rank in Bengali Culture: A History of Caste and Clan in Middle Period Bengal.
SOCIAL DIFFERENTIATION (*in part*)

R.Bl.   Raymond Bloch. *Professor, École Pratique des Hautes Études (Institute for Advanced Research), Paris. Author of* The Etruscans; The Origins of Rome.
ARCHITECTURE, THE HISTORY OF
WESTERN (*in part*)
GRECO-ROMAN CIVILIZATION, CLASSICAL
(*in part*)
PAINTING, THE HISTORY OF WESTERN
(*in part*)
SCULPTURE, THE HISTORY OF WESTERN
(*in part*)

R.B.L.   R. Bruce Lindsay (d. 1985). *Hazard Professor of Physics, Brown University, Providence, Rhode Island, 1936–71. Editor in Chief, Acoustical Society of America. Author of* Lord Rayleigh: The Man and His Work *and others.*
MECHANICS (*in part*)

RAYLEIGH, JOHN WILLIAM STRUTT, 3RD
BARON (Micropædia)
SOUND (*in part*)

R.B.M.   Raymond B. Manning. *Curator, Division of Crustacea, National Museum of Natural History, Smithsonian Institution, Washington, D.C. Author of* Stomatopod Crustacea of the Western Atlantic.
CRUSTACEANS (*in part*)

R.B.N.   Robert Bradford Newman (d. 1983). *Senior Vice President, Bolt Beranek and Newman Inc., Cambridge, Massachusetts. Adjunct Professor of Architecture, Massachusetts Institute of Technology, 1976–83. Professor of Architectural Technology, Harvard University, 1971–83.*
SOUND (*in part*)

R.B.Ni.   Robert Brayton Nichols. *Landscape architect.*
PARK (Micropædia)

R.Br.   Reginald Brill. *Free-lance writer and historian. Author of* Terror of the French: John, Lord Talbot, c. 1388–1453 *and several articles on the period of the Hundred Years' War.*
RICHEMONT, ARTHUR, CONSTABLE DE
(Micropædia)

R.B.S.   Richard B. Sewall. *Professor of English, Yale University. Author of* The Vision of Tragedy; *coeditor of* Tragedy: Modern Essays in Criticism.
LITERATURE, THE ART OF
(*in part*)

R.B.Se.   Robert Bertram Serjeant. *Sir Thomas Adams's Professor Emeritus of Arabic, University of Cambridge; Director, Middle East Centre, 1965–82. Author of* The Portuguese off the South Arabian Coast *and others.*
ARABIA (*in part*)

R.C.   René Coste. *President, French Institute of Coffee and Cocoa, Paris; General Director, 1958–78. Author of* Les Caféiers et les cafés dans le monde.
BEVERAGE PRODUCTION (*in part*)
FARMING AND AGRICULTURAL
TECHNOLOGY (*in part*)

R.Ca.   Raymond Carr. *Warden of St. Antony's College, University of Oxford. Author of* Spain, 1808–1939
SPAIN (*in part*)

R.C.A.   Raymond Clare Archibald (d. 1955). *Professor of Mathematics, Brown University, Providence, Rhode Island, 1923–43. Author of* Outline of the History of Mathematics *and others.*
GEOMETRY (*in part*)

R.C.Bi.   R.C. Bigalke. *Professor of Nature Conservation, University of Stellenbosch, South Africa. Coauthor of* The Evolution of Mammals on the Southern Continents.
MAMMALS (*in part*)

R.C.Bo.   Raj C. Bose. *Emeritus Professor of Mathematics and Statistics, Colorado State University, Fort Collins. Coeditor of* Proceedings

of the Conference on Combinatorial Mathematics and Its Applications.
COMBINATORICS AND COMBINATORIAL
GEOMETRY (*in part*)

R.C.Br.   Robert C. Brasted. *Professor of Chemistry; Director of General Chemistry Program, University of Minnesota, Minneapolis. Coauthor and editor of* Comprehensive Inorganic Chemistry, 8 vol.
CHEMICAL ELEMENTS (*in part*)

R.C.Bu.   Robin Caron Buss. *Lecturer in French, Woolwich College of Further Education, London. Author of* Vigny's Chatterton.
FRENCH LITERATURE (*in part*)

R.C.C.   Ralph C. Croizier. *Professor of History, University of Victoria, British Columbia. Author of* Traditional Medicine in Modern China.
CHENG CH'ENG-KUNG (Micropædia)

R.Ce.   Roberto Cessi (d. 1969). *Professor of History, University of Padua, Italy, 1922–60. Deputy in the Italian Parliament, 1948–53.*
ITALY (*in part*)
VENICE (*in part*)

R.C.E.   Robert C. Elliott (d. 1981). *Professor of English Literature, University of California, San Diego, 1964–81. Author of* The Power of Satire: Magic, Ritual, Art; The Shape of Utopia.
LITERATURE, THE ART OF (*in part*)

R.C.F.   Richard Charles Froeschner. *Curator, Hemiptera Section, Department of Entomology, Smithsonian Institution, Washington, D.C.*
INSECTS (*in part*)

R.C.H.   Reginald Crawshaw Honeybone. *Former Professor and Head, School of Education, University of the South Pacific, Suva, Fiji. Coauthor and editor of* World Geography.
PACIFIC ISLANDS (*in part*)

R.C.K.   Roy Clement Knight. *Emeritus Professor of French, University College of Swansea, University of Wales. Author of* Racine et la Grèce *and others.*
RACINE, JEAN (Micropædia)

R.C.L.   Richard C. Latham. *Partner, Seay & Latham Investments, Dallas, Texas. Coauthor of* United States Polo Association Annual.
POLO (*in part*) (Micropædia)

R.C.N.   Robert C. North. *Professor of Political Science, Stanford University, California. Author of* Moscow and Chinese Communists *and others.*
LIU SHAO-CH'I (Micropædia)

R.Co.   Robert Cornevin. *Permanent Secretary, Academy of Overseas Sciences, Paris. Head, Centre of Studies and Documentation on Africa and Overseas, Paris. Author of* Histoire de l'Afrique *and others.*
INDIAN OCEAN ISLANDS (*in part*)
WEST INDIES, THE (*in part*)
WESTERN AFRICA (*in part*)

R.Cog.   Raymond Cogniat (d. 1977). *Principal Inspector of Fine Arts, 1943–67. Head of the arts section, Le Figaro, Paris, 1957–77. Author of* Renoir *and other works on 20th-century artists of the school of Paris.*

RENOIR, PIERRE-AUGUSTE (Micropædia)

R.C.R.   Reed C. Rollins. *Asa Gray Professor Emeritus of Systematic Botany, Harvard University; Director, Gray Herbarium, 1948–78. Coauthor of* Edible Wild Plants of Eastern North America.

ANGIOSPERMS (*in part*)
UNITED STATES OF AMERICA (*in part*)

R.C.S.   Reginald C. Sutcliff. *Emeritus Professor of Meteorology, University of Reading, England. Author of* Weather and Climate.

CLIMATE AND WEATHER (*in part*)

R.C.Sm.   Robert C. Smith (d. 1975). *Professor of the History of Art, University of Pennsylvania, Philadelphia, 1956–75. Author of* The Art of Portugal *and others.*

DECORATIVE ARTS AND FURNISHINGS (*in part*)

R.C.Su.   Robert Carl Suggs. *Anthropologist. Conductor of anthropological and archaeological field research in Polynesia, 1956–58. Author of* Island Civilizations of Polynesia; The Hidden Worlds of Polynesia; *and others.*

PACIFIC ISLANDS (*in part*)

R.C.V.C.   Raoul Charles Van Caenegem. *Professor of Medieval History, State University of Ghent, Belgium. Author of* Guide to the Sources of Medieval History.

LOW COUNTRIES, THE (*in part*)

R.C.-W.   Rupert Crawshay-Williams (d. 1977) *Author of* Russell Remembered; Methods and Criteria of Reasoning.

RUSSELL, BERTRAND (Micropædia)

R.C.Y.   Richard Charles York. *Instructor of Ornamental Horticulture, McHenry County College, Crystal Lake, Illinois, Former Associate Editor, Biology,* Encyclopædia Britannica, *Chicago.*

PHILOSOPHIES OF THE BRANCHES OF KNOWLEDGE (*in part*)

R.D.   Robert Dorfman. *Professor of Economics, Harvard University. Author of* The Price System.

ECONOMIC THEORY (*in part*)

R.Da.   René David. *Professor of Comparative Law, University of Aix-Marseille III, Aix-en-Provence, France, 1970–76. Author of* Les Grands Systèmes de droit contemporains.

SOCIAL SCIENCES, THE (*in part*)

R.D.B.   Richard David Barnett (d. 1986). *Keeper, Department of Western Asiatic Antiquities, British Museum, London, 1955–74.*

LEBANON (*in part*)

R.D.D.G.   Robert Donald Davidson Gibson. *Professor of French, University of Kent at Canterbury, England. Author*

of Modern French Poets on Poetry.

VALÉRY, PAUL (Micropædia)

R.De.   Robert Descloitres. *President and Director of Research, Centre of Applied Human Sciences, Aix-en-Provence, France. Coauthor of* L'Algérie des bidonvilles.

NORTH AFRICA (*in part*)

R.D.F.   Ralph D. Feigin, M.D. *J.S. Abercrombie Professor and Chairman, Department of Pediatrics, Baylor College of Medicine, Houston. Physician-in-Chief, Texas Children's Hospital. Coeditor and coauthor of* Textbook of Pediatric Infectious Diseases.

INFECTIOUS DISEASES (*in part*)

R.D.Fo.   Raymond D. Fogelson. *Professor of Anthropology, University of Chicago. Editor of* Handbook of North American Indians, *vol. 14, Southeast.*

AMERICAN INDIANS (*in part*)

R.D.H.   Robert D. Herman. *Professor of Sociology, Pomona College, Claremont, California. Author of* Gamblers and Gambling.

LOTTERY (Micropædia)

R.D.L.   R. Duncan Luce. *Victor S. Thomas Professor of Psychology, Harvard University. Coauthor of* Foundations of Measurement.

MEASUREMENT THEORY (*in part*)

R.D.M.   Robert Douthat Meade (d. 1974). *Professor of History, Randolph-Macon Woman's College, Lynchburg, Virginia, 1939–71. Author of* Patrick Henry, Patriot in the Making *and others.*

HENRY, PATRICK (Micropædia)

R.D.Mi.   Robin David Middleton. *Librarian, Faculty of Architecture and History of Art, University of Cambridge. Head of General Studies, Architectural Association School of Architecture, London.*

ARCHITECTURE, THE HISTORY OF WESTERN (*in part*)

R.Do.   Ron Dorfman. *Editor,* The Quill. *Former Articles Editor,* Chicago *magazine.*

CHICAGO (*in part*)

Rd.T.   Rosalind Tolson. *Teacher, Antigua Girls' High School, The West Indies, 1954–56.*

WEST INDIES, THE (*in part*)

R.Du.   Raymond E. Durgnat. *Tutor in Cultural History, Royal College of Art, London. Author of* Films and Feelings; Buñuel; Jean Renoir; *and others.*

GODARD, JEAN-LUC (Micropædia)
RESNAIS, ALAIN (*in part*) (Micropædia)
TRUFFAUT, FRANÇOIS (*in part*) (Micropædia)

R.Dum.   René Dumesnil (d. 1967). *Literary and music critic. Member, Academy of Fine Arts, Institute of France, 1965–67. Author of* Gustave Flaubert, l'homme et l'oeuvre; Guy de Maupassant; *and others.*

FLAUBERT, GUSTAVE (*in part*) (Micropædia)

R.D.W.   Robert Deryck Williams (d. 1986). *Professor of Classics, University of Reading, England. Author of* Virgil; *editor of* Aeneid.

VIRGIL (*in part*)

R.E.Be.   Ronald E. Bedford. *Senior Research Officer, Division of Physics; Head, Heat Thermometry Section, National Research Council of Canada, Ottawa.*

MEASUREMENT AND OBSERVATION, PRINCIPLES, METHODS, AND INSTRUMENTS OF (*in part*)

Re.C.   René Crozet. *Professor of the History of Art, University of Poitiers, France, 1938–66; Director, Centre of Higher Studies on Medieval Civilization, 1954–66.*

FRANCE (*in part*)

R.E.C.   Roy Eugene Cameron. *Director, Energy Resources Training and Development, Environmental Impact Studies Division, Argonne National Laboratory, Illinois.*

NORTH AMERICA (*in part*)

R.E.Cr.   Raymond E. Crist. *Research Professor Emeritus of Geography, University of Florida, Gainesville. Author of* The Cauca Valley, Colombia.

HAVANA (*in part*)
SOUTH AMERICA (*in part*)
VENEZUELA (*in part*)
WEST INDIES, THE (*in part*)

R.E.D.   The Rev. Rupert E. Davies. *Principal, Wesley College, Bristol, England, 1967–73. Author of* Methodism *and others.*

PROTESTANTISM (*in part*)

R.E.Da.   Robert E. Davies. *Benjamin Franklin Professor of Molecular Biology and University Professor, School of Veterinary Medicine, University of Pennsylvania, Philadelphia.*

MUSCLES AND MUSCLE SYSTEMS (*in part*)

R.E.Di.   Robert Eric Dickinson. *Emeritus Professor of Geography, University of Arizona, Tucson.*

GERMANY (*in part*)

R.E.E.   Ronald Eric Emmerick. *Professor and Director, Department of Iranian Studies, University of Hamburg. Author of* Saka Grammatical Studies; *editor and translator of several Khotanese works.*

LANGUAGES OF THE WORLD (*in part*)

R.E.F.   Ralph E. Fuhrman. *Consultant. Manager, Washington Regional Office, Black & Veatch, consulting engineers, 1973–78. Special Assistant to the Director, Municipal Wastewater Systems Division, Environmental Protection Agency, 1972–73.*

PUBLIC WORKS (*in part*)

R.E.Fi.   Raymond E. Fielding. *Professor of Communications, University of Houston, Texas. Editor of* A Technological History of Motion

Pictures and Television.
DE FOREST, LEE (Micropædia)

Re.G. **Renu Garg, M.D.** *Resident in Pediatrics, Baylor College of Medicine, Houston, Texas.*
INFECTIOUS DISEASES (*in part*)

R.E.G. **Ralph E. Grim.** *Research Professor Emeritus of Geology, University of Illinois, Urbana. Scholar whose outstanding synthesis of clay mineralogy served as a guide for a generation of research scientists. Author of* Clay Mineralogy *and others.*
MINERALS AND ROCKS (*in part*)

R.E.Gi. **Reginald E. Gillmor** (d. 1960). *Vice-President, Sperry Gyroscope Company, Inc., Brooklyn, New York, 1932–45.*
NAVIGATION (*in part*)

Re.H. **Reinhold D. Hohl.** *Art historian. Author of* Giacometti *and others.*
GIACOMETTI, ALBERTO (Micropædia)

R.E.H. **Richard E. Holttum.** *Honorary Research Associate, Royal Botanic Gardens, Kew, England. Director, Botanic Gardens, Singapore, 1925–49. Professor of Botany, University of Malaya, Singapore, 1949–54. Author of* A Revised Flora of Malaya.
ANGIOSPERMS (*in part*)

R.E.H.M. **Roy E.H. Mellor.** *Professor of Geography, University of Aberdeen, Scotland. Author of* Eastern Europe *and others.*
GERMANY (*in part*)

R.E.K. **Rudolf E. Kalman.** *Graduate Research Professor of Mathematics; Director, Center for Mathematical System Theory, University of Florida, Gainesville. Professor of Mathematical System Theory, Swiss Federal Institute of Technology, Zürich, Switzerland. Coauthor of* Topics in Mathematical System Theory.
OPTIMIZATION, THE MATHEMATICAL THEORY OF (*in part*)

R.E.L.F **Robert E.L. Faris.** *Emeritus Professor of Sociology, University of Washington, Seattle. Editor of* Handbook of Modern Sociology.
SOCIAL SCIENCES, THE (*in part*)

R.E.O. **Ronald E. Osborn.** *Professor of American Church History, School of Theology at Claremont, California, 1973–82. Author of* The Spirit of American Christianity *and others.*
PROTESTANTISM (*in part*)

R.E.Or. **Richard Edmonds Orville.** *Professor and Chairman, Department of Atmospheric Science, State University of New York at Albany. Investigator of electrical phenomena in the atmosphere through photographs and their interpretation.*
CLIMATE AND WEATHER (*in part*)

Re.P. **Rebecca Posner.** *Professor of Romance Languages, University of Oxford. Author of* Consonantal Dissimilation in the Romance

Languages; The Romance Languages: A Linguistic Introduction.
LANGUAGES OF THE WORLD (*in part*)

R.E.P. **Rollie E. Poppino.** *Professor of History, University of California, Davis. Author of* Brazil; The Land and People *and others.*
BRAZIL (*in part*)
VARGAS, GETÚLIO (Micropædia)

R.E.Pi. **Richard E. Pipes.** *Frank B. Baird, Jr., Professor of History, Harvard University.*
NIKON (Micropædia)

R.Es. **Robert Escarpit.** *Professor of Information and Communication Sciences, University of Bordeaux III, France. Author of* L'Angleterre dans l'oeuvre de Madame de Staël *and others.*
STAËL-HOLSTEIN, ANNE-LOUISE-GERMAINE NECKER, BARONNE DE (Micropædia)

R.E.S. **Robert E. Stewart.** *Distinguished Professor of Agricultural Engineering, Texas A&M University, College Station.*
FARMING AND AGRICULTURAL TECHNOLOGY (*in part*)

R.E.Sh. **Robert E. Sheriff.** *Professor of Geophysics, University of Houston, Texas. Author of* Encyclopedic Dictionary of Exploration Geophysics *and others.*
EXPLORATION (*in part*)

R.F. **Robert L. Faherty.** *Managing Editor, Congressional Budget Office. Staff editor, Religion,* Encyclopædia Britannica, *1969–72.*
BIBLICAL LITERATURE AND ITS CRITICAL INTERPRETATION (*in part*)
RITES AND CEREMONIES, SACRED (*in part*)

R.F.B. **Robert F. Byrnes.** *Distinguished Professor of History, Indiana University, Bloomington. Author of* Pobedonostsev: His Life and Thought.
POBEDONOSTSEV, KONSTANTIN PETROVICH (Micropædia)

R.F.D. **Raymond F. Dasmann.** *Professor of Environmental Studies, University of California, Santa Cruz. Author of* Environmental Conservation.
CONSERVATION OF NATURAL RESOURCES (*in part*)

R.F.F. **Richard Foster Flint** (d. 1976). *Henry Barnard Davis Professor of Geology, Yale University, 1957–70. Author of* Glacial and Quaternary Geology.
GEOCHRONOLOGY (*in part*)

R.F.G.A. **R.F.G. Alford.** *Cassel Reader in Economics, London School of Economics and Political Science, University of London.*
MARKETS (*in part*)

R.F.H. **Sir Roy Forbes Harrod** (d. 1978). *Nuffield Reader in Economics, University of Oxford, 1952–67. Author of* International Economics *and others.*
INTERNATIONAL TRADE (*in part*)

R.F.-He. **Regina Flannery-Herzfeld.** *Emeritus Professor of Anthropology, Catholic University of America, Washington, D.C. Author of* The Gros Ventre of Montana, Part I, Social Life.
AMERICAN INDIANS (*in part*)

R.F.Hi. **Ronald Francis Hingley.** *Fellow of St. Antony's College, Oxford; University Lecturer in Russian, University of Oxford. Author of* Chekhov: A Biographical and Critical Study; Russian Writers and Society; Nihilists; *and others; editor and translator of* The Oxford Chekhov.
CHEKHOV, ANTON (*in part*) (Micropædia)
GORKY, MAKSIM (*in part*) (Micropædia)
STALIN

R.Fl. **Ronald Fletcher.** *Emeritus Professor of Sociology, University of Reading, England. Author of* Auguste Comte and the Making of Sociology *and others.*
COMTE, AUGUSTE (*in part*) (Micropædia)

R.F.L. **Robert Frederic Lawson.** *Professor of Education and Dean, Faculty of Education, University of Calgary, Alberta. Coauthor of* Studies in Educational Change.
EDUCATION, HISTORY OF (*in part*)

R.F.Li. **René Felix Lissens.** *Emeritus Professor of Dutch and General Literature, St. Ignatius University Faculty, Antwerp. Member, Royal Flemish Academy of Language and Literature. Author of* De Vlaamse letterkunde van 1780 tot heden.
BELGIAN LITERATURE (*in part*)

R.F.Lo. **Richard F. Logan.** *Professor of Geography, University of California, Los Angeles. Author of* Central Namib Desert.
AFRICA (*in part*)

R.-F.-M.A. **Roger-François-Marie Aubert.** *Professor of Church History, Catholic University of Louvain, Belgium. Author of* Le Pontificat de Pie IX *and others.*
LEO XIII (PAPACY) (Micropædia)

R.F.P. **Roland F.M. Pressat.** *Head, Department of Statistics, National Institute for Demographic Studies, Paris. Author of* Dictionnaire de démographie *and others.*
GEOGRAPHY (*in part*)

R.F.Pe. **Ronald Francis Peel** (d. 1985). *Professor of Geography, University of Bristol, England, 1957–77. Chairman, Commission on Arid Lands, International Geographical Union. Author of* Physical Geography.
AFRICA (*in part*)

R.F.S. **Robert F. Spencer.** *Professor of Anthropology, University of Minnesota, Minneapolis. Author of* The North Alaskan Eskimo.
ARCTIC, THE (*in part*)

R.F.T. **René Frédéric Thom.** *Mathematician, Institut des Hautes Études Scientifiques, Bures-sur-Yvette, France. Author of* Stabilité structurelle et

morphogénèse.
GEOMETRY (*in part*)

R.F.Th.   Robert Folger Thorne.
*Taxonomist and Curator, Rancho
Santa Ana Botanic Garden, Claremont,
California. Professor of Botany,
Claremont Graduate School.*
ANGIOSPERMS (*in part*)

R.F.Tr.   Reginald Francis Treharne (d.
1967). *Professor of History, University
College of Wales, Aberystwyth,
University of Wales, 1930–67. Author
of* The Baronial Plan of Reform, 1258–
1263 *and others.*
EDWARD I (ENGLAND AND GREAT
   BRITAIN) (Micropædia)
MONTFORT, SIMON DE, EARL OF
   LEICESTER (Micropædia)

R.G.   Roger Gibbins. *Professor
of Political Science, University of
Calgary, Alberta.*
POLITICAL SYSTEMS (*in part*)

R.G.A.   Raymond George Ayoub.
*Professor of Mathematics, Pennsylvania
State University, University Park. Author
of* An Introduction to the Analytic
Theory of Numbers.
NUMBER THEORY (*in part*)

**R.G.D.L.   Robert George Dalrymple
Laffan** (d. 1972). *University Lecturer,
University of Cambridge, 1927–53;
Fellow of Queen's College, Cambridge.
Author of* The Serbs, Guardians of the
Gate *and others.*
YUGOSLAVIA (*in part*)

R.G.G.   Robert G. Gallager. *Professor
of Electrical Engineering, Massachusetts
Institute of Technology, Cambridge.
Author of* Information Theory and
Reliable Communication *and others.*
INFORMATION THEORY (*in part*)

R.Gh.   Roman Ghirshman (d. 1979).
*Archaeologist. Director General, French
Archaeological Delegation to Iran,
1946–67.*
IRAN (*in part*)

R.G.H.   Ralph G. Hopkinson.
*Haden-Pilkington Professor Emeritus of
Environmental Design and Engineering,
University College, University of London.
Author of* Lighting *and others.*
LIGHTING AND LIGHTING DEVICES

R.Gi.   Robert W.V. Gittings. *Poet,
biographer, and playwright. Author of*
John Keats *and other works on Keats.*
KEATS, JOHN (Micropædia)

R.G.Lo.   Robert G. Logan. *Sportswriter,
Chicago Tribune. Author of* The
Bulls and Chicago: A Stormy Affair
and others.
SPORTS, MAJOR TEAM AND INDIVIDUAL
   (*in part*)

**R.G.M.   Robert Gwyn Macfarlane,
M.D.** *Emeritus Professor of Clinical
Pathology, University of Oxford.
Director, Medical Research Council
Blood Coagulation Research Unit,
Churchill Hospital, Oxford, 1959–67.
Coauthor of* Human Blood Coagulation

and Its Disorders; *editor of* Functions of
the Blood.
BLOOD (*in part*)

R.Gr.   Ronald Grimsley. *Emeritus
Professor of French, University of Bristol,
England. Author of* Jean d'Alembert.
ALEMBERT, JEAN LE ROND D'
   (Micropædia)

R.G.R.   Robert G. Richardson.
*Consultant medical editor. Former
Editor,* Abbottempo (*international
medical journal*). *Author of* Surgery: Old
and New Frontiers *and others.*
MEDICINE (*in part*)

R.G.S.   Ralph G. Sanger (d. 1968).
*Professor of Mathematics, Kansas State
University, Manhattan, 1946–68. Author
of* Synthetic Projective Geometry.
GEOMETRY (*in part*)

R.H.A.J.   Richard H.A. Jenkyns.
*Fellow of Lady Margaret Hall,
University of Oxford. Author of* Three
Classical Poets: Sappho, Catullus, and
Juvenal *and others.*
LATIN LITERATURE (*in part*)

R.H.B.   Roland H. Bainton (d. 1984).
*Titus Street Professor of Church History,
Yale University, 1936–62. Author of* The
Reformation of the Sixteenth Century
and others.
PROTESTANTISM (*in part*)

R.H.Bi.   R.H. Bing (d. 1986). *Professor
of Mathematics, University of Texas at
Austin. Author of* Elementary Point Set
Topology.
GEOMETRY (*in part*)

R.H.Br.   Robert Harold Brown.
*Professor of Geography, University
of Wyoming, Laramie. Author of*
Wyoming: A Geography *and others.*
UNITED STATES OF AMERICA (*in part*)

R.He.   Richard Hellie. *Professor of
Russian History, University of Chicago.
Author of* Enserfment and Military
Change in Muscovy *and others.*
ALEXANDER NEVSKY, SAINT
   (Micropædia)
UNION OF SOVIET SOCIALIST REPUBLICS
   (*in part*)

R.H.E.   Richard H. Eastman.
*Professor of Chemistry, Stanford
University, California. Author of* General
Chemistry—Experiment and Theory.
CHEMICAL COMPOUNDS (*in part*)

R.H.Ew.   Robert Harold Ewald.
*Professor of Anthropology, California
State University, Los Angeles.*
CENTRAL AMERICA (*in part*)

R.H.Fl.   Richard Howell Fleming.
*Emeritus Professor of Oceanography
and Marine Studies, University of
Washington, Seattle. Coauthor of*
The Oceans.
OCEANS (*in part*)

R.H.Fr.   Richard H. Freeborn.
*Professor of Russian Literature, School
of Slavonic and East European Studies,
University of London. Author of*
Turgenev, a Study *and others.*

TURGENEV, IVAN (*in part*) (Micropædia)
RUSSIAN LITERATURE (*in part*)

R.H.Fu.   Robert Henderson Fuson.
*Professor of Geography, University of
South Florida, Tampa. Author of* A
Geography of Geography *and others.*
UNITED STATES OF AMERICA (*in part*)

R.H.G.   Richard Harold Greenwood.
*Professor of Geography, University
College of Swansea, University of Wales,
1970–80. Professor of Geography,
University of Queensland, Brisbane,
Australia, 1958–70.*
AUSTRALIA (*in part*)

R.H.Ga.   Ralph Henry Gabriel. *Sterling
Professor Emeritus of History, Yale
University, New Haven, Connecticut.*
UNITED STATES OF AMERICA (*in part*)

R.H.H.   Robert H. Hardie. *Professor
of Physics and Astronomy, Vanderbilt
University, Nashville, Tennessee;
Director, Dyer Observatory, 1961–72.*
ANALYSIS AND MEASUREMENTS,
   PHYSICAL AND CHEMICAL (*in part*)
SOLAR SYSTEM, THE (*in part*)

R.H.I.   Ralph Hammond Innes. *Novelist
and writer on history and travel. Author
of* The Conquistadors *and many
others.*
CORTÉS, HERNÁN, MARQUES DEL VALLE
   DE OAXACA (Micropædia)

R.H.J.   Richard H. Jahns (d. 1983).
*Crook Professor of Geology and Applied
Earth Sciences, Stanford University,
California; Dean, School of Earth
Sciences, 1965–79. Editor and coauthor
of* Geology of Southern California.
MINERALS AND ROCKS (*in part*)

R.H.M.   Richard H. Manske (d. 1977).
*Director of Research, Dominion Rubber
Company Ltd., Guelph, Ontario, 1943–
66. Editor of* The Alkaloids.
CHEMICAL COMPOUNDS (*in part*)

R.H.O.   Richard Horsley Osborne.
*Professor of Geography, University
of Nottingham, England. Author of*
East-Central Europe: A Geographical
Introduction to Seven Socialist States.
CZECHOSLOVAKIA (*in part*)
PRAGUE (*in part*)

R.H.P.   Richard H. Popkin. *Professor
of Philosophy, Washington University,
St. Louis, Missouri. Author of* History of
Scepticism from Erasmus to Spinoza.
PHILOSOPHICAL SCHOOLS AND
   DOCTRINES, WESTERN (*in part*)

R.H.Po.   René Henry Pomeau.
*Professor of French Literature, University
of Paris IV. Author of* La Religion de
Voltaire *and others.*
VOLTAIRE

R.H.P.-W.   Ralph H. Pinder-Wilson.
*Former Deputy Keeper, Department of
Oriental Antiquities, British Museum,
London. Author of* Persian Painting in
the Fifteenth Century.
WRITING (*in part*)

R.H.Ra.   Robert H. Ralston. *Former
Senior Research Chemist, Hercules Inc.,*

Wilmington, Delaware.
FOOD PROCESSING (*in part*)

R.H.S.   Roger Henry Simpson.
Historian and lecturer.
MITHRADATES VI EUPATOR (PONTUS)
   (Micropædia)

R.H.St.   Roger H. Stuewer. *Professor of the History of Science and Technology, University of Minnesota, Minneapolis. Author of* The Compton Effect: Turning Point in Physics.
PLANCK

R.H.T.   Ralph H. Turner. *Professor of Sociology and Anthropology, University of California, Los Angeles. Coauthor of* Collective Behavior.
COLLECTIVE BEHAVIOUR (*in part*)

R.Hu.   René Huyghe. *Professor of Art, College of France, Paris. President, Council of Museums, Paris. Author of* Cézanne; Delacroix ou le combat solitaire; *and others.*
CÉZANNE, PAUL (Micropædia)
DELACROIX, EUGÈNE (Micropædia)

R.H.W.   Robert H. Whittaker (d. 1980). *Charles A. Alexander Professor of Biology, Cornell University, Ithaca, New York, 1976–80. Author of* Communities and Ecosystems; Ordination and Classification of Communities.
BIOSPHERE, THE (*in part*)

Ri.B.   Richard Beadle. *Fellow in English, St. John's College, University of Cambridge. Editor of* York Mystery Plays.
ENGLISH LITERATURE (*in part*)

Ri.G.   Richard David Greenfield.
Former Director of General Studies, University of Benin, Nigeria. Author of Ethiopia: A New Political History.
MENELIK II (*in part*) (Micropædia)

Ri.H.   Richard Hamilton Hobson.
Public Relations Officer, Zambia Appointments Ltd., London; formerly with Zambia Consolidated Copper Mines Ltd., Lusaka, Zambia.
SOUTHERN AFRICA (*in part*)

Ri.L.   Richard Lane. *Research Associate, Honolulu Academy of Arts. Author of* Masters of the Japanese Print; Hokusai and Hiroshige; *and many others.*
HIROSHIGE (Micropædia)
HOKUSAI (Micropædia)

Ri.M.L.   Richard M. Lerner. *Professor of Child and Adolescent Development; Director, Center for the Study of Child and Adolescent Development, Pennsylvania State University, University Park. Author of* Concepts and Theories of Human Development *and others.*
BEHAVIOUR, THE DEVELOPMENT OF
   HUMAN (*in part*)

Ri.P.   Richard Pittioni (d. 1985). *Emeritus Professor of Prehistory and Protohistory, University of Vienna. Author of* Ergebnisse und Probleme des urzeitlichen Metallhandels *and others.*
PREHISTORIC PEOPLES AND CULTURES
   (*in part*)

R.I.Ro.   Richard I. Rossbacher.
Consultant. Former Head, Warfare Analysis Department, U.S. Naval Weapons Laboratory, Dahlgren, Virginia.
MECHANICS (*in part*)

Ri.W.S.   Richard Walton Stephens.
Professor of Sociology, George Washington University, Washington, D.C. Coauthor of Power, Presidents, and Professors.
WASHINGTON, D.C.

R.J.A.   Richard J. Andrew. *Professor of Animal Behaviour, University of Sussex, Brighton, England. Author of numerous papers on behaviour of birds and primates.*
BEHAVIOUR, ANIMAL (*in part*)

R.J.Al.   Robert J. Alexander. *Professor of Economics and Political Science, Rutgers University, New Brunswick, New Jersey. Author of* Prophets of the Revolution: Profiles of Latin American Political Leaders.
CÁRDENAS, LÁZARO (Micropædia)

R.J.B.   Robert John Behnke. *Fisheries consultant. Part-time Associate Professor of Fishery Biology, Colorado State University, Fort Collins.*
FISHES (*in part*)

R.J.Br.   Robert J. Braidwood. *Emeritus Professor of Old World Prehistory, Oriental Institute, University of Chicago. Author of* Prehistoric Men *and others.*
PREHISTORIC PEOPLES AND CULTURES
   (*in part*)

R.J.C.   Robert John Clements.
Chairman, Department of Comparative Literature, New York University, New York City. Author of Michelangelo's Theory of Art; The Poetry of Michelangelo; *and others.*
MICHELANGELO (*in part*)

R.J.Ch.   Robert Jesse Charleston.
Keeper, Department of Ceramics, Victoria and Albert Museum, London, 1963–76. Author of "Glass," "Painted Enamels," *and* "Meissen and Other European Porcelain" *in* Waddesdon Manor Catalogues: James A. De Rothschild Collection.
DECORATIVE ARTS AND FURNISHINGS
   (*in part*)

R.J.Da.   R.J. Davies. *Professor of Geography, University of Cape Town.*
SOUTH AFRICA (*in part*)

R.J.F.   Robert J. Fernier (d. 1977). *President, The Friends of Gustave Courbet, Paris. Author of* Gustave Courbet, peintre de l'art vivant.
COURBET, GUSTAVE (Micropædia)

R.J.G.   Richard Johnson Goss.
Professor of Biology, Brown University, Providence, Rhode Island. Author of Principles of Regeneration.
GROWTH AND DEVELOPMENT,
   BIOLOGICAL (*in part*)

R.J.H.   Robert J. Havighurst. *Emeritus Professor of Education and of Human*

Development, University of Chicago. Specialist on the social pyschology of education and human development. Author of Comparative Perspectives on Education *and others.*
TEACHING (*in part*)

R.J.Ha.   Richard J. Harrison, M.D.
Emeritus Professor of Anatomy, University of Cambridge. Author of Reproduction and Man *and others.*
REPRODUCTION AND REPRODUCTIVE
   SYSTEMS (*in part*)

R.J.H.-C.   Ronald James Harrison-Church. *Emeritus Professor of Geography, London School of Economics and Political Science, University of London. Author of* West Africa.
AFRICA (*in part*)
WESTERN AFRICA (*in part*)

R.J.J.   Roland John Jackson. *Professor of Music, Claremont Graduate School, California. Editor of* Neapolitan Keyboard Composers c. 1600.
MUSIC, THE ART OF (*in part*)

R.J.M.   Ronald James Morley. *Former Technical Director, Coal Products Division, National Coal Board, Harrow, England.*
INDUSTRIES, EXTRACTION AND
   PROCESSING (*in part*)

R.J.M. De W.   Roger J.M. De Wiest.
Former Professor and Chairman, Water Resources Program, Princeton University, New Jersey. Author of Geohydrology.
HYDROSPHERE, THE (*in part*)

R.J.Me.   Robert James Menzies (d. 1976). *Professor of Oceanography, Florida State University, Tallahassee, 1967–76. Panel Chairman in Marine Biology, Gulf University Research Corporation.*
NORTH AMERICA (*in part*)

R.J.N.   Robert J. Nelson. *Professor of French and Comparative Literature, University of Illinois, Urbana. Author of* Corneille: His Heroes and Their Worlds *and others.*
CORNEILLE, PIERRE (Micropædia)

R.J.Ne.   R.J. Nelson. *Truman P. Handy Professor Emeritus of Philosophy, Case Western Reserve University, Cleveland. Author of* Introduction to Automata.
AUTOMATA THEORY (*in part*)

R.J.Q.   Ricardo J. Quinones. *Professor of English and Comparative Literature; Director, Center for Renaissance and Modernity, Claremont McKenna College, Califonia. Author of* Dante Alighieri *and others.*
DANTE

R.J.R.   Richard J. Russell (d. 1971). *Professor of Geography, Louisiana State University, Baton Rouge, 1930–71; Principal Investigator, Coastal Studies Institute, 1967–71. Author of* River Plains and Sea Coasts.
CONTINENTAL LANDFORMS (*in part*)

R.J.S.   R.J. Stephenson (d. 1973). *William F. Harn Professor of Physics, College of Wooster, Ohio, 1959–71.* NAVIGATION (*in part*)

R.J.Sm.   Ralph J. Smith. *Emeritus Professor of Electrical Engineering, Stanford University, California. Author of* Engineering as a Career. ENGINEERING (*in part*)

R.J.T.   Roger John Tayler. *Professor of Astronomy; Director, Astronomy Centre, University of Sussex, Brighton, England. Author of* The Origin of the Chemical Elements *and others.* CHEMICAL ELEMENTS (*in part*)

R.J.Th.   Robert James Thornton. *Senior Lecturer in Anthropology, University of Cape Town. Author of* The Iraqw of Northern Tanzania. EASTERN AFRICA (*in part*)

R.J.Z.   Roman J. Zorn. *Professor of History, University of Nevada, Las Vegas. Author of numerous articles on U.S. history and political science.* UNITED STATES OF AMERICA (*in part*)

R.J.Z.W.   R.J. Zwi Werblowsky. *Professor of Comparative Religion, Hebrew University of Jerusalem. Author of* Joseph Karo, Lawyer and Mystic *and others; coeditor of* The Encyclopaedia of the Jewish Religion. DOCTRINES AND DOGMAS, RELIGIOUS (*in part*)

R.K.   Rudolf Kingslake. *Professor of Optics, University of Rochester. Director of Optical Design, Eastman Kodak Company, Rochester, New York, 1939– 69. Author of* Lenses in Photography; *editor of* Applied Optics and Optical Engineering. OPTICS, PRINCIPLES OF (*in part*)

R.K.A.G.   Robert K.A. Gardiner. *Commissioner for Economic Planning, Ghana, 1975–78. Executive Secretary, United Nations Economic Commission for Africa, Addis Ababa, Ethiopia, 1962– 75. Author of* A World of Peoples. AFRICA (*in part*)

R.Ki.   Ralph Kirkpatrick (d. 1984). *Harpsichordist. Professor of Music, Yale University, 1965–76. Author of* Domenico Scarlatti *and others.* SCARLATTI, DOMENICO (Micropædia)

R.K.L.   Robert K. Lane. *Regional Director, Western and Northern Region, Environmental Protection Service, Environment Canada, Edmonton, Alberta. Head, Physical Limnology Section, Canada Centre for Inland Water, Burlington, Ontario, 1967–72.* LAKES (*in part*)

R.K.M.   Ronald K. Murton (d. 1978). *Senior Principal Scientific Officer, Institute of Terrestrial Ecology, Monks Wood Experimental Station, Huntingdon, England. Researcher on the population dynamics and behaviour of pigeons and doves. Author of* The Woodpigeon. BIRDS (*in part*)

R.Kr.   Richard Kroner (d. 1974). *Professor of the Philosophy of Religion, Union Theological Seminary, New York City, 1941–55. Author of* Von Kant bis Hegel. FICHTE, JOHANN GOTTLIEB (Micropædia)

R.K.U.   Reuben Kenrick Udo. *Professor of Geography, University of Ibadan, Nigeria. Author of* Geographical Regions of Nigeria *and others.* WESTERN AFRICA (*in part*)

R.L.   Robert Lekachman. *Distinguished Professor of Economics, Herbert H. Lehman College, City University of New York. Author of* The Age of Keynes *and others.* KEYNES, JOHN MAYNARD (*in part*) (Micropædia)

R.L.A.   Russell L. Ackoff. *Silberberg Professor of Systems Sciences, Wharton School, University of Pennsylvania, Philadelphia. Coauthor of* Fundamentals of Operations Research. INDUSTRIAL ENGINEERING AND PRODUCTION MANAGEMENT (*in part*)

R.Lay.   Robert Layton. *Producer, Music Talks, British Broadcasting Corporation, London. Author of* Sibelius; The World of Sibelius. SIBELIUS, JEAN (Micropædia)

R.L.B.   The Rev. Robert L. Bireley, S.J. *Professor of History, Loyola University, Chicago.* XAVIER, SAINT FRANCIS (Micropædia)

R.L.C.   Robert L. Collison. *Emeritus Professor of Library Science and Information Studies, University of California, Los Angeles. Author of* Encyclopaedias: Their History Throughout the Ages *and others.* ENCYCLOPAEDIAS AND DICTIONARIES (*in part*)

R.L.C.F.   Raymond-Louis-Charles Furon. *Former Professor of Geology, University of Paris. Author of* Géologie de l'Afrique *and others.* AFRICA (*in part*)

R.L.Ch.   Robert L. Christie. *Research Scientist, Geological Survey of Canada, Calgary, Alberta; Former Head, Arctic Islands Section. Author of numerous articles on the geology of Arctic islands.* ARCTIC, THE (*in part*)

R.L.D.   R.L. Dwivedi. *Professor and Head, Department of Geography, University of Allāhābād, Uttar Pradesh, India.* INDIA (*in part*)

R.Le.   Robert Lebel. *Art expert and critic. Author of* On Marcel Duchamp. DUCHAMP, MARCEL (Micropædia)

R.L.F.   Robert Louis Folk. *Dave P. Carlton Professor of Geology, University of Texas at Austin. An authority on the classification and interpretation of sedimentary rocks. Author of* Petrology of Sedimentary Rocks. MINERALS AND ROCKS (*in part*)

R.L.Fr.   Richard L. Frey. *Editor in Chief,* Official Encyclopedia of Bridge. *Associate Editor,* Bridge World *magazine; Emeritus Editor,* The Contract Bridge Bulletin; *Chief of Editorial Board, Charles H. Goren publications. President Emeritus and Chairman, International Bridge Press Association. Author of* According to Hoyle *and others.* CRIBBAGE (Micropædia)

R.L.G.   Roger Lancelyn Green. *Author of* Lewis Carroll *and others; editor of* The Diaries of Lewis Carroll. CARROLL, LEWIS (Micropædia)

R.L.Ge.   Robert Louis Gilmore. *Professor of History, University of Kansas, Lawrence.* COLOMBIA (*in part*)

R.L.Ha.   Rosemary Lois Harris. *Senior Lecturer in Social Anthropology, University College, University of London. Author of* The Political Organization of the Mbembe of South-East Nigeria. WESTERN AFRICA (*in part*)

R.L.He.   Robert L. Heilbroner. *Norman Thomas Professor of Economics, New School for Social Research, New York City. Author of* The Worldly Philosophers; An Inquiry into the Human Prospect; *and others.* SMITH, ADAM (*in part*)

R.L.Hi.   Richard Leslie Hill. *Professor of History, Abdullahi Bayero College, Ahmadu Bello University, Kano, Nigeria, 1968–69. Lecturer in Modern Near Eastern History, University of Durham, England, 1949–66. Author of* The Europeans in Sudan, 1834–78. MAHDI, AL- (Micropædia)

R.L.Ne.   Ray L. Newburn, Jr. *Leader, International Halley Watch and Cometary Science Team, Earth and Space Sciences Division, Jet Propulsion Laboratory, California Institute of Technology, Pasadena.* SOLAR SYSTEM, THE (*in part*)

R.L.N.S.   R.L.N. Sastri. *Research Officer, Teluga Academy, Hyderābād, India. Author of a series of studies of the* Laurales. ANGIOSPERMS (*in part*)

R.L.P.   Robert Lewis Parkinson. *Chief Librarian and Historian, Circus World Museum, Baraboo, Wisconsin. Author of* The First 100 Years of the Greatest Show on Earth. PAGEANTRY AND SPECTACLE (*in part*)

R.L.S.   Robert L. Scranton. *Emeritus Professor of Classical Art and Archaeology, University of Chicago. Author of* Aesthetic Aspects of Ancient Art; Corinth (*Vol. I, III, and XVI*); *and others.* ARCHITECTURE, THE HISTORY OF WESTERN (*in part*)

R.L.Sc.   Robert L. Scheina. *Historian, U.S. Coast Guard, Washington, D.C. Author of* U.S. Coast Guard Cutters and Craft of World War II; *coauthor of*

American Battleships, 1886–1923.
WAR, THE TECHNOLOGY OF (*in part*)

R.L.Se.   Robert L. Seale. *Professor of Nuclear and Energy Engineering, University of Arizona, Tucson. Coeditor of* Water Production Using Nuclear Energy.
ENERGY, THE CONCEPT OF (*in part*)

R.L.Sm.   Robert Leo Smith. *Professor of Wildlife Biology and Ecology, West Virginia University, Morgantown. Author of* Ecology and Field Biology.
BIOLOGICAL SCIENCES, THE (*in part*)

R.L.S.-R.   Reginald Leslie Smith-Rose (d. 1980). *Secretary General, Inter-Union Commission on Frequency Allocations for Radio Astronomy and Space Science, 1961–73. Director, Radio Research, Department of Scientific and Industrial Research, London, 1948–60.*
MARCONI, GUGLIELMO (Micropædia)
POPOV, ALEKSANDR STEPANOVICH (Micropædia)

R.L.Su.   Robert Lee Suettinger. *Author of* "The Political Process" in China: A Country Study.
CHINA (*in part*)

R.L.Sw.   Roland Lee Swink. *Director, Adult Evening Education Program, 10th Combat Support Group, United States Air Forces in Europe. Lecturer in Education, University of Maryland, Overseas Division. Author of* A Comparison of the Academic Achievement of English and American School Boys and Girls, Ages 12 and 17.
EDUCATION, HISTORY OF (*in part*)

R.L.Z.   Richard L. Zusi. *Associate Curator, Division of Birds, National Museum of Natural History, Smithsonian Institution, Washington, D.C. Author of* Structural Adaptations of the Head and Neck in the Black Skimmer, Rynchops nigra Linnaeus.
BIRDS (*in part*)

R.M.   Roger Manvell. *Biographer and film historian. Professor of Film, Boston University. Director, British Film Academy, 1947–59. Author of* Ellen Terry; *coauthor of* Hermann Göring; The Technique of Film Animation; *and many others.*
BROADCASTING (*in part*)
GÖRING, HERMANN (*in part*) (Micropædia)
MOTION PICTURES (*in part*)
TERRY, ELLEN (Micropædia)

R.Ma.   Roger Martinot. *Engineer in Chief, Rural Lands, Water, and Forests, National Institute of Agricultural Research, Paris. Coauthor of* La Stabulation libre des bovins Eyrolles.
FARMING AND AGRICULTURAL TECHNOLOGY (*in part*)

R.M.As.   Robert McCormick Adams. *Secretary, Smithsonian Institution, Washington, D.C. Provost, University of Chicago, 1982–84; Harold H. Swift Distinguished Service Professor of Anthropology, 1975–84; Director,*

Oriental Institute, 1962–68 and 1981–82.
PREHISTORIC PEOPLES AND CULTURES (*in part*)

R.M.B.   Ronald M. Berndt. *Emeritus Professor of Anthropology and Honorary Research Fellow, University of Western Australia, Nedlands. Coauthor of* The World of the First Australians.
AUSTRALIA (*in part*)

R.McD.   Raven I. McDavid, Jr. (d. 1984). *Professor of English and of Linguistics, University of Chicago, 1964–77. Coauthor of* The Pronunciation of English in the Atlantic States; *editor of* H.L. Mencken's The American Language.
LANGUAGE (*in part*)
WEBSTER, NOAH (Micropædia)

R.McK.MacI.   Robert McKinlay MacIntosh. *Former manager, Tin Research Institute, Inc., Columbus, Ohio. Author of numerous articles on tin, tin alloys, tin products, and tin processes.*
INDUSTRIES, EXTRACTION AND PROCESSING (*in part*)

R.McMu.   Roy Donald McMullen (d. 1984). *Art historian. Author of* Art, Affluence, and Alienation; The World of Marc Chagall; *and others.*
ARTS, STYLE IN THE
BRAQUE, GEORGES (Micropædia)
CHAGALL, MARC (Micropædia)
DAVID, JACQUES-LOUIS (Micropædia)
FOLK ARTS (*in part*)
KANDINSKY, WASSILY (*in part*) (Micropædia)
LÉGER, FERNAND (Micropædia)
MATISSE, HENRI (*in part*) (Micropædia)
POPULAR ARTS (*in part*)
ROUAULT, GEORGES (Micropædia)

R.M.D.   Richard M. Dorson (d. 1981). *Director, Folklore Institute; Professor of History and Folklore, Indiana University, Bloomington, 1957–81. Author of* American Folklore; Folklore and Fakelore; *and others; editor of* Journal of American Folklore.
FOLK ARTS (*in part*)

R.Me.   Reinhold Merkelbach. *Professor of Classics, University of Cologne. Author of* Roman und Mysterium in der Antike *and others.*
MYSTERY RELIGIONS

R.M.G.   Robert M. Grant. *Carl Darling Buck Professor of Humanities; Professor of Early Christian History, Divinity School, University of Chicago. Author of* Historical Introduction to the New Testament; Early Christianity and Society; *and others.*
BIBLICAL LITERATURE AND ITS CRITICAL INTERPRETATION (*in part*)

R.M.H.   Ragnhild Marie Hatton. *Professor of International History, London School of Economics and Political Science, University of London. Author of* Charles XII of Sweden *and others.*
CHARLES XII (SWEDEN) (Micropædia)

R.M.He.   Robert M. Henderson. *Chief, General Library and Museum of the Performing Arts, New York Public Library at Lincoln Center, New York City. Author of* D.W. Griffith, the Years at Biograph; D.W. Griffith, His Life and Times; *and others.*
GRIFFITH, D.W. (Micropædia)

R.M.Hi.   Richard M. Highsmith, Jr. *Professor and Chairman, Department of Geography, Oregon State University, Corvallis. Coauthor of* Conservation in the United States.
UNITED STATES OF AMERICA (*in part*)

R.M.Hl.   Ronald Max Hartwell. *Joint Director, Centre for Socio-Legal Studies, Wolfson College, University of Oxford, 1977–81; Reader in Recent Social and Economic History, 1956–77.*
AUSTRALIA (*in part*)

R.M.K   Robert M. Kingdon. *Professor of History; Director, Institute for Research in the Humanities, University of Wisconsin, Madison. Author of* Geneva and the Consolidation of the French Protestant Movement, 1564–1572 *and others.*
CALVINISM, CALVIN AND (*in part*)

R.M.L.   R.M. Lockley. *Naturalist. Author of* Shearwaters; Puffins; *and others; coauthor of* Sea Birds of the North Atlantic.
BIRDS (*in part*)

R.M.Le.   Richard M. Leighton. *Military historian and consultant. Professor of National Security Affairs, National Defense University, U.S. Department of Defense, Washington, D.C., 1965–78. Coauthor of* Global Logistics and Strategy 1940–45.
WAR, THE THEORY AND CONDUCT OF (*in part*)

R.M.Lu.   R.M. Lumiansky. *President Emeritus, American Council of Learned Societies. Professor of English, New York University, New York City. Author of* Of Sondry Folk: The Dramatic Principle in the Canterbury Tales *and others.*
CHAUCER (*in part*)

R.Mo.   Rudolf Morsey. *Professor of Modern History, Postgraduate School for Administrative Sciences, Speyer, West Germany. Author of* Die deutsche Zentrumspartei, 1917–1923 *and others.*
STRESEMANN, GUSTAV (Micropædia)

R.M.O.   Richard Marian Ogorkiewicz. *Senior Lecturer in Mechanical Engineering. Imperial College of Science and Technology, University of London. Honorary life member of the U.S. Armor Association. Author of* Armoured Forces *and others.*
WAR, THE TECHNOLOGY OF (*in part*)

R.M.Og.   Robert Maxwell Ogilvie (d. 1981). *Professor of Humanity, University of St. Andrews, Fife, Scotland. Editor of* A Commentary on Livy, Books 1–5.
LIVY (Micropædia)

R.M.P. Raghawendra Mukund Pai. *Professor and Head, Department of Botany, Marathwada University, Aurangabad, India.*
ANGIOSPERMS (*in part*)

R.M.S. Robert M. Saunders. *Professor of Electrical Engineering, University of California, Irvine. Coauthor of* Analysis of Feedback Control Systems.
ENERGY CONVERSION (*in part*)

R.M.Sa. Roger M. Savory. *Professor of Middle East and Islāmic Studies, University of Toronto. Translator of* The History of Shah 'Abbas.
'ABBĀS I (PERSIA) (Micropædia)

R.My. Rollo H. Myers (d. 1985). *Writer on music. Author of* Modern French Music; Ravel: Life and Works; *and others.*
RAVEL, MAURICE (Micropædia)

R.Na. Raghavan Narasimhan. *Professor of Mathematics, University of Chicago. Author of* Analysis on Real and Complex Manifolds; Several Complex Variables; *and others.*
ANALYSIS (IN MATHEMATICS) (*in part*)

R.N.Bu. Robert N. Burr. *Professor of History, University of California, Los Angeles. Coauthor of* Documents on Inter-American Cooperation, 1810–1948.
PERU (*in part*)

R.N.C. Richard N. Current. *University Distinguished Professor Emeritus of History, University of North Carolina, Greensboro. Author of* Daniel Webster and the Rise of National Conservatism; The Lincoln Nobody Knows; *and others.*
LINCOLN
WEBSTER, DANIEL (Micropædia)

R.N.DeJ. Russell N. DeJong, M.D. *Emeritus Professor of Neurology, University of Michigan Medical School, Ann Arbor. Author of* A History of American Neurology *and others.*
TISSUES AND FLUIDS (*in part*)

R.N.F. Richard N. Frye. *Aga Khan Professor of Iranian, Harvard University. Director, Asia Institute, Pahlavi University, Shīrāz, Iran, 1969–74. Author of* The Heritage of Persia.
CYRUS II (Micropædia)
KHOSROW I (Micropædia)

R.Ni. Romola Nijinsky (d. 1978). *Author of* Nijinsky; The Last Years of Nijinsky; *editor of* The Diary of Vaslav Nijinsky.
NIJINSKY, VASLAV (Micropædia)

R.N.S. The Rev. R. Norman Sharp. *Assistant Professor of Old Persian and Pahlavi, Pahlavi University, Shīrāz, Iran, 1962–67. Author of* The Inscriptions of the Achaemenian Emperors in Old Persian Cuneiform *and others.*
PERSEPOLIS (Micropædia)

Ro.A. Roberto Almagià (d. 1962). *Professor of Geography, University of Rome, 1915–59. Author of* Il mondo attuale *and many others.*
VESPUCCI, AMERIGO (Micropædia)

Ro.A.K. Roy A. Keller. *Professor of Chemistry, State University of New York College at Fredonia. Former Editor,* Journal of Chromatographic Science.
ANALYSIS AND MEASUREMENT, PHYSICAL AND CHEMICAL (*in part*)

Ro.Au. Robert Auty (d. 1978). *Professor of Comparative Slavonic Philology, University of Oxford, 1965–78; Fellow of Brasenose College, Oxford.*
CZECHOSLOVAK LITERATURE (*in part*)

R.O.C. Robert O. Collins. *Professor of History, University of California, Santa Barbara. Author of* Land Beyond the Rivers: The Southern Sudan, 1898–1918.
SUDAN (*in part*)

R.O.C.N. Richard O.C. Norman. *Professor of Chemistry, University of York, England. Author of* Principles of Organic Synthesis.
CHEMICAL COMPOUNDS (*in part*)

R.O.F. Raymond Oliver Faulkner (deceased). *Fellow of University College, London; Lecturer in Ancient Egyptian, University College, University of London, 1955–67. Author of* Egypt: From the Inception of the Nineteenth Dynasty to the Death of Ramesses III *and others.*
RAMSES II (Micropædia)

Ro.G. Robert Grudin. *Associate Professor of English, University of Oregon, Eugene. Author of* Time and the Art of Living *and others.*
HUMANISM

R.O.H. Raymond O. Harrison. *Architect. Former Director, Provincial Museum and Archives, Edmonton, Alberta.*
CANADA (*in part*)

Ro.H.R. Robert Henry Robins. *Professor of General Linguistics, University of London. Author of* General Linguistics: An Introductory Survey.
LANGUAGE (*in part*)

Ro.L. Robert Lechène. *Journalist and popular science writer. Author of* L'Imprimerie, de Gutenberg à l'électron.
PRINTING, TYPOGRAPHY, AND PHOTOENGRAVING (*in part*)

Ro.M. Robert Merle. *Novelist. Author of* Ahmed Ben Bella *and others.*
BEN BELLA, AHMED (Micropædia)

Ro.Ma. Robert L. Marshall. *Professor of Music, University of Chicago. Author of* The Compositional Process of J.S. Bach.
BACH (*in part*)

Ro.N. Robert Niklaus. *Emeritus Professor of French, University of Exeter, England. Author of* A Literary History of France: The Eighteenth Century; *editor of Diderot's* Pensées philosophiques; Lettre sur les aveugles.
DIDEROT, DENIS (Micropædia)

Ro.P. Roy Perrott. *Free-lance book editor and consultant. Fellow of the Royal Horticultural Society, London. Author of* The Aristocrats.
GARDENING AND HORTICULTURE (*in part*)

Ro.Pa. Roy Pascal (d. 1980). *Professor of German, University of Birmingham, England, 1939–69. Author of* The German Novel *and others.*
MANN, THOMAS (Micropædia)

Ro.P.B. Robert Percy Beckinsale. *Senior Lecturer in Geography, University of Oxford, 1945–75.*
SPAIN (*in part*)

Ro.Pe. Roger Pélissier (d. 1972). *Assistant Director, Centre for Far East Documentation, École Pratique des Hautes Études (Institute for Advanced Research), Paris. Author of* The Awakening of China, 1793–1949 *and others.*
CH'IEN-LUNG (Micropædia)

Ro.R. Rollin C. Richmond. *Professor and Chairman, Department of Biology, Indiana University, Bloomington.*
GENETICS AND HEREDITY, THE PRINCIPLES OF (*in part*)

Ro.Ri. Roberto Ridolfi. *Member of Accademia Nazionale dei Lincei. Director of* La Bibliofilia. *Director of "National Editions of the Works of Savonarola." Author of* Life of Machiavelli *and others.*
MACHIAVELLI, NICCOLÒ (*in part*) (Micropædia)
SAVONAROLA, GIROLAMO (Micropædia)

Ro.S. Ronald Strahan. *Research Fellow, Australian Museum, Sydney. Director, Taronga Zoological Park, Sydney, 1967–74. Coauthor of* The Biology of Myxine.
FISHES (*in part*)

Ro.Sc. Roger Scruton. *Professor of Aesthetics, Birkbeck College, University of London. Author of* The Aesthetics of Architecture *and others.*
AESTHETICS (*in part*)

Ro.Si. Roy Sieber. *Rudy Professor of Fine Art, Indiana University, Bloomington. Author of* African Textiles and Decorative Arts.
DECORATIVE ARTS AND FURNISHINGS (*in part*)

Ro.W. Robert L. Wilken. *Professor of the History of Christianity, University of Notre Dame, Indiana. Author of* The Myth of Christian Beginnings *and others.*
TERTULLIAN (Micropædia)

Ro.W.F. Robert W. Finley. *Emeritus Professor of Geography, University of Wisconsin, Madison. Author of* Geography of Wisconsin: A Content Outline.
UNITED STATES OF AMERICA (*in part*)

Ro.W.S. Robert Wooster Stallman (d. 1982). *Professor of English, University of Connecticut, Storrs, 1953–74. Author of* Stephen Crane: A Biography; Stephen Crane: A Critical Bibliography; *and others.*
CRANE, STEPHEN (Micropædia)

Ro.W.St.   Robert Walter Steel.
Principal, University College of Swansea, 1974–82; Vice-Chancellor, University of Wales, 1979–81. John Rankin Professor of Geography, University of Liverpool, 1957–74. Director, Commonwealth Geographical Bureau, 1972–81.
AFRICA (*in part*)
SOUTHERN AFRICA (*in part*)

R.O.Wt.   Sir Richard Olof Winstedt (d. 1966). *Reader in Malay, University of London, 1937–47. Author of* A History of Malay Literature; Malaya and Its History; *and others.*
SOUTHEAST ASIA, MAINLAND
   (*in part*)

R.P.   René Pélissier. *Authority on Portuguese and Spanish-speaking Africa. Author of* Los territorios españoles de Africa; Études hispano-guinéennes.
WESTERN AFRICA (*in part*)

R.Pa.   Reginald Passmore. *Former Reader in Physiology, University of Edinburgh. Coauthor of* Human Nutrition and Dietetics.
NUTRITION (*in part*)

R.P.A.   Richard Paul Aulie. *Former Lecturer in Natural Science, Loyola University, Chicago. Associate Editor,* Encyclopædia Britannica, *Chicago, 1971–72.*
EUDOXUS OF CNIDUS (Micropædia)

R.Pal.   Rodolfo Pallucchini. *Director, Institute of Art History, Giorgio Cini Foundation, Venice. Author of* Disegni di Giambattista Tiepolo; La giovinezza del Tintoretto; Veronese; *and others.*
TIEPOLO, GIOVANNI BATTISTA
   (Micropædia)
TINTORETTO (*in part*) (Micropædia)
VERONESE, PAOLO (Micropædia)

R.P.An.   Richard Paul Anschutz.
Emeritus Professor of Philosophy, University of Auckland, New Zealand. Author of Philosophy of J.S. Mill.
MILL, JOHN STUART (*in part*)

R.P.B.   Ronald Percy Bell. *Emeritus Professor of Chemistry, University of Stirling, Scotland. Honorary Research Professor of Physical Chemistry, University of Leeds, England, 1976–82. Author of* Acid-Base Catalysis.
CHEMICAL REACTIONS (*in part*)

R.P.Be.   Robert Pierce Beaver.
Emeritus Professor of Missions, Divinity School, University of Chicago.
CHRISTIANITY (*in part*)

R.P.B.P.   Robert P.B. Paine. *Professor of Anthropology, Memorial University of Newfoundland, St. John's. Author of* Coast Lapp Society.
ARCTIC, THE (*in part*)
FINLAND (*in part*)

R.P.C.M.   Reginald P.C. Mutter.
Emeritus Professor of English Literature, University of Sussex, Brighton, England. Editor of The History of Tom Jones.
DEFOE, DANIEL (Micropædia)
ENGLISH LITERATURE (*in part*)
STEELE, SIR RICHARD (Micropædia)

R.Pe.   Régine Pernoud. *Keeper, Joan of Arc Centre, Orléans, France. Author of* Aliénor d'Aquitaine; Héloïse and Abélard; Histoire de la bourgeoisie en France; *and others.*
ELEANOR OF AQUITAINE (Micropædia)
VILLON, FRANÇOIS (Micropædia)

R.P.H.   Richard P. Hall (d. 1969).
Professor of Biology, New York University, New York City, 1938–68. Author of Protozoology; Protozoa; Protozoan Nutrition.
PROTOZOA

R.P.He.   Robert Proulx Heaney, M.D.
Vice President for Health Sciences, Creighton University, Omaha, Nebraska. Coauthor of Skeletal Renewal and Metabolic Bone Diseases.
SUPPORTIVE AND CONNECTIVE
   TISSUES (*in part*)

R.Pi.   Robert Pick (d. 1978). *Free-lance writer and editor. Author of* Empress Maria Theresa.
MARIA THERESA (Micropædia)

R.P.M.   Robert P. Multhauf. *Senior Historian, Smithsonian Institution, Washington, D.C. Author of* The Origins of Chemistry; Neptune's Gift.
OCCULTISM (*in part*)

R.Po.   Raphael Powell (d. 1965).
Professor of Roman Law, University of London, 1955–64.
LEGAL SYSTEMS, THE EVOLUTION OF
   MODERN WESTERN (*in part*)

R.Pr.   Roy Pryce. *Visiting Professor, European Institute of Public Administration, Maastricht, The Netherlands. Director, Directorate General for Information, Commission of the European Communities, Brussels, 1973–78.*
EUROPE (*in part*)

R.P.S.   Robert P. Scharlemann.
Commonwealth Professor of Religious Studies, University of Virginia, Charlottesville. Author of Reflection and Doubt in the Thought of Paul Tillich.
PROTESTANTISM (*in part*)
SCHLEIERMACHER, FRIEDRICH
   (Micropædia)

R.P.Sp.   Robert Phillip Sharp.
Emeritus Professor of Geology, California Institute of Technology, Pasadena. Author of Glaciers.
GEOMORPHIC PROCESSES (*in part*)

R.Q.   Ricardo Quintana. *Emeritus Professor of English, University of Wisconsin, Madison. Author of* Mind and Art of Jonathan Swift; Oliver Goldsmith: A Georgian Study.
SWIFT, JONATHAN (*in part*) (Micropædia)

R.R.   Romney Robinson. *Professor of Economics, University of Toronto, 1967–70. Associate Professor of Economics, Brandeis University, Waltham, Massachusetts, 1955–67.*
INTERNATIONAL TRADE (*in part*)

R.R.B.   Richard R. Beeman. *Professor of History, University of Pennsylvania,*

Philadelphia. Author of The Old Dominion and the New Nation, 1788–1801 *and others.*
UNITED STATES OF AMERICA (*in part*)

R.R.D.   Ranjit Ramchandra Desai.
Agriculturist and writer. Author of Śrīmāna Yogi: the Life of Śivajī in Marathi *and others.*
ŚIVAJĪ (Micropædia)

R.Ri.   Raymond Ritter (d. 1974).
Attorney. Editor in Chief of the review Pyrénées. *Author of* Henry IV lui-même; *editor of* Lettres du cardinal de Florence sur Henri IV et sur la France (1596–1598).
HENRY IV (FRANCE) (Micropædia)

R.R.M.   Raymond R. Myers. *University Professor of Chemistry, Kent State University, Ohio. Editor, Journal of Rheology. Coeditor of* Treatise on Coatings.
INDUSTRIES, CHEMICAL PROCESS
   (*in part*)

R.R.Pr.   Richard Riseley Proud (d. 1975). *Lieutenant Colonel, Indian Army.*
NEPAL (*in part*)

R.R.R.   Richard R. Ring. *Former Assistant Professor of History, Ripon College, Wisconsin.*
ROME (*in part*)

R.R.S.   Robert R. Stoll. *Emeritus Professor of Mathematics, Cleveland State University. Author of* Set Theory and Logic.
SET THEORY (*in part*)

R.R.Sc.   Robert R. Schwanke. *Former member, Austrian Institute of Eastern and Southeastern European Studies, Vienna. Contributor of Albania section in P. Horecky,* Southeastern Europe.
ALBANIA (in part)

R.S.   Roger Sharrock. *Emeritus Professor of English Language and Literature, King's College, University of London. Author of* John Bunyan *and others; editor of* Oxford Bunyan.
BUNYAN, JOHN (Micropædia)

R.S.B.   Rupert Stevenson Bradley.
Former Reader in Inorganic and Structural Chemistry, University of Leeds, England. Coauthor and editor of High Pressure Physics and Chemistry.
BRIDGMAN, P.W. (Micropædia)

R.S.Be.   R. Stephen Berry. *Professor, Department of Chemistry and James Franck Institute, University of Chicago. Author of numerous papers on the interactions of light and electrons with atoms and molecules.*
CHEMICAL REACTIONS (*in part*)

R.Sc.   R.A.M. Schmidt. *Consulting geologist. Chairman, Geology Department, Anchorage Community College, University of Alaska. Geologist, Geological Survey, U.S. Department of the Interior, 1943–56; District Geologist, Anchorage, 1956–63.*
NORTH AMERICA (*in part*)

R.S.C.   Richard S. Cowan. *Senior Scientist, Department of Botany, National Museum of Natural History, Smithsonian Institution, Washington, D.C.*

ANGIOSPERMS (*in part*)

R.Sch.   Reiner Schürmann. *Professor of Philosophy, Graduate Faculty, New School for Social Research, New York City. Author of* Meister Eckhart, Mystic and Philosopher *and others.*

ECKEHART, MEISTER (Micropædia)

R.S.D.   Robert Sinclair Dietz. *Professor of Geology, Arizona State University, Tempe. Coauthor of* Seven Miles Down; The Story of the Bathyscaph Trieste.

OCEANS (*in part*)

R.S.De.   The Most Rev. Ralph Stanley Dean. *Theological Consultant, Christ Church, Greenville, South Carolina. Archbishop of Cariboo and Metropolitan of the Anglican Province of British Columbia, 1971–73. Author of* In the Light of the Cross.

PROTESTANTISM (*in part*)

R.S.Du.   Richard S. Dunn. *Professor of History, University of Pennsylvania, Philadelphia. Author of* Puritans and Yankees *and others.*

WINTHROP, JOHN (Micropædia)

R.S.F.S.   Richard S.F. Schilling. *Emeritus Professor of Occupational Health, University of London; Director, TUC Centenary Institute of Occupational Health, London School of Hygiene and Tropical Medicine, 1968–76. Coauthor and editor of* Occupational Health Practice.

OCCUPATIONAL DISEASES AND DISORDERS

R.Sh.   Robert Shackleton. *Marshal Foch Professor of French Literature, University of Oxford; Fellow of All Souls College, Oxford. Author of* Montesquieu: A Critical Biography.

MONTESQUIEU, CHARLES-LOUIS DE SECONDAT, BARON DE LA BREDE ET DE (*in part*) (Micropædia)

R.S.H.   Richard S. Hartenberg. *Emeritus Professor of Mechanical Engineering, Northwestern University, Evanston, Illinois. Coauthor of* Kinematic Synthesis of Linkages.

FULTON, ROBERT (Micropædia)
TOOLS (*in part*)

R.S.Ho.   Robert Stuart Hoyt (d. 1971). *Professor of History, University of Minnesota, Minneapolis, 1957–71. Author of* Europe in the Middle Ages.

EUROPE (*in part*)

R.Si.   Raymond Siever. *Professor of Geology, Harvard University. Coauthor of* Sand and Sandstone; Earth.

MINERALS AND ROCKS (*in part*)

R.Sk.   Robert A. Sklar. *Professor of Cinema Studies, New York University, New York City. Author of* F. Scott Fitzgerald: The Last Laocoön *and others;*

editor of The Plastic Age: 1917–1930.

UNITED STATES OF AMERICA (*in part*)

R.S.L.   Robert Sabatino Lopez (d. 1986). *Professor of History, Yale University, 1955–71. Author of* The Birth of Europe *and others.*

CONSTANTINE VII PORPHYROGENITUS (BYZANTINE EMPIRE) (Micropædia)

R.S.M.   Robert Slocumb Michaelsen. *Professor of Religious Studies, University of California, Santa Barbara. Author of* The Study of Religion in American Universities *and others.*

RELIGIOUS EDUCATION (*in part*)

R.So.   Robert W. Sowers. *Stained-glass artist. Author of* The Language of Stained Glass *and others.*

DECORATIVE ARTS AND FURNISHINGS (*in part*)

R.Sp.   Robert Spence (d. 1976). *Master of Keynes College; Professor of Applied Chemistry, University of Kent at Canterbury, England, 1968–73. Director, Atomic Energy Research Establishment, Harwell, England, 1964–68. Author of the obituary memoir on Otto Hahn for the Royal Society.*

HAHN, OTTO (Micropædia)

R.S.Q.   Robert S. Quimby. *Emeritus Professor of Humanities, Michigan State University, East Lansing. Author of* The Background of Napoleonic Warfare.

VAUBAN, SÉBASTIEN LE PRESTRE DE (Micropædia)

R.St.   Ralph Stephenson. *Former Director, Paris Pullman Cinema, London. Author of* The Animated Film; *coauthor of* The Cinema as Art.

MOTION PICTURES (*in part*)

R.St.J.   Robert St. John. *Journalist, lecturer, and foreign affairs radio commentator. Author of* The Boss *and others.*

NASSER, GAMAL ABDEL (Micropædia)

R.S.-U.   Rivka Schatz-Uffenheimer. *Edmonton Professor of Jewish Mysticism, Hebrew University of Jerusalem. Author of* ha-Ḥasidut ke-misṭiqa ("Ḥasidism as Mysticism") *and others.*

BAʿAL SHEM ṬOV (*in part*) (Micropædia)
LURIA, ISAAC BEN SOLOMON (*in part*) (Micropædia)

R.S.V.   René Santamaria Varela. *Director, R.V. y Asociados (management consultants), San Salvador, El Salvador.*

CENTRAL AMERICA (*in part*)

R.S.W.   Richard S. Westfall. *Professor of History of Science, Indiana University, Bloomington. Author of* The Construction of Modern Science; Never at Rest: A Biography of Isaac Newton *and others.*

NEWTON (*in part*)
RAY, JOHN (Micropædia)

R.S.Y.   Roland S. Young. *Consulting chemical engineer. Author of* Cobalt

in Biology and Biochemistry *and others; editor of* Cobalt: Its Chemistry, Metallurgy, Uses.

INDUSTRIES, EXTRACTION AND PROCESSING (*in part*)

R.T.   Robert Traub. *Colonel (retired), U.S. Army. Professor of Microbiology, University of Maryland, Baltimore. Author of numerous scientific papers, including many on fleas.*

INSECTS (*in part*)

R.T.An.   Roger T. Anstey (d. 1979). *Professor of Modern History, University of Kent at Canterbury, England. Author of* King Leopold's Legacy *and others.*

CENTRAL AFRICA (*in part*)

R.T.C.   Robert Thomas Coupland. *Professor and Head, Department of Plant Ecology, University of Saskatchewan, Saskatoon.*

ECOSYSTEMS (*in part*)

R.T.D.   Ralph Thomas Daniel (d. 1985). *Professor of Music History, Indiana University, Bloomington. Coauthor of* The Harvard Brief Dictionary of Music *and others.*

MUSIC, THE HISTORY OF WESTERN

Rt.H.   Robert Ho (d. 1972). *Senior Fellow, Department of Human Geography, Australian National University, Canberra. Author of* Farmers of Central Malaya; *editor of* Studies in the Geography of Southeast Asia.

SOUTHEAST ASIA, MAINLAND (*in part*)

R.Th.   Romila Thapar. *Professor of Ancient Indian History, Jawaharlal Nehru University, New Delhi. Author of* A History of India.

INDIA (*in part*)

R.T.H.   Robert Thomas Harms. *Professor of Linguistics, University of Texas at Austin. Author of* Estonian Grammar; Finnish Structural Sketch; *and others.*

LANGUAGES OF THE WORLD (*in part*)

R.T.J.   Richard T. Jackson. *Professor of Geography, University of Papua New Guinea, Port Moresby. Editor of* Introduction to the Urban Geography of Papua New Guinea.

EAST INDIES, THE (*in part*)

R.T.L.   Richard T. Lockhart. *President, Social Engineering Associates, Chicago; Editor,* Illinois Political Reporter.

UNITED STATES OF AMERICA (*in part*)

R.T.La.   Robert Terence Lange. *Reader in Botany, University of Adelaide, Australia. Coauthor of* Symbiosis.

AUSTRALIA (*in part*)

R.To.   Richard Tolson. The Times *(London) Correspondent, Leeward Islands, 1954–56.*

WEST INDIES, THE (*in part*)

R.T.S.   R. Thomas Sanderson. *Emeritus Professor of Chemistry, Arizona State University, Tempe. Author of* Chemical Bonds and Bond Energy *and others.*

CHEMICAL ELEMENTS (*in part*)

R.T.V. **Richard T. Vann.** *Professor of History and Letters, Wesleyan University, Middletown, Connecticut. Author of* The Social Development of English Quakerism.
PROTESTANTISM (*in part*)

R.T.We. **Richard Tilghman Weidner.** *Professor of Physics, Rutgers University, New Brunswick, New Jersey. Coauthor of* Elementary Modern Physics *and others.*
PHYSICAL SCIENCES, THE (*in part*)

Ru.M. **Russell Meiggs.** *Emeritus Fellow of Balliol College, Oxford; Lecturer in Ancient History, University of Oxford, 1939–70. Author of* Ostia; *editor of J.M. Bury's* History of Greece.
ALCIBIADES (Micropædia)
CLEISTHENES OF ATHENS (Micropædia)
GRECO-ROMAN CIVILIZATION, CLASSICAL (*in part*)

Ru.S. **Ruth Stephan** (d. 1974). *Writer. Author of* My Crown, My Love *and others.*
CHRISTINA (Micropædia)

Ru.V. **Rudolf Vierhaus.** *Professor and Director, Max Planck Institute for History, Göttingen, West Germany. Author of* Ranke und die soziale Welt *and others.*
RANKE, LEOPOLD VON (Micropædia)

R.V. **Randolph Vigne.** *Director, Stillit Books Ltd., London. Author of* The Transkei: A South African Tragedy.
SOUTH AFRICA (*in part*)

R.Va. **Richard Vaughan.** *Former Professor of History, University of Hull, England. Author of* Philip the Good; John the Fearless.
JOHN (BURGUNDY) (Micropædia)
PHILIP III (BURGUNDY) (Micropædia)

R.V.D. **Robert V. Daniels.** *Professor of History, University of Vermont, Burlington. Author of* Russia: Roots of Confrontation *and others.*
TROTSKY, LEON (*in part*) (Micropædia)
UNION OF SOVIET SOCIALIST REPUBLICS (*in part*)

R.V.F. **Richard V. Fisher.** *Professor of Geology, University of California, Santa Barbara.*
VOLCANISM (*in part*)

R.Vi. **Reino Virtanen.** *Emeritus Professor of Modern Languages, University of Nebraska, Lincoln. Author of* Claude Bernard and His Place in the History of Ideas.
BERNARD, CLAUDE (Micropædia)

R.V.R. **Robert Vincent Roosa.** *Partner, Brown Brothers, Harriman and Company, New York City. Under Secretary for Monetary Affairs, U.S. Department of the Treasury, 1961–64. Author of* Federal Reserve Operations in the Money and Government Securities Markets.
MARKETS (*in part*)

R.V.R.C.R. **R.V.R. Chandrasekhara Rao.** *Professor and Head, Department of Political Science; Dean, School of Social Sciences, University of Hyderabad, India. Author of* From Innocence to Strength: India Through Cold War, Detente and Entente.
INDIA (*in part*)

R.W. **Rex Wailes** (d. 1986). *Consultant, U.K. Department of the Environment and National Trust on Industrial Monuments. Author of* The English Windmill *and others.*
ENERGY CONVERSION (*in part*)

R.W.A. **R.W. Allard.** *Professor of Genetics, University of California, Davis. Author of* Principles of Plant Breeding.
FARMING AND AGRICULTURAL TECHNOLOGY (*in part*)

R.W.B. **Roger William Benedict.** *Managing Editor,* Petroleum Intelligence Weekly, *London.*
NORTH AMERICA (*in part*)

R.W.Ba. **Raymond William Baker.** *Associate Professor of Political Science, Williams College, Williamstown, Massachusetts. Author of* Egypt's Uncertain Revolution Under Nasser and Sadat.
EGYPT (*in part*)

R.W.Bd. **Raymond Walter Barnard** (d. 1962). *Associate Professor of Mathematics, University of Chicago, 1932–62.*
TRIGONOMETRY (*in part*)

R.W.C. **Robert W. Cahn.** *Former Professor of Materials Science, University of Sussex, Brighton, England. Editor of* Physical Metallurgy.
AGRICOLA, GEORGIUS (Micropædia)

R.W.Co. **Richard W. Cottle.** *Professor of Operations Research, Stanford University, California.*
OPTIMIZATION, THE MATHEMATICAL THEORY OF (*in part*)

R.W.D. **Ronald Walter Douglas.** *Emeritus Professor of Glass Technology, University of Sheffield, England. Editor of* Glass Technology; Physics and Chemistry of Glasses.
MATTER (*in part*)

R.W.D.E. **Robert Walter Dudley Edwards.** *Former Professor of Modern Irish History, University College, Dublin, National University of Ireland. Author of* Church and State in Tudor Ireland *and others.*
IRELAND (*in part*)

R.W.Di. **Robert William Ditchburn.** *Emeritus Professor of Physics, University of Reading, England. Author of* Light.
LIGHT (*in part*)

R.We. **Robert Werner.** *Professor of Ancient History, Friedrich Alexander University of Erlangen-Nürnberg, West Germany. Author of* Der Beginn der römischen Republik.
PTOLEMY I SOTER (Micropædia)

R.W.E. **Richard W. Everett.** *Vice President, Economic Research Division, Chase Manhattan Bank, New York City.*

ECONOMIC GROWTH AND PLANNING (*in part*)

R.W.F. **Rhodes W. Fairbridge.** *Professor of Geology, Columbia University. World authority on Quaternary history, events, and processes. Editor of* Encyclopedia of Geomorphology; Encyclopedia of World Regional Geology.
EARTH, THE (*in part*)
GEOCHRONOLOGY (*in part*)

R.W.Fi. **Sir Raymond William Firth.** *Emeritus Professor of Anthropology, University of London. Internationally known for his contributions in social anthropology. Author of* Man and Culture: An Evaluation of the Work of Bronislaw Malinowski.
MALINOWSKI, BRONISŁAW (*in part*) (Micropædia)

R.W.Fo. **Roland Wynfield Force.** *Director, Museum of the American Indian, New York City. Coeditor of* Polynesian Culture History.
PACIFIC ISLANDS (*in part*)

R.W.L. **Robert Warden Lee.** (d. 1958). *Rhodes Professor of Roman-Dutch Law, University of Oxford, 1921–56. Author of* Introduction to Roman-Dutch Law *and others.*
LEGAL SYSTEMS, THE EVOLUTION OF MODERN WESTERN (*in part*)

R.W.M. **Robert W. Marks.** *Former Lecturer, New School for Social Research, New York City. Author of* The Dymaxion World of Buckminster Fuller.
FULLER, R. BUCKMINSTER (Micropædia)

R.W.Ma. **Richard W. Macomber.** *Professor of Physics, Brooklyn Center, Long Island University, New York.*
LYELL, SIR CHARLES, BARONET (Micropædia)
SMITH, WILLIAM (Micropædia)

R.W.P. **Richard W. Pohl.** *Distinguished Professor of Botany; Curator of the Herbarium, Iowa State University, Ames. Author of* How to Know the Grasses *and others.*
ANGIOSPERMS (*in part*)

R.W.St. **Robert W. Storer.** *Professor of Zoology; Curator of Birds, Museum of Zoology, University of Michigan, Ann Arbor.*
BIRDS (*in part*)

R.W.S.-W. **Robert William Seton-Watson** (d. 1951). *Professor of Czechoslovak Studies, University of Oxford, 1945–49. Masaryk Professor of Central European History, King's College, University of London, 1922–45.*
YUGOSLAVIA (*in part*)

R.W.V. **Robert W. Vance.** *Consultant in cryogenic engineering. Member, National Research Council. Chairman, Board of Directors, Cryogenic Society of America. Editor of* Cryogenic Technology; *coeditor of* Applications of Cryogenic Technology.
REFRIGERATION (*in part*)

R.W.Y.   Ralph W. Yerger. *Professor of Biology, Florida State University, Tallahassee.*
FISHES (*in part*)

R.Y.C.   Roy Yorke Calne. *Professor of Surgery, University of Cambridge. Author of* Renal Transplantation.
TRANSPLANTS, ORGAN AND TISSUE

R.Y.T.   Robert Young Thomson. *Senior Lecturer in Biochemistry, University of Glasgow, Scotland.*
BIOCHEMICAL COMPONENTS OF ORGANISMS (*in part*)

S.A.   Stanley W. Angrist. *Columnist,* Forbes *magazine. Professor of Mechanical Engineering, Carnegie-Mellon University, Pittsburgh, 1971–82. Author of* Direct Energy Conversion.
ENERGY, THE CONCEPT OF (*in part*)

S.A.G.   Samuel A. Goudsmit (d. 1978). *Editor in Chief, American Physical Society, 1951–74. Senior Scientist, Brookhaven National Laboratory, Upton, New York, 1948–70. Coauthor of* Atomic Energy States.
ATOMS (*in part*)

S.A.K.   Samuel Alexander Kirk. *Professor of Special Education, University of Arizona, Tucson. Author of* Educating Exceptional Children *and others.*
EDUCATION, SPECIAL

S.A.Kr.   Stepan Andriyovich Kryzhanivsky. *Professor, Institute of Literature, Ukrainian S.S.R. Academy of Sciences, Kiev. Coauthor of* History of Ukrainian Literature, *vol. 8.*
UKRAINIAN LITERATURE (*in part*) (Micropædia)

S.A.M.   Samuel A. Matz. *President, Pocoloco, Inc., Villa Park, Illinois. Former Vice President, Research and Development, Ovaltine Food Products, Villa Park. Author of* Cookie and Cracker Technology.
FOOD PROCESSING (*in part*)

S.Ar.   Silvano Arieti, M.D. (d. 1981). *Clinical Professor of Psychiatry, New York Medical College, New York City, 1961–81. Author of* Interpretation of Schizophrenia *and others; editor of* American Handbook of Psychiatry.
MENTAL DISORDERS AND THEIR TREATMENT (*in part*)

S.A.R.   Sh. Abdur Rashid. *Adviser, Research Society of Pakistan, Lahore. Director, Historical Research Institute; Head, Department of History, University of the Punjab, Lahore, 1960–65. Author of* History of Muslims of India and Pakistan *and others.*
MUḤAMMAD IBN TUGHLUQ (Micropædia)

S.Ara.   Sinnappah Arasaratnam. *Professor of History, University of New England, Armidale, Australia. Author of* Ceylon *and others.*
SRI LANKA (*in part*)

S.A.Ri.   Stefan Albrecht Riesenfeld. *Emmanuel S. Heller Professor Emeritus of Law, University of California, Berkeley. Author of* Cases and Materials on Creditors' Remedies and Debtors' Protection.
BUSINESS LAW (*in part*)

S.A.S.   Stanley A. Schumm. *Professor of Geology, Colorado State University, Fort Collins.*
RIVERS (*in part*)

S.A.V.   Sergey Arsentyevich Vodovozov. *Head, Section of Economics of North Caucasus, Central Research Economic Institute of the R.S.F.S.R. Planning Committee.*
UNION OF SOVIET SOCIALIST REPUBLICS (*in part*)

S.A.W.   Stephen A. Wurm. *Professor of Linguistics, Research School of Pacific Studies, Australian National University, Canberra. Author of* Languages of Australia and Tasmania; Papuan Languages of Oceania.
LANGUAGES OF THE WORLD (*in part*)

S.A.Wo.   Stanley A. Wolpert. *Professor of History, University of California, Los Angeles. Author of* A New History of India *and others.*
INDIA (*in part*)

S.B.   Suri Balakrishna. *Assistant Director, National Geophysical Research Institute, Council of Scientific and Industrial Research, Hyderābād, India. Author of* Earth.
ASIA (*in part*)

S.Be.   Staffan Bergsten. *Novelist. Docent in Literary History, University of Uppsala, Sweden. Author of several works on 19th- and 20th-century Swedish poetry.*
SCANDINAVIAN LITERATURE (*in part*)

S.B.F.   Stuart Berg Flexner. *Editor-in-Chief, Reference Book Division, Random House, Inc., New York City. Coauthor and editor of* The Random House Dictionary of the American Language.
LANGUAGE (*in part*)

S.Bh.   The Rev. Sebastian Bullough, O.P. (d. 1967). *Lecturer in Hebrew, University of Cambridge.*
DOMINIC, SAINT (*in part*) (Micropædia)

S.Bl.   Solomon Bluhm. *Professor of Education, Hunter College, City University of New York, 1930–59.*
FROEBEL, FRIEDRICH (Micropædia)

S.B.O.   Sherry B. Ortner. *Professor of Anthropology, University of Michigan, Ann Arbor. Author of* Sherpas Through Their Rituals.
RITES AND CEREMONIES, SACRED (*in part*)

S.Br.   Savile Bradbury. *University Lecturer in Human Anatomy, University of Oxford; Fellow of Pembroke College, Oxford. Author of* The Evolution of the Microscope.

MEASUREMENT AND OBSERVATION, PRINCIPLES, METHODS, AND INSTRUMENTS OF (*in part*)

S.Bu.   Salvino Busuttil. *Director, Division of Human Settlements and Socio-cultural Environment,* UNESCO, *Paris. Former Professor and Head, Department of Economics, Royal University of Malta, Msida. Author of* Fiscal Policy in Malta.
MALTA

S.C.   Seymour Cain. *Fellow, National Endowment for the Humanities, Washington, D.C., 1979–80. Senior Editor, Religion,* Encyclopædia Britannica, *Chicago, 1967–73. Author of* Gabriel Marcel.
BIBLICAL LITERATURE AND ITS CRITICAL INTERPRETATION (*in part*)
MARCEL, GABRIEL (*in part*) (Micropædia)

S.C.E.   Søren Christian Egerod. *Professor of East Asian Languages, University of Copenhagen. Director, Scandinavian Institute of Asian Studies, Copenhagen. Editor,* Acta Orientalia. *Author of* The Lungtu Dialect *and others.*
LANGUAGES OF THE WORLD (*in part*)

S.Ch.   Sripati Chandrasekhar. *Distinguished Professor of Demography, University of Alaska, Fairbanks. Vice-Chancellor, Annamalai University, India, 1975–78. Member, Rajya Sabha (upper house of the Indian Parliament), 1964–70. Author of* Asia's Population Problems *and others.*
ASIA (*in part*)

S.C.K.   Stephen Cole Kleene. *Emeritus Dean of Letters and Science; Emeritus Professor of Mathematics and Computer Science, University of Wisconsin, Madison. Author of* Introduction to Metamathematics; Mathematical Logic.
MATHEMATICS, THE FOUNDATIONS OF (*in part*)

S.C.O.C.   Sten C.O. Carlsson. *Emeritus Professor of History, University of Uppsala, Sweden. Author of* Svensk historia *and others.*
CHARLES XIV JOHN (SWEDEN) (Micropædia)

S.D.   Stanley Dufford. *Film and theatre make-up artist. Make-up and Wig Designer, Lyric Opera of Chicago.*
THEATRICAL PRODUCTION (*in part*)

S.-d.C.   Sen-dou Chang. *Professor of Geography, University of Hawaii, Honolulu. Author of "Peking: The Growing Metropolis of Communist China" in* Geographical Review.
PEKING

S.Der N.   Sirarpie Der Nersessian. *Emeritus Professor of Byzantine Art, Dumbarton Oaks Research Library and Collection, Washington, D.C. Author of* L'Illustration des psautiers grecs du moyen-âge; L'Art arménien.
ARCHITECTURE, THE HISTORY OF WESTERN (*in part*)

PAINTING, THE HISTORY OF WESTERN
(*in part*)

S.Di. **Sven Dijkgraaf.** *Emeritus Professor of Comparative Physiology, Utrecht University, The Netherlands.*
SENSORY RECEPTION (*in part*)

Sd.K. **Sigmund Koch.** *Professor of Psychology and Philosophy, Boston University.*
PSYCHOLOGY (*in part*)

S.Dr. **Seymour Drescher.** *Professor of History, University of Pittsburgh. Author of* Tocqueville and England *and others.*
TOCQUEVILLE, ALEXIS DE (Micropædia)

S.E. **Samuel Eilon.** *Professor and Head, Department of Management Science, Imperial College of Science and Technology, University of London. Author of* Elements of Production Planning and Control *and others.*
INDUSTRIAL ENGINEERING AND
PRODUCTION MANAGEMENT (*in part*)

S.E.B. **Susan Elizabeth Benenson.** *Former Assistant Keeper, Department of Western Art, Ashmolean Museum, University of Oxford.*
HOGARTH, WILLIAM (*in part*)
(Micropædia)
PAINTING, THE HISTORY OF WESTERN
(*in part*)
SCULPTURE, THE HISTORY OF WESTERN
(*in part*)

S.E.C. **Sam E. Clagg.** *Professor of Geography, Marshall University, Huntington, West Virginia. Author of* West Virginia Historical Almanac *and others.*
UNITED STATES OF AMERICA (*in part*)

S.E.Cu. **Stanley Evan Curtis.** *Professor of Animal Science, University of Illinois, Urbana. Author of* Environmental Management in Animal Agriculture.
AGRICULTURAL SCIENCES (*in part*)

S.E.F. **Samuel Edward Finer.** *Gladstone Professor Emeritus of Government and Public Administration, University of Oxford. Author of* Anonymous Empire: A Study of the Lobby in Great Britian *and others.*
POLITICAL PARTIES AND INTEREST
GROUPS (*in part*)

Se.M. **Sengaku Mayeda.** *Professor of Indian Philosophy, University of Tokyo. Editor of Śaṅkara's* Upadeśasāhasrī.
ŚAṄKARA (Micropædia)

S.E.McG. **Samuel Emmett McGregor** (d. 1980). *Apiculturist, Bee Research Laboratory, U.S. Department of Agriculture, Tucson, Arizona. Coauthor of* Beekeeping in the United States.
FARMING AND AGRICULTURAL
TECHNOLOGY (*in part*)

S.Er. **Sirri Erinc.** *Director, Institute of Marine Sciences and Geography, University of Istanbul. Author of* Geography of Eastern Anatolia.
TURKEY AND ANCIENT ANATOLIA
(*in part*)

S.E.T. **Stephen E. Toulmin.** *Avalon Professor of the Humanities, Northwestern University, Evanston, Illinois. Author of* Philosophy of Science.
PHILOSOPHIES OF THE BRANCHES OF
KNOWLEDGE (*in part*)

S.F.Be. **Samuel Flagg Bemis** (d. 1973). *Sterling Professor of Diplomatic History and Inter-American Relations, Yale University, 1945–61. Author of* John Quincy Adams and the Foundations of American Foreign Policy *and others.*
ADAMS, JOHN QUINCY (Micropædia)
MONROE, JAMES (Micropædia)

S.Fe. **Solomon Feferman.** *Professor of Mathematics and Philosophy, Stanford University, California. Author of* The Number Systems: Foundations of Algebra and Analysis.
MATHEMATICS, THE FOUNDATIONS OF
(*in part*)

S.F.W. **S.F. Wise.** *Dean of Graduate Studies and Research, Carleton University, Ottawa. Coauthor of* Canada Views the United States: 19th Century Political Attitudes.
CANADA (*in part*)

S.F.We. **Stephen F. Weiss.** *Professor and Associate Chairman, Department of Computer Science, University of North Carolina at Chapel Hill.*
COMPUTERS (*in part*)

S.G. **Samy Gorgy.** *Former Director General, Institute of Oceanography and Fisheries, Alexandria. Author of numerous articles on oceanography.*
MEDITERRANEAN SEA (*in part*)

S.G.C. **Sir Stanley George Clayton, M.D.** (d. 1986). *Professor of Obstetrics and Gynecology, King's College Hospital Medical School, University of London, 1967–76.*
REPRODUCTION AND REPRODUCTIVE
SYSTEMS (*in part*)

S.G.F.B. **The Rev. Samuel G.F. Brandon** (d. 1971). *Professor of Comparative Religion, Victoria University of Manchester, 1951–71. Author of* Man and His Destiny in the Great Religions *and others.*
DOCTRINES AND DOGMAS, RELIGIOUS
(*in part*)
RITES AND CEREMONIES, SACRED
(*in part*)

S.Gh. **Sisirkumar Ghose.** *Professor of English, Visva-Bharati, Santiniketan, India. Author of* Mystics and Society.
RELIGIOUS EXPERIENCE (*in part*)

S.G.K. **Samir G. Khalaf.** *Professor of Sociology; Chairman, Department of Sociology and Anthropology, American University of Beirut. Coauthor of* Hamra of Beirut: A Case of Rapid Urbanization.
BEIRUT: *Bibliography*
LEBANON (*in part*)

S.Gl. **Sidney Glazer.** *Former Professor of History, Wayne State University, Detroit. Coauthor of* Michigan: From Primitive Wilderness to Industrial Commonwealth.

UNITED STATES OF AMERICA
(*in part*)

S.Go. **Stephen Gottschalk.** *Associate Professor of History, U.S. Naval Postgraduate School, Monterey, California, 1972–75. Author of* The Emergence of Christian Science in American Religious Life.
CHRISTIAN SCIENCE (Micropædia)

S.G.P. **Stanley G. Payne.** *Professor of History, University of Wisconsin, Madison. Author of* Franco's Spain *and others.*
FRANCO, FRANCISCO (Micropædia)

S.G.S. **Stanwyn G. Shetler.** *Curator, Department of Botany, Smithsonian Institution, Washington, D.C.*
ANGIOSPERMS (*in part*)

S.G.W. **Stephen Graham Wright.** *Former Adviser at the National Library of Ethiopia and at Haile Selassie I University, Addis Ababa.*
ETHIOPIAN LITERATURE (Micropædia)

S.H. **Samuel Handel** (d. 1972). *Member, Institution of Electrical Engineers. Author of* Dictionary of Electronics; The Electronic Revolution.
ELECTRONICS (*in part*)

S.Ha. **Shirō Hattori.** *Director, Tokyo Institute for Advanced Studies of Language. Emeritus Professor of Linguistics, University of Tokyo. Author of* Methods in Linguistics; Genealogy of Japanese; *and others.*
LANGUAGES OF THE WORLD (*in part*)

Sh.B. **Sh. Batbayar.** *Scientific Secretary, Institute of Economy, Academy of Sciences of the Mongolian People's Republic, Ulaanbaatar.*
MONGOLIA (*in part*)

S.H.B. **Samuel H. Baron.** *Professor of History, University of North Carolina at Chapel Hill. Author of* Plekhanov: The Father of Russian Marxism *and others.*
PLEKHANOV, GEORGY VALENTINOVICH
(Micropædia)

Sh.Bi. **Sh. Bira.** *Head of Section, Institute of History, Academy of Sciences of the Mongolian People's Republic, Ulaanbaatar.*
MONGOLIA (*in part*)

S.H.Bl. **Sheldon H. Blank.** *Emeritus Professor of Bible, Hebrew Union College-Jewish Institute of Religion, Cincinnati, Ohio. Author of* Prophetic Faith in Isaiah *and others.*
ISAIAH (Micropædia)

S.H.Br. **Stanley Henry Beaver.** *Professor of Geography, University of Keele, England, 1950–74.*
BALKANS (*in part*)

S.He. **Stanislaw Herbst** (d. 1973). *Professor of Pre-18th Century Polish History, University of Warsaw. President, Polish Historic Society, Warsaw. Coauthor of* A Thousand Years of Polish History.
KOŚCIUSZKO, TADEUSZ (Micropædia)

S.H.F.L. Seton H.F. Lloyd. *Emeritus Professor of Western Asiatic Archaeology, University of London. Author of* Art of the Ancient Near East; Early Highland Peoples of Anatolia; Twin Rivers; *and others.*

ASIA (*in part*)

INDIA (*in part*)

IRAQ (*in part*)

TURKEY AND ANCIENT ANATOLIA
  (*in part*)

Sh.H. Shigeru Hayashi. *Professor, Institute of Social Service, University of Tokyo. Author of* The Pacific War.

KONOE FUMIMARO, KOSHAKU
  (Micropædia)

S.H.J. Susan Heyner Joshi. *Professor of Biology, Philadelphia College of Pharmacy and Science.*

BIOLOGICAL SCIENCES, THE (*in part*)

Sh.M. Shula E. Marks. *Director, Institute of Commonwealth Studies; Reader in the History of Southern Africa, School of Oriental and African Studies and Institute of Commonwealth Studies, University of London. Author of* Reluctant Rebellion: The 1906–08 Disturbances in Natal *and others.*

SOUTHERN AFRICA (*in part*)

S.H.N. Seyyed Hossein Nasr. *Professor of Philosophy; Dean, Faculty of Letters and Humanities, University of Tehrān. Author of* Three Muslim Sages.

AVICENNA (Micropædia)

Sh.Nj. Sh. Natsagdorj. *Director, Institute of History, Academy of Sciences of the Mongolian People's Republic, Ulaanbaatar.*

MONGOLIA (*in part*)

S.H.O. Simeon Hongo Ominde. *Professor of Geography; Director, Population Studies and Research Institute, University of Nairobi, Kenya. Author of* Land and Population Movements in Kenya.

EASTERN AFRICA (*in part*)

S.H.P. Stewart Henry Perowne. *Orientalist, historian, and lecturer. Author of* The Life and Times of Herod the Great; The End of the Roman World; The Political Background of the New Testament; *and others.*

CLEOPATRA VII THEA PHILOPATOR
  (Micropædia)

HEROD I (Micropædia)

JERUSALEM (*in part*)

JULIAN (Micropædia)

S.H.St. S. Henry Steinberg (d. 1969). *Editor,* The Statesman's Year-Book, *1946–69. Author of* The Thirty Years' War and the Conflict for European Hegemony, 1600–1660 *and others.*

EUROPE (*in part*)

WALLENSTEIN, ALBRECHT WENZEL
  EUSEBIUS VON, HERZOG VON
  FRIEDLAND (Micropædia)

Sh.Ts. Sh. Tsevegmid. *Director, Institute of Geography and Geocryology, Academy of Sciences of the Mongolian*

People's Republic, Ulaanbaatar.

MONGOLIA (*in part*)

S.H.W. Stanley H. Weitzman. *Curator of Fishes, Division of Fishes, National Museum of Natural History, Smithsonian Institution, Washington, D.C. Author of numerous articles on fishes.*

FISHES (*in part*)

S.-I.A. Syun-Ichi Akasofu. *Professor of Geophysics, Geophysical Institute, University of Alaska, Fairbanks. Author of* Polar and Magnetospheric Substorms.

ATMOSPHERE (*in part*)

S.I.B. Solomon Ilich Bruk. *Deputy Director, Institute of Ethnography, Academy of Sciences of the U.S.S.R., Moscow. Coauthor and editor of* Ethnographic Maps of Asian Countries.

ASIA (*in part*)

UNION OF SOVIET SOCIALIST REPUBLICS
  (*in part*)

Si.M. Sidney Marrat. *Journalist, literary critic, and theatre historian.*

AFRICAN ARTS (*in part*)

Si.T. Sidney Thomas. *Professor of Fine Arts, Syracuse University, New York. Editor of* Images of Man; *coeditor of* The Nature of Art.

ARTS, PRACTICE AND PROFESSION OF
  THE (*in part*)

S.J.C. Selma Jeanne Cohen. *Editor,* International Encyclopedia of Dance. *Author of* Doris Humphrey: An Artist First; *editor of* The Modern Dance: Seven Statements of Belief.

DANCE, THE ART OF (*in part*)

S.J. de L. Sigfried Jan de Laet. *Former Professor of Archaeology, State University of Ghent. Author of* The Low Countries *and others.*

LOW COUNTRIES, THE
  (*in part*)

S.J.K.B. Samuel John Kenneth Baker. *Emeritus Professor of Geography, Makerere University, Kampala, Uganda. Honorary Lecturer in Geography, University of Leicester, England, 1968–74.*

AFRICA (*in part*)

S.J.S. Stanford Jay Shaw. *Professor of History, University of California, Los Angeles. Editor in Chief,* International Journal of Middle East Studies. *Author of* History of the Ottoman Empire and Modern Turkey *and others.*

TURKEY AND ANCIENT ANATOLIA
  (*in part*)

S.K. Shinzo Kiuchi. *Emeritus Professor of Geography, University of Tokyo. Coeditor of* Japanese Cities.

ŌSAKA-KŌBE METROPOLITAN AREA
  (*in part*)

TOKYO-YOKOHAMA METROPOLITAN
  AREA

S.Kh. Stella Kramrisch. *Curator, Indian and Himalayan Art, Philadephia Museum of Art. Professor of Indian Art, Institute of Fine Arts, New York University, New York City. Author of*

The Hindu Temple; Unknown India; The Art of Nepal; *and others.*

CENTRAL ASIAN ARTS (*in part*)

S.Kö. Stephan Körner. *Professor of Philosophy, University of Bristol, England, and Yale University. Author of* Conceptual Thinking; Categorical Frameworks; *and others.*

CLASSIFICATION THEORY

S.K.S. Sylvester K. Stevens (d. 1974). *Executive Director, Pennsylvania Historical and Museum Commission, Harrisburg, 1956–72. Author of* Pennsylvania: Birthplace of a Nation.

PHILADELPHIA (*in part*)

S.La. Sylvia Dorothy Lawler, M.D. *Professor of Human Genetics, Institute of Cancer Research, University of London. Honorary Consultant in Immunology and Cytogenetics, Royal Marsden Hospital, London. Coauthor of* Human Blood Groups and Inheritance.

BLOOD (*in part*)

S.L.D. S. Lawrence Dingman. *Professor of Water Resources, University of New Hampshire, Durham.*

ICE AND ICE FORMATIONS (*in part*)

S.Lr. Samuel Leiter. *Former Seminary Professor of Hebrew Literature, Jewish Theological Seminary of America, New York City. Editor of* Selected Stories of S.Y. Agnon.

HEBREW LITERATURE (*in part*)

S.L.R. Stanley L. Robbins, M.D. *Visiting Professor of Pathology, Harvard University. Senior Pathologist, Brigham and Womens Hospital, Boston. Author of* Pathologic Basis of Disease *and others.*

DISEASE (*in part*)

S.L.S. Shao L. Soo. *Professor of Mechanical Engineering, University of Illinois, Urbana. Author of* Fluid Dynamics of Multiphase Systems.

ENERGY CONVERSION (*in part*)

S.L.Sm. Sigmund L. Smith. *Emeritus Professor of Metallurgical Engineering, University of Arizona, Tucson. Author of* Ore Microscopy.

INDUSTRIES, EXTRACTION AND
  PROCESSING (*in part*)

S.M. Sonia Moore. *Founder and President, American Center for Stanislavski Theatre Art, Inc., New York City. Founder and Artistic Director, American Stanislavski Theatre. Author of* Training an Actor: The Stanislavski System in Class; The Stanislavski System.

STANISLAVSKY, KONSTANTIN
  (Micropædia)

S.Ma. Sibyl Marcuse. *Curator, Yale University Collection of Musical Instruments, 1952–60. Author of* Musical Instruments: A Comprehensive Dictionary; A Survey of Musical Instruments.

MUSICAL INSTRUMENTS (*in part*)

S.M.B. Surinder M. Bhardwaj. *Professor of Geography, Kent State*

University, Ohio.
ASIA (*in part*)

S.McD. Sheila D. McDonough.
*Professor of Religion, Sir George
Williams University, Montreal. Author
of* Muhammad Ali Jinnah, Maker of
Modern Pakistan *and others.*
IQBĀL, SIR MUḤAMMAD (Micropædia)

S.M.Ci. Sima M. Ćirković. *Professor
of the Medieval History of Yugoslavia,
University of Belgrade. Author of* Duke
Stefan Vukčić Kosača and His Time;
Istorija srednjovekovne bosanske države.
STEFAN, DUŠAN (Micropædia)

S.M.Co. Sonia M. Cole (d. 1982).
*Associate of the British Museum
(Natural History). Author of* The
Prehistory of East Africa; Leakey's Luck;
and others.
AFRICA (*in part*)

S.M.D. Stephanie Mary Dalley.
Independent researcher. Contributor to
Iraq (*journal*).
SARGON (AKKAD) (Micropædia)

S.M.G. Stanley M. Garn. *Professor of
Human Nutrition and of Anthropology;
Fellow of the Center for Human
Growth and Development, University
of Michigan, Ann Arbor. Author of*
Human Races.
EVOLUTION, HUMAN (*in part*)

S.M.H. Sigismund M. Herschdoerfer.
*Consultant and former Chief Chemist
and Quality Controller, T. Wall & Sons
Ltd. (ice cream), London. Editor of*
Quality Control in the Food Industry.
FOOD PROCESSING (*in part*)

S.Mi. Sandra Millikin. *Free-lance
architectural historian. Lecturer in the
History of Art, Open University, Walton,
England. 1971–73.*
ADAM, ROBERT (Micropædia)
ARCHITECTURE, THE HISTORY OF
  WESTERN (*in part*)

S.M.I. S.M. Ikram (d. 1973). *Director,
Institute of Islāmic Culture, Lahore,
Pakistan. Author of* History of Muslim
Civilisation in India and Pakistan
and others.
AHMAD KHAN, SIR SAYYID (Micropædia)

S.M.M. Sidnie M. Manton (d. 1979).
*Reader in Zoology, King's College,
University of London, 1949–60.*
SUPPORTIVE AND CONNECTIVE
  TISSUES (*in part*)

S.Mo. Sitanshu Mookerjee. *President,
Indian Institute of Geography. Principal,
Morris College, Nāgpur University,
India.*
INDIA (*in part*)

S.M.R. Sidney Martin Robbins.
*Chase Manhattan Professor Emeritus
of Financial Institutions, Columbia
University. Author of* Securities Markets
and others.
MARKETS (*in part*)

S.M.S. Shekou M. Sesay. *Deputy
Secretary-General, Mano River Union,
Freetown, Sierra Leone. Coauthor of*

Sierra Leone in Maps.
WESTERN AFRICA (*in part*)

S.M.Sn. Samuel Miklos Stern (d.
1969). *Fellow of All Souls College,
University of Oxford, 1957–69. Author
of* Les Chansons mozarabes; Fatimid
Decrees; *and others.*
COINS AND COINAGE (*in part*)

S.N.B. Steven N. Blair. *Director,
Epidemiology, Institute for Aerobics
Research, The Aerobics Center, Dallas,
Texas. Chair of the editorial committee,*
Guidelines for Exercise Testing and
Prescription.
EXERCISE AND PHYSICAL CONDITIONING
(*in part*)

S.N.M. S.N. Mukerji. *Director, Centre
for Advanced Studies in Education,
1962–65; Dean, Faculty of Education,
Maharaja Sayajirao University of
Baroda, India, 1949–65. Author of*
History of Education in India.
EDUCATION, HISTORY OF
  (*in part*)

**S.N.R. Sergey Nikolayevich
Ryazantsev.** *Professor of Economic
Geography, Moscow Pedagogical
Institute. Author of* Kirgizskaya S.S.R.
and many others.
UNION OF SOVIET SOCIALIST REPUBLICS
  (*in part*)

S.N.W. S. Nicholas Woodward.
*Fellow, Templeton College—the Oxford
Centre for Management Studies,
University of Oxford. Coauthor of*
Finance for Managers.
BUSINESS ORGANIZATION (*in part*)

So.T. Sol Tax. *Emeritus Professor of
Anthropology, University of Chicago.
Director, Center for the Study of Man,
Smithsonian Institution, Washington,
D.C., 1968–76. Editor,* Current
Anthropology, *1957–74. Authority
noted for his work in American Indian
ethnology and in the theory of social
anthropology.*
BOAS, FRANZ (Micropædia)

S.P. Simeon Potter (d. 1976). *Bains
Professor of English Language and
Philology, University of Liverpool, 1945–
65. Author of* Our Language; Changing
English; *and others.*
LANGUAGES OF THE WORLD (*in part*)

S.P.A. Sara P. Anastaplo. *Researcher.
Author of* Alexander The Great:
King of Asia.
GREECE (*in part*)

S.P.C. Shiba P. Chatterjee. *Emeritus
Professor of Geography, University of
Calcutta. Author of* Physiography of
India *and others; editor of* Selected
Papers of the 21st International
Geographical Congress, *vol. 1–4.*
ASIA (*in part*)
INDIA (*in part*)

S.P.D. Stephen Porter Dunn. *Director
of Research, Highgate Road Social
Science Research Station, Inc., Berkeley,
California. Coauthor of* The Peasants of
Central Russia.

UNION OF SOVIET SOCIALIST REPUBLICS
  (*in part*)

S.Pi. Shlomo Pines. *Former Professor
of General and Jewish Philosophy,
Hebrew University of Jerusalem. Author
of* Scholasticism after Thomas Aquinas
and the Teachings of Hasdai Crescas
and his Predecessors; *translator of*
Maimonides' Guide of the
Perplexed.
JUDAISM (*in part*)

S.P.J. S. Paul Johnston (d. 1985).
*Director, National Air and Space
Museum, Smithsonian Institution,
Washington, D.C., 1964–69. Author of*
Horizons Unlimited *and others.*
SIKORSKY, IGOR (Micropædia)
TRANSPORTATION (*in part*)

S.P.Jn. Stanley Percival Jackson.
*Emeritus Professor of Geography,
University of the Witwatersrand,
Johannesburg; Deputy Vice-Chancellor,
1965–73.*
SOUTHERN AFRICA (*in part*)

S.P.L. Stephen P. Ladas (d. 1976).
*Attorney. Partner, Ladas, Parry, Von
Gehr, Goldsmith & Deschamps, New
York City. Author of* The International
Protection of Industrial Property.
PROPERTY LAW (*in part*)

S.P.V. Shanti Prasad Varma. *Honorary
Director, Institute of Development
Studies, Jaipur, India. Former
Chairman, Department of Political
Science; former Director, South Asia
Studies Centre, University of Rājasthān,
Jaipur. Author of* A Study of Maratha
Diplomacy: Anglo-Maratha Relations,
1772–1783.
INDIA (*in part*)

S.R. Sydney Ross. *Professor of
Colloid Science, Rensselaer Polytechnic
Institute, Troy, New York. Coauthor of*
On Physical Adsorption; *editor of* The
Chemistry and Physics of Interfaces.
PRIESTLEY, JOSEPH (Micropædia)

S.Ra. Sheila Ralphs. *Former Senior
Lecturer in Italian, Victoria University of
Manchester, England.*
ITALIAN LITERATURE (*in part*)

S.R.M. S. Roy Meadow. *Professor
and Head, Department of Paediatrics
and Child Health, St. James's Hospital,
University of Leeds, England. Coauthor
of* The Child and His Symptoms
and others.
CHILDHOOD DISEASES AND DISORDERS
(*in part*)

S.Rs. Sir Sydney Roberts (d.
1966). *Vice Chancellor, University
of Cambridge, 1949–51; Master of
Pembroke College, Cambridge, 1948–
58. A noted Johnson scholar. Author
of* Doctor Johnson, and Others; *editor
of* Samuel Johnson, Writer; *and many
other works on Johnson.*
JOHNSON, SAMUEL (*in part*)

S.R.S. Stuart Reynolds Schram.
*Professor of Politics, School of Oriental
and African Studies, University of*

London. *Author of* Mao Tse-tung; Mao Zedong: A Political Reassessment; *and others.*
MAO TSE-TUNG

S.R.T.   Steven R. Tannenbaum. *Professor of Toxicology and Food Chemistry, Massachusetts Institute of Technology, Cambridge. Coeditor of* Single-Cell Protein *and others.*
FOOD PROCESSING (*in part*)

S.R.Ty.   Spencer Rowe Titley. *Professor of Geology, School of Earth Sciences, University of Arizona, Tucson. Coeditor of* Geology of the Porphyry Copper Deposits: Southwestern North America.
MINERALS AND ROCKS (*in part*)

S.S.A.   Stanislas Spero Adotevi. *Director, Institute of Applied Research, Porto-Novo, Benin. Author of* Demain la veille.
WESTERN AFRICA (*in part*)

S.S.C.   S.S. Chern. *Professor of Mathematics, University of California, Berkeley. Author of* Complex Manifolds Without Potential Theory.
GEOMETRY (*in part*)

S.S.Ch.   Sukhdev Singh Chib. *Reader and Head, Geography Department, Directorate of Correspondence Courses, Punjab University, Chandigarh, India. Author of* Nineteen Fateful Months: A Socio-economic Study *and others.*
INDIA (*in part*)

S.S.D.J.   S.S.D. Jones. *Navigation consultant. Former Head, Navigation and Guidance Division, Royal Aircraft Establishment, Farnborough, England. Author of* "Recent Developments in Radio Navigation" *in* Encyclopaedic Dictionary of Physics.
NAVIGATION (*in part*)

S.S.F.   Sheppard Sunderland Frere. *Emeritus Professor of the Archaeology of the Roman Empire, University of Oxford. Author of* Britannia: A History of Roman Britain *and others.*
UNITED KINGDOM (*in part*)

S.S.G.   Sergio Sepúlveda González. *Former Professor of Geography of Chile and Latin America, University of Chile, Santiago. Former Head, Department of Social Sciences, Centre of Experimental and Pedagogical Research. Author of* Regiones geográficas de Chile.
CHILE (*in part*)

S.S.H.   Syed Sajjad Husain. *Professor of English, Umm al-Qūrah University, Mecca, 1975–85. Vice-Chancellor, University of Rājshāhi, Bangladesh, 1969–71. Author of* Descriptive Catalogue of Bengali Manuscripts.
BANGLADESH (*in part*)

S.Sk.   Stephan Skalweit. *Professor of Modern History, Rhenish Friedrich Wilhelm University of Bonn. Author of* Frankreich und Friedrich der Grosse.
FREDERICK WILLIAM (BRANDENBURG) (Micropædia)
GERMANY (*in part*)

S.Sm.   Stephen Smale. *Professor of Mathematics, University of California, Berkeley. Coeditor of* Global Analysis.
ANALYSIS (IN MATHEMATICS) (*in part*)

S.Sp.   The Rev. Sidney Spencer (deceased). *Minister, Bath and Trowbridge Unitarian Churches, England. Principal of Manchester College, University of Oxford, 1951–56. Author of* Mysticism in World Religion.
CHRISTIANITY (*in part*)

S.St.   Sewell Stokes (d. 1979). *Author and dramatist. Author of* Isadora: An Intimate Portrait *and others.*
DUNCAN, ISADORA (Micropædia)

S.T.   Stith Thompson (d. 1976). *Distinguished Service Professor of English and Folklore, Indiana University, Bloomington, 1953–55. Author of* Motif-Index of Folk-Literature, 6 vol; The Folktale; *and others.*
FOLK ARTS (*in part*)

S.Ta.   Shin'ichi Tani. *Professor of the History of Japanese Art, Kyōritsu Women's University, Tokyo. Author of* Muromachi-jidai bijutsushiron (*"A Study on Arts of the Muromachi Period"*); Bijutsushi (*"History of Japanese Art"*).
EAST ASIAN ARTS (*in part*)

S.Th.   Sigurdur Thorarinsson. *Professor and Director, Division of Geosciences, Science Institute, University of Iceland, Reykjavik.*
ICELAND (*in part*)

S.Tr.   Stanley Trapido. *Lecturer in the Government of New States, University of Oxford.*
SOUTHERN AFRICA (*in part*)

S.V.G.   Stephen Vincent Grancsay (d. 1980). *Curator of Arms and Armor, Metropolitan Museum of Art, New York City, 1929–64. Author of classic studies on arms and metalwork.*
DECORATIVE ARTS AND FURNISHINGS (*in part*)

S.V.U.   Sergei Vasilievich Utechin. *Former Professor of Russian History, Pennsylvania State University, University Park. Author of* Everyman's Concise Encyclopædia of Russia *and others.*
UNION OF SOVIET SOCIALIST REPUBLICS (*in part*)

S.W.B.   Salo Wittmayer Baron. *Emeritus Professor of Jewish History, Literature, and Institutions, Columbia University. Author of* A Social and Religious History of the Jews.
JUDAISM (*in part*)

S.We.   Stanley Weintraub. *Research Professor of English; Director, Institute for the Arts and Humanistic Studies, Pennsylvania State University, University Park. Author of* Private Shaw and Public Shaw; A Dual Portrait of Lawrence of Arabia and G.B.S.; *editor of* Shaw: An Autobiography; *coeditor of* Evolution of a Revolt: Early Postwar Writings of T.E. Lawrence.
LAWRENCE, T.E. (*in part*) (Micropædia)
SHAW, GEORGE BERNARD (Micropædia)

S.W.F.   Sidney W. Fox. *Director, Institute for Molecular and Cellular Evolution; Research Professor, University of Miami, Coral Gables. Coauthor of* Molecular Evolution and the Origin of Life.
OPARIN, ALEKSANDR IVANOVICH (Micropædia)

S.W.J.   Stanley W. Jacob, M.D. *Associate Professor of Surgery, Oregon Health Sciences University, Portland. Author of* Structure and Function in Man.
CIRCULATION AND CIRCULATORY SYSTEMS (*in part*)

S.W.K.M.   Stephen William Kenneth Morgan. *Former Director, Imperial Smelting Processes Limited, Avonmouth, England.*
CHEMICAL ELEMENTS (*in part*)

S.W.M.   S.W. Mikhail. *Professor of Electrical Technology, Ryerson Polytechnical Institute, Toronto.*
ELECTRONICS (*in part*)

S.W.R.   Stephen Wentworth Roskill (d. 1982). *Captain, Royal Navy. Official Naval Historian, Cabinet Office of the United Kingdom, 1949–60. Author of* The War at Sea, 1939–1945 (*4 vol.*).
WAR, THE THEORY AND CONDUCT OF (*in part*)

S.Y.C.   Shou Yi Chen (d. 1978). *Professor of Chinese Culture, Pomona College, Claremont, California, 1941–67. Author of* Chinese Literature: A Historical Introduction.
CHINESE LITERATURE (*in part*)

S.-y.H.   Shan-yüan Hsieh. *Former Assistant Professor of Philosophy, Haverford College, Pennsylvania.*
TSENG KUO-FAN (Micropædia)

S.Z.L.   Sid Z. Leiman. *Professor of Jewish History and Literature; Chairman, Department of Judaic Studies, Brooklyn College, City University of New York.*
BA'AL SHEM ṬOV (*in part*) (Micropædia)
JUDAISM (*in part*)

T.A.J.   Thomas Athol Joyce (d. 1942). *Subkeeper, Department of Ethnography, British Museum, London, 1902–38.*
SOUTH AMERICA (*in part*)

T.A.S.   Thomas A. Schafer. *Professor of Church History, McCormick Theological Seminary, Chicago.*
EDWARDS, JONATHAN (Micropædia)

T.B.B.   Thomas B. Bottomore. *Professor of Sociology, University of Sussex, Brighton, England. Author of* Classes in Modern Society; Elites and Society.
SOCIAL DIFFERENTIATION (*in part*)

T.B.H.   Thomas B. Hinton (d. 1976). *Associate Professor of Anthropology, University of Arizona, Tucson. Author of* A Survey of Indian Assimilation in Eastern Sonora.
AMERICAN INDIANS (*in part*)

T.B.T. Terence Barrington Thomas.
*Director, Gladding International Ltd.
Angling correspondent,* The Field, *and
others. Presenter of "Angling Today,"
Associated Television, Birmingham,
England. Author of* Casting.
FISHING (*in part*) (Micropædia)

T.C. Theresa Clay. *Former Senior
Principal Scientific Officer, Department
of Entomology, British Museum (Natural
History), London.*
INSECTS (*in part*)

T.C.M. Terence Croft Mitchell. *Deputy
Keeper, Department of Western Asiatic
Antiquities, British Museum, London.*
HISTORY, THE STUDY OF (*in part*)

T.C.O. Tobias Chant Owen. *Professor
of Astronomy, State University of New
York at Stony Brook. Coauthor of* The
Search for Life in the Universe.
SOLAR SYSTEM, THE (*in part*)

T.C.P. Thomas C. Patterson. *Professor
of Anthropology, Temple University,
Philadelphia. Author of* Pattern and
Process in the Early Intermediate Period
Pottery of the Central Coast of Peru
and others.
PRE-COLUMBIAN CIVILIZATIONS (*in part*)

**T.Cr. The Rev. Theodore Crowley,
O.F.M.** *Emeritus Professor of Scholastic
Philosophy, Queen's University of
Belfast, Northern Ireland. Author of*
Roger Bacon: The Problem of the Soul
in His Philosophical Commentaries.
BACON, ROGER (Micropædia)

T.C.R. Thomas C. Reeves. *Professor
of History, University of Wisconsin,
Parkside. Author of* Freedom and the
Foundation: The Fund for the Republic
in the Era of McCarthyism *and
others.*
EISENHOWER, DWIGHT D. (Micropædia)

T.C.S. Thomas Clark Shedd. *Editorial
Director,* Modern Railroads, *Park
Ridge, Illinois.*
TRANSPORTATION (*in part*)

T.C.Y., Jr. T. Cuyler Young, Jr.
*Curator, West Asian Department, Royal
Ontario Museum, Toronto. Professor
of Near Eastern Studies, University of
Toronto. Author of "A Comparative
Ceramic Chronology for Western Iran,
1500–500 B.C." in* Iran.
IRAN (*in part*)

T.D. Theodosius Dobzhansky (d.
1975). *Professor of Biology, Rockefeller
University, New York City, 1962–
71. Adjunct Professor of Genetics,
University of California, Davis, 1971–75.
Author of* Mankind Evolving; Genetics
of the Evolutionary Process; *author
of numerous papers on evolutionary
genetics.*
GENETICS AND HEREDITY, THE
PRINCIPLES OF (*in part*)

T.d.A. The Rev. Tarsicio de Azcona.
*Former Professor of Theology, University
of Navarre, Pamplona, Spain. Author of*
Isabel la Católica.

FERDINAND II (SPAIN: ARAGON)
(Micropædia)

T.E.A. Thomas Edward Allibone.
*External Professor Emeritus of Electrical
Engineering, University of Leeds,
England. Robert Kitchin Research
Professor of Physics, City University,
London. Director, Research Laboratory,
Associated Electrical Industries,
Aldermaston, England, 1946–63. Author
of* The Release and Use of Nuclear
Energy *and others.*
RUTHERFORD

T.E.Ar. T.E. Armstrong. *Emeritus
Reader in Arctic Studies, Scott Polar
Research Institute, University of
Cambridge.*
ARCTIC, THE (*in part*)

T.E.G. T.E. Gudava. *Professor of
Linguistics, Tbilisi State University,
Georgian S.S.R.*
LANGUAGES OF THE WORLD (*in part*)

T.E.Je. Thomas Edmund Jessop (d.
1980). *Ferens Professor of Philosophy,
University of Hull, England, 1928–61.
Editor of* Bibliography of David Hume
and of Scottish Philosophy.
HUME (*in part*)

Te.K. Terrence Kaufman. *Associate
Professor of Anthropology, University of
Pittsburgh. Author of* Tzeltal Phonology
and Morphology.
LANGUAGES OF THE WORLD (*in part*)

T.E.K. Thomas Edward Keys.
*Emeritus Professor of the History of
Medicine, Mayo Graduate School of
Medicine, University of Minnesota,
Rochester. Emeritus Librarian, Mayo
Foundation. Author of* The History of
Surgical Anesthesia.
MAYO FAMILY (Micropædia)

T.E.O'T. Thomas E. O'Toole.
*Associate Professor of History, Western
Carolina University, Cullowhee, North
Carolina. Author of* Historical Dictionary
of Guinea.
WESTERN AFRICA (*in part*)

T.F.B. Thomas F. Budinger, M.D.
*Professor of Research Medicine,
Donner Laboratory, Lawrence
Berkeley Laboratory; Professor of
Bioinstrumentation, University of
California, Berkeley. Operations Officer,
International Ice Patrol, 1959–60.*
ICE AND ICE FORMATIONS (*in part*)

T.F.McG. Thomas F. McGann.
(deceased). *Professor of History,
University of Texas at Austin. Author
of* Argentina, the Divided Land;
Argentina, the United States, and the
Inter-American System, 1880–1914.
PERÓN, JUAN (*in part*) (Micropædia)

T.F.T. Thomas Frederick Tout (d.
1929). *President, Royal Historical
Society, 1925–28. Honorary Professor
and Professor of History, Victoria
University of Manchester, 1890–1925.
Author of* Edward the First; The Place
of the Reign of Edward II in English
History; *and others.*

EDWARD III (ENGLAND AND GREAT
BRITAIN) (*in part*) (Micropædia)

T.F.W.B. T.F.W. Barth (d. 1971).
*Professor of Geochemistry, University of
Oslo, 1936–46, 1949–71. Internationally
known for his work on igneous petrology
and geysers. Author of* Theoretical
Petrology.
VOLCANISM (*in part*)

T.G. Sir Tyrone Guthrie (d. 1971).
*Theatrical director. Chancellor, Queen's
University of Belfast, Northern Ireland,
1963–70. Author of* A Life in the
Theatre; New Theatre; *and others.*
THEATRE, THE ART OF (*in part*)

T.G.B. Thomas G. Benedek, M.D.
*Chief, Outpatient Department and
Rheumatology Section, Veterans
Administration Hospital, Pittsburgh.
Professor of Medicine, University of
Pittsburgh.*
SUPPORTIVE AND CONNECTIVE
TISSUES (*in part*)

**T.G.H.J. Thomas Garnet Henry
James.** *Keeper, Department of Egyptian
Antiquities, British Museum, London.
Editor of* The Hekanakhte Papers, and
Other Middle Kingdom Documents
and others.
EGYPT (*in part*)
EGYPTIAN ARTS AND ARCHITECTURE,
ANCIENT

T.G.Ms. Thomas G. Mathews.
*Secretary General, Association of
Caribbean Universities and Research
Institutes, San Juan, Puerto Rico.
Research Professor of History, University
of Puerto Rico, 1969–80.*
WEST INDIES, THE (*in part*)

T.G.P.S. T.G. Percival Spear (d. 1982).
*Fellow of Selwyn College, Cambridge;
Lecturer in History, University of
Cambridge, 1963–69. Author of* India:
A Modern History *and others; coauthor
and editor of* Oxford History of India
(3rd ed.).
AURANGZEB (Micropædia)
BĀBUR (Micropædia)
CLIVE, ROBERT, 1ST BARON CLIVE OF
PLASSEY (Micropædia)
INDIA (*in part*)

T.Gr. Theodore C. Grame. *President,
Study Center of American Musical
Pluralism, Tarpon Springs, Florida.
Author of* Folk Music; America's
Ethnic Music.
MUSICAL INSTRUMENTS (*in part*)

T.H. Thomas Herdman (d. 1970).
*Senior Lecturer in Geography and
Education, Training College, Dudley,
England. Author of* Geography for
To-Day—the World *and others.*
GERMANY (*in part*)

T.H.B. Thornton Howard Bridgewater.
*Chief Engineer, Television, British
Broadcasting Corporation, 1962–68.*
BROADCASTING (*in part*)

T.H.C. Theodore Hsi-en Chen.
*Emeritus Professor of Education and
Asian Studies, University of Southern*

California, Los Angeles. Author of Maoist Educational Revolution *and others.*

EDUCATION, HISTORY OF (*in part*)

T.H.D.   Tulio Halperin Donghi. *Professor of History, University of California, Berkeley. Author of* Historia contemporánea de América Latina *and others.*

ARGENTINA (*in part*)

T.H.E.   Thomas H. Everett. *Senior Horticulture Specialist, New York Botanical Garden, Bronx. Author of* Living Trees of the World.

TREES (*in part*)

T.H.G.   Theodor H. Gaster. *Emeritus Professor of Religion, Barnard College, Columbia University. Author of* Myth, Legend, and Custom in the Old Testament; Thespis: Ritual, Myth, and Drama in the Ancient Near East.

JUDAISM (*in part*)

Th.H.   Thor Heyerdahl. *Member, Norwegian Academy of Science and Letters, Oslo. Organizer and leader of Norwegian Archaeological Expedition to Easter Island and the East Pacific, 1955–56, and many other expeditions. Author of* Aku-Aku: The Secret of Easter Island; The Kon-Tiki Expedition; *and others.*

PACIFIC ISLANDS (*in part*)

Th.Ho.   Thomas Howarth. *Emeritus Professor of Architecture, University of Toronto.*

TORONTO

Th.M.   Thomas Munro (d. 1974). *Curator of Education, Cleveland Museum of Art, 1931–67. Professor of Art, Case Western Reserve University, Cleveland. Author of* The Arts and Their Interrelations *and others.*

AESTHETICS (*in part*)
ARTS, CLASSIFICATION OF THE

T.Hn.   Tom Harrisson (d. 1976). *Government Ethnologist and Curator, Sarawak Museum, 1947–66. Author of* The Malays of Sarawak *and others.*

EAST INDIES, THE (*in part*)
SOUTHEAST ASIA, MAINLAND (*in part*)

T.Ho.   Thomas Hodgkin (d. 1982). *Writer. Fellow of Balliol College, Oxford; Lecturer in the Government of New States, University of Oxford, 1965–70. Author of* Nationalism in Colonial Africa *and others.*

USMAN DAN FODIO (Micropædia)

T.Hor.   Theodore Hornberger (d. 1975). *John Welsh Centennial Professor of History and English Literature, University of Pennsylvania, Philadelphia, 1968–75. Author of* Benjamin Franklin.

FRANKLIN (*in part*)

T.H.v.A.   Tjeerd H. van Andel. *Wayne Loel Professor of Earth Sciences, Stanford University, California. Author of* New Views on an Old Planet: Continental Drift and the History of the Earth.

PLATE TECTONICS

Th.V.G.   Thomas V. Gamkrelidze. *Director, Oriental Institute, Academy of Sciences of the Georgian S.S.R., Tbilisi. Author of* Sibilant Correspondences and Some Questions of the Ancient Structure of the Kartvelian Languages; *coauthor of* The System of Sonants and Ablaut in the Kartvelian Languages.

LANGUAGES OF THE WORLD (*in part*)

T.I.   Toshihiko Izutsu. *Professor of Islāmic Studies, McGill University, Montreal, 1969–75. Author of* A Comparative Study of the Key Philosophical Concepts in Sufism and Taoism.

IBN AL'ARABĪ (Micropædia)

T.Ic.   Takashi Ichiye. *Professor of Oceanography, Texas A & M University, College Station.*

EKMAN, V. WALFRID (Micropædia)

T.Io.   Teiji Ichiko. *Former Director General, National Institute of Japanese Literature, Tokyo. Author of* History of Japanese Literature *and others.*

LITERATURE, THE ART OF (*in part*)

T.I.S.   Trevor Ian Shaw (d. 1972). *Professor of Zoology, Queen Mary College, University of London.*

NERVES AND NERVOUS SYSTEMS (*in part*)

T.J.   Thorkild Jacobsen. *Emeritus Professor of Assyriology, Harvard University. Author of* The Sumerian Kinglist; "Mesopotamia" *in* The Intellectual History of Ancient Man; *and others.*

MIDDLE EASTERN RELIGIONS, ANCIENT (*in part*)

T.J.B.   Trent J. Bertrand. *Professor of Economics, State University of New York at Binghamton. Senior Economist, World Bank, Washington, D.C.*

INTERNATIONAL TRADE (*in part*)

T.J.Br.   T. Julian Brown. *Professor of Palaeography, University of London. Coauthor of* Codex Lindisfarnensis.

WRITING (*in part*)

T.J.C.   Theodore John Cadoux. *Senior Lecturer in Ancient History, University of Edinburgh.*

CIMON (Micropædia)
SOLON (Micropædia)

T.J.Co.   Timothy John Connell. *Senior Lecturer in Hispanic Studies, Ealing College of Higher Education, London. Coauthor of* Spain after Franco *and others.*

BARCELONA
MADRID (*in part*)

T.J.H.   Theo Jozef Hermans. *Lecturer in Dutch, University College, University of London. Author of* The Structure of Modernist Poetry.

BELGIAN LITERATURE (*in part*)

T.Jn.   Thorkell Jóhannesson (deceased). *Professor of Icelandic History, University of Iceland, Reykjavik.*

ICELAND (*in part*)

T.Jo.   Thomas Jones (d. 1972). *Professor of Welsh Language and*

Literature, University College of Wales, Aberystwyth, University of Wales, 1952–70. Editor of Brut y Tywysogion; *cotranslator of* The Mabinogion.

CELTIC LITERATURE (*in part*)

T.Ka.   Thomas Kamanzi. *Research Assistant, National Institute of Scientific Research; Lecturer, National University of Rwanda, Butare. Coauthor of* Récits historiques Rwanda.

CENTRAL AFRICA (*in part*)

T.K.B.   T. Keilor Bentley. *Director, Owens Art Gallery, Mount Allison University, Sackville, New Brunswick. Superintendent, Alexander Graham Bell Museum, Baddeck. Nova Scotia, 1959–64.*

BELL, ALEXANDER GRAHAM (Micropædia)

T.Ke.   Tom Kemp. *Reader in Economic History, University of Hull, England. Author of* Economic Forces in French History *and others.*

EUROPE (*in part*)

T.K.F.   Thea K. Flaum. *Producer, WTTW (public television), Chicago. Former Editor, Urban Research Corporation, Chicago.*

UNITED STATES OF AMERICA (*in part*)

T.Kh.   Tarif Khalidi. *Associate Professor of History and Archaeology, American University of Beirut.*

'ABD AL-MALIK (Micropædia)
'ABD AR-RAḤMĀN III (Micropædia)

T.Kl.   Tibor Klaniczay. *Assistant Director, Institute for the History of Literature, Hungarian Academy of Sciences, Budapest.*

HUNGARIAN LITERATURE (*in part*)

T.Ku.   Tadachika Kuwata. *Emeritus Professor of Japanese History, Kokugakuin University, Tokyo. Author of* Toyotomi Hideyoshi *and others.*

TOYOTOMI HIDEYOSHI (Micropædia)

T.Ky.   Thin Kyi. *Emeritus Professor of Geography, University of Rangoon. Author of* Geography of Burma; Rangoon.

RANGOON (*in part*)

T.K.Z.   Tatyana Konstantinovna Zakharova. *Senior Science Editor,* Sovetskaya entsiklopediya *(publishing house).*

ASIA (*in part*)

T.L.K.   Thomas L. Karnes. *Professor of History, Arizona State University, Tempe. Author of* Failure of Union: Central America, 1824–1975 *and others.*

CENTRAL AMERICA (*in part*)

T.L.L.   Thomas L. Lentz, M.D. *Associate Professor of Cell Biology, School of Medicine, Yale University, New Haven, Connecticut. Author of* Primitive Nervous Systems.

NERVES AND NERVOUS SYSTEMS (*in part*)

T.L.Pe.   Troy L. Péwé. *Professor of Geology, Arizona State University, Tempe. Chairman, Fourth International Conference on Permafrost, National*

Academy of Sciences. An authority on the geomorphology of polar regions. Editor of The Periglacial Environment: Past and Present.

ICE AND ICE FORMATIONS (*in part*)

T.L.S.   T. Lynn Smith (d. 1976). *Graduate Research Professor of Sociology, University of Florida, Gainesville, 1959–74. Author of* Brazil: People and Institutions; Latin American Population Studies; *and others.*

BRAZIL (*in part*)
URUGUAY (*in part*)

T.M.   Tatsuro Matsumoto. *Emeritus Professor of Geology (Stratigraphy), Kyūshū University, Fukuoka, Japan. Authority on the Mesozoic history of Asia. Coauthor and editor of* Historical Geology.

GEOCHRONOLOGY (*in part*)

T.M.K.   Sir T. Malcolm Knox (d. 1980). *Principal of the University of St. Andrews, Scotland, 1953–66. Translator of Hegel's Political Writings, Early Theological Writings, and* Aesthetics.

HEGELIANISM, HEGEL AND (*in part*)

T.Mo.   Therald Moeller. *Professor of Chemistry, Arizona State University, Tempe. Author of* Inorganic Chemistry: A Modern Introduction.

CHEMICAL ELEMENTS (*in part*)

T.Na.   Takesi Nagata. *Director, National Institute of Polar Research, Tokyo. Author of* Rock Magnetism.

EARTH, THE (*in part*)

T.N.B.   Thomas N. Bisson. *Professor of History, University of California, Berkeley. Author of* Assemblies and Representation in Languedoc in the Thirteenth Century.

FRANCE (*in part*)

T.O.M.   Thomas Ollive Mabbott (d. 1968). *Professor of English, Hunter College, City University of New York, 1946–66. Editor of* Complete Works of Poe.

POE, EDGAR ALLAN (*in part*)
(Micropædia)

T.O'R.   Tarlach O'Raifeartaigh. *Chairman, Cultural Relations Committee, Dublin. Editor of* Genealogical Tracts I.

PATRICK, SAINT (Micropædia)

T.O.S.   Thomas O. Sloane. *Professor of Rhetoric, University of California, Berkeley. Author of* Donne, Milton, and the End of Humanist Rhetoric; *coeditor* The Rhetoric of Renaissance Poetry.

RHETORIC (*in part*)

To.Ya.   Tasaburo Yamada. *Senior Advisor, Japan Atomic Industrial Forum, Inc., Tokyo. Author of* Nuclear Power Generation.

ENERGY CONVERSION (*in part*)

T.P.   Tatiana Proskouriakoff (d. 1985). *Curator of Maya Art, Peabody Museum, Harvard University. Staff member, Carnegie Institution of Washington, D.C., 1939–58. Author of* An Album of Maya Architecture.

CALENDAR (*in part*)

T.P.M.   Terence Patrick Morris. *Professor of Social Institutions, London School of Economics and Political Science, University of London. Author of* The Criminal Area: A Study in Social Ecology *and others.*

CRIME AND PUNISHMENT (*in part*)

T.Po.   Tom Pocock. *Staff writer,* The Standard, *London. Author of* Nelson and His World; Remember Nelson.

NELSON, HORATIO NELSON, VISCOUNT (*in part*) (Micropædia)

T.P.v.B.   Theodorus P. van Baaren. *Former Professor of Science of Religions, State University of Groningen, The Netherlands. Author of* Menschen wie wir *and others.*

DOCTRINES AND DOGMAS, RELIGIOUS (*in part*)
RELIGIOUS AND SPIRITUAL BELIEF, SYSTEMS OF (*in part*)

T.R.H.   Theodore R. Higgins. *Director of Engineering and Research, American Institute of Steel Construction, New York City, 1943–69. Editor of* AISC Standard Specification for the Design, Fabrication and Erection of Structural Steel for Buildings.

BUILDING CONSTRUCTION (*in part*)

T.R.T.   Thomas R. Tregear. *Warden, Woodbrooke College, Selly Oak, Birmingham, England, 1959–63. Lecturer in Geography, University of Hong Kong, 1951–59. Author of* A Geography of China *and others.*

CHINA (*in part*)

T.S.   Tadao Sato. *Writer. Chairman, Japan Film P.E.N. Club. Author of* Kurosawa Akira no sekai *and others.*

KUROSAWA AKIRA (Micropædia)

T.Sa.   Taro Sakamoto. *Historian. Emeritus Professor, University of Tokyo. Author of* History of Japan *and others.*

JAPAN (*in part*)

T.S.B.   Truesdell S. Brown. *Emeritus Professor of History, University of California, Los Angeles. Author of* Ancient Greece *and others.*

HERODOTUS (Micropædia)

T.S.Bu.   Thomas S. Buechner. *President, Corning Museum of Glass, Corning, New York; Director, 1951–60. Chairman, Corning Glass Works Foundation and Steuben Glass, Inc. Author of* Guide to the Collections of the Corning Museum of Glass *and others.*

DECORATIVE ARTS AND FURNISHINGS (*in part*)

T.S.D.   T.S. Danowski, M.D. *Clinical Professor of Medicine, University of Pittsburgh. Director, Department of Medicine, Shadyside Hospital, Pittsburgh. Author of* Outline of Endocrine Gland Syndromes *and others.*

ENDOCRINE SYSTEMS (*in part*)

T.S.H.   Theodore S. Hamerow. *Professor of History, University of Wisconsin, Madison. Author of* The Social Foundations of German Unification, 1858–71 *and others.*

GERMANY (*in part*)

T.S.McL.   Thomas S. McLeod. *Former Director of Design Technology, Plessey Company Ltd., Ilford, England. Author of* Management of Research Development and Design in Industry.

INDUSTRIAL ENGINEERING AND PRODUCTION MANAGEMENT (*in part*)

T.Sp.   Terence John Bew Spencer (d. 1978). *Professor of English Language and Literature, 1958–78; Director, Shakespeare Institute, 1961–78, University of Birmingham, England. General Editor,* The New Penguin Shakespeare *and the* Penguin Shakespeare Library, *1964–78. Author of* The Tyranny of Shakespeare; Shakespeare: The Roman Plays.

SHAKESPEARE (*in part*)

T.T.   Takeshi Toyoda. *Historian. Professor, Tohoku University, Sendai, Japan, and Hōsei University, Tokyo. Author of* A History of Pre-Meiji Commerce in Japan *and others.*

JAPAN (*in part*)

T.-t.C.   Tse-tsung Chow. *Professor of East Asian Languages, Literature, and History, University of Wisconsin, Madison. Author of* The May Fourth Movement: Intellectual Revolution in Modern China *and others.*

CH'EN TU-HSIU (Micropædia)

T.T.M.   T.T. Macan. *Former Naturalist, Freshwater Biological Association, Windermere Laboratory, Ambleside, England. Author of* Freshwater Ecology.

ECOSYSTEMS (*in part*)

T.T.P.   Theodore Thomas Puck. *Director, Eleanor Roosevelt Institute for Cancer Research; Professor of Biochemistry, Biophysics, and Genetics, University of Colorado Health Sciences Center, Denver. Author of* The Mammalian Cell as a Microorganism: Genetic and Biochemical Studies in Vitro.

TISSUE CULTURE (*in part*)

T.T.R.   Tamara Talbot Rice. *Author of* Ancient Arts of Central Asia; The Scythians; Russian Art; *and others.*

CENTRAL ASIAN ARTS (*in part*)
EUROPE (*in part*)

T.V.W.   Turrell V. Wylie (d. 1984). *Professor of Tibetan Studies, University of Washington, Seattle, 1972–84. Author of* The Geography of Tibet According to the 'Dzam-gling-rgyas-bshad.

CENTRAL ASIAN ARTS (*in part*)
CHINA (*in part*)

T.W.   Thomas M. Woodard. *Writer and researcher. Instructor in Classics, Princeton University, 1962–64. Editor of* Sophocles: A Collection of Critical Essays.

GREEK DRAMATISTS, THE CLASSICAL (*in part*)

T.W.D.S. Tsepon W.D. Shakabpa. *Historian. Author of* Tibet: A Political History.
CHINA *(in part)*

T.W.J.G. Theodorus W.J. Gadella. *Lecturer in Systematic Botany, Utrecht University, The Netherlands. Author of* Cytotaxonomic Studies in the Genus Campanula.
ANGIOSPERMS *(in part)*

T.W.W. Thomas W. Whitaker. *Research Associate, University of California, San Diego. Collaborator, U.S. Department of Agriculture, La Jolla, California; Research Geneticist and Investigations Leader, Plant Science Research Division, Agricultural Research Service, 1961–73. Coauthor of* The Cucurbits: Botany, Cultivation and Utilization.
ANGIOSPERMS *(in part)*

T.Y. Takeo Yamane. *Former Professor of Food Manufacture, Showa Women's University, Tokyo. Author of* Cane Sugar Handbook.
FARMING AND AGRICULTURAL TECHNOLOGY *(in part)*
FOOD PROCESSING *(in part)*

T.-y.L. Tien-yi Li. *Mershon Professor of Chinese Literature and History, Ohio State University, Columbus. Editor of* Readings in Contemporary Chinese Literature; Chinese Historical Literature.
CHINESE LITERATURE *(in part)*

T.Z. Tayar Zavalani (deceased). *Program Assistant, Albanian Section, British Broadcasting Corporation, London.*
ALBANIA *(in part)*

U.A.U. Urho A. Uotila. *Professor and Chairman, Department of Geodetic Science and Surveying, Ohio State University, Columbus.*
EARTH, THE *(in part)*

U.B. Ugo Bianchi. *Professor of the History of Religions, University of Rome. Author of* Il dualismo religioso; *editor of* The Origins of Gnosticism.
RELIGIONS AND SPIRITUAL BELIEF, SYSTEMS OF *(in part)*

U.Ba. Umberto Baldini. *Art historian. Superintendent Director, Central Institute for the Restoration of Works of Art, Rome. Author of* Il Rinascimento nell' Italia centrale *and others.*
MASACCIO *(in part)* (Micropædia)

U.Be. Ulli Beier. *Former Director, Museum of Contemporary Art in the Third World, University of Bayreuth, West Germany. Research Professor and Director, Institute of African Studies, University of Ife, Ile-Ife, Nigeria, 1971–74. Founder of* Black Orpheus. *Author of* African Poetry *and others; editor of* Introduction to African Literature.
AFRICAN ARTS *(in part)*

U.M. Umberto Marcelli. *Lecturer in History, University of Bologna, Italy.*

Author of Cavour diplomatico.
CAVOUR, CAMILLO BENSO, CONTE DI *(Micropædia)*

U.M.D. Ulrich M. Drobnig. *Director, Max Planck Institute for Foreign Private and Private International Law, Hamburg. Author of* American-German Private International Law.
BUSINESS LAW *(in part)*

U.P.B. Ulick Peter Burke. *Lecturer in History, University of Cambridge; Fellow of Emmanuel College, Cambridge. Author of* The Renaissance Sense of the Past *and others.*
VALLA, LORENZO *(Micropædia)*

U.P.S. Umakant Premanand Shah. *Former Deputy Director, Oriental Institute, Maharaja Sayajirao University of Baroda, India. Author of* Studies in Jaina Art: Akota Bronzes.
JAINISM
MAHĀVĪRA *(in part)* *(Micropædia)*

V.A. Vernon Ahmadjian. *Professor of Botany, Clark University, Worcester, Massachusetts. Author of* The Lichen Symbiosis; *coeditor of* The Lichens.
PROTOPHYTES *(in part)*

Va.K. Valdimar Kristinsson. *Editor, Fjarmalatidindi (Financial Times), Central Bank of Iceland, Reykjavík.*
ICELAND *(in part)*

V.Al. Victor Alba. *Emeritus Professor of Political Science, Kent State University, Ohio. Author of* The Mexicans *and others.*
ZAPATA, EMILIANO *(Micropædia)*

V.A.U. Victor Andrade U. *Former Minister of Foreign Affairs of Bolivia. Ambassador of Bolivia to the U.S., 1944–46; 1952–58. Author of* Problemas sociales de Bolivia *and others.*
BOLIVIA *(in part)*

V.B. Victor Barna (d. 1972). *World table tennis champion, men's singles, 1930, 1932–35; men's doubles, 1929–35; mixed doubles, 1932, 1935. Author of* Table Tennis Today.
TABLE TENNIS *(in part)* *(Micropædia)*

V.Ba. Vladimir Bakarić (d. 1983). *Member, Council of the Federation, Socialist Federal Republic of Yugoslavia. Vice President of Yugoslavia, 1975–76. Prime Minister of the Socialist Republic of Croatia, 1953–63. Author of* Aktuelní problemi sadašnje etape revolucije.
YUGOSLAVIA *(in part)*

V.Bi. Victor J.P. Biel. *Attorney at Law, Luxembourg. Author of numerous articles on law.*
LOW COUNTRIES, THE *(in part)*

V.Br. Vincent Brome. *Biographer, novelist, playwright, and essayist. Author of* Freud and His Early Circle *and others.*
FREUD

V.B.W. Sir Vincent Brian Wigglesworth. *Emeritus Professor of Biology, University of Cambridge;*

Director, Agricultural Research Council Unit of Insect Physiology, 1943–67. Author of The Principles of Insect Physiology; The Life of Insects.
INSECTS *(in part)*

V.B.Z. Viktor Borisovich Zhmuida. *Head, Central Asian Section, Council for Research on Productive Forces, U.S.S.R. Planning Commission, Moscow. Author of numerous publications on Turkmen S.S.R.*
UNION OF SOVIET SOCIALIST REPUBLICS *(in part)*

V.C. Vincent Cronin. *Free-lance writer. Author of* The Flowering of the Renaissance *and others.*
SARPI, PAOLO *(Micropædia)*

V.Ca. Vernon Carstensen. *Emeritus Professor of History, University of Washington, Seattle.*
UNITED STATES OF AMERICA *(in part)*

V.C.F. Victor C. Falkenheim *Chairman, Department of East Asian Studies, University of Toronto. Editor of and contributor to* Citizens and Groups in Chinese Politics.
CHINA *(in part)*

V.D. Vilmos Diószegi (d. 1971). *Research Fellow, Hungarian Academy of Sciences, Budapest. Author of* Tracing Shamans in Siberia; *editor of* Popular Beliefs and Folklore Tradition in Siberia.
SACRED OFFICES AND ORDERS *(in part)*

V.D.B. Vasili Dmitrievitch Bykov. *Professor of Geography, Moscow M.V. Lomonosov State University. Author of* Hydrology *and others.*
HYDROSPHERE, THE *(in part)*

V.E.I. Verity Elizabeth Irvine. *Writer and researcher.*
ARABIA *(in part)*
SYRIA *(in part)*

V.E.McK. Vincent E. McKelvey. *Director, Geological Survey, U.S. Department of the Interior, Reston, Virginia, 1971–78; Senior Research Geologist, 1978–81. An authority on mineral deposits and energy needs of the United States.*
MINERALS AND ROCKS *(in part)*

V.F.K. Viktor Filipovich Kanayev. *Senior Scientist, Moscow M.V. Lomonosov State University. Coauthor of* Principal Features of the Structure of the Bottom of the Northeastern Part of the Indian Ocean.
OCEANS *(in part)*

V.F.Ko. Vladimir Fyodorovich Kosov. *Head, Kazakhstan Section, Scientific Council on the Location of U.S.S.R. Productive Forces, Academy of Sciences of the U.S.S.R., Moscow; Candidate of Sciences (Geography). Coauthor of* Development of National Economy of the U.S.S.R. Eastern Regions.
UNION OF SOVIET SOCIALIST REPUBLICS *(in part)*

V.G. Viktor Gutmann. *Professor of Inorganic Chemistry, Technical*

University of Vienna. Author of Halogen Chemistry *and others.*

CHEMICAL ELEMENTS (*in part*)

V.G.N.   Viktor Grigoryevich Neyman. *Senior Scientist, Institute of Oceanology, Academy of Sciences of the U.S.S.R., Moscow; Candidate of Sciences (Geography). Author of several articles on oceanology.*

OCEANS (*in part*)

V.G.S.   Victor G. Szebehely. *Professor of Aerospace Engineering, University of Texas at Austin. Coeditor of* Methods in Astrodynamics and Celestial Mechanics.

MECHANICS (*in part*)

V.I.S.   Victor Ilyich Seroff (d. 1979). *Writer. Author of* Rachmaninoff.

RACHMANINOFF, SERGEY (Micropædia)

V.J.C.   Valentine J. Chapman (deceased). *Professor of Botany, University of Auckland, New Zealand. Author of* The Algae *and others.*

PROTOPHYTES (*in part*)

V.J.M.   Vytautas J. Mažiulis. *Professor of Baltic Languages, Vilnius V. Kapsukas State University, Lithuanian S.S.R.*

LANGUAGES OF THE WORLD (*in part*)

V.J.P.   V.J. Parry (d. 1974). *Reader in the History of the Near and Middle East, School of Oriental and African Studies, University of London. Contributor to* The New Cambridge Modern History; Encyclopædia of Islam.

BAYEZID II (Micropædia)
SÜLEYMAN I (Micropædia)

V.J.T.   Vello Julius Tarmisto. *Head of Section, Institute of Economics, Estonian S.S.R. Academy of Sciences, Tallinn. Coauthor of* Estonian S.S.R.

UNION OF SOVIET SOCIALIST REPUBLICS (*in part*)

V.K.   Viola Klein (d. 1973). *Reader in Sociology, University of Reading, England, 1971–73. Coauthor of* Women's Two Roles: At Home and Work *and others.*

SOCIAL DIFFERENTIATION (*in part*)

V.Ka.   Vytautas Kavolis. *Charles A. Dana Professor of Comparative Civilizations and Professor of Sociology, Dickinson College, Carlisle, Pennsylvania. Author of* Artistic Expression: A Sociological Analysis; History on Art's Side: Social Dynamics in Artistic Efflorescences.

ARTS, PRACTICE AND PROFESSION OF THE (*in part*)

V.Lo.   Victor Lowe. *Emeritus Professor of Philosophy, Johns Hopkins University, Baltimore. Author of* Understanding Whitehead; The Life of Alfred North Whitehead.

WHITEHEAD, ALFRED NORTH (Micropædia)

V.L.S.   Victor L. Streeter. *Emeritus Professor of Civil Engineering, University of Michigan, Ann Arbor. Author of* Fluid Mechanics.

MECHANICS (*in part*)

V.L.S.P.R.   Vaddiparti Lova Surya Prakasa Rao. *Senior Fellow, Centre for Economic and Social Studies, Hyderabad, India.*

DELHI (*in part*)

V.L.T.   Victor-Lucien Tapié (d. 1974). *Member, Academy of Moral and Political Sciences, Institute of France, Paris, 1963–74. Professor of Modern History, University of Paris IV, 1949–70. Author of* La France de Louis XIII et de Richelieu *and others.*

COLBERT, JEAN-BAPTISTE (Micropædia)

V.M.   Valerio Mariani (deceased). *Professor of the History of Art, University of Naples. Author of* Pittori protagonisti della crisi del quattrocento; Giotto.

LIPPI, FRA FILIPPO (Micropædia)

V.M.S.   Vasily Mikhaylovich Sinitsyn. *Head, Laboratory of Paleography; Dean, Department of Geology, Leningrad A.A. Zhdanov State University.*

ASIA (*in part*)

V.M.St.   Valery Mikhailovich Strygin. *Head of Section, Geographical Books, Mysl Publishing House, Moscow. Author of numerous papers on the geography of the Soviet Union.*

UNION OF SOVIET SOCIALIST REPUBLICS (*in part*)

V.M.W.   Vera Muriel White. *Extramural Lecturer, University of Cambridge.*

PITT, WILLIAM, THE ELDER (Micropædia)

V.N.   Victor Nachtergaele. *Professor of French Literature, Catholic University of Louvain, Belgium.*

BELGIAN LITERATURE (*in part*)

V.N.D.   Vladimir Nikolaevich Dunaev. *Correspondent, Novosti Press Agency, Moscow. Author of numerous papers on administrative and social conditions in the Soviet Union.*

UNION OF SOVIET SOCIALIST REPUBLICS (*in part*)

V.N.K.   Victor Nikolaevich Kondratiev. *Assistant Director, Institute of Chemical Physics; Member, Academy of Sciences of the U.S.S.R., Moscow. Author of* Chemical Kinetics of Gas Reactions.

CHEMICAL REACTIONS (*in part*)

V.P.G.   Vladimir Petrovich Goncharov. *Head, Geology of the Southern Seas Laboratory, Southern Division, Institute of Oceanography, Academy of Sciences of the U.S.S.R., Gelendzhik. Coauthor of* Geomorphology of the Bottom and Tectonic Problems in the Black Sea.

EUROPE (*in part*)

V.P.P.   Victor P. Petrov. *Professor of Geography, California State University, Los Angeles, 1970–74, Author of* China: Emerging World Power *and others.*

AFGHANISTAN (*in part*)

V.P.U.   Vernon Philip Underwood. *Former Professor of French, University College, University of London. Author of* Verlaine et l'Angleterre; *editor of* Verlaine's Carnet personnel *and others.*

VERLAINE, PAUL (Micropædia)

V.P.Z.   Vsevolod Pavlovich Zenkovich. *Former Head of Shore Department, Institute of Oceanology, Academy of Sciences of the U.S.S.R., Moscow. An authority on near-shore oceanography and attendant physical processes.*

CONTINENTAL LANDFORMS (*in part*)
OCEANS (*in part*)

V.R.F.   Vernon R. Fryburger, Jr. *Professor of Advertising and Marketing; Chairman, Department of Advertising, Northwestern University, Evanston, Illinois. Coauthor of* Advertising Theory and Practice.

MARKETING AND MERCHANDISING (*in part*)

V.R.L.   Val R. Lorwin (d. 1982). *Professor of History, University of Oregon, Eugene, 1958–75.*

UNITED NATIONS (*in part*)

V.R.P.   V.R. Pillai. *Member, Kerala State Planning Board. Former Professor of Economics, University of Kerala, India. Coauthor of* Land Reclamation in Kerala *and others.*

INDIA (*in part*)

V.S.   Vera Sanford (deceased). *Professor of Mathematics, State University of New York College at Oneonta, 1943–59.*

MATHEMATICS, THE HISTORY OF (*in part*)

V.S.C.   Vasile S. Cucu. *Professor of Geography, University of Bucharest. Author of* Geografia României.

ROMANIA (*in part*)

V.S.M.   V. Standish Mallory. *Professor of Geological Sciences; Curator of Invertebrate Paleontology and Chairman, Geology and Paleontology Division, Burke Washington State Museum, University of Washington, Seattle.*

GEOCHRONOLOGY (*in part*)

V.T.C.   Ven Te Chow (d. 1981). *Professor of Civil and Hydrosystems Engineering, University of Illinois, Urbana. Editor in Chief and contributor to* Handbook of Applied Hydrology.

HYDROSPHERE, THE (*in part*)

V.T.P.   Vladimir T. Pashuto. *Corresponding member, Academy of Sciences of the U.S.S.R., Moscow. Author of* Vneshnyaya politika drevney Rusi *and others.*

ALGIRDAS (Micropædia)

V.U.   Valev Uibopuu. *Novelist. Editor, Estonian Writers' Co-operative, Lund, Sweden. Author of* Keegi ei kuule meid.

ESTONIAN LITERATURE (Micropædia)

V.V.I.   Vyacheslav Vsevolodovich Ivanov. *Head, Department of Structural Typology, Institute of Slavonic and Balkan Studies, Academy of Sciences of the U.S.S.R., Moscow.*

LANGUAGES OF THE WORLD (*in part*)

V.V.P.   Vladimir V. Pokhshishevsky. *Staff member, Institute of Ethnography,*

Academy of Sciences of the U.S.S.R., Moscow.

UNION OF SOVIET SOCIALIST REPUBLICS (*in part*)

V.V.Z.   Vladimir Viktorovich Zhdanov. *Literary critic. Assistant to the Chief Editor,* Kratkaya Literaturnaya Entsiklopediya, *Moscow. Author of* M. Yu. Lermontov *and other works on Russian writers.*

LERMONTOV, MIKHAIL (Micropædia)

V.W.v.H.   Victor Wolfgang von Hagen. *Director, Roman Road Expeditions in Europe and North Africa, 1961–70. Director, Inca Highway Expedition to Peru, Bolivia, and Ecuador, 1953–55. Author of* Realm of the Incas *and others; editor of* The Incas.

PRE-COLUMBIAN CIVILIZATIONS (*in part*)

V.Z.   Vice Zaninović. *Professor of Serbian Literature, University of Zagreb, Yugoslavia. Author of* August Cesarec, Life and Work.

YUGOSLAV LITERATURE (*in part*)

W.A.   Warren Andrew, M.D. (d. 1982). *Professor of Anatomy, Indiana University, Indianapolis, 1958–82. Author of* Textbook of Comparative Histology.

SUPPORTIVE AND CONNECTIVE TISSUES (*in part*)

Wa.B.   Walter Blair. *Emeritus Professor of English, University of Chicago. Author of* Mark Twain and "Huck Finn"; *coauthor of* America's Humor; Poor Richard to Doonesbury.

AMERICAN LITERATURE (*in part*)

W.A.B.   Warren A. Beck. *Professor of History, California State University, Fullerton. Author of* New Mexico: A History of Four Centuries; An Historical Atlas of New Mexico.

UNITED STATES OF AMERICA (*in part*)

Wa.E.M.   Wayne E. Manning. *Emeritus Professor of Botany, Bucknell University, Lewisburg, Pennsylvania. Author of numerous articles on the walnut family.*

ANGIOSPERMS (*in part*)

W.A.H.   Walter A. Harrison. *Professor of Applied Physics, Stanford University, California, Author of* Pseudopotentials in the Theory of Metals.

MATTER (*in part*)

W.A.Ha.   Willard A. Hanna. *Senior Associate, Universities Field Staff International, Hanover, New Hampshire. Author of* Bung Karno's Indonesia.

SUKARNO (Micropædia)

Wa.K.   Walter Kolneder. *Professor of Music, University of Karlsruhe, West Germany. Author of* Antonio Vivaldi *and others.*

VIVALDI, ANTONIO (Micropædia)

W.A.K.   Walid Ahmed Khalidi. *Professor of Political Studies and Public Administration, American University of Beirut.*

PALESTINE (*in part*)

W.Am.   Winslow Ames. *Associate Professor of Art, University of Rhode Island, Kingston, 1966–75. Curator, Gallery of Modern Art, New York City, 1957–61. Author of* Great Drawings of All Time, *vol. 1,* Italian Drawings *and others.*

CARICATURE, CARTOON, AND COMIC STRIP (*in part*)

Wa.M.   Wang Mingye. *Professor of Geomorphology, Ch'eng-tu Institute of Geography, Chinese Academy of Sciences. Author of* The Mountains in China *and others.*

CHUNGKING (*in part*)

W.A.N.   William Anderson Newman. *Professor of Biological Oceanography, Scripps Institution of Oceanography, University of California, San Diego. Coauthor of* "Cirripedia" in Treatise on Invertebrate Paleontology *and in* Antarctic Research Series.

CRUSTACEANS (*in part*)

W.A.P.   The Rev. William Arthur Purdy. *Secretary for Anglican and Methodist Relations, Secretariat for Promoting Christian Unity, Vatican. Author of* The Church on the Move: The Characters and Policies of Pius XII and John XXIII.

PIUS XII (Micropædia)

W.A.Po.   William A. Poucher. *Chief Perfumer, Yardley and Company, Ltd., London, 1929–59.*

DRESS AND ADORNMENT (*in part*)

Wa.R.   Walpola Rāhula. *Supervisor, University of Oxford. Chancellor, University of Kelaniya, Sri Lanka. Author of* What the Buddha Taught *and others.*

BUDDHISM, THE BUDDHA AND (*in part*)

W.A.R.   William Alexander Robson (d. 1980). *Professor of Public Administration, University of London, 1947–62. Author of* Justice and Administrative Law; *coauthor of* Great Cities of the World: Their Government, Politics and Planning.

CITIES (*in part*)

PUBLIC ADMINISTRATION (*in part*)

W.A.Ri.   William Andrew Ringler, Jr. *Emeritus Professor of English, University of Chicago. Senior Research Associate, Huntington Library, San Marino, California. Editor of* The Poems of Sir Philip Sidney.

SIDNEY, SIR PHILIP. (Micropædia)

W.A.S.   W.A. Swanberg. *Free-lance writer. Author of* Dreiser *and others.*

DREISER, THEODORE (Micropædia)

W.A.T.   Wilfred Asquith Townsley. *Chairman, Tasmanian Consumer Affairs Council. Professor of Political Science, University of Tasmania, Hobart, Australia, 1956–75.*

AUSTRALIA (*in part*)

W.A.W.   Warid A. Warid. *Former Professor of Agriculture, University of*

Al Fateh, Tripoli, Libya. Coauthor of Vegetable Production.

FARMING AND AGRICULTURAL TECHNOLOGY (*in part*)

W.B.B.   William B. Bean, M.D. *Sir William Osler Professor Emeritus of Medicine, University of Iowa, Iowa City. Editor in Chief,* Archives of Internal Medicine, *1962–67. Author of* Rare Diseases and Lesions: Their Contributions to Clinical Medicine.

DIAGNOSIS AND THERAPEUTICS (*in part*)

W.B.F.   W. Beall Fowler. *Professor of Physics, Lehigh University, Bethlehem, Pennsylvania.*

MATTER (*in part*)

W.B.Fi.   William B. Fisher (d. 1984). *Principal, Graduate Society, 1965–81; Professor of Geography, University of Durham, England, 1956–81. Author of* The Middle East; *editor of* Cambridge History of Iran, *vol. 1.*

AFRICA (*in part*)

IRAQ (*in part*)

W.B.F.R.   William B.F. Ryan. *Senior Research Scientist, Lamont-Doherty Geological Observatory, Columbia University.*

ASIA (*in part*)

W.Bi.   Walter Biemel. *Emeritus Professor of Philosophy, State Academy of Art of Düsseldorf, West Germany.*

PHILOSOPHICAL SCHOOLS AND DOCTRINES, WESTERN (*in part*)

W.B.K.   W. Barclay Kamb. *Professor of Geology and Geophysics, California Institute of Technology, Pasadena. A leading authority on the properties of Earth materials, including ice.*

MINERALS AND ROCKS (*in part*)

W.Bl.   Warren Blanding. *Chief Operating Executive, Marketing Publications Inc. Silver Spring, Maryland. Author of* Profit Opportunities in Physical Distribution *and others.*

HANDLING, PACKAGING, AND STORAGE (*in part*)

W.B.McM.   William B. McMahon. *Law enforcement and privacy consultant. Coeditor of* Law Enforcement Science and Technology III.

POLICE (*in part*)

W.B.N.B.   William B.N. Berry. *Professor of Paleontology, University of California, Berkeley. Author of* Growth of a Prehistoric Time Scale.

HUTTON, JAMES (Micropædia)

W.B.T.   William Bertram Turrill (d. 1961). *Keeper, Herbarium and Library, Royal Botanic Gardens, Kew, England, 1946–57. Author of* Plant Life of the Balkan Peninsula *and others.*

BALKANS (*in part*)

W.Bu.   William Burrows (d. 1978). *Professor of Microbiology, University of Chicago, 1947–73. Author of* Textbook of Microbiology.

DISEASE (*in part*)

W.B.W. Wilse B. Webb. *Graduate Research Professor of Psychology, University of Florida, Gainesville. Author of* Sleep: An Experimental Analysis.

SLEEP AND DREAMS (*in part*)

W.C. Warren Cowgill (d. 1985). *Professor of Indo-European Linguistics, Yale University, 1972–85. Author of several articles on Indo-European languages.*

LANGUAGES OF THE WORLD (*in part*)

W.C.A. William C. Atkinson. *Professor of Hispanic Studies, University of Glasgow, 1932–72; Director, Institute of Latin-American Studies, 1966–72. Author of* A History of Spain and Portugal; *translator of Camões'* The Lusiads.

PORTUGUESE LITERATURE (*in part*)
SPANISH LITERATURE (*in part*)

W.C.B. William Charles Brice. *Emeritus Professor of Geography, Victoria University of Manchester.*

BALKANS (*in part*)
NORTH AFRICA (*in part*)
PALESTINE (*in part*)
UNION OF SOVIET SOCIALIST REPUBLICS (*in part*)

W.C.Be. Wendell Clark Bennett (d. 1953). *Professor of Anthropology, Yale University, 1945–53.*

SOUTH AMERICA (*in part*)

W.C.Da. William C. Davis, Jr. *Firearms consultant. Former Chief, Small-Caliber-Ammunition Engineering Laboratory, U.S. Army, Frankford Arsenal, Philadelphia.*

WAR, THE TECHNOLOGY OF (*in part*)

W.C.Di. William C. Dilger. *Associate Professor of Ethology, Cornell University, Ithaca, New York. Author of* Psychobiology; 39 Steps to Biology; *and others.*

BEHAVIOUR, ANIMAL (*in part*)

W.C.F. Warren Curtis Freihofer. *Field Associate, Department of Ichthyology, California Academy of Sciences, San Francisco. Author of research papers on the anatomy and systematics of fishes.*

FISHES (*in part*)

W.C.H. Walther C. Hubatsch. *Professor of Medieval and Modern History, Rhenish Friedrich Wilhelm University of Bonn. Author of* Die Ära Tirpitz *and others.*

TIRPITZ, ALFRED VON (Micropædia)

W.C.McC. W. Cheyne McCallum. *Senior Research Fellow in Psychology, Burden Neurological Institute and University of Bristol, England. Coeditor of* The Responsive Brain.

ATTENTION

W.Cr. William Cruse. *Technical Consultant, Uris Theatre Complex, New York City, and New Orleans Cultural Center. Former Supervisor of Scenic Services, American Broadcasting Company, New York City. Former Technical Director, Ahmandson Theatre, Los Angeles.*

THEATRICAL PRODUCTION (*in part*)

W.C.S. William Cofield Summers, M.D. *Professor of Therapeutic Radiology, Molecular Biophysics and Biochemistry, and Human Genetics, Yale University.*

VIRUSES

W.C.Se. William C. Seitz (d. 1974). *George R. Kenan, Jr., Professor of the History of Art, University of Virginia, Charlottesville, 1971–74. Author of* Claude Monet.

MONET, CLAUDE (*in part*) (Micropædia)

W.C.St. William Campbell Steere. *Emeritus Professor of Botany, Columbia University. Emeritus President, New York Botanical Garden, Bronx. Editor of* Fifty Years of Botany.

BIOLOGICAL SCIENCES, THE (*in part*)

W.Cu. William Culican (d. 1984). *Reader in History, University of Melbourne, 1972–84. Author of* The Medes and Persians *and others.*

ARCHITECTURE, THE HISTORY OF WESTERN (*in part*)
HANNIBAL (Micropædia)
KHOSROW II (Micropædia)
PAINTING, THE HISTORY OF WESTERN (*in part*)
SCULPTURE, THE HISTORY OF WESTERN (*in part*)

W.D. Wilma Dykeman. *Free-lance writer. Author of* Seeds of Southern Change; *coauthor of* The Border States *and others.*

NORTH AMERICA (*in part*)
UNITED STATES OF AMERICA (*in part*)

W.D.B. Wayne D. Bray. *Attorney. Author of* The Common Law Zone in Panama; *compiler of* The Controversy Over a New Canal Treaty Between the United States and Panama.

CENTRAL AMERICA (*in part*)

W.De. Wilfrid Desan. *Emeritus Professor of Philosophy, Georgetown University, Washington, D.C. Author of* The Tragic Finale; The Marxism of Jean-Paul Sartre; *and others.*

SARTRE, JEAN-PAUL (Micropædia)

W.D.H. William Driver Howarth. *Professor of French, University of Bristol, England. Author of* Sublime and Grotesque: A Study of French Romantic Drama *and others.*

FRENCH LITERATURE (*in part*)

W.D.P. W. Douglas Piercey, M.D. (d. 1972). *Associate Professor of Hospital Administration, University of Toronto, 1954–65. Executive Director, Canadian Hospital Association, Toronto; Editor, The Canadian Hospital Journal, 1954–65.*

MEDICINE (*in part*)

W.D.R. Wayne D. Rasmussen. *Historian, Agricultural History Branch, Economic Research Service, U.S. Department of Agriculture, Washington, D.C., 1940–86. Editor of* Agriculture in the United States: A Documentary History.

AGRICULTURE, THE HISTORY OF (*in part*)

W.E. William Epstein. *Professor of Psychology, University of Wisconsin, Madison. Author of* Varieties of Perceptual Learning.

PERCEPTION, HUMAN (*in part*)

W.E.A. Walter E. Allen. *Professor of English Studies, New University of Ulster, Coleraine, Northern Ireland, 1968–73. Author of* The English Novel *and others.*

CONRAD, JOSEPH (*in part*) (Micropædia)
FIELDING, HENRY (Micropædia)
SMOLLETT, TOBIAS (Micropædia)

W.E.D. William E. Duellman. *Curator, Division of Herpetology, Museum of Natural History; Professor of Systematics and Ecology, University of Kansas, Lawrence. Researcher on the biology and systematics of frogs, with particular emphasis on the New World tropics. Author of* The Hylid Frogs of Middle America.

AMPHIBIANS (*in part*)

W.E.K. Walter Emil Kaegi, Jr. *Professor of Byzantine and Roman History, University of Chicago. Author of* Byzantine Military Unrest *and others.*

LEO III (BYZANTINE EMPIRE) (Micropædia)

W.Em. Walter Emery (d. 1974). *Director, Novello and Company Ltd., London. Specialist on the work of Bach. Author of* Bach's Ornaments.

BACH (*in part*)

W.E.M. William Edward May. *Commander, Royal Navy. Deputy Director, National Maritime Museum, Greenwich, England, 1951–68. Naval Assistant to the Director, Compass Department, Admiralty, 1929–51. Author of* Compass Adjustment.

NAVIGATION (*in part*)

W.E.Mo. W.E. Mosse. *Emeritus Professor of European History, University of East Anglia, Norwich, England. Author of* Alexander II and the Modernization of Russia *and others.*

ALEXANDER II (RUSSIA) (Micropædia)

W.E.P. Warren E. Preece. *Member, Board of Editors,* Encyclopædia Britannica, *Chicago; Vice Chairman, 1975–79; The Editor, 1964–75. Coauthor of* The Technological Order.

ENCYCLOPAEDIAS AND DICTIONARIES (*in part*)
PRINTING, TYPOGRAPHY, AND PHOTOENGRAVING (*in part*)

W.Er. Walter Erben (d. 1981). *Professor of Art Education, College of Education of the Ruhr, Dortmund, West Germany. Author of* Joan Miró; Chagall; *and others.*

MIRÓ, JOAN (*in part*) (Micropædia)

W.E.S. William Edward Stubbs. *Assistant Judge Advocate General, Office of the Judge Advocate General of the British Forces in Germany, London.*

WAR, THE THEORY AND CONDUCT OF
(*in part*)

W.E.T. William E. Thomson.
*Composer. Director, School of Music,
University of Southern California,
Los Angeles. Author of* Materials and
Structure of Music; Introduction to
Music as Structure.
MUSIC, THE ART OF (*in part*)

W.E.V. W. Edgar Vinacke. *Professor
of Psychology, State University of
New York at Buffalo. Author of* The
Psychology of Thinking.
THOUGHT AND THOUGHT PROCESSES
(*in part*)

W.F. Wallace Fowlie. *James B. Duke
Professor of French Literature, Duke
University, Durham, North Carolina.
Author of* Jean Cocteau; Stendhal;
A Guide to Contemporary French
Literature; Age of Surrealism.
COCTEAU, JEAN (Micropædia)
STENDHAL (Micropædia)

W.F.A. William Foxwell Albright (d.
1971). *Professor of Semitic Languages,
Johns Hopkins University, Baltimore,
Maryland, 1929–58. Author of*
Archæology of Palestine; From the Stone
Age to Christianity.
PALESTINE (*in part*)
PREHISTORIC PEOPLES AND CULTURES
(*in part*)

W.F.F. William F. Fratcher. *R.B. Price
Distinguished Professor Emeritus of
Law, University of Missouri, Columbia.
Author of* Perpetuities and Other
Restraints.
PROPERTY LAW (*in part*)

W.F.G. William F. Ganong, M.D.
*Lange Professor and Chairman,
Department of Physiology, University
of California, San Francisco. Author of*
Review of Medical Physiology; *coeditor
of* Frontiers in Neuroendocrinology.
ENDOCRINE SYSTEMS (*in part*)

W.F.K. William F. Kieffer. *Emeritus
Professor of Chemistry, Wooster College,
Ohio. Author of* The Mole Concept in
Chemistry; Chemistry Today; *and others.*
CHEMICAL COMPOUNDS (*in part*)

W.F.Kn. Wilfrid F. Knapp. *Dean,
Fellow, and Tutor in Politics, St.
Catherine's College, Oxford; Lecturer in
Politics, University of Oxford. Author of*
A History of War and Peace, 1939–65.
HITLER (*in part*)

W.Ft. Wesley Frost (d. 1968). *U.S.
Ambassador to Paraguay, 1942–44.*
SOUTH AMERICA (*in part*)

W.F.V. Walter F. Vella (d. 1984).
*Professor of History, University of
Hawaii, Honolulu. Author of* Siam under
Rama III, 1824–1851; A History of
Modern Thailand; *and others.*
SOUTHEAST ASIA, MAINLAND (*in part*)

W.F.W. Warren F. Walker, Jr.
*Professor of Biology, Oberlin College,
Ohio. Author of* Vertebrate Dissection.
MUSCLES AND MUSCLE SYSTEMS (*in part*)

W.F.Wh. William Foote Whyte.
*Emeritus Professor of Industrial and
Labour Relations, Cornell University,
Ithaca, New York. Author of*
Organizational Behavior: Theory and
Application *and others.*
WORK AND EMPLOYMENT (*in part*)

W. Ga. William Gaunt (d. 1980). *Art
historian. Special correspondent on art
subjects,* The Times, *London. Author
of* The Pre-Raphaelite Tragedy; The
Aesthetic Adventure.
ROSSETTI, CHRISTINA (Micropædia)
ROSSETTI, DANTE GABRIEL (Micropædia)
ROSSETTI, GABRIELE (Micropædia)
ROSSETTI, WILLIAM MICHAEL
(Micropædia)

W.G.A. W. Geoffrey Arnott. *Professor
of Greek Language and Literature,
University of Leeds, England.*
TERENCE (Micropædia)

W.G.B. Walter G. Bergmann. *Former
Editor, Schott and Co. Ltd., Music
Publishers, London. Author of several
articles on Telemann.*
TELEMANN, GEORG PHILIPP
(Micropædia)

W.G.C. William G. Constable (d.
1976). *Curator of Paintings, Boston
Museum of Fine Arts, 1938–57. Author
of* Canaletto: Giovanni Antonio Canal,
1697–1768.
CANALETTO (Micropædia)

W.G.E. W. Gordon East. *Emeritus
Professor of Geography, Birkbeck
College, University of London. Author of*
An Historical Geography of Europe.
EUROPE (*in part*)

W.G.Fi. Wolfgang G. Fischer. *Former
Director, Landesbibliothek, Oldenburg,
West Germany.*
GERMANY (*in part*)

W.G.I. W. Grant Inglis. *Director
General of Education for South
Australia, Adelaide. Author of "Patterns
of Evolution in Parasitic Nematodes" in*
Evolution of Parasites.
ASCHELMINTHS

W.G.J. Walton Glyn Jones. *Professor
of Scandinavian Studies, University of
Newcastle upon Tyne, England. Author
of* Denmark; Tove Jansson; *and others.*
SCANDINAVIAN LITERATURE (*in part*)

W.G.M. William George Mokray (d.
1974). *Editor and Publisher,* Basketball's
Best. *Writer for* Converse Basketball
Yearbook. *U.S. correspondent on
basketball for European publications.
Elected to the Basketball Hall of
Fame, 1965.*
SPORTS, MAJOR TEAM AND INDIVIDUAL
(*in part*)

W.G.Mo. Will G. Moore (d. 1978).
*Reader in French Literature, University
of Oxford. Author of* La Rochefoucauld:
His Mind and Art *and others.*
LA ROCHEFOUCAULD, FRANÇOIS VI,
DUC DE (Micropædia)
MOLIÈRE (*in part*)

W.Go. Walter Otto Julius Görlitz.
Journalist; Editorial Staff, Die Welt,
Hamburg. Author of History of the
German General Staff, 1657–1945.
LUDENDORFF, ERICH (Micropædia)
ROMMEL, ERWIN (Micropædia)

W.G.O. Willard Gurdon Oxtoby.
*Professor of Religious Studies; Director,
Centre for Religious Studies, University
of Toronto. Author of* Some Inscriptions
of the Safaitic Bedouin.
MIDDLE EASTERN RELIGIONS, ANCIENT
(*in part*)

W.G.Pr. W.G. Prout. *Consultant
Surgeon, Portsmouth Group Hospitals,
England.*
CIRCULATION AND CIRCULATORY
SYSTEMS (*in part*)

W.Gr. Werner Gross. *Professor,
Gustav Embden Centre of Biological
Chemistry, Johann Wolfgang Goethe
University of Frankfurt. Author
of* Transport Through Biological
Membranes.
CELLS (*in part*)

W.G.So. Wilhelm G. Solheim II.
*Professor of Anthropology, University
of Hawaii, Honolulu. Author of* The
Archaeology of Central Philippines.
EAST INDIES, THE (*in part*)

W.G.St. William Glenn Steiner.
*Professor of Psychology, Bradley
University, Peoria, Illinois.*
ALCOHOL AND DRUG CONSUMPTION
(*in part*)

W.G.U. William G. Urry (d.
1981). *Reader in Medieval Western
Paleography, University of Oxford;
Fellow of St. Edmund Hall, Oxford,
1969–81.*
HISTORY, THE STUDY OF (*in part*)

W.H. Wolfgang Helck. *Professor of
Egyptology, University of Hamburg.
Author of* Manetho und die ägyptischen
Königslisten *and others.*
HISTORY, THE STUDY OF
(*in part*)

W.Ha. Walter Harrelson.
*Distinguished Professor of Old
Testament, Vanderbilt University,
Nashville, Tennessee. Author of* From
Fertility Cult to Worship *and others.*
RITES AND CEREMONIES, SACRED
(*in part*)

W.H.B. William H. Baumer. *Major
General (retired), U.S. Army Reserve.
President, International General
Industries, Inc., Washington, D.C.,
1963–72. Coauthor of* The Little Wars of
the United States.
WAR, THE TECHNOLOGY OF (*in part*)

W.H.Br. Walter Henry Breen. *Former
Coeditor,* Standard Catalogue of United
States Coins. *Author of* Walter Breen's
Encyclopedia of U.S. and Colonial Proof
Coins, 1722–1977 *and others.*
COINS AND COINAGE (*in part*)

W.H.C. Walter Houston Clark.
Professor of the Psychology of Religion,

Andover Newton Theological School, Newton Centre, Massachusetts, 1962–67. Author of Chemical Ecstasy: Psychedelic Drugs and Religion.

ALCOHOL AND DRUG CONSUMPTION (*in part*)

W.H.C.F.   William Hugh Clifford Frend. *Professor of Ecclesiastical History, University of Glasgow. Author of* Martyrdom and Persecution in the Early Church *and others.*

CYPRIAN, SAINT (Micropædia)

W.H.D.   William Henry Dawbin. *Former Reader in Biology, University of Sydney, Australia. Author of papers on tuataras.*

REPTILES (*in part*)

W.He.   Walter Heinemeyer. *Professor of Medieval History, Philipps University of Marburg, West Germany. Coeditor of* Politisches Archiv des Landgrafen Philipps.

PHILIPP (HESSE) (Micropædia)

W.H.G.   W. Horsley Gantt, M.D. (d. 1980). *Associate Professor of Psychiatry, 1932–58; Director, Pavlovian Laboratory, School of Medicine, Johns Hopkins University, Baltimore. Senior Scientist, Pavlovian Laboratory, Veterans Administration Hospital, Perry Point, Maryland.*

PAVLOV, IVAN PETROVICH (Micropædia)

W.H.G.A.   Walter Harry Green Armytage. *Emeritus Professor of Education, University of Sheffield, England. Author of* A Social History of Engineering.

EADS, JAMES BUCHANAN (Micropædia)
EVANS, OLIVER (Micropædia)

W.H.I.   William Harold Ingrams (d. 1973). *Adviser on Overseas Information to the Secretary of State for the Colonies, United Kingdom, 1950–54. Author of* Arabia and the Isles *and others.*

ARABIA (*in part*)

W.H.M.   William H. Miller, M.D. *Professor of Ophthalmology and Visual Science, School of Medicine, Yale University.*

SENSORY RECEPTION (*in part*)

W.H.McL.   William Hewat McLeod. *Professor of History, University of Otago, Dunedin, New Zealand. Author of* Gurū Nānak and the Sikh Religion.

NĀNAK (Micropædia)

W.H.McN.   William H. McNeill. *Robert A. Millikan Distinguished Service Professor of History, University of Chicago. Author of* The Rise of the West *and others.*

BALKANS (*in part*)
STEPPE, THE HISTORY OF THE EURASIAN

W.Hn.   Walter B.O. Hansen. *University Professor Emeritus of Oceanography, University of Hamburg.*

MECHANICS (*in part*)

W.H.N.   William H. Nienhauser, Jr. *Professor of East Asian Languages and Literature, University of Wisconsin,*

Madison. Author of P'i Jih-hsiu; *editor of* Indiana Companion to Traditional Chinese Literature.

CHINESE LITERATURE (*in part*)

W.H.O.   William Hosking Oliver. *Editor, Dictionary of New Zealand Biography. Author of* The Story of New Zealand *and others.*

NEW ZEALAND (*in part*)

W.H.T.   William Homan Thorpe. *Emeritus Professor of Animal Ethology, University of Cambridge. Author of* Learning and Instinct in Animals.

BEHAVIOUR, ANIMAL (*in part*)

W.H.Th.   William Harford Thomas. *Journalist. Former Deputy Editor,* The Guardian, *London. Author of* Crisis in the British Press.

UNITED KINGDOM (*in part*)

W.H.v.A.   Wilhelm H. von Aulock. *Head, Bell Telephone Laboratories, Inc., Whippany, New Jersey. Coauthor of* Linear Ferrite Devices for Microwave Applications; *editor of* Handbook of Microwave Ferrite Materials.

ELECTRONICS (*in part*)

W.H.W.   William Henry Walsh (d. 1986). *Professor of Logic and Metaphysics, University of Edinburgh, 1960–79. Author of* Reason and Experience; Metaphysics.

METAPHYSICS (*in part*)

W.H.Wa.   Warren H. Wagner, Jr. *Professor of Botany; Curator of Pteridophytes, University Herbarium, University of Michigan, Ann Arbor. Author of* The Fern Genus Diellia.

FERNS

Wi.B.   William Back. *Research Hydrologist, Water Resources Division, Geological Survey, U.S. Department of the Interior, Reston, Virginia. An authority on the geochemistry of fresh waters.*

MINERALS AND ROCKS (*in part*)

Wi.G.M.   William G. Moulton. *Professor of Linguistics, Princeton University. Professor of Germanic Linguistics, Cornell University, Ithaca, New York, 1949–60. Author of* The Sounds of English and German.

LANGUAGES OF THE WORLD (*in part*)

Wi.M.   Wilhelm Matull. *Senior Civil Servant, National Centres for Political Education, Hannover, Bonn, and Düsseldorf, West Germany, 1954–68. Author of* Ferdinand Lassalle *and others.*

LASSALLE, FERDINAND (Micropædia)

W.J.   Walter John. *Research Scientist, Air and Industrial Hygiene Laboratory, California Department of Health Services, Berkeley.*

MECHANICS (*in part*)

W.J.Al.   Wybe Jappe Alberts. *Former Professor of History, University of Utrecht, The Netherlands.*

LOW COUNTRIES, THE (*in part*)

W.J.Ar.   W.J. Argyle. *Professor of Social Anthropology; Head, Department*

of African Studies, University of Natal, Durban, South Africa. Author of The Fon of Dahomey.

SOUTHERN AFRICA (*in part*)

W.J.B.   William J. Baumol. *Professor of Economics, Princeton University and New York University, New York City. Author of* Business Behavior, Value and Growth.

ECONOMIC THEORY (*in part*)

W.J.Bo.   William J. Bouwsma. *Sather Professor of History, University of California, Berkeley. Author of* Venice and the Defense of Republican Liberty.

ITALY (*in part*)

W.J.Bu.   The Rev. Walter John Burghardt, S.J. *Theologian in Residence, Georgetown University, Washington, D.C. Editor,* Theological Studies. *Author of* The Image of God in Man According to Cyril of Alexandria.

JEROME, SAINT (Micropædia)

W.J.C.   Willie J. Chevalier. *Journalist. Editor,* Le Droit (Ottawa), *1963–67. Managing Editor,* Le Petit Journal (Montreal), *1959–63.*

MONTREAL (*in part*)

W.J.E.   W.J. Eccles. *Emeritus Professor of History, University of Toronto. Author of* The Canadian Frontier, 1534–1760; Frontenac; *and others.*

CARTIER, JACQUES (Micropædia)
FRONTENAC, LOUIS DE BUADE, COMTE DE PALLUAU ET DE (Micropædia)

W.J.F.   W.J. Frank. *Senior Staff, Lawrence Livermore National Laboratory, University of California.*

WAR, THE TECHNOLOGY OF (*in part*)

W.J.G.   Willis John Gertsch. *Emeritus Curator, Arachnida, Department of Entomology, American Museum of Natural History, New York City. Author of* American Spiders.

ARACHNIDS (*in part*)

W.J.Gr.   William J. Griffith. *Emeritus Professor of History, University of Kansas, Lawrence; Director, Center of Latin American Studies, 1970–74. Author of* Empires in the Wilderness: Foreign Colonization and Development in Guatemala, 1834–1844.

CENTRAL AMERICA (*in part*)

W.J.H.   William James Hamilton, M.D. (d. 1975). *Professor of Anatomy, Charing Cross Hospital Medical School, University of London, 1947–70. Editor of* Textbook of Human Anatomy.

SUPPORTIVE AND CONNECTIVE TISSUES (*in part*)

W.J.He.   Wilfrid James Hemp (d. 1962). *Inspector of Ancient Monuments for Wales in H.M. Office of Works, United Kingdom. Secretary to the Royal Commission on Ancient Monuments for Wales and Monmouth.*

SPAIN (*in part*)

W.J.H.W.   Wolfgang J.H. Wickler. *Director, Max Planck Institute for*

Behavioral Physiology, Seewiesen, West Germany. Professor of Zoology, Ludwig Maximilian University of Munich. Author of Mimicry in Plants and Animals.
MIMICRY

W.J.LeV.   William Judson LeVeque. *Executive Director, American Mathematical Society, Providence, Rhode Island. Professor of Mathematics, Claremont Graduate School, California, 1970–77. Author of* Topics in Number Theory; Introduction to Number Theory; *and others.*
ARITHMETIC (*in part*)
MATHEMATICS, THE HISTORY OF
   (*in part*)

W.J.McC.   Willard J. McCarthy. *Associate Professor of Industrial Technology, Illinois State University, Normal. Coauthor of* Machine Tool Technology.
TOOLS (*in part*)

W.J.S.   W. John Smith. *Professor of Biology and Psychology, University of Pennsylvania, Philadelphia. Author of* The Behavior of Communicating *and others.*
BEHAVIOUR, ANIMAL (*in part*)

W.J.T.   William John Talbot. *Emeritus Professor of Geography, University of Cape Town. Coauthor of* Atlas of the Union of South Africa.
SOUTH AFRICA (*in part*)

W.J.Tu.   William Julian Tuttle. *Motion picture makeup artist. Adjunct Professor, School of Cinema-Television, University of Southern California, Los Angeles. President, Custom Color Cosmetics, Pacific Palisades, California. Winner of a special Academy Award, 1965.*
DRESS AND ADORNMENT (*in part*)

W.Jw.   Wadie Jwaideh. *Professor of History and Arabic; Chairman, Department of Near Eastern Languages and Literatures, Indiana University, Bloomington.*
IDRĪSĪ, ASH-SHARĪF AL- (Micropædia)

W.J.W.   Willem Johan Waworoentoe. *Professor of Regional and Urban Planning, Bandung Institute of Technology, Java, Indonesia. Rector, Sam Ratulangi University, Manado. Author of* Recent Urban Growth in Indonesia and Its Regional Development Implications.
JAKARTA

W.K.C.   Wilbert K. Carter. *Associate Professor of Anthropology; Cochairman, Department of Sociology and Anthropology, Tufts University, Medford, Massachusetts.*
ARCTIC, THE (*in part*)

W.K.D.D.   Wayne K.D. Davies. *Professor of Geography, University of Calgary, Alberta. Author of* The Conceptual Revolution in Geography: Selected Essays *and others.*
GEOGRAPHY (*in part*)

W.K.H.   William K. Holstein. *Professor of Management Science, State University of New York at Albany. Coauthor of* Casebooks in Production Management.
INDUSTRIAL ENGINEERING AND
   PRODUCTION MANAGEMENT (*in part*)

W.Ki.   William Kirk. *Professor and Head, Department of Geography, Queen's University of Belfast, Northern Ireland. Author of various articles on southern Asia.*
INDIA (*in part*)

W.K.M.   Woodville K. Marshall. *Professor of History, University of the West Indies, Cave Hill, Barbados.*
WEST INDIES, THE (*in part*)

W.K.R.M.   William K.R. Musgrave. *Emeritus Professor of Organic Chemistry, University of Durham, England. Author of numerous articles on halogen-containing organic compounds.*
CHEMICAL COMPOUNDS (*in part*)

W.L.J.   William Lee Jolly. *Professor of Chemistry, University of California, Berkeley. Author of* The Synthesis and Characterization of Inorganic Compounds *and others.*
CHEMICAL ELEMENTS (*in part*)
INDUSTRIES, EXTRACTION AND
   PROCESSING (*in part*)

W.L.M.   William Lewis Morton (d. 1980). *Vanier Professor of Canadian History, Trent University, Peterborough, Ontario, 1969–75. Author of* The Kingdom of Canada *and others.*
CANADA (*in part*)

W.L.O.   William L. Ochsenwald. *Professor of History, Virginia Polytechnic Institute and State University, Blacksburg. Author of* Religion, Society, and the State in Arabia.
ISRAEL (*in part*)
JORDAN (*in part*)
LEBANON (*in part*)
SYRIA (*in part*)

W.L.Re.   William L. Reese. *Professor of Philosophy, State University of New York at Albany. Author of* Dictionary of Philosophy and Religion: Eastern and Western Thought.
RELIGIOUS AND SPIRITUAL BELIEF,
   SYSTEMS OF (*in part*)

W.L.S.   William L. Schaaf. *Emeritus Professor of Mathematical Education, Brooklyn College, City University of New York. Author of* Bibliography of Recreational Mathematics.
NUMBER GAMES AND OTHER
   MATHEMATICAL RECREATIONS

W.L.Sc.   Waldo L. Schmitt (d. 1977). *Head Curator of Zoology, U.S. National Museum of Natural History, Washington, D.C., 1947–57. Author of* The Marine Decapod Crustacea of California.
CRUSTACEANS (*in part*)

W.L.St.   William Louis Stern. *Professor and Chairman, Department of Botany,*

University of Florida, Gainesville. Coauthor of Humanistic Botany.
ANGIOSPERMS (*in part*)

W.L.W.   Walter L. Weeks. *Professor of Electrical Engineering, Purdue University, West Lafayette, Indiana. Author of* Antenna Engineering *and others.*
ELECTRONICS (*in part*)

W.M.   William Montagna. *Professor of Dermatology, Oregon Health Sciences University, Portland. Author of* The Structure and Function of Skin.
INTEGUMENTARY SYSTEMS
   (*in part*)

W.Ma.   William Markowitz. *Adjunct Professor of Physics, Nova University, Fort Lauderdale, Florida. Astronomer, U.S. Naval Observatory, Washington, D.C., 1936–66; Director, Time Service, 1953–66. Coeditor of* Continental Drift, Secular Motion of the Pole, and Rotation of the Earth.
TIME (*in part*)

W.MacG.   Wyatt MacGaffey. *Professor of Anthropology, Haverford College, Pennsylvania. Author of* Custom and Government in the Lower Congo.
KINSHASA (*in part*)

W.Man.   William Manchester. *Adjunct Professor of History; Writer-in-Residence, Wesleyan University, Middletown, Connecticut. Author of* The Death of a President; The Arms of Krupp.
KENNEDY, JOHN F. (*in part*)
   (Micropædia)
KENNEDY, JOSEPH P. (*in part*)
   (Micropædia)
KENNEDY, ROBERT F. (*in part*)
   (Micropædia)

Wm.A.R.T.   William Archibald Robson Thomson, M.D. (d. 1983). *Editor,* The Practitioner, *1944–73. Author of* The Searching Mind in Medicine *and others; coeditor of* Black's Medical Dictionary.
MEDICINE (*in part*)

W.M.B.   W. Mary Bannerman (d. 1984). *Coauthor of* The Birds of the Atlantic Islands (*4 vol.*).
WESTERN AFRICA (*in part*)

W.M.Cl.   Wayne M. Clegern. *Professor of History, Colorado State University, Fort Collins. Author of* British Honduras: Colonial Dead End, 1859–1900.
CENTRAL AMERICA (*in part*)

W.M.E.   Walter M. Elsasser. *Adjunct Professor of Geophysics, Johns Hopkins University, Baltimore.*
SOLAR SYSTEM, THE (*in part*)

Wm.F.   William Fleming. *Emeritus Professor of Fine Arts, Syracuse University, New York.*
ARCHITECTURE, THE HISTORY OF
   WESTERN (*in part*)
PAINTING, THE HISTORY OF WESTERN
   (*in part*)

W.M.-F.   Wolfram Müller-Freienfels. *Professor of International Civil Law;*

Director, Institute of Foreign and International Civil Law, Albert Ludwig University of Freiburg, West Germany. Author of Die Vertretung beim Rechtsgeschäft *and others.*

BUSINESS LAW (*in part*)

W.Mi. Wesley Milgate. *Emeritus Professor of English, Australian National University, Canberra. Editor of* John Donne: The Satires, Epigrams and Verse Letters; John Donne: A Life.

DONNE, JOHN (Micropædia)

W.M. Warren Moran. *Professor of Geography, University of Auckland, New Zealand. Editor of* Auckland and the Central North Island.

NEW ZEALAND (*in part*)

W.Mr. William Miller (d. 1945). *Author of* Greece; The Ottoman Empire and Its Successors (1801–1936).

GREECE (*in part*)

W.M.S. William Merritt Sale, Jr. (d. 1981). *Goldwin Smith Professor of English, Cornell University, Ithaca, New York. Author of* Samuel Richardson: A Biographical Record; Samuel Richardson: Master Printer.

RICHARDSON, SAMUEL (Micropædia)

W.M.W. William Montgomery Watt. *Professor of Arabic and Islāmic Studies, University of Edinburgh, 1964–79. Author of* Muhammad: Prophet and Statesman; Muslim Intellectual: A Study of al-Ghazālī; *general editor of* Islāmic Surveys.

GHAZĀLĪ, AL- (Micropædia)
HĀRŪN AR-RASHĪD (Micropædia)
ISLĀM, MUḤAMMAD AND THE RELIGION OF (*in part*)

W.M.Wa. Willard M. Wallace. *Emeritus Professor of History, Wesleyan University, Middletown, Connecticut. Author of* Appeal to Arms: A Military History of the American Revolution *and others.*

UNITED STATES OF AMERICA (*in part*)

W.M.Wh. Walter Muir Whitehill (d. 1978). *Director and Librarian, Boston Athenaeum, 1946–73. Author of* Boston: A Topographical History *and others.*

BOSTON (*in part*)

W.M.Y. William Munro Yool (d. 1978). *Air Vice Marshal, Royal Air Force. Military writer. Assistant editor,* Brassey's Annual.

WAR, THE THEORY AND CONDUCT OF (*in part*)

W.N.D. William N. Dember. *Professor of Psychology, University of Cincinnati, Ohio. Author of* The Psychology of Perception.

PERCEPTION, HUMAN (*in part*)

W.N.H. Wilmot Norton Hess. *Director, National Center for Atmospheric Research, National Oceanic and Atmospheric Administration, U.S. Department of Commerce, Boulder, Colorado. Author of* The Radiation Belt and Magnetosphere.

ATMOSPHERE (*in part*)

W.O. Wilfred Owen. *Former Senior Fellow, Brookings Institution, Washington, D.C. Author of* The Accessible City *and others.*

UNITED STATES OF AMERICA (*in part*)

W.O.B. William O. Bright. *Professor of Linguistics and Anthropology, University of California, Los Angeles. Editor,* Language (*journal*). *Author of* American Indian Linguistics and Literature.

LANGUAGES OF THE WORLD (*in part*)

W.O.C. W. Owen Chadwick. *Former Regius Professor of Modern History, University of Cambridge. Author of* The Reformation *and others.*

GREGORY OF TOURS, SAINT (Micropædia)
NEWMAN, JOHN HENRY (Micropædia)
PROTESTANTISM (*in part*)

W.O.W. William Ogwen Williams (d. 1969). *Sir John Williams Professor of Welsh History, University College of Wales, Aberystwyth, 1967–69.*

UNITED KINGDOM (*in part*)

W.P. Wilhelm Pauck (d. 1981). *Professor of Church History, Union Theological Seminary, New York City, 1953–67. Author of* Harnack and Troeltsch *and others.*

HARNACK, ADOLF VON (Micropædia)

W.Pa. Władysław Parczewski (d. 1981). *Professor of Physics of the Atmosphere, Technical University of Warsaw. Director, National Institute for Hydrology and Meteorology, Warsaw, 1966–69.*

EUROPE (*in part*)

W.P.D. W. Phillips Davison. *Professor of Sociology and Journalism, Columbia University. Author of* International Political Communication.

PUBLIC OPINION

W.P.G. Wesley Patterson Garrigus. *Emeritus Professor of Animal Husbandry, University of Kentucky, Lexington. Author of* Introductory Animal Science.

FARMING AND AGRICULTURAL TECHNOLOGY (*in part*)

W.Ph.C. W.Ph. Coolhaas (deceased). *Professor of Colonial History, Utrecht University, The Netherlands. Coauthor of* Jan Pieterszoon Coen *and others.*

COEN, JAN PIETERSZOON (Micropædia)

W.P.M. William P. Malm. *Professor of Music, University of Michigan, Ann Arbor. Author of* Japanese Music and Musical Instruments; Music Cultures of the Pacific, the Near East, and Asia.

EAST ASIAN ARTS (*in part*)

W.P.McG. William Paul McGreevey. *Senior Economist, The World Bank, Washington, D.C. Author of* An Economic History of Colombia, 1845–1930.

COLOMBIA (*in part*)

W.P.Mn. Warren Perry Mason. *Senior Research Associate, Henry Krumb School of Mines, Columbia University, 1969–77. Head of Mechanics Research, Bell Telephone Laboratories, Inc., 1948–65. Author of* Piezoelectric Crystals and Their Application to Ultrasonics.

ELECTRONICS (*in part*)

W.R. Willi Reich (d. 1980). *Music critic. Author of* The Life and Work of Alban Berg *and many others.*

BERG, ALBAN (Micropædia)

W.Ra. William Ravenhill. *Reardon Smith Professor of Geography, University of Exeter, England. Author of* Ben Donn's Map of Devon, 1765; *coauthor of* South-West England.

UNITED KINGDOM (*in part*)

W.R.J. Wilbur R. Jacobs. *Professor of History, University of California, Santa Barbara. Editor of* The Letters of Francis Parkman.

PARKMAN, FRANCIS (Micropædia)
PRESCOTT, WILLIAM H. (Micropædia)

W.R.M. Wilhelm Rudolf Marquardt. *Member, Board of Curators, IFO-Institute for Economic Research, Munich. Author of* Seychellen, Komoren und Maskarenen.

INDIAN OCEAN ISLANDS (*in part*)

W.R.Me. William Richard Mead. *Emeritus Professor of Geography, University College, University of London. Author of* An Economic Geography of the Scandinavian States and Finland *and others.*

FINLAND (*in part*)

W.R.P. William Roe Polk. *Historian. Professor of Middle Eastern History, University of Chicago, 1965–75. Author of* The United States and the Arab World.

ISRAEL (*in part*)
SYRIA (*in part*)

W.R.S. Walter R. Sharp (d. 1977). *Professor of International Relations, Yale University, 1951–64. Author of* Field Administration in the United Nations System *and others.*

UNITED NATIONS (*in part*)

W.S. Wilfred Sircus, M.D. *Senior Consultant Physician, Gastrointestinal Unit; former Reader in Medicine, University of Edinburgh. Coeditor of* Scientific Foundations of Gastroenterology.

DIGESTION AND DIGESTIVE SYSTEMS (*in part*)

W.Sc. Walter Schulz. *Professor of Philosophy, Eberhard Karl University of Tübingen, West Germany. Member of the F.W.J. Schelling Commission of the Bavarian Academy of Sciences. Author of* Schelling.

SCHELLING, FRIEDRICH WILHELM JOSEPH VON (*in part*) (Micropædia)

W.S.-cg. Wu Shih-ch'ang. *Former Senior Lecturer in Chinese, University of Oxford.*

HISTORY, THE STUDY OF (*in part*)

W.S.F. **William S. Fyfe.** *Professor and Chairman, Department of Geology, University of Western Ontario, London. Coauthor of* The Earth.
MINERALS AND ROCKS (*in part*)

W.S.H. **Winthrop S. Hudson.** *Adjunct Professor of Religion, University of North Carolina at Chapel Hill. James B. Colgate Professor of the History of Christianity, Colgate Rochester Divinity School, Rochester, New York, 1948– 77. Author of* Baptists in Transition *and others.*
PROTESTANTISM (*in part*)

W.S.MacK. **William Scott MacKenzie.** *Professor of Petrology, Victoria University of Manchester.*
MINERALS AND ROCKS (*in part*)

W.S.MacNu. **W. Stewart MacNutt** (d. 1976). *Professor of History, University of New Brunswick, Fredericton. Author of* New Brunswick: A History, 1784–1867.
CANADA (*in part*)

W.S.N. **William S. Newman.** *Alumni Distinguished Professor Emeritus of Music, University of North Carolina at Chapel Hill. Author of* A History of the Sonata Idea *and others.*
MUSICAL FORMS AND GENRES (*in part*)

W.S.S. **William S. Sahakian.** *Professor of Psychology and Philosophy, Suffolk University, Boston. Author of* History and Systems of Psychology *and others.*
PSYCHOLOGY (*in part*)

W.S.Sh. **Wendy Stedman Sheard.** *Art historian. Author of* Antiquity in the Renaissance; *coeditor of* Collaboration in Italian Renaissance Art.
MANTEGNA, ANDREA (Micropædia)

W.T. **Walter Terry** (d. 1982). *Dance critic and editor,* Saturday Review *magazine;* New York Herald Tribune; *and others. Author of* The Dance in America *and many others.*
GRAHAM, MARTHA (Micropædia)

W.Ta. **William Taylor.** *Principal, University of London; Director, Institute of Education, 1973–83. Author of* Society and the Education of Teachers.
TEACHING (*in part*)

W.-t.C. **Wing-tsit Chan.** *Anna R.D. Gillespie Professor Emeritus of Philosophy, Chatham College, Pittsburgh. Emeritus Professor of Chinese Philosophy and Culture, Dartmouth College, Hanover, New Hampshire. Author of* A Source Book in Chinese Philosophy *and others.*
CONFUCIANISM, CONFUCIUS AND (*in part*)
OU-YANG HSIU (Micropædia)
WANG YANG-MING (Micropædia)

W.T.Ca. **William Thomas Calman** (d. 1952). *Lecturer in Zoology, University of St. Andrews, Scotland, 1940–46. Keeper, Department of Zoology, British Museum, London, 1927–36. Author of* The Life of Crustacea.
CRUSTACEANS (*in part*)

W.T.G. **Wassil Todorov Gjuzelev.** *Professor of Bulgarian Medieval History, University of Sofia. Author of* Knjaz Boris Parvi *and others.*
BORIS I (Micropædia)

W.T.I. **William T. Ingram.** *Consulting engineer. Adjunct Professor of Civil and Environmental Engineering, Polytechnic Institute of New York, New York City. Author of* "Environmental Engineering" *in* Standard Handbook for Civil Engineers.
BUILDING CONSTRUCTION (*in part*)

W.T.Ke. **William T. Keeton** (d. 1980). *Liberty Hyde Bailey Professor of Biology, Cornell University, Ithaca, New York, 1969–80. Author of* Biological Science; Elements of Biological Science.
DIGESTION AND DIGESTIVE SYSTEMS (*in part*)

W.T.Sa. **William T. Sanders.** *Professor of Anthropology, Pennsylvania State University, University Park. Coauthor of* Mesoamerica: The Evolution of a Civilization *and others.*
PRE-COLUMBIAN CIVILIZATIONS (*in part*)

W.T.v.S. **Wolfram Th. von Soden.** *Emeritus Professor of Ancient Semitic Philology and Ancient Oriental History, University of Münster, West Germany.*
IRAQ (*in part*)

W.U. **Walter Ullmann** (d. 1983). *Professor of Medieval History, University of Cambridge, 1972–78; Professor of Ecclesiastical History, 1965–72. Author of* The Growth of Papal Government in the Middle Ages *and others.*
LEO IX, SAINT (Micropædia)

W.V.D'A. **William Vincent D'Antonio.** *Executive Officer, American Sociological Association, Washington, D.C. Professor and Chairman, Department of Sociology, University of Connecticut, Storrs, 1971– 76. Coauthor of* Influentials in Two Border Cities.
UNITED STATES OF AMERICA (*in part*)

W.V.E. **Wolf Von Eckardt.** *Design Critic,* Time *magazine. Architecture Critic,* The Washington Post, *1963–81. Author of* A Place to Live: The Crisis of the Cities.
MIES VAN DER ROHE, LUDWIG (Micropædia)

W.V.M. **William Vernon Mayer.** *Emeritus Professor of Biology, University of Colorado, Boulder. Emeritus Director, Biological Sciences Curriculum Study. Author of* Hibernation.
BEHAVIOUR, ANIMAL (*in part*)

W.V.P. **William V. Porter.** *Associate Professor of Music History and Literature, Northwestern University, Evanston, Illinois.*
MUSICAL FORMS AND GENRES (*in part*)

W.V.S. **Walter V. Scholes** (d. 1975). *Professor of History, University of Missouri, Columbia, 1954–75. Author*

of Mexican Politics During the Juárez Regime, 1855–1872 *and others.*
JUÁREZ, BENITO (Micropædia)

W.W. **William Watson.** *Former Professor of Chinese Art and Archaeology; former Head, Percival David Foundation of Chinese Art, School of Oriental and African Studies, University of London. Author of* China Before the Han Dynasty *and others.*
HISTORY, THE STUDY OF (*in part*)

W.W.B. **William W. Brickman** (d. 1986). *Professor of Educational History and Comparative Education, University of Pennsylvania, Philadelphia, 1962–81. Author of* Educational Systems in the United States *and others.*
EDUCATION, SYSTEMS OF (*in part*)

W.W.C. **W. Walker Chambers.** *William Jacks Professor Emeritus of German, University of Glasgow. Coauthor of* A Short History of the German Language.
GERMAN LITERATURE (*in part*)

W.W.H. **Warren W. Hassler, Jr.** *Professor of American History, Pennsylvania State University, University Park. Author of* Commanders of the Army of the Potomac *and others.*
UNITED STATES OF AMERICA (*in part*)

W.Wi. **William Witte.** *Emeritus Professor of German, University of Aberdeen, Scotland. Author of* Schiller; *editor of several of Schiller's works.*
HÖLDERLIN, FRIEDRICH (Micropædia)
SCHILLER, FRIEDRICH VON (*in part*) (Micropædia)

W.W.R. **William Wallace Robson.** *Masson Professor of English Literature, University of Edinburgh. Author of* Critical Essays: Modern English Literature.
LAWRENCE, D.H. (*in part*) (Micropædia)
TENNYSON, ALFRED TENNYSON, 1ST BARON (Micropædia)

W.W.W. **William Walter Watts** (d. 1948). *Keeper, Department of Metal Work, Victoria and Albert Museum, London, 1879–1923. Author of* Old English Silver *and others.*
DECORATIVE ARTS AND FURNISHINGS (*in part*)

W.-Y.K. **Won-Yong Kim.** *Professor of Archaeology, Seoul National University. Author of* Treasures of Korean Art; History of Korean Art.
EAST ASIAN ARTS (*in part*)
WRITING (*in part*)

W.Y.W. **William Young Willetts.** *Former Curator, Museum of Asian Art, University of Malaya, Kuala Lumpur. Author of* Chinese Art.
DECORATIVE ARTS AND FURNISHINGS (*in part*)

W.Z. **Warren Zeiller.** *Vice President and General Manager, Miami Seaquarium. Author of* Tropical Marine Fishes of South Florida and the Bahamas *and others.*
FISHES (*in part*)

W.Ze. **Wilbur Zelinsky.** *Professor of Geography, Pennsylvania State University, University Park. Author of* Prologue to Population Geography.
UNITED STATES OF AMERICA (*in part*)

Y.A.C. **Yehudi A. Cohen.** *Professor of Anthropology, Rutgers University, New Brunswick, New Jersey. Editor of* Man in Adaptation.
RITES AND CEREMONIES, SACRED (*in part*)

Y.B. **Yvon Belaval.** *Professor of Philosophy, University of Paris I. Vice President, Leibniz Society, Hanover, West Germany. Honorary President, Society of Eighteenth Century Studies, Paris. Author of* Leibniz: Initiation à sa philosophie *and many others.*
LEIBNIZ, GOTTFRIED WILHELM (*in part*) (Micropædia)

Y.-c.K. **Yu-chin Kang.** *Professor of Atmospheric Sciences, National Taiwan University, Taipei.*
TAIWAN (*in part*)

Y.C.W. **Yi Chu Wang.** *Professor of History, Queens College, City University of New York. Author of* Chinese Intellectuals and the West.
CHANG CHIH-TUNG (Micropædia)
SUN YAT-SEN (Micropædia)

Y.-G.G.H. **Yueh-Gin Gung Hu.** *Researcher in Chinese studies. Assistant Librarian, University of Chicago, 1938–43.*
CHINA (*in part*)

Y.J. **Yette Jeandet.** *Former Editor,* Literary News, *Bayard-Presse, Paris. Author of* Blanche de Castille, reine de l'unité française *and others.*
BLANCHE OF CASTILE (Micropædia)

Y.K.Y. **Yury Konstantinovich Yefremov.** *Former Senior Scientist, Geographical Museum, Moscow M.V. Lomonosov State University.*
ASIA (*in part*)

Y.L. **Yvonne Lanhers.** *Curator, National Archives, Paris. Coeditor of* La Réhabilitation de Jeanne la Pucelle.
CHARLES VII (FRANCE) (Micropædia)
JOAN OF ARC (*in part*)

Y.M. **Yasuo Masai.** *Professor of Geography, Rissho University, Tokyo. Coeditor of* Japanese Geography 1966.
JAPAN (*in part*)

Y.M.A. **Yuri M. Ado.** *Chief of the Accelerator Division, Institute for High Energy Physics, State Committee for Utilization of Atomic Energy of the U.S.S.R., Serpukhov. Coauthor of* "Coherent Radiation from the Electrons in a Synchrotron" *in* Atomnaya energiya.
PARTICLE ACCELERATORS (*in part*)

Y.M.D. **Yelena Matveyevna Doroshinskaya.** *Journalist. Coauthor of* Leningrad.
LENINGRAD (*in part*)

Y.-m.Y. **Yue-man Yeung.** *Professor of Geography, Chinese University of Hong Kong.*
CHINA (*in part*)

Y.P.M. **Yi Pao Mei.** *Henry Luce Professor of Humanities, Tunghai University, T'ai-chung, Taiwan, 1973–77. Professor of Oriental Studies, University of Iowa, Iowa City, 1955–70. Author of* Motse: The Neglected Rival of Confucius.
CONFUCIANISM, CONFUCIUS AND (*in part*)
MENCIUS (Micropædia)
MO-TZU (Micropædia)

Y.T. **Yoshinori Takeuchi.** *Emeritus Professor of Philosophy of Religion, Kyōto University. Author of* Philosophy of Shinran; The Heart of Buddhism.
NISHIDA KITARŌ (Micropædia)

Y.T.T. **Youssef T. Toni.** *Professor of Geography, Laurentian University of Sudbury, Ontario.*
ARABIA (*in part*)

Y.V.Y. **Yevgeny Venyaminovich Yastrebov.** *Assistant Professor of Geography, Moscow Regional Pedagogical Institute.*
EUROPE (*in part*)

Y.Y.R. **Yelizaveta Yakovlevna Rantsman.** *Senior Scientist, Institute of Geography, Academy of Sciences of the U.S.S.R., Moscow. Author of numerous articles on geography.*
ASIA (*in part*)

Z.A.K. **Zafar Ahmad Khan.** *Professor of Geography, Government College, Rāwalpindi, Pakistan. Author of* Karachi: An Urban Profile.
KARĀCHI

Z.D.K. **Zimani David Kadzamira.** *Reader in Government; Principal, Chancellor College, University of Malawi, Zomba. Contributor to* Malawi Past and Present.
SOUTHERN AFRICA (*in part*)

Z.G. **Zhong Gongfu.** *Professor, Canton Institute of Geography, China.*
CANTON (*in part*)

Z.I.A. **Zafar Ishaq Ansari.** *Professor of History, University of Petroleum and Minerals, Dhahran, Saudi Arabia.*
ABŪ ḤANĪFAH (Micropædia)

Z.O. **Zoé Oldenbourg-Idalie.** *Novelist and free-lance writer. Author of* Catherine the Great *and others.*
CATHERINE II (Micropædia)

Z.V. **Zeno Vendler.** *Professor of Philosophy, University of California, San Diego, at La Jolla. Author of* Linguistics in Philosophy; Adjectives and Nominalizations; *and others.*
LINGUISTICS (*in part*)

Z.Z. **Zeng Zungu.** *Associate Professor of Geography, Nanking University, China. Coauthor of* World Geography.
NANKING (*in part*)

Names of
Contributors

Listed below, with initials that identify them, are the names of persons who have written articles or sections of articles. For brief summaries of their positions and the titles of all articles contributed, see under authors' initials in the list on pages 531–655.

Aaron, Richard I.   R.Aa.
Abbagnano, Nicola.   N.Ab.
Abbe, Ernst C.   E.C.A.
Abdo, Ass'ad Sulaiman.   A.S.A.
Abel-Smith, Brian.   B.A.-S.
Aberdare, Morys George Lyndhurst Bruce, 4th Baron.   A.
Abraham, Gerald E.H.   G.E.H.A.
Abrahams, Harold Maurice.   H.M.A.
Abrahams, John R.   J.R.A.
Abrahart, Edward Noah.   E.N.A.
Abramson, Glenda M.   G.M.A.
Abu Jaber, Kamel S.   K.S.A.J.
Abu-Lughod, Ibrahim A.   I.A.A.-L.
Abu-Lughod, Janet L.   J.L.A.-L.
Accordi, Bruno.   B.A.
Ackerman, James S.   J.S.Ac.
Ackoff, Russell L.   R.L.A.
Acton, Harry Burrows.   H.B.A.
Adamovich, Anthony.   A.Ad.
Adams, Charles Joseph.   C.J.A.
Adams, Preston.   P.Ad.
Adams, Robert McCormick.   R.M.As.
Adejuwon, James Oladipo.   J.O.A.
Adhémar, Jean.   J.Ad.
Adkins, Dorothy C.   D.C.A.
Adler, Jeremy D.   J.D.Ad.
Adler, John H.   J.H.A.
Ado, Yuri M.   Y.M.A.
Adotevi, Stanislas Spero.   S.S.A.
Agostino, Guido d'.   G.d'A.
Aguirre, Margarita.   M.Ag.
Aherne, Sister Consuelo Maria.   C.M.A.
Ahlström, Gösta W.   G.W.A.
Ahmad, Nafis.   N.A.
Ahmadjian, Vernon.   V.A.
Ahrweiler, Hélène.   H.Ah.
Aiyappan, Ayinipalli.   A.Ai.
Akasofu, Syun-Ichi.   S.-I.A.
Akdağ, Mustafa.   M.Ak.
Akita, George.   G.Ak.
Alavi, Hamza A.   H.A.A.
Alba, Victor.   V.Al.
Alberts, Wybe Jappe.   W.J.Al.
Albrecht-Carrié, René.   R.A.-C.
Albright, William Foxwell.   W.F.A.
Albritton, Claude C.   C.C.A.
Albury, E. Paul.   E.P.A.
Alden, John Richard.   J.R.Al.
Aleem, Anwar Abdel.   An.A.A.
Alexander, Frederick.   F.A.
Alexander, Lewis M.   L.M.A.
Alexander, Robert J.   R.J.Al.
Alexopoulos, Constantine John.   C.J.Al.
Alford, Alfred E.   A.E.A.

Alford, R.F.G.   R.F.G.A.
Ali, Mohammad.   M.Al.
Alip, Eufronio M.   Eu.M.A.
Allais, Maurice.   Ma.A.
Allan, John.   J.Al.
Allard, The Rev. Michel Adrien.   M.A.Al.
Allard, R.W.   R.W.A.
Allchin, Frank Raymond.   F.R.Al.
Allen, Francis A.   F.A.A.
Allen, Garland Edward.   G.E.Al.
Allen, Geoffrey Freeman.   G.F.A.
Allen, Walter E.   W.E.A.
Aller, Lawrence Hugh.   L.H.A.
Allibone, Thomas Edward.   T.E.A.
Allworth, Edward.   E.Al.
Almagià, Roberto.   Ro.A.
Alpers, Edward Alter.   E.A.A.
Al-Shahi, Ahmed S.   A.Al-Sh.
Alston, Rex.   R.Al.
Amadio, Anselm H.   A.H.Ao.
Amaral, Ilídio Melo Peres do.   I.M.P. do A.
Amengual, Barthélemy.   B.Am.
Amerine, Maynard A.   M.A.A.
Ames, Winslow.   W.Am.
Anastaplo, George.   G.An.
Anastaplo, Sara P.   S.P.A.
Anderson, Donald M.   D.An.
Anderson, Douglas M.W.   D.M.W.A.
Anderson, Edgar.   E.An.
Anderson, Edward M.   E.W.A.
Anderson, Franklin K.   F.K.A.
Anderson, Franz E.   F.E.A.
Andrade U., Victor.   V.A.U.
Andrew, Richard J.   R.J.A.
Andrew, Warren.   W.A.
Andreyev, Nikolay.   N.An.
Andrups, J.A.   J.A.A.
Angel, Pierre Robert.   P.R.A.
Angrist, Stanley W.   S.A.
Ansari, Zafar Ishaq.   Z.I.A.
Anschutz, Richard Paul.   R.P.An.
Anstey, Roger T.   R.T.An.
Anthony, Jean Daniel.   J.D.A.
Anweiler, Oskar.   O.A.
Aquilecchia, Giovanni.   G.A.
Arasaratnam, Sinnappah.   S.Ara.
Archibald, Raymond Clare.   R.C.A.
Aretin, Karl Otmar, Baron von.   K.O.v.A.
Arey, Leslie B.   L.B.A.
Arfa, Maj. Gen. Hassan.   H.Ar.
Argov, Daniel.   D.Ar.
Arguello, Rosendo.   R.A.
Argyle, Michael.   M.Ar.
Argyle, W.J.   W.J.Ar.
Arieti, Silvano.   S.Ar.
Arkhurst, Frederick S.   F.S.A.
Arlazorov, Mikhail S.   M.S.A.
Armitage, John.   J.Ar.
Armstrong, A. Hilary.   A.H.A.
Armstrong, Annette Elizabeth.   A.E.Ar.
Armstrong, David M.   D.M.A.

Armstrong, Lloyd Van Horn.   L.V.A.
Armstrong, T.E.   T.E.Ar.
Armytage, Walter Harry Green.   W.H.G.A.
Arnason, H. Harvard.   H.H.A.
Arnold, Denis Midgley.   D.M.Ar.
Arnold, Godfrey Edward.   G.E.A.
Arnott, W. Geoffrey.   W.G.A.
Arpigny, Claude.   C.A.
Arrington, Leonard James.   L.J.A.
Artsimovitch, Lev.   L.A.
Aruja, Endel.   E.Ar.
Arvon, Henri.   H.A.
Asanachinta, Col. Phoon Phon.   P.P.A.
Ashley, Maurice.   M.As.
Ashmole, Bernard.   B.As.
Ashmole, N. Philip.   N.P.As.
Asimov, Isaac.   I.A.
Aspinall, Arthur C.V.D.   A.As.
Asprey, Larned B.   L.B.As.
Asprey, Robert Brown.   R.B.A.
Atherden, Lewis Malcolm.   L.M.At.
Atherton, James Stephen.   J.S.A.
Atiyah, Sir Michael Francis.   M.F.A.
Atkinson, Bruce W.   B.W.A.
Atkinson, William C.   W.C.A.
Attwater, Donald.   D.At.
Aubert, Roger-François-Marie.   R.-F.-M.A.
Aubin, Hermann.   H.Au.
Auboyer, Jeannine.   J.Au.
Auclair, Marcelle.   M.A.
Auerbach, Charlotte.   C.Au.
Aulie, Richard Paul.   R.P.A.
Aulock, Wilhelm H. von.   W.H.v.A.
Aumann, Francis R.   F.R.A.
Aurenhammer, Hans.   Ha.A.
Austen, Ralph A.   R.A.A.
Austerlitz, Robert.   R.Au.
Austin, Oliver L., Jr.   O.L.A.
Auty, Phyllis.   P.Ay.
Auty, Robert.   Ro.Au.
Avery, Peter William.   P.W.A.
Avila, Héctor Fernando.   H.F.A.
Avila-Martel, Alamiro de.   A.de A.-M.
Avrich, Paul.   P.A.
Axelson, Eric.   E.A.
Ayoub, Raymond George.   R.G.A.
Ayres, John C.   J.C.A.
Ayyar, Nagarajan Panchapagesan.   N.P.A.
Azcona, The Rev. Tarsicio de.   T.d.A.

Baaren, Theodorus P. van.   T.P.v.B.
Back, George I.   G.I.Bk.
Back, William.   Wi.B.
Bacon, Frederick E.   F.E.B.
Badash, Lawrence.   L.Ba.
Badian, E.   E.Ba.
Badt, Kurt.   K.Ba.
Baigent, Margaret J.   M.J.B.
Bailey, John A.   J.A.Ba.
Bain, Joe S.   J.S.B.
Bainton, Roland H.   R.H.B.

Baird, A. Craig. A.C.B.
Bakarić, Vladimir. V.Ba.
Baker, Carl G. C.G.B.
Baker, D. James. D.J.Ba.
Baker, John Fleetwood Baker, Baron.
   J.F.Br.
Baker, Peter S. P.S.Ba.
Baker, Philip S. P.S.B.
Baker, Raymond William. R.W.Ba.
Baker, Samuel John Kenneth.
   S.J.K.B.
Balakrishna, Suri. S.B.
Balassa, Bela. B.B.
Baldini, Umberto. U.B.
Baldwin, A. Richard. A.R.B.
Baldwin, Marshall W. M.W.B.
Balfet, Hélène J. He.Ba.
Balfour, Michael Graham. M.G.B.
Balinsky, Boris Ivan. B.I.B.
Ballesteros Gaibrois, Manuel. M.B.G.
Ballhatchet, Kenneth A. K.A.B.
Ballinger, Ronald B. R.B.Ba.
Baloch, N.A. N.A.B.
Balon, Eugene Kornel. E.K.B.
Balsdon, John P.V. Dacre. J.P.V.D.B.
Baly, Denis. De.B.
Bannerman, W. Mary. W.M.B.
Bannister, Lawrence Howard. L.H.Ba.
Banton, Michael Parker. M.P.B.
Banzragch, D. D.Ba.
Barany, George. G.Ba.
Barblan, Guglielmo. Gu.B.
Barbour, Nevill. N.B.
Barbour, Ruth. R.Ba.
Barclay, Brig. Cyril Nelson. C.N.B.
Bargebuhr, Frederick P. F.P.B.
Barghoorn, Frederick C. F.C.B.
Barker, Clive. C.Ba.
Barker, Daniel Stephen. D.S.B.
Barker, John Walton, Jr. J.W.Ba.
Barlow, Frank. F.Ba.
Barlow, Jon Charles. J.C.B.
Barna, Victor. V.B.
Barnard, Raymond Walter. R.W.Bd.
Barnes, Clifford A. C.A.B.
Barnes, Ivan. I.B.
Barnes, John Arundel. Jo.A.B.
Barnes, Jonathan. J.B.
Barnett, Henry Lewis. H.L.B.
Barnett, Richard David. R.D.B.
Baron, Salo Wittmayer. S.W.B.
Baron, Samuel H. S.H.B.
Barraclough, Geoffrey. G.Bh.
Barrère, Jean-Bertrand. J.-B.Ba.
Barrington, Ernest J.W. E.J.W.B.
Barrow, Geoffrey Wallis Steuart.
   G.W.S.B.
Barth, T.F.W. T.F.W.B.
Barthakur, Minodhar. M.B.
Barton, Sir Derek Harold Richard.
   D.H.R.B.
Bar-Zohar, Michael. M.Ba.
Barzun, Jacques. J.Ba.
Basas Fernández, Manuel. M.B.F.
Basham, Arthur Llewellyn. A.L.B.
Bassham, James Alan. J.A.B.
Batbayar, Sh. Sh.B.
Bates, David V. D.V.B.
Battan, Louis J. L.J.B.
Bauer, Göran C.H. G.C.H.B.
Baumer, Maj. Gen. William H.
   W.H.B.
Baumol, William J. W.J.B.
Bawden, Charles R. C.R.B.
Baxter, Alexander D. A.D.B.
Baxter, Douglas C. D.C.B.

Baxter, Glen W. G.W.Ba.
Baxter, Ian F.G. I.F.G.B.
Bay, Howard. Ho.B.
Bayley, Charles Calvert. C.C.B.
Bazin, Germain René Michel.
   G.R.M.B.
Beadle, Richard. Ri.B.
Beale, Geoffrey H. G.H.B.
Bealer, Lewis W. L.W.B.
Beams, Jesse W. J.W.B.
Bean, Lowell John. Lo.J.B.
Bean, William B. W.B.B.
Beaufort, Lieven Ferdinand de.
   L.F. de B.
Beaufre, Gen. André. A.Be.
Beaujeu-Garnier, Jacqueline. J.B.-G.
Beaver, Robert Pierce. R.P.Be.
Beaver, Stanley Henry. S.H.Br.
Béchervaise, John Mayston. J.M.B.
Beck, Alfred C. A.C.Bk.
Beck, Curt W. F.E.Be.
Beck, Kevin Charles. K.C.B.
Beck, Leslie John. L.J.Be.
Beck, Warren A. W.A.B.
Becker, Alfons. Al.Be.
Beckerman, Bernard. B.Be.
Beckingsale, Bernard Winslow. B.W.B.
Beckinsale, Robert Percy. Ro.P.B.
Beckson, Karl. K.Be.
Bedford, Ronald E. R.E.Be.
Beegle, Dewey M. D.M.Be.
Beeman, Richard R. R.R.B.
Beer, John Bernard. J.B.B.
Beeton, Alfred M. A.M.B.
Behnke, Robert John. R.J.B.
Beier, Ulli. U.Be.
Belaval, Yvon. Y.B.
Bell, Eric Temple. E.T.B.
Bell, Ronald Percy. R.P.B.
Belshaw, Cyril S. C.S.B.
Belton, Michael J.S. M.J.S.B.
Bemis, Samuel Flagg. S.F.Be.
Benedek, Thomas G. T.G.B.
Benedict, Roger William. R.W.B.
Benedikz, Benedikt Sigurdur. B.S.B.
Benenson, Susan Elizabeth. S.E.B.
Ben-Gurion, David. D.B.-G.
Benítez, Fernando. F.Be.
Benneh, George. G.Be.
Bennett, John C. J.C.Be.
Bennett, Wendell Clark. W.C.Be.
Ben-Sasson, Haim Hillel. H.H.B.-S.
Bensing, Manfred. M.Be.
Benson, D. Mary. D.M.B.
Benson, Fred J. F.J.B.
Benson, Lyman. L.Be.
Bent, Ian D. I.Be.
Bentley, John Beresford. Jo.Be.
Bentley, T. Keilor. T.K.B.
Benz, Ernst Wilhelm. E.W.B.
Berengo, Marino. Ma.B.
Berenson, Louis Stanley. L.S.B.
Bergerol, Jane. Ja.Be.
Berghe, Pierre Louis van den.
   P.L.v.d.B.
Bergmann, Peter G. P.G.Be.
Bergmann, Walter G. W.G.B.
Bergsland, Knut. K.B.
Bergsten, Staffan. S.Be.
Berlyne, D.E. D.E.B.
Bernard, François. F.B.
Berndt, Ronald M. R.M.B.
Bernstein, Jeremy. J.Be.
Berrall, Julia S. Ju.S.B.
Berrill, N.J. N.J.B.
Berry, André. A.By.

Berry, R. Stephen. R.S.Be.
Berry, William B.N. W.B.N.B.
Bertram, C.K. C.K.B.
Bertram, G.C.L. G.C.L.B.
Bertrand, Trent J. T.J.B.
Bessac, Frank Bagnall. F.B.B.
Bessarabov, Georgy Dmitriyevich.
   G.D.B.
Best, Alan C.G. A.C.G.B.
Beuve-Méry, Hubert. H.B.-M.
Beven, Keith J. K.J.B.
Beynon, John Herbert. J.H.Be.
Bharati, Agehananda. A.Bh.
Bhardwaj, Surinder M. S.M.B.
Bianchi, Ugo. U.B.
Bibby, Cyril. C.Bi.
Bickerman, E.J. E.J.Bi.
Bieber, Margarete. M.Bi.
Biel, Victor J.P. V.Bi.
Bielenstein, Hans H.A. H.H.A.B.
Bieler, Ludwig G.J. L.G.J.B.
Biemel, Walter. W.Bi.
Bietenholz, Peter G. P.G.B.
Biezais, Haralds. H.Bi.
Bigalke, R.C. R.C.Bi.
Billingsley, Patrick Paul. P.P.B.
Bing, R.H. R.H.Bi.
Bira, Sh. Sh.Bi.
Bird, John Brian. J.B.Bd.
Bird, Otto Allen. O.A.B.
Bireley, The Rev. Robert L. R.L.B.
Birkhoff, Garrett. G.Bi.
Birmingham, David. D.Bi.
Birnbaum, Howard Kent. H.K.B.
Birnholz, Alan Curtis. A.C.Bi.
Bissell, Harold J. H.J.Bi.
Bisson, Thomas N. T.N.B.
Bivar, Adrian David Hugh. A.D.H.B.
Black, Clinton V. C.V.B.
Black, Sir Douglas A.K. D.A.K.B.
Blagoy, Dimitry Dimitriyevich.
   D.D.B.
Blair, Claude. C.Bl.
Blair, Steven N. S.N.B.
Blair, Walter. Wa.B.
Blake, Robert Norman William Blake,
   Baron. B.
Blanding, Warren. W.Bl.
Blank, Sheldon H. S.H.Bl.
Blanksten, George I. G.I.B.
Blanshard, Brand. B.Bl.
Blaug, Mark. M.Bg.
Blažek, Miroslav. M.Bl.
Bleaney, Brebis. B.Ble.
Blendinger, Friedrich. F.Br.
Bliss, Lawrence C. L.C.B.
Bliss, Milton E. M.E.Bl.
Bloch, Raymond. R.Bl.
Blond, Georges. G.Bl.
Bloom, Floyd E. F.E.Bl.
Bluhm, Solomon. S.Bl.
Blumenthal, Henry J. H.J.Bl.
Blyth, Conrad Alexander. C.A.Bl.
Boalt, Gunnar. G.Bo.
Boardman, John. Jo.Bo.
Boateng, Ernest Amano. E.A.B.
Bobek, Hans. H.B.
Bockris, John O'M. J.O'M.B.
Bode, Carl. Ca.B.
Bode, Hendrik W. H.W.B.
Bodin, D. Joseph. D.J.B.
Bogue, Allan G. A.G.Bo.
Bokser, Rabbi Ben Zion. B.Z.B.
Boland, Frederick Henry. F.H.B.
Bold, Harold C. H.C.B.
Bolle, Kees W. K.W.Bo.

Bollnow, Otto Friedrich. O.F.B.
Bolt, Bruce A. B.A.B.
Bond, Donald F. D.F.B.
Bonfante, Larissa. La.B.
Bonilla, José. Jo.B.
Bonilla, Luis. L.Bo.
Bonin, Gerhardt von. G.v.B.
Bonner, Charles Edmond Bradlaugh.
　　C.E.B.B.
Bonner, Gerald. Ge.B.
Bonner, John Tyler. J.T.Bo.
Boocock, Colin. C.B.
Borgatta, Edgar F. E.F.B.
Borgstrom, Georg A. G.A.B.
Boring, Edwin Garrigues. E.G.Bor.
Borko, Harold. H.Bo.
Borlaza, Gregorio C. G.C.B.
Bornecque, Jacques-Henry. J.-H.B.
Bornkamm, Günther. G.Bor.
Bornstein, Ira. I.Bo.
Bornstein, Marc H. M.H.Bo.
Borth, Paul F. P.F.B.
Bose, Raj C. R.C.Bo.
Bosellini, Alfonso. A.Bo.
Bosisio, Alfredo. Al.B.
Bottomore, Thomas B. T.B.B.
Boucot, Arthur James. A.J.Bo.
Boulding, Kenneth E. K.E.Bo.
Bouloiseau, Marc. M.Bo.
Bouvier, Jean. Je.B.
Bouwsma, William J. W.J.Bo.
Bowersock, G.W. G.W.Bo.
Bowle, John Edward. J.E.B.
Bowman, John S. J.S.Bo.
Bowness, Alan. Al.Bo.
Boxer, Baruch. B.Bo.
Boyden, Edward Allen. E.A.Bo.
Boyer, Carl B. C.B.B.
Boyer, Marjorie Nice. M.N.B.
Boyle, John Andrew. J.A.Bo.
Bradbury, Savile. S.Br.
Bradford, Ernle. E.Br.
Bradley, Harold Whitman. H.W.Br.
Bradley, John F.N. J.F.N.B.
Bradley, Sir Kenneth (Granville) K.G.B.
Bradley, Rupert Stevenson. R.S.B.
Brady, The Rev. Ignatius Charles.
　　I.C.B.
Braidwood, Robert J. R.J.Br.
Bramson, Leon. L.Br.
Brand, Donald Dilworth. D.D.Br.
Brandon, James R. J.R.B.
Brandon, The Rev. Samuel G.F.
　　S.G.F.B.
Brandt, Andres R.F.T. von. A.v.B.
Brant, Irving. I.Bt.
Brasted, Robert C. R.C.Br.
Brathwaite, Edward Kamau. E.Be.
Braun, Armin C. A.C.Br.
Bray, Wayne D. W.D.B.
Bready, James H. Ja.H.B.
Breen, Walter Henry. W.H.Br.
Brembeck, Cole S. Co.S.B.
Brett, Martin. Ma.Br.
Brice, William Charles. W.C.B.
Brickman, William W. W.W.B.
Bridges, Edward Bridges, 1st Baron.
　　E.B.
Bridgewater, Thornton Howard.
　　T.H.B.
Briggs, Asa Briggs, Baron. As.B.
Bright, John. Jo.Br.
Bright, William O. W.O.B.
Brill, Reginald. R.Br.
Brincourt, André. An.Br.
Brisby, Liliana. L.B.

Briskey, Ernest J. E.J.B.
Britt, Kenneth W. K.W.Br.
Britter, Eric V.B. E.V.B.B.
Brix, Andrew C. An.C.B.
Brock, John Fleming. J.F.B.
Brodie, Fawn McKay. F.M.B.
Broek, Jan O.M. J.O.M.Br.
Brogan, Hugh. H.Br.
Brome, Vincent. V.Br.
Bromiley, Geoffrey W. G.W.B.
Bromke, Adam. A.Br.
Brommelle, Norman Spencer. N.S.B.
Brookfield, Harold Chillingworth.
　　H.C.Br.
Brown, David. D.Bn.
Brown, David. Da.Br.
Brown, Elizabeth A.R. E.A.R.B.
Brown, Frank A., Jr. F.A.B.
Brown, G. Malcolm. G.M.B.
Brown, J.A.C. J.A.C.B.
Brown, J. Guthrie. J.G.B.
Brown, John Russell. J.R.Br.
Brown, L. Carl. L.C.Br.
Brown, Laurie M. L.M.B.
Brown, Leslie Hilton. L.H.B.
Brown, Maurice J.E. M.J.E.B.
Brown, Peter R.L. P.R.L.B.
Brown, Robert Harold. R.H.Br.
Brown, T. Julian. T.J.Br.
Brown, Truesdell S. T.S.B.
Browning, Robert. R.B.
Bruce, Frederick Fyvie. F.F.B.
Bruce, Michael I. M.I.B.
Brugière, Jean-Marie. Je.-M.B.
Bruhat, Jean. J.Bru.
Bruk, Solomon Ilich. S.I.B.
Brunnschweiler, Dieter. Di.B.
Bruschi, Arnaldo. Ar.B.
Brusher, The Rev. Joseph Stanislaus.
　　J.S.Br.
Bry, Doris. D.Br.
Bryant, Sir Arthur. Ar.Br.
Bryant, John H. J.H.Br.
Buchan, The Hon. Alastair Francis.
　　A.F.B.
Buchanan, Robert Angus. R.A.Bu.
Buckmaster, Barbara. B.Br.
Budden, Julian Medforth. J.M.Bu.
Budenholzer, Roland A. R.A.B.
Budinger, Thomas F. T.F.B.
Buechner, Thomas S. T.S.Bu.
Buettner-Janusch, John. J.B.-J.
Bugh, Glenn Richard. G.R.B.
Buitenen, J.A.B. van. J.A.B.v.B.
Bullock, Alan Bullock, Baron. A.B.
Bullough, The Rev. Sebastian. S.Bh.
Burdeau, Michel. Mi.B.
Burgess, Anthony. An.B.
Burghardt, The Rev. Walter John.
　　W.J.Bu.
Burke, Ulick Peter. U.P.B.
Burn, Andrew Robert. A.R.Bu.
Burnaby, The Rev. John. Jo.Bu.
Burns, Sir Alan Cuthbert. A.C.Bs.
Burr, Robert N. R.N.Bu.
Burrows, William W. W.Bu.
Burrus, John N. J.N.B.
Burton, Ivor F. I.F.B.
Burton, Maurice. M.Bn.
Burton, Milton. M.Bu.
Burtt, Edward Howland, Jr. E.H.B.
Buru, Mukhtar Mustafa. Mu.B.
Busch, Daryle H. D.H.B.
Bush, Douglas. D.B.
Bush-Brown, Albert. A.B.-B.
Bushman, Donald O. D.O.B.

Bushnell, Geoffrey H.S. G.H.S.B.
Buss, Robin Caron. R.C.Bu.
Busuttil, Salvino. S.Bu.
Butcher, H. John. H.J.B.
Butland, Gilbert James. G.J.B.
Butler, Joseph T. J.T.B.
Butler, M.H. M.H.B.
Butlin, Martin. Ma.Bu.
Butt, John Everett. J.E.Bu.
Butterfield, Lyman H. L.H.Bu.
Buttinger, Joseph. J.Bu.
Butts, Allison. A.Bu.
Butzer, Karl W. K.W.B.
Bykov, Vasili Dmitrievitch. V.D.B.
Byrnes, Robert F. R.F.B.

Cadbury, Henry J. H.J.C.
Cadoux, Theodore John. T.J.C.
Cahen, Claude. C.C.
Cahill, James F. J.F.C.
Cahn, Robert W. R.W.C.
Cain, A.J. A.J.Ca.
Cain, Seymour. S.C.
Cairns, James Ford. J.F.Ca.
Calkin, Carleton Ivers. C.I.C.
Calkins, Philip B. P.B.Ca.
Calman, William Thomas. W.T.Ca.
Calmon, Pedro. P.Ca.
Calnan, Charles D. C.D.C.
Calne, Roy Yorke. R.Y.C.
Calogero, Guido. G.C.
Camacho, Jorge A. J.A.Ca.
Camara, Camille. Ca.C.
Cameron, Kenneth Walter. K.W.C.
Cameron, Roy Eugene. R.E.C.
Campana, Pier Paolo del. P.P. del C.
Campbell, Alan K. A.K.Ca.
Campbell, Eila M.J. E.M.J.C.
Campbell, John R. J.R.C.
Cannon-Brookes, Peter. P.C.-B.
Canright, James Edward. J.E.Ca.
Cansdale, George S. Ge.C.
Capers, Gerald M. G.M.C.
Caponigri, A. Robert. A.R.C.
Capper, Comdr. Douglas Parodé.
　　D.P.C.
Cardona, George. Ge.Ca.
Cardoze, Nydia María. N.M.C.
Carey, Margret A. Ma.A.C.
Carli, Enzo. E.Ca.
Carlsson, Sten C.O. S.C.O.C.
Carluccio, Luigi. L.Ca.
Carmagnani, Marcello A. M.A.Ca.
Carpenter, Malcolm Breckenridge.
　　M.B.C.
Carr, Bruce Alan. B.A.C.
Carr, Edward H. E.H.C.
Carr, Raymond. R.Ca.
Carrington, Dorothy V. D.V.C.
Carruthers, John E. J.E.C.
Carsaniga, Giovanni. G.Car.
Carson, David. D.Ca.
Carson, Hampton L. H.L.C.
Carson, Michael Anthony. M.A.C.
Carstensen, Vernon. V.Ca.
Carter, Francis William. F.W.C.
Carter, Wilbert K. W.K.C.
Cartwright, Frederick F. F.F.C.
Cartwright, Janet M. J.M.Ca.
Cary, Max. M.Car.
Cary, Otis. O.C.
Cash, Arthur H. A.H.Ca.
Casolani, Lieut. Col. Charles Edward.
　　C.E.C.
Castañeda, Concepción E. C.E.Ca.

Castle, Peter Henry John. P.H.J.C.
Caswell, John Edwards. Jo.E.C.
Catalano, Eduardo F. E.F.C.
Caudle, Ben H. B.H.C.
Caughey, John W. J.W.C.
Caussou, Jean-Louis. J.-L.Ca.
Cavero Lataillade, Iñigo. I.C.L.
Cawkwell, George Law. G.L.Ca.
Cessi, Roberto. R.Ce.
Cestre, Charles. C.Ce.
Chadwick, Charles. C.Ch.
Chadwick, The Very Rev. Henry.
 H.Cha.
Chadwick, W. Owen. W.O.C.
Chaix-Ruy, Jules-Marie. J.C.-R.
Chambers, W. Walker. W.W.C.
Chambre, The Rev. Henri. H.C.
Chamot, Mary. M.Ch.
Chan, David B. D.B.C.
Chan, Hoklom. H.Ch.
Chan, Wing-tsit. W.-t.C.
Chanderli, Abdel Kader. A.K.Ch.
Chandler, David P. D.P.Ch.
Chandra, Pramod. P.Ch.
Chandrasekhar, Sripati. S.Ch.
Chang, Chen-tung. C.-t.C.
Chang, Sen-dou. S.-d.C.
Chao Lin. Ch.L.
Chapanis, Alphonse. Al.C.
Chapman, Brian. B.Ch.
Chapman, Floyd Barton. F.B.C.
Chapman, Frank. F.Ch.
Chapman, Valentine J. V.J.C.
Charles, Jean-Léon. J.-L.Ch.
Charleston, Robert Jesse. R.J.Ch.
Charlton, Donald Geoffrey. D.G.Ch.
Chastenet de Castaing, Jacques.
 J.C. de C.
Chatterjee, Shiba P. S.P.C.
Chen, Cheng-Siang. C.-S.Ch.
Ch'en, Jerome. Je.Ch.
Chen, Shou Yi. S.Y.C.
Chen, Theodore Hsi-en. T.H.C.
Cheng, Bin. Bi.C.
Cheng, Chu-yuan. C.-y.C.
Chenu, The Rev. Marie-Dominique.
 M.-D.Ch.
Chern, S.S. S.S.C.
Cherry, John. J.Ch.
Chevalier, Willie J. W.J.C.
Chevallier, Jean-Jacques. J.-J.C.
Chiang Yee. C.Y.
Chiappini, Luciano. L.Ch.
Chib, Sukhdev Singh. S.S.Ch.
Childers, Norman F. N.F.C.
Chilver, Guy Edward Farquhar.
 G.E.F.C.
Chisholm, Lawrence James. L.J.C.
Chissell, Joan. Jo.Ch.
Choay, Françoise. F.C.
Chong, Byong-Wuk. B.-W.C.
Chow, Tse-tsung. T.-t.C.
Chow, Ven Te. V.T.C.
Christensen, Aksel E. A.E.Cn.
Christensen, Dieter. Di.C.
Christensen, Jan. Ja.C.
Christie, Andrew Barnett. A.B.C.
Christie, Ian R. I.R.C.
Christie, Robert L. R.L.Ch.
Chuang Shang-yen. C.S.-y.
Ćirković, Sima M. S.M.Ci.
Clagg, Sam E. S.E.C.
Clark, Eugene. E.Cl.
Clark, George B. G.B.Cl.
Clark, John Grahame Douglas.
 J.G.D.C.

Clark, Walter Houston. W.H.C.
Clarke, Martin Lowther. M.L.C.
Clarke, Mary. M.Cl.
Clarkson, Jesse Dunsmore. J.D.C.
Classen, Peter. P.Cla.
Clay, Theresa. T.C.
Clayton, Raymond Brazenor. R.B.C.
Clayton, Sir Stanley George. S.G.C.
Clegern, Wayne M. W.M.Cl.
Clemence, Gerald M. G.M.Ce.
Clements, Robert John. R.J.C.
Clench, Mary Heimerdinger. M.H.C.
Clifford, Derek Plint. D.P.Cl.
Clifford, James Lowry. J.L.Cl.
Clifford, Paul R. P.R.Cd.
Cline, Barbara Lovett. B.L.C.
Cline, C.L. C.L.Cl.
Cline, Howard F. H.F.C.
Clingan, Ian C. I.C.C.
Closs, Gerhard L. G.L.C.
Cloud, Preston. P.C.
Cloudsley-Thompson, John Leonard.
 J.L.C.-T.
Clutton, Cecil. C.Cl.
Coates, J.E. J.E.Co.
Cochrane, The Rev. Arthur C. A.C.C.
Cockshut, A.O.J. A.O.J.C.
Codazzi, Angela. A.C.
Coe, Michael Douglas. M.D.C.
Cofer, Charles N. C.N.C.
Coffin, David R. D.R.C.
Coffin, Ivor Cecil. I.C.Cn.
Coggeshall, Ivan Stoddard. I.S.C.
Cogley, John. Jo.C.
Cogniat, Raymond. R.Cog.
Cohen, Arthur L. A.L.C.
Cohen, Gerson D. G.D.C.
Cohen, Jerome B. J.B.Co.
Cohen, Jozef. J.C.
Cohen, Selma Jeanne. S.J.C.
Cohen, Yehudi A. Y.A.C.
Cohn, Paul M. P.M.C.
Cole, Fay-Cooper. F.-C.Ce.
Cole, Dame Margaret I. M.I.C.
Cole, Sonia M. S.M.Co.
Coleman, James Malcolm. J.M.C.
Collins, George R. G.R.Co.
Collins, James Daniel. J.D.Co.
Collins, Peter. Pe.C.
Collins, Philip. Ph.C.
Collins, Robert O. R.O.C.
Collison, Robert L. R.L.C.
Comhaire, Jean L. L.Co.
Condliffe, J. B. J.B.C.
Condon, Edward U. E.U.C.
Cone, Carl B. C.B.Co.
Conley, C. Lockard. C.L.C.
Conn, J.F.C. J.F.C.C.
Connell, Timothy John. T.J.Co.
Connor, Ralph A. R.A.Co.
Conrad, Barnaby. B.C.
Constable, William G. W.G.C.
Contreras R., Jose Daniel. J.D.C.R.
Conversi, Leonard W. L.C.
Conybeare, Charles E.B. C.E.B.C.
Cook, Arthur Herbert. A.H.C.
Cook, James Gordon. J.G.Co.
Cook, L. Russell. L.R.C.
Cooke, Deryck V. D.V.Co.
Coolhaas, W.Ph. W.Ph.C.
Coon, Carleton Stevens. C.S.C.
Cooper, Douglas. D.C.
Cooper, G. Arthur. G.A.C.
Cooper, Kenneth H. K.H.C.
Cooper, Martin Du Pré. M. Du P.C.
Copp, J. Terry. J.T.C.

Corbet, Philip S. P.S.C.
Cordner, Michael. M.Co.
Cornelius, Charles E. C.E.Co.
Cornevin, Robert. R.Co.
Cornwall, John L. J.L.C.
Coser, Lewis A. L.A.C.
Coste, René. R.C.
Cotter, Charles Henry. C.H.C.
Cottle, Richard W. R.W.Co.
Cotton, F. Albert. F.A.C.
Coulson, Noel James. N.J.C.
Coupland, Robert Thomas. R.T.C.
Court, Nathan Altshiller. N.A.Ct.
Courthion, Pierre. P.Co.
Cousin, Jean. Je.C.
Couzens, Edward Gordon. E.G.C.
Cowan, Richard S. R.S.C.
Cowen, Denis Victor. D.V.Cn.
Cowgill, Warren. W.C.
Cowie, Alexander. A.Co.
Cowley, Malcolm. Ma.C.
Cox, Hiden T. H.T.C.
Cox, Maria S. M.Sc.
Coxe, Antony Dacres Hippisley.
 A.D.H.C.
Coxeter, H.S. MacDonald.
 H.S.MacD.C.
Crabb, David W. D.W.C.
Cragg, The Rt. Rev. Albert Kenneth.
 A.K.C.
Cranston, Maurice. M.C.
Cranstone, Bryan A.L. B.A.L.C.
Cratty, Bryant J. B.J.C.
Crawshay-Williams, Rupert. R.C.-W.
Creevey, Peter Raymond. P.R.C.
Cremin, Lawrence A. L.A.Cr.
Crews, Eli Rush. E.R.C.
Crews, Frederick C. F.C.C.
Crist, Raymond E. R.E.Cr.
Croizier, Ralph C. R.C.C.
Croll, Gerhard. G.Cr.
Cromer, George C. G.C.C.
Cromer, Orville C. O.C.C.
Crone, Gerald Roe. G.R.C.
Cronin, Vincent. V.C.
Cronquist, Arthur. A.Cr.
Crook, John Anthony. J.A.Cr.
Crook, Keith A.W. K.A.W.C.
Crossland, Norman. N.C.
Crossley-Holland, Peter. P.C.-H.
Crouzet, François Marie-Joseph. F.Ct.
Crowley, Daniel J. D.J.C.
Crowley, The Rev. Theodore. T.Cr.
Crowther, Bosley. B.Cr.
Crowther, J.G. J.G.Cr.
Crozet, René. Re.C.
Cruickshank, John. J.Cr.
Cruse, William. W.Cr.
Cucu, Vasile S. V.S.C.
Culican, William. W.Cu.
Cullen, James. J.Cul.
Cuninghame, John Garry. J.G.C.
Current, Richard N. R.N.C.
Curtin, Nancy A. N.A.C.
Curtin, Philip De Armond. P. De A.C.
Curtis, Alan S. A.S.Cu.
Curtis, Stanley Evan. S.E.Cu.
Cuthbert, Alan William. A.W.C.
Cuttler, Charles D. C.D.Cu.

Daiches, David. D.Da.
Dalley, Stephanie Mary. S.M.D.
Dalstrom, Harl Adams. H.A.D.
Daniel, Glyn Edmund. G.E.D.
Daniel, Ralph Thomas. R.T.D.

Daniels, Milton Rockwood. M.R.Da.
Daniels, Robert V. R.V.D.
Danowski, T.S. T.S.D.
Dansette, Adrien. A.Da.
D'Antonio, William Vincent.
  W.V.D'A.
Dantzig, George B. G.B.D.
Danzig, Allison. A.D.
Das, Hariprasanna. H.D.
Das, Manmath Nath. M.N.D.
Dashtseren, D. D.Dn.
Dasmann, Raymond F. R.F.D.
Dauer, A.M. A.M.D.
Dauster, Frank N. F.N.D.
David, René. R.Da.
Davidsohn, A.S. A.S.D.
Davidson, Eugene A. E.A.D.
Davidson, James Norman. J.N.D.
Davidson, Robert Bruce. R.B.D.
Davies, Ernest Albert John. E.A.J.D.
Davies, Hugh Alistair. H.A.Da.
Davies, The Rev. J. Gordon. J.G.D.
Davies, Norman. N.D.
Davies, Oliver. O.D.
Davies, R.J. R.J.Da.
Davies, Robert E. R.E.Da.
Davies, The Rev. Rupert E. R.E.D.
Davies, Wayne K.D. W.K.D.D.
Davis, Gwenda Louise. G.L.D.
Davis, Harry. Ha.D.
Davis, H. Grady. H.G.D.
Davis, M. Edward. M.E.D.
Davis, William C., Jr. W.C.Da.
Davison, P.H. P.H.D.
Davison, W. Phillips. W.P.D.
Davson, Hugh. H.Da.
Dawbin, William Henry. W.H.D.
Dawson, Andrew Hutchinson. A.H.D.
Dawson, Mary R. M.R.D.
Day, Michael H. M.H.D.
Dayal, P. P.D.
Dean, The Most Rev. Ralph Stanley.
  R.S.De.
DeBakey, Michael E. M.E.DeB.
de Beer, Sir Gavin. G. de B.
de Blij, Harm J. H.J. de B.
De Conde, Alexander. A. De C.
Dédéyan, Charles. C.De.
de Graft-Johnson, John Coleman.
  J.C. de G.-J.
DeJong, Russell N. R.N.DeJ.
Dekker, George G. G.De.
de la Mare, Peter B.D. P.B.D. de la M.
Delane, Mary. M.De.
Delebecque, Edouard. E.D.
Delmelle, Joseph-Edouard-Marie-
  Ghislain. J.-E.-M.-G.D.
DeLong, Dwight Moore. D.M.DeL.
Delporte, Henri J. H.J.De.
DeMaggio, Augustus E. A.E.D.
Dember, William N. W.N.D.
Demoz, Abraham. A.Dem.
Denecke, Ludwig. L.De.
Deraniyagala, Paul E. Pieris. P.E.P.D.
Der Nersessian, Sirarpie. S. Der N.
Desai, Ranjit Ramchandra. R.R.D.
Desan, Wilfrid. W.De.
de Santillana, Giorgio D. G. de S.
Descargues, Pierre. P.De.
Deschamps, Hubert Jules. H.J.D.
Descloitres, Robert. R.De.
Descola, Jean. J.De.
Despić, Aleksandar R. A.De.
Desrosier, Norman Wilfred. N.W.D.
Dethan, Georges. G.Det.
de Vleeschauwer, Herman Jean.

H.J. de V.
Devlin, John F. J.F.De.
de Vries, Johan G.W. J.G.W. de V.
Dewdney, John C. J.C.D.
De Wiest, Roger J.M. R.J.M. De W.
DeWoskin, Kenneth J. K.J.DeW.
Diakonoff, Igor Mikhailovich. I.M.D.
Diano, Carlo. C.D.
Dibner, Bern. B.Di.
Dickie, James. J.Di.
Dickinson, Harry T. H.T.D.
Dickinson, Robert Eric. R.E.Di.
Dickson, Kwamina Busumafi. K.B.D.
Dickson, Lovat. L.D.
Dienst, Heide. H.Di.
Diethrich, Edward Bronson. E.B.D.
Dietz, Robert Sinclair. R.S.D.
Diffloth, Gérard. G.Di.
Dijkgraaf, Sven. S.Di.
Dikaios, Porphyrios. P.Di.
Dilger, William C. W.C.Di.
Dillon, Myles. M.D.
Dimitrovsky, Haim Zalman. H.Z.D.
Dimock, Edward C., Jr. E.C.D.
Dimroth, Erich. E.Di.
Dingman, S. Lawrence. S.L.D.
Dinshaw, Fram E. F.E.D.
Diószegi, Vilmos. V.D.
Diringer, David. D.D.
Ditchburn, Robert William. R.W.Di.
Djibladze, Mikhail Leonidovich.
  M.L.D.
Djordjevic, Dimitrije V. D.V.D.
Dobzhansky, Theodosius. T.D.
Dockstader, Frederick J. F.J.D.
Dodson, Calaway H. C.H.D.
Dodson, Edward O. E.O.D.
Dölger, Franz. F.Dr.
Domanitsky, Anatoly Petrovich.
  A.P.D.
Domb, Cyril. Cy.Do.
Domingues, Mário José. M.J.D.
Domínguez, Jorge I. J.I.D.
Domke, Martin. M.Do.
Donald, David Herbert. D.H.D.
Donini, Filippo. F.Do.
Donnellan, Keith S. K.S.D.
Donoghue, Denis. D.Do.
Donovan, Bernard Thomas. B.T.D.
Dooling, David, Jr. Da.D.
Doorn, Jacques van. J.v.D.
Doresse, Jean P. J.P.Do.
Dorfman, Robert. R.D.
Dorfman, Ron. R.Do.
Doroshinskaya, Yelena Matveyevna.
  Y.M.D.
Dorpalen, Andreas. A.Do.
Dorson, Richard M. R.M.D.
Dorst, Jean P. J.P.D.
Doucy, Arthur J.M. Ar.D.
Douglas, A. Vibert. A.V.D.
Douglas, Ronald Walter. R.W.D.
Douie, Decima L. D.L.D.
Dowd, Douglas F. D.F.Do.
Dowdey, Clifford. C.Do.
Dowling, Herndon G. H.G.Do.
Dowsett, Charles James Frank.
  C.J.F.D.
Dresch, Jean. Je.D.
Drescher, Seymour. S.Dr.
Dresden, Mark J. M.J.Dr.
Driscoll, John S. J.S.D.
Drobnig, Ulrich M. U.M.D.
Drower, Margaret Stefana. M.S.D.
Drucker, Philip. P.Dr.
Drummond, Boyce A., Jr. B.A.D.

Dubois, Carlos Pablo. C.P.D.
Duchesne-Guillemin, Jacques. J.D.-G.
Duckett, Eleanor Shipley. E.S.D.
Dudley, Donald Reynolds. D.R.D.
Dudley, Elizabeth Corning. E.C.Du.
Due, John F. J.F.D.
Duellman, William E. W.E.D.
Dufford, Stanley. S.D.
Dufour, Pierre. P.Du.
Dugdale, Donald Stephen. D.S.D.
Dull, Jack L. J.L.D.
Dulles, The Rev. Avery. A.Du.
Dumesnil, René. R.Dum.
Dummett, Michael A.E. Mi.D.
Dunaev, Vladimir Nikolaevich. V.N.D.
Dunbar, Maxwell John. M.J.Du.
Dunbar, Moira. M.Dr.
Dunn, Ethel Deikman. E.D.D.
Dunn, L.C. L.C.D.
Dunn, Richard S. R.S.Du.
Dunn, Stephen Porter. S.P.D.
Dupree, Louis. L.Du.
Dupree, Nancy Hatch. N.H.D.
Durant, Frederick C., III. F.C.D.III.
Durgnat, Raymond E. R.Du.
Durham, J. Wyatt. J.W.Du.
Durko, Janusz. Ja.D.
Dury, George Harry. G.H.D.
Dussel, Enrique. E.Du.
Du Val, Patrick. P. Du V.
Duveen, Denis Ian. D.I.D.
Duverger, Maurice. M.Du.
Dwivedi, R.L. R.L.D.
Dworkin, Harvey J. H.J.Dw.
Dyck, Cornelius J. C.J.D.
Dyer, Denys G. D.G.D.
Dykeman, Wilma. W.D.
Dykhuizen, George. G.Dy.

Eardley, Armand J. A.J.E.
Earl, David Magarey. D.M.Ea.
Easby, Dudley Tate, Jr. D.T.E.
East, Robert A. R.A.E.
East, W. Gordon. W.G.E.
Eastman, Richard H. R.H.E.
Easton, Archie H. A.H.E.
Ebisawa, Arimichi. A.Eb.
Eccles, W.J. W.J.E.
Eckbo, Garrett. G.Ec.
Ede, David A. D.E.
Edel, Leon. L.Ed.
Edelmann, Chester Monroe, Jr. C.M.E.
Edlin, Herbert Leeson. H.L.E.
Edwards, Clive Arthur. C.A.E.
Edwards, Kenneth Charles. K.C.E.
Edwards, Robert Walter Dudley.
  R.W.D.E.
Edzard, Dietz O. D.O.E.
Egerod, Søren Christian. S.C.E.
Eggen, Olin Jeuck. O.J.E.
Egli, Emil. E.Eg.
Ehrlich, Blake. B.E.
Eibl-Eibesfeldt, Irenäus. I.E.-E.
Eilon, Samuel. S.E.
Ekstrom, George F. G.F.E.
Elath, Eliahu. E.E.
Elekes, Lajos. L.El.
Elftman, Herbert. H.El.
El Hamamsy, Laila Shukry. L.S.El H.
Eliade, Mircea. M.Ee.
El-Kammash, Magdi M. M.M.El-K.
Elkin, Adolphus Peter. A.P.E.
Eller, Ernest McNeill. E.McN.E.
Elliott, Geoffrey Kenyon. G.K.E.
Elliott, Sir Ivo D'Oyly. I.D'O.E.

Garden, Edward J.C. E.J.C.G.
Gardiner, Patrick Lancaster. P.L.G.
Gardiner, Robert K.A. R.K.A.G.
Gardner, Ernest Dean. E.D.G.
Garg, Renu. Re.G.
Gargi, Balwant. B.Ga.
Garigue, Philippe. P.Ga.
Garn, Stanley M. S.M.G.
Garrad, Kenneth. K.Ga.
Garrett, Alfred B. A.B.Ga.
Garrigus, Wesley Patterson. W.P.G.
Gash, Norman. N.G.
Gasking, Elizabeth Belmont. E.B.G.
Gasparini, Evel. E.G.
Gaster, Theodor H. T.H.G.
Gates, David M. D.M.G.
Gaunt, William. W.Ga.
Gavrilov, A.M. A.M.Ga.
Geanakoplos, Deno John. D.Ge.
Gebhard, Paul Henry. P.H.Ge.
Geerlings, Gerald K. G.K.Ge.
Geiringer, Karl. K.G.
Gelb, Arthur. A.Ge.
Gelb, Barbara. B.Ge.
Gelb, Ignace J. I.J.G.
Gelderman, Carol W. C.W.G.
Gelpi, Ettore. E.Ge.
Gelston, Arthur S., Jr. A.S.G.
Gentilli, Joseph. J.G.
Gentry, Alan William. A.W.G.
Gerasimov, Innokentii Petrovich.
   I.P.G.
Gerig, O. Benjamin. O.B.G.
Germani, Gino. G.Ge.
Gerow, Edwin. Ed.G.
Gerstenmaier, Eugen. Eu.G.
Gertsch, Willis John. W.J.G.
Geyer, Richard A. R.A.G.
Ghirshman, Roman. R.Gh.
Ghori, G.K. G.K.G.
Ghose, Sisirkumar. S.Gh.
Ghul, Mahmud Ali. M.A.G.
Gibb, Andrew Dewar. A.D.G.
Gibbins, Roger. R.G.
Gibbs, Frederick William. F.W.G.
Gibbs, Gerald V. G.V.G.
Gibbs-Smith, Charles Harvard.
   C.H.G.-S.
Gibney, Frank B. F.B.G.
Gibson, Robert Donald Davidson.
   R.D.D.G.
Giddings, J. Calvin. J.C.Gi.
Gies, Frances Carney. F.C.Gi.
Gifford, Ernest M., Jr. E.M.G.
Gilbert, Douglas Stuart. D.Gi.
Gilbert, M. Charles. M.C.G.
Gilbert, Robert Andrew. R.A.Gi.
Gilchrist, Peter Spence, Jr. Pe.S.G.
Giles, Charles Hugh. C.H.Gi.
Giles, James R. J.R.G.
Gill, The Rev. Joseph. J.Gi.
Gillies, Alexander. A.Gi.
Gillmor, Reginald E. R.E.Gi.
Gilmore, Robert Louis. R.L.Ge.
Gimbutas, Marija. M.G.
Gimm, Martin. M.Gi.
Gingerich, Owen. O.G.
Ginns, Harry Norwood. H.N.G.
Ginsberg, Donald M. D.M.Gi.
Ginsburg, Norton S. N.S.G.
Giorgetti, Giovanni Pietro. G.P.Gi.
Girvetz, Harry K. H.K.G.
Gittings, Robert W.V. R.Gi.
Gjuzelev, Wassil Todorov. W.T.G.
Glaessner, Martin F. M.F.G.
Glasz, Christiaan. C.G.

Glatzer, Nahum N. N.N.G.
Glazer, Sidney. S.Gl.
Gleeson, Leo John. L.J.G.
Glendon, Mary Ann. M.A.Gl.
Glubb, Sir John Bagot. J.B.Gl.
Godechot, Jacques. J.Go.
Godman, Peter. P.Go.
Goethals, Peter R. P.R.Go.
Goetz, Hermann. H.Go.
Gogolák, Ludwig von. L.v.G.
Goin, Coleman Jett. C.J.G.
Goldammer, Kurt Moritz Artur.
   K.M.A.G.
Goldbeck, Frederick. F.Go.
Goldblatt, Howard C. H.C.G.
Goldin, Judah. J.Gol.
Goldscheider, Ludwig. L.Go.
Gollin, Gillian Lindt. G.L.Go.
Gomillion, Charles Goode. C.G.G.
Gomme, Arnold Wycombe. A.W.Ge.
Gömöri, George. G.G.
Gonçalves Pereira, António Armando.
   A.A.G.P.
Goncharov, Vladimir Petrovich.
   V.P.G.
González, Nancie L. N.L.G.
González Casanova, Pablo. P.G.C.
González Díaz, Emilio Fernando.
   E.F.G.D.
Gooberman, George L. G.L.G.
Goodall, David W. D.W.G.
Goodbody, Ivan M. I.M.G.
Goode, Richard B. R.B.G.
Goodman, George J. G.J.G.
Goodman, Morris F. M.F.Go.
Goodnight, Clarence James. C.J.Go.
Goodnight, Marie Louise. M.L.Go.
Goodrich, Leland Matthew. L.M.G.
Goodwin, Albert. Al.G.
Goodwin, Noël. N.Go.
Gorbman, Aubrey. Au.G.
Gordon, Cyrus H. C.H.G.
Gordon, David Frank. D.F.G.
Gordon, George N. G.N.G.
Gordon, Isabella. I.G.
Gordon-Walker, Patrick Chrestien
   Gordon Walker, Baron. P.G.W.
Gorgy, Samy. S.G.
Görlitz, Walter Otto Julius. W.Go.
Gorman, George C. G.C.G.
Gosling, L.A. Peter. L.A.P.G.
Goss, Richard Johnson. R.J.G.
Gottschalk, Stephen. S.Go.
Goudsmit, Samuel A. S.A.G.
Goult, Herman W. H.W.G.
Gourou, Pierre. P.Gu.
Goveia, Elsa Vesta. E.V.G.
Gowans, Alan. Al.Go.
Gowing, Sir Lawrence. La.G.
Grabar, Oleg. O.Gr.
Graf, Alfred Byrd. A.B.Gr.
Grame, Theodore C. T.Gr.
Grancsay, Stephen Vincent. S.V.G.
Grant, Michael. M.Gr.
Grant, Peter R. P.R.G.
Grant, Robert M. R.M.G.
Grastyán, Endre. E.Gr.
Graue, Jerald C. J.C.Gr.
Gray, Alic William. A.W.Gr.
Gray, Eric William. E.W.G.
Gray, Jane. J.Gr.
Gray, Peter. Pe.G.
Grayling, A.C. A.C.G.
Green, Benny. B.Gr.
Green, Edna R. E.R.G.
Green, Estill I. E.I.G.

Green, J. J.Gre.
Green, Peter S. P.S.G.
Green, Roger Lancelyn. R.L.G.
Greenaway, Frank. F.Gre.
Greenberg, Moshe. Mo.Gr.
Greene, David. D.Gr.
Greene, Mark Richard. M.R.G.
Greenfield, Richard David. Ri.G.
Greenspan, Morris. M.Gre.
Greenwood, Peter Humphry. P.H.G.
Greenwood, Richard Harold. R.H.G.
Greer, Henry Kirk. H.K.Gr.
Gregg, Alan. Al.Gr.
Gregorietti, Guido. G.Gr.
Gregory, Derek Peter. D.P.G.
Greisen, Kenneth I. K.Gr.
Grenand, Pierre. P.Gd.
Grenville, John A.S. J.A.S.G.
Gressitt, Judson Linsley. J.L.G.
Griffith, Guy Thompson. G.T.G.
Griffith, William J. W.J.Gr.
Grim, Ralph E. R.E.G.
Grimsley, Ronald. R.Gr.
Groen, Pier. P.Gr.
Groover, Mikell P. M.P.G.
Gross, Harvey S. Ha.G.
Gross, M. Grant. M.G.G.
Gross, Werner. W.Gr.
Grudin, Robert. Ro.G.
Gruijters, Johannes P.A. J.P.A.G.
Grünbaum, Branko. B.G.
Gspan, Alfonz. A.Gn.
Gudava, T.E. T.E.G.
Gudzii, Nikolai Kallinikovich. N.K.G.
Guenther, Herbert V. H.G.
Guerello, The Rev. Franco. F.Gu.
Guest, Ann Hutchinson. A.H.Gt.
Guiart, Jean. J.Gt.
Guichonnet, Paul. P.G.
Guiguemde, Pierre H. P.H.Gu.
Guillemin, Henri. He.Gu.
Guimarães, Alberto Passos. A.P.G.
Guitton, Henri. H.Gu.
Gulliver, P.H. P.H.Gul.
Gulyan, Pyotr Vatslavovich. P.V.G.
Gundermann, Karl-Dietrich. K.-D.G.
Gungaadash, B. B.Gu.
Gunstone, Frank Denby. F.D.G.
Gunther, Erna. E.Gu.
Gurney, Ashley B. A.B.G.
Gurney, Oliver Robert. O.R.G.
Gusdorf, Georges Paul. G.P.G.
Gustafson, Neil C. N.C.G.
Güterbock, Hans G. H.G.G.
Gutherz, Elmer J. E.J.G.
Guthke, Karl S. K.S.G.
Guthrie, Douglas James. D.J.G.
Guthrie, Sir Tyrone. T.G.
Gutmann, Viktor. V.G.
Gutsche, C. David. C.D.G.
Gvozdetsky, Nikolay Andreyevich.
   N.A.G.
Gwynn, Denis Rolleston. D.R.G.
Gyftopoulos, Elias Panayiotis.
   E.P.G.
Gyllensvärd, Bo Vilhelm. B.V.Gy.

Haaf, Ernst ten. E.t.H.
Haar, Dirk ter. D.t.H.
Hackett, John. Jo.Hac.
Haedeke, Hanns-Ulrich. H.-U.H.
Haekel, Josef. Jo.H.
Hagely, John R. J.R.Ha.
Haggerty, James J. J.J.Ha.
Hahn, Bae-ho. B.-h.H.

Haight, Gordon S.   G.S.Ha.
Hainsworth, F. Reed.   F.R.H.
Hájek, Igor.   I.H.
Haley, K.H.D.   K.H.D.H.
Halfpenny, Eric.   E.Hy.
Hall, The Rev. Basil.   B.H.
Hall, Marshall, Jr.   Ma.H.
Hall, Richard P.   R.P.H.
Hall, Robert A., Jr.   R.A.H.
Halm, George N.   G.N.H.
Halperin Donghi, Tulio.   T.H.D.
Halpern, Jack.   J.Ha.
Halstead, Bruce W.   B.W.H.
Hambly, Gavin R.G.   G.R.G.H.
Hamelin, Louis-Edmond.   L.-E.H.
Hamerow, Theodore S.   T.S.H.
Hamidé, Abdul-Rahman.   A.-R.H.
Hamilton, Bernice Margaret.
   B.M.H.
Hamilton, William James.   W.J.H.
Hamman, The Rev. Adalbert G.
   A.G.Ha.
Hammen, Oscar J.   O.J.H.
Hammer, A. Gordon.   A.G.H.
Hammond, Mason.   M.Ha.
Hammond, Nicholas G.L.   N.G.L.H.
Hammond Innes, Ralph.   R.H.I.
Hamp, Eric P.   E.P.H.
Hamzah Sendut.   Ha.Se.
Hanahan, Donald J.   D.J.H.
Hancock, Keith J.   K.J.H.
Hand, Cadet H., Jr.   C.H.Ha.
Handel, Samuel.   S.H.
Hanna, Willard A.   W.A.Ha.
Hansen, Arlen J.   A.J.H.
Hansen, Gladys Cox.   G.C.Ha.
Hansen, Walter B.O.   W.Hn.
Hanshaw, Bruce B.   B.B.H.
Hanson, A.H.   A.H.H.
Hanson, Carl.   C.H.
Hanson, Earl Dorchester.   E.D.H.
Hanson, Earl Parker.   E.P.Ha.
Harbaugh, John W.   J.W.Ha.
Harbison, Craig S.   C.S.Ha.
Hardie, Robert H.   R.H.H.
Hardy, Sir Alister C.   A.C.Ha.
Hardy, Arthur C.   A.C.Hy.
Hardy, Edward R.   E.R.Ha.
Hare, F. Kenneth.   F.K.H.
Hargrave, John G.   J.G.H.
Harler, Campbell Ronald.   C.R.H.
Harmel, Claude.   C.H.
Harmon, Mamie.   Ma.Ha.
Harms, Robert Thomas.   R.T.H.
Harrelson, Walter.   W.Ha.
Harris, David.   Da.H.
Harris, David Russell.   D.R.Ha.
Harris, Enriqueta.   E.Ha.
Harris, James T.   J.T.H.
Harris, Leslie.   L.H.
Harris, Rosemary Lois.   R.L.Ha.
Harrison, Anna J.   A.J.Ha.
Harrison, John A.   J.A.Ha.
Harrison, Raymond O.   R.O.H.
Harrison, Richard J.   R.J.Ha.
Harrison, Walter A.   W.A.H.
Harrison-Church, Ronald James.
   R.J.H.-C.
Harriss, C. Lowell.   C.L.Ha.
Harrisson, Tom.   T.Hn.
Harrod, Sir Roy Forbes.   R.F.H.
Harroy, Jean-Paul.   Je.-P.H.
Hart, Harold.   H.Ha.
Hart, Herbert Lionel Adolphus.
   H.L.A.H.
Hartenberg, Richard S.   R.S.H.

Hartwell, Ronald Max.   R.M.Hl.
Hashisaki, Joseph.   Jo.Ha.
Haskell, Arnold Lionel.   A.L.H.
Hassler, Warren W., Jr.   W.W.H.
Hastings, Margaret.   M.Has.
Hatsopoulos, George N.   G.N.Ha.
Hatt, Jean-Jacques.   J.-J.H.
Hatton, Ragnhild Marie.   R.M.H.
Hattori, Shirō.   S.Ha.
Haugen, Einar.   Ei.H.
Haurowitz, Felix.   F.Ha.
Häuser, Karl H.   K.Hä.
Hauser, Philip M.   P.M.H.
Havard, C. William H.   C.W.H.H.
Havard, John David Jayne.   J.D.J.H.
Havelock, Eric Alfred.   E.A.Ha.
Haverschmidt, François.   F.H.
Havighurst, Alfred F.   A.F.H.
Havighurst, Robert J.   R.J.H.
Hawkins, Gerald S.   G.S.H.
Hawkins, Joseph E., Jr.   J.E.H.
Hawting, G.R.   G.R.H.
Hayashi, Shigeru.   Sh.H.
Hayford, Charles W.   C.W.H.
Hayne, David M.   D.M.Ha.
Hayward, Charles Harold.   C.H.H.
Hayward, John F.   J.F.Ha.
Haywood, H. Carl.   H.C.H.
Haywood, John A.   J.A.H.
Hazai, Georg.   G.Ha.
Hazard, John N.   J.N.H.
Healy, Nicholas Joseph.   N.J.H.
Heaney, Robert Proulx.   R.P.He.
Heath, Dwight B.   D.B.H.
Heaton, Pauline.   Pa.H.
Hecht, Charles E.   C.E.He.
Hecht, Melvin E.   M.E.H.
Heelan, Patrick Aidan.   P.A.H.
Heerden, Ernst van.   E.v.H.
Heezen, Bruce C.   B.C.H.
Heiber, Helmut.   H.Hei.
Heilbroner, Robert L.   R.L.He.
Heine, Hermann-Heino.   H.-H.He.
Heinemeyer, Walter.   W.He.
Heinen, Heinz.   He.H.
Heinz, Erich.   E.H.
Heirtzler, J.R.   J.R.H.
Heiser, Charles B., Jr.   C.B.He.
Held, Julius S.   Ju.H.
Heldrich, Andreas F.A.   A.F.A.H.
Heller, Peter.   Pe.H.
Hellie, Richard.   R.He.
Hemp, Wilfrid James.   W.J.He.
Hempel, Carl G.   C.G.H.
Henderson, Philip Prichard.   P.P.H.
Henderson, Robert M.   R.M.He.
Hendricks, George.   G.He.
Hendrickson, James B.   J.B.He.
Hendy, Sir Philip.   P.He.
Heneghan, Maureen.   M.H.
Henfrey, Norman V.   N.V.He.
Hensel, Herbert.   H.He.
Henson, Ronald A.   R.A.He.
Herbert, H.W.   H.W.H.
Herbst, Stanislaw.   S.He.
Herde, Peter.   Pe.He.
Herdman, Thomas.   T.H.
Herget, Paul.   P.H.
Herivel, John.   J.He.
Herklots, Geoffrey A.C.   G.A.C.H.
Herman, Robert D.   R.D.H.
Hermans, Theo Jozef.   T.J.H.
Herschdoerfer, Sigismund M.   S.M.H.
Hertzberg, Rabbi Arthur.   Ar.H.
Herzfeld, Hans.   Ha.He.

Herzog, Marvin Irving.   M.I.H.
Herzog, Peter E.   P.E.H.
Heslop, D. Alan.   D.A.He.
Heslop-Harrison, John.   J.H.-H.
Hess, Eckhard H.   E.H.H.
Hess, Wilmot Norton.   W.N.H.
Heston, The Most Rev. Edward
   Louis.   E.L.H.
Hey, Max H.   M.H.H.
Heydenreich, Ludwig Heinrich.   L.H.H.
Heyerdahl, Thor.   Th.H.
Heywood, John B.   J.B.H.
Hibbert, Christopher.   C.Hi.
Hickey, Gerald C.   G.C.H.
Hieatt, A. Kent.   A.K.H.
Higgins, David J.M.   D.J.M.H.
Higgins, Reynold Alleyne.   R.A.Hi.
Higgins, Theodore R.   T.R.H.
Higgs, Eric S.   E.S.H.
Highet, Gilbert.   G.Hi.
Highfield, J.R.L.   J.R.L.H.
Highsmith, Richard M., Jr.   R.M.Hi.
Hightower, Nicholas Carr.   N.C.H.
Higonnet, Patrice Louis-René.   P.Hi.
Hill, Dorothy.   D.Hi.
Hill, J.E. Christopher.   J.E.C.H.
Hill, John Hugh.   J.H.Hi.
Hill, Laurita L.   L.L.H.
Hill, Richard Leslie.   R.L.Hi.
Hiller, Lejaren.   L.Hi.
Hillers, Delbert R.   D.R.H.
Hills, John M.   J.M.Hi.
Hilton, Peter John.   P.J.H.
Hines, Colin O.   C.O.H.
Hingley, Ronald Francis.   R.F.Hi.
Hintikka, K. Jaakko J.   K.J.Hi.
Hinton, Thomas B.   T.B.H.
Hiorthøy, Finn.   F.Hi.
Hirai, Naofusa.   N.H.
Hitchins, Keith Arnold.   K.A.H.
Hjelmqvist, Hakon.   H.Hj.
Ho, Robert.   Rt.H.
Hoaglin, David C.   D.C.H.
Hobbs, F.D.   F.D.H.
Hobson, Richard Hamilton.   Ri.H.
Hodge, Harold C.   H.C.Ho.
Hodge, Paul W.   P.W.H.
Hodges, James A.   J.A.Ho.
Hodgkin, Thomas.   T.Ho.
Hofer, Kenneth E., Jr.   K.E.H.
Hoffmann, Herbert.   H.Hn.
Hofmann, Michel-Rostislav.   M.-R.Ho.
Hogetsu, Keigo.   K.Ho.
Hogg, Helen Sawyer.   H.S.H.
Hohl, Reinhold D.   Re.H.
Hölder, Helmut.   H.H.
Holderbaum, James.   J.Hm.
Hollister, C. Warren.   C.W.Ho.
Holm, Donald August.   D.A.H.
Holmes, Arthur F.   A.F.Ho.
Holmes, Ralph.   Ra.Ho.
Holstein, William K.   W.K.H.
Holt, Edgar Crawshaw.   E.C.H.
Holt, J.C.   J.C.H.
Holt, Peter M.   P.M.Ho.
Holthusen, Hans Egon.   H.E.H.
Holttum, Richard E.   R.E.H.
Holtzman, Jerome.   Je.Ho.
Honeybone, Reginald Crawshaw.
   R.C.H.
Honeycutt, Baxter D.   B.D.H.
Honigmann, John J.   J.J.Ho.
Honko, Lauri O.   L.O.H.
Hood, M. Sinclair F.   M.S.F.H.
Hoogstraten, Jan S.F. van.   J.v.H.
Hopkins, John Francis Price.   J.F.P.H.

Hopkinson, Ralph G. R.G.H.
Hornberger, Theodore. T.Hor.
Horne, R.A. R.A.Ho.
Hose, Charles. C.Ho.
Hoskin, Michael Anthony. M.A.H.
Hosking, Geoffrey Alan. G.A.H.
Hospers, John. Jo.Ho.
Houghton, Lois Chapman. L.C.H.
Houlton, Sir John Wardle. Jo.W.H.
Hourani, Albert Habib. A.H.Ho.
House, Michael R. M.R.H.
Houston, James. J.Ho.
Houtgast, Jakob. J.H.
Houtte, Baron Jean M.J. van.
  J.M.J.v.H.
Houwink ten Cate, Philo H.J.
  Ph.H.J.H.t.C.
Howard, Ian P. I.P.H.
Howard, John Lawrence. J.L.H.
Howard, Perry H. P.H.H.
Howarth, Thomas. Th.Ho.
Howarth, William Driver. W.D.H.
Howell, F. Clark. F.C.H.
Howie, Alan Crawford. A.C.H.
Hoy, Cyrus Henry. C.H.Ho.
Hoyt, Joseph Bixby. J.B.Ho.
Hoyt, Robert Stuart. R.S.Ho.
Hrbek, Ivan. I.Hr.
Hsia, David Yi-Yung. D.Y.-Y.H.
Hsiao, Kung-chuan. K.-c.H.
Hsieh, Chiao-Min. C.-M.H.
Hsieh, Shan-yüan. S.-y.H.
Hsu, Cho-yun. C.-y.H.
Htin Aung, Maung. M.H.Au.
Hu, Charles Y. C.Hu.
Hu, Yueh-Gin Gung. Y.-G.G.H.
Hubatsch, Walther C. W.C.H.
Hübscher, Arthur. Ar.Hü.
Hucker, Charles O. C.O.Hu.
Hudnut, Joseph. J.Hud.
Hudson, Winthrop S. W.S.H.
Huffman, John W. J.W.Hu.
Hughes, David C. D.C.Hu.
Hughes, The Rev. G.E. G.E.H.
Hughes, Graham McK. G.McK.H.
Huizing, Peter J. P.Hu.
Hultkrantz, Åke Gunnar Birger.
  Å.G.B.H.
Humphrey, John H. J.H.Hy.
Hung, Frederick Fu. F.Hu.
Hunt, Charles B. C.B.H.
Hunt, Earl B. E.B.H.
Hunt, Herbert James. H.J.H.
Hunt, Inez Whitaker. I.W.H.
Hunten, Donald M. D.M.H.
Huot, Jean-Louis. J.-L.Hu.
Huq, Muhammad Shamsul. M.S.H.
Husain, Mahmud. M.Hu.
Husain, Syed Sajjad. S.S.H.
Hussey, Dyneley. D.Hus.
Hussey, Joan Mervyn. J.M.H.
Hutter, Heribert R. H.R.H.
Huxley, Herbert Henry. H.H.Hu.
Huygens, Gerard Willem. G.W.H.
Huyghe, René. R.Hu.
Hyatt, J. Philip. J.P.Hy.
Hyde, Earl K. E.K.H.
Hyman, Isabelle. I.Hy.

Iakovos, Archbishop (James A.
  Coucouzes). I.
Ichiko, Teiji. T.Io.
Ichiye, Takashi. I.Ic.
Ihde, Aaron J. A.J.I.
IJsewijn, Jozef A.M.K. J.A.M.K.I.

Ike, Nobutaka. N.I.
Ikram, S.M. S.M.I.
Illick, Joseph E. J.E.I.
Imshenetsky, Aleksandr Ilyich. A.I.I.
Inalcik, Halil. H.I.
Inden, Ronald B. R.B.I.
Ingham, Kenneth. K.In.
Inglis, David Rittenhouse. D.R.I.
Inglis, W. Grant. W.G.I.
Ingram, William T. W.T.I.
Ingrams, William Harold. W.H.I.
Insall, Donald W. D.W.I.
Ipfling, Heinz-Jürgen. H.-J.I.
Irmscher, Hans Dietrich. H.D.I.
Irvine, Keith. K.I.
Irvine, Verity Elizabeth. V.E.I.
Irwin, David. D.I.
Irwin, John B. J.B.I.
İsnard, Hildebert. H.İs.
Issawi, Charles. C.I.
Ivanov, Vyacheslav Vsevolodovich.
  V.V.I.
Ivić, Pavle. P.I.
Iwasawa, Kenkichi. K.Iw.
İz, Fahir. F.İ.
Izenour, George C. G.C.I.
Izutsu, Toshihiko. T.I.

Jackson, Christopher Stewart. C.S.J.
Jackson, Joy Juanita. J.J.J.
Jackson, Richard T. R.T.J.
Jackson, Roland John. R.J.J.
Jackson, Stanley Percival. S.P.Jn.
Jacob, Stanley W. S.W.J.
Jacobs, Wilbur R. W.R.J.
Jacobsen, Thorkild. T.J.
Jacobson, Bernard. B.Ja.
Jacoby, Oswald. O.J.
Jaffe, Bernard. Be.J.
Jaffe, Hans L.C. H.L.C.J.
Jaffé, Michael. Ml.J.
Jahns, Richard H. R.H.J.
Jairazbhoy, Nazir Ali. N.A.J.
James, A. Walter. A.W.J.
James, C.L.R. C.L.R.J.
James, D. Clayton. D.C.J.
James, The Rev. Edwin Oliver. E.O.J.
James, Preston E. P.E.J.
James, Thomas Garnet Henry.
  T.G.H.J.
Jamieson, John Calhoun. J.C.J.
Jan, Helmut von. H.v.J.
Janick, Jules. J.J.
Jansen, Marius B. M.B.J.
Janson, H.W. H.W.J.
Jarry, Madeleine. M.J.
Järvinen, E. Jaakko. E.J.J.
Jayne, Kingsley Garland. K.G.J.
Jeandet, Yette. Y.J.
Jeffares, Alexander Norman. A.N.J.
Jefferson, Alan R. A.R.J.
Jelavich, Barbara. B.Je.
Jelavich, Charles. C.J.
Jellett, John Holmes. J.H.J.
Jenkins, The Rev. Daniel T. D.T.J.
Jenkins, Elizabeth. E.Je.
Jenks, C. Wilfred. C.W.J.
Jenkyns, Richard H.A. R.H.A.J.
Jennings, Burgess H. B.H.J.
Jerphagnon, Lucien. L.J.
Jescheck, Hans-Heinrich. H.-H.J.
Jessop, Thomas Edmund. T.E.Je.
Jóhannesson, Thorkell. T.Jn.
Johansson, Ivar K. I.J.
John, Walter. W.J.

Johnson, D. Gale. D.G.J.
Johnson, Dorothy M. D.M.J.
Johnson, John J. J.J.Jo.
Johnson, Norman Gardner. N.G.J.
Johnston, Marshall C. M.C.J.
Johnston, S. Paul. S.P.J.
Jolly, William Lee. W.L.J.
Jolowicz, Herbert Felix. H.F.J.
Jones, The Rev. A.M. A.M.J.
Jones, Abeodu Bowen. A.B.J.
Jones, Arnold Hugh Martin. A.H.M.J.
Jones, Benjamin A., Jr. B.A.J.
Jones, Douglas Henry. D.H.J.
Jones, Emrys. E.J.
Jones, Frederick L. F.L.J.
Jones, Gareth H. G.H.J.
Jones, J. Knox, Jr. J.K.J.
Jones, Marsden. Ma.J.
Jones, S.S.D. S.S.D.J.
Jones, Thomas. T.Jo.
Jones, Walton Glyn. W.G.J.
Jongkees, Adriaan G. A.G.J.
Jonsson, Inge. I.Jo.
Jonsson, Ingrid Margareta. I.M.J.
Jordan, David Starr. D.S.J.
Jordan, Karl H.E. K.J.
Jordan, Pascual W. P.W.J.
Josephson, Matthew. M.Jo.
Joshi, Susan Heyner. S.H.J.
Joy, Bernard. B.Jo.
Joyce, Thomas Athol. T.A.J.
Joys, Charles. C.Jo.
Judson, Jay Richard. J.R.J.
Jutikkala, Eino Kaarlo Ilmari. E.K.I.J.
Jwaideh, Wadie. W.Jw.

Kadzamira, Zimani David. Z.D.K.
Kaegi, Walter Emil, Jr. W.E.K.
Kaeppler, Adrienne L. A.Ka.
Kalinin, Gennadi Pavlovitch. G.P.Ka.
Kallen, Horace M. H.M.K.
Kalman, Rudolf E. R.E.K.
Kalmbach, Olin. O.K.
Kalven, Harry, Jr. H.Ka.
Kamanzi, Thomas. T.Ka.
Kamb, W. Barclay. W.B.K.
Kanayev, Viktor Filipovich. V.F.K.
Kanda, Nobuo. N.Ka.
Kang, Yu-chin. Y.-c.K.
Kann, Robert A. R.A.K.
Kanya-Forstner, Alexander Sydney.
  A.S.K.-F.
Kapelrud, Arvid S. A.S.K.
Kaplan, James L. J.L.K.
Kaplan, Lawrence. L.K.
Kaplansky, Irving. I.K.
Karan, P.P. P.P.K.
Karasek, Francis W. F.W.K.
Karger, Barry L. B.L.K.
Karlen, Delmar. D.K.
Karnes, Thomas L. T.L.K.
Katritzky, Alan Roy. A.R.K.
Kaufman, Hyman. Hy.K.
Kaufman, Terrence. Te.K.
Kaufmann, Edgar, Jr. E.K.
Kavolis, Vytautas. V.Ka.
Kay, John Anderson. J.A.Ka.
Kay, Marshall. M.K.
Kazimour, Jan. Ja.K.
Keating, Frank E. F.E.K.
Kedourie, Elie. E.Ke.
Keen, Benjamin. B.K.
Keenan, Edward Louis. E.L.K.
Keenan, Joseph Henry. J.H.K.

Lavender, David Sievert. D.S.Lr.
Laver, James. Ja.L.
Lavondès, Henri. H.La.
Lavrencic, Karl. Ka.La.
Lavrin, Janko. Ja.La.
Lawler, Sylvia Dorothy. S.La.
Lawrence, Carl Adam. C.A.L.
Lawrence, Joseph Collins. J.C.L.
Lawson, Joan. Jo.L.
Lawson, Robert Frederic. R.F.L.
Laya, Diouldé. Di.L.
Layton, Robert. R.Lay.
Lea, Sir Frederick M. F.M.L.
Lea, Kathleen Marguerite. K.M.L.
Leary, Lewis. L.Le.
Lebel, Robert. R.Le.
Lecco, Alberto. A.L.
Lechène, Robert. Ro.L.
Lechevalier, Hubert Arthur. H.A.L.
Lee, Chan. C.Le.
Lee, James A. J.A.Le.
Lee, Ki-baik. K.-b.L.
Lee, Kwang-rin. K.-r.L.
Lee, Peter H. P.H.L.
Lee, Robert Warden. R.W.L.
Leech, Clifford. Cl.L.
Leeming, Frank Andrew. F.A.L.
Legge, Dominica. D.Le.
Legge, John David. J.D.L.
Legum, Colin. Co.L.
Legum, Margaret Jean. M.J.L.
Lehman, Mildred K. M.K.L.
Lehman, Milton. M.Ln.
Lehmann, Andrew George. A.G.L.
Lehmann-Haupt, Hellmut E.
    H.E.L.-H.
Leicester, Henry M. H.M.L.
Leichter, Otto. O.L.
Leighton, Richard M. R.M.Le.
Leiman, Sid Z. S.Z.L.
Leite, Aureliano. A.Le.
Leiter, Samuel. S.Lr.
Lejeune, Michel. M.Le.
Lejewski, Czeslaw. Cz.L.
Lekachman, Robert. R.L.
Lenk, Leonhard. L.Lk.
Lenti, Libero. Li.L.
Lentz, Thomas L. T.L.L.
Leonard, Justin W. J.W.L.
Leone, Lucile P. L.P.Le.
Leontiev, Oleg Konstantinovich.
    O.K.L.
Leprohon, Pierre. P.Le.
Lerner, Richard M. Ri.M.L.
Lernet-Holenia, Alexander. A.L.-Ho.
Lessing, Lawrence P. L.P.L.
Leung, Chi-Keung. C.-K.L.
Le Vay, David. D. Le V.
LeVeque, William Judson. W.J.LeV.
Levi, Albert William. A.W.L.
Levi, Herbert W. H.W.L.
Levi, Lorna R. L.R.L.
Levie, Col. Howard S. H.S.L.
Levron, Jacques. J.Le.
Lewis, David L. D.L.Le.
Lewis, David Malcolm. D.M.L.
Lewis, Geoffrey D. G.D.L.
Lewis, George Knowlton. G.K.L.
Lewis, Hywel David. H.D.L.
Lewis, I.M. I.M.L.
Lewis, John Wilson. J.W.Le.
Lewis, Peirce F. P.F.L.
Leyser, K.J. K.J.L.
Li, Fang Kuei. F.K.L.
Li, Tien-yi. T.-y.L.
Libin, Laurence Elliot. La.L.

Lieberich, Heinz. H.Li.
Lieberthal, Kenneth G. K.G.L.
Liebeschütz, Hans. H.Lz.
Lien, Chan. C.Li.
Liess, Otto. O.Li.
Lieuwen, Edwin. E.Li.
Lifson, David S. D.S.L.
Liley, Bruce Sween. B.S.L.
Lin, Maung Wai. M.W.L.
Lindars, Barnabas. B.L.
Lindauer, Martin. M.Li.
Lindbeck, Assar. A.Li.
Lindbeck, George Arthur. G.A.L.
Lindsay, R. Bruce. R.B.L.
Lindström, Maurits. M.L.
Link, Arthur Stanley. A.S.L.
Lippold, Adolf. A.Lip.
Lisitsin, Aleksandr Petrovich. A.P.L.
Lissens, René Felix. R.F.Li.
Little, Donald P. D.P.L.
Liu, James T.C. J.T.C.L.
Livermore, Harold V. H.V.L.
Livet, Georges. G.Li.
Livi-Bacci, Massimo. M.L.-B.
Livingstone, Daniel A. D.A.L.
Llwellyn, Karl Nickerson. K.N.L.
Lloyd, Albert Lancaster. A.L.Ll.
Lloyd, Seton H.F. S.H.F.L.
Lloyd-Jones, David Mathias. D.M.L.-J.
Lloyd-Jones, Hugh. H.L.-J.
Lo, Jung-pang. J.-p.L.
Lockhart, Richard T. R.T.L.
Lockley, R.M. R.M.L.
Lockspeiser, Edward. E.L.
Loeffler, M. John. M.J.Lo.
Loewe, Fritz P. F.P.L.
Logan, Richard F. R.F.Lo.
Logan, Robert G. R.G.Lo.
Lohuizen, Johanna E. van. J.E.v.L.
Lombardo, Antonino. An.L.
Long, Charles H. C.H.Lo.
Long, Edward Ernest. E.E.L.
Longford, Elizabeth Pakenham,
    Countess of. E.Lo.
Longworth, Philip. P.L.
Lonsdale, Dame Kathleen. K.Lo.
Loomis, Charles P. C.P.L.
Loon, Maurits N. van. M.N.v.L.
Loosli, John K. J.K.L.
Lopez, Robert Sabatino. R.S.L.
Lorig, Clarence H. C.H.L.
Lortz, Joseph. J.L.
Lorwin, Val R. V.R.L.
Losey, George S. G.S.Lo.
Low, D. Anthony. D.A.Lo.
Low, David Morrice. D.M.Lo.
Lowe, Victor. V.Lo.
Lowenthal, Constance. C.Lo.
Lozinsky, Mikhail Grigoriyevich.
    M.G.L.
Luard, Evan. E.Lu.
Lucas, Donald William. D.W.L.
Luce, R. Duncan. R.D.L.
Luck, Georg Hans. G.Lu.
Lucker, Joseph M. J.M.Lu.
Lui, Ante. A.Lu.
Lukoff, Fred. F.L.
Lüling, Karl Heinz. K.H.L.
Lumiansky, R.M. R.M.Lu.
Luscombe, David Edward. D.E.L.
Lustig, Lawrence K. L.K.L.
Lutfi al-Sayyid Marsot, Afaf.
    A.L.al-S.M.
Luttrell, Anthony Thornton. A.T.L.
Lyman, John. J.Ly.
Lynch, John. Jo.Ly.

Lyne, A. Gordon. A.G.Ly.
Lyons, John. J.Lyo.

Mabbott, Thomas Ollive. T.O.M.
Mabbutt, J.A. J.A.M.
Mabee, Carleton. C.Ma.
Mabogunje, Akinlawon Ladipo.
    A.L.M.
Macan, T.T. T.T.M.
Macartney, Carlile Aylmer. C.A.M.
McAuley, Mary. M.McA.
McBirney, Alexander R. A.R.McB.
McBride, George M. G.McC.McB.
McBryde, F. Webster. F.W.McB.
McCallum, W. Cheyne. W.C.McC.
McCarthy, Patrick. P.McC.
McCarthy, Willard J. W.J.McC.
McChesney, Malcolm. M.McC.
Macchia, Giovanni. Gi.M.
McClelland, Charles A. C.A.McC.
McClintock, Elizabeth. E.McC.
McComb, Arthur Kilgore. A.K.McC.
MacConaill, Michael A. M.A.MacC.
McDavid, Raven I., Jr. R.McD.
McDivitt, James F. J.F.McD.
McDonald, Alexander Hugh.
    A.H.McD.
MacDonald, Charles B. C.B.MacD.
McDonald, Forrest. F.McD.
McDonough, Sheila D. S.McD.
MacDuffee, C.C. C.C.MacD.
Maceda, José. Jé.Ma.
McElroy, Frank E. F.E.McE.
McEwen, The Rev. James Stevenson.
    J.S.McE.
McFarlane, James Walter. J.W.McF.
Macfarlane, Robert Gwyn. R.G.M.
MacGaffey, Janet. J.MacG.
MacGaffey, Wyatt. W.MacG.
McGann, Thomas F. T.F.McG.
McGeough, Joseph A. J.A.McG.
McGreevey, William Paul. W.P.McG.
McGregor, Samuel Emmett. S.E.McG.
Machlis, Joseph. J.Ma.
McHugh, Christine. C.McH.
McIntosh, Christopher Angus.
    C.A.McI.
MacIntosh, Robert McKinlay.
    R.Mck.MacI.
McIntyre, Donald. D.McI.
McKelvey, Vincent E. V.E.McK.
Mackenzie, Fred T. F.T.M.
McKenzie, The Rev. John L. J.L.McK.
MacKenzie, William Scott. W.S.MacK.
Mackie, J. Alan. J.A.Ma.
Mackintosh, Nicholas John. N.J.M.
McKnight, Brian E. B.E.McK.
Mackridge, Peter A. P.A.M.
Mack Smith, Denis. De.M.S.
McLaughlin, John. J.McL.
MacLeod, Murdo J. M.J.MacL.
McLeod, Thomas S. T.S.McL.
McLeod, William Hewat. W.H.McL.
McLintock, Peter. P.McL.
McMahon, William B. W.B.McM.
McMullen, Roy Donald. R.McMu.
McMurtrey, James Edward, Jr.
    J.E.McM.
McNeill, William H. W.H.McN.
McNickle, D'Arcy. D'A.McN.
MacNutt, W. Stewart. W.S.MacNu.
Macomber, Richard W. R.W.Ma.
MacRae, Donald Gunn. D.G.MacR.
Maeno, Naoaki. Na.Mo.
Magarshack, David. Da.Ma.

Magda, Matthew S.   M.S.Ma.
Magdoff, Harry.   Ha.Ma.
Magnus, Bernd.   Be.M.
Magoun, Horace Winchell.   H.W.M.
Mahdi, Muhsin S.   M.S.M.
Majeska, George P.   G.P.M.
Makdisi, George.   G.M.
Maksoud, Clovis F.   C.F.M.
Malcolm, Norman A.   N.A.M.
Malia, Martin E.   M.E.Ma.
Malik, Liliya Konstantinovna.   L.K.M.
Malin, Michael C.   M.C.Ma.
Malina, Frank J.   F.J.Ma.
Mallett, Michael Edward.   Mi.Ma.
Mallory, V. Standish.   V.S.M.
Mallowan, Sir Max.   M.Mn.
Malm, William P.   W.P.M.
Maloney, Francis J. Terence.   Fr.J.M.
Manchester, William.   W.Man.
Mann, Golo.   G.Ma.
Mannheim, Hermann.   H.M.
Mannheim, L. Andrew.   L.A.Ma.
Manning, Raymond B.   R.B.M.
Manning, Wayne E.   Wa.E.M.
Manschreck, Clyde L.   C.L.Ma.
Manske, Richard H.   R.H.M.
Mantell, Charles L.   C.L.M.
Manton, Sidnie M.   S.M.M.
Manuel, Frank Edward.   F.E.M.
Manvell, Roger.   R.M.
Maraini, Fosco.   F.M.
Marcelli, Umberto.   U.M.
March, Benjamin.   B.Ma.
Marc'hadour, The Rev. Germain P.
   G.P.Ma.
Marchand, Leslie A.   L.A.M.
Marcus, Leonard M.   L.M.M.
Marcuse, Sibyl.   S.Ma.
Margenau, Henry.   H.Ma.
Margolis, Joseph.   J.Ms.
Mariani, Valerio.   V.M.
Mark, Herman F.   H.F.M.
Markovitz, Hershel.   He.M.
Markowitz, William.   W.Ma.
Marks, Robert W.   R.W.M.
Marks, Shula E.   Sh.M.
Marlowe, John.   Jo.Ma.
Marquard, Leopold.   L.Ma.
Marquardt, Wilhelm Rudolf.   W.R.M.
Marrat, Sidney.   Si.M.
Marriott, McKim.   Mc.M.
Marrou, Henri-Irénée.   H.-I.M.
Marsh, Christopher Marriage.   C.M.
Marshall, Joe T.   J.T.M.
Marshall, John S.   J.S.Ma.
Marshall, P.J.   P.J.M.
Marshall, Robert L.   Ro.Ma.
Marshall, Woodville K.   W.K.M.
Martin, Boyd A.   B.A.M.
Martin, Gene E.   G.E.Ma.
Martin, Laurence Woodward.   L.W.M.
Martindale, Andrew Henry Robert.
   A.Ma.
Martin-Demézil, Jean.   J.M.-D.
Martini, Giuseppe.   Gi.Ma.
Martinot, Roger.   R.Ma.
Martins, Luciano.   L.Ms.
Marty, Martin E.   M.E.M.
Marwick, Maxwell Gay.   M.G.Ma.
Masai, Yasuo.   Y.M.
Mascarenhas, Adolfo C.   A.C.M.
Mason, Sir Basil John.   B.J.M.
Mason, Brian H.   B.H.M.
Mason, Charles T., Jr.   C.T.M., Jr.
Mason, Haydn T.   H.T.M.
Mason, J. Alden.   J.A.Mn.

Mason, Leonard E.   L.E.M.
Mason, Philip.   P.Ma.
Mason, Warren Perry.   M.P.Mn.
Massevitch, Alla Genrikhovna.
   A.G.Ma.
Massey, Alan Gibbs.   A.G.M.
Mast, Gerald.   Ge.M.
Masutani Fumio.   Ma.Fu.
Mathew, The Most Rev. David.   D.Ma.
Mathews, Thomas G.   T.G.Ms.
Mathis, John S.   J.S.M.
Matloff, Maurice.   Ma.M.
Matsumoto, Nobuhiro.   N.M.
Matsumoto, Tatsuro.   T.M.
Matthews, G.V.T.   G.V.T.M.
Matthews, J.F.   J.F.Ma.
Matthias, Erich.   E.Ma.
Matthíasson, Björn.   B.M.
Mattuck, Arthur Paul.   A.P.Ma.
Matull, Wilhelm.   Wi.M.
Matz, Samuel A.   S.A.M.
Maurer, The Rev. Armand.   A.A.Ma.
Maxwell, D.E.S.   D.E.S.M.
May, Comdr. William Edward.
   W.E.M.
Mayeda, Sengaku.   Se.M.
Mayer, Harold M.   H.M.M.
Mayer, William Vernon.   W.V.M.
Mays, John Barron.   J.B.M.
Mažiulis, Vytautas J.   V.J.M.
Mazur, B.W.   B.W.Ma.
Mead, William Richard.   W.R.Me.
Meade, Robert Douthat.   R.D.M.
Meadow, S. Roy.   S.R.M.
Medina, José Ramón.   J.R.Me.
Medina, Manuel.   M.Me.
Mee, John F.   J.F.Me.
Meerheaghe, M.A. van.   M.A.v.M.
Meeuse, Bastiaan J.D.   B.J.D.M.
Mehren, Arthur Taylor von.   A.T.v.M.
Mei, Yi Pao.   Y.P.M.
Meier, Mark F.   M.F.M.
Meiggs, Russell.   Ru.M.
Meischner, Dieter.   D.M.
Meisner, Maurice J.   M.J.M.
Meland, Bernard E.   B.E.M.
Mellonby, Kenneth.   K.Me.
Mellor, Roy E.H.   R.E.H.M.
Melsen, Andrew G.M. van.
   A.G.M.v.M.
Meltzer, Julian Louis.   J.L.Me.
Ménager, Daniel.   D.Mé.
Mendeloff, Albert I.   A.I.M.
Mendenhall, George Emery.   G.E.Me.
Mendoza, Eric.   E.M.
Mensching, Gustav.   G.Me.
Menzies, Robert James.   R.J.Me.
Mercier, Paul.   Pa.M.
Merdinger, Capt. Charles John.   C.J.M.
Merkelbach, Reinhold.   R.Me.
Merlan, Philip.   Pp.M.
Merle, Robert.   Ro.M.
Mernagh, Laurence Reginald.   L.R.M.
Mero, John Lawrence.   J.L.M.
Merritt, H. Houston.   H.H.M.
Mertz, Barbara G.   B.G.M.
Mertz, Pierre.   P.Me.
Meškauskas, Kazimieras Antano.
   K.A.M.
Messenger, P.S.   P.S.M.
Metford, John Callan James.   J.C.J.M.
Meyendorff, The Rev. John.   J.M.
Meyer, Adolphe Erich.   A.E.M.
Meyer, John Richard.   J.R.M.
Meyer, Michael C.   M.C.M.
Mezei, Kathy.   K.M.

Michael, Franz H.   F.H.M.
Michaelsen, Robert Slocumb.   R.S.M.
Michel, Michel.   M.Ml.
Michelena, Luis.   L.M.
Michelmore, Peter.   P.Mi.
Middlehurst, Barbara Mary.   B.M.M.
Middleton, Dorothy.   D.Mi.
Middleton, Gerard V.   G.V.M.
Middleton, John F.M.   J.F.M.
Middleton, Robin David.   R.D.Mi.
Miège, Jacques.   J.Mi.
Miers, Earl Schenck.   E.S.Mi.
Mikhail, S.W.   S.W.M.
Mikhaylov, Nikolay Ivanovich.   N.I.M.
Mikoletzky, Hanns Leo.   H.L.M.
Milgate, Wesley.   W.Mi.
Milkov, Fyodor Nikolayevich.   F.N.M.
Miller, George Leslie.   G.L.M.
Miller, James Grier.   Ja.G.M.
Miller, John Donald Bruce.   J.D.B.M.
Miller, Mark D.H.   M.D.H.M.
Miller, Max.   Mx.M.
Miller, Maynard Malcolm.   M.M.M.
Miller, William.   W.Mr.
Miller, William H.   W.H.M.
Millikin, Sandra.   S.Mi.
Millman, Peter Mackenzie.   P.M.M.
Millner, Maurice Alfred.   M.A.M.
Millon, Henry A.   H.A.M.
Millot, Jacques.   Ja.M.
Mills, Gladstone E.M.   G.E.M.M.
Minarcik, Elbert John.   E.J.M.
Minifie, Bernard W.   B.W.M.
Minio-Paluello, Lorenzo.   L.M.-P.
Minkel, C.W.   C.W.M.
Mints, Aleksey Aleksandrovich.
   A.A.M.
Mirreh, Hassan Ali.   H.A.Mi.
Mirsky, Jeannette.   J.Mir.
Misner, Gordon E.   G.E.Mi.
Mitchell, Andrew Ronald.   A.R.Mi.
Mitchell, G.A.G.   G.A.G.M.
Mitchell, James Clyde.   J.C.Mi.
Mitchell, Jean Brown.   J.B.Mi.
Mitchell, John.   Jo.M.
Mitchell, Mairin.   M.Mi.
Mitchell, Terence Croft.   T.C.M.
Mitford, Nancy.   Na.M.
Mitry, Jean.   Je.M.
Mitzman, Arthur.   Ar.M.
Mizener, Arthur.   A.Mi.
Moeller, Therald.   T.Mo.
Moen, Arve Sverre.   A.S.M.
Mohanty, Jitendra N.   J.N.M.
Mohr, Paul.   Pa.Mo.
Mokray, William George.   W.G.M.
Moldenhauer, Hans.   Ha.M.
Mollat, Michel J.   M.J.Mo.
Moltmann, Jürgen D.   J.D.M.
Momigliano, Arnaldo Dante.   A.D.Mo.
Momo, Hiroyuki.   Hi.Mo.
Momtchiloff, Nicholas Ivan.   N.I.Mo.
Moncada R., J. Roberto.   J.R.M.R.
Monet, The Rev. Jacques.   J.Mo.
Mongan, Agnes.   Ag.M.
Mongrédien, Georges.   G.Mn.
Monick, John A.   J.A.Mo.
Monk, C.B., Jr.   C.B.Mo.
Monnerville, Gaston.   G.Mo.
Monroy, Alberto.   A.Mo.
Montagna, William.   W.M.
Montross, Lynn.   L.Mo.
Moog, Florence.   Fl.M.
Mookerjee, Sitanshu.   S.Mo.
Moore, Gerald.   Ge.Mo.
Moore, Gordon E.   G.E.Mo.

Moore, Harold E., Jr.   H.E.Mo.
Moore, John Preston.   J.P.M.
Moore, Patrick.   P.Mo.
Moore, Sonia.   S.M.
Moore, Will G.   W.G.Mo.
Moraes, Frank R.   F.R.M.
Morales-Carrión, Arturo.   A.M.-C.
Moran, Francis.   F.Mo.
Moran, Warren.   W.Mo.
Morgan, Neil.   N.Mo.
Morgan, Stephen William Kenneth.
   S.W.K.M.
Morley, Cyril John.   C.J.Mo.
Morley, Ronald James.   R.J.M.
Morrey, Charles B., Jr.   C.B.My.
Morris, Charles Nicholas.   C.N.M.
Morris, Donald R.   D.R.M.
Morris, H.S.   H.S.M.
Morris, Terence Patrick.   T.P.M.
Morrison, Hugh Sinclair.   Hu.M.
Morrissey, Charles Thomas.
   C.T.Mo.
Morsey, Rudolf.   R.Mo.
Mortensen, Brita Maud Ellen.
   B.Mo.
Morton, John Edward.   J.E.Mo.
Morton, William Lewis.   W.L.M.
Moseley, Maynard F., Jr.   M.F.Mo.
Mosher, Frederick C.   F.C.M.
Mosley, J. Philip.   J.P.Mo.
Mosley, Leonard.   Le.M.
Mosse, W.E.   W.E.Mo.
Mosteller, Frederick.   Fr.M.
Mostofi, Khosrow.   Kh.Mo.
Mostow, George Daniel.   G.D.M.
Moulton, Matthew James.   Ma.J.M.
Moulton, William G.   Wi.G.M.
Moumouni, Abdou.   A.M.
Movius, Hallam L., Jr.   H.L.Ms.
Mozumder, Asokendu.   A.Moz.
Mueller, David Livingstone.   D.L.M.
Mukerji, S.N.   S.N.M.
Mulholland, J. Derral.   J.D.Mu.
Müller, Claudius Cornelius.   C.C.M.
Müller, Edith A.   E.A.M.
Müller, Joachim.   J.Mu.
Müller-Brockmann, Josef.   J.M.-Br.
Müller-Freienfels, Wolfram.   W.M.-F.
Multhauf, Robert P.   R.P.M.
Mundel, Marvin E.   M.E.Mu.
Munn-Rankin, J.M.   J.M.M.-R.
Munro, Thomas.   Th.M.
Munroe, John A.   J.A.Mu.
Munson, J. Ronald.   J.R.Mn.
Munsterberg, Hugo.   H.Mu.
Munz, Peter.   P.Mu.
Muranov, Aleksandr Pavlovich.
   A.P.M.
Murphy, Arthur D.   A.D.M.
Murphy, The Rev. Francis Xavier.
   F.X.M.
Murphy, James J.   J.J.M.
Murra, John V.   J.V.M.
Murray, Anne Wood.   A.W.M.
Murray, Francis J.   F.J.M.
Murray, Peter J.   P.J.Mu.
Murton, Ronald K.   R.K.M.
Musgrave, William K.R.   W.K.R.M.
Muskie, Edmund S.   E.S.M.
Mutter, Reginald P.C.   R.P.C.M.
Mutton, Alice F.A.   A.F.A.M.
Myachin, Ivan Kirillovich.   I.K.M.
Myers, Alexander Reginald.   A.R.M.
Myers, Raymond R.   R.R.M.
Myers, Rollo H.   R.My.
Myint, Hla.   H.My.

Nachod, Frederick C.   F.C.N.
Nachtergaele, Victor.   V.N.
Nadeau, Maurice.   M.Na.
Naess, Arne D.   A.D.N.
Nagahara, Keiji.   K.N.
Nagata, Takesi.   T.Na.
Nagel, Heinrich.   H.N.
Nagler, Alois M.   A.M.N.
Naim, C.M.   C.M.N.
Nair, Kusum.   K.Na.
Nair, N. Chandrasekharan.
   N.C.N.
Naisbitt, John.   Jo.N.
Naka, Arata.   A.Na.
Nakamura, Hajime.   H.Na.
Nakosteen, Mehdi K.   M.K.N.
Namias, Jerome.   J.Na.
Nanda, B.R.   B.R.N.
Nangeroni, Giuseppe.   G.Na.
Napier, B. Davie.   B.D.N.
Napier, J.R.   J.R.N.
Narasimhan, Chakravarthi V.   C.V.N.
Narasimhan, Raghavan.   R.Na.
Narayana, H.S.   H.S.N.
Narr, Karl J.   K.J.N.
Nash, Manning.   Ma.N.
Nash, Paul.   Pa.N.
Nash, Ray.   Ra.N.
Nasr, Seyyed Hossein.   S.H.N.
Natsagdorj, Sh.   Sh.Nj.
Neal, James T.   J.T.Ne.
Nel, Andries.   A.Ne.
Nelson, E. Clifford.   E.C.N.
Nelson, Gareth Jon.   G.J.N.
Nelson, R.J.   R.J.Ne.
Nelson, Robert J.   R.J.N.
Nemerov, Howard.   H.Ne.
Nestyev, Israel Vladimirovich.
   I.V.N.
Nettl, Bruno.   B.N.
Neumann, Gerhard.   G.N.
Neumark, Fritz.   F.N.
Nevins, Allan.   Al.N.
Newbigin, Marion I.   M.I.N.
Newburn, Ray L., Jr.   R.L.Ne.
Newcombe, Curtis L.   C.N.
Newhall, Beaumont.   Be.N.
Newlin, Dika.   D.N.
Newman, Graeme R.   G.Ne.
Newman, Robert Bradford.   R.B.N.
Newman, William Anderson.   W.A.N.
Newman, William S.   W.S.N.
Newton, Brian E.   B.E.N.
Neyman, Viktor Grigoryevich.
   V.G.N.
Nicholas, Herbert G.   H.G.N.
Nichols, Robert Brayton.   R.B.Ni.
Nicholson, Norman L.   N.L.N.
Nicol, Davidson S.H.W.   D.S.H.W.N.
Nicol, Donald MacGillivray.   D.M.N.
Nicolaï, Henri.   He.Ni.
Nicolet, Marcel.   M.N.
Nicolle, Jacques-M.-R.   J.-M.-R.N.
Niddrie, David Lawrence.   D.L.N.
Niederer, Arnold.   A.Ni.
Nielsen, Kai E.   K.E.N.
Nienhauser, William H., Jr.   W.H.N.
Nijim, Basheer K.   B.K.N.
Nijinsky, Romola.   R.Ni.
Nikiforov, Leonid Alekseyevich.
   L.A.N.
Niklaus, Robert.   Ro.N.
Nisbet, Robert A.   R.A.N.
Niven, Alastair N.R.   A.N.R.N.
Noback, Charles R.   C.R.N.
Noble, Clyde Everett.   C.E.N.

Noble, J. Jeremy.   J.J.No.
Noble, Joseph Veach.   J.V.N.
Noller, Carl R.   C.R.No.
Norbeck, Edward.   E.N.
Nordhagen, Per Jonas.   P.J.N.
Nordtvedt, Kenneth L., Jr.   K.L.N.
Nörlund, Niels Erik.   N.E.N.
Norman, A.V.B.   A.V.B.N.
Norman, Lennart T.   L.T.N.
Norman, Richard O.C.   R.O.C.N.
Norris, David A.   D.A.N.
Norris, Kenneth Stafford.   K.S.N.
North, Robert C.   R.C.N.
Norwich, John Julius Cooper, 2nd
   Viscount.   N.
Nove, Alexander.   A.No.
Novick, Alvin.   A.N.
Nowell, Charles E.   C.E.No.
Nuwinkware, Pierre-Claver.   P.-C.N.

Oakley, Francis Christopher.   F.C.O.
Oakley-Hill, Dayrell Reed.   D.R.O.-H.
Oates, E.E. David M.   E.E.D.M.O.
Oberg, Kalervo.   K.Ob.
O'Brien, Conor Cruise.   C.C.O'B.
O'Callaghan, Joseph F.   J.F.O'C.
Occhialino, Mario E.   Ma.E.O.
Ochsenwald, William L.   W.L.O.
O'Connell, Daniel Patrick.   D.P.O'C.
O'Connor, Daniel William.   D.W.O'C.
O'Connor, Francis Valentine.
   F.V.O'C.
Oddone, Juan A.   J.A.O.
Odlozilik, Otakar.   O.O.
Odum, Eugene P.   E.P.O.
Oehser, Paul H.   P.H.O.
Ogden, Horace Russell.   H.R.O.
Ogilvie, Robert Maxwell.   R.M.Og.
Ogorkiewicz, Richard Marian.
   R.M.O.
O'Gorman, James Francis.   J.F.O'G.
O'Grady, Brendan Anthony.   B.O'G.
O'Kelly, Bernard.   B.O'K.
Olah, George A.   G.A.O.
Oldenbourg-Idalie, Zoé.   Z.O.
Oldroyd, Harold.   H.O.
Oliver, Jack E.   J.E.O.
Oliver, William Hosking.   W.H.O.
Olivier, Daria.   D.Ol.
Ollier, Clifford David.   C.D.O.
Olson, Edwin A.   E.A.O.
Olson, Everett C.   E.C.O.
Olson, Jerry S.   J.S.O.
Olson, Maynard V.   M.V.O.
Oman, Carola (Lady Lenanton).
   C.O.
Omar, Farouk.   F.Om.
Ominde, Simeon Hongo.   S.H.O.
Ommanney, Francis D.   F.D.O.
O'Neill, Denis.   D.O'N.
Ooi Jin Bee.   O.J.B.
Oppenheimer, Jane M.   J.M.O.
O'Raifeartaigh, Tarlach.   T.O'R.
Orcibal, Jean.   J.Or.
Ordish, George.   G.O.
Ore, Oystein.   O.Or.
Ornati, Oscar A.   O.A.O.
Orne, Martin T.   M.T.O.
Ortner, Sherry B.   S.B.O.
Orton, Glenn S.   G.S.O.
Orville, Richard Edmonds.   R.E.Or.
Orvin, Anders Kristian.   A.K.O.
Osborn, Frederick Henry.   F.H.O.
Osborn, Ronald E.   R.E.O.
Osborne, John W.   J.W.O.

Osborne, Milton Edgeworth.   M.E.O.
Osborne, Richard Horsley.   R.H.O.
Osler, Margaret J.   M.J.O.
Ostenso, Ned Allen.   N.A.O.
O'Toole, James Joseph.   J.O'T.
O'Toole, Thomas E.   T.E.O'T.
Otto, Christian F.   C.F.O.
Otto, Eberhard.   E.O.
Outler, Albert Cook.   A.C.O.
Overbeek, Jan Theodoor Gerard.
   J.T.G.O.
Overdijkink, Gerrit Willem.   G.W.O.
Overton, Leonard C.   L.C.O.
Owen, D.D.R.   D.D.R.O.
Owen, Peter D.   P.D.O.
Owen, Tobias Chant.   T.C.O.
Owen, Wilfred.   W.O.
Owens, The Rev. Joseph.   J.O.
Oxtoby, Willard Gurdon.   W.G.O.

Pacaut, Marcel.   M.Pa.
Padelford, Norman J.   N.J.P.
Pagel, Bernard E.J.   B.E.J.P.
Pai, Raghawendra Mukund.   R.M.P.
Paine, Frank A.   F.A.P.
Paine, Robert P.B.   R.P.B.P.
Painter, George Duncan.   G.D.P.
Pal, Indra.   I.P.
Palerm, Angel.   An.Pa.
Pallis, Christopher A.   C.A.P.
Pallucchini, Rodolfo.   R.Pal.
Palmer, Allison R.   A.R.P.
Palmer, Ralph Anthony.   R.A.Pr.
Pálsson, Hermann.   He.P.
Pannain, Guido.   G.Pan.
Paoletti, John T.   J.T.Pa.
Papadakis, Juan.   J.Pa.
Papike, J.J.   J.J.Pa.
Paproth, Eva.   E.P.
Parczewski, Władysław.   W.Pa.
Park, George Kerlin.   G.K.P.
Parke, Herbert William.   H.W.P.
Parker, Alexander A.   A.A.P.
Parker, Franklin D.   F.D.P.
Parkes, Henry Bamford.   H.B.P.
Parkes, Kenneth C.   K.C.P.
Parkin, Charles William.   C.W.Pa.
Parkinson, Robert Lewis.   R.L.P.
Parrot, André.   A.Pa.
Parry, John Horace.   J.H.Py.
Parry, V.J.   V.J.P.
Parsons, James Bayard.   J.B.Pa.
Pascal, Roy.   Ro.Pa.
Pashuto, Vladimir T.   V.T.P.
Passavant, Günter.   G.Pa.
Passmore, Reginald.   R.Pa.
Pastor, José M.F.   J.M.F.P.
Pathak, Devavrat Nanubhai.   D.N.P.
Patrick, Hugh T.   H.T.P.
Patterson, Colin.   C.P.
Patterson, Thomas C.   T.C.P.
Patze, Hans.   H.Pa.
Patzig, Günther.   Gü.P.
Pauck, Wilhelm.   W.P.
Pauling, Linus C.   L.C.P.
Pavelić, Ante S.   A.S.Pa.
Pavlowitch, Kosta Stevan.   K.St.P.
Pawley, Andrew K.   A.K.Pa.
Pawson, David Leo.   D.L.P.
Payanzo, Ntsomo.   N.Pa.
Payne, Stanley G.   S.G.P.
Pearson, Charles G.   C.G.P.
Pearson, H.F.   H.F.P.
Pedanou, Macaire K.   M.K.P.
Peel, Edwin A.   E.A.P.

Peel, Ronald Francis.   R.F.Pe.
Peiser, H. Steffen.   H.S.P.
Pelczar, Michael J., Jr.   M.J.P.
Pelikan, Jaroslav Jan.   J.J.Pe.
Pélissier, René.   R.P.
Pélissier, Roger.   Ro.Pe.
Pellat, Charles L.P.   C.L.P.P.
Pelletier, Michel B.   M.B.P.
Pen, Jan.   J.P.
Penčev, Peter Georgiev.   P.G.P.
Pendle, George.   G.Pe.
Penner, Hans H.   Ha.P.
Pennington, D.H.   D.H.P.
Penny, Nicholas B.   N.B.P.
Pepelasis, Adamantios A.   A.A.Ps.
Perelman, Chaim.   C.Pe.
Perham, Dame Margery.   M.Pm.
Perkins, Edward S.   E.S.P.
Pernoud, Régine.   R.Pe.
Perowne, Stewart Henry.   S.H.P.
Perrin, Norman.   N.P.
Perrott, Roy.   Ro.P.
Perry, Harry.   H.Pe.
Peruta, Franco della.   F.d.Pe.
Pessen, Edward.   E.Pe.
Péter, László.   L.P.
Peterdi, Gabor F.   G.F.P.
Peters, James A.   J.A.P.
Peterson, James T.   J.T.P.
Petit, Paul.   P.P.
Petrov, Mikhail Platonovich.   M.P.Pe.
Petrov, Victor P.   V.P.P.
Petterson, Donald Rahl.   D.R.P.
Pettitt, George A.   G.A.P.
Péwé, Troy L.   T.L.Pe.
Peyre, Henri M.   H.M.P.
Pfaffmann, Carl.   C.Pf.
Phelps Brown, Ernest Henry.   E.H.P.B.
Philby, Harry St. John Bridger.
   H.St.J.B.P.
Philips, Sir Cyril Henry.   C.H.Ps.
Phillips, Courtenay Stanley Goss.
   G.S.G.P.
Phillips, Joseph D.   J.D.P.
Phillips, Melba.   M.Ph.
Phiri, Kings Mbacazwa G.   K.M.G.P.
Pichon, Jean-Charles.   J.-C.P.
Pick, Robert.   R.Pi.
Pickering, Sir George.   G.Pi.
Pickersgill, John Whitney.   Jo.W.P.
Pickles, Dorothy M.   D.M.P.
Pielke, Roger A.   R.A.Pi.
Pieper, Josef.   Jf.Pi.
Pierce, A. Keith.   A.K.P.
Pierce, Francis S.   F.S.P.
Pierce, John R.   J.R.P.
Piercey, W. Douglas.   W.D.P.
Pieri, David C.   D.C.P.
Pike, Douglas Henry.   D.H.Pe.
Pilikian, Hovhanness Israel.   Ho.I.P.
Pillai, V.R.   V.R.P.
Pincus, Alexis G.   A.G.P.
Pinder-Wilson, Ralph H.   R.H.P.-W.
Pine, Leslie Gilbert.   L.G.P.
Pines, Shlomo.   S.Pi.
Pingree, David E.   D.E.P.
Pinker, Robert A.   R.A.P.
Pipes, Richard E.   R.E.Pi.
Pirsig, Maynard E.   M.E.P.
Pittioni, Richard.   Ri.P.
Piveteau, Jean.   J.Piv.
Plamenatz, John P.   J.P.Pl.
Platnauer, Maurice.   M.Pl.
Playfair, Giles William.   G.W.P.
Plischke, Hans.   Hs.P.
Pluckhahn, J. Bruce.   J.B.P.

Plumb, Sir John.   Jo.Pl.
Pocock, Tom.   T.Po.
Podhajsky, Alois Wilhelm.   A.W.P.
Podlecki, Anthony J.   A.J.P.
Poelhekke, Jan J.   J.J.P.
Pogue, Forrest C.   F.C.P.
Pohl, Frederik.   F.Po.
Pohl, Richard W.   R.W.P.
Pokhshishevsky, Vladimir V.   V.V.P.
Polk, William Roe.   W.R.P.
Pollack, Peter J.   P.J.P.
Pollard, John Graham.   J.G.P.
Pollard, John Richard Thornhill.
   J.R.T.P.
Polmar, Norman C.   N.C.P.
Polunin, Nicholas.   N.Po.
Pomeau, René Henry.   R.H.Po.
Pontecorvo, Guido.   G.Po.
Pontieri, Ernesto.   E.Po.
Poole, Gary William.   Ga.P.
Poole, Gray Johnson.   G.J.P.
Poole, Kenyon Edwards.   K.E.P.
Poonawala, Ismail K.   I.K.P.
Pope, Clifford Hillhouse.   C.H.P.
Pope-Hennessy, Sir John.   J.P.-H.
Popkin, Richard H.   R.H.P.
Popov, Igor Vladimirovich.   I.V.P.
Poppino, Rollie E.   R.E.P.
Porter, William V.   W.V.P.
Posner, Rebecca.   Re.P.
Potter, David Morris.   D.M.Po.
Potter, George Richard.   G.R.P.
Potter, Simeon.   S.P.
Potthoff, Heinrich.   H.P.
Potts, Malcolm.   M.P.
Poucher, William A.   W.A.Po.
Pounder, Cuthbert Coulson.   C.C.P.
Pournaras, Dimitris.   D.P.
Powell, James M.   J.M.Po.
Powell, Raphael.   R.Po.
Powers, Philip N.   P.N.P.
Pozo Vélez, Homero.   H.P.V.
Prakasa Rao, Vaddiparti Lova Surya.
   V.L.S.P.R.
Prausnitz, John M.   J.M.P.
Prawer, Joshua.   Jo.Pr.
Preece, Warren E.   W.E.P.
Preidel, Helmut.   H.Pr.
Prescott, J.R.V.   J.R.V.P.
Pressat, Roland F.M.   R.F.P.
Preuschen, Gerhardt.   G.P.
Prevost, Jean.   J.Pr.
Price, Arnold H.   A.H.P.
Price, Cecil John Layton.   C.J.L.P.
Priestley, Charles Henry Brian.
   C.H.B.P.
Prieto, Justo Pastor.   J.P.P.
Pringle, John Douglas.   J.D.Pr.
Proskouriakoff, Tatiana.   T.P.
Proud, Lieut. Col. Richard Riseley.
   R.R.Pr.
Proudlove, James Alan.   J.Pro.
Prout, W.G.   W.G.Pr.
Prown, Jules David.   J.D.Pro.
Pruchnicki, Jerzy.   Je.P.
Prudhoe, John Edgar.   Jo.P.
Pryce, Roy.   R.Pr.
Puck, Theodore Thomas.   T.T.P.
Puhvel, Jaan.   J.Pl.
Pulgar-Vidal, Javier.   J.P.-V.
Pullen, Andrew M.   A.M.P.
Pulleyblank, Edwin G.   E.G.P.
Purdy, Ken W.   K.W.P.
Purdy, The Rev. William Arthur.
   W.A.P.
Puri, Baij Nath.   B.N.P.

Purković, Miodrag Al. M.A.P.
Purrington, Philip F. P.F.P.
Pye, E. Michael. M.Py.

Quimby, Robert S. R.S.Q.
Quinn, John Francis. J.F.Q.
Quinones, Ricardo J. R.J.Q.
Quintana, Ricardo. R.Q.
Quinton, Anthony M. Quinton,
    Baron. A.M.Q.
Quittmeyer, Charles Loreaux. C.L.Q.

Rabie, Hassanein Muhammad. H.Ra.
Rabin, Chaim. Ch.R.
Raby, Frederic James Edward. F.J.E.R.
Rae, John Bell. J.B.Ra.
Raeff, Marc. M.Ra.
Raghavan, Chakravarthi. C.Ra.
Rahman, Fazlur. F.R.
Rāhula, Walpola. Wa.R.
Ralphs, Sheila. S.Ra.
Ralston, Robert H. R.H.Ra.
Ramanujan, A.K. A.K.R.
Ramm, Agatha. A.Ra.
Ramsay, James Arthur. J.A.R.
Ramsey, The Rt. Rev. Ian Thomas.
    I.T.R.
Rand, Austin L. Au.L.R.
Rang, Humphrey P. H.P.R.
Rankin, Bayard. B.R.
Ransom, Harry Howe. H.H.R.
Rantsman, Yelizaveta Yakovlevna.
    Y.Y.R.
Rao, R.V.R. Chandrasekhara.
    R.V.R.CR.
Rashid, Sh. Abdur. S.A.R.
Rasmussen, John O., Jr. J.O.R.
Rasmussen, Wayne D. W.D.R.
Ravenhill, William. W.Ra.
Rawlings, Arthur Lionel. A.L.Ra.
Rawlinson, John Lang. J.L.Ra.
Rawski, Evelyn S. E.S.R.
Rawson, Philip S. P.S.R.
Rea, Donald G. D.G.R.
Rea, Kenneth Grahame. K.G.R.
Rea, Kenneth John. K.J.R.
Read, Allen Walker. A.W.Re.
Read, Donald. D.Re.
Rebelo, Luís de Sousa. L.de S.R.
Rechnitzer, Andreas B. A.B.R.
Reddick, DeWitt C. DeW.C.R.
Reed, Alan. A.Re.
Reese, William L. W.L.Re.
Reeves, Marjorie E. M.E.R.
Reeves, Thomas C. T.C.R.
Reich, Willi. W.R.
Reichardt, Hans. H.Re.
Reid, John Cowie. J.C.Rd.
Reilly, John C., Jr. J.C.Re.
Reindel, Kurt. Ku.R.
Reinhard, Marcel. M.Re.
Reish, Donald J. D.J.R.
Reiss, Hans Siegbert. H.S.R.
Reiter, Elmar Rudolf. E.R.R.
Renger, Johannes M. J.M.R.
Rentz, George S. G.Re.
Rescher, Nicholas. N.R.
Resis, Albert. Al.Re.
Rexroth, Kenneth. K.Re.
Reynolds, Charles Edward. C.E.R.
Reynolds, Christopher Hanby Baillie.
    C.H.B.R.
Reynolds, Frank E. F.E.R.
Reynolds, Graham. G.R.

Rheinstein, Max. M.Rh.
Rhoads, Edward J.M. E.J.M.R.
Rhode, Gotthold K.S. G.K.S.R.
Riasanovsky, Nicholas V. N.V.R.
Rich, Alan. A.Ri.
Richard, Jean B. J.B.R.
Richards, Alan Westcott. A.W.R.
Richards, Paul Westmacott. P.W.R.
Richardson, Hugh E. H.E.R.
Richardson, Margaret Ann. M.A.R.
Richardson, Robert G. R.G.R.
Riché, Pierre. P.R.
Richey, Michael William. M.W.Ri.
Richmond, Rollin C. Ro.R.
Richter, Gisela Marie Augusta.
    G.M.A.R.
Richtering, Helmut. He.Ri.
Ridolfi, Roberto. Ro.Ri.
Riesenfeld, Stefan Albrecht. S.A.Ri.
Rightmire, G. Philip. G.P.Ri.
Riley, Edward C. E.C.R.
Riley, Matilda White. M.W.R.
Ring, Klaus. K.R.
Ring, Richard R. R.R.R.
Ringer, Alexander L. A.L.R.
Ringer, Barbara A. B.A.R.
Ringgren, Helmer. H.R.
Ringler, William Andrew, Jr. W.A.Ri.
Ringwood, Alfred Edward. A.E.R.
Ripin, Edwin M. E.M.R.
Ritchie, C.T. C.T.R.
Ritter, Raymond. R.Ri.
Ritterbush, Philip C. P.C.R.
Riva, Alfredo. Al.R.
Riva, Joseph P., Jr. J.P.Ri.
Rivlin, Helen Anne B. H.A.B.R.
Rizley, John H. J.H.R.
Robb, Nesca A. N.A.R.
Robbins, Jonathan H. J.H.Ro.
Robbins, Sidney Martin. S.M.R.
Robbins, Stanley L. S.L.R.
Roberts, Michael. M.Ro.
Roberts, Sir Sydney. S.Rs.
Robertson, Bruce Carlisle. B.C.R.
Robineau, Claude. C.R.
Robins, Robert Henry. Ro.H.R.
Robinson, Arthur. Ar.R.
Robinson Arthur Napoleon Raymond.
    A.N.R.R.
Robinson, Christopher. C.Ro.
Robinson, Daniel Sommer. D.S.R.
Robinson, David J. D.J.Ro.
Robinson, Edgar Eugene. E.E.R.
Robinson, Edward. E.Rn.
Robinson, Elwyn B. E.B.R.
Robinson, Frank Neville H. F.N.H.R.
Robinson, George Clarence. G.C.R.
Robinson, Gloria. G.Ro.
Robinson, J. Lewis. J.L.Ro.
Robinson, Joan Violet. J.Ro.
Robinson, Romney. R.R.
Robson, James Scott. J.S.Ro.
Robson, William Alexander. W.A.R.
Robson, William Wallace. W.W.R.
Rockwell, Anne F. A.F.R.
Rodgers, H.B. H.B.Ro.
Rodnan, Gerald P. G.P.R.
Rodríguez-Monegal, Emir. E.R.-M.
Roe, Michael. Ml.R.
Roey, Jan L.R. Van. J.V.R.
Rogers, C. Ambrose. C.A.Ro.
Rogers, Leonard R. L.R.R.
Rogg, Lionel A. L.A.R.
Rogge, Helmuth. He.R.
Rohan-Csermak, G. de. G. de R.-C.
Rohde, Peter P. P.P.R.

Rollins, Reed C. R.C.R.
Rolt, L.T.C. L.T.C.R.
Romas, Nicholas A. N.A.Ro.
Romer, Alfred S. A.S.R.
Ronan, Colin Alistair. C.A.R.
Ronen, Dov. D.Ro.
Rood, Arnold. A.Ro.
Roos, Hans. Ha.Ro.
Roosa, Robert Vincent. R.V.R.
Rose, Leo E. L.E.R.
Rosen, Edward. Ed.R.
Rosenberg, Pierre M. P.M.R.
Rosenfeld, Arthur H. A.H.Ro.
Rosenthal, Erwin I.J. E.I.J.R.
Roseveare, Henry Godfrey. H.G.R.
Roskill, Capt. Stephen Wentworth.
    S.W.R.
Ross, C.D. C.D.R.
Ross, Marvin Chauncey. M.C.R.
Ross, Peter McGregor. P.McG.R.
Ross, Sydney. S.R.
Rossbacher, Richard I. R.I.Ro.
Rossi, Mario. M.R.
Rostovtsev, Mikhail Ivanovich. M.I.R.
Rothschild, The Hon. Miriam Louisa.
    M.L.R.
Rouch, Jean Pierre. J.P.R.
Roud, Brian James. B.J.R.
Rouse, Irving. I.Re.
Rouzé, Michel. Mi.Ro.
Rowe, James Wilmot. J.W.R.
Rowe, John A. Jo.R.
Rowe, Margaret Ann. M.A.Ro.
Rowen, Herbert H. H.Ro.
Rowlatt, Mary. Ma.R.
Rowlinson, John Shipley. Jo.S.R.
Rowton, Michael B. M.B.R.
Royde-Smith, John Graham. J.R.-S.
Rubinstein, Nicolai. N.Ru.
Rudwick, Elliott. El.R.
Ruggles, Eleanor. E.Ru.
Ruhmer, Eberhard. Eb.R.
Ruiter, Leendert de. L. de R.
Rumney, George Richard. G.R.R.
Rupp, The Rev. Ernest Gordon.
    E.G.R.
Russell, Charles R. C.R.R.
Russell, Don. D.R.
Russell, Norman H. N.H.R.
Russell, Peter Edward. P.E.R.
Russell, Richard J. R.J.R.
Russon, Allien R. A.R.R.
Ryalls, Alan. A.R.
Ryan, The Rev. Edward A. E.A.R.
Ryan, William B.F. W.B.F.R.
Ryazantsev, Sergey Nikolayevich.
    S.N.R.
Ryder, John D. J.D.R.
Rylaarsdam, J. Coert. J.C.Ry.
Ryland, John S. J.S.R.

Sabr, Mohy el Din. M.e.D.S.
Sacher, George A. G.A.Sa.
Sadek, Dawlat Ahmed. D.A.Sa.
Sadler, John E. J.E.Sa.
Sáez, Emilio. E.Sa.
Sagan, Carl. C.Sn.
Saggs, Henry W.F. H.W.F.S.
Sahakian, William S. W.S.S.
St. John, Robert. R.St.J.
Sakamoto, Taro. T.Sa.
Salah, Mostafa Moh. M.M.Sa.
Sale, William Merritt, Jr. W.M.S.
Salibi, Kamal Suleiman. K.S.S.
Salisbury, Sir Edward James. E.J.S.

Salisbury, Neil E. N.E.S.
Salita, Domingo C. D.C.S.
Salmi, Mario. M.Sal.
Salmon, Edward. E.Sn.
Salmon, Edward Togo. E.T.S.
Salmon, John Hearsey McMillan.
 J.H.McM.S.
Sammons, Jeffrey L. J.L.Sa.
Samuel, Alan Edouard. A.E.S.
Samuel, Pierre. P.S.
Samuels, Michael Anthony. M.A.Sa.
Sandeen, Ernest R. E.R.S.
Sandelin, Carl Fredrik. C.F.S.
Sander, Emilie T. E.T.Sa.
Sanders, William T. W.T.Sa.
Sanderson, R. Thomas. R.T.S.
Sandvik, Gudmund. G.Sa.
Saner, Hans. Ha.S.
Sanford, Vera. V.S.
Sanger, Clyde William. C.W.S.
Sanger, Ralph G. R.G.S.
Sarà, Michele. M.Sà.
Sarason, Irwin G. I.G.S.
Sarna, Nahum M. N.M.Sa.
Sartori, Claudio. C.Sa.
Sasaki, Genjun H. G.H.S.
Sastri, R.L.N. R.L.N.S.
Sato, Tadao. T.S.
Satter, Heinrich. H.Sa.
Saunders, Jason Lewis. Ja.L.S.
Saunders, Robert M. R.M.S.
Sautter, Gilles François. G.F.S.
Savage, George. Ge.S.
Savile, Douglas B.O. D.B.O.S.
Saville, James Patrick. J.P.S.
Savory, Roger M. R.M.Sa.
Sawer, Geoffrey. G.S.
Sawyer, John Stanley. J.S.S.
Scarne, John. J.S.
Scarpelli, Dante G. D.G.Sc.
Schaaf, William L. W.L.S.
Schaden, Egon. Eg.S.
Schaeffer, Bobb. B.Sc.
Schaeffer, Claude Frédéric Armand.
 C.F.A.S.
Schafer, Thomas A. T.A.S.
Schaper, Eva. Ev.S.
Schapera, Isaac. I.S.
Schapiro, Leonard Bertram. L.B.S.
Scharf, Aaron. A.Sc.
Scharlemann, Robert P. R.P.S.
Schatz-Uffenheimer, Rivka. R.S.-U.
Schawlow, Arthur L. Ar.L.S.
Scheepers, Johannes Nicolaas. J.N.S.
Scheer, Bradley Titus. B.T.S.
Scheina, Robert L. R.L.Sc.
Schell, Herbert S. H.S.Sc.
Schiffers, Heinrich. H.Sc.
Schilling, Richard S.F. R.S.F.S.
Schimmel, Annemarie. An.Sc.
Schirmann, Jefim H. J.Sc.
Schirokauer, Conrad. C.Sc.
Schlechten, Albert Wilbur. A.W.S.
Schmale, Franz-Josef. F.-J.Se.
Schmidt, Carl Frederic. C.F.Sc.
Schmidt, John D. J.D.Sc.
Schmidt, Karl Patterson. K.P.S.
Schmidt, R.A.M. R.Sc.
Schmitt, Hans Otto. H.O.Sc.
Schmitt, Waldo L. W.L.Sc.
Schnath, Georg. Gg.S.
Scholes, Walter V. W.V.S.
Schram, Stuart Reynolds. S.R.S.
Schreiber, B. Charlotte. B.C.S.
Schreyvogl, Friedrich. F.Sc.
Schubert, Bernice Giduz. B.G.S.

Schudson, Michael S. Mi.S.
Schultz, Alarich R. A.R.S.
Schulz, Walter. W.Sc.
Schumach, Murray. Mu.S.
Schumacher, Alvin J. A.J.Sc.
Schumm, Stanley A. S.A.S.
Schürmann, Reiner. R.Sch.
Schwanke, Robert R. R.R.Sc.
Schwartz, Jacob T. J.T.Sc.
Schwartz, Mark F. M.F.S.
Schwartz, Mischa. M.Sch.
Schwartz, Paul A. P.A.S.
Schwarzenberger, Georg. G.Sc.
Scott, Alfred Eric. A.E.Sc.
Scott, The Rev. Guthrie Michael.
 G.M.S.
Scott, Joseph Frederick. J.F.S.
Scott, Peter. P.Sc.
Scranton, Robert L. R.L.S.
Screech, M.A. M.A.S.
Scruton, Roger. Ro.Sc.
Scullard, Howard Hayes. H.H.S.
Seaborg, Glenn T. G.T.S.
Seabury, Paul. P.Se.
Seale, Robert L. R.L.Se.
Sealey, B. Raphael. B.R.S.
Searle, Humphrey. H.Se.
Šega, Drago. D.Še.
Segre, Claudio G. C.G.Se.
Seibert, Jakob. J.Se.
Seidel, Anna K. A.K.Se.
Seiff, Alvin. A.S.
Seitz, William C. W.C.Se.
Sellwood, David Grenville John.
 D.G.J.S.
Selz, Jean. Je.S.
Sen, Amulya Chandra. A.Se.
Sen, D.M. D.M.S.
Sena, Jorge de. J. de S.
Sepúlveda González, Sergio. S.S.G.
Sequera de Segnini, Isbelia M.
 I.S. de S.
Serjeant, Robert Bertram. R.B.Se.
Seroff, Victor Ilyich. V.I.S.
Serventy, D.L. D.L.Se.
Service, Elman R. E.R.Se.
Sesay, Shekou M. S.M.S.
Seton-Watson, Hugh. H.S.-W.
Seton-Watson, Robert William.
 R.W.S.-W.
Severin, Giles Timothy. G.T.Se.
Sewall, Richard B. R.B.S.
Seymour, Charles. C.Se.
Seznec, Jean J. J.J.Se.
Shackleton, Robert. R.Sh.
Shadbolt, Maurice Francis Richard.
 M.F.R.S.
Shaffer, Jerome A. J.A.Sh.
Shagdarsuren, O. O.Sh.
Shah, Umakant Premanand. U.P.S.
Shakabpa, Tsepon W.D. T.W.D.S.
Shambaugh, George E., Jr. G.E.S.
Sharlin, Harold I. H.I.S.
Sharp, Aaron J. A.J.Sh.
Sharp, The Rev. R. Norman. R.N.S.
Sharp, Robert Phillip. R.P.Sp.
Sharp, Walter R. W.R.S.
Sharrock, Roger. R.S.
Shaw, Byron Thomas. B.T.Sh.
Shaw, Ivan Peter. I.P.S.
Shaw, Stanford Jay. S.J.S.
Shaw, Trevor Ian. T.I.S.
Sheard, Wendy Stedman. W.S.Sh.
Shearman, John K.G. J.K.Sh.
Shedd, Thomas Clark. T.C.S.
Sheehy, Ann. An.Sh.

Shelton, John E. J.E.S.
Shennan, J.H. J.H.Sh.
Shepard, Francis P. F.P.S.
Shepherd, The Rev. Massey H., Jr.
 M.H.S.
Sheppard, Richard A. R.A.S.
Shepperson, George Albert. G.A.S.
Shercliff, Jose. J.Sh.
Sheridan, Lionel Astor. L.A.S.
Sheriff, Robert E. R.E.Sh.
Sherman, Franklin. F.S.
Sherrington, Sir Charles Scott. C.S.S.
Shetler, Stanwyn G. S.G.S.
Shiel, James. J.Shi.
Shih, The Rev. Joseph Hsing-san.
 J.H.-s.S.
Shillinglaw, Gordon. G.Sh.
Shiloah, Amnon. A.Sh.
Shiloh, Ailon. An.S.
Shimahara, Nobuo. N.S.
Shinoda, Minoru. M.Sh.
Shipman, Frank M. F.M.S.
Shirendev, B. B.Sv.
Shirley-Smith, Sir Hubert. H.S.-Sm.
Shock, Nathan Wetherill. N.W.S.
Shoemaker, Frank C. F.C.S.
Shore, Arthur Frank. A.F.Sh.
Short, The Rev. Harry Lismer. H.L.S.
Short, Lester L. L.L.S.
Shrimpton, Nicholas. N.Sh.
Shu, Frank H. F.H.Sh.
Shurtleff, Malcolm C. M.C.S.
Sibley, David C.G. D.C.G.S.
Sick, Helmut. H.S.
Siebens, Arthur A. A.A.S.
Sieber, Roy. Ro.Si.
Siever, Raymond. R.Si.
Silaev, Evgeny Dmitrievich. E.D.S.
Silber, Kate. K.Si.
Silberbauer, George Bertrand. G.Si.
Silbergeld, Jerome. Je.Si.
Silberman, Lou Hackett. L.H.S.
Sillery, Anthony. Ay.Sy.
Silverstein, Josef. J.Si.
Simmons, Adele Smith. Ad.S.
Simmons, Ernest J. E.J.Si.
Simmons, Gustavus J. G.J.Si.
Simmons, Pauline. Pa.S.
Simon, Akiba Ernst. A.E.Si.
Simon, Edith. E.Si.
Simon, John Y. J.Y.S.
Simons, Eric Norman. E.N.S.
Simpson, Dale R. D.R.S.
Simpson, John M. J.M.S.
Simpson, Roger Henry. R.H.S.
Sinclair, Andrew Annandale. A.A.Si.
Sinclair, Keith. Ke.S.
Singer, Isaac Bashevis. I.B.S.
Singer, Peter. P.Si.
Singh, H.K. Manmohan. H.K.M.S.
Singh, Khushwant. K.S.
Singh, Madan Mohan. M.M.S.
Singleton, Frederick Bernard. F.B.S.
Sinha, N.K. N.K.S.
Sinitsyn, Vasily Mikhaylovich. V.M.S.
Sinor, Denis. D.Si.
Sippl, Charles J. C.J.S.
Siragusa, Alfredo. A.Si.
Sircus, Wilfred. W.S.
Sivaramamurti, Calambur. C.S.
Skalweit, Stephan. S.Sk.
Sklar, Robert A. R.Sk.
Sloane, Thomas O. T.O.S.
Slobin, Mark S. M.S.S.
Sløk, Axel Mose. A.M.Sl.
Slonimsky, Nicolas. N.Sl.

Sloss, L.L. L.L.Sl.
Smailes, Arthur Eltringham. A.E.Sm.
Smale, Stephen. S.Sm.
Smart, John Jamieson Carswell. J.J.C.S.
Smart, Ninian. N.Sm.
Smethurst, Colin. C.Sm.
Smith, Anna Hester. A.H.S.
Smith, Bruce Lannes. B.L.S.
Smith, Charles Gordon. C.G.S.
Smith, Dale M. D.M.Sm.
Smith, David Eugene. D.E.S.
Smith, Donald Arnold. D.A.S.
Smith, Gabriel. Ga.S.
Smith, George Alan. G.A.Sm.
Smith, Harlan James. H.Sm.
Smith, James Irvine. J.I.S.
Smith, J. Beverley. J.B.Sm.
Smith, John Edwin. J.E.Sm.
Smith, Jonathan Zittell. J.Z.S.
Smith, Joseph V. J.V.S.
Smith, L.P. L.P.S.
Smith, Lacey Baldwin. La.B.S.
Smith, Lyman B. L.B.Sm.
Smith, Neal Griffith. N.G.S.
Smith, Norman Obed. N.O.S.
Smith, Peter A.S. P.A.S.S.
Smith, Ralph J. R.J.Sm.
Smith, Robert C. R.C.Sm.
Smith, Robert Leo. R.L.Sm.
Smith, Sigmund L. S.L.Sm.
Smith, T. Lynn. T.L.S.
Smith, W. John. W.J.S.
Smith-Rose, Reginald Leslie. R.L.S.-R.
Smogorzewski, Kazimierz Maciej. K.M.S.
Smykay, Edward W. E.W.S.
Smylie, The Rev. James Hutchinson. J.H.Sm.
Smyth, James Desmond. J.D.Sm.
Sneddon, Ian Naismith. I.N.S.
Snell, Esmond E. E.E.Sn.
Snellgrove, David Llewelyn. D.L.S.
Snyder, Irvin S. I.S.S.
Snyder, James E. J.E.Sn.
Soboul, Albert M. Al.S.
Soden, Wolfram Th. von. W.T.v.S.
Sokoloff, Leon. L.S.
Solem, G. Alan. G.A.So.
Solheim, Wilhelm G., II. W.G.So.
Solinger, Jacob. J.So.
Solmi, Angelo. A.So.
Solmsen, Friedrich. F.So.
Solomon, Arthur K. A.K.S.
Solt, Leo F. L.F.S.
Somers, Harold M. H.M.S.
Soo, Shao L. S.L.S.
Sorley Walker, Kathrine. K.S.W.
Sourdel, Dominique. D.So.
Soustelle, Jacques. Ja.S.
Southall, Aidan William. Ai.S.
Southam, Brian C. B.C.So.
Southgate, Donald. Do.S.
Southward, Alan James. A.J.So.
Sowers, Robert W. R.So.
Spalding, David A.E. D.A.E.S.
Spalding, Fred L. F.L.S.
Spalding, James C. J.C.S.
Spaulding, Jay L. J.L.Sp.
Speaight, George. G.St.
Spear, T.G. Percival. T.G.P.S.
Spears, Monroe K. M.K.Sp.
Spedding, Frank Harold. F.H.S.
Spekke, Arnold. Ar.Sp.
Spence, Robert. R.Sp.
Spencer, J. Brookes. J.B.Sp.

Spencer, John R. J.R.Sp.
Spencer, Joseph E. Jo.E.S.
Spencer, Robert F. R.F.S.
Spencer, The Rev. Sidney. S.Sp.
Spencer, Terence John Bew. T.Sp.
Spengler, Joseph J. J.J.Sp.
Spiegel, Henry William. H.W.S.
Spiegelberg, Herbert. H.Sp.
Spilhaus, Athelstan. A.Sp.
Spinka, Matthew. M.Sp.
Spiro, Herbert John. H.J.Sp.
Spring, David. D.Sp.
Squires, James Duane. J.D.S.
Srivastava, A.L. A.L.S.
Stacey, The Rev. John. Jo.S.
Stadler, Karl R. K.R.St.
Stafford-Clark, David. D.S.-C.
Stains, Howard James. H.J.S.
Stallman, Robert Wooster. Ro.W.S.
Stamp, Sir Laurence Dudley. L.D.S.
Štampar, Emil. Em.Š.
Standen, Anthony. A.St.
Standley, Barbara A. B.A.St.
Stannard, Jerry. Je.St.
Stannard, Lewis Judson, Jr. L.J.S.
Stant, Margaret Yvonne. M.Y.S.
Stanzione, Kaydon Al. K.A.St.
Stark, Craig L. C.L.S.
Stark, John E. J.E.St.
Starke, Helmut Dietmar. H.D.S.
Starkey, Lawrence H. L.H.St.
Starkey, Otis P. O.P.S.
Starkie, Enid. En.S.
Starr, Chester G. C.G.St.
Steel, Robert Walter. Ro.W.St.
Steere, William Campbell. W.C.St.
Stehkämper, Hugo. H.Sr.
Stein, Jane J. J.J.St.
Stein, Peter G. P.G.S.
Steinberg, Alfred. A.Sg.
Steinberg, S. Henry. S.H.St.
Steiner, H. Arthur. H.A.S.
Steiner, William Glenn. W.G.St.
Steingräber, Erich. Er.St.
Stendahl, The Rev. Krister. K.St.
Stengers, Jean. Jr.S.
Stephan, Ruth. Ru.S.
Stephens, Richard Walton. Ri.W.S.
Stephenson, Ralph. R.St.
Stephenson, R.J. R.J.S.
Stern, Henri. He.S.
Stern, Joshua. J.Sn.
Stern, Samuel Miklos. S.M.Sn.
Stern, William Louis. W.L.St.
Sternstein, Lawrence. La.S.
Steudel, Johannes. J.Ste.
Stevens, Courtenay Edward. C.E.S.
Stevens, Denis William. D.W.S.
Stevens, Halsey. H.Ss.
Stevens, Sylvester K. S.K.S.
Stevenson, James. J.St.
Stevenson, Lloyd Grenfell. L.G.S.
Stewart, David B. D.B.S.
Stewart, John Harris. J.H.St.
Stewart, John I.M. J.I.M.S.
Stewart, Robert E. R.E.St.
Stibitz, George R. G.R.St.
Stigler, George J. G.J.S.
Stilwell, Rear Adm. James Joseph. Ja.J.S.
Stock, Noel. N.St.
Stokes, Sewell. S.St.
Stolberg, Irving J. I.J.S.
Stoll, Robert R. R.R.S.
Stone, F. Gordon A. F.G.A.S.
Stone, Julius. Ju.S.

Stoner, John Oliver, Jr. J.O.S.
Storer, Robert W. R.W.St.
Størmer, Leif. L.St.
Stotz, Elmer H. E.H.St.
Stoudt, John J. J.J.S.
Strahan, Ronald. Ro.S.
Strand, Kaj Aa. K.A.S.
Strange, Edward Fairbrother. E.F.S.
Strasberg, Lee. Le.S.
Stratford, Alan Howard. A.H.St.
Street, Brian Vincent. B.V.S.
Streeter, Victor L. V.L.S.
Streng, Frederick J. F.J.S.
Strickmann, Michel. M.St.
Strode, Hudson. Hu.S.
Strugnell, John. Jo.St.
Struik, Dirk Jan. D.J.S.
Strygin, Valery Mikhailovich. V.M.St.
Stubbs, William Edward. W.E.S.
Stuewer, Roger H. R.H.St.
Sturley, Kenneth Reginald. K.R.S.
Sturmberger, Hans. H.St.
Sturmthal, Adolf F. A.F.St.
Styan, J.L. J.L.S.
Suárez, Jorge A. J.A.S.
Suárez Fernández, Luis. L.S.Fe.
Suckling, Eustace E. E.E.S.
Suettinger, Robert Lee. R.L.Su.
Suggs, Robert Carl. R.C.Su.
Sukhopara, Fyodor Nikolayevich. F.N.S.
Sullivan, Michael. M.Su.
Summers, William Cofield. W.C.S.
Summerson, Sir John. J.Sum.
Sumner, Margaret Ann. M.A.Su.
Sundaram, K.V. K.V.Su.
Suppes, Patrick. P.Su.
Suryadinata, Leo. L.Sur.
Süsskind, Charles. Ch.S.
Sutcliffe, Reginald C. R.C.S.
Sutherland, Carol Humphrey Vivian. C.H.V.S.
Sutherland, James Kenneth. J.K.S.
Sutherland, James R. J.R.Su.
Sutherland, N.M. N.M.Su.
Sutton, Denys. D.Su.
Sutton, John. J.Su.
Suzuki, Chusei. C.Su.
Sverdrup, Harald Ulrik. H.U.S.
Swain, Frederick M. F.M.Sw.
Swan, Bradford Fuller. B.F.S.
Swanberg, W.A. W.A.S.
Swanson, Don R. D.R.Sw.
Sweet-Escott, Bickham A.C. B.S.-E.
Swenson, J. Patricia Morgan. J.P.M.S.
Swink, Roland Lee. R.L.Sw.
Sykes, Gresham M'Cready. G.M'C.S.
Sylvain, Edmond. E.Sy.
Synge, Patrick Millington. P.M.Sy.
Szebehely, Victor G. V.G.S.

Tahmankar, Dattatraya Vishwanath. D.V.T.
Tait, Hugh. H.Ta.
Takeuchi, Yoshinori. Y.T.
Takhtajan, Armen Leonovich. A.T.
Talbi, Mohamed. M.Ta.
Talbot, William John. W.J.T.
Talbot Rice, David. D.T.R.
Talbot Rice, Tamara. T.T.R.
Tanenbaum, Morris. M.T.
Tani, Shin'ichi. S.Ta.
Tannenbaum, Steven R. S.R.T.
Tanner, James M. J.M.T.
Tapié, Victor-Lucien. V.L.T.

Taplin, Oliver. O.T.
Tarmisto, Vello Julius. V.J.T.
Tate, Allen. A.Ta.
Tax, Sol. So.T.
Tayler, Roger John. R.J.T.
Taylor, A.J.P. A.J.P.T.
Taylor, Alfred Edward. A.E.Ta.
Taylor, B.N. B.N.T.
Taylor, Gordon Ernest. G.E.T.
Taylor, Sir Hugh S. H.S.Ta.
Taylor, John Russell. J.R.T.
Taylor, John W.R. J.W.R.T.
Taylor, William. W.Ta.
Teall, John L. J.L.Te.
Tebeau, Charlton W. C.W.T.
Teichert, Curt. C.T.
Teitelbaum, Michael S. M.S.T.
Temir, Ahmet. A.Te.
Temperley, Nicholas. N.T.
Tepper, Frederick. F.T.
Terrasse, Henri-Louis-Étienne.
    H.-L.-É.T.
Terry, Walter. W.T.
Thapar, Romila. R.Th.
Thayer, H.S. H.S.T.
Thelen, David P. D.P.T.
Thesleff, Holger. H.T.
Thielicke, Helmut. H.Th.
Thieret, John W. J.W.Th.
Thin Kyi. T.Ky.
Thom, René Frédéric. R.F.T.
Thomas, David Christopher Traherne.
    D.C.Th.
Thomas, Harold E. H.E.T.
Thomas, John A. J.A.T.
Thomas, John Gareth. J.G.Th.
Thomas, John L. J.L.T.
Thomas, John Patrick. J.Th.
Thomas, Sidney. Si.T.
Thomas, Terence Barrington. T.B.T.
Thomas, William Harford. W.H.Th.
Thomasson, Gordon Conrad. G.C.T.
Thompson, Brian J. B.J.T.
Thompson, Carol Lewis. C.L.T.
Thompson, E.A. E.A.T.
Thompson, Sir Eric. E.Th.
Thompson, George Raynor. G.R.T.
Thompson, John. J.Tn.
Thompson, Laura. L.Th.
Thompson, Leonard Monteath. L.M.T.
Thompson, Stith. S.T.
Thomsen, Helmuth. He.Th.
Thomson, Sir A. Landsborough.
    A.L.T.
Thomson, David. D.Tn.
Thomson, Derick S. D.S.T.
Thomson, Sir George Paget. G.P.T.
Thomson, Robert Young. R.Y.T.
Thomson, William Archibald Robson.
    Wm.A.R.T.
Thomson, William E. W.E.T.
Thöne, Friedrich. F.Th.
Thorarinsson, Sigurdur. S.Th.
Thorne, Robert Folger. R.F.Th.
Thornton, Robert James. R.J.Th.
Thorpe, Lewis. L.T.
Thorpe, William Homan. W.H.T.
Tikhotskiy, Constantine Gennadiyevich.
    C.G.T.
Tiles, Mary Elizabeth. M.E.T.
Tilley, Cecil Edgar. C.E.T.
Timmers, Jan Joseph Marie. J.J.M.T.
Tinker, Hugh Russell. H.R.T.
Tinkle, Donald W. D.W.T.
Titley, Spencer Rowe. S.R.Ty.
Tobias, Cornelius A. C.A.T.

Tobias, Phillip Vallentine. P.V.T.
Todd, John Walford. J.W.T.
Toffoletto, Ettore. E.T.
Tolson, Richard. R.To.
Tolson, Rosalind. Rd.T.
Toni, Youssef T. Y.T.T.
Tooker, Elisabeth. E.To.
Toomer, Gerald J. G.J.T.
Totman, Conrad D. C.D.T.
Toulmin, Stephen E. S.E.T.
Toupet, Charles Henri. C.H.T.
Toussaint, Auguste. Au.T.
Tout, Thomas Frederick. T.F.T.
Townsend, Clifford Charles. C.C.T.
Townsley, Wilfred Asquith. W.A.T.
Toynbee, Arnold Joseph. A.J.T.
Toynbee, Jocelyn M.C. J.M.C.T.
Toyoda, Takeshi. T.T.
Tracey, Andrew. A.Ty.
Tracey, Hugh. H.Ty.
Trapido, Stanley. S.Tr.
Traub, Hamilton P. H.P.Tr.
Traub, Col. Robert. R.T.
Travis, Martin Bice, Jr. M.B.T.
Tregear, Thomas R. T.R.T.
Tregonning, Kennedy G. K.G.T.
Treharne, Reginald Francis. R.F.Tr.
Treves, François. F.Tr.
Treves, Piero. P.T.
Tricker, Ronald A.R. R.A.R.T.
Trigg, George L. G.L.T.
Trinterud, L.J. L.J.T.
Trunkey, Donald D. D.D.T.
Trussell, John B.B. J.B.B.T.
Trypanis, Constantine Athanasius.
    C.A.Tr.
Tsevegmid, Sh. Sh.Ts.
Tsoumis, George Thomas. G.Ts.
Tucci, Giuseppe. Gi.T.
Tucker, A.W. A.W.T.
Tucker, David Gordon. D.G.T.
Tucker, Glenn. G.Tu.
Tuma, Elias H. E.H.T.
Turkevich, Anthony Leonid. A.L.Tu.
Turnell, Martin. M.Tu.
Turner, B.L. B.L.T.
Turner, Edward Lewis. E.L.T.
Turner, Sir Eric Gardner. E.G.T.
Turner, Ralph H. R.H.T.
Turnock, David. D.T.
Turrill, William Bertram. W.B.T.
Turville-Petre, E.O.G. E.O.G.T.-P.
Tuttle, William Julian. W.J.Tu.
Tweedie, Michael Willmer Forbes.
    M.W.F.T.
Twersky, Isadore. I.T.
Twidale, Charles Rowland. C.R.T.
Twitchett, Denis C. D.C.T.
Tyler, James Chase. J.C.T.

Uda, Michitaka. M.U.
Udo, Reuben Kenrick. R.K.U.
Uibopuu, Valev. V.U.
Ullmann, Walter. W.U.
Ulrich, Homer. H.U.
Underwood, Benton J. B.J.U.
Underwood, E. Ashworth. E.A.U.
Underwood, Vernon Philip. V.P.U.
Unhjem, Arne. A.U.
Untermann, Jürgen. J.U.
Unwin, George. G.U.
Unwin, Philip Soundy. P.U.
Uotila, Urho A. U.A.U.
Upton, Caroline Jean. C.J.U.
Urbach, Peter Michael. P.M.U.

Urry, William G. W.G.U.
Utechin, Sergei Vasilievich. S.V.U.

Vaizey, John Vaizey, Baron. J.V.
Vajda, Georges. G.V.
Vale, Malcolm G.A. M.G.A.V.
Valentine, Frederick Albert. F.A.V.
Valgiglio, Ernesto. E.Va.
Vallier, Dora. D.V.
van Andel, Tjeerd H. T.H.v.A.
Van Caenegem, Raoul Charles.
    R.C.V.C.
Vance, Robert W. R.W.V.
Vandenbosch, Amry. A.Va.
Vanderpool, Eugene. E.V.
Van Deusen, Glyndon G. G.G.V.D.
Van Deusen, Hobart Merritt.
    H.M.V.D.
Vanger, Milton I. M.I.V.
Van Horn, Kent R. K.R.V.H.
Vann, Richard T. R.T.V.
Van Steenberghen, Fernand. F.V.Sn.
Varela, René Santamaria. R.S.V.
Varma, Shanti Prasad. S.P.V.
Vaughan, Richard. R.Va.
Vázquez, Josefina Zoraida. J.Z.V.
Velásquez, M. Tulio. M.T.V.
Vella, Walter F. W.F.V.
Vendler, Zeno. Z.V.
Venkataramanan, Lalgudi S. L.S.V.
Vennesland, Birgit. B.V.
Verlinden, J. Charles. J.C.V.
Vernet Ginés, Juan. J.V.G.
Verniers, Louis. L.Ve.
Veyret, Paul. P.V.
Viallaneix, Paul. P.Vi.
Vidalenc, Jean. J.Vi.
Vidyarthi, Lalita P. L.P.V.
Viereck, Peter. Pe.V.
Vierhaus, Rudolf. Ru.V.
Vignaux, Paul D. P.D.V.
Vigne, Randolph. R.V.
Villari, Letterio Carlo. L.C.V.
Villari, Luigi. L.Vi.
Villee, Claude A. C.A.V.
Villiers, Alan John. A.J.V.
Vinacke, Harold M. Hd.M.V.
Vinacke, W. Edgar. W.E.V.
Vinaver, Eugène. E.Vi.
Vincent, Paul F. P.F.V.
Vioux, Marcelle. M.Vi.
Virtanen, Reino. R.Vi.
Viscovo, Mario Del. M. Del V.
Vishny, Michele. Mi.V.
Vita-Finzi, Claudio. C.V.-F.
Vodovozov, Sergey Arsentyevich.
    S.A.V.
Voegelin, Charles F. C.F.V.
Voegelin, Florence M. F.M.V.
Vogt, Hans K. H.K.V.
Volkmann, Hans. H.V.
Von Eckardt, Wolf. W.V.E.
von Hagen, Victor Wolfgang.
    V.W.v.H.
Voous, Karel Hendrik. K.H.V.
Voss, Gilbert L. G.L.V.
Vowles, Jack. J.Vo.
Voyce, Arthur. A.Vo.
Vroman, Leo. L.V.

Waage, Frederick O. F.O.Wa.
Waage, Karl M. K.M.W.
Waddams, A.L. A.L.W.
Waddington, Conrad H. C.H.W.

Wormley, Edward J. E.J.Wo.
Worthy, Edmund H., Jr. E.H.W., Jr.
Wright, Almon Robert. A.R.W.
Wright, Arthur F. A.F.W.
Wright, Georg Henrik von.
  G.H. von W.
Wright, Gordon. G.Wr.
Wright, John Wilfrid. J.W.Wr.
Wright, Quincy. Q.W.
Wright, Stephen Graham. S.G.W.
Wurfel, David O.D. D.O.D.W.
Wurm, Stephen A. S.A.W.
Wu Shih-ch'ang. W.S.-cg.
Wylie, Turrell V. T.V.W.
Wyllie, Peter John. P.J.W.

Yale, David Eryl Corbet. D.E.C.Y.
Yamada, Tasaburo. To.Ya.
Yamane, Takeo. T.Y.
Yapp, Malcolm Edward. M.E.Y.
Yastrebov, Yevgeny Venyaminovich.
  Y.V.Y.
Yefremov, Yury Konstantinovich.
  Y.K.Y.
Yerger, Ralph W. R.W.Y.
Yerofeyev, Ivan Alekseyevich. I.A.Y.
Yeung, Yue-man. Y.-m.Y.
Yiannopoulos, A.N. A.N.Y.
Yinger, J. Milton. J.M.Yi.

Yoder, Hatten Schuyler, Jr. H.S.Y.
Yoffey, Joseph M. J.M.Y.
Yoingco, Angel Quintana. A.Q.Y.
Yonge, Sir C. Maurice. C.M.Y.
Yool, Air Vice Marshal William
  Munro. W.M.Y.
York, Richard Charles. R.C.Y.
Yoshida, Atsuhiko. A.Y.
Youlten, Lawrence J.F. L.J.F.Y.
Young, Ellen Louise. E.L.Y.
Young, Ernest P. E.P.Y.
Young, Jay A. J.A.Y.
Young, Percy Marshall. P.M.Y.
Young, Philip. P.Y.
Young, Roland S. R.S.Y.
Young, T. Cuyler, Jr. T.C.Y., Jr.

Zakharova, Tatyana Konstantinovna.
  T.K.Z.
Zangwill, Oliver Louis. O.L.Z.
Zaninović, Vice. V.Z.
Záruba, Quido. Q.Z.
Zasenko, Oleksa Eliseyovich. O.E.Z.
Zavalani, Tajar. T.Z.
Zeeden, Ernst Walter. E.W.Z.
Zeiller, Warren. W.Z.
Zeisel, Hans. H.Z.
Zelinsky, Wilbur. W.Ze.
Zeng Zungu. Z.Z.

Zenkovich, Vsevolod Pavlovich.
  V.P.Z.
Zernov, Nicolas M. N.Z.
Zetlin, Lev. L.Z.
Zgusta, Ladislav. L.Zg.
Zhdanov, Vladimir Viktorovich.
  V.V.Z.
Zhmuida, Viktor Borisovich.
  V.B.Z.
Zhong Gongfu. Z.G.
Ziadeh, Nicola Abdo. N.A.Z.
Ziman, J.M. J.M.Z.
Zimmermann, Martin Huldrych.
  M.H.Z.
Zirkel, Conway. C.Z.
Zöllner, Erich. E.Zö.
Zoltán, Imre. I.Z.
Zorn, Roman J. R.J.Z.
Zuberi, Matinuzzaman. M.Zu.
Zucker, Moses. M.Z.
Zuckerman, J.J. J.J.Z.
Zudaire Huarte, E. E.Z.H.
Zug, George R. G.R.Z.
Zumberge, James Herbert.
  J.H.Z.
Zürcher, Erik. E.Z.
Zusi, Richard L. R.L.Z.
Zvelebil, Kamil V. K.V.Z.
Zygmund, Antoni. A.Zy.

Authorities for the Micropædia

volumes 1–12

Material in these volumes was written by or is based on material or advice submitted by the following authorities.

Part One. Matter and Energy

George Ogden Abell. *Professor of Astronomy, University of California, Los Angeles.*

Anatole Abragam. *Professor of Nuclear Magnetism, Collège de France, Paris.*

Roger Adams (d. 1971). *Professor of Organic Chemistry, University of Illinois, Urbana, 1919–57.*

Henry Gavin Alexander. *Headmaster, Hampton Grammar School, England. Editor of the Leibniz-Clarke correspondence.*

Lawrence Hugh Aller. *Emeritus Professor of Astronomy, University of California, Los Angeles.*

Douglas M.W. Anderson. *Reader in Chemistry, University of Edinburgh.*

Edward Neville da Costa Andrade (d. 1971). *Quain Professor of Physics, University of London, 1928–50.*

Isaac Asimov. *Science writer. Professor of Biochemistry, Boston University.*

Larned B. Asprey. *Staff Member, Los Alamos National Laboratory, New Mexico.*

Lawrence Badash. *Professor of the History of Science, University of California, Santa Barbara.*

Donald Baim. *Free-lance writer on physics.*

Robert Horace Baker (d. 1964). *Professor of Astronomy, University of Illinois, 1923–51.*

Virginia Bartow. *Associate Professor Emerita of Chemistry, University of Illinois, Urbana.*

Curt W. Beck. *Matthew Vassar, Jr., Professor of Chemistry, Vassar College, Poughkeepsie, N.Y.*

J.M. Beckers. *Director, Multiple Mirror Telescope Observatory, University of Arizona, Tucson.*

Jeremy Bernstein. *Professor of Physics, Stevens Institute of Technology, Hoboken, N.J.*

Robert H. Bernstein. *Research Assistant, Department of Physics, Columbia University.*

R. Byron Bird. *Vilas Research Professor of Chemical Engineering, University of Wisconsin, Madison.*

William John Bishop (d. 1961). *Editor, Medical History. Librarian, Wellcome Historical Medical Library, London, 1946–53.*

Bart Bok (d. 1983). *Professor of Astronomy, University of Arizona, Tucson, 1966–74.*

Rupert Stevenson Bradley. *Former Reader in Inorganic and Structural Chemistry, University of Leeds, Eng.*

John C. Brandt. *Chief, Laboratory for Astronomy and Solar Physics, Goddard Space Flight Center, National Aeronautics and Space Administration, Greenbelt, Md.*

J.W. Buchta (d. 1966). *Professor of Physics, University of Minnesota, Minneapolis, 1938–62.*

Anton B. Burg. *Emeritus Professor of Chemistry, University of Southern California, Los Angeles.*

Joseph A. Burns. *Professor of Mechanics and Astronomy, Cornell University, Ithaca, N.Y.*

Horace R. Byers. *Emeritus Professor of Meteorology, Texas A & M University, College Station.*

Eric Dungan Carlson. *Senior Astronomer, Adler Planetarium, Chicago.*

Michael H. Carr. *Member, Voyager and Galileo Imaging Teams, Geological Survey, U.S. Department of the Interior, Menlo Park, Calif.*

Joseph M. Chamberlain. *Director, Adler Planetarium, Chicago.*

James W. Christy. *Astronomer, U.S. Naval Observatory, Washington, D.C.*

Francis Edward Cislak. *Director of Research, Reilly Tar and Chemical Corporation, Indianapolis, Ind., 1937–73.*

Norman Clarke. *Secretary and Registrar, Institute of Mathematics and Its Applications, Southend-on-Sea, Eng.*

Paul R. Clifford. *Department Head, Environmental Chemistry and Biology, Metrek Division, Mitre Corporation, McLean, Va.*

Barbara Lovett Cline. *Biology teacher. Author of* The Questioners: Physicists and the Quantum Theory.

Gerhard L. Closs. *A.A. Michelson Distinguished Service Professor of Chemistry, University of Chicago.*

J.E. Coates (d. 1973). *Professor of Chemistry, University College of Swansea, University of Wales, 1920–48.*

Alexander Cowie. *Emeritus Professor of Mechanical and Aerospace Engineering, Illinois Institute of Technology, Chicago. Associate Editor, Technology, Encyclopædia Britannica, Chicago, 1967–72.*

Frank Donald Drake. *Goldwin Smith Professor of Astronomy, Cornell University, Ithaca, N.Y.*

Raynor Duncombe. *Professor of Aerospace Sciences, University of Texas at Austin.*

Edward W. Dunham. *Research Associate, Department of Earth, Atmospheric, and Planetary Sciences, Massachusetts Institute of Technology, Cambridge.*

Richard H. Eastman. *Professor of Chemistry, Stanford University, Calif.*

Olin Jeuck Eggen. *Senior Astronomer, Cerro Tololo Interamerican Observatory, La Serena, Chile.*

Farouk El-Baz. *Research Director for Earth and Planetary Studies, National Air and Space Museum, Smithsonian Institution, Washington, D.C.*

James L. Elliot. *Associate Professor of Astronomy and Physics; Director, Wallace Astrophysical Observatory, Massachusetts Institute of Technology, Cambridge.*

Paul P. Ewald (d. 1985). *Professor of Physics, Polytechnic Institute of Brooklyn, N.Y., 1949–59.*

Henry Eyring (d. 1981). *Distinguished Professor of Chemistry and Professor of Metallurgy, University of Utah, Salt Lake City, 1967–81.*

Henry Feuer. *Emeritus Professor of Chemistry, Purdue University, West Lafayette, Ind.*

Henry Michael Foley (d. 1982). *Professor of Physics, Columbia University, 1954–82.*

Alfred B. Garrett. *Emeritus Professor of Chemistry, Ohio State University, Columbus.*

Tom Gehrels. *Professor, Lunar and Planetary Laboratory, University of Arizona, Tucson.*

Thomas R.P. Gibb, Jr. *Emeritus Professor of Chemistry, Tufts University, Medford, Mass.*

Frederick William Gibbs (d. 1966). *Deputy Secretary and Editor, Royal Institute of Chemistry, London.*

Henry Lee Giclas. *Astronomer, Lowell Observatory, Flagstaff, Ariz., 1942–81.*

Peter J. Gierasch. *Professor of Astronomy, Cornell University, Ithaca, N.Y.*

Owen Gingerich. *Professor of Astronomy and of the History of Science, Harvard University. Astrophysicist, Smithsonian Astrophysical Observatory, Cambridge, Mass.*

Leo Goldberg. *Emeritus Director, Kitt Peak National Observatory, Tucson, Ariz. Higgins Professor Emeritus of Astronomy, Harvard University.*

Donald Goldsmith. *President, Interstellar Media, Berkeley, Calif.*

Murray Goodman. *Professor of Chemistry, University of California, San Diego.*

Lois Graham. *Professor of Mechanical Engineering, Illinois Institute of Technology, Chicago.*

Frank Greenaway. *Keeper, Department of Chemistry, Science Museum, London, 1967–80.*

Edward F. Greene. *Professor of Chemistry, Brown University, Providence, R.I.*

Earle Covington Gregg (d. 1983). *Professor of Radiology, School of Medicine, Case Western Reserve University, Cleveland.*

Dirk ter Haar. *Reader in Theoretical Physics, University of Oxford; Fellow of Magdalen College, Oxford.*

Wayne B. Hadley. *Engineering Scientist, AMP Incorporated, Harrisburg, Pa.*

Dalziel Llewellyn Hammick (d. 1966). *Fellow of Oriel College, Oxford, 1921–52; Aldrichian Praelector in Chemistry, University of Oxford, 1949–52.*

Edward Robert Harrison. *Professor of Astrophysics, University of Massachusetts, Amherst.*

William K. Hartmann. *Senior Scientist, Planetary Science Institute, Science Applications, Inc., Tucson, Ariz.*

George N. Hatsopoulos. *President, Thermo Electron Corporation, Waltham, Mass.*

Gerald S. Hawkins. *Physicist and Astronomer, U.S. Information Agency, Washington, D.C.*

Eleanor Kay Helin. *Member of the technical staff, Jet Propulsion Laboratory, California Institute of Technology, Pasadena.*

Wilfried Heller. *Emeritus Professor of Chemistry, Wayne State University, Detroit.*

James B. Hendrickson. *Professor of Chemistry, Brandeis University, Waltham, Mass.*

G.H. Herbig. *Professor of Astronomy, Lick Observatory, University of California, Santa Cruz.*

John Herivel. *Former Reader in the History and Philosophy of Science, Queen's University of Belfast, N.Ire.*

Reuben Hersh. *Professor of Mathematics, University of New Mexico, Albuquerque.*

Max H. Hey. *Senior Principal Scientific Officer, Department of Mineralogy, British Museum (Natural History), London, 1951–69.*

Christopher T. Hill. *Associate Scientist, Fermi National Accelerator Laboratory, Batavia, Ill.*

William B. Hubbard. *Professor of Planetary Sciences, University of Arizona, Tucson.*

Maurice Loyal Huggins. *Research consultant. Senior Research Associate, Arcadia Institute for Scientific Research, Woodside, Calif., 1968–75.*

Earl K. Hyde. *Deputy Director, Lawrence Berkeley Laboratory, University of California, Berkeley.*

Merkel Henry Jacobs (d. 1970). *Professor of General Physiology, University of Pennsylvania, Philadelphia, 1923–35.*

Stanley Eric Janson (d. 1974). *Keeper, Department of Astronomy and Geophysics, Science Museum, London, 1967–69; Keeper, Department of Chemistry, 1959–67.*

Hamilton Moore Jeffers (d. 1976). *Astronomer, Lick Observatory, Mount Hamilton, Calif., 1938–61.*

Flora Johnson. *Free-lance writer on technical subjects.*

William J. Kaufmann. *Adjunct Professor of Physics, San Diego State University, Calif.*

Richard Kimmel. *Free-lance writer on physics.*

George B. Kistiakowsky (d. 1982). *Abbot and James Lawrence Professor of Chemistry, Harvard University.*

Martin Jesse Klein. *Eugene Higgins Professor of the History of Physics, Yale University.*

Charles T. Kowal. *Member of the professional staff, California Institute of Technology, Pasadena.*

Sonja Krause. *Professor of Physical Chemistry, Rensselaer Polytechnic Institute, Troy, N.Y.*

Polykarp Kusch. *Eugene McDermott Professor of Physics, University of Texas at Dallas. Cowinner, Nobel Prize for Physics, 1955.*

Juliet Lee-Franzini. *Professor of Physics; Director, Lepton-Photon Spectrometer Group, State University of New York at Stony Brook.*

Henry M. Leicester. *Emeritus Professor of Biochemistry, University of the Pacific, San Francisco.*

Dame Kathleen Lonsdale (d. 1971). *Professor of Chemistry, University of London, 1949–68.*

Raymond Arthur Lyttleton. *Emeritus Professor of Theoretical Astronomy, University of Cambridge; Fellow of St. John's College, Cambridge.*

Douglas McKie (d. 1967). *Professor of History and Philosophy of Science, University of London, 1957–64.*

William Marshall MacNevin (deceased). *Professor and Chairman, Department of Chemistry, Ohio State University, Columbus.*

William Markowitz. *Adjunct Professor of Physics, Nova University, Fort Lauderdale, Fla. Astronomer, U.S. Naval Observatory, Washington, D.C., 1936–66; Director, Time Service, 1953–66.*

Ladislaus L. Marton (d. 1979). *Chief, Office of International Relations, National Bureau of Standards, Washington, D.C., 1962–70; Chief, Electron Physics Section, 1948–62.*

Alla Genrikhovna Massevitch. *Vice President, Astronomical Council, Academy of Sciences of the U.S.S.R., Moscow.*

Gary Mechler. *Astronomy consultant and writer.*

Henry Jay Melosh. *Associate Professor of Geophysics, State University of New York at Stony Brook.*

Eric Mendoza. *Professor of Science Teaching, Hebrew University of Jerusalem.*

Paul Willard Merrill (d. 1961). *President, American Astronomical Society. Member of Staff, Mt. Wilson and Palomar Observatories, Pasadena, Calif., 1929–52.*

Allan M. Morrish. *Professor and Head, Department of Physics, University of Manitoba, Winnipeg.*

Frederick C. Nachod. *Consultant. Director of Special Projects, Sterling-Winthrop Research Institute, Rensselaer, N.Y., 1974–78; Chemical Liaison Staff Director, 1964–74.*

Gerald C. Nelson. *Member of the Technical Staff, Sandia Laboratories, Albuquerque, N.M.*

Francis Netter. *Head, Department of the Linear Accelerator, Nuclear Research Centre, Saclay, Fr.*

The Rev. Daniel J.K. O'Connell, S.J. (d. 1982). *Director of the Vatican Observatory, Castel Gandolfo, 1952–70.*

Charles Robert O'Dell. *Space Telescope Project Scientist, National Aeronautics and Space Administration, Marshall Space Flight Center, Ala.*

Peter Oesper. *Professor of Chemistry, St. Lawrence University, Canton, N.Y.*

Ralph Edward Oesper (d. 1977). *Professor of Analytical Chemistry, University of Cincinnati, Ohio, 1937–51.*

John A. O'Keefe. *Astronomer, Laboratory for Astronomy and Solar Physics, Goddard Space Flight Center, National Aeronautics and Space Administration, Greenbelt, Md.*

George A. Olah. *Professor of Chemistry, University of Southern California, Los Angeles.*

Donald E. Osterbrock. *Professor of Astronomy, Lick Observatory, University of California, Santa Cruz.*

Thornton Leigh Page. *Research Astrophysicist, Lyndon B. Johnson Space Center, National Aeronautics and Space Administration, Houston, Texas. Professor of Astronomy, Wesleyan University, Middletown, Conn., 1958–68.*

Bernard E.J. Pagel. *Deputy Chief Scientific Officer, Royal Greenwich Observatory, Herstmonceux, Eng. Visiting Professor of Astronomy, University of Sussex, Brighton, Eng.*

James Bayard Parsons (d. 1985). *Professor of Chemistry, University of Chicago, 1958–61.*

H. Steffen Peiser. *Chief, Office of International Relations, National Bureau of Standards, U.S. Department of Commerce, Washington, D.C., 1969–79.*

Melba Phillips. *Emerita Professor of Physics, University of Chicago.*

Herman Pines. *Vladimir Ipatieff Professor Emeritus of Chemistry, Northwestern University, Evanston, Ill.*

Michael Polanyi, M.D. (d. 1976). *Professor of Social Studies, 1948–58; Professor of Physical Chemistry, 1933–48, Victoria University of Manchester.*

Ernest Rabinowicz. *Professor of Mechanical Engineering, Massachusetts Institute of Technology, Cambridge.*

John O. Rasmussen, Jr. *Professor of Chemistry, University of California, Berkeley.*

Donald G. Rea. *Assistant Laboratory Director, Technology and Space Programs Development, Jet Propulsion Laboratory, California Institute of Technology, Pasadena.*

Franklin Evans Roach. *Affiliate Astronomer, University of Hawaii, Honolulu. Physicist, U.S. National Bureau of Standards, 1954–65.*

Frank Neville H. Robinson. *Senior Research Officer, Clarendon Laboratory, University of Oxford.*

Colin Alistair Ronan. *Science writer and lecturer. Editor, Journal of the British Astronomical Association.*

Carl (Edward) Sagan. *Director, Laboratory for Planetary Studies; David Duncan Professor of Astronomy, Cornell University, Ithaca, N.Y.*

Edwin Ernest Salpeter. *J.G. White Distinguished Professor of Physical Science, Cornell University, Ithaca, N.Y.*

Bernard G. Saunders. *Associate Editor, Physics, Encyclopædia Britannica, Chicago, 1970–73; Physicist, Lawrence Radiation Laboratory, University of California, Livermore, 1959–70.*

Arthur L. Schawlow. *Professor of Physics, Stanford University, Calif. Cowinner, Nobel Prize for Physics, 1981.*

Aurelia Keith Townes Schawlow (Mrs. Arthur L. Schawlow).

Hermann I(rving) Schlesinger (d. 1960). *Professor of Chemistry, University of Chicago.*

Maarten Schmidt. *Professor of Astronomy, California Institute of Technology, Pasadena.*

Robert L. Seale. *Professor of Nuclear and Energy Engineering, University of Arizona, Tucson.*

Frederick Hanley Seares (d. 1964). *Assistant Director, Mount Wilson Observatory of the Carnegie Institution of Washington, Pasadena, Calif., 1925–40.*

Emilio Gino Segrè. *Emeritus Professor of Physics, University of California, Berkeley. Nobel Prize for Physics, 1959.*

Ralph Pray Seward. *Emeritus Professor of Chemistry, Pennsylvania State University, University Park.*

Charles Donald Shane (d. 1983). *Director, Lick Observatory, University of California, Santa Cruz, 1945–58.*

Steven Soter. *Senior Research Associate, Center for Radiophysics and Space Research, Cornell University, Ithaca, N.Y.*

Robert Spence (d. 1976). *Master of Keynes College; Professor of Applied Chemistry, University of Kent at Canterbury, Eng., 1968–73. Director, Atomic Energy Research Establishment, Harwell, Eng., 1964–68.*

Steven W. Squyres. *National Research Associate, Ames Research Center, National Aeronautics and Space Administration, Moffett Field, Calif.*

Vernon Arthur Stenger. *Consultant, Dow Chemical Company, Midland, Mich.*

Kaj Aa. Strand. *Scientific Director, U.S. Naval Observatory, Washington, D.C., 1963–77.*

Yervant Terzian. *Professor and Chairman, Department of Astronomy, Cornell University, Ithaca, N.Y.*

Saul Arno Teukolsky. *Associate Professor of Physics, Cornell University, Ithaca, N.Y.*

Sir George Paget Thomson (d. 1975). *Professor of Physics, University of London, 1930–52. Cowinner, Nobel Prize for Physics, 1937.*

Ethel Truman. *Formerly Senior Science Tutor, Queen's College, London.*

Peter van de Kamp. *Professor of Astronomy, Swarthmore College, Pa., 1940–72.*

Birgit Vennesland. *Head, Vennesland Research Laboratory, Max Planck Society, 1970–81; Director, Max Planck Institute for Cell Physiology, Berlin, 1968–70.*

Joseph Veverka. *Associate Professor of Astronomy, Cornell University, Ithaca, N.Y.*

Robert Vernon Wagoner, Jr. *Professor of Physics, Stanford University, Calif.*

Robert M. Wald. *Professor of Physics, University of Chicago.*

Cheves T. Walling. *Distinguished Professor of Chemistry, University of Utah, Salt Lake City.*

Charles A. Wert. *Professor of Metallurgy; Head, Department of Metallurgy and Mining Engineering, University of Illinois, Urbana.*

Gunther K. Wertheim. *Member, Chemical Physics Research Laboratory, AT&T Bell Laboratories, Murray Hill, N.J.*

F. Wesemael. *Research Assistant in Physics, University of Montreal.*

George Willard Wheland (d. 1972). *Professor of Chemistry, University of Chicago.*

Donald H. White. *Professor of Physics, Western Oregon State College, Monmouth.*

Gerald James Whitrow. *Emeritus Professor of the History and Applications of Mathematics, Imperial College of Science and Technology, University of London.*

Edward Wichers (d. 1984). *Associate Director, National Bureau of Standards, U.S. Department of Commerce, Washington, D.C., 1958–62; Chief, Division of Chemistry, 1948–58.*

John A. Wood, Jr. *Geologist, Smithsonian Astrophysical Observatory, 1972–76.*

Sir Richard Woolley. *Director, South African Astronomical Observatory, 1972–76.*

Fritz Zwicky (d. 1973). *Professor of Astrophysics, California Institute of Technology, Pasadena, 1942–68. Staff Astronomer, Mt. Wilson and Palomar Observatories.*

Part Two. The Earth

Ernst (Valdemar) Antevs. *Private research geologist.*

Clifford A. Barnes. *Emeritus Professor of Oceanography, University of Washington, Seattle.*

Michel J. Batisse. *Director, Department of Environmental Sciences and Natural Resources Research, Unesco, Paris.*

Louis J. Battan. *Professor of Atmospheric Sciences, University of Arizona, Tucson.*

Werner A. Baum. *Chancellor and Professor of Geography, University of Wisconsin, Milwaukee.*

Kenneth O. Bennington. *Research Chemist, Thermodynamics Laboratory, Albany Metallurgy Research Center, Bureau of Mines, U.S. Department of the Interior, Albany, Ore.*

Marland P. Billings. *Emeritus Professor of Geology, Harvard University.*

F. Donald Bloss. *Alumni Distinguished Professor of Mineralogy, Virginia Polytechnic Institute and State University, Blacksburg.*

William Frank Bradley (d. 1973). *Professor of Chemical Engineering, University of Texas at Austin.*

George William Brindley (d. 1983). *Professor of Mineral Sciences, Pennsylvania State University, University Park, 1962–73.*

Max Edwin Britton. *Consultant on environmental science. Biological Scientist, Geological Survey, U.S. Department of the Interior, Reston, Va., 1974–80.*

Edward Morgan Brooks. *Professor of Geology and Geophysics, Boston College, Chestnut Hill, Mass.*

Arthur C. Barrington Brown. *Consulting oil geologist.*

Franklin Becker Brown. *Director of Research and Development, Union Carbide Corporation, Chemicals and Plastics Operations Division, South Charleston, W.Va.*

Wesley Carr Calef. *Professor of Geography, Illinois State University, Normal.*

Carleton Abramson Chapman. *Professor of Geology, University of Illinois, Urbana.*

Felix Chayes. *Petrologist, Geophysical Laboratory, Carnegie Institution of Washington, D.C.*

Robert Griffin Coleman. *Professor of Geology, Stanford University, Calif.*

Paul E. Damon. *Professor of Geosciences; Chief Scientist, Laboratory of Isotope Geochemistry, University of Arizona, Tucson.*

Hubert G. Davis. *Staff Scientist and Principal Investigator, Energy and Environment Division, Lawrence Berkeley Laboratory, University of California.*

George A. Dawson. *Professor of Atmospheric Sciences, University of Arizona, Tucson.*

George W. DeVore. *Professor of Geology, Florida State University, Tallahassee.*

Ernest George Ehlers. *Professor of Mineralogy, Ohio State University, Columbus.*

Richard Kempton Estelow. *Business Manager, Columbian Carbon Company, Princeton, N.J.*

George Tobias Faust. *Former Mineralogist–Petrologist, Division of Experimental Geochemistry and Mineralogy, Geological Survey, U.S. Department of the Interior, Washington, D.C.*

Carroll Lane Fenton (d. 1969). *Author of* Our Amazing Earth *and others.*

Mildred Adams Fenton. *Coauthor of* Story of the Great Geologists *and others.*

Robert G. Fleagle. *Professor of Atmospheric Sciences, University of Washington, Seattle.*

Robert Louis Folk. *Dave P. Carlton Professor of Geology, University of Texas at Austin.*

Clifford Frondel. *Professor of Mineralogy, Harvard University, 1954–77.*

Fritiof Melvin Fryxell. *Emeritus Professor of Geology, Augustana College, Rock Island, Ill.*

Julian R. Goldsmith. *Charles E. Merriam Distinguished Service Professor of Geochemistry, University of Chicago.*

Allan Grierson. *Senior Lecturer in Mining, Royal School of Mines, Imperial College of Science and Technology, University of London.*

John W. Harbaugh. *Professor of Geology, Stanford University, Calif.*

Walter Brian Harland. *Fellow of Gonville and Caius College, Cambridge; Reader in Tectonic Geology, University of Cambridge.*

Herbert Edwin Hawkes, Jr. *Consulting geologist. Professor of Mineral Exploration, University of California, Berkeley, 1957–65.*

E. William Heinrich. *Professor of Geological Science, University of Michigan, Ann Arbor.*

Donald Munro Henderson. *Professor of Geology, University of Illinois, Urbana.*

Benjamin M. Herman. *Professor of Atmospheric Sciences, University of Arizona, Tucson.*

Jörgen Holmboe. *Emeritus Professor of Meteorology, University of California, Los Angeles.*

Floyd Allen Hummel. *Emeritus Professor of Ceramic Science, Pennsylvania State University, University Park.*

Charles B(utler) Hunt. *Professor of Geology, Johns Hopkins University, Baltimore, Md., 1961–73.*

Cornelius Searle Hurlbut. *Emeritus Professor of Mineralogy, Harvard University.*

Takashi Ichiye. *Professor of Oceanography, Texas A & M University, College Station.*

Richard H. Jahns (d. 1983). *Crook Professor of Geology and Applied Earth Sciences, Stanford University, Calif.*

George Clayton Kennedy. *Professor of Geology and Geochemistry, University of California, Los Angeles, 1969–80.*

Léo F. Laporte. *Professor of Earth Sciences, University of California, Santa Cruz.*

Austin Long. *Associate Professor of Geosciences, University of Arizona, Tucson.*

Duncan McConnell. *Emeritus Professor of Dentistry and of Mineralogy, Ohio State University, Columbus.*

Wayne Anthony McCurdy. *Head, Division of Mining and Preparation, Office of Coal Research, U.S. Department of the Interior, Washington, D.C.*

D. Clay McDowell. *Professor of Meteorology; Director, Institute of Tropical Meteorology, University of Puerto Rico, Río Piedras.*

Wayne E. McGovern. *Meteorologist, Environmental Monitoring and Prediction, National Oceanic and Atmospheric Administration, U.S. Department of Commerce, Rockville, Md.*

Richard W. Macomber. *Professor of Physics, Brooklyn Center, Long Island University, Brooklyn, N.Y.*

Rolland Lee Mays. *Director of Research, Linde Division, Union Carbide Corporation, Tarrytown, N.Y., 1978–81.*

J. Robert Moore. *Director, Marine Science Institute; Professor of Marine Studies, University of Texas at Austin.*

Paul B. Moore. *Professor of Mineralogy and Crystallography, University of Chicago.*

Morris Neiburger. *Emeritus Professor of Meteorology, University of California, Los Angeles.*

Jehuda Neumann. *Emeritus Professor of Atmospheric Sciences, Hebrew University of Jerusalem.*

Bert E. Nordlie. *Professor and Chairman, Department of Geology, Iowa State University, Ames.*

Frederick J. North. *Formerly Keeper of the Department of Geology, National Museum of Wales.*

John Claud Trewinard Oates. *Emeritus Reader in Historical Bibliography, University of Cambridge; Emeritus Fellow of Darwin College, Cambridge.*

Gerald D. O'Brien. *Staff Geologist, Shell Oil Company.*

Charles W. Ott. *Free-lance writer.*

Robert Joseph Pafford, Jr. *Regional Director, Bureau of Reclamation, U.S. Department of the Interior, Sacramento, Calif., 1963–73.*

Hans Arnold Albert Panofsky. *Evan Pugh Research Professor of Atmospheric Sciences, Pennsylvania State University, University Park.*

Kenneth Macaulay Papworth. *Brigadier (retired). Chief Survey Officer, Ordnance Survey, Northern Ireland, 1949–57.*

Ralph Brazelton Peck. *Emeritus Professor of Foundation Engineering, University of Illinois, Urbana.*

Márton Pécsi. *Director, Geographical Research Institute, Hungarian Academy of Sciences, Budapest.*

F.J. Pettijohn. *Emeritus Professor of Geology, Johns Hopkins University, Baltimore.*

Hans Ramberg. *Professor and Head, Department of Mineralogy and Petrology, University of Uppsala, Swed.*

Lewis S. Ramsdell (d. 1975). *Professor of Mineralogy, University of Michigan, Ann Arbor, 1945–61.*

Kelvin S. Rodolfo. *Associate Professor of Geological Sciences, University of Illinois at Chicago.*

Edwin (Woods) Roedder. *Geologist, Experimental Geochemistry and Mineralogy Branch, Geological Survey, U.S. Department of the Interior, Reston, Va.*

James Romanes. *Petroleum geologist.*

Della Roy. *Professor of Materials Science, Pennsylvania State University, University Park.*

Rustum Roy. *Evan Pugh Professor of the Solid State; Director, Materials Research Laboratory, Pennsylvania State University, University Park.*

George Richard Rumney. *Professor of Geography, University of Connecticut, Storrs.*

Maurice L. Schwartz. *Professor of Geology, Western Washington University, Bellingham.*

William D. Sellers. *Professor of Atmospheric Sciences, University of Arizona, Tucson.*

Nicholas M. Short. *Research Scientist, Geophysics Branch, Laboratory for Earth Sciences, Goddard Space Flight Center, National Aeronautics and Space Administration, Greenbelt, Md.*

Sol Robert Silverman. *Senior Research Associate, Chevron Oil Field Research Company, La Habra, Calif.*

Joseph V. Smith. *Louis Block Professor of Physical Sciences, University of Chicago.*

Ian M. Steele. *Senior Research Associate, Department of Geophysical Sciences, University of Chicago.*

John S. Sumner. *Professor of Geosciences and Mining and Geological Engineering, University of Arizona, Tucson.*

Reginald C. Sutcliffe. *Emeritus Professor of Meteorology, University of Reading, Eng.*

Sir Graham Sutton (d. 1977). *Vice President, University College of Wales, Aberystwyth, 1967–77. Director General, Meteorological Office, London, 1953–65.*

George S. Switzer. *Emeritus Curator, Department of Mineral Sciences, Smithsonian Institution, Washington, D.C.*

John M. Teal. *Senior Scientist, Woods Hole Oceanographic Institution, Mass.*

Thomas Prence Thayer. *Geologist, Eastern Mineral Resources Branch, Geological Survey, U.S. Department of the Interior, Washington, D.C.*

James Burleigh Thompson, Jr. *Sturgis Hooper Professor of Geology, Harvard University.*

Charles Warren Thornthwaite (d. 1963). *Director, Laboratory of Climatology, Centerton, N.J. Principal Climatologist, U.S. Soil Conservation Service, 1935–46.*

Cecil Edgar Tilley (d. 1973). *Professor of Mineralogy and Petrology, University of Cambridge, 1931–61.*

Karl M. Waage. *Professor of Geology; Curator of Invertebrate Paleontology, Peabody Museum of Natural History, Yale University.*

Howel Williams. *Emeritus Professor of Geology, University of California, Berkeley.*

Richard F. Wilson. *Associate Professor of Geosciences, University of Arizona, Tucson.*

Donald Wolberg. *Paleontologist, New Mexico Bureau of Mines and Mineral Resources, Socorro.*

W.A. Wooster. *Director, Crystal Structures Ltd., Cambridge, Eng.*

Jerome J. Wright. *Chief Hydrologist, Metropolitan Utilities Management Agency, Tucson, 1974–78. Associate Professor of Geosciences, University of Arizona, Tucson, 1966–74.*

Vsevolod Pavlovich Zenkovich. *Former Head of Shore Department, Institute of Oceanology, Academy of Sciences of the U.S.S.R., Moscow.*

Part Three. Life on Earth

Constantine John Alexopoulos (d. 1986). *Professor of Botany, University of Texas at Austin, 1962–77.*

Garland Edward Allen. *Professor of Biology, Washington University, St. Louis, Mo.*

Angeles Alvariño. *Fishery Research Biologist, National Marine Fisheries Service, National Oceanic and Atmospheric Administration, U.S. Department of Commerce, La Jolla, Calif.*

George Sherman Avery. *Emeritus Director, Brooklyn Botanic Garden, N.Y.*

Edward William Baker. *Acarologist, Agricultural Research Service, U.S. Department of Agriculture, Beltsville, Md.*

Fred Alexander Barkley. *Former Professor of Biology, Northeastern University, Boston.*

J. Laurens Barnard. *Curator, Division of Crustacea, Smithsonian Institution, Washington, D.C.*

Roger Lyman Batten. *Professor of Geology, Columbia University. Curator, American Museum of Natural History, New York City.*

Dmitri Konstantinovich Belyaev. *Director, Institute of Cytology and Genetics; Chief of the Laboratory of Evolution Genetics, Siberian Department, Academy of Sciences of the U.S.S.R., Novosibirsk.*

Lyman Benson. *Emeritus Professor of Botany; Director of the Herbarium, Pomona College, Claremont, Calif.*

Victor Rickman Boswell. *Assistant Director, Crops Research Division, U.S. Department of Agriculture, Plant Industry Station, Beltsville, Md., 1965–68.*

Andrew Gavin Brown. *Former Senior Experimental Officer, Department of Applied Genetics, John Innes Institute, Norwich, Eng.*

Frank A. Brown, Jr. (d. 1983). *Morrison Professor of Biology, Northwestern University, Evanston, Ill., 1956–76.*

John Bonner Buck. *Chief, Section of Comparative Physiology, National Institutes of Health, Bethesda, Md.*

John Walford Bundy. *Company Agricultural General Manager, Birds Eye Foods Ltd., England.*

F.M. Carpenter. *Fisher Professor Emeritus of Natural History, Harvard University; Curator of Fossil Insects, Museum of Comparative Zoology, 1936–72.*

Jackson Leaphart Cartter. *Director, U.S. Regional Soybean Laboratory, U.S. Department of Agriculture, Urbana, Ill., 1950–65.*

Robert H. Catlett. *Former Associate Professor of Zoology, San Diego State College, Calif.*

Ailsa McGowan Clark. *Principal Scientific Officer, Department of Zoology, British Museum (Natural History), London.*

Phil Clark. *Free-lance writer on botany.*

Arthur L. Cohen. *Emeritus Professor of Botany and of Biological Sciences, Washington State University, Pullman; Director, Electron Microscope Center, 1962–79.*

Ira Judson Condit (d. 1981). *Professor of Subtropical Horticulture, University of California, Citrus Research Center, Riverside.*

Patricia L. Cook. *Principal Scientific Officer, Department of Zoology, British Museum (Natural History), London.*

Charles E. Cornelius. *Director, California Primate Research Center, University of California, Davis. Dean, College of Veterinary Medicine, University of Florida, Gainesville, 1971–81.*

Paul F.S. Cornelius. *Principal Scientific Officer, Department of Zoology, British Museum (Natural History), London.*

Donovan Stewart Correll. *Program Director, Division of Biological and Medical Sciences, National Science Foundation. Chief Botanist; Head of Botanical Laboratory, Texas Research Foundation, Renner, Texas, 1956–71.*

Francis E.G. Cox. *Professor of Zoology, King's College, University of London.*

Alistair Cameron Crombie. *Senior Lecturer in the History of Science, University of Oxford.*

Frank P. Cullinan. *Collaborator, U.S. National Arboretum, Washington, D.C.*

R.L. Cushing. *Vice President and Secretary, Hawaiian Sugar Planters Association, Honolulu; Director, Experiment Station, 1963–79.*

George McMillan Darrow. *Consultant, U.S. Department of Agriculture, Beltsville, Md.; Principal Horticulturist in Charge of Small Fruit Investigations, 1954–57.*

Charles C. Davis. *Professor of Biology, Memorial University of Newfoundland, St. John's, 1968–77.*

Sir Gavin de Beer (d. 1972). *Professor of Embryology, University College, University of London, 1945–50. Director, British Museum (Natural History), London, 1950–60.*

Robert H. Denison. *Associate, Museum of Comparative Zoology, Harvard University. Curator of Fossil Fishes, Field Museum of Natural History, Chicago, 1948–71.*

Bernard Dixon. *Science writer. Editor,* New Scientist, *1969–79.*

Elizabeth C. Dudley. *Research Associate, Zoology, University of Maryland, College Park.*

L.C. Dunn (d. 1974). *Professor of Zoology, 1928–62; Senior Research Associate in Biological Sciences, 1962–74, Columbia University.*

Stephen Porter Dunn. *Director of Research, Highgate Road Social Science Research Station, Inc., Berkeley, Calif.*

O.J. Eigsti. *Emeritus Professor of Botany, Chicago State University.*

Alfred E. Emerson (d. 1976). *Professor of Biology, University of Chicago, 1934–62.*

Richard Fifield. *Managing Editor,* New Scientist.

Claudio Gilberto Froehlich. *Associate Professor of Zoology, Institute of Biosciences, University of São Paulo, Braz.*

Marshall Gates. *Charles Frederick Houghton Professor of Chemistry, University of Rochester, N.Y.*

J. Whitfield Gibbons. *Associate Director, Savannah River Ecology Laboratory, University of Georgia, Aiken, S.C.*

David Ian Gibson. *Principal Scientific Officer, Department of Zoology, British Museum (Natural History), London.*

Ray Gibson. *Senior Lecturer in Biology, Liverpool Polytechnic, Eng.*

Ernest M. Gifford, Jr. *Professor of Botany, University of California, Davis.*

Clarence James Goodnight. *Professor of Biology, Western Michigan University, Kalamazoo.*

Marie Louise Goodnight. *Free-lance writer and researcher. Instructor in Biological Sciences, Purdue University, West Lafayette, Ind., 1946–65.*

Andres Goth, M.D. *Former Professor of Pharmacology, University of Texas Southwestern Medical School at Dallas.*

Edna R. Green. *Former Head, Science Department, Philadelphia High School for Girls.*

J. Green. *Professor of Zoology, Westfield College, University of London.*

Per H.H. Halldal. *Professor of Plant Physiology, University of Oslo.*

Yata Haneda. *Curator, Yokosuka City Museum, Japan. Coeditor of* Bioluminescence in Progress.

Sir Alister C. Hardy (d. 1985). *Linacre Professor of Zoology, University of Oxford; 1946–61.*

Ellwood Scott Harrar (d. 1975). *James B. Duke Professor of Wood Science, Duke University, Durham, N.C., 1967–74.*

Hudson Thomas Hartmann. *Professor of Pomology, University of California, Davis.*

Joel W(alker) Hedgpeth. *Emeritus Professor of Oceanography, Oregon State University, Newport; Head, Yaquina Biological Laboratory, Marine Science Center, 1965–74.*

Edward Hindle (d. 1973). *Scientific Director, Zoological Society of London, 1944–51. Regius Professor of Zoology, University of Glasgow, 1935–43.*

Cecil Arthur Hoare (d. 1984). *Wellcome Research Fellow, Wellcome Laboratories of Tropical Medicine, London, 1957–70; Head, Protozoological Department, 1923–57.*

Walter Henricks Hodge. *Section Head for Ecological and Systematic Botany, National Science Foundation, Washington, D.C., 1970–73.*

Richard Lawrence Hoffman. *Professor of Biology, Radford University, Va.*

Turner Harcourt Hopper. *Chief, Oilseed Crops Laboratory, Southern Utilization Research and Development Division, Agricultural Research Service, New Orleans, 1958–65.*

Carl L. Hubbs (d. 1979). *Professor of Biology, Scripps Institution of Oceanography, University of California, San Diego, at La Jolla, 1944–69.*

Clark Hubbs. *Professor of Zoology, University of Texas at Austin.*

Hilary Mary Hughes. *Horticulturalist, Ministry of Agriculture, Wolverhampton, Great Britain.*

Laurence Irving (d. 1979). *Professor of Zoophysiology, University of Alaska, Fairbanks, 1962–74; Advisory Scientific Director, Institute of Arctic Biology, 1966–74.*

Artemy V. Ivanov. *Head, Laboratory of Evolutionary Morphology, Zoological Institute, Academy of Sciences of the U.S.S.R., Leningrad. Former Professor of Zoology, Leningrad A.A. Zhdanov State University.*

David Starr Jordan, M.D. (d. 1931). *Chancellor, Stanford University, Calif., 1913–16; President, 1891–1913. President, Indiana University, Bloomington, 1885–91; Professor of Zoology, 1879–85.*

Theodor (Karl) Just (d. 1960). *Chief Curator, Department of Botany, Field Museum of Natural History, Chicago.*

Chester Scott Keefer, M.D. (d. 1972). *Wade Professor of Medicine, Boston University, 1940–64.*

Keith R. Kelson. *Former Acting Assistant Director for Education and Executive Assistant, National Science Foundation, Washington, D.C. Coauthor of* The Mammals of North America.

Vera V. Khvostova (d. 1977). *Chief, Laboratory of Cytogenetics, Institute of Cytology and Genetics, Siberian Department, Academy of Sciences of the U.S.S.R., Novosibirsk.*

James Edward Knott. *Emeritus Professor of Vegetable Crops, University of California, Davis; Chairman of the Department, 1940–64.*

Paulden Ford Knowles. *Professor of Agronomy, University of California, Davis.*

Barry Koffler. *Free-lance writer on zoology and ecology.*

Sir Hans (Adolf) Krebs (d. 1981). *Whitley Professor of Biochemistry, University of Oxford, 1954–67. Cowinner, Nobel Prize for Physiology or Medicine, 1953.*

Christine Laning. *Free-lance writer on botany.*

Carl Adam Lawrence (d. 1972). *Director, Bureau of Laboratories, Los Angeles County Health Department, Calif., 1953–70.*

Hubert Arthur Lechevalier. *Professor of Microbiology, Rutgers University, New Brunswick, N.J.*

Morris Cecil Leikind (d. 1976). *Scientist Administrator, National Clearinghouse for Mental Health Information, National Institutes of Health, Bethesda, Md., 1963–66.*

Roger John Lincoln. *Principal Scientific Officer, Department of Zoology, British Museum (Natural History), London.*

Thomas D. Luckey. *Professor of Biochemistry, University of Missouri, Columbia.*

Joseph Colvin McDaniel. *Former Assistant Professor of Horticulture (Research), University of Illinois, Urbana.*

John Robert Magness. *Chief, Fruit and Nut Crops Research Branch, U.S. Department of Agriculture, U.S. Plant Industry Station, Beltsville, Md., 1953–59.*

Leonard Harrison Matthews. *Scientific Director, Zoological Society of London, 1951–66. Fellow of the Royal Society.*

Florence Moog. *Rebstock Professor of Biology, Washington University, St. Louis, Mo.*

Thomas Edwin Moore. *Curator of Insects, Museum of Zoology; Professor of Zoology, University of Michigan, Ann Arbor.*

Ernst Trier Mörch, M.D. *Anesthesiologist, Nassau General Hospital, Fernandina Beach, Fla. Former Clinical Professor of Surgery, University of Illinois, Chicago.*

James William Moulder. *Professor of Microbiology, University of Chicago.*

Walter Conrad Muenscher (d. 1963). *Professor of Botany, Cornell University, Ithaca, N.Y.*

Carl F.W. Muesebeck. *Honorary Collaborator, U.S. Department of Agriculture and U.S. National Museum, 1954–65. Chief, Division of Insect Identification, U.S. Department of Agriculture, 1935–54.*

John Spangler Nicholas (d. 1963). *Sterling Professor of Biology, Yale University, 1939–63.*

George Torao Okita. *Professor of Pharmacology, Northwestern University, Chicago.*

Everett C. Olson. *Emeritus Professor of Zoology, University of California, Los Angeles.*

Jane M. Oppenheimer. *Emeritus Professor of the History of Science, Bryn Mawr College, Pa.*

Gilbert Fred Otto. *Professor of Zoology, University of Maryland, College Park, 1966–72.*

Thomas G. Overmire. *Head, Office of Project Management, Kuwait Institute for Scientific Research. Author of* Homeostatic Regulation.

Gordon Paterson. *Higher Scientific Officer, Department of Zoology, British Museum (Natural History), London.*

Fernandus Payne (deceased). *Professor of Zoology, Indiana University, Bloomington, 1919–51.*

Michael J. Pelczar, Jr. *Emeritus Vice President for Graduate Studies and Research; Emeritus Professor of Microbiology, University of Maryland, College Park.*

Bernard George Peters (d. 1967). *Professor of Parasitology, Imperial College of Science and Technology, University of London, 1955–67.*

Sir Rudolph Albert Peters (d. 1982). *Whitley Professor of Biochemistry, University of Oxford, 1923–54. Head, Biochemistry Department, Agricultural Research Council, Institute of Animal Physiology, Babraham, Cambridge, Eng., 1954–59.*

Richard W. Pohl. *Distinguished Professor of Botany; Curator of the Herbarium, Iowa State University, Ames.*

(Frederick) Wilson Popenoe. *Director Emeritus, Escuela Agrícola Panamericana, Tegucigalpa, Honduras, Author of* Manual of Tropical and Subtropical Fruits *and others.*

John Ramsbottom (d. 1974). *Keeper, Department of Botany, British Museum (Natural History), London, 1930–50.*

Austin L. Rand (d. 1982). *Research Associate, Archbold Biological Station, Lake Placid, Fla. Chief Curator of Zoology, Field Museum of Natural History, Chicago, 1955–70.*

Gloria Robinson. *Research Affiliate in the History of Medicine, Yale University.*

Alfred S. Romer (d. 1973). *Alexander Agassiz Professor of Zoology, Harvard University, 1947–65.*

Anthony H. Rose. *Professor of Microbiology, University of Bath, Eng.*

Herbert Holdsworth Ross (d. 1978). *Professor of Entomology, University of Georgia, Athens.*

Bradley Titus Scheer. *Emeritus Professor of Biology, University of Oregon, Eugene.*

Aaron J. Sharp. *Alumni Distinguished Service Professor Emeritus of Botany, University of Tennessee, Knoxville.*

Malcolm C. Shurtleff, Jr. *Professor of Plant Pathology; Extension Plant Pathologist, University of Illinois, Urbana.*

Reginald W. Sims. *Head, Annelida Section, Department of Zoology, British Museum (Natural History), London.*

Walton B. Sinclair. *Emeritus Professor of Biochemistry, University of California, Riverside.*

Robert Leo Smith. *Professor of Wildlife Biology and Ecology, West Virginia University, Morgantown.*

Howard James Stains. *Professor of Zoology, Southern Illinois University, Carbondale.*

William Campbell Steere. *Emeritus Professor of Botany, Columbia University. Emeritus President, New York Botanical Garden, Bronx.*

C.D. Stein, V.M.D. (d. 1965). *Consultant, Animal Disease Eradication Division, Agricultural Research Service, U.S. Department of Agriculture.*

William Louis Stern. *Professor and Chairman, Department of Botany, University of Florida, Gainesville.*

Robert W. Storer. *Professor of Zoology; Curator of Birds, Museum of Zoology, University of Michigan, Ann Arbor.*

William Cofield Summers, M.D. *Professor of Therapeutic Radiology, Molecular Biophysics and Biochemistry, and Human Genetics, Yale University.*

William H. Taliaferro (d. 1973). *Eliakim Hastings Moore Distinguished Service Professor of Microbiology, University of Chicago, 1954–60. Senior Immunologist, Division of Biological and Medical Research, Argonne National Laboratory, Argonne, Ill., 1960–69.*

John David Taylor. *Head, Mollusca Section, Zoology Department, British Museum (Natural History), London.*

Norman Taylor (d. 1967). *Assistant Curator, New York Botanical Garden, 1905–11. Author of* Guide to Garden Flowers *and others.*

John W. Thieret. *Professor of Botany, Northern Kentucky University, Highland Heights.*

Frederick Ichiro Tsuji. *Research Biochemist, Marine Biology Research Division, Scripps Institution of Oceanography, University of California, San Diego, at La Jolla.*

Robert Templeton Van Tress. *Former Horticulturist, Chicago Park District.*

Paul Dirks Voth. *Emeritus Professor of Botany, University of Chicago.*

David B. Wake. *Director, Museum of Vertebrate Zoology; Professor of Zoology, University of California, Berkeley.*

Lionel A. Walford (d. 1979). *Director, Sandy Hook Marine Laboratory, Highlands, N.J., 1960–71; Senior Scientist, 1971–74.*

Stanley H. Weitzman. *Curator of Fishes, Division of Fishes, National Museum of Natural History, Smithsonian Institution, Washington, D.C.*

Rupert L. Wenzel. *Emeritus Curator of Insects, Field Museum of Natural History, Chicago; Chairman, Department of Zoology, 1970–77.*

Geoffrey Buckle West. *Honorary Fellow in Pharmacology, North East London Polytechnic.*

G(eorge) W(illard) Wharton. *Emeritus Professor of Entomology, Ohio State University, Columbus; Director, Acarology Laboratory, 1969–76.*

Donald Walter Wilkie. *Director, Aquarium-Museum, Scripps Institution of Oceanography, University of California, San Diego.*

Gordon Roy Williams. *Head, New Zealand Wildlife Service, Department of Internal Affairs, Wellington.*

Louis O. Williams. *Emeritus Curator of Botany, Field Museum of Natural History, Chicago.*

A.J. Winkler. *Emeritus Professor of Viticulture and Emeritus Viticulturist, College of Agriculture, University of California, Davis.*

Keith Arthur John Wise. *Entomologist, Auckland Institute and Museum, N.Z.*

Dorothea Woodruff. *Herbarium Associate and Research Assistant, Department of Biology, University of Utah, Salt Lake City.*

A.H. Wright (d. 1966). *Professor of Agronomy, University of Wisconsin, Madison, 1931–57.*

Kanichiro Yashiroda. *Proprietor, Yashiroda Acclimatization Garden, Tonosho, Japan. Author of* Bonsai: Japanese Miniature Trees.

Richard Charles York. *Instructor of Ornamental Horticulture, McHenry County College, Crystal Lake, Ill. Former Associate Editor, Biology, Encyclopædia Britannica, Chicago.*

Wolfram Winfried Zillig. *Director, Max Planck Institute for Biochemistry, Munich.*

Martin Huldrych Zimmermann (d. 1984). *Charles Bullard Professor of Forestry, Harvard University; Director, Harvard Forest, Petersham, 1970–84.*

Conway Zirkle (d. 1972). *Professor of Biology, University of Pennsylvania, Philadelphia, 1937–66.*

Solly Zuckerman, Baron Zuckerman. *Sands Cox Professor Emeritus of Anatomy, University of Birmingham, Eng. President, Zoological Society of London, 1977–84.*

Part Four. Human Life

Fred Lyman Adair, M.D. (d. 1972). *Mary Campau Ryerson Professor of Obstetrics and Gynecology, University of Chicago, 1931–42.*

Rodolfo Almeida Pintos (deceased). *Phthisiologist, Institute of Epidemiology and Contagious Diseases, School of Medicine, University of Montevideo, Uruguay.*

W.A.D. Anderson, M.D. *Emeritus Professor of Pathology, School of Medicine, University of Miami.*

Alfred Alvin Angrist, M.D. (d. 1984). *Professor of Pathology, Albert Einstein College of Medicine, Yeshiva University, Bronx, N.Y.*

(Edith Kathleen) Charlotte Banks. *Former Lecturer in Psychology, University College, University of London.*

M. Robert Barnett. *Consultant, American Foundation for the Blind, Inc., New York City; Executive Director, 1949–74.*

Edward W. Barrett. *Consultant and writer on communications.*

Frank X. Barron. *Professor of Psychology, University of California, Santa Cruz.*

Sir Frederic Charles Bartlett (d. 1969). *Professor of Experimental Psychology, University of Cambridge, 1931–52; Director, Psychological Laboratory, 1922–52.*

S. Howard Bartley. *Distinguished Research Professor Emeritus of Psychology, Memphis State University, Tenn. Emeritus Professor of Psychology, Michigan State University, East Lansing; Director, Laboratory for the Study of Vision and Related Sensory Processes, 1966–71.*

David V. Bates, M.D. *Professor of Medicine and Physiology, University of British Columbia, Vancouver.*

William B. Bean, M.D. *Sir William Osler Professor Emeritus of Medicine, University of Iowa, Iowa City. Editor in Chief, Archives of Internal Medicine, 1962–67.*

Marc Oliver Beem, M.D. *Professor of Pediatrics, University of Chicago.*

Walter Reginald Bett. *Medical Editor, Wm. Douglas McAdams, Inc., New York City. Author of* The Infirmities of Genius *and others.*

Emma Mary Birch. *Head Occupational Therapist, Royal Free Hospital Group, London.*

Edwin Garrigues Boring (d. 1968). *Edgar Pierce Professor of Psychology, Harvard University, 1956–57; Professor of Psychology, 1928–56.*

Arthur Hills Brayfield. *Emeritus Professor of Psychology, Claremont Graduate School, Calif.*

Henry W. Brosin, M.D. *Professor of Psychiatry, University of Arizona, Tucson.*

Carroll L. Bryant. *Director, Office of Publications, American National Red Cross, 1954–60.*

William Burrows (d. 1978). *Professor of Microbiology, University of Chicago, 1947–73.*

Sir Cyril Lodowic Burt (d. 1971). *Professor of Psychology, University College, University of London, 1931–50.*

Douglas E. Busby, M.D. *Medical Director, Downtown Healthcare Services, Lutheran Medical Center, Cleveland.*

Donald E. Cassels, M.D. (d. 1981). *Professor of Pediatrics, University of Chicago.*

Andrew Barnett Christie, M.D. *Honorary Physician, Fazakerly Hospital, Liverpool. Former Head, Department of Infectious Diseases, University of Liverpool.*

Conrad Chyatte. *Associate Professor of Psychology, De Paul University, Chicago, 1952–76.*

Leighton E. Cluff, M.D. *Executive Vice President, Robert Wood Johnson Foundation, Princeton, N.J. Professor and Chairman, Department of Medicine, University of Florida, Gainesville, 1966–76.*

Robert Coope, M.D. *Honorary Consulting Physician, Liverpool United Hospitals, Eng.*

David W. Crabb. *Associate Professor of Anthropology, Princeton University.*

Paul Frederic Cranefield. *Professor of Physiology, Rockefeller University, New York City.*

Jean-Marie Crépin. *Electroradiologist, Léopold Bellan Hospital, Paris.*

Edward P. Crowell, D.O. *Former Executive Director, American Osteopathic Association, Chicago.*

Liza Dahlby. *Translator and free-lance writer.*

Robert Croly Darling, M.D. *Simon Baruch Professor Emeritus of Rehabilitation Medicine, Columbia University.*

Henry P. David. *Director, Transnational Family Research Institute, Bethesda, Md. Associate Clinical Professor of Psychology, School of Medicine, University of Maryland, Baltimore.*

Peter P.H. De Bruyn, M.D. *Emeritus Professor of Anatomy, University of Chicago.*

Susan J. Decker. *Free-lance writer on medical topics. Electron Microscopist, Department of Biology, University of Illinois, Chicago.*

William N. Dember. *Professor of Psychology, University of Cincinnati, Ohio.*

Helen Aird Dickie, M.D. *Professor of Medicine, University of Wisconsin, Madison.*

John Holmes Dingle, M.D. (d. 1973). *Elisabeth Severance Prentiss Professor of Preventive Medicine and Professor of Medicine, Case Western Reserve University, Cleveland.*

Joseph Lewi Donhauser (d. 1964). *Professor of Surgery, Albany Medical College, N.Y. Senior Surgeon, Albany Medical Center Hospital.*

Roy Melvin Dorcus (d. 1968). *Professor of Psychology, 1944–65; Dean, Division of Life Sciences, University of California, Los Angeles, 1950–63.*

James Russell Eckman. *Senior Consultant, Section of Publications, Mayo Clinic, Rochester, Minn.*

Lillian Eichelberger. *Emeritus Professor of Biochemistry, Department of Surgery, University of Chicago.*

Kendall Emerson, Jr., M.D. *Emeritus Professor of Medicine, Harvard Medical School, Harvard University.*

William Fisher Enneking, M.D. *Distinguished Service Professor of Orthopaedic Surgery, University of Florida, Gainesville.*

George Hoben Estabrooks (d. 1974). *Professor of Psychology, Colgate University, Hamilton, N.Y., 1935–64.*

Hans Jurgen Eysenck. *Professor of Psychology, University of London.*

Ernest Carroll Faust (d. 1978). *Professor of Parasitology, Tulane University, New Orleans.*

Louis B. Flexner, M.D. *Professor of Anatomy, University of Pennsylvania, Philadelphia.*

Anna Freud (d. 1982). *Director of the Hampstead Child Therapy Course and Clinic, London, 1952–82. Author of* The Ego and the Mechanisms of Defence *and others.*

William F. Ganong, M.D. *Lange Professor and Chairman, Department of Physiology, University of California, San Francisco.*

Esther Garvey. *Registered Nurse, specializing in geriatric care.*

Jacob Warren Getzels. *R. Wendell Harrison Distinguished Service Professor Emeritus of Educational Psychology, University of Chicago.*

Edward Girden. *Emeritus Professor of Psychology, Brooklyn College, City University of New York.*

Francis Byron Gordon, M.D. (d. 1973). *Director, Department of Microbiology, Naval Medical Research Institute, Bethesda, Md., 1962–72.*

Ashton Graybiel, M.D. *Chief Scientific Advisor, Naval Aerospace Medical Research Laboratory, Naval Air Station, Pensacola, Fla.; Director of Research, 1945–70.*

Douglas James Guthrie, M.D. (d. 1975). *Medical historian. Lecturer on the History of Medicine, University of Edinburgh, 1945–56.*

Ward Campbell Halstead (d. 1969). *Professor, Department of Psychology and Medicine, University of Chicago, 1946–69.*

A. Gordon Hammer. *Emeritus Professor of Psychology, Macquarie University, North Ryde, Australia.*

Henry Nelson Harkins, M.D. (d. 1967). *Professor of Surgery, University of Washington, 1947–67; Surgeon-in-Chief, University Hospital, Seattle, 1957–64.*

Donald F.N. Harrison, M.D. *Professor of Laryngology and Otology, University of London.*

Réjane M. Harvey, M.D. *Professor of Medicine, Columbia University. Director, Pulmonary Division, Department of Medicine, Presbyterian Hospital, New York City.*

A. Waller Hastings. *Medical writer and editor.*

R.L. Hay. *Professor of Geology, University of California, Berkeley. Author of* Geology of the Olduvai Gorge.

Ralph William Heine. *Emeritus Professor of Psychology, University of Michigan, Ann Arbor; Director, Institute for Human Adjustment, 1974–78.*

Roger Moss Herriott. *Professor of Biochemistry, School of Hygiene and Public Health, Johns Hopkins University, Baltimore.*

Nicholas Carr Hightower, M.D. *Senior Consultant, Department of Gastroenterology, Scott and White Clinic and Scott and White Memorial Hospital, Temple, Texas.*

Constance Holden. *Staff writer,* Science *magazine.*

Howard Francis Hunt. *Professor of Psychology in Psychiatry, New York Hospital—Cornell University Medical Center, White Plains, New York.*

Stanley W. Jacob, M.D. *Associate Professor of Surgery, Oregon Health Sciences University, Portland.*

Saul Jarcho, M.D. *Associate Attending Physician, Mt. Sinai Hospital, New York City. Consultant to the Surgeon General of the U.S. Army and to the National Institute of Health, Bethesda, Md.*

Herbert Henry Jasper, M.D. *Emeritus Professor of Neurophysiology, University of Montreal. Consultant in Neurophysiology, Montreal Neurological Institute, McGill University.*

Franklin Davis Johnston, M.D. (d. 1971). *Professor of Internal Medicine, University of Michigan, Ann Arbor.*

J.R. Kantor (d. 1984). *Professor of Psychology, Indiana University, Bloomington, 1923–59.*

George Alexander Kelly (d. 1967). *Professor of Psychology, Brandeis University, Waltham, Mass., 1965–67.*

Pearl L(uella) Kendrick. *Emeritus Lecturer, Department of Epidemiology, School of Public Health, University of Michigan, Ann Arbor.*

Meave Kenny, M.D. *Former University Reader in Obstetrics and Gynecology, Postgraduate Medical School of London.*

John Franklin Kenward, M.D. *Associate Professor Emeritus of Pediatrics and Psychiatry, University of Chicago.*

Thomas Edward Keys. *Emeritus Professor of the History of Medicine, Mayo Graduate School of Medicine, University of Minnesota, Rochester.*

Joseph Barnett Kirsner, M.D. *Louis Block Distinguished Service Professor of Medicine, University of Chicago.*

Arthur Paul Klotz, M.D. *Staff Physician, Boswell Memorial Hospital, Sun City, Ariz. Professor of Medicine, University of Kansas, Kansas City, 1962–75; Head of Section of Gastroenterology, 1954–75.*

Heinrich Klüver (d. 1979). *Sewell L. Avery Distinguished Service Professor of Biological Psychology, University of Chicago, 1957–62.*

John Knowelden, M.D. *Professor of Community Medicine, University of Sheffield, Eng.*

Helen Lois Koch (d. 1977). *Professor of Child Psychology, University of Chicago, 1945–60.*

Sigmund Koch. *Professor of Psychology and Philosophy, Boston University.*

Dieter Koch-Weser, M.D. *Professor of Preventive and Social Medicine; Associate Dean for International Programs, Medical School, Harvard University.*

Sheldon Jerome Korchin. *Professor of Psychology, University of California, Berkeley.*

Raymond G. Kuhlen (d. 1967). *Professor of Psychology, Syracuse University, N.Y.*

Karen Landahl. *Assistant Professor of Linguistics, University of Chicago.*

Olof Larsell (d. 1964). *Professor of Neuroanatomy, University of Minnesota, Minneapolis.*

Gabriel W(ard) Lasker. *Professor of Anatomy, School of Medicine, Wayne State University, Detroit.*

Richard Last. *Television critic,* Daily Telegraph (London).

James P. Leake, M.D. (d. 1973). *Medical Director, U.S. Public Health Service, Washington, D.C., 1935–45.*

Mary Leakey. *Director of Research, Olduvai Gorge, Tanzania.*

W.R. Lee, M.D. *Professor of Occupational Health, Victoria University of Manchester, Eng.*

Benedict Leerburger. *Free-lance science writer.*

Edwin Herman Lennette, M.D. *Emeritus Chief, Viral and Rickettsial Disease Laboratory, California State Department of Public Health. Lecturer in Epidemiology and Virology, University of California, Berkeley, 1948–78.*

David Le Vay. *Consultant Surgeon, National Health Service, United Kingdom.*

Max Levin, M.D. (d. 1974). *Neurologist and psychiatrist. Clinical Professor of Neurology, New York Medical College, New York City.*

Dorothy C.H. Ley, M.D. *Director, Palliative Care Foundation, Toronto. Former Director, Laboratory Certification and Proficiency Testing Program, Ontario Medical Association.*

Allan L. Lorincz, M.D. *Professor of Dermatology, University of Chicago.*

Douglas McAlpine, M.D. (d. 1981). *Consulting Physician, Middlesex Hospital and Maida Vale Hospital, London.*

Morton McCutcheon, M.D. (d. 1962). *Professor of Pathology, University of Pennsylvania, Philadelphia.*

William J. McGuire. *Professor of Psychology, Yale University.*

Ralph Hermon Major, M.D. (d. 1970). *Professor of Medicine and of the History of Medicine, University of Kansas, Kansas City.*

Judd Marmor, M.D. *Franz Alexander Professor Emeritus of Psychiatry, University of Southern California, Los Angeles.*

Jonathan Meader. *Free-lance writer on entertainment.*

Harold Merskey, M.D. *Professor of Psychiatry, University of Western Ontario, London.*

Heino F.L. Meyer-Bahlburg. *Associate Clinical Professor of Medical Psychology, Columbia University.*

William James Mills, Jr., M.D. *Orthopedic Surgeon. Professor and Director, Center of High Latitude Health Research, University of Alaska, Anchorage. Rear Admiral (retired), Medical Corps, U.S. Naval Reserve.*

John Edgar Morison, M.D. *Honorary Professor of Histopathology, Queen's University of Belfast, N.Ire. Consultant in Histopathology, Belfast City Hospital.*

John Douglas Newth. *Former Honorary Secretary, British Council for Doctor Schweitzer's Hospital.*

Charles R. Noback. *Professor of Anatomy, College of Physicians and Surgeons, Columbia University.*

Norman H. Olsen, D.D.S. *Dean, Dental School, Northwestern University, Chicago.*

Charles Donald O'Malley (d. 1970). *Professor of Medical History, University of California Medical Center, Los Angeles.*

Martin T. Orne, M.D. *Professor of Psychiatry, University of Pennsylvania, Philadelphia; Director, Unit for Experimental Psychiatry, Institute of Pennsylvania Hospital.*

Thomas Parran, M.D. (d. 1968). *Surgeon General, U.S. Public Health Service, 1936–48. Dean, Graduate School of Public Health, University of Pittsburgh, 1948–58. President, Avalon Foundation, New York City, 1958–61.*

Donald G. Paterson (d. 1961). *Professor of Psychology; Member of Staff, Industrial Relations Center, University of Minnesota, Minneapolis.*

Sir George (White) Pickering, M.D. (d. 1980). *Master of Pembroke College, Oxford, 1968–74; Regius Professor of Medicine, University of Oxford, 1956–68.*

Fred Plum, M.D. *Anne Parrish Titzell Professor of Neurology, Medical College, Cornell University, New York City. Neurologist in Chief, New York Hospital.*

C. Stanford Read, M.D. *Former Lecturer in Psychological Medicine, Bethlem Royal Hospital, London. Former Clinical Psychologist, West End Hospital for Nervous Diseases, London.*

Robert G. Richardson. *Consultant medical editor. Former Editor, Abbottempo (international medical journal).*

J. Alfred Rider, M.D. *Director, Gastrointestinal Research Laboratory, Franklin Hospital, San Francisco.*

Walther Riese, M.D. (d. 1976). *Associate Professor of the History of Medicine and of Neurology and Psychiatry, Medical College of Virginia, Richmond, 1958–60.*

Austin Herbert Riesen. *Emeritus Professor of Psychology, University of California, Riverside.*

H. Rocke Robertson, M.D. *Principal and Vice Chancellor, McGill University, Montreal, 1962–70.*

Arthur Robinson, M.D. *Professor of Biochemistry, Biophysics, and Genetics and of Pediatrics, University of Colorado, Denver.*

Nicholas A. Romas, M.D. *Director of Urology, St. Luke's-Roosevelt Hospital Center, New York City.*

Arturo Stearns Rosenblueth, M.D. *Former Director, Centre for Investigation and Advanced Studies, National Polytechnic Institute, Mexico City.*

Paul Farr Russell, M.D. (d. 1983). *Visiting Professor, Harvard University School of Public Health, 1960–63. Staff member, Rockefeller Foundation, 1923–59.*

Heinrich Satter. *Free-lance writer. Author of Paul Ehrlich, Begründer der Chemotherapie and others.*

T.C. Schneirla (d. 1968). *Curator of Animal Behaviour, American Museum of Natural History, New York City, 1947–68.*

Sidney Schulman, M.D. *Ellen C. Manning Professor of Neurology, University of Chicago.*

Laurance F. Shaffer (d. 1976). *Professor of Psychology and Education, Teachers College, Columbia University.*

Leon Sokoloff, M.D. *Professor of Pathology, State University of New York at Stony Brook.*

Walter Graham Spector (d. 1982). *Professor of Pathology, St. Bartholomew's Hospital Medical College, University of London, 1962–82.*

William Spector. *Senior Editor, Human Life, Encyclopædia Britannica, Chicago, 1967–72. Editor of Handbook of Biological Data and others.*

Wesley William Spink, M.D. *Regents' Professor Emeritus of Medicine, University of Minnesota, Minneapolis.*

Howard Burnham Sprague, M.D. (d. 1970). *Honorary Physician to the Massachusetts General Hospital. Lecturer in Medicine, Harvard University, 1956–59.*

Ross Stagner. *Emeritus Professor of Psychology, Wayne State University, Detroit.*

Mario Stefanini, M.D. *Director of the Laboratories, St. Elizabeth's Hospital, Danville, Ill.*

Robert Henry Thouless (d. 1984). *Reader in Educational Psychology, University of Cambridge, 1945–61; Fellow of Corpus Christi College, Cambridge.*

Bettey Tomasi. *Free-lance writer on medical topics. Scuba Diving Instructor, Northern Michigan University, Marquette.*

Richard Tuttle. *Researcher, Trudeau Institute, Saranac Lake, N.Y.*

Leroy Vail. *Free-lance writer.*

Ilza Veith. *Emeritus Professor of Psychiatry and the History of Health Sciences, University of California, San Francisco.*

Reino Virtanen. *Emeritus Professor of Modern Languages, University of Nebraska, Lincoln.*

Nancy Theilgaard Watts. *Assistant Professor of Physical Therapy, Bouvé-Boston School, Tufts University, Medford, Mass.*

Louis Weinstein, M.D. *Professor of Medicine, Tufts University, Medford, Mass., 1957–75.*

Michael M. Wertheimer. *Professor of Psychology, University of Colorado, Boulder. Consultant, Veterans Administration Hospital, Denver.*

Emil Witschi (d. 1971). *Senior Scientist, Bio-Medical Division of the Population Council, Rockefeller University, New York City, 1967–71.*

Henry D. von Witzleben, M.D. *Emeritus Director of Professional Education, Veterans Administration Hospital, Palo Alto, Calif. Associate Clinical Professor Emeritus of Psychiatry, Stanford University, Calif.*

Rose Wolfson. *Clinical psychologist. Author of* A Study in Handwriting Analysis *and others.*

John H. Wykert. *Medical and psychiatric writer.*

Robert Henry Yager, V.M.D. *Executive Secretary, Institute on Laboratory Animal Resources, National Research Council, National Academy of Sciences, Washington, D.C.*

Leo M. Zimmerman, M.D. (d. 1980). *Professor of Surgery, Chicago Medical School, 1948–80. Senior Attending Surgeon, Michael Reese Hospital, Chicago.*

Imre Zoltán, M.D. *Professor of Gynecology and Obstetrics, Semmelweis Medical University, Budapest, Hung.*

Joseph Zubin. *Emeritus Professor of Psychology, Columbia University. Chief, Psychiatric Research (Biometrics), New York State Psychiatric Institute and Hospital, 1960–75.*

Part Five. Human Society

John C. Abbott. *Deputy Director, Economic Analysis Division, Food and Agriculture Organization of the United Nations, Rome.*

George Plimpton Adams, Jr. *Emeritus Professor of Economics, Cornell University, Ithaca, N.Y.*

John H. Adler (d. 1980). *Director, Programming and Budgeting Department, International Bank for Reconstruction and Development, Washington, D.C., 1968–76.*

Joseph C. Agrella. *Correspondent,* The Blood-Horse *magazine.*

Leslie Ronald Aldous. *Head of Information Department, United Nations Association of Great Britain and Northern Ireland, 1947–66. Editor,* United Nations Association Yearbook *and* New World.

Maurice Allais. *Professor of Economic Analysis, National College of Mines of Paris. Professor of Monetary Analysis, University of Paris.*

Francis A. Allen. *Edson R. Sunderland Professor of Law, University of Michigan, Ann Arbor.*

Rex Alston. *Broadcaster and journalist. Staff Sports Commentator and Reporter, British Broadcasting Corporation, 1942–61. Cricket Reporter,* Daily *and* Sunday Telegraph (*London*), 1961–83.

John Thomas Amber. *Emeritus Editor in Chief, D.B.I. Books, Inc., Northfield, Illinois; editor of* Gun Digest, Handloader's Digest, Single Shot Actions and Rifles, *and others.*

Robert T. Anderson. *Professor of Anthropology, Mills College, Oakland, Calif.*

Jack Andresen. *Consulting Engineer. Underwater Photographer. World Champion Trick Water Skier, 1950.*

Pierre Robert Angel. *Professor and Head, Department of Classical and Modern Languages, Literature and Civilizations, University of Tours, Fr.*

John Armitage (d. 1980). *London Editor,* Encyclopædia Britannica, *1949–65, President, Rugby Fives Association, London, 1955–60.*

Michael Austin. *Rugby and cricket writer,* Daily Telegraph (*London*).

Robert Auty (d. 1978). *Professor of Comparative Slavonic Philology, University of Oxford, 1965–78.*

Paul Avrich. *Distinguished Professor of History, Queens College, City University of New York, Flushing.*

Hans Herman Baerwald. *Professor of Political Science, University of California, Los Angeles; Director, Study Center of the University of California, Tokyo, 1965–67; 1969–70.*

B. Devereux Barker III. *Associate, Brewer & Lord (insurance), Boston. Former Associate Editor,* Yachting *magazine.*

Victor Barna (d. 1972). *World table tennis champion, men's singles, 1930, 1932–35; men's doubles, 1929–35; mixed doubles, 1932, 1935. Author of* Tennis Today.

Harry Elmer Barnes (d. 1968). *Historian, sociologist, and writer. Author of* A History of Historical Writing *and others.*

Samuel H. Baron. *Professor of History, University of North Carolina at Chapel Hill.*

Howard Bass. *Winter sports correspondent,* Daily Telegraph *and* Sunday Telegraph (*London*). *Sports broadcaster, British Broadcasting Corporation World Service.*

Richard Reeve Baxter (d. 1980). *Judge, International Court of Justice, The Hague, 1979–80. Professor of Law, Harvard University, 1959–80.*

Lowell John Bean. *Professor of Anthropology, California State University, Hayward.*

Charles-Louis de Beaumont (d. 1972). *President, Amateur Fencing Association of Great Britain. President, British Commonwealth Fencing Federation. Deputy Chairman, British Olympic Association.*

John Matthew Beck. *Executive Director, Chicago Consortium of Colleges and Universities.*

Cyril S(hirley) Belshaw. *Professor of Anthropology, University of British Columbia, Vancouver.*

Ernest Bender. *Professor of Indo-Aryan Languages and Literatures, University of Pennsylvania, Philadelphia. General Editor,* Journal of the American Oriental Society.

George C.S. Benson. *Emeritus President and Professor of Political Science, Claremont Men's College, Calif.*

Ellen M. Bentsen. *Director for Development Communications, Northwestern University. Former Assistant Director for One Design Racing, U.S. Yacht Racing Union, Evanston, Ill.; Former Editor,* USYRU News.

Louis Stanley Berenson. *Owner and President, Berensons' Hartford Jai-Alai, Conn.*

Stanley F. Bergstein. *Executive Vice President, Harness Tracks of America, Morristown, N.J. Vice President, Publicity—Public Relations, U.S. Trotting Association, and Executive Editor,* Hoof Beats *magazine, 1968–75.*

Ronald M. Berndt. *Emeritus Professor of Anthropology and Honorary Research Fellow, University of Western Australia, Nedlands.*

Siegfried F. Bethke. *Marketing Economist, Food and Agriculture Organization of the United Nations, Rome.*

David Bidney. *Emeritus Professor of Anthropology and of Education, Indiana University, Bloomington.*

George W. Bishop, Jr. (d. 1974). *Professor and Head, Department of Finance, Northern Illinois University, De Kalb, 1965–74.*

Max Black. *Susan Linn Sage Professor of Philosophy, Cornell University, Ithaca, N.Y., 1946–77.*

Mark Blaug. *Professor of the Economics of Education, Institute of Education, University of London.*

Friedrich Blendinger. *Director of Archives, Augsburg, W.Ger., 1966–77.*

Solomon Bluhm. *Professor of Education, Hunter College, City University of New York, 1930–59.*

George Gleason Bogert (d. 1977). *James Parker Hall Professor of Law, University of Chicago.*

Marc Bouloiseau. *Former Secretary, Commission for the Economic and Social History of the French Revolution. Emeritus Teaching Assistant in the History of the French Revolution, University of Paris.*

Marjorie Boulton. *Principal, Charlotte Mason College, Ambleside, Eng., 1962–70. Member of the Esperanto Academy, Author of* Zamenhof, Creator of Esperanto *and others.*

Jean Bouvier. *Professor of Economics, University of Paris I.*

Lloyd Vernet Bridges. *Actor. Author of* Masks and Flippers.

William O(liver) Bright. *Professor of Linguistics and Anthropology, University of California, Los Angeles. Editor,* Language *(journal).*

Colin Fraser Brockington, M.D. *Emeritus Professor of Social and Preventive Medicine, Victoria University of Manchester, Eng.*

Dorothy Margaret Brodie. *Editor of Edmund Dudley's* Tree of Commonwealth.

Martin Bronfenbrenner. *Kenan Professor Emeritus of Economics, Duke University, Durham, N.C.*

Arthur Joseph Brown. *Emeritus Professor of Economics, University of Leeds, Eng.*

Lionel Neville Brown. *Professor of Comparative Law, University of Birmingham, Eng.*

William Francis Brown. *Editor,* American Field, *Chicago. Author of* How to Train Hunting Dogs *and others.*

James Robert Browning. *Chief Judge, United States Court of Appeals for the Ninth Circuit, San Francisco.*

Jean Bruhat. *Professor, Institute of Political Science; Instructor, University of Paris VIII.*

Avery Brundage (d. 1975). *President, International Olympic Committee, 1952–72.*

The Hon. Alastair Francis Buchan (d. 1976). *Montague Burton Professor of International Relations, University of Oxford, 1972–76. Founder and Director, International Institute for Strategic Studies, London, 1958–69.*

Arthur F. Burns. *U.S. Ambassador to the Federal Republic of Germany. John Bates Clark Professor Emeritus of Economics, Columbia University. Chairman, Board of Governors, Federal Reserve System, Washington, D.C., 1970–78.*

Thomas Ferrier Burns. *Chairman of Burns and Oates Ltd., Publishers, London, 1948–67. Editor,* The Tablet.

Asa S. Bushnell (d. 1975). *Commissioner, Eastern College Athletic Conference, 1938–70.*

Robin Buss. *Lecturer in French, Woolwich College of Further Education, London.*

R. Freeman Butts. *William F. Russell Professor Emeritus in the Foundations of Education, Teachers College, Columbia University; Associate Dean for International Studies, 1964–75.*

Raoul C. van Caenegem. *Professor of Medieval History, State University of Ghent, Belgium.*

Joseph R. Caldwell. *Professor of Anthropology, University of Georgia, Athens.*

Robert Graham Caldwell. *Professor of Criminology, University of Iowa, Iowa City, 1948–72.*

Charles Clifford Callahan. *Professor of Law, Ohio State University, Columbus.*

Schuyler van Rensselaer Cammann. *Professor of East Asian Studies, University of Pennsylvania, Philadelphia.*

Archibald Hunter Campbell. *Regius Professor of Public Law, University of Edinburgh, 1945–72.*

Guillaume Cardascia. *Professor of the History of Ancient Private Law, University of Paris II.*

George Cardona. *Professor of Linguistics, University of Pennsylvania, Philadelphia.*

Michael Carey. *Cricket writer,* Daily Telegraph *(London).*

Edward H. Carr (d. 1982). *Wilson Professor of International Politics, University College of Wales, Aberystwyth, 1936–47.*

George Barr Carson, Jr. *Professor of History, Oregon State University, Corvallis.*

John Philip Carter. *Emeritus Professor of Business Administration, University of California, Berkeley.*

Joseph Cataio. *Free-lance writer.*

David Gawen Champernowne. *Professor of Economics and Statistics, University of Cambridge, 1969–78; Fellow of Trinity College, Cambridge.*

Brian Chapman (d. 1981). *Professor of Government, Victoria University of Manchester, 1961–81.*

Floyd Barton Chapman. *Ecologist, Metropolitan Park District, Columbus, Ohio.*

Elliott E. Cheatham (d. 1972). *Charles Evans Hughes Professor of Law, Columbia University, 1950–57. Research Professor of Law, Vanderbilt University, Nashville, Tenn., 1968–72.*

Charles Edward Clark (d. 1963). *Judge, 1939–63. Chief Judge, U.S. Court of Appeals, 2nd Circuit, 1954–59. Dean, Law School, Yale University, 1929–39.*

James D. Clarkson. *Research Associate, Center for South and Southeast Asian Studies, University of Michigan, Ann Arbor.*

Inis Lothair Claude, Jr. *Edward R. Stettinius, Jr., Professor of Government and Foreign Affairs, University of Virginia, Charlottesville.*

Susan Clinton. *Free-lance writer on public administration.*

Luella Cole (Mrs. R.H. Lowie) (deceased). *Author of* History of Education, from Socrates to Montessori *and others.*

Dame Margaret I. Cole (d. 1980). *Honorary President, Fabian Society, England. Author of* Beatrice Webb *and others.*

J(ohn) B. Condliffe (d. 1981). *Senior Economist, Stanford Research Institute, Menlo Park, Calif., 1961–67. Author of* The Commerce of Nations *and others.*

Bernard Earl Conor. *Corporate Vice President and President, AMF International Trade Operations, AMF, Incorporated, Stamford, Conn.*

Barnaby Conrad. *Free-lance writer. Student of bullfighting with Juan Belmonte, 1943–46; bullfighter, 1946. Author of* Encyclopedia of Bullfighting *and others.*

William Stewart Cornyn (d. 1971). *Professor of Slavic and Southeast Asian Linguistics, Yale University.*

Frank A. Cowell. *Lecturer in Economics, London School of Economics and Political Science, University of London.*

Denis Victor Cowen. *Former Professor of Law, University of Chicago. Former Professor of Comparative Law, University of Cape Town, S.Af.*

Robert Cowen. *Senior Lecturer in Comparative Education, Institute of Education, University of London.*

Warren Cowgill (d. 1985). *Professor of Indo-European Linguistics, Yale University, 1972–85.*

Robert L. Crain. *Senior Social Scientist, Rand Corporation, at the Center for the Social Organization of Schools, Johns Hopkins University, Baltimore.*

Lawrence A. Cremin. *Frederick A.P. Barnard Professor of Education, Teachers College, Columbia University.*

Robert A. Cromie. *Host,* Book Beat, *National Educational Television. Daily Columnist,* Chicago Tribune, *1969–74.*

Brainerd Currie (d. 1965). *Professor of Law, Duke University, Durham, N.C., 1961–65.*

Stanley James Curtis (deceased). *Reader in Education, University of Leeds, Eng., 1955–58; Honorary Lecturer in Medieval Philosophy, 1934–58.*

Allison Danzig. *Sportswriter.* The New York Times, *1923–68. Author of* The History of American Football *and others.*

Bernard Darwin (d. 1961). *Golf Correspondent,* Country Life, *1907–61, and* The Times *(London), 1919–58.*

John P. Davis (d. 1973). *Editor of Special Publications, Phelps-Stokes Fund, N.Y. Editor of* The American Negro Reference Book.

Alan Charles Lynn Day. *Professor of Economics, London School of Economics and Political Science, University of London.*

George Henry John Daysh. *Emeritus Professor of Geography, University of Newcastle upon Tyne, Eng.*

Martin Dell (d. 1966). *Cartoonist and Puzzle Maker, Chicago Tribune Syndicate.*

Carl Thomas Devine. *Professor of Accounting, Florida State University, Tallahassee.*

Dudley Dillard. *Professor and Head, Department of Economics, University of Maryland, College Park.*

Mary Earhart Dillon. *Emerita Professor of Political Science, Queens College, City University of New York.*

William H. Dodge. *Professor of Business, University of Wisconsin, Madison.*

Michael Hugh Donovan. *Free-lance economic journalist. Former Editor, Retail Business (monthly), Economist Intelligence Unit, London.*

Joseph Dorfman. *Emeritus Professor of Economics, Columbia University.*

Robert Dorfman. *Professor of Economics, Harvard University.*

Douglas F. Dowd. *Professor of Economics, San Jose State University, Calif.*

Harold Edson Driver. *Emeritus Professor of Anthropology, Indiana University, Bloomington.*

John W. Dudderidge. *President of Honour, British Canoe Union. Honorary Member, International Canoe Federation. Vice President, British Olympic Association.*

Ralph Craigon Dudrow, Jr. *Former Director for the Red Cross Centenary, League of Red Cross Societies, Geneva.*

John F. Due. *Professor of Economics, University of Illinois, Urbana.*

Allison Dunham. *Arnold I. Shure Professor Emeritus of Urban Law, University of Chicago.*

Charles Émile Durand. *Former Professor of Constitutional Law, University of Aix-Marseille, Aix-en-Provence, France.*

Isidore Dyen. *Professor of Comparative Linguistics and Austronesian Languages, Yale University.*

John K. Dyer, Jr. *Independent Actuary.*

George Dykhuizen. *Emeritus Professor of Philosophy, University of Vermont, Burlington.*

Karl August Eckhardt. *Former Professor of Law, University of Berlin.*

John Percy Eddy (d. 1975). *Queen's Counsel; Recorder of West Ham, 1936–49; Stipendiary Magistrate for East and West Ham, 1949–54.*

Robert Romain Edge. *Former Associate Editor,* Sports Afield. *Outdoor Editor, American Broadcasting Company.*

Fred R. Eggan. *Harold H. Swift Distinguished Service Professor Emeritus of Anthropology; Director, Philippine Studies Program, University of Chicago.*

Paul Einzig (d. 1973). *London Correspondent,* The Commercial and Financial Chronicle. *(New York), 1945–73.*

Daniel Judah Elazar. *Director, Center for the Study of Federalism; Professor of Political Science, Temple University, Philadelphia. Senator N.M. Paterson Professor of Intergovernmental Relations, Bar-Ilan University, Ramat Gan, Israel.*

Adolphus Peter Elkin (d. 1979). *Professor of Anthropology, University of Sydney, 1934–56.*

Norman Robson Elliott. *Senior Lecturer in Geography, University of Edinburgh.*

Manuel C(onrad) Elmer (deceased). *Professor and Head, Department of Sociology, University of Pittsburgh.*

Alex Elson. *Attorney. Coauthor of* Illinois Civil Practice Forms *and others.*

Linn Emrich. *Manager, Skyport Airfield, Issaquah, Washington. Professional balloonist, parachutist, and pilot.*

Ralph Erickson. *Physical Education Instructor; Swimming and Water Polo Coach, Loyola University, Chicago.*

Emory Gibbons Evans. *Professor and Chairman, Department of History, University of Maryland, College Park.*

Gordon Page Evans. *Secretary, Standing Conference on the Economic and Social Work of the United Nations.*

Gwynfor Evans. *Member of Parliament for Carmarthen, Wales, 1966–70; 1974–79. President, Plaid Cymru, 1945–81.*

Frank Fairfax. *Visiting Lecturer, Center for Afro-American and African Studies, University of Michigan, Ann Arbor.*

Charles Fairman. *Emeritus Professor of Law, Harvard University.*

David I. Fand. *Professor of Economics, Wayne State University, Detroit.*

Dan Farley. *Managing Editor,* The Thoroughbred Record.

Louis C. Faron. *Professor of Anthropology, State University of New York at Stony Brook.*

David Fellman. *Vilas Professor Emeritus of Political Science, University of Wisconsin, Madison.*

Charles G. Fenwick (d. 1973). *Director, Department of International Law, Pan American Union, Washington, D.C., 1948–62. Professor of Political Science, Bryn Mawr College, Pa., 1918–40.*

Cornelia Van Hook Ferber. *Economist, Office of Programs and Research, Export-Import Bank of the United States.*

John Henry Webb Fingleton (d. 1981). *Journalist. International Cricketer, 1931–38. Author of* Cricket Crisis *and others.*

Lawrence E. Fisher. *Director of Graduate Studies, Department of Anthropology, Loyola University, Chicago.*

Ossip K. Flechtheim. *Emeritus Professor of Political Science, Free University, Berlin.*

Henry Hubbard Foster, Jr. *Emeritus Professor of Law, New York University, New York City.*

Robert Allen Fowkes. *Emeritus Professor of Germanic Languages, New York University, New York City.*

Henry Waller Fowler, Jr. *Securities trader. Author of* Kites *and others.*

Michel François. *Professor of the History of French Institutions, École Nationale des Chartes, Paris. Secretary General, International Committee of Historical Sciences.*

Phyllis Frederick. *Toy and game designer, Mattel Inc., Hawthorne, Calif.*

Richard L(incoln) Frey. *Editor in Chief,* Official Encyclopaedia of Bridge. *Associate Editor,* Bridge World *magazine; Emeritus Editor,* The Contract Bridge Bulletin; *Chief of Editorial Board, Charles H. Goren publications. Emeritus President and Chairman, International Bridge Press Association.*

(Jerome) Ed(ison) Friel. *Sportswriter, Newark (N.J.) News. Former President, New York Track Writers Association.*

Harold T. Friermood. *Chairman, Education Council, United States Olympic Committee. Editor of* When Volleyball Began *and others.*

Lon L. Fuller (d. 1978). *Carter Professor of General Jurisprudence, Harvard University, 1948–72.*

Joseph William Garbarino. *Professor of Business Administration, University of California, Berkeley.*

Charles Garratt-Holden. *Former Secretary, The Building Societies Association, London.*

Paul Henry Gebhard. *Professor of Anthropology, Indiana University, Bloomington; former Director, Institute for Sex Research.*

Ignace J. Gelb (d. 1985). *Frank P. Hixon Distinguished Service Professor, Oriental Institute and Departments of Linguistics and of Near Eastern Languages and Civilizations, University of Chicago, 1965–79.*

David George. *Journalist and free-lance writer on sports.*

O. Benjamin Gerig (d. 1976). *Director, Office of Dependent Area Affairs, U.S. Department of State, 1945–62.*

Colin Gibson. *Rugby League writer, Daily Telegraph (London).*

Douglas Stuart Gilbert (d. 1979). *Sports columnist, Edmonton Sun, 1978–79. Sports reporter, Montreal Gazette, 1970–78.*

Peter Robin Gimbel. *Film Producer and Director, Blue Water, White Death and others.*

Alexander Hayden Girard. *Architect.*

Geoffrey R. Gleeson. *International judo consultant. Executive Officer, British Association of National Coaches. Author of Judo for the West and others.*

Oscar R. Goodman (d. 1985). *Professor of Ecomonics and Finance, Roosevelt University, Chicago, 1966–85.*

Charles H. Goren. *Author and lecturer. Bridge Editor, Chicago Tribune-New York News Syndicate. Author of Contract Bridge Complete and others.*

E. Kathleen Gough Aberle. *Research Associate in Anthropology, University of British Columbia, Vancouver. Professor of Anthropology, Simon Fraser University, Burnaby, B.C., 1967–70.*

Frank Graner. *Professor of Finance, University of Wisconsin, Madison.*

Leo Gross. *Emeritus Professor of International Law, Tufts University, Medford, Mass.*

David Lawrence Grove. *President, U.S. Council, International Chamber of Commerce. Vice President and Chief Economist, International Business Machines Corp., Armonk, N.Y., 1969–78.*

Seli Groves. *Free-lance writer.*

Claude William Guillebaud (d. 1971). *Lecturer in Economics, University of Cambridge, 1926–56.*

Lealand Roger Gustavson (d. 1966). *Artist and illustrator. Author of Winning Badminton and others.*

Harry G. Guthmann. *Morrison Professor Emeritus of Finance, Northwestern University, Evanston, Ill.*

Gottfried Haberler. *Emeritus Professor of International Trade, Harvard University.*

Green H. Hackworth (d. 1973). *Judge, International Court of Justice, The Hague, 1946–61.*

Eric P. Hamp. *Robert Maynard Hutchins Distinguished Service Professor of Linguistics and of Behavioral Sciences; Director, Center for Balkan and Slavic Studies, University of Chicago.*

Moffatt Hancock. *Kirkwood Professor Emeritus of Law, Stanford University, Calif.*

Frank Hamilton Hankins (d. 1970). *Professor of Sociology, Smith College, Northampton, Mass., 1922–46.*

Jerry F. Hardy. *Coordinator for Gymnastics, Amateur Athletic Union of the United States. Member, Board of Directors, U.S. Gymnastics Federation. Member, U.S. Men's Olympic Gymnastic Committee, 1940; 1952–72.*

Fred Harvey Harrington. *Vilas Research Professor of American Diplomatic History, University of Wisconsin, Madison; President of the University of Wisconsin, 1962–70.*

Herbert Lionel Adolphus Hart. *Principal of Brasenose College, Oxford, 1973–78; Professor of Jurisprudence, University of Oxford, 1952–68.*

Joseph R. Hartley. *Professor of Business Administration, Indiana University, Bloomington.*

Nancy Kymn Harvin. *Free-lance writer.*

Harlan Henthorne Hatcher. *President Emeritus, University of Michigan, Ann Arbor.*

Robert J. Havighurst. *Emeritus Professor of Education and of Human Development, University of Chicago.*

Robert D. Herman. *Professor of Sociology, Pomona College, Claremont, Calif.*

D. Alan Heslop. *Director, Rose Institute of State and Local Government, Claremont McKenna College, Calif.*

Forest Garrett Hill. *Professor of Economics, University of Texas at Austin.*

J. E. Christopher Hill. *Master, Balliol College, University of Oxford, 1965–78.*

Norman Llewellyn Hill (d. 1976). *Professor of International Law and Relations, University of Nebraska, Lincoln, 1935–63.*

Finn Hiorthøy. *Judge of the Supreme Court of Norway, Oslo, 1955–73.*

Frank Hole. *Professor and Chairman, Department of Anthropology, Yale University.*

(George) Kenneth Holland (d. 1977). *President, Institute of International Education, Inc., New York City, 1950–73.*

Bert Frank Hoselitz. *Emeritus Professor of the Social Sciences and Economics, University of Chicago.*

Cyril O. Houle. *Emeritus Professor of Education, University of Chicago.*

Ralph Gordon Hoxie. *President, Center for the Study of the Presidency, New York City. Chancellor, Long Island University, Greenvale, N.Y., 1964–68.*

Edward M. Hutchinson. *Educational consultant. Secretary, National Institute of Adult Education, London, 1947–71; Editor, Adult Education journal, 1949–71.*

Ford Hutchinson. *Free-lance writer.*

Terence Wilmot Hutchison. *Emeritus Professor of Economics, University of Birmingham, Eng.*

John Henry Hutton (d. 1968). *William Wyse Professor of Social Anthropology, University of Cambridge, 1937–50.*

James Nevins Hyde. *Lawyer.*

Jozef A.M.K. IJsewijn. *Professor of Neo-Latin, Catholic University of Louvain, Belg.*

Jacques André Istel. *President, Parachutes Incorporated, Orange, Mass. Captain, U.S. parachuting team, 1956 and 1958.*

Elmore Jackson. *Vice President, United Nations Association of the U.S.A., 1966–73. Special Assistant for Policy Planning to the Assistant Secretary of State for International Organization Affairs, U.S. Department of State, 1961–64.*

William Turrentine Jackson. *Professor of American History, University of California, Davis.*

Per Jacobsson (d. 1963). *Managing Director, International Monetary Fund, Washington, D.C., 1956–63.*

Oswald Jacoby (d. 1984). *Author of Oswald Jacoby's Complete Canasta and many other works on card playing.*

Fred W. Jameson (deceased). *Manager of Educational Services, Public Relations Department, Montgomery Ward and Company, Chicago.*

Philip C. Jessup (d. 1986). *Judge, International Court of Justice, The Hague, The Netherlands, 1961–70.*

John E. Jeuck. *Robert Law Professor of Business Administration, University of Chicago.*

Gareth H. Jones. *Downing Professor of the Laws of England, University of Cambridge; Fellow of Trinity College, Cambridge.*

Bernard Joy. *Former football correspondent, Evening Standard, London. Author of Soccer Tactics.*

Milton Z. Kafoglis. *Professor of Economics, Emory University, Atlanta, Ga.*

Jerome Kagan. *Professor of Human Development, Harvard University.*

Nicholas deBelleville Katzenbach. *Vice President and General Counsel, International Business Machines Corporation, Armonk, N.Y. Attorney General, U.S. Department of Justice, 1965–66. Under Secretary, U.S. Department of State, 1966–68.*

Terrence Kaufman. *Associate Professor of Anthropology, University of Pittsburgh.*

Frank E. Keating. *Fishing Editor, Newsday, Garden City, N.Y.*

George Williams Keeton. *President, London Institute of World Affairs. Emeritus Professor of English Law, University of London.*

William H. Kelly (d. 1980). *Professor of Anthropology, University of Arizona, Tucson, 1952–74.*

Howard H. Kendler. *Professor of Psychology, University of California, Santa Barbara.*

Raymond P. Kent (d. 1983). *Professor of Finance and Business Economics, University of Notre Dame, Ind.*

Marshall D. Ketchum. *Emeritus Professor of Finance, University of Chicago.*

V.O. Key, Jr. (d. 1963). *Jonathan Trumbull Professor of American History and Government, Harvard University, 1955–63.*

Frank Leroy Kidner. *Vice President of Educational Relations; Professor of Economics, University of California, Berkeley.*

Hans Kiefner. *Professor of German Civil Law, Roman Law and Canon Law, University of Münster, W.Ger.*

Carol D. Kiesinger. *Arts consultant. Hiker and mountain climber. Coeditor of* The Armchair Mountaineer.

Charles P. Kindleberger. *Emeritus Professor of Economics, Massachusetts Institute of Technology, Cambridge.*

Vernon Kinietz. *Educator. Author of* Chippewa Village *and others.*

Clyde Vernon Kiser. *Former Senior Research Demographer, Office of Population Research, Princeton, N. J.*

Lawrence R. Klein. *Benjamin Franklin Professor of Economics, University of Pennsylvania, Philadelphia. Nobel Prize for Economics, 1980.*

Paul Lincoln Kleinsorge. *Emeritus Professor of Economics, University of Oregon, Eugene.*

Paul E. Klopsteg. *Emeritus Professor of Applied Science, Northwestern University, Evanston, Ill.*

George Frederick Kneller. *Emeritus Professor of Education, University of California, Los Angeles.*

Ole Ferdinand Knudsen. *Editor, Export Council of Norway, Oslo.*

Herman Kogan. *Corporate Historian, Field Enterprises, Inc. Author of* The Great EB.

Omari Kokole. *Lecturer in Political Science, University of Michigan, Ann Arbor.*

Walter Korn. *Author of* The Brilliant Touch in Chess; Modern Chess Openings; *and others.*

John Richard Krueger. *Former Professor of Uralic and Altaic Studies, Indiana University, Bloomington.*

Philip B. Kurland. *William R. Kenan, Jr., Distinguished Service Professor of Law, University of Chicago. Editor of* The Supreme Court Review.

Peter N. Ladefoged. *Professor of Phonetics, University of California, Los Angeles.*

Harry Wellington Laidler (d. 1970). *Executive Director, League for Industrial Democracy.*

Clay Lancaster. *Author of* Japanese Influence in America; Architectural Follies in America; *and others.*

Gerard Eduard Langemeijer. *Attorney General, Supreme Court of the Netherlands, The Hague, 1957–73.*

Luce-Andrée Langevin. *Honorary Professor; former teacher of physical science, Lycée Fénelon, Paris. Author of* Lomonossov.

George E. Lardner (deceased). *Associate Editor, Bell-McClure Syndicate, Inc., New York City.*

Richard C. Latham. *Partner, Seay & Latham Investments, Dallas, Texas. Coauthor of* United States Polo Association Annual.

Gilbert P. Laue. *Chief Copy Editor, Richard D. Irwin, Inc., Homewood, Ill. Former Associate Editor, Sports, Encyclopædia Britannica, Chicago.*

Elihu Lauterpacht. *Barrister-at-Law. Fellow of Trinity College, Cambridge; Reader in International Law, University of Cambridge.*

Sir Edmund Ronald Leach. *Provost of King's College, Cambridge, 1966–79; Professor of Social Anthropology, University of Cambridge, 1972–78.*

James Elzar Lebensohn, M.D. *Associate Professor Emeritus of Ophthalmology, Northwestern University, Chicago.*

Colin Legum. *Associate Editor,* The Observer, *London, 1949–82. Editor,* Africa Contemporary Record, *1968–83.*

Richard M. Leighton. *Military historian and consultant. Professor of National Security Affairs, National Defense University, U.S. Department of Defense, Washington, D.C., 1965–78.*

George Eidt Lent. *Assistant Director, Tax Policy Division, International Monetary Fund, Washington, D.C., 1964–75.*

Don Divance Lescohier (d. 1961). *Professor of Economics, University of Wisconsin, Madison, 1918–61.*

Robert Alan LeVine. *Roy E. Larsen Professor of Education and Human Development, Harvard University.*

David L. Lewis. *Professor of History, Howard University, Washington, D.C.*

Choh-Ming Li. *Emeritus Professor of Business Administration, University of California, Berkeley. Vice Chancellor, Chinese University of Hong Kong, 1964–78.*

Fang Kuei Li. *Emeritus Professor of Chinese Linguistics and Anthropology, University of Washington, Seattle. Emeritus Professor of Asian Linguistics, University of Hawaii, Honolulu.*

Alfred Lief. *Biographer and business historian.*

Joseph Colville Lincoln. *Author of* Soaring for Diamonds.

Genevieve Collins Linebarger. *Associate Professor of Political Science, Trinity College, Washington, D.C., 1967–68.*

Paul M.A. Linebarger (d. 1966). *Professor of Asiatic Politics, School of Advanced International Studies, Johns Hopkins University, Washington, D.C., 1946–66.*

Kwang-Ching Liu. *Professor of History, University of California, Davis.*

Karl Nickerson Llewellyn (d. 1962). *Professor of Law, University of Chicago, 1951–62.*

Laurence Lockhart (d. 1975). *Member of the Faculty of Oriental Studies, University of Cambridge.*

Erwin Hugo Loewenfeld (deceased). *Solicitor of the Supreme Court, Great Britain. Member of the Faculty of Law, University of Cambridge. Legal Adviser, Liechtenstein Government.*

James Rubert Longstreet. *Professor of Finance, University of South Florida, Tampa.*

Jo Desha Lucas. *Arnold I. Shure Professor of Law, University of Chicago.*

Alma Lutz (d. 1973). *Author of* Susan B. Anthony, Rebel, Crusader, Humanitarian *and others.*

John P. Lyall. *Marine Information Specialist and Sailing Directions Writer, Sailing Directions Branch, U.S. Naval Oceanographic Office, Washington, D.C.*

John Lyons. *Master of Trinity Hall, University of Cambridge. Professor of Linguistics, University of Sussex, Brighton, Eng., 1976–84.*

John Dennis McCallum. *Author of* That Kelly Family; The Tiger Wore Spikes; Big Eight Football; *and others.*

Wendell McClean. *Research Assistant, Institute of Social and Economic Research, University of the West Indies, Kingston, Jamaica.*

John McDowell (d. 1974). *Director for Social Welfare, National Council of the Churches of Christ in the U.S.A., 1967–73.*

Joseph E. McGrath. *Professor of Psychology, University of Illinois, Urbana.*

James Angell MacLachlan (d. 1967). *Professor of Law, Harvard University, 1927–60.*

Charles R. McLoud. *Head, Sailing Directions Branch, U.S. Naval Oceanographic Office, Washington, D.C.*

(Ardee) Wayne McMillen. *General Consultant, Bay Area Social Planning Council, Oakland, Calif. Professor of Social Service Administration, University of Chicago, 1936–60.*

Arnold Duncan McNair, 1st Baron McNair (d. 1975). *President, International Court of Justice, 1952–55; Judge, 1946–55.*

Edward McWhinney. *Queen's Counsel. Professor of International Law and Relations, Simon Fraser University, Burnaby, B.C.*

Norris Dewar McWhirter. *Television commentator, Olympic Games, British Broadcasting Corporation, 1960–72. Compiler,* Guinness Book of World Records; Dunlop Book of Facts.

Philip Maher. *Free-lance writer.*

Janice Grow Maienza. *Free-lance writer.*

Reginald Francis Malcolmson. *Professor of Architecture, University of Michigan, Ann Arbor.*

Martin E. Malia. *Professor of History, University of California, Berkeley.*

Yakov Malkiel. *Professor of Linguistics and Romance Philology, University of California, Berkeley.*

Sir James Gow Mann (d. 1962). *Surveyor of the Queen's Works of Art, 1946–62. Master of the Armouries, The Tower of London, 1939–62.*

Benigno Mantilla Pineda. *Professor of the Sociology and Philosophy of Law, University of Antioquia, Medellín, Colom.*

Julius Margolis. *Professor of Economics, University of California, Irvine.*

McKim Marriott. *Professor, Department of Anthropology and Social Sciences, Collegiate Division, University of Chicago.*

John C. Martin. *Director, Navigational Information Services Division, U.S. Naval Oceanographic Office, Washington, D.C.*

Roscoe C. Martin (d. 1972). *Professor of Political Science, Syracuse University, N.Y., 1949–72.*

Erich Matthias (d. 1983). *Professor of Contemporary History and Political Science, University of Mannheim, W.Ger.*

Wilhelm Matull. *Senior Civil Servant, National Centres for Political Education, Hannover, Bonn, and Düsseldorf, W.Ger., 1954–68.*

Harold M. Mayer. *Professor of Geography, University of Wisconsin, Milwaukee. Vice President, Milwaukee Harbor Commission.*

John F. Mee (d. 1985). *Mead Johnson Professor of Management, Indiana University, Bloomington.*

Ben Scudder Meeker. *Chief U.S. Probation Officer and Director of Training Center, Chicago.*

Patrick Denis Mehigan (deceased). *Author of* History of Hurling; History of Irish Athletics; *and others.*

Lois Bannister Merk. *Lecturer in History, Northeastern University, Boston, 1956–68.*

Ford Messamore (d. 1962). *Professor of Stockton College, Canton, Mo.*

Michael Charles Meston. *Professor of Scots Law, University of Aberdeen, Scot.*

Adolphe Erich Meyer. *Emeritus Professor of Educational History, New York University, New York City.*

Karl W. Meyer. *Chancellor, University of Wisconsin, Superior.*

Karl B. Michael. *Emeritus Swimming Coach, Dartmouth College, Hanover, N.H. U.S. Olympic Team Men's Diving Coach, 1956.*

John Francis Marchment Middleton. *Professor of Anthropology, Yale University.*

Elmer Mayse Million. *Professor of Law, University of Oklahoma, Norman.*

Aron Leonard Minkes. *Professor of Business Organization, University of Birmingham, Eng.*

Broadus Mitchell. *Emeritus Professor of Economics, Rutgers University, New Brunswick, N.J.*

Laura Molzahn. *Free-lance writer.*

Ashley Montagu. *Biological and cultural anthropologist. Professor and Chairman, Department of Anthropology, Rutgers University, New Brunswick, N.J., 1949–55.*

Patrick Wykeham Montague-Smith. *Consulting Editor,* Debrett's Peerage; *Editor, 1962–80.*

John Michael Montias. *Professor of Economics, Yale University.*

Lynn Montross (d. 1961). *Historian, United States Marine Corps, 1950–61.*

The Rev. E. Garth Moore. *Barrister-at-Law. Chancellor, Dioceses of Durham, Southwark and Gloucester. Fellow of Corpus Christi College, University of Cambridge.*

Albert H. Morehead (d. 1966). *Writer and editor. Bridge editor,* The New York Times, *1935–63.*

Hans J. Morgenthau (d. 1980). *Albert A. Michelson Distinguished Service Professor of Political Science and Modern History, University of Chicago, 1963–68. Leonard Davis Distinguished Professor of Political Science, City College, City University of New York, 1968–74.*

Cyril John Morley. *Former Honorary Secretary, British Falconers' Club and International Association of Falconry and Conservation of Birds of Prey.*

James William Morley. *Professor of Government, Columbia University.*

Geoffrey Mott-Smith (d. 1960). *Editor,* The Bridge World, *1936–46;* Games Digest, *1938–39, Author of* Book of Hobbies *and others.*

Nicos Panayiotou Mouzelis. *Senior Lecturer in Sociology, London School of Economics and Political Science, University of London.*

George Peter Murdock (d. 1985). *Andrew Mellon Professor of Social Anthropology, University of Pittsburgh, 1960–73.*

Lawrence Nabers. *Professor of Economics, University of Utah, Salt Lake City.*

Manning Nash. *Professor of Anthropology, University of Chicago.*

Phil Caldwell Neal. *Harry A. Bigelow Professor Emeritus of Law, University of Chicago.*

Bert Nelson. *Editor,* Track & Field News.

Carl Leroy Nelson. *George O. May Professor of Financial Accounting, Columbia University.*

Jeannette Paddock Nichols. *Historian, University of Pennsylvania, Philadelphia, 1969–78; Associate Professor of History, 1957–61.*

Maurice Nockles. *Press and Information Officer, Board of Customs and Excise, London.*

Val Nolan, Jr. *Professor of Law and of Zoology, Indiana University, Bloomington.*

Jan P. Norbye. *Free-lance writer on automobiles. Former International Editor,* Automotive News.

Douglass Cecil North. *Professor of Economics, University of Washington, Seattle.*

Robert C. North. *Professor of Political Science, Stanford University, Calif.*

D.P. O'Brien. *Professor of Economics, University of Durham, Eng.*

A.C. Olshen. *Actuarial consultant. Former Senior Vice President and Director, West Coast Life Insurance Company, San Francisco.*

Ron Olver. *British correspondent,* The Ring. *Former Assistant Editor,* Boxing World *and* Boxing News.

Morris Edward Opler. *Emeritus Professor of Anthropology, Cornell University, Ithaca, N.Y.*

Keith Langford Osborne. *Honorary Editor of* British Rowing Almanack.

Herbert L. Packer (d. 1972). *Professor of Law, Stanford University, Calif.*

Roland Palmedo (d. 1977). *President, Amateur Ski Club of New York. Cofounder, National Ski Patrol.*

Robert Parienté. *Editor in Chief,* L'Équipe (*daily sports newspaper*), *Paris.*

Ralph Halstead Parker. *Emeritus Dean, School of Library and Information Science, University of Missouri, Columbia.*

Charles William Parkin. *Fellow and Lecturer of Clare College, University of Cambridge.*

Cyril Northcote Parkinson. *Raffles Professor of History, University of Malaya, 1950–58.*

Maureen L.P. Patterson. *Former Associate Professor of South Asian Languages and Civilizations; former South Asia Bibliographic Specialist, University of Chicago.*

Kosta Stevan Pavlowitch. *Librarian, Department of Slavonic Studies, University of Cambridge. Yugoslav diplomat, 1928–45.*

Andrew K. Pawley. *Associate Professor of Linguistics, University of Auckland, New Zealand.*

Adamantios A. Pepelasis. *Former Professor of Economics, Virginia Polytechnic Institute and State University, Blacksburg.*

R. Scott Perry. *Free-lance writer on education.*

Frederick William Pethick-Lawrence, 1st Baron Pethick-Lawrence (d. 1961). *Secretary of State for India and Burma, 1945–47. Privy Councillor.*

James L. Phillips. *Associate Professor of Archaeology; Director, Graduate Studies in Archaeology, University of Illinois, Chicago.*

Joseph Dexter Phillips. *Research Professor, Bureau of Economic and Business Research, University of Illinois, Urbana.*

Donald L. Piccard. *Balloon designer and manufacturer.*

Jean Felix Piccard (d. 1963). *Professor of Aeronautical Engineering, University of Minnesota, Minneapolis. F.A.I. Balloon Pilot.*

Jeannette Piccard (d. 1981). *Consultant to the Director, National Aeronautical and Space Administration Manned Spacecraft Center, Houston, Texas, 1964–70.*

Francis S. Pierce. *Editor, Congressional Budget Office, Washington, D.C. Associate Editor, Economics, Encyclopædia Britannica, Chicago, 1967–73.*

George Wilson Pierson. *Larned Professor Emeritus of History, Yale University.*

John Pincus. *Economic consultant. Former Manager, California Program, Rand Corporation, Santa Monica.*

William M. Pinkerton. *News Officer for the University, Harvard University.*

Frederick P. Pittera. *Chairman, International Exposition Consultants Co. President, Frederick Pittera and Associates, Inc. Author of* The Art and Science of International Fairs and Exhibitions *and others.*

Cecil Wilson Plant. *Honorary Secretary, International Water Polo Board.*

Earl Edward Pollock. *Member of the law firm of Sonnenschein, Carlin, Nath & Rosenthal, Chicago.*

David Morris Potter (d. 1971). *William R. Coe Professor of American History, Stanford University, Calif., 1961–71.*

Pitman Benjamin Potter (d. 1981). *Grozier Professor of International Law, American University, Washington, D.C., 1944–57.*

Raphael Powell (d. 1965). *Professor of Roman Law, University of London, 1955–64.*

Arnold H. Price. *Bibliographer, American Historical Association, Washington, D.C. Former Area Specialist for Central Europe, Library of Congress, Washington, D.C.*

Francis Douglas Price. *Lecturer in Modern History, University of Oxford; Fellow and Tutor, Keble College, Oxford.*

Jack H. Prost. *Associate Professor of Physical Anthropology, University of Illinois, Chicago.*

Roy Pryce. *Visiting Professor, European Institute of Public Administration, Maastricht, Neth. Director, Directorate General for Information, Commission of the European Communities, Brussels, 1973–78.*

Jean Puhvel. *Professor of Classics and Indo-European Studies, University of California, Los Angeles.*

Ernst Pulgram. *Hayward Keniston Distinguished Professor of Romance and Classical Linguistics, University of Michigan, Ann Arbor.*

Peter George Julius Pulzer. *Lecturer in Politics, University of Oxford; Official Student and Tutor in Politics, Christ Church, Oxford.*

Nathan Marsh Pusey. *President of Harvard University, 1953–71.*

Robert Mantle Rattenbury (d. 1970). *Registrary, University of Cambridge, 1953–69.*

Helen B. Redl. *Professor of Early Child Education, North Adams State College, Mass.*

Jerry Reedy. *Free-lance writer.*

David Allen Revzan. *Professor of Marketing, University of California, Berkeley.*

Max Rheinstein (d. 1977). *Max Pam Professor of Comparative Law, University of Chicago, 1942–68.*

Madeleine Hooke Rice. *Emeritus Professor of History, Hunter College, City University of New York.*

Ivor Armstrong Richards (d. 1979). *Professor of English, Harvard University, 1944–63.*

John Henry Richardson (d. 1970). *United Nations Technical Assistance Adviser (International Labour Office), 1956–65. President, Aden Industrial Court, 1960–66. Professor of Industrial Relations, University of Leeds, Eng., 1930–55.*

Jack L. Roach. *Professor of Sociology, University of Connecticut, Storrs.*

Janet K. Roach. *Instructor in Sociology, Eastern Connecticut State College, Willimantic.*

Allen Roberts. *Professor of Anthropology, University of Michigan, Ann Arbor.*

Benjamin Charles Roberts. *Professor of Industrial Relations, London School of Economics and Political Science, University of London.*

John Morris Roberts. *Vice-Chancellor, University of Southampton, Eng.*

Sir Dennis Holme Robertson (d. 1963). *Professor of Political Economy, University of Cambridge, 1944–57.*

William H.P. Robertson (deceased). *Editor-Publisher, The Thoroughbred Record; Chairman, Record Publishing Company, Inc., Lexington, Kentucky.*

Robert Robson. *Fellow and Tutor of Trinity College, University of Cambridge. Author of* The Attorney in Eighteenth Century England.

William Alexander Robson (d. 1980). *Professor of Public Administration, University of London, 1947–62.*

C.H. Rolph. *Legal and sociological correspondent,* New Statesman, *London. Author of* Law and the Common Man *and others.*

Raymond de Roover (d. 1972). *Professor of History, Brooklyn College, City University of New York. Foreign Member, Royal Flemish Academy of Science, Section of Letters, Brussels.*

Samuel Rosenblatt. *Professor of Oriental Languages, Johns Hopkins University, Baltimore.*

Margaret Keeney Rosenheim. *Helen Ross Professor of Social Service Administration, University of Chicago.*

Elliot Rudwick (d. 1985). *Professor of Sociology and of History; Senior Research Fellow, Center for Urban Regionalism, Kent State University, Ohio.*

Raymond A. Ruge. *President, Eastern Ice Yachting Association, 1948, 1959–60; Secretary, 1938–42.*

Don Russell (d. 1986). *Free-lance writer. Author of* The Wild West: A History of the Wild West Shows *and others.*

Alan Ryalls. *Former Editor,* Camping and Caravanning *magazine, Camping Club of Great Britain and Ireland. Author of* Modern Camping *and others.*

M.J. Ryan. *Former Professor of Constitutional Law, University College, Dublin.*

John E. Sadler. *Head, Education Department, City of Birmingham College of Education, University of Birmingham, Eng., 1950–67.*

Wolfgang Sauer. *Professor of History, University of California, Berkeley.*

Donald Sayenga. *Author of "The Oldest Sport," a series of articles on the history of wrestling, in* Amateur Wrestling News.

John Scarne (d. 1985). *President, John Scarne Games, Inc., North Bergen, N.J. Author of* Scarne's Complete Guide to Gambling *and others.*

Joseph B. Schechtman (d. 1970). *President, United Zionist Revisionists of America.*

Donald Schiffer (d. 1964). *Editor, Sport and Outdoor Book Division, Thos. Nelson and Sons, New York City.*

Elmer Schmierer. *Colonel, U.S. Army, Infantry (retired).*

Helmut Schoeck. *Professor of Sociology, Johannes Gutenberg University, Mainz, W.Ger.*

Albert Schoenfield. *Swimmer.*

G. Richard Schreiber. *President, National Automatic Merchandising Association, Chicago.*

Gerhard Schulz. *Professor of Contemporary History; Director, Seminar of Contemporary History, University of Tübingen, W.Ger.*

Georg Schwarzenberger. *Emeritus Professor of International Law, University of London. Vice President, London Institute of World Affairs.*

Egon Schwelb (d. 1979). *Principal Officer, Office of Legal Affairs, United Nations, New York City; Deputy Director, Division of Human Rights, 1947–62. Senior Fellow and Lecturer in Law, Yale University, 1962–68.*

Austin Wakeman Scott, Jr. (d. 1966). *Professor of Law, University of Colorado, Boulder.*

Thomas A. Sebeok. *Distinguished Professor of Linguistics; Professor of Anthropology and of Uralic and Altaic Studies; Chairman, Research Center for the Language Sciences, Indiana University, Bloomington.*

Melvin Seeman. *Professor of Sociology, University of California, Los Angeles.*

Odell Shepard (d. 1967). *Author of* Pedlar's Progress, The Life of Bronson Alcott *and others.*

Kate Silber (deceased). *Senior Lecturer in German, University of Edinburgh, 1963–73.*

David L. Sills. *Executive Associate, Social Science Research Council, New York City.*

Stanley C. Silverberg. *Director of Research, Federal Deposit Insurance Corporation, Washington, D.C.*

Helen Silving. *Professor of Law, University of Puerto Rico, 1957–76.*

Edwin Howard Simmons. *Brigadier General, U.S. Marine Corps; Director, Marine Corps History and Museums, Arlington, Va.*

Denis Sinor. *Distinguished Professor of Uralic and Altaic Studies and of History, Indiana University, Bloomington.*

Gabriel Smith. *Barrister-at-Law. Lecturer in Industry and Finance, City of London College. Departmental Editor,* Journal of Business Law.

George Alan Smith. *Arts consultant. Hiker and mountain climber. Author of* Introduction to Mountaineering.

Jack Smith. *Senior Editor,* Yachting *magazine, Cos Cobb, Conn.*

Theodore H. Smith. *Emeritus Professor of Marketing, California State College, Fullerton.*

Pincus Sober (d. 1980). *Chairman, National A.A.U. Law and Legislation Committee; Track and Field Committee, 1956–61. Chairman, U.S. Olympic Track and Field Committee, 1957–61.*

Ernst Frithiof Söderlund. *Emeritus Professor of Economic History, University of Stockholm.*

Wallace Sokolsky. *Associate Professor of History, Bronx Community College, City University of New York. Lecturer, New York University and New School for Social Research, New York City.*

Ezra Solomon. *Dean Witter Professor of Finance, Graduate School of Business, Stanford University, Calif.*

Dorothy Mary Spencer. *Visiting Lecturer in South Asia Regional Studies, University of Pennsylvania, Philadelphia.*

Joseph J. Spengler. *James B. Duke Professor Emeritus of Economics, Duke University, Durham, N.C.*

Edward H. Spicer (d. 1983). *Professor of Anthropology, University of Arizona, Tucson.*

Sybille van der Sprenkel. *Former Lecturer in Sociology, University of Leeds, Eng.*

Mysore Narasimhachar Srinivas. *Professor and Head, Department of Sociology, Institute for Social and Economic Change, Bangalore, India.*

W.J. Stankiewicz. *Professor of Political Science, University of British Columbia, Vancouver.*

Helmut Dietmar Starke. *Free-lance writer on modern European history.*

Oscar State. *Former General Secretary, International Weightlifting Federation and Commonwealth Weightlifting Federation.*

Michael Steed. *Senior Lecturer in Government, Victoria University of Manchester.*

Erwin Stengel, M.D. (d. 1973). *Professor of Psychiatry, University of Sheffield, Eng.*

Wilson Stephens. *Former Editor,* The Field, *London. Coeditor of* In Praise of Hunting.

Walter Marcel Stern. *Former Senior Lecturer in Economic History, London School of Economics and Political Science, University of London.*

Henry Noel Cochrane Stevenson. *Managing Director, Scottish Television Ltd., 1961–66. Lecturer in Social Anthropology, University of Glasgow, 1950–57. Burma Frontier Service, 1926–47.*

Omer C. Stewart. *Emeritus Professor of Anthropology, University of Colorado, Boulder.*

Marcel Henri Stijns (d. 1967). *President of Honour, International Federation of Journalists. Editor in Chief,* Het Laatste Nieuws, *Brussels.*

John E. Stoner. *Emeritus Professor of Government, Indiana University, Bloomington.*

John Ford Stover. *Emeritus Professor of History, Purdue University, West Lafayette, Ind.*

Ruth Strang (d. 1971). *Professor of Education, Teachers College, Columbia University, 1940–60.*

Robert Strausz-Hupé. *U.S. Ambassador to Turkey. Emeritus Professor of Political Science, University of Pennsylvania, Philadelphia.*

Donald Stuart Strong. *Emeritus Professor of Political Science, University of Alabama, Tuscaloosa.*

Roland Stucki. *Emeritus Professor of Banking and Finance, University of Utah, Salt Lake City.*

William C. Sturtevant. *Curator, Department of Anthropology, Smithsonian Institution, Washington, D.C.*

Ernst W. Swanson. *Emeritus Professor of Economics, North Carolina State University at Raleigh.*

L.E. Sweet. *Professor of Anthropology, University of Manitoba, Winnipeg.*

Philip Taft (d. 1976). *Professor of Economics, Brown University, Providence, R.I.*

Lawrence Edward Tanner (d. 1979). *Librarian, Westminster Abbey, London, 1956–72; Keeper of the Muniments, 1926–66.*

Sol Tax. *Emeritus Professor of Anthropology, University of Chicago. Director, Center for the Study of Man, Smithsonian Institution, Washington, D.C., 1968–76.*

Sheldon Tefft. *James Parker Hall Professor Emeritus of Law, University of Chicago.*

Georges Tessier (d. 1967). *Professor of Diplomacy, École Nationale des Chartes (School of Paleography), Paris, 1930–61.*

Brinley Thomas. *Professor of Economics, University College, Cardiff, University of Wales, 1946–73.*

Bruce R. Thomas. *Free-lance writer on labour matters.*

Joseph Anthony Charles Thomas (d. 1981). *Professor of Roman Law, University of London, 1965–81.*

Terence Barrington Thomas. *Director, Gladding International Ltd. Angling correspondent,* The Field *and others. Presenter of "Angling Today," Associated Television, Birmingham, Eng.*

William Miles Webster Thomas, Baron Thomas (d. 1980). *Chairman, Britannia Airways Ltd.; Neumo Ltd.; and other companies. Director, Sun Insurance Office, Ltd. President, National Savings Committee, 1965–72.*

David Thomson (d. 1970). *Master, Sidney Sussex College, University of Cambridge, 1957–70. Author of* Europe Since Napoleon *and others.*

Lynn Thorndike (d. 1965). *Professor of History, Columbia University, 1924–52.*

Samuel Edmund Thorne. *Fairchild Professor Emeritus of Legal History, Harvard University.*

Fred J. Tickner (d. 1980). *Professor of Political Science, State University of New York at Albany.*

Nicholas S. Timasheff (d. 1970). *Professor of Sociology, Fordham University, New York City, 1949–57.*

Mischa Titiev. *Emeritus Professor of Anthropology, University of Michigan, Ann Arbor.*

Bursley Howland Titus. *Former Analyst, Department of the Army, Washington, D.C.*

Frederick Porter Todd (d. 1977). *Colonel, U.S. Army Reserve. Director, West Point Museum, U.S. Military Academy, 1953–65.*

Frederick B. Tolles (d. 1975). *Howard M. Jenkins Professor of Quaker History, Swarthmore College, Pa., 1954–70; Director, Friends Historical Library, 1941–70.*

Stanley Trapido. *Lecturer in the Government of New States, University of Oxford.*

Philip N(orton) Tucker. *Military Intelligence Research Specialist, Office of Assistant Chief of Staff, Intelligence, Department of the Army, Washington, D.C.*

Will C. Turnbladh. *Former Commissioner of Corrections, State of Minnesota.*

Lorenzo Dow Turner (d. 1972). *Professor of English, Roosevelt University, Chicago, 1946–69.*

Arthur Walter Tyler. *Former President, TYCO, Inc., Waltham, Mass.*

Frederick John Underhill. *Secretary, National Greyhound Racing Club Ltd., London.*

Dorothy Firman Van Ess (Mrs. John Van Ess) (d. 1975). *Missionary, Arabian Mission of the Reformed Church in America; Educational and social worker, Basra, Iraq, 1909–55.*

Harold Goodhue Vatter. *Professor of Economics, Portland State University, Ore.*

Francis Joseph Violich. *Professor of City Planning and of Landscape Architecture, University of California, Berkeley.*

Charles De Visscher (d. 1973). *Honorary President of the Institute of International Law. Judge, International Court of Justice, 1945–52.*

Sir Claud Humphrey Meredith Waldock (d. 1981). *Chichele Professor of Public International Law, University of Oxford, 1947–72.*

Pat Ward-Thomas. *Writer on golf.*

Donovan William Mockford Waters. *Professor of Law, University of Victoria, B.C.*

Nathan A. Waxman. *Scholar of Caucasian languages.*

Hans W. Weigert (d. 1983). *Director, Georgetown Research Project; Research Professor of Political Geography, Georgetown University, Washington, D.C.*

Joseph Sidney Weiner (d. 1982). *Professor of Environmental Physiology, 1965–80; Director, Medical Research Council Environmental Physiology Unit, 1962–80, London School of Hygiene and Tropical Medicine, University of London.*

William Thomas Wells. *Queen's Counsel. Member of Parliament for Walsall, Eng., 1945–55; Walsall North, 1955–74. General Staff Officer, 2nd Grade, Directorate of Military Training, War Office, London, 1942–45.*

Hans Fritz Welzel (deceased). *Professor of Penal Law and of the Philosophy of Law, Rhenish Friedrich Wilhelm University of Bonn, W.Ger.*

Roger J.R. Whistler. *Major; Regimental Secretary, Regimental Headquarters, Royal Military Police, Roussillon Barracks, Chichester, Eng.*

Harry George Whiteman. *Writer and critic.*

Trevor Williamson. *Chief Sports Subeditor,* Daily Telegraph (*London*).

Neill Compton Wilson. *Author of* Treasure Express: Epic Days of Wells Fargo *and others.*

Robert Renbert Wilson. *James B. Duke Professor Emeritus of Political Science, Duke University, Durham, N.C.*

Hans Julius Wolff (d. 1983). *Professor of Roman Law, Albert Ludwig University of Freiburg, Freiburg im Breisgau, W.Ger.*

William Lower Wonderly. *Translations Coordinator for Latin America, United Bible Societies, Mexico City.*

Arthur Evans Wood (d. 1960). *Professor of Sociology, University of Michigan, Ann Arbor.*

Michael Henry Woodford. *Secretary, British Falconers' Club, London, 1956–60.*

Ruth Frances Woodsmall (d. 1963). *United Nations Representative of International Alliance of Women. Chief of Women's Affairs, U.S. High Commission of Germany, 1948–52. General Secretary, World YWCA, 1934–48.*

Quincy Wright (d. 1970). *Professor of International Law, University of Chicago, 1931–56.*

Frederick S. Wyle. *Attorney.*

David Eryl Corbet Yale. *Reader in English Legal History, University of Cambridge; Fellow of Christ's College, Cambridge.*

Dale Yoder. *Professor and Director, Bureau of Business Services and Research, California State University, Long Beach, 1967–75. Professor of Industrial Relations, Stanford University, California, 1959–66.*

Kimball Young (d. 1973). *Professor of Sociology, Northwestern University, Evanston, Ill., 1947–62.*

Carle Clark Zimmerman (deceased). *Associate Professor of Sociology, Harvard University.*

Robert Walter Zimmermann. *Retired foreign service officer, U.S. Department of State; Director, East Coast Affairs, 1976–79.*

George William Zinke. *Emeritus Professor of Economics, University of Colorado, Boulder.*

Roman J. Zorn. *Professor of History, University of Nevada, Las Vegas.*

Part Six. Art

Gerald E.H. Abraham. *President, Royal Musical Association, 1970–74. Assistant Controller of Music, British Broadcasting Corporation, London, 1962–67. James and Constance Alsop Professor of Music, University of Liverpool, England, 1947–62.*

Irving Abrahamson. *Associate Professor of English, Kennedy-King College, City Colleges of Chicago.*

Percy G. Adams. *Professor of English, University of Tennessee, Knoxville.*

Jean Adhémar. *Curator of Prints, Bibliothèque Nationale, Paris.*

Margarita Aguirre. *Writer. Author of* Las vidas de Pablo Neruda *and others.*

Walter E. Allen. *Professor of English Studies, New University of Ulster, Coleraine, N.Ire., 1968–73.*

Barthélemy Amengual. *Editor,* Études Cinématographiques. *Author of* René Clair; Clés pour le cinéma.

Reed Anderson. *Assistant Professor of Spanish and Portuguese, University of California, Davis.*

J.A. Andrups. *Author of* Latvian Literature *and others.*

Noel Gilroy Annan, Baron Annan. *Vice-Chancellor, University of London, 1978–81; Provost of University College, 1966–78. Author of* Leslie Stephen.

Joseph Anthony. *Former Special Assignments Editor,* Encyclopædia Britannica, *Chicago.*

Giovanni Aquilecchia. *Professor of Italian, University College, University of London.*

Arthur John Arberry (d. 1969). *Sir Thomas Adams Professor of Arabic, University of Cambridge, 1947–69.*

Annette Elizabeth Armstrong. *Former Fellow and Tutor in Modern Languages, Somerville College, Oxford; former Lecturer in French Literature, University of Oxford.*

H. Harvard Arnason (d. 1986). *Art historian. Vice President for Art Administration, Solomon R. Guggenheim Foundation, New York City, 1961–69.*

Denis Midgley Arnold (d. 1986). *Heather Professor of Music, University of Oxford, 1975–86.*

Steven Arnold. *Free-lance writer on African literature.*

W. Geoffrey Arnott. *Professor of Greek Language and Literature, University of Leeds, Eng.*

Elizabeth Mary Aslin. *Keeper, Bethnal Green Museum, Victoria and Albert Museum, London, 1974–81.*

James Stephen Atherton (deceased). *Lecturer in English Literature, Wigan and District Mining and Technical College, England. Author of* The Books at the Wake.

Marcelle Auclair (d. 1983). *Writer. Author of* Enfances et mort de Garcia Lorca *and others.*

Hans Aurenhammer. *Former Director, Austrian State Gallery, Vienna.*

Kurt Badt (deceased). *Art historian. Author of* Die Kunst des Nicolas Poussin *and others.*

Anthony Cuthbert Baines. *Curator of the Bate Collection of historical wind instruments, University of Oxford, 1970–80.*

A. Craig Baird (d. 1979). *Professor of Speech, University of Iowa, Iowa City, 1928–52.*

Peter P. Baldass. *Author of* Romanische Kunst in Österreich *and others.*

Umberto Baldini. *Art historian. Superintendent Director, Central Institute for the Restoration of Works of Art, Rome.*

The Rev. John Francis Bannon, S.J. (d. 1986). *Professor of History, St. Louis University, Mo., 1949–73.*

Eric Arthur Barber (d. 1965). *Rector of Exeter College, University of Oxford, 1943–56.*

Guglielmo Barblan (d. 1978). *Professor of Music History, University of Milan. Director of the Library, G. Verdi Conservatory of Music, Milan.*

Frederick P. Bargebuhr (d. 1978). *Professor of Religion, University of Iowa, Iowa City, 1962–70.*

William Barr. *Senior Lecturer in Latin, University of Liverpool.*

Jean-Bertrand Barrère (d. 1985). *Professor of French Literature, University of Cambridge, 1954–82; Fellow of St. John's College, Cambridge.*

Eleanor Dodge Barton. *Former Professor and Chairman, Department of Art History, University of Hartford, West Hartford, Conn. Professor and Chairman, Department of Art, Sweet Briar College, Va., 1952–71.*

Jacques Barzun. *University Professor Emeritus, Columbia University; Dean of Faculties and Provost, 1958–67.*

Annette K. Baxter. *Professor of History, Barnard College, Columbia University. Author of* Henry Miller, Expatriate.

Germain René Michel Bazin. *Research Professor Emeritus of Fine Arts, York University, Toronto. Emeritus Curator, the Louvre Museum, Paris.*

William Beare (d. 1963). *Professor of Latin, University of Bristol, Eng., 1931–63.*

Alexander Munro Beattie. *Emeritus Professor of English, Carleton University, Ottawa.*

Bernard Beckerman (d. 1985). *Brander Matthews Professor of Dramatic Literature, Columbia University, 1977–85.*

Karl Beckson. *Professor of English, Brooklyn College, City University of New York.*

John Bernard Beer. *Fellow of Peterhouse, Cambridge; Reader in English Literature, University of Cambridge.*

Charles G. Bell. *Poet and novelist. Tutor, St. John's College, Santa Fe, N.M. Author of* Delta Return; The Married Land; *and others.*

Benedikt Sigurdur Benedikz. *Head of Special Collections, Library, University of Birmingham, Eng.*

Susan Elizabeth Benenson. *Former Assistant Keeper, Department of Western Art, Ashmolean Museum, University of Oxford.*

Michel N. Benisovich (d. 1963). *Art historian. Instructor, New York University.*

Albert S. Bennett. *Free-lance writer. Senior Editor and Biographies Editor,* The American Heritage Dictionary of the English Language, *1966–68.*

Joan Bennett (d. 1986). *Fellow of Girton College, Cambridge; Lecturer in English, University of Cambridge, 1936–64.*

Ian D. Bent. *Professor of Music, University of Nottingham, Eng.*

Walter G. Bergmann. *Former Editor, Schott and Co. Ltd., Music Publishers, London.*

John Dagfinn Bergsagel. *Musicologist, Institute of Musicology, University of Copenhagen.*

Joshua Berrett. *Assistant Professor of Humanities, Wayne State University, Detroit.*

Brenda Berrian. *Free-lance writer on African literature.*

André Berry. *Author of* Florilège des troubadours; Anthologie de la poésie occitane; *and others.*

Albert Bettex. *Author and lecturer. Editor,* Librarium.

Alan Curtis Birnholz. *Associate Professor of Art History, State University of New York at Buffalo.*

Easley Blackwood. *Professor of Music, University of Chicago.*

James Blades. *Lecturer on music. Professional Timpanist, formerly with the English Opera Group and English Chamber Orchestra.*

Dimitry Dimitriyevich Blagoy. *Correspondent Member, Academy of Sciences of the U.S.S.R., Moscow. Member, Academy of Pedagogical Sciences of the U.S.S.R., Moscow.*

Claude Blair. *Keeper of Metalwork, Victoria and Albert Museum, London, 1972–82.*

Walter Blair. *Emeritus Professor of English, University of Chicago.*

José Manuel Blecua. *Professor of the History of Spanish Language and Literature, University of Barcelona.*

Carl Bode. *Professor of English, University of Maryland, College Park.*

Joseph Sullivan Bolt. *Professor of Art History, University of Alabama, Tuscaloosa.*

Donald F. Bond. *Emeritus Professor of English, University of Chicago.*

Jacques-Henry Bornecque. *Professor of Modern and Contemporary French Literature, University of Paris XIII.*

Marvin Sidney Borowsky (d. 1969). *Professor of Theatre Arts, University of California, Los Angeles.*

Umberto Bosco. *Emeritus Professor of Italian Language and Literature, University of Rome. Director, Enciclopedia italiana.*

Margaret Innes Bouton. *Curator in Charge of Educational Work, National Gallery of Art, Washington, D.C.*

Alan Bowness. *Director, Tate Gallery, London.*

Charles Ralph Boxer. *Camoens Professor Emeritus of Portuguese, King's College, University of London.*

Muriel Clara Bradbrook. *Professor of English Literature, University of Cambridge, 1965–76; Mistress of Girton College, Cambridge, 1968–76.*

Johannes Christiaan Brandt Corstius. *Former Professor of Comparative Literature, State University of Utrecht, Neth.*

Edward Kamau Brathwaite. *Poet and critic. Professor of History, University of the West Indies, Mona (Kingston), Jamaica.*

Otto J. Brendel (d. 1973). *Professor of Art History and Archaeology, Columbia University, 1956–69.*

André Brincourt. *Director of Cultural Services, Le Figaro, Paris.*

Liliana Brisby. *Editor,* The World Today. *Author of* Les Relations russo-bulgares, 1878–1886.

Oscar Gross Brockett. *Waggener Professor of Drama, University of Texas at Austin.*

Bernard Jocelyn Brooke (d. 1966). *Author of* The Military Orchid *and others.*

Anita Brookner. *Reader in the History of Art, Courtauld Institute of Art, University of London.*

Conrad Brown. *Chief Editor, Adult Books, Grosset and Dunlap Inc., New York City.*

David Brown. *Professor of Musicology, University of Southampton, Eng.*

Maurice J.E. Brown (d. 1975). *Author of* Schubert: A Critical Biography; Essays on Schubert.

Reginald Francis Brown (d. 1985). *Cowdray Professor of Spanish Language and Literature, University of Leeds, Eng., 1953–75.*

Robert Browning. *Emeritus Professor of Classics and Ancient History, Birkbeck College, University of London.*

Charlotte H. Bruner. *Professor of French, Iowa State University, Ames.*

Arnaldo Bruschi. *Professor of the History of Architecture, University of Rome.*

Doris Bry. *Writer on photography, art history, and natural science. Representative for the paintings of Georgia O'Keeffe.*

Sir Arthur Bryant (d. 1985). *Author of* Samuel Pepys *and many others.*

J.A.B. Van Buitenen (d. 1979). *Distinguished Service Professor of Sanskrit and Indic Studies, University of Chicago, 1974–79.*

Donald Burness. *Professor of English, Franklin Pierce College, Rindge, N.H.*

John Burton-Page. *Reader in the Art and Archaeology of South Asia, School of Oriental and African Studies, University of London.*

Douglas Bush (d. 1983). *Gurney Professor of English Literature, Harvard University, 1957–66.*

Joseph T. Butler. *Curator, Sleepy Hollow Restorations, Tarrytown, N.Y. Adjunct Associate Professor of Architecture, Columbia University.*

Martin Butlin. *Keeper of the British Collection, Tate Gallery, London.*

John Everett Butt (d. 1965). *Regius Professor of Rhetoric and English Literature, University of Edinburgh, 1959–65.*

James F. Cahill. *Professor of the History of Art, University of California, Berkeley.*

Kenneth Walter Cameron. *Emeritus Associate Professor of English, Trinity College, Hartford, Conn.*

Henry Seidel Canby (d. 1961). *Literary critic. Founder and Editor, Saturday Review of Literature, 1924–36.*

Peter Cannon-Brookes. *Keeper, Department of Art, National Museum of Wales, Cardiff.*

Harry Caplan (d. 1980). *Goldwin Smith Professor of the Classical Languages and Literature, Cornell University, Ithaca, N.Y., 1941–67.*

Sir Neville Cardus (d. 1975). *Music Critic,* The Guardian *(London).*

Margret A. Carey. *Former Assistant Keeper, Department of Ethnography, British Museum, London.*

Enzo Carli. *Director, Cathedral Museum, Siena, Italy.*

Luigi Carluccio. *Member of the arts editorial staff,* La Gazzetta del popolo, *Turin, Italy.*

Arthur H. Cash. *Professor of English, State University of New York, College at New Paltz.*

Pierre-Georges Castex. *Emeritus Professor of Modern French Literature, University of Paris.*

Homero Castillo. *Professor of Spanish, University of California, Davis.*

James Caswell. *Associate Professor of Art History, University of British Columbia, Vancouver.*

Eduardo F. Catalano. *Emeritus Professor of Architecture, Massachusetts Institute of Technology, Cambridge.*

Jean-Louis Caussou. *Former Editor,* Opéra *(journal), Paris. Author of* Rossini.

Charles Cestre (d. 1959). *Professor of American Literature and Civilization, University of Paris, 1917–42.*

Charles Chadwick. *Carnegie Professor of French, University of Aberdeen, Scot.*

John Chalker. *Professor of English Language and Literature, Westfield College, University of London.*

Mary Chamot. *Assistant Keeper, Tate Gallery, London, 1950–65.*

Moti Chandra. *Former Director, Prince of Wales Museum of Western India, Bombay.*

Pramod Chandra. *George P. Bickford Professor of Indian Art, Harvard University.*

Frank Chapman. *Former Senior English Master, High School for Boys, Oswestry, Eng. Author of "Hardy the Novelist" in* Scrutiny.

Joan Chissell. *Assistant Music Critic,* The Times, *London, 1947–79.*

Françoise Choay. *Professor of Urban Studies, University of Paris VIII. Author of* Le Corbusier *and others.*

Chuang Shang-yen. *Former Deputy Director, National Palace Museum, Taipei, Taiwan.*

Charles Manning Hope Clark. *Emeritus Professor of History, Australian National University, Canberra.*

James Midgley Clark (d. 1961). *Professor of German, University of Glasgow, 1951–54.*

Derek Plint Clifford. *Free-lance writer. Author of* A History of Garden Design *and others.*

C.L. Cline. *Ashbel H. Smith Professor Emeritus of English, University of Texas at Austin.*

Raymond Cogniat (d. 1977). *Principal Inspector of Fine Arts, 1943–67. Head of the arts section, Le Figaro, Paris, 1957–77.*

Pierre Cogny. *Senior Lecturer in French Literature, University of Caen, France.*

John Michael Cohen. *Writer, critic, and translator. Editor of* More Comic and Curious Verse; A History of Western Literature; *and others.*

George R. Collins. *Professor of Art History, Columbia University.*

Peter Collins (d. 1981). *Professor of Architecture, McGill University, Montreal.*

Carl Wilbur Condit. *Professor of Art and Urban Affairs, Northwestern University, Evanston, Ill.*

William G. Constable (d. 1976). *Curator of Paintings, Boston Museum of Fine Arts, 1938–57.*

Deryck V. Cooke (d. 1976). *Musicologist. Music Presentation Editor, British Broadcasting Corporation, London, 1965–76.*

Douglas Cooper (d. 1984). *Art historian and critic. Author of* Courtauld Collection, a Catalogue *and others.*

Martin Du Pré Cooper (d. 1986). *Music Editor,* Daily Telegraph, *London, 1954–76.*

Wayne F. Cooper. *Free-lance writer. Editor of* The Passion of Claude McKay.

Gertrude Mary-Anne Coor (d. 1962). *Art historian. Assistant, Institute for Advanced Study, Princeton, N.J., 1959–62.*

Solange Corbin. *Professor of Musicology, University of Poitiers, Fr.*

Charles Philip Corney. *Deputy Librarian, British Library of Political and Economic Science, University of London.*

Robert B. Costello. *Publications Editor, Museum of Modern Art, New York City.*

Pierre Courthion. *Vice President, Syndicate of the French Artistic Press. Author of* Klee; Manet; *and many other monographs on modern European artists.*

David Cowan. *Senior Lecturer in Arabic, School of Oriental and African Studies, University of London.*

Malcolm Cowley. *Literary Adviser, The Viking Press. President, National Institute of Arts and Letters, New York City, 1956–59, 1961–64.*

Edward Croft-Murray (d. 1980). *Keeper, Department of Prints and Drawings, British Museum, London, 1954–73.*

Gerhard Croll. *Professor of Musicology, University of Salzburg, Austria.*

Anthony Cronin. *Poet and critic.*

Bosley Crowther (d. 1981). *Creative consultant, Columbia Pictures, New York City, 1968–73. Screen critic and editor,* The New York Times, *1940–68.*

John Cruickshank. *Professor of French, University of Sussex, Brighton, Eng.*

Margaret Campbell Crum. *Assistant, Department of Western Manuscripts, Bodleian Library, University of Oxford.*

Charles Cudworth (d. 1977). *Curator, Pendlebury Library of Music, University of Cambridge.*

Alan S. Curtis. *Professor of Music, University of California, Berkeley.*

Charles D. Cuttler. *Emeritus Professor of Art History, University of Iowa, Iowa City.*

David Daiches. *Emeritus Professor of English, University of Sussex, Brighton, Eng.*

Mary L. Daniel. *Professor of Portuguese, University of Wisconsin, Madison.*

William Aubrey Darlington (d. 1979). *Chief Drama Critic,* London Daily Telegraph, *1920–68. London Theatre Correspondent,* The New York Times, *1939–60.*

O.R. Dathorne. *Professor of English and Director, Caribbean, African, and Afro-American Studies, University of Miami, Coral Gables, Florida.*

Ronald Austin Davey. *Professor of Art, University of Alberta, Edmonton.*

Donald Alfred Davie. *Andrew W. Mellon Professor of Humanities, Vanderbilt University, Nashville, Tenn.*

Harold Hess Davis (d. 1964). *Phebe Estelle Spalding Professor of English Literature, Pomona College, Claremont, Calif.*

J. Cary Davis. *Emeritus Professor of Romance Languages, Southern Illinois University, Carbondale.*

Margaret Josephine Dean-Smith. *Author of* A Guide to English Folk Song Collections *and others.*

William A. De Gregorio. *Writer on American history.*

George G. Dekker. *Professor of English, Stanford University, Calif.*

Joseph-Edouard-Marie-Ghislain Delmelle. *Poet, essayist, and critic of art and literature. Member, International Academy of French Culture.*

Frederic Paul Deloffre. *Professor of French Literature, University of Paris III.*

Ludwig Denecke. *Director, Murhard Library of the City of Kassel and State Library; Head of the Brothers Grimm Museum, Kassel, W.Ger., 1959–68.*

Bernard Denvir. *Principal Lecturer, Ravensbourne College of Art and Design, Bromley, Eng.*

Wilfrid Desan. *Emeritus Professor of Philosophy, Georgetown University, Washington, D.C.*

Pierre Descargues. *Art historian and critic. Author of* Frans Hals; Jan Vermeer; *and other monographs.*

Hugues de Varine-Bohan. *Director, France-Portuguese Institute, Lisbon. Former Director, International Council of Museums, Paris.*

Leon Townsend Dickinson. *Professor of English, University of Missouri, Columbia.*

Lovat Dickson. *Writer. Director, Macmillan & Company Ltd., London, 1941–64. Author of* H.G. Wells *and others.*

Paul Dinnage. *Free-lance writer, translator, and book reviewer. Formerly reviewer for literature,* The Times *(London)* Literary Supplement, *and for art,* The Spectator.

Maurice Willson Disher (d. 1969). *Author of* Blood and Thunder; Clowns and Pantomimes; *and others.*

Armel Hugh Diverres. *Professor of French; Head, Department of Romance Studies, University College of Swansea, University of Wales, 1974–81.*

Frederick J. Dockstader. *Museum consultant and art historian. Director, Museum of the American Indian, Heye Foundation, New York City, 1960–75.*

John V. Dodge. *Vice-President Emeritus, International Editorial, Encyclopædia Britannica, Inc., Chicago; Assistant and Managing Editor, 1938–60; Executive Editor, 1960–64.*

Charles Reginald Dodwell. *Pilkington Professor of the History of Art; Director, Whitworth Art Gallery, Victoria University of Manchester.*

Frank Doeringer. *Assistant Professor of History, Lawrence University, Appleton, Wis.*

Robert Donington. *Musician and musicologist. Professor of Music, University of Iowa, Iowa City, 1966–73.*

Filippo Donini. *Cultural Expert, Cultural Relations Department, Italian Ministry of Foreign Affairs, Rome, 1972–76. Director, Italian Institute, London, 1961–72.*

Denis Donoghue. *Henry James Professor of Letters, New York University, New York City.*

David F. Dorsey, Jr. *Associate Dean, School of Arts and Sciences, Atlanta University, Ga.*

Richard M. Dorson (d. 1981). *Director, Folklore Institute; Professor of History and Folklore, Indiana University, Bloomington, 1957–81.*

Brian Westerdale Downs (d. 1984). *Master of Christ's College, Cambridge, 1950–63; Professor of Scandinavian Studies, University of Cambridge, 1950–60.*

Kandioura Drame. *Free-lance writer on African literature.*

Philip Drew. *Professor of English Literature, University of Glasgow.*

Laura Dru. *Records and Archives Department, Madame Tussaud's Ltd., London.*

Donald Reynolds Dudley (d. 1972). *Professor of Latin, University of Birmingham, Eng., 1955–72.*

Anne Schley Duggan (d. 1973). *Professor and Dean, College of Health, Physical Education and Recreation, Texas Woman's University, Denton.*

René Dumesnil (d. 1967). *Literary and music critic. Member, Academy of Fine Arts, Institute of France, 1965–67.*

Archibald A.M. Duncan. *Professor of Scottish History and Literature, University of Glasgow.*

Lowell Dunham. *Distinguished Regents Professor of Modern Languages, University of Oklahoma, Norman.*

Raymond E. Durgnat. *Tutor in Cultural History, Royal College of Art, London. Author of* Films and Feelings; Jean Renoir; *and others.*

Wilma Robb Ebbitt. *Professor of English, Pennsylvania State University, University Park.*

Edwin Harold Eby. *Emeritus Professor of English, University of Washington, Seattle.*

Leon Edel. *Henry James Professor Emeritus of English and American Letters, New York University, New York City. Citizens Professor Emeritus of English, University of Hawaii, Honolulu.*

Christopher Edmunds. *Composer. Examiner for the Trinity College of Music, London, 1940–78.*

Hugh Edwards. *Former Curator of Photography and Associate Curator, Department of Prints and Drawings, Art Institute of Chicago.*

Tudor Edwards. *Formerly Investigating Officer of Historic Buildings, Ministry of Town and Country Planning, England.*

Lorenz E.A. Eitner. *Professor and Chairman, Department of Art, Stanford University, Calif.*

Sverker Ek. *Emeritus Professor of Literary History, Göteborg University, Swed.*

Charles Grant Ellis. *Research Associate, The Textile Museum, Washington, D.C.*

Elmer Ellis. *Emeritus President; Emeritus Professor of History, University of Missouri, Columbia.*

Angna Enters. *Dancer, mime, and artist. Originator of phase dance mime. Author of* On Mime.

Joaquín de Entrambasaguas. *Former Professor of Spanish Literature, University of Madrid.*

Walter Erben (d. 1981). *Professor of Art Education, College of Education of the Ruhr, Dortmund, W.Ger.*

Robert Escarpit. *Professor of Information and Communication Sciences, University of Bordeaux III, France.*

Martin J. Esslin. *Professor of Drama, Stanford University, Calif. Head of Radio Drama, British Broadcasting Corporation, London, 1963–77.*

Joan Evans (d. 1977). *President, Society of Antiquaries, London, 1959–64. Author of* John Ruskin *and many others.*

David Fagan. *Former Assistant Professor of Spanish and Portuguese, Indiana University, Bloomington.*

Alison (Anna Bowie) Fairlie. *Professorial Fellow of Girton College, Cambridge; Professor of French, University of Cambridge.*

Dennis Larry Ashwell Farr. *Director, Courtauld Institute Galleries, London.*

Suzanne Pier Fauteux. *Free-lance writer.*

John Bailey Fernald (d. 1985). *Theatre Director. Principal, Royal Academy of Dramatic Art, London, 1955–65. Professor of Dramatic Art, Oakland University, Rochester, Mich., 1966–70.*

Robert J. Fernier (d. 1977). *President, The Friends of Gustave Courbet, Paris. Author of* Gustave Courbet, peintre de l'art vivant.

Andrew Field. *Professor of Comparative Literature, Griffith University, Brisbane, Australia.*

Roger Elwyn Fiske. *Musicologist and composer. Author of* Listening to Music; Ballet Music; *and others.*

Constantine FitzGibbon (d. 1983). *Writer. Author of* The Life of Dylan Thomas.

Ian Fletcher. *Professor of English Literature, University of Reading, Eng.*

Louis-Fernand Flutre. *Emeritus Professor of Old French Language and Literature, University of Lyon.*

John Stuart Forbes. *Deputy Warden, The Worshipful Company of Goldsmiths, London.*

Patrick K. Ford. *Director, Center for the Study of Comparative Folklore and Mythology, University of California, Los Angeles.*

Nigel Fortune. *Reader in Music, University of Birmingham, Eng.*

Wallace Fowlie. *James B. Duke Professor of French Literature, Duke University, Durham, N.C.*

George Sutherland Fraser (d. 1980). *Poet and critic. Reader in Modern English Literature, University of Leicester, Eng., 1964–79.*

Richard H. Freeborn. *Professor of Russian Literature, School of Slavonic and East European Studies, University of London.*

Marion Valerie Friedmann. *Editor and translator. Author of* The Slap; *editor of* I Will Still Be Moved: Reports from South Africa.

Oluf Anker Friis (d. 1979). *Professor of Literature, University of Copenhagen, 1957–64.*

Holger Elof Uno Frykenstedt. *Lecturer in Literary History with Poetics, University of Stockholm.*

David Fuller. *Professor of Music, State University of New York at Buffalo.*

Jean Overton Fuller. *Codirector, Fuller d'Arch Smith Ltd., Rare Books, London. Author of* Swinburne: A Critical Biography *and others.*

Richard Clair Gabriel. *Senior History Master, King's School, Worcester, Eng. Former Research Assistant, Institute of Historical Research, University of London.*

Hans Gal. *Composer and musicologist. Lecturer on Music, University of Edinburgh, 1945–65. Director of Municipal College of Music, Mainz, Ger., 1929–33.*

Edward J.C. Garden. *Professor and Head, Department of Music, University of Sheffield, Eng.*

John F. Garganigo. *Professor of Spanish and Chairman, Department of Latin American Studies, Washington University, St. Louis, Mo.*

William Gaunt (d. 1980). *Art historian. Special correspondent on art subjects, The Times (London).*

Robert Gayre of Gayre and Nigg. *Editor, Armorial, Edinburgh.*

Karl Geiringer. *Emeritus Professor of Music, University of California, Santa Barbara.*

Willi Geismeier. *Former Director, National Gallery, National Museum of Berlin.*

Arthur Gelb. *Deputy Managing Editor, The New York Times. Coauthor of* O'Neill.

Barbara Gelb. *Writer. Coauthor of* O'Neill.

Margaret Oliver Gentles. *Former Keeper of the Buckingham Collection of Japanese Prints; former Associate Curator of Oriental Art, Art Institute of Chicago.*

Albert S. Gerard. *Professor of Comparative Literature, State University of Liège, Belg.*

Edwin Gerow. *Frank L. Sulzberger Professor of Civilizations; Professor of Sanskrit, University of Chicago.*

Giuseppe Giangrande. *Professor of Classics, Birkbeck College, University of London.*

Robert Donald Davidson Gibson. *Professor of French, University of Kent at Canterbury, Eng.*

Alexander Gillies (d. 1977). *Professor of German Language and Literature, University of Leeds, Eng., 1945–72.*

Giovanni Pietro Giorgetti. *Lecturer in Italian, Birkbeck College, University of London.*

Cuthbert Morton Girdlestone (d. 1975). *Professor of French, Universities of Durham and Newcastle upon Tyne, Eng., 1926–60.*

Robert W.V. Gittings. *Poet, biographer, and playwright. Author of* John Keats *and numerous other works on Keats.*

Nina C. Gitz. *Free-lance writer and translator.*

Kurt Moritz Artur Goldammer. *Professor of Comparative History of Religions and of the History of Religious Art, Philipps University of Marburg, W.Ger.*

Frederick Goldbeck (d. 1981). *Critic and musicologist. Adviser for Music, Radiotélévision Française.*

Ludwig Goldscheider. *Art historian. Former director and designer of books for Phaidon Press Ltd., London. Author of* Kokoschka *and many others.*

Dale Good. *Editor,* Compton's Encyclopedia. *Librarian, Music Division, New York Public Library's Research Center for the Performing Arts at Lincoln Center, New York City, 1970–77.*

Robert Marshall Goodwin. *Racing correspondent, London.*

Sydney Charles Gould. *Former Reader in French and Comparative Literature, University of Bristol, Eng.*

Andrew Sydenham Farrar Gow (d. 1978). *Fellow of Trinity College, University of Cambridge; Brereton Reader in Classics, 1947–51.*

Alan Gowans. *Professor of History in Art, University of Victoria, B.C.*

Philip Graham (d. 1967). *Professor of American Literature, University of Texas at Austin.*

Theodore C. Grame. *President, Study Center of American Musical Pluralism, Tarpon Springs, Fla.*

Serge Grandjean. *Keeper, Department of Objets d'Art, Louvre Museum, Paris.*

Benny Green. *Record reviewer, British Broadcasting Corporation. Jazz Critic,* The Observer, *London, 1958–77.*

Roger Lancelyn Green. *Author of* Lewis Carroll *and others; editor of* The Diaries of Lewis Carroll.

David Greene (d. 1981). *Senior Professor, School of Celtic Studies, Dublin Institute for Advanced Studies.*

Mark Gridley. *Lecturer in Music, Case Western Reserve University, Cleveland, Ohio.*

F. Grossmann (d. 1984). *Senior Professor of Art History, University of Washington, Seattle.*

Henri Guillemin. *Emeritus Professor of History of French Literature, University of Geneva.*

Masakatsu Gunji. *Professor of Kabuki Drama, Waseda University, Tokyo.*

Karl S. Guthke. *Professor of German Literature, Harvard University.*

Gordon S. Haight (d. 1985). *Professor of English, Yale University, 1950–68.*

Eric Halfpenny (d. 1979). *Editor,* The Galpin Society Journal, *1963–70.*

Frieda F. Halpern. *Consultant on needlework.*

Charles E. Hamm. *Composer. Arthur Virgin Professor of Music, Dartmouth College, Hanover, N.H.*

Craig S. Harbison. *Associate Professor of Art, University of Massachusetts, Amherst.*

Enriqueta Harris. *Honorary Fellow of the Warburg Institute, University of London. Author of* Spanish Painting; Goya.

Francis Llewellyn Harrison. *Emeritus Professor of Ethnomusicology, University of Amsterdam. Reader in the History of Music, University of Oxford, 1962–70.*

William J. Harrison. *Consultant on industrial design.*

Kenneth Harrow. *Professor of Humanities, Michigan State University, East Lansing.*

Arnold Lionel Haskell (d. 1980). *Director, 1946–65, and Governor, 1966–77, Royal Ballet School; Governor, Royal Ballet, London, 1957–80.*

David Hately. *Critic and consultant on literature.*

Eric Alfred Havelock. *Sterling Professor Emeritus of Classics, Yale University.*

David M. Hayne. *Professor of French, University of Toronto.*

John A. Haywood. *Reader in Arabic, University of Durham, Eng., 1967–78.*

Ernst van Heerden. *Poet. Emeritus Professor of Afrikaans and Netherlands, University of the Witwatersrand, Johannesburg.*

Julius S. Held. *Emeritus Professor of Art History, Barnard College, Columbia University.*

Peter Heller. *Professor of German and Comparative Literature, State University of New York at Buffalo.*

Ruth P. Hellman. *Consultant on lace, Metropolitan Museum of Art, New York City.*

Philip Prichard Henderson (d. 1977). *Free-lance writer and editor. Author of* William Morris: His Life, Work and Friends.

Robert M. Henderson. *Chief, General Library and Museum of the Performing Arts, New York Public Library at Lincoln Center, New York City.*

Sir Philip Hendy (d. 1980). *Adviser to the Israel Museum, Jerusalem, 1968–71. Director, National Gallery, London, 1946–67.*

Julian Herbage (d. 1976). *Free-lance musicologist, broadcaster, and writer.*

Don Herdeck. *Free-lance writer on African literature.*

Barnard Hewitt. *Emeritus Professor of Theatre, University of Illinois, Urbana.*

Howard Hibbard (d. 1984). *Professor of Art History, Columbia University, 1966–84.*

A. Kent Hieatt. *Professor of English, University of Western Ontario, London.*

David J.M. Higgins (d. 1975). *Associate Professor of English, Monmouth College, West Long Branch, N.J., 1973–75.*

Gilbert Highet (d. 1978). *Anthon Professor of Latin Language and Literature, Columbia University, 1950–72.*

Ronald Francis Hingley. *Fellow of St. Antony's College, Oxford; University Lecturer in Russian, University of Oxford.*

André Hodeir. *Composer, conductor, and writer. Author of* Jazz: Its Evolution and Its Essence.

Michel-Rostislav Hofmann. *Musicologist. Author of* Moussorgski; Histoire de la musique en Russie.

Reinhold D. Hohl. *Art historian. Author of* Giacometti *and others.*

Christina Stanley Hole. *Honorary Editor,* Folklore. *Author of* English Custom and Usage; English Folklore; *and others.*

Hans Egon Holthusen. *Professor of German, Northwestern University, Evanston, Ill., 1968–81.*

Yasuji Honda. *Former Professor of Drama, Waseda University, Tokyo. Member, Japanese Society for Theatre Research.*

Kenneth Hopkins. *Novelist and poet. Professor of English, Southern Illinois University, Carbondale, 1964–72.*

John Horden. *Author of* Francis Quarles: A Bibliography of His Works to the Year 1800.

Paul Horgan. *Emeritus Professor of English; Author in Residence, Wesleyan University, Middleton, Conn.*

Louis Horst (d. 1964). *Teacher of Dance Composition, Juilliard School of Music. Managing Editor,* Dance Observer.

William Driver Howarth. *Professor of French, University of Bristol, Eng.*

Alan Crawford Howie. *Lecturer in Music, Victoria University of Manchester.*

Ivan Hrbek. *Member, Oriental Institute, Czechoslovak Academy of Sciences, Prague.*

Garfield Hopkin Hughes (d. 1969). *Senior Lecturer in Welsh Language and Literature, University College of Wales, Aberystwyth, 1960–69.*

Herbert James Hunt (d. 1973). *Professor of French Language and Literature, Royal Holloway College, University of London, 1944–66.*

G(eorge) Haydn Huntley. *Emeritus Professor of Art, Northwestern University, Evanston, Ill.*

Jethro Hurt. *Former Instructor in the History of Art and Architecture, University of Illinois, Chicago.*

Dyneley Hussey (d. 1972). *Music Critic, The Times (London), 1923–46; The Listener, 1946–60. Author of* Verdi; Some Composers of Opera.

Hans Huth (d. 1977). *Curator of Decorative Arts, Art Institute of Chicago, 1958–63.*

Herbert Henry Huxley. *Emeritus Professor of Classics, University of Victoria, B.C. Supervisor in Classics, St. John's College, University of Cambridge.*

Gerard Willem Huygens. *Professor of History and Dutch Literature, Rotterdam Lyceum.*

René Huyghe. *Professor of Art, College of France, Paris. President, Council of Museums, Paris.*

Stuart Wallace Hyde. *Professor of Broadcast Communication Arts, San Francisco State University.*

Isabelle Hyman. *Professor of Fine Arts, Washington Square and University College of Arts and Science, New York University, New York City.*

Catherine Mills Ing (d. 1983). *Fellow of St. Hilda's College, Oxford; Senior Lecturer in English Literature, University of Oxford.*

Hans Dietrich Irmscher. *Professor of Modern German Literary Criticism, University of Cologne.*

John H.B. Irving. *Director, Education Division, WGBH Educational Foundation, Boston.*

David Irwin. *Chairman, Department of History of Art, University of Aberdeen, Scot.*

Elizabeth Jachimowicz. *Curator of Costumes, Chicago Historical Society.*

Ian Jack. *Fellow of Pembroke College, Cambridge; Professor of English Literature, University of Cambridge.*

Stephen W. Jacobs. *Professor of Architecture, Cornell University, Ithaca, N.Y.*

Hans L.C. Jaffé. *Professor of Modern Art History, University of Amsterdam.*

Michael Jaffé. *Professor of the History of Western Art; Director, Fitzwilliam Museum, University of Cambridge; Fellow of King's College, Cambridge.*

Richard Edward Warwick James. *Assistant Curator, Barber Institute of Fine Arts; Lecturer in History of Art, University of Birmingham, Eng.*

William Louis G. James. *Reader in English, University of Kent at Canterbury, Eng.*

H.W. Janson (d. 1982). *Professor of Fine Arts, Washington Square College of Arts and Science, New York University, New York City, 1949–79.*

Alexander Norman Jeffares. *Professor of English, University of Stirling, Scot.*

Alan R. Jefferson. *Light Orchestral Manager, British Broadcasting Corporation, London, 1968–73. Professor of Vocal Interpretation, Guildhall School of Music and Drama, London, 1967–74.*

Harold Jenkins. *Emeritus Professor of Rhetoric and English Literature, University of Edinburgh.*

Romilly James Heald Jenkins (d. 1969). *Professor of Byzantine History and Director of Studies, Harvard University Dumbarton Oaks Research Library and Collection, 1960–69.*

Frederick L. Jones (d. 1973). *Professor of English, University of Pennsylvania, Philadelphia.*

Joseph Jay Jones. *Emeritus Professor of English, University of Texas at Austin.*

Bertram Leon Joseph (d. 1981). *Professor of Drama; Chairman, Department of Theatre, Queens College, City University of New York, 1970–81.*

Wayne Kamin. *Research Associate in African and Afro-American Studies, University of Texas at Austin.*

Maxine Kanter. *Free-lance writer on music.*

Ben Zion Kaplan. *President, Universal Hairpieces, New York City.*

Edgar Kaufmann, Jr. *Emeritus Professor of the History of Architecture, Columbia University. Director, Department of Industrial Design, Museum of Modern Art, New York City, 1946–50.*

Martin J. Kemp. *Professor of Fine Arts, University of St. Andrews, Scot.*

Elspeth Mary Kennedy. *Lecturer in French, University of Oxford; Fellow of St. Hilda's College, Oxford.*

Edward John Kenney. *Kennedy Professor Emeritus of Latin, University of Cambridge; Fellow of Peterhouse, Cambridge.*

Herbert Leon Kessler. *Professor and Chairman, Department of the History of Art, Johns Hopkins University, Baltimore.*

Arnold Charles Kettle. *Former Professor of Literature, Open University, Walton, Eng.*

Heinz Kindermann (d. 1985). *Professor of Drama, University of Vienna. Chairman, Commission for the History of the Austrian Theatre, Austrian Academy of Sciences, Vienna. Vice President, International Institute for Theatrical Research, Vienna.*

Donald King. *Deputy Keeper, Victoria and Albert Museum, London.*

Peter K. King. *Director, Institute of Modern Dutch Studies, University of Hull, Eng.*

A.M. Kinghorn. *Professor of English. University of Qatar, Doha.*

Romas Kinka. *Former Lecturer in Lithuanian, University of Chicago. Vice Director of the Lithuanian Institute of Education, Chicago.*

The Rev. James Kinsley (d. 1984). *Professor and Head, Department of English Studies, University of Nottingham, Eng., 1961–84. General Editor, Oxford English Novels, 1967–77.*

F.E. Kirby. *Professor of Music, Lake Forest College, Ill.*

Ralph Kirkpatrick (d. 1984). *Harpsichordist. Professor of Music, Yale University, 1965–76.*

Lincoln Edward Kirstein. *General Director, New York City Ballet Company.*

Michael William Lely Kitson. *Deputy Director and Professor of the History of Art, Courtauld Institute of Art, University of London.*

Tibor Klaniczay. *Assistant Director, Institute for the History of Literature, Hungarian Academy of Sciences, Budapest.*

Margaret Brown Klapthor. *Former Associate Curator, Division of Political History, National Museum of History and Technology, Smithsonian Institution, Washington, D.C.*

Carl Frederick Klinck. *Emeritus Professor of Canadian Literature, University of Western Ontario, London.*

Jan Knappert. *Lecturer in Bantu, School of Oriental and African Studies, University of London.*

Arthur Knight. *Professor of Cinema, University of Southern California, Los Angeles. Film Critic, The Hollywood Reporter.*

Roy Clement Knight. *Emeritus Professor of French, University College of Swansea, University of Wales.*

Dorothy Knowles. *Historian of modern French drama. Honorary Research Fellow, Bedford College, University of London.*

H.F. Koeper. *Professor of Architectural History, California State Polytechnic University, Pomona.*

Walter Kolneder. *Professor of Music, University of Karlsruhe, W.Ger.*

Leonie Judith Kramer. *Professor of Australian Literature, University of Sydney.*

Sven Møller Kristensen. *Professor of Scandinavian Literature, University of Copenhagen, Den., 1964–79.*

Stepan Andriyovich Kryzhanivsky. *Professor, Institute of Literature, Ukrainian S.S.R. Academy of Sciences, Kiev.*

George Alexander Kubler. *Sterling Professor of the History of Art, Yale University.*

Daniel P. Kunene. *Professor of African Languages and Literature, University of Wisconsin, Madison.*

David M. Kunzle. *Professor of Art, University of California, Los Angeles.*

Ado Kyrou. *Writer, motion-picture and television director. Author of* Luis Buñuel *and others.*

Kai L.K. Laitinen. *Associate Professor of Finnish Literature, University of Helsinki.*

Basil Raymond Lam (d. 1984). *Conductor and harpsichordist. Organizer of Pre-Classical Music Programmes, British Broadcasting Corporation.*

Norman Jones Lamb. *Former Senior Lecturer in Portuguese and Spanish, University of Liverpool.*

Richard Lane. *Research Associate, Honolulu Academy of Arts. Author of* Masters of the Japanese Print.

Paul M. Laporte. *Emeritus Professor of Art History, Immaculate Heart College, Los Angeles.*

Mary Madge Lascelles. *Fellow of the British Academy. Reader in English Literature, University of Oxford, 1966–67.*

Jan Lauts. *Director, Karlsruhe Art Gallery, W.Ger., 1956–73.*

Pierre Lavedan. *Director, Institute of Town Planning, University of Paris, 1940–65; Professor, Faculty of Letters, 1930–55.*

Janko Lavrin (d. 1986). *Professor of Russian Literature, University of Nottingham, Eng., 1923–53.*

Reginald Norcom Lawrence (d. 1967). *Playwright. Lecturer in Speech, City College, City University of New York.*

Frederick Laws (d. 1976). *Free-lance journalist and art critic.*

Robert Layton. *Producer, Music Talks, British Broadcasting Corporation, London.*

Luis Leal. *Emeritus Professor of Spanish, University of Illinois, Urbana.*

Lewis Leary. *William Rand Kenan, Jr., Professor Emeritus of English, University of North Carolina at Chapel Hill.*

Raymond Lebègue. *Emeritus Professor of 16th- and 17th-Century French Literature, University of Paris. Officer of the Legion of Honour.*

Robert Lebel. *Art expert and critic. Author of* On Marcel Duchamp *and others.*

Eileen Le Breton. *Reader in French, Bedford College, University of London.*

Clifford Leech (d. 1977). *Professor of English, University of Toronto, 1963–74.*

Trevor LeGassick. *Professor of Arabic, University of Michigan, Ann Arbor.*

(Mary) Dominica Legge. *Emeritus Professor of Anglo-Norman Studies, University of Edinburgh.*

Andrew George Lehmann. *Professor, School of European Studies, University of Buckingham, Eng.*

Richard Lepine. *Free-lance writer on African literature.*

Pierre Leprohon. *Writer and journalist. Author of* Jean Renoir; Charles Chaplin; Antonioni; *and others.*

Laurence Elliot Libin. *Curator of Musical Instruments, Metropolitan Museum of Art, New York City.*

Ronald William Lightbown. *Keeper of the Library, Victoria and Albert Museum, London; Assistant Keeper, Department of Metalwork, 1964–73.*

Bernth Lindfors. *Professor of English and African Literatures, University of Texas at Austin.*

Sten Hjalmar Lindroth. *Professor of the History of Science and Ideas, University of Uppsala, Swed.*

Anne Lippert. *Professor of French, Ohio Northern University, Ada.*

René Felix Lissens. *Emeritus Professor of Dutch and General Literature, St. Ignatius University Faculty, Antwerp.*

David Mathias Lloyd-Jones. *Musicologist and conductor. Artistic Director, Opera North, Leeds, Eng.*

Edward Lockspeiser (d. 1973). *Writer and broadcaster on music. Author of* Debussy: His Life and Mind *and others.*

David Loshak. *Assistant Professor of Art History, University of Wisconsin, Madison, 1958–64.*

John Evelyn Lowe. *Director, Weald and Downland Open Air Museum, Sussex, Eng., 1969–74. Principal, West Dean College, 1972–78.*

Constance Lowenthal. *Assistant Museum Educator, Department of Public Education, Metropolitan Museum of Art, New York City.*

Bates Lowry. *Director, National Building Museum, Washington, D.C. Professor of Art History, University of Massachusetts, Boston, 1971–80.*

Wilfrid Irvine Lucas (d. 1973). *Professor of German, University of Southampton, Eng., 1954–71.*

Georg Hans Luck. *Professor of Classics, Johns Hopkins University, Baltimore.*

Kenneth Schuyler Lynn. *Professor of History, Johns Hopkins University, Baltimore.*

Henry Julius Philip Maas. *Joint Head of Academic Staff and Tutor in Classics, Moreton Hall, Oswestry, Eng. Coeditor of* The Letters of Ernest Dowson *and others.*

Thomas Ollive Mabbott (d. 1968). *Professor of English, Hunter College, City University of New York, 1946–66.*

Richard Dyer MacCann. *Professor of Film, University of Iowa, Iowa City.*

Giovanni Macchia. *Professor of French Language and Literature, University of Rome.*

Ivy Lilian McClelland. *Former Reader in Spanish, University of Glasgow.*

Arthur Kilgore McComb (deceased). *Author of* The Baroque Painters of Italy *and others.*

Raven I. McDavid, Jr. (d. 1984). *Professor of English and of Linguistics, University of Chicago, 1964–77.*

The Rev. Eric McDermott, S.J. *Associate Professor Emeritus of History, Georgetown University, Washington, D.C.*

Sheila D. McDonough. *Professor of Religion, Sir George Williams University, Montreal.*

Robert Law McDougall. *Professor of English; Carleton University, Ottawa; General Editor,* The Carleton Library.

James Walter McFarlane. *Professorial Fellow in European Literature, University of East Anglia, Norwich, Eng.*

Sheila Roberts McGuire. *Professor of English and African Studies, Michigan State University, East Lansing.*

Joseph Machlis. *Emeritus Professor of Music, Queens College, City University of New York.*

Christine McHugh. *Associate, Joseph D. Kaplan & Son, P.C.* (law firm) *Trenton, N.J.*

Roy Donald McMullen (d. 1984). *Art historian, Author of* Art, Affluence, and Alienation; The World of Marc Chagall; *and others.*

Hugo A. McPherson. *Professor of English, McGill University, Montreal. Chairman and Commissioner, National Film Board of Canada, Montreal, 1967–70.*

Walter James Macqueen-Pope (d. 1960). *Writer on the theatre. Author of* Haymarket: Theatre of Perfection *and others.*

David Magarshack (d. 1977). *Author of* Chekhov the Dramatist; Dostoevsky; Pushkin: A Biography *and many other works on Russian writers.*

Claude-Edmonde Magny (d. 1966). *Teacher of Philosophy, University of Paris.*

Francis Peabody Magoun, Jr. (d. 1979). *Professor of English, Harvard University, 1951–61.*

Jean Mallion. *Lecturer, Faculty of Literature and Humane Studies, University of Grenoble, France.*

William P. Malm. *Professor of Music, University of Michigan, Ann Arbor.*

Charles Mancuso. *Associate Professor of the Performing Arts, State University of New York College at Buffalo.*

William Somervell Mann. *Music Critic, The Times* (*London*).

Roger Manvell. *Biographer and film historian. Professor of Film, Boston University. Director, British Film Academy, 1947–59.*

Leslie A. Marchand. *Emeritus Professor of English, Rutgers University, New Brunswick, N.J.*

Valerio Mariani (deceased). *Professor of the History of Art, University of Naples.*

Sidney Marrat. *Journalist, literary critic, and theatre historian.*

Leonard Cyril Martin (d. 1976). *King Alfred Professor of English Literature, University of Liverpool, 1929–51.*

Colin Mason (d. 1971). *Music critic. Editor, Tempo, 1964–71.*

D.E.S. Maxwell. *Professor of English, York University, Toronto.*

Claude Albert Mayer. *Former Professor and Head, Department of French, University of Liverpool.*

Ralph Mayer (d. 1979). *Painter. Director, Artists Technical Research Institute. Lecturer in Painting, Columbia University, 1944–64.*

El-Hadji Mbengue. *Associate Professor of African Studies, Howard University, Washington, D.C.*

Wesley Milgate. *Emeritus Professor of English, Australian National University, Canberra.*

John Miller. *Researcher and writer on music.*

Sandra Millikin. *Free-lance architectural historian. Lecturer in the History of Art, Open University, Walton, Eng., 1971–73.*

Henry A. Millon. *Dean, Center for Advanced Study in the Visual Arts, National Gallery of Art, Washington, D.C.*

William Mishler. *Associate Professor of Scandinavian, University of Minnesota, Minneapolis.*

Donald (Charles Peter) Mitchell. *Music critic and publisher. Chairman, Faber Music Ltd., London.*

Jean Mitry. *Professor and Director, Cinema Division, Institute of Art and Archaeology, University of Paris I.*

Arthur Mizener. *Mellon Foundation Professor Emeritus of Humanities, Cornell University, Ithaca, N.Y.*

Arve Sverre Moen (d. 1976). *Cultural Editor,* Arbeiderbladet (*newspaper*) *Oslo. Member of the Board, Edvard Munch Museum, Oslo.*

Hans Moldenhauer. *Musicologist. Director, Moldenhauer Archives. President, Spokane Conservatory of Music and Allied Arts, Inc., Wash.*

Agnes Mongan. *Emeritus Curator of Drawings, Fogg Art Museum, Harvard University.*

Lillian Moore (d. 1967). *Dancer. Member of Faculty, American Ballet Center, New York City.*

Sonia Moore. *Founder and President, American Center for Stanislavski Theatre Art, Inc., New York City. Founder and Artistic Director, American Stanislavski Theatre.*

Will G. Moore (d. 1978). *Reader in French Literature, University of Oxford.*

Albert Mordell (deceased). *Author of* Quaker Militant: John Greenleaf Whittier *and others.*

Anne-Marie de Moret. *Free-lance writer on African literature.*

Edwin George Morgan. *Poet. Titular Professor of English, University of Glasgow, 1975–80.*

Brita Maud Ellen Mortensen (d. 1958). *Lecturer in Swedish, University of Cambridge, 1950–58.*

Charles Moseley. *Free-lance writer.*

Frank Luther Mott (d. 1964). *Dean, School of Journalism, University of Missouri, Columbia, 1942–51.*

Joachim Müller. *Professor of German Literature, Friedrich Schiller University of Jena, E.Ger.*

Hugo Munsterberg. *Professor of Oriental Art, Bard College, Annandale-on-Hudson, New York.*

Peter J. Murray. *Emeritus Professor of the History of Art, Birkbeck College, University of London.*

Reginald P.C. Mutter. *Emeritus Professor of English Literature, University of Sussex, Brighton, Eng.*

Bernard S. Myers. *Art historian. Editor in Chief and Manager, Art Books Department, McGraw-Hill Book Company, New York City, 1958–70.*

Rollo H. Myers (d. 1985). *Writer on music. Author of* Music in the Modern World; Ravel: Life and Works *and others.*

Maurice Nadeau. *Editor,* Lettres Nouvelles *and* La Quinzaine Littéraire, *Paris.*

Alois M. Nagler. *Henry McCormick Professor Emeritus of Dramatic History and Criticism, Yale University.*

James Thompson Nardin. *Professor of English, Louisiana State University, Baton Rouge.*

Ray Nash (d. 1982). *Professor of Art, Dartmouth College, Hanover, N.H., 1949–70.*

Robert J. Nelson. *Professor of French and Comparative Literature, University of Illinois, Urbana.*

Israel Vladimirovich Nestyev. *Chief Scientist, Research Institute of History of Arts, Moscow.*

Arthur Hobart Nethercot. *Franklyn Bliss Snyder Professor Emeritus of English, Northwestern University, Evanston, Ill.*

Dika Newlin. *Composer. Professor of Music, Virginia Commonwealth University, Richmond.*

Robert Brayton Nichols. *Landscape architect.*

Norman Cornthwaite Nicholson. *Poet and critic. Author of* H.G. Wells *and others.*

Romola Nijinsky (d. 1978). *Author of* Nijinsky; The Last Years of Nijinsky.

Robert Niklaus. *Emeritus Professor of French, University of Exeter, Eng.*

Arnoldus Noach (d. 1976). *Professor of the History of Art and Architecture, University of Leeds, Eng.*

J. Jeremy Noble. *Associate Professor of Music, State University of New York at Buffalo.*

Linda Weinberg Nochlin. *Distinguished Professor of Art History, Graduate Center, City University of New York.*

Paul F. Norton. *Professor of Art, University of Massachusetts, Amherst.*

Bonnie Oberman. *Free-lance writer.*

Francis Valentine O'Connor. *Director, Raphael Research Enterprises* (*fine arts consultants*), *New York City. Editor, Federal Art Patronage Notes.*

Donald Mitchell Oenslager (d. 1975). *Designer of scenery and theatre consultant. Professor of Scene Design, Yale University.*

James Francis O'Gorman. *Grace Slack McNeil Professor of American Art, Wellesley College, Mass.*

Kenneth O'Leary. *Former Associate Professor of English, Seton Hall University, South Orange, N. J.*

Aladar Olgyay (d. 1963). *Architect. Author of* Solar Control and Shading Devices *and others.*

Carola Oman (Lady Lenanton) (d. 1978). *Biographer. Author of* David Garrick *and others.*

Peter M. Opie (d. 1982). *Coauthor of* The Oxford Dictionary of Nursery Rhymes; The Lore and Language of Schoolchildren; Children's Games in Street and Playground.

Masako Osako. *Free-lance writer on Japanese literature and affairs.*

Christian F. Otto. *Professor of Architecture, Cornell University, Ithaca, N.Y.*

Peter D. Owen. *Painter and printmaker. Former Senior Lecturer, Croydon College of Design and Technology, Eng.*

Oyekan Owomoyela. *Professor of Literature and Drama, University of Nebraska, Lincoln.*

(William Cyril) Desmond Pacey (d. 1975). *Vice President; Professor of English, University of New Brunswick, Fredericton.*

Sir Denys (Lionel) Page (d. 1978). *Regius Professor of Greek, University of Cambridge, 1950–73.*

George Duncan Painter. *Assistant Keeper in charge of incunabula, Department of Printed Books, British Library, London, 1954–74.*

Rodolfo Pallucchini. *Director, Institute of Art History, Giorgio Cini Foundation, Venice.*

Guido Pannain (d. 1977). *Professor of the History of Music, S. Pietro a Maiella Conservatory of Music, Naples.*

John T. Paoletti. *Professor of Art History, Wesleyan University, Middletown, Conn.*

Alexander A. Parker. *Emeritus Professor of Spanish Literature, University of Texas at Austin.*

Robert Lewis Parkinson. *Chief Librarian and Historian, Circus World Museum, Baraboo, Wis.*

Dorothy Margaret Partington. *Literary historian and critic.*

Roy Pascal (d. 1980). *Professor of German, University of Birmingham, Eng., 1939–69.*

Günter Passavant. *Editor, Journals of the German Institute for the History of Art, Florence.*

David Patterson. *President, Oxford Centre for Post-Graduate Hebrew Studies; Cowley Lecturer in Post-Biblical Hebrew, University of Oxford; Fellow of St. Cross College, Oxford.*

Damião António Peres. *Former Professor of History, University of Coimbra, Port. Member, Portuguese Academy of History.*

Roy Perrott. *Free-lance book editor and consultant. Author of* The Aristocrats.

Lino Pertile. *Reader in Italian, University of Sussex, Brighton, Eng.*

Gabor F. Peterdi. *Painter and printmaker. Professor of Printmaking, Yale University.*

Helene Peters. *Professor of French, Macalester College, St. Paul, Minn.*

Edwin Burr Pettet. *Former Schulman Professor of Theatre Arts, Brandeis University, Waltham, Mass.*

Friedrich Pfister (deceased). *Professor of Classical Philology, University of Würzburg, W.Ger.*

James Smith Pierce. *Professor of Art History, University of Kentucky, Lexington.*

André Pierre (d. 1966). *Member of Editorial Staff,* Le Monde, *Paris, 1944–58.*

Hovhanness Israel Pilikian. *Theatre director. Founder and Artistic Director of Hana-no Mask-Theatre Company.*

Vivian de Sola Pinto (d. 1969). *Professor of English, University of Nottingham, Eng., 1938–61.*

Henry C. Pitz (d. 1976). *Writer and painter. Professor of Art, Philadelphia College of Art, 1934–60.*

Adolf K. Placzek. *Avery Librarian Emeritus, Columbia University.*

Giles William Playfair. *Free-lance writer. Professor of Drama, Williams College, Williamstown, Mass., 1956–63.*

Henry A. Pochmann (d. 1973). *Professor of English, University of Wisconsin, Madison, 1938–71.*

Georg Poensgen. *Formerly Director of the Palatinate Museum, Heidelberg, W.Ger.*

Peter J. Pollack (d. 1978). *Photographer and lecturer. Author of* The Picture History of Photography *and others.*

Sir John Pope-Hennessy. *Consultative Chairman, Department of European Paintings, Metropolitan Museum of Art, New York City. Professor of Fine Arts, New York University.*

William V. Porter. *Associate Professor of Music History and Literature, Northwestern University, Evanston, Ill.*

Frederick A(lbert) Pottle. *Sterling Professor Emeritus of English, Yale University.*

John Povey. *Professor of English, University of California, Los Angeles.*

Anthony Powell. *Novelist, playwright, and literary critic.*

Mario Praz (d. 1982). *Professor of English Language and Literature, University of Rome, 1934–66.*

Joseph Prescott. *Emeritus Professor of English, Wayne State University, Detroit.*

Cecil John Layton Price. *Emeritus Professor of English Language and Literature, University College of Swansea, University of Wales.*

Brian Priestman. *Orchestral conductor. Dean, Faculty of Music, University of Cape Town.*

Jules David Prown. *Professor of the History of Art, Yale University.*

Ricardo Quintana. *Emeritus Professor of English, University of Wisconsin, Madison.*

Regula B. Qureshi. *Mactaggart Fellow, Department of Music, University of Alberta, Edmonton.*

Chaim Rabin. *Former Professor of Hebrew Language, Hebrew University of Jerusalem.*

Frederic James Edward Raby (d. 1966). *Fellow and Lecturer, Jesus College, University of Cambridge, 1948–54. Author of* A History of Christian Latin Poetry *and others.*

Kathleen Raine. *Poet and scholar. Author of* Collected Poems; Blake and Tradition; *and others.*

Gilbert Reaney. *Professor of Musicology, University of California, Los Angeles.*

Frederick Stephen Reckert. *Camoens Professor of Portuguese, King's College, University of London.*

Willi Reich (d. 1980). *Music critic. Author of* The Life and Work of Alban Berg *and many others.*

John Cowie Reid (d. 1972). *Professor of English, University of Auckland, New Zealand.*

Hans Siegbert Reiss. *Professor of German, University of Bristol, Eng.*

Graham Reynolds. *Keeper, Departments of Prints and Drawings, 1961–74, and of Paintings, 1959–74, Victoria and Albert Museum, London.*

Edgar Preston Richardson (d. 1985). *President, Pennsylvania Academy of the Fine Arts, 1968–70. Director, Detroit Institute of Arts, 1945–62, and Winterthur Museum, Wilmington, Del., 1962–66.*

Margaret Ann Richardson. *Deputy Curator, Drawings Collection, Royal Institute of British Architects, London.*

Gisela Marie Augusta Richter (d. 1972). *Curator, Greek and Roman Department, Metropolitan Museum of Art, New York City.*

Christopher Bruce Ricks. *Professor of English, University of Cambridge.*

Alexander L. Ringer. *Professor of Musicology, University of Illinois, Urbana.*

William Andrew Ringler, Jr. *Emeritus Professor of English, University of Chicago. Senior Research Associate, Huntington Library, San Marino, Calif.*

Charles Martin Robertson. *Lincoln Professor of Classical Archaeology and Art, University of Oxford, 1961–78.*

Jean Robertson. *Former Senior Lecturer in English Literature, University of Southampton, Eng.*

Charles Alan Robson. *Former Reader in French Philology and Old French Literature, University of Oxford.*

William Wallace Robson. *Masson Professor of English Literature, University of Edinburgh.*

Jerome Laurence Alexander Roche. *Senior Lecturer in Music, University of Durham, Eng.*

Anne F. Rockwell. *Free-lance writer and illustrator. Author of* Glass, Stones and Crown: The Abbé Suger and the Building of St. Denis *and others.*

Emir Rodríguez-Monegal. *Professor of Latin American and Comparative Literature, Yale University.*

Leonard R. Rogers. *Sculptor and writer. Former Head, Faculty of Three-Dimensional Design, College of Art and Design, Loughborough, Eng.*

Arnold Rood. *Professor of Dramatic Art, Dowling College, Oakdale, N.Y.*

Pierre M. Rosenberg. *Curator, Department of Paintings, Louvre Museum, Paris.*

Sybil (Marion) Rosenfeld. *Former Joint Editor,* Theatre Notebook; *former Joint Honorary Secretary, Society for Theatre Research.*

Marion Dean Ross. *Emeritus Professor of Architecture, University of Oregon, Eugene.*

Ronald Rossner. *Free-lance writer on African literature.*

Cecil Roth (d. 1970). *Editor in Chief,* Encyclopaedia Judaica. *Reader in Jewish Studies, University of Oxford, 1939–64.*

The Rev. Erik Reginald Routley (d. 1982). *Professor of Church Music, Westminster Choir College, Princeton, N.J., 1975–82.*

Eleanor Ruggles. *Biographer. Author of* Prince of Players: Edwin Booth *and others.*

Eberhard Ruhmer. *Former Curator in Chief, Bavarian State Painting Collection, Munich.*

Harold Rutland (d. 1977). *Music critic.* Examiner, *Trinity College of Music, London. Editor,* The Musical Times, *1957–60.*

Elizabeth Sabiston. *Academic Adviser, Stong College, York University, Downsview, Ont.*

Stanley John Sadie. *Music critic,* The Times (*London*). *Editor of* The Musical Times; The New Grove Dictionary of Music and Musicians.

William Merritt Sale, Jr. (d. 1981). *Goldwin Smith Professor of English, Cornell University, Ithaca, N.Y.*

Mario Salmi (d. 1980). *Professor of the History of Medieval and Modern Art, University of Rome.*

Kaarlo Salo. *Former Attaché for Press and Cultural Affairs, Finnish Embassy, London.*

Lionel Salter. *Harpsichordist, pianist, and conductor. Assistant Controller of Music, British Broadcasting Corporation, London, 1967–74.*

Jeffrey L. Sammons. *Professor of German, Yale University.*

Claudio Sartori. *Chief, Office of Research and Indexing of the Italian Musical Funds, Braidense National Library, Milan.*

Angiola Sartorio. *Choreographer. Director of International Summer Dance School, Corona Del Mar, Calif. Former Head of the Dance Department, Sullins College, Bristol, Va.*

Tadao Sato. *Writer. Chairman, Japan Film P.E.N. Club. Author of* Kurosawa Akira no sekai *and others.*

Richard Anthony Sayce (d. 1977). *Fellow of Worcester College, Oxford; Reader in French Literature, University of Oxford.*

Byron Schaeffer, Jr. *Free-lance writer.*

Aaron Scharf. *Professor of Art History, Open University, Milton Keynes, Eng., 1969–82.*

Jefim H. Schirmann (d. 1981). *Professor of Hebrew Literature, Hebrew University of Jerusalem.*

Paul Schlueter. *Writer, editor, and lecturer on literary topics.*

Laurence E. Schmeckebier. *Emeritus Professor of Fine Arts and Emeritus Dean, School of Art, Syracuse University, N.Y.*

Nancy Schmidt. *Free-lance writer on African literature.*

Paul Waldo Schwartz. *Art Critic in Paris for* The New York Times *and* Studio International. *Author of* The Sculptor in His Studio.

Alexander Mackie Scott. *Reader in Scottish Literature, University of Glasgow.*

M.A. Screech. *Fielden Professor of French Language and Literature, University College, University of London.*

Humphrey Searle (d. 1982). *Composer. Professor of Composition, Royal College of Music, London.*

Nancy Seeger. *Free-lance writer on visual arts.*

Edward G. Seidensticker. *Professor of Japanese, Columbia University.*

William C. Seitz (d. 1974). *George R. Kenan, Jr., Professor of the History of Art, University of Virginia, Charlottesville, 1971–74.*

Charles Coleman Sellers. *Librarian, Dickinson College, Carlisle, Pa., 1956–68. Author of* Charles Willson Peale *and others.*

Jean Selz. *Art historian and critic. Member, International Association of Art Critics, Paris.*

Jorge de Sena (d. 1978). *Professor of Portuguese and Comparative Literature, University of California, Santa Barbara, 1970–78.*

Victor Ilyich Seroff (d. 1979). *Writer. Author of* Rachmaninoff *and others.*

Alexandrino E. Severino. *Professor of Portuguese, Vanderbilt University, Nashville, Tenn.*

Charles Seymour, Jr. (d. 1977). *Professor of the History of Art, Yale University, 1954–77.*

Isaac Avi Shapiro. *Honorary Fellow, Shakespeare Institute, University of Birmingham, Eng.; former Senior Lecturer in English.*

Claude L. Shaver. *Alumni Professor Emeritus of Speech, Louisiana State University, Baton Rouge.*

Donald Leslie Shaw. *Professor of Latin American Studies, University of Edinburgh.*

Wendy Stedman Sheard. *Art historian. Author of* Antiquity in the Renaissance.

John K.G. Shearman. *Chairman, Department of Art and Archaeology, Princeton University.*

Sin-yan Shen. *President, Chinese Music Society of North America, Woodridge, Ill.*

David Julian Silverman. *Former Lecturer on Music, University of London.*

João Gaspar Simões. *Literary Critic,* Diario de Noticias, *Lisbon.*

Denis Sinor. *Distinguished Professor of Uralic and Altaic Studies and of History, Indiana University, Bloomington.*

Otto Skutsch. *Emeritus Professor of Latin, University College, University of London.*

Nicolas Slonimsky. *Conductor, composer, writer, and editor. Lecturer in Music, University of California, Los Angeles, 1964–67.*

F. Basil R. Smallman. *Alsop Professor Emeritus of Music, University of Liverpool.*

Arthur J(ames) M(arshall) Smith (d. 1980). *Professor of English and Poet-in-Residence, Michigan State University, East Lansing, 1960–72.*

Gilbert G. Smith. *Associate Professor of Spanish, North Carolina State University, Raleigh.*

Sheila Mary Smith. *Senior Lecturer in English, University of Nottingham, Eng.*

Whitney Smith. *Executive Director, Flag Research Center; Editor,* The Flag Bulletin, *Winchester, Mass.*

William Stevenson Smith (d. 1969). *Curator, Department of Egyptian Art, Museum of Fine Arts, Boston, 1956–69. Lecturer in Fine Arts, Harvard University, 1948–69.*

Craig Hugh Smyth. *Director, Villa I Tatti, Harvard Center for Italian Renaissance Studies, Florence; Professor of Fine Arts, Harvard University.*

M.R. Snodin. *Curatorial staff member, Department of Metalwork, Victoria and Albert Museum, London.*

Wilbert Snow (d. 1977). *Professor of English, Wesleyan University, Middletown, Conn., 1929–72.*

James E. Snyder. *Professor of Art History, Bryn Mawr College, Pa.*

David Sokol. *Professor of the History of Art and Architecture, University of Illinois, Chicago.*

Angelo Solmi. *Film critic,* Oggi (*weekly literary periodical*). *Former Managing Editor, Rizzoli Editore, Milan.*

Friedrich Solmsen. *Moses Slaughter Professor Emeritus of Classical Studies, University of Wisconsin, Madison.*

Kathrine Sorley Walker. *Free-lance writer, editor, and dance critic. Author of* Dance and Its Creators *and others.*

Brian C. Southam. *Publisher, Athlone Press, London. Author of* Jane Austen's Literary Manuscripts *and others.*

John Sparrow. *Warden of All Souls College, University of Oxford, 1952–77.*

George Speaight. *Former Editorial Director, George Rainbird Ltd. Author of* The History of the English Puppet Theatre *and others.*

Robert (William) Speaight (d. 1976). *Actor, biographer, critic, and fiction writer. Author of* Life of Hilaire Belloc *and others.*

Monroe K. Spears. *Moody Professor of English, Rice University, Houston, Texas.*

John R. Spencer. *Professor of Art, Duke University, Durham, N.C.*

Albert Sperisen. *Vice President in Charge of Production, Foote, Cone & Belding, San Francisco.*

Radcliffe Squires. *Poet. Professor of English, University of Michigan, Ann Arbor, 1963–81.*

Robert Wooster Stallman (d. 1982). *Professor of English, University of Connecticut, Storrs, 1953–74.*

William Bedell Stanford (d. 1984). *Chancellor, University of Dublin, 1982–84; Regius Professor of Greek, 1940–80.*

Jerry Stannard. *Professor of History of Science and Medicine, University of Kansas, Lawrence.*

Enid Starkie (d. 1970). *Reader in French Literature, University of Oxford; Fellow, Somerville College, Oxford, 1934–65.*

Wolfgang Stechow (d. 1974). *Professor of Fine Arts, Oberlin College, Ohio, 1940–63.*

Richard G. Stern. *Professor of English, University of Chicago.*

Frederick William Sternfeld. *Former Reader in the History of Music, University of Oxford.*

Denis William Stevens. *Professor of Musicology, Columbia University, 1964–76.*

Halsey Stevens. *Composer. Emeritus Professor of Music, University of Southern California, Los Angeles.*

John I.M. Stewart. *Reader in English Literature, University of Oxford, 1969–73.*

Noel Stock. *Professor of English, University of Toledo, Ohio.*

Göran Stockenström. *Professor and Chairman, Department of Scandinavian, University of Minnesota, Minneapolis.*

Sewell Stokes (d. 1979). *Author and dramatist. Author of* Isadora: An Intimate Portrait *and others.*

Eric Stone. *Lecturer in Modern History, University of Oxford; Fellow and Tutor in Medieval History, Keble College, Oxford.*

Gleb Struve (d. 1985). *Professor of Slavic Languages and Literatures, University of California, Berkeley, 1947–67.*

Michael Sullivan. *Christensen Professor of Oriental Art, Stanford University, Calif.*

Sir John Summerson. *Curator, Sir John Soane's House and Museum, London.*

James R. Sutherland. *Emeritus Professor of Modern English Literature, University of London.*

Denys Sutton. *Editor,* Apollo *magazine. Art Critic,* Financial Times. *Author of* The Art of James McNeill Whistler *and others.*

W.A. Swanberg. *Free-lance writer. Author of* Dreiser *and others.*

Frederick A. Sweet. *Curator of American Painting and Sculpture, Art Institute of Chicago, 1952–68.*

Jean-Guy Sylvestre. *National Librarian of Canada, Library of Parliament, Ottawa.*

Charles Johnson Taggart. *Free-lance writer.*

Stanley Taikeff. *Playwright and poet.*

James S. Tassie. *Adjunct Professor of French, Carleton University, Ottawa.*

Allen Tate (d. 1979). *Poet and critic. Regents' Professor of English, University of Minnesota, Minneapolis, 1966–68.*

Abdallah at-Tayib. *Vice-Chancellor; Professor of Arabic, University of Khartoum, Sudan.*

John Russell Taylor. *Art Critic,* The Times *(London); Film Critic, 1962–73. Professor of Cinema, University of Southern California, Los Angeles, 1972–78.*

Owen Reece Taylor (d. 1983). *Professor of French, Queen Mary College, University of London, 1969–77.*

Ronald Jack Taylor. *Professor of German, University of Sussex, Brighton, Eng.*

Walter Terry (d. 1982). *Dance critic and editor,* Saturday Review *magazine;* New York Herald Tribune; *and others.*

David Christopher Traherne Thomas. *Former Assistant Director of Art, Arts Council of Great Britain, London. Joint compiler of* The First Hundred Years of the Royal Academy, 1769–1868 (*catalog of Royal Academy Winter Exhibition, London, 1951–52*).

Lawrance R. Thompson (d. 1973). *Holmes Professor of Belles-Lettres, Princeton University, 1968–73; Professor of English, 1951–73.*

Friedrich Thöne (deceased). *Art historian. Author of* Lucas Cranach der Ältere *and others.*

Anthony Thwaite. *Poet and critic. Coeditor,* Encounter. *Author of* Contemporary English Poetry *and others.*

Marion Rose Tinling. *Coeditor of* The Secret Diary of William Byrd of Westover *and others.*

Joyce M.S. Tompkins. *Reader in English, University of London, 1948–65.*

Louis Tremaine. *Free-lance writer on African literature.*

Brian Lewis Trowell. *King Edward Professor of Music, King's College, University of London.*

C.H. Truman. *Curatorial staff member, Victoria and Albert Museum, London.*

Constantine Athanasius Trypanis. *Minister of Culture and Science, Government of Greece, 1974–77. Professor of Classical Languages and Literatures, University of Chicago, 1968–74.*

Martin Turnell (d. 1979). *Writer. Head, Programme Contracts Department, BBC, London, 1959–69.*

Arlin Turner (d. 1980). *James B. Duke Professor of English, Duke University, Durham, N.C., 1974–79.*

Darwin T. Turner. *Professor of English; Director, Afro-American Studies, University of Iowa, Iowa City.*

Valev Uibopuu. *Novelist. Editor, Estonian Writers' Co-operative, Lund, Sweden.*

Vernon Philip Underwood. *Former Professor of French, University College, University of London.*

Dora Vallier. *Art critic. Author of* Henri Rousseau: Catalogue raisonné de l'oeuvre; Henri Rousseau; *and others.*

Eugene Vanderpool. *Professor of Archaeology, American School of Classical Studies at Athens.*

Milos Velimirovic. *Professor of Music, University of Virginia, Charlottesville.*

Paul Viallaneix. *Professor of French Literature; Director, Centre for Romantic Research, University of Clermont-Ferrand, Fr.*

Michele Vishny. *Art historian and critic. Contributor to* Arts Magazine.

Wolf Von Eckardt. *Design Critic,* Time *magazine. Architecture Critic,* The Washington Post, *1963–81.*

Klaus Philipp Wachsmann. *Emeritus Professor of Music, Northwestern University, Evanston, Ill.*

Hyatt H. Waggoner. *Emeritus Professor of English, Brown University, Providence, R.I.*

John Wain. *Novelist, poet, and critic. Professor of Poetry, University of Oxford, 1973–78.*

Hugh Wakefield (d. 1984). *Keeper, Department of Circulation, Victoria and Albert Museum, London, 1960–75.*

Frank Walker (d. 1962). *Musicologist and broadcaster.*

David Harold Wallace. *Chief, Branch of Reference Services, National Park Service, U.S. Department of the Interior, Harpers Ferry, W.Va., 1974–80.*

Irving Wallace. *Novelist and biographer. Author of* The Fabulous Showman: The Life and Times of P.T. Barnum; The Man; *and many others.*

Francis James Warne. *Former Senior Lecturer in French, University of Bristol, Eng.*

Sir Ellis K. Waterhouse (d. 1985). *Director of Studies, Paul Mellon Centre for Studies in British Art, London, 1970–73. Barber Professor of Fine Arts; Director, Barber Institute of Fine Arts, University of Birmingham, Eng., 1952–70.*

Sir F.J.B. Watson. *Director of the Wallace Collection, London, 1963–74. Surveyor of the Queen's Works of Art, 1963–72.*

Paul F. Watson. *Associate Professor of the History of Art, University of Pennsylvania, Philadelphia.*

Max Wehrli. *Professor of the History of German Literature, University of Zürich.*

Sharon Weiner. *Free-lance writer.*

Stanley Weintraub. *Research Professor of English; Director, Institute for the Arts and Humanistic Studies, Pennsylvania State University, University Park.*

John S. Weissmann. *Musicologist.*

David Welch. *Assistant Professor of Music, Ramapo College, Mahwah, N.J.*

Arthur Frederick Wells (d. 1966). *Praelector in Classics, University College, University of Oxford.*

James M. Wells. *Former Vice President and Custodian Emeritus, John M. Wing Foundation on the History of Printing, Newberry Library, Chicago.*

Enid Elder Hancock Welsford (d. 1981). *Lecturer in English, University of Cambridge, 1923–59. Author of* The Court Masque; The Fool; *and others.*

Francis William Wentworth-Sheilds (d. 1969). *Artist. Principal Lecturer, Department of Printing and Graphic Design, Twickenham College of Technology, Middlesex, Eng., 1966–69.*

Algot Werin (d. 1975). *Professor of Literature, University of Lund, Sweden.*

Carroll W. Westfall. *Associate Professor of the History of Art and Architecture, University of Illinois, Chicago.*

Geoffrey Weston. *Editorial staff member,* The Times (*London*). *Former Senior Sub-editor,* Country Life.

Sir Jack Allan Westrup (d. 1975). *Professor of Music, University of Oxford, 1946–71; Fellow of Wadham College, Oxford, 1947–71.*

Harold E. Wethey (d. 1984). *Professor of the History of Art, University of Michigan, Ann Arbor, 1946–72.*

Margaret Dickens Whinney (d. 1975). *Reader in the History of Art, University of London, 1950–64.*

D. Maxwell White. *Professor and Head, Department of Italian Language and Literature, University of Leeds, Eng.*

David White. *Faculty member, Department of Visual Arts, Trinity College, University of Dublin.*

E.B. White (d. 1985). *Writer. Contributing Editor,* The New Yorker.

Eric Walter White. *Former Assistant Secretary and Literature Director, Arts Council of Great Britain, London.*

Dorothy Whitelock (d. 1982). *Elrington and Bosworth Professor of Anglo-Saxon, University of Cambridge; Fellow of Newnham College, Cambridge, 1957–69.*

John Humphreys Whitfield. *Serena Professor Emeritus of Italian Language and Literature, University of Birmingham, Eng.*

Richard Whittingham. *Free-lance writer.*

David S. Wiley. *Director, African Studies Program, Michigan State University, East Lansing.*

John Ritchie Wilkie. *Emeritus Professor of German, University of Aberdeen, Scot.*

Frank Willett. *Director and Titular Professor, Hunterian Museum and Art Gallery, University of Glasgow.*

John William Mills Willett. *Writer and editor. Planning Editor,* The Times (*London*) *Literary Supplement, 1969–71.*

Basil Willey (d. 1978). *King Edward VII Professor of English Literature, University of Cambridge, 1946–64.*

Geoffrey Wills. *Free-lance writer on antiques. Author of "Automata" in* The Concise Encyclopedia of Antiques.

Marjorie Winters. *Free-lance writer on African literature.*

William Witte. *Emeritus Professor of German, University of Aberdeen, Scot.*

Rudolf Wittkower (d. 1971). *Professor of the History of Art, Columbia University, 1956–68.*

Friedrich Wilhelm Wodtke (d. 1973). *Professor of German Literature, Kiel University, W.Ger., and Athens University, Greece.*

Mary Woodall. *Director, City Museum and Art Gallery, Birmingham, Eng., 1956–64.*

George Woodcock. *Free-lance writer. Editor,* Canadian Literature (*quarterly*), *University of British Columbia, Vancouver, 1959–77.*

Raymond Bernard Wood-Jones. *Reader in Architecture, Victoria University of Manchester.*

John E. Woods. *Associate Professor of History, University of Chicago.*

John Woodward. *Former Keeper, Birmingham City Museum and Art Gallery, Eng.*

Edward J. Wormley. *Products and interior designer. Former Design Director, Dunbar Furniture Corporation of Indiana, New York City.*

Robert M. Wren. *Professor of English, University of Houston, Texas.*

Stephen Graham Wright. *Former Adviser at the National Library of Ethiopia and at Haile Selassie I University, Addis Ababa.*

Patrick Maurice Yarker. *Former Senior Lecturer in English Literature, King's College, University of London.*

Percy Marshall Young. *Composer. Director of Music, Wolverhampton College of Technology, Eng., 1944–66.*

Philip Young. *Evan Pugh Professor of English, Pennsylvania State University, University Park.*

Oleksa Eliseyovich Zasenko. *Head, Department of the History of Ukrainian Prerevolutionary Literature, Institute of Literature, Ukrainian S.S.R. Academy of Sciences, Kiev.*

Nicolas M. Zernov (d. 1980). *Spalding Lecturer in Eastern Orthodox Culture, University of Oxford, 1947–66.*

Vladimir Viktorovich Zhdanov. *Literary critic. Assistant to the Chief Editor, Kratkaya Literaturnaya Entsiklopediya, Moscow.*

Leon M. Zolbrod. *Professor of Asian Studies, University of British Columbia, Vancouver.*

Part Seven. Technology

Samuel Roy Aldrich. *Emeritus Professor of Agronomy, University of Illinois, Urbana.*

Robert Theodore Alexander. *Captain, U.S. Coast Guard (retired); former Chief, Civil Engineering Division, U.S. Coast Guard Headquarters, Washington, D.C.*

Bruce E. Anderson. *Former Head, (gun) Propellant Research, U.S. Army Ordnance, Research and Development Division.*

Joseph Chapman Anderson. *Professor of Electrical Materials, Imperial College of Science and Technology, University of London.*

Walter Harry Green Armytage. *Emeritus Professor of Education, University of Sheffield, Eng. Author of* A Social History of Engineering.

A. Richard Baldwin. *Vice President and Executive Director of Research, Cargill, Inc., Minneapolis, Minn., 1964–73. Editor,* Journal of the American Oil Chemists' Society.

Stanley S. Ballard. *Distinguished Service Professor of Physics, University of Florida, Gainesville.*

Karl A. Bauer. *Former President, Carl Zeiss, Inc., New York City.*

Sir Frederick Charles Bawden (d. 1972). *Director of Rothamsted Experimental Station, Harpenden, Eng., 1958–72.*

Roy E. Beal. *Manager, Welding Research, Illinois Institute of Technology Research Institute, Chicago.*

Jesse W. Beams (d. 1977). *Professor of Physics, University of Virginia, Charlottesville, 1930–69.*

T. Keilor Bentley. *Director, Owens Art Gallery, Mount Allison University, Sackville, N.B. Superintendent, Alexander Graham Bell Museum, Baddeck, Nova Scotia, 1959–64.*

Don H. Berkebile. *Associate Curator, Division of Transportation, Smithsonian Institution, Washington, D.C., 1974–81.*

Henry H. Billings. *Free-lance writer, illustrator, and mural painter. Author of* Bridges *and others.*

Raymond C. Binder (d. 1978). *Professor of Mechanical Engineering, University of Southern California, Los Angeles, 1960–78.*

Orlan William Boston. *Emeritus Professor of Mechanical and Production Engineering, University of Michigan, Ann Arbor.*

John Boyd. *Consulting Engineer, Electro Mechanical Division, Westinghouse Electric Corporation, Cheswick, Pa.*

John E. Brekke. *Head, Hawaii Fruit Laboratory, U.S. Department of Agriculture, University of Hawaii, Honolulu.*

Benjamin Arthur Brock. *Director and Factory Manager, Brock's Fireworks Ltd., England.*

Matthew Joseph Bruccoli. *Jefferies Professor of English, University of South Carolina, Columbia.*

Nelson Hitchcock Budd. *Former Information and Public Relations Director, National Canners Association.*

Willem Burger. *Former Senior Lecturer in Maritime Studies, University of Wales Institute of Science and Technology, Cardiff.*

Thomas Burnett. *Research Officer, Ottawa Research Station, Canada Department of Agriculture.*

Henry R. Clauser. *Consultant,* Materials Engineering *magazine; Editor-Publisher, 1965–69; Editor, 1958–64; Associate Editor and Managing Editor, 1946–57.*

Donald George Coleman. *Compiler, Computerized Information Retrieval System,* Wood Science and Forest Products Journal, *Forest Products Research Society, Madison, Wis.*

John Paul Comstock. *Former Naval Architect, Newport News Shipbuilding and Dry Dock Company, Va.*

Grace Rogers Cooper. *Museum consultant. Curator, Division of Textiles, Smithsonian Institution, Washington, D.C., 1946–76.*

André George Corbet. *Lecturer in Maritime Studies, University of Wales Institute of Science and Technology, Cardiff.*

Edwin Alfred Course. *Senior Lecturer in Adult Education, University of Southampton, Eng. Author of* London Railways.

Alden S. Crafts. *Emeritus Professor of Botany, University of California, Davis.*

Daniel B. Dallas. *Editorial Director, Society of Manufacturing Engineers, Dearborn, Mich.; Editor-in-chief,* The Tool and Manufacturing Engineers Handbook.

Milton Rockwood Daniels (deceased). *Commodore, U.S. Coast Guard.*

C.W. Dannatt (d. 1962). *Professor, Royal School of Mines, University of London.*

Donald de Carle. *Author of* Horology; Practical Watch Repairing; *and many others.*

Nigel T.M. Dennis. *Technical Manager, Edwards High Vacuum (Division of BOC Ltd.), Crawley, Eng.*

Charles Dollfus (d. 1981). *Aeronautical historian. Founder and Director, Museum of the Air, Paris.*

Francis Donaldson (d. 1970). *Vice President, Mason & Hanger—Silas Mason, Inc., New York City. Author of* Practical Shaftsinking.

George Dubpernell. *Consultant, M & T Chemicals Inc., Southfield, Mich.; technical adviser, 1955–66.*

Peter Duff. *Former Editor,* The Shipping World, *London.*

LeRoy Dugan. *Professor of Food Science, Michigan State University, East Lansing.*

Frederick C. Durant III. *Aerospace historian. Assistant Director, Astronautics, National Air and Space Museum, Smithsonian Institution, Washington, D.C., 1965–81.*

Ernst R.G. Eckert. *Regents' Professor Emeritus of Mechanical Engineering, University of Minnesota, Minneapolis; Director, Thermodynamics and Heat Transfer Division, 1955–73.*

John F. Elliott. *Professor of Metallurgy, Massachusetts Institute of Technology, Cambridge.*

Victor A. Endersby. *Consulting civil engineer.*

Barbara Ensrud. *Writer and editor on food and wine.*

Daniel Snell Eppelsheimer. *Emeritus Professor of Metallurgical and Nuclear Engineering, University of Missouri, Rolla.*

Valeska Evertsbusch. *Biochemist and Technical Editor, Biomedical Research Division, Lawrence Radiation Laboratory, University of California, Livermore.*

Gordon Maskew Fair (d. 1970). *Abbott and James Lawrence Professor of Engineering; Gordon McKay Professor of Sanitary Engineering, Harvard University.*

Raymond E. Fielding. *Professor of Communications, University of Houston, Texas.*

Gerald Reginald Mansel Garratt. *Keeper, Department of Aeronautics and Marine Transport, Science Museum, London, 1966–71.*

Wesley Patterson Garrigus. *Emeritus Professor of Animal Husbandry, University of Kentucky, Lexington.*

Alan H. Gayfer. *Editorial consultant and technical adviser,* Cycling World, *London. Editor,* Cycling, *1964–69.*

Lucien Albert Gerardin. *Research Director, Future Studies, Groupe Thomson, Paris.*

Frank Gerrard. *President, Institute of Meat, London, 1960–62. Head of Department, National College of Food Technology, Smithfield, London, 1947–61.*

George Sweet Gibb. *Director of Communications, Balfour Company, Attleboro, Mass.*

Charles Harvard Gibbs-Smith (d. 1981). *Research Fellow, Science Museum, London, 1976–81. Keeper, Public Relations and Education Department, Victoria and Albert Museum, London, 1947–71.*

Keith Reginald Gilbert (d. 1973). *Keeper, Department of Mechanical and Civil Engineering, Science Museum, London.*

John B. Gordon (d. 1964). *Secretary, Bureau of Raw Materials for American Vegetable Oils and Fats Industries, Washington, D.C.*

Linton E. Grinter. *Emeritus Dean, Graduate School, University of Florida, Gainesville; Executive Vice President, 1969–70. Author of* Design of Modern Steel Structures *and others.*

Harold James Grossman (d. 1967). *Marketing consultant on beverages. Author of* Grossman's Guide to Wines, Spirits and Beers *and others.*

Hagiwara Takahiro. *Emeritus Professor of Earthquake Research Institute, University of Tokyo.*

Andrew Edward Hahn. *Former Managing Editor,* Quality of Sheffield, *Sheffield, Eng.*

Robert W. Hamilton. *Consultant in environmental physiology. Research Supervisor, Research and Development Laboratory, Ocean Systems, Inc., Tarrytown, N.Y., 1969–74.*

Stanley Baines Hamilton. *Chartered civil and structural engineer. Writer and editor on engineering history.*

Francis Hamit. *Free-lance writer.*

Carl Hanson (d. 1985). *Pro-Vice-Chancellor; Professor of Chemical Engineering, University of Bradford, Eng.*

Wayne V. Harsha. *Editor,* Inland Printer/American Lithographer, *1951–70; Executive Editor, 1970–75.*

Richard S. Hartenberg. *Emeritus Professor of Mechanical Engineering, Northwestern University, Evanston, Ill.*

Alden Hatch (d. 1975). *Novelist, biographer, and historian. Author of* Remington Arms in American History *and others.*

John M. Hayes. *Emeritus Professor of Structural Engineering, Purdue University, West Lafayette, Ind.*

John F. Hayward (d. 1983). *Associate Director, Sotheby Parke-Bernet and Company, London and New York City. Deputy Keeper, Victoria and Albert Museum, London, 1946–65.*

Phyllis West Heathcote. *Former Paris correspondent for women's topics,* The Guardian (*Manchester*) *and* Glasgow Herald.

John B. Heffernan. *Rear Admiral, U.S. Navy (retired). Secretary, Naval Historical Foundation, Washington, D.C. Director of Naval History, Navy Department, 1946–56.*

Philip Heiberger. *Research Associate, E.I. du Pont de Nemours & Company, Inc., Philadelphia.*

Russell W. Henke. *Consulting engineer. Education Consultant, Institute for Fluid Power Education.*

David Himmelfarb. *Former Superintendent, U.S. Navy Ropewalk, Boston Naval Shipyard, Charlestown, Mass.*

Frederick Anthony Holland. *Professor and Chairman, Department of Chemical Engineering, University of Salford, Eng. Partner in Saldrem Associates (consulting chemical engineers).*

Solomon Cady Hollister (d. 1982). *Professor of Civil Engineering, Cornell University, Ithaca, N.Y.; Dean of Engineering, 1937–59.*

W.E. Howland. *Emeritus Professor of Sanitary Engineering, Purdue University, West Lafayette, Ind.*

Inez Whitaker Hunt (d. 1983). *Lecturer and free-lance writer. Teacher of creative writing, University of Colorado, Colorado Springs, 1963–66.*

John Cyril Herbert Hurd. *Textiles consultant. Former Head, School of Textiles, Leicester College of Technology and Commerce, Eng.*

William G. Ibberson. *Chairman, Sheffield Testing Works Ltd. and Sheffield Assay Office, Eng. Former Chairman, George Ibberson and Company Ltd., Sheffield, Eng.*

Miles Hopkins Imlay. *Rear Admiral (retired), U.S. Coast Guard.*

William Thorton Innes (d. 1969). *Founder and Director, Typothetae Printing Trade School, Philadelphia.*

Emerson C. Itschner. *Lieutenant General, U.S. Army (retired); Chief of Engineers, U.S. Army Corps of Engineers, 1956–61.*

Jules Janick. *Professor of Horticulture, Purdue University, West Lafayette, Ind.*

S. Paul Johnston (d. 1985). *Director, National Air and Space Museum, Smithsonian Institution, Washington, D.C., 1964–69.*

C. Clyde Jones. *Professor of Business Administration, Kansas State University, Manhattan.*

Ralph Kenyon Kilbon. *Director, Creative Services, RCA Corporation, New York City.*

John Louis King, Jr. *Assistant Professor of History, University of the District of Columbia, Washington, D.C.*

Peter W. Kingsford. *Tutor, Extra Mural Department, University of London. Author of* Engineers, Inventors, and Workers.

Rudolf Kingslake. *Professor of Optics, University of Rochester. Director of Optical Design, Eastman Kodak Company, Rochester, N.Y., 1939–69.*

D.C. Kiplinger (deceased). *Professor of Horticulture, Ohio State University, Columbus.*

Arthur Koehler (d. 1967). *Wood consultant, 1948–67. Chief, Division of Silvicultural Relations, Forest Products Laboratory, U.S. Forest Service, 1927–48. Lecturer, School of Forestry, Yale University, 1951–53.*

Dietrich Küchemann (d. 1976). *Consultant, Aerodynamics Department, Royal Aircraft Establishment, Farnborough, Eng.; Head of Department, 1966–71.*

George Lang. *International hotel, restaurant, and food consultant. Columnist,* Travel & Leisure *magazine.*

Pierre de Latil. *Scientific Editor,* Le Figaro, *Paris. Coauthor of* Le Professeur Auguste Piccard *and others.*

Mildred K. Lehman. *Associate Administrator, Alcohol, Drug Abuse, and Mental Health Administration, U.S. Department of Health and Human Services, Rockville, Md.*

Milton Lehman (d. 1966). *Free-lance writer. Author of* This High Man: The Life of Robert H. Goddard.

Hellmut E. Lehmann-Haupt. *Emeritus Professor of Bibliography and Rare Book Consultant, University of Missouri, Columbia.*

Irwin Solomon Lerner. *President, Lerner Laboratories, New Haven, Conn.*

Lawrence P. Lessing. *Member, Board of Editors,* Fortune *magazine, New York City, 1941–52; 1965–74.*

Donald S. Lopez. *Chairman, Department of Aeronautics, National Air and Space Museum, Smithsonian Institution, Washington, D.C.*

Carleton Mabee. *Professor of History, State University of New York College at New Paltz.*

Alexander McDonald (d. 1968). *Secretary, The Institution of Civil Engineers, London, 1954–67.*

James McDonald. *Free-lance writer.*

Fred Devereux McHugh. *Editor for the Office, Chief of Ordnance (Army), Washington, D.C.*

Donald LeCrone McMurry. *Author of* The Great Burlington Strike of 1888 *and others.*

L. Andrew Mannheim. *Technical editor, writer, and consultant. Author of* Leica Way *and others; editor of* Focal Encyclopedia of Photography.

Clarence Thomas Marek. *Former Professor of Metal Processing, School of Materials Science and Metallurgical Engineering, Purdue University, West Lafayette, Ind.*

Robert W. Marks. *Former Lecturer, New School for Social Research, New York City.*

George Peterkin Meade (d. 1975). *Vice President, International Commission for Uniform Methods of Sugar Analysis. Manager, Colonial Sugars Company, Gramercy, La., 1928–56.*

John Lawrence Mero. *President, Ocean Resources, Inc., La Jolla, Calif.*

Peter Michelmore. *Roving Editor,* Reader's Digest. *Author of* Einstein: Profile of the Man.

Jeannette Mirsky. *Visiting Fellow, Department of East Asian Studies, Princeton University, 1970–74. Coauthor of* The World of Eli Whitney.

Malcolm Monroe. *Former Vice President, Monroe Calculating Machine Company, Orange, N.J.*

John D. Moorhead. *Free-lance writer on military and technical subjects.*

James Charles Moran. *Former Editor,* Graphic Technology (*London*).

Michael James Moylan. *Director, Moylubes Ltd., Farnham, Eng.*

William Alvin Mudge. *Assistant to the President, International Nickel Company, Inc., New York City, 1955–58; Director, Technical Service, 1947–55.*

Herbert Lownds Nichols, Jr. *Publisher, Greenwich, Conn. Author of* Moving the Earth *and others.*

St. John Cousins Nixon. *Author of* The Invention of the Automobile; Wolseley: A Saga of the Motor Industry; *and others.*

Richard Marian Ogorkiewicz. *Senior Lecturer in Mechanical Engineering, Imperial College of Science and Technology, University of London.*

William David Ollis. *Professor of Organic Chemistry, University of Sheffield, Eng.*

Christabel Susan Orwin. *Coauthor of* The Open Fields; History of British Agriculture, 1846–1914.

A.S. Osley. *Consultant, Engineering Council, London. Former Head of Naval Scientific Administration Department, Ministry of Defence, United Kingdom.*

Robert P. Pace. *Account Executive, R. Hoe & Company, Inc., New York City.*

John Bingham Parkinson. *Former Chief, Aerodynamics, Aeronautical Vehicles, National Aeronautics and Space Administration, Washington, D.C.*

John W. Parry (d. 1976). *Author of* Spices; The Spice Handbook.

Harold Leslie Peterson (d. 1978). *Chief Curator, National Park Service, U.S. Department of the Interior, 1964–77. Author of* Arms and Armor in Colonial America, 1526–1783 *and others.*

William G. Pfann (d. 1982). *Department Head, Materials Research Laboratory, Bell Telephone Laboratories, Inc., Murray Hill, N.J.*

Jack Pickthall. *Consultant to International Flavours and Fragrances Ltd., Enfield, Eng. Former President, Society of Cosmetic Chemists, Great Britain, and British Society of Perfumers.*

Norman C. Polmar. *Consultant. Editor, U.S. section,* Jane's Fighting Ships, 1967–77.

John Bell Rae. *Emeritus Professor of the History of Technology, Harvey Mudd College, Claremont, Calif.*

Deborah Robbins. *Free-lance writer.*

L.T.C. Rolt (d. 1974). *Member, Executive Committee, American Society for the History of Technology. Chairman, Talyllyn Railway Company, England, 1963–68.*

John Kerr Rose (d. 1974). *Senior Specialist in Natural Resources and Conservation, Library of Congress, 1955–73.*

Richard D. Ross. *President, Four Nines, Inc., Haddonfield, N.J. Coauthor of* Industrial Waste Disposal Handbook.

Hunter Rouse. *Carver Professor Emeritus of Hydraulics, University of Iowa, Iowa City.*

Michel Rouzé. *Former producer in French broadcasting. Author of* Robert Oppenheimer: The Man and His Theories.

Charles R. Russell. *Former Professor of Mechanical Engineering, California Polytechnic State University, San Luis Obispo.*

Sir (Edward) John Russell (d. 1965). *Director, Rothamsted Experimental Station, Harpenden, Eng., 1912–43.*

Harold Eugene Saunders (d. 1961). *Captain, U.S. Navy; Technical Assistant to Chief of Bureau of Ships, Navy Department.*

James Patrick Saville. *Former Manager, Information Services, The Metals Society, London.*

Julian L. Schueler (d. 1962). *Consultant, Continental Steel Corporation, Kokomo, Ind.*

Bernard Sylvester Schweigert. *Professor and Chairman, Department of Food Science and Technology, University of California, Davis.*

Donald Shannon. *Former Manager, Public Relations Department, Otis Elevator Company, New York City.*

Mitchell R. Sharpe. *Science writer and rocketry historian. Author of* Living in Space: The Astronaut and His Environment *and others.*

Orson Cutler Shepard. *Emeritus Professor of Metallurgy, Stanford University, Calif.*

Charles Ely Rose Sherrington. *Secretary, British Railways Research Service, 1924–62.*

Thomas Mortimer Simmons. *Deputy Keeper, Department of Transport and Mining, Science Museum, London.*

Alec Westley Skempton. *Emeritus Professor of Civil Engineering, Imperial College of Science and Technology, University of London.*

Albert Lewis Slover. *Former Technical Assistant to the Chief, Naval Engineering Division, U.S. Coast Guard.*

F.D. Smith. *Consultant, Monsanto Chemical Company, St. Louis, Mo.; Manager, University Development, Research and Engineering Division, 1956–63.*

Reginald Leslie Smith-Rose (d. 1980). *Secretary General, Inter-Union Commission on Frequency Allocations for Radio Astronomy and Space Science, 1961–73. Director, Radio Research, Department of Scientific and Industrial Research, London, 1948–60.*

Edward W. Smykay. *Professor and Chairman, Department of Marketing, University of Baltimore.*

Harry J. Solberg. *Director of Corporate Planning, American Express Company. Former Associate Professor of Commerce, University of Wisconsin, Madison.*

Hereward Philip Spratt. *Deputy Keeper, Science Museum, London, 1930–67.*

Anthony Standen. *Executive Editor,* Kirk-Othmer Encyclopedia of Chemical Technology, *New York City, 1963–70.*

Joshua Stern. *Lecturer in Physics, University of Maryland, College Park. Associate Editor,* Review of Scientific Instruments.

Robert E. Stewart. *Distinguished Professor of Agricultural Engineering, Texas A & M University, College Station.*

Arthur Stowers (d. 1977). *Keeper, Department of Mechanical and Civil Engineering, Science Museum, London, 1950–62.*

George R. Strakosch. *Associate, Jaros, Baum and Bolles (consulting engineers), New York City. Former Manager, Elevators, General Sales, Otis Elevator Company, New York City.*

Frank Whitworth Stubbs, Jr. (d. 1967). *Professor of Civil Engineering, Purdue University, West Lafayette, Ind.*

Charles Süsskind. *Professor of Engineering Science, University of California, Berkeley.*

Harry C. Thomson. *Former Chairman, Political Science Department, De Paul University, Chicago. Assistant Editor, Encyclopædia Britannica, Chicago, 1959–66.*

Samuel Tolansky (d. 1973). *Professor of Physics, Royal Holloway College, University of London, 1947–73.*

Forrest Glenn Tucker. *Emeritus Professor of Physics, Oberlin College, Ohio.*

William Arthur Vine (d. 1966). *Professor and Head, Department of Mining Engineering, Montana College of Mineral Science and Technology.*

Francis Walley. *Under Secretary, Director of Civil Engineering Development, Department of the Environment, London, 1973–78.*

J. Garth Watson. *Secretary, Institution of Civil Engineers, London, 1967–79.*

Leon H. Weaver. *Professor of Criminal Justice, Michigan State University, East Lansing.*

Frederick Victor Wells. *Former Editor,* Soap, Perfumery and Cosmetics, *London. Founder-President, Society of Cosmetic Chemists of Great Britain.*

Charles S. Whewell. *Emeritus Professor of Textile Industries, University of Leeds, Eng.*

Theodore J. Williams. *Professor of Engineering; Director, Purdue Laboratory for Applied Industrial Control, Purdue University, West Lafayette, Ind.*

Harold Francis Williamson. *Professor of Economics, Northwestern University, Evanston, Ill., 1948–69. Author of* Winchester: The Gun That Won the West.

Charles Morrow Wilson (d. 1977). *Free-lance writer. Author of* Diesel: His Engine Changed the World *and others.*

George Bulkeley Laird Wilson. *Former Deputy Keeper, Department of Mechanical and Civil Engineering, Science Museum, London.*

Mitchell Wilson (d. 1973). *Science writer and novelist. Author of* American Science and Invention *and others.*

Melville Lawrence Wolfrom (d. 1969). *Regents' Professor of Chemistry, Ohio State University, Columbus, 1965–69.*

Ellen Louise Young. *Historical research specialist (manufactures).*

R. Eric Young. *Consultant in high technology systems engineering and instrumentation.*

Lev Zetlin. *President, Zetlin-Argo Structural Investigations, Inc., New York City.*

Part Eight. Religion

Nigel James Abercrombie. *Chief Regional Adviser, Arts Council of Great Britain, London, 1968–73; Secretary General, 1963–68.*

Charles Joseph Adams. *Professor of Islāmic Studies, McGill University, Montreal.*

The Rev. Joseph Denis Agius, O.S.B. *Monk of Downside Abbey, England.*

Sister Consuelo Maria Aherne. *Professor of History, Chestnut Hill College, Philadelphia. Assistant Staff Editor for Mediaeval Church History; Contributor to the* New Catholic Encyclopedia.

Sydney Eckman Ahlstrom (d. 1984). *Professor of Modern Religious History and American History, Yale University, 1964–83.*

Kye-hyon Ahn. *Director, Dong-kook University Museum, Seoul.*

Kurt Aland. *Professor of Church History, University of Münster, W.Ger.*

Hamilcar S. Alivisatos (d. 1969). *State Procurator of the Holy Synod of the Church of Greece. Professor of Canon Law and Pastoral Theology, University of Athens, 1918–56.*

The Rev. Michel Adrien Allard, S.J. (d. 1976). *Director, Institute of Oriental Studies, St. Joseph University, Beirut.*

The Rev. Arthur MacDonald Allchin. *Residentiary Canon of Canterbury Cathedral, Eng.*

Robert W. Allison. *Former Manuscript Research Specialist, Department of Special Collections, University of Chicago Library.*

Anselm H. Amadio. *Chaplain; Instructor in Philosophy, Illinois Institute of Technology, Chicago. Staff Writer, Philosophy and Religion,* Encyclopædia Britannica, *Chicago, 1970–73.*

Milton Vasil Anastos. *Emeritus Professor of Byzantine Greek and History, University of California, Los Angeles.*

The Rev. George Wishart Anderson, D.D. *Professor of Hebrew and Old Testament Studies, University of Edinburgh.*

The Very Rev. Laurence Thomas Anderson, C.R.P. *President, St. Norbert's College, Kilnacrott, Cavan, Ire.*

William Scovil Anderson. *Professor of Latin and Comparative Literature, University of California, Berkeley.*

Zafar Ishaq Ansari. *Professor of History, University of Petroleum and Minerals, Dhahran, Saudi Arabia.*

Michio Araki. *Professor of Asian Studies, Tokyo Science University.*

Henri Arvon. *Professor, University of Paris X.*

Max Arzt (d. 1975). *Vice Chancellor, Jewish Theological Seminary of America, New York City, 1951–75.*

Donald Attwater (d. 1977). *Author of* Penguin Dictionary of Saints; St. John Chrysostom, Pastor and Preacher.

Roger-François-Marie Aubert. *Professor of Church History, Catholic University of Louvain, Belg.*

Peter William Avery. *Lecturer in Persian; Director, Middle East Centre, University of Cambridge; Fellow of King's College, Cambridge.*

Roland H. Bainton (d. 1984). *Titus Street Professor of Church History, Yale University, 1936–62.*

The Rev. Msgr. Joseph W. Baker. *Officialis, Archdiocese of Saint Louis, Mo.*

Ernst Bammel. *Reader in Early Christian and Jewish Studies, University of Cambridge.*

The Rev. Wade Crawford Barclay (d. 1965). *Historian, Board of Missions, Methodist Church, New York City.*

The Rt. Rev. Msgr. John Mackintosh Tilney Barton (d. 1977). *Priest-in-Charge, S.S. Peter and Edward, London, 1950–75. English Consultor, Pontifical Biblical Commission.*

František M. Bartoš (d. 1972). *Professor of Church History, Comenius Protestant Theological Faculty, Prague.*

Robert Pierce Beaver. *Emeritus Professor of Missions, Divinity School, University of Chicago.*

The Very Rev. Msgr. Henry G.J. Beck. *Emeritus Professor of Church History, Immaculate Conception Seminary, Darlington, N.J.*

Alfons Becker. *Professor of Medieval History, Johannes Gutenberg University of Mainz, W.Ger.*

David Ben-Gurion (d. 1973). *Prime Minister and Minister of Defense, government of Israel, 1948–53, 1955–63.*

John C. Bennett. *Emeritus President, Union Theological Seminary, New York City.*

Haim Hillel Ben-Sasson (d. 1977). *Professor of Jewish Medieval History, Hebrew University of Jerusalem.*

Manfred Bensing. *Professor of History, Karl Marx University, Leipzig.*

Alan Lewis Berger. *Instructor in Religion, Miami University, Oxford, Ohio.*

Reginald Robert Betts (d. 1961). *Masaryk Professor of Central European History, University of London, 1946–61.*

The Rev. Maurice Bévenot, S.J. (d. 1980). *Professor of Ecclesiology, Heythrop College, University of London.*

Stephen Beyer. *Free-lance writer.*

Agehananda Bharati. *Professor and Chairman, Department of Anthropology, Syracuse University, N.Y.*

Jean Elfride Bickersteth. *Lecturer in Theology, University of Hull, Eng.*

Ludwig G.J. Bieler (d. 1981). *Professor of Palaeography and Late Latin, University College, Dublin, National University of Ireland.*

The Rev. Anselm Gordon Biggs, O.S.B. *Professor of History, Belmont Abbey College, N.C.*

Katharine Bird. *Free-lance writer on religion.*

The Rev. Robert L. Bireley, S.J. *Professor of History, Loyola University, Chicago.*

The Rev. Nicholas Frederick Bisheimer, S.V.D. (d. 1966). *President, Society of the Divine Word, Western Province.*

Ernst Bizer (d. 1975). *Professor of Church History, Rhenish Friedrich Wilhelm University of Bonn.*

William Barnett Blakemore (d. 1975). *Professor of Ecumenical Christianity, 1971–75; Dean, Disciples Divinity House, University of Chicago.*

Sheldon H. Blank. *Emeritus Professor of Bible, Hebrew Union College–Jewish Institute of Religion, Cincinnati, Ohio.*

Edwin Boardman (d. 1968). *Professor of Church History and Senior Counselor, Ashland Theological Seminary, Ohio.*

Pieter Arie Hendrik de Boer. *Former Professor of Old Testament, State University of Leiden, Neth.*

Rabbi Ben Zion Bokser (d. 1984). *Rabbi, Forest Hills Jewish Center, Forest Hills, N.Y. Adjunct Professor of Political Science, Queens College, City University of New York.*

Arthur Stanley Bolster, Jr. *Professor of Education, Harvard University.*

Gerald Bonner. *Reader in Church History, University of Durham, Eng.*

The Rev. William Joseph Bosch, S.J. *Associate Professor of History, LeMoyne College, Syracuse, N.Y.*

Carroll Julian Bourg. *Associate Professor of Sociology, Fisk University, Nashville, Tenn. Director, Office of Social Research, Maryland Province of Jesuits, Baltimore, 1966–68.*

The Rev. Charles Samuel Braden (d. 1970). *Resident Scholar, Perkins School of Theology, Southern Methodist University. Professor of History and Literature of Religions, Northwestern University, Evanston, Ill., 1943–54.*

The Rev. Ignatius Charles Brady, O.F.M. *Former Director of the theological section, College of St. Bonaventura, Grottaferrata, Italy.*

Paul Breidenbach. *Associate Professor of Anthropology, Loyola University, Chicago.*

Keith Richard Bridston. *Professor of Systematic Theology, Pacific Lutheran Theological Seminary and the Graduate Theological Union, Berkeley, Calif.*

John Bright. *Emeritus Professor of Hebrew and the Interpretation of the Old Testament, Union Theological Seminary, Richmond, Va.*

Harmon Hartzell Bro. *Director, History of Religions Research Project, Virginia Beach, Va.*

The Rev. John Francis Broderick, S.J. *Emeritus Professor of Ecclesiastical History, Weston College, Mass.*

The Rev. James Patrick Brodrick, S.J. *Author of* Origin of the Jesuits *and others.*

Geoffrey W. Bromiley. *Senior Professor of Church History and Historical Theology, Fuller Theological Seminary, Pasadena, Calif.*

The Rev. Victor John Knight Brook (d. 1974). *Fellow of All Souls College, Oxford, 1938–59; Lecturer in Reformation Theology, University of Oxford, 1929–34.*

Christopher Nugent Lawrence Brooke. *Dixie Professor of Ecclesiastical History, University of Cambridge.*

Peter R.L. Brown. *Professor of History and Classics, University of California, Berkeley.*

Frederick Fyvie Bruce. *Rylands Professor Emeritus of Biblical Criticism and Exegesis, Victoria University of Manchester, Eng.*

The Rev. Joseph Stanislaus Brusher, S.J. (d. 1972). *Professor of History, University of San Francisco, 1968–72.*

The Rev. Erwin Buck. *Pastor, St. Peter Lutheran Church, Medicine Hat, Alberta.*

Robert J. Buck. *Professor of Classics, University of Alberta, Edmonton.*

J.A.B. van Buitenen (d. 1979). *Distinguished Service Professor of Sanskrit and Indic Studies, University of Chicago, 1974–79.*

The Rev. Sebastian Bullough, O.P. (d. 1967). *Lecturer in Hebrew, University of Cambridge.*

The Rev. Walter John Burghardt, S.J. *Theologian in Residence, Georgetown University, Washington, D.C. Editor,* Theological Studies.

The Rev. Ernest Joseph Burrus, S.J. *Historian of Jesuit Order, Jesuit Historical Institute, Rome, Italy, and St. Louis, Mo.*

Harold Butcher. *Free-lance writer.*

Theodore Vern Buttrey, Jr. *Professor of Classics, University of Michigan, Ann Arbor.*

Charles Robert Byrnes. *Former Executive Director, International Association of Auditorium Managers, Chicago Heights, Ill.*

The Rev. William James Byron, S.J. *President, Catholic University of America, Washington, D.C.*

Henry J. Cadbury (d. 1974). *Hollis Professor of Divinity, Harvard University, 1934–54. Chairman, American Friends Service Committee, 1928–34; 1944–60.*

The Rev. Carnegie Samuel Calian. *President and Professor of Theology, Pittsburgh Theological Seminary.*

Mother Louise Callan, R.S.C.J. (d. 1966). *Professor of History, Maryville College of the Sacred Heart, St. Louis, Mo.*

Pier Paolo del Campana. *Professor of Comparative Religion, Sophia University, Tokyo.*

The Rev. Philip Caraman, S.J. *Editor,* The Month, *1948–63.*

Clifford M. Carey. *Assistant Executive Director, National Council of the Young Men's Christian Associations, New York City.*

John Carey. *Merton Professor of English Literature, University of Oxford.*

William David James Cargill Thompson (d. 1978). *Professor of Ecclesiastical History, King's College, University of London, 1976–78.*

The Rev. Edward Wilson Carlile. *Liaison Officer, East Africa Appeal, Church Army, London; Chief Secretary, 1949–60.*

Henry Stewart Carter (deceased). *Minister, Memorial Church, Cambridge, Eng.*

Ernest Cassara. *Professor of History, George Mason University, Fairfax, Va.*

The Very Rev. Henry Chadwick. *Regius Professor Emeritus of Divinity, University of Cambridge.*

Nora Kershaw Chadwick (d. 1972). *University Lecturer, University of Cambridge, 1950–58. Editor and contributor,* Studies in Early British History *and others.*

W. Owen Chadwick. *Former Regius Professor of Modern History, University of Cambridge.*

Wing-tsit Chan. *Emeritus Professor of Chinese Philosophy and Culture, Dartmouth College, Hanover, N.H. Anna R.D. Gillespie Professor Emeritus of Philosophy, Chatham College, Pittsburgh.*

Helen McCaig Chandra. *Free-lance writer on Asian religions.*

Byong-gil Chang. *Professor of Religion, Seoul National University.*

Kenneth K.S. Chen. *Emeritus Professor of Oriental Languages, University of California, Los Angeles.*

The Rev. Sok-u Choe. *Pastor, Myong-dong Catholic Cathedral, Seoul.*

Francis P(almer) Clarke. *Emeritus Professor of Philosophy, University of Pennsylvania, Philadelphia.*

The Rev. Arthur C. Cochrane. *Emeritus Professor of Systematic Theology, Dubuque Theological Seminary, Iowa.*

A.O.J. Cockshut. *G.M. Young Lecturer in 19th Century English Literature, University of Oxford; Fellow of Hertford College, Oxford. Author of* Anglican Attitudes: A Study of Victorian Religious Controversies *and others.*

John Cogley (d. 1976). *Senior Fellow, Center for the Study of Democratic Institutions, Santa Barbara, Calif., 1967–76; Editor,* The Center Magazine, *1967–74. Author of* The Layman and the Council *and others.*

The Rev. Louis Cognet. *Director of Studies, Collège de Juilly, France.*

Gerson D. Cohen. *Jacob H. Schiff Professor of History, The Jewish Theological Seminary of America, New York City; Chancellor, 1972–85.*

The Very Rev. Francis J. Connell (d. 1967). *Dean for Religious Communities, Catholic University of America, Washington, D.C., 1957–67; Professor of Moral Theology, 1949–58.*

Thomas L. Coonan. *Former Professor of History, St. Louis University, Mo.*

Patricia Louise Cox. *Free-lance writer on religion.*

Vincent Cronin. *Free-lance writer. Author of* The Flowering of the Renaissance *and others.*

The Rev. Frank Leslie Cross (d. 1968). *Lady Margaret Professor of Divinity, University of Oxford, 1944–68. Editor of* The Oxford Dictionary of the Christian Church.

Alice Curtayne (d. 1981). *Author of* St. Catherine of Siena; The Irish Story; *and others.*

Jean Dagens. *Former Professor of Classical French Literature, University of Strasbourg, Fr.*

Horton Marlais Davies. *Henry W. Putnam Professor of the History of Christianity, Princeton University.*

The Rev. J. Gordon Davies. *Edward Cadbury Professor and Head, Department of Theology, University of Birmingham, Eng.*

The Rev. Victor Cyril De Clercq, C.I.C.M. *Former Professor of Patrology and Church History, Pontifical College Josephinum, Worthington, Ohio.*

Count Michael de la Bedoyere (d. 1973). *Editor,* Search *newsletter, 1962–68;* Catholic Herald, *1934–62.*

The Rt. Rev. Carl Gustav Diehl. *Bishop of Tranquebar, Tamil Evangelical Lutheran Church, South India, 1967–72.*

The Rev. Godfrey Leo Diekmann, O.S.B. *Regents Professor of Theology, St. John's University, Collegeville, Minn. Editor of* Worship.

George Edward Dimock, Jr. *Professor of Classical Languages and Literatures, Smith College, Northampton, Mass.*

Decima L. Douie. *Former Reader in Medieval History, University of Hull, Eng.*

Jacques Duchesne-Guillemin. *Emeritus Professor of Indo-Iranian Studies, State University of Liège, Belg.*

The Rev. George H. Dunne, S.J. *Secretary, Committee on Society, Development and Peace, World Council of Churches and the Pontifical Commission for Justice and Peace, Ecumenical Centre, Geneva, Switz., 1967–72.*

The Very Rev. Joseph William Dunne (deceased). *Canon of Metropolitan Chapter of Birmingham; Parish Priest, St. Mary's, The Mount, Walsall, Eng.*

Donald F. Durnbaugh. *Professor of Church History, Bethany Theological Seminary, Oak Brook, Ill.*

Cornelius J. Dyck. *Professor of Anabaptist and Sixteenth-century Studies, Mennonite Biblical Seminary, Elkhart, Ind.*

H. Byron Earhart. *Professor of Religion, Western Michigan University, Kalamazoo.*

David A. Ede. *Associate Professor of Religion, Western Michigan University, Kalamazoo.*

E. Earle Ellis. *Research Professor of New Testament Literature, New Brunswick Theological Seminary, N.J.*

The Rt. Rev. John Tracy Ellis. *Emeritus Professor of Church History, University of San Francisco.*

Gracia Fay Ellwood. *Free-lance writer on religion, mythology, and the occult.*

Robert S. Ellwood, Jr. *Bishop James W. Bashford Professor of Oriental Studies, University of Southern California, Los Angeles.*

The Rev. John Adney Emerton. *Regius Professor of Hebrew, University of Cambridge.*

Marc Marie Escholier (d. 1972). *Judge, Supreme Court of Appeal, Paris. Author of* Port-Royal *and others.*

Josef van Ess. *Professor of Islamic Studies and Semitic Languages, Eberhard Karl University of Tübingen, W.Ger.*

The Rev. Carl Evans. *Pastor, Door Village United Methodist Church, La Porte, Ind.*

The Rev. Edward Every. *Canon, St. George's Collegiate Church, Jerusalem.*

Brother George Every, S.S.M. (deceased). *Lecturer, Kelham Theological College, Newark, Eng. Lay brother of the Society of the Sacred Mission.*

The Rev. Eugene Rathbone Fairweather. *Keble Professor of Divinity, Trinity College, University of Toronto.*

Andrea Faste. *Free-lance writer on religion.*

J.W. Fiegenbaum. *Professor of Religion, Mount Holyoke College, South Hadley, Mass.*

Floyd V. Filson. *Emeritus Dean and Emeritus Professor of New Testament, McCormick Theological Seminary, Chicago.*

Louis Finkelstein. *Emeritus Chancellor, Jewish Theological Seminary of America, New York City.*

Thomas Fish. *Professor of Mesopotamian Studies, University of Manchester, 1948–60.*

The Rev. Joseph Augustine Fitzmyer, S.J. *Professor of New Testament, Catholic University of America, Washington, D.C.*

The Ven. Charles Robert Forder. *Emeritus Archdeacon of York, Eng.; Canon and Prebendary of Fenton in York Minster, 1957–72.*

A. Durwood Foster. *Professor of Christian Theology, Pacific School of Religion, Berkeley, Calif.*

The Rev. Kenelm Francis Foster, O.P. (d. 1986). *Reader in Italian, University of Cambridge.*

Brian Fothergill. *Author of* The Cardinal King; Nicholas Wiseman; *and others.*

Linwood Fredericksen. *Undersecretary and Manager, Program Development Division, Rotary International. Associate Editor, Religion,* Encyclopædia Britannica, *Chicago, 1969–73.*

The Rev. Walter Freitag. *Professor of the Church in Historic Witness and Biblical Interpretation, Lutheran Theological Seminary, University of Saskatchewan, Saskatoon.*

The Rev. Reginald Michael French. *Vicar of St. James', London, 1930–55.*

William Hugh Clifford Frend. *Professor of Ecclesiastical History, University of Glasgow.*

Rabbi Albert H. Friedlander. *Dean of Rabbinic Studies, Leo Baeck College, London. Minister, Westminster Synagogue, London.*

Asaf Ali-Asghar Fyzee. *Vice Chancellor, University of Jammu and Kashmir, Srinagar, India, 1957–58. Indian Ambassador to Egypt, 1949–51.*

John G. Gallaher. *Associate Professor of History, Southern Illinois University, Edwardsville.*

The Rev. Maynard Joseph Geiger, O.F.M. *Former Historian of the Franciscan Fathers of the Pacific Coast and Archivist of Mission, Santa Barbara, Calif.*

The Rev. Joseph Gill, S.J. *Former Professor of Byzantine Greek Language and of Byzantine History, Pontifical Oriental Institute, Rome.*

Nahum N. Glatzer. *Samuel Lane Professor Emeritus of Jewish History and Social Ethics, Brandeis University, Waltham, Mass.*

Judah Goldin. *Professor of Oriental Studies and Post-Biblical Hebrew Literature, University of Pennsylvania, Philadelphia.*

Gillian Lindt Gollin. *Professor of Sociology of Religion, Columbia University.*

Cyrus H. Gordon. *Professor of Hebraic Studies; Director, Center for Ebla Research; New York University, New York City. Emeritus Professor of Mediterranean Studies, Brandeis University, Waltham, Mass.*

Stephen Gottschalk. *Associate Professor of History, U.S. Naval Postgraduate School, Monterey, Calif., 1972–75. Author of* The Emergence of Christian Science in American Religious Life.

John Grace (d. 1972). *National Chief Secretary, The Salvation Army, New York City, 1961–70.*

Hilda Charlotte Graef. *Author of* The Light and the Rainbow; Mary, A History of Doctrine and Devotion; *and others.*

Ernest (Eugene) Graf (d. 1962). *Monk of Buckfast Abbey, England.*

Robert M. Grant. *Carl Darling Buck Professor of Humanities; Professor of Early Christian History, Divinity School, University of Chicago.*

John Evelyn Bury Gray. *Reader in Sanskrit, School of Oriental and African Studies, University of London.*

The Rev. Paul Grosjean, S.J. (d. 1964). *Bollandist. Author of* Henrici VI Angliae Regis Miracula Postuma *and others.*

G.E. von Grunebaum (d. 1972). *Professor of History; Director, Near Eastern Center, University of California, Los Angeles, 1957–72.*

The Rev. Pierre Joseph G'sell, O.S.B. (deceased). *Monk at Solesmes Abbey, France.*

Herbert V. Guenther. *Emeritus Professor of Far Eastern Studies, University of Saskatchewan, Saskatoon.*

The Rev. Franco Guerello, S.J. *Professor of Italian Literature, Social Institute, Turin, Italy.*

The Rev. Walter George Gumbley, O.P. (d. 1968). *Occasional Lecturer at Blackfriars, Oxford, 1942–45; 1950–61. Author of* Parish Priests Among the Saints *and others.*

Oliver Robert Gurney. *Emeritus Professor of Assyriology, University of Oxford.*

Oskar Halecki (d. 1973). *Professor of Eastern European History, Graduate School, Fordham University, New York City, 1944–61. Honorary President, Polish Institute of Arts and Science, New York City.*

Edward Elton Young Hales (d. 1986). *Author of* Revolution and Papacy *and others.*

The Rev. François Halkin, S.J. *Bollandist. Author of* Bibliotheca Hagiographica Graeca *and others.*

The Rev. Basil Hall. *Fellow and Dean, St. John's College, University of Cambridge, 1974–79. Professor of Ecclesiastical History, Victoria University of Manchester, 1968–74.*

Bernice Margaret Hamilton. *Associate of St. Edmund's House, University of Cambridge. Former Senior Lecturer in Politics, University of York, Heslington, Eng.*

Robert Theodore Handy. *Henry Sloane Coffin Professor of Church History, Union Theological Seminary, New York City.*

Edward R. Hardy (d. 1981). *Lecturer in Early Church History, University of Cambridge, 1969–75. Professor of Church History, Berkeley Divinity School, New Haven, Conn., 1947–69.*

Ruth Mulvey Harmer. *Professor of English and Modern Languages, California State Polytechnic University, Pomona.*

The Rev. Carl John Hemmer, S.J. *Former Research Assistant of Ecclesiastical History, Colegio de San Estanislao, Salamanca, Spain.*

Carl F.H. Henry. *Theologian. Lecturer-at-Large, World Vision International. Writer and editor on religion.*

The Rev. Ben Mohr Herbster (d. 1984). *President, United Church of Christ, 1961–69.*

Ferdinand Aloys Hermens. *Emeritus Professor of Political Science, University of Cologne.*

The Most Rev. Edward Louis Heston, C.S.C. (d. 1973). *Chairman, Pontifical Social Communications Commission, Vatican City, 1971–73.*

Naofusa Hirai. *Professor of Shinto Studies, Kokugakuin University, Tokyo.*

H.Z. Hirschberg (d. 1976). *Professor of Jewish History in Muslim Countries, Bar-Ilan University, Ramat Gan, Israel.*

The Rev. Ian Hislop, O.P. *Former Provincial of the English Dominican Province.*

John Thayer Hitchcock. *Professor of Anthropology and South Asian Studies, University of Wisconsin, Madison.*

Philip Khuri Hitti (d. 1978). *Professor of Semitic Literature, Princeton University, 1936–54.*

Lauri O. Honko. *Professor of Folkloristics and Comparative Religion, University of Turku, Fin.*

Winthrop S. Hudson. *Adjunct Professor of Religion, University of North Carolina at Chapel Hill. James B. Colgate Professor of the History of Christianity, Colgate Rochester Divinity School, Rochester, N.Y., 1948–77.*

The Rev. Gordon Huelin. *Vicar, St. Margaret Pattens, London. Lecturer in Ecclesiastical History, King's College, University of London.*

William Robert Hutchison. *Charles Warren Professor of the History of Religion in America, Harvard University.*

J. Philip Hyatt (d. 1972). *Professor of Old Testament, Vanderbilt University, Nashville, Tenn., 1944–72.*

S.M. Ikram (d. 1973). *Director, Institute of Islāmic Culture, Lahore, Pak.*

Toshihiko Izutsu. *Professor of Islāmic Studies, McGill University, Montreal, 1969–75.*

Carl T. Jackson. *Professor of History, University of Texas at El Paso.*

Edmond Jacob. *Professor of Old Testament Exegesis, Evangelical Theological Faculty, University of Strasbourg, France.*

The Rev. Jerome Vincent Jacobsen, S.J. (d. 1970). *Professor of History, Loyola University, Chicago.*

Thorkild Jacobsen. *Emeritus Professor of Assyriology, Harvard University.*

The Rev. Edwin Oliver James (d. 1972). *Chaplain of All Souls College, University of Oxford. Professor of the History and Philosophy of Religion, University of London.*

The Rev. Daniel T. Jenkins. *Weyerhaeuser Professor of Systematic Theology, Princeton Theological Seminary, N.J., 1981–84.*

Eric John. *Reader in History, Victoria University of Manchester, Eng.*

Sherman Elbridge Johnson. *Dean, Church Divinity School of the Pacific, Berkeley, Calif., 1951–72.*

Inge Jonsson. *Professor of Comparative Literature, University of Stockholm. Author of* Emanuel Swedenborg *and others.*

J. Stillson Judah. *Emeritus Professor of the History of Religions, Pacific School of Religion and Graduate Theological Union, Berkeley, Calif.*

Mark Juergensmeyer. *Associate Professor of Religious Studies, Graduate Theological Union and University of California, Berkeley.*

Max Kaltenmark. *Director of Studies, École Pratique des Hautes Études (Institute for Advanced Research), Paris, 1957–78.*

Arvid S. Kapelrud. *Professor of Old Testament, University of Oslo.*

Firuz Kazemzadeh. *Professor of History, Yale University. Former Chairman, National Spiritual Assembly of the Bahá'í's of the United States.*

Elie Kedourie. *Professor of Politics, London School of Economics and Political Science, University of London.*

The Rev. John N.D. Kelly. *Principal of St. Edmund Hall, Oxford, 1951–79; Lecturer in Patristic Studies, University of Oxford, 1948–76.*

The Rev. John Arthur Kemp, S.J. (d. 1963). *Professor of Medieval History, Loyola University, Chicago, 1959–63.*

Malcolm H. Kerr (d. 1984). *President, American University of Beirut, 1982–84. Professor of Political Science, University of California, Los Angeles, 1967–82.*

The Rt. Rev. Sylvester Michael Killeen, O. Praem. *Former Chancellor, Saint Norbert College, De Pere, Wis.*

Joseph M. Kitagawa. *Emeritus Professor of the History of Religions and of Far Eastern Languages and Civilizations, University of Chicago.*

George Angus Fulton Knight. *President, Pacific Theological College, Suva, Fiji, 1965–72.*

The Rev. Michael David Knowles, O.S.B. (d. 1974). *Regius Professor of Modern History, University of Cambridge, 1954–63.*

The Most Rev. Franz Cardinal König. *Archbishop of Vienna.*

Gottfried Georg Krodel. *Professor of History and Church History, Valparaiso University, Ind.*

Bruno Kroker. *Free-lance writer on American Protestantism.*

Hans Kühner. *Historian and free-lance writer. Specialist on the history of the Roman Catholic Church and the Papacy. Author of* Encyclopedia of the Papacy *and others.*

Werner Georg Kümmel. *Emeritus Professor of New Testament, Philipps University of Marburgh, W.Ger.*

Stephan George Kuttner. *Emeritus Professor of Canon Law, University of California, Berkeley. President, Institute of Research and Study in Medieval Canon Law.*

Gerhart B. Ladner. *Emeritus Professor of History, University of California, Los Angeles.*

The Most Rev. Pio Laghi. *Ambassador of the Vatican to the United States.*

Helen B. Lamb (d. 1975). *Author of* Economic Development of India.

The Rev. John William Lamb. *Former Canon of York. Member, National Church Assembly, England. Author of* The Archbishopric of Lichfield *and others.*

Eugene N. Lane. *Professor of Classics, University of Missouri, Columbia.*

Henri Laoust. *Emeritus Professor of Sociology of Islām, College of France, Paris.*

Harriet Pratt Lattin. *Historian. Author of* The Peasant Boy Who Became Pope.

The Rev. M.-H. Laurent, O.P. (deceased). *Keeper of the Vatican Library.*

Clifford Hugh Lawrence. *Professor of Medieval History, Bedford College, University of London.*

Du-hyon Lee. *Professor, Teacher's College, Seoul National University.*

Sid Z. Leiman. *Professor of Jewish History and Literature; Chairman, Department of Judaic Studies, Brooklyn College, City University of New York.*

The Rev. Augustin Pierre Léonard, O.P. *Professor of Theology, Dominican College of La Sarte, Belg., and University of Notre Dame, Ind.*

The Rev. Joseph Leonard, C.M. (deceased). *Lecturer at St. Mary's College, London. Author of* Saint Vincent de Paul and Mental Prayer.

The Rev. William Paul Le Saint, S.J. *Professor of Theology; President of the Faculty, St. Mary of the Lake Seminary, Mundelein, Ill., 1965–70.*

Sir Shane Leslie (d. 1971). *Author of* Memoir of Cardinal Gasquet *and others.*

Fairy von Lilienfeld. *Professor of the Theology of the Christian East, Friedrich Alexander University of Erlangen-Nürnberg, W.Ger.*

The Rev. Poul Georg Lindardt. *Professor of Church History, University of Århus, Den., 1942–80.*

Franklin Hamlin Littell. *Professor of Religion, Temple University, Philadelphia.*

The Rev. Charles Patrick Loughran, S.J. *Emeritus Professor of European History, Fordham University, New York City.*

Frederick Stanley Lusby. *Professor of Religious Studies, University of Tennessee, Knoxville.*

The Rev. Thomas Timothy McAvoy, C.S.C. (d. 1969). *Archivist and Professor of History, University of Notre Dame, Ind.*

George Englert McCracken. *Emeritus Professor of Classical Languages, Drake University, Des Moines, Iowa.*

The Rev. James Stevenson McEwen. *Professor of Church History, University of Aberdeen, Scot., 1958–77.*

Sister Mary Emmanuel McIver, O.S.U. *Former Professor of Theology, College of New Rochelle, N.Y.*

The Rev. John L. McKenzie, S.J. *Emeritus Professor of Theology, De Paul University, Chicago.*

Joseph Cumming McLelland. *Professor of Philosophy of Religion; Dean, Faculty of Religious Studies, McGill University, Montreal.*

William Hewat McLeod. *Professor of History, University of Otago, Dunedin, New Zealand.*

William Gerald McLoughlin. *Professor of History, Brown University, Providence, R.I. Author of* Modern Revivalism: C.G. Finney to Billy Graham.

John F. McMahon. *General and Commander in Chief, Volunteers of America, New York City, 1958–80.*

The Rev. Francis Gerard McManamin, S.J. *Former Associate Professor of History, Loyola College, Baltimore.*

The Rev. Robert Edward McNally, S.J. (d. 1977). *Professor of Historical Theology, Fordham University, New York City, 1966–77.*

The Very Rev. Joseph McSorley (d. 1963). *Superior General of the Paulist Fathers, 1924–29.*

The Right Rev. Msgr. Richard C. Madden. *Former Pastor, St. John the Beloved, Summerville, S.C.*

William Mahony. *Professor of Religion, Davidson College, N.C.*

George Makdisi. *Professor of Arabic and Islamic Studies; Director, Center of Medieval Studies, University of Pennsylvania, Philadelphia.*

Cyril Alexander Mango. *Bywater and Sotheby Professor of Byzantine and Modern Greek, University of Oxford.*

The Rev. William W. Manross. *Emeritus Professor of Church History, Philadelphia Divinity School, Pa.*

Clyde L. Manschreck. *Chavanne Professor of Religious Studies, Rice University, Houston, Texas. Emeritus Professor of the History of Christianity, Chicago Theological Seminary.*

The Rev. Joseph M.-F. Marique, S.J. (deceased). *Director, Institute of Early Christian Iberian Studies, College of the Holy Cross, Worcester, Mass.*

John S. Marshall (d. 1979). *Professor of Philosophy, University of the South, Sewanee, Tenn., 1946–68.*

Ira Jay Martin III (d. 1983). *Henry Mixter Penniman Professor of Philosophy and Religion, Berea College, Ky., 1966–77.*

Martin E. Marty. *Fairfax M. Cone Distinguished Service Professor, Divinity School, University of Chicago. Associate Editor,* The Christian Century.

Masutani Fumio. *Professor of the History of Religion, Taisho University, Tokyo.*

The Rev. Vivian John Manley Matthews. *Priest of the London Oratory, Eng.*

Sengaku Mayeda. *Professor of Indian Philosophy, University of Tokyo.*

Louis Mazoyer. *Former Teacher at the Lycée Condorcet, Paris.*

Sidney Earl Mead. *Professor of History and of Religion, University of Iowa, Iowa City, 1964–72.*

Bernard E. Meland. *Emeritus Professor of Constructive Theology, University of Chicago.*

The Rev. William Moelwyn Merchant. *Professor of English Language and Literature, University of Exeter, Eng., 1961–74. Emeritus Canon of Salisbury Cathedral.*

Reinhold Merkelbach. *Professor of Classics, University of Cologne.*

The Rev. John Meyendorff. *Dean, St. Vladimir's Orthodox Theological Seminary, Tuckahoe, N.Y. Professor of Byzantine and East European History, Fordham University, New York City.*

John Richard Meyer. *Associate Professor of Education, University of Windsor, Ont.*

Rabbi Eugene Mihaly. *Professor of Homiletics and Midrash, Hebrew Union College–Jewish Institute of Religion, Cincinnati, Ohio.*

The Rev. Raymond Joseph Miller, C.SS.R. *Former Pastor, St. Leo's Church, Versailles, Ky.*

Nicholas Byram Millet. *Professor of Near Eastern Studies, University of Toronto.*

Kyong-bae Min. *Professor of Religion, Yonsei University, Seoul.*

Christine Mohrmann. *Former Professor of Early Christian Greek and Latin, and Medieval Latin, Catholic University of Nijmegen, Neth.*

Mary Moriarty. *Benedictine of Stanbrook Abbey, Worcester, Eng. Author of* The Saints in Silhouette; *translator and editor of* A Capuchin Chronicle.

The Rev. Claude Beaufort Moss (d. 1964). *Lecturer at Bishop's College, Cheshunt, Eng.*

David Livingstone Mueller. *Professor of Christian Theology, Southern Baptist Theological Seminary, Louisville, Ky.*

James DeForest Murch (d. 1973). *Member, Board of Administration, 1958–71; Publications Director, 1945–58, National Association of Evangelicals.*

The Rev. Francis Xavier Murphy, C.SS.R. *Emeritus Professor of Patristic Moral Theology, Academia Alfonsiana, Rome. Staff editor for* Patrology, *New Catholic Encyclopedia.*

A. Victor Murray (d. 1967). *President of Cheshunt College, Cambridge, 1945–59. Professor of Education, University of Hull, Eng., 1933–45.*

Tiruppattur Ramaseshayyar Venkatachala Murti. *Emeritus Professor of Philosophy, Banaras Hindu University, Varanasi, India.*

The Rev. Wilfrid Myatt, C.J.M. *Coeditor of* Saint John Eudes: a Spiritual Portrait *and others.*

B. Davie Napier. *Professor of Bible, Yale University. President, Pacific School of Religion, Berkeley, Calif., 1972–78.*

Seyyed Hossein Nasr. *Professor of Philosophy; Dean, Faculty of Letters and Humanities, University of Tehrān.*

The Rt. Rev. Stephen Charles Neill (d. 1984). *Professor of Philosophy and Religious Studies, University of Nairobi, Kenya, 1969–73.*

James D. Nelson. *Professor of Church History, United Theological Seminary, Dayton, Ohio.*

David Hay Newsome. *Master of Wellington College, Crowthorne, Eng. Fellow of Emmanuel College, University of Cambridge, 1959–70.*

John Thomas Nichol. *Professor of History; Vice President for Academic Affairs, Bentley College, Waltham, Mass.*

The Rev. Richard Patrick Noonan, S.J. *Alumni Director, McQuaid Jesuit High School, Rochester, N.Y.*

John B(oyer) Noss (d. 1980). *Professor of Philosophy, Franklin and Marshall College, Lancaster, Pa. Adjunct Professor of World Religions and the Christian Faith, Lancaster Theological Seminary, Pa.*

Morgan Phelps Noyes (d. 1972). *Associate Professor of Practical Theology, Union Theological Seminary, New York City, 1945–51. Minister, Central Presbyterian Church, Montclair, N.J., 1932–57.*

Geoffrey Fillingham Nuttall. *Lecturer in Church History, New College, University of London, 1945–77.*

The Rev. Austin Oakley (d. 1977). *Secretary, Anglican and Eastern Orthodox Churches Association, London, 1945–53. Vicar of St. Johns, London, 1944–62.*

Dimitri Obolensky. *Professor of Russian and Balkan History, University of Oxford.*

The Rev. Elmer O'Brien, S.J. *Writer in Residence, Ignatius College, Guelph, Ont. Research Professor of Theology, Loyola College, Montreal, 1966–73.*

The Rev. Thomas Gerald O'Callaghan, S.J. *Associate Professor of Religious Studies, Fairfield University, Conn.*

Daniel William O'Connor. *Charles A. Dana Professor of Religious Studies, Saint Lawrence University, Canton, N.Y.*

Tarlach O'Raifeartaigh. *Chairman, Cultural Relations Committee, Dublin. Editor of* Genealogical Tracts I.

The Rev. William James O'Shea. *Former Professor of Church History and Liturgy, St. Mary's Seminary, Baltimore.*

Eberhard Otto (d. 1974). *Professor of Egyptology, Rupert Charles University of Heidelberg, W.Ger.*

The Rev. Paul F. Palmer, S.J. (d. 1982). *Professor of Theology, Fordham University, New York City.*

Pascal P. Parente (d. 1971). *Professor of Ascetical and Mystical Theology, Catholic University of America, Washington, D.C., 1938–60.*

Herbert William Parke (d. 1986). *Professor of Ancient History, Trinity College, University of Dublin, 1934–73.*

The Rev. Thomas Maynard Parker (d. 1985). *Fellow of University College, Oxford; University Lecturer in Theology, University of Oxford, 1950–73.*

André Parrot (d. 1980). *Archaeologist. Director of the Louvre, Paris, 1968–72.*

Wilhelm Pauck (d. 1981). *Professor of Church History, Union Theological Seminary, New York City, 1953–67.*

The Rev. Ernest Alexander Payne (d. 1980). *President, World Council of Churches, 1968–75.*

Jaroslav Jan Pelikan. *Sterling Professor of History, Yale University.*

Norman Perrin (d. 1976). *Professor of New Testament, University of Chicago, 1969–76.*

Gerald Bernard Phelan (d. 1965). *Professor of Philosophy, St. Michael's College, University of Toronto, and Pontifical Institute of Medieval Studies, Toronto.*

The Rev. Arthur Carl Piepkorn (d. 1973). *Graduate Professor of Systematic Theology, Concordia Seminary, St. Louis, Mo., 1963–73.*

The Rev. Martin Pierce. *Vicar of St. John's Mickleover, Derby, Eng.*

John Richard Thornhill Pollard. *Former Senior Lecturer in Classics, University College of North Wales, University of Wales, Bangor.*

Harry Culverwell Porter. *Lecturer in History, University of Cambridge.*

Eli Daniel Potts. *Associate Professor of History, Monash University, Clayton, Australia. Author of* British Baptist Missionaries in India, 1793–1837.

The Rev. Leon Pouliot, S.J. *Former Teacher of Church History, Collège Sainte-Marie, Montreal.*

James M(atthew) Powell. *Professor of Medieval History, Syracuse University, N.Y.*

Henri-Charles Puech (d. 1986). *Professor of History of Religions, College of France, Paris, 1952–72. Director of Religious Studies, École Pratique des Hautes Études (Institute for Advanced Research), Paris.*

The Rev. William Arthur Purdy. *Secretary for Anglican and Methodist Relations, Secretariat for Promoting Christian Unity, Vatican.*

John Francis Quinn. *Professor of Philosophy, Pontifical Institute of Medieval Studies, Toronto.*

The Very Rev. Msgr. William Joseph Quinn. *Former Executive Secretary, Bishops' Committee for Migrant Workers, Chicago, Ill. Former Codirector, Latin American Bureau, National Catholic Welfare Conference, Washington, D.C.*

Gilles Quispel. *Professor of Early Church History, State University of Utrecht, Neth.*

Fazlur Rahman. *Professor of Islāmic Philosophy, University of Chicago.*

Helen Louise Redpath (Sister Dominic) (d. 1965). *Bridgettine Nun of Syon Abbey, Devon, Eng.*

Marjorie E. Reeves. *Honorary Fellow and former Vice-Principal, St. Anne's College, Oxford; former Lecturer in Modern History, University of Oxford.*

Ernest Edwin Reynolds. *Author of* Baden-Powell; Three Cardinals; *and others.*

The Rev. James A. Reynolds. *Former Professor of Church History, St. Joseph's Seminary, Yonkers, N.Y.*

The Rev. Joseph Alfred Richard. *Society of Missionaries of Africa, the White Fathers.*

James T. Richardson. *Professor of Sociology, University of Nevada, Reno.*

Theodore Henry Robinson (d. 1964). *Professor of Semitic Languages, University College of South Wales and Monmouthshire, Cardiff, 1927–44.*

The Very Rev. Gerard Rooney, C.P. *Former Director, Department of Education, Diocese of Worcester, Mass.*

Herbert Jennings Rose (d. 1961). *Professor of Greek, University of St. Andrews, Scot., 1927–53.*

Henry Rosemont, Jr. *Professor of Philosophy, St. Mary's College of Maryland.*

Erwin I.J. Rosenthal. *Emeritus Reader in Oriental Studies, University of Cambridge.*

Franz Rosenthal. *Sterling Professor of Near Eastern Languages, Yale University.*

Judah M. Rosenthal. *Emeritus Professor of Biblical Exegesis, College of Jewish Studies, Chicago.*

Anne Ross. *Free-lance writer on Celtic mythology.*

The Rev. Ernest Gordon Rupp. *Dixie Professor Emeritus of Ecclesiastical History, University of Cambridge.*

The Rev. Edward A. Ryan, S.J. (d. 1964). *Rector, Our Lady of Martyrs Tertianship, Auriesville, N.Y., 1962–64. Professor of Church History, Woodstock College, Md., 1936–62.*

The Rt. Rev. Msgr. J(ohn) Joseph Ryan. *Emeritus Professor of Church History, St. John's Seminary, Brighton, Mass. Emeritus Professor of Medieval History, Pontifical Institute of Medieval Studies, Toronto.*

J. Coert Rylaarsdam. *Emeritus Professor of Old Testament Theology, University of Chicago. Emeritus Professor of Theology, Marquette University, Milwaukee.*

William Merritt Sale III. *Professor of Classics and Comparative Literature, Washington University, St. Louis, Mo.*

Matti Salo. *Former Assistant Professor of Anthropology, Northern Illinois University, DeKalb.*

Ernest R. Sandeen (d. 1982). *Professor of History, Macalester College, St. Paul, Minn., 1973–82.*

Dittakavi Subrahmanya Sarma. *Principal Emeritus of Vivekananda College, Madras.*

Genjun H. Sasaki. *Professor of Buddhism, Otani University, Kyōto, Japan.*

Thomas A. Schafer. *Professor of Church History, McCormick Theological Seminary, Chicago.*

Eva Schaper. *Professor of Philosophy, University of Glasgow, Scot.*

Robert P. Scharlemann. *Commonwealth Professor of Religious Studies, University of Virginia, Charlottesville.*

Rivka Schatz-Uffenheimer. *Edmonton Professor of Jewish Mysticism, Hebrew University of Jerusalem.*

Joseph Herman Schauinger. *Professor of History, College of St. Thomas, St. Paul, Minn.*

Annemarie Schimmel. *Professor of Indo-Muslim Culture, Harvard University.*

The Rt. Rev. Alexander Schmemann (d. 1983). *Dean, St. Vladimir's Orthodox Theological Seminary, Crestwood, N.Y.*

Reiner Schürmann. *Professor of Philosophy, Graduate Faculty, New School for Social Research, New York City.*

Amulya Chandra Sen. *Former Editor, The Indo-Asian Culture. Author of Asoka's Edicts and others.*

Umakant Premanand Shah. *Former Deputy Director, Oriental Institute, Maharaja Sayajirao University of Baroda, India.*

Roger Sharrock. *Emeritus Professor of English Language and Literature, King's College, University of London.*

The Rev. Ronald Duncan Mackintosh Shaw (d. 1972). *Missionary Professor, Central Theological College, Rikkyo University, Tokyo, 1922–37.*

The Rt. Rev. Msgr. George William Shea. *Pastor Emeritus, Our Lady of Sorrows Church, South Orange, N.J.*

The Most Rev. Fulton John Sheen (d. 1979). *Bishop of the Diocese of Rochester, N.Y., 1966–69.*

Lancelot Capel Sheppard (d. 1971). *Editor, "Faith and Fact Series,"* Twentieth Century Encyclopaedia of Catholicism.

Franklin Sherman. *Professor of Christian Ethics; Dean of the Faculty, Lutheran School of Theology at Chicago.*

The Rev. Joseph Hsing-san Shih. *Professor of Missions and Sinology, Pontifical Gregorian University, Rome.*

Ailon Shiloh. *Professor and Director of Graduate Studies, Department of Anthropology, University of South Florida, Tampa.*

David Clark Shipley. *Emeritus Professor of Theology, Methodist Theological School, Delaware, Ohio.*

Donald Howard Shively. *Professor of Japanese History and Literature, Harvard University.*

Lou Hackett Silberman. *Hillel Professor Emeritus of Jewish Literature and Thought, Vanderbilt University, Nashville, Tenn.*

Akiba Ernst Simon. *Emeritus Professor of Education, Hebrew University of Jerusalem.*

The Rev. Joachim Frederick Smet, O.Carm. *Editor of Philippe de Mézières's* The Life of St. Peter Thomas.

The Rev. B.T.D. Smith. *Lecturer in Divinity, University of Cambridge, 1915–50.*

Jonathan Zittell Smith. *Robert O. Anderson Distinguished Service Professor of the Humanities, University of Chicago.*

The Rev. James Hutchinson Smylie. *Professor of American Church History, Union Theological Seminary, Richmond, Va.*

The Rev. Norman Henry Snaith (d. 1982). *Principal, 1954–61; Tutor in Old Testament Languages and Literature, 1936–61, Wesley College, Leeds, Eng.*

Ida Sloan Snyder. *Associate and News Director, Bureau of Communications, National Board of the Young Women's Christian Association, New York City.*

The Rev. John Songster, S.J. *Assistant Professor Emeritus of History, Georgetown University, Washington, D.C.*

Jacques Soustelle. *Professor of Social Anthropology, School of Advanced Studies in the Social Sciences, Paris.*

James C. Spalding. *Professor of Protestant Theology; Administrative Director, School of Religion, University of Iowa, Iowa City.*

Matthew Spinka (d. 1972). *Professor of Church History, Hartford Seminary Foundation, Conn., 1943–58.*

The Rev. John Stacey. *Secretary, Local Preachers' Office, British Methodist Church, London; Editor, Epworth Press.*

James Stevenson. *Emeritus Fellow of Downing College, Cambridge; formerly University Lecturer in Divinity, University of Cambridge.*

John J. Stoudt. *Professor of Philosophy, Kutztown State College, Pennsylvania, 1965–70. Free-lance writer and researcher.*

Frederick J. Streng. *Professor of the History of Religions, Southern Methodist University, Dallas, Texas.*

The Rev. Dom Anselm Strittmatter, O.S.B. (d. 1978). *Prior, St. Anselm's Abbey, Washington, D.C., 1961–67.*

John Strugnell. *Professor of Christian Origins, Harvard University.*

Herbert P. Sullivan. *Professor of Religion and Dean, Vassar College, Poughkeepsie, N.Y.*

The Very Rev. Norman Sykes (d. 1961). *Dean of Winchester, Eng., 1958–61.*

The Rev. William Telfer (d. 1968). *Canon of Ely. Master of Selwyn College, University of Cambridge, 1947–56.*

Sydney A. Temple, Jr. *Lecturer in Classical Languages, University of Hawaii, Honolulu.*

Mary Frances Thelen. *Professor of Religion, Randolph-Macon Woman's College, Lynchburg, Va.* Author of Man as Sinner in Contemporary American Realistic Theology.

The Rev. Antonine Severin Tibesar, O.F.M. *Emeritus Professor of History, Catholic University of America, Washington, D.C. Former Director, Academy of American Franciscan History, Washington, D.C.*

L.J. Trinterud. *Emeritus Professor of Church History, San Francisco Theological Seminary, San Anselmo, Calif.*

Jacques Truchet. *Professor of French Literature, University of Paris IV.*

Harold Walter Turner. *Director, Study Centre for New Religious Movements in Primal Societies, Selly Oak Colleges, Birmingham, Eng.*

Isadore Twersky. *Littauer Professor of Hebrew Literature and Philosophy, Harvard University.*

Walter Ullmann (d. 1983). *Professor of Medieval History, University of Cambridge, 1972–78; Professor of Ecclesiastical History, 1965–72.*

James Herman Van der Veldt (d. 1977). *Professor of Psychology, Catholic University of America, Washington, D.C., 1945–62.* Coauthor of Psychiatry and Catholicism.

The Rev. Alexander Roper Vidler. *Fellow and Dean of King's College, Cambridge, 1956–66; Lecturer in Divinity, University of Cambridge, 1959–67.*

The Rev. Aubrey Russell Vine (d. 1973). *General Secretary, Free Church Federal Council.*

Arthur Vööbus. *Emeritus Professor of New Testament and Church History, Lutheran School of Theology at Chicago.*

The Rev. Canon Herbert Montague Waddams (d. 1972). *Residentiary Canon of Canterbury Cathedral, Eng., 1962–72.*

David Waines. *Lecturer in Arabic and Islamic Studies, University of Lancaster, Eng.*

Francis Redding Walton. *Emeritus Director of the Gennadius Library, American School of Classical Studies, Athens.*

The Rt. Rev. and Rt. Hon. John William Charles Wand (d. 1977). *Canon and Treasurer of St. Paul's Cathedral, and Editor,* Church Quarterly Review, *1956–69. Bishop of London, 1944–55.*

James Hamilton Ware, Jr. *Professor of Philosophy and Religion; Chairman, Asian Studies Program, Austin College, Sherman, Texas.*

Edward Ingram Watkin (d. 1981). Author of Neglected Saints *and others.*

The Very Rev. Hugh Watt (d. 1968). *Professor of Church History, New College, 1919–50; University of Edinburgh, 1935–50.*

William Montgomery Watt. *Professor of Arabic and Islāmic Studies, University of Edinburgh, 1964–79.*

Rabbi Meyer Waxman (d. 1969). *Professor, Hebrew Theological College, Skokie, Ill.*

The Rev. Gustave Weigel, S.J. (d. 1964). *Professor of Ecclesiology, Woodstock College, Md., 1948–64.*

Egon Joseph Wellesz (d. 1974). *Composer. Reader in Byzantine Music, University of Oxford, 1948–56.*

R.J. Zwi Werblowsky. *Professor of Comparative Religion, Hebrew University of Jerusalem.*

James King West. *Professor of Religion and Philosophy, Catawba College, Salisbury, N.C.*

William J. Whalen. *Associate Professor of Communication, Purdue University, West Lafayette, Ind.; Director of Publications and University Editor; Director, Purdue University Press.* Author of Minority Religions in America *and others.*

The Rev. John Lloyd White, S.M. *Former Provincial Director of Education, Washington Province of the Society of Mary.*

The Very Rev. Henry Charles Whitley (d. 1976). *Minister of St. Giles' Cathedral, Edinburgh, 1954–72.*

Allen Paul Wikgren. *Emeritus Professor of New Testament Language and Literature, University of Chicago.*

Hellmut Wilhelm. *Emeritus Professor of Chinese History and Literature, University of Washington, Seattle.*

Robert L. Wilken. *Professor of the History of Christianity, University of Notre Dame, Ind.*

George Huntston Williams. *Hollis Professor of Divinity, Harvard University.*

J. Paul Williams (d. 1973). *Professor of Religion, Mt. Holyoke College, South Hadley, Mass., 1945–66.*

John Alden Williams. *Professor of Arab Studies, American University in Cairo. Professor of Art and Islamic Studies, University of Texas at Austin.*

Bryan R. Wilson. *Reader in Sociology, University of Oxford.*

Gustaf Wingren. *Emeritus Professor of Systematic Theology, University of Lund, Swed.*

The Rev. Allan Bernard Wolter, O.F.M. *Professor of Philosophy, Catholic University of America, Washington, D.C.*

Douglas Woodruff (d. 1978). *Editor,* The Tablet, *London, 1936–67.* Author of Church and State in History *and others.*

Donald Ernest Wilson Wormell. *Professor of Latin, University of Dublin, 1942–78.*

Franklin Woodrow Young. *Amos Ragan Kearns Professor of New Testament and Patristic Studies; Director of Graduate Studies in Religion, Duke University, Durham, N.C.*

Ying-shih Yu. *Charles Seymour Professor of History, Yale University.*

Sa-sun Yun. *Professor, Teacher's College, Seoul National University.*

The Rev. John H. Ziegler, C.S.P. *Former Chaplain to Catholic Students, University of Connecticut, Storrs.*

Larzer Ziff. *Caroline Donovan Professor of English, Johns Hopkins University, Baltimore.*

Part Nine. The History of Mankind

William Wright Abbot. *James Madison Professor of History, University of Virginia, Charlottesville.*

Thomas Perkins Abernethy (d. 1975). *Richmond Alumni Professor of History, University of Virginia, Charlottesville, 1930–61.*

Hélène Ahrweiler. *Chancellor, University of Paris; Professor of the History of Byzantine Civilization, University of Paris I.*

George Akita. *Professor of History, University of Hawaii, Honolulu.*

Victor Alba. *Emeritus Professor of Political Science, Kent State University, Ohio.*

John Richard Alden. *James B. Duke Professor Emeritus of History, Duke University, Durham, N.C.*

Anthony Dolphin Alderson. *Historian and translator. Director of Transouth Ltd., Fareham, Eng.*

Robert J. Alexander. *Professor of Economics and Political Science, Rutgers University, New Brunswick, N.J.*

Mohammad Ali (deceased). *Professor and Head, Department of History, Kābul University, Afg.*

Frank Raymond Allchin. *Reader in Indian Studies, University of Cambridge.*

Mary L. Allison. *Free-lance writer.*

Roberto Almagià (d. 1962). *Professor of Geography, University of Rome, 1915–59.*

Antony Andrewes. *Wykeham Professor of Ancient History, University of Oxford, 1953–77.*

Nikolay Andreyev (d. 1982). *Reader in Russian Studies, University of Cambridge; Fellow of Clare Hall, Cambridge.*

Roy Edgar Appleman. *Lieutenant Colonel, U.S. Army (retired). Historian, National Park Service, U.S. Department of the Interior, Washington, D.C., 1936–70.*

Karl Otmar, Baron von Aretin. *Professor of Contemporary History, Technical University of Darmstadt, W.Ger.*

Hassan Arfa. *Major General, Iranian Army (retired). Author of* Under Five Shahs *and others.*

Daniel Argov. *Former Lecturer in Modern Indian History, Institute of Asian and African Studies, Hebrew University of Jerusalem.*

Maurice Ashley. *Research Fellow, Loughborough University of Technology, Eng., 1967–70. Author of* England in the Seventeenth Century *and others.*

Arthur C.V.D. Aspinall (d. 1972). *Professor of Modern History, University of Reading, Eng., 1947–65.*

Clement Richard Attlee, 1st Earl Attlee (d. 1967). *Prime Minister of Great Britain, 1945–51. Labour Party Leader, 1935–56.*

Jacques, Comte d'Avout (d. 1978). *Historian. Author of* La Querelle des Armagnacs et des Bourguignons *and others.*

The Rev. Tarsicio de Azcona. *Former Professor of Theology, University of Navarre, Pamplona, Spain.*

Michael Graham Balfour. *Emeritus Professor of European History, University of East Anglia, Norwich, Eng.*

Evan Whyte-Melville Balfour-Melville (deceased). *Senior Lecturer in History, University of Edinburgh.*

Manuel Ballesteros Gaibrois. *Professor and Head, Section of American History, University of Madrid.*

Kenneth A. Ballhatchet. *Professor of the History of South Asia, School of Oriental and African Studies, University of London.*

John P.V. Dacre Balsdon (d. 1977). *Fellow of Exeter College, University of Oxford, 1928–69.*

Margaret Amelia Banks. *Law Librarian, University of Western Ontario, London.*

Cyril Nelson Barclay (d. 1979). *Brigadier, The Cameronians (Scottish Rifles). Editor,* The Army Quarterly and Defence Journal, *1950–66; coeditor,* Brassey's Annual: The Armed Forces Year Book, *1950–69.*

Thomas Swain Barclay. *Emeritus Professor of Political Science, Stanford University, Calif.*

William Eldon Baringer. *Historical writer. Professor of History, University of Florida, Gainesville, 1977–81.*

John Walton Barker, Jr. *Professor of History, University of Wisconsin, Madison.*

Frank Barlow. *Emeritus Professor of History, University of Exeter, Eng.*

Geoffrey Wallis Steuart Barrow. *Sir William Fraser Professor of Scottish History and Palaeography, University of Edinburgh.*

Dieter Bartels. *Instructor in Social Sciences/Humanities, Yavapai College, Clarkdale, Ariz.*

Michael Bar-Zohar. *Free-lance writer. Member of the Knesset. Former Lecturer in Political Science, Haifa University, Israel.*

Arthur Llewellyn Basham (d. 1986). *Professor of Asian Civilizations, Australian National University, Canberra.*

Charles R. Bawden. *Former Professor of Mongolian, University of London.*

Douglas C. Baxter. *Associate Professor of History, Ohio University, Athens.*

John Cawte Beaglehole (d. 1971). *Professor of British Commonwealth History, Victoria University of Wellington, N.Z., 1963–66.*

Hubert Irving Beatty. *Professor of History, West Virginia State College, Institute.*

Bernard Winslow Beckingsale. *Former Senior Lecturer in Modern History, University of Newcastle upon Tyne, Eng.*

Samuel Flagg Bemis (d. 1973). *Sterling Professor of Diplomatic History and Inter-American Relations, Yale University, 1945–61.*

D. Mary Benson. *Writer. Author of* Chief Albert Lutuli of South Africa *and others.*

Norman de Mattos Bentwich (d. 1971). *Professor of International Relations, Hebrew University of Jerusalem, 1932–51.*

Marvin David Bernstein. *Professor of History, State University of New York at Buffalo.*

Guillaume de Bertier de Sauvigny. *Professor of History, Catholic Institute of Paris, 1949–76.*

Hans H.A. Bielenstein. *Professor of Chinese History, Columbia University.*

Wilfred E. Binkley (d. 1965). *Professor of Political Science, Ohio Northern University, Ada.*

Thomas N. Bisson. *Professor of History, University of California, Berkeley.*

Adrian David Hugh Bivar. *Lecturer in Iranian and Central Asian Art and Archaeology, School of Oriental and African Studies, University of London.*

Robert Norman William Blake, Baron Blake. *Provost, Queen's College, University of Oxford.*

Georges Blond. *Novelist and historian. Author of* Pétain, 1856–1951 *and others.*

Martin Blumenson. *Historian, Office of Chief of Military History, Department of the Army, Washington, D.C., 1952–67.*

John Boardman. *Lincoln Professor of Classical Art and Archaeology, University of Oxford.*

Derk Bodde. *Emeritus Professor of Chinese, University of Pennsylvania, Philadephia.*

Robert Ralph Bolgar. *Fellow and Director of Studies in Modern Languages, King's College, University of Cambridge.*

Hans A. Bornewasser. *Professor at the Theologian Faculty, Catholic University of Tilburg, Neth.*

Alfredo Bosisio. *Professor of Medieval History, University of Pavia, Italy.*

Jean Bourdon. *Emeritus Professor of Modern History, University of Nancy, Fr.*

Robert Boutruche (d. 1975). *Professor of Economic History of the Middle Ages, University of Paris, 1958–73.*

William J. Bouwsma. *Sather Professor of History, University of California, Berkeley.*

G.W. Bowersock. *Professor of Ancient History, Institute for Advanced Study, Princeton, N.J.*

Mary Boyce. *Professor of Iranian Studies, School of Oriental and African Studies, University of London.*

Sir (John) Francis Boyd. *Political Correspondent,* The Guardian (*Manchester and London*), *1945–72; Political Editor, 1972–75.*

John Andrew Boyle (d. 1978). *Professor of Persian Studies, Victoria University of Manchester, 1966–78.*

Ernle Bradford (d. 1986). *Author of* The Wind Commands Me: A Life of Sir Francis Drake *and others.*

Harold Whitman Bradley. *Emeritus Professor of History, Vanderbilt University, Nashville, Tenn. Member, Tennessee House of Representatives, 1964–72.*

Robert J. Braidwood. *Emeritus Professor of Old World Prehistory, Oriental Institute, University of Chicago; Field Director, Oriental Institute Prehistoric Projects.*

Irving Brandt (d. 1976). *Member, Advisory Board, James Madison Papers, University of Chicago. Council Member, Institute of Early American History and Culture, 1959–62.*

Elias Lunn Bredsdorff. *Reader and Head, Department of Scandinavian Studies, University of Cambridge, 1960–79.*

Sidney Reed Brett. *Second Master, King Edward VI School, Nuneaton, Eng., 1921–54. Author of* British History, 1485–1939; John Pym, 1583–1643; *and others.*

Asa Briggs, Baron Briggs. *Provost of Worcester College, University of Oxford.*

Reginald Brill. *Free-lance writer and historian. Author of* Terror of the French: John, Lord Talbot, *c. 1388–1453.*

Fawn McKay Brodie (d. 1981). *Professor of History, University of California, Los Angeles, 1971–77.*

Adam Bromke. *Professor of Political Science, McMaster University, Hamilton, Ont.*

Thomas Robert Shannon Broughton. *Paddison Professor Emeritus of Classics, University of North Carolina at Chapel Hill.*

B. Katherine Brown. *Historian.*

Delmer M. Brown. *Emeritus Professor of History, University of California, Berkeley.*

Elizabeth A.R. Brown. *Professor of History, Brooklyn College and the Graduate Center, City University of New York.*

Andrew Browning (d. 1972). *Professor of History, University of Glasgow, 1931–57.*

Eleanor Stephens Bruchey. *Seminar Associate, Columbia University.*

Peter Astbury Brunt. *Camden Professor of Ancient History, University of Oxford; Fellow of Brasenose College, Oxford.*

Barbara Buckmaster (The Hon. Mrs. Barbara Miller) (d. 1966). *Writer on Balkan affairs. Member of the Staff, Foreign Research and Press Service, Royal Institute of International Affairs, London.*

Daniel Meredith Bueno de Mesquita. *Former Lecturer in Modern History, University of Oxford; former Student and Tutor of Christ Church, Oxford.*

Andrew Robert Burn. *Visiting Professor, A College Year in Athens, Inc., 1969–72. Reader in Ancient History, University of Glasgow, 1965–69.*

Sir Alan Cuthbert Burns (d. 1980). *Permanent Representative of the United Kingdom on the United Nations Trusteeship Council, 1947–56. Governor and Commander in Chief, Gold Coast, 1941–47.*

Alfred Leroy Burt (d. 1971). *Professor of History, University of Minnesota, Minneapolis, 1930–57.*

Ivor F. Burton. *Professor of Social Policy, Bedford College, University of London.*

Claude A. Buss. *Professor of History, U.S. Naval Postgraduate School, Monterey, Calif. Emeritus Professor of History, Stanford University, Calif.*

Sir James Ramsay Montagu Butler (d. 1975). *Regius Professor of Modern History, University of Cambridge, 1947–54. Chief Historian,* Official United Kingdom History of the Second World War *(military series).*

Robert F. Byrnes. *Distinguished Professor of History, Indiana University, Bloomington.*

Theodore John Cadoux. *Senior Lecturer in Ancient History, University of Edinburgh.*

Claude Cahen. *Emeritus Professor of Islāmic History, University of Paris.*

James Ford Cairns. *Member, House of Representatives, for the Division of Lalor, Victoria, 1969–77. Lecturer in Economic History, University of Melbourne, 1946–55.*

North Callahan. *Emeritus Professor of History, New York University, New York City.*

Wilfrid Hardy Callcott (d. 1969). *Professor of History, University of South Carolina, Columbia.*

Pedro Calmon. *President, Brazilian Historical and Geographical Institute, Rio de Janeiro.*

George Glenn Cameron (d. 1979). *Professor of Near Eastern Cultures, University of Michigan, Ann Arbor, 1948–75; Chairman, Department of Near Eastern Languages and Literatures, 1948–71.*

Manoel Cardozo (d. 1985). *Professor of History, 1954–78; Curator, Oliveira Lima Library, Catholic University of America, Washington, D.C.*

J.M.S. Careless. *Professor of History, University of Toronto.*

Sten C.O. Carlsson. *Emeritus Professor of History, University of Uppsala, Swed.*

André Castelot. *Biographer and historical scriptwriter for radio and television.*

Frank Catania. *Free-lance writer on Southeast Asia.*

John W. Caughey. *Professor of American History, University of California, Los Angeles, 1946–70.*

Raymond Cazelles. *Curator, Condé Museum, Chantilly, Fr.*

David B. Chan. *Professor of History, California State University, Hayward.*

Jean-Léon Charles. *Professor of Military History, Belgian Royal Military Academy, Brussels.*

Jacques Chastenet de Castaing (d. 1978). *Historian and journalist. Author of* Léon Gambetta *and others.*

B.D. Chattopadhyaya. *Associate Professor of History, Jawaharlal Nehru University, New Delhi.*

Jerome Ch'en. *Professor of East Asian History, York University, Toronto.*

Jean-Jacques Chevallier. *Emeritus Professor of the History of Political Thought, University of Paris.*

Luciano Chiappini. *Teacher. President, Ferrarese Delegation for the History of Italy. Committeeman, Antonio Frizzi Institute for the History of Ferrara.*

Marquis William Childs. *Columnist, reporter, and biographer.*

Guy Edward Farquhar Chilver (d. 1982). *Professor of Classical Studies, University of Kent at Canterbury, Eng., 1964–76.*

Tse-tsung Chow. *Professor of East Asian Languages, Literature, and History, University of Wisconsin, Madison.*

Ian R. Christie. *Astor Professor of British History, University College, University of London.*

Sima M. Ćirković. *Professor of the Medieval History of Yugoslavia, University of Belgrade.*

William Bell Clark (d. 1968). *Naval biographer. Vice President, N.W. Ayer & Son, 1939–50. Editor,* Documentary Naval History of the American Revolution.

Jesse Dunsmore Clarkson (d. 1973). *Professor of History, Brooklyn College, City University of New York, 1945–67.*

Sheldon S. Cohen. *Professor of U.S. and Colonial History, Loyola University, Chicago.*

Henry Jacob Cohn. *Senior Lecturer in History, University of Warwick, Coventry, Eng.*

Hugh Marshal Cole. *Vice President, Research Analysis Corporation, McLean, Va. Author of* The Lorraine Campaign; The Ardennes: Battle of the Bulge.

Douglas Colyer (d. 1978). *Air Marshal. Civil Aviation Representative, Western Europe, Ministry of Transport and Civil Aviation, 1952–60.*

James Richard Connor. *Chancellor and Professor of History, University of Wisconsin, Whitewater.*

F. Hilary Conroy. *Professor of Far Eastern History, University of Pennsylvania, Philadelphia.*

Sarah Gibbard Cook. *Free-lance writer on history and geography.*

W. Mercer Cook. *Emeritus Professor of Romance Languages, Howard University, Washington, D.C.*

W. Ph. Coolhaas (deceased). *Professor of Colonial History, Utrecht University, Neth.*

J. Terry Copp. *Professor of History, Wilfrid Laurier University, Waterloo, Ont.*

James A(rthur) Corbett. *Emeritus Professor of Medieval History, University of Notre Dame, Ind.*

Cornelius P. Cotter. *Professor of Political Science, University of Wisconsin, Milwaukee.*

Jean Cousin. *Former Professor of Latin Language and Literature, University of Besançon, Fr.*

James Coyle. *Free-lance writer on Vietnamese history.*

Peter Craumer. *Consultant and writer on Polish history and affairs.*

Avery Craven (d. 1980). *Professor of American History, University of Chicago, 1927–72.*

Ralph C. Croizier. *Professor of History, University of Victoria, B.C.*

John Anthony Crook. *Professor of Ancient History, University of Cambridge, 1979–84.*

François Marie-Joseph Crouzet. *Professor of Economic History, University of Paris.*

William Culican (d. 1984). *Reader in History, University of Melbourne, 1972–84.*

Noble E. Cunningham, Jr. *Professor of History, University of Missouri, Columbia.*

Richard N. Current. *University Distinguished Professor Emeritus of History, University of North Carolina, Greensboro.*

Douglas Dakin. *Former Professor and Head, Department of History, Birkbeck College, University of London.*

Stephanie Mary Dalley. *Independent researcher. Contributor to* Iraq *(journal).*

Robert V. Daniels. *Professor of History, University of Vermont, Burlington.*

Adrien Dansette (d. 1976). *Member of the Academy of Moral and Political Sciences, Paris.*

Cuthbert Collin Davies (d. 1974). *Reader in Indian History, University of Oxford, 1936–63.*

Ernest Albert John Davies. *Publisher,* Traffic Engineering and Control; *Editor, 1960–76. Member of Parliament for Enfield East, Eng., 1945–59. Chairman, Labour Party Transport Committee, 1945–59.*

William Robert Davies. *Secretary, Liberal Party Organization, 1936–55.*

Warren Royal Dawson (d. 1968). *Hon. Fellow, Imperial College of Science. Hon. Member, Egypt Exploration Society.*

Istvan Deak. *Professor of History, Columbia University.*

Ann Dearden. *Author of* Jordan.

Alexander De Conde. *Professor of History, University of California, Santa Barbara.*

Juliette C. Decreus. *Former Senior Lecturer in French, Queen Mary College, University of London.*

John Coleman de Graft-Johnson (d. 1977). *Editor,* Economic Bulletin of Ghana. *Research Associate Professor of Economics, University of Ghana.*

Herbert Stanley Deighton. *Lecturer in International Politics, Brunel University, Uxbridge, Eng., 1967–73.*

John Duncan Martin Derrett. *Professor of Oriental Laws, University of London.*

Ranjit Ramchandra Desai. *Agriculturist and writer. Author of* Srīmāna Yogī: the Life of Śivajī in Marathi *and others.*

Jean Descola (d. 1981). *Historian. Director, Ibero-American Center for Study and Research, Paris.*

Georges Dethan. *Archivist, French Foreign Ministry Archives, Paris. Chief Editor,* Revue d'Histoire Diplomatique.

Jean Devisse. *Lecturer, University of Paris VIII.*

Harry T. Dickinson. *Professor of History, University of Edinburgh.*

Heide Dienst. *Assistant, Institute of Austrian History Research, University of Vienna.*

Porphyrios Dikaios (d. 1971). *Professor, Archaeological Institute, Rupert Charles University of Heidelberg, W.Ger. Director of Antiquities, Nicosia, Cyprus, 1960–63.*

Dimitrije V. Djordjevic. *Professor of History, University of California, Santa Barbara.*

Mário José Domingues. *Author of* O Marquês de Pombal *and others.*

Jorge I. Domínguez. *Professor of Government; Member, Center for International Affairs, Harvard University.*

David Herbert Donald. *Charles Warren Professor of American History and Professor of American Civilization, Harvard University.*

Gordon Donaldson. *Emeritus Professor of Scottish History and Palaeography, University of Edinburgh.*

Andreas Dorpalen (d. 1982). *Professor of History, Ohio State University, Columbus, 1958–78.*

Clifford Dowdey (d. 1979). *Lecturer in Creative Writing, University of Richmond, Va., 1958–69. Author of* Lee *and others.*

Glanville Downey. *Distinguished Professor Emeritus of History and of Classical Studies, Indiana University, Bloomington.*

Margaret Stefana Drower. *Former Reader in Ancient History, University College, University of London.*

Joaquin Milton Duarte, Jr. *Dom Pedro II Professor of Luso-Brazilian and Hispanic American Studies; Chairman, Department of International Studies, American Graduate School of International Management, Glendale, Ariz.*

Eleanor Shipley Duckett (d. 1976). *Professor of Classical Languages and Literature, Smith College, Northampton, Mass., 1928–49.*

Jack L. Dull. *Associate Professor of History; Chairman, China Program, School of International Studies, University of Washington, Seattle.*

Richard S. Dunn. *Professor of History, University of Pennsylvania, Philadelphia.*

Trevor Nevitt Dupuy. *Colonel, U.S. Army (retired). President and Executive Director, Historical Evaluation and Research Organization, McLean, Va.*

Enrique Dussel. *Professor of Ethics, National Autonomous University of Mexico, Mexico City.*

Brainerd Dyer. *Emeritus Professor of History, University of California, Los Angeles.*

Denys G. Dyer. *University Lecturer in German, University of Oxford; Fellow of Exeter College, Oxford.*

Robert Harris Dyson, Jr. *Professor of Anthropology; Curator, Near Eastern Section, University Museum, University of Pennsylvania, Philadelphia.*

David Magarey Earl. *Former Professor of History, Eastern Michigan University, Ypsilanti.*

Robert A. East. *Emeritus Professor of History, Brooklyn College, City University of New York.*

Arimichi Ebisawa. *Guest Professor of History, International Christian University, Tokyo. President, Society of Historical Studies of Christianity, Japan.*

W.J. Eccles. *Emeritus Professor of History, University of Toronto.*

Robert Walter Dudley Edwards. *Former Professor of Modern Irish History, University College, Dublin, National University of Ireland.*

Lajos Elekes. *Professor of the Medieval History of Hungary, Eötvös Loránd University, Budapest.*

Nikita Elisséeff. *Professor of Islamic History and Archaeology, University of Lyon II.*

Sir Ivo D'Oyly Elliott (d. 1961). *Indian Civil Service, 1906–32.*

Sir Geoffrey R. Elton. *Regius Professor of Modern History, University of Cambridge.*

Marcel Emerit. *Emeritus Professor of History; Member, Academy of Ethics and Politics, Institute of France.*

William Richard Emerson. *Director, Franklin D. Roosevelt Library, Hyde Park, N.Y.*

Henrik Enander. *Former Lecturer in History, University of Stockholm.*

Jens Engberg. *Professor of History, University of Arhus, Den.*

Philippe Erlanger. *Minister Plenipotentiary. Former Director of Cultural Activities, Ministry of Foreign Affairs, Paris.*

Heinrich Gustav Euler. *Professor of Modern History, University of Würzburg, W.Ger.*

(Henry) Outram Evennett (d. 1964). *Fellow of Trinity College, Cambridge; Lecturer in History, University of Cambridge, 1930–55.*

John E. Fagg. *Emeritus Professor of History, New York University, New York City.*

Stanley Lawrence Falk. *Deputy Chief Historian, Southeast Asia, U.S. Army Center of Military History, Washington, D.C.*

Cyril Bentham Falls (d. 1971). *Military Correspondent of* The Times *(London), 1939–53. Chichele Professor of the History of War, University of Oxford, 1946–53.*

Raymond Oliver Faulkner (deceased). *Fellow of University College, London; Lecturer in Ancient Egyptian, University College, University of London, 1955–67.*

Lee Nathan Feigon. *Associate Professor of History and Asian Studies, Colby College, Waterville, Maine. Staff Writer, East Asian Affairs,* Encyclopædia Britannica, *Chicago, 1970–73.*

Isaac M. Fein. *Emeritus Professor of Jewish History, Baltimore Hebrew College.*

John Lister Illingworth Fennell. *Professor of Russian, University of Oxford.*

Michael de Ferdinandy. *Emeritus Professor of Humanities, University of Puerto Rico, Río Piedras.*

John Ferguson. *President, Selly Oak Colleges, Birmingham, Eng. Professor, Dean, and Director of Studies in Arts, The Open University, Milton Keynes, Eng., 1969–79.*

William Ferguson. *Reader in Scottish History, University of Edinburgh.*

Sir James Fergusson of Kilkerran, 8th Bart. (d. 1973). *Keeper of the Records of Scotland, 1949–69.*

Ronald Whitaker Ferrier. *Assistant Professor and Head, Department of English, Pahlavi University, Iran, 1963–65.*

Charles Patrick FitzGerald. *Emeritus Professor of Far Eastern History, Australian National University, Canberra.*

Russell H. Fitzgibbon (d. 1979). *Professor of Political Science, University of California, Santa Barbara, 1964–72.*

Geoffrey Bernard Abbott Fletcher. *Professor of Latin, University of Newcastle upon Tyne, Eng., 1963–69. Author of* Annotations on Tacitus.

Michael T. Florinsky (d. 1981). *Professor of Economics, Columbia University, 1956–63.*

David Floyd. *Special correspondent on Communist affairs,* The Daily Telegraph *and* The Sunday Telegraph, *London.*

Philip S. Foner. *Independence Foundation Professor Emeritus of History, Lincoln University, Pennsylvania.*

Michael Richard Daniell Foot. *Professor of History, Victoria University of Manchester, 1967–73.*

William George Forrest. *Fellow of New College, Oxford; Wykeham Professor of Ancient History, University of Oxford.*

Heinrich Fraenkel (d. 1986). Free-lance writer. *Author of* The Other Germany; *coauthor of* Hermann Göring *and many others.*

Enno Franzius. *Historian. Author of* History of the Byzantine Empire *and others.*

Lady Antonia Fraser. *Writer. Author of* Mary, Queen of Scots *and others.*

Greville Stewart Parker Freeman-Grenville. *Honorary Fellow, University of York, Heslington, Eng. Former Professor of African History, State University of New York College at New Paltz.*

Frank Freidel. *Professor of History, University of Washington, Seattle. Emeritus Professor of History, Harvard University.*

Michael Freund (d. 1973). *Professor of Political Theory and History, Christian Albrecht University of Kiel, W.Ger.*

Jean Claude Froelich (d. 1972). *Director, Center for Advanced Studies on Modern Africa and Asia, University of Paris.*

Richard N. Frye. *Aga Khan Professor of Iranian, Harvard University.*

André Fugier. *Former Professor of Modern History, University of Lyon, Fr.*

Fujimura Michio. *Professor of History, Sophia University, Tokyo.*

Sir Roger Fulford (d. 1983). *Author of* Royal Dukes *and others; coeditor of* The Greville Memoirs.

Edmund Fuller. *Writer and editor. Book Reviewer,* Wall Street Journal. *Coeditor of* Four American Biographies *and others.*

Cyril John Gadd (d. 1969). *Professor of Ancient Semitic Languages and Civilizations, University of London, 1955–60. Keeper, Egyptian and Assyrian Antiquities, British Museum, London, 1948–55.*

Vivian Hunter Galbraith (d. 1976). *Regius Professor of Modern History, University of Oxford, 1947–57.*

Kenneth Garrad. *Professor of Spanish, Flinders University of South Australia, Bedford Park (Adelaide).*

Noel George Garson. *Professor of History, University of the Witwatersrand, Johannesburg.*

Raymond Leonard Garthoff. *U.S. foreign service officer (retired); U.S. Ambassador to Bulgaria, 1977–79.*

Norman Gash. *Emeritus Professor of History, University of St. Andrews, Scot.*

Deno John Geanakoplos. *Professor of History and Religious Studies, Yale University.*

Lucien Genet. *Inspector General of Public Instruction, Paris.*

Eugen Gerstenmaier (d. 1986). *President, Bundestag (lower house of the Federal Assembly), Federal Republic of Germany, 1954–69.*

Sir Hamilton Alexander Rosskeen Gibb (d. 1971). *University Professor and J.R. Jewett Professor of Arabic, Harvard University, 1955–64.*

Frank B. Gibney. *Vice Chairman, Board of Editors, Encyclopædia Britannica, Inc., Chicago. Vice Chairman, TBS-Britannica Company Ltd., Tokyo. Author of* The Khrushchev Pattern *and others.*

Frederick Wellington Gibson. *Professor of History, Queen's University at Kingston, Ont.*

Aleksander Gieysztor. *Professor of Medieval History, University of Warsaw.*

Sara D. Gilbert. *Free-lance writer.*

Robert Louis Gilmore. *Professor of History, University of Kansas, Lawrence.*

Marija Gimbutas. *Professor of European Archaeology, University of California, Los Angeles.*

Martin Gimm. *Professor of Sinology, University of Cologne.*

Wassil Todorov Gjuzelev. *Professor of Bulgarian Medieval History, University of Sofia.*

Sir John Bagot Glubb (d. 1986). *Lieutenant General; Chief of General Staff, The Arab Legion, Amman, Jordan, 1939–56.*

Jacques Godechot. *Emeritus Professor of Modern and Contemporary History; Honorary Dean, Faculty of Letters, University of Toulouse II, Fr.*

Ludwig von Gogolák. *Author of* Csehszlovákia *and others.*

Alfred Goldberg. *Senior Social Scientist, Rand Corporation, Washington, D.C. Chief, Current History Branch, U.S. Department of the Air Force, 1944–65.*

L. Carrington Goodrich. *Dean Lung Professor Emeritus of Chinese, Columbia University.*

Albert Goodwin. *Emeritus Professor of Modern History, Victoria University of Manchester.*

Cyrus H. Gordon. *Professor of Hebraic Studies; Director, Center for Ebla Research, New York University, New York City. Emeritus Professor of Mediterranean Studies, Brandeis University, Waltham, Mass.*

Walter Otto Julius Görlitz. *Journalist; Editorial Staff,* Die Welt, *Hamburg.*

Norman A. Graebner. *Edward R. Stettinius Professor of History, University of Virginia, Charlottesville.*

William Roger Graham. *Douglas Professor of Canadian History, Queen's University at Kingston, Ont.*

Bruce Grant (d. 1977). *Author of* Isaac Hull: Captain of Old Ironsides *and others.*

Michael Grant. *President and Vice Chancellor, Queen's University of Belfast, Northern Ireland, 1959–66.*

Eric William Gray. *Lecturer in Ancient History, University of Oxford; Official Student and Tutor in Roman History, Christ Church, Oxford, 1939–77.*

Richard L. Greaves. *Professor of History, Florida State University, Tallahassee.*

Constance McLaughlin Green (d. 1975). *Director, Washington History Project, American University, Washington, D.C., 1954–60. Pulitzer Prize for History, 1963.*

Fletcher Melvin Green (d. 1978). *Kenan Professor of History, University of North Carolina at Chapel Hill.*

George William Greenaway. *Former Senior Lecturer in History, University of Exeter, Eng.*

Jonas Carl Greenfield. *Professor of Ancient Semitic Languages, Hebrew University of Jerusalem.*

Richard David Greenfield. *Former Director of General Studies, University of Benin, Nigeria.*

Thomas Hoag Greer. *Emeritus Professor of Humanities, Michigan State University, East Lansing.*

John A.S. Grenville. *Professor of Modern History, University of Birmingham, Eng.*

Ian Grey. *Author of* Catherine the Great; The First Fifty Years: Soviet Russia 1917–67; *and others.*

Guy Thompson Griffith (d. 1985). *Laurence Reader in Classics, University of Cambridge, 1951–75; Fellow of Gonville and Caius College, Cambridge.*

Géza Grosschmid. *Professor of Economics, Duquesne University, Pittsburgh; Director, Institute of African Affairs, 1959–70.*

Hans G. Güterbock. *Tiffany and Margaret Blake Distinguished Service Professor Emeritus of Hittitology, Oriental Institute, University of Chicago.*

Denis Rolleston Gwynn (d. 1971). *Research Professor of Modern Irish History, University College, Cork, National University of Ireland, 1946–63.*

Richard Carleton Haines (d. 1977). *Field Architect, 1930–42 and 1949–72; Assistant Professor, 1963–71, Oriental Institute, University of Chicago.*

K.H.D. Haley. *Emeritus Professor of Modern History, University of Sheffield, Eng.*

John Whitney Hall. *Griswold Professor of History, Yale University.*

Theodore S. Hamerow. *Professor of History, University of Wisconsin, Madison.*

Mary Agnes Hamilton (d. 1966). *Editor, English-Speaking World. Author of* Sidney and Beatrice Webb *and others.*

The Rev. Raphael Noteware Hamilton, S.J. (d. 1980). *Professor of History, Marquette University, Milwaukee, 1932–64; Archivist, 1960–73.*

Oscar J. Hammen. *Emeritus Professor of History, University of Montana, Missoula.*

Mason Hammond. *Pope Professor Emeritus of Latin Language and Literature; former Professor of Roman History, Harvard University.*

Nicholas G.L. Hammond. *Henry Overton Wills Professor Emeritus of Greek, University of Bristol, Eng.*

Ralph Hammond Innes. *Novelist and writer on history and travel. Author of* The Conquistadors *and many others.*

Eric Walter Handley. *Professor of Greek, University College, University of London.*

Cyril Francis James Hankinson (d. 1984). *Editor,* Debrett's Peerage, *London, 1935–62.*

Willard A. Hanna. *Senior Associate, Universities Field Staff International, Hanover, New Hampshire.*

Sidney Harcave. *Emeritus Professor of History, State University of New York at Binghamton.*

Peter Hardy. *Reader in the History of Islām in South Asia, School of Oriental and African Studies, University of London.*

Claude Harmel. *Editor,* Les Études Sociales et Syndicales, *Paris. Former Secretary, Institute for Social History, Paris.*

John A. Harrison. *Emeritus Professor of History, University of Miami, Coral Gables, Fla. Editor,* The Journal of Asian Studies, *1969–72.*

John Bennett Harrison. *Reader in the History of South Asia, School of Oriental and African Studies, University of London.*

Erich Hugo Hassinger. *Emeritus Professor of Modern History, Albert Ludwig University of Freiburg, Freiburg im Breisgau, W.Ger.*

Warren W. Hassler, Jr. *Professsor of American History, Pennsylvania State University, University Park.*

Ragnhild Marie Hatton. *Professor of International History, London School of Economics and Political Science, University of London.*

Alfred F. Havighurst. *Emeritus Professor of History, Amherst College, Mass.*

Zenos Eric Myhren Hawkinson. *Professor of History, North Park College, Chicago.*

G.R. Hawting. *Lecturer in the History of the Near and Middle East, School of Oriental and African Studies, University of London.*

Shigeru Hayashi. *Professor, Institute of Social Science, University of Tokyo.*

Charles W. Hayford. *Associate, Department of History, Northwestern University, Evanston, Ill., and Center for Far Eastern Studies, University of Chicago.*

Stephen Heder. *Free-lance writer and consultant on Cambodia.*

Helmut Heiber. *Assistant, Institute for Contemporary History, Munich. Author of* Joseph Goebbels *and others.*

Walter Heinemeyer. *Professor of Medieval History, Philipps University of Marburg, W.Ger.*

Heinz Heinen. *Professor of Ancient History, University of Trier, W.Ger.*

Richard Hellie. *Professor of Russian History, University of Chicago.*

Charles Alistair Hennessy. *Professor of History, University of Warwick, Coventry, Eng.*

Stanislaw Herbst (d. 1973). *Professor of Pre-18th Century Polish History, University of Warsaw. President, Polish Historic Society, Warsaw.*

Hans Herzfeld (d. 1982). *Professor of Modern History, Free University of Berlin, 1950–60.*

William B. Hesseltine (d. 1963). *Professor of History, University of Wisconsin, 1940–63.*

Christopher Hibbert. *Historian and biographer. Author of* Benito Mussolini; The Rise and Fall of Il Duce; *and others.*

Agnes H. Hicks. *Member and Honorary Consultant on Scandinavian Affairs, Royal Institute of International Affairs.*

Jay Higginbotham. *Head, Local History Department, Mobile Public Library, Ala.*

J.R.L. Highfield. *Fellow of Merton College, Oxford; Lecturer in Modern History, University of Oxford.*

Patrice Louis-René Higonnet. *Professor of History, Harvard University.*

John Hugh Hill. *Emeritus Professor of Medieval History, University of Houston, Texas.*

Laurita L. Hill (deceased). *Writer and editor. Instructor in History, University of Texas, Austin, 1963–68.*

Richard Leslie Hill. *Professor of History, Abdullahi Bayero College, Ahmadu Bello University, Kano, Nigeria, 1968–69. Lecturer in Modern Near Eastern History, University of Durham, Eng., 1949–66.*

Thomas Hodgkin (d. 1982). *Writer. Fellow of Balliol College, Oxford; Lecturer in the Government of New States, University of Oxford, 1965–70.*

Fritz L(eo) Hoffmann. *Emeritus Professor of Latin-American History, University of Colorado, Boulder.*

Keigo Hogetsu. *Honorary Professor of Literature, University of Tokyo.*

C. Warren Hollister. *Professor of History, University of California, Santa Barbara.*

Edgar Crawshaw Holt (d. 1975). *Author and journalist. Author of* The Making of Italy, 1815–1870 *and others.*

J.C. Holt. *Professor of Medieval History, University of Cambridge.*

Shan-Yüan Hsieh. *Former Assistant Professor of Philosophy, Haverford College, Pa.*

Walther C. Hubatsch. *Professor of Medieval and Modern History, Rhenish Friedrich Wilhelm University of Bonn.*

Jean Hubert. *Emeritus Professor of Medieval Archaeology, École Nationale des Chartes (School of Paleography), Paris.*

Charles O(scar) Hucker. *Emeritus Professor of Chinese and of History, University of Michigan, Ann Arbor.*

Harri Llwyd Hudson-Williams. *Emeritus Professor of Greek, University of Newcastle upon Tyne, Eng.*

Jean-Louis Huot. *Professor of Oriental Archaeology, University of Paris I.*

Joel Hurstfield (d. 1980). *Astor Professor of English History, University College, University of London, 1962–79.*

Mahmud Husain (d. 1975). *Vice Chancellor, University of Karāchi, Pakistan.*

Joan Mervyn Hussey. *Emeritus Professor of History, Royal Holloway College, University of London.*

Richard Wyatt Hutchinson (d. 1970). *Lecturer in Classical Archaeology, University of Cambridge, 1952–55, and University of Liverpool, 1948–57.*

William Thomas Hutchinson (d. 1976). *Preston and Sterling Morton Professor of American History, University of Chicago, 1955–62.*

Nobutaka Ike. *Professor of Political Science, Stanford University, Calif.*

Joseph E. Illick. *Professor of History, San Francisco State University.*

Halil Inalcik. *Professor of History, University of Chicago.*

Denis Liddell Ireland. *Senator, Republic of Ireland, 1948–51. Author of* Patriot Adventure *and others.*

Keith Irvine. *President, Reference Publications, Inc., Algonac, Michigan. Principal Editor, Geography, Encyclopædia Britannica, Chicago, 1969–72. Research Officer, Permanent Mission of Ghana to the United Nations, New York City, 1958–69.*

Fahir İz. *Professor of Turkish Literature, Boğaziçi University, Istanbul.*

D. Clayton James. *Professor of History, Mississippi State University, Mississippi State.*

Marius B. Jansen. *Professor of History, Princeton University.*

Wilhelmina Feemster Jashemski. *Emeritus Professor of Ancient History, University of Maryland, College Park.*

Yette Jeandet. *Former Editor,* Literary News, *Bayard-Presse, Paris. Author of* Blanche de Castille, reine de l'unité française *and others.*

Barbara Jelavich. *Professor of History, Indiana University, Bloomington.*

Dafydd Jenkins. *Former Reader in Law, University College of Wales, Aberystwyth, University of Wales.*

Robert Thomas Jenkins (d. 1969). *Professor of Welsh History, University College of North Wales, Bangor, University of Wales, 1945–48.*

Rt. Hon. Roy Jenkins. *Member of Parliament. President of the European Commission, 1977–81. Chancellor of the Exchequer, 1967–70.*

John J. Johnson. *Emeritus Professor of History, Stanford University, Calif. Author of* Political Change in Latin America *and others.*

Robert Carl Johnson. *Associate Professor of History, Temple University, Philadelphia.*

Arnold Hugh Martin Jones (d. 1970). *Professor of Ancient History, University of Cambridge, 1951–70.*

Frits de Jong. *Professor of Modern and Contemporary History, University of Amsterdam.*

Adriaan G. Jongkees. *Professor of Medieval History, State University of Groningen, Neth.*

Karl H.E. Jordan. *Emeritus Professor of Medieval and Modern History, Christian Albrecht University of Kiel, W.Ger.*

Albert Jourcin. *Professor agrégé honoraire. Author of* Les Médicis *and others.*

Eino Kaarlo Ilmari Jutikkala. *Professor of Finnish History, University of Helsinki, 1947–50; 1954–74.*

Wadie Jwaideh. *Professor of History and Arabic; Chairman, Department of Near Eastern Languages and Literatures, Indiana University, Bloomington.*

Walter Emil Kaegi, Jr. *Professor of Byzantine and Roman History, University of Chicago.*

Nobuo Kanda. *Professor of East Asian History, Meiji University, Tokyo.*

Robert A. Kann (d. 1981). *Professor of History, Rutgers University, New Brunswick, N.J., 1956–76.*

Alexander Sydney Kanya-Forstner. *Professor of History, York University, Downsview, Ont.*

Enver Ziya Karal. *President, Turkish Historical Society. Former Professor of Contemporary History, University of Ankara.*

Thomas L(indas) Karnes. *Professor of History, Arizona State University, Tempe.*

Hugh Francis Kearney. *Former Richard Pares Professor of History, University of Edinburgh.*

Benjamin Keen. *Emeritus Professor of History, Northern Illinois University, De Kalb.*

John L.H. Keep. *Professor of Russian History, University of Toronto.*

Harper Kelley (deceased). *Head of Research, National Center for Scientific Research, Paris. Head, Department of Prehistory, Musée de l'Homme, Paris.*

Jerold Kellman. *Free-lance writer.*

Annajane Kennard. *Former Librarian, Straits Times Press, Malaysia.*

John P. Kenyon. *Professor of Modern History, University of St. Andrews, Scot.*

Dame Kathleen Mary Kenyon (d. 1978). *Principal, St. Hugh's College, University of Oxford, 1962–73. Director, British School of Archaeology, Jerusalem, 1951–66.*

George Briscoe Kerferd. *Emeritus Professor of Greek, Victoria University of Manchester, Eng.*

Tarif Khalidi. *Associate Professor of History and Archaeology, American University of Beirut.*

Stefan Kieniewicz. *Emeritus Professor of 19th and 20th Century Polish History, University of Warsaw.*

Martin Kilson. *Professor of Government, Harvard University; Research Associate, Harvard Center for International Affairs.*

P.D. King. *Senior Lecturer in History, University of Lancaster, Eng.*

Jay Kinsbruner. *Professor of History, Queens College, City University of New York.*

Russell Amos Kirk. *Author and lecturer. Editor,* The University Bookman.

Donald W. Klein. *Lecturer in Political Science, Tufts University, Medford, Mass.*

Wilfrid F. Knapp. *Dean, Fellow, and Tutor in Politics, St. Catherine's College, Oxford; Lecturer in Politics, University of Oxford.*

George Harmon Knoles. *Margaret Byrne Professor Emeritus of American History, Stanford University, Calif.*

Bernhard Knollenberg (d. 1973). *Fellow of Saybrook College, Yale University; Yale Librarian, 1938–44. Author of* Origin of the American Revolution *and others.*

Lionel Kochan. *Bearsted Reader in Jewish History, University of Warwick, Eng.*

Helmut Georg Koenigsberger. *Emeritus Professor of History, King's College, University of London.*

Hans Kohn (d. 1971). *Professor of History, City College, City University of New York, 1949–62.*

Frank P. Kolb. *Professor of Ancient History, Christian Albrecht University of Kiel, W.Ger.*

E.H. Kossmann. *Professor of Modern History, State University of Groningen, Neth.*

E.A. Kracke, Jr. (d. 1976). *Professor of Chinese Literature and Institutions, University of Chicago, 1960–73.*

Carl H(ermann) Kraeling (d. 1966). *Professor of Archaeology, 1950–62; Director, Oriental Institute, 1950–60, University of Chicago.*

Daniel Wilhelmus Kruger. *Professor of History, University of the Transkei, Umtata.*

Hyman Kublin. *Emeritus Professor of History, Brooklyn College, City University of New York.*

Harold Kurtz (d. 1972). *Author of* The Trial of Marshal Ney: His Last Years and Death *and others.*

Tadachika Kuwata. *Emeritus Professor of Japanese History, Kokugakuin University, Tokyo.*

Jean Lacouture. *Former Professor, Institute for Political Studies, University of Paris. Adviser, Éditions du Seuil, Paris.*

Jorgen Laessoe. *Professor of Assyriology, University of Copenhagen.*

Robert George Dalrymple Laffan (d. 1972). *University Lecturer, University of Cambridge, 1927–53; Fellow of Queen's College, Cambridge.*

Charles-André Laffargue. *General, French Army (retired). Author of* Foch et la Bataille de 1918 *and others.*

Ursula Schaefer Lamb. *Professor of History, University of Arizona, Tucson.*

Gustave Lanctot (d. 1975). *Dominion Archivist and Deputy Minister of the Canadian Archives, 1937–48.*

Aubrey C(hristian) Land. *Research Professor of History, University of Georgia, Athens.*

Yvonne Lanhers. *Curator, National Archives, Paris.*

Taft Alfred Larson. *Member, House of Representatives, Wyoming State Legislature. William Robertson Coe Distinguished Professor Emeritus of American Studies, University of Wyoming, Laramie.*

Agnes M.C. Latham. *Former Reader in English, Bedford College, University of London.*

Hugh Talmage Lefler. *Kenan Professor Emeritus of History, University of North Carolina at Chapel Hill.*

George Alexander Lensen (d. 1980). *Professor of History, Florida State University, Tallahassee, 1959–80.*

Alexander Marie Norbert Lernet-Holenia (d. 1976). *Novelist and playwright. Author of* Prinz Eugen *and others.*

Jacques Levron. *Honorary Chief Curator, Archives of France, Paris.*

Reuben Levy (d. 1966). *Professor of Persian, University of Cambridge, 1950–58.*

Bernard Lewis. *Cleveland E. Dodge Professor of Near Eastern Studies, Princeton University.*

David Malcolm Lewis. *Student and Tutor in Ancient History, Christ Church, Oxford; Lecturer in Greek Epigraphy, University of Oxford.*

Lucjan Ryszard Lewitter. *Professor and Head, Department of Slavonic Studies, University of Cambridge; Fellow of Christ's College, Cambridge.*

K.J. Leyser. *Fellow and Tutor in Modern History, Magdalen College, Oxford; Lecturer in Modern History, University of Oxford.*

Alphons Lhotsky (d. 1968). *Professor of Austrian History, University of Vienna, 1951–68.*

Li Chi. *Emeritus Director, Institute of History and Philology, Academia Sinica, Tapei. Director of Excavations at An-yang.*

Heinz Lieberich. *General Director, Bavarian State Archives, Munich.*

Kenneth G. Lieberthal. *Professor of Political Science; Research Associate, Center for Chinese Studies, University of Michigan, Ann Arbor.*

Hans Liebeschütz (d. 1978). *Reader in Medieval History, University of Liverpool, 1955–59.*

Chan Lien. *Professor of Political Science, National Taiwan University, Taipei.*

Adolf Lippold. *Professor of History, University of Regensburg, W.Ger.*

Donald P. Little. *Professor and Director, Institute of Islāmic Studies, McGill University, Montreal.*

Harold V. Livermore. *Former Professor of Spanish and Portuguese, University of British Columbia, Vancouver.*

Charles Christopher Lloyd (d. 1986). *Professor of History, Royal Naval College, Greenwich, Eng., 1962–66.*

Robert Bruce Lloyd. *Mary Frances Williams Professor of Humanities, Randolph-Macon Woman's College, Lynchburg, Va.*

Jung-pang Lo (d. 1981). *Professor of History, University of California, Davis, 1969–76.*

Henry Cabot Lodge (d. 1985). *Personal Envoy of the President to the Vatican, 1970–77. United States Ambassador to South Vietnam, 1963–64, 1965–67. Representative of the United States to the United Nations, 1953–60.*

Leo Loewenson. *Deputy Librarian and Tutor in Russian History, School of Slavonic Studies, University of London, 1939–56.*

Antonino Lombardo. *Inspector General of National Archives, Rome. Professor of the Study of Archives, University of Rome.*

Stephen Hemsley Longrigg (d. 1979). *Historian and orientalist. Author of* Four Centuries of Modern Iraq *and others.*

Philip Longworth. *Associate Professor of History, McGill University, Montreal.*

Robert Sabatino Lopez (d. 1986). *Professor of History, Yale University, 1955–71.*

Donald William Lucas (d. 1985). *P.M. Laurence Reader in Classics, University of Cambridge, 1952–69.*

Afaf Lutfi al-Sayyid Marsot. *Professor of History, University of California, Los Angeles.*

James G. Lydon. *Professor of History, Duquesne University, Pittsburgh.*

John Lynch. *Professor of Latin American History; Director, Institute of Latin American Studies, University of London.*

Carlile Aylmer Macartney (d. 1978). *Research Fellow, All Souls College, University of Oxford, 1936–65. Montagu Burton Professor of International Relations, University of Edinburgh, 1951–57.*

Charles A. McClelland. *Emeritus Professor of International Relations, University of Southern California, Los Angeles.*

Alexander Hugh McDonald (d. 1979). *Lecturer in Ancient History, University of Cambridge, 1952–73.*

Forrest McDonald. *Professor of History, University of Alabama, University.*

Robert Brendan McDowell. *Associate Professor of History, Trinity College, University of Dublin.*

Thomas F. McGann (deceased). *Professor of History, University of Texas at Austin.*

Daniel Doyle McGarry. *Professor of Medieval History, St. Louis University, Mo.*

Clarence Fredric McIntosh. *Professor of History, California State University, Chico.*

Denis Mack Smith. *Senior Research Fellow and Dean of Visiting Fellows, All Souls College, University of Oxford.*

Edward Anthony MacLysaght. *Chairman, Irish Manuscripts Commission, 1956–73. Keeper of Manuscripts, National Library of Ireland, 1949–55.*

Philip Magnus (Sir Philip Magnus-Allcroft). *Fellow of the Royal Society of Literature. Author of* Kitchener *and others.*

Michael Edward Mallett. *Professor of History, University of Warwick, Eng.*

Sir Max Mallowan (d. 1978). *Professor of Western Asiatic Archaeology, University of London, 1947–62. President, British School of Archaeology in Iraq, 1970–78. Archaeologist on staff of the British Museum Expedition to Nineveh, 1931–32; later led many other archaeological expeditions.*

William Manchester. *Adjunct Professor of History; Writer-in-Residence, Wesleyan University, Middletown, Conn.*

Robert Mandrou (d. 1984). *Professor of History, University of Paris X.*

Golo Mann. *Writer. Professor of History and Political Science, Technical University, Stuttgart, W.Ger., 1960–64.*

(Philip) Nicholas Seton Mansergh. *Smuts Professor of the History of the British Commonwealth, University of Cambridge, 1953–70; Master of St. John's College, Cambridge, 1969–79.*

Fosco Maraini. *Lecturer in Japanese, University of Florence.*

Umberto Marcelli. *Lecturer in History, University of Bologna, Italy.*

The Rev. Germain P. Marc'hadour. *Professor of Philology, Catholic University of the West, Angers, Fr.*

John Marlowe. *Free-lance writer. Author of* Anglo-Egyptian Relations, 1800–1953; Cromer in Egypt; *and others.*

Leopold Marquard (deceased). *Publisher. President, South African Institute of Race Relations, 1957–58, 1968. Author of* The Story of South Africa *and others.*

P.J. Marshall. *Rhodes Professor of Imperial History, King's College, University of London.*

Thomas Powderly Martin (d. 1963). *Assistant Chief and Acting Chief, Manuscript Division, Library of Congress, 1928–48.*

J. Alden Mason (d. 1967). *Curator, American Section, University Museum, University of Pennsylvania, 1926–55.*

Paul T. Mason. *Professor of History, Duquesne University, Pittsburgh.*

Philip Mason. *Writer. Director, Institute of Race Relations, London, 1958–69. Indian Civil Service, 1928–47.*

Donald Campbell Charles Masters. *Emeritus Professor of Canadian History, University of Guelph, Ont.*

Gerhard Strassmann Masur (d. 1975). *Professor of History, Sweet Briar College, Lynchburg, Va., 1948–66.*

The Most Rev. David Mathew (d. 1975). *Archbishop of Apamea; Assistant at the Pontifical Throne. Author of* James I.

Therkel Mathiassen (d. 1967). *Curator, Prehistoric Department, National Museum, Copenhagen.*

Neville Maxwell. *Senior Research Officer, Institute of Commonwealth Studies, University of Oxford. South Asia correspondent,* The Times *(London), 1959–67.*

Robert Douthat Meade (d. 1974). *Professor of History, Randolph-Macon Woman's College, Lynchburg, Va., 1939–71.*

Russell Meiggs. *Emeritus Fellow of Balliol College, Oxford; Lecturer in Ancient History, University of Oxford, 1939–70.*

Julian Louis Meltzer. *Executive Vice Chairman, Yad Chaim Weizmann National Memorial, and Director, Weizmann Archives, Rehovot, Israel, 1966–75.*

Lucy Shoe Meritt. *Archaeologist. Visiting Scholar, University of Texas at Austin. Editor of Publications, American School of Classical Studies at Athens, 1950–72. Member, Institute for Advanced Study, Princeton, N.J., 1948–73.*

Robert Merle. *Novelist. Author of* Ahmed Ben Bella *and others.*

Barbara G. Mertz. *Historian and writer. Author of* Temples, Tombs and Hieroglyphs *and others.*

John Callan James Metford. *Emeritus Professor of Spanish, University of Bristol, Eng.*

Franz H. Michael. *Emeritus Professor of Far Eastern History and International Affairs, George Washington University, Washington, D.C.*

Earl Schenck Miers (d. 1972). *Historian, editor, and writer. Author of* The American Civil War *and many others.*

Hanns Leo Mikoletzky (d. 1978). *General Director, Austrian State Archives, Vienna. Professor of History, University of Vienna.*

Vladimir F. Minorsky (d. 1966). *Professor of Persian, University of London, 1938–44. Fellow of the British Academy, 1943–66.*

Mairin Mitchell. *Free-lance writer. Author of* The Odyssey of Acurio Who Sailed with Magellan *and others.*

Nancy Mitford (d. 1973). *Writer. Author of* Madame de Pompadour *and others.*

Michel J. Mollat. *Emeritus Professor of History, University of Paris.*

Arnaldo Dante Momigliano. *Alexander White Visiting Professor, University of Chicago. Professor of Ancient History, University College, University of London, 1951–75.*

Nicholas Ivan Momtchiloff (d. 1964). *Economic Adviser, Industrial and Commercial Finance Corporation, London.*

The Rev. Jacques Monet, S.J. *President, Regis College, Toronto School of Theology, University of Toronto.*

Georges Mongrédien (d. 1980). *Historian. Director of the Municipal Council of Paris and General Council of the Seine, 1947–67.*

Gaston Monnerville. *Member, Constitutional Council of France, 1974–83. President, Senate of France, 1958–68.*

The Rev. Joseph Nestor Moody. *Emeritus Professor of French History, Catholic University of America, Washington, D.C.*

Frank R. Moraes (d. 1974). *Editor in Chief,* The Indian Express, *New Delhi, 1957–72.*

Dale Lowell Morgan (d. 1971). *Historian. Specialist, Bancroft Library, University of California, Berkeley.*

Donald R. Morris. *News analyst,* The Houston *(Texas)* Post.

John Robert Morris (d. 1977). *Senior Lecturer in Ancient History, University College, University of London.*

Rudolf Morsey. *Professor of Modern History, Postgraduate School for Administrative Sciences, Speyer, W.Ger.*

Louis Morton (d. 1976). *Daniel Webster Professor of History, Dartmouth College, Hanover, N.H., 1968–76.*

William Lewis Morton (d. 1980). *Vanier Professor of Canadian History, Trent University, Peterborough, Ont., 1969–75.*

Leonard Mosley. *Author of* Curzon: The End of an Epoch *and others.*

W.E. Mosse. *Emeritus Professor of European History, University of East Anglia, Norwich, Eng.*

Charles Loch Mowat (d. 1970). *Professor of History, University College of North Wales, Bangor, University of Wales, 1958–70.*

Claudius Cornelius Müller. *Head, East Asian Department, State Museum of Ethnology, Munich.*

Stephanie Mullins. *Free-lance writer.*

Joan Margaret Munn-Rankin (d. 1981). *Lecturer in Near Eastern History, University of Cambridge, 1949–81.*

Jean Mary Munro (Jean Dunlop). *Author of* Clan Mackenzie; Clan Gordon *and others.*

Peter Munz. *Professor of History, Victoria University of Wellington, New Zealand.*

James J. Murphy. *Professor and Chairman, Department of Rhetoric, University of California, Davis.*

Raymond Muse. *Professor and Chairman, Department of History, Washington State University, Pullman, 1956–79.*

Alexander Reginald Myers (d. 1980). *Professor of Medieval History, University of Liverpool, 1967–80.*

Keiji Nagahara. *Professor of History, Hitotsubashi University, Tokyo.*

A.K. Narain. *Professor of History and Indian Studies, University of Wisconsin, Madison.*

Herbert Blair Neatby. *Professor of History, Carleton University, Ottawa.*

Allan Nevins (d. 1971). *Historian. Senior Research Associate, Henry E. Huntington Library and Art Gallery, San Marino, Calif., 1958–69. Dewitt Clinton Professor of History, Columbia University, 1931–58.*

Herbert G. Nicholas. *Rhodes Professor Emeritus of American History and Institutions, University of Oxford.*

Roy Franklin Nichols (d. 1973). *Professor of History; Vice Provost, 1953–66; and Dean of the Graduate School of Arts and Sciences, 1952–66, University of Pennsylvania, Philadelphia.*

Donald MacGillivray Nicol. *Koraës Professor of Byzantine and Modern Greek History, Language, and Literature, King's College, University of London.*

Louis Nicolas. *Former Professor of Naval History, Naval School, Lanvéoc-Poulmic, Fr.*

Lennart T. Norman. *Archivist and historian.*

John Julius Cooper, 2nd Viscount Norwich. *Writer and broadcaster. Author of* The Normans in the South; The Kingdom in the Sun.

Charles E. Nowell. *Emeritus Professor of History, University of Illinois, Urbana.*

Russel Blaine Nye. *Distinguished Professor of English, Michigan State University, East Lansing, 1965–79.*

Conor Cruise O'Brien. *Pro-Chancellor, University of Dublin. Editor in Chief,* The Observer, *London, 1978–81. Member, Seanad Eireann, Dublin, 1977–79; Dáil Eireann, 1969–77.*

Daniel Patrick O'Connell (d. 1979). *Chichele Professor of International Law, University of Oxford, 1972–79.*

Zoé Oldenbourg-Idalie. *Novelist and free-lance writer. Author of* Catherine the Great *and others.*

Roland Anthony Oliver. *Professor of the History of Africa, School of Oriental and African Studies, University of London.*

Daria Olivier. *Writer, translator, book reviewer, and historian. Author of* Alexandre Ier *and others.*

William J. O'Malley. *Research Fellow on Political and Social Change, Research School of Pacific Studies, Australian National University, Canberra.*

Farouk Omar. *Professor of History, College of Arts, University of Baghdad, Iraq.*

Francis D. Ommanney (d. 1980). *Reader in Marine Biology, University of Hong Kong, 1957–60.*

George Coleman Osborn. *Emeritus Professor of History and Social Sciences, University of Florida, Gainesville.*

John W. Osborne. *Professor of History, Rutgers University, New Brunswick, N.J.*

Andrei Otetea (d. 1977). *Director, Institute of History, Academy of the Socialist Republic of Romania, Bucharest. Professor of Medieval Universal History, University of Bucharest.*

Marcel Pacaut. *Professor of the History of the Middle Ages; Emeritus Director, Institute of Political Studies, University of Lyon.*

Joseph Howard Parks. *Emeritus Professor of History, University of Georgia, Athens.*

V.J. Parry (d. 1974). *Reader in the History of the Near and Middle East, School of Oriental and African Studies, University of London.*

Vladimir T. Pashuto. *Corresponding member, Academy of Sciences of the U.S.S.R., Moscow.*

Hans Patze. *Professor of German History; Director, Institute for Historical Research, Georg August University of Göttingen, W.Ger.*

George M. Paul. *Professor of Classics, McMaster University, Hamilton, Ont.*

Ante S. Pavelić. *Author of* Dr. Ante Trumbić: Problemi hrvatsko-srpskih odnosa *and others.*

Stanley G. Payne. *Professor of History, University of Wisconsin, Madison.*

H.F. Pearson (deceased). *Author of* A Popular History of Singapore; This Other India: A Biography of Sir Thomas Stamford Raffles.

Howard Henry Peckham. *Director, William L. Clements Library of Americana; Professor of History, University of Michigan, Ann Arbor, 1953–77.*

Roger Pélissier (d. 1972). *Assistant Director, Centre for Far East Documentation, École Pratique des Hautes Études (Institute for Advanced Research), Paris.*

D.H. Pennington. *Former Fellow and Tutor in History, Balliol College, Oxford; Former Lecturer in Modern History, University of Oxford.*

Dame Margery Perham (d. 1982). *Fellow of Nuffield College, Oxford, 1939–63; Reader in Colonial Administration, University of Oxford, 1939–48.*

Luis Pericot García (d. 1978). *Professor of Prehistory, University of Barcelona, Spain.*

Régine Pernoud. *Keeper, Joan of Arc Centre, Orléans, Fr.*

Stewart Henry Perowne. *Orientalist, historian, and lecturer. Author of* The Life and Times of Herod the Great *and others.*

Charles-Edmond Perrin (d. 1974). *Member, Institute of France. Professor of Medieval History, University of Paris, 1937–58.*

Jean Perrot. *Director of the French Archaeological Delegation in Iran.*

Edward Pessen. *Distinguished Professor of History, Baruch College and the Graduate Center, City University of New York.*

Ann Petry. *Novelist. Author of* Harriet Tubman: Conductor on the Underground Railroad *and others.*

Edward Hake Phillips. *Bryan Professor of History, Austin College, Sherman, Texas.*

Jean-Charles Pichon. *Author of* Saint-Néron; Historie des mythes; *and others.*

Robert Pick (d. 1978). *Free-lance writer and editor. Author of* Empress Maria Theresa.

John Whitney Pickersgill. *President, Canadian Transport Commission, Ottawa, 1967–72. Member, House of Commons, Parliament of Canada, 1953–67.*

Dorothy M. Pickles. *Writer, lecturer, and broadcaster. Author of* The Fifth French Republic; The Government and Politics of France; *and others.*

Thomas Jones Pierce (deceased). *Professor of Medieval Welsh History, University College of Wales, Aberystwyth.*

Josephine Ketcham Piercy. *Emeritus Professor of English, Indiana University, Bloomington.*

Francis Stewart Gilderoy Piggott (d. 1966). *Major General, British Army. Author of* Broken Thread; The Elements of Sosho.

Stuart Piggott. *Abercromby Professor of Prehistoric Archaeology, University of Edinburgh, 1946–77.*

Richard E. Pipes. *Frank B. Baird, Jr., Professor of History, Harvard University.*

Richard Pittioni (d. 1985). *Emeritus Professor of Prehistory and Protohistory, University of Vienna.*

Sir John Plumb. *Master of Christ's College, Cambridge, 1978–82; Professor of Modern English History, University of Cambridge, 1966–74.*

Tom Pocock. *Staff writer,* The Standard, *London. Author of* Nelson and His World *and others.*

Jan J. Poelhekke. *Emeritus Professor of Modern History, Catholic University of Nijmegen, Neth.*

Forrest C. Pogue. *Director, Dwight D. Eisenhower Institute for Historical Research, Smithsonian Institution, Washington, D.C.*

Frederik Pohl. *Author of* Tiberius *(under the pseudonym Ernst Mason) and of many works of science fiction.*

Ernesto Pontieri (deceased). *Professor of Medieval and Modern History, University of Naples.*

Gary William Poole. *Associate Editor,* Encyclopædia Britannica, *Chicago, 1970–72.*

The Rev. Stanley Burke-Roche Poole. *Vicar of Littlebourne, Eng., 1948–70. Former Assistant Editor,* Debrett's Peerage.

Ismail K. Poonawala. *Professor of Arabic and Islāmic Studies, University of California, Los Angeles.*

Rollie Edward Poppino. *Professor of History, University of California, Davis.*

George Richard Potter (d. 1981). *Professor of Medieval History, University of Sheffield, Eng.*

Heinrich Potthoff. *Contributor, Commission for the History of Parliamentarism and Political Parties, Bonn.*

Dimitris Pournaras. *Former Publisher and Editor of* Eleutheros *(newspaper), Athens. Former Chairman, Greek Broadcasting Corporation.*

Helmut Preidel. *Historian. Author of* Handel und Handwerk im frühgeschichtlichen Mitteleuropa *and others.*

Morgan Philips Price (d. 1973). *Member of Parliament, 1929–31 and 1935–59. Author of* A History of Turkey *and others.*

Thomas Brynmor Pugh. *Reader in History, University of Southampton, Eng.*

Edwin G. Pulleyblank. *Professor of Chinese, University of British Columbia, Vancouver.*

Baij Nath Puri. *Emeritus Professor of Ancient Indian History and Archaeology, University of Lucknow, India.*

Sergei Germanovich Pushkarev. *Historian. Author of* The Emergence of Modern Russia, 1801–1917 *and others.*

Robert S. Quimby. *Emeritus Professor of Humanities, Michigan State University, East Lansing.*

Robert Emmett Quirk. *Professor of History, Indiana University, Bloomington.*

Horst Rabe. *Professor of History, University of Constance, W.Ger.*

Hassanein Muhammad Rabie. *Professor of History, University of Cairo.*

Sh. Abdur Rashid. *Adviser, Research Society of Pakistan, Lahore. Director, Historical Research Institute; Head, Department of History, University of the Punjab, Lahore, Pak., 1960–65.*

John Lang Rawlinson. *Professor of History, Hofstra University, Hempstead, N.Y.*

Philip S. Rawson. *Curator, Gulbenkian Museum of Oriental Art and Archaeology, University of Durham, Eng., 1960–79.*

Donald Read. *Professor of Modern English History, University of Kent at Canterbury, Eng.*

Ann Lindsey Reber. *Researcher, Department of History, Duke University, Durham, N.C.*

Thomas C. Reeves. *Professor of History, University of Wisconsin, Parkside.*

Juan Reglá (d. 1973). *Professor of Modern History, University of Valencia, Spain.*

Kurt Reindel. *Professor of History, University of Regensburg, W.Ger.*

Marcel Reinhard (d. 1973). *Professor of History, University of Paris.*

Robert Vincent Remini. *Professor of History, University of Illinois, Chicago.*

Johannes M. Renger. *Professor of Assyriology, Free University of Berlin, West Berlin.*

Yves Renouard (d. 1965). *Professor of Medieval History, University of Paris.*

Frank E. Reynolds. *Professor of Buddhist Studies and History of Religions, University of Chicago.*

Edward J.M. Rhoads. *Associate Professor of History, University of Texas at Austin.*

Gotthold K.S. Rhode. *Professor of East European and Russian History; Director, Institute for East European Research, Johannes Gutenberg University of Mainz, W.Ger.*

Nicholas V. Riasanovsky. *Sidney Hellman Ehrman Professor of European History, University of California, Berkeley.*

Jean B. Richard. *Honorary Dean, Faculty of Letters and Human Sciences, University of Dijon, Fr.*

Sir Ian Archibald Richmond (d. 1965). *Professor of the Archaeology of the Roman Empire, University of Oxford, 1956–65.*

C.T. Ritchie. *Historian, writer, and artist. Author of* The First Canadian: The Story of Champlain *and others.*

Raymond Ritter (d. 1974). *Attorney. Editor in Chief of the review* Pyrénées. *Author of* Henry IV lui-même.

Helen Anne B. Rivlin. *Professor of History, State University of New York at Binghamton.*

Nesca A. Robb (d. 1976). *Free-lance writer and lecturer, Author of* William of Orange: A Personal Portrait *and others.*

Michael Roberts. *Professor of Modern History, Queen's University of Belfast, N.Ire., 1954–73.*

Bruce Carlisle Robertson. *Specialist in Oriental studies. Former Instructor in Philosophy and Religion, Towson State College, Md.*

Edgar Eugene Robinson (d. 1977). *Margaret Byrne Professor of American History, Stanford University, Calif., 1931–52.*

George Clarence Robinson (d. 1976). *Professor of Political Science, University of Northern Iowa, Cedar Falls.*

George William Robinson. *Professor and Chairman, Department of History, Eastern Kentucky University, Richmond.*

Judith Mary Rodden. *Research Student, Department of Archaeology and Anthropology, University of Cambridge.*

Michael Roe. *Professor of History, University of Tasmania, Hobart, Australia.*

William R. Roff. *Professor of History, Columbia University.*

Helmuth Rogge. *Chief Archivist, National Records Office, Potsdam, Germany, 1921–45.*

Andrew Frank Rolle. *Robert Glass Cleland Professor of History, Occidental College, Los Angeles.*

Hans Roos (d. 1984). *Professor of East European History, University of the Ruhr, Bochum, W.Ger.*

Eugene Holloway Roseboom, Sr. *Emeritus Professor of History, Ohio State University, Columbus.*

Henry Godfrey Roseveare. *Reader in History, King's College, University of London.*

Ralph J. Roske. *Professor of History, University of Nevada, Las Vegas.*

C.D. Ross (d. 1986). *Professor of Medieval History, University of Bristol, Eng.*

Stanley Robert Ross (d. 1985). *Professor of History, University of Texas at Austin, 1968–85.*

Emanuel Rostworowski. *Professor of Modern History, Historical Institute, Polish Academy of Sciences, Cracow.*

Gordon Oliver Rothney. *Professor of History, University of Manitoba, Winnipeg.*

Jean Pierre Rouch. *Director of Research, National Centre for Scientific Research, Paris.*

John A. Rowe. *Associate Professor of African History, Northwestern University, Evanston, Ill.*

Herbert H. Rowen. *Professor of History, Rutgers University, New Brunswick, N.J.*

Nicolai Rubinstein. *Emeritus Professor of History, Westfield College, University of London.*

Peter Edward Russell. *King Alfonso XIII Professor Emeritus of Spanish Studies, University of Oxford; Fellow of Exeter College, Oxford.*

Nils Göran Rystad. *Professor of History, University of Lund, Swed.*

Emilio Sáez. *Former Professor of Medieval Spanish History, University of Barcelona, Spain.*

Leland Livingston Sage. *Emeritus Professor of History, University of Northern Iowa, Cedar Falls.*

Henry W.F. Saggs. *Emeritus Professor of Semitic Languages, University College, Cardiff, University of Wales.*

Robert St. John. *Journalist, lecturer, and foreign affairs radio commentator. Author of* The Boss *and others.*

Edward Togo Salmon. *Messecar Professor Emeritus of History, McMaster University, Hamilton, Ont.*

Theodore Saloutos (d. 1980). *Professor of History, University of California, Los Angeles, 1956–78.*

Roger M. Savory. *Professor of Middle East and Islāmic Studies, University of Toronto.*

Claude Frédéric Armand Schaeffer (d. 1982). *Professor of the Archaeology of Western Asia, College of France, Paris, 1954–69. Director of the French Archaeological Expeditions to Ras Shamra-Ugarit, Syria and Enkomi-Alasia, Cyprus.*

Leonard Bertram Schapiro (d. 1983). *Professor of Political Science (Russian Studies), London School of Economics and Political Science, University of London, 1963–75.*

Theodor Schieffer. *Professor of Medieval and Modern History, University of Cologne, W.Ger.*

Franz-Josef Schmale. *Professor of Medieval History, University of the Ruhr, Bochum, W.Ger.*

Karl Michael Schmitt. *Professor of Government, University of Texas at Austin.*

Ronald Milton Schneider. *Professor of Political Science, Queens College, City University of New York.*

Walter V. Scholes (d. 1975). *Professor of History, University of Missouri, Columbia, 1954–75.*

Friedrich Schreyvogl (d. 1976). *Novelist and free-lance writer. Vice Director, Vienna Burgtheater, 1954–59.*

Alvin J. Schumacher. *Author of* Thunder on Capitol Hill: The Life of Chief Justice Roger B. Taney.

Lee Schwartz. *Free-lance writer and consultant on Polish history.*

The Rev. Guthrie Michael Scott (d. 1983). *Anglican Clergyman, Diocese of Chichester, Eng. Coauthor of* Attitude to Africa *and others.*

Robert L. Scranton. *Emeritus Professor of Classical Art and Archaeology, University of Chicago.*

Howard Hayes Scullard (d. 1983). *Professor of Ancient History, King's College, University of London, 1959–70.*

B. Raphael Sealey. *Professor of History, University of California, Berkeley.*

Jakob Seibert. *Professor of Ancient History, Ludwig Maximilian University of Munich.*

M.V. Seton-Williams. *Former Lecturer in Western Asiatic Archaeology, University of London. Former director of archaeological expeditions in Turkey, Syria, Jordan, Egypt, and Cyprus.*

Charles Seymour (d. 1963). *President, Yale University, 1937–50; Professor of History, 1918–37.*

Irfan Arif Shahîd. *Professor of Arabic, Georgetown University, Washington, D.C.*

David Allen Shannon. *Commonwealth Professor of History, University of Virginia, Charlottesville; Vice President and Provost, 1971–81.*

The Rev. R. Norman Sharp. *Assistant Professor of Old Persian and Pahlavi, Pahlavi University, Shīrāz, Iran, 1962–67.*

Ivan Peter Shaw. *Former Fellow and Secretary, King's College, University of London. Author of* Nationality and the Western Church Before the Reformation.

Hugh Shearman. *Historian and writer on politics and world affairs. Author of* Modern Ireland; Ulster; *and others.*

Eric William Sheppard. *Major, British Army (retired). Author of* A Short History of the British Army *and others.*

George Albert Shepperson. *William Robertson Professor of Commonwealth and American History, University of Edinburgh.*

Adrian N. Sherwin-White. *Reader in Ancient History, University of Oxford, 1966–78.*

James Henry Shideler. *Professor of History, University of California, Davis.*

Minoru Shinoda. *Professor of History, University of Hawaii, Honolulu.*

David C.G. Sibley. *Free-lance writer and artist.*

Winant Sidle. *Brigadier General, U.S. Army.*

Julie Siegel. *Free-lance writer.*

Henry Harrison Simms. *Emeritus Professor of History, Ohio State University, Columbus.*

John Y. Simon. *Professor of History, Southern Illinois University, Carbondale. Executive Director, Ulysses S. Grant Association.*

Eric Norman Simons (d. 1983). *Author of* The Queen and the Rebel: Mary Tudor and Wyatt the Younger *and others.*

John M. Simpson. *Senior Lecturer in Scottish History, University of Edinburgh.*

Roger Henry Simpson. *Historian and lecturer.*

Andrew Annandale Sinclair. *Historian and filmmaker. Author of* Guevara *and others.*

Khushwant Singh. *Free-lance journalist. Member, Rajya Sabha (upper house of the Indian Parliament).*

Otis Arnold Singletary. *President, University of Kentucky, Lexington.*

N.K. Sinha (d. 1974). *Professor and Head, Department of History, University of Calcutta, 1955–68.*

Stephan Skalweit. *Professor of Modern History, Rhenish Friedrich Wilhelm University of Bonn.*

Fridlev Skrubbeltrang. *Lecturer in Agricultural History, University of Copenhagen, 1956–71.*

Bradford Smith (d. 1964). *Author of* Bradford of Plymouth; Captain John Smith; *and others.*

Lacey Baldwin Smith. *Peter B. Ritzma Professor of Humanities, Northwestern University, Evanston, Ill.*

Robert Ross Smith. *Chief, General History Branch, U.S. Army Center of Military History, Washington, D.C.*

Thomas C. Smith. *Ford Professor of History and Comparative Studies, University of California, Berkeley.*

Kazimierz Maciej Smogorzewski. *London Correspondent,* Kurier Polski *(Warsaw), 1957–81. Founder and Editor,* Free Europe, *1939–45. Foreign correspondent, 1919–39.*

Albert M. Soboul (d. 1982). *Professor of the History of the French Revolution, University of Paris I.*

Ramón Solís Llorente (d. 1978). *Novelist and historian. Corresponding member, Royal Academy of History, Madrid.*

Albert Somit. *President, Southern Illinois University, Carbondale.*

Dominique Sourdel. *Professor of Muslim Civilization, University of Paris IV.*

Donald Southgate. *Former Reader in Political and Constitutional History, University of Dundee, Scot.*

T.G. Percival Spear (d. 1982). *Fellow of Selwyn College, Cambridge; Lecturer in History, University of Cambridge, 1963–69.*

Arnold Spekke (d. 1972). *Author of* History of Latvia *and others.*

David Spring. *Professor of History, Johns Hopkins University, Baltimore.*

Chester G. Starr. *Bentley Professor of Ancient History, University of Michigan, Ann Arbor.*

Alfred Steinberg. *Free-lance writer. Author of* Man from Missouri: The Life and Times of Harry S. Truman *and others.*

S. Henry Steinberg (d. 1969). *Editor,* The Statesman's Year-Book, *1946–69.*

Doris Mary Stenton (d. 1971). *Reader in History, University of Reading, Eng.*

Ruth Stephan (d. 1974). *Writer. Author of* My Crown, My Love *and others.*

George R. Stewart (d. 1980). *Professor of English, University of California, Berkeley, 1942–62.*

Arndt Mathis Stickles (deceased). *Professor of History, Western Kentucky University, Bowling Green.*

Hudson Strode (d. 1976). *Professor of English, University of Alabama, Tuscaloosa, 1924–63.*

David Brian Stronach. *Professor of Near Eastern Studies, University of California, Berkeley.*

Hans Sturmberger. *Former Director, Upper Austrian Provincial Archives, Linz.*

Leo Suryadinata. *Former Research Associate, Centre for Southeast Asian Studies, Kyōto University, Japan.*

N.M. Sutherland. *Reader in Early Modern History, Royal Holloway College, University of London.*

Harald Ulrik Sverdrup (d. 1957). *Director, Norwegian Polar Institute, Oslo, 1948–57. Director, Scripps Institution of Oceanography, University of California, La Jolla, 1936–48.*

Dattatraya Vishwanath Tahmankar. *London Editor,* Deccan Herald, *Bangalore, India. Author of* Lokamanya Tilak *and others.*

Victor-Lucien Tapié (d. 1974). *Member, Academy of Moral and Political Sciences, Institute of France, Paris, 1963–74. Professor of Modern History, University of Paris IV, 1949–70.*

John Taylor. *Reader in Medieval History, University of Leeds, Eng.*

Robert H. Taylor. *Lecturer in Political Studies, School of Oriental and African Studies, University of London.*

Geoffrey Templeman. *Vice Chancellor, University of Kent at Canterbury, Eng., 1963–80.*

Henri-Louis-Étienne Terasse (d. 1971). *Curator, Historic Monuments of Morocco, 1935–57. Director, Institute for Advanced Moroccan Studies, Rabat, Mor., 1941–57. Chairman, Department of Islāmic Archaeology, University of Algiers, 1945–57. Director, Casa de Velázquez, Ciudad University, Madrid, 1957–65.*

Romila Thapar. *Professor of Ancient Indian History, Jawaharlal Nehru University, New Delhi.*

David P. Thelen. *Professor of History, University of Missouri, Columbia.*

Alfred Barnaby Thomas. *Emeritus Professor of History, University of Alabama, Tuscaloosa.*

John L. Thomas. *Professor of History, Brown University, Providence, R.I.*

Nicholas de L'Eglise Wolferstan Thomas. *Former Keeper, Department of Archaeology, City Museum, Birmingham, Eng.*

Arthur Frederick Thompson. *Fellow and Tutor of Wadham College, Oxford; Lecturer in Modern History, University of Oxford.*

E.A. Thompson. *Professor of Classics, University of Nottingham, Eng., 1948–79.*

Lewis Thorpe (d. 1977). *Professor of French, University of Nottingham, Eng., 1958–77.*

Roy Gilbert Thurburn. *Brigadier, the Cameronians (Scottish Rifles) (retired). Secretary, Army Museums Ogilby Trust, Ministry of Defence, London, 1957–72.*

Conrad D. Totman. *Professor of History, Northwestern University, Evanston, Ill.*

Hans Louis Trefousse. *Professor of History, Brooklyn College, City University of New York.*

Reginald Francis Treharne (d. 1967). *Professor of History, University College of Wales, Aberystwyth, University of Wales, 1930–67.*

Piero Treves. *Professor of Ancient History, University of Venice, Italy.*

Glenn Tucker (d. 1976). *Free-lance writer and historian. Author of* Tecumseh: Vision of Glory *and others.*

Sir Eric Gardner Turner (d. 1983). *Professor of Papyrology, University College, University of London, 1950–78; Director, Institute of Classical Studies, 1953–63.*

Edward Ullendorff. *Professor of Semitic Languages, School of Oriental and African Studies, University of London.*

Esta Ungar. *Researcher, Department of Far Eastern History, Research School of Pacific Studies, Australian National University, Canberra.*

Ernesto Valgiglio. *Professor of Greek and Latin Grammar, University of Genoa.*

Glyndon G. Van Deusen. *Research Professor Emeritus of History, University of Rochester, N.Y.*

Frank Everson Vandiver. *President, Texas A & M University, College Station.*

Richard Vaughan. *Former Professor of History, University of Hull, Eng.*

J. Charles Verlinden. *Emeritus Professor of History, State University of Ghent, Belg.*

Jean Vidalenc. *Former Professor of Contemporary History, University of Rouen, Fr.*

Alan John Villiers (d. 1982). *Free-lance writer. President, Society for Nautical Research, London. Author of* Captain James Cook *and many others.*

Marcelle Vioux. *Free-lance writer. Author of* François I; Henri IV; *and others.*

Hans Volkmann (deceased). *Professor of Ancient History, University of Cologne.*

The Rev. Edward Robert Vollmar, S.J. (d. 1976). *Professor of History and Associate Director of Libraries, St. Louis University, Mo.*

John Waechter. *Former Senior Lecturer in Paleolithic Archaeology, Institute of Archaeology, University of London.*

Peter Busby Waite. *Professor of History, Dalhousie University, Halifax, Nova Scotia.*

Frank W. Walbank. *Rathbone Professor Emeritus of Ancient History and Classical Archaeology, University of Liverpool.*

Paul E. Walker. *Executive Director, American Research Center in Egypt, Columbia University.*

William Stewart Wallace (d. 1970). *Librarian, University of Toronto. Author of* A History of the Canadian People.

John Michael Wallace-Hadrill (d. 1985). *Chichele Professor of Modern History, University of Oxford, 1974–83; Fellow of All Souls College, Oxford.*

Immanuel Wallerstein. *Distinguished Professor of Sociology, State University of New York at Binghamton.*

Friedrich Walter (d. 1968). *Extraordinary Professor of Modern Austrian History, University of Vienna, 1955–67.*

Yi Chu Wang. *Professor of History, Queens College, City University of New York.*

William Reginald Ward. *Professor of Modern History, University of Durham, Eng.*

John Bryan Ward-Perkins (d. 1981). *Director, British School at Rome, 1946–74.*

Brian H. Warmington. *Reader in Ancient History, University of Bristol, Eng.*

Oliver Martin Wilson Warner (d. 1976). *Naval historian. Member, Council of the Society of Nautical Research, 1955–60; Council of the Navy Records Society, 1969–70.*

John Steven Watson. *Principal and Vice Chancellor, University of St. Andrews, Scot.*

William Watson. *Former Professor of Chinese Art and Archaeology; former Head, Percival David Foundation of Chinese Art, School of Oriental and African Studies, University of London.*

Bruce Webster. *Senior Lecturer in History, University of Kent at Canterbury, Eng.*

Dame C.V. Wedgwood. *Free-lance writer and historian. Fellow, University College, University of London. Fellow, Lady Margaret Hall, University of Oxford.*

Saul S. Weinberg. *Emeritus Professor of Classical Archaeology, University of Missouri, Columbia.*

Lynn Weiner. *Free-lance writer.*

Edward Weintal (d. 1973). *Diplomatic Correspondent, Chief European Correspondent, and Contributing Editor,* Newsweek *magazine, 1944–69.*

C. Bradford Welles (d. 1969). *Professor of Ancient History, Yale University, 1940–69.*

Manly Wade Wellman (d. 1986). *Novelist and writer on American history. Author of* Giant in Gray: A Biography of Wade Hampton of South Carolina *and others.*

Edward F. Wente. *Professor of Egyptology, Oriental Institute and Department of Near Eastern Languages and Civilizations, University of Chicago.*

Robert Werner. *Professor of Ancient History, Friedrich Alexander University of Erlangen-Nuremberg, W.Ger.*

Richard Bruce Wernham. *Emeritus Professor of Modern History, University of Oxford; Fellow of Worcester College, Oxford, 1951–72.*

H. van Werveke (d. 1974). *Professor of the History of Belgium, State University of Ghent.*

William C. West. *Consultant on Russian literature and Soviet affairs.*

Gunnar Torvald Westin. *Emeritus Professor of History, University of Stockholm.*

Vera Muriel White. *Extramural Lecturer, University of Cambridge.*

Matthew Immanuel Wiencke. *Professor of Classics, Dartmouth College, Hanover, N.H.*

Hermann Wiesflecker. *Professor of Austrian History, University of Graz, Austria.*

Donald N. Wilber. *Free-lance writer and consultant on the Middle East and Southeast Asia. Author of* Iran Past and Present *and others.*

Ivor G. Wilks. *Melville J. Herskovits Professor of African Studies, Northwestern University, Evanston, Ill.*

Charles Henry Wilson. *Professor of Modern History, University of Cambridge, 1965–79; Fellow of Jesus College, Cambridge.*

John A. Wilson (d. 1976). *Andrew MacLeish Distinguished Service Professor of Egyptology, University of Chicago, 1953–68.*

Oscar O. Winther (d. 1970). *University Professor of History, Indiana University, Bloomington, 1965–70.*

Donald John Wiseman. *Emeritus Professor of Assyriology, School of Oriental and African Studies, University of London.*

Elizabeth Wiskemann (d. 1971). *Montague Burton Professor of International Relations, University of Edinburgh, 1958–61. Tutor in Modern History, University of Sussex, Eng., 1961–64.*

Gunther Wolf. *Lecturer in History, Rupert Charles University of Heidelberg, W.Ger.*

James Madison Wood, Jr. *Professor of History, Santa Monica College, Calif.*

Sir Leonard Woolley (d. 1960). *Archaeologist; excavated at Ur, 1922–34, and many other sites. Author of* Digging Up the Past *and others.*

Brian Harvey Goodwin Wormald. *Emeritus Fellow of Peterhouse, Cambridge; Lecturer in History, University of Cambridge, 1948–79.*

Edmund H. Worthy, Jr. *Associate Director, Resident Associate Program, Smithsonian Institution, Washington, D.C.*

Arthur F. Wright (d. 1976). *Charles Seymour Professor of History, Yale University, 1961–76.*

Gordon Wright. *William H. Bonsall Professor Emeritus of History, Stanford University, Calif.*

David K. Wyatt. *Professor of History, Cornell University, Ithaca, N.Y.*

Malcolm Edward Yapp. *Senior Lecturer in the History of the Near and Middle East, School of Oriental and African Studies, University of London.*

John Howard Young (d. 1978). *W.H. Collins Vickers Foundation Professor of Archaeology, Johns Hopkins University, Baltimore, 1956–78.*

Mary Elizabeth Young. *Professor of History, University of Rochester, N.Y.*

T(heodore) Cuyler Young (d. 1976). *Horatio Whitridge Garrett Professor of Persian Language and History, 1952–69; Chairman, Oriental Studies Department, Princeton University, 1954–69.*

Andrzej Zahorski. *Professor of Modern History, University of Warsaw.*

Ernst Walter Zeeden. *Professor of Modern and Medieval History, Eberhard Karl University of Tübingen, W.Ger.*

Herbert Zeiden. *Free-lance writer in the area of history.*

Nicola Abdo Ziadeh. *Emeritus Professor of Arab History, American University of Beirut.*

E. Zudaire Huarte. *Instructor, Good Counsel Academy, Lecaroz, Spain. Author of* El conde-duque y Cataluña *and others.*

Part Ten. The Branches of Knowledge

Harry Burrows Acton (d. 1974). *Professor of Moral Philosophy, University of Edinburgh, 1964–74.*

Alexander Altmann. *Philip W. Lown Professor Emeritus of Jewish Philosophy, Brandeis University, Waltham, Mass.*

Mikhail S. Arlazorov. *Staff member, Union of Cinematographers, Moscow.*

A. Hilary Armstrong. *Gladstone Professor Emeritus of Greek, University of Liverpool.*

Richard Paul Aulie. *Former Lecturer in Natural Science, Loyola University, Chicago. Associate Editor, Encyclopædia Britannica, Chicago, 1971–72.*

Edward J. Barbeau. *Associate Professor of Mathematics, University of Toronto.*

George Alfred Barnard. *Emeritus Professor of Mathematics, University of Essex, Eng.*

Glen W. Baxter. *Senior Lecturer on East Asian Studies, Harvard University, 1956–80; Associate Director, Harvard-Yenching Institute, 1964–80.*

Geoffrey H. Beale. *Royal Society Research Professor of Genetics, University of Edinburgh, Scot., 1963–78.*

Yvon Belaval. *Professor of Philosophy, University of Paris I. Vice President, Leibniz Society, Hanover, W.Ger.*

Eric Temple Bell (d. 1960). *Professor of Mathematics, California Institute of Technology, Pasadena, 1926–60.*

Leonard D. Berkovitz. *Professor of Mathematics, Purdue University, West Lafayette, Ind.*

Simeon Berman. *Professor of Mathematics, Courant Institute of Mathematical Sciences, New York University, New York City.*

William B.N. Berry. *Professor of Paleontology, University of California, Berkeley.*

Cyril Bibby. *Principal, Kingston upon Hull College of Education, University of Hull Institute of Education, Eng., 1959–76.*

Peter G. Bietenholz. *Professor of History, University of Saskatchewan, Saskatoon.*

Otto Allen Bird. *Emeritus Professor of Arts and Letters, University of Notre Dame, Ind.*

Haig Bohigian. *Professor of Mathematics and Operations Research, John Jay College of Criminal Justice, City University of New York.*

Otto Friedrich Bollnow. *Emeritus Professor of Philosophy and Education, Eberhard Karl University of Tübingen, W.Ger.*

Carl B. Boyer (d. 1976). *Professor of Mathematics, Brooklyn College, City University of New York, 1952–76.*

Felix E. Browder. *Max Mason Distinguished Service Professor of Mathematics, University of Chicago.*

Delwin Brown. *Professor of Religious Studies, Arizona State University, Tempe.*

Truesdell S. Brown. *Emeritus Professor of History, University of California, Los Angeles.*

David L. Buckley. *Free-lance writer on philosophy and music.*

Ulick Peter Burke. *Lecturer in History, University of Cambridge; Fellow of Emmanuel College, Cambridge.*

Martin D. Burrow. *Professor of Mathematics, Courant Institute of Mathematical Sciences, New York University, New York City.*

Lyman H. Butterfield (d. 1982). *Editor in Chief,* The Adams Papers, *Massachusetts Historical Society, Boston, 1954–75.*

Robert W. Cahn. *Former Professor of Materials Science, University of Sussex, Brighton, Eng.*

Seymour Cain. *Fellow, National Endowment for the Humanities, Washington, D.C., 1979–80. Senior Editor, Religion,* Encyclopædia Britannica, *Chicago, 1967–73.*

A. Robert Caponigri (d. 1983). *Professor of Philosophy, University of Notre Dame, Ind.*

Frederick F. Cartwright. *Emeritus Senior Lecturer in the History of Medicine, King's College Hospital, University of London.*

George Law Cawkwell. *Lecturer in Ancient History, University of Oxford; Fellow of University College, Oxford.*

Jules-Marie Chaix-Ruy. *Professor of Philosophy, University of Nice, Fr., 1965–67.*

Donald Geoffrey Charlton. *Professor of French; Chairman, Department of French Studies, University of Warwick, Coventry, Eng.*

Chung-hwan Chen. *Emeritus Professor of Philosophy, University of South Florida, Tampa.*

Alonzo Church. *Professor of Mathematics and Philosophy, University of California, Los Angeles.*

Martin Lowther Clarke. *Former Professor of Latin, University College of North Wales, Bangor, University of Wales.*

Gerald M. Clemence (d. 1974). *Professor of Astronomy, Yale University, 1966–74.*

I. Bernard Cohen. *Victor S. Thomas Professor of the History of Science, Harvard University.*

Frederick Coppotelli. *Free-lance writer on mathematics.*

H.S. MacDonald Coxeter. *Emeritus Professor of Mathematics, University of Toronto.*

Rupert Crawshay-Williams (d. 1977). *Author of* Russell Remembered; Methods and Criteria of Reasoning; *and others.*

The Rev. Theodore Crowley, O.F.M. *Emeritus Professor of Scholastic Philosophy, Queen's University of Belfast, N.Ire.*

J.G. Crowther. *Author of* Famous American Men of Science; Science in Modern Society; *and others.*

Glyn Edmund Daniel. *Disney Professor Emeritus of Archaeology, University of Cambridge; Fellow of St. John's College, Cambridge.*

Joseph Dauben. *Professor of the History of Science, Herbert H. Lehman College, City University of New York, Bronx.*

Charles De Prima. *Professor of Mathematics, California Institute of Technology, Pasadena.*

Carlo Diano (d. 1974). *Professor of Greek Literature, University of Padua, Italy.*

Bern Dibner. *Director, Burndy Library, Norwalk, Conn. Author of* Heralds of Science.

Paul Dibon. *Former Director, École Pratique des Hautes Études, Paris.*

A. Vibert Douglas. *Emeritus Professor of Astronomy, Queen's University at Kingston, Ont.*

Seymour Drescher. *Professor of History, University of Pittsburgh.*

Michael A.E. Dummett. *Wykeham Professor of Logic, University of Oxford; Fellow of New College, Oxford.*

James H. Earle. *Professor and Head, Department of Engineering Design Graphics, Texas A & M University, College Station.*

William R. Eckhardt. *Free-lance writer on mathematics.*

Dorothy Mary Emmet. *Emeritus Professor of Philosophy, Victoria University of Manchester.*

Robert A. Fefferman. *Professor of Mathematics, University of Chicago.*

Louis H. Feldman. *Professor of Classics, Yeshiva University, New York City.*

Raphael Finkel. *Assistant Professor of Computer Science, University of Wisconsin, Madison.*

Sir Raymond William Firth. *Emeritus Professor of Anthropology, University of London.*

Ronald Fletcher. *Emeritus Professor of Sociology, University of Reading, Eng.*

Marcel Florkin, M.D. (d. 1979). *Professor of Biochemistry, State University of Liège, Belg.*

Frieda Fordham. *Training analyst, Society of Analytical Psychology, London.*

Michael S.M. Fordham. *Analytical psychologist. Co-editor of* The Collected Works of C.G. Jung.

Sidney W. Fox. *Director, Institute for Molecular and Cellular Evolution; Research Professor, University of Miami, Coral Gables, Fla.*

Andrew M. Gallant. *Free-lance writer on mathematics.*

W. Horsley Gantt, M.D. (d. 1980). *Associate Professor of Psychiatry, 1932–58; Director, Pavlovian Laboratory, School of Medicine, Johns Hopkins University, Baltimore.*

Elizabeth Belmont Gasking (d. 1973). *Senior Lecturer in the History and Philosophy of Science, University of Melbourne, Australia.*

Frances Carney Gies. *Co-author of* Leonard of Pisa and the New Mathematics of the Middle Ages *and others.*

Boris Vladimirovich Gnedenko. *Professor of Physics and Mathematics; Head, Faculty of Mathematics, Moscow M.V. Lomonosov State University.*

Kenneth P. Goldberg. *Associate Professor of Mathematics Education, New York University, New York City.*

Arnold Wycombe Gomme (d. 1959). *Professor of Greek, University of Glasgow, 1946–57.*

Samuel L. Greitzer. *Emeritus Professor of Mathematics, Rutgers University, New Brunswick, N.J.*

Ronald Grimsley. *Emeritus Professor of French, University of Bristol, Eng.*

William Keith Chambers Guthrie (d. 1981). *Laurence Professor of Ancient Philosophy, University of Cambridge, 1952–73; Master of Downing College, Cambridge, 1957–72.*

John G. Hargrave (d. 1982). *Author of* The Life and Soul of Paracelsus *and others.*

Melvin Hausner. *Professor of Mathematics, Courant Institute of Mathematical Sciences, New York University, New York City.*

Carl G. Hempel. *Stuart Professor Emeritus of Philosophy, Princeton University. University Professor of Philosophy, University of Pittsburgh, Pa.*

Norman V. Henfrey. *Lecturer in English, University of Bristol, Eng.*

Eckhard H. Hess (d. 1986). *Professor of Psychology, University of Chicago, 1959–86.*

Roland John Hill. *London Correspondent, Stuttgarter Zeitung, Stuttgart, W.Ger.*

Peter John Hilton. *Fellow of Battelle Research Center, Seattle, Wash. Distinguished Professor of Mathematics, State University of New York at Binghamton.*

Harry Hochstadt. *Professor of Mathematics, Polytechnic Institute of New York, Brooklyn.*

Banesh Hoffman (d. 1986). *Professor of Mathematics, Queen's College, City University of New York, Flushing.*

Dewey J. Hoitenga, Jr. *Professor of Philosophy, Calvin College, Grand Rapids, Mich.*

Constantin Ludwig Adolph Rudolph Hope. *Vicar, St. Michael's and All Angels, New Marston, Oxford, Eng.*

Michael Anthony Hoskin. *Lecturer in History of Science, University of Cambridge; Fellow of Churchill College, Cambridge.*

Kung-chuan Hsiao (d. 1981). *Professor of the History of Chinese Thought, University of Washington, Seattle, 1959–68.*

Arthur Hübscher. *Former Director, Schopenhauer Archives, Frankfurt. Senior President, International Schopenhauer Society, Frankfurt.*

Aaron J. Ihde. *Professor of Chemistry and History of Science, University of Wisconsin, Madison.*

Yasuke Ikari. *Instructor, Seminar for Indology, Kyōto University.*

Charles Issawi. *Bayard Dodge Professor of Near Eastern Studies, Princeton University.*

Bernard Jaffe. *Free-lance science writer. Chairman, Science Department, James Madison High School, Brooklyn, New York, 1944–58.*

A. Walter James. *Principal, St. Catharine's, Windsor, England, 1974–82. Editor,* The Times *(London)* Educational Supplement, *1952–69.*

Horace M. Kallen (d. 1974). *Professor of Social Philosophy, New School for Social Research, New York City, 1919–52.*

Irving Kaplansky. *Director, Mathematical Sciences Research Institute, Berkeley, Calif.*

Charlotte L. Kellner. *Former Lecturer in Physics, Imperial College of Science and Technology, University of London.*

Joan Kelly-Gadol (d. 1982). *Professor of History, City College, City University of New York, 1972–82.*

Jim Kenevan. *Free-lance writer on mathematics.*

Lester S. King, M.D. *Professorial Lecturer in the History of Medicine, University of Chicago.*

Stephen Cole Kleene. *Emeritus Dean of Letters and Science; Emeritus Professor of Mathematics and Computer Science, University of Wisconsin, Madison.*

David Marcus Knight. *Senior Lecturer in History of Science, University of Durham, Eng.*

Sir T. Malcolm Knox (d. 1980). *Principal, University of St. Andrews, Scot., 1953–66; Professor of Moral Philosophy, 1936–53.*

Richard Kroner (d. 1974). *Professor of the Philosophy of Religion, Union Theological Seminary, New York City, 1941–55.*

Ludwig M. Landgrebe. *Professor of Philosophy, University of Cologne. Director of the Husserl Archives, Cologne.*

Anneli Lax. *Professor of Mathematics, Washington Square and University College of Arts and Science, New York University, New York City.*

Robert Lekachman. *Distinguished Professor of Economics, Herbert H. Lehman College, City University of New York.*

Casimir Lewy. *Fellow of Trinity College, Cambridge; Emeritus Reader in Philosophy, University of Cambridge.*

R. Bruce Lindsay (d. 1985). *Hazard Professor of Physics, Brown University, Providence, R.I., 1936–71.*

Antony Charles Lloyd. *Professor of Philosophy, University of Liverpool.*

David Morrice Low (d. 1972). *Classical Lecturer and Subdean, Arts Faculty, King's College, University of London, 1945–57.*

Victor Lowe. *Emeritus Professor of Philosophy, Johns Hopkins University, Baltimore.*

David Edward Luscombe. *Professor of Medieval History, University of Sheffield, Eng.*

John David Mabbott. *President, St. John's College, University of Oxford, 1963–69. Author of* An Introduction to Ethics *and others.*

Donald Gunn MacRae. *Martin White Professor of Sociology, London School of Economics and Political Science, University of London.*

Norman A. Malcolm. *Susan Linn Sage Professor Emeritus of Philosophy, Cornell University, Ithaca, N.Y.*

Frank J. Malina (d. 1981). *Trustee, International Academy of Astronautics, Paris, 1963–81; President, 1963. Founder-Editor,* Leonardo *(international journal of the contemporary artist).*

Kishore B. Marathe. *Associate Professor of Mathematics, Brooklyn College, City University of New York.*

Herbert S. Matsen. *Associate Professor of Philosophy, University of South Carolina, Columbia, 1972–82.*

Yi Pao Mei. *Henry Luce Professor of Humanities, Tunghai University, T'ai-chung, Taiwan, 1973–77. Professor of Oriental Studies, University of Iowa, Iowa City, 1955–70.*

Philip Merlan (d. 1968). *Professor of German Philosophy and Literature, Scripps College, Claremont, Calif., 1942–68.*

Lorenzo Minio-Paluello. *Emeritus Reader in Mediaeval Philosophy, University of Oxford; Fellow of Oriel College, Oxford, 1962–75. Director of Aristoteles Latinus, 1959–72.*

Arthur Mitzman. *Professor of History, University of Amsterdam.*

M.L. Modica. *Free-lance writer on mathematics.*

Arne D. Naess. *Emeritus Professor of Philosophy, University of Oslo.*

Hajime Nakamura. *Director, Eastern Institute, Inc., Tokyo. Emeritus Professor of Indian and Buddhist Philosophy, University of Tokyo.*

Otto E. Neugebauer. *Emeritus Professor of the History of Mathematics, Brown University, Providence, R.I.*

Robert Maxwell Ogilvie (d. 1981). *Professor of Humanity, University of St. Andrews, Fife, Scot.*

Oystein Ore (d. 1968). *Sterling Professor of Mathematics, Yale University, 1931–68.*

James Joseph O'Toole. *University Associates' Professor of Management and Organization, University of Southern California, Los Angeles.*

George A. Pettitt (d. 1976). *Assistant to the President, University of California, Berkeley, 1936–66; Lecturer in Anthropology, 1940–66.*

Henri M. Peyre. *Distinguished Professor Emeritus, Graduate Center, City University of New York. Sterling Professor Emeritus of French, Yale University.*

Jean Piveteau. *Professor of Palaeontology, University of Paris.*

John P. Plamenatz (d. 1975). *Chichele Professor of Social and Political Theory, University of Oxford, 1967–75; Fellow of All Souls College, Oxford.*

Carl Pomerance. *Associate Professor of Mathematics, University of Georgia, Athens.*

Guido Pontecorvo. *Member of research staff, Imperial Cancer Research Fund, London, 1968–75. Professor of Genetics, University of Glasgow, 1955–68.*

Gray Johnson Poole. *Free-lance writer. Coauthor of* Men Who Dig Up History *and others.*

Murray Protter. *Professor of Mathematics, University of California, Berkeley.*

The Rt. Rev. Ian Thomas Ramsey (d. 1972). *Lord Bishop of Durham, Eng., 1966–72. Nolloth Professor of the Philosophy of the Christian Religion, University of Oxford, 1951–66.*

D.D. Raphael. *Emeritus Professor of Philosophy, Imperial College of Science and Technology, University of London.*

The Rev. Charles Earle Raven (d. 1964). *Regius Professor of Divinity, University of Cambridge, 1932–50. Canon of Liverpool, 1924–32.*

Roberto Ridolfi. *Member of Accademia Nazionale dei Lincei. Director of* La Bibliofilia. *Director of "National Editions of the Works of Savonarola."*

Philip C. Ritterbush. *Historian of science. Program Director, Institute for Cultural Progress, Washington, D.C.*

Alfredo Riva. *Assistant Professor of Industrial Chemistry, University of Bologna, Italy.*

Peter P. Rohde. *Free-lance writer. Editor, Kierkegaard's Collected Works (in progress). Author of* Søren Kierkegaard.

Sydney Ross. *Professor of Colloid Science, Rensselaer Polytechnic Institute, Troy, N.Y.*

Joan Saberhagen. *Free-lance writer on mathematics.*

Sir Edward James Salisbury (d. 1978). *Director, Royal Botanic Gardens, Kew, Eng., 1943–56.*

V.C. Samuel. *Former Dean, Theological College, University of Addis Ababa, Eth.*

Francis Henry Sandbach. *Fellow of Trinity College, Cambridge; Professor of Classics, University of Cambridge, 1967–70.*

Hans Saner. *Free-lance writer. Personal assistant to Professor Karl Jaspers, 1962–69. Author of* Karl Jaspers.

Vera Sanford (deceased). *Professor of Mathematics, State University of New York College at Oneonta, 1943–59.*

Arthur Schlissel. *Professor and Chairman, Department of Mathematics, John Jay College of Criminal Justice, City University of New York.*

Walter Schulz. *Professor of Philosophy, Eberhard Karl University of Tübingen, W.Ger.*

Jacob T. Schwartz. *Chairman, Department of Computer Science, Courant Institute of Mathematical Sciences, New York University, New York City.*

Joseph Frederick Scott (d. 1971). *Vice Principal; Principal Lecturer in Mathematics, St. Mary's College, Strawberry Hill, Eng.*

Abraham Seidenberg. *Professor of Mathematics, University of California, Berkeley.*

Jean J. Seznec (d. 1983). *Marshal Foch Professor of French Literature, University of Oxford, 1950–72.*

Robert Shackleton. *Marshal Foch Professor of French Literature, University of Oxford; Fellow of All Souls College, Oxford.*

Harold I. Sharlin. *Consultant on science policy. Former Professor of History, Iowa State University, Ames.*

James Shiel. *Former Reader in the History of Hellenic Thought, University of Sussex, Brighton, Eng.*

Stephen Smale. *Professor of Mathematics, University of California, Berkeley.*

Gertrude Smith. *Edward Olson Professor Emeritus of Greek, University of Chicago.*

Ian Naismith Sneddon. *Simson Professor of Mathematics, University of Glasgow.*

Murray R. Spiegel. *Free-lance writer on mathematics.*

Martin K. Starr. *Professor of Management Science, Columbia University.*

Johannes Steudel (d. 1973). *Professor of the History of Medicine, Rhenish Friedrich Wilhelm University of Bonn.*

Lloyd Grenfell Stevenson, M.D. *William H. Welch Professor of the History of Medicine; Director, Institute of the History of Medicine, Johns Hopkins University, Baltimore.*

Brian Vincent Street. *Lecturer in Social Anthropology, University of Sussex, Brighton, Eng.*

Dirk Jan Struik. *Emeritus Professor of Mathematics, Massachusetts Institute of Technology, Cambridge.*

Yoshinori Takeuchi. *Emeritus Professor of Philosophy of Religion, Kyōto University.*

Tang Chun-i. *Former Professor of Philosophy, New Asia College, Chinese University of Hong Kong.*

Brian Tierney. *Bowmar Professor of Humanistic Studies, Cornell University, Ithaca, N.Y.*

Ettore Toffoletto, M.D. *President of the Administration Council, Arts Academy, Bologna, Italy.*

Alan C. Tucker. *Professor of Applied Mathematics and Statistics, State University of New York at Stony Brook.*

Walter Tuvell. *Free-lance writer on mathematics.*

E. Ashworth Underwood, M.D. (d. 1980). *Director, Wellcome Institute of the History of Medicine, London, 1946–64.*

Peter Ungar. *Former Professor of Mathematics, Courant Institute of Mathematical Sciences, New York University, New York City.*

Arne Unhjem. *Professor of Philosophy, Wagner College, Staten Island, N.Y.*

Rudolf Vierhaus. *Professor and Director, Max Planck Institute for History, Göttingen, W.Ger.*

Paul D. Vignaux. *Professor and former President, Section of Religious Sciences, École Pratique des Hautes Études (Institute for Advanced Research), Paris.*

Bartel Leendert van der Waerden. *Emeritus Professor of Mathematics, University of Zürich.*

William Henry Walsh (d. 1986). *Professor of Logic and Metaphysics, University of Edinburgh, 1960–79.*

Yi-T'ung Wang. *Professor of Classical Chinese, University of Pittsburgh.*

Harold W. Wardman. *Professor of French Studies, University of Lancaster, Eng.*

Fritz Wehrli. *Professor of Classical Philology, University of Zürich.*

Richard S. Westfall. *Professor of History of Science, Indiana University, Bloomington.*

Gerald James Whitrow. *Emeritus Professor of the History and Applications of Mathematics, Imperial College of Science and Technology, University of London.*

Lothar F.K. Wickert. *Emeritus Professor of Ancient History, University of Cologne.*

Dallas Willard. *Associate Professor of Philosophy, University of Southern California, Los Angeles.*

Stephen S. Willoughby. *Professor and Chairman, Department of Mathematics Education, New York University, New York City.*

Paul August Wilpert (d. 1967). *Professor of Philosophy and Director of the Thomas Institute, University of Cologne.*

Lien-sheng Yang. *Former Harvard-Yenching Professor of Chinese History, Harvard University.*

Theodore F. Zelman. *Free-lance writer on mathematics.*

Moses Zucker. *Professor of Biblical Exegesis, Jewish Theological Seminary of America, New York City.*

Geography

Jan Achterstraat. *Director, Sociografisch Bureau, Haarlemmermeer, Neth.*

Evelyn Martha Acomb-Walker. *Emeritus Professor of History, State University of New York College at New Paltz.*

Ebenezer Acquaah-Harrison. *Managing Director and Chairman, Obonoma Press, Ghana.*

André Adam. *Emeritus Professor of Muslim Sociology, University of Paris V.*

Elizabeth S. Adams. *Member, Michigan Historical Commission.*

Frederick Wayne Adrian. *Emeritus Professor of History, University of Nebraska at Omaha.*

Mikhail Mikhaylovich Adrov. *Former Chief Manager, Laboratory of Oceanology, Polar Research Institute of Marine Fisheries and Oceanography, Murmansk, U.S.S.R.*

Dwight Luther Agnew. *Professor of History; Emeritus Dean, School of Liberal Studies, University of Wisconsin-Stout, Menomonie.*

Enayat Ahmad. *Professor and Head, Department of Geography; Dean, Faculty of Arts, University of Ranchi, India.*

Kazi Saied-Uddin Ahmad (d. 1970). *Professor of Geography, University of the Punjab, Lahore, Pak.*

Syed Ahmed (deceased). *Reader and Head of the Department of Geography, Osmania University, Hyderabad, India.*

Frank Oswald Ahnert. *Professor of Physical Geography, Rhenish-Westphalian Technical University, Aachen, W.Ger. Professor of Geography, University of Maryland, College Park, 1966–74.*

Henrik S. Ahnlund. *Curator of Antiquities of Älvsborg, Swed. Former Director, Archaeological Department, Stockholm Municipal Museum.*

Ayinipalli Aiyappan. *Special Officer, Tribal Research and Training Centre, Chevayur, Calicut, India.*

Hyacinth Iheanyichuku Ajaegbu. *Professor and Head, Department of Geography, University of Jos, Nigeria.*

Robert Edwin Albright (d. 1969). *Professor of Social Studies, State University of New York College at Buffalo.*

William Thomas Alderson. *Director of Museum Studies, University of Delaware, Newark.*

Natalia Vitalyevna Aleksandrovskaya. *Associate Professor of Geography, Moscow M.V. Lomonosov State University.*

Lewis M. Alexander. *Professor of Geography, University of Rhode Island, Kingston.*

John Edmund Allison. *Supervisor, Department of Education, University of Liverpool, 1959–64. Head, Department of Geography, Birkenhead Institute, Eng., 1921–58.*

Roland Allison. *Senior tutor, College of St. Mark and St. John, Plymouth, Eng.*

David Nelson Alloway. *Professor of Sociology, Montclair State College, N.J.*

Ilídio Melo Peres do Amaral. *Rector; Professor of Geography, University of Lisbon.*

Frank Angelo. *Associate Executive Editor, Detroit Free Press, 1971–81.*

Roger M. Anthoine. *Public Information Officer, CERN (European Organization for Nuclear Research), Geneva.*

John Conrad Appel. *Professor of History, East Stroudsburg State College, Pa.*

Rosendo Arguello. *Former President, Academy of the Geography and History of Nicaragua, Managua.*

Donald Ecklund Armagost. *Former Chairman, Department of Anthropology-Sociology, State University of New York College at Potsdam.*

T.E. Armstrong. *Emeritus Reader in Arctic Studies, Scott Polar Research Institute, University of Cambridge.*

Ethel Stephens Arnett. *Author of* Greensboro, North Carolina, the County Seat of Guilford; Confederate Guns Were Stacked [at] Greensboro, North Carolina; *and others.*

Nina Yakovlevna Arsenyeva. *Senior Member in Science, Leningrad Department, State Institute of Oceanography.*

Bruce W. Atkinson. *Professor of Geography, Queen Mary College, University of London.*

Jack Nelson Averitt. *Professor of History; Emeritus Dean, Graduate School, Georgia Southern College, Statesboro.*

G.H.P. Aymans. *Professor of Applied Geography, Rhenish Friedrich Wilhelm University of Bonn.*

Paul Bachetta. *Director of Administrative Services, Office of the Mayor, Chambéry, Fr.*

E. Badian. *John Moors Cabot Professor of History, Harvard University.*

Leslie Henry Baines. *Former Clerk of the Peace and Clerk of the County Council, Isle of Wight.*

Albert Wilford Baisler. *Education Consultant, Heald Hobson & Associates, New York City. President, Jamestown Community College, N.Y., 1957–69.*

Frederick Thomas Baker. *Former Director, Lincoln Public Library, City and County Museum, and Usher Gallery, Lincoln, Eng.*

Samuel John Kenneth Baker. *Emeritus Professor of Geography, Makerere University, Kampala, Uganda. Honorary Lecturer in Geography, University of Leicester, Eng., 1968–74.*

Frank Arnold Barnes. *Senior Lecturer in Geography, University of Nottingham, Eng.*

Lucy Goodell Barnes. *Former Research Associate, Massachusetts Institute of Technology, Cambridge.*

Norman Farley James Batchelor. *Former Public Relations Officer, London Borough of Haringey, Eng.*

Merrill D. Beal. *Emeritus Professor of History, Idaho State University, Pocatello.*

Jacqueline Beaujeu-Garnier. *Professor of Geography, University of Paris I; Director, Centre for Space Analysis Research.*

J. Murray Beck. *Emeritus Professor of Political Science, Dalhousie University, Halifax, Nova Scotia.*

Virginia Beck. *Emeritus Professor of History, Millersville State College, Pa.*

Alfred M. Beeton. *Professor of Natural Resources and Atmospheric and Oceanic Science; Director, Great Lakes and Marine Waters Center, University of Michigan, Ann Arbor.*

Natalia Maree Belting. *Associate Professor of History, University of Illinois, Urbana.*

Roger William Benedict. *Managing Editor, Petroleum Intelligence Weekly, London.*

S. Ann Berich. *Former Instructor in Geography, Youngstown State University, Ohio.*

Simone Bertrand. *Former Director of the Library and of the Tapestry, Bayeux, Fr.*

Jozef Marie Nicolas Beugels. *Senior Official, Kerkrade Municipality, Neth.*

George Athan Billias. *Professor of American History, Clark University, Worcester, Mass.*

Louis Robert Binding. *Committee Clerk, Luanshya Municipal Council, Zambia.*

Claude T. Bissell. *Professor of English, University of Toronto; President, 1958–71.*

Lloyd Deacon Black. *Professor of Geography, Northern Illinois University, De Kalb.*

Vladimir Alekseyevich Blagoobrazov. *Senior Science Editor, Soviet Encyclopaedia Publishing House, Moscow.*

Phyllis Ruth Blakeley. *Associate Archivist, Province of Nova Scotia, Halifax.*

Mary Joyce Boast. *Administration Officer of the Libraries, Southwark, London.*

Ernest Amano Boateng. *Environmental and educational consultant. Executive Chairman, Environmental Protection Council of Ghana, Accra, 1973–81. Vice Chancellor, University of Cape Coast, Ghana, 1971–73.*

Hans Bobek. *Emeritus Professor of Geography, University of Vienna.*

Eugene Reeves Bock. *Former Editor of the Editorial Page, Anderson (Ind.) Daily Bulletin.*

Norbert Bodenstedt. *Chief Director of Archives, Freising, W.Ger.*

Hans H. Boesch. *Former Professor of Geography, University of Zürich.*

Victor Morton Bogle. *Chancellor; Professor of History, Indiana University, Kokomo.*

Boris Borisovich Bogoslovsky. *Professor of Physical Geography of the U.S.S.R., Belorussian V.I. Lenin State University, Minsk, U.S.S.R.*

Allan G. Bogue. *Frederick Jackson Turner Professor of History, University of Wisconsin, Madison.*

Janis A. Bokalders. *Former Professor of Economics, University of Latvia, Riga.*

Jan Bollema. *Director, Public Relations and Information Department, Municipality of The Hague.*

Juan M. Bonelli Rubio (d. 1981). *Permanent Secretary, Royal Geographical Society, Madrid.*

Paul Yvan Bonnard. *Municipal Archivist, Aix-en-Provence, Fr.*

James Calvin Bonner. *Professor and Chairman, Department of History and Political Science, Georgia College, Milledgeville, 1944–69.*

Ernst Borchorst. *Town Clerk of Esbjerg, Den.*

Vishnu Vinayak Borkar. *Professor and Head, Department of Economics, Marathwada University, Aurangabad, India.*

Otto Borst. *Professor of History, Esslingen College of Education, W.Ger.*

Clara Boscaglia. *Executive Officer, Secretariat of State for Foreign Affairs, San Marino.*

Gérard Boulet. *Schoolteacher, Nîmes, Fr.*

Baruch Boxer. *Professor of Geography and Human Ecology, Rutgers University, New Brunswick, N.J.*

Keith Brace. *Literary Editor and Chief Feature Writer,* The Birmingham Post, *Eng.*

John P. van Brakel. *Municipal Works Officer and President, Historical Society, Katwijk, Neth.*

Peter Alexander Brannon (d. 1967). *Director, Alabama Department of Archives and History, Montgomery.*

Moshe Brawer. *Professor of Geography; Dean, Faculty of Humanities, Tel Aviv University, Israel.*

James Shober Brawley. *Telegraph Editor,* Salisbury (*N.C.*) Post.

Edward Joseph Breen. *Lawyer. Editor of* History of Early Fort Dodge and Webster County, *Iowa.*

John Otis Brew. *Peabody Professor Emeritus of American Archaeology and Ethnology, Harvard University.*

William Charles Brice. *Emeritus Professor of Geography, Victoria University of Manchester.*

Harold Edward Briggs (deceased). *Professor of History, Southern Illinois University, Carbondale, 1945–65.*

George Mercer Brooke, Jr. *Professor of History, Virginia Military Institute, Lexington, 1958–80.*

Harold Chillingworth Brookfield. *Professor of Human Geography, Australian National University, Canberra.*

Alfred Edward Brown. *Former Director, Enfield Public Library, London Borough of Enfield, Eng.*

Chester Sidney Brown. *Former Director of Parks and Conservation, Department of Natural Resources, Government of Saskatchewan, Regina.*

Richard Holbrook Brown. *Director of Research and Education, Newberry Library, Chicago.*

Robert Eugene Burke. *Professor of History, University of Washington, Seattle. Managing Editor,* Pacific Northwest Quarterly.

Devereux Butcher. *Author and photographer. Author of* Exploring Our National Parks and Monuments *and others.*

Gilbert James Butland. *Emeritus Professor of Geography, University of New England, Armidale, Australia.*

Robin Alan Butlin. *Professor of Geography, Loughborough University of Technology, Eng.*

Felix Buttersack. *Editor of* Münchner Merkur *(newspaper), Munich.*

Victor Harrison Cahalane. *President, Defenders of Wildlife, 1962–71. Assistant Director, New York State Museum, Albany, 1955–67. Collaborator, National Park Service, 1955–70.*

George H. Callcott. *Professor of History, University of Maryland, College Park; Vice Chancellor for Academic Affairs, 1970–76.*

Eila M.J. Campbell. *Emeritus Professor of Geography, Birkbeck College, University of London.*

Erminio Canova. *Schoolmaster and journalist, Guastalla, Italy.*

Gerald M. Capers. *Emeritus Professor of History, Tulane University, New Orleans.*

Albert Sigfrid Carlson (d. 1975). *Professor of Geography, Dartmouth College, Hanover, N.H., 1944–73.*

Juan de M. Carriazo. *Professor of Ancient and Medieval Spanish History, University of Seville, 1927–69.*

Francisco Machado Carrion. *Professor of Geography, Federal University of Rio Grande do Sul, Pôrto Alegre, Braz.*

Carole-Ann Carter. *Tutor in geography.*

Harvey Lewis Carter. *John and Harriet Parker Campbell Professor Emeritus of American History, Colorado College, Colorado Springs; Curator of the Archer B. Hulbert Memorial Collection of Western Americana, 1960–73.*

José Candido de Melo Carvalho. *Professor, National Museum, Rio de Janeiro.*

Theodore J. Cassady. *Former Director, Illinois State Archives, Springfield.*

John Edwards Caswell. *Emeritus Professor of History, California State College, Stanislaus, Turlock, Calif.*

Abdel Kader Chanderli. *Senior Adviser, the Arab Fund, Kuwait. President and General Manager, C.A.M.E.L. Petroleum Company, Algiers, 1969–75. Ambassador of Algeria to the United Nations, 1962.*

Shiba P. Chatterjee. *Emeritus Professor of Geography, University of Calcutta.*

Jan Christensen. *Financial Editor,* Verdens Gang, *Oslo.*

Charles B. Clark. *Professor and Chairman, Department of Political Science and History, Salisbury State College, Md.*

Ira Granville Clark. *Emeritus Professor of History, New Mexico State University, Las Cruces.*

Thomas D. Clark. *Emeritus Professor of History, University of Kentucky. Distinguished Service Professor Emeritus of History, Indiana University, Bloomington.*

Frans de Clercq. *Community Official, Roosendaal en Nispen, Neth.*

Carolyn M. Clewes. *Professor of History, Wheaton College, Norton, Mass., 1954–81.*

Morris Harold Cohen. *Professor of Government, Clark University, Worcester, Mass.*

Saul Bernard Cohen. *President, Queens College, City University of New York, Flushing. Director, Graduate School of Geography, Clark University, 1965–78.*

John Peter Cole. *Professor of Regional Geography, University of Nottingham, Eng.*

John M. Coleman. *Professor of History, Lafayette College, Easton, Pa.*

J(ohn) Winston Coleman, Jr. *Author of* Slavery Times in Kentucky; Lexington During the Civil War; *and others.*

David de Lancey Condon. *Former Assistant Superintendent, Grand Canyon National Park, Arizona.*

Paul Keith Conkin. *Distinguished Professor of History, Vanderbilt University, Nashville, Tenn.*

James Robert Constantine. *Professor of History, Indiana State University, Terre Haute.*

Michael Garnet Cook. *University Archivist; Lecturer in Medieval History, University of Liverpool.*

John Terence Coppock. *Ogilvie Professor of Geography, University of Edinburgh.*

Jean Coppolani. *State Town Planner, Toulouse, Fr.*

Edmund Victor Corbett. *Former Librarian, Wandsworth Public Library, London Borough of Wandsworth, Eng.*

Paul Grant Cornell. *University Archivist; Professor of History, University of Waterloo, Ont.*

William Ainsworth Cornell. *Assistant Executive Secretary, Pennsylvania State Education Association, Harrisburg.*

Robert Cornevin. *Permanent Secretary, Academy of Overseas Sciences, Paris. Head, Centre of Studies and Documentation on Africa and Overseas, Paris.*

E. Merton Coulter (d. 1981). *Professor of History, University of Georgia, Athens, 1923–58.*

John Wesley Coulter (d. 1968). *Professor of Geography, University of Cincinnati, Ohio.*

Joseph Francis Courtney. *Attorney. Lecturer in Public Administration, Northeastern University, Boston.*

Raymond Gibson Cowherd. *Emeritus Professor of History, Lehigh University, Bethlehem, Pa.*

James Stevens Cox. *Editor,* Proceedings of the Dorset Natural History and Archaeological Society, *and others.*

Clark Nixon Crain. *Former Professor of Geography and Regional Development, University of Denver, Colo.*

Albert Charles Crane. *Former Clerk, Border Rural District Council, England.*

Leland Hargrave Creer. *Emeritus Professor of History, University of Utah, Salt Lake City.*

Bernarr Cresap. *Professor of History, University of North Alabama, Florence, 1951–77.*

John Clark Crighton. *Professor of History, Stephens College, Columbia, Mo., 1935–70.*

Virgil Charles Crisafulli. *Emeritus Professor of Economics, Utica College of Syracuse University, N.Y.*

Gerald Roe Crone. *Librarian and Map Curator, Royal Geographical Society, London, 1945–66.*

Jesse Crawford Crowe. *Professor of History, Western Kentucky University, Bowling Green.*

Kenneth Brailey Cumberland. *Former Professor of Geography, University of Auckland, New Zealand.*

Décio Neves da Cunha. *Professor, Centre for General Education, Federal University of Espírito Santo, Vitória, Braz.*

Pedro Cunill. *Professor of Historical Geography, Central University of Venezuela, Caracas.*

Alden (Denzel) Cutshall. *Emeritus Professor of Geography, University of Illinois, Chicago.*

Ernest Rockwell Dalton (d. 1984). *Dean of Instruction, Centenary College for Women, Hackettstown, N.J.*

Arthur Davies. *Reardon-Smith Professor of Geography, University of Exeter, Eng., 1948–71.*

Wayne K.D. Davies. *Professor of Geography, University of Calgary, Alberta.*

James Treadwell Davis. *Emeritus Professor of History, University of Southern Mississippi, Hattiesburg.*

John Armstrong Davison (d. 1966). *Professor of Greek Language and Literature, University of Leeds, Eng., 1951–66.*

Raul d'Eça. *Lecturer on Latin-American affairs. Assistant Career Planning Officer, U.S. Information Agency, 1959–61. Branch Public Affairs Officer, Recife and Belo Horizonte, Braz., Office of International Information and Cultural Affairs, 1947–58.*

John Alvin Decker. *Former Professor of Political Science, Stephens College, Columbia, Mo.*

Gerhard Deissmann. *Former Collaborator and Assistant Director, Bremen Committee for Economic Research, W.Ger.*

Henry Delmont. *Former Curator, J.B. Rames Museum, Aurillac, Fr.*

Abraham Demoz. *Professor of Linguistics; Director, Program of African Studies, Northwestern University, Evanston, Ill.*

René Julien C. De Roo. *Curator, Royal Museums of Art and History, Brussels. Archivist and Museum Director, Mechelen, Belg., 1949–63.*

Hans Otto Jerphaas de Ruyter de Wildt. *Chief of Educational and Cultural Affairs, Hoorn, Neth.*

P.B. Desai. *Former Professor and Head, Department of Ancient Indian History and Culture, Karnatak University, Dharwar, India.*

Pedro Neiva de Santana. *Governor of Maranhão State. Former Rector, University of Maranhão, São Luis, Braz.*

Jean-Jacques Despois (d. 1978). *Professor of Geography, University of Paris, 1957–69.*

Jack J. Detzler. *Professor of History, Saint Mary's College, Notre Dame, Ind.*

Caio Benjamin Dias. *Former Rector, University of Brasília.*

Samuel Newton Dicken. *Emeritus Professor of Geography, University of Oregon, Eugene.*

Robert Eric Dickinson. *Emeritus Professor of Geography, University of Arizona, Tucson.*

Kwamina Busumafi Dickson. *Vice-Chancellor, University of Cape Coast, Ghana.*

Alonzo Thomas Dill. *Public Relations Director, Chesapeake Corporation of Virginia, West Point, Va., 1958–80.*

Ernest H.G. Dobby (d. 1981). *Professor of Geography, University of Malaya, Singapore.*

William Mann Dobriner. *Charles A. Dana Professor of Sociology, Lafayette College, Easton, Pa.*

Anatoly Petrovich Domanitsky. *Senior Scientist, Leningrad Hydrological Institute.*

J. Don. *Archivist, Kampen, Neth.*

Desmond Thomas Donovan. *Former Yates-Goldsmid Professor of Geology, University College, University of London.*

Arthur J.M. Doucy. *Professor of Social Economics; former Director, Institute of Sociology, Free University of Brussels.*

Garland Downum. *Emeritus Professor of History, Northern Arizona University, Flagstaff.*

Jean Dresch. *Emeritus Professor of Geography, University of Paris VII.*

Robert Roland Drummond. *Professor of Geography, Indiana State University, Terre Haute.*

Raymond Dubé. *Former Editor in Chief, Le Soleil, Quebec City.*

George Harry Dury. *Emeritus Professor of Geography and Geology, University of Wisconsin, Madison.*

André Duval. *Former Deputy Mayor, Clichy, Fr.*

Denis John Dwyer. *Professor of Geography, University of Keele, Eng.*

Donald Ray Dyer. *Regional Geographic Attaché, U.S. Department of State, Washington, D.C.*

Wilma Dykeman. *Author of* The French Broad (Rivers of America Series); The Border States; *and others.*

David Livingstone Dykstra. *Emeritus Professor of History, Hofstra University, Hempstead, N.Y.*

Armand J. Eardley (d. 1972). *Professor of Geology, University of Utah, Salt Lake City, 1965–70; Dean, College of Mines and Mineral Industries, 1954–65.*

The Rev. George Herbert Eastman. *Principal of the London Missionary Society's Training College at Beru, Gilbert and Ellice Islands, 1918–48.*

Herbert Leeson Edlin (d. 1976). *Publications Officer, Forestry Commission of Great Britain, London.*

Kenneth Charles Edwards (d. 1982). *Professor of Geography, University of Nottingham, Eng., 1948–70.*

Emil Egli. *Professor of Geography, Zürich Gymnasium. Lecturer, University of Zürich and Swiss Federal Institute of Technology, Zürich.*

Blake Ehrlich (d. 1974). *Free-lance writer. Author of* Paris on the Seine; London on the Thames; *and many others.*

H.W. Eldermans. *Journalist. Former Editor*, Rotterdamsch Nieuwsblad.

Dorothy M. Ellicott. *Justice of the Peace. Member, City Council of Gibraltar, 1947–55; House of Assembly, 1959–64.*

Robert Neal Elliott. *Associate Professor of History, North Carolina State University, Raleigh.*

Joseph Waldo Ellison (deceased). *Professor of History, Oregon State University, Corvallis.*

Antonia Déa Erdens. *Professor of Geography, Federal University of Bahia, Salvador, Braz.*

Sirri Erinc. *Director, Institute of Marine Sciences and Geography, University of Istanbul.*

Sir Robert Charles Evans. *Principal, University College of North Wales, Bangor, University of Wales. Author of* Kangchenjunga: The Untrodden Peak *and others.*

Russell Charles Ewing (d. 1972). *Professor of History, University of Arizona, Tucson, 1948–72.*

J.D. Eyles. *Lecturer in Geography, Queen Mary College, University of London.*

John Douglas Eyre. *Professor of Geography, University of North Carolina at Chapel Hill.*

John Donnelly Fage. *Pro-Vice-Chancellor, Vice-Principal, and Professor of African History, University of Birmingham, Eng.*

Albert Leonard Farley. *Professor of Geography, University of British Columbia, Vancouver.*

Bertram Hughes Farmer. *Fellow of St. John's College, Cambridge; Reader in South Asian Geography; Director, Centre of South Asian Studies, University of Cambridge.*

Francis Peloubet Farquhar (d. 1975). *Author of* Place Names of the High Sierra *and others.*

Irmgard Feldhaus. *Director, Clemens Sels Museum, Neuss, W.Ger.*

João Epitácio Fernandes Pimenta (d. 1972). *Judge, First District of Natal, Braz., 1954–57. Member, Electoral Tribunal of Rio Grande do Norte, 1953–57.*

A.M. Ferrar. *Map Curator, University of Hull, Eng.*

Milton Gonçalves Ferreira. *Former Vice Rector and Director of the Faculty of Economics, Federal University of Alagoas, Maceió, Braz.*

George Leonard Fersh. *Associate Director, Joint Council on Economic Education, New York City.*

José Carlos de Figueiredo. *Emeritus Professor of Geography of Brazil, Federal University of Paraná, Curitiba, Braz.*

José de Silva Ribeiro Filho. *Professor of Criminal Law, Federal University of Sergipe, Aracaju, Braz. Secretary, Public Security of the State of Sergipe.*

Ingo Findenegg (d. 1974). *Head, International Biological Program Laboratory, Austrian Academy of Sciences, Klagenfurt.*

George Michael Fitzpatrick. *Emeritus Editor*, New Mexico Magazine.

Betty Lorraine Fladeland. *Professor of History, Southern Illinois University, Carbondale.*

Allen Richard Foley (d. 1978). *Professor of History, Dartmouth College, Hanover, N.H.*

Martin Otto Walter Folkerts. *Assistant Scientist, Institute of Geography and Economic Geography, University of Hamburg.*

Lachlan Maxwell Forbes. *Former Editor*, Polar Record, *Scott Polar Research Institute, University of Cambridge.*

Arthur B. Ford. *Geologist, Branch of Alaskan Geology, Geological Survey, U.S. Department of the Interior, Menlo Park, Calif.*

Enid R.A. Forde. *Associate Professor of Geography, Fourah Bay College, University of Sierra Leone, Freetown.*

Charles Nelson Forward. *Professor of Geography, University of Victoria, B.C.*

Abram John Foster. *Professor of History, Millersville State College, Pa., 1952–79.*

Catharine Osgood Foster. *Teacher of English and American Literature, Bennington College, Vt., 1934–68.*

Lucien Fourez. *Judge, Tribunal of First Instance, Belgium.*

Thomas Walter Freeman. *Former Professor of Geography, Victoria University of Manchester.*

Marion R. Fremont-Smith. *Attorney, Choate, Hall & Stewart, Boston. Assistant Attorney General, Commonwealth of Massachusetts, 1959–63.*

Richard Antony French. *Senior Lecturer in the Geography of the U.S.S.R., University College and School of Slavonic and East European Studies, University of London.*

Hermann Friedrich. *Former Director, Overseas Museum, Bremen, W.Ger.*

Robert F. Fries. *Emeritus Professor of History, De Paul University, Chicago.*

Grigory Ivanovich Galazy. *Director, Institute of Limnology, Siberian Department, Academy of Sciences of the U.S.S.R., Irkutsk.*

Edward John Gallagher (d. 1978). *Publisher*, Laconia (N.H.) Evening Citizen.

Maureen L. Gallery. *Free-lance writer on Middle Eastern geography.*

Hans Gamma. *Editor. Former Mayor, Altdorf, Switz.*

Vico Garbesi. *Assistant Librarian, Library of Imola, Italy.*

Elizabeth Gard. *Copy Editor,* Hispanic American Historical Review, *Albuquerque, N.M. Editorial Assistant,* Geography, Encyclopædia Britannica, Chicago, 1970–71.

John H. Garland. *Emeritus Professor of Geography, University of Illinois, Urbana.*

Richard Gascon. *Professor of Local History, University of Lyon II.*

Werner Gatz. *Director, Bremen Society for Economic Research, W.Ger.*

Aleksandr Mikhaylovich Gavrilov. *Senior Scientist, Leningrad Hydrological Institute.*

George Roosevelt Gayler. *Professor of History, Northwest Missouri State University, Maryville.*

Alastair George Geddes. *Former Lecturer in Adult Education, University of Southampton, Eng.*

Clyde Christian Gelbach. *Professor of History, Indiana State University, Pa., 1955–82.*

Susannah C. Gentry. *Associate Editor,* Independence (Mo.) Examiner.

Arch C. Gerlach (d. 1972). *Chief Geographer, Geological Survey, U.S. Department of the Interior, 1967–72. Incumbent, Chair of Geography, Library of Congress.*

Percy Amorey Beufort Gethin. *Tutor in English and Political Institutions, Lennox Cook School of English, Cambridge, Eng.*

Huricihan Ghaznavi. *Teaching Assistant in Middle Eastern History and Turkish, University of Wisconsin, Madison.*

G.K. Ghori. *Visiting Professor of Geography, University of Benin, Nigeria.*

Arrell Morgan Gibson. *Professor of History; Curator, Western History Collection, University of Oklahoma, Norman.*

Frans Gijzels. *Mayor of Heerlen, Neth.*

Malaquias Gil Arantegui. *Professor of History and Geography, "Pedro Henriquez Urena" National University, Santo Domingo, Dominican Republic.*

Robert Creighton Gilmore. *Associate Professor of History, University of New Hampshire, Durham.*

Marcel Gingras. *Secretary, Public Service Commission of Canada, Ottawa.*

Norton S. Ginsburg. *Director, Environment and Policy Institute, East-West Center, Honolulu.*

Francesco Giunta. *Professor of Medieval History, University of Palermo.*

Charles Nelson Glaab. *Professor of History, University of Toledo, Ohio.*

Robert Morton Glendinning. *Emeritus Professor of Geography, University of California, Los Angeles.*

Stephen Goddard. *Deputy Librarian, School of Oriental and African Studies, University of London.*

António Armando Gonçalves Pereira. *Professor of Commercial and Maritime Law, Technical University of Lisbon.*

George Goodwin, Jr. *Professor of Politics, University of Massachusetts, Boston.*

Arnold L. Gordon. *Professor of Oceanography, Lamont-Doherty Geological Observatory, Columbia University, Palisades, N.Y.*

Jean Grandmaison. *Keeper of the Archives and Library, Tarascon, Fr.*

Lee Albert Graver. *Emeritus Professor of History and Political Science, Kutztown University, Pa.*

Mabel Green. *Former Lecturer in Geography, College of Education, Hull, Eng.*

Donald Paul Greene. *Former Associate Professor of History and Anthropology, Adams State College, Alamosa, Colo.*

Richard A. Greene. *Columnist and Editorial Writer,* Muncie *(Ind.)* Star.

Gwilym David Gregory. *Principal Assistant, London Borough of Camden Public Libraries, Eng.*

Jack Irving Grenfell. *Justice of the Peace; Town Clerk and Treasurer, City of Ararat, Australia.*

Edward Frederick Greve. *Associate Professor of Library Science, University of Wisconsin, Superior.*

Thomas Melvin Griffiths. *Emeritus Professor of Geography, University of Denver, Colo.*

Theodore Gregory Gronert (d. 1966). *Chairman, Department of History, Wabash College, Crawfordsville, Ind.*

Alberto Passos Guimarães. *Geography Editor,* Enciclopédia Mirador Internacional, *Rio de Janeiro.*

Bernard Victor Gutsell. *Former Professor of Geography, York University, Toronto. Editor,* Cartographica.

LeRoy R. Hafen. *Emeritus Professor of History, Brigham Young University, Provo, Utah. State Historian of Colorado, 1924–54.*

Daniel George Edward Hall (d. 1979). *Professor of the History of South-East Asia, University of London, 1949–59.*

J.M. Hall. *Lecturer in Geography, Queen Mary College, University of London.*

Ray Hall. *Lecturer in Geography, Queen Mary College, University of London.*

Robert Burnett Hall (d. 1975). *Colonel, U.S. Army. Professor of Geography, University of Michigan, Ann Arbor; Director, Center for Japanese Studies, 1947–57.*

Louis-Edmond Hamelin. *Geographer, University of Quebec at Trois-Rivières; Rector, 1978–83.*

Edward Hamming. *Professor of Geography, Augustana College, Rock Island, Ill.*

John W. Hanson. *Professor of Geography, Michigan State University, East Lansing.*

F. Kenneth Hare. *University Professor of Geography and of Physics; Provost, Trinity College, University of Toronto.*

George Dewey Harmon. *Emeritus Professor of American History, Lehigh University, Bethlehem, Pa.*

John Lauren Harr. *Emeritus Professor of History, Northwest Missouri State University, Maryville.*

Ronald James Harrison-Church. *Emeritus Professor of Geography, London School of Economics and Political Science, University of London.*

Mary Harvey. *Lecturer in Geography, Goldsmiths' College, University of London.*

Maria van Hasselt. *Former Curator, History of The Hague Department, Municipal Museum of The Hague.*

Raymond Hastey. *Teacher, Lycée, Cherbourg, Fr.*

Athan(assios) D. Hatzikakidis. *General Director, Institute of Oceanographic and Fisheries Research, Athens.*

Richard Walter Haupt. *Former Director, The Cincinnati Historical Society, Ohio.*

H. Bowman Hawkes. *Emeritus Professor of Geography, University of Utah, Salt Lake City.*

Hubert Howard Hawkins. *Director, Indiana Historical Bureau and Indiana Historical Society, Indianapolis, 1953–76.*

Hermann-Heino Heine. *Taxonomic Botanist, Kew Gardens, London.*

Herbert Lynn Heller. *Emeritus Professor of Education, Baldwin-Wallace College, Berea, Ohio.*

Walter Brookfield Hendrickson. *Emeritus Professor of History, MacMurray College, Jacksonville, Ill.*

Henri Henneguelle. *Mayor of Boulogne, Fr., 1945–47; 1953–77.*

Roger Chatsey Heppell. *Professor of Geography, State University of New York College at Cortland.*

Thomas Herdman (d. 1970). *Senior Lecturer in Geography and Education, Training College, Dudley, Eng.*

Herman Heupers. *Manager, Public Relations Office, Enschede, Neth.*

Sanford Wilson Higginbotham. *Professor of History, Rice University, Houston, Texas. Editor,* Journal of Southern History.

Ernest Gotthold Hildner, Jr. *Professor of History, Illinois College, Jacksonville, 1938–72.*

Marie-Elisabeth Hilger. *Professor of Social and Economic History, Institute for Social and Economic History, University of Hamburg.*

Dorothy Hill. *Research Professor Emeritus of Geology, University of Queensland, St. Lucia, Brisbane, Australia.*

Neal O. Hines. *Former Staff Associate, Laboratory of Radiation Biology, University of Washington, Seattle.*

Mark David Hirsch. *Emeritus Professor of History, Bronx Community College, City University of New York.*

Edward Henry Hobbs. *Dean of Arts and Sciences, Auburn University, Ala.*

Walter Hoffelner. *Official of the Municipal Council, Steyr, Austria.*

Hans Högn (d. 1980). *Mayor of Hof, W.Ger.*

Stanley Charles Holliday. *Former Chief Librarian, Kensington and Chelsea Public Libraries, London.*

Madhusudan Shriniwas Honrao. *Former Reader and Head, Department of Geography, Karnatak University, Dharwar, India.*

Reginald Horsman. *Distinguished Professor of American History, University of Wisconsin, Milwaukee.*

Jack Luin Hough. *Emeritus Professor of Meteorology and Oceanography and of Geology and Mineralogy, University of Michigan, Ann Arbor.*

James Houston. *Chancellor, Regent College, Vancouver, B.C.*

Henry Forbush Howe, M.D. *Author of* Salt Rivers of the Massachusetts Shore; Massachusetts: There She Is—Behold Her; *and others.*

Lewis Grenfell Huddy. *Former Town Clerk, London Borough of Hackney, Eng.*

Jean Hugli. *Teacher, Technical College, Lausanne, Switz.*

Robert Edward Huke. *Professor of Geography, Dartmouth College, Hanover, N.H.*

Arjuna Hulugalle. *Publishing company director. Coeditor and cotranslator of* Reiseführer von Sri Lanka *("Guide to Ceylon").*

Herbert A.J. Hulugalle. *Chairman, Advisory Committee, National and Grindlays Bank, Sri Lanka Branch, Colombo. Ambassador of Ceylon to Italy, 1954–59.*

John Owen Hunt. *Former Clerk, Urban District Council, Matlock, Eng.*

Thomas John Hunt. *Chairman, Somerset Archaeological Society and Somerset Record Society, Eng.*

J.O. Hunwick. *Professor of History, Northwestern University, Evanston, Ill.*

Jacob C. Hurewitz. *Professor of Political Science, Columbia University.*

Georg Illert. *Former Director, State Library, Archives, and Museum, Worms, W.Ger.*

Giuseppe Imbo. *Emeritus Professor of Earth Sciences, University of Naples. Director, Vesuvian Observatory, Naples, 1935–70.*

Robert Henry Irrmann. *Emeritus Professor of History, Beloit College, Wis.; Archivist, 1953–80.*

William Harold Irvine. *Secretary General, Nigerian Tourist Association, Lagos, 1963–68.*

Norman Itzkowitz. *Professor of Near Eastern Studies, Princeton University.*

John David Ives. *Professor of Geography; Director, Institute of Arctic and Alpine Research, University of Colorado, Boulder.*

Phil Rowland Jack. *Professor of History, California State College, Pa.*

Wilbur R. Jacobs. *Professor of History, University of California, Santa Barbara.*

Orville John Jaebker. *Professor and Head, Department of History, University of Evansville, Ind.*

Karel Frederik Otto James. *President, Central Committee of Regional Gasboards, Amerongen. Former Burgomaster, Gouda, Neth.*

Preston E. James (d. 1986). *Maxwell Professor of Geography, Syracuse University, N.Y., 1964–70.*

Neil L. Jamieson, III. *Acting Assistant Professor of Anthropology, Freshman Seminar Program, University of Hawaii at Manoa, Honolulu.*

Brian Michael Jenkins. *Senior Staff Member, The RAND Corporation, Santa Monica, Calif.*

John Leonard Jennewein (d. 1968). *Associate Professor of History, Dakota Wesleyan University, Mitchell, S.D.*

Dorothy O. Johansen. *Emeritus Professor of History, Reed College, Portland, Ore.*

John Edwin Johns. *President, Furman University, Greenville, S.C.*

Bert Willard Johnson. *County Manager, Arlington, Va., 1962–76. City Manager, Evanston, Ill., 1953–62.*

William Stephen Kwesi Johnston (Nana Amoah IV). *Vice Chairman, Ghana Boy Scouts Association, Central Region. Senior Divisional Chief of Ognaa (Cape Coast) Traditional Area; Local Court Magistrate, Cape Coast, Ghana, 1960–66.*

Clarence F. Jones. *Emeritus Professor of Geography, Northwestern University, Evanston, Ill.*

Lewis Pinckney Jones. *Kenan Professor of History, Wofford College, Spartanburg, S.C.*

Meirion T. Jones. *Principal Scientific Officer, Marine Information and Advisory Service, Institute of Oceanographic Sciences, Birkenhead, Eng.*

Robert Leslie Jones. *Emeritus Professor of History, Marietta College, Ohio.*

Ronald Jones. *Reader in Geography, Queen Mary College, University of London.*

Stanley Llewellyn Jones. *Professor of History; Vice Chancellor of Academic Affairs, University of North Carolina at Greensboro.*

Weymouth Tyree Jordan (d. 1968). *Professor, 1949–68, and Head of the Department of History, 1955–68, Florida State University, Tallahassee.*

Derrick Neville Edwin Kain. *Industrial and Business Editor, Natal Witness, Pietermaritzburg, S.Af.*

James Samuel Kaleem. *Former Principal Education Officer, Ministry of Education, Tamale, Ghana.*

Samuel Richey Kamm (deceased). *Professor of History and Social Science, Wheaton College, Ill., 1942–73.*

Otto Kandler. *Professor of Geography, Johannes Gutenberg University of Mainz, W.Ger.*

Suk Oh Kang. *Former Professor of Geography, Ewha Woman's University, Seoul.*

Helene Juliet Kantor. *Professor of Near Eastern Archaeology, University of Chicago.*

P.P. Karan. *Professor of Geography, University of Kentucky, Lexington.*

John Haskell Kemble. *Emeritus Professor of History, Pomona College, Claremont, Calif.*

Peter Alexander Kennedy. *Former County Archivist, Devon County Council, England.*

Joan Margaret Kenworthy. *Principal, St. Mary's College; Honorary Lecturer in Geography, University of Durham, Eng.*

Hendrik Jakob Keuning. *Former Professor of Economics and Social Geography, State University of Groningen, Neth.*

Huỳnh Kim Khánh. *Research Fellow, Institute of Social Studies, The Hague.*

Rudolf Kiepke. *Publisher of* Die Warte, *Paderborn, W.Ger.*

Harold Godfrey King. *Librarian and Information Officer, Scott Polar Research Institute, University of Cambridge.*

Spencer Bidwell King, Jr. (d. 1977). *Professor of History, Mercer University, Macon, Ga., 1948–73.*

George Kish. *Professor of Geography, University of Michigan, Ann Arbor.*

Anna Alekseyevna Klyukanova. *Junior Scientist, Institute of Geography, Academy of Sciences of the U.S.S.R., Moscow.*

Anton C.F. Koch. *Former Town archivist and librarian, Deventer, Neth.*

John Kolars. *Professor of Geography, University of Michigan, Ann Arbor.*

Rudolf Koller. *Director of the Municipal Department of Culture and the Arts, Ingolstadt, W.Ger.*

John G.J. Koreman. *Chief Assistant, Municipal Record Office, Maastricht, Neth.*

Dimiter Konstantinov Kossev. *Editor in Chief,* Bulgarian Historical Review. *Rector, University of Sofia, 1962–67.*

Hans-Joachim Kramm. *Professor of Economic Geography, College of Education, Potsdam, E.Ger.*

Walter Kranz. *Former Director, Press and Information Office of the Liechtenstein Government.*

Hermann Kresse. *Editor in Chief, Saarland Edition,* Rhein-Saar-Spiegel. *Reporter,* Saarbrücker Zeitung.

Werner Kugler (d. 1973). *Burgomaster of Schleswig, W.Ger.*

Werner Th. Kuhn (d. 1973). *Professor of Geography, Staedtisches Gymnasium, Bern. Lecturer, State College, Bern.*

Wiebren Hendrik Kuipers. *Public Relations Officer, Community of Leeuwarden, Neth.*

Eeva-Sinikka Kurikka. *Chief Correspondent, Werner Söderström Osakeyhtiö, Publishers, Helsinki.*

Wilhelm von Kürten. *Professor of Geography, University of Wuppertal, W.Ger.*

Pieter Th.J. Kuyer. *Keeper of Municipal Records, 's Hertogenbosch, Neth.*

Nikolay Timofeyevich Kuznetsov. *Senior Scientist, Institute of Geography, Academy of Sciences of the U.S.S.R., Moscow.*

Alexander Atta Yaw Kyerematen. *Director, Ghana National Cultural Centre, Kumasi.*

Howard Lackman. *Professor of History, University of Texas at Arlington.*

Ernest McPherson Lander, Jr. *Alumni Professor of History, Clemson University, S.C.*

Elfrieda Wilhelmina Henrietta Lang. *Curator of Manuscripts, Lilly Library, Indiana University, Bloomington, 1965–74.*

Robert Millard Langdon (d. 1967). *Associate Professor of History, Civilian Faculty, U.S. Naval Academy.*

Richard W. Lariviere. *Assistant Professor of Sanskrit, University of Texas at Austin.*

Helge Larsen. *Minister of Education, Danish Government, 1968–71.*

François Lasserre. *Emeritus Professor of Classical Greek, University of Lausanne, Switz.*

Geoffrey Charles Last. *Adviser, Imperial Ethiopian Ministry of Education and Fine Arts, Addis Ababa.*

Louis-Noël Latour. *Curator, Museum of the Hôtel-Dieu, Beaune, Fr.*

Keith Eric Lauder. *Former Town Clerk, London Borough of Barking, Eng.*

Heinz Lauenroth. *Chief City Official and Director, Cultural and Sport Department, Hanover, W.Ger.*

Joseph J. Lauer. *Africana Librarian, University of California, Los Angeles.*

J.H.G. Lebon (d. 1969). *Reader in Geography, School of Oriental and African Studies, University of London, 1966–69.*

Enoch Lawrence Lee. *Emeritus Professor of History, The Citadel, Charleston, S.C.*

Roger Kendrick Lee. *Lecturer in Geography, Queen Mary College, University of London.*

Aureliano Leite (d. 1976). *President of the São Paulo Historical and Geographical Institute. Member of the São Paulo Academy of Letters. Member of the Brazilian Historical and Geographical Institute.*

Celso de Paiva Leite. *Professor, Centre of Applied Social Sciences, Federal University of Paraíba, João Pessoa, Braz.*

Robert Lemaire. *Librarian of the Municipal Library, Beauvais, Fr.*

Walter John Lemke (d. 1968). *Professor of Journalism, University of Arkansas, Fayetteville.*

John Herbert Le Patourel (d. 1981). *Research Professor of Medieval History, University of Leeds, Eng., 1970–74.*

Edith Veronica Lewis. *Reference Librarian, Finsbury Library, London Borough of Islington, Eng.*

George Knowlton Lewis. *Professor of Geography, Boston University.*

Reginald George Lickfold. *Former Town Clerk, Weston-super-Mare, Eng.*

George Lighton. *Principal of Stevenage College of Further Education, Stevenage, Eng. Former Senior Geography Master, Queen's College, Georgetown, British Guiana.*

José Lourenço de Lima. *Professor of Romance Languages, Federal University of Pernambuco, and Catholic University of Pernambuco, Recife, Braz.*

Miguel Alves de Lima. *Professor of Physical Geography, State University of Rio de Janeiro; former Director, Earth Sciences Institute.*

Steffen Linvald. *Director of Copenhagen City Museum, 1952–79.*

Aleksandr Petrovich Lisitsin. *Head, Laboratory of Physical Methods of Research, Institute of Oceanology, Academy of Sciences of the U.S.S.R., Moscow.*

Georges Livet. *Professor of Modern History, University of Strasbourg II, Fr.*

Donald Lloyd. *Former Deputy Clerk, Urban District Council of Winsford, Eng.*

Seton H.F. Lloyd. *Emeritus Professor of Western Asiatic Archaeology, University of London.*

W. Duane Lockard. *Professor of Political Science, Princeton University.*

M. John Loeffler. *Professor of Geography, University of Colorado, Boulder.*

Julius Loennechen. *British Vice Consul, Kristiansund, Nor.*

Rayford Whittingham Logan (d. 1982). *Professor of History, Howard University, Washington, D.C., 1938–72.*

Richard F. Logan. *Professor of Geography, University of California, Los Angeles.*

Alan R. Longhurst. *Director-General, Atlantic Ocean Science and Surveys, Bedford Institute of Oceanography, Dartmouth, Nova Scotia.*

Richard Lowitt. *Former Professor of History, University of Kentucky, Lexington.*

Myron Harper Luke. *Emeritus Professor of History, C.W. Post College, Long Island University, Greenvale, N.Y.*

Gustav Johannes Luntowski. *Town Archivist, Dortmund. Former Town Archivist and Chief Librarian, Lüneburg, W.Ger.*

Anthony Thornton Luttrell. *Former Assistant Director, British School at Rome.*

Vasily Yosifovich Lymarev. *Professor of Geography, Kaliningrad State University, U.S.S.R.*

Charles Maas. *Director, Cultural Office, Villach, Austria.*

John Morris McClelland, Jr. *Former Editor and Publisher,* Longview (*Wash.*) Daily News.

Margaret McDerby. *Librarian in Charge, Reference and Museum Services, London Borough of Barnet, Eng.*

William Duff Mackay. *Town Clerk and Treasurer, Richmond, S.Af. Town Clerk, Ladysmith, S.Af., 1946–61.*

Henry Miller Madden. *Adjunct Professor of Bibliography, California State University, Fresno; Librarian, 1949–79.*

Desiderio Maggioni. *Former Member for Milano-Pavia, Chamber of Deputies, Italy.*

William Richard Maidment. *Former Borough Librarian, London Borough of Camden, Eng.*

Vasile Malinschi. *Governor, National Bank of the Socialist Republic of Romania, 1963–77. Member, Section of Economics and Sociological Research, Academy of the Socialist Republic of Romania, Bucharest.*

Ulrich W. Mammey. *Research Associate, Federal Institute for Population Research, Wiesbaden, W.Ger. Associate of the Geographical Institute, Johann Wolfgang Goethe University of Frankfurt.*

Gordon Manley (d. 1980). *Professor of Environmental Sciences, University of Lancaster, Eng., 1964–68.*

Luis Marden. *Former Chief, Foreign Editorial Staff,* National Geographic Magazine, *Washington, D.C.*

Aleksandr Mefodyevich Marinich. *Director, Department of Geography, C.I. Subotin Institute of Geophysics, Ukrainian S.S.R. Academy of Sciences, Kiev.*

Albert John Marino. *Assistant City Editor,* New Britain (*Conn.*) Herald.

Nemesio Marqués. *General Secretary to the Bishop of Urgel, Coprince of Andorra.*

Hendrik Michiel Martens. *Burgomaster, Ermelo, Neth., 1938–62.*

Jean Martin-Demézil. *Archivist, Département de Loir-et-Cher, France, 1941–78.*

M.E. Marts. *Professor of Geography, University of Washington, Seattle.*

Kenneth Mason (d. 1976). *Lieutenant Colonel, Royal Engineers. Professor of Geography, University of Oxford, 1932–53.*

Philip Parker Mason. *Professor of History, Wayne State University, Detroit.*

Matsui Taketoshi. *Former Professor of Human Geography, Nagoya University, Japan.*

Eberhard Matthes. *Former Town Archivist, Eisenach, E.Ger.*

John E. Mawby. *Associate Professor of Geology, California State University, Fresno.*

William Richard Mead. *Emeritus Professor of Geography, University College, University of London.*

Howard Brett Melendy. *Professor of History, San Jose State University, Calif.*

Ralph Robertson Mellon, M.D. (deceased). *Director, Institute of Pathology, Western Pennsylvania Hospital, Pittsburgh, 1927–53.*

Roy E.H. Mellor. *Professor of Geography, University of Aberdeen, Scot.*

Alberto Mennella. *Archivist and Departmental Head, Municipality of Torre del Greco, Italy.*

Jean Michel Mercadier. *Director, Honoré de Balzac College of Secondary Education, Albi, Fr.*

(Ethel) Doris Mercer. *Head Archivist, Greater London Council.*

Horst Messerschmidt. *Burgomaster of Bernburg, E.Ger.*

Patricia Meyer. *Reference Librarian, Borough of Wandsworth, Eng.*

Dorothy Middleton. *Assistant Editor, Geographical Journal, 1953–71. Author of* Baker of the Nile *and others.*

R.E. Millard. *Former Clerk of the Peace and Clerk of the County Council, Buckinghamshire, Eng.*

Maynard Malcolm Miller. *Professor of Geology; Dean, College of Mines and Earth Resources; Chief, Idaho Bureau of Mines and Geology, University of Idaho, Moscow.*

Paul Eugene Million, Jr. *Associate Professor of History, Purdue University, West Lafayette, Ind.*

Norah Mitchell. *Teacher at the Kodaï School, Madurai District, Tamil Nadu, India.*

Mario Modiano. *Athens Correspondent,* The Times (*London*).

Maurice P. Moffatt. *Former Professor and Chairman, Department of Social Studies, Montclair State College, N.J.*

Jay Monaghan (d. 1981). *Consultant, Wyles Collection of Lincolniana and Western Americana, University of California, Santa Barbara. State Historian of Illinois, 1946–51.*

Robert Scott Monahan. *Former Forester and Manager of Outing Properties, Dartmouth College, Hanover, N.H.*

Annie Monginoux. *Librarian, Saint-Étienne Municipal Library, Fr.*

Francis John Monkhouse (d. 1975). *Professor of Geography, University of Southampton, Eng., 1954–66.*

Powell A. Moore (d. 1967). *Professor of History, Indiana University, Bloomington.*

Amélia A. Norgueira Moreira (deceased). *Professor of Geography, Federal University of Ceará, Fortaleza, Braz.*

Gladys Margery Morris. *Former Clerk, Ashburton Urban District Council, Eng.*

James Davidson Morrison. *Emeritus Professor of History, Southeastern State College, Durant, Okla.*

Ralph Ernest Morrow. *Professor of History, Washington University, St. Louis, Mo.*

Richard Lee Morton (d. 1974). *Professor of History, College of William and Mary, Williamsburg, Va., 1921–59.*

Heinz Motel. *Chief of Tourist Office, Göttingen, W.Ger.*

Malcolm Herbert Moule. *Professor of English History, University of the Pacific, Stockton, Calif.*

Alan Bertram Mountjoy. *Reader in Geography, Bedford College, University of London.*

Pieter Mourik. *Municipal Economic Adviser, Haarlem, Neth.*

Ottheinz Münch. *City Archivist, Kaiserslautern, W.Ger.*

John A. Munroe. *H. Rodney Sharp Professor Emeritus of History, University of Delaware, Newark.*

Aleksey Mikhaylovich Muromtsev. *Assistant Director, State Institute of Oceanography, Moscow.*

Keith A. Murray. *Emeritus Professor of History, Western Washington University, Bellingham.*

Maurice Murzeau. *Director, Information Bureau, Angers, Fr.*

Alice F.A. Mutton (d. 1979). *Reader in Geography, Queen Mary College, University of London.*

Geoffrey Myers. *Former United Nations Correspondent,* The London Daily Telegraph.

Merle Wentworth Myers. *Emeritus Professor of Geology and Geography, Mississippi State University, Starkville.*

Sarah K. Myers. *Editor,* The Geographical Review, *1973–78.*

Dnyandeo Giraji Narkhede. *Lecturer in Geography, Nagpur Mahavidyalaya, Nagpur University, India.*

Maria Teresa Anzidei Natali. *Teacher of Literature, Scuola Media Statale Petrocchi, Rome.*

Philippus Rudolph Nell. *Town Clerk, Boksburg, S.Af.*

Werner Neugebauer. *Former Director, Office for Prehistory and Early History, Office of the Mayor of Lübeck, W.Ger.*

Edward J. Nichols. *Emeritus Professor of English Composition, Pennsylvania State University, University Park.*

Joan Nicklin. *Free-lance writer on geography.*

Henri Nicolaï. *Professor of Applied Geography, Free University of Brussels.*

Willem Petrus van Niekerk. *Town Clerk and Treasurer, Jagersfontein, S.Af.*

Ursula Niemann. *Curator of Bielefeld Town Archives, W.Ger.*

Yevgeny Gurevich Nikiforov. *Senior Scientist, Arctic and Antarctic Scientific Research Institute, Leningrad.*

Nancy Paine Norton. *Professor of History, Wheaton College, Norton, Mass.*

Boniface Ihewunwa Obichere. *Professor of History, University of California, Los Angeles.*

John Gerard O'Connor. *Former Instructor of Art, University of New Mexico. Director, Gallup Museum of Indian Arts and Crafts, N.M., 1956–60.*

Andrew Charles O'Dell (d. 1966). *Professor of Geography, University of Aberdeen, 1951–66.*

Herman Martinus Oldenhof. *Burgomaster of Ede, Neth., 1952–62.*

Kjeld Olsen. *Municipal Official of Randers, Den.*

Frederick Irving Olson. *Professor of History, University of Wisconsin, Milwaukee.*

Simeon Hongo Ominde. *Professor of Geography; Director, Population Studies and Research Institute, University of Nairobi, Kenya.*

Gordon Oosterman. *Principal, Middletown Christian School, Pa. Former Professor of Geography, Calvin College, Grand Rapids, Mich.*

Leonard Edwin Ortzen. *Normandy Correspondent, French Radio's English-Language Service, 1949–64. Author of* The Gallic Land *and others.*

George Augustus Osborn (d. 1972). *Editor, Sault Ste. Marie (Mich.) Evening News.*

David Oteiza. *Professor of Geography of the Western Hemisphere, National University of La Plata, Arg.*

Fred Mallery Packard. *International Specialist, National Park Service, U.S. Department of the Interior, 1963–78. Secretary, International Commission on National Parks, International Union for Conservation of Nature and Natural Resources, 1958–69; 1975–78.*

Reinhard E. Paesler. *Lecturer, Institute for Economic Geography, Ludwig Maximilian University of Munich.*

Elwin Lawrence Page (deceased). *Lawyer. Author of* Judicial Beginnings in New Hampshire, 1640–1700 *and others.*

Clarke Jaye Pahlas. *General Manager, The A.N. Palmer Company, Publishers, Schaumburg, Ill.*

Manohar Ramchandra Palande (deceased). *Chief Editor, Gujarat District Gazetteers, Government of Gujarat, India, 1960–64.*

S. Pandey. *Head, Cartography Division, National Bureau of Soil Survey and Land Use Planning, Indian Agricultural Research Institute, New Delhi.*

Clifton W. Pannell. *Professor of Geography, University of Georgia, Athens.*

William Henry Parker. *Former Lecturer in Geography of the U.S.S.R., University of Oxford. Author of* Canada: A Travel Guide *and others.*

Edward Caffrey Parr. *Former Town Clerk and Chief Executive Officer, Teesside County Borough Council, Eng.*

James Jerome Parsons. *Emeritus Professor of Geography, University of California, Berkeley.*

John Harris Paterson. *Professor of Geography, University of Leicester, Eng.*

Ntsomo Payanzo. *Former Assistant Professor of Sociology, National University of Zaire, Lubumbashi.*

Dick N. Pazen. *Research Analyst, Wisconsin Legislative Reference Bureau, Madison.*

Anne Merriman Peck. *Writer, illustrator, and painter. Former Instructor of Creative Writing, Extension Department, University of Arizona, Tucson.*

Mary Tunstall Pedoe (d. 1965). *Lecturer, University of Sudan, Khartoum.*

George Pendle (d. 1977). *Managing Director, Pendle & Rivett Ltd., London. Author of* Pelican History of Latin America *and others.*

Pietro Perin. *Assistant Secretary, Commune of Pordenone (Udine), Italy.*

Maurice Perret (deceased). *Chief Editor, Académie International du Tourisme: Revue. Director, Syndicat d'Initiative de Grenoble, Fr., 1945–56.*

Eugene Thor Petersen. *Superintendent, Mackinac Island State Park Commission, Mich.*

Harry St. John Bridger Philby (d. 1960). *Explorer in Arabia. Author of* The Heart of Arabia *and others.*

Walter Fernando Piazza. *Professor of History, Federal University of Santa Catarina, Florianópolis, Braz.*

David Joshua Pittman. *Professor and Chairman, Department of Sociology, Washington University, St. Louis.*

Forrest Pitts. *Professor of Geography, University of Hawaii at Manoa.*

Cyril Ernest Charles Reginald Platten. *Former Town Clerk, London Borough of Enfield, Eng.*

Henri Polge. *Town Archivist, Gers, Fr.*

Philip Wayland Porter. *Professor of Geography, University of Minnesota, Minneapolis.*

Bernard A. Pothier. *Research Editor,* Dictionary of Canadian Biography, *1967–69.*

Merritt Bloodworth Pound (d. 1970). *Professor of Political Science, University of Georgia, Athens, 1941–64.*

William Stevens Powell. *Professor of History, University of North Carolina at Chapel Hill.*

Charles Aloysius Paul Prangers. *Information Officer, City of The Hague, Neth.*

Pierre du Prey. *Novelist and journalist. Technical Adviser to the Minister of State, Abidjan, Ivory Coast.*

Dalias Adolph Price. *Professor and Head, Department of Geography, Eastern Illinois University, Charleston.*

Colette Prieur. *Keeper, Jean de la Fontaine Museum; Keeper, Library and Archives, Château Thierry, Fr.*

Joseph Prinz. *Director of City Archives, Münster, W.Ger.*

Ralph Mansell Prothero. *Professor of Geography, University of Liverpool.*

Merle C. Prunty, Jr. (d. 1982). *Alumni Foundation Distinguished Professor of Geography, University of Georgia, Athens, 1969–82.*

Friedrich (Johann Diedrich) Prüser. *Director, Bremen State Archives, Bremen, W.Ger., 1937–57.*

Zain ol-Abedin Rahnema. *Secretary General of the P.E.N. Club of Iran, Teherān. Former Member of the Parliament of Iran.*

Giuseppe Raimondi. *Official in the Press Office, City House, Rapallo, Italy.*

William Francis Raney (d. 1962). *Professor of European History, Lawrence College, Appleton, Wis.*

R.V.R. Chandrasekhara Rao. *Professor and Head, Department of Political Science; Dean, School of Social Sciences, University of Hyderabad, India.*

Wilhelm Felix Rausch. *City Archivist, Linz, Austria.*

Charles Wyatt Raymond. *Director, Maritime Resource Management Service, Amherst, Nova Scotia.*

Leo Franklyn Redfern. *Former President, Keene State College, N.H.*

John Rice. *Professor of Geography, University of Minnesota, Minneapolis.*

Robert William Richmond. *Assistant Executive Director and Treasurer, Kansas State Historical Society, Topeka.*

Dorothy Lois Riker. *Editor, Indiana Historical Bureau, Indianapolis, 1946–71.*

Brian Birley Roberts (d. 1978). *Research Associate, Scott Polar Research Institute, University of Cambridge, 1960–78.*

Blackwell Pierce Robinson. *Associate Professor of History, University of North Carolina at Greensboro.*

J. Lewis Robinson. *Professor of Geography, University of British Columbia, Vancouver.*

Öivind Rödevand. *Lecturer in Geography Teaching, University of Oslo.*

Rolland C. Rogers. *Emeritus Professor of History, San Jose State University, Calif.*

Irmentraud Rohrmayr. *Town Archivist, Straubing, W.Ger.*

Guido Rotthoff. *Director of Municipal Archives, Krefeld, W.Ger.*

Joseph S. Roucek. *Professor of Social Science, Queensborough Community College, City University of New York, Bayside, 1967–72.*

Jean-Maurice Rouquette. *Curator of the Museum, Arles, Fr.*

B.B. Roy. *Professor of Agricultural Chemistry; Head, Department of Agriculture, University of Calcutta.*

Erich Ruckgaber. *Editor,* Fellbacher Zeitung, *W.Ger.*

William Willis Ruff. *Former Clerk of the Surrey County Council, Eng.*

Karl Ruppert. *Professor and Head, Institute for Economic Geography, Ludwig Maximilian University of Munich.*

A. Bower Sageser. *Professor of American History, Kansas State University, Manhattan, 1941–73.*

Henry de Surirey de Saint-Remy. *Chief Librarian, Historical Library of the City of Paris, 1953–74.*

Leslie Arthur Sallnow. *Former Public Relations and Information Officer, Waltham Forest, Eng.*

Carl Fredrik Sandelin. *Novelist. Former General Manager and Editor in Chief, Finnish News Agency, Helsinki.*

Irwin Taylor Sanders. *Emeritus Professor of Sociology, Boston University.*

Jonathan Sanger. *Former Associate Editor,* Américas *magazine.*

Paul Jean Sanlaville. *Research Associate, National Centre for Scientific Research, Lyon.*

Ann Margaret Savours. *Assistant Keeper, National Maritime Museum, London.*

Michael Schattenhofer. *Former Director, Munich State Archives.*

James Ralston Scobie (d. 1981). *Professor of History, University of California, San Diego, 1977–81.*

Thomas Morris Hornby Scott. *Former Town Clerk, London Borough of Sutton, Eng.*

Se-Il Sonn. *Senior editorial writer,* Dong-A Ilbo *newspaper, Seoul.*

Tsepon W.D. Shakabpa. *Historian. Author of* Tibet: A Political History.

Abd el Aziz Torayah Sharaf. *Professor of Geography, Islamic University of Imam Muhammad Ibn Saud, Riyadh, Saudi Arabia.*

Abdu Aly Shata. *Director, Desert Research Institute, Cairo.*

Donald Henry Sheehan (d. 1974). *President and Professor of History, Whitman College, Walla Walla, Wash., 1968–74.*

Arseny Vladimirovich Shnitnikov. *Senior Scientist, Limnology Laboratory, Academy of Sciences of the U.S.S.R., Leningrad.*

Hugh de Sausmarez Shortt. *Former Curator, Salisbury and South Wiltshire Museum, Eng.*

Alfred Osipovich Shpaykher. *Senior Scientist, Arctic and Antarctic Scientific Research Institute, Leningrad.*

Phillip Raymond Shriver. *Emeritus President; Professor of History, Miami University, Oxford, Ohio.*

Francis Butler Simkins (d. 1966). *Professor of History, Longwood College, Farmville, Va.*

David Stanley Simonett. *Director, Land Evaluation and Land Use Studies, Earth Satellite Corporation, Washington, D.C.*

Edward Smethurst Simpson. *Professor of Geography, University of Newcastle upon Tyne, Eng.*

Frederick Bernard Singleton. *Honorary Senior Visiting Research Fellow, Postgraduate School of Yugoslav Studies, University of Bradford, Eng.*

Karl Aemilian Sinnhuber. *Professor of Economics; Head, Geographical Institute, University of Vienna.*

Raleigh Ashlin Skelton (d. 1970). *Superintendent, Map Room, British Museum, 1950–67.*

Vladimir Ilich Slavin. *Professor, Moscow M.V. Lomonosov State University.*

Axel Mose Sløk. *Managing Director and Editor, Confederation of Danish Agricultural Employers' Associations, Copenhagen.*

Arthur Eltringham Smailes (d. 1984). *Professor of Geography, Queen Mary College, University of London, 1955–73.*

Gerald Wayne Smith. *Academic Dean; Professor of History, Waynesburg College, Pa.*

Helen L. Smith. *Associate Professor of Geography, Middle Tennessee State University, Murfreesboro, 1970–74.*

Walter Charles Dudley Smith. *Town Engineer, Boksburg, S.Af.*

Felix Eugene Snider. *Former Librarian and former Director, Department of Library Science, Southeast Missouri State College, Cape Girardeau.*

Aleksey Aleksandrovich Sokolov. *Former Director, Leningrad Hydrological Institute.*

Jacob Spelt. *Professor of Geography, University of Toronto.*

Joseph E. Spencer. *Emeritus Professor of Geography, University of California, Los Angeles.*

Karl R. Stadler. *Professor and Head, Institute of Modern and Contemporary History, Johannes Kepler University of Linz, Austria.*

Sir Laurence Dudley Stamp (d. 1966). *Professor of Social Geography, University of London, 1948–58.*

Dan Stanislawski. *Research Associate in Geography, University of California, Berkeley.*

William Richard Stanley. *Professor of Geography, University of South Carolina, Columbia.*

Martin Purefoy Statham. *Former County Archivist, West Suffolk, Eng.*

Robert Walter Steel. *Principal, University College of Swansea, 1974–82; Vice-Chancellor, University of Wales, 1979–81.*

Harriet Grace Steers. *Lecturer in Geography, University of Cambridge, 1936–66.*

Hugo Steneberg. *Municipal Official, Witten, W.Ger.*

Cj Stevens. *Professor and Chairman, Department of Speech and Theatre, Herbert H. Lehman College, City University of New York.*

David Stick. *Author of* Outer Banks of North Carolina; The Cape Hatteras Seashore; *and others.*

Joseph Stocker. *Author of* Arizona: A Guide to Easier Living.

Henry Gordon Stokes. *Author of* English Place-Names *and others.*

James Herbert Stone. *Emeritus Professor of Humanities, San Francisco State University.*

Goffe Struiksma. *Municipal Official, Heerenveen, Neth.*

Alfred Donald Sumberg. *Associate General Secretary, American Association of University Professors. Professor of Social Studies, East Stroudsburg State College, Pa., 1956–67.*

Charles Grayson Summersell. *Emeritus Professor of History, University of Alabama, University.*

Tatyana Yosifovna Supranovich. *Senior Scientist and Head, Division of Sea Dynamics, Far Eastern Hydrometeorological Research Institute, Vladivostok, U.S.S.R.*

Robert M. Sutton. *Professor of History; Director of the Illinois Historical Survey, University of Illinois, Urbana.*

Arthur Ronald Taffs. *Former Public Relations Officer, London Borough of Lewisham, Eng.*

Tamotsu Takahashi. *Senior Researcher, Institute of Developing Economies, Tokyo.*

Charles Antoine Peter Takes. *Former Director, International Institute for Land Reclamation and Improvement, Wageningen, Neth.*

Mohamed Talbi. *Professor, Faculty of Letters and Human Sciences, University of Tunis.*

Ken-Chi Tanabe. *Professor of Geography, University of Tokyo.*

Charlton W. Tebeau. *Emeritus Professor of History, University of Miami, Coral Gables, Fla.*

Tenzing Norgay (d. 1986). *Field Director of Training, Himalayan Mountaineering Institute, Darjeeling, India. The first man (with Edmund Hillary) to reach the summit of Mount Everest.*

Johannes Theodoor Thijsse. *Professor of Hydraulics, Technological University of Delft, Neth., 1938–63.*

John Thompson. *Professor of Geography, University of Illinois, Urbana.*

Robert Ribblesdale Thornton. *Former Town Clerk, Leicester, Eng.*

Harry Thorpe (d. 1977). *Professor and Head, Department of Geography, University of Birmingham, Eng.*

Robert H. Thorsbro. *Chief of Production, Danish Tourist Board, Copenhagen.*

Arthur E. Tiedemann. *Professor of History, City College, City University of New York.*

James L. Tigner. *Professor of History, University of Nevada, Reno.*

Robert Tinthoin. *Chief Archivist, Deux-Sèvres, Fr., 1959–63. Chief Archivist, Department of Oran, 1938–56, and Director of Museum of Oran, Alg., 1941–56.*

Hong Djin Tjia. *Professor of Geology, National University of Malaysia, Bangi.*

Augusto Torre (d. 1977). *Professor and Chairman, Department of Modern and Contemporary History, University of Bologna, Italy, 1956–60.*

Pietro Torrione. *Director of Biella Library and Museum, Italy.*

J. Allen Tower (d. 1961). *Professor of Geography, Birmingham-Southern College, Birmingham, Ala.*

Mary Curry Tresidder. *Honorary Chairman of the Board, Yosemite Park & Curry Company, Yosemite National Park, Calif.*

Jean-Léon-François Tricart. *Professor and Director, Centre of Applied Geography, University of Strasbourg I, Fr.*

Raymond Thérèse Troprès. *Clerk, Town Hall, Avranches, Fr.*

Hsu-pai Tseng. *Chairman of the Board, Central News Agency, Taipei. Professor of Journalism, National Chengchi University, Taipei. Dean, Sun Yat-sen Memorial Research Institute, College of Chinese Culture, Taipei.*

The Rt. Rev. Cyril James Tucker. *Former Anglican Bishop of the Falkland Islands and in Argentina.*

Erol Tümertekin. *Former Professor of Geography, University of Istanbul.*

Necdet Tunçdilek. *Associate Professor of Geography, University of Istanbul.*

David Turnock. *Reader in Geography, University of Leicester, Eng.*

Denis C. Twitchett. *Gordon Wu Professor of Chinese Studies, Princeton University.*

Roger Henry Van Bolt. *Director, Sloan Museum, Flint, Mich., 1965–81.*

Burke G. Vanderhill. *University Service Professor of Geography, Florida State University, Tallahassee.*

Albert Edward Van Dusen. *Professor of History, University of Connecticut, Storrs. State Historian.*

Milton I. Vanger. *Professor of History, Brandeis University, Waltham, Mass.; Chairman of Latin American Studies, 1971–81.*

R. Suzanne Van Meter. *Professor of History, Clarion State College, Pa.*

Milorad Vasović. *Professor of Regional Geography, University of Belgrade.*

Gustave Vaucher. *State Archivist, Geneva, Switz., 1940–66.*

Christiaan van Veen. *President, Federation of Netherlands Industry. Minister of Education and Science, Government of the Netherlands, 1971–73.*

Anna Johanna Versprille. *Keeper of the Public Records, Leiden, Neth.*

Hermann Wahl. *Town Archivist, Pforzheim, W.Ger.*

Frank Walker. *Former Senior Lecturer in Geography, University of Bristol, Eng.*

Peter Franklin Walker. *Professor of History, University of North Carolina at Chapel Hill.*

Bernard J. Wall (d. 1974). *Free-lance writer. Author of* Report on the Vatican; A City and a World; *and many others.*

Joseph Frazier Wall. *Rosenfield Professor of History, Grinnell College, Iowa.*

Ernest Wallace. *Horn Professor Emeritus of History, Texas Tech University, Lubbock.*

Helen Margaret Wallis. *Map Librarian, British Library, London.*

Mildred Marie Walmsley. *Associate Professor of Geography, Case Western Reserve University, Cleveland.*

Peter Walne. *County Archivist, Hertfordshire County Council, England.*

Clyde C. Walton. *Director of Libraries, University of Colorado, Boulder.*

Herbert Ward. *Former Borough Librarian, London Borough of Tower Hamlets, Eng.*

Judson Clements Ward, Jr. *Executive Vice President, Emory University, Atlanta, Ga., 1970–79; Dean of the Faculties, 1957–79.*

William Stanley Alphonsus Warren. *Town Clerk, Blantyre, Malawi.*

Burton DeWitt Watson. *Free-lance translator. Professor of Chinese, Columbia University, 1967–73.*

Richard John Waygood. *Former Municipal Committee Clerk, Romsey, Eng.*

Glenn Weaver. *Professor of History, Trinity College, Hartford, Conn.*

Herbert Weaver (d. 1985). *Professor of History, Vanderbilt University, Nashville, Tenn., 1952–74.*

Kempton E. Webb. *Professor of Geography, Columbia University.*

Wilfrid Webster. *Executive Editor,* Atlas of the Marine Environment, *American Geographical Society, New York City.*

Russell Frank Weigley. *Professor of History, Temple University, Philadelphia.*

Ernst Weigt. *Emeritus Professor of Economic Geography, Friedrich Alexander University of Erlangen-Nuremberg, W.Ger.*

John H. Wellington. *Emeritus Professor of Geography, University of the Witwatersrand, Johannesburg.*

Merle William Wells. *Historian and Archivist, Idaho State Historical Society, Boise.*

Geoffrey Edleston Wheeler. *Lieutenant Colonel, Indian Army (retired). Director, Central Asian Research Centre, London, 1953–68.*

Paul Frank Wheeler. *Professor of Sociology, State University of New York at Albany.*

Nathan Laselle Whetten (d. 1984). *Professor of Sociology, University of Connecticut, Storrs, 1938–71; Dean of the Graduate School, 1940–71.*

Edward Stanley White. *Former Town Clerk, Bulawayo, Rhodesia.*

(Charles) Langdon White. *Emeritus Professor of Geography, Stanford University, Calif.*

Maurice Leslie White. *Former Public Relations Officer, London Borough of Hillingdon, Eng.*

Daniel Jay Whitener. *Former Dean, Appalachian State Teachers College, Boone, N.C.; Head, Social Studies Department, 1932–57.*

Vincent Heath Whitney. *Emeritus Professor of Sociology, University of Pennsylvania, Philadelphia; Director, Population Studies Center, 1962–76.*

John Byron Whittow. *Senior Lecturer in Geography, University of Reading, Eng.*

Willard Chester Wichers. *Director, Midwestern Division, Netherlands Information Service; Director, Netherlands Museum, Holland, Mich.*

Johan de Widt. *Burgomaster, Amersfoort, Neth.*

Fritz Wiegand. *Former Director of the Municipal Archives, Erfurt, E.Ger.*

David Willey. *Rome correspondent, British Broadcasting Corporation.*

Eliot Churchill Williams, Jr. *Professor of Zoology, Wabash College, Crawfordsville, Ind.*

Frank B. Williams, Jr. *Emeritus Professor of History, East Tennessee State University, Johnson City.*

Richmond Dean Williams. *Director, Eleutherian Mills Historical Library, Greenville, Del.*

George Ernest Willis. *Justice of the Peace, Newbury, Eng. Former Alderman, Newbury Borough Council.*

Harold Fisher Wilson. *Former Professor of History, Glassboro State College, N.J.*

Arthur N.L. Wina. *Member of Parliament, 1962–68 and 1973– ; Minister of Finance, 1963–67; Minister of Education, 1967–68, Government of Northern Rhodesia, renamed Zambia in 1964.*

Conrad L. Wirth. *Former Director, National Park Service, U.S. Department of the Interior, Washington, D.C.*

Malverne Ray Wolfe. *Emeritus Professor of History, California State College, Pa.; Director of Guidance Services, 1957–69.*

Robert Coldwell Wood. *Professor of Political Science, University of Massachusetts, Boston; President, University of Massachusetts, Amherst, 1970–77.*

A. Geoffrey Woodhead. *Fellow of Corpus Christi College, Cambridge; Emeritus Lecturer in Classics, University of Cambridge. Adjunct Professor of Classics, Ohio State University, Columbus.*

Christopher Montague Woodhouse. *Member of Parliament for Oxford, 1959–66, 1970–74. Fellow of Trinity Hall, University of Cambridge.*

L.W. Wright. *Lecturer in Geography, Queen Mary College, University of London.*

Paul Zabel. *Former Public Relations Officer, Gelsenkirchen, W.Ger.*

Clifford Maynard Zierer (deceased). *Professor of Geography, University of California, Los Angeles, 1945–65.*

Joseph Francis Zimmerman. *Professor of Political Science, State University of New York at Albany.*

Friedrich Zollhoefer. *Town Archivist, Kempten, W.Ger.*

Staff of the Encyclopædia Britannica

Editorial Staff

EDITORS

Donald Duncanson, *Deputy Editor, Chicago*
Charles Mosley, *Deputy Editor, London*
Robert F. Rauch, *Deputy Editor, Chicago*
Yutorio C. Hori, *Senior Editor*
Raymond Dennerstein
Charles Hills
John Killheffer
Kathleen Kuiper
George Kenneth Leivers
Erdmut Lerner
Janet S. McDonald
Marvin Martin
Gary Masters
Paul Mendelson
Kenneth R. Pletcher
Jane Toomey

RESEARCHERS

Robert Curley
Edith A. Johnson

BIBLIOGRAPHERS

Leah Hotimlanska
Anne-Marie Schroeder

CORRESPONDENCE AND RESEARCH

Helen L. Carlock, *Supervisor*
Lars Mahinske

ART DEPARTMENT

Cynthia Peterson, *Director*
Barbara Epstein, *Senior Picture Editor*
Anne H. Becker
Kathryn Creech
Daniel M. Delgado
John L. Draves
Patricia A. Henle
Dale Horn
La Bravia Jenkins
Raul Rios
Richard A. Roiniotis
Lillian Simcox
William T. Soltis

CARTOGRAPHY

Gerzilla Leszczynski, *Coordinator*
Steven Bogdan
Amelia R. Gintautas
Chandrika Kaul
Emma A. Kowalenko

LIBRARY

Terry Miller, *Head Librarian*
David W. Foster
Shantha Uddin

Production Staff

Karen M. Barch, *Executive Director*

COPY DEPARTMENT

Anita Wolff, *Manager*
Marilyn Klein, *Senior Copy Editor*
Sylvia Wallace, *Senior Copy Editor*
Patricia Bauer
Elizabeth A. Blowers
Lisa Braucher
Carol Burwash
Glenn Jenne
Patrick Joyce
Lilia W. Kulas
Joan Lackowski
Gerilee Martens-Hundt
Julian Ronning
John E. Scanlon
Melinda Shepherd
Dennis Skord
Carol Smith
Ann Wambach
Judith West

PRODUCTION CONTROL

Mary C. Srodon, *Manager*
Marilyn L. Barton
Mayme R. Cussen
Timothy A. Phillips

COMPOSITION AND PAGE MAKEUP

Melvin Stagner, *Manager*
Duangnetra Debhavalya
Morna Freund
Van Jones
John Krom, Jr.
Thomas Mulligan
Gwen Rosenberg
Tammy Tsou
Marsha Check, *Supervisor, Page Makeup*
Michael Born, Jr.
Griselda Chaidez
Arnell Reed
Philip Rehmer
Danette Wetterer

INDEX DEPARTMENT

Frances E. Latham, *Manager*
Rosa E. Casas, *Assistant Manager*
Mansur G. Abdullah
Margaret A. Berger
Angela P. Boone
Christopher G. Boucek
Carmen-Maria Hetrea
Virginia M. LaFleur
Steven Monti
Edward Paul Moragne
Valerie J. Munei
Susan Marts Myers
Helen A. Peterson
Mary L. Reynolds
John G. Scanlon
Lisa Strubin
Martin L. White
Gayl E. Williams

Editorial Planning and Technology Staff

Nathan Taylor, *Executive Director*
Carl D. Holzman, *Director of Editorial Budgets*
Ines Baptist
Kenneth R. Huff
William M. Webb

EDITORIAL COMPUTER SERVICES

Michael J. Brandhorst, *Director*
Steven Bosco
Clark Elliot
Richard Frye
Daniel Johnsen
Vincent Starr
I. Dean Washington

Administrative and Editorial Support Staff

Anne Long Dimopoulos, *Manager*
Ana Maria Blanco
Sophia Chang
Eunice Magnus
Velia Palomar
Holly Whitten